Organizational Behavior

Organizational Behavior

Mary Uhl-Bien
Texas Christian University

Ron Piccolo
University of Central Florida

John Schermerhorn
Ohio University

A WileyPLUS Learning Space Course

VICE PRESIDENT, EDUCATION	Tim Stookesbury
VICE PRESIDENT & EXECUTIVE PUBLISHER	George Hoffman
EDITORIAL DIRECTOR	Veronica Visentin
EXECUTIVE EDITOR	Lisé Johnson
SPONSORING EDITOR	Jennifer Manias
ASSOCIATE DEVELOPMENT EDITOR	Emma Townsend-Merino
EXECUTIVE MARKETING MANAGER	Christopher DeJohn
DESIGN DIRECTOR	Harry Nolan
SENIOR CONTENT MANAGER	Dorothy Sinclair
SENIOR PRODUCTION EDITOR	Valerie Vargas
PRODUCT DESIGN MANAGER	Allison Morris
PRODUCT DESIGN ASSOCIATE	Rebecca Costantini
SENIOR DESIGNER	Thomas Nery
COVER PHOTO	©ULTRA.F/Getty Images, Inc.

This book was typeset in 9.5/11.5 Source Sans Pro at Aptara®, Inc. and printed and bound by Strategic Content Imaging. The cover was printed by Strategic Content Imaging.

This book is printed on acid free paper. ∞

Founded in 1807, John Wiley & Sons, Inc. has been a valued source of knowledge and understanding for more than 200 years, helping people around the world meet their needs and fulfill their aspirations. Our company is built on a foundation of principles that include responsibility to the communities we serve and where we live and work. In 2008, we launched a Corporate Citizenship Initiative, a global effort to address the environmental, social, economic, and ethical challenges we face in our business. Among the issues we are addressing are carbon impact, paper specifications and procurement, ethical conduct within our business and among our vendors, and community and charitable support. For more information, please visit our website: www.wiley.com/go/citizenship.

Evaluation copies are provided to qualified academics and professionals for review purposes only, for use in their courses during the next academic year. These copies are licensed and may not be sold or transferred to a third party. Upon completion of the review period, please return the evaluation copy to Wiley. Return instructions and a free of charge return shipping label are available at www.wiley.com/go/returnlabel. If you have chosen to adopt this textbook for use in your course, please accept this book as your complimentary desk copy. Outside of the United States, please contact your local representative.

ISBN 13 978-1-119-09168-4

Printed in the United States of America.

TO THE STUDENT

Your *WileyPLUS Learning Space* course includes video lessons that bring the chapter concepts to life through high-interest stories and vivid, real-world examples. The individual video lectures, expert interviews, and interactive media are enhanced by additional engaging visual elements—such as graphics and definitions—to help activate your curiosity and deepen your understanding of the material.

The video lessons and the chapter reading content are coupled together to provide you with a more meaningful learning experience. In general, video lessons present an overview of the major concepts as well as real-world examples and applications. The accompanying etext provides greater detail and more in-depth coverage of the chapter concepts and may include media like videos and animations. For the best course experience and mastery of the concepts you will want to utilize the video and media materials alongside the etext and this printed course companion.

The video player allows you to experience the material at your own speed, stopping the video delivery to study graphics and media more closely, and then resuming the lesson when you're ready. The player also includes an editing tool that allows your instructor to customize your course, by adding additional questions, comments, and even more video.

How to Use this Print Companion

This Print Companion includes all of the text passages in the online course and will direct you on where to find more information in *WileyPLUS Learning Space*. This study tool, a secondary source for the reading, will reinforce your conceptual understanding and will help you make a deeper connection to the content. For ease of use, you'll find the following elements throughout:

- **Boldface type** is used to indicate figures, tables, and other elements.
- Marginal notes and small, "thumbnail" images help you know where you can find art, figures, additional media, and Concept Check questions.
- Icons help direct you to all the resources in *WileyPLUS Learning Space*.

 View the large version of the figure.

 See the table or boxed feature.

 Play the video or animation.

 Answer the Concept Check questions.

TO THE INSTRUCTOR

Organizational Behavior, a *WileyPLUS Learning Space* course, couples comprehensive core content with a wealth of engaging digital assets to provide a dynamic teaching and learning environment for you and your students. The carefully crafted original video segments for each chapter's learning objectives use the power of personal storytelling via current examples to bring the chapter concepts to life for students. This model gives professors an excellent framework for flipping the class and providing a more interactive in-class experience. By assigning these videos, instructors will make the content personally relevant to their students and increase their motivation in the course.

Video segments feature academic and professional contributors who coach students through various topics using memorable examples and study tips. Each chapter also features a business professional who tells a story about a real business situation, showing students how the material relates to their future careers. In addition, the embedded video player includes an editing tool that allows you to customize your course, by adding your own questions, comments, and even more video.

Designed to engage today's student, *WileyPLUS Learning Space* will transform any course into a vibrant, collaborative, learning community.

WileyPLUS Learning Space is class tested and ready-to-go for instructors. It offers a flexible platform for quickly organizing learning activities, managing student collaboration, and customizing courses—including choice of content as well as the amount of interactivity between students. An instructor using *WileyPLUS Learning Space* is able to easily:

- Assign activities and add special materials
- Guide students through what's important by easily assigning specific content
- Set up and monitor group learning
- Assess student engagement
- Gain immediate insights to help inform teaching

WileyPLUS Learning Space now includes ORION, a personal, adaptive learning experience so that students can build their proficiency on learning objectives and use their study time more effectively especially before quizzes and exams. By tracking students' work, ORION provides instructors with insights into students' work, without having to ask. Efficacy research shows that *WileyPLUS Learning Space* improves student outcomes by as much as one letter grade.

Organizational Behavior also includes:

- Key Term Flashcards and Crossword Puzzles
- Lecture Launcher Videos
- Interactive Self-Assessments
- Learning Styles Survey
- Wiley Management Weekly Updates
- Business Hot Topics

CONTENTS

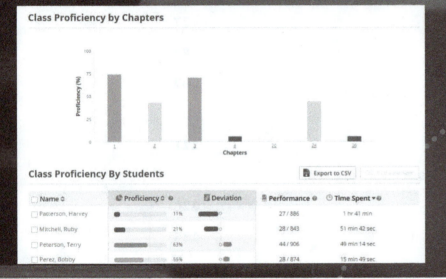

Reading for
INTRODUCING ORGANIZATIONAL BEHAVIOR

WP LS Go to your WileyPLUS Learning Space course for video episodes, examples, art, tables, Concept Checks, practice, and resources that will help you succeed in this course.

Introducing Organizational Behavior

What Is Organizational Behavior?

If you pause to consider the vast effects of our recent economic and social turmoil, there shouldn't be any doubt that organizations and their members face huge challenges. Talk to friends and follow the news headlines. Preferred jobs are still hard to come by for new college graduates, and unemployment remains high, especially for candidates without strong career skills. Those with jobs often struggle to support a desired lifestyle while balancing conflicting demands of work and family responsibilities. Like it or not, this is your world. It's the one you'll have to master for both career and personal success.

In this challenging era, the body of knowledge we call organizational behavior offers many insights of great value. **Organizational behavior (OB)** is the study of human behavior in organizations. It is an academic discipline devoted to understanding individuals, teams, interpersonal processes, and organizational dynamics. Learning about OB can help you build solid job skills and expand your potential for career success in the dynamic, shifting, and complex workplaces of today . . . and tomorrow.

Importance of Organizational Behavior

Think OB and great jobs! Think OB and career success! Think OB and overall life satisfaction! Don't think—OB and another course completed for my degree!

The real importance of OB boils down to how it helps you develop the skills needed for a successful career in our ever-changing world. This is a time in which the normal complexities of human behavior in organizations are ramped up by an environment of constant change and the growing influence of social technology. Take the OB relevance test. How prepared are you to excel in jobs with fashion-forward titles like these?[1]

- Relationship champion
- Logistics ringmaster
- Innovation game changer
- Collaboration pioneer
- Market trends virtuoso

If you can describe in your own words what these job holders would be doing, you're already moving in the right direction. You're starting to get a real sense of what it takes to succeed in this emerging new workplace and why it pays to learn what OB can teach us about human behavior in organizations.

Behind each of the prior job titles is a common foundation that comes to life as "networking," "connecting," "ideating," "collaborating," "helping," "linking," "supporting," "seeking," and "performing." These and other similar behaviors drive what can be called a **smart workforce**, one in which you must be prepared to excel.[2] Smart workforces are communities of action whose members tackle constantly shifting projects while sharing knowledge and skills to solve real and often complex problems. Smart workforces are built through connections activated by relational skills and social technologies and used to forge a powerful collective brain that keeps growing and adapting over time.

This text helps you bridge the gap between OB as a body of knowledge and OB as a pathway to career and life success. Our book is about people, everyday people like you and like us, who work and pursue careers in today's demanding settings. It's about people who seek fulfillment in their lives and jobs in a variety of ways and in uncertain times. It's about the challenges of leadership, ethics, globalization, technology, diversity, work–life balance, and many social issues. And it is about how our complex ever-changing environment requires people and organizations to continuously adapt and improve in the quest for promising futures.

There is no doubt that success with our life and career goals requires ongoing learning and continuous attention to new trends, practices, and opportunities. The following changes in what people expect and value in terms of human behavior in organizations are of special interest in the study of OB.[3]

- *Importance of connections and networks.* Work is increasingly being done through personal connections and networks. In this environment, building effective relationships face to face and online is a must-have career skill.
- *Commitment to ethical behavior.* Highly publicized scandals involving unethical and illegal practices prompt concerns for ethical behavior in the workplace; growing intolerance for breaches of public faith by organizations and those who run them are drawing new attention to business ethics.
- *Broader views of leadership.* New pressures and demands mean organizations can no longer rely on just managers for leadership. Leadership is valued from all members, found at all levels, and flows in all directions—not just top-down.
- *Emphasis on human capital and teamwork.* Success is earned through knowledge, experience, and commitments to people as valuable human assets; work is increasingly team based with a focus on peer contributions.
- *Demise of command-and-control.* Traditional hierarchical structures and practices are being replaced by shared leadership, flexible structures, and participatory work settings that engage human and social capital.
- *Influence of information technology.* As new technologies—including social media— penetrate the workplace, implications for work arrangements, organizational systems and processes, and individual behavior are continuously evolving.
- *Respect for new workforce expectations.* The new generation is less tolerant of hierarchy, more high tech, and less concerned about status. Balance of work and nonwork responsibilities is a top-priority value.
- *Changing concept of careers.* New economy jobs require special skill sets and a continuous development. More people now work as independent contractors and freelancers who shift among employers rather than hold full-time jobs.
- *Concern for sustainability.* Issues of sustainability are top priorities. Decision making and goal setting increasingly give attention to the environment, climate justice, and preservation of resources for future generations.

Organizational Behavior as a Science

How do we find out what a new generation of graduates really wants and needs from work and in careers? How do we learn how to integrate multigenerational workforces around common goals and high performance expectations? How do we gain solid insights into how these and other important issues of human behavior play out in day-to-day organizational practice? The answer is found in one word: *science.*

Scientific Foundations of Organizational Behavior

More than a century ago, consultants and scholars were already giving attention to the systematic study of management and organizational practices. Although the early focus was on physical working conditions, principles of administration, and industrial engineering, interest soon broadened to include the human factor. This led to research dealing with individual attitudes, group dynamics, and the relationships between managers and workers. Organizational behavior then emerged as a scholarly discipline devoted to scientific understanding of individuals and groups in organizations, and of the performance implications of organizational processes, systems, and structures.[4]

Interdisciplinary Body of Knowledge Organizational behavior is an interdisciplinary body of knowledge with strong ties to the behavioral sciences—psychology, sociology, and anthropology—

as well as to allied social sciences such as economics and political science. What makes OB unique is its desire to integrate the diverse insights of these other disciplines and apply them to real-world organizational problems and opportunities. The ultimate goal of OB is to improve the performance of people, groups, and organizations, and to improve the quality of work life overall.

Use of Scientific Methods The field of organizational behavior uses scientific methods to develop and empirically test generalizations about behavior in organizations. OB scholars often propose and test **models**—simplified views of reality that attempt to identify major factors and forces underlying real-world phenomena. These models link **independent variables**—presumed causes—with **dependent variables**—outcomes of practical value and interest. For example, the following model describes one of the findings of OB research: Job satisfaction (independent variable) influences, absenteeism (dependent variable). The "+" and "−" signs indicate that as job satisfaction increases absenteeism is expected to go down, and as job satisfaction decreases, absenteeism should go up.

As you look at the above model, you might ask what dependent variables other than absenteeism are also important to study in OB—perhaps things like task performance, ethical behavior, work stress, incivility, team cohesion, and leadership effectiveness. Think also about job satisfaction as a dependent variable in its own right. What independent variables do you believe might explain whether satisfaction will be high or low for someone doing a service job, such as an airline flight attendant, or a managerial job, such as a school principal?

Figure 1.1 describes methods commonly used by OB researchers to study models and the relationships among variables. These research methods are based on scientific thinking. This means (1) the process of data collection is controlled and systematic, (2) proposed explanations are carefully tested, and (3) only explanations that can be rigorously verified are accepted.

See **FIGURE 1.1** Common scientific research methods in organizational behavior

Focus on Application The science of organizational behavior focuses on applications that can make a real difference in how organizations and people in them perform. Some examples of the many practical research questions addressed by the discipline of OB and reviewed in this book are:

- What causes unethical and socially irresponsible behavior by people in organizations?
- How should rewards such as pay raises be allocated?
- How can jobs be designed for both job satisfaction and high performance?
- What are the ingredients of successful teamwork?
- How can a manager deal with resistance to change?
- Should leaders make decisions by individual, consultative, or group methods?
- How can win–win outcomes be achieved in negotiations?

Contingency Thinking Rather than assuming that there is one best or universal answer to questions such as those just posed, OB recognizes that behavior and practices must be tailored to fit the exact nature of each situation—this is called **contingency thinking**. In fact, one of the most accepted conclusions of scientific research to date is that there is no single best way to handle people and the situations that develop as they work together in organizations.

Stated a bit differently, contingency thinking recognizes that cookie-cutter solutions cannot be universally applied to solve organizational problems. Responses must be crafted to best fit the circumstances and people involved. As you might expect, this is where solid scientific findings in organizational behavior become very helpful. Many examples are provided in the "Research Insight" feature found in each chapter.

Quest for Evidence An essential responsibility of any science is to create and test models that offer evidence-based foundations for decision making and action. A book by scholars Jeffrey Pfeffer and Robert Sutton defines **evidence-based management** as making decisions on "hard facts"—that is, about what really works, rather than on "dangerous half-truths"—what sounds good but lacks empirical substantiation.[5] One of the ways evidence-based thinking manifests itself in OB is through a contingency approach in which researchers identify how different situations can best be understood and handled.

Cross-Cultural Awareness In a time of complex globalization, it's important for everyone, from managers and employees to government leaders, to understand how OB theories and concepts apply in different countries.[6] Although it is relatively easy to conclude that what works in one culture may not work as well in another, it is far more difficult to describe how specific cultural differences can affect such things as ethical behavior, motivation, job satisfaction, leadership style, and negotiating tendencies. OB is now rich with empirically based insights into cross-cultural issues.

Learning about Organizational Behavior

Today's knowledge-based world and smart workforces place a great premium on learning. Only the learners, so to speak, will be able to keep the pace and succeed in a connected, high-tech, global, and constantly changing environment. But just what are we talking about here?

Think of **learning** as an enduring change of behavior that results from experience. Think also of **lifelong learning** as a process of learning continuously from day-to-day experiences. When it comes to learning about OB, this book and your course are starting points and launch platforms to make your experiences more meaningful. There also is a rich and ever-expanding pool of learning experiences available in the work events and activities, conversations with colleagues and friends, counseling and advice provided by mentors, success models, training seminars and workshops, and other daily opportunities that consume your time. What is learned from all such experiences—now and in the future—will in many ways be the key to your personal and career success. The "Bringing OB to Life" feature helps you make these connections between OB and our everyday experiences.

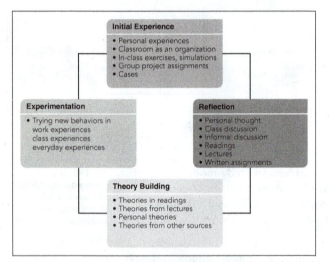

See **FIGURE 1.2**
Experiential learning in an OB course

■ **Figure 1.2** shows how the content and activities of the typical OB course fit together in an experiential learning cycle.[7] The learning sequence begins with initial experience and subsequent reflection. It grows as theory building takes place to try to explain what has happened. Theory is then tested in behavior. Textbooks, readings, class discussions, and other course assignments and activities should help you practice the phases of the learning cycle.

Notice that Figure 1.2 assigns to you a substantial responsibility for learning. Along with your instructor, our author team can offer examples, cases, and exercises to provide you with initial experience. We can even stimulate your reflection and theory building by presenting concepts and discussing their research and practical implications. Sooner or later, however, you must become an active participant in the process; you and only you can do the work required to take full advantage of the learning cycle.

At the end of this book you'll find the rich and useful *OB Skills Workbook*. It provides a variety of active learning opportunities that can help you better understand the practical applications of OB concepts, models, and theories. The workbook contains cases for analysis, team and experiential exercises, and a portfolio of self-assessments that includes the popular Kouzes and Posner "Student Leadership Practices Inventory."

Finally, don't forget that opportunities to learn more about OB and yourself abound in everyday living. Every team project, part-time work experience, student co-curricular activity, or visit to the store is rich in learning potential. Even our leisure pastimes from sports to social interactions to television, movies, and online games offer learning insights—if we tune in. The "OB in Popular Culture" feature in each chapter is a reminder to keep your learning dialed in all the time.

The Context of Organizational Behavior

Organizations and the External Environment

In order to understand the complex forces that influence human behavior in organizations, we need to begin with the nature of the "organization" itself. Simply stated, an **organization** is a collection of people working together in a division of labor to achieve a common purpose. This definition describes everything from clubs, voluntary organizations, and religious bodies to entities such as small and large businesses, schools, hospitals, and government agencies.

▣ **Figure 1.3** shows that organizations are dynamic **open systems**. They obtain resource inputs from the environment and transform them into finished goods or services that are returned to the environment as product outputs. If everything works right, suppliers value the organization and continue to provide needed resources, employees infuse work activities with their energies and intellects, and customers and clients value the organization's outputs enough to create a continuing demand for them.

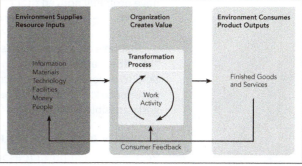

See **FIGURE 1.3 Organizations are open systems that create value while interacting with their environments**

Organizations are also **complex adaptive systems**. Because the environments they interact with are constantly evolving and changing, organizations must adapt to survive. And in a world that is increasingly complicated—socially, politically, and economically—this process of adaptation is never ending. Organizations today are embedded in environments whose components are so highly interconnected that changes in one have consequences—sometimes unpredictable and even uncontrollable—for other parts. A recent IBM Global Chief Executive Officer Study identifies this rise of complexity as the biggest challenge facing world leaders today. One CEO says: "The time available to capture, interpret and act on information is getting shorter and shorter."[8]

It can be useful to describe and analyze the external environments of organizations in terms of **stakeholders**—people, groups, and institutions that are affected by and thus have an interest or stake in an organization's performance. Key stakeholders from an OB perspective include an organization's customers, owners, employees, suppliers, regulators, and local communities, as well as future generations.

Although an organization should ideally operate in ways that best serve all stakeholders, the realities are that conflicting interests add to the complexity faced by decision makers. Consider possibilities such as these. Customers want value pricing and high-quality products, owners want profits and returns on investments. Employees want secure jobs with good pay and benefits, suppliers want reliable contracts and on-time payments. Regulators want compliance with laws, local communities want good organizational citizenship and community support. Present generations want the benefits of available natural resources, future generations want preserved and protected for long-term sustainability.

The Internal Environment of Organizations

The internal environment of organizations also creates an important context for human behavior. Think about it. Do you act differently when you are with your friends, at school, or at work? In many cases the answer is probably "yes," and the question then becomes "Why?" The answer is that the context is different. To understand behavior in any setting, we must always ask how contextual factors influence it and in what ways. And, we must also consider how we or other people are affecting the context. The question in this respect is: How do our behaviors contribute to what is happening to us and around us, and in both positive and negative ways?

One of the strongest contextual influences on human behavior is **organizational culture**—the shared beliefs and values that influence the behavior of organizational members. Former eBay CEO Meg Whitman calls it the "character" of the organization. She says organization culture is "the set of values and principles by which you run a company" and becomes the "moral center" that helps every member understand what is right and wrong in terms of personal behavior.[9]

Organizational cultures influence the way we feel and act as members. In more authoritarian and hierarchical cultures, people are hesitant to make decisions and take action on their own. So, they withhold initiative and wait for approval. In competitive cultures, people can be extremely aggressive in the quest for rewards. Still other cultures are known for their emphasis on speed and agility in dealing with markets and environments, and in generating new ideas and innovations.

There is also something called **organizational climate**—the shared perceptions among members regarding what the organization is like in terms of management policies and practices. You have probably noticed that relations among managers and employees are relaxed and communication is free-flowing in some climates. But in others, managers act distant and communication is restricted.

Just how an organization's culture and climate affect members depends on something called "fit"—the match of internal environment and individual characteristics. People who find a good fit tend to experience confidence and satisfaction. Those with a bad fit may be prone to withdraw, experience stress, and even become angry and aggressive due to dissatisfaction. The sidebar suggests possible fit preferences for today's graduates.

Diversity and Multiculturalism in Organizations

People are an important aspect of the internal environment of any organization. Consultant R. Roosevelt Thomas makes the point that positive organizational cultures tap the talents, ideas, and creative potential of *all* members.[10] This focuses attention on **workforce diversity**, the presence of individual differences based on gender, race and ethnicity, age, able-bodiedness, and sexual orientation.[11] It also highlights **multiculturalism** as an attribute of organizations that emphasize pluralism, and genuine respect for diversity and individual differences.[12] And in respect to Thomas's point again, organizations benefit when the variety of ideas and perspectives of a diverse workforce help them deal with complexity through innovation and adaptability.

Demographic trends driving workforce diversity in American society are well recognized. There are more women working than ever before. They earn 60 percent of college degrees and fill a bit more than half of managerial jobs.[13] The proportion of African Americans, Hispanics, and Asians in the population is now above 43 percent and increasing. By the year 2060, six out of every 10 Americans will be a person of color, and close to 30 percent of the population overall will be Hispanic.[14]

A key issue in any organization is **inclusion**—the degree to which the culture embraces diversity and is open to anyone who can perform a job, regardless of their diversity attributes.[15] In practice, however, valuing diversity must still be considered a work in progress. Women still earn only about 75 cents per dollar earned by men; female CEOs earn 85 cents per dollar earned by males. At *Fortune* 500 companies women hold only 15 CEO jobs and 6.2 percent of top-paying positions; women of color hold only 1.7 percent of corporate officer positions and 1 percent of top-paying jobs.[16] Indeed, when Ursula Burns was named CEO of Xerox, she became the first African-American woman to head a Fortune 500 firm.[17]

Management and Organizational Behavior

Effective Managers

A **manager** is someone whose job it is to directly support the work efforts of others. Being a manager is a unique challenge with responsibilities that link closely with the field of organizational behavior. At the heart of the matter, managers help other people get important things done in timely, high-quality, and personally satisfying ways. And in the workplaces of today, this is accomplished more through "helping" and "supporting" than through traditional notions of "directing" and "controlling." You'll find that the word *manager* is increasingly being replaced in conversations by such terms as *coordinator*, *coach*, or *team leader*.

Whatever the label used, someone who is an **effective manager** helps other people achieve both high performance and job satisfaction. This definition focuses attention on two key outcomes, or dependent variables, that are important in OB. The first is **task performance**. Think of this as the quality and quantity of the work produced or the services provided by an individual, team or work unit, or organization as a whole. The second is **job satisfaction**. It indicates how people feel about their work and the work setting.

OB is quite clear that managers and team leaders should be held accountable for both task performance and job satisfaction. Performance pretty much speaks for itself. Satisfaction might give you some pause for thought. But just as a valuable machine should not be allowed to break down for lack of proper maintenance, the talents and enthusiasm of an organization's workforce should never be lost or compromised for lack of proper care. In this sense, taking care of job satisfaction today can be considered an investment in tomorrow's performance potential.

The Management Process

Anyone serving as a manager or team leader faces a challenging and complicated job. The nature of managerial work is often described and taught through the four functions shown in ▦ **Figure 1.4**—planning, organizing, leading, and controlling. These functions make up the **management process** and involve the following responsibilities.

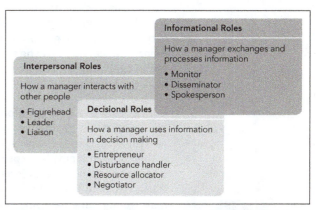

Four functions of management

- **Planning.** Defining goals, setting specific performance objectives, and identifying the actions needed to achieve them.
- **Organizing.** Creating work structures and systems, and arranging resources to accomplish goals and objectives.
- **Leading.** Instilling enthusiasm by communicating with others, motivating them to work hard, and maintaining good interpersonal relations.
- **Controlling.** Ensuring that things go well by monitoring performance and taking corrective action as necessary.

See **FIGURE 1.4**
The management process of planning, organizing, leading, and controlling

In what has become a classic study, Henry Mintzberg described how managers enact the management process in a busy, hectic, and challenging work context where they are move among many tasks and face many interruptions.[18] He went on to point out that the four management functions are fulfilled more simultaneously than step-by-step. They are also accomplished while a manager acts out the set of ten managerial roles shown in ▦ **Figure 1.5**.

A manager's *interpersonal roles* involve working directly with other people, hosting and attending official ceremonies (figurehead), creating enthusiasm and serving people's needs (leader), and maintaining contacts with important people and groups (liaison). The *informational roles* involve managers exchanging information with other people, seeking relevant information (monitor), sharing it with insiders (disseminator), and sharing it with outsiders (spokesperson). A manager's *decisional roles* involve making decisions that affect other people, seeking problems to solve and opportunities to explore (entrepreneur), helping to resolve conflicts (disturbance handler), allocating resources to various uses (resource allocator), and negotiating with other parties (negotiator).

See **FIGURE 1.5**
Mintzberg's ten roles of effective managers

Essential Managerial Skills

We all need skills to do well in work and life. It's no different for managers and team leaders—it takes skill to perform well. Formally stated, a **skill** is an ability to translate knowledge into action that results in a desired performance. Robert Katz divides the essential managerial skills into three categories: technical, human, and conceptual.[19]

Technical Skills A **technical skill** is an ability to perform specialized tasks using knowledge or expertise gained from education or experience. A good example is skill in using the latest communication and information technologies. In the high-tech workplaces of today, technical proficiency in database management, spreadsheet analysis, presentation software, video chats and conferencing, and social media is often a hiring prerequisite. It's also helpful to think "skills" in respect to your college major. Recruiters today don't just want to know that you are a marketing or finance or MIS major with high grades. They want to know what skills in the major you are going to bring with you to the job.

Human Skills Central to all aspects of managerial work and team leadership are **human skills**, or the ability to work well with other people. They show up as a spirit of trust, enthusiasm, and genuine involvement in interpersonal relationships. A person with good human skills will have a high degree of self-awareness and a capacity for understanding or empathizing with the feelings of others. People with this skill are able to interact well with others, engage in persuasive communications, and deal successfully with disagreements and conflicts.

A manager or team leader's human skills should contain a strong base of **emotional intelligence** (EI). As defined by Daniel Goleman, EI is the ability to understand and manage emotions well, both personally and in relationships with others.[20] The building blocks for emotional intelligence are:

- *Self-awareness*—ability to understand your own moods and emotions
- *Self-regulation*—ability to think before acting and to control bad impulses
- *Motivation*—ability to work hard and persevere
- *Empathy*—ability to understand the emotions of others
- *Social skill*—ability to gain rapport with others and build good relationships

Human skills in emotional intelligence and interpersonal relationships are essential to success in each of the managerial activities and roles previously discussed. If you don't have the human skills you can't connect with other people in a positive way. Managers and team leaders need these skills to develop, maintain, and work well with a wide variety of people, both inside and outside the organization.[21] These include *task networks* of specific job-related contacts, *career networks* of career guidance and opportunity resources, and *social networks* of trustworthy friends and peers.[22] It can be said in this sense that strong human skills are the pathways to obtain **social capital** in the form of relationships and networks that can be called upon as needed to get work done through other people.

Conceptual Skills In addition to technical and human skills, managers should be able to view the organization or situation as a whole so that problems are always solved for the benefit of everyone concerned. This capacity to think analytically and solve complex and sometimes ambiguous problems is a **conceptual skill**. It involves the ability to see and understand how systems work and how their parts are interrelated, including human dynamics. Conceptual skill is used to identify problems and opportunities, gather and interpret relevant information, and make good problem-solving decisions.

One final point about Katz's model of essential managerial skills is worth thinking about. He suggests that the relative importance of these skills varies across the different levels of management. Technical skills are considered more important at entry levels, where supervisors and team leaders must deal with job-specific problems. Senior executives require more conceptual skills as they face more complex problems and deal with strategic issues related to organizational mission and fitness. Human skills, which are strongly grounded in the foundations of organizational behavior, are consistently important across all managerial levels.

Ethical Management

Having managerial and leadership skills is one thing; using them correctly to get things done in organizations is quite another. And when it comes to ethics and morality, scholar Archie B. Carroll draws a distinction between immoral managers, amoral managers, and moral managers.[23]

The **immoral manager** essentially chooses to behave unethically. She or he doesn't subscribe to any ethical principles, making decisions and acting to gain best personal advantage. Perhaps the best examples are disgraced executives such as Bernard Madoff, whose unethical acts made national and world headlines. The **amoral manager**, by contrast, acts unethically at times but does so unintentionally. This manager fails to consider the ethics of a decision or behavior. Unintentional ethical lapses that we all must guard against include prejudice from unconscious stereotypes and attitudes, showing bias based on in-group favoritism, and claiming too much personal credit for performance accomplishments.[24] The **moral manager** incorporates ethical principles and goals into his or her personal behavior. Ethical behavior is a goal, a standard, and even a matter of routine; ethical reasoning is part of every decision, not just an occasional afterthought.

Carroll believes that the majority of managers tend to act amorally. If this is true, and because we also know immoral managers are around, it is very important to understand personal responsibilities for everyday ethical behavior and leadership. All organization members can and should be ethical leaders. This includes always acting as ethical role models and being willing to take stands in the face of unethical behavior by those above, below, and around them.

A review article by Terry Thomas and his colleagues describes how the "ethics center of gravity" shown in ▣ **Figure 1.6** can be moved positively through moral leadership or negatively through amoral leadership.[25] In this view, a moral manager or moral leader always sets an ethics example, communicates ethics values, and champions **ethics mindfulness**. This is defined as an "enriched awareness" that causes one to behave with an ethical consciousness from one decision or behavioral event to another.

Moral managers and moral leaders contribute to the "virtuous shift" shown in Figure 1.6. They help create an organizational culture in which people encourage one another to act ethically as a matter of routine. One of the themes of this book, as reflected in the "Ethics in OB" feature in each chapter, is that ethics is the responsibility of everyone in the organization.

See **FIGURE 1.6 Moral leadership, ethics mindfulness, and the virtuous shift**

Source: Developed from Terry Thomas, John R. Schermerhorn Jr., and John W. Dinehart, "Strategic Leadership of Ethical Behavior in Business," *Academy of Management Executive* 18 (May 2004), pp. 56–66.]

Leadership and Organizational Behavior

The Leadership Process

The job of a manager or team leader has never been more demanding than it is in today's dynamic and hypercompetitive work environments. But the fact is, not all managers are good leaders. And even if they were, the challenges facing organizations are too complex for managers alone to resolve. Organizations today require leadership at all levels, not just from those holding the formal titles.

Leadership occurs when leaders and followers work together to advance change that benefits the mission and vision of the organization. Leadership is a *process*, not just the leader's behavior. As shown in ▣ **Figure 1.7**, it requires leaders and followers to partner in jointly producing leadership outcomes. Effective following is an essential—perhaps the most important part—of the **leadership process**. Without followers there can be no leaders.

See **FIGURE 1.7 The leadership process**

Interestingly, leadership doesn't always have to be intentional. Sometimes others follow because they see leadership potential in someone, or they like what a person says and how they say it. This means that leadership is not only downward influence, it also involves influencing upward and side to side. You can be a leader by convincing higher management to adopt new practices suggested from your level. You can be a leader among your peers by becoming the person people turn to for advice, support, or direction. And, remember the notion of the manager as "coach" and "coordinator"? Every time you act in ways that fit these descriptions, there's no doubt you're being a leader.

Effective Leaders

Effective leaders contribute to the leadership process by using their influence to advance positive outcomes. Leaders are those who are willing to proactively envision new ways of doing things and take initiative in promoting needed changes in organizations. Organizations are full of leaders, managers and non-managers alike. These are people who get listened to by their peers, their bosses, and people below and higher up in the organization.

Leaders know that competence and reputation, being an effective communicator, and developing relationships and influence are vital to their success. Therefore they work to develop these skills. Effective leaders, for example, frame communication in ways that others will listen. **Framing** in this setting means tailoring communication in ways to encourage certain interpretations and discourage others. An effective leader recognizes that focusing on organizational interest (e.g., "We can increase productivity if we give people more time to rest and rejuvenate") will be a more effective frame than focusing on self-interest (e.g., "We've been working too hard and want time off").

Effective leaders also know how to build relationships. They do what they can to be trustworthy, reliable, and respectful in not sharing or spreading information inappropriately. They understand that relationships are developed through **social exchange**, so they manage exchange processes and reciprocity to build partnerships and networks. They help others out when needed because they know that the **law of reciprocity** will invoke a sense of obligation by the other to return the favor ("if I do something for you, you will do something for me later if I need it"). This helps them build networks and relationships that serve as a key source of leadership influence.

Leaders succeed when people follow them not because they have to, but because they *want* to. They are followed because others see the value of their ideas and suggestions. This positive influence emerges from leaders' competence, persuasiveness, and human skills. Managers and team leaders, by virtue of their positions of authority, have the opportunity to act as leaders. But they don't always do so, or do so successfully. The "Finding the Leader in You" feature in each chapter is designed to provide role models and get you thinking about developing your leadership potential.

Effective Followers

Effective followers are those who work *with* leaders to produce positive outcomes. They support leaders by being willing to collaborate and defer when needed, rather than working against leaders or trying to undermine their power. At the same time, effective followers are not blindly obedient or subservient and passive. You are being an effective follower when you assume responsibility for telling leaders information they need to know, and not avoiding responsibility for passing along the "bad" news as well as the "good" news.

The best followers do not have to be micromanaged. They take responsibility for their own attitudes and behaviors and view themselves as partners with leaders in the leadership process. They help the manager by avoiding engaging in **upward delegation**, or passing their problems on to managers and burdening them with even more work. The best followers bring solutions along with problems. Overall, they try to identify things that could cause problems for leaders and then work to seek solutions before the problems escalate into big issues.

Organizations today are undergoing major transitions. They require successful leadership at all levels, and the need for more effective followership is on the rise. Followers today cannot get away with shrugging off responsibility or passing along blame as they might have in the past. They are expected to question and challenge leaders when needed, and to bring new ideas and creativity to their work. But to do so effectively they must act with respect, and keep the higher purpose in mind—the focus is on working with leaders in ways that advance the mission and purpose of the organization. And when leaders and followers partner effectively together, the result is a more meaningful, engaging and fulfilling work experience.

WP LS Go to your WileyPLUS Learning Space course for video episodes, examples, art, tables, Concept Checks, practice, and resources that will help you succeed in this course.

DIVERSITY, PERSONALITY, AND VALUES

2

WP LS Go to your WileyPLUS Learning Space course for video episodes, examples, art, tables, Concept Checks, practice, and resources that will help you succeed in this course.

Individual Differences and Diversity

People are complex. You approach a situation one way, and someone else may approach it quite differently. These differences among people can make it difficult to predict and understand individual behavior in relationships, teams, and organizations. They also contribute to what makes the study of organizational behavior so fascinating. The term **individual differences** refers to the ways in which people are similar and dissimilar in personal characteristics.

The mix of individual differences in organizations creates workforce diversity. Some of these differences are easily observable and often demographic. They represent **surface-level diversity** based on quite visible physical attributes such as ethnicity, race, sex, age, and abilities. Other individual differences—such as personalities, values, and attitudes—are more psychologically innate and less immediately visible. They represent **deep-level diversity** that may take time and effort to understand.[1]

Regardless of the level, diversity issues are of great interest in OB. Women, for example, now lead global companies such as PepsiCo, Xerox, IBM, and Kraft. But they still hold only 3 percent of top jobs in American firms.[2] Why have so few women so far made it to the top?[3] Society is becoming more diverse in its racial and ethnic makeup. But a research study found that résumés of people with white-sounding first names—such as Brett—received 50 percent more responses from potential employers than those with black-sounding first names—such as Kareem.[4] How can these results be explained given that the résumés were created equal?

Self-Concept, Self-Awareness, and Awareness of Others

To best understand and deal well with individual differences and diversity, it only makes sense that it's important to have a strong sense of self. The **self-concept** is the view individuals have of themselves as physical, social, and spiritual or moral beings.[5] It is a way of recognizing oneself as a distinct human being. Two factors that increase awareness of individual differences—our own and others—are self-awareness and awareness of others. **Self-awareness** means being aware of our own behaviors, preferences, styles, biases, personalities, and so on. **Awareness of others** means being aware of these same things in others.

A person's self concept shows up in **self-esteem**, a belief about one's own worth based on an overall self-evaluation.[6] People high in self-esteem see themselves as capable, worthwhile, and acceptable; they tend to have few doubts about themselves. People who are low in self-esteem are full of self-doubt and are often afraid to act because of it. Someone's self-concept is also displayed in **self-efficacy**, sometimes called the *effectance motive*, which is a more specific version of self-esteem. It is an individual's belief about the likelihood of successfully completing a specific task. You could have high self-esteem and yet have a feeling of low self-efficacy about performing a certain task, such as public speaking.

What determines the development of the self? How, for example, can we explain **prejudice** in the form of negative, irrational, and superior opinions and attitudes toward persons who are different from ourselves? Perhaps you have heard someone say "She acts like her mother," or "Bobby is the way he is because of the way he was raised." These two comments illustrate the *nature/nurture controversy*: Are we the way we are because of *heredity*—genetic endowment, or because of *environment*—the cultural places and situations in which we have been raised and live? It is most likely that these two forces act in combination, with heredity setting the limits and environment determining how a person develops within them.[7]

Valuing–or Not Valuing–Diversity

The U.S. population is not just getting bigger; it is more racially and ethnically diverse, and it is getting older. The U.S. Census Bureau predicts that the country will become a true plurality by 2060, with no one ethnic or racial group being in the majority. Hispanics are now the fastest growing community and by 2060 will constitute one-third of the population. America is also growing demographically older; by 2050 one in five people will be aged 65-plus.[8] What do these and other such demographic trends mean for everyday living, for our personal relationships, for the way we work?

More and more organizations are embracing policies and practices to value diversity in their workforces as a way to increase competitiveness, build talent, expand organizational capabilities, and enhance access to diverse customers.[9] Individual differences are fast becoming valued for the strengths that diversity can bring to a workforce.[10] If you need creativity, for example, do you turn to people who think like you or to people who can help you think differently? Moreover, when you need to understand something you have never encountered before, such as another culture or an emerging market, do you turn to people who are the same as you or would you want access to co-workers familiar with those cultures?

The flip side of valuing diversity is outright **discrimination** against women and minorities in the workplace. It occurs when minority members are unfairly treated and denied the full benefits of organizational membership. An example is when a manager fabricates reasons not to interview a minority job candidate, or refuses to promote a working mother on the belief that "she has too many parenting responsibilities to do a good job at this level." Such thinking underlies a form of discrimination called the **glass ceiling effect**, an invisible barrier or "ceiling" that prevents women and minorities from rising above a certain level of organizational responsibility.[11]

Diversity Issues in the Workplace

Race and Ethnicity The value of heterogeneous perspectives within teams and organizations can be gained from multicultural workforces with a rich mix of racial and ethnic diversity. And **Title VII of the Civil Rights Act of 1964** protects individuals against employment discrimination on the basis of race and ethnicity, as well as national origin, sex, and religion. It applies to employers with 15 or more employees, including state and local governments.

According to Title VII, equal employment opportunity cannot be denied any person because of his/her racial group or perceived racial group, his/her race-linked characteristics (e.g., hair texture, color, facial features), or because of his/her marriage to or association with someone of a particular race or color. It also prohibits employment decisions based on stereotypes and assumptions about abilities, traits, or the performance of individuals of certain racial groups. But, as noted earlier in the research showing prejudice in job searches against person's with black-sounding first names, it's still an imperfect world.[12]

Gender Women are bringing not just task expertise but valuable interpersonal skills and styles to the workplace, such as listening and collaborative skills, and abilities to multitask and synthesize alternative viewpoints effectively and quickly. Research shows that companies with a higher percentage of female board directors and corporate officers, on average, financially outperform companies with the lowest percentages by significant margins.[13] The presence of women leaders is also beneficial because they encourage more women in the pipeline and act as role models and mentors for younger women. Moreover, the presence of women leaders sends important signals that an organization has a broad and deep talent pool, and offers an inclusive workplace.

Despite these benefits to organizations and anti-discrimination protections afforded them under Title VII of the U.S. Civil Rights Act of 1964, women have not penetrated the highest level of organizational leadership to the extent we would expect. Even worse, many are still abandoning corporate careers just as they are positioned to attain higher-level responsibilities. The term **leaking pipeline** was coined by Professor Lynda Gratton and colleagues of the London Business School to describe this phenomenon.[14] In one study of 61 organizations operating in 12 European countries, they found that the number of women decreases the more senior the roles become.

The nonprofit research organization Catalyst reports that women consistently identify gender stereotypes as a significant barrier to advancement and cause for the leaking pipeline.[15] They describe a "think-leader-think-male" mind-set in which men are largely seen as leaders by default because of stereotypically masculine "take charge" skills such as influencing superiors and problem solving. Women, by contrast are stereotyped for "caretaking skills" such as supporting and encouraging others. This creates what is called a **leadership double bind** for women. If they conform to the stereotype they are seen as weak, and if they go against the stereotype they are breaking norms of femininity. As some describe it, female leaders are "damned if they do, doomed if they don't."[16] Organizations can help address these stereotypes by creating workplaces that are more meaningful and satisfying to successful women, such as cultures that are less command-and-control and status-based. As *Catalyst* reports, "Ultimately, it is not women's leadership styles that need to change but the structures and perceptions that must keep up with today's changing times."[17]

Sexual Orientation The first U.S. corporation to add sexual orientation to its nondiscrimination policy did so 30 years ago. That company was AT&T and its chairman, John DeButts, said that his company would "respect the human rights of our employees."[18] Although employment discrimination based on sexual orientation or gender identity is not yet protected by federal legislation, such legislation has been proposed to Congress (the Employment Non-Discrimination Act), and individuals are protected from sexual harassment bullying at work and school.[19] Also, many states now have executive orders protecting the rights of lesbian, gay, bisexual, and transgender workers.[20]

Regardless of weak and incomplete legislative support, the workplace is beginning to improve for gay Americans. Harris polling shows that 78 percent of heterosexual adults in the United States agree that how an employee performs at his or her job should be the standard for judging an employee, not one's sexual orientation, while 62 percent agree that all employees are entitled to equal benefits on the job, such as health insurance for partners or spouses.[21]

Age Age or generational diversity is affecting the workplace like never before. Population demographics and economic trends have created a workforce where Millennials, Gen Xers, and Baby Boomers have to work and get along together. Nonetheless, there are points of conflict based on age stereotypes. Baby Boomers may view Millennials as feeling a sense of entitlement and not being hard working due to the way they dress and their interest in flexible hours. Millennials may view Baby Boomers and Gen Xers as more concerned about the hours they work than what they produce.[22]

The generational mix in organizations provides an excellent example of how diversity can deliver benefits. For example, Millennials seem to embrace gender equality and sexual, cultural, and racial diversity more than any previous generation, and they bring these values to work. Millennials also have an appreciation for community and collaboration. They can help create a more relaxed workplace that reduces some of the problems that come from too much focus on status and hierarchy. At the same time, Boomers and Gen Xers bring a wealth of experience, dedication, and commitment that contribute to productivity, and a sense of professionalism that is benefiting their younger counterparts.[23]

Ability In recent years the "disability rights movement" has been working to bring attention and support to the needs of disabled workers.[24] Estimates indicate that over 50 million Americans have one or more physical or mental disabilities, and studies show these workers do their jobs as well as, or better than, nondisabled workers. Despite this, nearly three-quarters of severely disabled persons are reported to be unemployed, and almost 80 percent of those with disabilities say they want to work.[25]

The passage of the **Americans with Disabilities Act** (ADA) in 1990 has been a significant catalyst in advancing their efforts. The focus of the ADA is to eliminate employers' practices that treat people with disabilities unnecessarily different. The ADA has helped to generate a more inclusive climate in which organizations are reaching out more to people with disabilities. The most visible changes from the ADA have been in issues of **universal design**—the practice of designing products, buildings, public spaces, and programs to be usable by the greatest number of people. You may see this in your own college or university's actions to make their campus and classrooms more accessible.[26]

The disability rights movement is working passionately to advance a redefinition of what it means to be disabled in U.S. society. The goal is to overcome the stigmas attached to disability. A **stigma** is a phenomenon whereby an individual with an attribute that is deeply discredited by his or her society is rejected as a result of the attribute. Because of stigmas, many are reluctant to seek coverage under the ADA because they do not want to experience discrimination in the form of stigmas.

Diversity and Social Identity

Although in the past many organizations addressed the issue of diversity from the standpoint of compliance with legal mandates, the focus is now on policies and practices of inclusion.[27] This new focus represents a shift in thinking about how organizations can create inclusive cultures for everyone.[28]

The move from compliance to inclusion occurred primarily because employers began to learn that although they were able to recruit diverse individuals, they were not able to retain them. In work settings where upper ranks of organizations continued to be mostly composed of white males, difficult questions started to be asked and answered: Do employees in all groups and categories feel comfortable and welcomed in the organization? Do they feel included, and do they experience the environment as inclusive?[29]

Questions like those just posed are the focus of **social identity theory** as developed by social psychologists Henri Tajfel and John Turner in their quest to understand the psychological basis of discrimination.[30] According to the theory, individuals have not one but multiple "personal selves." Which self is activated depends on the group with which the person identifies. The mere act of identifying, or "categorizing," oneself as a member of a group will generate favoritism toward that group, and this favoritism is displayed in the form of "in-group" enhancement. This in-group favoritism occurs *at the expense of* the out-group. In terms of diversity, social identity theory suggests that simply having diversity in groups makes that identity salient in peoples' minds. Individuals engage these identities and experience feelings of **in-group membership** and **out-group membership**.

The implications of social identity theory are straightforward. When organizations have strong identities formed around in-group and out-group categorizations based on diversity, this will work against a feeling of inclusion. Such in-group and out-group categorizations can be subtle but powerful, and they may be most noticeable to those in the "out-group" category. Organizations may not intend to create discriminatory environments, but when only a few members of a group are present, this may evoke a strong out-group identity. They may end up feeling uncomfortable and less a part of the organization. Managers and organizations try to deal with all this by creating work cultures and environments that welcome and embrace inclusion. The concept of valuing diversity emphasizes an appreciation of differences while creating a workplace where everyone feels valued and accepted.[31]

Personality

The term **personality** encompasses the overall combination of characteristics that capture the unique nature of a person as that person reacts to and interacts with others. It combines a set of physical and mental characteristics that reflect how a person looks, thinks, acts, and feels. Think of yourself, and of your family and friends. A key part of how you interact with others depends on your own and their personalities, doesn't it? If you have a friend who has a sensitive personality, do you interact with that person differently than you do with a friend or family member who likes to joke around?

Sometimes attempts are made to measure personality with questionnaires or special tests. Frequently, personality can be inferred from behavior alone. Either way, personality is an important individual characteristic to understand. It helps us identify predictable interplays between people's individual differences and their tendencies to behave in certain ways.

Big Five Personality Traits

Numerous lists of **personality traits**—enduring characteristics describing an individual's behavior—have been developed, and used in OB research. A key starting point is to consider the personality dimensions known as the "Big Five Model":[32]

- *Extraversion*—the degree to which someone is outgoing, sociable, and assertive. An extravert is comfortable and confident in interpersonal relationships; an introvert is more withdrawn and reserved.
- *Agreeableness*—the degree to which someone is good-natured, cooperative, and trusting. An agreeable person gets along well with others; a disagreeable person is a source of conflict and discomfort for others.
- *Conscientiousness*—the degree to which someone is responsible, dependable, and careful. A conscientious person focuses on what can be accomplished and meets commitments; a

person who lacks conscientiousness is careless, often trying to do too much and failing, or doing little.

- *Emotional stability*—the degree to which someone is relaxed, secure, and unworried. A person who is emotionally stable is calm and confident; a person lacking in emotional stability is anxious, nervous, and tense.

- *Openness to experience*—the degree to which someone is curious, open to new ideas, and imaginative. An open person is broad-minded, receptive to new things, and comfortable with change; a person who lacks openness is narrow-minded, has few interests, and is resistant to change.

A considerable body of literature links the personality dimensions of the Big Five model with behavior at work and in life overall. For example, conscientiousness is a good predictor of job performance for most occupations, and extraversion is often associated with success in management and sales. Indications are that extraverts tend to be happier than introverts in their lives overall, that conscientious people tend to be less risky, and that those more open to experience are more creative.[33]

You can easily spot the Big Five personality traits in people with whom you work, study, and socialize. But don't forget that they also apply to you. Others form impressions of your personality, and respond to it, just as you do in response to theirs. Managers often use these and other personality judgments when making job assignments, building teams, and otherwise engaging in the daily social give-and-take of work.

Social Traits

Social traits are surface-level traits that reflect the way a person appears to others when interacting in various social settings. A person's **problem-solving style**, based on the work of noted psychologist Carl Jung, is a good example. It reflects the way someone goes about gathering and evaluating information in solving problems and making decisions. Problem-solving styles are most frequently measured by the typically 100-item *Myers-Briggs Type Indicator (MBTI)*, which asks individuals how they usually act or feel in specific situations. The MBTI is often used by organizations to improve self-awareness of participants in management development programs.[34]

The first component in Jung's typology, information gathering, involves getting and organizing data for use. Styles of information gathering vary from sensation to intuitive. *Sensation-type individuals* prefer routine and order and emphasize well-defined details in gathering information; they would rather work with known facts than look for possibilities. By contrast, *intuitive-type individuals* prefer the "big picture." They like solving new problems, dislike routine, and would rather look for possibilities than work with facts.

The second component of problem solving, evaluation, involves making judgments about how to deal with information once it has been collected. Styles of information evaluation vary from an emphasis on feeling to an emphasis on thinking. *Feeling- type individuals* are oriented toward conformity and try to accommodate themselves to other people. They try to avoid problems that may result in disagreements. *Thinking-type individuals* use reason and intellect to deal with problems and downplay emotions.

When the two dimensions of information gathering and evaluation are combined, four basic problem-solving styles can be identified. As shown in ■ **Figure 2.1**, people can be classified into combinations of sensation-feeling (SF), intuitive-feeling (IF), sensation-thinking (ST), and intuitive-thinking (IT).

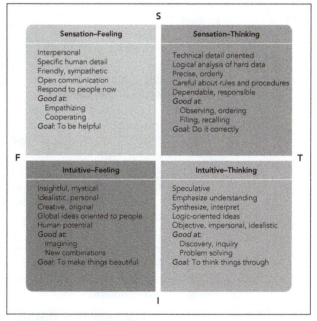

Research indicates that there is a fit between the styles of individuals and the kinds of decisions they prefer. For example, STs (sensation-thinkers) prefer analytical strategies—those that emphasize detail and method. IFs (intuitive-feelers) prefer intuitive strategies—those that emphasize an overall pattern and fit. Not surprisingly, mixed styles (sensation-feelers or intuitive-thinkers) select both analytical and intuitive strategies. Other findings also indicate that

 See **FIGURE 2.1 Four problem-solving styles of the Jungian typology**

15

thinkers tend to have higher motivation than do feelers, and that individuals who emphasize sensations tend to have higher job satisfaction than do intuitives. These and other findings suggest a number of basic differences among different problem-solving styles, emphasizing the importance of fitting such styles with a task's information processing and evaluation requirements.[35]

Personal Conception Traits

What are known as **personal conception traits** represent various ways people think about their social and physical setting, their major beliefs, and personal orientations toward a range of issues. Personal conception traits often discussed in the work context include locus of control, proactive personality, authoritarianism/dogmatism, Machiavellianism, and self-monitoring.

Information processing	Internals make more attempts to acquire information, are less satisfied with the amount of information they possess, and are better at utilizing information.
Job satisfaction	Internals are generally more satisfied, less alienated, less rootless, and there is a stronger job satisfaction/performance relationship for them.
Performance	Internals perform better on learning and problem-solving tasks when performance leads to valued rewards.
Self-control, risk, and anxiety	Internals exhibit greater self-control, are more cautious, engage in less risky behavior, and are less anxious.
Motivation, expectancies, and results	Internals display greater work motivation, see a stronger relationship between what they do and what happens to them, expect that working hard leads to good performance, and feel more control over their time.
Response to others	Internals are more independent, more reliant on their own judgment, and less susceptible to the influence of others; they are more likely to accept information on its merit.

See **FIGURE 2.2 Ways in which internal locus of control differs from external locus of control**

Locus of Control The extent to which a person feels able to control his or her own life is known as **locus of control**.[36] People have personal conceptions about whether events are controlled primarily by themselves, which indicates an internal orientation, or by outside forces, such as their social and physical environment, which indicates an external orientation. *Internals*, or persons with an internal locus of control, believe that they control their own fate or destiny. In contrast, *externals*, or persons with an external locus of control, believe that much of what happens to them is beyond their control and is determined by environmental forces (such as fate).

In general, externals are more extraverted in their interpersonal relationships and are more oriented toward the world around them. Internals tend to be more introverted and are more oriented toward their own feelings and ideas. **Figure 2.2** suggests that internals tend to do better on tasks requiring complex information processing and learning as well as initiative.

Proactive Personality Some people in organizations are passive recipients when faced with constraints, whereas others take direct and intentional action to change their circumstances. The disposition that identifies whether or not individuals act to influence their environments is known as **proactive personality**. Individuals with high proactive personalities identify opportunities and act on them, show initiative, take action, and persevere until meaningful change occurs. Those low in proactivity are the opposite. They fail to identify—let alone seize—opportunities to change things. They tend to be passive and reactive, preferring to adapt to circumstances rather than change them.[37]

In the ever more demanding world of work, many employers are seeking individuals with more proactive qualities—individuals willing to take initiative and engage in proactive problem solving. Research supports this, showing that proactive personality is positively related to job performance, creativity, leadership, and career success. Other studies have shown that proactive personality is related to team effectiveness and entrepreneurship. Moreover, when organizations try to make positive and innovative change, these changes have more positive effects for proactive individuals—they are more involved and more receptive to change. This research is showing that proactive personality is an important and desirable element in today's work environment.

Authoritarianism/Dogmatism Both authoritarianism and dogmatism as personal conception traits deal with the rigidity of someone's beliefs. A person high in **authoritarianism** tends to adhere rigidly to conventional values and to obey recognized authority. This person is concerned with toughness and power and opposes the use of subjective feelings. Highly authoritarian individuals present a special problem because they can be so eager to comply with directives from authority figures that they end up willing to behave unethically.[38]

An individual high in **dogmatism** sees the world as a threatening place. This person regards legitimate authority as absolute, and accepts or rejects others according to how much they agree with accepted authority. Superiors who possess these latter traits tend to be rigid and closed. At the same time, dogmatic subordinates tend to want certainty imposed on them.

Machiavellianism The very name of the sixteenth-century author Niccolo Machiavelli often evokes visions of someone who acts with guile, deceit, and opportunism. Machiavelli earned his place in history by writing *The Prince*, a nobleman's guide to the acquisition and use of power.[39] The subject of Machiavelli's book is manipulation as the basic means of gaining and keeping control of others. From its pages emerges the personality profile of **Machiavellianism**—the practice of viewing and manipulating others purely for personal gain.

Persons high in Machiavellianism approach situations logically and thoughtfully, and are even capable of lying to achieve personal goals.[40] They are rarely swayed by loyalty, friendships, past promises, or the opinions of others, and they are skilled at influencing others. They can also be expected to take control and try to exploit loosely structured environmental situations but will perform in a perfunctory, even detached, manner in highly structured situations. Where the situation permits, they might be expected to do or say whatever it takes to get their way. Those low in Machiavellianism, by contrast, tend to be more strongly guided by ethical considerations and are less likely to lie, cheat, or get away with lying or cheating.

Self-Monitoring **Self-monitoring** reflects a person's ability to adjust his or her behavior to external, situational (environmental) factors.[41] High self-monitors are sensitive to external cues and tend to behave differently in different situations. High self-monitors can present a very different appearance from their true self. In contrast, low self-monitors, are less able to disguise their behaviors—"What you see is what you get." There is also evidence that high self-monitors are closely attuned to the behavior of others and conform more readily than do low self-monitors.[42] Thus, they appear flexible and may be especially good at adjusting their behavior to fit different kinds of situations and the people in them.

Personality and Stress

An individual's personality can also be described in terms of **emotional adjustment traits** that indicate how one handles emotional distress or displays unacceptable acts, such as impatience, irritability, or aggression.[43] Among these, a personality with **Type A orientation** is characterized by impatience, desire for achievement, and perfectionism. In contrast, those with a **Type B orientation** are characterized as more easygoing and less competitive in relation to daily events.[44] Type A people tend to work fast and to be abrupt, uncomfortable, irritable, and aggressive. Such tendencies may show up as "obsessive" behavior. When carried to the extreme, it may lead to greater concerns for details than for results, resistance to change, and overzealous attempts to exert control. In contrast, Type B people tend to be much more laid back and patient in their relationships with others.

Type A Orientation and Stress

In one survey of college graduates, 31 percent reported working over 50 hours per week, 60 percent rushed meals and 34 percent ate lunches "on the run," and 47 percent of those under 35 and 28 percent of those over 35 had feelings of job burnout. A study by the Society for Human Resources Management found that 70 percent of those surveyed worked over and above scheduled hours, including putting in extra time on the weekends; over 50 percent said that the pressure to do the extra work was "self-imposed."[45]

The situations just described all evidence the presence of **stress** as a state of internal tension experienced by individuals who perceive themselves as facing extraordinary demands, constraints, or opportunities.[46] If you look back to the discussion of Type A and Type B personalities, the fact is that Type As often bring stress upon themselves. They may even do this in situations others may find relatively stress free. You can spot Type A personality tendencies in yourself and others through the following patterns of behavior:

- Always moving, walking, and eating rapidly
- Acting impatient, hurrying others, put off by waiting
- Doing, or trying to do, several things at once
- Feeling guilty when relaxing
- Hurrying or interrupting the speech of others[47]

Work and Life Stressors

Not all stress that we experience is personality driven. Any variety of things can cause stress for individuals. Some stressors can be traced directly to what people experience in the workplace, whereas others derive from life situations and nonwork factors.

Work Stressors There is no doubt that work can be stressful and job demands can sometimes disrupt one's work–life balance. Work stressors can arise from excessively high or low task demands, role conflicts or ambiguities, poor interpersonal relations, career progress that is either too slow or too fast, and more. The following is a list of common stressors:

- *Task demands*—being asked to do too much or being asked to do too little
- *Role ambiguities*—not knowing what one is expected to do or how work performance is evaluated
- *Role conflicts*—feeling unable to satisfy multiple, possibly conflicting, performance expectations
- *Ethical dilemmas*—being asked to do things that violate the law or personal values
- *Interpersonal problems*—experiencing bad relationships or working with others with whom one does not get along
- *Career developments*—moving too fast and feeling stretched; moving too slowly and feeling stuck on a plateau
- *Physical setting*—being bothered by noise, lack of privacy, pollution, or other unpleasant working conditions

Life Stressors Life stressors such as family events (e.g., the birth of a new child), economic difficulties (e.g., loss of income by a spouse), and personal affairs (e.g., a separation or divorce) can all be extremely stressful. That pretty much goes without saying. But it's also true that people can easily suffer from *spillover effects* that result when forces in their personal lives spill over to affect them at work or when forces at work spill over to affect their personal lives. Because it is often difficult to completely separate work and nonwork lives, especially in this age of smart devices that keep us continually in touch with work and personal affairs, life stressors and spillover effects are highly significant.

Outcomes of Stress

The stress we experience at work or in personal affairs isn't always negative. Scholars talk about two types of stress.[48] The first is **eustress**—constructive stress that results in positive outcomes. It occurs when moderate—not extreme—stress levels prompt things like increased work effort, greater creativity, and more diligence. You may know such stress as the tension that causes you to study hard before exams, pay attention in class, and complete assignments on time. The second type of stress is **distress**—destructive stress that turns out to be dysfunctional for both the individual. Key symptoms of individuals suffering distress are changes from regular attendance to absenteeism, from punctuality to tardiness, from diligent work to careless work, from a positive attitude to a negative attitude, from openness to change to resistance to change, or from cooperation to hostility.

One possible outcome of extended distress, for example, is the **job burnout** that shows up as loss of interest in and satisfaction with a job due to stressful working conditions. Someone who is "burned out" feels emotionally and physically exhausted, and is less able to deal positively with work responsibilities and opportunities. More extreme reactions to distress include bullying of co-workers and even workplace violence. It is also clear that too much stress can overload and break down a person's physical and mental systems, resulting in absenteeism, turnover, errors, accidents, dissatisfaction, reduced performance, unethical behavior, and even illness.[49]

Approaches to Managing Stress

Coping Mechanisms Along with rising sensitivities to stress in the workplace, interest is also growing in how to manage, or *cope*, with distress. **Coping** is a response or reaction to distress that has occurred or is threatened. It involves cognitive and behavioral efforts to master, reduce, or tolerate the demands created by the stressful situation.

There are two major types of coping mechanisms. **Problem-focused coping** strategies try to manage the problem that is causing the distress. Indicators of this type of coping are comments like "I'll get the person responsible to change his or her mind," "I'll make a new plan of action and follow it," and "I'm going to stand my ground and fight for what I need." **Emotion-focused coping** strategies try to regulate the emotions drawn forth by stress. Indicators of this type of coping include comments like "I'll look for the silver lining, try to look on the bright side of things," "I'll accept the sympathy and understanding offered by others," and "I'll just try to forget the whole thing."[50]

People with different personalities tend to cope with stress in different ways. In respect to the Big Five, emotional stability has been found linked with increased use of hostile reaction, escapism/fantasy, self-blame, withdrawal, wishful thinking, passivity, and indecisiveness. People high in extraversion and optimism tend to show rational action, positive thinking, substitution, and restraint. And individuals high in openness to experience are likely to use humor in dealing with stress.

Stress Prevention Stress prevention is the best first-line strategy in the battle against stress. It involves taking action to present stress from reaching destructive levels. Work and life stressors must be recognized before one can take action to prevent their occurrence or to minimize their adverse impacts. Persons with Type A personalities, for example, may exercise self-discipline, whereas supervisors of Type A employees may try to model a lower-key, more relaxed approach to work. Family problems may be partially relieved by a change of work schedule; simply knowing that your supervisor understands your situation may also help to reduce the anxiety caused by pressing family concerns.

Personal Wellness To keep stress from reaching a destructive point, special techniques of stress management can be implemented. This process begins with the recognition of stress symptoms and continues with actions to maintain a positive performance edge. The term *wellness* is increasingly used these days. **Personal wellness** involves the pursuit of one's job and career goals with the support of a personal health promotion program. The concept recognizes individual responsibility to enhance and maintain wellness through a disciplined approach to physical and mental health. It requires attention to such factors as smoking, weight management, diet, alcohol use, and physical fitness.

Values

Values are broad preferences concerning appropriate courses of action or outcomes. They reflect a person's sense of right and wrong or what "ought" to be.[52] Statements like "Equal rights for all" and "People should be treated with respect and dignity" are indicators of values. And we recognize that values tend to influence attitudes and behavior.

Sources of Values

Parents, friends, teachers, siblings, education, experience, and external reference groups are all possible influences on individual values. Our values develop as a product of the learning and experience we encounter in the cultural setting in which we live, as learning and experiences differ from one person to another. Value differences result. Such differences are likely to be deep seated and difficult (though not impossible) to change. Many have their roots in early childhood and the way a person has been raised.[53]

Personal Values

The noted psychologist Milton Rokeach classified values into two broad categories.[54] **Terminal values** reflect a person's pref-

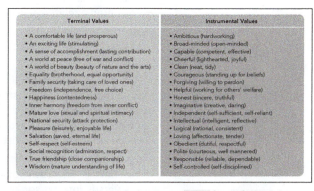

See **FIGURE 2.3 Terminal and Instrumental Values in the Rokeach value survey**

erences concerning the "ends" to be achieved; they are the goals an individual would like to achieve during his or her lifetime. **Instrumental values** reflect the "means" for achieving desired ends. They represent *how* you might go about achieving your important goals. Rokeach identifies the eighteen terminal values and eighteen instrumental values shown in ▣ **Figure 2.3**. Take a look at the list. Then ask this: What are my top five values, and what do they say about me and how I relate or work with others?

Bruce Meglino and colleagues discuss the importance of value congruence between leaders and followers.[55] It occurs when individuals express positive feelings upon encountering others who exhibit values similar to their own. When values differ, or are incongruent, conflicts over such things as goals and the means to achieve them may result. Research finds that satisfaction with a leader is greater when there is congruence among the four values of achievement, helping, honesty, and fairness.[56]

- *Achievement*—getting things done and working hard to accomplish difficult things in life
- *Helping and concern for others*—being concerned for other people and with helping others
- *Honesty*—telling the truth and doing what you feel is right
- *Fairness*—being impartial and doing what is fair for all concerned

Cultural Values

Values can also be discussed for their presence at the level of national or societal culture. In this sense, **culture** can be defined as the learned, shared way of doing things in a particular society. It is the way, for example, in which its members eat, dress, greet and treat one another, teach their children, solve everyday problems, and so on.[57] Geert Hofstede, a Dutch scholar and consultant, refers to culture as the "software of the mind," making the analogy that the mind's "hardware" is universal among human beings.[58] But the software of culture takes many different forms. We are not born with a culture; we are born into a society that teaches us its culture. And because culture is shared among people, it helps to define the boundaries between different groups and affect how their members relate to one another.

Cultures are known to vary in their underlying patterns of values, and these differences are important in OB. The way people think about such matters as achievement, wealth and material gain, risk, and change, for example, may influence how they approach work and their relationships with organizations. Increasingly now you will hear the term **cultural quotient (CQ)** used to describe someone's ability to work effectively across cultures. And it's a point well worth considering in terms of personal growth and professional development.

See **FIGURE 2.4 Sample country clusters on Hofstede's five dimensions of national values**

India	Malaysia		Japan	USA	Australia
High power distance				**Low power distance**	
Japan	Costa Rica	France		USA	Sweden
High uncertainty avoidance				**Low uncertainty avoidance**	
USA	Australia		Japan	Mexico	Thailand
Individualism				**Collectivism**	
Japan	Mexico	USA	Thailand		Sweden
Masculinity				**Femininity**	
USA	Netherlands		India		Japan
Short-term thinking				**Long-term thinking**	

One framework for understanding how value differences across national cultures was developed by the cross-cultural psychologist Hofstede. His framework is shown in **Figure 2.4** and includes these five dimensions of national culture:

- **Power distance** is the willingness of a culture to accept status and power differences among its members. It reflects the degree to which people are likely to respect hierarchy and rank in organizations. Indonesia is considered a high-power-distance culture, whereas Sweden is considered a relatively low-power-distance culture.

- **Uncertainty avoidance** is a cultural tendency toward discomfort with risk and ambiguity. It reflects the degree to which people are likely to prefer structured versus unstructured organizational situations. France is considered a high-uncertainty-avoidance culture, whereas Hong Kong is considered a low-uncertainty-avoidance culture.

- **Individualism–collectivism** is the tendency of a culture to emphasize either individual or group interests. It reflects the degree to which people are likely to prefer working as individuals or working together in groups. The United States is a highly individualistic culture, whereas Mexico is a more collectivist one.

- **Masculinity–femininity** is the tendency of a culture to value stereotypical masculine or feminine traits. It reflects the degree to which organizations emphasize competition and assertiveness versus interpersonal sensitivity and concerns for relationships. Japan is considered a very masculine culture, whereas Thailand is considered a more feminine culture.

- **Long-term/short-term orientation** is the tendency of a culture to emphasize values associated with the future, such as thrift and persistence, or values that focus largely on the present. It reflects the degree to which people and organizations adopt long-term or short-term performance horizons. South Korea is high on long-term orientation, whereas the United States is a more short-term-oriented country.[59]

The first four dimensions in Hofstede's framework were identified in an extensive study of thousands of employees of a multinational corporation operating in more than forty countries.[60] The fifth dimension, long-term/short-term orientation, was added from research using the Chinese Values Survey conducted by cross-cultural psychologist Michael Bond and his colleagues.[61] Their research suggested the cultural importance of a value they called *Confucian dynamism*, with its emphasis on persistence, the ordering of relationships, thrift, sense of shame, personal steadiness, reciprocity, protection of "face," and respect for tradition.[62]

When using the Hofstede framework, it is important to remember that the five cultural value dimensions are interrelated, not independent.[63] National cultures may best be understood in terms of cluster maps or collages that combine multiple dimensions. For example, high power distance and collectivism are often found together, as are low power distance and individualism. Whereas high collectivism may lead us to expect a work team in Indonesia to operate by consensus, the high power distance may cause the consensus to be heavily influenced by the desires of a formal leader. A similar team operating in more individualist and low-power-distance Great Britain or America might make decisions with more open debate, including expressions of disagreement with a leader's stated preferences.

Hofstede also warns against falling prey to the **ecological fallacy**. This is acting with the mistaken assumption that a generalized cultural value, such as individualism in American culture or masculinity in Japanese culture, applies equally to all members of the culture.[64] And, finally, this model is just one starting point for developing cross-cultural awareness of values and value differences, and other frameworks of interest are available.[65]

 Go to your WileyPLUS Learning Space course for video episodes, examples, art, tables, Concept Checks, practice, and resources that will help you succeed in this course.

3

Reading for

PERCEPTION, ATTRIBUTION, AND LEARNING

The Perception Process

Perception is the process by which people select, organize, interpret, retrieve, and respond to information from the world around them.[1] It is a way of forming impressions about ourselves, other people, and daily life experiences. It also serves as a screen or filter through which information passes before it has an effect on people. Because perceptions are influenced by many factors, different people may perceive the same situation quite differently. Since people behave according to their perceptions, the consequences of these differences can be great in terms of what happens next.

Consider the example shown in ▣ **Figure 3.1**. It shows substantial differences in how performance-review discussions are perceived by managers and members of their work teams. The managers here may end up not giving much attention to things like career development, performance goals, and supervisory support since they perceive that these issues were adequately addressed at performance-review time. However, the team members may end up frustrated and unsatisfied because they perceive that less attention was given and they want more.

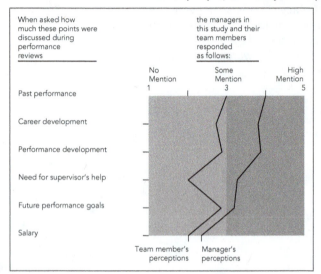

 See **FIGURE 3.1** Contrasting perceptions between managers and subordinates regarding performance appraisal interviews

Factors Influencing Perception

We can think of perception as a bubble that surrounds us and influences significantly the way we receive, interpret, and process information received from our environments. As the perception process varies, so too can things like decisions made and actions taken. When someone does things that we don't understand or in ways that we don't understand or that surprise us, the reason may well be due to the fact that their perceptions in the situation differed from ours or what we would normally expect. The many factors influencing perception include characteristics of the *perceiver*, the *setting*, and the *perceived*.

Characteristics of the Perceiver A person's past experiences, needs or motives, personality, values, and attitudes may all influence the perceptual process. Someone with a strong need for achievement need tends to perceive a situation in terms of that need. If doing well in class is perceived as a way to help meet your achievement need, for example, you will tend to emphasize that aspect when choosing classes to take. In the same way, a person with a negative attitude toward younger workers may react poorly when asked to work for a young, newly hired but very competent team leader.

Characteristics of the Setting The physical, social, and organizational context can influence the perception process. A teammate perceived by peers as temperamental may well be tolerated on the team. But take that person and make them the team leader and the same temperamental behavior may be perceived as bullying or intimidating.

Characteristics of the Perceived Characteristics of the perceived person, object, or event are also important in the perception process. We talk about them in terms of contrast, intensity, figure–ground separation, size, motion, and repetition or novelty. In respect to contrast, for example, one iPad among six Android tablets or one man among six women will be perceived differently than one of six iPad computers or one of six men. In respect to intensity, a bright red sports car stands out from a group of gray sedans; whispering or shouting stands out from ordinary conversation. This links with a concept known as *figure–ground separation*. Look, for example, at the margin illustration. What do you see, faces or a vase? It depends on which image is perceived as the background and which as the figure or object of our attention.

In the matter of size, very small or very large objects or people tend to be perceived differently. In terms of motion, moving objects and people are perceived differently than stationary ones. In addition, repetition or frequency can also influence perceptions. Television advertisers well know that the more they put something in front of us the more likely we are to give it attention. Finally, the novelty of a situation affects its perception. A college student who enters class with streaks of hair dyed purple may be perceived quite differently by an instructor than others with a more common hair color.

Information Processing and the Perception Process

The ways we process information during the perception process affect how we respond to experiences through feelings, thoughts, and actions taken. The four stages of this information processing are attention and selection, organization, interpretation, and retrieval. A good understanding of these stages can help us manage our own perceptions better, as well as both understand and influence the perceptions of others.

Attention and Selection Our senses are constantly bombarded with so much information that if we don't screen it, we quickly become incapacitated with information overload. We tend to deal with this through **selective screening** that lets in only a tiny portion of all the information available.

Some of the selective screening that we do comes from controlled processing: consciously deciding what information to pay attention to and what to ignore. Think, for example, about the last time you were at a noisy restaurant and screened out all the sounds but those of the person with whom you were talking. Some screening also takes place without conscious awareness. We often drive cars without thinking about the process; we're aware of things like traffic lights and other cars, but we don't pay conscious attention to them. This selectivity of attention and automatic information processing works well most of the time. But if a nonroutine event occurs, such as an animal darting in front of your vehicle, you may have an accident unless you quickly shift to controlled processing.

Organization Even when selective screening takes place in the attention stage, it's still necessary for us to organize information efficiently. This is done to some extent through **schemas**. These are cognitive frameworks that represent organized knowledge developed through experience about a concept or stimulus.[2] The schemas most commonly used are script schemas, person schemas, and person-in-situation schemas.

A *script schema* is a knowledge framework that describes the appropriate sequence of events in a given situation.[3] For example, an experienced team leader might use a script schema to think about the appropriate steps involved in running a meeting. A *self schema* contains information about a person's own appearance, behavior, and personality. For instance, people with decisiveness schemas tend to perceive themselves in terms of that aspect, especially in circumstances calling for leadership.

Person schemas sort people into categories—types or groups, in terms of similar perceived features. They include **prototypes** which are pre-set bundles of features expected to be characteristic of people in certain categories or roles. An example might be the prototype of a "good teammate" as someone who is intelligent, dependable, and hard-working. Once formed, person schemas are stored in long-term memory and retrieved only when needed for a comparison of how well a person matches the schema's features.[4]

Interpretation Once your attention has been drawn to certain stimuli and you have grouped or organized this information, the next step is to uncover the reasons behind the actions. Even if your attention is called to the same information and you organize it in the same way your friend does, you may still interpret it differently or make different assumptions about what you have perceived. As a team leader, for example, you might interpret compliments from a team member as due to his being eager and enthusiastic about a task; your friend might interpret the team member's behavior as an attempt at insincere flattery.

Retrieval Each stage of the perception process becomes part of memory. This information stored in our memory must be retrieved if it is to be used. But all of us at times have trouble retrieving stored information. Memory decays, so that only some of the information may be retrieved. Schemas can make it difficult for people to remember things not included in them. If you hold the prototype of a "good worker" as someone showing lots of effort, punctuality, intelligence, articulateness, and decisiveness, you may emphasize these traits and overlook others when evaluating the performance of a team member whom you generally consider good.

Perception, Impression Management, and Social Media

Richard Branson, CEO of the Virgin Group, is one of the richest and most famous executives in the world. He may also be the ultimate master of **impression management**, the systematic attempt to behave in ways that will create and maintain desired impressions in the eyes of others.[5] One of Branson's early business accomplishments was the successful start-up of Virgin Airlines, now a global competitor to the legacy airlines. In a memoir, the former head of British Airways, Lord King, said, "If Richard Branson had worn a shirt and tie instead of a goatee and jumper, I would not have underestimated him."[6]

Don't you wonder if creating a casual impression was part of Branson's business strategy? Whether intended or not, the chances are he's used this persona to very good advantage in other business dealings as well. It's an example of how much our impressions can count, both positive and negative, in how others perceive us. And it's not a new lesson; we've all heard it before. Who hasn't been told when heading off to a job interview "Don't forget to make a good first impression"?

The fact is that we already practice a lot of impression management as a matter of routine in everyday life. Impression management is taking place when we dress, talk, act, and surround ourselves with what reinforces a desirable self-image and helps to convey that image to other persons. When well done, that can help us to advance in jobs and careers, form relationships with people we admire, and even create pathways to group memberships. We manage impressions by such activities as associating with the "right" people, "dressing up" and "dressing down" at the right times, making eye contact when introduced to someone, doing favors to gain approval, flattering others to impress them, taking credit for a favorable event and apologizing for a negative one, and agreeing with the opinions of others.[7]

One of the most powerful forces in impression management today might be the one least recognized—how we communicate our presence in the online world of social media. It might even be the case that this short message deserves to go viral: User beware! The brand you are building through social media may last a lifetime. For tips to remember, check the sidebar on "How to Build Your Personal Brand Through Impression Management in Social Networks."

It's no secret that more and more employers are intensely scouring the Web to learn what they can about job candidates. What they are gathering are impressions left in the trails of the candidates' past social media journeys. One bad photo, one bad nickname, or one bad comment sends the wrong impression and can kill a great job opportunity. We are creating impressions of ourselves whenever we are active in the online world. The problem is that those impressions may be fun in social space but harmful in professional space. There's a lot to learn about impression management and social media. At a minimum it pays to keep the two social media spaces—the social and the professional—separated with a good firewall between them.

Common Perceptual Distortions

Given the complexity of the information streaming toward us from various environments, we use various means of simplifying and organizing our perceptions. However, these simplifications can cause inaccuracies in our impressions and in the perception process more generally. Common perceptual distortions trace to the use of stereotypes, halo effects, selective perception, projection, contrast effects, and self-fulfilling prophecies.

Stereotypes

One of the most common simplifying devices in perception is the **stereotype**. It occurs when we identify someone with a group or category, and then use the attributes perceived to be associated with the group or category to describe the individual. Although this makes matters easier for us by reducing the need to deal with unique individual characteristics, it is an oversimplification. Because stereotypes obscure individual differences, we can easily end up missing the real individual. For managers this means not accurately understanding the needs, preferences, and abilities of others in the workplace.

Some of the most common stereotypes, at work and in life in general, relate to such factors as gender, age, race, and physical ability. Why are so few top executives in industry African Americans or Hispanics? Legitimate questions can be asked about *racial and ethnic stereotypes* and about the slow progress of minority managers into America's corporate mainstream.[8] Why is it that women constitute only a small percentage of American managers sent abroad to work on international business assignments? A Catalyst study of opportunities for women in global business points to *gender stereotypes* that place women at a disadvantage compared to men for these types of opportunities. The tendency is to assume women lack the ability and/or willingness to work abroad.[9] Gender stereotypes may cause even everyday behavior to be misconstrued. For example, consider "He's talking with co-workers" (Interpretation: He's discussing a new deal) and "She's talking with co-workers" (Interpretation: She's gossiping).[10]

Ability stereotypes and *age stereotypes* also exist in the workplace. Physically or mentally challenged candidates may be overlooked by a recruiter even though they possess skills that are perfect for the job. A talented older worker may not be promoted because a manager assumes older workers are cautious and tend to avoid risk.[11] Yet a Conference Board survey of workers age 50 and older reports that 72 percent felt they could take on additional responsibilities, and two-thirds were interested in further training and development.[12] Then there's the flip side: Can a young person be a real leader, even a CEO? Facebook's founder and CEO Mark Zuckerberg is still in his twenties. When current CEO Sheryl Sandberg was being recruited from Google, she admits to having had this thought: "Wow, I'm going to work for a CEO who is quite young." "Mark is a great leader," she now says. After working for him, her perception has changed. "Mark has a real purity of vision. . . . He brings people along with him."[13]

Halo Effects

A **halo effect** occurs when one attribute of a person or situation is used to develop an overall impression of that individual or situation. Like stereotypes, these distortions are more likely to occur in the organization stage of perception. Halo effects are common in our everyday lives. When meeting a new person, for example, a pleasant smile can lead to a positive first impression of an overall "warm" and "honest" person. The result of a halo effect is the same as that associated with a stereotype, however, in that individual differences are obscured.

Halo effects are particularly important in the performance appraisal process because they can influence a manager's evaluations of subordinates' work performance. For example, people with good attendance records may be viewed as intelligent and responsible while those with poor attendance records are considered poor performers. Such conclusions may or may not be valid. It is the manager's job to try to get true impressions rather than allowing halo effects to result in biased and erroneous evaluations.

Selective Perception

Selective perception is the tendency to single out those aspects of a situation, person, or object that are consistent with one's needs, values, or attitudes. Its strongest impact occurs in the attention stage of the perceptual process. This perceptual distortion was identified in a classic research study involving executives in a manufacturing company.[14] When asked to identify the key problem in a comprehensive business policy case, each executive selected a problem consistent with his or her functional area work assignments. Most marketing executives viewed the key problem area as sales, whereas production people tended to see the problem as one of production and organization. These differing viewpoints would likely affect how each executive would approach the problem; they might also create difficulties as the executives tried to work together to improve things.

Projection

Projection is the assignment of one's personal attributes to other individuals. It is especially likely to occur in the interpretation stage of perception. A classic error is projecting your needs, values, and views onto others. This causes their individual differences to get lost. Such projection errors can be controlled through a high degree of self-awareness and empathy—the ability to view a situation as others see it.

Suppose, for example, that you enjoy responsibility and achievement in your work. Suppose, too, that you are the newly appointed leader of a team whose jobs seem dull and routine. You may move quickly to expand these jobs so that members get increased satisfaction from more challenging tasks. Basically, you want them to experience what you value in work. However, this may not be a good decision. Instead of designing team members' jobs to best fit their needs, you have designed their jobs to best fit yours.

Contrast Effects

We mentioned earlier how a bright red sports car would stand out from a group of gray sedans. This shows a **contrast effect** in which the meaning or interpretation of something is arrived at by contrasting it with a recently occurring event or situation. This form of perceptual distortion can occur, say, when a person gives a talk following a strong speaker or is interviewed for a job following a series of mediocre applicants. A contrast effect occurs when an individual's characteristics are contrasted with those of others recently encountered who rank higher or lower on the same characteristics.

Self-Fulfilling Prophecies

A final perceptual distortion is the **self-fulfilling prophecy**: the tendency to create or find in another situation or individual that which you expected to find in the first place. A self-fulfilling prophecy is sometimes referred to as the "Pygmalion effect," named for a mythical Greek sculptor who created a statue of his ideal mate and then made her come to life.[15]

Self-fulfilling prophecies can have both positive and negative outcomes. In effect, they may create in work and personal situations that which we expect to find. Suppose you assume that team members prefer to satisfy most of their needs outside the work setting and want only minimal involvement with their jobs. Consequently, you assign simple, highly structured tasks designed to require little involvement. Can you predict what response they will have to this situation? In fact, they may show the very same lack of commitment you assumed they would have in the first place. In this case your initial expectations get confirmed as a negative self-fulfilling prophecy.

Self-fulfilling prophecies can also have a positive side. In a study of army tank crews, one set of tank commanders was told that some members of their assigned crews had exceptional abilities whereas others were only average. However, the crew members had been assigned randomly so that the two test groups were equal in ability. The commanders later reported that the so-called "exceptional" crew members performed better than the "average" ones. The study also revealed that the commanders had given more attention and praise to the crew members for whom they had the higher expectations.[16] Don't you wonder what might happen with students and workers in general if teachers and managers adopted more uniformly positive and optimistic approaches toward them?

Perception, Attribution, and Social Learning

One of the ways in which perception exerts its influence on behavior is through **attribution**. This is the process of developing explanations or assigning perceived causes for events. It is natural for people to try to explain what they observe and what happens to them. What happens when you perceive that someone in a job or student group isn't performing up to expectations? How do you explain this? And, depending on the explanation, what do you do to try and correct things?

Importance of Attributions

Attribution theory helps us understand how people perceive the causes of events, assess responsibility for outcomes, and evaluate the personal qualities of the people involved.[17] It is especially concerned with whether the assumption is that an individual's behavior, such as poor performance, has been internally or externally caused. Internal causes are believed to be under an individual's control—you believe Jake's performance is poor because he is lazy. External causes are seen as coming from outside a person—you believe Kellie's performance is poor because the software she's using is out of date.

According to attribution theory, three factors influence this internal or external determination of causality: distinctiveness, consensus, and consistency. *Distinctiveness* considers how consistent a person's behavior is across different situations. If Jake's performance is typically low, regardless of the technology with which he is working, we tend to assign the poor performance to an internal attribution—there's something wrong with Jake. If the poor performance is unusual, we tend to assign an external cause to explain it—there's something happening in the work context. *Consensus* takes into account how likely all those facing a similar situation are to respond in the same way. If all the people using the same technology as Jake perform poorly, we tend to assign his performance problem to an external attribution. If others do not perform poorly, we attribute Jake's poor performance to internal causation. *Consistency* concerns whether an individual responds the same way across time. If Jake performs poorly over a sustained period of time, we tend to give the poor performance an internal attribution. If his low performance is an isolated incident, we may well attribute it to an external cause.

Cause of Poor Performance by Others	Most Frequent Attribution	Cause of Poor Performance by Themselves
Many	Lack of *ability*	Few
Many	Lack of *effort*	Few
Few	Lack of *support*	Many

Attribution Errors

People often fall prey to perception errors when making attributions about what caused certain events.[18] Look, for example, at the data reported in **Figure 3.2**. When executives were asked to attribute causes of poor performance among their subordinates, they most often blamed internal deficiencies of the individual—lack of ability and effort, rather than external deficiencies in the situation—lack of support. This demonstrates what is known as **fundamental attribution error**—the tendency to underestimate the influence of situational factors and to overestimate the influence of personal factors when evaluating someone else's behavior. When asked to identify causes of their own poor performance, however, the executives mostly cited lack of support—an external, or situational, deficiency. This demonstrates **self-serving bias**—the tendency to deny personal responsibility for performance problems but to accept personal responsibility for performance success.

See **FIGURE 3.2 Attribution errors by executives when explaining poor performance by others and themselves**

The managerial implications of attribution errors trace back to the fact that perceptions influence behavior.[19] For example, a team leader who believes that members are not performing well and perceives the reason to be an internal lack of effort is likely to respond with attempts to "motivate" them to work harder. The possibility of changing external, situational factors that may remove job constraints and provide better organizational support may be largely ignored. This oversight could sacrifice major performance gains for the team.

Attribution and Social Learning

Perception and attribution are important components in **social learning theory**, which describes how learning takes place through the reciprocal interactions among people, behavior, and environment. According to the work of Albert Bandura, an individual uses modeling or vicarious learning to acquire behavior by observing and imitating others.[20] In a work situation, the model may be a higher manager or co-worker who demonstrates desired behaviors. Mentors or senior workers who befriend younger and more inexperienced protégés can also be important models. Indeed, some have argued that a shortage of mentors for women in senior management has been a major constraint to their progression up the career ladder.[21]

See **FIGURE 3.3 Simplified model of social learning**

The symbolic processes shown in **Figure 3.3** are important in social learning. Words and symbols used by managers and others in the workplace help communicate values, beliefs, and goals and thus serve as guides to an individual's behavior. For example, a "thumbs up" or other signal from the boss lets you know your behavior is appropriate. At the same time, the person's self-control is important in influencing his or her own behavior. And self-efficacy—the person's belief that he or she can perform adequately in a situation—is an important part of such self-control. Closely associated with the concept of self-efficacy are such terms as confidence, competence, and ability.[22]

People with high self-efficacy believe that they have the necessary abilities for a given job, that they are capable of the effort required, and that no outside events will hinder them from attaining their desired performance level.[23] In contrast, people with low self-efficacy believe that no matter how hard they try, they cannot manage their environment well enough to be successful. If you feel high self-efficacy as a student, a low grade on one test is likely to encourage you to study harder, talk to the instructor, or do other things to enable you to do well the next time. In contrast, a person low in self-efficacy would probably drop the course or give up studying. Of course, even people who are high in self-efficacy do not control their environment entirely.

Learning by Reinforcement

When it comes to learning, the concept of reinforcement is very important in OB. It has a very specific meaning that has its origin in some classic studies in psychology.[24] **Reinforcement** is the administration of a consequence as a result of a behavior. Managing reinforcement properly can change the direction, level, and persistence of an individual's behavior. This idea is best understood through the concepts of conditioning and reinforcement that you may have already learned in a basic psychology course.

Classical Conditioning

Ivan Pavlov described **classical conditioning** as a form of learning through association that involves the manipulation of stimuli to influence behavior. The Russian psychologist "taught" dogs to salivate at the sound of a bell by ringing the bell when feeding the dogs. The sight of the food naturally caused the dogs to salivate. The dogs "learned" to associate the bell ringing with the presentation of food and to salivate at the ringing of the bell alone.

The key here is to understand stimulus and conditioned stimulus. A stimulus is something that incites action and draws forth a response, such as food for the dogs. The trick is to associate one neutral stimulus—the bell ringing—with another stimulus that already affects behavior—the food. The once-neutral stimulus is called a conditioned stimulus when it affects behavior in the same way as the initial stimulus. Such learning through association is so common in organizations that it is often ignored until it causes considerable confusion.

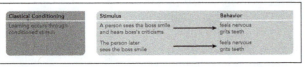

See **FIGURE 3.4**
Classical conditioning in the workplace

Take a look at **Figure 3.4** for an example of how **classical conditioning** might occur in the workplace. Here, the boss's smiling has become a conditioned stimulus because of its association with his criticisms. The employee has learned to feel nervous and grit her teeth whenever the boss smiles.

Operant Conditioning and the Law of Effect

The well-known psychologist B. F. Skinner extended the applications of learning by reinforcement to include more than just conditioned stimulus and response behavior.[25] He focused on operant conditioning as the process of controlling behavior by manipulating its consequences. You may think of operant conditioning as learning by reinforcement. In a work setting the goal is to use reinforcement principles to systematically reinforce desirable behavior and discourage undesirable behavior.[26]

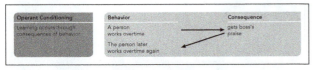

See **FIGURE 3.5**
Operant conditioning in the workplace

Operant conditioning occurs by linking behavior and consequences. **Figure 3.5** uses the example of an agreement with the boss to work overtime. When the employee actually does work overtime, this is the *behavior*. The *consequence* in the example is receiving the boss's praise. In operant conditioning, this consequence strengthens the behavior and makes it more likely to reoccur when the boss next requests overtime work.

The basis for operant conditioning rests in E. L. Thorndike's **law of effect**.[27] It is simple but powerful: Behavior that results in a pleasant outcome is likely to be repeated, whereas behavior that results in an unpleasant outcome is not likely to be repeated. The implications of this law are rather straightforward. If you want more of a behavior—say the willingness of someone to stay and work overtime when things are rushed—you must make sure the consequences of performing the desired behavior are positive for the individual.

The consequences that reinforce behavior under the Law of Effect are **extrinsic rewards**—positively valued work outcomes given to the individual by another person.[28] Some of these are *contrived rewards* like pay increases and cash bonuses. These rewards have direct costs and budgetary implications. Other outcomes could be *natural rewards* such as verbal praise and recognition. These have no real cost other than the time and effort expended to deliver them.

The use of extrinsic rewards to systematically reinforce desirable work behavior and to discourage unwanted work behavior is known as **organizational behavior modification**, or OB Mod for short. It involves the use of four basic reinforcement strategies: positive reinforcement, negative reinforcement (or avoidance), punishment, and extinction.[29]

Positive Reinforcement

B. F. Skinner and his followers place great emphasis on the power of **positive reinforcement** in operant conditioning. This is the administration of positive consequences that tend to increase the likelihood that desirable behavior will be repeated. An example is when a team leader nods to a team member to express approval after she makes a useful comment during a sales meeting. For example, this increases the likelihood of future useful comments from the team member, something that might not happen if the useful comments went unrecognized when first offered in the meeting.

It's easy to waste rewards by giving them in ways that have little impact on future desired behaviors. In order to have maximum reinforcement value, a reward should be delivered only when a desired behavior—such as giving constructive comments in a meeting—is exhibited. That is, the reward must be contingent on the desired behavior. This principle is known as the **law of contingent reinforcement**. In addition, the reward should be given as soon as possible after the desired behavior. This is known as the **law of immediate reinforcement**.[30] If a team leader waits for the annual performance review to praise a team member for providing constructive comments during meetings, the law of immediate reinforcement would be violated.

Shaping The power of positive reinforcement can be mobilized through a process known as **shaping**: the creation of a new behavior by the positive reinforcement of successive approximations to it. For example, new machine operators in the Ford Motor casting operation in Ohio must learn a complex series of tasks in pouring molten metal into castings in order to avoid gaps, overfills, or cracks.[31] The molds are filled in a three-step process, with each step progressively more difficult than its predecessor. Astute master craftspersons first show newcomers how to pour as the first step and give praise based on what they did right. As the apprentices gain experience, they are given praise only when all of the elements of the first step are completed successfully. Once the apprentices have mastered the first step, they move to the second. Reinforcement is given only when the entire first step and an aspect of the second step are completed successfully. Over time, apprentices learn all three steps and are given contingent positive rewards immediately upon completing a casting that has no cracks or gaps. In this way behavior is shaped gradually rather than changed all at once.

Scheduling Positive Reinforcement Positive reinforcement can be given on either continuous or intermittent schedules. **Continuous reinforcement** administers a reward each time a desired behavior occurs, whereas **intermittent reinforcement** rewards behavior only periodically. In general, continuous reinforcement draws forth a desired behavior more quickly than does intermittent reinforcement. However, it is easily extinguished when reinforcement is no longer present. Behavior acquired under intermittent reinforcement is more resistant to extinction and lasts longer upon the discontinuance of reinforcement. This is why shaping typically begins with a continuous reinforcement schedule and then gradually shifts to an intermittent one.

	Interval	Ratio
Fixed	**Fixed interval** Reinforcer given after a given time Weekly or monthly paychecks Regularly scheduled exams	**Fixed ratio** Reinforcer given after a given number of behavior occurrences Piece-rate pay Commissioned salespeople: certain amount is given for each dollar of sales
Variable	**Variable interval** Reinforcer given at random times Occasional praise by boss on unscheduled visits Unspecified number of pop quizzes to students	**Variable ratio** Reinforcer given after a random number of behavior occurrences Random quality checks with praise for zero defects Commissioned salespeople: a varying number of calls are required to obtain a given sale
	Time-based	Behavior occurrence–based

 See **FIGURE 3.6 Alternative ways to schedule positive reinforcement**

■ **Figure 3.6** shows that intermittent reinforcement can be given according to fixed or variable schedules. *Variable schedules* typically result in more consistent patterns of desired behavior than do fixed reinforcement schedules. *Fixed-interval schedules* provide rewards at the first appearance of a behavior after a given time has elapsed. *Fixed-ratio schedules* result in a reward each time a certain number of the behaviors have occurred. A *variable-interval schedule* rewards behavior at random times, whereas a *variable-ratio schedule* rewards behavior after a random number of occurrences.

Negative Reinforcement

A second reinforcement strategy in operant conditioning is **negative reinforcement** or avoidance learning. It uses the withdrawal of negative consequences to increase the likelihood of desirable behavior being repeated. An example might be the manager regularly nags a worker about being late for work and then doesn't nag when the worker next shows up on time. The term *negative reinforcement* comes from this withdrawal of the negative consequences. The strategy is also called *avoidance learning* because its intent is for the person to avoid the negative consequence by performing the desired behavior. Think of it this way. Even when the streets are deserted, we still stop at red lights to avoid getting a traffic ticket.

Punishment

Unlike positive reinforcement and negative reinforcement which are intended to encourage desired behavior, **punishment** intends to discourage undesirable behavior. It is the administration of negative consequences or the withdrawal of positive consequences to reduce the likelihood of a behavior being repeated.

Evidence does show that punishment administered for poor performance can lead to better performance. Yet, when punishment is perceived as arbitrary and capricious, it leads to low satisfaction and low performance.[32] The lesson here and highlighted in the "How to Make Positive Reinforcement and Punishment Work for You" sidebar is that punishment can be handled poorly, or it can be handled well. If it is necessary to use punishment as a reinforcement strategy, be sure to do it well.

It's also worth noting that punishment may be offset by positive reinforcement received from another source. Take the case of someone being positively reinforced by peers at the same time as he or she is receiving punishment from a boss, parent, or teacher. Sometimes the positive value of peer support is so great that the individual chooses to put up with punishment and continues the bad behavior. As many times as a child may be verbally reprimanded by a teacher for playing jokes, for example, the "grins" offered by classmates may keep the jokes flowing in the future.

Extinction

The final reinforcement strategy is **extinction**—the withdrawal of reinforcing consequences in order to weaken undesirable behavior. For example, Enya is often late for work and co-workers provide positive reinforcement by covering for her. The manager instructs Enya's co-workers to stop covering, thus withdrawing the positive consequences of her tardiness. This is a use of extinction to try and get rid of an undesirable behavior. Still, even though a successful extinction strategy decreases the frequency of or weakens behavior, the behavior is not "unlearned." It simply is not exhibited and will reappear if reinforced again.

Reinforcement Pros and Cons

The effective use of the four reinforcement strategies presented in these pages can help in the management of human behavior at work, but their use is not without criticism.[33] A major criticism is that using reinforcement to influence human behavior is demeaning and dehumanizing.[34] Another criticism is that it becomes too easy for managers to abuse the power of their positions when they exert this type of external control over individual behavior.

Advocates of the reinforcement approach attack its critics head on. They agree that behavior modification involves the control of behavior, but they also argue that such control is an irrevocable part of every manager's job. The real question, they say, is how to ensure that the reinforcement strategies are done in positive and constructive ways.[35]

WP LS Go to your **WileyPLUS Learning Space** course for video episodes, examples, art, tables, Concept Checks, practice, and resources that will help you succeed in this course.

EMOTIONS, ATTITUDES, AND JOB SATISFACTION

4

WP LS Go to your WileyPLUS Learning Space course for video episodes, examples, art, tables, Concept Checks, practice, and resources that will help you succeed in this course.

Understanding Emotions and Moods

How do you feel when . . . You are driving a car and are halted by a police officer? You are in class and receive a poor grade on an exam? A favorite pet passes away? You check e-mail and discover that you are being offered a job interview? A good friend walks right by without speaking? A parent or sibling or child loses his job? You get this SMS from a new acquaintance: "Ur gr8!"?

These are examples of things that draw out feelings of many forms, such as happy or sad, angry or pleased, anxious or elated. Such feelings constitute what scholars call **affect**, the range of emotions and moods that people experience in their life context.[1] Our affects have important implications not only for our lives in general but also our work experiences and careers.[2]

The Nature of Emotions

Anger, excitement, apprehension, attraction, sadness, elation, grief are all **emotions** that appear as strong positive or negative feelings directed toward someone or something.[3] Emotions are usually intense and not long-lasting. They are always associated with a source. That is, someone or something makes us feel the way we do. You might feel the positive emotion of elation when an instructor congratulates you on a fine class presentation; you might feel the negative emotion of anger when an instructor criticizes you in front of the class. In both situations the object of your emotion is the instructor, but the impact of the instructor's behavior on your feelings is quite different in each case. And your response to the aroused emotions is likely to differ as well—perhaps breaking into a wide smile after the compliment, or making a nasty side comment or withdrawing from further participation after the criticism.

Emotional Intelligence

All of us are familiar with the notions of cognitive ability and intelligence, or IQ, which have been measured for many years. A related concept is **emotional intelligence**, or EI as it is often called. It is defined by scholar Daniel Goleman as an ability to understand emotions in ourselves and others and to use that understanding to manage relationships effectively.[4] EI is demonstrated in the ways in which we deal with affect—for example, by knowing when a negative emotion is about to cause problems and being able to control that emotion so that it doesn't become disruptive.

Goleman's point about emotional intelligence is that we perform better when we are good at recognizing and dealing with emotions in ourselves and others. When high in EI, we are more likely to behave in ways that avoid having our emotions "get the better of us." Knowing that an instructor's criticism causes us to feel anger, for example, EI might help us control that anger, maintain a positive face, and perhaps earn the instructor's praise when we make future class contributions. If the unchecked anger caused us to act in a verbally aggressive way—creating a negative impression in the instructor's eyes—or to withdraw from all class participation—causing the instructor to believe we have no interest in the course, our course experience would likely suffer.

If you are good at knowing and managing your emotions and are good at reading others' emotions, you may perform better while interacting with other people. This applies to life in

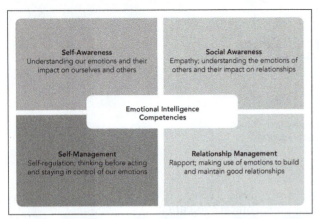

See **FIGURE 4.1**
Four key emotional
intelligence
competencies for
success in leadership
and relationships

general, as well as to work leadership situations.[5] ■ **Figure 4.1** identifies four essential *emotional intelligence competencies* that can and should be developed for leadership success and success more generally in all types of interpersonal situations.[6] The competencies are self-awareness, social awareness, self-management, and relationship management.

Self-awareness in emotional intelligence is the ability to understand our emotions and their impact on our work and on others. You can think of this as a continuing appraisal of your emotions that results in a good understanding of them and the capacity to express them naturally. **Social awareness** is the ability to empathize, to understand the emotions of others, and to use this understanding to better relate to them. It involves continuous appraisal and recognition of others' emotions, resulting in better perception and understanding of them.

Self-management in emotional intelligence is the ability to think before acting and to be in control of otherwise disruptive impulses. It is a form of *self-regulation* in which we stay in control of our emotions and avoid letting them take over. **Relationship management** is an ability to establish rapport with others in ways that build good relationships and influence their emotions in positive ways. It shows up as the capacity to make good use of emotions by directing them toward constructive activities and improved relationships.

Types of Emotions

Researchers have identified six major types of emotions: anger, fear, joy, love, sadness, and surprise. The key question from an emotional intelligence perspective is this: Do we recognize these emotions in ourselves and others, and can we manage them well? Anger, for example, may involve disgust and envy, both of which can have very negative consequences. Fear may contain alarm and anxiety; joy may contain cheerfulness and contentment; love may contain affection, longing, and lust; sadness may contain disappointment, neglect, and shame.

It is also common to differentiate between **self-conscious emotions** that arise from internal sources and **social emotions** that are stimulated by external sources.[7] Shame, guilt, embarrassment, and pride are examples of internal emotions. Understanding self-conscious emotions helps individuals regulate their relationships with others. Social emotions such as pity, envy, and jealousy derive from external cues and information. An example is feeling envious or jealous upon learning that a co-worker received a promotion or job assignment that you were hoping to get.

The Nature of Moods

Whereas emotions tend to be short term and clearly targeted at someone or something, **moods** are more generalized positive and negative feelings or states of mind that may persist for some time. Everyone seems to have occasional moods, and we each know the full range of possibilities they represent. How often do you wake up in the morning and feel excited and refreshed and just happy, or wake up feeling grouchy and depressed and generally unhappy? And what are the consequences of these different moods for your behavior with friends and family, and at work or school?

The field of OB is especially interested in how moods influence someone's likeability and relationships at work. When it comes to CEOs, for example, it often pays to be viewed as in a positive mood, one that makes them seem more personable and caring in the eyes of others. If a CEO goes to a meeting in a good mood and gets described as "cheerful," "charming," "humorous," "friendly," and "candid," she or he may be viewed as on the upswing. If the CEO goes into a meeting in a bad mood and is perceived as "prickly," "impatient," "remote," "tough," "acrimonious," or even "ruthless," the perception will more likely be of a CEO on the downslide.[8]

See **FIGURE 4.2**
Emotions and
moods are different,
but they can also
influence one another

■ **Figure 4.2** offers a brief comparison of emotions and moods. In general, emotions are intense feelings directed at someone or something; they always have rather specific triggers; and they come in many types: anger, fear, happiness, and the like. Moods tend to be more generalized positive or negative feelings. They are less intense than emotions and most often seem to lack a clear source; it's often hard to identify how or why we end up in a particular mood.[9] In addition, moods tend to be more long lasting than emotions. When someone says or does something that causes a quick and intense positive or negative reaction from you, that emotion will probably quickly pass. However, a bad or good mood is likely to linger for hours or even days and influence a wide range of behaviors.

How Emotions and Moods Influence Behavior

Although emotions and moods are influenced by different events and situations, each of us may display some relatively predictable tendencies.[10] Some people seem almost always positive and upbeat about things. For these *optimists* we might say the glass is nearly always half full. Others, by contrast, seem to be often negative or downbeat. They tend to be *pessimists* viewing the glass as half empty. Such tendencies toward optimism and pessimism influence the individual's behavior. They can also influence the people with whom he or she interacts.

Emotion and Mood Contagion

Researchers are increasingly interested in **emotion and mood contagion**—the spillover effects of one's emotions and mood onto others.[11] You might think this as a bit like catching a cold from someone. Such contagion can have up and down effects on the emotions and moods of co-workers and teammates as well as family and friends.

Daniel Goleman and his colleagues studying emotional intelligence believe leaders should manage emotion and mood contagion with care. "Moods that start at the top tend to move the fastest," they say, "because everyone watches the boss."[12] When mood contagion is positive, followers report being more attracted to their leaders and rate the leaders more highly.[13] In teams, one study found, team members shared good and bad moods within two hours of being together. Interestingly, the contagion of bad moods traveled person to person in teams faster than good moods did.[14]

Emotional Labor

The concept of **emotional labor** relates to the need to show certain emotions in order to perform a job well.[15] Good examples come from service settings such as airline check-in personnel or flight attendants. Persons in such jobs are supposed to appear approachable, receptive, and friendly while taking care of the things you require as a customer. Some airlines, such as Southwest, go even further in asking service employees to be "funny" and "caring" and "cheerful" while doing their jobs.

Emotional labor isn't always easy; it can be hard to be consistently "on" in displaying the desired emotions in one's work. If you're having a bad mood day or have just experienced an emotional run-in with a neighbor, for example, being "happy" and "helpful" with a demanding customer might seem a little much to ask. Such situations can cause **emotional dissonance** in which the emotions we actually feel are inconsistent with the emotions we try to project.[16] That is, we are expected to act with one emotion while we actually feel quite another.

It often requires a lot of self-regulation to display organizationally desired emotions in one's job. Imagine, for example, how often service workers struggling with personal emotions and moods experience dissonance when having to act positive toward customers.[17] *Deep acting* occurs when someone tries to modify his or her feelings to better fit the situation—such as putting yourself in the position of the air travelers whose luggage went missing and feeling the same sense of loss. *Surface acting* occurs when someone hides true feelings while displaying very different ones—such as smiling at a customer even though the words they used to express a complaint just offended you.

Emotional Empathy

It was noted previously that empathy is an important component of emotional intelligence. Although empathy itself can be thought of as a generalized sensitivity to other persons and their states of mind, it can be further considered at both the cognitive and emotional levels.[18] Daniel Goleman differentiates between **cognitive empathy**—an ability to know how others are viewing things—and **emotional empathy**—an ability to feel what the other person is experiencing in a particular situation.[19]

Emotional empathy is considered important in how relationships play out, be they relationships between spouses and family members, friends, or co-workers. Simply the perception that a partner is putting forth the effort to seek emotional empathy has been linked to relationship satisfaction among spouses.[20] In the work context, emotional empathy and management affect trust and collaboration in interpersonal relationships.[21] And when it comes to the distribution of empathic emotional skills, Goleman cites research showing that women score better than men.[22]

Cultural Aspects of Emotions and Moods

Issues of emotional intelligence, emotion and mood contagion, and emotional labor can be complicated in cross-cultural situations. General interpretations of emotions and moods appear similar across cultures, with the major emotions of happiness, joy, and love all valued positively.[23] However, the frequency and intensity of emotions are known to vary somewhat. In China, for example, research suggests that people report fewer positive and negative emotions as well as less intense emotions than in other cultures.[24] Norms for emotional expression also vary across cultures. In collectivist cultures that emphasize group relationships such as Japan, individual emotional displays are less likely to occur and less likely to be accepted than in individualistic cultures.[25]

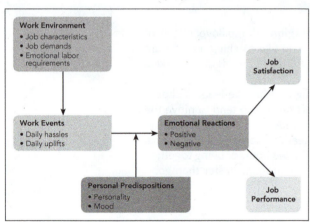

See **FIGURE 4.3**
Figurative summary of affective events theory

Informal cultural standards called **display rules** govern the degree to which it is appropriate to show emotions. The display rules of British culture, for example, tend to encourage downplaying emotions. Those of Mexican culture tend to allow emotions to be more publicly demonstrative. Overall, the lesson is that the way emotions are displayed in one culture may not be the same in another culture. When Walmart first went to Germany, its executives found that an emphasis on friendliness embedded in its U.S. roots didn't work as well in the local culture. The more serious German shoppers did not respond well to Walmart's friendly greeters and helpful personnel.[26]

Emotions and Moods as Affective Events

The affective events theory (AET) shown in **Figure 4.3** is one way of summarizing how emotions and moods end up influencing human behavior in organizations.[27] The basic notion of the theory is that day-to-day events involving other people and situations end up having an impact on our emotions and moods . They, in turn, influence our job performance and satisfaction.

The left-hand side of the figure shows how the work environment—including the job and its emotional labor requirements, daily work events, everyday hassles and uplifts—elicit positive and negative emotional reactions. These reactions affect one's job satisfaction and performance.[28] Notice that personal predispositions in the form of personality and moods also affect the connection between work events and emotional reactions. Someone's mood at the time can exaggerate the emotions experienced as a result of an event. If you have just been criticized by your boss, for example, you are likely to feel worse than you would otherwise when a colleague makes a joke about the length of your coffee breaks.

How Attitudes Influence Behavior

At one time Challis M. Lowe was one of only two African-American women among the five highest-paid executives in U.S. companies.[29] Her 25-year career included several changes of employers and lots of stressors—working-mother guilt, a failed marriage, gender bias on the job, and an MBA degree earned part time. Looking back she said: "I've never let being scared stop me from doing something. Just because you haven't done it before doesn't mean you shouldn't try." That, simply put, is what we would call a "can-do" attitude.

What Is an Attitude?

An **attitude** is a predisposition to respond in a positive or negative way to someone or something in one's environment. When you say, for example, that you "like" or "dislike" someone or something, you are expressing an attitude. It's important to remember that an attitude, like a value, is a hypothetical construct; one never sees, touches, or actually isolates an attitude. Rather, attitudes are *inferred* from the things people say or through their behavior.

Attitudes are influenced by values and are acquired from the same sources—friends, teachers, parents, role models, and culture. Attitudes, however, focus on specific people or objects. The notion that shareholders should have a voice in setting CEO pay is a value. Your positive or negative feeling about a specific company due to the presence or absence of shareholder inputs on CEO pay is an attitude.

Components of Attitudes

The three components of an attitude are shown in 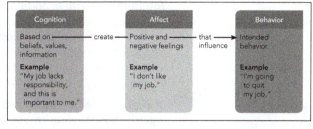 **Figure 4.4**: cognitive, affective, and behavioral.[30] The *cognitive component* of an attitude reflects underlying beliefs, opinions, knowledge, or information a person possesses. It represents a person's ideas about someone or something and the conclusions drawn about them. The statement "My job lacks responsibility" is a belief as shown in the figure. The statement "and this is important to me" reflects an underlying value. Together they comprise the cognitive component of an attitude toward one's work or workplace.

See **FIGURE 4.4** A work-related example of the three components of attitudes

The *affective component* of an attitude is a specific feeling regarding the personal impact of the antecedent conditions evidenced in the cognitive component. In essence this becomes the actual attitude, such as the feeling "I don't like my job." Notice that the affect in this statement displays a negative attitude; "I don't like my job" is a very different condition than "I do like my job."

The *behavioral component* is an intention to behave in a certain way based on the affect in one's attitude. It is a predisposition to act, but may or may not be implemented. The example in the figure shows behavioral intent expressed as "I'm going to quit my job." Yet even with such intent, it remains to be seen whether or not the person really quits.

As just pointed out, the link between attitudes and behavior is tentative. An attitude expresses an intended behavior that may or may not be carried out. In general, the more specific attitudes are, the stronger the relationship with eventual behavior. A person who feels "I don't like my job" may be less likely to actually quit than someone who feels "I can't stand another day with Alex harassing me at work." For an attitude to actually influence behavior, it's also necessary to have the opportunity or freedom to behave in the intended way. There are lots of people who stick with their jobs while still holding negative job attitudes, perhaps you know some. The fact is they may not have any other choice.[31]

Attitudes and Cognitive Consistency

Social psychologist Leon Festinger used the term **cognitive dissonance** to describe a state of inconsistency between an individual's attitudes and/or between attitudes and behavior.[32] This is an important issue. Perhaps you have the attitude that recycling is good for the economy. You also realize you aren't always recycling everything you can. Festinger points out that such cognitive inconsistency between attitude and behavior is uncomfortable. We tend to deal with the discomfort by trying to do things to reduce or eliminate the dissonance: (1) changing the underlying attitude, (2) changing future behavior, or (3) developing new ways of explaining or rationalizing the inconsistency.

The way we respond to cognitive dissonance is influenced by the degree of control we seem to have over the situation and the rewards involved. In the case of recycling dissonance, for example, the lack of convenient recycling containers would make rationalizing easier and changing the positive attitude less likely. A reaffirmation of intention to recycle in the future might also reduce the dissonance.

Attitudes and the Workplace

Even though attitudes do not always predict behavior, the link between attitudes and potential or intended behavior is an important workplace issue. Think about your daily experiences or conversations with other people about their work. It isn't uncommon to hear concerns expressed about a co-worker's "bad attitude" or another's "good attitude." Such feelings get reflected in things like job satisfaction, job involvement, organizational commitment, organizational identification, and employee engagement.

Job Satisfaction You often hear the term *morale* used to describe how people feel about their jobs and employers. It relates to the more specific notion of **job satisfaction**, an attitude reflecting a person's positive and negative feelings toward a job, co-workers, and the work environment. Indeed, you should remember that helping others realize job satisfaction is considered one hallmark of effective team leaders and managers—those who create work environments in which people achieve high performance and experience high job satisfaction.

Job Involvement In addition to job satisfaction, OB scholars and researchers are interested in **job involvement**. This is the extent to which an individual feels dedicated to a job. Someone with high job involvement psychologically identifies with her or his job and, for example, shows willingness to work beyond expectations to complete a special project. A high level of job involvement is generally linked with lower tendencies to withdraw from work, either physically by quitting or psychologically by reducing one's work efforts.

Organizational Commitment and Organizational Identification Another work attitude is **organizational commitment**, or the degree of loyalty an individual feels toward the organization. Individuals with a high organizational commitment want to maintain their membership in the organization. Just as persons with a high sense of job involvement, their inclination is to stay and contribute rather than withdraw either physically or psychologically.

Two types of organizational commitment are often discussed. *Rational commitment* reflects feelings that the job serves one's financial, and career development, interests—in other words, "I am committed because I need what the organization offers in return for my labor." *Emotional commitment* reflects feelings that what one does is important, valuable, and of real benefit to others—in other words, "I am committed because of the self-satisfaction I experience from my membership in the organization." Research shows that strong emotional commitments to the organization are more powerful than rational commitments in positively influencing performance.[33]

The concept of emotional commitment is linked in OB research to something called **organizational identification**, or OID. It is the extent to which one feels personally identified with one's membership organization to the point that it becomes part of the self-concept. This notion derives from social identity theory and the premise that the memberships individuals maintain contribute to their feelings of self-esteem.[34]

When organizational identification is positive for one's esteem, the expectation is that the individual will strive to be a good team player, a responsible organizational citizen, and generally a positive work contributor and performer.[35] It's also recognized that positive identification can work to the negative if it causes someone to commit unethical acts perceived as necessary to maintain organizational membership.[36] But, organizational identification can be negative as well as positive. Think of a person saying "I belong to this organization, and I don't feel good about myself because of it." In such cases individuals may struggle to psychologically balance their self-concept with the reality of the organizational membership.[37]

Employee Engagement A survey of 55,000 American workers by the Gallup, Inc., suggests that profits for employers rise when workers' attitudes reflect high levels of job involvement, organizational commitment, and organizational identification. This combination creates a high sense of **employee engagement**—defined by Gallup as feeling "a profound connection" with the organization and "a passion" for one's job.[38] Scholar Jeffrey Pfeffer describes it as a "conceptual cousin" of job satisfaction.[39]

A highly engaged individual tends to have an enthusiastic attitude toward work as well as being willing to help others, to always try to do something extra to improve performance, and to speak positively about the organization. Individuals with high employee engagement also report more positive moods and better handling of workplace stress.[40] The drivers of high engagement in the Gallup research held the beliefs that one has the opportunity to do one's best every day, one's opinions count, fellow workers are committed to quality, and a direct connection exists between one's work and the organization's mission.[41]

Given all this, do you have a sense of how engaged most people are in their work? The fact is that recent Gallup research shows that 52 percent of American workers are "not engaged"—think "mentally checked out"—and another 18 percent are "actively disengaged"—think "undermining and disrupting." Even though high employee engagement is good for organizations and probably for the individual, only about 30 percent of American workers on the average report experiencing it.[42]

Job Satisfaction Trends and Issues

There is no doubt that job satisfaction—a person's feelings toward his or her job or job setting at a particular point in time—is one of the most talked about of all job attitudes.[43] And when it comes to job satisfaction, several good questions can be asked. What are the major components of job satisfaction? What are the main job satisfaction findings and trends? What is the relationship between job satisfaction and job performance?

Components of Job Satisfaction

It is possible to infer the job satisfaction of others by careful observation and interpretation of what they say and do while going about their jobs. Interviews and questionnaires can also be used to more formally assess levels of job satisfaction on a team or in an organization.[44] Two of the more popular job satisfaction questionnaires used over the years are the Minnesota Satisfaction Questionnaire (MSQ) and the Job Descriptive Index (JDI).[45] The MSQ measures satisfaction with working conditions, chances for advancement, freedom to use one's own judgment, praise for doing a good job, and feelings of accomplishment, among others. The JDI measures these five job satisfaction facets:

- *The work itself*—responsibility, interest, and growth
- *Quality of supervision*—technical help and social support
- *Relationships with co-workers*—social harmony and respect
- *Promotion opportunities*—chances for further advancement
- *Pay*—adequacy of pay and perceived equity vis-á -vis others

Job Satisfaction Trends

If you watch or read the news, you'll regularly find reports on the job satisfaction of workers. You'll also find lots of job satisfaction studies in the academic literature. The results don't always agree, but they usually fall within a common range. Until recently, we generally concluded that the majority of U.S. workers are at least somewhat satisfied with their jobs. Now, the trend has turned down.[46]

Surveys conducted by The Conference Board showed in 1987 that about 61 percent of American workers said they were satisfied; in 2009 only 45 percent were reporting job satisfaction.[47] The report states, "Fewer Americans are satisfied with all aspects of employment, and no age or income group is immune. In fact, the youngest cohort of employees (those currently under age 25) expresses the highest level of dissatisfaction ever recorded by the survey for that age group." In terms of other patterns, just 51 percent of workers surveyed in 2009 said their jobs were interesting versus 70 percent in 1987. And, only 51 percent said they were satisfied with their bosses versus 60 percent in 1987.

A global survey in 2011 by Accenture contacted 3,400 professionals from 29 countries around the world.[48] Results showed less than one-half were satisfied with their jobs, and that the percentage of job satisfaction was about equal between women (43 percent) and men (42 percent). But about three-quarters of the respondents said they had no plans to leave their current jobs. These data prompt an important question: What are the implications for both employees and employers when people stick with jobs that give them little satisfaction?

Both men and women in the Accenture survey generally agreed on the least satisfying things about their jobs: being underpaid, lacking career advancement opportunities, and feeling trapped in their jobs. Gender differences were also evident. Women are less likely than men to ask for pay raises (44 percent vs. 48 percent) and for promotions (28 percent vs. 39 percent). Women are more likely to believe their careers are not fast tracked (63 percent vs. 55 percent) and more likely to report that getting ahead in careers is due to hard work and long hours (68 percent vs. 55 percent). In respect to generational differences, Gen Y workers ranked pay higher as a source of motivation (73 percent) than either Gen Xers (67 percent) or Baby Boomers (58 percent).

How Job Satisfaction Influences Work Behavior

Would you agree that people deserve to have satisfying work experiences? You probably do. But, is job satisfaction important in other than a "feel good" sense? How does it impact work behaviors and job performance? In commenting on the Conference Board data just summarized, for example, Lynn Franco, the director of the organization's Consumer Research Center, said, "The downward trend in job satisfaction could spell trouble for the engagement of U.S. employees and ultimately employee productivity."[49]

Physical Withdrawal There is a strong relationship between job satisfaction and physical withdrawal behaviors of absenteeism and turnover. Workers who are more satisfied with their jobs are absent less often than those who are dissatisfied. Satisfied workers are also more likely to remain with their present employers, and dissatisfied workers are more likely to quit or at least be on the lookout for other jobs.[50] Withdrawal through absenteeism and turnover can be very costly in terms of lost experience and the expenses for recruiting and training of replacements.[51]

A survey by Salary.com showed that employers tend not only to overestimate the job satisfaction of their employees; they also underestimate the amount of job seeking they are doing.[52] Whereas employers estimated that 37 percent of employees were on the lookout for new jobs, 65 percent of the employees said they were job seeking by networking, Web surfing, posting résumés, or checking new job possibilities. Millennials in their twenties and early thirties were most likely to engage in these "just-in-case" job searches. The report concluded that "most employers have not placed enough emphasis on important retention strategies."

Psychological Withdrawal There is also a relationship between job satisfaction and psychological withdrawal behaviors. Think of the employee engagement concept introduced previously and discussed in the positive sense. Now we are talking about work disengagement as the negative side of things. It shows up in such forms as daydreaming, cyber-loafing via Internet surfing or personal electronic communications, excessive socializing, and even just giving the appearance of being busy when one is not. These disengagement behaviors are something that Gallup researchers say as many as 71 percent of workers report feeling at times.[53]

Organizational Citizenship Job satisfaction is also linked with **organizational citizenship behaviors**.[54] These are discretionary behaviors, sometimes called OCBs, that represent a willingness to "go beyond the call of duty" or "go the extra mile" in one's work.[55] A person who is a good organizational citizen does extra things that help others—*interpersonal OCBs*—or advance the performance of the organization as a whole—*organizational OCBs*.[56] You might observe interpersonal OCBs in a service worker who is extraordinarily courteous while taking care of an upset customer, or a team member who takes on extra tasks when a co-worker is ill or absent. Examples of organizational OCBs are co-workers who are always willing volunteers for special committee or task force assignments, and those whose voices are always positive when commenting publicly on their employer.

Counterproductive Behavior The flip side of organizational citizenship shows up as **counterproductive work behaviors**.[57] Often associated with a lack of job satisfaction, they purposely disrupt relationships, processes, satisfaction and/or performance in the workplace.[58] Counterproductive workplace behaviors cover a wide range of behaviors from work avoidance, to physical and verbal aggression, to bad-mouthing, to outright work sabotage and even theft. **Workplace bullying** is a special type of counterproductive behavior that manifests itself as one person acting in an abusive, demeaning, intimidating, and/or violent manner toward another on a continuing basis. It is continuing occurrence rather than one-off or occasional behavior that differentiates "bullying" from essentially "bad" behavior. Although bullying has roots in the personality of the perpetrator and power differentials between perpetrator and victim, it can also reflect the bully's personal lack of satisfaction with work.[59]

Work-Home Spillover OB scholars are very aware that what happens to us at home can affect our attitudes and behaviors at work. They also recognize that job satisfaction can spill over to influence **at-home affect**, basically how we feel at home as represented by emotions and moods. Research finds that people with higher daily job satisfaction show more positive affect after work.[60] In a study that measured spouse or significant-other evaluations, more positive at-home affect scores were reported on days when workers experienced higher job satisfaction.[61] This issue of the job satisfaction and at-home affect link is proving especially significant as workers in today's high-tech and always-connected world struggle with work–life balance.

Linking Job Satisfaction and Job Performance

We might say that people make two key decisions about their employment and organizational memberships—the *decision to belong* and the *decision to perform*. But, we also know that not everyone who belongs to an organization—whether it's a classroom or workplace or sports team or voluntary group—performs up to expectations. So, just how does the relationship between job satisfaction and performance enter into this puzzle?[62]

Three different positions have been advanced about causality in the satisfaction–performance relationship. The first is that job satisfaction causes performance; in other words, a happy worker is a productive worker. The second is that performance causes job satisfaction. The third is that job satisfaction and performance influence one another, and they are mutually affected by other factors such as the availability of rewards. Perhaps you can make a case for one or more of these positions based on your work experiences.

Satisfaction Causes Performance If job satisfaction causes high levels of performance, the message is clear. To increase someone's work performance, make them happy. But, research hasn't found a simple and direct link between individual job satisfaction at one point in time and later work performance. A sign once posted in a tavern near one of Ford's Michigan plants helps tell the story: "I spend 40 hours a week here. Am I supposed to work, too?" Even though some evidence exists for the satisfaction-causes-performance relationship among professional or higher-level employees, the best conclusion is that job satisfaction alone is not a consistent predictor of individual work performance.

Performance Causes Satisfaction If high levels of performance cause job satisfaction, the message is quite different. Instead of focusing on job satisfaction as the precursor to performance, try to create high performance as a pathway to job satisfaction. It generally makes sense that people should feel good about their jobs when they perform well. And, research does find a link between individual performance measured at one time and later job satisfaction. ■ **Figure 4.5** shows this relationship using a model from the work of Edward E. Lawler and Lyman Porter. It suggests that performance leads to rewards that, in turn, lead to satisfaction.[63]

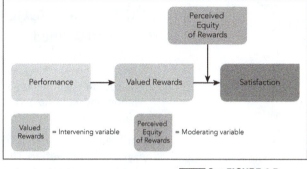

See **FIGURE 4.5 Simplified Porter-Lawler model of the performance → satisfaction relationship**

Rewards are intervening variables in the Porter-Lawler model. When valued by the recipient, they link performance with later satisfaction. The model also includes perceived equity of rewards as a moderator variable. This indicates that performance leads to satisfaction only if rewards are perceived as fair and equitable. Although this model is insightful, we also know from experience that some people may perform well but still not like the jobs that they have to do.

Rewards Cause Both Satisfaction and Performance The third alternative in the job satisfaction–performance discussion suggests that the right rewards allocated in the right ways will positively influence both performance and satisfaction. A key issue here is *performance contingency* in the allocation of rewards. This means that the size of the reward varies in proportion to the level of performance.

Research generally finds that rewards in general influence satisfaction, while performance-contingent rewards influence performance.[64] The prevailing advice is to make good use of performance contingency when giving out rewards. A high performer receiving a large reward is likely to strive for more of the same in the future. And although giving a low performer a small reward may lead to dissatisfaction at first, the expectation is that he or she will make efforts to improve performance in order to obtain higher rewards in the future.[65]

WP LS Go to your WileyPLUS Learning Space course for video episodes, examples, art, tables, Concept Checks, practice, and resources that will help you succeed in this course.

Reading for
MOTIVATION

WP LS Go to your WileyPLUS Learning Space course for video episodes, examples, art, tables, Concept Checks, practice, and resources that will help you succeed in this course.

What Is Motivation?

Motivation Defined

Parable: Once upon a time there was a horse standing knee deep in a field of carrots, contentedly munching away. A farmer wanted the horse to pull a wagon to another field, but she couldn't get the horse to come over to the fence and be harnessed. So, she stood by the wagon and held up a bunch of carrots for the horse to see. But, the horse continued to munch away on the carrots in the field.[1]

"What," you might be asking, "do horses and carrots have to do with human behavior in organizations?" The answer is **motivation**. Think of it as the forces within the individual that account for the direction, level, and persistence of effort expended at work. *Direction* refers to an individual's choice among alternative ends or goals. *Level* refers to the amount of effort put forth. *Persistence* refers to the length of time a person sticks with a path of action, even in face of difficulty.

With our co-workers and teammates, and with those we supervise and those who supervise us, we are often like the farmer in our opening parable: We'd really like someone to do something for us or for the team or organization, and we reach for some sort of incentive to try and "motivate" them to do so. All too often these attempts aren't any more successful than that of the farmer in the field.

Motivation Theories

Many years of OB scholarship have created a rich foundation of research and thinking about motivation. Even as that research continues to evolve, a number of core "content" and "process" theories help us to think more rigorously and systematically about what turns people on and off in their work.[2] Although no single theory offers an absolutely best explanation, each is valuable in its own way. By combining insights from the available theories with wisdom gained through our experiences, we have a good chance of developing personal models of motivation that work well for us in most situations.

The **content theories** of motivation focus primarily on individual needs—physiological or psychological deficiencies that we feel a compulsion to reduce or eliminate. These theories try to explain the behaviors people display at work as a search for pathways to satisfy important needs or as reactions to blocked needs. Examples to be discussed in this chapter are Maslow's hierarchy of needs theory, Alderfer's ERG theory, McClelland's acquired needs theory, and Herzberg's two-factor theory.

The **process theories** of motivation focus on how cognitive processes—individual thoughts and decision tendencies—influence work behavior. The focus is on understanding how and why certain factors influence people's decisions to work hard or not in certain situations. Three process theories discussed in this chapter are equity theory, expectancy theory, and goal-setting theory.

Motivation and Human Needs

The premise of the content or needs theories is that motivation results from our attempts to satisfy important needs. They suggest that once an individual's needs are understood, it should be possible to create situations—work, family, sport, or otherwise—that respond positively to them.

Hierarchy of Needs Theory

Perhaps the most well-known of the content approaches to motivation is Abraham Maslow's **hierarchy of needs theory**. As depicted in ▣ **Figure 5.1**, this theory identifies five levels of individual needs. They range from self-actualization and esteem needs at the top, to social, safety, and physiological needs at the bottom.[3] The concept of a needs "hierarchy" assumes that some needs are more important than others and must be satisfied before the other needs can serve as motivators. For example, physiological needs must be satisfied before safety needs are activated; safety needs must be satisfied before social needs are activated; and so on.

Maslow's model is easy to understand and has been quite popular for many years. However, it needs to be considered with caution. Research fails to support the existence of a precise five-step hierarchy of needs. If anything, the needs are more likely to operate in a flexible rather than in a strict, step-by-step sequence. The **higher-order needs** of self-actualization and esteem, for example, may grow more important than the **lower-order needs**—physiological, safety, and social, as one moves to higher levels of work responsibility.[4]

Studies report that needs may vary according to a person's career stage, the size of the organization, and even geographic location.[5] There is also no consistent evidence that the satisfaction of a need at one level decreases its importance and increases the importance of the next-higher need.[6] In addition, the presumed hierarchy of needs may vary across cultures. Findings suggest, for instance, that social needs tend to take on higher importance in more collectivist societies, such as Mexico, than in individualistic ones, such as the United States.[7]

HIGHER-ORDER NEEDS

Self-Actualization
Highest need level; need to fulfill oneself; to grow and use abilities to fullest and most creative extent

Esteem
Need for esteem of others; respect, prestige, recognition, need for self-esteem, personal sense of competence, mastery

LOWER-ORDER NEEDS

Social
Need for love, affection, sense of belongingness in one's relationships with other persons

Safety
Need for security, protection, and stability in the physical and inter-personal events of day-to-day life

Physiological
Most basic of all human needs; need for biological maintenance; need for food, water, and sustenance

See **FIGURE 5.1** Pathways to satisfaction of Maslow's higher-order and lower-order needs

ERG Theory

Clayton Alderfer's **ERG theory** is also based on needs, but it differs from Maslow's theory in important ways.[8] To begin, the theory collapses Maslow's five needs categories into three. **Existence needs** are desires for physiological and material well-being. **Relatedness needs** are desires for satisfying interpersonal relationships. **Growth needs** are desires for continued personal growth and development. ERG theory also abandons Maslow's strict hierarchy and contends that more than one of these needs need may be active at the same time.

One of the most unique aspects of ERG theory is its allowance for *frustration–regression* in how needs become activated. Alderfer believes an already satisfied lower-level need can become reactivated when a higher-level need cannot be satisfied. When someone is continually frustrated in attempts to satisfy growth needs, for example, relatedness and existence needs can again surface as key motivators.[9] This frustration-regression dynamic might explain why complaints about wages, benefits, and working conditions are often heard in many work settings. In addition to possible absolute deficiencies in these matters, concerns for them may also get exaggerated attention due to a lack of opportunities for workers to satisfy their relatedness and growth needs.

Acquired Needs Theory

In the late 1940s psychologist David I. McClelland and his co-workers began experimenting with the Thematic Apperception Test (TAT) as a way of measuring human needs.[10] The TAT is a projective technique that asks people to view pictures and write stories about what they see, and its use proved historic in motivation theory. Consider, for example, these differences when McClelland showed three executives a photograph of a man looking at family photos arranged on his work desk. One executive wrote of an engineer who was daydreaming about a family outing scheduled for the next day. Another described a designer who had picked up an idea for a new gadget from remarks made by his family. The third described an engineer who was intently working on a bridge stress problem that he seemed sure to solve because of his confident look.[11]

McClelland identified themes in the TAT stories that he believed correspond to needs that are acquired over time as a result of our life experiences. **Need for achievement (nAch)** was evident in the executive who spoke of an engineer working on a bridge stress problem. It is the desire to do something better or more efficiently, to solve problems, or to master complex tasks. **Need for affiliation (nAff)** is the desire to establish and maintain friendly and warm relations with others. This need may be more represented in the executives who mentioned family in regards to the TAT photos. Yet another need identified in McClelland's work is **need for power (nPower).** You can think of it as the desire to control others, to influence their behavior, or to be responsible for others.

Because each of the acquired needs can be linked with a set of work preferences, McClelland encouraged managers to identify in themselves and in others the strengths of nAch, nAff, and nPower. Armed with this understanding, it is possible to create work environments that will satisfy people with different need profiles. Someone with a high need for achievement, for example, will prefer individual responsibilities, challenging goals, and performance feedback. Someone with a high need for affiliation is drawn to interpersonal relationships and opportunities for communication. Someone with a high need for power seeks influence over others and likes attention and recognition.

Since these three needs are acquired, McClelland also believed it may be possible to teach people to develop need profiles required for success in various types of jobs. His research indicated, for example, that a moderate-to-high need for power that is stronger than a need for affiliation is linked with success as a senior executive. The high nPower creates the willingness to exercise influence and control over others; the lower nAff allows the executive to make difficult decisions without undue worry over being disliked.[12]

Two-Factor Theory

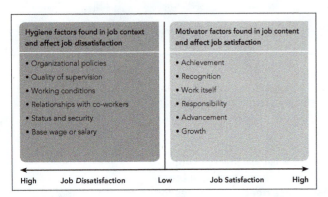

Hygiene factors found in job context and affect job *dissatisfaction*	Motivator factors found in job content and affect job satisfaction
• Organizational policies • Quality of supervision • Working conditions • Relationships with co-workers • Status and security • Base wage or salary	• Achievement • Recognition • Work itself • Responsibility • Advancement • Growth

High   Job *Dissatisfaction*   Low   Job Satisfaction   High

See **FIGURE 5.2 Sources of dissatisfaction and satisfaction in Herzberg's two-factor theory**

As scholarship on work motivation continued to develop, Frederick Herzberg took yet another approach that proved insightful to some and controversial to many. He began by asking workers to report the times they felt exceptionally good about their jobs and the times they felt exceptionally bad about them.[13] Results showed that people talked about very different things when they reported feeling good or bad about their jobs. Herzberg explained these results using what he called the **two-factor theory**, also known as the motivator–hygiene theory. This theory identifies motivator factors as primary causes of job satisfaction and hygiene factors as primary causes of job dissatisfaction.

Hygiene factors, shown to the left in ▣ **Figure 5.2**, are sources of job dissatisfaction, and they are found in the *job context* or work setting. They relate more to the setting in which people work than to the nature of the work itself. The two-factor theory suggests that job dissatisfaction occurs when hygiene is poor. It also suggests that improving the hygiene factors will not increase job satisfaction; it will only decrease job dissatisfaction. Among the hygiene factors, perhaps the most surprising is salary. Herzberg found that paying a low base salary or wage makes people dissatisfied, but paying more does not necessarily satisfy or motivate them.

Motivator factors, shown on the right in Figure 5.2, are sources of job satisfaction. These factors are found in *job content*—what people actually do in their work. They include such things as a sense of achievement, opportunities for personal growth, recognition, and responsibility. According to two-factor theory, the presence or absence of satisfiers or motivators in people's jobs is the key to satisfaction, motivation, and performance. When motivator factors are minimal, low job satisfaction decreases motivation and performance. When motivator factors are substantial, high job satisfaction raises motivation and performance.

A controversial point in the two-factor theory is Herzberg's belief that job satisfaction and job dissatisfaction are separate dimensions. Taking action to improve a hygiene factor, such as by giving pay raises or creating better physical working conditions, will not make people satisfied and more motivated in their work; it will only prevent them from being less dissatisfied on these matters. To improve job satisfaction, Herzberg believes job content must be enriched by adding more motivator factors. His technique of **job enrichment** is given special attention in the next chapter as a job design alternative. For now, the implication is well summarized in this statement by Herzberg: "If you want people to do a good job, give them a good job to do."[14]

OB scholars have long debated the merits of the two-factor theory.[15] It is criticized as being method bound, or replicable only when Herzberg's original methods are used. This is a serious criticism, since the scientific approach valued in OB requires that theories be verifiable under different research methods.[16] Yet, the distinction between hygiene and motivator factors has been a useful contribution to OB. As will be apparent in the discussions of job designs and alternative work schedules in the next chapter, the notion of two factors—job content and job context—has a practical validity that adds useful discipline to management thinking.

Emotional Drives or Needs Model

An example of continuing attention to the link between human needs and motivation is found in the emotional drives or needs model described by Harvard scholars Paul Lawrence and Nitin Nohria. Their model of motivation identifies four emotional drives or needs that people seek to satisfy at work and in daily living. The *drive to acquire* is the need to obtain physical and psychological gratification. The *drive to bond* is the need to connect with other people individually and in groups. The *drive to comprehend* is the need to understand things and gain a sense of mastery. And, the *drive to defend* is the need to be protected from threats and obtain justice.[17]

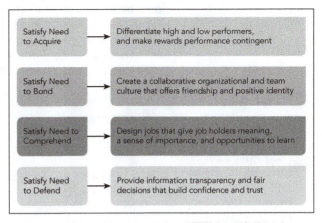

The emotional drives or needs model ties each of the four drives with specific things that organizations and managers can do to satisfy them as ways to gain a positive impact on motivation. As shown in ■ **Figure 5.3**, the drive to acquire is satisfied through reward systems that clearly distinguish between high and low performers and that distribute rewards contingently based on performance. The drive to bond is satisfied through a collaborative organizational and team culture that encourages friendship and positive social identity. The drive to comprehend is satisfied by job designs that provide a sense of meaning and importance in work being done, as well as the opportunity to learn and improve in one's competencies. The drive to defend is satisfied by information transparency and fair practices that build confidence and trust, especially in relation to rewards and resource allocations.

When the four emotional drives or needs were examined in empirical studies of 685 workers in major businesses, researchers found that their satisfaction explained 60 percent of the motivation workers experienced in their organizations.[18] Perhaps more important, they also reached this conclusion: "Employees in our study attributed as much importance to their boss's meeting their four drives as to the organization's policies."[19]

See **FIGURE 5.3 Reward systems for high and low performers**

Motivation and Equity

What happens when you get a grade back on a written assignment or test? How do you interpret your results, and what happens to your future motivation in the course? Such questions fall in the motivational domain of process theory, specifically **equity theory**. As known in OB through the writing of J. Stacy Adams, equity theory argues that any perceived inequity becomes a motivating state. In other words, people are motivated to behave in ways that restore or maintain a sense of balance—perceived equity—in their minds. These tendencies are found in work situations and the full variety of our personal affairs.[20]

Equity and Social Comparisons

The act of social comparison is a basic foundation of equity theory. Think back to the earlier questions. When you receive a grade, do you quickly try to find out what others received as well? When you do, does the interpretation of your grade depend on how well your grade compared to those of others? Equity theory predicts that your behavior upon receiving a grade—working less or harder in the course—will be based on whether or not you perceive it as fair and equitable. Furthermore, that determination is made only after you compare your results with those received by others.

Adams argues that the motivational consequences of rewards are a function of how one evaluates rewards received relative to efforts made, and as compared to the rewards received by others relative to their efforts made. A key issue in this comparison is "fairness." **Perceived inequity** occurs when someone believes that he or she has been under-rewarded or over-rewarded for work contributions in comparison to other people. As you might expect, any feelings of unfairness or perceived inequity are uncomfortable. They create a state of mind that equity theory says we are motivated to eliminate.

Equity Theory Predictions and Findings

The basic equity comparison can be summarized as follows:

$$\frac{\text{Individual Outcomes}}{\text{Individual Efforts}} =? \frac{\text{Others' Outcomes}}{\text{Others' Efforts}}$$

The preceding equity comparison shows that **felt negative inequity** exists when an individual believes that he or she has received relatively less than others in proportion to work efforts. Think of this as *under-reward inequity*. By contrast, **felt positive inequity** exists when an individual believes that he or she has received relatively more than others. Think of this as *over-reward inequity*. When either felt negative or positive inequity exists, the theory suggests that people will be motivated to act in ways that remove the cognitive discomfort and restore a sense of perceived equity to the situation. In both cases the motivational value of rewards is determined by social comparison. It isn't the reward giver's intentions that count in terms of motivational impact. What counts is how the recipient perceives the reward in his or her social context. In ■ **Figure 5.4**:

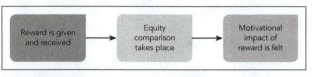

See **FIGURE 5.4 The perception of a given reward**

Research on equity theory indicates that people who feel they are overpaid (perceived positive inequity) are likely to try to increase the quantity or quality of their work, whereas those who feel they are underpaid (perceived negative inequity) are likely to try to decrease the quantity or quality of their work.[21] The research is most conclusive with respect to felt negative inequity. It appears that people are less comfortable when they are under-rewarded than when they are over-rewarded.[22] And it is important to understand how people may react, particularly in felt negative inequity situations. In these cases, an individual might engage one of the following alternatives as a way of restoring a sense of perceived equity to the situation.

- Reduce work inputs (e.g., don't do anything extra in future: "If that is all I'm going to get, this is all I'm going to do.").
- Change the outcomes received (e.g., ask for a bigger raise: "Given my contributions and what I see others getting for their work, I believe I deserve more.").
- Leave the situation (e.g., quit: "That's it, I'm out of here.").
- Change the comparison points (e.g., compare to a different co-worker: "Perhaps I'm looking at this the wrong way. My situation is more similar to Henry's than Alicia's.").
- Psychologically distort things (e.g., rationalize the inequity as temporary: "The boss has been under a lot of pressure and misses a lot of things going on in the office. Things should improve in the future.").
- Try to change the efforts of the comparison person (e.g., get a teammate to accept more work: "Look, Miranda, I know you've had a hard time at home, but it's only fair that you do a bit more to justify the raises that were just given out.").

Equity and Organizational Justice

Fairness is a basic element of equity theory. It raises an issue in organizational behavior known as **organizational justice**—how fair and equitable people view the practices and outcomes of their workplace.[23]

Procedural justice is the degree to which the process, such as rules and procedures specified by policies, is properly followed in all cases to which it applies. In a sexual harassment case, for example, this may mean that required formal hearings are held for every case submitted for administrative review. **Distributive justice** is the degree to which all people are treated the same, regardless of race, ethnicity, gender, age, or any other demographic characteristic. In a sexual harassment case, this might mean that a complaint filed by a man against a woman would receive the same consideration as one filed by a woman against a man.

Interactional justice is the degree to which the people affected by a decision are treated with dignity and respect. Interactional justice in a sexual harassment case, for example, may mean that both the accused and accusing parties believe they have received a complete explanation of any decision made. **Commutative justice** is the degree to which exchanges and transactions among parties is considered free and fair. In the sexual harassment example again, commutative justice is present when everyone involved perceives themselves as having full access to all the available facts and information.[24]

Motivation and Expectancy

Another of the process theories of motivation achieving substantial scholarly impact is Victor Vroom's **expectancy theory**.[25] It's legacy value rests with the suggestion that motivation is a result of a rational calculation—people will do what they can do when they want to do it. In other words, work motivation is determined by individual beliefs regarding effort–performance relationships and work outcomes.

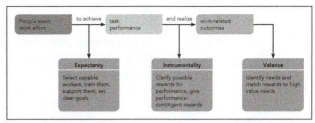

Expectancy Terms and Concepts

In expectancy theory, and as summarized in ▣ **Figure 5.5** a person is motivated to the degree that he or she believes that (1) effort will yield acceptable performance (expectancy), (2) performance will be rewarded (instrumentality), and (3) the value of the rewards is highly positive (valence). Each of the key terms is defined as follows:

▣ See **FIGURE 5.5 Key terms and managerial implications of Vroom's expectancy theory**

- **Expectancy** is the probability assigned by an individual that work effort will be followed by a given level of achieved task performance. Expectancy would equal zero if the person felt it were impossible to achieve the given performance level; it would equal one if a person were 100 percent certain that the performance could be achieved.
- **Instrumentality** is the probability assigned by the individual that a given level of achieved task performance will lead to various work outcomes. Instrumentality also varies from 0 to 1. Strictly speaking, Vroom's treatment of instrumentality would allow it to vary from −1 to +1. We use the probability definition here and the 0 to +1 range for pedagogical purposes; it is consistent with the instrumentality notion.
- **Valence** is the value attached by the individual to various work outcomes. Valences form a scale from −1 (very undesirable outcome) to +1 (very desirable outcome).

Expectancy Theory Predictions

Vroom posits that motivation, expectancy, instrumentality, and valence are related to one another in multiplicative fashion.

$$\text{Motivation} = \text{Expectancy} \times \text{Instrumentality} \times \text{Valence}$$

You can remember this expectancy equation simply as M × E × I × V, and the multiplier effect described by the "×" signs is significant. It means that the motivational appeal of a work path is sharply reduced whenever any one or more of these factors—E, I, or V—diminishes and at the extreme approaches the value of zero. In order for a reward to have a high and positive motivational impact as a work outcome, the expectancy, instrumentality, and valence associated with it must each be high and positive.

Suppose, for example, that a team leader is wondering whether or not the prospect of earning a merit pay raise will be motivational to employee team member. Expectancy theory predicts that motivation to work hard to earn the merit pay will be low if *expectancy* is low: a person feels that he or she cannot achieve the necessary performance level. Motivation will also be low if *instrumentality* is low—the person is not confident that a high level of task performance will result in a high merit pay raise. Motivation will also be low if *valence* is low: the person places little value on a merit pay increase. Finally, motivation will be low if any combination of these exists.

Expectancy Theory Implications and Research

The logic of expectancy theory suggests that work situations should be adjusted or created to maximize expectancies, instrumentalities, and valences for people in their jobs.[26] To influence expectancies, the advice is to select people with proper abilities, train them well, support them with needed resources, and identify clear performance goals. To influence instrumentality, the advice is to clarify performance–reward relationships, and then live up to them when rewards are actually given for performance accomplishments. To influence valences, the advice is to identify the needs that are important to each individual and adjust available rewards to match these needs.

A great deal of research on expectancy theory has been conducted.[27] Even though the theory has received substantial support, specific details, such as the operation of the multiplier effect, remain subject to some question. In addition, expectancy theory has proven interesting in terms of helping to explain some apparently counterintuitive findings in cross-cultural management situations. For example, one study found that a pay raise motivated a group of Mexican workers to work fewer hours. Why? They wanted a certain amount of money in order to enjoy things other than work, rather than just getting more money in general. And, a Japanese sales representative's promotion to sales manager at a U.S. company adversely affected his performance. Why? His superiors did not realize that the promotion embarrassed him and distanced him from his colleagues.[28]

Motivation and Goals

Every so often a defensive football player makes a dramatic error—scooping up an opponent's fumble and then with obvious effort and delight running the ball into the wrong end zone. These players don't lack motivation, but they fail by not focusing their energies toward the right goal. Less dramatic but similar goal and goal-setting problems occur regularly in work settings. People work hard, but end up disappointing themselves and their bosses because they pursued the wrong goals. When goals are clear and properly set, motivation is both activated and directed toward the right accomplishments.

Motivational Properties of Goals

Goal setting is the process of developing, negotiating, and formalizing the targets or objectives that a person is responsible for accomplishing.[29] Over a number of years Edwin Locke, Gary Latham, and their associates have developed a comprehensive framework linking goals to performance. They say: "Purposeful activity is the essence of living action. If the purpose is not clear, not challenging, very little gets accomplished."[30]

Goal-Setting Guidelines

Although the theory has its critics, the basic precepts of goal setting remain a respected source of advice for managing human behavior in the work setting.[31] The major implications of research are highlighted in the "How to Make Goal Setting Work for You" sidebar and can be summarized as follows:[32]

- *Difficult goals are more likely to lead to higher performance than are less difficult ones.* If the goals are seen as too difficult or impossible, however, the relationship with performance no longer holds. For example, you will likely perform better as a financial services agent if you have a goal of selling six annuities a week than if you have a goal of selling three. But if your goal is selling fifteen annuities a week, you may consider that impossible to achieve, and your performance may well be lower than what it would be with a more realistic goal.

- *Specific goals are more likely to lead to higher performance than are no goals or vague or very general ones.* All too often people work with very general goals such as the encouragement of "Do your best." Research indicates that more specific goals, such as selling six annuities a week, are much more motivational than a simple "Do your best" goal.

- *Task feedback, or knowledge of results, is likely to motivate people toward higher performance by encouraging the setting of higher performance goals.* Feedback lets people know where they stand and whether they are on course or off course in their efforts. Think, for example, about how eager you may be to find out how well you did on an examination. Think also about the instructor who often waits until the end of the course to find out how well students really liked his or her approach.

- *Goals are most likely to lead to higher performance when people have the abilities and the feelings of self-efficacy required to accomplish them.* The individual must be able to accomplish the goals and feel confident in those abilities. To take the financial services example again, you may be able to do what is required to sell six annuities a week and feel confident that you can. If your goal is to sell fifteen, however, you may believe that your abilities are insufficient to the task, and thus you may lack the confidence to work hard enough to accomplish it.

- *Goals are most likely to motivate people toward higher performance when they are accepted and there is commitment to them.* Participating in the goal-setting process helps build acceptance and commitment; it creates a sense of "ownership" of the goals that is motivating. However, even when goals are assigned, they can still be motivating if they come from a respected authority figure and are perceived as attainable. Assigned goals are most likely to lose motivational value when they are curtly or inadequately explained, and/or seem impossible to achieve.

Goal Setting and the Management Process

The entire management process is affected by goal setting. Goals set during planning provide the focus for organizing and leading, and they also facilitate controlling by identifying desired outcomes that can then be measured. One approach that tries to integrate goals across these management functions is known as **management by objectives (MBO)**. MBO is essentially a process of joint goal setting between managers or team leaders and those who report to them.[33]

An example is the team leader who works with team members to set performance goals consistent with higher-level organizational objectives.

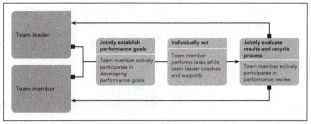

■ **Figure 5.6** shows how the MBO process can take advantage of goal-setting principles. The joint team leader and team member discussions are designed to extend participation from the point of setting initial goals all the way to evaluating results in terms of goal attainment. As team members work to achieve their goals, the team leader's role is to actively coach them.

See **FIGURE 5.6 How a management by objectives process works**

Researchers identify a number of common difficulties with MBO in practice.[34] These include overemphasizing paperwork to document goals and accomplishments, and focusing on top-down goals, goals that are easily stated and achieved, and individual instead of team goals. When these issues are resolved, however, an MBO-type approach can help bring the many benefits and insights of goal-setting theory to life.

WP LS Go to your WileyPLUS Learning Space course for video episodes, examples, art, tables, Concept Checks, practice, and resources that will help you succeed in this course.

6 Reading for
MOTIVATION AND PERFORMANCE

WP LS Go to your WileyPLUS Learning Space course for video episodes, examples, art, tables, Concept Checks, practice, and resources that will help you succeed in this course.

Motivation, Rewards, and Performance

Motivation is defined as forces within the individual that account for the level and persistence of an effort expended at work. And because motivation is a property of the individual, we basically motivate ourselves. All managers and team leaders or parents and teachers can do is try to create environments that offer other individuals appealing sources of motivation. Whether they respond positively or not is up to them. But, one way to unlock this motivational potential is to provide opportunities to earn rewards that match well with individual needs and goals.

Employee Value Proposition and Fit

Perhaps the best place to start any discussion of the link between motivation, rewards, and performance is the concept of an **employee value proposition**, or EVP. Think of it as an exchange of value, what the organization offers the employee in return for his or her work contributions.[1] The value offered by the individual includes things like effort, loyalty, commitment, creativity, and skills. The value offered by the employer includes things like pay, benefits, meaningful work, flexible schedules, and personal development opportunities. It is common to call this exchange of values the *psychological contract*.

When everything comes together in an EVP and the psychological contract is in balance, the foundations for motivation are well set—not perfect yet, but well set. The key starting point is that each party perceives the exchange of values as fair and that it is getting what it needs from the other. Any perceived imbalance is likely to cause problems. From the individual's side, a perceived lack of inducements from the employer may reduce motivation and ultimately poor performance. From the employer's side, a perceived lack of contributions from the individual may cause a loss of confidence in and commitment to the employee, and reduced rewards for work delivered.

The foundation for a healthy and positive employee value proposition is "fit." **Person–job fit** is the extent to which an individual's skills, interests, and personal characteristics match well with the requirements of the job. **Person–organization fit** is the extent to which an individual's values, interests, and behaviors are consistent with the culture of the organization. A poor fit in either case increases the likelihood that imbalance will creep into the EVP. The importance of a good fit to the employee value proposition is highlighted to the extreme at Zappos.com. Believe it or not, if a new employee is unhappy with the firm after going through initial training, Zappos pays them to quit. At last check the "bye-bye bounty" was $4,000, and between 2 and 3 percent of new hires were taking it each year.[2]

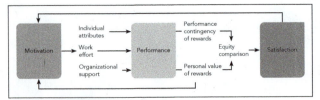

See **FIGURE 6.1 An integrated model of individual motivation to work**

Integrated Model of Motivation

Wouldn't it be nice if we all worked with a great employee value proposition and could connect with our jobs and organizations in positive and inspirational ways? In fact, there are lots of great workplaces out there. And, they become great because people and practices throughout the organization turn members on to their jobs rather than off of them. Making this happen requires a good understanding of motivation, a true appreciation for diversity and individual differences, and the ability to make rewards for good work truly meaningful.

Figure 6.1 outlines an integrated model of motivation that ties together the basic effort–performance–rewards relationship. The figure shows job performance and satisfaction as separate but interdependent work results. Performance is influenced by *individual attributes* such as ability and experience; *organizational support* comes from things such as goals, resources, and technology; and *effort* is the willingness of people to work hard at what they are doing. The individual experiences satisfaction when the rewards received for work accomplishments are perceived as both performance contingent and equitable.

Double-check Figure 6.1 and locate where various motivation theories come into play. Reinforcement theory highlights performance contingency and immediacy in determining how rewards affect future performance. Equity theory points to the influence on behavior of the perceived fairness of rewards. Content theories offer insight into individual needs that can give motivational value to the possible rewards. And, expectancy theory is central to the effort–performance–rewards linkage.

Intrinsic and Extrinsic Rewards

The typical reward systems of organizations offer a mix both intrinsic and extrinsic rewards. **Intrinsic rewards** are positively valued work outcomes that the individual receives directly as a result of task performance. Think of them as the reasons we do things just to enjoy them—play a sport, listen to certain music, and even do certain jobs. A feeling of achievement after completing a particularly challenging task is an example. Yves Chouinard, founder and CEO of Patagonia, Inc., puts it this way: "It's easy to go to work when you get paid to do what you love to do."[3] One of the most important things to remember about intrinsic rewards is that we give them to ourselves. Their positive impact doesn't require anyone else—boss or team leader included—to be involved.

Extrinsic rewards are positively valued work outcomes that are given to an individual or a group by another person. We don't get them by ourselves; someone else has to be the provider. Common extrinsic rewards include symbolic gestures, such as praise for a job well done, or material perks, such as pay raises or bonuses and so on. All such rewards have to be well managed if they are to have positive motivational impact. And the process can be tricky. How often have you heard someone say, "I'll do the minimum to keep the pay and benefits of this job, but that's it," or "For what I get paid with not even a thank-you, this job is hardly worth the effort I put into it."

Pay for Performance

Pay is a common and often talked about extrinsic reward. It's also an especially complex one that may not always deliver the hoped-for results. When pay functions well, it can help an organization attract and retain highly capable workers. It can also help satisfy and motivate these workers to work hard to achieve high performance. But when something goes wrong with pay, the results may decrease motivation performance. Pay dissatisfaction often shows up as bad attitudes, increased absenteeism, intentions to leave and actual turnover, poor organizational citizenship, and even adverse impacts on employees' physical and mental health.

The research of scholar and consultant Edward Lawler generally concludes that pay only serves as a motivator when high levels of job performance are viewed as the paths through which high pay can be achieved.[4] This is the logic of **performance-contingent pay**, or pay for performance, where you earn more when you produce more and earn less when you produce less. Organizations pursue various options when implementing performance-contingent pay systems.

Merit Pay It is most common to talk about pay for performance in respect to **merit pay**, a compensation system that directly ties an individual's salary or wage increase to measures of performance accomplishments during a specified time period.

Although the concept of merit pay is compelling, a survey by the Hudson Institute demonstrates that it is more easily said than done. When asked if employees who perform better really get paid more, only 48 percent of managers and 31 percent of nonmanagers responded with agreement. When asked if their last pay raise had been based on performance, 46 percent of managers and just 29 percent of nonmanagers said yes.[5] In fact, surveys often show that people do not believe their pay is an adequate reward for a job well done.[6]

In order to work well a merit pay plan should create a belief among employees that the way to achieve high pay is to perform at high levels. This means that the merit system should be based on realistic and accurate measures of work performance. It means that the merit system should clearly discriminate between high and low performers in the amount of pay increases awarded. It also means that any "merit" aspects of a pay increase are clearly and contingently linked with the desired performance.

Bonuses Some employers award cash **bonuses** as extra pay for performance that meets certain benchmarks or is over and above expectations. The bonus becomes "cash in hand" without raising the base salary or wage rate. This practice is especially common in senior executive ranks. However, a current trend is to extend bonus opportunities to workers at all levels. Employees at Applebee's, for example, may earn "Applebucks"—small cash bonuses that are given to reward performance and increase loyalty to the firm.[7]

Gain Sharing and Profit Sharing Another way to link pay with performance is **gain sharing**. This gives workers the opportunity to earn more by receiving shares of any productivity gains that they help to create at the team or work unit levels. An alternative is **profit sharing**, which rewards workers for contributions to increased organizational profits.[8] Both gain-sharing and profit-sharing plans are supposed to create a greater sense of personal responsibility for performance improvements and increase motivation to work hard. They are also supposed to encourage cooperation and teamwork to increase productivity.[9]

Stock Options and Employee Stock Ownership Some companies offer employees **stock options** that give the owner the right to buy shares of stock at a future date at a fixed or "strike" price.[10] The expectation is that because employees gain financially as the stock price increases, those with stock options will be highly motivated to do their best so that the firm performs well. In **employee stock ownership plans (ESOPs)**, companies allow stock to be purchased by employees at a price below market value. The incentive value is like the stock options: Employee owners are expected to work hard so that the organization will perform well, the stock price will rise, and, as owners, they will benefit from the gains. Of course, there are risks to both options and stock ownership since a firm's stock prices can fall in the future as well as rise.[11]

Skill-Based Pay **Skill-based pay** rewards people for acquiring and developing job-relevant skills. Pay systems of this sort pay people for the mix and depth of skills they have, not for the particular job assignment they hold. The expected motivational advantages include more willingness to engage in cross-training to learn other jobs in a team or work unit as well as to take on more self-management responsibilities, thus reducing the need to pay for more supervisors.[12]

Motivation and Performance Management

If you want to get hired by Procter & Gamble and get rewarded by advancements to upper management, you had better be good. Not only is the company highly selective in hiring; it also carefully tracks the performance of every manager in every job they are asked to do. The firm always has at least three performance-proven replacements ready to fill any vacancy that occurs. By linking performance to career advancement, motivation to work hard is built into the P&G management model.[13]

The approach followed by P&G can be highly motivating to those who want to work hard, advance in rank, and have successful top executive careers. However, we shouldn't underestimate the challenge of implementing this type of performance-based reward system. Such systems falter and fail to deliver desired results when the process and/or the performance measurement isn't respected by everyone involved.

Performance Management Process

The foundations for performance management are shown in **Figure 6.2**. And if the process is to work well, everyone involved must have good answers to both the "Why?" and the "What?" questions.

The "Why?" question in performance management is "What is the purpose?" Performance management serves an *evaluation purpose* when it lets people know where their actual performance stands relative to objectives and standards. Such an evaluation feeds into decisions that allocate rewards and otherwise administer the organization's human resource management

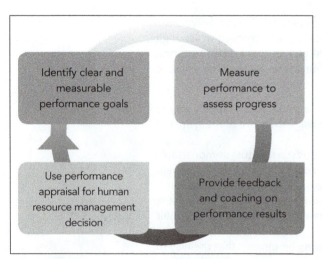

See **FIGURE 6.2**
Four steps in the performance management process

systems. Performance management serves a *developmental purpose* when it provides insights into individual strengths and weaknesses. This can be used to plan helpful training and career development activities.

The "What?" question in performance management is "What is being measured?" It takes us back to the adage "What gets measured happens"—that is, people tend to do what they know is going to be measured. Given this, we have to make sure we are measuring the right things in the right ways in the performance management process. If a dean wants faculty members to be great teachers, for example, teaching has to be measured in valid ways and rewards tied to the results. Of course, the definition of "great" teaching and the measurement of it are both open to controversy. This is one reason we often talk about the importance of teaching while rewarding faculty members for easier-to-measure research output.

Performance Measurement Approaches and Errors

Performance measurements should be based on clear criteria, be accurate and defensible in differentiating between high and low performance, and be useful as feedback that can help improve performance in the future. Yet, talking about good measurement is easier than actually doing it. It's good to use **output measures** that assess what is accomplished in respect to concrete work results. But when measuring outputs is hard, **activity measures** that assess work inputs in respect to activities tried and efforts expended are often used as replacements. An example might be to use the number of customer visits made per day—an activity measure—to assess a salesperson, instead of or in addition to counting the number of actual sales made—an output measure.

Regardless of the method being employed, any performance assessment system should satisfy two criteria. First, the measures should past the test of **reliability**. This means they provide consistent results each time they are used for the same person and situation. Second, the measures should pass the test of **validity**. This means that they actually measure something of direct relevance to job performance. The following are examples of measurement errors that can reduce the reliability or validity of any performance assessment.[14]

- *Halo error*—results when one person rates another person on several different dimensions and gives a similar rating for each dimension.
- *Leniency error*—just as some professors are known as "easy A's," some managers tend to give relatively high ratings to virtually everyone under their supervision; the opposite is *strictness error*—giving everyone a low rating.
- *Central tendency error*—occurs when managers lump everyone together around the average, or middle, category; this gives the impression that there are no very good or very poor performers on the dimensions being rated.
- *Recency error*—occurs when a rater allows recent events to influence a performance rating over earlier events; an example is being critical of an employee who is usually on time but shows up one hour late for work the day before his or her performance rating.
- *Personal bias error*—displays expectations and prejudices that fail to give the jobholder complete respect, such as showing racial bias in ratings.

Performance Assessment Methods

The formal procedure or event that evaluates a person's work performance is often called *performance review*, *performance appraisal*, or *performance assessment*. A variety of methods can be used. But, each has strengths and weaknesses that may make it a better choice in some situations than in others.[15]

Comparative Methods Comparative methods of performance assessment identify one worker's standing relative to others. **Ranking** is the simplest approach and is done by rank ordering each individual from best to worst on overall performance or on specific performance dimensions. Although relatively simple to use, this method can be difficult when many people must be considered. An alternative is the **paired comparison** in which each person is directly compared with every other one. A person's final ranking is determined by the number of pairs for which she or he emerges as the "winner." Yet another alternative is **forced distribution**. It forces a set percentage of all persons being assessed into predetermined performance categories, such as outstanding, good, average, and poor. For example, it might be that a team leader

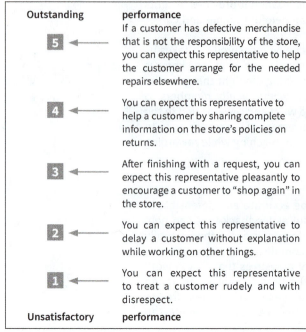

Outstanding	performance
5	If a customer has defective merchandise that is not the responsibility of the store, you can expect this representative to help the customer arrange for the needed repairs elsewhere.
4	You can expect this representative to help a customer by sharing complete information on the store's policies on returns.
3	After finishing with a request, you can expect this representative pleasantly to encourage a customer to "shop again" in the store.
2	You can expect this representative to delay a customer without explanation while working on other things.
1	You can expect this representative to treat a customer rudely and with disrespect.
Unsatisfactory	performance

See **FIGURE 6.3 Sample behaviorally anchored rating scale (BARS) for a customer service representative**

must assign 10 percent of members to "outstanding," another 10 percent to "poor," and another 40 percent each to "good" and "average." One goal of this method is to eliminate tendencies to rate everyone about the same.

Rating Scales Graphic rating scales list a variety of performance dimensions, such as quality or quality of work, or personal traits, such as punctuality or diligence that an individual is expected to exhibit. The scales allow the manager to easily assign the individual scores on each dimension, but the descriptions are often very generalized and lack solid performance links to a given job. The **behaviorally anchored rating scale (BARS)** adds more sophistication by linking ratings to specific and observable job-relevant behaviors. These include descriptions of superior and inferior performance. The sample BARS for a customer service representative in ▣ **Figure 6.3** shows a focus on discriminating among very specific work behaviors. This specificity makes the BARS more valuable for both evaluation and development purposes.[16]

Critical Incident Diary Critical incident diaries are written records that give examples of a person's work behavior that leads to either unusual performance success or failure. The incidents are typically recorded in a diary-type log that is kept daily or weekly according to predetermined dimensions. This approach is excellent for employee development and feedback. However, because it consists of qualitative statements rather than quantitative ratings, it is more debatable as an evaluation tool. This is why the critical incident technique is often used in combination with one of the other methods.

360° Review Many organizations now make assessments based on a combination of feedback from a person's bosses, peers, and subordinates, internal and external customers, and self-ratings. Known as the **360° review**, or *360° assessment,* it is quite common in today's team-oriented organizations. A typical approach asks the jobholder to complete a self rating and meet with a set of 360° participants to discuss it as well as their ratings. The jobholder learns from how well one's self-rating compares with the viewpoints of others, and the results are useful for both evaluation and development purposes.

New technologies allow 360° feedback to be continuous rather than periodic. Accenture uses a computer program called Performance Multiplier that allows users to post projects, goals, and status updates for review by others. And Microsoft-Rypple software allows users to post assessment questions in 140 characters or less. Examples might be—"What did you think of my presentation?" or "How could I have run that meeting better?" Anonymous responses are compiled by the program, and the 360° feedback is then sent to the person posting the query.[17]

Motivation and Job Design

When it comes to motivation, we might say that nothing beats a good person–job fit. A match of job requirements with individual abilities and needs is often a high satisfaction and high performance combination. By contrast, a bad person–job fit is likely to result in poor motivation and performance problems. You might think of the goal this way:

Person + Good Job Fit = High Motivation

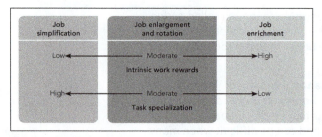

See **FIGURE 6.4 A continuum of job design strategies**

Job design is the process of planning and specifying job tasks and work arrangements.[18] ▣ **Figure 6.4** shows how three alternative job design approaches differ in the way tasks are defined and availability of intrinsic rewards. The "best" job design is one that meets organizational performance requirements, offers a good fit with individual skills and needs, and provides opportunities for job satisfaction.

Scientific Management

The history of scholarly interest in job design can be traced in part to Frederick Taylor's work with **scientific management** in the early 1900s.[19] Taylor and his contemporaries wanted to create management and organizational practices that would increase people's efficiency at work. Their approach was to study a job carefully, break it into its smallest components, establish exact time and motion requirements for each task to be done, and then train workers to do these tasks in the same way over and over again. Taylor's principles of scientific management can be summarized as follows:

1. Develop a "science" for each job that covers rules of motion, standard work tools, and supportive work conditions.
2. Hire workers with the right abilities for the job.
3. Train and motivate workers to do their jobs according to the science.
4. Support workers by planning and assisting their work using the job science.

Today, the term **job simplification** is used to describe a scientific management approach that standardizes work procedures and employs people in routine, clearly defined, and highly specialized tasks. The machine-paced automobile assembly line is a classic example. Why is it used? The answer is to increase operating efficiency. Job simplification reduces the number of skills required, allows for hiring low-cost labor, keeps the need for job training to a minimum, and focuses expertise on repetitive tasks. Why is it often criticized? Jobs designed this way come with potential disadvantages—lower work quality, high rates of absenteeism and turnover, and demands for ever-higher wages to compensate for unappealing work. One response is more automation to replace people with technology. In automobile manufacturing, for example, robots now do many different kinds of work previously accomplished with human labor.

Job Enlargement and Job Rotation

Although job simplification makes the limited number of tasks easier to master, the repetitiveness of the work can reduce motivation. This has prompted alternative job design approaches that try to make jobs more interesting by adding breadth to the variety of tasks performed.

Job enlargement increases task variety by combining into one job two or more tasks that were previously assigned to separate workers. Sometimes called *horizontal loading*, this approach increases job breadth by having the worker perform more and different tasks, but all at the same level of responsibility and challenge.

Job rotation increases task variety by periodically shifting workers among jobs involving different tasks. Also a form of horizontal loading, the responsibility level of the tasks stays the same. The rotation can be arranged according to almost any time schedule, such as hourly, daily, or weekly schedules. An important benefit of job rotation is training. It allows workers to become more familiar with different tasks and increases the flexibility with which they can be moved from one job to another.

Job Enrichment

When it comes to job rotation and enlargement, psychologist Frederick Herzberg asks: "Why should workers become motivated when one or more 'meaningless' tasks are added to previously existing ones or when work assignments are rotated among equally 'meaningless' tasks?"[20] He recommends **job enrichment**. It designs job that create opportunities to experiene responsibility, achievement, recognition, and personal growth. This is done by *vertical loading* that moves into a job many planning and evaluating tasks normally performed by supervisors. The increased job depth provides pathways to higher-order need satisfaction, and is supposed to increase both motivation and performance.

Job Characteristics Model

OB scholars have been reluctant to recommend job enrichment as a universal approach to job design. There are just too many individual differences among people at work for it to solve all performance and satisfaction problems. Their answer to the question "Is job enrichment for everyone?" is a clear "No." Present thinking focuses more on a diagnostic and contingency approach to job design. A good example is the job characteristics model developed by Richard Hackman and Greg Oldham.[21]

Core Job Characteristics

- Skill variety
- Task identity
- Task significance
- Autonomy
- Feedback

Job Outcomes

- Motivation
- Job Satisfaction
- Job Performance

Individual Moderator Variables

- Growth-need strength
- Knowledge and skill
- Context satisfaction

See **FIGURE 6.5 Job design considerations according to the job characteristics model**

Core Characteristics ▣ **Figure 6.5** shows how the Hackman and Oldham model informs the process of job design. The higher a job scores on each of the following five core characteristics, the higher its motivational potential and the more it is considered to be enriched:[22]

- *Skill variety*—the degree to which a job includes a variety of different activities and involves the use of a number of different skills and talents
- *Task identity*—the degree to which the job requires completion of a "whole" and identifiable piece of work, one that involves doing a job from beginning to end with a visible outcome
- *Task significance*—the degree to which the job is important and involves a meaningful contribution to the organization or society in general
- *Autonomy*—the degree to which the job gives the employee substantial freedom, independence, and discretion in scheduling the work and determining the procedures used in carrying it out
- *Job feedback*—the degree to which carrying out the work activities provides direct and clear information to the employee regarding how well the job has been done

A job's motivating potential can be raised by combining tasks to create larger jobs, opening feedback channels to enable workers to know how well they are doing, establishing client relationships to experience such feedback directly from customers, and employing vertical loading to create more planning and controlling responsibilities. When the core characteristics are enriched in these ways, the job creates what is often called psychological empowerment—a sense of personal fulfillment and purpose that arouses one's feelings of competency and commitment to the work.[23] Figure 6.5 identifies three critical psychological states that have a positive impact on individual motivation, performance, and satisfaction: experienced meaningfulness of the work, experienced responsibility for the outcomes of the work, and knowledge of actual results of the work.

Moderator Variables The five core job characteristics do not affect all people in the same way. Rather than accept the notion that enriched jobs should be good for everyone, Hackman and Oldham take a contingency view that suggests enriched jobs will lead to positive outcomes only for those persons who are a good match for them—the person–job fit issue again.

"Fit" in the job characteristics model is based on the three moderators shown in Figure 6.5. The first is *growth-need strength*, or the degree to which a person desires the opportunity for self-direction, learning, and personal accomplishment at work. The expectation here is that people high in growth-need strengths will respond positively to enriched jobs, whereas people low in growth-need strengths will find enriched jobs to be sources of anxiety. The second moderator is *knowledge and skill*. People whose capabilities fit the demands of enriched jobs are predicted to feel good about them and perform well. Those who are inadequate or who feel inadequate in this regard are likely to experience difficulties. The third moderator is *context satisfaction*, or the extent to which an employee is satisfied with aspects of the work setting such as salary, quality of supervision, relationships with co-workers, and working conditions. In general, people who are satisfied with job context are more likely to do well in enriched jobs.

Research Concerns and Questions Experts generally agree that the job characteristics model and its diagnostic approach are useful but not perfect, guides to job design.[24] One concern is whether or not jobs have stable and objective characteristics to which individuals will respond predictably and consistently over time.[25] It's quite possible that individual needs and task perceptions are a result of socially constructed realities. Suppose, for example, that several of your friends tell you that the instructor for a course is bad, the content is boring, and the requirements involve too much work. You may then think that the critical characteristics of the class are the instructor, the content, and the workload, and that they are all bad. All of this may substantially influence the way you perceive your instructor and the course, and the way you deal with the class—regardless of the core characteristics discussed in the Hackman and Old-ham model.

Finally, research provides the following answers for three common questions about job enrichment and its applications. (1) *Should everyone's job be enriched?* The answer is clearly "No." The logic of individual differences suggests that not everyone will want an enriched job. Individuals most likely to have positive reactions to job enrichment are those who need achievement, who exhibit a strong work ethic, or who are seeking higher-order growth-need satisfaction at work. Job enrichment also appears to work best when the job context is positive and when workers have the abilities needed to do the enriched job. Costs, technological constraints, and workgroup or union opposition may also make it difficult to enrich some jobs. (2) *With so much attention on teams in organizations today, can job enrichment apply to groups?* The answer is "Yes." The result is called a self managing team. (3) *For those who don't want an enriched job, what can be done to make their work more motivating?* One answer rests in the following section and its focus on alternative work schedules. Even if the job content can't be changed, a redesign of the job context or setting may have a positive impact on motivation and performance.

Alternative Work Schedules

Another way that organizations are reshaping employee value propositions is through alternative work arrangements that do away with the traditional forty-hour weeks and nine-to-five schedules where work is done at the place of business. New alternatives are designed to improve satisfaction by helping employees balance the demands of work with their nonwork lives.[26] The value from the employee side is more support for work–life balance by a "family-friendly" employer.

If you have any doubts at all about the forces at play, consider these facts: 78 percent of American couples are dual wage earners; 63 percent believe they don't have enough time for spouses and partners; 74 percent believe they don't have enough time for their children; 35 percent are spending time caring for elderly relatives. Furthermore, both Baby Boomers and Gen Ys believe flexible work is important and want opportunities to work remotely at least part of the time.[27]

Compressed Workweeks

A **compressed workweek** is any schedule that allows a full-time job to be completed in fewer than the standard five days. The most common form is the "4/40"—40 hours of work accomplished in four 10-hour days, leaving a 3-day break. The additional time off gives workers longer weekends, free weekdays to pursue personal business, and lower commuting costs. In return, the organization hopes for less absenteeism, greater work motivation, and improved recruiting of new employees.[28] However, scheduling compressed workweeks can be more complicated, overtime pay for time over 8 hours in one day may be required by law, and union opposition to the longer workday is also a possibility.

Flexible Working Hours

Another alternative is some form of **flexible working hours** or *flextime* that gives individuals daily choice in work hours. A common flex schedule requires certain hours of "core" time but leaves employees free to choose their remaining hours from flexible time blocks. One person, for example, may start early and leave early, whereas another may start later and leave later.

All top 100 companies in *Working Mother* magazine's list of best employers for working moms offer flexible scheduling. Reports indicate that the flexibility gained to deal with nonwork obligations can lower turnover, absenteeism, and tardiness for the organization while reducing stress and raising commitment and performance by workers.[29] Flexible hours help employees manage children's schedules, fulfill elder care responsibilities, and attend to personal affairs such as medical and dental appointments, home emergencies, banking, and so on.

Job Sharing

In **job sharing**, two or more persons split one full-time job. This can be done, for example, on a half day, weekly, or monthly basis. Organizations benefit from job sharing when they can attract talented people who would otherwise be unable to work. Some job sharers report less burnout and claim that they feel recharged each time they report for work. The tricky part of this arrangement is finding two people who will stay coordinated and work well with each other.

Job sharing should not be confused with something called **work sharing**. This occurs when workers agree to cut back on the number of hours they work in order to protect against layoffs. In the recent economic crisis, for example, workers in some organizations agreed to voluntarily reduce their paid hours worked so that others would not lose their jobs.

Telecommuting

Technology has enabled yet an-other alternative work arrangement that is now highly visible in employment sectors ranging from higher education to government, and from manufacturing to services.[30] **Telecommuting** is work done at home or in a remote location via the use of computers, tablets, and smart phone connections with bosses, co-workers, and customers. And it's popular. About four out of five employees say they would like the option and consider it a "significant job perk."[31]

When asked what they like, telecommuters report increased productivity, fewer distractions, the freedom to be their own boss, and the benefit of having more time for themselves. They also like the added flexibility, comforts of home, and being able to live and work in locations consistent with personal lifestyles. Potential negatives are reported as well. Some telecommuters say they end up working too much while having difficulty separating work and personal life. Other complaints include not being considered as important as on-site workers, feeling isolated from co-workers and less identified with the work team, and even having trouble managing interruptions from everyday family affairs. One telecommuter says, "You have to have self-discipline and pride in what you do, but you also have to have a boss that trusts you enough to get out of the way."[32]

Employers that allow telecommuting expect it to help improve work–life balance and job satisfaction for employees. But, some also worry that too much telecommuting disrupts schedules and reduces important face-to-face time among co-workers. Yahoo CEO Marissa Mayer, for example, was willing to face criticism when she decided to disallow it. Her reasoning was that working from home detracted from Yahoo!'s collaborative culture and ability to innovate.[33]

Part-Time Work

Part-time work is an increasingly prominent and controversial work arrangement. One of the big downsides is that part-timers often fail to qualify for fringe benefits such as health care insurance and retirement plans. In addition, they may be paid less than their full-time counterparts. Because part-timers are easily released and hired as needs dictate, they are also likely to be laid off before full-timers during difficult business times.

The number of part-time workers is growing as today's employers try to stay flexible and manage costs in a demanding global economy. This is reflected in what you might hear called a "permanent temp economy," one where working as a permanent part timer—or—*permatemp* is a new reality for many job hunters.[34] Some choose this schedule voluntarily. Recent data, for example, show that many Millennials are opting for a shifting portfolio of freelance jobs that give them flexibility while still providing earning power.[35] But, there's no doubt that part-time work is an involuntary alternative for many who would prefer full-time work but are unable to get it.

WP LS Go to your WileyPLUS Learning Space course for video episodes, examples, art, tables, Concept Checks, practice, and resources that will help you succeed in this course.

Reading for
THE NATURE OF TEAMS

Teams in Organizations

When we hear the word *team*, a variety of popular sports teams often comes to mind, perhaps a favorite from the college ranks or the professional leagues. For a moment, let's stick with basketball. *Scene—NBA Basketball:* Scholars find that both good and bad basketball teams win more games the longer the players have been together. Why? They claim it's a "teamwork effect" that creates wins because players know each other's moves and playing tendencies.[1]

Let's not forget that teams are important in work settings as well. And whether or not a team lives up to expectations can have a major impact on how well its customers and clients are served. *Scene—Hospital Operating Room:* Scholars notice that the same heart surgeons have lower death rates for similar procedures when performed in hospitals where they do more operations. They claim it's because the doctors spend more time working together with members of these surgery teams. The scholars argue it's not only the surgeon's skills that count: "The skills of the team, and of the organization, matter."[2]

Teams and Teamwork

What is going on in the prior examples? Whereas a group of people milling around a coffee shop counter is just that—a "group" of people, teams like those in the examples are supposed to be something more—"groups +" if you will. That "+" factor is what distinguishes the successful NBA basketball teams from the also-rans and the best surgery teams from all the others.

In OB we define a **team** as a group of people brought together to use their complementary skills to achieve a common purpose for which they are collectively accountable.[3] Real **teamwork** occurs when team members accept and live up to their collective accountability by actively working together so that all of their respective skills are best used to achieve team goals.[4] Of course, there is a lot more to teamwork than simply assigning members to the same group, calling it a team, appointing someone as team leader, and then expecting everybody to do a great job.[5] The responsibilities for building high-performance teams rest not only with the team leader, manager, or coach, but also with the team members. If you look now at the "Heads Up: Don't Forget" sidebar, you'll find a checklist of several team must-haves, the types of contributions that team members and leaders can make to help their teams achieve high performance.[6]

What Teams Do

One of the first things to understand about teams in organizations is that they do many things and make many types of performance contributions. In general, we can describe them as teams that recommend things, run things, and make or do things.[7]

Teams that recommend things are set up to study specific problems and recommend solutions for them. These teams typically work with a target completion date and often disband once the purpose has been fulfilled. The teams include task forces, ad hoc committees, special project teams, and the like. Members of these teams must be able to learn quickly how to pool talents, work well together, and accomplish the assigned task.

Teams that run things lead organizations and their component parts. A good example is a top-management team composed of a CEO and other senior executives. Key issues addressed by top-management teams include identifying overall organizational purposes, goals, and values as well as crafting strategies and persuading others to support them.[8]

Teams that make or do things are work units that perform ongoing tasks such as marketing, sales, systems analysis, manufacturing, or working on special projects with assigned due dates.

Members of these action teams must have good working relationships with one another, the right technologies and operating systems, and the external support needed to achieve performance effectiveness over the long term or within an assigned deadline.

Organizations as Networks of Teams

The many **formal teams** found in organizations are created and officially designated to serve specific purposes. Some are permanent and appear on organization charts as departments (e.g., market research department), divisions (e.g., consumer products division), or teams (e.g., product-assembly team). Such teams can vary in size from very small departments or teams consisting of just a few people to large divisions employing 100 or more people. Other formal teams are temporary and short lived. They are created to solve specific problems or perform defined tasks and are then disbanded once the purpose has been accomplished. Examples include temporary committees and task forces.[9]

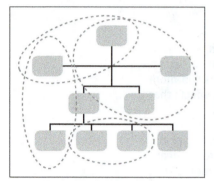

See **FIGURE 7.1 An interlocking network of an informal group**

Interlocking networks of formal teams create the basic structure of an organization. On the vertical dimension, the team leader at one level is a team member at the next higher level.[10] On the horizontal dimension, a team member may also serve on organization-wide task forces and committees.

Organizations also have vast networks of **informal groups**, which emerge and coexist as a shadow to the formal structure and without any assigned purpose or official endorsement. As shown in ▣ **Figure 7.1**, these informal groups develop through personal relationships and create their own interlocking networks within the organization. *Friendship groups* consist of persons who like one another. Their members tend to work together, sit together, take breaks together, and even do things together outside of the workplace. *Interest groups* consist of persons who share job-related interests, such as an intense desire to learn more about computers, or non work interests, such as community service, sports, or religion.

Although informal groups can be places where people meet to complain, spread rumors, and disagree with what is happening in the organization, they can also be quite helpful. The personal connections activated within informal networks can speed up workflows as people assist each other in ways that cut across the formal structures. They also create interpersonal relationships that can satisfy individual needs, such as by providing companionship (meeting a social need) or a sense of personal importance (meeting an ego need).

A tool known as **social network analysis** is used to identify the informal groups and networks of relationships that are active in an organization. The analysis typically asks people to identify co-workers who most often help them, who communicate with them regularly, and who motivate and demotivate them. When these social networks are mapped, you learn a lot about how work really gets done and who communicates most often with whom. The results often contrast markedly with the formal arrangements depicted on organization charts. And, this information can be used to redo the charts and reorganize teamwork for better performance.

Cross-Functional and Problem-Solving Teams

A **cross-functional team** consists of people brought together from different functional departments or work units to achieve more horizontal integration and better lateral relations. Members of cross-functional teams are supposed to work together with a positive combination of functional expertise and integrative team thinking. The expected result is higher performance driven by the advantages of better information and faster decision making.

Cross-functional teams are a way of trying to beat the **functional silos problem**, also called the *functional chimneys problem*. It occurs when members of functional units stay focused on internal matters and minimize their interactions and cooperation with other functions. In this sense, the functional departments or work teams create artificial boundaries, or "silos," that discourage rather than encourage interaction with other units. The result is poor integration and poor coordination with other parts of the organization. The cross-functional team helps break down these barriers by creating a forum in which members from different functions work together as one team with a common purpose.[11]

Organizations also use any number of **problem-solving teams**, which are created temporarily to serve a specific purpose by dealing with a specific problem or opportunity. The president of a company, for example, might convene a task force to examine the possibility of implementing flexible work hours; a human resource director might bring together a committee to advise her on changes in employee benefit policies; a project team might be formed to plan and implement a new organization-wide information system.

The term **employee involvement team** applies to a wide variety of teams whose members meet regularly to collectively examine important workplace issues. They might discuss, for example, ways to enhance quality, better satisfy customers, raise productivity, and improve the quality of work life. Such employee involvement teams are supposed to mobilize the full extent of workers' know-how and experiences for continuous improvements. An example is what some organizations call a **quality circle**, a small team of persons who meet periodically to discuss and make proposals for ways to improve quality.[12]

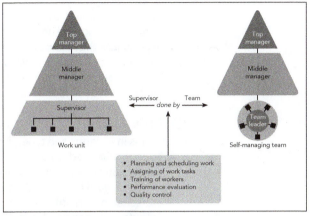

Self-Managing Teams

The **self-managing team** is a high-involvement workgroup design that is becoming increasingly well established. Sometimes called *self-directed work teams*, these teams are empowered to make the decisions needed to manage themselves on a day-to-day basis.[13] They basically replace traditional work units with teams whose members assume duties otherwise performed by a manager or first-line supervisor. **Figure 7.2** shows that members of true self-managing teams make their own decisions about scheduling work, allocating tasks, training for job skills, evaluating performance, selecting new team members, and controlling the quality of work.

See **FIGURE 7.2** **Organizational and management implications of self-managing teams**

Most self-managing teams include between five and fifteen members. They need to be large enough to provide a good mix of skills and resources but small enough to function efficiently. Because team members have a lot of discretion in determining work pace and in distributing tasks, **multiskilling** is important. This means that team members are expected to perform many different jobs—even all of the team's jobs—as needed. Pay is ideally skill based: The more skills someone masters, the higher the base pay.

The expected benefits of self-managing teams include better work quality, faster response to change, reduced absenteeism and turnover, and improved work attitudes and quality of work life. As with all organizational changes, however, the shift from traditional work units to self-managing teams may encounter difficulties. It may be hard for some team members to adjust to the "self-managing" responsibilities, and higher-level managers may have problems dealing with the absence of a first-line supervisor. Given all this, self-managing teams are probably not right for all organizations, situations, and people. They have great potential, but they also require the right setting and a great deal of management support. At a minimum, the essence of any self-managing team—high involvement, participation, and empowerment—must be consistent with the values and culture of the organization.

Virtual Teams

It used to be that teamwork was confined in concept and practice to those circumstances in which members could meet face to face. Information technology has changed all that. The **virtual team**, one whose members work together through computer mediation rather than face to face, is now common.[14] Working in electronic space and free from the constraints of geographical distance, members of virtual teams do the same things members of face-to-face groups do. They share information, make decisions, and complete tasks together. And just like face-to-face teams, they have to be set up and managed well to achieve their full benefits. Some steps to successful teams are summarized in the "Don't Neglect These Steps to Successful Virtual Teams" sidebar.[15]

The potential advantages of virtual teams begin with the cost and time efficiencies of bringing together people located at some, perhaps great, distance from one another.[16] The electronic rather than face-to-face environment of the virtual team can help keep things on task by focusing attention and decision making on objective issues rather than emotional considerations and distracting interpersonal problems. Discussions and information shared among team members can also be stored electronically for continuous access and historical record keeping.

The potential downsides to virtual teams are also real. Members of virtual teams may find it hard to get up to speed and work well with one another. When the computer is the go-between, relationships and interactions can be different and require special attention. The lack of face-to-face interaction limits the role of emotions and nonverbal cues in the communication process, perhaps depersonalizing relations among team members.

Team Effectiveness

There is no doubt that teams are pervasive and important in organizations. They accomplish important tasks and help members achieve satisfaction in their work. We also know from personal experiences that teams and teamwork have their difficulties; not all teams perform well, and not all team members are always satisfied. Surely you've heard the sayings "A camel is a horse put together by a committee" and "Too many cooks spoil the broth." They raise an important question: Just what are the foundations of team effectiveness?[17]

Criteria of an Effective Team

Teams in all forms and types, just like individuals, should be held accountable for their performance. To do this we need to have some understanding of team effectiveness. In OB we describe an **effective team** as one that achieves high levels of task performance, member satisfaction, and team viability.

With regard to *task performance*, an effective team achieves its performance goals in the standard sense of quantity, quality, and timeliness of work results. For a formal work unit such as a manufacturing team, this may mean meeting daily production targets. For a temporary team such as a new policy task force, this may involve meeting a deadline for submitting a new organizational policy to the company president.

With regard to *member satisfaction*, an effective team is one whose members believe that their participation and experiences are positive and meet important personal needs. They are satisfied with their team tasks, accomplishments, and interpersonal relationships. And, with regard to *team viability*, the members of an effective team are sufficiently satisfied to continue working well together on an ongoing basis. When one task is finished, they look forward to working on others in the future. Such a team has all-important long-term performance potential.

Synergy and Team Benefits

Effective teams offer the benefits of **synergy**—the creation of a whole that is greater than the sum of its parts. Synergy works within a team, and it works across teams as their collective efforts are harnessed to serve the organization as a whole. It creates the great beauty of teams: people working together and accomplishing more through teamwork than they ever could by working alone.

The performance advantages of teams over individuals are most evident in three situations.[18] First, when there is no clear "expert" for a particular task or problem, teams tend to make better judgments than does the average individual alone. Second, teams are typically more successful than individuals when problems are complex and require a division of labor and the sharing of information. Third, because they tend to make riskier decisions, teams can be more creative and innovative than individuals.

Teams are interactive settings where people learn from one another and share job skills and knowledge. The learning environment and the pool of experience within a team can be used to solve difficult and unique problems. This is especially helpful to newcomers, who often need help in their jobs. When team members support and help each other in acquiring and improving job competencies, they may even make up for deficiencies in organizational training systems.

Teams are also important sources of need satisfaction for their members. Opportunities for social interaction within a team can provide individuals with a sense of security through work assistance and technical advice. Team members can also provide emotional support for one another in times of special crisis or pressure. The many contributions individuals make to teams can help members experience self-esteem and personal involvement.

Social Facilitation

Teams are also settings for something known as **social facilitation**—the tendency for one's behavior to be influenced by the presence of others in a group or social setting.[19] In a team context it can be a boost or a detriment to an individual member's performance contributions.

Social facilitation theory suggests that working in the presence of others creates an emotional arousal or excitement that stimulates behavior and affects performance. The effect is positive and stimulates extra effort when one is proficient with the task at hand. An example is the team member who enthusiastically responds when asked to do something she is really good at, such as making slides for a team presentation. But the effect of social facilitation can be negative when the task is unfamiliar or a person lacks the necessary skills. A team member might withdraw, for example, when asked to do something he or she isn't very good at.

Social Loafing and Team Problems

Although teams have enormous performance potential, one of their problems is **social loafing**. Also known as the *Ringlemann effect*, it is the tendency of people to work less hard in a group than they would individually.[20] Max Ringlemann, a German psychologist, pinpointed the phenomenon by asking people to pull on a rope as hard as they could, first alone and then as part of a team.[21] Average productivity dropped as more people joined the rope-pulling task. Ringlemann suggested that people may not work as hard in groups because their individual contributions are less noticeable in the group context and because they prefer to see others carry the workload.

You may have encountered social loafing in your work and study teams, and been perplexed in terms of how to best handle it. Perhaps you have even been surprised at your own social loafing in some performance situations. Rather than give in to the phenomenon and its potential performance losses, you can often reverse or prevent social loafing. Steps that team leaders can take include keeping group size small and redefining roles so that free-riders are more visible and peer pressures to perform are more likely, increasing accountability by making individual performance expectations clear and specific, and making rewards directly contingent on an individual's performance contributions.[22]

Other common problems and difficulties can easily turn the great potential of teams into frustration and failure. Personality conflicts and differences in work styles can disrupt relationships and create antagonisms. Task uncertainties and competing goals or visions may cause some team members to withdraw and reduce their participation. Ambiguous agendas or ill-defined problems can also cause fatigue and loss of motivation when teams work too long on the wrong things with little to show for it. Finally, not everyone is always ready to do group work. This might be due to lack of motivation, but it may also stem from conflicts with other work deadlines and priorities. Low enthusiasm may also result from perceptions of poor team organization or progress, as well as from meetings that seem to lack purpose.

Stages of Team Development

There is no doubt that the pathways to team effectiveness are often complicated and challenging. One of the first things to consider—whether we are talking about a formal work unit, a task force, a virtual team, or a self-managing team—is the fact that the team passes through a series of life cycle stages.[23] Depending on the stage the team has reached, the leader and members can face very different challenges and the team may be more or less effective.

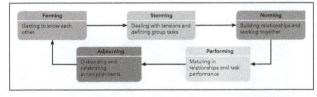

🖼 **Figure 7.3** describes the five stages of team development as forming, storming, norming, performing, and adjourning.[24]

See **FIGURE 7.3 Five stages of team development**

Forming Stage

In the **forming stage** of team development, a primary concern is the initial entry of members to a group. During this stage, individuals ask a number of questions as they begin to identify with other group members and with the team itself. Their concerns may include "What can the group offer me?" "What will I be asked to contribute?" "Can my needs be met at the same time that I contribute to the group?" Members are interested in getting to know each other and discovering what is considered acceptable behavior, in determining the real task of the team, and in defining group rules.

Storming Stage

The **storming stage** of team development is a period of high emotionality and tension among the group members. During this stage, hostility and infighting may occur, and the team typically experiences many changes. Coalitions or cliques may form as individuals compete to impose their preferences on the group and to achieve a desired status position. Outside demands such as premature performance expectations may create uncomfortable pressures. In the process, membership expectations tend to be clarified, and attention shifts toward obstacles standing in the way of team goals. Individuals begin to understand one another's interpersonal styles, and efforts are made to find ways to accomplish team goals while also satisfying individual needs.

Norming Stage

The **norming stage** of team development, sometimes called initial integration, is the point at which the members really start to come together as a coordinated unit. The turmoil of the storming stage gives way to a precarious balancing of forces. While enjoying a new sense of harmony, team members will strive to maintain positive balance, but holding the team together may become more important to some than successfully working on the team tasks. Minority viewpoints, deviations from team directions, and criticisms may be discouraged as members experience a preliminary sense of closeness. Some members may mistakenly perceive this stage as one of ultimate maturity.

In fact, a premature sense of accomplishment at this point needs to be carefully managed in order to reach the next level of team development: performing.

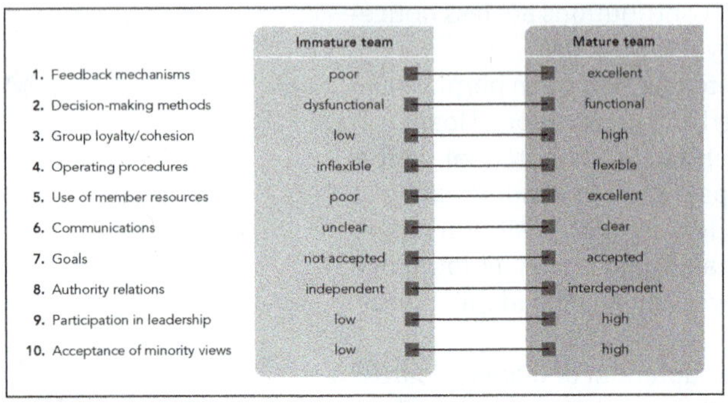

Performing Stage

The **performing stage** of team development, sometimes called total integration, marks the emergence of a mature, organized, and well-functioning team. Team members are now able to deal with complex tasks and handle internal disagreements in creative ways. The structure is stable, and members are motivated by team goals and are generally satisfied. The primary challenges are continued efforts to improve relationships and performance. Team members should be able to adapt successfully as opportunities and demands change over time. A team that has achieved the level of total integration typically scores high on the criteria of team maturity as shown in 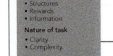 **Figure 7.4**.

See **FIGURE 7.4** **Ten criteria for measuring the maturity of a team**

Adjourning Stage

A well-integrated team is able to disband, if required, when its work is accomplished. The **adjourning stage** of team development is especially important for the many temporary teams such as task forces, committees, project teams, and the like. Their members must be able to convene quickly, do their jobs on a tight schedule, and then adjourn—often to reconvene later if needed. Their willingness to disband when the job is done and to work well together in future responsibilities, team or otherwise, is an important long-term test of team success.

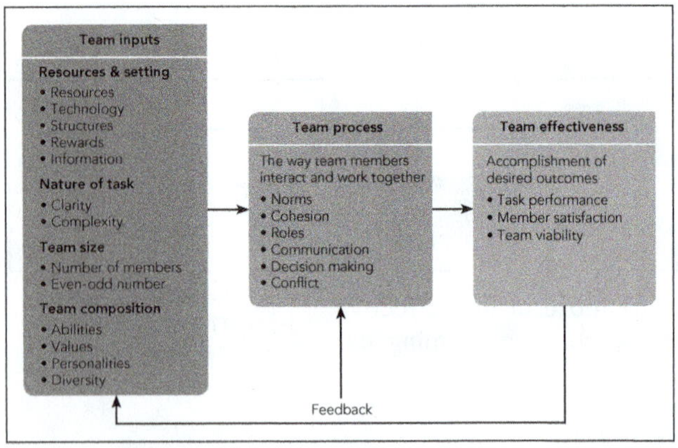

Input Foundations for Teamwork

It's common for managers and consultants to speak about the importance of having "the right players in the right seats on the same bus, headed in the same direction."[25] This wisdom is quite consistent with the findings of OB scholars. One of the ways to put it into practice is to understand the open systems model presented in **Figure 7.5**. It shows team effectiveness being influenced by both team inputs—"right players in the right seats"—and team processes—"on the same bus, headed in the same direction."[26] You can remember the point with this equation:

See **FIGURE 7.5** **An open systems model of team effectiveness**

$$\text{Team effectiveness} = \text{Quality of inputs} \times (\text{Process gains} - \text{Process losses})$$

As shown in the above equation, team inputs establish the initial foundations for team performance. They set the stage for how processes like communication, conflict, and decision making play out in action. And the fact is that the stronger the input foundations of a team, the more likely it is that processes will be smooth and performance will be effective. Key team inputs include resources and setting, the nature of the task, team size, and team composition.

Team Resources and Setting

Appropriate goals, well-designed reward systems, adequate resources, and appropriate technology are all essential to support the work of teams. Performance can suffer when team goals are unclear, insufficiently challenging, or arbitrarily imposed. It can also suffer if goals and rewards are focused too much on individual-level instead of group-level accomplishments. In addition, it can suffer when resources—information, budgets, work space, deadlines, rules and procedures, technologies, and the like—are insufficient to accomplish the task. By contrast, getting the right resources in place sets a strong launching pad for team success.

The importance of physical setting to teamwork is evident in the attention now being given to office architecture. Simply said, putting a team in the right workspace can go a long way toward nurturing teamwork. At SEI Investments, for example, employees work in a large, open space without cubicles or dividers. Each person has a private set of office furniture and fixtures, but everything is on wheels. Technology easily plugs and unplugs from suspended power beams that run overhead. This makes it easy for project teams to convene and disband as needed and for people to meet and converse intensely within the ebb and flow of daily work.[27]

Team Task

The nature of the task is always an important team input because different tasks place different demands on teamwork. When tasks are clear and well defined, it's quite easy for members to both know what they are trying to accomplish and work together while doing it. But, team effectiveness is harder to achieve with complex tasks.[28] Such tasks require lots of information exchange and intense interaction, and everything takes place under conditions of some uncertainty. To deal well with complexity and achieve desired results, team members have to fully mobilize their talents and use the available resources well. When teams succeed with complex tasks, however, members tend to experience high satisfaction.

One way to analyze the nature of the team task is in terms of its technical and social demands. The *technical demands* of a task include the degree to which it is routine or not, the level of difficulty involved, and the information requirements. The *social demands* of a task involve the degree to which issues of interpersonal relationships, egos, controversies over ends and means, and the like come into play. Tasks that are complex in technical demands require unique solutions and more information processing. Those that are complex in social demands pose difficulties for reaching agreement on goals and methods to accomplish them.

Team Size

The size of a team can have an impact on team effectiveness. As a team becomes larger, more people are available to divide up the work and accomplish needed tasks. This can boost performance and member satisfaction, but only up to a point. Communication and coordination problems arise at some point because of the sheer number of linkages that must be maintained. Satisfaction may dip, and turnover, absenteeism, and social loafing may increase. Even logistical matters, such as finding time and locations for meetings, become more difficult for larger teams.[29]

The ideal size of creative and problem-solving teams is probably between five and seven members, or just slightly larger. Those with fewer than five may be too small to adequately share all the team responsibilities. With more than seven, individuals may find it harder to join in the discussions, contribute their talents, and offer ideas. Larger teams are also more prone to possible domination by aggressive members and have tendencies to split into coalitions or subgroups.[30] Amazon.com's founder and CEO, Jeff Bezos, is a great fan of teams. But he also has a simple rule when it comes to the size of Amazon's product development teams: No team should be larger than two pizzas can feed.[31]

When voting is required, odd-numbered teams are preferred to help rule out tie votes. When careful deliberations are required and the emphasis is more on consensus, such as in jury duty or very complex problem solving, even-numbered teams may be more effective. The even number forces members to confront disagreements and deadlocks rather than simply resolve them by majority voting.[32]

Team Composition

"If you want a team to perform well, you've got to put the right members on the team to begin with." It's advice we hear a lot. There is no doubt that one of the most important input factors is the **team composition**. You can think of this as the mix of abilities, personalities, backgrounds, and experiences that the members bring to the team. The basic rule of thumb for team composition is to choose members whose talents and interests fit well with the tasks to be accomplished, and whose personal characteristics increase the likelihood of being able to work well with others.

Ability counts in team composition, and it's a top priority when selecting members. The team is more likely to perform better when its members have skills and competencies that best fit task demands. Although talents alone cannot guarantee desired results, they do establish an important baseline of high performance potential. Let's not forget, however, that it takes more than raw talent to generate team success. Surely you've been on teams or observed teams where there was lots of talent but very little teamwork. A likely cause is that the blend of members caused relationship problems over everything from needs to personality to experience to age and other background characteristics.

Needs count too. The **FIRO-B theory** (FIRO = fundamental interpersonal relations orientation) identifies differences in how people relate to one another in groups based on their needs to express and receive feelings of inclusion, control, and affection.[33] Developed by William Schultz, the theory suggests that teams whose members have compatible needs are likely to be more effective than teams whose members are more incompatible. Symptoms of incompatibilities include withdrawn members, open hostilities, struggles over control, and domination by a few members. Schultz states the management implications of the FIRO–B theory this way: "If at the outset we can choose a group of people who can work together harmoniously, we shall go far toward avoiding situations where a group's efforts are wasted in interpersonal conflicts."[34]

Another issue in team composition is status in terms relative rank, prestige, or social standing. **Status congruence** occurs when a person's position within the team is equivalent in status to positions the individual holds outside of it. Any status incongruence may create problems. Consider something that is increasingly common today—generationally blended teams. Things may not go smoothly, for example, when a young college graduate is asked to head a project team on social media and whose members largely include senior and more experienced workers.

Membership Diversity and Team Performance

Diversity is always an important aspect of team composition. The presence of different values, personalities, experiences, demographics, and cultures among members can bring both opportunities and problems.[35]

Teamwork usually isn't much of a problem in **homogeneous teams** where members are very similar to one another. The members typically find it quite easy to work together and enjoy the team experience. Yet, researchers warn about the risks of homogeneity. Although it may seem logical that having members similar to one another is an asset, it doesn't necessarily work out that way. Research points out that teams composed of members who are highly similar in background, training, and experience often underperform even though the members may enjoy a sense of harmony and feel very comfortable with one another.[36]

Teamwork problems are likely in **heterogeneous teams** where members are very dissimilar to one another. The mix of diverse personalities, experiences, backgrounds, ages, and other personal characteristics may create difficulties as members try to define problems, share information, mobilize talents, and deal with obstacles or opportunities. Nevertheless, if—and this is a big "if"—members can work well together, the diversity can be a source of advantage and enhanced performance potential.[37]

Team process and performance difficulties due to diversity issues are especially likely to occur in the initial stages of team development. The so-called **diversity–consensus dilemma** is the tendency for diversity to make it harder for team members to work together, especially in the early stages of their team lives, even though the diversity itself expands the skills and perspectives available for problem solving.[38] These dilemmas may be most pronounced in the critical zone of the storming and norming stages of development as described in ■ **Figure 7.6**. Problems may occur as interpersonal stresses and conflicts emerge from the heterogeneity. The challenge to team effectiveness is to take advantage of diversity without suffering process disadvantages.[39]

Working through the diversity–consensus dilemma can slow team development and impede relationship building, information sharing, and problem solving.[40] Some teams get stuck here and

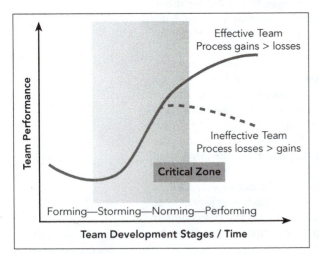

See **FIGURE 7.6 Member diversity, stages of team development, and team performance**

can't overcome their process problems. If and when such difficulties are resolved, diverse teams can emerge from the critical zone with effectiveness and often outperform less diverse ones. Research also shows that the most creative teams include a mix of old-timers and newcomers.[41] The old-timers have the experience and connections; the newcomers bring in new talents and fresh thinking.

The diversity and performance relationship is evident in research on **collective intelligence**— the ability of a group or team to perform well across a range of tasks.[42] Researchers have found only a slight correlation between average or maximum individual member intelligence and the collective intelligence of teams. But, they find strong correlations between collective intelligence and two process variables—social sensitivities within the teams and absence of conversational domination by a few members. Furthermore, collective intelligence is associated with gender diversity, specifically the proportion of females on the team. This finding also links to process, with researchers pointing out that females in their studies scored higher than males on social sensitivity.

 Go to your WileyPLUS Learning Space course for video episodes, examples, art, tables, Concept Checks, practice, and resources that will help you succeed in this course.

Reading for
TEAMWORK AND TEAM PERFORMANCE

High-Performance Teams

Are you an iPad, Kindle Fire, Samsung Galaxy, or Google Nexus user? Have you ever wondered why the companies behind these products keep giving us a stream of innovative and trend-setting choices?

In many ways today's smartphone and tablet stories started years ago with Apple, Inc., its co-founder Steve Jobs, the first Macintosh computer, and a very special team. The "Mac" was Jobs's brainchild. To create it, he put together a team of high achievers who were excited and motivated by a highly challenging task. They worked all hours and at an unrelenting pace free from Apple's normal bureaucracy. Team members combined high talent with commitment to an exciting goal: change the world through computing. They ended up setting a benchmark for high-tech product innovation as well as new standards for what makes for a high-performance team.[1]

The smartphone, tablet, and notebook computer industry today is crowded and very competitive. But you can bet that all the players follow some version of the original Apple model, making their firms hotbeds of high-performing teams that harness great talents to achieve innovation. But even as we celebrate great teams and the teamwork that drives them, scholar J. Richard Hackman warns that many teams in organizations underperform and fail to live up to their potential. He says that they simply "don't work."[2] The question for us is: What differentiates high-performing teams from the also-rans?

Characteristics of High-Performance Teams

It's quite easy to agree on must-have team leadership skills like those described in the "Teams Gain from Great Leaders . . ." sidebar. It also makes sense that having a leader set a clear and challenging team direction is at the top of the list.[3] Again, Apple's original Macintosh story gives us an example. After getting a sneak look at what he had been told was the "machine that was supposed to change the world," *Wired* magazine's Steven Levy wrote: "I also met the people who created that machine. They were groggy and almost giddy from three years of creation. Their eyes blazed with Visine and fire. They told me that with Macintosh, they were going to "put a dent in the Universe." Their leader, Steven P. Jobs, told them so. They also told me how Jobs referred to this new computer: 'Insanely Great.'"[4]

High-performing teams have members who believe in team goals and are motivated to work hard to accomplish them. They feel "collectively accountable" for moving in what Hackman calls "a compelling direction." Getting to this point isn't always easy. All too often a team's members don't agree on the goal and don't share an understanding of what the team is supposed to accomplish.[5]

Whereas a shared sense of purpose gives general direction to a team, commitment to targeted—not general or vague—performance results makes this purpose truly meaningful. High-performance teams turn a general sense of purpose into specific performance objectives. They set standards for taking action, measuring results, and gathering performance feedback. They also provide a clear focus when team members have to find common ground to solve problems and resolve conflicts.

Talent is essential. High-performance teams have members with the right mix of skills—technical, problem-solving, and interpersonal. Values count too. High-performance teams have strong core values that help guide team members' attitudes and behaviors in consistent directions. These values act as an internal control system that keeps team members on track without outside direction and supervisory attention.

The concept of **collective intelligence** applies in a high-performance team. Think of it as the ability of a team to do well on a wide variety of tasks. It fuels a team to excel not just once, but over and over again. Researchers point out that collective intelligence is higher in teams whose processes are not dominated by one or a few members. Collective intelligence is also higher on teams having more female members, a finding researchers link to higher social sensitivity in team dynamics.[6]

The Team-Building Process

Coaches and managers in the sports world spend a lot of time at the start of each season joining new members with old ones and forming a strong team. Yet, we all know that even the most experienced teams can run into problems as a season progresses. Members slack off or become disgruntled with one another; some have performance "slumps," and others criticize them for it; some are traded gladly or unhappily to other teams.

Even world-champion teams have losing streaks. At times even the most talented players can lose motivation, quibble among themselves, and end up contributing little to team success. When such things happen, concerned owners, managers, and players are apt to examine their problems, take corrective action to rebuild the team, and restore the teamwork needed to achieve high-performance results.[7]

Work teams face similar challenges. When newly formed, they must master many challenges as members learn how to work together while passing through the stages of team development. Even when mature, most work teams encounter problems of insuffi-cient teamwork at different points in time. At the very least we can say that teams sometimes need help to perform well and that teamwork always needs to be nurtured.

The occasional need for a performance "tune up" is why a pro-cess known as **team building** is so important. It is a sequence of planned activities designed to gather and analyze data on the func-tioning of a team and to initiate changes designed to improve team-work and increase team effectiveness.[8] When done well and at the right times, team building can be a good way to deal with actual or potential teamwork problems.

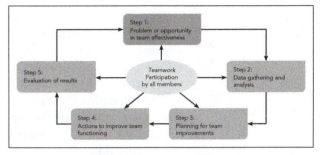

The action steps for team building are highlighted in ▣ **Figure 8.1**. Although it is tempting to view the process as something that consultants or outside experts are hired to do, the fact is that it can and should be part of any team leader and manager's skill set.

See **FIGURE 8.1 Steps in the team-building process**

Team building begins when someone notices an actual or a potential problem with team effectiveness. Data are gathered to examine the problem. This can be done by questionnaire, interview, nominal group meeting, or other creative methods. The goal is to get good answers to such questions as "How well are we doing in terms of task accomplishment?" "How satisfied are we as individuals with the group and the way it operates?" After the answers to such questions are analyzed by team members, they then work together to plan for and accomplish improve-ments. This team-building process is highly collaborative and participation by all members is essential.

Team-Building Alternatives

One fall day, a team of employees from American Electric Power (AEP) went to an outdoor camp. They worked on problems such as how to get six members through a spider-web maze of bungee cords strung 2 feet above the ground. When her colleagues lifted Judy Gallo into their hands to pass her over the obstacle, she was nervous. A trainer addressed her anxiety by telling the team this was just like solving a problem together at the office. The spider web was just another perfor-mance constraint, like the difficult policy issues or financial limits they might face at work. After high-fives for making it through the web, Judy's team jumped tree stumps together, passed hula hoops while holding hands, and more. Says one outdoor team trainer, "We throw clients into situ-ations to try and bring out the traits of a good team."[9]

This was an example of the *outdoor experience approach* to team building. It is increasingly popular and can be done on its own or in combination with other approaches. The outdoor experience places teams in a variety of physically challenging situations. By having to work together to master difficult obstacles, team members are supposed to grow in self-confidence, gain more respect for each others' capabilities, and leave with a greater capacity for and commitment to teamwork.

In the *formal retreat approach*, team building takes place during an off-site retreat. The agenda, which may cover one or more days, is designed to engage team members in the variety of assessment and planning tasks. Formal retreats are often held with the assistance of a consultant, who is either hired from the outside or made available from in-house staff. Team-building retreats are opportunities to take time away from the job to assess team accomplishments, operations, and future potential.

In a *continuous improvement approach*, the manager, team leader, or group members themselves take responsibility for regularly engaging in the team-building process. This method can be as simple as periodic meetings that implement the team-building steps; it can also include self-managed formal retreats. In all cases, the goal is to engage team members in a process that leaves them more capable and committed to continuous performance assessment and improved teamwork.

Improving Team Processes

Team building should be an ongoing concern for leaders and members alike. It's a way of updating and strengthening the processes through which people work together in teams, something often called **team or group dynamics**. These are forces operating in teams that affect the way members relate to and work with one another.[10] They are especially important and at risk when teams are taking on new members, addressing disagreements on goals and responsibilities, resolving decision-making delays and disputes, reducing personality friction, and managing conflicts.

Entry of New Members

Special team process difficulties are likely to occur when members first get together in a new group or team, or when new members join an existing team. Problems arise as new members try to understand what is expected of them while dealing with the anxiety and discomfort of a new social setting. New members, for example, may worry about any of the following:

- *Participation*—"Will I be allowed to participate?"
- *Goals*—"Do I share the same goals as others?"
- *Control*—"Will I be able to influence what takes place?"
- *Relationships*—"How close do people get?"
- *Processes*—"Are conflicts likely to be upsetting?"

Scholar and consultant Edgar Schein points out that people may try to cope with individual entry problems in self-serving ways that may hinder team development and performance.[11] He identifies three behavior profiles that are common in such situations.

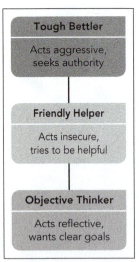

Tough Battler   The *tough battler* is frustrated by a lack of identity in the new group and may act aggressively or reject authority. This person wants answers to this question: "Who am I in this group?" The best team response may be to allow the new member to share his or her skills and interests, and then have a discussion about how these qualities can best be used to help the team.

Friendly Helper   The *friendly helper* is insecure, suffering uncertainties of intimacy and control. This person may show extraordinary support for others, behave in a dependent way, and seek alliances in subgroups or cliques. The friendly helper needs to know whether he or she will be liked. The best team response may be to offer support and encouragement while encouraging the new member to be more confident in joining team activities and discussions.

Objective Thinker   The *objective thinker* is anxious about how personal needs will be met in the group. This person may act in a passive, reflective, and even single-minded manner while struggling with the fit between individual goals and group directions. The best team response may be to engage in a discussion to clarify team goals and expectations, and to clarify member roles in meeting them.

Roles and Role Dynamics

New and old team members alike need to know what others expect of them and what they can expect from others. A **role** is a set of expectations associated with a job or position on a team. We know that teams tend to perform better when their members have clear and realistic expectations about one another's tasks and responsibilities. When team members are unclear about their roles or face conflicting role demands, process problems are likely and team effectiveness can suffer. Although this is a common situation, it can be managed with proper attention to role dynamics and their causes.

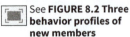
See **FIGURE 8.2 Three behavior profiles of new members**

Role ambiguity occurs when a person is uncertain about his or her role or job on a team. Role ambiguities may create problems as team members find that their work efforts are wasted or unappreciated. This can even happen in mature groups if team members fail to share expectations and listen to one another's concerns.

Being asked to do too much or too little as a team member can also create problems. **Role overload** occurs when too much is expected and someone feels overwhelmed. **Role underload** occurs when too little is expected and the individual feels underused. Both role overload and role underload can cause stress, dissatisfaction, and performance problems.

Role conflict occurs when a person is unable to meet the expectations of others. The individual understands what needs to be done but for some reason cannot comply. The resulting tension is stressful and can reduce satisfaction. It can affect an individual's performance and relationships with other group members. People at work and in teams can experience four common forms of role conflict:

- *Intrasender role conflict* occurs when the same person sends conflicting expectations. Example: Team leader—"You need to get the report written right away, but now I need you to help me get the PowerPoints ready."

- *Intersender role conflict* occurs when different people send conflicting and mutually exclusive expectations. Example: Team leader (to you)—"Your job is to criticize our decisions so that we don't make mistakes." Team member (to you)—"You always seem so negative. Can't you be more positive for a change?"

- *Person–role conflict* occurs when a person's values and needs come into conflict with role expectations. Example: Other team members (showing agreement with each other)—"We didn't get enough questionnaires back, so let's each fill out five more and add them to the data set." You (to yourself)—"Mmm, I don't think this is right."

- *Inter-role conflict* occurs when the expectations of two or more roles held by the same individual become incompatible, such as the conflict between work and family demands. Example: Team leader—"Don't forget the big meeting we have scheduled for Thursday evening." You (to yourself)—"But my daughter is playing in her first little-league soccer game at that same time."

A technique known as **role negotiation** is a helpful way of managing role dynamics. It's a process whereby team members meet to discuss, clarify, and agree on the role expectations each holds for the other. Such a negotiation might begin, for example, with one member writing down this request of another: "If you were to do the following, it would help me to improve my performance on the team." Her list of requests might include such specifics as "Respect it when I say that I can't meet some evenings because I have family obligations to fulfill"—indicating role conflict; "Stop asking for so much detail when we are working hard with tight deadlines"—indicating role overload; and "Try to make yourself available when I need to speak with you to clarify goals and expectations"—indicating role ambiguity.

Task and Maintenance Leadership

Research in social psychology suggests that teams have both task needs and maintenance needs, and that both must be met for teams to be successful.[12] Even though a team leader should be able to meet these needs at the appropriate times, each team member is responsible as well. This sharing of responsibilities for making task and maintenance contributions to move a team forward is called **distributed leadership**. And, it is well evidenced in high-performance teams.

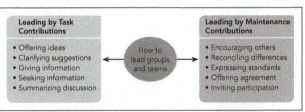

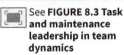

See **FIGURE 8.3 Task and maintenance leadership in team dynamics**

▣ **Figure 8.3** describes **task activities** as what team members and leaders do that directly contribute to the performance of important group tasks. They include initiating discussion, sharing information, asking information of others, clarifying something that has been said, and summarizing the status of a deliberation.[13] A team will have difficulty accomplishing its objectives when task activities are not well performed. In an effective team, by contrast, all members pitch in to contribute important task leadership as needed.

Figure 8.2 also shows that **maintenance activities** support the social and interpersonal relationships among team members. They help a team stay intact and healthy as an ongoing and well-functioning social system. A team member or leader can contribute maintenance leadership by encouraging the participation of others, trying to harmonize differences of opinion, praising the contributions of others, and agreeing to go along with a popular course of action. When maintenance leadership is poor, members become dissatisfied with one another, the value of their group membership diminishes, and emotional conflicts may drain energies otherwise needed for task performance. In an effective team, by contrast, maintenance activities support the relationships needed for team members to work well together over time.

In addition to helping meet a group's task and maintenance needs, team members share additional responsibility for avoiding and eliminating any **disruptive behaviors** that harm the group process. These dysfunctional activities include bullying and being overly aggressive toward other members, showing incivility and disrespect, withdrawing and refusing to cooperate, horsing around when there is work to be done, using meetings as forums for self-confession, talking too much about irrelevant matters, and trying to compete for attention and recognition. *Incivility* or *antisocial behavior* by members can be especially disruptive of team dynamics and performance. Research shows that persons who are targets of harsh leadership, social exclusion, and harmful rumors often end up working less hard, performing less well, being late and absent more, and reducing their commitment.[14]

Team Norms

The entry issues, role dynamics, and task and maintenance needs we have just discussed all relate to what team members expect of one another and of themselves. This brings up the issue of team **norms**—beliefs about how members are expected to behave. They can be considered as rules or standards of team conduct.[15] Norms help members to guide their own behavior and predict what others will do. When someone violates a team norm, other members typically respond in ways that are aimed at enforcing it and bring behavior back into alignment with the norm. These responses may include subtle hints, direct criticisms, and even reprimands. At the extreme, someone violating team norms may be ostracized or even expelled.

Types of Team Norms A key norm in any team setting is the **performance norm**. It conveys expectations about how hard team members should work and what the team should accomplish. In some teams, the performance norm is high and strong. There is no doubt that all members are expected to work very hard and that high performance is the goal. If someone slacks off, they get reminded to work hard or end up removed from the team. In other teams, the performance norm is low and weak; members are left to work hard or not as they like, with little concern shown by the other members.

Many other norms also influence the day-to-day functioning of teams. Norms regarding attendance at meetings, punctuality, preparedness, criticism, and social behavior are important. So, too, are norms on how members deal with supervisors, colleagues, and customers, as well as norms about honesty and ethical behavior. Consider the following examples of norms that can have positive and negative implications for team processes and effectiveness:[16]

- *Ethics norms*—"We try to make ethical decisions, and we expect others to do the same" (positive); "Don't worry about inflating your expense account; everyone does it here" (negative).

- *Organizational and personal pride norms*—"It's a tradition around here for people to stand up for the company when others criticize it unfairly" (positive); "In our company, they are always trying to take advantage of us" (negative).

- *High-achievement norms*—"On our team, people always want to win or be the best" (positive); "No one really cares on this team whether we win or lose" (negative).

- *Support and helpfulness norms*—"People on this committee are good listeners and actively seek out the ideas and opinions of others" (positive); "On this committee it's dog-eat-dog and save your own skin" (negative).

- *Improvement and change norms*—"In our department people are always looking for better ways of doing things" (positive); "Around here, people hang on to the old ways even after they have outlived their usefulness" (negative).

How to Influence Team Norms Team leaders and members can do several things to help their teams develop positive norms that foster high performance as well as membership satisfaction. The first thing is to always *act as a positive role model*. In other words, be the exemplar of the norm, always living up to the norm in everyday behavior. It is helpful to hold meetings where time is set aside to *discuss team goals* and also *discuss team norms* that can best contribute to their achievement.

Norms are too important to be left to chance. The more directly they are discussed and confronted in the early stages of team development, the better.

It's always best to *select members who can and will live up to the desired norms*. They should be given the *right training and support*, and their *rewards should positively reinforce desired behaviors*. Finally, teams should remember the power of team building and *hold regular meetings to discuss team performance and plan how to improve* it in the future. This is a full-cycle approach to developing positive team norms: select the right people, provide them support, give positive reinforcement for doing things right, and continuously review progress and make constructive adjustments.

Team Cohesiveness

The **cohesiveness** of a group or team is the degree to which members are attracted to and motivated to remain part of it.[17] We might think of it as the feel-good factor that causes people to value their membership on a team, positively identify with it, and strive to maintain positive relationships with other members. Feelings of cohesion can be a source of need satisfaction, often providing a source of loyalty, security, and esteem for team members. Because cohesive teams are such a source of personal satisfaction, their members tend to be energetic when working on team activities, less likely to be absent, less likely to quit the team, and more likely to be happy about performance success and sad about failures.

Team Cohesiveness and Conformity to Norms Even though cohesive teams are good for their members, they may or may not be good for the organization. The question is this: Will the cohesive team also be a high-performance team? The answer to this question depends on the match of cohesiveness with conformity to norms.

The **rule of conformity** in team dynamics states that the greater the cohesiveness of a team, the greater the conformity of members to team norms. So when the performance norms are positive in highly cohesive teams, the resulting conformity to the norm should have a positive effect on both team performance and member satisfaction. This is a best-case situation for team members, the team leader, and the organization.

When the performance norms are negative in a highly cohesive team, as shown in **Figure 8.4**, the rule of conformity creates a worst-case situation for the team leader and the organization. Although the high cohesiveness leaves the team members feeling loyal and satisfied, they are also highly motivated to conform to the negative performance norm. In between these two extremes are two mixed-case situations for teams low in cohesion. Because there is little conformity to either the positive or negative norms, team performance will most likely fall on the moderate or low side.

See **FIGURE 8.4 How cohesiveness and conformity to norms influence team performance**

How to Influence Team Cohesiveness What can be done to tackle the worst-case and mixed-case scenarios just described? The answer rests with the factors influencing team cohesiveness. Cohesiveness tends to be high in teams that are homogeneous in makeup—that is, when members are similar in age, attitudes, needs, and backgrounds. Cohesiveness also tends to be high in teams of small size, where members respect one another's competencies, agree on common goals, and like to work together rather than alone on team tasks. Cohesiveness tends to rise when groups are physically isolated from others and when they experience performance success or crisis.

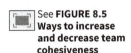
See **FIGURE 8.5 Ways to increase and decrease team cohesiveness**

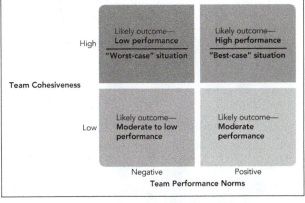 **Figure 8.5** shows how team cohesiveness can be increased or decreased by making changes in goals, membership composition, interactions, size, rewards, competition, location, and duration. When the team norms are positive but cohesiveness is low, the goal is to take actions to increase cohesion and gain more conformity to the positive norms. When team norms are negative and cohesiveness is high, just the opposite may have to be done. If efforts to change the norms fail, it may be necessary to reduce cohesiveness and thus reduce conformity to the negative norms.

Inter-Team Dynamics

Organizations ideally operate as cooperative systems in which the various groups and teams support one another. In the real world, however, competition and inter-team problems often develop. Their consequences can be good or bad for the host organization and the teams themselves. This raises the issue of what happens between, not just within, teams. We call this **inter-team dynamics**.

On the positive side of inter-team dynamics, competition among teams can stimulate them to become more cohesive, work harder, become more focused on key tasks, develop more internal loyalty and satisfaction, or achieve a higher level of creativity in problem solving. This effect is demonstrated at virtually any intercollegiate athletic event, and it is common in work settings as well.[18] On the negative side, such as when manufacturing and sales units don't get along, inter-team dynamics may drain and divert work energies. Members may spend too much time focusing on their animosities or conflicts with another team and too little time focusing on their own team's performance.[19]

A variety of steps can be taken to avoid negative and achieve positive effects from inter-team dynamics. Teams engaged in destructive competition, for example, can be refocused on a common enemy or a common goal. Direct negotiations can be held among the teams. Members can be engaged in intergroup team building that encourages positive interactions and helps members of different teams learn how to work more cooperatively together. Reward systems can also be refocused to emphasize team contributions to overall organizational performance and on how much teams help out one another.

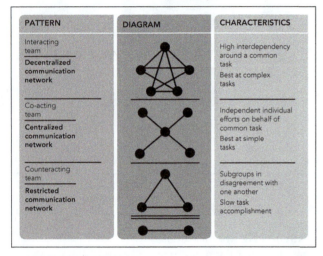

PATTERN	DIAGRAM	CHARACTERISTICS
Interacting team **Decentralized communication network**		High interdependency around a common task. Best at complex tasks
Co-acting team **Centralized communication network**		Independent individual efforts on behalf of common task. Best at simple tasks
Counteracting team **Restricted communication network**		Subgroups in disagreement with one another. Slow task accomplishment

See **FIGURE 8.6 Interaction patterns and communication networks found in teams**

Improving Team Communications

It is important in teams to make sure that every member is strong and capable in basic communication and collaboration skills. In addition, however, teams must address questions like these: What communication networks are being used by the team and why? How does space affect communication among team members? Is the team making good use of the available communication technologies?

Interaction Patterns and Communication Networks

Three interaction patterns are common when team members work with one another on team tasks. We call these patterns the interacting team, the co-acting team, and the counteracting team as shown in **Figure 8.6**.

One of the most common teamwork mistakes is that members are not using the right interaction patterns. An example might be a student project team whose members believe every member must always be present when any work gets done on the project; in other words, no one works on his own and everything is done together. Team effectiveness requires that the interaction pattern should fit the task at hand. Because tasks vary, a team ideally shifts among the alternative interaction patterns as task demands emerge and change over time.

Figure 8.5 links interaction patterns with team communication networks.[20] Tasks that require intense interaction among team members are best done with a **decentralized communication network**. Also called the *star network* or *all-channel network*, it operates with everyone communicating and sharing information with everyone else. Information flows back and forth constantly, with no one person serving as the center point.[21] Decentralized communication networks work well when team tasks are complex and nonroutine, perhaps tasks that involve uncertainty and require creativity. Member satisfaction on such interacting teams is usually high.

Tasks that allow team members to work independently are best done using a **centralized communication network**. Also called the *wheel network* or *chain network*, it operates with a central hub through which one member—often a formal or informal team leader—collects and distributes information. Members of such coacting teams work on assigned tasks independently while the hub keeps everyone and everything coordinated. Work is divided among members, and results are pooled to create the finished product. The centralized network works well when team tasks are routine and easily subdivided. It is usually the hub member who experiences the most satisfaction on successful co-acting teams.

Counteracting teams form when subgroups emerge within a team due to issue-specific disagreements, such as a temporary debate over the best means to achieve a goal, or emotional disagreements, such as personality clashes. This creates a **restricted communication network** in which the subgroups contest each other's positions and restrict interactions with one another. The poor communication often creates problems but can be useful at times. Counteracting teams might be set up to stimulate conflict and criticism to help improve creativity or double-check decisions about to be implemented.

Proxemics and Use of Space

An important but sometimes neglected part of communication in teams involves **proxemics**, or the use of space as people interact.[22] We know, for example, that office or workspace architecture is an important influence on communication behavior. It only makes sense that communication in teams might be improved by arranging physical space to best support it. This might be done by moving chairs and tables closer together, or by choosing to meet in physical spaces that are most conducive to communication. Meeting in a small conference room at the library, for example, may be a better choice than meeting in a busy coffee shop.

Some architects and consultants specialize in office design for communication and teamwork. When Sun Microsystems built its facility in San Jose, California, public spaces were designed to encourage communication among persons from different departments. Many meeting areas had no walls, and most walls were glass.[23] At Google headquarters, often called Googleplex, specially designed office "tents" are made of acrylics to allow both the sense of private personal space and transparency.[24]

Communication Technologies

It hardly seems necessary in the age of Facebook, Twitter, and Skype to mention that teams now have access to many useful technologies that can facilitate communication and reduce the need to be face to face. We live and work in an age of instant messaging, tweets and texting, online discussions, video chats, videoconferencing, and more. We are networked socially 24/7 to the extent we want, and there's no reason the members of a team can't utilize the same technologies to good advantage.

Think of technology as empowering teams to use **virtual communication networks** in which members communicate electronically all or most of the time. Technology in virtual teamwork acts as the "hub member" in the centralized communication network and as an ever-present "electronic router" that links members in decentralized networks on an as-needed and always-ready basis. New developments with social media keep pushing these capabilities forward. General Electric, for example, started a "Tweet Squad" to advise employees how social networking could be used to improve internal collaboration. The insurer MetLife has its own social network, Connect MetLife, which facilitates collaboration through a Facebook-like setting.[25] Of course, certain steps need to be taken to ensure that virtual teams and communication technologies are as successful as possible. This means doing things like online team building so that members get to know one another, learn about and identify team goals, and otherwise develop a sense of cohesiveness.[26]

Improving Team Decisions

One of the most important activities for any team is **decision making**, the process of choosing among alternative courses of action. The quality and timeliness of decisions and the processes through which they are made can have an important impact on how teams work and what they achieve.

Ways Teams Make Decisions

Consider the many teams of which you have been and are a part. Just how do major decisions get made? Most often there's a lot more going on than meets the eye. Edgar Schein has worked extensively with teams to identify, analyze, and improve their decision processes.[27] He observes

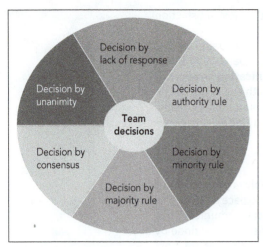

See **FIGURE 8.7** **Alternative ways that teams can make decisions**

that teams may make decisions through any of the six methods shown in 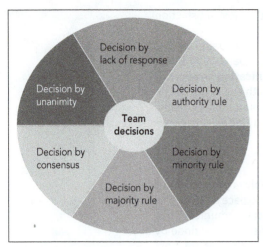 **Figure 8.7**. Although Schein doesn't rule out any method, he does point out their advantages and disadvantages.

Lack of Response In *decision by lack of response,* one idea after another is suggested without any discussion taking place. When the team finally accepts an idea, all others have been bypassed and discarded by simple lack of response rather than by critical evaluation. This may happen early in a team's development when new members are struggling for identities and confidence. It's also common in teams with low-performance norms and when members just don't care enough to get involved in what is taking place. Whenever lack of response drives decisions, it's relatively easy for a team to move off in the wrong, or at least not the best, direction.

Authority Rule In *decision by authority rule,* the chairperson, manager, or leader makes a decision for the team. This is very time efficient and can be done with or without inputs by other members. Whether the decision is a good one or a bad one depends on whether or not the authority figure has the necessary information and if other group members accept this approach. When an authority decision is made without expertise or member commitment, problems are likely.

Minority Rule In *decision by minority rule,* two or three people are able to dominate, or railroad, the group into making a decision with which they agree. This is often done by providing a suggestion and then forcing quick agreement. The railroader may challenge the group with statements such as "Does anyone object? . . . No? Well, let's go ahead then." Although such forcing and bullying may get the team moving in a certain direction, member commitment to making the decision successful will probably be low. Kickback and resistance, especially when things get difficult, aren't unusual in these situations.

Majority Rule One of the most common ways that groups make decisions is through *decision by majority rule*. This usually takes place as a formal vote to find the majority viewpoint. When team members get into disagreements that seem irreconcilable, for example, voting is seen to be an easy way out of the situation. Nonetheless, majority rule is often used without awareness of its potential problems. The very process creates coalitions, especially when votes are taken and results are close. Those in the minority—the "losers"—may feel left out or discarded without having had a fair say. They may not be enthusiastic about implementing the decision of the "winners." Lingering resentments may hurt team effectiveness in the future if they become more concerned about winning the next vote than doing what is best for the team.

Consensus Another of the decision alternatives is **consensus**. It results when discussion leads to one alternative being favored by most team members and other members agree to support it. When a consensus is reached, even those who may have opposed the chosen course of action know that they have been listened to and have had a fair chance to influence the outcome. Consensus does not require unanimity. What it does require is the opportunity for any dissenting members to feel that they have been able to speak and that their voices have been heard.[28] Because of the extensive process involved in reaching a consensus decision, it may be inefficient from a time perspective. Still, consensus is very powerful in terms of generating commitments among members to making the final decision work best for the team.

Unanimity A *decision by unanimity* may be the ideal state of affairs. Here, all team members wholeheartedly agree on the course of action to be taken. This "logically perfect" decision situation is extremely difficult to attain in actual practice. One reason that teams sometimes turn to authority decisions, majority voting, or even minority decisions, in fact, is the difficulty of managing the team process to achieve decisions by consensus or unanimity.

Assets and Liabilities of Team Decisions

The best teams don't limit themselves to any one of the decision methods just described. Instead, they move back and forth among them. Each method is used in circumstances for which it is a best fit. As professors, for example, we never complain when a department head makes an authority decision to have a welcome reception for new students at the start of the academic year or calls for a faculty vote on a proposed new travel policy. Yet we'd quickly disapprove if a department head made an authority decision to hire a new faculty member—something we believe should be made by faculty consensus.

It's important for any team leader to use the right decision method for the situation at hand. Without doubt, there are many times when the best choice is to go with the more team-oriented decisions. However, even they have potential disadvantages as well as advantages.[29] On the positive side, team decisions by consensus and unanimity offer the advantages of bringing more information, knowledge, and expertise to bear on a problem. Extensive discussion tends to create broader understanding of the final decision, and this increases acceptance. It also strengthens the commitments of members to follow through and support the decision.

On the negative side, we all know that team decisions can be imperfect. It usually takes a team longer to make a decision than it does an individual. Then too, social pressures to conform might make some members unwilling to go against or criticize what appears to be the will of the majority. Furthermore, in the guise of a so-called team decision, a team leader or a few members might railroad or force other members to accept their preferred decision.

Groupthink Symptoms and Remedies

One important problem that sometimes occurs when teams try to make decisions is **groupthink**—the tendency of members in highly cohesive groups to lose their critical evaluative capabilities.[30] As identified by social psychologist Irving Janis, groupthink is a property of highly cohesive teams, and it occurs because team members are so concerned with harmony that they become unwilling to criticize each other's ideas and suggestions. Desires to hold the team together, feel good, and avoid unpleasantries bring about an overemphasis on agreement and an underemphasis on critical discussion. This often results in a poor decision.

By way of historical examples, Janis suggests that groupthink played a role in the U.S. forces' lack of preparedness at Pearl Harbor before the United States entered World War II. It has also been linked to flawed U.S. decision making during the Vietnam War, to events leading up to the space shuttle disasters, and, most recently, to failures of American intelligence agencies regarding the status of weapons of mass destruction in Iraq. Perhaps you can think of other examples from your own experiences where otherwise well-intentioned teams end up doing the wrong things.

The following symptoms of teams displaying groupthink should be well within the sights of any team leader and member:[31]

- *Illusions of invulnerability*—Members assume that the team is too good for criticism or beyond attack.
- *Rationalizing unpleasant and disconfirming data*—Members refuse to accept contradictory data or to thoroughly consider alternatives.
- *Belief in inherent group morality*—Members act as though the group is inherently right and above reproach.
- *Stereotyping competitors as weak, evil, and stupid*—Members refuse to look realistically at other groups.
- *Applying direct pressure to deviants to conform to group wishes*—Members refuse to tolerate anyone who suggests the team may be wrong.
- *Self-censorship by members*—Members refuse to communicate personal concerns to the whole team.
- *Illusions of unanimity*—Members are quick to accept consensus prematurely, without testing its completeness.
- *Mind guarding*—Members try to protect the team from hearing disturbing ideas or outside viewpoints.

Even though groupthink is a serious threat to teams at all levels and in all types of organizations, it can be managed. To do so, team leaders and members must stay alert to the preceding symptoms and be quick to take action when they are spotted.[32] The sidebar offers a number of steps that can be taken to prevent or minimize groupthink. During the Cuban missile crisis, for example, President John F. Kennedy chose to absent himself from certain strategy discussions conducted by his cabinet. This made it easier for them to engage in critical discussion and avoided tendencies for cabinet members to try to figure out what the president wanted and then give it to him. The result was an open and expansive decision process, and the crisis was successfully resolved.

Team Decision Techniques

What can be done to improve decision making in teams that are having problems? It's not just things like groupthink and premature rush to agreement that can harm decision making. Decision deficits often occur, for example, when meetings are poorly structured or poorly led as members try to work together. Decisions can easily get bogged down or go awry when tasks are complex, information is uncertain, creativity is needed, time is short, "strong" voices are dominant, and debates turn emotional and personal. These are times when special team decision techniques can be helpful.[33]

Brainstorming In the time-tested technique of **brainstorming**, team members actively generate as many ideas and alternatives as possible. They are supposed to do so relatively quickly and without inhibitions. But scholar Leigh Thompson points out that you have to be careful because brainstorming doesn't always work as intended. She recommends a period of "solo thinking" before brainstorming begins, keeping the brainstorming groups small, and making sure that rules are clear and followed.[34]

You are surely familiar with the rules of brainstorming. First, all criticism is ruled out. No one is allowed to judge or evaluate any ideas until they are all on the table. Second, freewheeling is welcomed. The emphasis is on creativity and imagination; the wilder or more radical the ideas, the better. Third, quantity is a goal. The assumption is that the greater the number, the more likely a superior idea will appear. Fourth, piggybacking is good. Everyone is encouraged to suggest how others' ideas can be turned into new ideas or how two or more ideas can be joined into still another new idea.

Nominal Group Technique At times teams get so large that open discussion and brainstorming are awkward to manage. It's also common for teams to get into situations where the opinions of members differ so much that discussions become antagonistic and argumenative. In such cases, using the structured **nominal group technique** for face-to-face or virtual decision making may be helpful.[35]

The nominal group technique begins by asking team members to respond individually and in writing to a *nominal question*, such as "What should be done to improve the effectiveness of this work team?" Everyone is encouraged to list as many alternatives or ideas as they can. Next, participants in round-robin fashion are asked to read or post their responses to the nominal question. Each response is recorded on large newsprint or in a computer database as it is offered. No criticism is allowed. The recorder asks for any questions that may clarify specific items on the list, but no evaluation is allowed. The goal is simply to make sure that everyone fully understands each response. A structured voting procedure is then used to prioritize responses to the nominal question and identify the choice or choices having most support. This procedure allows ideas to be evaluated without risking the inhibitions, hostilities, and distortions that may occur in an open and less structured team meeting.

Delphi Technique The **Delphi technique** has evolved as a useful decision-making technique when team members are unable to meet face to face. It's virtual version basically collects online responses to a set of questions posed to a panel of decision makers. A coordinator summarizes responses, then sends the summary plus follow-up questions back to the panel. This process is repeated until a consensus is reached and a clear decision emerges.

WP LS Go to your WileyPLUS Learning Space course for video episodes, examples, art, tables, Concept Checks, practice, and resources that will help you succeed in this course.

Reading for
DECISION MAKING

> **WP LS** Go to your WileyPLUS Learning Space course for video episodes, examples, art, tables, Concept Checks, practice, and resources that will help you succeed in this course.

The Decision-Making Process

The world of the manager is the world of choice. It is also no wonder that a Graduate Management Admissions Council survey reports that 25 percent of business school alumni would like more training in managing the decision-making process.[1] Even in your first job, making the appropriate decisions to solve problems will be a key to success.

Steps in the Decision-Making Process

A common definition of **decision making** is the process of choosing a course of action for dealing with a problem or an opportunity.[2] The process is usually described in five steps that constitute the ideal or so-called *rational decision model*.

1. *Recognize and define the problem or opportunity*—gather information and deliberate in order to specify exactly why a decision is needed and what it should accomplish. Three mistakes are common in this critical first step in decision making. First, we may define the problem too broadly or too narrowly. Second, we may focus on problem symptoms instead of causes. Third, we may choose the wrong problem to deal with.

2. *Identify and analyze alternative courses of action*—evaluate possible alternative courses of action and their anticipated consequences for costs and benefits. Decision makers at this stage must be clear on exactly what they know and what they need to know. They should identify key stakeholders and consider the effects of each possible course of action on them.

3. *Choose a preferred course of action*—a choice is made to pursue one course of action rather than others. Criteria used in making the choice typically involve costs and benefits, timeliness of results, impact on stakeholders, and ethical soundness. Another issue is who makes the decision: team leader, team members, or some combination?

4. *Implement the preferred course of action*—actions are taken to put the preferred course of action into practice. This is a point where teams may suffer from **lack-of-participation error** because they haven't included certain people in the decision-making process whose support is necessary for its implementation. Teams that use participation and involvement successfully gather information and insights for better decision making, and commitments from team members to put choices into action. Some of the participation techniques are quite simple, such as a checklist for an emergency room surgery team.

5. *Evaluate results and follow up as necessary*—performance results are measured against initial goals and both anticipated and unanticipated outcomes are examined. This is where decision makers exercise control over their actions, being careful to ensure that the desired results are achieved and undesired side effects are avoided. It is a stage that many individuals and teams often neglect, with negative implications for their performance effectiveness.

The Decision to Decide

The reality is that making and implementing the right choices is complicated. And one of the most critical aspects of the decision-making process is setting priorities. Not every problem requires an immediate response and the best decision may be the one not made. Asking and answering the following questions can sometimes help with the decision to decide.

- *What really matters?* Small and less significant problems should not get the same time and attention as bigger ones.

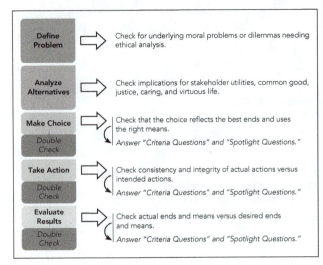

| Define Problem | ⟹ | Check for underlying moral problems or dilemmas needing ethical analysis. |

| Analyze Alternatives | ⟹ | Check implications for stakeholder utilities, common good, justice, caring, and virtuous life. |

| Make Choice / Double Check | ⟹ | Check that the choice reflects the best ends and uses the right means. Answer "Criteria Questions" and "Spotlight Questions." |

| Take Action / Double Check | ⟹ | Check consistency and integrity of actual actions versus intended actions. Answer "Criteria Questions" and "Spotlight Questions." |

| Evaluate Results / Double Check | ⟹ | Check actual ends and means versus desired ends and means. Answer "Criteria Questions" and "Spotlight Questions." |

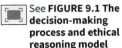

See **FIGURE 9.1 The decision-making process and ethical reasoning model**

- *Might the problem resolve itself?* Putting problems in rank order leaves the less significant for last. Surprisingly, many of these less important problems resolve themselves or are solved by others before you get to them.
- *Is this my, or our, problem?* Many problems can be handled by other people. These should be delegated to people who are best prepared to deal with them. Ideally, they should be delegated to people whose work they most affect.
- *Will time spent make a difference?* A really effective decision maker recognizes the difference between problems that realistically can be solved and those that are simply not solvable.

Ethical Reasoning and Decision Making

Choices at each step in the decision-making process often have moral issues that can easily be overlooked. ▣ **Figure 9.1** links the steps in the decision-making process with corresponding issues of ethical reasoning.[3] As suggested in the figure, we are advocating that an ethical reasoning approach be followed when decisions are made and that this approach be linked with steps in the decision-making process. In other words, decision making is incomplete without including ethical analysis.

Moral Problems and Dilemmas Ethics is the philosophical study of morality or standards regarding good character and conduct.[4] When we apply ethical reasoning to decisions made by individuals and teams in organizations, the focus is on moral problems and dilemmas that are associated with the decision-making process.

A **moral problem** poses major ethical consequences for the decision maker or for others. It is possible to address a personal, management, or business problem and not properly consider any moral problems that might be associated with it, but the preferred approach is to carefully examine the ethics of each alternative for all stakeholders, and make choices that minimize negative impact and maximize respect for everyone's rights.

During the recession, for example, job layoffs were commonplace. For the manager or executive teams involved, layoffs may seem straightforward and necessary solutions to a business problem—there are insufficient sales to justify the payroll and some jobs must be cut. But this situation also involves a moral problem. The people who lose their jobs may have families, debts, and perhaps limited alternative job options. They will be hurt even if the business benefits from lowering its costs. Although addressing the moral problem might not change the business decision, it might change how the business decision is reached and implemented. This includes addressing whether or not better alternatives to job eliminations exist and what support is offered to those who do lose jobs.

Sometimes decision makers face **moral dilemmas** and need to decide between two or more ethically uncomfortable alternatives. An example might be having to make the decision to sign an outsourcing contract with a less expensive supplier in a country where employment discrimination exists but where the country is poor and new jobs are necessary for economic development, or contracting a local supplier whose high cost will affect the bottom line. A situation like this involves the uncomfortable position of choosing between alternatives that contain both potential benefits and harm.

Although such moral dilemmas are difficult to resolve, ethical reasoning helps ensure that the decisions will be made with rigor and thoughtful consideration. A willingness to pause to examine the ethics of a proposed decision may well result in a better decision, preservation of respect and reputation, and avoidance of costly litigation.

Ethics Double-Checks In the preceding example of job layoffs, business executives who have been criticized for making job cuts might scramble to provide counseling and job search help to affected employees. This is after the fact, and moral conduct does not result from after-the-fact embarrassment. As ethicist Stephen Fineman suggests, "If people are unable to anticipate shame or guilt before they act in particular ways, then moral codes are invalid."[5] When you are the decision maker, decision making is not just a process followed for the good of the organization; it involves your values and your morality, and potential adverse impact on them should be anticipated.[6]

If you look at Figure 9.1, you will see that "ethics double-checks" are built into the ethical reasoning framework. This is a way of testing to make sure our decisions meet personal moral standards. The recommended ethics double-checks ask and answer two sets of questions: criteria questions and spotlight questions. Ethicist Gerald Cavanagh and his associates identify these four **criteria questions** for assessing ethics in decision making:[7]

- *Utility*—Does the decision satisfy all constituents or stakeholders?
- *Rights*—Does the decision respect the rights and duties of everyone?
- *Justice*—Is the decision consistent with the canons of justice?
- *Caring*—Is the decision consistent with my responsibilities to care?

The **spotlight questions** expose a decision to public scrutiny and force us to consider a decision in the context of full transparency.[8] They include:

- "How would I feel if my family found out about this decision?"
- "How would I feel if this decision were published in the local newspaper or posted on the Internet?"
- "What would the person you know or know of who has the strongest character and best ethical judgment do in this situation?"

Alternative Decision Environments

Decisions in organizations are typically made under the three conditions or environments—uncertainty, risk, and certainty—providing the decision maker with *nonprogrammed* or programmed types of decisions.[9] Combinations of these environments and types of decision are depicted in ▣ **Figure 9.2**. A quick examination of these combinations reveals interesting differences in the speed, accuracy, and efficiency of decision making.

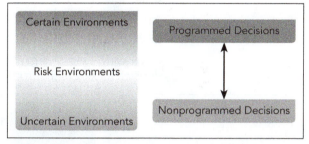

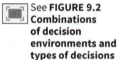

See **FIGURE 9.2 Combinations of decision environments and types of decisions**

Certain Environments and Programmed Decisions **Certain environments** exist when information is sufficient to predict the results of each alternative in advance of implementation. When a person invests money in a savings account, for example, absolute certainty exists about the interest that will be earned on that money in a given period of time.

Programmed decisions are choices made as standardized responses to recurring situations and routine problems. They deal with things a decision maker or team already has experience with. Although it appears the choice has been made, there remains the question of implementation and tailoring the implementation to the exact problem at hand. For instance, even programmed decisions that deal with employee absences, compensation, or other standard human resource issues call for care in implementation.

The combination of a certain decision environment and programmed decisions appears trivial because it represents well established standard operating practice in a well-known setting. Choices should be activated when a choice is made for fast, accurate, and efficient choices. The astute manager also realizes there is an opportunity to delegate implementation, simplify decision rules, and/or investigate if new alternatives have arisen.

Uncertain Environments and Nonprogrammed Decisions **Uncertain environments** exist when managers have so little information that they cannot even assign probabilities to various alternatives and their possible outcomes. This is the most difficult decision environment. As we will see in the rest of this chapter, uncertainty forces decision makers to rely heavily on unique, novel, and often totally innovative alternatives. This environment calls on managers to use their intuition, educated guesses, and even hunches to develop nonprogrammed decisions.

Nonprogrammed decisions are specifically crafted or tailored to fit a unique situation. They address novel or unexpected problems that demand a special response— one not available from a decision inventory. An example is a marketing team that has to respond to the introduction of a new product by a foreign competitor. Although past experience may help deal with this competitive threat, the immediate decision requires a creative solution based on the unique characteristics of the present market situation.

Risk Environments and Programmed Decisions **Risk environments** exist when decision makers are aware of the probabilities associated with their likely occurrence. Decision makers often attempt to eliminate uncertainty by assigning probabilities to alternatives. The assignment can be made through objective statistical procedures or through personal intuition. For instance, a senior production manager can make statistical estimates of quality rejects in production runs or make similar estimates based on personal past experience. Managers believe risk is a common decision environment.

In risk environments, decision makers often implement programmed decisions to gain speed and the appearance of efficiency. However, to the degree that the risk is manufactured from managerial estimates of conditions that are really uncertain, the accuracy of the choices could decline substantially.

Decision Environment and Decision Type Mismatches The presence of unusual combinations of decision environments and types signals potentially serious decision-making deficiencies. When organizations rely on unprogrammed decisions in certain and risk environments, there is a potential loss of efficiency. Conversely, use of programmed decisions in an uncertain environment often fails because choices made don't solve the problem or match the opportunity. The use of programmed decisions in uncertain environments is perhaps more common than you might first think. This combination indicates that decision makers are unresponsive to changing, dynamic conditions.

Decision-Making Models

Historically, field of organizational behavior has emphasized two alternative approaches to decision making as shown in ▣ **Figure 9.3**—classical and behavioral.[15] The classical decision model views rational people acting in a world of complete certainty, whereas the behavioral decision model accepts the notion of bounded rationality and suggests that people act only in terms of what they perceive about a given situation.

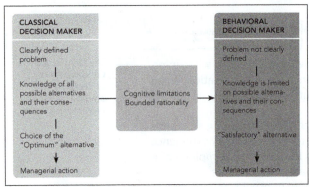

See **FIGURE 9.3 Decision making viewed from the classical and behavioral perspectives**

Classical Decision Model

The **classical decision model** views the manager or team as acting rationally and in a fully informed manner. In a certain environment, the problem is clearly defined, all possible action alternatives are known, and their consequences are clear. This allows for an **optimizing decision** that gives the best solution to the problem. This model fits the five-step decision-making process described earlier. It is an ideal situation of complete information where the decision maker moves through the steps one by one in a logical fashion. And it nicely lends itself to various forms of quantitative decision analysis as well as to computer-based applications.[16]

Behavioral Decision Model

As Nobel laureate Herbert Simon noted, the reality is that many, perhaps most, decision situations faced by individuals and teams in organizations don't fit the assumptions of the model. Recognizing this, the premise of the alternative **behavioral decision model** is that people act only in terms of their perceptions, which are frequently imperfect.[17]

Behavioral scientists recognize that human beings have *cognitive limitations*—limits on what we are able to know at any point in time. These limitations restrict our information-processing capabilities. The result is that information deficiencies and overloads compromise the ability of decision makers to operate according to the classical model. Instead, they end up acting with *bounded rationality*, where things are interpreted and made sense of as perceptions and only within the context of the situation. They engage in decision making within the box of a simplified view of a more complex reality.

Armed with only partial knowledge about the available action alternatives and their consequences, decision makers in the behavioral model are likely to choose the first alternative that appears satisfactory to them. Herbert Simon calls this the tendency to make **satisficing decisions**. He states, "Most human decision making, whether individual or organizational, is concerned with the discovery and selection of satisfactory alternatives; only in exceptional cases is it concerned with the discovery and selection of optimal decisions."[18]

Systematic and Intuitive Thinking

Individuals and teams may be described as using both comparatively slow "systematic" and quick "intuitive" thinking as they make decisions and try to solve problems. **Systematic thinking** is consistent with the rational model where a decision is approached in step-by-step and analytical fashion. You might recognize this style in a team member who tries to break a complex problem into smaller components that can be addressed one by one. Teams engaged in systematic thinking will try to make a plan before taking action, and to search for information and proceed with problem solving in a fact-based and logical fashion. Systematic thinking is also known as an analytical approach and is often recommended for superior decision making.[19]

We think of *intuition* as the ability to know or recognize quickly and readily the possibilities of a given situation.[20] Individuals and teams using **intuitive thinking** are more flexible and spontaneous in decision making.[21] You might observe this pattern in someone who always seems to come up with an imaginative response to a problem, often based on a quick and broad evaluation of the situation. Decision makers in this intuitive mode tend to deal with many aspects of a problem at once, search for the big picture, jump quickly from one issue to another, and act on hunches from experience or on spontaneous ideas. This approach is common under conditions of risk and uncertainty. Because intuitive thinkers take a flexible and spontaneous approach to decision making, their presence on a team adds potential for creative problem solving and innovation.

When US Airways Flight 1549 hit a flock of birds on takeoff from LaGuardia Airport, lost engine power, and was headed for a crash, Pilot Chesley "Sully" Sullenberger III made the decision to land in the Hudson River. The landing was successful, and no lives were lost. Called a hero for his efforts, Sullenberger described his thinking this way.[22]

> I needed to touch down with the wings exactly level. I needed to touch down with the nose slightly up. I needed to touch down at . . . a descent rate that was survivable. And I needed to touch down just above our minimum flying speed but not below it. And I needed to make all these things happen simultaneously.

Sullenberger did the right thing—he made the decision himself, betting on his training and experience and, stood behind it with his own life on the line.

Does this mean that we should always favor the more intuitive and less systematic approach? Most likely not—teams, like individuals, should use and combine the two approaches to solve complex problems. In other words, there's a place for both systematic and intuitive thinking in management decision making.

Decision-Making Traps and Issues

The pathways to good decisions can seem like a minefield of challenging issues and troublesome traps. Whether working individually or as part of a team, it is important to understand the influence of judgmental heuristics and other potential decision biases, as well as be capable of making critical choices regarding if, when, and how decisions get made.

Judgmental Heuristics

Judgment, or the use of intellect, is important in all aspects of decision making. When we question the ethics of a decision, for example, we are questioning the judgment of the person making it. Work by Nobel laureate Daniel Kahneman, his colleagues, and many others shows that people are prone to mistakes and biases that often interfere with the quality of decision making.[23] Many of these mistakes and biases can be traced back to the use of **heuristics**. Heuristics serve a useful purpose by making it easier to deal with uncertainty and the limited information common to problem situations. However, they can also lead us toward systematic errors that affect the quality, and perhaps the ethical implications, of any decisions made.[24]

Availability Heuristic The **availability heuristic** involves assessing a current event based on past occurrences that are easily available in one's memory. An example is the product development specialist who decides not to launch a new product because of a recent failure launching another one. In this case, the existence of a past product failure has negatively, and perhaps inappropriately, biased judgment regarding how best to handle the new product.

Representativeness Heuristic The **representativeness heuristic** involves assessing the likelihood that an event will occur based on its similarity to one's stereotypes of similar occurrences. An example is the team leader who selects a new member, not because of any special qualities of the person but because the individual comes from a department known to have produced high performers in the past. In this case, the individual's current place of employment—not job qualifications—is the basis for the selection decision.

Anchoring and Adjustment Heuristic   The **anchoring and adjustment heuristic** involves assessing an event by taking an initial value from historical precedent or an outside source and then incrementally adjusting this value to make a current assessment. An example is the executive who makes salary increase recommendations for key personnel by simply adjusting their current base salaries by a percentage. In this case, the existing base salary becomes an "anchor" that limits subsequent salary increases. This anchor may be inappropriate, such as in the case of an individual whose market value has become substantially higher than what is reflected by the base salary plus increment approach.

Decision Biases

In addition to the common judgmental heuristics, decision makers are also prone to more general biases in decision making. One bias is **confirmation error**, whereby the decision maker seeks confirmation for what is already thought to be true and neglects opportunities to acknowledge or find disconfirming information. A form of selective perception, this bias involves seeking only information and cues in a situation that support a preexisting opinion.

A second bias is the **hindsight trap** where the decision maker overestimates the degree to which he or she could have predicted an event that has already taken place. One risk of hindsight is that it may foster feelings of inadequacy or insecurity in dealing with future decision situations.

A third bias is the **framing error**. It occurs when managers and teams evaluate and resolve a problem in the context in which they perceive it—either positive or negative. Suppose research data show that a new product has a 40 percent market share. What does this really mean to the marketing team? A negative frame views the product as deficient because it is missing 60 percent of the market. Discussion and problem solving within this frame would likely focus on "What are we doing wrong?" If the marketing team used a positive frame and considered a 40 percent share as a success, the conversation might have been quite different: "How can we do even better?" By the way, we are constantly exposed to framing in the world of politics; the word used to describe it is *spin*.

Knowing When to Quit

After the process of making a decision is completed and implementation begins, it can be hard for decision makers to change their minds and admit they made a mistake even when things are clearly not going well. Instead of backing off, the tendency is to press on to victory. This is called **escalating commitment**—continuing and renewing efforts on a previously chosen course of action, even though it is not working.[25] The tendency toward escalating commitment is reflected in the popular adage "If at first you don't succeed, try, try again."

Escalating commitments are a form of decision entrapment that leads people to do things that the facts of a situation do not justify. This is one of the most difficult aspects of decision making to convey to executives because so many of them rose to their positions by turning losing courses of action into winning ones.[26] Managers should be proactive in spotting "failures" and more open to reversing decisions or dropping plans that are not working. But this is easier said than done.

The tendency to escalate commitments often outweighs the willingness to disengage from them. Decision makers may rationalize negative feedback as a temporary condition, protect their egos by not admitting that the original decision was a mistake, or characterize any negative results as a "learning experience" that can be overcome with added future effort.

Perhaps you have experienced an inability to call it quits or been on teams with similar reluctance. It's hard to admit to a mistake, especially when a lot of thought and energy went into the decision in the first place; it can be even harder when one's ego and reputation are tied up with the decision. Fortunately, researchers suggest the following to avoid getting trapped in escalating commitments:

- Set advance limits on your involvement and commitment to a particular course of action; stick with these limits.
- Make your own decisions; don't follow the lead of others because they are also prone to escalation.
- Carefully determine just why you are continuing a course of action; if there are insufficient reasons to continue, don't.
- Remind yourself of the costs of a course of action; consider saving these costs as a reason to discontinue.

Knowing Who to Involve

In practice, good organizational decisions are made by individuals acting alone, by individuals consulting with others, and by people working together in teams.[27] In true contingency fashion, no one option is always superior to the others; who participates and how decisions are to be made should reflect the issues at hand.[28]

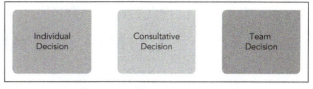

See **FIGURE 9.4 Three scenarios for successful decision making**

🖼 **Figure 9.4** shows three scenarios for successful decision making. When **individual decisions**, also called *authority decisions*, are made, the manager or team leader uses information gathered and decides what to do without involving others. This decision method assumes that the decision maker is an expert on the problem at hand. In **consultative decisions**, by contrast, inputs are gathered from other persons and the decision maker uses this information to arrive at a final choice. In **team decisions**, group members work together to make the final choice, hopefully by consensus or unanimity.

Victor Vroom, Phillip Yetton, and Arthur Jago developed the framework shown in 🖼 **Figure 9.5** for helping managers choose the right decision-making methods for various problem situations.[29] They identify these variants of the individual, consultative, and team decision options just described.

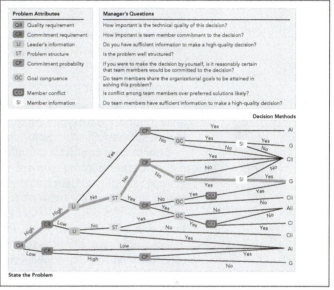

- *AI (first variant on the authority decision):* The manager solves the problem or makes the decision alone, using information available at that time.

- *AII (second variant on the authority decision):* The manager obtains the necessary information from team members and then decides on the problem's solution. The team members provide the necessary information but do not generate or evaluate alternatives.

- *CI (first variant on the consultative decision):* The manager shares the problem with team members individually, getting their ideas and suggestions without bringing them all together. The manager then makes a decision.

- *CII (second variant on the consultative decision):* The manager shares the problem with team members, collectively obtaining their ideas and suggestions. The manager then makes a decision.

- *G (the team or consensus decision):* The manager shares the problem with team members as a total group and engages them in consensus seeking to arrive at a final decision.

See **FIGURE 9.5 The Vroom-Jago model for a manager's use of alternative decision-making methods**

Figure 9.4 is a decision tree developed from the research of Vroom and his colleagues. Though complex, it helps to illustrate how decision makers can choose among the individual, consultative, and team decision options by considering these factors: (1) required quality of the decision, (2) commitment needed from team members to implement the decision, (3) amount of information available to the team leader, (4) problem structure, (5) chances team members will be committed if the leader makes the decision, (6) degree to which the team leader and members agree on goals, (7) conflict among team members, and (8) information available to team members.

Consultative and team decisions are recommended by this model when the leader lacks sufficient expertise and information to solve this problem alone; the problem is unclear and help is needed to clarify the situation; acceptance of the decision and commitment by others are necessary for implementation; and adequate time is available to allow for true participation. By contrast, authority decisions work best when team leaders have the expertise needed to solve the problem; they are confident and capable of acting alone; others are likely to accept and implement the decision they make; and little or no time is available for discussion. When problems must be resolved immediately, the authority decision made by the team leader may be the only option.[30]

WP LS Go to your WileyPLUS Learning Space course for video episodes, examples, art, tables, Concept Checks, practice, and resources that will help you succeed in this course.

10

Reading for
CONFLICT AND NEGOTIATION

Conflict in Organizations

We all need skills to work well with others who don't always agree with us, even in situations that are complicated and stressful.[1] **Conflict** occurs whenever disagreements exist in a social situation over issues of substance, or whenever emotional antagonisms create frictions between individuals or groups.[2] Team leaders and members can spend considerable time dealing with conflicts. Sometimes they are direct participants, and other times they act as mediators or neutral third parties to help resolve conflicts between other people.[3] The fact is that conflict dynamics are inevitable in the workplace, and it's best to know how to handle them.[4]

Types of Conflict

Conflicts in teams, at work, and in our personal lives occur in at least two basic forms: substantive and emotional. Both types are common, ever present, and challenging. How well prepared are you to deal successfully with them?

Substantive conflict is a fundamental disagreement over ends or goals to be pursued and the means for their accomplishment.[5] A dispute with one's boss or other team members over a plan of action to be followed, such as the marketing strategy for a new product, is an example of substantive conflict. When people work together every day, it is only normal that different viewpoints on a variety of substantive workplace issues will arise. At times people will disagree over such things as team and organizational goals, the allocation of resources, the distribution of rewards, policies and procedures, and task assignments.

Emotional conflict involves interpersonal difficulties that arise over feelings of anger, mistrust, dislike, fear, resentment, and the like.[6] This conflict is commonly known as a "clash of personalities." How many times, for example, have you heard comments such as "I can't stand working with him" or "She always rubs me the wrong way" or "I wouldn't do what he asked if you begged me"? When emotional conflicts creep into work situations, they can drain energies and distract people from task priorities and goals. Yet, they emerge in a wide variety of settings and are common in teams, among co-workers, and in superior–subordinate relationships.

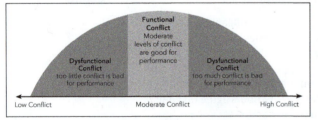

See **FIGURE 10.1 The two faces of conflict: functional conflict and dysfunctional conflict.**

Functional and Dysfunctional Conflict

Any type of conflict in teams and organizations can be upsetting both to the individuals directly involved and to others affected by its occurrence. It can be quite uncomfortable, for example, to work on a team where two co-workers are continually hostile toward each other, or where your team is constantly battling another to get resources from top management attention. As **Figure 10.1** points out, however, it's important to recognize that conflict can have a functional or constructive side as well as a dysfunctional or destructive side.

Functional conflict, also called *constructive conflict*, results in benefits to individuals, the team, or the organization. This positive conflict can bring important problems to the surface so they can be addressed. It can cause decisions to be considered carefully and perhaps reconsidered to ensure that the right path of action is being followed. It can increase the amount of information used for decision making. It can offer opportunities for creativity that can improve performance. Indeed, an effective manager or team leader is able to stimulate constructive conflict in situations in which satisfaction with the status quo is holding back needed change and development.

Dysfunctional conflict, or *destructive conflict*, works to the disadvantage of an individual or team. It diverts energies, hurts group cohesion, promotes interpersonal hostilities, and creates an overall negative environment for workers. This type of conflict occurs, for example, when two team members are unable to work together because of interpersonal differences—a destructive emotional conflict—or when the members of a work unit fail to act because they cannot agree on task goals—a destructive substantive conflict. Destructive conflicts of these types can decrease performance and job satisfaction as well as contribute to absenteeism and job turnover. Managers and team leaders should be alert to destructive conflicts and be quick to take action to prevent or eliminate them—or at least minimize any harm done.

Culture and Conflict

Society today shows many signs of cultural wear and tear in social relationships. We experience difficulties born of racial tensions, homophobia, gender gaps, and more. They arise from tensions among people who are different from one another in some way. They are also a reminder that cultural differences must be considered for their conflict potential. Consider the cultural dimension of time orientation. When persons from short-term cultures such as the United States try to work with persons from long-term cultures such as Japan, the likelihood of conflict developing is high. The same holds true when individualists work with collectivists and when persons from high-power-distance cultures work with those from low-power-distance cultures.[7]

People who are not able or willing to recognize and respect cultural differences can cause dysfunctional conflicts in multicultural teams. On the other hand, members with cultural intelligence and sensitivity can help the team to unlock its performance advantages. Consider these comments from members of a joint European and American project team at Corning. *American engineer:* "Something magical happens. Europeans are very creative thinkers; they take time to really reflect on a problem to come up with the very best theoretical solution. Americans are more tactical and practical—we want to get down to developing a working solution as soon as possible." *French teammate:* "The French are more focused on ideas and concepts. If we get blocked in the execution of those ideas, we give up. Not the Americans. They pay more attention to details, processes, and time schedules. They make sure they are prepared and have involved everyone in the planning process so that they won't get blocked. But it's best if you mix the two approaches. In the end, you will achieve the best results."[8]

Conflict Management

Conflict can be addressed in many ways, but true **conflict resolution**—a situation in which the underlying reasons for dysfunctional conflict are eliminated—can be elusive. When conflicts go unresolved, the stage is often set for future conflicts of the same or related sort. Rather than trying to deny the existence of conflict or settle on a temporary resolution, it is always best to deal with important conflicts in such ways that they are completely resolved.[9] This requires a good understanding of the stages of conflict, the potential causes of conflict, and indirect and direct approaches to conflict management.

Stages of Conflict

Most conflicts develop in the stages shown in ▪ **Figure 10.2**. *Conflict antecedents* establish the conditions from which conflicts are likely to emerge. When the antecedent conditions become the basis for substantive or emotional differences between people or groups, the stage of *perceived conflict* exists. Of course, this perception may be held by only one of the conflicting parties.

There is quite a difference between perceived and *felt conflict*. When conflict is felt, it is experienced as tension that motivates the person to take action to reduce feelings of discomfort. For conflict to be resolved, all parties should perceive the conflict and feel the need to do something about it.

Manifest conflict is expressed openly in behavior. At this stage removing or correcting the antecedents results in *conflict resolution*, whereas failing to do so results in *conflict suppression*. With suppression, no change in antecedent conditions occurs even though the manifest conflict behaviors may be temporarily controlled. This occurs, for example, when one or both parties choose to ignore conflict in their dealings with one another. Conflict suppression is a superficial and often temporary state that leaves the situation open to future conflicts over similar issues. Only true conflict resolution establishes conditions that eliminate an existing conflict and reduce the potential for it to recur in the future.

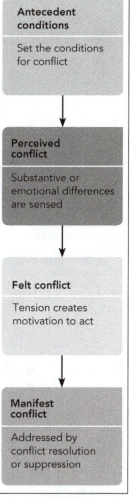

Antecedent conditions

Set the conditions for conflict

Perceived conflict

Substantive or emotional differences are sensed

Felt conflict

Tension creates motivation to act

Manifest conflict

Addressed by conflict resolution or suppression

 See **FIGURE 10.2 Stages of conflict development**

Hierarchical Causes of Conflict

The nature of organizations as hierarchical systems provides a convenient setting for conflicts as individuals and teams try to work with one another. *Vertical conflict* occurs between levels and commonly involves supervisor–subordinate and team leader–team member disagreements over resources, goals, deadlines, or performance results. *Horizontal conflict* occurs between persons or groups working at the same organizational level.

Hierarchical conflicts commonly arise from goal incompatibilities, resource scarcities, or purely interpersonal factors. *Line–staff conflict* involves disagreements between line and staff personnel over who has authority and control over decisions on matters such as budgets, technology, and human resource practices. Also common are *role ambiguity conflicts* that occur when the communication of task expectations is unclear or upsetting in some way, such as a team member receiving different expectations from the leader and other members. Conflict is always likely when people are placed in ambiguous situations where it is hard to understand who is responsible for what, and why.

Contextual Causes of Conflict

The context of the organization as a complex network of interacting subsystems is a breeding ground for conflicts. *Task and workflow interdependencies* cause disputes and open disagreements among people and teams who are required to cooperate to meet challenging goals.[10] Conflict potential is especially great when interdependence is high—that is, when a person or group must rely on or ask for contributions from one or more others to achieve its goals. Conflict escalates with *structural differentiation*, when different teams and work units pursue different goals with different time horizons as shown in  **Figure 10.3**. Conflict also develops out of *domain ambiguities*, when individuals or teams lack adequate task direction or goals and misunderstand such things as customer jurisdiction or scope of authority.

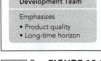

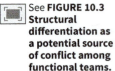
See **FIGURE 10.3** Structural differentiation as a potential source of conflict among functional teams.

Actual or perceived *resource scarcity* can foster destructive conflict. Working relationships are likely to suffer as individuals or teams try to position themselves to gain or retain maximum shares of a limited resource pool. They are also likely to resist having their resources redistributed to others.

Power or value asymmetries in work relationships can also create conflict. They exist when interdependent people or teams differ substantially from one another in status and influence or in values. Conflict resulting from asymmetry is likely, for example, when a low-power person needs the help of a high-power person who does not respond, when people who hold dramatically different values are forced to work together on a task, or when a high-status person is required to interact with and perhaps be dependent on someone of lower status.

Indirect Conflict Management Strategies

Most people will tell you that not all conflict in teams and organizations can be resolved by getting everyone involved to adopt new attitudes, behaviors, and stances toward one another. Think about it. Aren't there likely to be times when personalities and emotions prove irreconcilable? In such cases an indirect or structural approach to conflict management can often help. It uses such strategies as reduced interdependence, appeals to common goals, hierarchical referral, and alterations in the use of mythology and scripts to deal with the conflict situation.

Managed Interdependence When workflow conflicts exist, managers can adjust the level of interdependency among teams or individuals.[11] One simple option is *decoupling*, or taking action to eliminate or reduce the required contact between conflicting parties. In some cases, team tasks can be adjusted to reduce the number of required points of coordination. The conflicting parties are separated as much as possible from one another.

Buffering is another approach that can be used when the inputs of one team are the outputs of another. The classic buffering technique is to build an inventory, or buffer, between the teams so that any output slowdown or excess is absorbed by the inventory and does not directly pressure the target group. Although it reduces conflict, this technique is increasingly out of favor because it increases inventory costs.

Conflict can sometimes be reduced by assigning people to serve as liaisons between groups that are prone to conflict.[12] Persons in these *linking-pin roles* are expected to understand the operations, members, needs, and norms of their host teams. They are supposed to use this knowledge to help the team work better with others in order to accomplish mutual tasks.

Appeals to Common Goals An *appeal to common goals* can focus the attention of conflicting individuals and teams on one mutually desirable conclusion. This elevates any dispute to the level of common ground where disagreements can be put in perspective. In a course team where members are arguing over content choices for a PowerPoint presentation, for example, it might help to remind everyone that the goal is to impress the instructor and get an "A" for the presentation and that this is only possible if everyone contributes their best.

Upward Referral *Upward referral* uses the chain of command for conflict resolution.[13] Problems are moved up from the level of conflicting individuals or teams for more senior managers to address. Although tempting, this has limitations. If conflict is severe and recurring, the continual use of upward referral may not result in true conflict resolution. Higher managers removed from day-to-day affairs may fail to see the real causes of a conflict, and attempts at resolution may be superficial. In addition, busy managers may tend to blame the people involved and perhaps act quickly to replace them.

Altering Scripts and Myths In some situations, conflict is superficially managed by scripts, or behavioral routines, that are part of the organization's culture.[14] The scripts become rituals that allow the conflicting parties to vent their frustrations and to recognize that they are mutually dependent on one another. An example is a monthly meeting of department heads that is held presumably for purposes of coordination and problem solving but actually becomes just a polite forum for agreement.[15] Managers in such cases know their scripts and accept the difficulty of truly resolving any major conflicts. For instance, by sticking with the script, expressing only low-key disagreement, and then quickly acting as if everything has been taken care of, the managers can leave the meeting with everyone feeling a superficial sense of accomplishment.

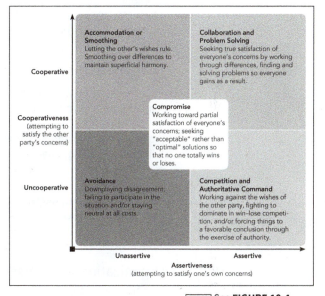

Direct Conflict Management Strategies

In addition to the indirect conflict management strategies just discussed, it is also very important to understand how conflict management plays out in face-to-face fashion. **Figure 10.4** shows five direct conflict management strategies that vary in their emphasis on cooperativeness and assertiveness in the interpersonal dynamics of the situation. Although true conflict resolution can occur only when a conflict is dealt with through a solution that allows all conflicting parties to "win," the reality is that direct conflict management may also pursue lose–lose and win–lose outcomes.[16]

See **FIGURE 10.4 Five direct conflict management strategies.**

Lose–Lose Strategies *Lose–lose conflict* occurs when nobody really gets what he or she wants in a conflict situation. The underlying reasons for the conflict remain unaffected, and a similar conflict is likely to occur in the future. Lose–lose outcomes are likely when the conflict management strategies involve little or no assertiveness. **Avoidance** is the extreme where no one acts assertively and everyone simply pretends the conflict doesn't exist and hopes it will go away. **Accommodation** (or **smoothing**) as it is sometimes called, involves playing down differences among the conflicting parties and highlighting similarities and areas of agreement. This peaceful coexistence ignores the real essence of a conflict and often creates frustration and resentment. **Compromise** occurs when each party shows moderate assertiveness and cooperation and is ultimately willing to give up something of value to the other. Because no one gets what they really wanted, the antecedent conditions for future conflicts are established.

Win–Lose Strategies In *win–lose conflict*, one party achieves its desires at the expense and to the exclusion of the other party's desires. This is a high-assertiveness and low-cooperativeness situation. It may result from outright **competition** in which one party achieves a victory through force, superior skill, or domination. It may also occur as a result of **authoritative command**, whereby a formal authority such as manager or team leader simply dictates a solution and specifies what is gained and what is lost by whom. Win–lose strategies fail to address the root causes of the conflict and tend to suppress the desires of at least one of the conflicting parties. As a result, future conflicts over the same issues are likely to occur.

Win–Win Strategies *Win-win conflict* is achieved by a blend of both high cooperativeness and high assertiveness.[17] **Collaboration and problem solving** involve recognition by all conflicting parties that something is wrong and needs attention. It stresses gathering and evaluating information in solving disputes and making choices. All relevant issues are raised and openly discussed. Win–win outcomes eliminate the reasons for continuing or resurrecting the conflict because nothing has been avoided or suppressed.

The ultimate test for collaboration and problem solving is whether or not the conflicting parties see that the solution to the conflict: (1) achieves each party's goals, (2) is acceptable to both parties, and (3) establishes a process whereby all parties involved see a responsibility to be open and honest about facts and feelings. When success in each of these areas is achieved, the likelihood of true conflict resolution is greatly increased. However, this process often takes time and consumes lots of energy, to which the parties must be willing to commit. Collaboration and problem solving aren't always feasible, and the other strategies are sometimes useful if not preferred.[18] As the "You Should Know . . ." features points out, each of the conflict management strategies may have advantages under certain conditions.

Negotiation

Picture yourself trying to make a decision. *Situation:* You are about to order a new tablet device for a team member in your department. Then another team member submits a request for one of a different brand. Your boss says that only one brand can be ordered. *Situation:* You have been offered a new job in another city and want to take it, but you are disappointed with the salary. You've heard friends talk about how they "negotiated" better offers when taking jobs. You are concerned about the costs of relocating and would like a signing bonus as well as a guarantee of an early salary review.

The preceding examples are just two of the many situations that involve **negotiation**—the process of making joint decisions when the parties involved have different preferences.[19] Negotiation has special significance in teams and work settings, where disagreements are likely to arise over such diverse matters as wage rates, task objectives, performance evaluations, job assignments, work schedules, work locations, and more.

Organizational Settings for Negotiation

Managers and team leaders should be prepared to participate in at least four major action settings for negotiations. In a *two-party negotiation*, the manager negotiates directly with one other person. In a *group negotiation,* the manager is part of a team or group whose members are negotiating to arrive at a common decision. In an *intergroup negotiation*, the manager is part of a team that is negotiating with another group to arrive at a decision regarding a problem or situation affecting both. In a *constituency negotiation*, each party represents a broader constituency—for example, representatives of management and labor negotiating a collective bargaining agreement.

Negotiation Goals and Outcomes

Two important goals are at stake in any negotiation: substance goals and relationship goals. *Substance goals* deal with outcomes that relate to the content issues under negotiation. The dollar amount of a salary offer in a recruiting situation is one example. *Relationship goals* deal with outcomes that relate to how well people involved in the negotiation and any constituencies they may represent are able to work with one another once the process is concluded. An example is the ability of union members and management representatives to work together effectively after a labor contract dispute has been settled.

Effective negotiation occurs when substance issues are resolved and working relationships are maintained or even improved. In practice, think of this in terms of two criteria for effective negotiation:

- *Quality of outcomes*—The negotiation results in a "quality" agreement that is wise and satisfactory to all sides.
- *Harmony in relationships*—The negotiation is "harmonious" and fosters rather than inhibits good interpersonal relations.

Ethical Aspects of Negotiation

It would be ideal if everyone involved in a negotiation followed high ethical standards of conduct, but this goal can get sidetracked by an overemphasis on self-interests. The motivation to behave ethically in negotiations can be put to the test by each party's desire to get more than the other from the negotiation and/or by a belief that there are insufficient resources to satisfy all parties.[20] After the heat of negotiations dies down, the parties may try to rationalize or explain away questionable ethics as unavoidable, harmless, or justified. Such after-the-fact rationalizations can have long-run negative consequences, such as not being able to achieve one's wishes again the next time. At the very least, the unethical party may be the target of revenge tactics by those who were disadvantaged. Once some people have behaved unethically in one situation, furthermore, they may become entrapped by such behavior and may be more likely to display it again in the future.[21]

Negotiation Strategies

When we think about negotiating for something, perhaps cars and salaries are the first things that pop into mind. But people in organizations are constantly negotiating over not only just pay and raises, but also such things as work rules or assignments, rewards, and access to any variety of scarce resources—money, time, people, facilities, equipment, and so on. The strategy used can have a major influence on how the negotiation transpires and its outcomes.

Two broad negotiation strategies differ markedly in approach and possible outcomes. **Distributive negotiation** focuses on positions staked out or declared by conflicting parties. Each party tries to claim certain portions of the available "pie" whose overall size is considered fixed. **Integrative negotiation**, sometimes called *principled negotiation*, focuses on the merits of the issues. Everyone involved tries to enlarge the available pie and find mutually agreed-on ways of distributing it, rather than stake claims to certain portions of it.[22] Think of the conversations you overhear and are part of in team situations. The notion of "my way or the highway" is analogous to distribution negotiation; "Let's find a way to make this work for both of us" is more akin to integrative negotiation.

Approaches to Distributive Negotiation

Participants in distributive negotiation usually approach it as a win–lose episode. Things tend to unfold in one of two directions—a hard battle for dominance or a soft and quick concession. Neither one nor the other delivers great results.

"Hard" distributive negotiation takes place when each party holds out to get its own way. This leads to competition, whereby each party seeks dominance over the other and tries to maximize self-interests. The hard approach may lead to a win–lose outcome in which one party dominates and gains, or it can lead to an impasse.

"Soft" distributive negotiation takes place when one party or both parties make concessions just to get things over with. This soft approach leads to accommodation—in which one party gives in to the other—or to compromise—in which each party gives up something of value in order to reach agreement. In either case at least some latent dissatisfaction is likely to remain.

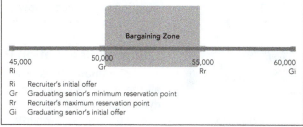

Ri — Recruiter's initial offer
Gr — Graduating senior's minimum reservation point
Rr — Recruiter's maximum reservation point
Gi — Graduating senior's initial offer

■ **Figure 10.5** illustrates classic two-party distributive negotiation by the example of the graduating senior negotiating a job offer with a recruiter.[23] Look at the situation first from the graduate's perspective. She has told the recruiter that she would like a salary of $60,000; this is her initial offer. However, she also has in mind a minimum reservation point of $50,000—the lowest salary that she will accept for this job. Thus she communicates a salary request of $60,000 but is willing to accept one as low as $50,000. The situation is somewhat the reverse from the recruiter's perspective. His initial offer to the graduate is $45,000, and his maximum reservation point is $55,000; this is the most he is prepared to pay.

The **bargaining zone** is the range between one party's minimum reservation point and the other party's maximum reservation point. In Figure 10.4, the bargaining zone is $50,000 to $55,000. This is a positive bargaining zone since the reservation points of the two parties overlap.

Whenever a positive bargaining zone exists, bargaining has room to unfold. Had the graduate's minimum reservation point been greater than the recruiter's maximum reservation point (for example, $57,000), no room would have existed for bargaining. Classic two-party bargaining

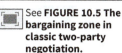

See **FIGURE 10.5 The bargaining zone in classic two-party negotiation.**

always involves the delicate tasks of first discovering the respective reservation points—one's own and the other's. Progress can then be made toward an agreement that lies somewhere within the bargaining zone and is acceptable to each party.

How to Gain Integrative Agreements

The integrative approach to negotiation is less confrontational than the distributive, and it permits a broader range of alternatives to be considered in the negotiation process. From the outset there is much more of a win–win orientation. Even though it may take longer, the time, energy, and effort needed to negotiate an integrated agreement can be well worth the investment. Always, the integrative or principled approach involves a willingness to negotiate based on the merits of the situation. The foundations for gaining truly integrative agreements can be described as supportive attitudes, constructive behaviors, and good information.[24]

Attitudinal Foundations There are three attitudinal foundations of integrative agreements. First, each party must approach the negotiation with a *willingness to trust* the other party. This is a reason why ethics and maintaining relationships are so important in negotiations. Second, each party must convey a *willingness to share* information with the other party. Without shared information, effective problem solving is unlikely to occur. Third, each party must show a *willingness to ask concrete questions* of the other party. This further facilitates information sharing.

Behavioral Foundations All behavior during a negotiation is important for both its actual impact and the impressions it leaves behind. This means the following behavioral foundations of integrative agreements must be carefully considered and included in any negotiator's repertoire of skills and capabilities:

- Separate people from the problem.
- Don't allow emotional considerations to affect the negotiation.
- Focus on interests rather than positions.
- Avoid premature judgments.
- Keep the identification of alternatives separate from their evaluation.
- Judge possible agreements by set criteria or standards.

Information Foundations The information foundations of integrative agreements are substantial. They involve each party becoming familiar with the best alternative to a negotiated agreement (BATNA). That is, each party must know what he or she will do if an agreement cannot be reached. Both negotiating parties must identify and understand their personal interests in the situation. They must know what is really important to them in the case at hand and, they must come to understand what the other party values.

Common Negotiation Pitfalls

The negotiation process is admittedly complex on ethical and many other grounds. It is subject to all the possible confusions of complex, and sometimes even volatile, interpersonal and team dynamics. And as if this isn't enough, negotiators need to guard against some common negotiation pitfalls as shown in ▤ **Figure 10.6**.[25]

One common pitfall is the tendency to stake out your negotiating position based on the assumption that in order to gain your way, something must be subtracted from the gains of the other party. This *myth of the fixed pie* is a purely distributive approach to negotiation. The whole concept of integrative negotiation is based on the premise that the pie can sometimes be expanded or used to the maximum advantage of all parties, not just one.

Second, the possibility of *escalating commitment* is high when negotiations begin with parties stating extreme demands. Once demands have been stated, people become committed to them and are reluctant to back down. Concerns for protecting one's ego and saving face may lead to the irrational escalation of a conflict. Self-discipline is needed to spot tendencies toward escalation in one's own behavior as well as in the behavior of others.

Third, negotiators often develop *overconfidence* that their positions are the only correct ones. This can lead them to ignore the other party's needs. In some cases negotiators completely fail to see merits in the other party's position—merits that an outside observer would be sure to spot. Such overconfidence makes it harder to reach a positive common agreement.

Fixed pie myth

Escalating commitment

Over-confidence

Too much telling

Too little listening

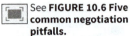
See **FIGURE 10.6 Five common negotiation pitfalls.**

Fourth, communication problems can cause difficulties during a negotiation. It has been said that "negotiation is the process of communicating back and forth for the purpose of reaching a joint decision."[26] This process can break down because of a *telling problem*—the parties don't really talk to each other, at least not in the sense of making themselves truly understood. It can also be damaged by a *hearing problem*—the parties are unable or unwilling to listen well enough to understand what the other is saying. Indeed, positive negotiation is most likely when each party engages in active listening and frequently asks questions to clarify what the other is saying. Each party occasionally needs to "stand in the other party's shoes" and to view the situation from the other's perspective.[27]

Third-Party Roles in Negotiation

Negotiation may sometimes be accomplished through the intervention of third parties, such as when stalemates occur and matters appear to be irresolvable under current circumstances. In a process called *alternative dispute resolution*, a neutral third party works with persons involved in a negotiation to help them resolve impasses and settle disputes. There are two primary forms through which it is implemented.

In **arbitration**, such as the salary arbitration now common in professional sports, the neutral third party acts as a "judge" and has the power to issue a decision that is binding on all parties. This ruling takes place after the arbitrator listens to the positions advanced by the parties involved in a dispute. In **mediation**, the neutral third party tries to engage the parties in a negotiated solution through persuasion and rational argument. This is a common approach in labor–management negotiations, where trained mediators acceptable to both sides are called in to help resolve bargaining impasses. Unlike an arbitrator, the mediator is not able to dictate a solution.

 Go to your WileyPLUS Learning Space course for video episodes, examples, art, tables, Concept Checks, practice, and resources that will help you succeed in this course.

11

Reading for
COMMUNICATION

The Nature of Communication

Communication is the lifeblood of the organization. All organizational behavior—good and bad—stems from communication. Yet, despite the fact that we spend most of our lives communicating, we are not always very good at it.

In this chapter we examine communication in organizational and relational contexts to identify factors associated with effective and ineffective communication. A basic premise of this chapter is that to communicate effectively we need to have good relationships, and to have good relationships we need to communicate effectively.

Importance of Communication

Communication has always been important, but the nature of communication is changing in organizations and in the world. Widely available information is empowering people and societies in unprecedented ways. For example, the Egyptian Revolution of 2012 was called the "Facebook Revolution" because Egyptian citizens used Facebook to organize a revolution behind the scenes. In organizations, managers are not able to control information like they once could, and this is changing the nature of power in organizations. When Yahoo! announced that it would no longer allow employees to work at home, employees rebelled by anonymously posting company memos online. What managers had intended to be private company policy quickly snowballed into a major international news story and critique.

Communication is the glue that holds organizations together. It is the way we share information, ideas, and expectations as well as display emotions to coordinate action. Therefore we need to make effective communication a top priority in organizations.

The Communication Process

Although we all know what communication is, it is useful to review the basic communication model to set up a discussion of how and why communication breakdowns occur. As illustrated in ▣ **Figure 11.1**, **communication** is a process of sending and receiving messages with attached meanings. The key elements in the communication process include a source, which encodes an intended meaning into a message, and a receiver, which decodes the message into a perceived meaning. The receiver may or may not give feedback to the source.

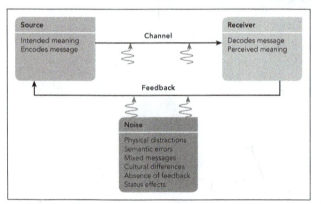

See **FIGURE 11.1**
The communication process

The information source, or **sender**, is a person or group trying to communicate with someone else. The source seeks to communicate, in part, to change the attitudes, knowledge, or behavior of the receiver. A team leader, for example, may want to communicate with a division manager in order to explain why the team needs more time or resources to finish an assigned project. This involves **encoding**—the process of translating an idea or thought into a message consisting of verbal, written, or nonverbal symbols (such as gestures), or some combination of these. Messages are transmitted through various **communication channels**, such as face-to-face meetings, e-mail, texts, videoconferencing, Skype, blogs, and newsletters. The choice of channel can have an important impact on the communication process. Some people are better at particular channels, and certain channels are better able to handle some types of messages. In the case of the team leader communicating with the division manager, for example, it can make quite a difference whether the message is delivered in person or electronically.

The communication process is not complete even though a message is sent. The **receiver** is the individual or group of individuals to whom a message is directed. In order for meaning to be assigned to any received message, its contents must be interpreted through decoding. This process of translation is complicated by many factors, including the knowledge and experience of the receiver and his or her relationship with the sender. A message may also be interpreted with the added influence of other points of view, such as those offered by co-workers, colleagues, or family members. Problems can occur in receiving when the decoding results in the message being interpreted differently from what was originally intended.

Feedback is the process through which the receiver communicates with the sender by returning another message. Feedback represents two-way communication, going from sender to receiver and back again. Compared to one-way communication, which flows from sender to receiver only, two-way communication is more accurate and effective, although it may also be more costly and time consuming. Because of their efficiency, one-way forms of communication—mass e-mails, reports, newsletters, division-wide meetings, and the like—are frequently used in work settings. Although one-way messages are easy for the sender, they might be more time consuming in the long run when receivers are unsure what the sender means or wants done.

Although this process appears to be elementary, it is not as simple as it looks. Many factors can inhibit effective transmission of a message. One of these is noise. **Noise** is the term used to describe any disturbance that disrupts communication and interferes with the transference of messages within the communication process. If your stomach is growling because your class is right before lunch, or if you are worried about an exam later in the day, it can interfere with your ability to pay attention to what your professor and classmates are saying. In addition, if you don't like a person, your emotions may trigger a "voice" in your head that you can't turn off, disrupting your ability to hear and listen effectively. These are all *noise* in the communication process.

Nonverbal Communication

Nonverbal communication is communication through means other than words. The most common forms are facial expressions, body position, eye contact, and other physical gestures. Studies show that when verbal and nonverbal communication do not match, receivers pay more attention to the nonverbal. This is because the nonverbal side of communication often holds the key to what someone is really thinking or meaning. Do you know how to tell if someone is lying? Watch for avoidance of eye contact and signs of stress, such as fidgeting, sweating, and, in more serious cases, dilated pupils.

Nonverbal communication affects the impressions we make on others. Because of this, we should pay careful attention to both verbal and nonverbal aspects of our communication, including dress, timeliness, and demeanor. It is well known that interviewers tend to respond more favorably to job candidates whose nonverbal cues are positive, such as eye contact and erect posture, than to those displaying negative nonverbal cues, such as looking down or slouching. The way we choose to design or arrange physical space also has

"I am the boss."   "I am the boss, but let's talk."   "Forget I'm the boss, let's talk."

See **FIGURE 11.2 Furniture placement and nonverbal communication in the office**

powerful effects on how we interpret one another.[1] This can be seen in choice of workspace designs, such as that found in various office layouts or buildings. ▣ **Figure 11.2** shows three different office arrangements and the messages they may communicate to visitors. Check the diagrams against the furniture arrangement in your office or that of your instructor or a person with whom you are familiar. What are you or they saying to visitors by the choice of furniture placement?[2]

Because nonverbal communication is so powerful, those who are more effective at communication are careful to use it to their advantage. For some, this means recognizing the importance of **presence**, or the act of speaking without using words. Analysis of Adolf Hitler's speeches shows he was a master at managing presence. Hitler knew how to use silence to great effect. He would stand in front of large audiences in complete silence for several minutes, all the while in total command of the room. Steve Jobs of Apple used the same technique during product demonstrations. In fact, Jobs was so good at managing presence that it made it more difficult for his successor, Tim Cook, who pales in comparison.

Communication Barriers

In interpersonal communication, it is important to understand the barriers that can easily create communication problems. The most common barriers in the workplace include interpersonal issues, physical distractions, meaning (or "semantic") barriers, and cultural barriers.

Interpersonal Barriers

Interpersonal barriers occur when individuals are not able to objectively listen to the sender due to things such as lack of trust, personality clashes, a bad reputation, or stereotypes/ prejudices. Interpersonal barriers are reflected in a quote paraphrased from Ralph Waldo Emerson: "I can't hear what you say because who you are rings so loudly in my ears." When strong, interpersonal barriers are present, receivers and senders often distort communication by evaluating and judging a message or failing to communicate it effectively. Think of how you communicate with someone you don't like, or a co-worker or a classmate who rubs you the wrong way. Do you listen effectively, or do you ignore them? Do you share information, or do you keep your interactions short, and perhaps even evasive?

Such problems are indicative of selective listening and filtering. In **selective listening**, individuals block out information or only hear things that match preconceived notions. Someone who does not trust will assume that the other is not telling the truth, or may "hear" things in the communication that are not accurate. An employee who believes a co-worker is incompetent may disregard important information if it comes from that person. Individuals may also **filter** information by conveying only some of the information. If we don't like a co-worker, we may decide to leave out critical details or pointers that would help him or her to be more successful in getting things done.

Another major problem in interpersonal communication is avoidance. **Avoidance** occurs when individuals choose to ignore or deny a problem or issue, rather than confront it. It is a major barrier to openness and honesty in communication. Avoidance occurs because individuals fear the conversation will be uncomfortable, or worry that trying to talk about the problem will only make it worse. This fear often comes with a lack of understanding about how to approach difficult conversations. Avoidance can be overcome by learning to use supportive communication principles, as described in a later section.

Physical Barriers

Physical distractions are another barrier that can interfere with the effectiveness of a communication attempt. Some of these distractions are evident in the following conversation between an employee, George, and his manager.[3]

> Okay, George, let's hear your problem (phone rings, boss picks it up, promises to deliver the report "just as soon as I can get it done"). Uh, now, where were we—oh, you're having a problem with marketing. So (the manager's secretary brings in some papers that need immediate signatures; he scribbles his name and the secretary leaves) . . . you say they're not cooperative? I tell you what, George, why don't you (phone rings again, lunch partner drops by) . . . uh, take a stab at handling it yourself. I've got to go now.

Besides what may have been poor intentions in the first place, George's manager allowed physical distractions to create information overload. As a result, the communication with George suffered. Setting priorities and planning can eliminate this mistake. If George has something to say, his manager should set aside adequate time for the meeting. In addition, interruptions such as telephone calls, drop-in visitors, and the like should be prevented. At a minimum, George's manager could start by closing the door to the office and instructing his secretary not to disturb them.

Semantic Barriers

Semantic barriers involve a poor choice or use of words and mixed messages. When in doubt regarding the clarity of your written or spoken messages, the popular KISS principle of communication is always worth remembering: "*Keep it short and simple.*" Of course, that is often easier said than done. The following illustrations of the "bafflegab" that once tried to pass as actual "executive communication" are a case in point.[4]

> A. "We solicit any recommendations that you wish to make, and you may be assured that any such recommendations will be given our careful consideration."

B. "Consumer elements are continuing to stress the fundamental necessity of a stabilization of the price structure at a lower level than exists at the present time."

One has to wonder why these messages weren't stated more understandably: (A) "Send us your recommendations; they will be carefully considered." (B) "Consumers want lower prices."

Cultural Barriers

We all know that globalization is here to stay. What we might not realize is that the success of international business often rests with the quality of cross-cultural communication. A common problem in cross-cultural communication is **ethnocentrism**, the tendency to believe one's culture and its values are superior to those of others. It is often accompanied by an unwillingness to try to understand alternative points of view and to take the values they represent seriously. Another problem in cross-cultural communication arises from **parochialism**—assuming that the ways of your culture are the only ways of doing things. It is parochial for traveling American businesspeople to insist that all of their business contacts speak English, whereas it is ethnocentric for them to think that anyone who dines with a spoon rather than a knife and fork lacks proper table manners.

The difficulties with cross-cultural communication are perhaps most obvious in respect to language differences. Advertising messages, for example, may work well in one country but not when translated into the language of another. Problems accompanied the introduction of Ford's European small car model, the "Ka," into Japan (in Japanese, *ka* means "mosquito"). Gestures may also be used quite differently in the various cultures of the world. For example, crossed legs are quite acceptable in the United Kingdom but are rude in Saudi Arabia if the sole of the foot is directed toward someone. Pointing at someone to get his or her attention may be acceptable in Canada, but in Asia it is considered inappropriate and even offensive.[5]

The role of language in cross-cultural communication has additional and sometimes even more subtle sides. The anthropologist Edward T. Hall notes important differences in the ways different cultures use language, and he suggests that these differences often cause misunderstanding.[6] Members of **low-context cultures** are very explicit in using the spoken and written word. In these cultures, such as those of Australia, Canada, and the United States, the message is largely conveyed by the words someone uses, and not particularly by the context in which they are spoken. In contrast, members of **high-context cultures** use words to convey only a limited part of the message. The rest must be inferred or interpreted from the context, which includes body language, the physical setting, and past relationships—all of which add meaning to what is being said. Many Asian and Middle Eastern cultures are considered high context, according to Hall, whereas most Western cultures are low context.

International business experts advise that one of the best ways to gain understanding of cultural differences is to learn at least some of the language of the country with which one is dealing. Says one global manager: "Speaking and understanding the local language gives you more insight; you can avoid misunderstandings." A former American member of the board of a German multinational says: "Language proficiency gives a [non-German] board member a better grasp of what is going on . . . not just the facts and figures but also texture and nuance."[7] Although the prospect of learning another language may sound daunting, there is little doubt that it can be well worth the effort.

Communication in Organizational Contexts

Communication Channels

Organizations are designed based on bureaucratic organizing principles; that is, jobs are arranged in hierarchical fashion with specified job descriptions and formal reporting relationships. However, much information in organizations is also passed along more spontaneously through informal communication networks. These illustrate two types of information flows in organizations: formal and informal communication channels.

Formal channels follow the chain of command established by an organization's hierarchy of authority. For example, an organization chart indicates the proper routing for official messages passing from one level or part of the hierarchy to another. Because formal channels are recognized as authoritative, it is typical for communication of policies, procedures, and other official announcements to adhere to them. On the other hand, much "networking" takes place through the use of **informal channels** that do not adhere to the organization's hierarchy of authority. They coexist with the formal channels but frequently diverge from them by skipping levels in the hierarchy or cutting across divisional lines. Informal channels help to create open communications in organizations and ensure that the right people are in contact with one another.

A common informal communication channel is the **grapevine**, or network of friendships and acquaintances through which rumors and other unofficial information are passed from person to person. Grapevines have the advantage of being able to transmit information quickly and efficiently. They also help fulfill the needs of people involved in them. Being part of a grapevine can provide a sense of security that comes from "being in the know" when important things are going on. It also provides social satisfaction as information is exchanged interpersonally. The primary disadvantage of grapevines arises when they transmit incorrect or untimely information. Rumors can be very dysfunctional, both to people and to organizations. One of the best ways to avoid rumors is to make sure that key persons in a grapevine get the right information from the start.

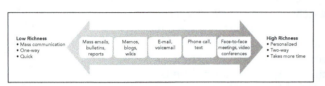

See **FIGURE 11.3 Richness of communication channels**

Channel richness indicates the capacity of a channel to convey information. And as indicated in **Figure 11.3**, the richest channels are face to face. Next are telephone, videoconferences and text, followed by e-mail, reports, and letters. The leanest channels are posted notices and bulletins. When messages get more complex and open ended, richer channels are necessary to achieve effective communication. Leaner channels work well for more routine and straightforward messages, such as announcing the location of a previously scheduled meeting.

Communication Flows

Information in organizations flows in many directions: downward, laterally, and upward. **Downward communication** follows the chain of command from top to bottom. Lower-level personnel need to know what higher levels are doing and be reminded of key policies, strategies, objectives, and technical developments. Of special importance are feedback and information on performance results. Sharing such information helps minimize the spread of rumors and inaccuracies regarding higher-level intentions, as well as create a sense of security and involvement among receivers who believe they know the whole story.

Lateral communication is the flow of information across the organization. The biggest barrier to lateral communication is **organizational silos**, units that are isolated from one another by strong departmental or divisional lines. In siloed organizations, units tend to communicate more inside than outside, and they often focus on protecting turf and information rather than sharing it. This is in direct contrast to what we need in today's organizations, which is timely and accurate information in the hands of workers.

Inside organizations, people must communicate across departmental or functional boundaries and listen to one another's needs as "internal customers." More effective organizations design lateral communication into the organizational structure, in the form of cross-departmental committees, teams, or task forces as well as matrix structures. There is also growing attention to organizational ecology—the study of how building design may influence communication and productivity by improving lateral communications.

The flow of messages from lower to higher organizational levels is **upward communication**. Upward communication keeps higher levels informed about what lower-level workers are doing and experiencing in their jobs. A key issue in upward communication is status differences. **Status differences** create potential communication barriers between persons of higher and lower ranks.

Communication is frequently biased when flowing upward in organizational hierarchies. Subordinates may filter information and tell their superiors only what they think the bosses want to hear. They do this out of fear of retribution for bringing bad news, an unwillingness to identify personal mistakes, or just a general desire to please. Regardless of the reason, the result is the same: The higher-level decision maker may end up taking the wrong actions because of biased and inaccurate information supplied from below.

This is sometimes called the mum effect, in reference to tendencies to sometimes keep "mum" from a desire to be polite and a reluctance to transmit bad news.[8] One of the best ways to counteract the mum effect is to develop strong trusting relationships. Therefore, organizations that want to enhance upward communication and reduce the mum effect work hard to develop high-quality relationships and trusting work climates throughout the organization.

Voice and Silence

The choice to speak up (i.e., to confront situations) rather than remain silent is known as **voice**.[9] Employees engage in voice when they share ideas, information, suggestions, or concerns upward in organizations. Voice is important because it helps improve decision making and promote responsiveness in dynamic business conditions. It also facilitates team performance by encouraging team members to share concerns if they think the team is missing information or headed in the wrong direction—correcting problems before they escalate.[10]

Despite this, many employees choose to remain silent rather than voice.[11] **Silence** occurs when employees have input that could be valuable but choose not to share it. Research shows that two key factors play into the choice to voice or remain silent. The first is the *perceived efficacy* of voice, or whether the employee believes their voice will make a difference. If perceived efficacy is low, employees will think "Why bother? No one will listen and nothing will change."

The second is *perceived risk*. Employees will be less likely to voice if they believe speaking up to authority will damage their credibility and/or relationships. Consistent with the mum effect, many employees deliberately withhold information from those in positions of power because they fear negative consequences, such as bad performance evaluations, undesirable job assignments, or even being fired.

Employees are more likely to remain silent in hierarchical or bureaucratic structures, and when they work in a fear climate. Therefore, organizations should create environments that are open and supportive. Formal structural channels for employees to provide information, such as hotlines, grievance procedures, and suggestion systems, are also helpful.

Communication in Relational Contexts

Much of the work that gets done in organizations occurs through relationships. Surprisingly, although we live our lives in relationships, most of us are not aware of, or ever taught, how to develop good-quality relationships. Many times people think relationships just happen. When relationships develop poorly, we have a tendency to blame the other: "There is something wrong with the other person," or "They are just impossible to deal with." But relationships are much more manageable than we might think . . . it comes down to how we communicate in relational contexts.

Relationship Development

Relationships develop through a **relational testing** process. This begins when one person makes a **disclosure**—an opening up or revelation about oneself—to another. For example, a simple disclosure is sharing one's likes or dislikes with another.

Once a disclosure is made, the other automatically begins to form a judgment. If the other shares the like or dislike, the individuals experience a sense of bonding, or attachment, with one another. If the other does not share the likes or dislikes, a positive connection is not felt and the relationship may remain at arm's length.

A deeper disclosure is a more intensely personal revelation, such as an intimate detail about one's personal history. Deeper disclosures are typically appropriate only in very high-quality relationships in which individuals know and trust one another. Inappropriate disclosures made too early in exchanges can derail the process and result in ineffective relationship development.

This sequential process represents the active "scorekeeping" stage of the testing process. If a test is passed, the relationship progresses, and disclosures may become more revealing. If a test is failed, individuals begin to hold back, and interactions may even take on a negative tone. This process is much like the classic game of Chutes and Ladders (see ■ **Figure 11.4**). When relational tests go well they can act like "ladders," escalating the relationship to higher levels. When relational violations occur they can act like "chutes," dropping the relationship back down to lower levels.

Relational testing is really easy to see in the context of going out with someone. When you first hang out you share information with the other and watch for a reaction; you also listen for what

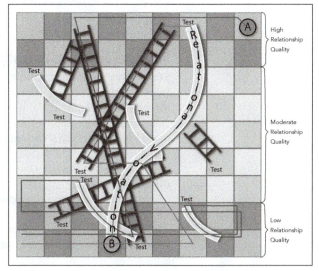

See **FIGURE 11.4 Relational Testing Process**

the other shares with you. When things go well, you "hit it off" and things flow smoothly—you enjoy the interaction, and you like what the other person has to say. This leads you to share more information. When things go poorly, tests are not being passed for at least one individual and the interactions can become awkward and uncomfortable.

Because we are taught to be polite, sometimes it can be hard to tell how things are really going if individuals are covering up their true feelings or reactions. In professional settings, we engage in testing without even thinking about it. We don't do it on purpose—it's a natural part of how humans interact. Oftentimes, opinions get formed on a very trivial or limited information.

The key point is to understand that testing processes are going on around us all of the time, and if you want to more carefully manage your relationships, you need to be more consciously aware of when and how testing is occurring. When it is happening, you have to pay attention so you can manage the process more effectively. This does not mean being dishonest or fake; in fact, being fake is a quick way to fail a test! It does mean being careful how you engage with others with whom you have not yet established a relationship (e.g., a new boss).

Relationship Maintenance

Once relationships are established, testing processes take on a different form. They go from active testing to watching for relational violations.[12] A **relational violation** is a violation of the "boundary" of acceptable behavior in a relationship. These boundaries will vary depending on the nature of the relationship. In marriage, infidelity is a boundary violation. In a high-quality manager–subordinate relationship, breaking trust is a boundary violation. In a poor-quality manager–subordinate relationship, it may take more serious offense, such as sabotage or a work screwup, to constitute a boundary violation. The point is that the testing process is now not active "score-keeping," or evaluating nearly every interaction, but rather one of noticing testing only when the relationship has been violated.[13]

As long as violations don't occur, individuals interact in the context of the relational boundaries, and the relationship proceeds just fine. When violations do occur, however, testing kicks back. If the relationship survives the violation—and some don't—it is now at a lower quality, or even in a negative state. For it to recover, it must go through relational repair.

Relational repair involves actions to return the relationship to a positive state. Relational repair is again a testing process, but this time the intention is to rebuild or reestablish the relationship quality. For example, a violation of trust can be repaired with a sincere apology, followed by actions demonstrating trustworthiness. A violation of professional respect can be repaired with strong displays of professional competence.

In most cases, relational repair requires effective communication. As you can imagine, not everyone has these skills, and those who have them often use them intuitively—not quite aware of what they are doing. One set of principles that can help individuals engage in relational repair, as well as in relationships, is *supportive communication principles*.

Supportive Communication Principles

Supportive communication principles focus on joint problem solving. They are especially effective in dealing with relational breakdowns or in addressing problematic behaviors before they escalate into relational violations.[14]

Supportive communication principles help us avoid problems of *defensiveness* and *disconfirmation* in interpersonal communication. We all know these problems. You feel defensive when you think you are being attacked and need to protect yourself. Signs of **defensiveness** are people beginning to get angry or aggressive in a communication, or lashing out. You have a feeling of **disconfirmation** when you sense that you are being put down and your self-worth is being questioned. When people are disconfirmed they withdraw from a conversation or engage in show-off behaviors to try to build themselves back up.

Relationships under stress are particularly susceptible to problems of defensiveness and disconfirmation. Therefore, in situations of relational repair it is doubly important to watch for and diffuse defensiveness and disconfirmation by stopping and refocusing the conversation as soon as these problems begin to appear.

The first, and most important, technique to consider in supportive communication is to *focus on the problem and not the person*. If you focus on the person, the most likely reaction is for the other to become defensive or disconfirmed. A trick many people use to remember this is "I" statements rather than "you" statements. "You" statements are like finger pointing: "You screwed up the order I sent you" or "You undermined me in the meeting." An "I" statement, and a focus on the problem, would be "I had a problem with my order the other day and would like to talk with you about what went wrong with it" or "I felt undermined in the meeting the other day when I was interrupted in the middle of my presentation and not able to continue."

The second technique is to focus on a problem that the two of you can do something about. Remember that the focus should be on *joint problem solving*. This means the framing of the message should be on a shared problem, and the tone should be on how you can work together to fix it and both benefit in the process. It helps in this part of the conversation if you can make it clear to the other person how you care about him or her or the relationship and that the other person trusts your motives. If another perceives that you are out for yourself or out to attack, the conversation will break down. For example, "I'd like to talk with you about how we can manage the budget more effectively so we can avoid problems in the future" rather than "You overspent on the budget and now I have to fix your mess."

Beyond this, the other techniques help you think about the kinds of words you should choose to make the conversation more effective. For example, you should be *specific/not global*, and *objective/not judgmental*. Specific/not global means not using words like *never* or *always*. These words are easy to argue, and you will quickly find the other person saying "It's not true." Try to be more factual and objective. Instead of saying "You never listen to me," say "The other day in the meeting you interrupted me three times and that made it hard for me to get my point across."

The principles also tell you to *own the communication* and make sure to *be congruent*. Owning the communication means you take responsibility for what you say rather than place it on a third party. A manager who says, "Corporate tells us we need to better document our work hours," sends a weaker message than one who says, "I believe that better documenting our work hours will help us be more effective in running our business." Being congruent means matching the words (verbal) and the body language (nonverbal). If your words say, "No, I'm not mad," but your body language conveys anger, then you are not being honest or forthright. The other person will know it, and this may cause him or her to be less open and committed to the conversation in return.

Active Listening

Supportive communication principles emphasize the importance of **active listening**. Active listening again focuses on problem solving, but this time from the standpoint of trying to help another person. For example, active listening is often used in counseling situations. In these situations, your intent is to help the other person sort through problems involving emotions, attitudes, motivation, personality issues, and so on. To do this effectively, you need to keep the focus on the counselee and his or her issue(s) and not you and your issue(s).

The biggest mistake people make in this kind of listening is jumping to advice too early or changing the focus of the conversation onto themselves. A good principle to keep in mind during active listening is "We have two ears and one mouth, so we should listen twice as much as we speak."[15] When you are engaged in active listening, your goal is to keep the focus on the other person, and to help that other person engage in effective self-reflection and problem solving.

Active listening involves understanding the various types of listening responses and matching your response to the situation. What is most important to remember is that to counsel someone, you want to use *reflecting* and *probing* more often than *advising* or *deflecting*. Reflecting and probing are "opening" types of responses that encourage others to elaborate and process. Advising and deflecting are "closed" types of responses and should only be used sparingly, and at the end of the conversation rather than the beginning.[16]

Reflecting means paraphrasing back what the other said. Reflecting can also mean summarizing what was said or taking a step further by asking a question for clarification or elaboration. Reflecting allows us to show we are really listening and to give the speaker a chance to correct any misunderstanding we may have. **Probing** means asking for additional information. In probing you want to be careful about the kinds of questions you ask so you do not come across as judgmental (e.g., "How could you have done that?"). You also don't want to change the subject before the current subject is resolved. Effective probing flows from what was previously said, and asks for elaboration, clarification, and repetition if needed.

Deflecting means shifting to another topic. When we deflect to another topic we risk coming across as uninterested in what is being said or being too preoccupied to listen. Many of us unwittingly deflect by sharing our own personal experiences. While we think this is being helpful in letting the speaker know he or she is not alone, it can be ineffective if it diverts the conversation to us and not them. The best listeners keep deflecting to a minimum.[17]

Advising means telling someone what to do. This is a closed response, because once you tell someone what to do that typically can end a conversation. While we think we are helping others by advising them, we actually may be hurting because doing so can communicate a position of superiority rather than mutuality. Again, the best listeners work to control their desire to advise unless specifically asked to do so and to deliver the advice in the context of supportiveness rather than presumptuousness.

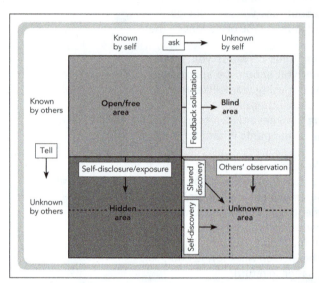

See **FIGURE 11.5 The Johari Window**

Developmental Feedback

In most workplaces, there is too little feedback rather than too much. This is particularly the case for negative feedback. People avoid giving unpleasant feedback because they fear heightening emotions in the other that they will not know how to handle. For example, words intended to be polite and helpful can easily be interpreted as unpleasant and hostile. This risk is especially evident in the performance appraisal process. To serve a person's developmental needs, feedback—both the praise and the criticism—must be well communicated.

Feedback Giving

Feedback is vital for human development. Therefore, giving another person honest and **developmental feedback** in a sensitive and caring way is critically important. It lets us know what we are doing well and not so well, and what we can do to improve.

One tool that helps us understand this is the **Johari Window** (see ▣ **Figure 11.5**). The Johari Window shows us that we know some things about ourselves that others know ("open") and some things about ourselves that others don't know ("hidden"). But there are also some things about ourselves that we don't know but others do—this is our blind spot. The blind spot is blind to us but not to others. As you can imagine, this is a problem because it means others are aware of something about us, but we are in the dark! The only way to reduce blind spots is through feedback from others—which is why feedback is so important. It helps us reduce our blind spots.

Despite this, giving feedback is perhaps one of the most avoided activities in organizations. It doesn't have to be, however. When delivered properly, giving feedback can be a rewarding experience. It helps build relationships and strengthens trust. As with supportive communication principles, you should keep in mind certain important techniques when giving feedback:[18]

1. *Make sure it is developmental:* Be positive and focus on improvement.
2. *Be timely:* Provide feedback soon after the issue occurs so it is fresh in mind.
3. *Prepare ahead of time:* Be clear about what you want to say so you stick to the issue.
4. *Be specific:* Don't use generalities, as that will just leave them wondering.
5. *Do it in private:* Have the discussion in a safe and comfortable place for the other.
6. *Limit the focus:* Stick to a behavior the person can do something about.
7. *Reinforce:* Don't bring the person down—make sure he or she knows there are good things about them too.
8. *Show caring:* Convey a sense of caring and that you are trying to help.

Feedback Seeking

The Johari Window implies we should not only give feedback—*we should also seek it*. Pursuing feedback allows us to learn more about ourselves and how others perceive us. In organizations, people engage in **feedback seeking** for multiple reasons: (1) to gather information for increasing performance, (2) to learn what others think about them, and (3) to regulate one's behavior.[19]

Because feedback can be emotionally charged, people typically like to see feedback involving favorable information. But this is not always the case. If individuals are more self-confident, they are more willing to seek feedback regarding performance issues, even if that feedback may be bad. The premise is that people prefer to know what they are doing wrong than perform poorly on a task. This seems to be less the case the longer that employees are in a job. Research shows that feedback seeking is lower for those who have been in a job longer, even though these employees find feedback just as valuable as newer employees do. This may be due to employees feeling they should be able to assess their own performance without needing to ask.[20]

When individuals fear that performance feedback will hurt their image, they are more likely to forego feedback seeking and therefore won't gain the benefits it can provide. Safe environments, where employees can trust others and there is little risk to their image or ego, can help overcome avoidance.[21]

Feedback Orientation

A concept that can help us understand individual differences in how people receive feedback is **feedback orientation**. Feedback orientation describes one's overall receptivity to feedback. Those with a higher feedback orientation are better able to control and overcome their emotional reactions to feedback. They also process feedback more meaningfully by avoiding common attribution errors such as externalizing blame. This helps them to successfully apply feedback in establishing goals that will help them improve performance.[22]

Feedback orientation is composed of four dimensions. *Utility* represents the belief that feedback is useful in achieving goals or obtaining desired outcomes. *Accountability* is the feeling that one is accountable to act on feedback he or she receives (e.g., "It is my responsibility to utilize feedback to improve my performance"). *Social awareness* is consideration of others' views of oneself and being sensitive to these views. *Feedback self-efficacy* is an individual's perceived competence in interpreting and responding to feedback appropriately (e.g., "I feel self-assured when dealing with feedback").[23]

Those with feedback orientation tend to be higher in feedback-seeking behavior and have better relationships. They also tend to receive higher performance ratings from their managers. An important role for managers, however, is enhancing climates for developmental feedback. They can do this by being accessible, encouraging feedback seeking, and consistently providing credible, high-quality feedback in a tactful manner.[24]

 Go to your WileyPLUS Learning Space course for video episodes, examples, art, tables, Concept Checks, practice, and resources that will help you succeed in this course.

12

Reading for
POWER AND POLITICS

WP LS Go to your WileyPLUS Learning Space course for video episodes, examples, art, tables, Concept Checks, practice, and resources that will help you succeed in this course.

Understanding Power

Power and politics are among the most important, yet least understood, concepts in organizational behavior. When you hear the words *power* and *politics*, how do you feel? Do you want power?

If you say you don't want power you are likely missing out on important opportunities. Without power and influence you will be less effective in organizations. Did you know that the modern computer was first invented by Xerox in 1975? But name Xerox is not associated with computers because the engineers who designed it were not able to influence Xerox executives who saw themselves as a "paper company" to adopt their innovation. Instead, as we now know, Xerox showed it to Steve Jobs of Apple, who went on to commercialize it to great success.

The point is this: If you want to get things done, you have to be able to influence others. And influence comes from power and political skill. But engaging in power and politics is not what many people think. As you will see in this chapter, the key lies in building power for yourself while expanding the power of those around you.

What Is Power and Why Is It Important?

"The fundamental concept in social science is Power, in the same sense in which Energy is the fundamental concept in physics."

Bertrand Russell

Power is the ability of a person or group to influence or control some aspect of another person or group.[1] In organizations, it is often associated with control over resources others need, such as money, information, decisions, work assignments, and so on.

Most people assume that power comes from hierarchical positions—that because managers have positions with authority embedded in them they have all the power. But this isn't always true. Can you think of a manager who was not very effective because no one listened to her, or a teacher who had no control over his classroom? When others do not comply with a person's authority that person doesn't really have power. In other words, power is not an absolute. It has to be *given* by others who are willing to be influenced.

For this reason, most of the power we study in organizations is social power. **Social power** is used to recognize that power comes from the ability to influence another in a social relation. It differs from **force**, which describes power that occurs against another's will. Social power is *earned* through relationships, and if it isn't used properly, it can be taken away. We see teenagers take their parents' power away when they don't listen or do as they are told. Employees remove managers' power when they do not act respectfully or badmouth managers to others in the organization.

Power and Dependence

Power is based on dependence. This means that to understand power, we need to understand the nature of dependence. **Dependence** means that one person or group relies on another person or group to get what they want or need.[2] If dependence can be easily removed then an individual has power only as long as the other is willing to give it to him or her. If dependence cannot be easily removed individuals have little choice and must comply.

Dependence in organizations is most often associated with **control** over access to things other people need, such as information, resources, and decision-making.[3] For this reason, major organizational powerholders are usually those who have important competencies (e.g., influential executives, top salespeople, skilled technicians). Power is also associated with key decision-making functions, such as budgets, schedules, performance appraisals, organizational strategy, and the like.

Because power is based on dependence, we need to manage dependencies in order to manage power. We do this by increasing others' dependence on us and reducing our dependence on others. We increase others' dependence on us by establishing competence and being indispensable. Individuals who are highly competent are in great demand. They are seen as irreplaceable and organizations will work hard to keep them.

We reduce our dependence on others by increasing employability. This means that if we lose our job today we can soon get another. Individuals reduce dependence by keeping their options open, such as being willing to relocate if necessary to take another job. We reduce dependence on employers by not getting overextended financially, which can make us overly dependent on a particular organization for our livelihood. And, we reduce dependency and increase power and self-control by removing another's power over us. The decision to give someone or something power over us is a choice. Sometimes the choice to remove a dependency is difficult. It may mean changing jobs, leaving an organization, or blowing the whistle. But when we allow others to abuse power, we are complicit in their unethical and inappropriate behavior.

The Problem of Powerlessness

One of the biggest problems associated with power and dependence is the perception of power-lessness. **Powerlessness** is a lack of autonomy and participation.[4] It occurs when power imbalances make people feel that they have no option but to do what others say. When we experience powerlessness we feel little control over ourselves and our work processes. Research shows that when we feel powerless we display it in our body language—for example, by shrinking in, caving in our chests, physically withdrawing, or using less forceful hand gestures.[5]

In organizations, powerlessness has debilitating effects. Perceptions of powerlessness create spirals of helplessness and alienation. Think for a minute about a situation in which you feel power*less*. How does it make you feel? Frustrated? Anxious? Angry? Afraid? Resentful? Isolated? These are destructive emotions in relationships and in organizations. When we feel power*ful*, on the other hand, we view power in a positive way. We feel energized, engaged, excited, and fulfilled by work.

Powerless people often try to regain some sense of control over themselves and their work environment. But the result can be extremely damaging to organizations (e.g., absenteeism, tardiness, theft, vandalism, grievances, shoddy workmanship, and counterproductive behavior).[6] Contrary to what we think, therefore, the problem in organizations *is not power, but powerlessness*. And this means that to gain and use power responsibly, we need to work to *expand* the power of others rather than restrict it to a few.

Power as an Expanding Pie

The idea that social power can be an expanding pie is the basis for the trend in organizations over the past decades toward empowerment. **Empowerment** involves sharing power, information, and rewards with employees to make decisions and solve problems in their work. More than ever, managers in progressive organizations are expected to be good at and comfortable with empowering others. Rather than considering power to be something held only at higher levels in the traditional pyramid of organizations, this view considers power to be something that can be shared by everyone working in flatter and more collegial structures. When managers empower others, they also empower themselves by gaining a more dedicated and engaged workforce.

Although many firms want empowerment, it is extremely difficult to accomplish. It requires individuals to change their understanding of power away from it being a zero sum game. A **zero sum game** means one person's gain is equal to another person's loss ("I win, you lose"). It represents a belief that "for me to gain power, you must lose power." Viewing power as a zero sum game causes you to lose power in the long run.

This is because increasing your own power while others lose power leads to power imbalances. When power imbalances get bad, they trigger forces that rise up to take power away to restore the balance. This is known as the **Iron Law of Responsibility**. An example is when lobbying groups work to take an organizations' power away by passing regulations.

The idea that force is met with countervailing force is also described by psychological reactance theory, which says that people rebel against constraints and efforts to control their behavior. The extent to which we do this varies, but for some of us, when we feel overpowered it will trigger us to push back very hard in an effort to maintain our autonomy—perhaps without even realizing we are doing it![7]

Empowerment views, therefore, change our understanding of power away from a focus on "power over" others to a focus on "power with" others.[8] It recognizes that the more power we allow others, the more power we will be given in return (e.g., treat people with respect and they will respect you back). The most sustainable way to gain and use power, therefore, is by increasing positive power all around.

Sources of Power and Influence

Over fifty years ago, John French and Bertram Raven identified a typology of five bases of power that is still used today.[9] These bases are classified into two main categories: position power and personal power. **Position power** stems from the formal hierarchy or authority vested in a particular role or position. **Personal power** resides in the individual and is independent of position; it is generated in relationships with others.

We can tell if the power a person holds is positional or personal because when a person leaves a position, their personal power goes with them. Have you ever had a really good boss or teacher who left a position and, when they did, it felt like a vacuum? This is because they had a lot of personal power. In the case of position power, however, the power stays with the position. For example, when the president of the United States leaves office, the daily security briefings that are a key source of information power are transferred to the new president.

Position Power

There are three main types of position power in organizations: *legitimate power*, *reward power*, and *coercive power*.

Legitimate Power **Legitimate power** represents the formal hierarchical authority that comes from a position. It is called legitimate because it represents a belief that those holding certain positions have a legitimate right to prescribe behavior, and those reporting to the position have a legitimate obligation to follow (e.g., "After all, I am your supervisor, and you should feel some obligation to do what I ask").[10] In organizations, legitimate power is hierarchically structured. Managers have authority, and subordinates are expected to comply with that authority. This power is associated with offices (i.e., positions) rather than between persons, and remains in the office regardless of who the occupant is.[11]

Managers who rely only on legitimate power are not likely to be powerful for very long. This is the mistake made by many first-time managers when they assume they are "the boss" but then find out that others are not willing to go along. Chester Barnard described an unwillingness to automatically comply with legitimate power as the **zone of indifference**. It represents the range of requests to which a person is willing to respond without subjecting the directives to critical evaluation or judgment.[12] When directives fall within the zone they are obeyed routinely, but when they fall outside the zone of indifference or are not considered legitimate, they are not necessarily obeyed, as is shown in ▣ **Figure 12.1**.

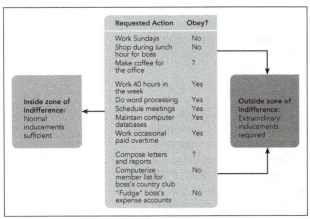

Requested Action	Obey?
Work Sundays	No
Shop during lunch hour for boss	No
Make coffee for the office	?
Work 40 hours in the week	Yes
Do word processing	Yes
Schedule meetings	Yes
Maintain computer databases	Yes
Work occasional paid overtime	Yes
Compose letters and reports	?
Computerize member list for boss's country club	No
"Fudge" boss's expense accounts	No

Inside zone of indifference: Normal inducements sufficient

Outside zone of indifference: Extraordinary inducements required

See **FIGURE 12.1** Hypothetical psychological contract for a secretary.

Because the mere possession of formal authority can generate power distance that isolates managers from employees, overuse of legitimate power is often accompanied by hierarchical thinking in organizations. **Hierarchical thinking** occurs when hierarchical systems create environments of superiority among managers (i.e., "superiors") and inferiority among employees (i.e., "subordinates"). Hierarchical thinking is a problem because it can lead employees to defer responsibility and initiative-taking, and cripple an organization that needs to be flexible and adaptive to survive.[13]

Reward Power **Reward power** comes from the ability to administer outcomes that have positive valence (i.e., provide positive rewards) and remove or decrease outcomes that have negative valence (i.e., remove negative rewards). Examples of rewards include money, promotions, kudos, enriched jobs, or not assigning unpleasant task duties or undesirable work schedules. For rewards to be effective, they must be perceived as equitable. Problems arise in the use of reward power when rewards do not match expectations.

Coercive Power **Coercive power** involves the use of threat or punishment. It stems from the expectation that one will be punished if he or she fails to conform to the influence attempt. For example, coercive power can involve the threat that one will be transferred, demoted, or fired if they do not act as desired. Pay can become a form of coercive power when a manager threatens to withhold a pay raise. Although coercive power is sometimes needed to correct performance or behavioral problems, when not used carefully and sparingly, it can reduce the strength and quality of relationships. For this reason, organizations often have policies on employee treatment to protect employees from abuses of coercive power.

Personal Power

Personal power resides in the individual and comes from personal qualities distinct from position power, such as a person's reputation, charm, charisma, perceived worth, and right to respect from others.[14] Because it resides in the person and not the position, it is available to anyone in the organization, not just those in formal or managerial roles. Sources of personal power include *expert power* and *referent power*.

Expert Power **Expert power** comes from special skills and abilities that others need but do not possess themselves. It can include knowledge, experience, and judgment. Expert power is often determined by the individual's performance record over time and the alternative sources of knowledge available. It also is highly influenced by the importance of the area of expertise. People who have expertise in steam engines have little expert power today compared to those with expertise in biotechnology. Expert power is also relative, not absolute. If you are the best cook in the kitchen, you have expert power until a real chef enters, and then the chef has the expert power.

Referent Power **Referent power** is the ability to alter another's behavior because the person wants to identify with you as the power source. Identification comes from a feeling of oneness with another, and it is based on the sense of wanting to be associated with another person or to feel part of a group.[15] Identification acts as a source of referent power because it causes individuals to want to behave, believe, and perceive in ways similar to the leader. Individuals holding referent power are respected and looked up to by others. Although referent power is an invaluable source of power for individuals, it can be variable. To retain referent power, its holders are under constant pressure to maintain their exemplary images and live up to other's expectations.

Information Power

Another form of power that plays an important role in organizations—and can be either positional or personal—is information power. **Information power** is possession of or access to information that is valuable to others.[16] It can come from one's position in the organization, such as the information a manager has because he or she is in the chain of command. Or it can come from one's informal networks and being "in the know," such as personal relationships with others who have access to information. Individuals who have information power have wide discretion in how to use it. Some will guard it, and others will share it to build more personal relationships and more substantive networks in organization.

Information power comes with a cautionary note. Individuals who use information power must be very careful not to share or spread proprietary information. Violating confidentiality and trust can lead to loss of relationships, which is damaging to all forms of power an individual may hold in organizations.

Connection Power

In today's interconnected society and knowledge-based organizations, connection power from networks and relationships is becoming increasingly important. **Connection power** is the ability to call on connections and networks both inside and outside the organization for support in getting things done and in meeting one's goals.[17] It is another form of power that crosses both positional and personal power. Two forms of connection power are *association power* and *reciprocal alliances*.

Association Power **Association power** arises from influence with a powerful person on whom others depend. Individuals have association power when they know people in key positions or have networks of relationships with higher-ups who connect them to influential others. Association power is reflected in the expression "It's not what you know but who you know." It is valuable because so many things in organizations happen through personal connections and relationships. Association power can help you cut through bureaucracy, provide greater access to sponsorship and promotions, and allow you to gain access to positions and resources needed to get things done.

Reciprocal Alliances **Reciprocal alliances** describe a form of power arising from connections with others developed through reciprocity. Reciprocity is based on the concept that if one person does something for another, it will invoke an obligation to return the favor. For example, if your friend goes out of his way to give you a ride and you respond with "I owe you one," you are recognizing that you are now indebted to that friend until you can pay him back in some way. These bonds of indebtedness link individuals together in networks of relationships.

Effective networkers recognize that reciprocity and reciprocal alliances are a powerful way to form strong networks in organizations. Research shows that executives who consistently rank in the top 20 percent of their companies in both performance and well-being have developed strong networks made up of high-quality relationships from diverse areas and up and down the corporate hierarchy. Such networks are characterized by an exchange of resources and support, including access to information, expertise, best practices, mentoring, developmental feedback, and political support.[18]

Responses to Power and Influence

Power is relational. Whether you have power depends on how others respond to your influence attempts. If individuals do not defer to your influence attempt, then you have no power. This means that to understand power you need to keep in mind how individuals respond to you and your influence.

Conformity

In the earliest formal research into power and influence, Herbert Kelman identified three levels of conformity one can make to another's influence attempt: *compliance*, *identification*, and *internalization*.

Compliance **Compliance** occurs when individuals accept another's influence because of the positive or negative outcomes tied to it. When individuals comply, they go along not because they want to but because they have to. When you take a required class for a subject you are not interested in or study only because you have to, you are complying. The motivation here is purely instrumental—it is done to obtain the specific reward or avoid the punishment associated with not complying.

Because compliance is an extrinsic form of motivation, it results in minimal effort (proportional to the reward or punishment). Because of this, it is not a very effective influence strategy in the long run. Moreover, it requires surveillance by management. For example, employees who are not committed to excellent customer service will typically slack off when the supervisor is not monitoring their behavior.

Commitment **Commitment** occurs when individuals accept an influence attempt out of duty or obligation. Committed individuals agree with the desired action and show initiative and persistence in completing it. Kelman identified two forms of commitment in response to influence attempts: *identification* and *internalization*.

Identification is displayed when individuals accept an influence attempt because they want to maintain a positive relationship with the person or group making the influence request.[19] Students who join a fraternity or sorority accept the influence of their peers because they identify with the organization and want to be part of the group. **Internalization** occurs when an individual accepts influence because the induced behavior is congruent with their value system. Internalization means you believe in the ideas and actions you are being asked to undertake. For example, members of religious organizations follow the dictates of the church because they truly believe in the principles and philosophies being advocated.

Resistance

Responses to power include not only conformity but also resistance. Resistance involves individuals saying no, making excuses, stalling or even arguing against the initiative. There are two main types of resistance strategies used by individuals when they perceive an impractical request from their supervisor: constructive resistance and dysfunctional resistance.[20]

Constructive Resistance **Constructive resistance** is characterized by thoughtful dissent aimed at constructively challenging the manager to rethink the issue. Individuals who use constructive resistance make suggestions for alternative actions accompanied by reasons for noncompliance. They do so in the hope of opening a dialogue to try to find a more appropriate solution to a problem.[21]

Dysfunctional Resistance **Dysfunctional resistance** involves ignoring or dismissing the request of the influencing agent.[22] Employees who engage in dysfunctional resistance attempt to thwart and undermine the manager by disrupting workflows (e.g., ignoring requests, making only a half-hearted effort, or simply refusing to comply by just saying "no").

Studies of dysfunctional resistance show that employees are more likely to refuse when their supervisors are abusive, but that these effects depend on the employee's personality. Conscientious employees are more likely to use constructive resistance, whereas less conscientious employees are more likely to use dysfunctional resistance.[23] Moreover, employees who use constructive resistance are more likely to receive positive performance ratings from managers, whereas employees who use dysfunctional resistance are more likely to receive negative ratings from managers.[24]

How Power Corrupts

We have all heard the expression "Power corrupts, and absolute power corrupts absolutely." The question is why? What is it about power that causes people to lose perspective and do terrible things that cause great harm to themselves and others?

Dean Ludwig and Clinton Longenecker describe the problem as the **Bathsheba syndrome**.[25] The Bathsheba syndrome is based on the story of King David, a once great and revered leader who got caught up in a downward spiral of unethical decisions when his success led him to feel so privileged and self-indulgent that he took another man's wife (Bathsheba), and then covered it up through murder and deception. It describes what happens to men and women of otherwise strong personal integrity and intelligence, who just at the moment of seemingly "having it all"—and despite the fact that they know it is wrong—engage in unethical and selfish behavior with the mistaken belief that they have the power to conceal it.

The lesson from the Bathsheba syndrome is that power can have corruptive effects that, if not prepared for, may lead to devastating outcomes. To avoid the Bathsheba syndrome, individuals should prepare themselves for success. Success often leads to complacency—it can make those who have it too comfortable and inflate their ego, causing one to lose perspective. Power can have an intoxicating allure that makes people crave more and more of it.

A key to being powerful, therefore, is to manage yourself in the face of power. Maintaining humility and being around others who will push back on you can help keep you grounded and maintain perspective. Being powerful also means taking responsibility in the face of others' power. Responsibly managing power means acting to keep power in check.

Understanding Organizational Politics

For many, the word *politics* conjures up thoughts of illicit deals, favors, and advantageous personal relationships. It is important, however, to understand the importance of organizational politics and how they can help the workplace function in a much broader capacity.[26]

Why Do We Have Organizational Politics?

Politics occur because we have both formal and informal systems in organizations.[27] **Formal systems** tell us what is to be done in organizations and how work processes are to be coordinated and structured. They represent the "rational" side of organizations that controls behavior and reduces uncertainty. Not all behaviors in organizations can be prescribed, however, so informal systems arise to fill in the blanks. **Informal systems** are patterns of activity and relationships that arise in everyday activities when individuals and groups work to get things done. They are highly changeable and occur through personal connections. For example, when a salesperson uses a personal connection with someone in operations to help speed up an order for a customer, this is an example of the informal system.

Organizational politics involve efforts by organizational members to seek resources and achieve desired goals through informal systems and structures. Politics represent how people get ahead, how they gain and use power, and how they get things done (for good and bad) in organizations.

The Role of Self-Interest

Like power, organizational politics are neutral. Whether they are good or bad depends on how they are used. They are positive when they advance the interests of the organization and do not intentionally harm individuals. They are negative when they involve self-interested behaviors of individuals and groups who work to benefit themselves in ways that disadvantage others and the organization.

Self-interested politics occur when people work to shift otherwise ambiguous outcomes to their personal advantage. What makes this tricky is that individuals often disagree as to whose self-interests are most valuable. Self-interested politics are those that benefit, protect, or enhance self-interests without consideration of the welfare of co-workers or the organization.[28] They include illegitimate political activities such as coalition building, favoritism-based pay and promotions, scapegoating, backstabbing, and using information as a political tool to enhance one's self or harm others.

Political Climates

Political climate refers to whether people in organizations work "within" or "around" formal policies and procedures in getting their work done.[29] When people work around formal policies and procedures, the climate is perceived as more political. Less political climates involve more direct and straightforward activities, where there is less need to interpret and watch out for the behaviors happening behind the scenes.

Informal Systems and Workarounds Consistent with the idea that politics manifest in and through informal systems, organizational political climates are seen in the extent to which people engage in **workarounds**. Workarounds occur when people go around rules to accomplish a task or goal because the normal process or method isn't producing the desired result.[30] Workarounds can involve seeking assistance from influential people in one's network, exploiting loopholes in a system, or using one's connections to access potentially useful information or influence decisions.

How the political climate is seen depends on the nature and motivation of workarounds. Workarounds that benefit oneself or one's work unit at the expense of others will likely trigger copycat behaviors, fueling dysfunctional political climates. When workarounds are used to benefit the organization, however, such as when a policy loophole is used to make a process more efficient or to contribute to an innovative new service, they contribute to advancing organizational interests. In this case they serve a functional purpose.[31]

Connections and Perceptions Two people in the same work group may experience a political climate very differently. The difference depends on one's status and power in the political system. For someone in the know and highly connected, the political climate will likely be perceived as quite positive. For an individual who is disadvantaged or not well connected, the political climate can be seen as very negative.

People who are connected with powerful others see the political climate as a vital and important part of their career and professional advancement. Those who are in the "out group" and without access to organizational power and status, have much more negative perceptions of organizational politics. They see political climates as rewarding employees who engage in manipulative influence tactics, which can include things like taking credit for others' work, coalition building, and using connections to create unfair advantage. Those who report stronger perceptions of organizational politics often experience greater job stress and strain, reduced job satisfaction and organizational commitment, and, ultimately, increased turnover.[32]

Navigating the Political Landscape

Power and politics are facts of life in organizations. They are necessary for getting things done in social systems. So to be effective we need to manage our power successfully in political environments. Those who don't navigate politics in organizations are at a disadvantage not only in terms of winning raises and promotions, but maybe even in keeping their jobs.

A key to navigating power and politics is managing one's own attitude and behavior. People who are nonpolitical or cynical about power may find themselves not getting promoted and being left out of key decisions and activities in the organization. Those who are overly political and abuse their power may be perceived as Machiavellian, or self-serving. Ultimately these people may lose credibility and influence. A moderate amount of prudent political behavior, therefore, is a survival tool. It involves understanding how to establish power bases, develop political skills, and build strong and effective networks.

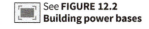

Building Power Bases

You have to establish your power bases—position, personal, information, connection—to do well at managing power and politics. **Power bases** are the sources of power (position, personal, information, connection) that individuals and subunits develop in organizations. As can be seen in ▣ **Figure 12.2**

See **FIGURE 12.2 Building power bases**

shows these sources of power can help in navigating political climates in organizations. Individuals without established power bases are more susceptible to powerlessness. A lack of power limits ability to have real influence. Persons with power are able to advance important initiatives and gain access to key resources. They are also better able to protect themselves from powerful others. Power bases must be established before you need them, however. If you wait to develop them when needed, it is probably too late.

There are two main ways to build power bases in organizations. The first involves establishing competence and value added to the organization. This builds personal and position power by proving your ability to perform at higher levels and having competencies that are hard to replace. High competency and value added make an individual or work unit non-substitutable. They increase others' dependency on you. The goal for individuals and teams is to increase **non-substitutability** by making their work more critical, relevant, visible, and central to organizational performance.

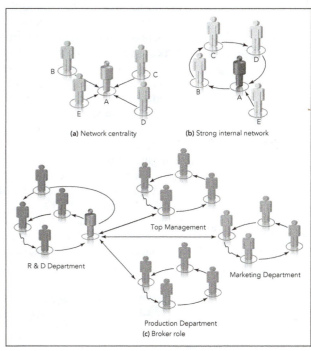

The second way to build power bases is through developing information and connection power. You do this by building relationships and networks. Information comes from formal access to information (e.g., meetings, task forces, e-mails, policy documents), informal access to information (e.g., grapevine, hall talk) and the opportunity to distribute or share information with others (e.g., being the first to tell others about an organizational change).[33] Individuals who want to build information power often spend a lot of time making connections that let them be "in the know." They can use this information in various (positive or negative) ways, such as telling others the "real" story, withholding information, filtering communication, and even selectively leaking key information to suit their purposes.

Connection power comes from internal networks, external networks, and being central in a network. The sample connection and network scenarios in ▣ **Figure 12.3** show how you can build your connection power by aligning with others to gain advice, friendship, alliances, collaborations, information flows, and access to job opportunities.

See **FIGURE 12.3 Sample scenarios for connections and networks in organizations**

Developing Political Skills

Rarely in organizational politics are things as they appear. Instead they are more like those 3D hidden stereogram images in which, on the surface, you see a bunch of dots, but when you peer deeply into the image a hidden picture emerges. Individuals who are successful at politics are like this. They know how to read political situations and uncover the real motivations and connections going on behind the scenes. They have what can be described as **political savvy**—skill and adroitness at reading political environments and understanding how to influence effectively in these environments.

Another term for political savvy is **political skill,** defined as the ability to understand and influence others to act in ways that enhance personal and/or organizational objectives.[35] Individuals who are high in political skill have the ability to read and understand people and get them to act in desired ways. They use connections to skillfully align themselves with others to attain goals. They adapt their behavior to the situation, but with authenticity and genuineness to build trust and credibility rather than suspicion or disdain.

Developing political savvy involves learning to read the situation, increasing awareness of self and others, negotiating with rather than negating others and framing messages so that others will listen (e.g., a focus on organizational interest rather than self-interest). One of the best ways you can build these skills is to learn from and watch others who have them. It is also helpful to find mentors or sponsors who can provide developmental feedback and coaching in how to interpret and respond to political environments.

Networking

What you know is not enough. You also need connections, or social capital, to get ahead. **Social capital** is resources that come from networks of relationships.[36] It differs from **human capital**, which is knowledge, skills, and intellectual assets employees bring to the workplace. Whereas human capital represents *what* you know, social capital represents *who* you know. The importance of social capital is understanding that being smart, or having great ideas and information, is not sufficient—it is only beneficial if you are able to get the ideas communicated and implemented.

Networking helps individuals find better jobs and enjoy greater occupational success. If you have more network ties, you have greater opportunity to gain access to resources and influence others. Research has found that for many things—such as finding jobs or getting ahead—weak "acquaintance" ties work better than strong "friendship" ties. Individuals have greater access to more and different job opportunities when relying on weak ties.[37] This is good news because strong ties are costly to maintain—they require more time than weak associations.

Another way individuals can provide an advantage to themselves and to organizations is by acting as a **broker,** someone who bridges **structural holes** which exist as gaps between individuals and groups without connections in networks.[38] Brokers develop relationships that link formerly unconnected actors by building bridges that provide greater access to information, resources, and opportunities. Bridging ties provide access to a diverse set of opinions, which is important for creativity. Networking is vital to the performance of both individuals and organizations.

The most beneficial networks come from acquaintances one makes through everyday work activities and professional events, as well as from reciprocity in the exchange of resources. Skilled networkers know that a request for a favor is a great opportunity. If you do a favor for someone else, he or she will now feel obligated to pay you back when needed. People who get ahead keep themselves open to opportunities, continually develop their competencies and skills sets, and build connections and relationships that benefit both individual and organizational success.

WP LS Go to your WileyPLUS Learning Space course for video episodes, examples, art, tables, Concept Checks, practice, and resources that will help you succeed in this course.

Reading for
THE LEADERSHIP PROCESS

WP LS Go to your WileyPLUS Learning Space course for video episodes, examples, art, tables, Concept Checks, practice, and resources that will help you succeed in this course.

Leadership

When we think of leadership, we often think of leaders. But leaders are only one element of leadership. Other key elements are followers, leader–follower relationships, and context. It is only when all these elements come together effectively that leadership is produced. For this reason, leadership should be thought of as a process.

The leadership process shown in ▦ **Figure 13.1** is co-created by leaders and followers acting in context. **Leadership** is generated when acts of leading (e.g., influencing) are combined with acts of following (e.g., deferring). It represents an influence relationship between two or more people who depend on one another for attainment of mutual goals.[1] The implication of this is that leadership is not only about the actions of leaders. It also involves the actions of followers who contribute to, or detract from, leaders' attempts to influence.

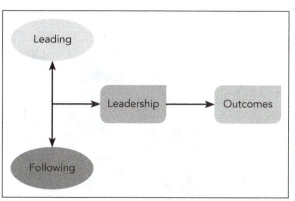

See **FIGURE 13.1 The Leadership Process. Leadership is co-created in context**

Because following is so important to leading, we could almost say that it is in following that leadership is created. If others do not follow then, even if a person has a leadership position, he or she is not really a leader. The person may be a manager—but not a leader. For example, when students in a class act up and do not respect the teacher, they are not following and the teacher is not leading. The teacher may try to use position power to manage the situation, but in this case the teacher is acting as a manager rather than a leader.

Leadership influence can be located in one person (i.e., a "leader") or be distributed throughout the group (i.e., collective leadership). For example, some teams have one project leader who everyone follows. Other groups may be more self-managing, where team members share the leadership function and responsibilities. While in the past leadership was largely the domain of formal managerial leaders, in today's environments leadership is broadly distributed more throughout organizations, with everyone expected to play their part.

Formal and Informal Leadership

Leadership processes occur both inside and outside of formal positions and roles. When leadership is exerted by individuals appointed or elected to positions of formal authority, it is called **formal leadership**. Managers, teachers, ministers, politicians, and student organization presidents are all formal leaders. Leadership can also be exerted by individuals who do not hold formal roles but become influential due to special skills or their ability to meet the needs of others. These individuals are **informal leaders**.[2] Informal leaders can include opinion leaders, change agents, and idea champions.

Whereas formal leadership involves top-down influence flows, informal leadership can flow in any direction: up, down, across, and even outside the organization. Informal leadership allows us to recognize the importance of upward leadership (or "leading-up"). **Upward leadership** occurs when individuals at lower levels act as leaders by influencing those at higher levels. This concept of leadership flowing upward is often missed in discussions of leadership in organizations, but it is absolutely critical for organizational change and effectiveness.

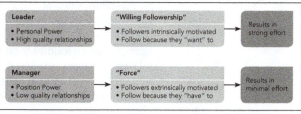

See **FIGURE 13.2 The role of "willing followership" in leadership**

Regardless of whether it is formal or informal, a key to effective leadership is "willing followership," as shown in ▦ **Figure 13.2**. Willing followership means that others follow because they *want* to, not because they have to. This is closely related to the concept of power. When leaders operate from a willing followership model, others follow out of intrinsic motivation and power comes from personal sources. This differs from more compliance-based approaches-common to managers who aren't leaders, where others follow out of extrinsic motivation and power is more position based. Managers who are also effective leaders have *both* position and personal power. On the other hand, informal leaders who do not have formal positions can only operate through personal power.

Leadership as Social Construction

Understanding leadership as a process helps us see that leadership is socially constructed. The **social construction of leadership** means that leadership is co-created in relational interactions among people acting in context. Because of this, it cannot be meaningfully separated from context. Each leadership situation is unique, having its own particular dynamics, variables, and players. There is no one-size-fits-all solution in leadership.

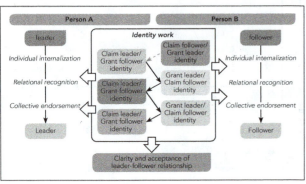

See **FIGURE 13.3** **DeRue and Ashford Leadership Identity Construction Process**

Social construction approaches see leadership as socially defined. They recognize leaders and followers as relational beings who "constitute" each other in dynamic, unfolding relational contexts.[3] In other words, whether you are a leader or a follower depends on the nature of the interactions you have with other people. Because of this, communication and the everyday interactions of people are a key element of constructionist approaches to leadership.

Leadership as Identity Construction An example of social construction can be seen in DeRue and Ashford's model of the **leadership identity construction process**. This model shows how individuals negotiate identities as leaders and followers.[4] As seen in ■ **Figure 13.3**, the identity construction process involves individuals "claiming" an identity (as a leader or follower) and others affirming or "granting" that identity by going along with the claim. **Claiming** refers to actions people take to assert their identity as a leader or follower. **Granting** refers to actions people take to bestow an identity of a leader or follower onto another person.[5]

We can see the identity construction process occurring every time a new group is formed. When there is no designated leader, group members negotiate who will be leaders and who will be followers. For example, some might say, "I am willing to take the leader role," or "Leadership is not really my thing, so I prefer to follow." It may also be more implicit, with some people doing more influencing and organizing and others doing more deferring and performing.

This process occurs even when there is a designated leader. In these cases it may be more subtle, however, such as when individuals choose not to follow the designated leader (i.e., when they do not grant the leader claim). In groups we often see informal norms emerging around leader and follower grants and claims in the form of people supporting or resisting each other's claims.

Leader identity construction has important implications, particularly for those who are high in **motivation to lead**.[6] Although these individuals may want to lead, if others do not grant them a leadership identity their efforts will not succeed. It also helps us understand why some individuals seem to find themselves in a leader role even if they don't want to be. For these "natural leaders," leadership is thrust upon them by others who grant them leadership identities regardless of their desire to claim leadership (see the "OB in Popular Culture" feature on *Forrest Gump*).

The leadership identity construction process brings a new understanding to the importance of followership. Contrary to views that depict followers as passive bystanders to leaders, identity construction shows that followers play an important role in leadership by (a) granting claims to leaders and (b) claiming roles as followers. When these grants and claims do not align—for example, when followers do not grant leaders' claims or when followers do not accept their own role as followers—the result is conflict and lack of legitimacy. Unless the problems are worked through, individuals will not be able to negotiate compatible identities. In these cases conflict will prevail, and the leadership process will break down.

Implicit Leadership Theories

A key element affecting whether leadership claims will be granted lies in the "implicit theories" we hold about leadership. **Implicit leadership theories** are beliefs or understanding about the attributes associated with leaders and leadership.[7] They can vary widely depending on our experiences and understandings of leadership. For example, some people believe leaders are charismatic, so they look for charismatic traits and behaviors in those vying for leadership status. Others believe leaders are directive and assertive, so they grant leadership status to those who take charge. Still others believe leaders are confident and considerate, so they identify leaders as those who have innovative and interesting ideas and involve others in bringing the idea to fruition.

Implicit theories cause us to naturally classify people as leaders or nonleaders. We are often not aware this process is occurring. It is based in the cognitive categorization processes associated with perception and attribution. These processes help us quickly and easily handle the overwhelming amounts of information we receive from our environments every day. The categorization process is often particularly salient when we are faced with new information. For example, on the first day of class did you look around the room and find yourself making assessments of the teacher, and even your classmates? If so, you did this using your cognitive categories and implicit theories.

To understand your own implicit leadership theories, think about the factors you associate with leadership. What traits and characteristics come to mind? Take a minute and make a list of those attributes. Now look at the sidebar on spotting implicit leadership prototypes.[8] How does your list compare? Did you identify the same prototypical leader behaviors as found in research? What is the nature of your implicit theory? Is it more positive, such as sensitivity, dedication, intelligence, and strength, or is it more negative, involving leaders' tendencies to dominate, control, or manipulate others? Why do you think you have the implicit theory you do? What experiences you've had make you see leadership in this way?

Followership

Until very recently, followership has not been given serious consideration in leadership research. We are infatuated with leaders, but often disparage followers. Think about how often you are told the importance of being an effective leader. Now think about the times when you have been told it is important to be an effective follower—has it ever happened? If you are like most people, you have received recognition and accolades for leadership but rarely have you been encouraged or rewarded for being a follower.

What Is Followership?

Followership represents the capacity or willingness to follow a leader. It is a process through which individuals choose how they will engage with leaders to co-produce leadership and its outcomes. These co-productions can take many forms. For example, it may be heavily leader dominated, with passive followers who comply or go along. Or it may be a partnership, in which leaders and followers work collaboratively to produce leadership outcomes.

Our infatuation with leaders at the expense of followers is called the **romance of leadership**: the tendency to attribute all organizational outcomes—good or bad—to the acts and doings of leaders.[9] The romance of leadership reflects our needs and biases for strong leaders who we glorify or demonize in myths and stories of great and heroic leaders. We see it in our religious teachings, our children's fairy tales, and in news stories about political and business leaders.

The problem with the romance of leadership is that its corollary is the "subordination of followership."[10] The subordination of followership means that while we heroize (or demonize) leaders, we almost completely disregard followers. Leo Tolstoy's description of the French Revolution provides an excellent example. According to Tolstoy, the French Revolution was the product of the "spectacle of an extraordinary movement of millions of men" all over Europe and crossing decades, but "historians . . . lay before us the sayings and doings of some dozens of men in one of the buildings in the city of Paris," and the detailed biography and actions of *one* man, to whom it is all attributable: Napoleon. To overcome the problem of the romance of leadership, we need to better understand the role of followership in the leadership process.

How Do Followers See Their Roles?

Followers have long been considered in leadership research, but mainly from the standpoint of how they see leaders. The question we need to consider is this: How do followers see their own role? And how do leaders see the follower role? Research is now beginning to offer new insight into these issues.

The Social Construction of Followership One of the first studies to examine follower views was a qualitative investigation in which individuals were asked to describe the characteristics and behaviors they associate with a follower (subordinate) role.[11] The findings support the socially constructed nature of followership and leadership in that, according to followers, they hold certain

	Authoritarian climate	Empowering climate
Passive beliefs	Passive followers act as traditional "obedient" followers	Passive followers uncomfortable—experience stress
Proactive beliefs	Proactive followers act passively, but this creates dissonance and dissatisfaction	Proactive followers act as constructive partners in co-producing leadership

See **FIGURE 13.4** **Followership in Context**

beliefs about how they should act in relation to leaders but whether they can act on these beliefs depends on context as shown in ▣ **Figure 13.4**.

Some followers hold *passive beliefs*, viewing their roles in the classic sense of following—that is, passive, deferential, and obedient to authority. Others hold *proactive beliefs*, viewing their role as expressing opinions, taking initiative, and constructively questioning and challenging leaders. Proactive beliefs are particularly strong among "high potentials"—those identified by their organizations as demonstrating strong potential to be promoted to higher-level leadership positions in their organization.

Because social construction is dependent on context, individuals are not always able to act according to their beliefs. For example, individuals holding proactive beliefs reported not being able to be proactive in authoritarian or bureaucratic work climates. These environments suppress their ability to take initiative and speak up, often leaving them feeling frustrated and stifled—not able to work to their potential. In empowering climates, however, they work with leaders to co-produce positive outcomes. Individuals with passive beliefs are often uncomfortable in empowering climates because their natural inclination is to follow rather than be empowered. In these environments they report feeling stressed by leaders' demands, and uncomfortable with requests to be more proactive. Passive followers are more comfortable in authoritarian climates where they receive more direction from leaders.

Follower Role Orientation Follower beliefs are also being studied in research on follower role orientation. **Follower role orientation** represents the beliefs followers hold about the way they should engage and interact with leaders to meet the needs of the work unit.[12] It reflects how followers define their role, how broadly they perceive the tasks associated with it, and how to approach a follower role to be effective.

Findings show that followers with hierarchical, **power distance orientation** believe leaders are in a better position than followers to make decisions and determine direction.[13] These individuals have lower self-efficacy, meaning they have less confidence in their ability to execute on their own, and they demonstrate higher obedience to leaders. They depend on leaders for structure and direction, which they follow without question. These followers report working in contexts of greater hierarchy of authority and lower job autonomy. This may be because these contexts are attractive to them, or it may be because those with more proactive follower orientations are less likely to remain in these environments.

Individuals with a **proactive follower orientation** approach their role from the standpoint of partnering with leaders to achieve goals.[14] These individuals are higher in proactive personality and self-efficacy. They believe followers are important contributors to the leadership process and that a strong follower role (e.g., voice) is necessary for accomplishing the organizational mission. Proactive followers tend to work in environments that support and reinforce their followership beliefs—that is, lower hierarchy of authority, greater autonomy, and higher supervisor support. These environments are important because proactive followers need support for their challenging styles. They need to trust leaders and to know that they will not be seen as overstepping their bounds.

The issue that is less clear is what managers want from followers. It seems that managers want voice, as long as that voice is provided in constructive ways. However, findings with obedience are not significant, indicating that managers may be mixed on whether obedience is positive or negative. This is true regardless of whether it comes from those with a power distance or proactive follower orientation. Therefore, we are not quite sure how obedience plays into followership. Do managers want obedience? Do only some managers want it, or do managers want only certain types of obedience? It turns out that although we have spent decades learning about what followers want from leaders, we still know very little about what leaders prefer in terms of follower behaviors and styles. Research is now underway to better investigate the manager side of the leadership story.

How Do Leaders See Follower Roles?

One area that helps us understand the manager's view is the study of **implicit followership theories**.[15] Research on implicit followership theories takes the approach described in implicit leadership theory research but reverses it—asking *leaders* (i.e., managers) to describe characteristics associated with *followers* (e.g., effective followers, ineffective followers). It then analyzes the data to identify prototypical and anti-prototypical follower characteristics.

Findings shown in the sidebar on the next page indicate that characteristics associated with good followers include being industrious, having enthusiasm, and being a good organizational citizen.[16] Characteristics associated with ineffective followers (i.e., anti-prototypical characteristics) include conformity, insubordination, and incompetence. Of these anti-prototypical traits, it appears that incompetence is the most impactful. In other words, leaders see incompetence as the greatest factor associated with ineffective followership.

What is interesting about the findings on prototypes and antiprototypes (see the sidebar) is that they may show why we are uncertain of what managers desire from followers. What managers see as insubordination and incompetence, followers may see as proactive follower behaviors. There can be a fine line between these behaviors as provided by followers, and whether leaders are ready and able to effectively receive them. Although it hasn't been studied yet in research, we can be pretty sure that a key factor in influencing how managers view and receive proactive follower behaviors is the quality of the relationship between the manager and the subordinate.

The Leader–Follower Relationship

Among the strongest findings in leadership research are studies showing that the nature of leader–follower relationships matter. When relationships are good, outcomes are positive. When relationships are bad, outcomes are negative, and potentially even destructive.

Leader–Member Exchange (LMX) Theory

The underlying premise of **leader–member exchange (LMX)** theory is that leaders (i.e., managers) have differentiated relationships with followers (i.e., subordinates).[17] With some subordinates, managers have high-quality LMX relationships, characterized by trust, respect, liking, and loyalty. With other subordinates, managers have low-quality LMX relationships, characterized by lack of trust, respect, liking, and loyalty. Whereas the former (high LMX relationships) are more like partnerships between managers and subordinates in co-producing leadership, the latter (low LMX relationships) are more like traditional supervision, with managers supervising and monitoring and subordinates complying (or maybe resisting).

Leader–follower relationships are important because they are differentially related to leadership and work outcomes. As you would expect, when relationship quality is high it has all kinds of benefits: Performance is better, subordinates are more satisfied and feel more supported, commitment and citizenship are higher, and turnover is reduced. When relationship quality is low, outcomes are not only negative, they can also be destructive. At the very least, workers in low LMX relationships are less productive and have more negative job attitudes. At their worst, relationships are hostile, leading to abuse or even sabotage.[18]

The implications of leader–member exchange theory are very clear. Bad relationships are counterproductive for individuals and organizations, whereas good relationships bring tremendous benefits. If you have a bad relationship with your boss, you can expect it to negatively impact your work and possibly your career. In organizations, bad relationships create negative environments and poor morale. They drain organizations of the energy needed to perform, adapt, and thrive.

Social Exchange Theory

To avoid these problems, we need to work to develop better-quality relationships throughout the organization. The question is, how?

Social exchange theory helps explain the social dynamics behind relationship building. According to social exchange theory, relationships develop through *exchanges*—actions contingent upon rewarding reactions. We engage in exchanges every day when we say something or do something for another and those actions are rewarded or not rewarded. Relationships develop when exchanges are mutually rewarding and reinforcing. When exchanges are one sided or not satisfactory, relationships will not develop effectively, and will likely deteriorate or extinguish.

At the core of social exchange is the **norm of reciprocity**, the idea that when one party does something for another an obligation is generated, and that party is indebted to the other until the obligation is repaid.[19] We see this all the time when someone does us a favor and then, depending on how close we are to them, we feel indebted to pay them back. If the relationship is close (e.g., family) we don't worry about paying back right away because we know it will be repaid in some way in the future. If the exchange is with someone we don't know as well (e.g., a classmate we just met), we are more anxious to repay so that the other knows we are "good" for it.

The norm of reciprocity can be seen as involving three components.[20] **Equivalence** represents the extent to which the amount of what is given back is roughly the same as what was received (e.g., the exact same or something different). **Immediacy** refers to the *time span of reciprocity*—how quickly the repayment is made (e.g., immediately or an indeterminate length of time). **Interest** represents the motive the person has in making the exchange. Interest can range from pure self-interest, to mutual interest, to other interest (pure concern for the other person).

The way in which these components work together varies by the quality of leader-follower relationships. When relationships are first forming, or if they are low quality, reciprocity involves greater equivalence (we want back what we give), immediacy is low (we expect payback relatively quickly), and exchanges are based on self-interest (we are watching out for ourselves). As relationships develop and trust is built, equivalence reduces (we don't expect exact repayment), the time span of reciprocity extends (we aren't concerned about payback—we may bank it for when we need it at some time in the future), and exchanges become more mutually or other (rather than self) interested.

What makes this process social and not economic is that it is based on trust. **Trust** is based on the belief regarding the intention and ability of the other to repay. Economic exchanges are necessarily devoid of trust. The reason we make economic contracts is to create a legal obligation in case one party breaks the contract. In social exchange, trust is the foundational element upon which exchanges occur. If one party demonstrates that they are not trustworthy, the other party will see this and stop exchanging—and the relationship will degenerate.

If we want to build effective relationships, therefore, we need to pay attention to reciprocity and social exchange processes. We need to make sure that we are engaging in exchanges, that we are doing so based on reciprocity, and that the exchanges are mutually satisfying and rewarding for all involved.

Hollander's Idiosyncrasy Credits

Another way to view the nature of exchange in relationships is idiosyncrasy credit theory, developed by social psychologist Edwin Hollander in the 1950s.[21] **Idiosyncrasy credits** represent our ability to violate norms with others based on whether we have enough "credits" to cover the violation. If we have enough credits, we can get away with idiosyncrasies (i.e., deviations from expected norms) as long as the violation does not exceed the amount of credits. If we do not have enough credits, the violation will create a deficit. When deficits become large enough, or go on for too long, our account becomes "bankrupt," and the deviations will no longer be tolerated, resulting in deterioration of relationships.

Idiosyncrasy credits offer a fun and simple way to think about some key concepts we need to keep in mind in relationship building. The main point is to manage your balances. If you are expending credits by behaving in idiosyncratic ways (deviating from expected norms), then you have to stop spending and start building. If you have a rich account and the relationship is flying high, you can afford to expend some credits by acting in a quirky way or doing things that might not be seen as positively in the other's eyes. Others will be willing to stick with you—as long as you don't go into a deficit.

Collective Leadership

Relational interactions are the foundation of leadership, and relational approaches have allowed us to understand that leadership is more aptly described as a collective rather than an individual process. **Collective leadership** considers leadership not as a property of individuals and their behaviors but as a social phenomenon constructed in interaction. It advocates a shift in focus from traits and characteristics of leaders to a focus on the shared activities and interactive processes of leadership.

Distributed Leadership

One of the first areas to recognize leadership as a collective process was **distributed leadership** research, distinguishing between "focused" and "distributed" forms of leadership. This research draws heavily on systems and process theory, and locates leadership in the relationships and interactions of multiple actors and the situations in which they are operating.[22]

Distributed leadership is based on three main premises. First, leadership is an emergent property of a group or network of interacting individuals, i.e., it is co-constructed in interactions among people. Second, distributed leadership is not clearly bounded. It occurs in context, and therefore it is affected by local and historical influences. Third, distributed leadership draws from the variety of expertise across the many, rather than relying on the limited expertise of one or a few leaders. In this way it is a more democratic and inclusive form of leadership than hierarchical models.[23]

Leadership from this view is seen in the day-to-day activities and interactions of people working in organizations. Rather than simply being a hierarchical construct, it occurs in small, incremental, and emergent everyday acts that go on in organizations. These emergent acts, interacting with large-scale change efforts from the top, can be mutually reinforcing to produce emergence and adaptability in organizations. Hence, leadership is about learning together and constructing meaning and knowledge collaboratively and collectively. For this to happen, though, formal leaders must let go of some of their authority and control and foster consultation and consensus over command and control.[24]

Co-Leadership

Another form of collective leadership is co-leadership. **Co-leadership** occurs when top leadership roles are structured in ways that no single individual is vested with the power to unilaterally lead.[25] Co-leadership can be found in professional organizations (e.g., law firms that have partnerships), the arts (the artistic side and administrative side), and healthcare (where power is divided between the community, administration, and medical sectors). Co-leadership has been used in some very famous and large businesses (e.g., Google, Goldman-Sachs).

Co-leadership helps overcome problems related to the limitations of a single individual and of abuses of power and authority. It is more common today because challenges facing organizations are often too complex for one individual to handle. Co-leadership allows organizations to capitalize on the complementary and diverse strengths of multiple individuals. These forms are sometimes referred to as constellations, or collective leadership in which members play roles that are *specialized* (i.e., each operates in a particular area of expertise), *differentiated* (i.e., avoiding overlap that would create confusion), and *complementary* (i.e., jointly cover all required areas of leadership).[26]

Shared Leadership

According to **shared leadership** approaches, leadership is a dynamic, interactive influence process among individuals in groups for which the objective is to lead one another to the achievement of group or organizational goals, or both.[27] This influence process occurs both laterally—among team members—and vertically, with the team leader. Vertical leadership is formal leadership; shared leadership is distributed leadership that emerges from within team dynamics. The main objective of shared leadership approaches is to understand and find alternate sources of leadership that will impact positively on organizational performance.

In shared leadership, leadership can come from outside or inside the team. Within a team, leadership can be assigned to one person, rotate across team members, or be shared simultaneously as different needs arise across time. Outside the team, leaders can be formally designated. Often these nontraditional leaders are called coordinators or facilitators. A key part of their job is to provide resources to their unit and serve as a liaison with other units.

According to the theory, the key to successful shared leadership and team performance is to create and maintain conditions for that performance. This occurs when vertical and shared leadership efforts are complementary. Although a wide variety of characteristics may be important for the success of a specific effort, five important characteristics have been identified across projects: (1) efficient, goal-directed effort; (2) adequate resources; (3) competent, motivated performance; (4) a productive, supportive climate; and (5) a commitment to continuous improvement.[28] The distinctive contribution of shared leadership approaches is in widening the notion of leadership to consider participation of all team members while maintaining focus on conditions for team effectiveness.

WP LS Go to your WileyPLUS Learning Space course for video episodes, examples, art, tables, Concept Checks, practice, and resources that will help you succeed in this course.

Reading for
LEADER TRAITS AND BEHAVIORAL STYLES

WP LS Go to your WileyPLUS Learning Space course for video episodes, examples, art, tables, Concept Checks, practice, and resources that will help you succeed in this course.

Leader Traits and Behaviors

We all have experience with many different kinds of leaders. Some are task oriented and authoritarian. Others are inspirational and motivating. Still others are hands off, with laissez-faire or ineffectual styles that can make it frustrating when situations require strong leadership.

These characteristics represent traits and behavioral styles of leaders. Trait and behavioral approaches help us understand how characteristics of leaders are associated with their effectiveness. The basic premise is that we can identify more and less effective leadership styles by studying how followers perceive and react to different kinds of leaders.

As any of us who have worked in organizations know, managers play a crucial role in creating the climates in which we work. When a manager fosters a supportive and motivating climate, our work is meaningful and going to work is fun. But when we have a bad manager, morale plummets and we are drained of the energy we need to be productive in work—and in life. Research has shown us what makes some managers more effective than others. In this chapter we build from this knowledge to understand how we can become more effective managers and leaders in the workplace.

Early Trait Approaches

For over a century, scholars have been on a quest to identify the elusive qualities that separate leaders from non-leaders. Based on the assumption that leaders are endowed with certain traits or characteristics, much of the early work focused on identifying qualities that predict who is a leader and who is not. These studies, collectively called **trait approaches**, assumed that if we could identify leadership qualities, we could select individuals for leadership positions based on their leadership traits.

The focus in this early work was on personality, needs, motives, values, and even physical characteristics such as height and sex. For this reason, these theories were often called "great man theories" because one of the key traits they associated with leadership was being male.

Early review were discouraging. Scholars concluded that traits were not significantly associated with leadership. A primary reason was the failure to look for situational and mediating variables, such as communication or interpersonal behaviors, that would help explain how leader traits are causally linked to outcomes.[1] Instead, researchers looked for significant correlations between traits and leadership outcomes, such as group performance or leader advancement. When they failed to find strong relationships, they concluded that traits were not a significant predictor of leadership or its effectiveness.

Later Trait Approaches

These early reviews saying there was not a pattern of significant correlations caused trait approaches to fall out of favor. In recent years, however, trait approaches have experienced a comeback as management scholars are developing new measures and new ways to analyze the relationship between a manager's traits and his or her leadership effectiveness.

Some scholars are using the Big Five dimensions of personality in an attempt to predict leader emergence (i.e., who is recognized as leader of a group) and leader effectiveness (i.e., how well a leader performs in the role). Findings show significant but small relationships for four of the Big Five traits: extraversion, conscientiousness, emotional stability, and openness to experience.[2] This means that effective leaders seem to have a bit more of these traits than ineffective and non-leaders.

Other scholars are pulling from evolutionary psychology to identify genetic factors associated with leadership that have evolved through natural selection. These scholars argue that our predilections toward leadership and followership are likely due to natural selection that caused certain traits and behaviors to be retained because they solved adaptive problems faced by our ancestors.[3] According to evolutionary psychology approaches, it may be engrained in some of us to voluntarily subordinate to others because our ancestors learned that, in certain situations, it is better to defer to a central command.

Behavioral Leadership Approaches

If you want to know whether a leader has a certain trait—that is, intelligence, extraversion, or persuasiveness—how would you find out? The answer is that you would look at his or her *behaviors*. Not surprisingly, then, when the early trait approaches failed to produce meaningful results, researchers began considering other types of leader characteristics, such as what leaders did, or how they behaved.

This led to what is known as the **behavioral approach** in management research. The behavioral approach focuses on identifying categories of relevant leadership behavior and examining their relationships with outcomes. It does this primarily through the use of interviews and questionnaires that gather subordinates' perceptions of the supervisors' behaviors.

Much of the early work on behavioral approaches was centered at two universities, so they became known as the Ohio State and Michigan studies.[4] These studies discovered that the majority of a manager's leadership behaviors could be divided into two meta-categories: relations-oriented and task-oriented behavior. **Relations-oriented behavior**, or *consideration*, involves concern for relationships and interpersonal support. It focuses on employee-centered, or socioemotional, concerns. **Task-oriented behavior**, or *initiating structure*, involves directive behavior focused on providing clarity and task focus. It addresses production-centered, or task-related, concerns of management.

These two behavioral categories form the foundation for much of the management research that was to follow. Relations-oriented behavior focuses on the human relations aspects of management. It shows that highly considerate managers are sensitive to people's feelings and try to make things pleasant for followers. They do this by listening to subordinates and treating them as respected colleagues, defending subordinates when needed, being willing to accept suggestions, and consulting with subordinates on important matters.[5]

Task-oriented behavior focuses on production. Its key concern is to provide structure for subordinates by defining task requirements and specifying the work agenda. Task-oriented behaviors include maintaining performance standards, assigning tasks, identifying standard procedures, enforcing deadlines, correcting performance problems, and coordinating activities.[6]

Are Leaders Born or Made?

The focus on traits and behaviors raises another issue at the center of leadership. Is leadership restricted to those who are *born* with leadership ability, or can anyone be *made* into a leader? This is known as the "born/made" argument in leadership. The "born" argument aligns with trait theory, which says that leaders have certain traits—that they are natural-born leaders. The "made" argument aligns with the behavior approaches, which say that leadership is associated with behaviors (i.e., if you behave like a leader you are a leader). The made argument implies that anyone can be made into a leader through training and development.

Where do you fall on this issue? Do you think anyone can be made into a leader? Or do you think people have to have certain skills to be a leader? If the born argument is right, then we should focus on *selection* by screening new hires for leadership traits and skills. If the made argument is correct then we should focus on *development* by training individuals to better demonstrate leadership behaviors.

Potential insight into the answer can be found in a series of research studies by Rich Arvey and colleagues based on samples of fraternal and identical twins from the Minnesota Twin Registry. Examining how much leadership is determined by nature (i.e., genetics) and how much by nurture (i.e., environment), they found that 30 percent to 32 percent of the variance in role occupancy among twins could be accounted for by genetic factors. This means that roughly 70 percent can be developed.[7] The implication of these findings is that not everyone can be a leader. Instead, individuals must possess at least some set of basic leadership skills and abilities. In other words, just like being a musician or a star athlete, leadership is a talent—and some people have it more than others.

Contingency Theories

Common sense would tell us that not all traits or behaviors of leaders are positively related to effectiveness all of the time. Instead, whether a leader behavior is effective will depend on the situation. On the first day of class, what do you want from your professor: Do you want more considerate behavior, or do you want more structuring behavior? Most students want more

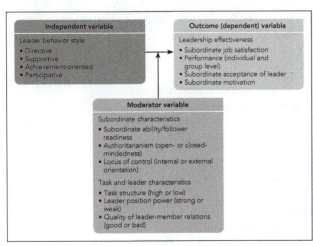

Independent variable	Outcome (dependent) variable
Leader behavior style • Directive • Supportive • Achievement-oriented • Participative	Leadership effectiveness • Subordinate job satisfaction • Performance (individual and group level) • Subordinate acceptance of leader • Subordinate motivation

Moderator variable

Subordinate characteristics
• Subordinate ability/follower readiness
• Authoritarianism (open- or closed-mindedness)
• Locus of control (internal or external orientation)

Task and leader characteristics
• Task structure (high or low)
• Leader position power (strong or weak)
• Quality of leader-member relations (good or bad)

See **FIGURE 14.1**
A comprehensive contingency model

structuring behavior. If your professor comes in and is nice and friendly (i.e., consideration) but does not hand out a syllabus (i.e., initiating structure), the response will likely not be very positive. In other words, some situations call for certain types of behaviors more than others.

This is the premise behind the **contingency approaches** in leadership theory. Contingency approaches state that whether a leader style or behavior is positively associated with leadership effectiveness depends on (i.e., is *contingent* upon) the situation. In situations requiring more direction and structure, task-oriented behavior will be more effective and desired. In situations requiring more support and consideration, relations-oriented behavior will be more effective.

The Contingency Model

A general contingency model is shown in ▣ **Figure 14.1**. It indicates that a manager's leadership behavior or style (e.g., the independent variable) is related to leadership effectiveness (e.g., the outcome variable) depending on the situation (e.g., the moderator variable).

Contingency theories start with a manager's behavioral style. The most common leadership behaviors used by managers are task oriented and relations oriented. In contingency approaches, these are often referred to as **directive leadership** and **supportive leadership** styles. Two additional behavioral styles were added later: achievement-oriented and participative leadership.[8] **Achievement-oriented leadership** focuses on building subordinates' confidence in their ability to achieve high standards of performance through a focus on excellence and goal setting. **Participative leadership** focuses on consulting with subordinates and taking their suggestions into account before making decisions.

Contingency theories try to predict leadership effectiveness. The most common effectiveness variables are subordinate job satisfaction and performance. As described in previous chapters, job satisfaction is the positive feelings one has about the work and work setting. Performance is the quality and quantity of work produced. Performance can be measured at the individual level (i.e., the performance of a particular subordinate) or at the group level (i.e., the performance of a work unit).

The central argument of contingency theories is that situational factors moderate the association between a manager's leadership style and his or her effectiveness. Situational variables are assessed in a variety of ways. They include characteristics of the follower, such as **follower readiness**, or ability to do the task. They can be characteristics of the task, such as **task structure** (e.g., high or low task structure). Or they can be characteristics of the organizational structure, such as **leader position power** (e.g., formal or informal authority system).

Findings from Contingency Theories

Findings from contingency approaches show, in general, that certain situations favor certain leadership styles. Managers, therefore, need to understand, what the situation is and how to adjust their style to fit it.

Directive Leadership Directive leadership is needed when subordinates want guidance and direction in their jobs. It helps increases role clarity, self-efficacy, effort, and performance. When the task is clear, directive leadership will have a negative impact, as it will be seen as overly domineering—a "micromanaging" style—by subordinates.

Supportive Leadership Supportive leadership is needed when subordinates want emotional, not task, support. Supportive leadership is beneficial for highly repetitive or unpleasant tasks. It helps reduce stress by letting employees know the organization cares and will provide help.

Achievement-Oriented Leadership Achievement-oriented leadership is needed for challenging tasks or when subordinates need to take initiative. It helps employees gain confidence and strive for higher standards. It increases expectations that effort will lead to desired performance.

Participative Leadership Participative leadership is best when subordinates need limited direction and support. It allows employees to provide input. When tasks are repetitive, nonauthoritarian subordinates appreciate being involved to help break up the monotony.

Fiedler's Leader-Match

One contingency theory that differs from the others in how it handles the issue of fit between leader style and the situation is Fiedler's LPC (least-preferred co-worker) model. Fiedler's LPC model suggests that a manager's leadership style does not change. A manager has a certain style and that is the style he or she has to work with. Therefore, instead of modifying their style, managers need to match (i.e., **leader-match)** the situation to their style.

A match can be achieved in two ways: by selecting managers with the appropriate style to fit the situation, or by training managers to change the situation to make it fit their leadership style. In the latter case, Fiedler developed leader-match training, which Sears, Roebuck and Co. and other organizations used for training managers to diagnose the situation and match their style to it. A number of studies have been designed to test this leader match training. Although they are not uniformly supportive, more than a dozen such tests found increases in work unit effectiveness following the training.[9]

Problems with Contingency Approaches

Although contingency approaches focus managers on the importance of matching their styles to the situation, they do not describe exactly how to do this. The problem is that the guidelines coming out of contingency approaches are broad, and therefore not very informative. In the workplace, managers face leadership situations that are complex and dynamic, and each situation is unique in its own way. There is no "magic toolbox" we can give managers for how to deal with these situations. Leaders need to understand the basic concepts but then be able to adapt their style to fit the needs of the particular situation.

Frustration with these limitations led to what some refer to as the "doom and gloom" period in leadership research. This period (the 1970s to 1980s) was characterized by disillusionment and criticism from scholars that leadership research had told us very little.[10] To address these criticisms, scholars turned to a new way to think about leadership. Instead of focusing on leadership contexts, they focused on leaders. This led to visionary, charismatic, and transformational approaches in leadership.

Charismatic/Transformational Views

Charismatic Leadership

We are all familiar with charismatic leadership. We have been witness to the powerful effects, both good and bad, charismatic leaders can have on those around them. But what exactly is charisma, and how does it operate in leadership?

Charisma **Charisma** is a special personal quality or attractiveness that enables an individual to influence others. It is often characterized as personal magnetism or charm. Charisma evokes enthusiasm and commitment among followers. For example, John F. Kennedy, Oprah Winfrey, and Nelson Mandela are often described as charismatic leaders.

Charisma has its roots in Christianity. The earliest usage depicts leaders set apart from ordinary people by their divine calling, personal sacrifice, and devotion to a spiritual mission and duty.[11] People follow out of a sense of obedience and trust in the leader and his or her revelation. Mother Theresa and Gandhi were able to amass large followings because of their self-sacrifice and dedication to their mission. Their calling had broad appeal to the needs and hopes of the people around them.

Although charisma is often considered an individual trait, it is more aptly described as a relational process involving a leader, followers, and a situation. Katherine Klein and Robert House describe charisma as "a fire" produced by three elements: (1) a "spark"—a leader with charismatic qualities, (2) "flammable material"—followers who are open or susceptible to charisma, and (3) "oxygen"—an environment, such as a crisis or a situation of unrest among followers, that is conducive to charisma.[12] For example, Martin Luther King was a leader with charismatic qualities (a skilled communicator), who tapped into the needs of followers hungry for change (protestors for equality), in a time of great unrest (the Civil Rights Movement).

Charismatic Traits and Behaviors What most distinguishes charismatic leaders is their skill as communicators. Charismatic leaders connect with followers on a deep, emotional level. They use metaphors and symbols to articulate their vision in ways that captivate followers and build identification. Their vision may offer promises that otherwise appear impossible. For many, this was the appeal of Barack Obama's 2008 election platform of "Change We Can Believe In" and "Yes We Can."

Charismatic leaders often use unconventional behavior to demonstrate their exceptional qualities. Virgin Group founder Richard Branson is often described as a charismatic leader, and his record-breaking crossing of the Pacific Ocean in a hot air balloon certainly qualifies as unconventional and exceptional behavior.

Consequences of Charisma For charisma to achieve positive outcomes, it needs to be used from a **socialized charismatic** power orientation, where power is used for collective rather than personal benefit. When used for personal interests, or a **personalized charismatic** power orientation it can have destructive consequences. Personalized charismatics dominate followers and keep them weak and dependent on the leader. For example, many dictators oppress their people by not allowing access to schooling or meaningful employment. In organizations, personalized charismatics reduce followers' power by centralizing decision making, restricting information, and doing what they can to make themselves look more important than others.[13]

Research findings suggest that charisma is not a beneficial attribute for most chief executives.[14] Studies of CEO charisma have shown that financial performance was predicted by past performance but not by CEO charisma. Although charismatics are often able to persuade boards of directors to give them higher compensation, there is no evidence that these CEOs improve financial performance for their companies. One exception is in times of crisis or change management. For example, Steve Jobs's charisma was critical to the turnaround of Apple Computer in the late 1990s.

Dangers of Charismatic Leadership Charisma is a powerful force, and can be a dangerous one. Because charismatic leaders arouse strong emotions among followers, they can produce radical behaviors, even when that is not their intention. This occurs because followers often have psychological needs causing them to want hero figures who make them feel motivated, special, or secure.[15] This can lead followers to interpret leaders as wanting them to do things even when leaders do not. For example, in the movie *Dead Poet's Society*, Robin Williams plays a charismatic teacher, John Keating, who inspires students in a conservative and aristocratic boarding school in Vermont to "seize the day" and live their lives to the fullest. His charisma goes out of control, however, when one of the students, Neil Perry, interprets Keating's message to mean he should rebel against his parents. When that doesn't work, Neil is so distraught that he commits suicide.

Followers' heroizing of charismatic leaders can also lead to disbelief and frustration when leaders don't live up to their expectations. Followers of charismatic leaders often put the leader on a pedestal and expect superhuman behavior. But the problem is all leaders are human, and rarely will they live up to these expectations.

Charismatic leaders can try to address these problems by reducing **power distance**. Power distance is the extent to which followers see the leader as having much higher status than them.[16] When power distance is high, followers are reluctant to speak up or question because they believe the leader knows best. Leaders can address these problems by empowering followers to think critically and encouraging them to push back when they have concerns. They can also share in the credit for success, letting followers know that it is the combined actions that allowed the success— not the leader acting alone.

Burns's Transforming Leadership Theory

Transformational leadership theory is another approach that helped lift leadership out of the doom and gloom period in leadership studies. It began with publication of a book by political scientist James MacGregor Burns in 1978 analyzing the leadership styles of prominent political leaders.[17] Burns's approach focused on leadership from the standpoint of power, purpose, and relationships.[18] Key to his analysis was the distinction between leaders and power wielders.

According to Burns, leaders take followers' goals, motivations, needs, and feelings into consideration and use power for good. **Power wielders**, on the other hand, are egocentric and Machiavellian. They use power to advance their own interests without considering followers' needs. Whereas leaders elevate followers (and themselves) to new heights, power wielders gain power *over* followers in ways that cause followers to engage in behaviors they otherwise would not. In Burns's view, power wielders are not leaders.

Through his analysis, Burns noticed different styles and approaches used by leaders. Some used **transactional leadership** styles, in which they focused on exchanging valued goods in return for something they want (e.g., economic, political, or social exchanges, such as exchange of money for goods or support for votes). The focus here is purely instrumental. There is no expectation beyond the exchange. Other leaders—the ones Burns was most interested in learning about—used what he called **transformational leadership** styles. Transformational leaders developed inspirational relationships with followers in which both leaders and followers were positively transformed in the process. This transformation raised human conduct and enhanced the moral aspirations of both leaders and followers. In Burns's transforming leadership theory, the transformation is based on both leaders and followers attaining higher levels of moral purpose as they accomplished common goals.

The key element of Burns's theory is the moral foundation upon which transforming leadership rests.[19] A transforming leader is one who, though initially impelled by the quest for individual recognition, ultimately advances collective purpose by being attuned to the aspirations and needs of his or her followers. In Burns's theory, the transformation is a moral accomplishment because its outcome raises human conduct. According to Burns, Mao and Gandhi were quintessential transforming leaders. Instead of exploiting power they remained sensitive to higher purposes and aspirations.[20] Hitler, on the other hand, was not a leader in Burns's analysis, but a power wielder who used his power for selfish and destructive purpose.

Bass's Transactional/Transformational Leadership Theory

Bernard Bass drew from Burns's theory of political leadership to develop a theory of leadership for organizations. He called his approach "performance beyond expectations." Contrary to Burns's focus on transformation as a higher moral purpose and values, Bass's focus on transformation was on organizational performance. In his theory, the transformation occurs when followers are inspired to set aside their self-interest for organizational interest. In other words, they accept the purpose is attainment of pragmatic task objectives for the good of the organization.[21]

Bass's Transformational Leadership Bass's **transformational leadership** styles move the follower beyond immediate self-interests by using four types of leader behaviors shown in ▣ **Figure 14.2**. *Idealized influence* and *inspirational leadership* are similar to charismatic leadership, described earlier in this chapter. They are displayed when the leader envisions a desirable future, articulates how it can be reached, sets an example to be followed, sets high standards of performance, and shows determination and confidence. *Intellectual stimulation* is displayed when the leader helps followers to become more innovative and creative. *Individualized consideration* is displayed when leaders pay attention to the developmental needs of followers by providing support, encouragement, and coaching.[22]

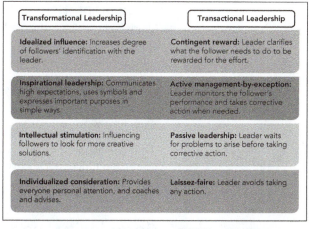

See **FIGURE 14.2 Key Differences in Transformational and Transactional Leadership Styles**

Transformational leaders articulate a shared vision of the future, intellectually stimulate subordinates, provide a great deal of support to individuals, recognize individual differences, and set high expectations for the work unit.[23] They increase followers' social identity by enhancing pride in contributing to a higher purpose, and make followers feel more secure in their membership and status in the group.

Bass's Transactional Leadership Bass's **transactional leadership** is based in self-interest, and use exchanges between leaders and followers to attain desired behavior and outcomes. The transactional leadership styles shown in Figure 14.2 are associated with several kinds of behavior. *Contingent rewards* involve exchanging rewards for mutually agreed-upon goal accomplishment. *Active management by exception* involves watching for deviations from rules and standards and taking corrective action. *Passive management by exception* involves intervening only if standards are not met. And *laissez-faire* leadership involves abdicating responsibilities and avoiding decisions.[25]

Findings from Bass's Approach Bass's transactional and transformational leadership theory is one of the most prominent theories in organizational leadership research. To advance his work, Bass began by developing a measure known as the Multifactor Leadership Questionnaire (MLQ). This measure assesses transformational and transactional leadership styles.[24] Hundreds of studies have used the MLQ to investigate transformational and transactional styles of managerial leaders as perceived by their subordinates. Findings largely support Bass's premise that transformational leadership is associated with increased follower motivation and performance (more so than transactional leadership) and that effective leaders use a combination of both types of leadership.

Meta-analyses show that composite measures of transformational and transactional leadership are related to leadership effectiveness, particularly when ratings are provided by subordinates (e.g., subordinate satisfaction). One likely reason for this is that transformational leadership is highly correlated with trust. In other words, much of the relationship between transformational leaders and outcomes is likely due to the trust subordinates have in transformational leaders.[26]

One criticism of Bass's approach is that in focusing on organizational performance as the ultimate goal, Bass lost the moral underpinnings upon which Burns's theory is based. Burns's theory is based on the leader's allegiance to followers and to uplifting society. Bass's theory is based on allegiance to the organization and performance. Some argue that this makes the approach susceptible to problems of narcissism and exploitation when leaders interpret the transformation from self-interest to organizational interest to mean their wishes take precedence over others.[27] It is also morally questionable to ask subordinates to put aside their self-interest for organizational good.

Problems of "Heroic" Leadership Views

Charismatic and transformational approaches were key to revitalizing leadership studies after the doom and gloom period, so they hold a prominent place in leadership theory and practice. One side effect of these approaches, however, is the rise of **heroic leadership views**. Heroic views see leadership as the acts of great leaders who inspire and motivate others to accomplish extraordinary things. Heroic views create pictures of leaders as white knights swooping in to save the day, and followers as weak and passive subordinates who are fully reliant on leaders for direction, trust and hope.[28]

In so doing, heroic views overlook the significance of everyday leaders influencing throughout the organization. They also miss the importance of process, and the key role of followers in the leadership process. They overestimate the influence of the leader and underestimate the importance of context and timing. To address these issues and others, new approaches such as complexity leadership theory are being introduced to leadership research.

Complexity Leadership Views

Complexity leadership approaches draw from complexity science to bring a more dynamic and contextual view to leadership.[29] Complexity science originates in fields such as biology, physics, mathematics, economics, and meteorology. It is the study of **complex adaptive systems**—systems that adapt and evolve in the process of interacting with dynamic environments.[30]

Complex adaptive systems offer a valuable lens for organizational behavior because, contrary to bureaucratic organizing approaches, complex systems have no centralized coordination and control. Coordination comes from within the system, occurring through interactive dynamics and emergence among system components.[31] Many are beginning to see complex adaptive systems as powerful mechanisms for explaining phenomena in the physical and economic world, including weather (e.g., hurricanes, tornadoes), anthills, swarming fish, bee colonies, economies, and markets.

Complex adaptive systems help us think about how organizations can make themselves more adaptive rather than bureaucratic. They emphasize that a key goal of organizations and criteria for leadership effectiveness should be the extent to which they are able to adapt to survive.

Today's Complex Environments

Interest in complexity approaches is increasing because our environments today are radically different from those of the industrial era when management theories first developed.[32] In the Industrial Age managers were trying to figure out how to organize semiskilled laborers in assembly lines and factories. To do this they turned to **bureaucracy**, which allowed managers to use hierarchy and control to achieve efficiency and results.[33]

In today's environments these approaches are no longer working. Managers no longer have control over information, and employees are less willing to just go along or do what they are told. They expect to be engaged at work and to be treated as active partners in the leadership process. Moreover, problems are too complex to be solved by one person. They require teams of people and distributed intelligence, rather than the limited intelligence of the leader at the top.

As seen in Figure 14.2, these changes are requiring radical differences in assumptions about what leaders need to do to be effective in today's workplace. We are gradually moving away from a hierarchical world into a more connectionist one. In this highly connected world leaders need to rely more on personal power than position power, and we need both "bottom up" and "top down" influence and information flows in organizations. This requires more proactive than passive followership, and leadership responsibility needs to be distributed throughout the organization. It is no longer just the responsibility of leaders (i.e., accountability up) but instead the responsibility of all (i.e., accountability all).

The major differences in complexity and bureaucratic assumptions are shown in ▣ **Figure 14.3**.[34] Perhaps the biggest difference lies in the nature of control. Unlike the Industrial Age when managers could control events, today's interconnected world means that things happen unexpectedly and without our ability to stop them. Managers today operate in workplaces where they are expected to think on their feet and respond quickly and creatively. And they can't respond to complex problems by themselves. All of this requires that leaders enable their organizations to cope with complexity by being more adaptive.

Bureaucratic Assumptions	Complexity Assumptions
Environments stable, controllable	Environments dynamic, uncontrollable
Hierarchical organizing systems using centralized control	Self-organizing systems with no centralized control
Coordination from hierarchy, formal rules, regulations	Coordination from interactions within system, simple rules
Change is linear, predictable	Change is nonlinear, unpredictable
Value = efficiency and reliability	Value = adaptability and responsiveness
Direction set by a few leaders	Direction set by participation of many
Leaders are experts, authorities	Leaders are facilitators, supporters

See **FIGURE 14.3 Major Differences Between Bureaucratic and Complexity Assumptions**

Complexity Leadership Theory

Today's leaders enable adaptability by fostering innovation, flexibility, and learning. These characteristics are the key to survival in complex (ever-changing) environments. That said, organizations are still bureaucracies: They still have hierarchical organizing systems, and they still need efficiency and control. Therefore, the key lies in effectively combining bureaucratic organizing structures with complex adaptive systems.[35]

Complexity leadership theory says we can do this by understanding three types of leadership systems in organizations.[36] The first, **administrative leadership**, focuses on how we can gain efficiency and meet the financial and performance needs of the organization. The goal of administrative leadership is to drive business results through tools such as policy, efficiency, strategic planning, resource allocation, budgeting, and scheduling. It occurs in formal roles (i.e., the administrative system) and is mainly performed by managers.

Entrepreneurial leadership represents the bottom-up, emergent forces that drive innovation, learning, and change in organizations. This form of leadership can be subtle, such as when people develop new ways of working as part of their day-to-day functioning and these changes dissipate into the system. Or it can be more intentional, as in the case of entrepreneurial leaders acting as intrapreneurs: individuals who work to create and actively champion new ideas and innovations. These types of entrepreneurial leaders are often highly proactive, self-motivated, and action oriented in the pursuit of innovative products or services.

Top-down and bottom-up forces alone are not sufficient, however. They need to function together effectively to make the overall system adaptive. Therefore, complexity leadership adds a third function called adaptive leadership. **Adaptive leadership** operates in the interface between administrative and entrepreneurial systems.[37] Its job is to foster the conditions for productive emergence by helping generate new ideas and then enabling them within the formal administrative system to produce results (i.e., innovation). It does this by sponsoring ideas from the entrepreneurial system, providing critical resources, and helping innovations to flow into the formal administrative system to increase fitness for the firm.

Research findings provide support for complexity leadership models. They offer evidence for emergence and the importance of adaptive leadership in organizations. One of the most significant findings, however, is the overwhelming predominance of stifling bureaucratic leadership in organizations. This is because traditional leadership theories have socialized managers and organizational members into control-oriented approaches that respond to complexity with order and stability. Findings are beginning to show that traditional top-down approaches are not only insufficient in complex environments—they may even be harmful to organizational health when they stifle the adaptive dynamics needed to respond in complex environments.

Challenges of Complexity Leadership Approaches

Because complexity leadership is a new approach, more study is needed. Early findings are supportive, but we need greater understanding of how these processes work in organizations, particularly with respect to the adaptive system. Complexity is a broad and technical field so it needs to be translated appropriately for business leaders. It also represents a paradigm shift that will be uncomfortable to many. Although research findings show that leaders who use complexity approaches are successful in driving business results and adaptability, these approaches are so different that some individuals may not be recognized as leaders because they are not as directive and controlling as described in predominant thinking about leadership. As we continue to transition from a hierarchical to a complex world, however, these styles will not only be more recognized, they will be more expected.

Leadership Ethics

At the core of leadership is the issue of the moral and ethical dilemmas that arise in leadership contexts. And leadership contexts are ripe for moral challenges. Leaders can be seduced by power, and pressure for results can tempt achievement-oriented leaders to cheat to avoid failure. The hierarchical nature of manager–subordinate relationships can make followers afraid to speak up, and the lack of checks and balances on leaders can lead to devastating outcomes.[38]

To address these challenges, scholars are focusing more seriously on leadership ethics. **Leadership ethics** is the study of ethical problems and challenges distinctive to and inherent in the processes, practices, and outcomes of leading and following.[39] It is concerned with the ethical use of power and the morality of leadership outcomes (e.g., fairness, equality, liberty). Paralleling the study of ethics more generally, leadership ethics examines right, wrong, good, evil, virtue, duty, obligation, rights, justice, and fairness as they apply to leadership relationships and leader and follower behaviors.

Shared Value View

In organizational contexts, a challenge to leadership ethics comes from the way we socialize individuals into the purpose of business. Nearly all businesspeople have been indoctrinated in to Milton Friedman's dictum that the "social responsibility of business is to increase its profits."[40] This is known as the **profit motive**, and it drives the belief that the sole purpose of business is to make money.

The profit motive is being seriously questioned in today's environment. Leaders such as John Mackey, the CEO of Whole Foods, and Michael Porter of Harvard University are offering alternative views based on conscious capitalism and creating shared value. These views, developed from purpose-driven mind-sets, argue that the problem is not profit but profit at what cost? To address this issue, recent discussions of the role of profit in business are arguing for a **shared value view**, stating that organizations should create economic value in a way that also creates value for society by addressing societal needs and challenges.[41] In a shared value view, the focus is on both profit and societal gain.

This more modern take advocates the need for business to reconnect company success with social progress. In the process, it addresses the issue at the very core of the debate in leadership ethics: Whose interests matter more . . . those of the individual (or company) or the collective (i.e., the "greater good")? Shared value argues that the answer is both.

Servant Leadership

Servant leadership, developed by Robert K. Greenleaf, is based on the notion that the primary purpose of business should be to create a positive impact on the organization's employees as well as the community. In an essay that Greenleaf wrote about servant leadership in 1970, he stated, "The servant-leader *is* servant first. . . . It begins with the natural feeling that one wants to serve, to serve *first*. Then conscious choice brings one to aspire to lead."[42]

The core characteristic of servant leadership as described by Greenleaf is "going beyond one's self-interest." Compared to other leadership styles, such as transformational leadership where the primary allegiance is to the organization, the servant leader emphasizes how the organization can create opportunities for followers to grow. It is a person-oriented approach focused on building safe and strong relationships in organizations. Leaders use power not for self-interest but for the growth of employees, survival of the organization, and responsibility to the community.[43]

The servant leader is attuned to basic spiritual values and in serving these assists others, including colleagues, the organization, and society. Servant leaders see their responsibility as increasing the autonomy of followers and encouraging them to think for themselves. They complement their focus on followers with a leadership style that places primary emphasis on humility and remaining true to themselves and their moral convictions in the face of power. Servant leaders accomplish this by empowering and developing people, having high integrity, accepting people for who they are, and being stewards who work for the good of the whole.[44]

Empowering Leadership

Empowering leadership is similar to servant leadership in its focus on valuing and developing people. Although it was not developed as an ethical leadership theory, it is consistent with leadership ethics in its core premise that employees should be treated with dignity and respect.

Empowering leadership is in direct contrast to **authoritarian (or autocratic) leadership** styles that involve leaders dictating policies and procedures, making all decisions about what goals are to be achieved, and directing and controlling all activities without any meaningful participation by subordinates. **Empowering leadership** focuses instead on conveying the significance of the work, allowing participation in decision making, removing bureaucratic constraints, and instilling confidence that performance will be high.[45] Empowering leadership emphasizes the importance of leaders delegating authority and employees assuming responsibility. It argues that by sharing knowledge and information, and allowing employees responsibility and self-control, organizations will be rewarded with a more dedicated and intrinsically motivated workforce.

Research findings show that empowering leadership is related to increased employee creativity and, to some extent, performance.[46] Most views assume that empowering leadership is most appropriate for those with high follower readiness (e.g., high ability and experience). Interestingly, however, research findings have shown the opposite. A study of sales representatives showed that, contrary to expectations, empowering leadership was most beneficial for those with *low* levels of product and industry knowledge and *low* experience rather than those with high readiness. For those with high knowledge and experience, empowering leadership appeared to reap no benefits. Perhaps experienced individuals have little to gain from leader efforts toward empowerment.

Ethical Leadership Theory

Ethical leadership theory is a normative theory focused on understanding how ethical leaders behave. A **normative theory** implies or prescribes a norm or standard. Ethical leadership theory prescribes that leaders should be role models of appropriate behavior—such as openness, honesty, and trustworthiness—who are motivated by altruism, meaning they are unselfish and concerned for others (e.g., treating employees fairly and considerately). Ethical leaders should (1) communicate to followers what is ethical and allow followers to ask questions and provide feedback regarding ethical issues; (2) set clear ethical standards, and ensure followers comply with those standards by rewarding ethical conduct and disciplining those who don't follow standards; and (3) take into account ethical principles in making decisions and ensure that followers observe and follow this process.[47]

Ethical leaders create ethical climates by allowing followers voice and ensuring that processes are fair. **Ethical climates** are the ethical values, norms, attitudes, feelings, and behaviors of employees in an organization.[48] Ethical leaders foster such climates by creating moral awareness and concern, enhancing moral reasoning, clarifying moral values, and encouraging moral responsibility. They consider the consequences of their decisions and make principled and fair choices that can be observed and emulated by others.[49]

Research shows that ethical leadership is linked to higher levels of follower performance and innovative behavior. Evidence also suggests a mitigating effect of ethical leadership on followers' misconduct, unethical behaviors, and workplace bullying.[50] Despite this, ethical leadership theory is limited in that it focuses primarily on leaders' responsibilities for ethics. For ethical leadership to truly take hold in organizations, it needs to be the responsibility of both leaders and followers.

WP LS Go to your **WileyPLUS Learning Space** course for video episodes, examples, art, tables, Concept Checks, practice, and resources that will help you succeed in this course.

15

Reading for
ORGANIZATIONAL CULTURE

WP LS Go to your WileyPLUS Learning Space course for video episodes, examples, art, tables, Concept Checks, practice, and resources that will help you succeed in this course.

Organizational Culture

Organizational culture is the system of shared actions, values, and beliefs that develops within an organization and guides the behavior of its members.[1] In the business setting, this system is often referred to as the **corporate culture**. Each organization has its own unique culture. Just as no two individual personalities are the same, no two organizational cultures are identical. Yet, there are some common cultural elements that yield stability and meaning for organizations.[2]

Functions of Organizational Culture

It is important to recognize that the organizational culture of a firm emerges from (1) the dialogue and discourse among its members and their collective experience over time, (2) the attempts by managers to influence subordinates, and (3) pressures from the larger environment in which the members, the managers, and the organization operate. In this chapter we will examine the functions of organizational culture and various levels of cultural analysis to understand the powerful force of organizational culture. We will then turn to innovation and link innovation to managing organizational culture.

External Adaptation An important function of organizational culture is to provide historically successful answers to external adaptation.[3] Issues of **external adaptation** deal with ways of reaching goals, tasks to be accomplished, methods used to achieve the goals, and cope with success and failure. Through their shared experiences, members can develop common views that help guide their day-to-day activities toward commonly shared goals.

Although managers attempt to influence members and the organization in many ways, they have an important influence by emphasizing a limited number of goals that shape the shared actions, values, and beliefs of all organizational members and key external contributors.

For managers, this goal-setting aspect of external adaptation involves answering important instrumental or goal-related questions concerning reality: How do we (the organization) contribute? What is the real mission? What are our goals? How do we reach our goals? Organizational members need to know the real mission of the organization, not just the pronouncements to key constituencies, such as stockholders. If they know and accept organizational goals, members will develop an understanding of how they contribute to the mission.

Each group of individuals in an organization tends to (1) separate more important from less important external forces, (2) develop ways to measure accomplishments, and (3) create explanations for why goals are not always met. At Dell, for example, managers have moved away from judging their progress against specific targets to estimating the degree to which they are moving a development process forward. They work on improving participation and commitment.[4]

The final issues in external adaptation deal with two important, but often neglected, aspects of coping with external reality. First, individuals need to develop ways of promoting the firm and themselves. At 3M, for example, employees talk about the quality of their products and the many new, useful products the organization has brought to the market. Second, individuals must collectively know when and how to admit defeat. At the beginning of 3M's development process, team members establish "drop" points where they will quit the development effort and redirect it if necessary. When the decision is made to quit, project managers are careful not to suggest that the group has failed but stress that what they have learned increases the chances that the next project will succeed to market.[5]

In sum, external adaptation involves answering important instrumental or goal—related questions concerning coping with reality: What is the real mission? How do we contribute? What are our goals? How do we reach our goals? What external forces are important? How do we measure results? What do we do if we do not meet specific targets? When do we quit?

Internal Integration A second important function of the organizational culture, **internal integration**, centers on the collective identity of members and how they live and work together.[6] The process of internal integration often begins with the establishment of a unique identity. Through dialogue and interaction, members begin to characterize their world. They may see it as malleable or fixed, filled with opportunities or threats. As with external adaptation, there are important issues. These include a series of membership issues: Who is a group member, what behavior is acceptable, who is a friend?

For all organizational members, the three most important aspects of working together are (1) deciding who is a member of the group and who is not, (2) developing an informal understanding of acceptable and unacceptable behavior, and (3) separating friends from enemies. Aetna, one of the nation's leading health care benefits companies, describes its corporate culture as one in which employees "work together openly, share information freely and build on each other's ideas to continually create the next better way. Nothing is impossible to our Aetna team. We are eager, ambitious learners and continuous innovators. And we are succeeding. Every day."[7]

To work together effectively, individuals need to decide collectively how to allocate power, status, and authority. They need to establish a shared understanding of who will get rewards and sanctions for specific types of actions. Too often, managers fail to recognize these important aspects of internal integration. A manager may fail, for example, to explain the basis for a promotion and to show why this reward, the status associated with it, and the power given to the newly promoted individual are consistent with commonly shared beliefs.

Organizations with More Engaged Employees Perform Better

The Gallup organization uses an "engagement ratio" as an indicator of organizational health. And research finds that engagement can have a big performance impact.

Data show that in the best organizations, actively engaged employees outnumber the disengaged ones by a ratio of 9.57 to 1. By contrast, the ratio falls to 1. 83 to 1 in average organizations.

The benefits derived from an actively engaged workforce extend to profitability, safety records, employee retention, and customer orientation. Gallup points out that in high-performing organizations "engagement is more than a human resources initiative—it is a strategic foundation for the way they do business."

Individuals also need to work out acceptable ways to communicate and develop guidelines for relationships at work. Although these aspects of internal integration may appear esoteric, they are vital. For example, to function effectively as a team, all must recognize that some members will be closer than others; friendships are inevitable.[8]

Resolving the issues of internal integration helps individuals develop a shared identity and a collective commitment. It may well lead to longer-term stability and provide a lens for members to make sense of their part of the world. In sum, internal integration involves answers to important questions associated with living together. What is our unique identity? How do we allocate power, status, and authority? How do we communicate? Answering these questions is important to organizational members because the organization is more than just a place to work.

Subcultures and Countercultures

Whereas smaller firms often have a single dominant culture with a universal set of shared actions, values, and beliefs, most larger organizations contain several subcultures as well as one or more countercultures.[9]

Subcultures **Subcultures** are groups of individuals who exhibit a unique pattern of values and a philosophy that is consistent with the organization's dominant values and philosophy.[10] Although subcultures are unique, their members' values do not clash with those of the larger organization. Strong subcultures are often found in task forces, teams, and special-project groups in organizations. The subculture emerges, binding individuals to work together intensely to accomplish a specific task. For example, there are strong subcultures of stress engineers and liaison engineers in the Boeing plant in Renton, Washington. These highly specialized groups must solve technical issues to ensure that Boeing planes are safe. Although they are distinct, these groups of engineers share in the core values at Boeing.

Countercultures In contrast, **countercultures** are groups whose patterns of values and philosophies reject those of the larger organization or social system.[11] The infamous story of Steve Jobs's return to Apple illustrates a counterculture. When Jobs returned to Apple as its CEO, he formed a counterculture within the company that did not follow the values and philosophies of the former CEO, Gil Amelio. Numerous clashes occurred as the followers of the former CEO fought to maintain their place in Apple and maintain the old culture. Job's counterculture took off and so did Apple. His counterculture became dominant, and the company has continued to thrive, even after his death.[12]

Every large organization imports subcultural groupings when it hires employees from the larger society. In North America, for instance, subcultures and countercultures may naturally form based on ethnic, racial, gender, generational, or locational similarities. In Japanese organizations, subcultures often form based on the date of graduation from a university, gender, or geographic location. In European firms, ethnicity and language play an important part in developing subcultures, as does gender.

Within an organization, mergers and acquisitions may produce adjustment problems for established subcultures and countercultures.[13] Employers and managers of an acquired firm may hold values and assumptions that are inconsistent with those of the acquiring firm. This is known as the "clash of corporate cultures." One example of culture clash occurred at Bank of America when it acquired Merrill Lynch, the Wall Street trading firm. Old-line bank employees objected to the huge bonuses given to traders in its new Merrill Lynch unit.[14]

National Culture and Corporate Culture

Most organizations originate in one national culture and incorporate many features from this host culture even when they expand internationally. The difference between Toyota's corporate emphasis on group achievements and Ford's emphasis on individual engineering excellence, for example, can be traced to the Japanese emphasis on collective action versus the U.S. emphasis on individualism. National cultural values may also become embedded in the expectations of organizational constituencies and in generally accepted solutions to problems.

When moving across cultures, managers need to be sensitive to cultural differences so that their actions do not violate common assumptions in the underlying national culture. To improve morale at General Electric's French subsidiary, Chi. Générale de Radiologie, American managers invited the European managers to a get-acquainted meeting near Paris. The Americans gave out colorful T-shirts for everyone to wear, embellished with the GE slogan "Go for One." One outspoken employee said, "It was like Hitler was back, forcing us to wear uniforms. It was humiliating."[15] Firms often face problems like this in developing strong ethical standards, particularly when they import societal subgroups.

Importing Societal Subgroups Beyond culturally sensitivity, difficulties often arise with importing groupings from the larger society. Some of these groupings are relevant to the organization, whereas others may be quite destructive. At the one extreme, senior managers can merely accept societal divisions and work within the confines of the larger culture. This approach presents three primary difficulties. First, subordinated groups, such as members of a specific religion or ethnic group, may form into a counterculture and to work more diligently to change their status than to better the firm. Second, the firm may find it difficult to cope with broader cultural changes. For instance, in the United States the treatment of women, ethnic minorities, and the disabled has changed dramatically over the last 20 years. Firms that don't change with the times and accept old customs and prejudices have experienced a greater loss of key personnel and increased communication difficulties, as well as greater interpersonal conflict, than have their more progressive counterparts. Third, firms that accept and build on natural divisions from a single larger culture may find it challenging to develop sound international operations. For example, some Japanese firms continue to experience difficulties adjusting to the equal treatment of women in their U.S. operations.[16]

Building on National Cultural Diversity At the other extreme, managers can work to eradicate all naturally occurring national subcultures and countercultures. Firms are struggling to develop what Taylor Cox calls the **multicultural organization**, a firm that values diversity but systematically works to block the transfer of societally based subcultures into the fabric of the organization.[17] Because Cox focuses on some problems unique to the United States, his prescription for change may not apply to organizations located in other countries with more homogeneous populations.

Cox suggests a five-step program for developing the multicultural organization. First, the organization should develop pluralism with the objective of multibased socialization. To accomplish this objective, members of different occurring groups need to educate one another to increase knowledge and information and to help eliminate stereotyping. Second, the firm should fully integrate its structure so that there is no direct relationship between a naturally occurring group and any particular job—for instance, there are no distinct male or female jobs. Third, the firm must integrate the informal networks by eliminating barriers and increasing participation— that is, it must break down existing societally based informal groups. Fourth, the organization should break the linkage between naturally occurring group identity and the identity of the firm. Finally, the organization must actively work to eliminate interpersonal conflict based on either the group identity or the backlash of the largest societally based grouping.

Understanding Organizational Cultures

Some aspects of organizational culture are easy to see. But not all aspects of organizational culture are readily apparent because they are buried deep in the shared experience of organizational members. It may take years to understand some deeper aspects of the culture. This complexity has led researchers to examine different layers of analysis ranging from easily observable to deeply hidden aspects of corporate culture.

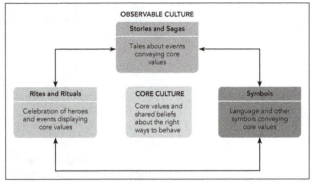

Layers of Cultural Analysis

■ **Figure 15.1** illustrates the observable aspects of culture, shared values, and underlying assumptions as three layers.[18] The deeper one digs, the more difficult it is to discover the culture but the more important an aspect becomes.

See **FIGURE 15.1 Three levels of analysis in studying organizational culture**

The first layer concerns **observable culture**, or "the way we do things around here." Important parts of an organization's culture emerge from the collective experience of its members. These emergent aspects of the culture help make it unique and may well provide a competitive advantage for the organization. Some of these aspects may be observed directly in day-to-day practices. Others may have to be discovered—for example, by asking members to tell stories of important incidents in the history of the organization. We often learn about the unique aspects of the organizational culture through descriptions of specific events.[19] By observing employee actions, listening to stories, and asking members to interpret what is going on, one can begin to understand the organization's culture. The observable culture includes the unique stories, ceremonies, and corporate rituals that make up the history of the firm or a group within the firm.

The second layer recognizes that shared values can play a critical part in linking together people and can provide a powerful motivational mechanism for members of the culture. Many consultants suggest that organizations should develop a "dominant and coherent set of shared values."[20] The term *shared* in cultural analysis implies that the group is a whole. Not every member of an organization may agree with the shared values, however, but they will continue to be exposed to them. At Microsoft, for example, a shared culture value is a passion for technology.

At the deepest layer of cultural analysis are common cultural assumptions. These are the taken-for-granted truths that collections of corporate members share as a result of their joint experience. It is often difficult to isolate these patterns, but doing so can help explain why culture invades every aspect of organizational life.

Stories, Rites, Rituals, and Symbols

To understand a corporate culture, it is often easiest to start with stories. Organizations are rich with tales of winners and losers, successes and failures. Perhaps one of the most important stories concerns the founding of the organization. The founding story often contains the lessons learned from the heroic efforts of an embattled entrepreneur, whose vision may still guide the firm. The story of the founding may be so embellished that it becomes a **saga**—a heroic account of accomplishments.[21] Sagas are important because they are used to tell new members the mission of the organization, how the organization operates, and how individuals can fit into the company. Rarely is the founding story totally accurate, and it often glosses over some of the more negative aspects of the founders.

Such is the case with Monterey Pasta[22] before it was purchased by a Korea-based holding company and its name was changed to Monterey Gourmet Foods. "The Monterey Pasta Company was launched from a 400-square-foot storefront on Lighthouse Avenue in Monterey, California in

1989. . . . The founders started their small fresh pasta company in response to the public's growing interest in healthy gourmet foods. Customers were increasingly excited about fresh pasta given its superior quality and nutritional value, as well as ease of preparation. . . . The company soon accepted its first major grocery account. . . . In 1993, the company completed its first public offering." An unsuccessful venture into the restaurant business in the mid-1990s provided a significant distraction, and substantial losses were incurred before the company refocused on its successful retail business. But why ruin a good founding story?

If you have job experience, you may have heard stories that address the following questions: How will the boss react to a mistake? Can someone move from the bottom to the top of the company? What will get me fired?[23] Often, the stories provide valuable but hidden information about who has the most power, whether or not jobs are secure, and how things are controlled within the organization. In essence, the stories begin to suggest how organizational members view the world and work together.

Some of the most obvious aspects of organizational culture are rites and rituals.[24] **Rites** are standardized and recurring activities that are used at special times to influence the behaviors and understanding of organizational members; **rituals** are systems of rites. It is common for Japanese workers and managers to start their workdays with group exercises and singing of the "company song." Separately, the exercises and song are rites. Together, they form part of a ritual. Another example is, Mary Kay Cosmetics, where scheduled ceremonies are reminiscent of the Miss America pageant (a ritual) and are used to spotlight positive work achievements and reinforce high-performance expectations with awards, including gold and diamond pins, and top performers are rewarded with a pink Cadillac.

Rituals and rites may be unique to particular groups within the organization. Subcultures often arise from the type of technology deployed by the unit, the function being performed, and the collection of specialists in the unit. A unique language may well maintain the boundaries of the subculture. Often, the language of a subculture, and its rituals and rites, emerge from the group as a form of jargon. In some cases, the special language starts to move outside the firm and begins to enter the larger society. For instance, look at Microsoft Word's specialized language, with such words as hyperlink, frames, and quick parts, that has become commonplace outside of the organization.

Another observable aspect of corporate culture centers on the symbols found in organizations. A **cultural symbol** is any object, act, or event that serves to transmit cultural meaning. Examples are the uniforms worn by UPS and Federal Express delivery personnel.

Cultural Rules and Roles

Organizational culture often specifies when various types of actions are appropriate and where individual members stand in the social system. These cultural rules and roles are part of the normative controls of the organization and emerge from its daily routines.[25] For instance, the timing, presentation, and methods of communicating authoritative directives are often quite specific to each organization. In one firm, meetings may follow a set rigid agenda. The manager could go into meetings to tell subordinates what to do and how to accomplish tasks. Private conversations prior to the meeting might be the place for any new ideas or critical examination. In other firms, meetings might be forums for dialogue and discussion, for which managers set agendas and then let others offer new ideas, critically examine alternatives, and fully participate.

Shared Values, Meanings, and Organizational Myths

To describe an organization's culture more fully, it is necessary to go deeper than the observable aspects. To many researchers and managers, shared common values lie at the very heart of organizational culture.

Shared Values Shared values help turn routine activities into valuable and important actions, tie the corporation to the important values of society, and possibly provide a distinctive source of competitive advantage. Important values are then attributed to these solutions to everyday problems. By linking values and actions, the organization taps into some of the strongest and deepest realms of the individual. The tasks a person performs are given not only meaning but also value.

Successful organizations often share common cultural characteristics.[26] Those with "strong cultures" possess a broad and deeply shared value system. Unique, shared values can provide a strong corporate identity, enhance collective commitment, provide a stable social system, and reduce the need for formal and bureaucratic controls. When consultants suggest that organizations develop strong cultures, they basically mean the following:[27]

- A widely shared understanding of what the organization stands for, often embodied in slogans
- A concern for individuals over rules, policies, procedures, and adherence to job duties
- A recognition of heroes whose actions illustrate the company's shared philosophy and concerns
- A belief in ritual and ceremony as important to members and to building a common identity
- A well-understood sense of the informal rules and expectations so that employees and managers understand what is expected of them
- A belief that what employees and managers do is important and that it is important to share information and ideas

A strong culture and value system can reinforce a singular and sometimes outdated view of the organization and its environment. If dramatic changes are needed, it may be very difficult to change the organization. For years General Motors had a strong culture. But as the global auto industry changed, GM did not. It took bankruptcy to shake it to its foundations and provide the impetus for radical change.

Shared Meanings When you are observing the actions within an organization, it is important to keep in mind the three levels of analysis discussed earlier. What you see as an outside observer may not be what organizational members experience because members may link actions to values and unstated assumptions. For instance, in the aftermath of the 9/11 terrorist attacks, a new building and its meaning are contested. Is it just another gleaming office tower or the Freedom Tower symbolizing the resilience of the American people and New York City's ability to recover from the attacks?[28]

In this sense, organizational culture is a "shared" set of meanings and perceptions. The members of most organizations create and learn a deeper aspect of their shared culture.[29] Often one finds a series of common assumptions known to most everyone: "We are different." "We are better at. . . ." "We have unrecognized talents." Cisco Systems provides an excellent example. Senior managers often share common assumptions, such as "We are good stewards" and "We are competent managers" and "We are practical innovators." Like values, such assumptions become reflected in the organizational culture. Of course, shared meanings and perceptions can create a double-edged sword. In his book *How Do the Mighty Fall,* consultant Jim Collins notes that organizations may begin to decline if managers share an unrealistic positive perception of them.[30]

Organizational Myths In many firms, a key aspect of the shared common assumptions involves organizational myths. **Organizational myths** are unproven and frequently unstated beliefs that are accepted without criticism. Often corporate mythology focuses on cause–effect relationships and assertions by senior management that cannot be empirically supported.[31] Although some may scoff at organizational myths and want to see rational analysis replace mythology, each firm needs a series of managerial myths.[32] Myths allow executives to redefine impossible problems into more manageable components. Myths can facilitate experimentation and creativity, and they allow managers to govern.

Managing Organizational Culture

The process of managing organizational culture is a complex challenge of the first order. A leader or manager must first understand the subculture at the top of the system be it the whole organization or just a department. A series of cascading goals from the societal contribution of the organization to the expectations for each unit and individual must be put into place. Once these goals are shared by all, reward systems consistent with the goals must be developed and consistently used to reward groups and individuals for the appropriate actions. This top-down view must also be accompanied by an understanding of the emergent aspects of organizational culture and a focus on helping individuals cope with the challenges of external adaptation and internal integration.

Direct Attempts to Change Values

Early research on culture and cultural change often emphasized direct attempts by senior management to alter the values and shared meanings of individuals by resocializing them—that is, trying to change their hearts so that their minds and actions would follow the desires of senior management.[33] Many top-level managers wanted all employees to adopt the organization's subculture in order to establish one clear, consistent organization-wide consensus. Key aspects of the top-down management subculture are often referred to in the OB literature by the term *management philosophy*. A **management philosophy** links important goals with key collaboration issues and comes up with a series of general ways by which the firm will manage its affairs.[34] Specifically, it (1) establishes generally understood boundaries for all members of the firm, (2) provides a consistent way of approaching new and novel situations, and (3) helps bond employees by ensuring them of a path toward success. In other words, it is the way in which top management addresses the questions of external adaptation.

More recent work suggests that this unified approach of working through the values of the top management subculture may not possible.[35] Although there are many reasons, two stand out. The first is that shared values and meanings evolve from the shared experiences, dialogue, and discussion of members, and that the "world" of top executives is often fundamentally different from the "world" of other employees. The second reason is that trying to change people's values from the top down without changing how the organization operates and rewards individuals and groups usually doesn't work.

In addition a narrowly diverse culture may not be desirable.[36] As the diversity of opinions values, and meaning in an organization narrows, it becomes more vulnerable to external change and less able to capitalize on external opportunities. The management philosophy at the top is often too narrow. For instance, recent research on the link between corporate culture and financial performance reaffirms the importance of helping employees adjust to the environment. And it suggests that a narrow emphasis is not sufficient. Neither is an emphasis solely on stockholders or customers associated with long-term economic performance. Instead, managers must emphasize responsiveness to competitive pressures, stockholder demands, and customer desires simultaneously.

Developing Shared Goals

One of the most powerful ways managers influence organizational culture is through commonly shared goals that are specific to the organization. The choice of specific goals often begins with the type of contribution the firm makes to society and the types of outputs it seeks.[37] Astute managers recognize that they should specify a desired set of internal conditions that can be used to evaluate progress.

Societal Goals, Output Goals, and Mission Statements Organizations normally serve a specific function or an enduring need of society. By emphasizing their contributions to the larger society, organizations gain legitimacy, a social right to operate, discretion to adopt non—societal goals, and freedom for operating practices. **Societal goals** represent an organization's intended contributions to the broader society.[38] By claiming to provide specific societal contributions, an organization can also make legitimate claims over resources, individuals, markets, and products. And a clear articulation of the organization's societal contribution can become a foundation for positively shared meanings and values.

For most organizations, the societal goals are just the beginning and lead to more detailed statements concerning their products and services. These product and service goals provide not only an important basis for judging the firm but also a common basis for members to evaluate the organization's progress. **Output goals** define the type of business an organization is in and provide some substance to the more general social contribution.

Often, the social contribution of the firm and its stated output goals are part of its mission statement. **Mission statements** are written statements of organizational purpose. Weaving a mission statement together with an emphasis on implementation to provide direction and motivation is an executive order of the first magnitude. A good mission statement, in addition to specifying outcomes, also includes whom the firm will serve and how it will go about accomplishing its societal purpose.[39]

We would expect to see the mission statement of a political party linked to generating and allocating power for the betterment of citizens. Mission statements for universities often profess to both develop and disseminate knowledge. Courts are expected to integrate the interests and activities of citizens. Finally, business firms are expected to provide economic sustenance and material well-being.[40] As managers consider how they will accomplish their firm's mission, many begin by clarifying with refined output goals which business they are in.[41] This refinement spells out how managers hope to deal with external adaptation. The refined mission often targets efforts toward a very specific group and recognizes secondary contributions to powerful outsiders[42]—that is, organizations have a primary beneficiary, but the refined mission also recognizes the interests of many other parties. For example, business mission statements often stress profitability to shareholders but recognize the organization's obligations to customers as well as its intention to support the community.

Systems Goals Managers also recognize that regardless of the mission or output goals, the organization needs to survive. **Systems goals** are concerned with the conditions within the organization that are expected to increase the organization's survival potential.[43] The list of systems goals is almost endless. For many organizations, however, the list includes growth, productivity, stability, harmony, flexibility, prestige, innovation, quality, and human-resource maintenance. Although technically market share and current profitability are not internal conditions, many businesses analysts consider them as important systems goals because of the link from profitability and market share to survival.

Systems goals must be balanced against one another and collectively present members with a natural tension among competing desires. For instance, a productivity and efficiency drive, if taken too far, may reduce the flexibility of an organization. To effectively manage the culture, systems goals must be well-defined, practical, and easy to understand. They must help focus attention on what should be done and provide a basis for employees to understand their contributions.

Modifying Visible Aspects of Culture

Beyond focusing on goals and reward systems, managers can modify the visible aspects of culture, such as the language, stories, rites, rituals, and sagas. Because of their positions, senior managers can interpret situations in new ways and can adjust the meanings attached to important corporate events. They can create new rites and rituals. Executives can support these initiatives with both words and actions. All of this takes time and an enormous amount of energy, but the long-run benefits can be great. For example, examine the actions of Christine Specht of Cousins Subs in the "Finding the Leader in You" feature.

Reinforcing Ethical Standards Although it seems obvious that managers at all levels need to establish and reinforce ethical cultural standards, in far too many cases this has not happened. The need to provide an ethics emphasis in managing culture can be seen when executives violate ethical and legal standards, as in the case of firms publishing misleading earning statements. One key study found that whereas the fines levied for "cooking the books" may appear small, other costs were far more substantial. The real costs to these firms came from a loss of their reputation in the business community. Customers lost confidence, suppliers demanded greater assurances, and the financial community undervalued the firm so that loan costs were higher, stock prices were lower, and scrutiny was more extensive. How big is big? The fines averaged about $23 million a firm. But the financial cost from the loss of reputation was estimated at 7.5 times the average fine. That yielded a loss of an average of $196 million.[44]

Modifying Reward Systems To change the culture, managers need to develop a new, powerful, and meaningful reward system. In many larger U.S.-based firms, the reward system matches the overall way the firm competes and reinforces the culture emerging from day-to-day activities. Two patterns are common. The first is a steady-state way of competing matched with hierarchical rewards and consistent with what can be labeled a clan culture. Specifically, rewards emphasize and reinforce a culture characterized by long-term commitment, fraternal relationships, mutual interests, and collegiality with heavy pressures to conform from peers, and with superiors acting as mentors. Firms with this pattern are in power generation, chemicals, mining, and pharmaceuticals industries.

In contrast is a second pattern in which the firm competes by stressing evolution and change. Here the rewards emphasize and reinforce a more market culture. That is, rewards emphasize a contractual link between employee and employer, focus on short-term performance, and stress individual initiative with little pressure from peers to conform, and with supervisors acting as resource allocators. Firms with this pattern are often in restaurants, consumer products, and industrial services industries.[45]

WP LS Go to your WileyPLUS Learning Space course for video episodes, examples, art, tables, Concept Checks, practice, and resources that will help you succeed in this course.

16

Reading for

ORGANIZATIONAL STRUCTURE AND DESIGN

Formal Organizational Structure

Once the goals of an organization are clear, managers must decide how to organize work to accomplish these goals.[1] The static aspect of the process is known as organizational structure. Specifically, the formal structure of an organization outlines the jobs to be done, the people who are to perform specific activities, and the ways the tasks of the organization are to be accomplished. In other words, the formal structure is the skeleton of the firm.[2]

The formal structure shows the planned pattern of positions, job duties, and the lines of authority among different parts of the company. Traditionally, the formal structure of the firm also has been called the division of labor. This terminology is still used to isolate decisions concerning formal structure from choices regarding the division of markets and/or technology. We will deal with environmental and technology issues after we discuss the structure as a foundation for managerial action.

Organizations as Hierarchies

In most organizations, there is a clear separation of authority and duties by rank. How authority is specialized is known as vertical specialization. **Vertical specialization** is an organization's hierarchical division of labor that distributes formal authority and establishes where and how critical decisions will be made. This division creates a hierarchy of authority—an arrangement of work positions in order of increasing authority.[3]

See **FIGURE 16.1 A partial organization chart for a state university**

The Organization Chart Organization charts are diagrams that depict the formal structures of organizations. A typical chart shows the various positions, the position holders, and the lines of authority that link them to one another. **Figure 16.1** presents a partial organization chart for a large university. The chart allows university employees to locate their positions in the structure and to identify the lines of authority linking them with others in the organization. For instance, in this figure, the treasurer reports to the vice president of administration, who, in turn, reports to the president of the university.

Although an organization chart may indicate who each employee reports to, it is also important to recognize that it does not show how work is completed, who exercises the most power over specific issues, or how the firm will respond to its environment. However, organization charts can be important to the extent that they accurately represent the chain of command, a listing of who reports to whom up and down the firm's hierarchy and shows how executives, managers, and supervisors are connected. Traditional management theory suggests that each individual should have one boss, and each unit should have one leader. Under these circumstances, there is a unity of command which is necessary to avoid confusion, assign accountability to specific individuals, and provide clear channels of communication throughout the organization.

Span of Control The number of individuals reporting to a supervisor is called the **span of control**. Narrower spans of control are expected when tasks are complex, when subordinates are inexperienced or poorly trained, or when tasks call for team effort. Unfortunately, narrow spans of control yield many organizational levels. The excessive number of levels is not only expensive, but it also makes the organization unresponsive to necessary change. Communications often becomes less effective because information is successively screened and modified and subtle but important changes can be ignored. When organizations have many levels, managers can get too far removed from the action and become isolated. Conversely with too few levels, organizations may experience coordination and control problems and managers are subject to burnout.

Line and Staff Units A useful way to examine the vertical division of labor is to separate line and staff units. **Line units** and personnel conduct the major business of the organization. The production and marketing functions are two examples. In contrast, **staff units** and personnel assist the line units by providing specialized expertise and services, such as accounting and public relations. For example, the vice president of administration in a university (see Figure 16.1) heads a staff unit, as does the vice president of student affairs.

Staff units can be assigned predominantly to senior-, middle-, or lower-level managers. When staff is assigned predominantly to senior management, the capability of senior management to develop alternatives and make decisions and monitor progress is expanded.

Centralization and Decentralization

Organizations differ in how vertical specialization plays out in everyday practices. An important point of difference is the distribution of authority to make important decisions. Is it concentrated at the top of the hierarchy or more broadly distributed among organizational levels?[4]

Centralization The farther up the hierarchy of authority the discretion to spend money, to hire people, and to make similar decisions is moved, the greater the degree of **centralization**. Greater centralization is often adopted when an organization faces a single major threat to its survival. It is little wonder that armies tend to be centralized and that firms facing bankruptcy increase centralization. Recent research even suggests that governmental agencies may improve their performance via centralization when in a defensive mode.[5]

Decentralization The more decisions are delegated, or moved down the hierarchy of authority, the greater the degree of **decentralization**. Greater decentralization generally provides higher subordinate satisfaction and a quicker response to a diverse series of unrelated problems. Decentralization also assists in the on-the-job training of subordinates for higher-level positions. Decentralization is now a popular approach in many industries.[6] For instance, Union Carbide is pushing responsibility down the chain of command, as are SYSCO and Hewlett-Packard. In each case, the senior managers hope to improve both performance quality and organizational responsiveness.

Closely related to decentralization is the notion of participation. Many people want to be involved in making decisions that affect their work. Participation results when a manager delegates some authority for such decision making to subordinates. For example, Macy's has successfully experimented with moving decisions down the chain of command and increasing employee participation. In many cases, employees want a say both in what the unit objectives should be and in how they can be achieved.

Organizing and Coordinating Work

Managers must divide the total task into separate duties and group similar people and resources together.[7] Organizing work is formally known as **horizontal specialization**, which is a division of labor that establishes specific work units or groups within an organization. This aspect of the organization is also called departmentation. Whatever is divided horizontally into two or more departments must also be integrated.[8] **Coordination** is the set of mechanisms that an organization uses to link the actions of its units into a consistent pattern. This includes mechanisms to connect managers and staff units, operating units, and divisions with each other. Managers use a mix of personal and impersonal methods of coordination to tie together the efforts of departments.

Traditional Types of Departments

Since the pattern of departmentation is so visible and important in a firm, managers often refer to their pattern of departmentation as the departmental structure. Although most firms use a mix of various types of departments, it is important to look at the traditional types and what they do and do not provide the firm.[9]

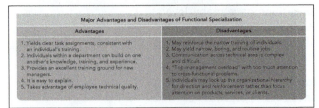

Major Advantages and Disadvantages of Functional Specialization

Advantages	Disadvantages
1. Yields clear task assignments, consistent with an individual's training.	1. May reinforce the narrow training of individuals.
2. Individuals within a department can build on one another's knowledge, training, and experience.	2. May yield narrow, boring, and routine jobs.
3. Provides an excellent training ground for new managers.	3. Communication across technical area is complex and difficult.
4. It is easy to explain.	4. "Top-management overload" with too much attention to cross-functional problems.
5. Takes advantage of employee technical quality.	5. Individuals may look up the organizational hierarchy for direction and reinforcement rather than focus attention on products, services, or clients.

See **FIGURE 16.2**
Major advantages and disadvantages of functional specialization

Functional Departments Grouping individuals by skill, knowledge, and action yields a pattern of **functional departmentation**. Recall that Figure 16.1 shows the partial organization chart for a large university in which each department has a technical specialty. Marketing, finance, production, and personnel are important functions in business. In many small companies, this functional pattern dominates. Even large organizations use this pattern in technically demanding areas. 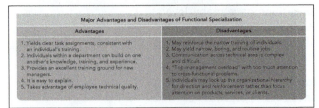 **Figure 16.2** summarizes the advantages and disadvantages of the functional pattern.

With all of these advantages, it is not surprising that the functional form is popular. It is used in most organizations, particularly toward the bottom of the hierarchy. The extensive use of functional departments does have some disadvantages. Organizations that rely heavily on functional specialization may expect the following tendencies to emerge over time: an emphasis on quality from a technical standpoint, rigidity to change, and difficulty in coordinating the actions of different functional areas.

Divisional Departments With **divisional departments**, individuals and resources are grouped by products, territories, services, clients, or legal entities. A divisional pattern is often used to meet diverse external threats and opportunities. As shown in 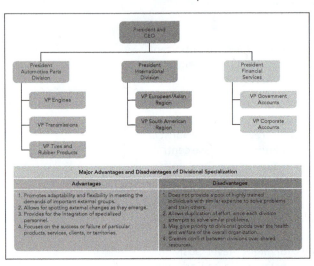 **Figure 16.3**, the major advantages of the divisional pattern are its flexibility in meeting external demands, spotting external changes, integrating specialized individuals deep within the organization, and focusing on the delivery of specific products to specific customers. Among its disadvantages are duplication of effort by function, the tendency for divisional goals to be placed above corporate interests, and conflict among divisions. It is also not the structure most desired for training individuals in technical areas. Firms relying on this pattern may fall behind technically to competitors with a functional pattern.

Major Advantages and Disadvantages of Divisional Specialization

Advantages	Disadvantages
1. Promotes adaptability and flexibility in meeting the demands of important external groups.	1. Does not provide a pool of highly trained individuals with similar expertise to solve problems and train others.
2. Allows for spotting external changes as they emerge.	2. Allows duplication of effort, since each division attempts to solve similar problems.
3. Provides for the integration of specialized personnel.	3. May give priority to divisional goods over the health and welfare of the overall organization.
4. Focuses on the success or failure of particular products, services, clients, or territories.	4. Creates conflict between divisions over shared resources.

See **FIGURE 16.3**
A divisional pattern of departmentation and the advantages and disadvantages of divisional specialization

Many larger, geographically dispersed organizations that sell to national and international markets may rely on departmentation by geography. The savings in time, effort, and travel can be substantial, and each territory can adjust to regional differences. Organizations that rely on a few major customers may organize their people and resources by client. Here, the idea is to focus attention on the needs of the individual customer. To the extent that customer needs are unique, departmentation by customer can also reduce confusion and increase synergy. Organizations expanding internationally may also form divisions to meet the demands of complex host-country ownership requirements. For example, NEC, Sony, Nissan, and many other Japanese corporations have developed U.S. divisional subsidiaries to service their customers in the U.S. market. Some European-based corporations such as Philips and Nestlé have also adopted a divisional structure in their expansion to the United States.

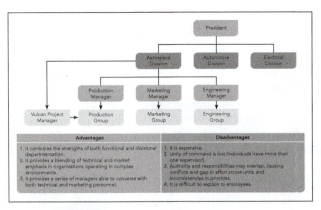

Advantages	Disadvantages
1. It combines the strengths of both functional and divisional departmentation.	1. It is expensive.
2. It provides a blending of technical and market emphasis in organizations operating in complex environments.	2. Unity of command is lost (individuals have more than one supervisor).
3. It provides a series of managers able to converse with both technical and marketing personnel.	3. Authority and responsibilities may overlap, causing conflicts and gap in effort across units and inconsistencies in priorities.
	4. It is difficult to explain to employees.

See **FIGURE 16.4**
A matrix pattern of departmentation in an aerospace division

Matrix Structures Originally from the aerospace industry, a third unique form of departmentation is called the matrix structure.[10] In aerospace efforts, projects are technically complex, involving hundreds of subcontractors located throughout the world. Precise integration and control are needed across many functional specialties and corporations. This is often more than a functional or divisional structure can provide, for many firms do not want to trade the responsiveness of the divisional form for the technical emphasis provided by the functional form. Therefore, **matrix departmentation** uses both the functional and divisional forms simultaneously. 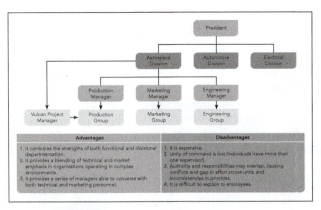 **Figure 16.4** shows the basic matrix arrangement for an aerospace program. Note the functional departments on one side and the project efforts on the other. Workers and supervisors in the middle of the matrix have two bosses—one functional and one project manager.

Figure 16.4 summarizes the major advantages and disadvantages of the matrix form of departmentation. The key disadvantage of the matrix method is the loss of unity of command. Individuals can be unsure as to what their jobs are, who they report to for specific activities, and how various managers are to administer the effort. It can also be an expensive method because it relies on individual managers to coordinate efforts deep within the firm. Despite these limitations, the matrix structure provides a balance between functional and divisional concerns. Many problems can be resolved at the working level, where the balance among technical, cost, customer, and organizational concerns can be dealt with effectively.

Which form of departmentation should be used? As the matrix concept suggests, it is possible to departmentalize by two different methods at the same time. Actually, companies often use a mixture of departmentation forms. It is often desirable to divide the effort (group people and resources) by two methods at the same time in order to balance the advantages and disadvantages of each. These mixed forms help organizations use their division of labor to capitalize on environmental opportunities, capture the benefits of larger size, and realize the potential of new technologies in pursuit of its strategy.

Coordination

Whatever is divided up horizontally in two departments should also be integrated.[11] Coordination, as noted previously, is the set of mechanisms that an organization uses to link the actions of its units into a consistent pattern. Coordination is needed at all levels of management, not just across a few scattered units. Much of the coordination within a unit is handled by its manager. Smaller organizations may rely on their management hierarchy to provide the necessary consistency and integration.

Personal Methods of Coordination Personal methods of coordination produce synergy by promoting dialogue and discussion, innovation, creativity, and learning, both within and across organizational units. Personal methods allow the organization to address the needs of distinct units and individuals simultaneously. There is a wide variety of personal methods of coordination.[12] Perhaps the most popular is direct contact between and among organizational members. As new information technologies have moved into practice, the potential for developing and maintaining effective contact networks has expanded. For example, many executives use electronic communication to supplement direct personal communication. Direct personal contact is also associated with the ever—present "grapevine." Although the grapevine is notoriously inaccurate in its role as a rumor mill, it is often accurate and quick enough that managers cannot ignore it. Instead, managers need to work with and supplement the rumor mill with accurate information.

Managers are often assigned to committees in order to improve coordination across departments. Committees can be effective in communicating complex qualitative information and in helping managers whose units must work together to adjust schedules, workloads, and work assignments to increase productivity.

The appropriate mix of personal coordination methods, and tailoring them to the individual skills, abilities, and experience of subordinates, also varies with the type of task. As the "Research Insight" feature suggests, a variety of personal methods can be tailored to match different individuals and the settings in which they operate. Personal methods are only one important part of coordination. The manager may also establish a series of impersonal mechanisms.

Impersonal Methods of Coordination Impersonal methods of coordination produce synergy by stressing consistency and standardization so that individual pieces fit together. Impersonal coordination methods are often refinements and extensions of process controls with an emphasis on formalization and standardization. Organizations often have written policies and procedures, such as schedules, budgets, and plans that are designed to mesh the operations of several units into a whole by providing predictability and consistency.

Managers often institute controls under the title of coordination. Since some of the techniques are used for both, many managers suggest that all efforts at control are for coordination. It is extremely important to separate these two functions because the reactions to controls and coordination are different. The underlying logic of control involves setting targets, measuring performance, and taking corrective action to meet goals normally assigned by higher management. Many employees see an increase in controls as a threat based on a presumption that they have been doing something wrong. The logic of coordination is to get unit actions and interactions meshed together into a unified whole. Although control involves the vertical exercise of formal authority, coordination stresses cooperative problem solving. Experienced employees recognize the difference between controls and coordination regardless of what their manager calls it.[13] Increasing controls rarely solves problems of coordination, and emphasizing coordination to solve control issues rarely works.

Organizational Design

Organizational design is the process of choosing and implementing a structural configuration.[14] It goes beyond indicating who reports to whom and what types of jobs are contained in each department. The design process takes the basic structural elements and molds them to the company's desires, demands, constraints, and choices. When managers chose their overall approach to reaching their mission, the choice of an appropriate organizational design is contingent on several factors, including the size of the organization, its operations and information technology, and its environment.

An effective organizational design reflects powerful external forces as well as size and technological factors. Organizations, as open systems, need to receive input from the environment and in turn to sell output to their environment. Therefore, understanding the environment is important.[15]

Environment and Organizational Design

The general environment is the set of cultural, economic, legal–political, and educational conditions found in the areas in which the organization operates. Firms expanding globally encounter multiple general environments.

The owners, suppliers, distributors, government agencies, and competitors with which an organization must interact in order to grow and survive constitute its specific environment. A firm typically has much more choice in the composition of its specific environment than its general environment. Although it is often convenient to separate the general and specific environmental influences on the firm, managers need to recognize the combined impact of both.

Environmental Complexity A basic concern to address when analyzing the environment of the organization is its complexity. A more complex environment provides an organization with more opportunities and more problems. **Environmental complexity** refers to the magnitude of the problems and opportunities in the organization's environment, as evidenced by three main factors: the degree of richness, the degree of interdependence, and the degree of uncertainty stemming from both the general and the specific environment.

Environmental Richness Overall, the environment is richer when the economy is growing, when individuals are improving their education, and when everyone that the organization relies on is prospering. For businesses, a richer environment means that economic conditions are improving, customers are spending more money, and suppliers (especially banks) are willing to invest in the organization's future. In a rich environment, more organizations survive, even if they have poorly functioning organizational designs. A richer environment is also filled with more opportunities and dynamism—the potential for change. The organizational design must allow the company to recognize these opportunities and capitalize on them. The opposite of richness is decline. For most business firms, recession is a good example of a leaner environment.

Environmental Interdependence The link between external interdependence and organizational design is often subtle and indirect. The organization may co-opt powerful outsiders by including them. For instance, many large companies have financial representatives from banks and insurance companies on their boards of directors.

The organization may also adjust its overall design strategy to absorb or buffer the demands of a more powerful external element. Perhaps the most common adjustment is the development of a centralized staff department to handle an important external group. Few large U.S. corporations lack some type of centralized governmental relations group.[16]

Uncertainty and Volatility Environmental uncertainty and volatility can be particularly damaging to large organizations. In times of change, investments quickly become outmoded, and internal operations no longer work as expected. The organizational design response to uncertainty and volatility is to opt for a more flexible organic form. At the extremes, movement toward an adhocracy may be important. However, these pressures may run counter to those that come from large size and operations technology. In these cases, it may be too hard or too time consuming for some organizations to make the design adjustments. The organization may continue to struggle while adjusting its design just a little bit at a time. Some firms can deal with the conflicting demands from environmental change and need for internal stability by developing alliances.

Bureaucracy and Mechanistic Structures

Modern complex societies are not just dominated by organizations but contain a number of large powerful organizations know as *bureaucracies*. In OB this term has a special meaning, beyond its negative connotation. The German sociologist Max Weber suggested that organizations would thrive if they became bureaucracies by emphasizing legal authority, logic, and order.[17] Ideally, **bureaucracies** rely on a division of labor, hierarchical control, promotion by merit with career opportunities for employees, and administration by rule.

Weber argued that the rational and logical idea of bureaucracy was superior to building the firm based on charisma or cultural tradition. The "charismatic" ideal-type organization was overly reliant on the talents of one individual and could fail when the leader leaves. Too much reliance on cultural traditions blocked innovation, stifled efficiency, and was often unfair. Since the bureaucracy prizes efficiency, order, and logic, Weber hoped that it could also be fair to employees and provide more freedom for individual expression than is allowed when tradition dominates or dictators rule. Many interpreted Weber as suggesting that bureaucracy or some variation of this ideal form, although far from perfect, would dominate modern society.[18] For large organizations, the bureaucratic form is predominant. Yet, the bureaucracy poses a series of challenges for managers, including the following:

- Overspecialization with conflicts between highly specialized units
- Overreliance on the chain of command rather than bottom-up problem solving
- Objectification of senior executives as rulers rather than problem solvers for others
- Overemphasis on conformity
- Rules as ends in and of themselves

Just as interpretations of Weber have evolved over time, so has the notion of a bureaucracy.[19] We will discuss some popular basic types of bureaucracies: the mechanistic structure and machine bureaucracy, the organic structure and professional bureaucracy, and some hybrid approaches. Each type is a different mix of the basic elements discussed in this chapter, and each mix yields firms with a slightly different blend of capabilities and natural tendencies.

The **mechanistic (or machine) type of bureaucracy** emphasizes vertical specialization and control.[20] Organizations of this type stress rules, policies, and procedures; specify techniques for decision making; and emphasize developing well-documented control systems backed by a strong middle management and supported by a centralized staff. There is often extensive use of the functional pattern of departmentation throughout the company. Henry Mintzberg uses the term *machine bureaucracy* to describe an organization structured in this manner.[21]

The mechanistic design results in a management emphasis on routine for efficiency. Firms often used this design in pursuing a strategy of becoming a low-cost leader. Until the implementation of new information systems, most large-scale firms in basic industries were machine bureaucracies. Included in this long list were all of the auto firms, banks, insurance companies, steel mills, large retail establishments, and government offices. Efficiency was achieved through extensive vertical and horizontal specialization tied together with elaborate controls and impersonal coordination mechanisms.

There are, however, limits to the benefits of specialization backed by rigid controls. Employees generally do not like rigid designs, so motivation becomes a problem. Unions further solidify narrow job descriptions by demanding fixed work rules and regulations to protect employees from the extensive vertical controls. In short, using a machine bureaucracy can hinder an organization's capacity to adjust to subtle external changes or new technologies.

Organic Structures and the Professional Bureaucracy

The **organic (or professional) type of bureaucracy** is less vertically oriented than its mechanistic counterpart is; it emphasizes horizontal specialization. Procedures are minimal, and those that do exist are not as formalized. The organization relies on the judgments of experts and personal means of coordination. When controls are used, they are often based on professional standards, training, and individual reinforcement. Staff units are placed toward the middle of the organization. Because this is a popular design in professional firms, Mintzberg calls it a professional bureaucracy.[22]

Your university is probably a professional bureaucracy that looks like a broad, flat pyramid with a large bulge in the center for the professional staff. Power in this ideal type rests with knowledge. Other examples of organic types include most hospitals and social service agencies.

Compared to the machine bureaucracy, the professional bureaucracy is better for problem solving and for serving individual customer needs. Since lateral relations and coordination are emphasized, centralized direction by senior management is less intense. This type is good at detecting external changes and adjusting to new technologies, but at the sacrifice of responding to central management direction. Firms using this pattern have found it easier to pursue product quality, quick response to customers, and innovation as strategies.

Hybrid Structures

Many large firms have found that neither the mechanistic nor the organic approach is suitable for all of their operations. Adopting a machine bureaucracy overloads senior management and yields too many levels of management. Yet, adopting an organic type would mean losing control and becoming too inefficient. Senior managers may opt for one of a number of hybrid types.

We have briefly introduced two of the more common hybrid types. One is an extension of the divisional pattern of departmentation and is sometimes called a divisional firm. Here, the firm is composed of quasi-independent divisions so that different divisions can be more or less organic or mechanistic. Although the divisions may be treated as separate businesses, they often share a similar mission and systems goals.[23] When adopting this hybrid type, each division can pursue a different strategy.

A second hybrid is the true conglomerate. A **conglomerate** is a single corporation that contains a number of unrelated businesses. On the surface, these firms look like divisionalized firms, but when the various businesses of the divisions are unrelated, the term *conglomerate* is applied.[24] For instance, General Electric is a conglomerate that has divisions in unrelated businesses and industries, ranging from producing light bulbs, to designing and servicing nuclear reactors, to building jet engines. Most state and federal entities are also, by necessity, conglomerates. For instance, a state governor is the chief executive officer of those units concerned with higher education, welfare, prisons, highway construction and maintenance, police, and the like.

The conglomerate type illustrates three important points about organization structures. First, all structures are combinations of the basic elements. Second, no one structure is always best. What is best is situational and depends on a number of factors such as the size of the organization, its environment, its technology, and, of course, the goals it pursues. Third, no organization stands alone. It is always part of a larger complex network of other organizations and stakeholders.

WP LS Go to your **WileyPLUS Learning Space** course for video episodes, examples, art, tables, Concept Checks, practice, and resources that will help you succeed in this course.

Endnotes

Chapter 1

[1] "Unlock the Potential in All Your People," *Bloomberg BusinessWeek* (January 28–February 3, 2013), p. 63.

[2] "The Rise of Social Business," *Wall Street Journal* (January 30, 2013), p. A14.

[3] For historical foundations see Jay A. Conger, *Winning 'Em Over: A New Model for Managing in the Age of Persuasion* (New York: Simon & Schuster, 1998), pp. 180–181; Stewart D. Friedman, Perry Christensen, and Jessica DeGroot, "Work and Life: The End of the Zero-Sum Game," *Harvard Business Review* (November/December 1998), pp. 119–129; and C. Argyris, "Empowerment: The Emperor's New Clothes," *Harvard Business Review* (May/June 1998), pp. 98–105.

[4] For a general overview see Jay W. Lorsch (ed.), *Handbook of Organizational Behavior* (Englewood Cliffs, NJ: Prentice Hall, 1987); and Julian Barling, Cary Li Cooper, and Stewart Clegg (eds.), *The Sage Handbook of Organizational Behavior,* Volumes 1 and 2 (San Francisco: Sage, 2009).

[5] Jeffrey Pfeffer and Robert I. Sutton, *Hard Facts, Dangerous Half-Truths, and Total Nonsense: Profiting from Evidence-Based Management* (Boston: Harvard Business School Press, 2006). See also Jeffrey Pfeffer and Robert I. Sutton, "Management Half-Truths and Nonsense," *California Management Review* 48.3 (2006), pp. 77–100; and Jeffrey Pfeffer and Robert I. Sutton, "Evidence-Based-Management," *Harvard Business Review* (January 2006), R0601E.

[6] Geert Hofstede, "Cultural Constraints in Management Theories," *Academy of Management Executive* 7 (1993), pp. 81–94.

[7] For a discussion of experiential learning, see D. Christopher Kayes, "Experiential Learning and Its Critics: Preserving the Role of Experience in Management Learning and Education," *Academy of Management Learning and Education* 1.2 (2002), pp. 137–149.

[8] "Leading through Connections," IBM Institute for Business Value, accessed June 5, 2013, at www-01.ibm.com/software/solutions/soa/newsletter/june12/leading_connections.html.

[9] Rajiv Dutta, "eBay's Meg Whitman on Building a Company's Culture," *Business Week* (March 27, 2009), accessed June 5, 2013, at www.businessweek.com/managing/content/mar2009/ca20090327_626373.htm.

[10] R. Roosevelt Thomas Jr., *Beyond Race and Gender* (New York: AMACOM, 1992), p. 10. See also R. Roosevelt Thomas Jr., "From 'Affirmative Action' to 'Affirming Diversity,'" *Harvard Business Review* (November/December 1990), pp. 107–117; and R. Roosevelt Thomas Jr., with Marjorie I. Woodruff, *Building a House for Diversity: A Fable About a Giraffe & an Elephant Offers New Strategies for Today's Workforce* (New York: AMACOM, 1999).

[11] A baseline report on diversity in the American workplace is *Workforce 2000: Work and Workers in the 21st Century* (Indianapolis, IN: Hudson Institute, 1987). For comprehensive discussions, see Martin M. Chemers, Stuart Oskamp, and Mark A. Costanzo, *Diversity in Organization: New Perspectives for a Changing Workplace* (Beverly Hills, CA: Sage, 1995); and Robert T. Golembiewski, *Managing Diversity in Organizations* (Tuscaloosa: University of Alabama Press, 1995).

[12] See Taylor Cox Jr., "The Multicultural Organization," *Academy of Management Executive* 5 (1991), pp. 34–47; *Cultural Diversity in Organizations: Theory, Research and Practice* (San Francisco: Berrett-Koehler, 1993).

[13] "In CEO Pay, Another Gender Gap." *BusinessWeek* (November 24, 2008), p. 22; "The View from the Kitchen Table," *Newsweek* (January 26, 2009), p. 29; Del Jones, "Women Slowly Gain on Men," *USA Today* (January 2, 2009), p. 6B; Catalyst research reports at www.catalyst.org; and "Nicking the Glass Ceiling," *BusinessWeek* (June 9, 2009), p. 18.

[14] "We're Getting Old," *Wall Street Journal* (March 26, 2009), p. D2; and Les Christie, "Hispanic Population Boom Fuels Rising U.S. Diversity," accessed June 5, 2013, at www.cnn.com/2009/US/05/14/money.census.diversity; and Betsy Towner, "The New Face of 501 America," *AARP Bulletin* (June 2009), p. 31. "Los U.S.A.: Latino Population Grows Faster, Spreads Wider," *Wall Street Journal* (March 25, 2011), p. A1; and, Laura Meckler, "Hispanic Future in the Cards," *Wall Street Journal* (December 13, 2012), p. A3. See also U.S. Census Bureau reports at www.factfinder.census.gov.

[15] Thomas and Woodruff, *Building a House for Diversity* (1999).

[16] Conor Dougherty, "Strides by Women, Still a Wage Gap," *Wall Street Journal* (March 1, 2011), p. A3; Jones, op. cit.; Catalyst research reports, op. cit.; Women in Top Jobs; Information from Del Jones, "Women Slowly Gain on Corporate America," *USA Today* (January 2, 2009), p. 6B; "Catalyst 2008 Census of the Fortune 500 Reveals Women Gained Little Ground Advancing to Business Leadership Positions," *Catalyst Press Release* (December 8, 2008).

[17] William M. Bulkeley, "Xerox Names Burns Chief as Mulcahy Retires Early," *Wall Street Journal* (May 22, 2009), pp. B1, B2.

[18] Henry Mintzberg, The Nature of Managerial Work (New York: Harper & Row, 1973). See also Henry Mintzberg, *Mintzberg on Management* (New York: Free Press, 1989); and Henry Mintzberg, "Rounding Out the Manager's Job," *Sloan Management Review* (Fall 1994), pp. 11–26.

[19] Robert L. Katz, "Skills of an Effective Administrator, *Harvard Business Review* 52 (September/October 1974), p. 94. See also Richard E. Royatzis, *The Competent Manager: A Model for Effective Performance* (New York: Wiley, 1982).

[20] Daniel Goleman, *Emotional Intelligence* (New York: Bantam, 1995); Daniel Goleman, *Working with Emotional Intelligence* (New York: Bantam, 1998). See also Daniel Goleman, "What Makes a Leader," *Harvard Business Review* (November/December 1998), pp. 93–102; and Daniel Goleman, "Leadership That Gets Results," *Harvard Business Review* (March/April 2000), pp. 79–90, quote from p. 80.

[21] John P. Kotter, "What Effective General Managers Really Do," *Harvard Business Review* 60 (November/December 1982), p. 161.

[22] Herminia Ibarra, "Managerial Networks," Teaching Note: 9-495-039, Boston: Harvard Business School Publishing.

[23] Archie B. Carroll, "In Search of the Moral Manager," *Business Horizons* (March/April 2001), pp. 7–15.

[24] See Mahzarin R. Banagji, Max H. Bazerman, and Dolly Chugh, "How (Un)ethical Are You?" *Harvard Business Review* (December 2003), pp. 56–64.

[25] Terry Thomas, John R. Schermerhorn Jr., and John W. Dinehart, "Strategic Leadership of Ethical Behavior in Business," *Academy of Management Executive* (2004), pp. 56–66.

Chapter 2

[1] See, for example, S. E. Jackson, K. E. May, and K. Whitney, "Understanding the Dynamics of Diversity in Decision-Making Teams," pp. 204–261, in Richard A. Guzzo and Eduardo Salas (eds.) *Team Decision-Making Effectiveness in Organizations* (San Francisco: Jossey-Bass, 2005); Kenneth H. Price, and Myrtle P. Bell, "Beyond Relational Demography: Time and the Effects of Surface- and Deep-Level Diversity on Work Group Cohesion," *Academy of Management Journal*. 41 (1998), pp. 96–107; and Kenneth H. Price, Joanne H. Gavin, and Anna T. Florey, "Time, Teams, and Task Performance: Changing Effects of Surface- and Deep-Level Diversity on Group Functioning," *Academy of Management Journal* 45 (2002), pp. 1029–1045.

[2] Information from "Women and Work: We Did It!" *Economist* (December 31, 2009).

[3] Information from Eric Shurenberg, "Salary Gap: Men vs. Women," March 10, 2010, accessed June 10, 2013, at www.cbsnews.com/video/watch/?id=10397821n.

[4] Information from "Racism in Hiring Remains, Study Says," *The Columbus Dispatch* (January 17, 2003), p. B2.

[5] Viktor Gecas, "The Self-Concept," in *Annual Review of Sociology* 8, Ralph H. Turner and James F. Short Jr. (eds.), (Palo Alto, CA: Annual Review, 1982), p. 3. Also see Arthur P. Brief and Ramon J. Aldag, "The Self in Work Organizations: A Conceptual Review," *Academy of Management Review* (January 1981), pp. 75–88; and Jerry J. Sullivan, "Self Theories and Employee Motivation," *Journal of Management* (June 1989), pp. 345–363.

[6] Based in part on a definition in Gecas, 1982, p. 3.

[7] See N. Brody, *Personality: In Search of Individuality* (San Diego, CA: Academic Press, 1988), pp. 68–101; and C. Holden, "The Genetics of Personality," *Science* (August 7, 1987), pp. 598–601.

[8] Laura B. Shrestha and Elayne J. Heisler, *The Changing Demographic Profile of the United States*, CRS Report for Congress (Washington, DC: Congressional Research Service 7-5700, March 31, 2011); "Los USA: Latin Population Grows Faster, Spreads Wider," *Wall Street Journal* (March 25, 2011), p. A1; and, Laura Melcker, "Hispanic Future in the Cards," *Wall Street Journal* (December 13, 2012), p. A3.

[9] Rob McInnes, "Workforce Diversity: Changing the Way You Do Business," (1999), accessed June 10, 2013, at www.diversityworld.com/Diversity/workforce_diversity.htm.

[10] Ibid.

[11] See for example Judith B. Rosener, "Women Make Good Managers. So What?" *BusinessWeek* (December 11, 2000), p. 24. Also see P. E. Jacob, J. J. Flink, and H. L. Schuchman, "Values and Their Function in Decision Making," *American Behavioral Scientist* 5, suppl. 9 (1962), pp. 6–38.

[12] "Racism in Hiring Remains, Study Says," op. cit., 2003.

[13] See Lois Joy, "Advancing Women Leaders: The Connection Between Women Corporate Board Directors and Women Corporate Officers." Catalyst.org (July 15, 2008), accessed June 10, 2013, at www.catalyst.org/knowledge/advancing-women-leaders-connection-between-women-board-directors-and-women-corporate.

[14] See Lynda Gratton, Elisabeth Kelan, and Lamia Walker, "Inspiring Women: Corporate Best Practice in Europe," London: London Business School, The Lehman Brothers Centre for Women in Business (2007), accessed June 10, 2013, at http://communications.london.edu/aem/clients/LBS001/docs/lehman/May_2007_Corporate_Best_Practice.pdf.

[15] See "The Double-Bind Dilemma for Women in Leadership: Damned if You Do, Doomed if You Don't" (July 15, 2007), accessed June 10, 2013, at http://www.catalyst.org/knowledge/double-bind-dilemma-women-leadership-damned-if-you-do-doomed-if-you-dont-0.

[16] Ibid.

[17] Ibid. Also see Global Human Capital Gender Advisory Council, "The Leaking Pipeline: Where Are Our Female Leaders? 79 Women Share Their Stories," PricewaterhouseCoopers (March 2008), accessed June 10, 2013, at www.pwc.com/en_GX/gx/women-at-pwc/assets/leaking_pipeline.pdf.

[18] See "The Workplace Improves for Gay Americans," GFN News (December 17, 2007), accessed May 5, 2009 from www.gfn.com/recordDetails.php?page_id=19&section_id=22&pcontent_id=18.

[19] www.eeoc.gov/facts/fs-orientation_parent_marital_political.html.

[20] See "The Workplace Improves for Gay Americans," op. cit.

[21] "Same-Sex Marriage, Gay Rights," Polling report.com (2013), accessed June 10, 2013, at www.pollingreport.com/civil.htm.

[22] See Carol Mithers, "Workplace Wars," in *Ladies' Home Journal* (May 2009), pp. 104–109.

[23] Ibid.

[24] "The Americans with Disabilities Act," The Center for an Accessible Society (n.d.), accessed June 11, 2013, at www.accessiblesociety.org/topics/ada/index.htm.

[25] Patricia Digh, "Finding New Talent in a Tight Market," *Mosaics* 4.3 (March–April, 1998), pp. 1, 4–6.

[26] "The Americans with Disabilities Act," op. cit.

[27] www.shrm.org/.../Diversity_CLA_Definitions_of_Diversity_Inclusion.ppt.

[28] "The Americans with Disabilities Act," op. cit.

[29] See Katharine Esty, "From Diversity to Inclusion," Northeast Human Resources Association (April 30, 2007), accessed June 11, 2013, at www.boston.com/jobs/nehra/043007.shtml

[30] See Henri Tajfel and John Turner, "An Integrative Theory of Intergroup Conflict," in G. William Austin and Stephen Worchel, *The Social Psychology of Intergroup Relations,* Monterey, CA: Brooks-Cole (1979), pp. 94–109.

[31] www.catalystwomen.org/press_room/factsheets/factwoc3.htm. Accessed May 4, 2009.

[32] M. R. Barrick and M. K. Mount, "The Big Five Personality Dimensions and Job Performance: A Meta Analysis," *Personnel Psychology* 44 (1991), pp. 1–26; and M. R. Barrick and M. K. Mount, "Autonomy as a Moderator of the Relationships Between the Big Five Personality Dimensions and Job Performance," *Journal of Applied Psychology* (February 1993), pp. 111–118.

[33] "The Big Five Personality Dimensions and Job Performance: A Meta-Analysis," op. cit.

[34] Some examples of firms using the Myers-Briggs Type Indicators are given in J. M. Kunimerow and L. W. McAllister, "Team Building with the Myers-Briggs Type Indicator: Case Studies," *Journal of Psychological Type* 15 (1988), pp. 26–32; G. H. Rice Jr. and D. P. Lindecamps, "Personality Types and Business Success of Small Retailers," *Journal of Occupational Psychology* 62 (1989), pp. 177–182; and B. Roach, *Strategy Styles and Management Types: A Resource Book for Organizational Management Consultants* (Stanford, CA: Balestrand, 1989).

[35] Raymond G. Hunt, Frank J. Kryzstofiak, James R. Meindl, and Abdalla M. Yousry, "Cognitive Style and Decision Making," *Organizational Behavior and Human Decision Processes* 44.3 (1989), pp. 436–453. For additional work on problem-solving styles, see Ferdinand A. Gul, "The Joint and Moderating Role of Personality and Cognitive Style on Decision Making," *Accounting Review* (April 1984), pp. 264–277; Brian H. Kleiner, "The Interrelationship of Jungian Modes of Mental Functioning with Organizational Factors: Implications for Management Development," *Human Relations* (November 1983), pp. 997–1012; and James L. McKenney and Peter G. W. Keen, "How Managers' Minds Work," *Harvard Business Review* (May–June 1974), pp. 79–90.

[36] J. B. Rotter, "Generalized Expectancies for Internal versus External Control of Reinforcement," *Psychological Monographs* 80 (1966), pp. 1–28.

[37] See J. Michael Crant, "Proactive Behavior in Organizations," *Journal of Management* 26 (2000), pp. 435–462. See also T. S. Bateman, and J. M. Crant, "The Proactive Component of Organizational Behavior," *Journal of Organizational Behavior* 14 (1993), pp. 103–118.

[38] Don Hellriegel, John W. Slocum Jr., and Richard W. Woodman, *Organizational Behavior*, 5th ed. (St. Paul, MN: West, 1989), p. 46.

[39] Niccolo Machiavelli, *The Prince*, trans. George Bull (Middlesex, UK: Penguin, 1961).

[40] Richard Christie and Florence L. Geis, *Studies in Machiavellianism* (New York: Academic Press, 1970).

[41] See M. Snyder, *Public Appearances/Private Realities: The Psychology of Self-Monitoring* (New York: Freeman, 1987).

[42] Ibid.

[43] Adapted from R. W. Bonner, "A Short Scale: A Potential Measure of Pattern A Behavior," *Journal of Chronic Diseases* 22 (1969). Used by permission.

[44] See Meyer Friedman and Ray Roseman, *Type A Behavior and Your Heart* (New York: Knopf, 1974). For another view, see Walter Kiechel III, "Attack of the Obsessive Managers," *Fortune* (February 16, 1987), pp. 127–128.

[45] Data from Michael Mandel, "The Real Reasons You're Working So Hard," *BusinessWeek* (October 3, 2005), pp. 60–70; "Many U.S. Employees Have Negative Attitudes to Their Jobs, Employers and Top Managers," The Harris Poll #38 (May 6, 2005), accessed June 11, 2013, at www.thefreelibrary.com/PR+Newswire/2005/May/6-p51926.

[46] Arthur P. Brief, Randall S. Schuler, and Mary Van Sell, *Managing Job Stress* (Boston: Little, Brown, 1981).

[47] The classic work is Meyer Friedman and Ray Roseman, *Type A Behavior and Your Heart*, op. cit.

[48] See H. Selye, *The Stress of Life*, rev. ed. (New York: McGraw-Hill, 1976).

[49] See John D. Adams, "Health, Stress and the Manager's Life Style," *Group and Organization Studies* 6 (1981), pp. 291–301.

[50] See Susan Folkman "Personal Control and Stress and Coping Processes: A Theoretical Analysis," *Journal of Personality and Social Psychology* 46(4) (1984), p. 844.

[51] See Mayo Clinic, "Stress Relief: When and How to Say No" (July 23, 2010), accessed June 11, 2013, at www.riversideonline.com/health_reference/Stress/SR00039.cfm.

[52] See P. E. Jacob, J. J. Flink, and H. L. Schuchman, "Values and Their Function in Decision Making," *American Behavioral Scientist* 5, suppl. 9 (1962), pp. 6–38.

[53] See M. Rokeach and S. J. Ball Rokeach, "Stability and Change in American Value Priorities, 1968–1981," *American Psychologist* (May 1989), pp. 775–784.

[54] Milton Rokeach, *The Nature of Human Values* (New York: Free Press, 1973).

[55] Bruce M. Meglino and Elizabeth C. Ravlin, "Individual Values in Organizations: Concepts, Controversies and Research," *Journal of Management* 24 (1998), pp. 351–389.

[56] Ibid.

[57] Geert Hofstede, *Culture's Consequences: International Differences in Work-Related Values*, 2nd ed. (Beverly Hills, CA: Sage, 2001). See also Peter B. Smith and Michael Harris Bond, "Culture: The Neglected Concept," in *Social Psychology Across Cultures*, 2nd ed. (Boston: Allyn & Bacon, 1998); Michael H. Hoppe, "An Interview with Geert Hofstede," *Academy of Management Executive* 18 (2004), pp. 75–79; and Harry C. Triandis, "The Many Dimensions of Culture," *Academy of Management Executive* 18 (2004), pp. 88–93.

[58] Geert Hofstede, *Culture and Organizations: Software of the Mind* (London: McGraw-Hill, 1991).

[59] Hofstede, *Culture's Consequences*, op. cit.; Geert Hofstede and Michael H. Bond, "The Confucius Connection: From Culture Roots to Economic Growth," *Organizational Dynamics* 16 (1988), pp. 4–21.

[60] Hofstede, *Culture's Consequences*, op. cit.

[61] Chinese Culture Connection, "Chinese Values and the Search for Culture-Free Dimensions of Culture," *Journal of Cross-Cultural Psychology* 18 (1987), pp. 143–164.

[62] Hofstede and Bond, "The Confucius Connection," op. cit.; Geert Hofstede, "Cultural Constraints in Management Theories," *Academy of Management Executive* 7 (1993), pp. 81–94. For a further discussion of Asian and Confucian values, see also Jim Rohwer, *Asia Rising: Why America Will Prosper as Asia's Economies Boom* (New York: Simon & Schuster, 1995).

[63] For an example, see John R. Schermerhorn Jr. and Michael H. Bond, "Cross-Cultural Leadership Dynamics in Collectivism 1 High Power Distance Settings," *Leadership and Organization Development Journal* 18 (1997), pp. 187–193.

[64] Hofstede, *Culture and Organizations*, op. cit.

[65] See, for example, Edward T. Hall, *The Silent Language* (New York: Anchor Books, 1959); Fons Trompenaars, *Riding the Waves of Culture: Understanding Cultural Diversity in Business* (London: Nicholas Brealey Publishing, 1993); Steven H. Schwartz, "A Theory of Cultural Values and Some Implications for Work," *Applied Psychology: An International Review* 48 (1999), pp. 23–47; Robert J. House, Paul J. Hanges, Mansour Javidan, Peter W. Dorfman, and Vipin Gupta (eds.), *Culture, Leadership and Organizations: The GLOBE Study of 62 Societies* (Thousand Oaks, CA: Sage, 2004); and Michele J. Gelfand et al. (42 co-authors), "Differences Between Tight and Loose Cultures: A 33 Nation Study," *Science* 332 (May 2011), pp. 100–1104.

Chapter 3

[1] H. R. Schiffmann, *Sensation and Perception: An Integrated Approach*, 3rd ed. (New York: Wiley, 1990).

[2] See Georgia T. Chao and Steve W. J. Kozlowski, "Employee Perceptions on the Implementation of Robotic Manufacturing Technology," *Journal of Applied Psychology* 71 (1986), pp. 70–76; Steven F. Cronshaw and Robert G. Lord, "Effects of Categorization, Attribution, and Encoding Processes in Leadership Perceptions," *Journal of Applied Psychology* 72 (1987), pp. 97–106.

[3] See Robert G. Lord, "An Information Processing Approach to Social Perceptions, Leadership, and Behavioral Measurement in Organizations," in *Research in Organizational Behavior* 7, ed. B. M. Staw and L. L. Cummings (Greenwich, CT: JAI Press, 1985), pp. 87–128; T. K. Srull and R. S. Wyer, *Advances in Social Cognition* (Hillsdale, NJ: Erlbaum, 1988); and U. Neisser, *Cognition and Reality* (San Francisco: Freeman, 1976), p. 112.

[4] See J. G. Hunt, *Leadership: A New Synthesis* (Newbury Park, CA: Sage, 1991), ch. 7; R. G. Lord and R. J. Foti, "Schema Theories, Information Processing, and Organizational Behavior," in *Thinking Organization*, ed. H. P. Simms Jr. and D. A. Gioia (San Francisco: Jossey-Bass, 1986), pp. 20–48; and S. T. Fiske and S. E. Taylor, *Social Cognition* (Reading, MA: Addison-Wesley, 1984).

[5] See William L. Gardner and Mark J. Martinko, "Impression Management in Organizations," *Journal of Management* (June 1988), p. 332.

[6] Quotation from Sheila O'Flanagan, "Underestimate Casual Dressers at Your Peril," *Irish Times* (July 22, 2005).

[7] See B. R. Schlenker, *Impression Management: The Self-Concept, Social Identity, and Interpersonal Relations* (Monterey, CA: Brooks/Cole, 1980); W. L. Gardner and M. J. Martinko, "Impression Management in Organizations," *Journal of Management* (June 1988), p. 332; R. B. Cialdini, "Indirect Tactics of Image Management: Beyond Banking" in *Impression Management in the Organization*, ed. R. A. Giacolini and P. Rosenfeld (Hillsdale, NJ: Erlbaum, 1989), pp. 45–71; and Sandy Wayne and Robert Liden, "Effects of Impression Management on Performance Ratings," *Academy of Management Journal* 38:1 (1995), pp. 232–260.

[8] See, for example, Stephan Thernstrom and Abigail Thernstrom, *America in Black and White* (New York: Simon & Schuster, 1997); and David A. Thomas and Suzy Wetlaufer, "A Question of Color: A Debate on Race in the U.S. Workspace," *Harvard Business Review* 2 (September–October 1997), pp. 118–132.

[9] Information from "Misconceptions about Women in the Global Arena Keep Their Number Low," accessed June 24, 2013, at www.catalyst.org/media/misconceptions-about-women-global-arena-keep-their-numbers-low.

[10] These examples are from Natasha Josefowitz, *Paths to Power* (Reading, MA: Addison-Wesley, 1980), p. 60. For more on gender issues, see Gray N. Powell (ed.), *Handbook of Gender and Work* (Thousand Oaks, CA: Sage, 1999).

[11] For a recent report on age discrimination, see Joseph C. Santora and William J. Seaton, "Age Discrimination: Alive and Well in the Workplace?" *The Academy of Management Perspectives* 22 (May 2008), pp. 103–104.

[12] Survey reported in Kelly Greene, "Age Is Still More Than a Number," *Wall Street Journal* (April 10, 2003), p. D2.

[13] "Facebook Gets Down to Business," *BusinessWeek* (April 20, 2009), p. 30.

[14] Dewitt C. Dearborn and Herbert A. Simon, "Selective Perception: A Note on the Departmental Identification of Executives," *Sociometry* 21 (1958), pp. 140–144.

[15] J. Sterling Livingston, "Pygmalion in Management," *Harvard Business Review* (July–August 1969), pp. 81–89.

[16] D. Eden and A. B. Shani, "Pygmalion Goes to Boot Camp," *Journal of Applied Psychology* 67 (1982), pp. 194–199.

[17] See H. H. Kelley, "Attribution in Social Interaction," in E. Jones et al. (eds.), *Attribution: Perceiving the Causes of Behavior* (Morristown, NJ: General Learning Press, 1972).

[18] See Terence R. Mitchell, S. G. Green, and R. E. Wood, "An Attribution Model of Leadership and the Poor Performing Subordinate," in *Research in Organizational Behavior*, ed. Barry Staw and Larry L. Cummings (New York: JAI Press, 1981), pp. 197–234; and John H. Harvey and Gifford Weary, "Current Issues in Attribution Theory and Research," *Annual Review of Psychology* 35 (1984), pp. 427–459.

[19] See F. Fosterling, "Attributional Retraining: A Review," *Psychological Bulletin* (November 1985), pp. 496–512.

[20] Albert Bandura, *Social Learning Theory* (Englewood Cliffs, NJ: Prentice-Hall, 1977); and Albert Bandura, *Self-Efficacy: The Exercise of Control* (New York: W. H. Freeman, 1997).

[21] See, for example, A. M. Morrison, R. P. White, and E. Van Velsor, *Breaking the Glass Ceiling* (Reading, MA: Addison-Wesley, 1987); J. D. Zalesny and J. K. Ford, "Extending the Social Information Processing Perspective: New Links to Attitudes, Behaviors and Perceptions," *Organizational Behavior and Human Decision Processes* 47 (1990), pp. 205–246; M. E. Gist, C. Schwoerer, and B. Rosen, "Effects of Alternative Training Methods of Self-Efficacy and Performance in Computer Software Training," *Journal of Applied Psychology* 74 (1989), pp. 884–891; D. D. Sutton and R. W. Woodman, "Pygmalion Goes to Work: The Effects of Supervisor Expectations in a Retail Setting," *Journal of Applied Psychology* 74 (1989), pp. 943–950; and M. E. Gist, "The Influence of Training Method on Self-Efficacy and Idea Generation among Managers," *Personnel Psychology* 42 (1989), pp. 787–805.

[22] Bandura (1977 and 1997), op. cit.

[23] See M. E. Gist, "Self Efficacy: Implications in Organizational Behavior and Human Resource Management," *Academy of Management Review* 12 (1987), pp. 472–485; and A. Bandura, "Self-Efficacy Mechanisms in Human Agency," *American Psychologist* 37 (1987), pp. 122–147.

[24] For good overviews of reinforcement-based views, see W. E. Scott Jr. and P. M. Podsakoff, *Behavioral Principles in the Practice of Management* (New York: Wiley, 1985); and Fred Luthans and Robert Kreitner, *Organizational Behavior Modification and Beyond* (Glenview, IL: Scott Foresman, 1985).

[25] For some of B. F. Skinner's work, see *Walden Two* (New York: Macmillan, 1948); *Science and Human Behavior* (New York: Macmillan, 1953); and *Contingencies of Reinforcement* (New York: Appleton-Century-Crofts, 1969).

[26] Fred Luthans and Robert Kreitner, *Organizational Behavior Modification* (Glenview, IL: Scott Foresman, 1975); Fred Luthans and Robert Kreitner (1985), op cit.; and Fred Luthans and Alexander D. Stajkovic, "Reinforce for Performance: The Need to Go Beyond Pay and Even Rewards," *Academy of Management Executive* 13 (1999), pp. 49–57.

[27] E. L. Thorndike, *Animal Intelligence* (New York: Macmillan, 1911), p. 244.

[28] Example adapted from Luthans and Kreitner (1985), op. cit.

[29] Luthans and Kreitner (1985), op. cit.

[30] Both laws are stated in Keith L. Miller, *Principles of Everyday Behavior Analysis* (Monterey, CA: Brooks/Cole, 1975), p. 122.

[31] This example is based on a study by Barbara Price and Richard Osborn, "Shaping the Training of Skilled Workers," working paper (Detroit: Department of Management, Wayne State University, 1999).

[32] A. R. Korukonda and James G. Hunt, "Pat on the Back versus Kick in the Pants: An Application of Cognitive Inference to the Study of Leader Reward and Punishment Behavior," *Group and Organization Studies* 14 (1989), pp. 199–234.

[33] Edwin A. Locke, "The Myths of Behavior Mod in Organizations," *Academy of Management Review* 2 (October 1977), pp. 543–553. For a counterpoint, see Jerry L. Gray, "The Myths of the Myths about Behavior Mod in Organizations: A Reply to Locke's Criticisms of Behavior Modification," *Academy of Management Review* 4 (January 1979), pp. 121–129.

[34] Robert Kreitner, "Controversy in OBM: History, Misconceptions, and Ethics," in Lee Frederiksen (ed.), *Handbook of Organizational Behavior Management* (New York: Wiley, 1982), pp. 71–91.

[35] W. E. Scott Jr. and P. M. Podsakoff, *Behavioral Principles in the Practice of Management* (New York: Wiley, 1985); also see W. Clay Hamner, "Reinforcement Theory and Contingency Management in Organizational Settings," in Richard M. Steers and Lyman W. Porters (eds.), *Motivation and Work Behavior*, 4th ed. (New York: McGraw-Hill, 1987), pp. 139–165; Luthans and Kreitner (1985), op. cit.; and Charles C. Manz and Henry P. Sims Jr., *Superleadership* (New York: Berkeley, 1990).

Chapter 4

[1] These concept definitions and discussions are based in J. M. George, "Trait and State Affect," in K. R. Murphy (ed.), *Individual Differences in Behavior in Organizations,* (San Francisco: Jossey-Bass, 1996), p. 45; N. H. Frijda, "Moods, Emotion Episodes and Emotions," in M. Lewis and J. M. Haviland (eds.), *Handbook of Emotions* (New York: Guilford Press, 1993), pp. 381–403; H. M. Weiss and R. Cropanzano, "Affective Events Theory: A Theoretical Discussion of the Structure, Causes, and Consequences of Affective Experiences at Work," in B. M. Staw and L. L. Cummings (eds.), *Research in Organizational Behavior,* 18 (Greenwich, CT: JAI Press, 1996), pp. 17–19; and P. Ekman and R. J. Davidson (eds.), *The Nature of Emotions: Fundamental Questions* (Oxford, UK: Oxford University Press, 1994).

[2] For an example, see Mary Ann Hazen, "Grief and the Workplace," *Academy of Management Perspective* 22 (August 2008), pp. 78–86.

[3] J. A. Fuller, J. M. Stanton, G. G. Fisher, C. Spitzmuller, S. S. Russell, and P. C. Smith, "A Lengthy Look at the Daily Grind: Time Series Analysis of Events, Mood, Stress, and Satisfaction," *Journal of Applied Psychology* 88 (2003), pp. 1019–1033; C. J. Thoreson, S. A. Kaplan, A. P. Barsky, C. R. Warren, and K. de Chermont, "The Affective Underpinnings of Job Perceptions and Attitudes: A Meta-Analytic Review and Integration," *Psychological Bulletin* 129 (2003), pp. 914–925.

[4] Daniel Goleman, "Leadership That Gets Results," *Harvard Business Review* (March–April 2000), pp. 78–90. See also his books *Emotional Intelligence* (New York: Bantam Books, 1995) and *Working with Emotional Intelligence* (New York: Bantam Books, 1998).

[5] See Davies L. Stankow and R. D. Roberts, "Emotion and Intelligence: In Search of an Elusive Construct," *Journal of Personality and Social Psychology* 75 (1998), pp. 989–1015; and I. Greenstein, *The Presidential Difference: Leadership Style from FDR to Clinton* (Princeton, NJ: Princeton University Press, 2001); Goleman (2000), op. cit.

[6] Goleman (1998), op. cit.

[7] J. P. Tangney and K. W. Fischer (eds.), "*Self-Conscious Emotions: The Psychology of Shame, Guilt, Embarrassment and Price* (New York: Guilford Press, 1995); J. L. Tracy and R. W. Robbins, "Putting the Self into Self-Conscious Emotions: A Theoretical Model," *Psychological Inquiry* 15 (2004), pp. 103–125; D. Keltner and C. Anderson, "Saving Face for Darwin: The Functions and Uses of Embarrassment," *Current Directions in Psychological Science* 9 (2000), pp. 187–192; J. S. Beer, E. A. Heery, D. Keltner, D. Scabini, and R. T. Knight, "The Regulatory Function of Self-Conscious Emotion: Insights from Patients with Orbitofrontal Damage," *Journal of Personality and Social Psychology* 85 (2003), pp. 594–604; R. P. Vecchio, "Explorations of Employee Envy: Feeling Envious and Feeling Envied," *Cognition and Emotion* 19 (2005), pp. 69–81; and C. F. Poulson II, "Shame and Work," in N. M. Ashkanasy, W. Zerby, and C. E. J. Hartel (eds.), *Emotions in the Workplace: Research, Theory, and Practice* (Westport, CT: Quorum Books), pp. 490–541.

[8] Diane Brady, "Charm Offensive," *BusinessWeek* (June 26, 2006), pp. 76–80.

[9] Lewis and Haviland (1993), op. cit.

[10] R. E. Lucas, A. E. Clark, Y. Georgellis, and E. Deiner, "Unemployment Alters the Set Points for Life Satisfaction," *Psychological Science* 15 (2004), pp. 8–13; C. Graham, A. Eggers, and S. Sukhtaner, "Does Happiness Pay? An Exploration Based on Panel Data from Russia," *Journal of Economic Behavior and Organization* 55 (November 2004), pp. 319–342; G. L. Clore, N. Schwartz, and M. Conway, "Affective Causes and Consequences of Social Information Processing," in R. S. Wyer Jr. and T. K. Srull (eds.), *Handbook of Social Cognition,* Vol. 1, (Hillsdale, NJ: Erlbaum, 1994), pp. 323–417; K. D. Vohs, R. F. Baumeister, and G. Lowenstein, *Do Emotions Help or Hurt Decision Making?* (New York: Russell Sage Foundation Press, 2007; H. M. Weiss, J. P. Nicholas, and C. S. Daus, "An Examination of the Joint Effects of Affective Experiences and Job Beliefs on Job Satisfaction and Variations in Affective Experiences over Time," *Organizational Behavior and Human Decision Processes* 78 (1999), pp. 1–24; and N. M. Ashkanasy, "Emotion and Performance," *Human Performance* 17 (2004), pp. 137–144.

[11] See Robert G. Lord, Richard J. Klimoski, and Ruth Knafer (eds.), *Emotions in the Workplace: Understanding the Structure and Role of Emotions in Organizational Behavior* (San Francisco: Jossey-Bass, 2002); Roy L. Payne and Cary L. Cooper (eds.), *Emotions at Work: Theory Research and Applications for Management* (Chichester, UK: John Wiley & Sons, 2004); and Daniel Goleman and Richard Boyatzis, "Social Intelligence and the Biology of Leadership," *Harvard Business Review* (September 2008), Reprint R0809E.

[12] Daniel Goleman, Richard Boyatzis, and Annie McKie, *Primal Leadership: Realizing the Power of Emotional Intelligence* (Boston: Harvard Business School Publishing, 2002); quote from "Managing the Mood Is Crucial When Times Are Tough," *Financial Times* (March 24, 2009).

[13] Joyce K. Bono and Remus Ilies, "Charisma, Positive Emotions and Mood Contagion," *Leadership Quarterly* 17 (2006), pp. 317–334; Goleman and Boyatzis (2008), op. cit.

[14] Caroline Bartel and Richard Saavedra, "The Collective Construction of Work Group Moods," *Administrative Science Quarterly* 45 (June 2000), pp. 197–231.

[15] S. M. Kruml and D. Geddes, "Catching Fire Without Burning Out: Is There an Ideal Way to Perform Emotional Labor?" in N. M. Ashkanasy, C. E. J. Hartel, and W. J. Zerby, *Emotions in the Workplace* (New York: Quorum, 2000), pp. 177–188.

[16] A. Grandey, "Emotional Regulation in the Workplace: A New Way to Conceptualize Emotional Labor, "*Journal of Occupational Health Psychology* 5.1 (2000), pp. 95–110; and R. Cropanzano, D. E. Rupp, and Z. S. Byrne, "The Relationship of Emotional Exhaustion to Work Attitudes, Job Performance and Organizational Citizenship Behavior," *Journal of Applied Psychology* (2003), pp. 160–169.

[17] W. Tasi and Y. Huang, "Mechanisms Linking Employee Affective Delivery and Customer Behavioral Intentions," *Journal of Applied Psychology* 87 (2002), pp. 1001–1008.

[18] See Adam Smith, "Cognitive Empathy and Emotional Empathy in Human Behavior and Evolution," *The Psychological Record*, Vol. 56 (2006), pp. 3–21.

[19] Daniel Goleman, "Are Women More Emotionally Intelligent than Men?" accessed June 26, 2013, at www.psychologytoday.com/blog/the-brain-and-emotional-intelligence/201104/are-women-more-emotionally-intelligent-men.

[20] Shiri Cohen, Marc S. Shulz, Emily Weiss, and Robert J. Waldinger, "Eye of the Beholder: The Individual and Dyadic Contributions of Empathic Accuracy and Perceived Effort to Relationship Satisfaction," *Journal of Family Psychology* 26 (2012), pp. 236–245.

[21] Michele Williams, "Building Genuine Trust Through Interpersonal Emotion Management: A Threat Regulation Model of Trust and Collaboration across Boundaries," *Academy of Management Review* 32 (2007), pp. 595–621.

[22] Goleman (2011), op. cit.

[23] M. Eid and E. Diener, "Norms for Experiencing Emotions in Different Cultures: Inter- and Intranational Differences," *Journal of Personality and Social Psychology* 81.5 (2001), pp. 869–885.

[24] Ibid.

[25] B. Mesquita, "Emotions in Collectivist and Individualist Contexts," *Journal of Personality and Social Psychology* 80.1 (2001), pp. 68–74.

[26] D. Rubin, "Grumpy German Shoppers Distrust the Wal-Mart Style," *Seattle Times* (December 30, 2001), p. a15; and A. Rafaeli, "When Cashiers Meet Customers: An Analysis of Supermarket Cashiers," *Academy of Management Journal* (1989), pp. 245–273.

[27] H. M. Weiss and R. Cropanzano, "An Affective Events Approach to Job Satisfaction," in B. M. Staw and L. L. Cummings (eds.), *Research in Organizational Behavior*, vol. 18 (Greenwich, CT: JAI Press, 1996), pp. 1–74; and N. M. Ashkanasy and C. S. Daus, "Emotion in the Workplace: New Challenges for Managers," *Academy of Management Executive* 16 (2002), pp. 76–86.

[28] A. G. Miner and C. L. Hulin, *Affective Experience at Work: A Test of Affective Events Theory.* Poster presented at the 15th annual conference of the Society for Industrial and Organizational Psychology (2000).

[29] Information and quote from Joann S. Lublin, "How One Black Woman Lands Her Top Jobs: Risks and Networking," *Wall Street Journal* (March 4, 2003), p. B1.

[30] Compare Martin Fishbein and Icek Ajzen, *Belief, Attitude, Intention and Behavior: An Introduction to Theory and Research* (Reading, MA: Addison-Wesley, 1973).

[31] See A. W. Wicker, "Attitude Versus Action: The Relationship of Verbal and Overt Behavioral Responses to Attitude Objects," *Journal of Social Issues* (Autumn 1969), pp. 41–78.

[32] L. Festinger, *A Theory of Cognitive Dissonance* (Palo Alto, CA: Stanford University Press, 1957).

[33] See "The Things They Do for Love," *Harvard Business Review* (December 2004), pp. 19–20.

[34] See Henry Tajfel and John C. Turner, "The Social Identity Theory of Intergroup Behavior," in S. Worchel and W. Austin (eds.), *Psychology of Intergroup Relations* (Chicago: Nelson, 1986).

[35] See for example, Blake E. Ashforth, Spencer H. Harrison, and Kevin G. Corely, "Identification in Organizations: An Examination of Four Fundamental Questions," *Journal of Management* 34 (2008), pp. 325–274.

[36] Ibid.

[37] Glen E. Kreiner and Blake E. Ashforth, "Evidence Toward an Expanded Model of Organizational Identification," *Journal of Organizational Behavior* 25 (2004), pp. 1–27.

[38] Tony DiRomualdo, "The High Cost of Employee Disengagement" (2004, July 7), accessed June 26, 2013, at http://wtnnews.com/articles/983.

[39] Jeffrey Pfeffer, "Building Sustainable Organizations: The Human Factor," *Academy of Management Perspectives* 24 (2010, February), pp. 34–45.

[40] Jim Harter, "Mondays Not So 'Blue' for Engaged Employees," Gallup Wellbeing (2012, July 23), accessed June 26, 2013, at www.gallup.com/poll/155924/mondays-not-blue-engaged-employees.aspx.

[41] Information from Sue Shellenbarger, "Employers Are Finding It Doesn't Cost Much to Make a Staff Happy," *Wall Street Journal* (November 19, 1977), p. B1; see also "Special Consumer Survey Report: Job Satisfaction on the Decline," *The Conference Board* (July 2002).

[42] "Majority of American Workers Not Engaged in Their Jobs," Gallup news release (Washington, DC: October 28, 2011): gallup.com (accessed January 24, 2013); Melissa Korn, "Employed, but Not Engaged on the Job," *The Wall Street Journal* (June 11, 2013): www.wsj.com (accessed July 3, 2013).

[43] See, for example, Remus Ilies, Kelly Schwind Wilson, and David T. Wagner, "The Spillover of Daily Job Satisfaction onto Employees' Family Lives: The Facilitating Role of Work-Family Integration," *Academy of Management Journal* 52 (February 2009), pp. 87–102.

[44] See W. E. Wymer and J. M. Carsten, "Alternative Ways to Gather Opinions," *HR Magazine* 37.4 (April 1992), pp. 71–78.

[45] The Job Descriptive Index (JDI) is available from Dr. Patricia C. Smith, Department of Psychology, Bowling Green State University; the Minnesota Satisfaction Questionnaire (MSQ) is available from the Industrial Relations Center and Vocational Psychology Research Center, University of Minnesota.

[46] See Ibid.; Timothy A. Judge, "Promote Job Satisfaction through Mental Challenge," Chapter 6 in Edwin A. Locke (ed.), *The Blackwell Handbook of Principles of Organizational Behavior* (Malden, MA: Blackwell, 2004); "U.S. Employees More Dissatisfied with Their Jobs," *Associated Press* (February 28, 2005), www.msnbc.com; "U.S. Job Satisfaction Keeps Falling, The Conference Board Reports Today," *The Conference Board* (February 28, 2005), www.conference-board.org; and Salary.com, "Survey Shows Impact of Downturn on Job Satisfaction," *OH&S: Occupational Health and Safety* (February 7, 2009), www.ohsonline.com.

[47] Data reported in Jeannine Aversa, "Happy Workers Harder to Find," *Columbus Dispatch* (January 5, 2010), pp. A1, A4. Data from "U.S. Job Satisfaction the Lowest in Two Decades," press release, The Conference Board (January 5, 2010), accessed January 6, 2010 at www.conference-board.org.

[48] Accenture, "Despite Low Job Satisfaction, Employees Unlikely to Seek New Jobs, Accenture Research Reports, Prefer to Focus on Creating Opportunities with Current Employers" (2011, March 4), accessed June 26, 2013, at newsroom.accenture.com/article_display.cfm?article_id=5163.

[49] The Conference Board (2005), op. cit.

[50] For historical research, see B. M. Staw, "The Consequences of Turnover," *Journal of Occupational Behavior* 1 (1980), pp. 253–273; and J. P. Wanous, *Organizational Entry* (Reading, MA: Addison-Wesley, 1980).

[51] C. N. Greene, "The Satisfaction-Performance Controversy," *Business Horizons* 15 (1972), pp. 31–41; M. T. Iaffaldano and P. M. Muchinsky, "Job Satisfaction and Job Performance: A Meta-Analysis," *Psychological Bulletin* 97 (1985), pp. 251–273; D. Organ, "A Reappraisal and Reinterpretation of the Satisfaction-Causes-Performance Hypothesis," *Academy of Management Review* 2 (1977), pp. 46–53; and P. Lorenzi, "A Comment on Organ's Reappraisal of the Satisfaction-Causes-Performance Hypothesis," *Academy of Management Review* 3 (1978), pp. 380–382.

[52] Salary.com (2009), op. cit.

[53] Tony DiRomualdo, "The High Cost of Employee Disengagement" (July 7, 2004), www.wistechnology.com.

[54] Dennis W. Organ, *Organizational Citizenship Behavior: The Good Soldier Syndrome* (Lexington, MA: Lexington Books, 1988); and Dennis W. Organ, "Organizational Citizenship Behavior: It's Constructive Cleanup Time," *Human Performance* 10 (1997), pp. 85–97.

[55] See Mark C. Bolino and William H. Turnley, "Going the Extra Mile: Cultivating and Managing Employee Citizenship Behavior," *Academy of Management Executive* 17 (August 2003), pp. 60–67.

[56] See Venetta I. Coleman and Walter C. Borman, "Investigating the Underlying Structure of the Citizenship Performance Domain," *Human Resource Management Review* 10 (2000), pp. 115–126.

[57] Sandra L. Robinson and Rebecca J. Bennett, "A Typology of Deviant Workplace Behaviors: A Multidimensional Scaling Study," *Academy of Management Journal* 38 (1995), pp. 555–572.

[58] Reeshad S. Dalal, "A Meta-Analysis of the Relationship Among Organizational Citizenship Behavior and Counterproductive Work Behavior," *Journal of Applied Psychology* 90 (2005), pp. 1241–1255.

[59] HealthForceOntario, *Bullying in the Workplace: A Handbook for the Workplace* (Toronto: Ontario Safety Association for Community and Health Care, 2009).

[60] Timothy A. Judge and Remus Ilies, "Affect and Job Satisfaction: A Study of Their Relationship at Work and at Home," *Journal of Applied Psychology* 89 (2004), pp. 661–673.

[61] Ilies et al. (2009), op. cit.

[62] See Benjamin Schneider, Paul J. Hanges, D. Brent Smith, and Amy Salvaggio, "Which Comes First: Employee Attitudes or Organizational, Financial, and Market Performance?" *Journal of Applied Psychology* 88.5 (2003), pp. 836–851.

[63] L. W. Porter and E. E. Lawler III, *Managerial Attitudes and Work Performance* (Homewood, IL: Irwin, 1968).

[64] Schneider, Hanges, Smith, and Salvaggio (2003), op. cit.

[65] Ibid.

Chapter 5

[1] Adaped from Dale McConkey, "The 'Jackass Effect' in Management Compensation," *Business Horizons* 17 (June, 1974), pp. 81–91.

[2] See John P. Campbell, Marvin D. Dunnette, Edward E. Lawler III, and Karl E. Weick Jr., *Managerial Behavior Performance and Effectiveness* (New York: McGraw-Hill, 1970), ch. 15.

[3] Abraham Maslow, *Eupsychian Management* (Homewood, IL: Irwin, 1965); Abraham Maslow, *Motivation and Personality*, 2nd ed. (New York: Harper & Row, 1970).

[4] Lyman W. Porter, "Job Attitudes in Management: Perceived Importance of Needs as a Function of Job Level," *Journal of Applied Psychology* 47 (April 1963), pp. 141–148.

[5] Douglas T. Hall and Khalil E. Nougaim, "An Examination of Maslow's Need Hierarchy in an Organizational Setting," *Organizational Behavior and Human Performance* 3 (1968), pp. 12–35; and John M. Ivancevich, "Perceived Need Satisfactions of Domestic versus Overseas Managers," *Journal of Applied Psychology* 54 (August 1969), pp. 274–278.

[6] Mahmoud A. Wahba and Lawrence G. Bridwell, "Maslow Reconsidered: A Review of Research on the Need Hierarchy Theory," *Academy of Management Proceedings* (1974), pp. 514–520; and Edward E. Lawler III and J. Lloyd Shuttle, "A Causal Correlation Test of the Need Hierarchy Concept," *Organizational Behavior and Human Performance* 7 (1973), pp. 265–287.

[7] Nancy J. Adler, *International Dimensions of Organizational Behavior*, 2nd ed. (Boston: PWS-Kent, 1991), p. 153; and Richard M. Hodgetts and Fred Luthans, *International Management* (New York: McGraw-Hill, 1991), ch. 11.

[8] Clayton P. Alderfer, "An Empirical Test of a New Theory of Human Needs," *Organizational Behavior and Human Performance* 4 (1969), pp. 142–175; Clayton P. Alderfer, *Existence, Relatedness, and Growth* (New York: Free Press, 1972); and Benjamin Schneider and Clayton P. Alderfer, "Three Studies of Need Satisfaction in Organizations," *Administrative Science Quarterly* 18 (1973), pp. 489–505.

[9] Lane Tracy, "A Dynamic Living Systems Model of Work Motivation," *Systems Research* 1 (1984), pp. 191–203; and John Rauschenberger, Neal Schmidt, and John E. Hunter, "A Test of the Need Hierarchy Concept by a Markov Model of Change in Need Strength," *Administrative Science Quarterly* 25 (1980), pp. 654–670.

[10] Sources pertinent to this discussion are David C. McClelland, *The Achieving Society* (New York: Van Nostrand, 1961); David C. McClelland, "Business, Drive and National Achievement," *Harvard Business Review* 40 (July/August 1962), pp. 99–112; David C. McClelland, "That Urge to Achieve," *Think* (November/December 1966), pp. 19–32; and G. H. Litwin and R. A. Stringer, *Motivation and Organizational Climate* (Boston: Division of Research, Harvard Business School, 1966), pp. 18–25.

[11] George Harris, "To Know Why Men Do What They Do: A Conversation with David C. McClelland," *Psychology Today* 4 (January 1971), pp. 35–39.

[12] David C. McClelland and David H. Burnham, "Power Is the Great Motivator," *Harvard Business Review* 54 (March/April 1976), pp. 100–110; and David C. McClelland and Richard E. Boyatzis, "Leadership Motive Pattern and Long-Term Success in Management," *Journal of Applied Psychology* 67 (1982), pp. 737–743.

[13] The complete two-factor theory is well explained by Herzberg and his associates in Frederick Herzberg, Bernard Mausner, and Barbara Bloch Synderman, *The Motivation to Work*, 2nd ed. (New York: Wiley, 1967); and Frederick Herzberg, "One More Time: How Do You Motivate Employees?" *Harvard Business Review* 46 (January/February 1968), pp. 53–62.

[14] From Herzberg (1968), op. cit.

[15] See Robert J. House and Lawrence A. Wigdor, "Herzberg's Dual-Factor Theory of Job Satisfaction and Motivation: A Review of the Evidence and a Criticism," *Personnel Psychology* 20 (Winter 1967), pp. 369–389.

[16] Adler (1991), op. cit.; Nancy J. Adler and J. T. Graham, "Cross Cultural Interaction: The International Comparison Fallacy," *Journal of International Business Studies* (Fall 1989), pp. 515–537; and Frederick Herzberg, "Workers' Needs: The Same Around the World," *Industry Week* (September 27, 1987), pp. 29–32.

[17] Paul R. Lawrence and Nitin Nohria, *Drive: How Human Nature Shapes Our Choices* (San Francisco: Jossey-Bass, 2002); and Nitin Nohria, Bors Groysberg, and Linda-Eling Lee, "Employee Motivation: A Powerful New Model," *Harvard Business Review* (July–August, 2008), pp. 78–84.

[18] Nohria et al. (2008), op. cit.

[19] Ibid, p. 83.

[20] See, for example, J. Stacy Adams, "Toward an Understanding of Inequality," *Journal of Abnormal and Social Psychology* 67 (1963), pp. 422–436; and J. Stacy Adams, "Inequity in Social Exchange," in L. Berkowitz (ed.), *Advances in Experimental Social Psychology* 2 (New York: Academic Press, 1965), pp. 267–300.

[21] Adams (1965), op. cit.

[22] These issues are discussed in C. Kagitcibasi and J. W. Berry, "Cross-Cultural Psychology: Current Research and Trends," *Annual Review of Psychology* 40 (1989), pp. 493–531.

[23] See Blair Sheppard, Roy J. Lewicki, and John Minton, *Organizational Justice: The Search for Fairness in the Workplace* (New York: Lexington Books, 1992); Jerald Greenberg, *The Quest for Justice on the Job: Essays and Experiments* (Thousand Oaks, CA: Sage, 1995); Robert Folger and Russell Cropanzano, *Organizational Justice and Human Resource Management* (Thousand Oaks, CA: Sage, 1998); and Mary A. Konovsky, "Understanding Procedural Justice and Its Impact on Business Organizations," *Journal of Management* 26 (2000), pp. 489–511.

[24] Interactional justice is described by Robert J. Bies, "The Predicament of Injustice: The Management of Moral Outrage," in L. L. Cummings and B. M. Staw (eds.), *Research in Organizational Behavior* 9 (Greenwich, CT: JAI Press, 1987), pp. 289–319. The example is from Carol T. Kulik and Robert L. Holbrook, "Demographics in Service Encounters: Effects of Racial and Gender Congruence on Perceived Fairness," *Social Justice Research* 13 (2000), pp. 375–402. On commutative justice see Marion Fortin and Martin Fellenz, "Hypocrisies of Fairness: Towards a More Reflexive Ethical Base in Organizational Justice Research and Practice," *Journal of Business Ethics*, vol. 78 (2008), pp. 415–433.

[25] Victor H. Vroom, *Work and Motivation* (New York: Wiley, 1964).

[26] Ibid.

[27] See Terence R. Mitchell, "Expectancy Models of Job Satisfaction, Occupational Preference and Effort: A Theoretical, Methodological, and Empirical Appraisal," *Psychological Bulletin* 81 (1974), pp. 1053–1077; Mahmoud A. Wahba and Robert J. House, "Expectancy Theory in Work and Motivation: Some Logical and Methodological Issues," *Human Relations* 27 (January 1974), pp. 121–147; Terry Connolly, "Some Conceptual and Methodological Issues in Expectancy Models of Work Performance Motivation," *Academy of Management Review* 1 (October 1976), pp. 37–47; and Terrence Mitchell, "Expectancy-Value Models in Organizational Psychology," in N. Feather (ed.), *Expectancy, Incentive and Action* (New York: Erlbaum & Associates, 1980).

[28] See Adler (1991), op. cit.

[29] Edwin A. Locke, Karyll N. Shaw, Lise M. Saari, and Gary P. Latham, "Goal Setting and Task Performance: 1969–1980," *Psychological Bulletin* 90 (July/November 1981), pp. 125–152; Edwin A. Locke and Gary P. Latham, "Work Motivation and Satisfaction: Light at the End of the Tunnel," *Psychological Science* 1.4 (July 1990), pp. 240–246; and Edwin A. Locke and Gary Latham, *A Theory of Goal-Setting and Task Performance* (Englewood Cliffs, NJ: Prentice Hall, 1990).

[30] Edwin A. Locke and Gary P. Latham, "Has Goal Setting Gone Wild, or Have Its Attackers Abandoned Good Scholarship?" *The Academy of Management Perspective* 23 (February 2009), pp. 17–23.

[31] For recent debate on goal setting, see Lisa D. Ordóñez, Maurice E. Schwitzer, Adam D. Galinsky, and Max H. Bazerman, "Goals Gone Wild: The Systematic Side Effects of Overprescribing Goal Setting," *The Academy of Management Perspective* 23 (February 2009), pp. 6–16; Locke and Latham (2009), op. cit.

[32] Ibid.

[33] For a good review of MBO, see Anthony P. Raia, *Managing by Objectives* (Glenview, IL: Scott Foresman, 1974).

[34] Ibid. Steven Kerr summarizes the criticisms well in "Overcoming the Dysfunctions of MBO," *Management by Objectives* 5.1 (1976).

Chapter 6

[1] For a good overview see Adrienne Fox, "Make a 'Deal,'" *HR Magazine* (January, 2012), pp. 37–42.

[2] Information from Adam Lashinsky, "Zappos: Life After Acquisition," tech.fortune.cnn.com (November 24, 2010); and Nicholas Boothman, "Will You Be My Friend?" *BloombergBusinessWeek* (January 7–January 13, 2013), pp. 63–65.

[3] Steve Hamm, "A Passion for the Plan," *BusinessWeek* (August 21, 2B 2006), pp. 92–94. See also Yvon Chouinard, *Let My People Go Surfing: The Education of a Reluctant Businessman* (New York: Penguin, 2006).

[4] For complete reviews of theory, research, and practice see Edward E. Lawler III, *Pay and Organizational Effectiveness* (New York: McGraw-Hill, 1971); Edward E. Lawler III, *Pay and Organizational Development* (Reading, MA: Addison-Wesley, 1981); and Edward E. Lawler III, "The Design of Effective Reward Systems," in Jay W. Lorsch (ed.), *Handbook of Organizational Behavior* (Englewood Cliffs, NJ: Prentice-Hall, 1987), pp. 255–271.

[5] "Reasons for Pay Raises," *BusinessWeek* (May 29, 2006), p. 11.

[6] As an example, see D. B. Balkin and L. R. Gómez-Mejia (eds.), *New Perspectives on Compensation* (Englewood Cliffs, NJ: Prentice-Hall, 1987).

[7] Erin White, "How to Reduce Turnover," *Wall Street Journal* (November 21, 2005), p. B5.

[8] S. E. Markham, K. D. Scott, and B. L. Little, "National Gainsharing Study: The Importance of Industry Differences," *Compensation and Benefits Review* (January/February 1992), pp. 34–45.

[9] See Brian Graham-Moore, "Review of the Literature," in Brian Graham-Moore and Timothy L. Ross (eds.), *Gainsharing* (Washington, DC: Bureau of National Affairs, 1990), p. 20.

[10] Jeffrey Pfeffer and John F. Veiga, "Putting People First for Organizational Success," *Academy of Management Executive* 13 (May 1999), pp. 37–48.

[11] L. R. Gómez-Mejia, D. B. Balkin, and R. L. Cardy, *Managing Human Resources* (Englewood Cliffs, NJ: Prentice-Hall, 1995), pp. 410–411.

[12] N. Gupta, G. E. Ledford, G. D. Jenkins, and D. H. Doty, "Survey Based Prescriptions for Skill-Based Pay," *American Compensation Association Journal* 1.1 (1992), pp. 48–59; and L. W. Ledford, "The Effectiveness of Skill-Based Pay," *Perspectives in Total Compensation* 1.1 (1991), pp. 1–4.

[13] Mina Kines, "P&G's Leadership Machine," *Fortune* (April 14, 2009).

[14] For discussion of many of these errors, see David L. Devries, Ann M. Morrison, Sandra L. Shullman, and Michael P. Gerlach, *Performance Appraisal on the Line* (Greensboro, NC: Center for Creative Leadership, 1986), ch. 3.

[15] For more details, see G. P. Latham and K. N. Wexley, *Increasing Productivity through Performance Appraisal* (2nd ed.); and Stephen J. Carroll and Craig E. Schneier, *Performance Appraisal and Review Systems* (Glenview, IL: Scott Foresman, 1982).

[16] See George T. Milkovich and John W. Boudreau, *Personnel/Human Resource Management: A Diagnostic Approach*, 5th ed. (Plano, TX: Business Publications, 1988).

[17] Examples are from Jena McGregor, "Job Review in 140 Keystrokes," *Business Week* (March 23 and 30, 2009), p. 58.

[18] For an overall discussion see Greg R. Oldham and J. Richard Hackman, "Not What It Was and Not What It Will Be: The Future of Job Design Research," *Journal of Organizational Behavior* 31 (2010), pp. 463–479.

[19] Frederick W. Taylor, *The Principles of Scientific Management* (New York: Norton, 1967).

[20] Frederick Herzberg, "One More Time: How Do You Motivate Employees?" *Harvard Business Review* 46 (January/February 1968), pp. 53–62.

[21] For a complete description, see J. Richard Hackman and Greg R. Oldham, *Work Redesign* (Reading, MA: Addison-Wesley, 1980).

[22] See J. Richard Hackman and Greg Oldham, "Development of the Job Diagnostic Survey," *Journal of Applied Psychology* 60 (1975), pp. 159–170.

[23] See, for example, Kenneth D. Thomas and Betty A. Velthouse, "Cognitive Elements of Empowerment: An 'Interpretive' Model of Intrinsic Task Motivation," *Academy of Management Review*, 15.4 (1990), pp. 666–681.

[24] For forerunner research, see Charles L. Hulin and Milton R. Blood, "Job Enlargement, Individual Differences, and Worker Responses," *Psychological Bulletin* 69 (1968), pp. 41–55; and Milton R. Blood and Charles L. Hulin, "Alienation, Environmental Characteristics and Worker Responses," *Journal of Applied Psychology* 51 (1967), pp. 284–290.

[25] Gerald Salancik and Jeffrey Pfeffer, "An Examination of Need-Satisfaction Models of Job Attitudes," *Administrative Science Quarterly* 22 (1977), pp. 427–456; Gerald Salancik and Jeffrey Pfeffer, "A Social Information Processing Approach to Job Attitude and Task Design," *Administrative Science Quarterly* 23 (1978), pp. 224–253.

[26] For overviews, see Allan R. Cohen and Herman Gadon, *Alternative Work Schedules: Integrating Individual and Organizational Needs* (Reading, MA: Addison-Wesley, 1978); and Jon L. Pearce, John W. Newstrom, Randall B. Dunham, and Alison E. Barber, *Alternative Work Schedules* (Boston: Allyn & Bacon, 1989). See also Sharon Parker and Toby Wall, *Job and Work Design* (Thousand Oaks, CA: Sage, 1998).

[27] Data reported in "A Saner Workplace," *BusinessWeek* (June 1, 2009), pp. 66–69, and based on excerpt from Claire Shipman and Katty Kay, *Womenomics: Write Your Own Rules for Success* (New York: Harper Business, 2009); and "A to Z of Generation Y Attitudes," *Financial Times* (June 18, 2009).

[28] See Sue Shellenbarger, "What Makes a Company a Great Place to Work," *Wall Street Journal* (October 4, 2007), p. D1.

[29] Olga Kharif, "Chopping Hours, Not Heads," *BusinessWeek* (January 5, 2009), p. 85.

[30] See Wayne F. Cascio, "Managing a Virtual Workplace," *Academy of Management Executive* 14 (2000), pp. 81–90.

[31] Claire Suddath, "Work-from-Home Truths, Half-Truths, and Myths," *BloombergBusinessWeek* (March 4–March 10, 2013), p. 75.

[32] Quote from Phil Porter, "Telecommuting Mom Is Part of a National Trend," *Columbus Dispatch* (November 29, 2000), pp. H1, H2.

[33] Ibid.

[34] *Times*, opinionator.blogs.nytimes.com (January 26, 2013): (accessed August 8, 2013).

[35] Heesun Wee, "Why More Millennials Go Part Time for Full Time Pay" (October 1, 2013), accessed June 29, 2013, at www.cnbc.com/id/49181054.

Chapter 7

[1] Information from Scott Thurm, "Teamwork Raises Everyone's Game," *Wall Street Journal* (November 7, 2005), p. B7.

[2] Ibid.

[3] See, for example, Jon R. Katzenbach and Douglas K. Smith, "The Discipline of Teams," *Harvard Business Review* (March/April 1993a), pp. 111–120; and Jon R. Katzenbach and Douglas K. Smith, *The Wisdom of Teams: Creating the High-Performance Organization* (Boston: Harvard Business School Press, 1993b).

[4] For a good overview, see Greg L. Stewart, Charles C. Manz, and Henry P. Sims, *Team Work and Group Dynamics* (New York: Wiley, 1999).

[5] Katzenbach and Smith (1993a, 1993b), op. cit.

[6] Katzenbach and Smith (1993a), op. cit., p. 112.

[7] Katzenbach and Smith (1993a, 1993b), op. cit.

[8] See Jon R. Katzenbach, "The Myth of the Top Management Team," *Harvard Business Review* 75 (November/December 1997), pp. 83–91.

[9] See Stewart, Manz, and Sims (1999), pp. 43–44.

[10] Rensis Likert, *New Patterns of Management* (New York: McGraw-Hill, 1961).

[11] See Jay R. Galbraith, *Designing Organizations* (San Francisco: Jossey-Bass, 1998).

[12] Robert P. Steel, Anthony J. Mento, Benjamin L. Dilla, Nestor Ovalle, and Russell F. Lloyd, "Factors Influencing the Success and Failure of Two Quality Circles Programs," *Journal of Management* 11.1 (1985), pp. 99–119; and Edward E. Lawler III and Susan A. Mohrman, "Quality Circles: After the Honeymoon," *Organizational Dynamics* 15.4 (1987), pp. 42–54.

[13] See, for example, Paul S. Goodman, Rukmini Devadas, and Terri L. Griffith Hughson, "Groups and Productivity: Analyzing the Effectiveness of Self-Managing Teams," ch. 11, in John R. Campbell and Richard J. Campbell (eds.), *Productivity in Organizations* (San Francisco: Jossey-Bass, 1988); Jack Orsbrun, Linda Moran, Ed Musslewhite, and John H. Zenger, with Craig Perrin, *Self-Directed Work Teams: The New American Challenge* (Homewood, IL: Business One Irwin, 1990); and Dale E. Yeatts and Cloyd Hyten, *High Performing Self-Managed Work Teams* (Thousand Oaks, CA: Sage, 1997).

[14] See D. Duarte and N. Snyder, *Mastering Virtual Teams: Strategies, Tools, and Techniques that Succeed* (San Francisco: Jossey-Bass, 1999); and Jessica Lipnack and Jeffrey Stamps, *Virtual Teams: Reaching Across Space, Time, and Organizations with Technology* (New York: Wiley, 1997).

[15] For reviews see Wayne F. Cascio, "Managing a Virtual Workplace," *Academy of Management Executive* 14 (2000), pp. 81–90; and Sheila Simsarian Webber, "Virtual Teams: A Meta-Analysis" (2002), paper presented at the Academy of Management Conference, Denver, CO.

[16] Stacie A. Furst, Martha Reeves, Benson Rosen, and Richard S. Blackburn, "Managing the Life Cycle of Virtual Teams," *Academy of Management Executive* 18.2 (2004), pp. 6–11; Ibid.; Duarte and Schneider (1999), op. cit.; Lipnack and Stamps (1997), op. cit.; and J. Richard Hackman by Diane Coutu, "Why Teams Don't Work," *Harvard Business Review* (May 2009), pp. 99–105.

[17] See, for example, J. Richard Hackman and Nancy Katz, "Group Behavior and Performance," ch. 32, pp. 1208–1251, in Susan T. Fiske, Daniel T. Gilbert, and Gardner Lindzey (eds.), *Handbook of Social Psychology,* 5th ed. (Hoboken, NJ: Wiley, 2010).

[18] Marvin E. Shaw, *Group Dynamics: The Psychology of Small Group Behavior*, 2nd ed. (New York: McGraw-Hill, 1976).

[19] Bib Latané, Kipling Williams, and Stephen Harkins, "Many Hands Make Light the Work: The Causes and Consequences of Social Loafing," *Journal of Personality and Social Psychology* 37 (1978), pp. 822–832; E. Weklon and G. M. Gargano, "Cognitive Effort in Additive Task Groups: The Effects of Shared Responsibility on the Quality of Multi-Attribute Judgments," *Organizational Behavior and Human Decision Processes* 36 (1985), pp. 348–361; John M. George, "Extrinsic and Intrinsic Origins of Perceived Social Loafing in Organizations," *Academy of Management Journal* (March 1992), pp. 191–202; and W. Jack Duncan, "Why Some People Loaf in Groups While Others Loaf Alone," *Academy of Management Executive* 8 (1994), pp. 79–80.

[20] D. A. Kravitz and B. Martin, "Ringelmann Rediscovered," *Journal of Personality and Social Psychology* 50 (1986), pp. 936–941.

[21] John M. George (1992), op. cit.; and W. Jack Duncan (1994), op. cit.

[22] A classic article by Richard B. Zajonc, "Social Facilitation," *Science* 149 (1965), pp. 269–274.

[23] See, for example, Leland P. Bradford, *Group Development*, 2nd ed. (San Francisco: Jossey-Bass, 1997).

[24] J. Steven Heinen and Eugene Jacobson, "A Model of Task Group Development in Complex Organizations and a Strategy of Implementation," *Academy of Management Review* 1 (October 1976), pp. 98–111; Bruce W. Tuckman, "Developmental Sequence in Small Groups," *Psychological Bulletin* 63 (1965), pp. 384–399; and Bruce W. Tuckman and Mary Ann C. Jensen, "Stages of Small Group Development Revisited," *Group & Organization Studies* 2 (1977), pp. 419–427.

[25] Quote from Alex Markels, "Money & Business," usnews.com (October 22, 2006).

[26] Ibid.

[27] Example from Jessica Sung, "Designed for Interaction," *Fortune* (January 8, 2001), p. 150.

[28] David M. Herold, "The Effectiveness of Work Groups," in Steven Kerr (ed.), *Organizational Behavior* (New York: Wiley, 1979), p. 95. See also the discussion of group tasks in Stewart, Manz, and Sims (1999), op. cit., pp. 142–143.

[29] F. J. Thomas and C. F. Fink, "Effects of Group Size," in Larry L. Cummings and William E. Scott (eds.), *Readings in Organizational and Human Performance* (Homewood, IL: Irwin, 1969), pp. 394–408.

[30] Thomas and Fink (1969), op. cit.

[31] Robert D. Hof, "Amazon's Risky Bet," *BusinessWeek* (November 13, 2006), p. 52.

[32] Shaw (1976), op. cit.

[33] William C. Schultz, *FIRO: A Three-Dimensional Theory of Interpersonal Behavior* (New York: Rinehart, 1958).

[34] William C. Schultz, "The Interpersonal Underworld," *Harvard Business Review* 36 (July/August 1958), p. 130.

[35] See Daniel, R. Ilgen, Jeffrey A. LePiner, and John R. Hollenbeck, "Effective Decision Making in Multinational Teams," in P. Christopher Earley and Miriam Erez (eds.), *New Perspectives on International Industrial/Organizational Psychology* (San Francisco: New Lexington Press, 1997), pp. 377–409.

[36] Matt Golosinski, "Teamwork Takes Center Stage," *Northwestern* (Winter 2005), p. 39.

[37] Ilgen, LePine, and Hollenbeck (1997), op. cit.; and Warren Watson, "Cultural Diversity's Impact on Interaction Process and Performance," *Academy of Management Journal* 16 (1993).

[38] L. Argote and J. E. McGrath, "Group Processes in Organizations: Continuity and Change," in C. L. Cooper and I. T. Robertson (eds.), *International Review of Industrial and Organizational Psychology* (New York: Wiley, 1993), pp. 333–389.

[39] See Ilgen, LePiner, and Hollenbeck (1997), op. cit.

[40] Golosinski (2005), op. cit., p. 39.

[41] "Dream Teams," *Northwestern* (Winter 2005), p. 10; and Golosinski (2005), op. cit.

[42] Anita Williams Woolley, Christopher F. Chabris, Alex Pentland, Nada Hasmi, and Thomas W. Malone, "Evidence for a Collective Intelligence Factor in the Performance of Human Groups," *Science* 330 (October 29, 2010), pp. 686–688.

Chapter 8

[1] See Owen Linzmeyer and Owen W. Linzmeyer, *Apple Confidential 2.0: The Definitive History of the World's Most Colorful Company* (San Francisco: No Starch Press, 2004); and Jeffrey L. Cruikshank, *The Apple Way* (New York: McGraw-Hill, 2005).

[2] Diane Coutu, "Why Teams Don't Work," *Harvard Business Review* (May 2009), pp. 99–105.

[3] Ibid.

[4] Steven Levy, "Insanely Great," *Wired* (February 1994), accessed July 1, 2013, at www.wired.com/wired/archive/2.02/macintosh_pr.html.

[5] Ibid.

[6] Anita Williams Woolley, Christopher F. Chabris, Alex Pentland, Nada Hasmi, and Thomas W. Malone, "Evidence for a Collective Intelligence Factor in the Performance of Human Groups," *Science* 330 (October) 29, 2010), pp. 686–688.

[7] For an interesting discussion of sports teams, see Ellen Fagenson-Eland, "The National Football League's Bill Parcells on Winning, Leading, and Turning around Teams," *Academy of Management Executive* 15 (August 2001), pp. 48–57; and Nancy Katz, "Sport Teams as a Model for Workplace Teams: Lessons and Liabilities," *Academy of Management Executive* 15 (August 2002), pp. 56–69.

[8] See William D. Dyer, *Team Building*, 3rd ed. (Reading, MA: Addison-Wesley, 1995).

[9] Dennis Berman, "Zap! Pow! Splat!" *BusinessWeek*, Enterprise Issue (February 9, 1998), p. ENT22.

[10] The classic work in this area is George Homans, *The Human Group* (New York: Harcourt Brace, 1950).

[11] Developed from a discussion by Edgar H. Schein, *Process Consultation* (Reading, MA: Addison-Wesley, 1969), pp. 32–37; and Edgar H. Schein, *Process Consultation,* Vol. 1 (Reading, MA: Addison-Wesley, 1988), pp. 40–49.

[12] The classic work is Robert F. Bales, "Task Roles and Social Roles in Problem-Solving Groups," in Eleanor E. Maccoby, Theodore M. Newcomb, and E. L. Hartley (eds.), *Readings in Social Psychology* (New York: Holt, Rinehart & Winston, 1958).

[13] For a good description of task and maintenance functions, see John J. Gabarro and Anne Harlan, "Note on Process Observation," Note 9-477-029 (Harvard Business School, 1976).

[14] Christine Porath and Christine Pearson, "How Toxic Colleagues Corrode Performance," *Harvard Business Review* (April 2009), p. 24.

[15] See Daniel C. Feldman, "The Development and Enforcement of Group Norms," *Academy of Management Review* 9 (1984), pp. 47–53.

[16] See Robert F. Allen and Saul Pilnick, "Confronting the Shadow Organization: How to Select and Defeat Negative Norms," *Organizational Dynamics* (Spring 1973), pp. 13–17; and Alvin Zander, *Making Groups Effective* (San Francisco: Jossey-Bass, 1982), ch. 4; Feldman (1984), op. cit.

[17] For a summary of research on group cohesiveness, see Marvin E. Shaw, *Group Dynamics* (New York: McGraw-Hill, 1971), pp. 110–112, 192.

[18] See Jay R. Galbraith, *Designing Organizations* (San Francisco: Jossey-Bass, 1998).

[19] Jerry Yoram Wind and Jeremy Main, *Driving Change: How the Best Companies Are Preparing for the 21st Century* (New York: Free Press, 1998), p. 135.

[20] The concept of interacting, coaching, and counteracting groups is presented in Fred E. Fiedler, *A Theory of Leadership Productivity* (New York: McGraw-Hill, 1967).

[21] Research on communication networks is found in Alex Bavelas, "Communication Patterns in Task-Oriented Groups," *Journal of the Acoustical Society of America* 22 (1950), pp. 725–730. See also "Research on Communication Networks," as summarized in Shaw (1971), op. cit., pp. 137–153.

[22] A classic work on proxemics is Edward T. Hall's book, *The Hidden Dimension* (Garden City, NY: Doubleday, 1986).

[23] Mirand Wewll, "Alternative Spaces Spawning Desk-Free Zones," *Columbus Dispatch* (May 18, 1998), pp. 10–11.

[24] "Tread: Rethinking the Workplace," *BusinessWeek* (September 25, 2006), p. IN.

[25] Michelle Conlin and Douglas MacMillan, "Managing the Tweets," *BusinessWeek* (June 1, 2009), pp. 20–21.

[26] See Wayne F. Cascio, "Managing a Virtual Workplace," *Academy of Management Executive* 14 (2000), pp. 81–90; Sheila Simsarian Webber, "Virtual Teams: A Meta-Analysis," www.shrm.org/foundation/findings.asp; and Stacie A. Furst, Martha Reeves, Benson Rosen, and Richard S. Blackburn, "Managing the Life Cycle of Virtual Teams," *Academy of Management Executive* 18 (2004), pp. 6–20.

[27] The discussion is developed from Sch ein (1988), op. cit., pp. 69–75.

[28] Developed from guidelines presented in the classic article by Jay Hall, "Decisions, Decisions, Decisions," *Psychology Today* (November 1971), pp. 55–56.

[29] Norman R. F. Maier, "Assets and Liabilities in Group Problem Solving," *Psychological Review* 74 (1967), pp. 239–249.

[30] Irving L. Janis, "Groupthink," *Psychology Today* (November 1971), pp. 33–36; and Irving L. Janis. *Groupthink*, 2nd ed. (Boston: Houghton Mifflin, 1982). See also J. Longley and D. G. Pruitt, "Groupthink: A Critique of Janis' Theory," in L. Wheeler (ed.), *Review of Personality and Social Psychology* (Beverly Hills, CA: Sage, 1980); and Carrie R. Leana, "A Partial Test of Janis's Groupthink Model: The Effects of Group Cohesiveness and Leader Behavior on Decision Processes," *Journal of Management* 1.1 (1985), pp. 5–18. See also Jerry Harvey, "Managing Agreement in Organizations: The Abilene Paradox," *Organizational Dynamics* (Summer 1974), pp. 63–80.

[31] See Janis (1971, 1982), op. cit.

[32] Gayle W. Hill, "Group versus Individual Performance: Are Two Leads Better Than One?" *Psychological Bulletin* 91 (1982), pp. 517–539.

[33] These techniques are well described in George P. Huber, *Managerial Decision Making* (Glenview, IL: Scott, Foresman, 1980); Andre L. Delbecq, Andrew L. Van de Ven, and David H. Gustafson, *Group Techniques for Program Planning: A Guide to Nominal Groups and Delphi Techniques* (Glenview, IL: Scott, Foresman. 1975); and William M. Fox, "Anonymity and Other Keys to a Successful Problem-Solving Meeting," *National Productivity Review* 8 (Spring 1989), pp. 145–156.

[34] Anne Stein, "On Track," *Kellogg* (Winter, 2012), pp. 14–27. See also Leigh Thompson, *The Creative Conspiracy: The New Rules of Breakthrough Collaboration* (Cambridge, MA: Harvard Business Review Press, 2013).

[35] Delbecq et al. (1975), op. cit.

Chapter 9

[1] "Skills Stakeholders Want," *Biz-Ed* (May/June 2009), p. 11.

[2] For concise overviews, see Susan J. Miller, David J. Hickson, and David C. Wilson, "Decision-Making in Organizations" in Steward R. Clegg, Cynthia Hardy, and Walter Nord (eds.), *Handbook of Organizational Studies* (London: Sage, 1996); and George P. Huber, *Managerial Decision Making* (Glenview, IL: Scott Foresman, 1980), pp. 293–312.

[3] This figure and the related discussion are developed from conversations with Dr. Alma Acevedo of the University of Puerto Rico at Rio Piedras and from her articles "Of Fallacies and Curricula: A Case of Business Ethics," *Teaching Business Ethics* 5 (2001), pp. 157–170, and "Business Ethics: An Introduction," working paper (2009).

[4] Acevedo (2009), op. cit.

[5] Stephen Fineman, "Emotion and Organizing," in Clegg, Hardy, and Nord (eds.) (1996) op. cit., pp. 542–580.

[6] For discussion of ethical frameworks for decision making, see Joseph R. Desjardins, *Business, Ethics and the Environment* (Upper Saddle River, NJ: Pearson Education, 2007); Linda A. Trevino and Katherine A. Nelson, *Managing Business Ethics* (New York: Wiley, 1995); Saul W. Gellerman, "Why 'Good' Managers Make Bad Ethical Choices," *Harvard Business Review* 64 (July/August 1986), pp. 85–90; and Barbara Ley Toffler, *Tough Choices: Managers Talk Ethics* (New York: Wiley, 1986).

[7] Based on Gerald F. Cavanagh, *American Business Values*, 4th ed. (Upper Saddle River, NJ: Prentice-Hall, 1998).

[8] The Josephson Institute, www.josephsoninstitute.org.

[9] This section stems from the classic work on decision making found in Michael D. Cohen, James G. March, and Johan P. Olsen, "The Garbage Can Model of Organizational Choice," *Administrative Science Quarterly* 17 (1972), pp. 1–25; and James G. March and Herbert A. Simon, *Organizations* (New York: Wiley, 1958), pp. 137–142.

[10] See, for example, Jonathan Rosenoer and William Scherlis, "Risk Gone Wild," *Harvard Business Review* (May 2009), p. 26.

[11] See KPMG, "Enterprise Risk Management," www.kpmg.com/global/en/topics/climate-change-sustainability-services/pages/enterprise-risk-management.aspx, accessed July 3, 2013.

[12] For scholarly reviews, see Dean Tjosvold, "Effects of Crisis Orientation on Managers' Approach to Controversy in Decision Making," *Academy of Management Journal* 27 (1984), pp. 130–138; and Ian I. Mitroff, Paul Shrivastava, and Firdaus E. Udwadia, "Effective Crisis Management," *Academy of Management Executive* 1 (1987), pp. 283–292.

[13] Ibid.

[14] Mitroff et. al (1987), op. cit.

[15] This traditional distinction is often attributed to Herbert Simon, *Administrative Behavior* (New York: Free Press, 1945); see also Herbert Simon, *The New Science of Management Decision* (New York: Harper and Row, 1960).

[16] For a historical review, see Leight Buchanan and Andrew O'Connell, "Thinking Machines," *Harvard Business Review* 84.1 (2006), pp. 38–49. For recent applications, see Jiju Antony, Raj Anand, Maneesh Kumar, and M. K. Tiwari, "Multiple Response Optimization Using Taguchi Methodology and Nero-Fuzzy Based Model," *Journal of Manufacturing Technology Management* 17.7 (2006), pp. 908–112; and Craig Boutilier, "The Influence of Influence Diagrams on Artificial Intelligence," *Decision Analysis* 2.4 (2005), pp. 229–232.

[17] Simon, *Administrative Behavior* (1945), op. cit. See also Mary Zey (ed.), *Decision Making: Alternatives to Rational Choice Models* (Thousand Oaks, CA: Sage, 1992).

[18] March and Simo (1958), op. cit.

[19] For a comprehensive discussion see Daniel Kahneman, *Thinking, Fast and Slow* (New York: Random House), 2011.

[20] For a good discussion, see Watson H. Agor, *Intuition in Organizations: Leading and Managing Productively* (Newbury Park, CA: Sage, 1989); Herbert A. Simon, "Making Management Decisions: The Role of Intuition and Emotion," *Academy of Management Executive* 1 (1987), pp. 57–64; Orlando Behling and Norman L. Eckel, "Making Sense Out of Intuition," *Academy of Management Executive* 1 (1987), pp. 57–64; and Orlando Behling and Norman L. Eckel, "Making Sense Out of Intuition," *Academy of Management Executive* 5 (1991), pp. 46–54.

[21] Agor (1989), op. cit.

[22] Quote from Susan Carey, "Pilot 'in Shock' as He Landed Jet in River," *Wall Street Journal* (February 9, 2009), p. A6.

[23] The classic work in this area is found in a series of articles by D. Kahneman and A. Tversky, "Subjective Probability: A Judgment of Representativeness," *Cognitive Psychology* 3 (1972), pp. 430–454; "On the Psychology of Prediction," *Psychological Review* 80 (1973), pp. 237–251; "Prospect Theory: An Analysis of Decision under Risk,"

Econometrica 47 (1979), pp. 263–291; "Psychology of Preferences," *Scientific American* (1982), pp. 161–173; and "Choices, Values, Frames," *American Psychologist* 39 (1984), pp. 341–350. Alsop see Kahneman (2011), op. cit.

[24] See Max H. Bazerman, *Judgment in Managerial Decision Making*, 6th ed. (New York: Wiley, 2005).

[25] Barry M. Staw, "The Escalation of Commitment to a Course of Action," *Academy of Management Review* 6 (1981), pp. 577–587; Barry M. Staw and Jerry Ross, "Knowing When to Pull the Plug," *Harvard Business Review* 65 (March/April 1987), pp. 68–74. See also Glen Whyte, "Escalating Commitment to a Course of Action: A Reinterpretation," *Academy of Management Review* 11 (1986), pp. 311–321; Joel Brockner, "The Escalation of Commitment to a Failing Course of Action: Toward Theoretical Progress," *Academy of Management Review* 17 (1992), pp. 39–61; and J. Ross and B. M. Staw, "Organizational Escalation and Exit: Lessons from the Shoreham Nuclear Power Plant," *Academy of Management Journal* 36 (1993), pp. 701–732.

[26] Joel Brockner, "The Escalation of Commitment to a Failing Course of Action: Toward Theoretical Progress," *Academy of Management Review* 17 (1992), pp. 39–61; and Ross and Staw (1993), op. cit.

[27] They may also try to include too many others, as shown by Phillip G. Clampitt and M. Lee Williams in "Decision Downsizing," *MIT Sloan Management Review* 48.2 (2007), pp. 77–89.

[28] Victor H. Vroom and Arthur G. Jago, *The New Leadership: Managing Participation in Organizations* (Englewood Cliffs, NJ: Prentice-Hall, 1988). This is based on earlier work by Victor H. Vroom, "A New Look in Managerial Decision-Making," *Organizational Dynamics* (Spring 1973), pp. 66–80; and Victor H. Vroom and Phillip Yetton, *Leadership and Decision-Making* (Pittsburgh, PA: University of Pittsburgh Press, 1973).

[29] Vroom and Yetton (1973), op. cit.; and Vroom and Jago (1988), op. cit.

[30] See the discussion by Victor H. Vroom, "Leadership and the Decision Making Process," *Organizational Dynamics* 28 (2000), pp. 82–94.

Chapter 10

[1] See, for example, Henry Mintzberg, *The Nature of Managerial Work* (New York: Harper & Row, 1973); and John R. P. Kotter, *The General Managers* (New York: Free Press, 1982).

[2] One of the classic discussions is by Richard E. Walton, *Interpersonal Peacemaking: Confrontations and Third-Party Consultation* (Reading, MA: Addison-Wesley, 1969).

[3] Kenneth W. Thomas and Warren H. Schmidt, "A Survey of Managerial Interests with Respect to Conflict," *Academy of Management Journal* 19 (1976), pp. 315–318.

[4] For a good overview, see Richard E. Walton, *Managing Conflict: Interpersonal Dialogue and Third Party Roles*, 2nd ed. (Reading, MA: Addison-Wesley, 1987); and Dean Tjosvold, *The Conflict-Positive Organization: Stimulate Diversity and Create Unity* (Reading, MA: Addison-Wesley, 1991).

[5] Walton (1969), op. cit.

[6] Ibid.

[7] Geert Hofstede, *Culture's Consequences: International Differences in Work-Related Values* (Beverly Hills, CA: Sage, 1980); and Geert Hofstede, "Cultural Constraints in Management Theories," *Academy of Management Executive* 7 (1993), pp. 81–94.

[8] Information from "Capitalizing on Diversity: Navigating the Seas of the Multicultural Workforce and Workplace," *BusinessWeek*, Special Advertising Section (December 4, 1998).

[9] These stages are consistent with the conflict models described by Alan C. Filley, *Interpersonal Conflict Resolution* (Glenview, IL: Scott Foresman, 1975); and Louis R. Pondy, "Organizational Conflict: Concepts and Models," *Administrative Science Quarterly* (September 1967), pp. 269–320.

[10] Information from Ken Brown and Gee L. Lee. "Lucent Fires Top China Executives," *Wall Street Journal* (April 7, 2004), p. A8.

[11] Walton and Dutton (1969), op. cit.

[12] Rensis Likert and Jane B. Likert, *New Ways of Managing Conflict* (New York: McGraw-Hill, 1976).

[13] See Jay Galbraith, *Designing Complex Organizations* (Reading, MA: Addison-Wesley, 1973); and David Nadler and Michael Tushman, *Strategic Organizational Design* (Glenview, IL: Scott Foresman, 1988).

[14] E. M. Eisenberg and M. G. Witten, "Reconsidering Openness in Organizational Communication," *Academy of Management Review* 12 (1987), pp. 418–426.

[15] R. G. Lord and M. C. Kernan, "Scripts as Determinants of Purposeful Behavior in Organizations," *Academy of Management Review* 12 (1987), pp. 265–277.

[16] See Filley (1975), op. cit.; and L. David Brown, *Managing Conflict at Organizational Interfaces* (Reading, MA: Addison-Wesley, 1983).

[17] Ibid., pp. 27, 29.

[18] For discussions, see Robert R. Blake and Jane Strygley Mouton, "The Fifth Achievement," *Journal of Applied Behavioral Science* 6 (1970), pp. 413–427; Kenneth Thomas, "Conflict and Conflict Management," in M. D. Dunnett (ed.), *Handbook of Industrial and Organizational Behavior* (Chicago: Rand McNally, 1976), pp. 889–935; and Kenneth W. Thomas, "Toward Multi-Dimensional Values in Teaching: The Examples of Conflict Behaviors," *Academy of Management Review* 2 (1977), pp. 484–490.

[19] See Roger Fisher and William Ury, *Getting to Yes: Negotiating Agreement Without Giving In* (New York: Penguin, 1983). See also James A. Wall Jr., *Negotiation: Theory and Practice* (Glenview, IL: Scott Foresman, 1985).

[20] Roy J. Lewicki and Joseph A. Litterer, *Negotiation* (Homewood, IL: Irwin, 1985), pp. 315–319.

[21] Ibid., pp. 328–329.

[22] The following discussion is based on Fisher and Ury (1983), op. cit.; and Lewicki and Litterer (1985), op. cit.

[23] This example is developed from Max H. Bazerman, *Judgment in Managerial Decision Making*, 2nd ed. (New York: Wiley, 1991), pp. 106–108.

[24] For a detailed discussion, see Fisher and Ury (1983), op. cit.; and Lewicki and Litterer (1985), op. cit.

[25] Developed from Bazerman (1991), pp. 127–141.

[26] Fisher and Ury (1983), p. 33.

[27] Lewicki and Litterer (1985), pp. 177–181.

Chapter 11

[1] Edward T. Hall, *The Hidden Dimension* (Garden City, NY: Doubleday, 1966).

[2] See D. E. Campbell, "Interior Office Design and Visitor Response," *Journal of Applied Psychology* 64 (1979), pp. 648–653; P. C. Morrow and J. C. McElroy, "Interior Office Design and Visitor Response: A Constructive Replication," *Journal of Applied Psychology* 66 (1981), pp. 646–650.

[3] Information from "Chapter 2.2," *Kellogg* (Winter 2004), p. 6; "Room to Read," *Northwestern* (Spring 2007), pp. 32–33.

[4] The statements are from *BusinessWeek* (July 6, 1981), p. 107.

[5] See C. Bamum and N. Woliansky, "Taking Cues from Body Language," *Management Review* (78) 1989, p. 59; S. Bochner (ed.), *Cultures in Contact: Studies in Cross-Cultural Interaction* (London: Pergamon, 1982); A. Furnham and S. Bochner, *Culture Shock: Psychological Reactions to Unfamiliar Environments* (London: Methuen, 1986); "How Not to Do International Business," *Business Week* (April 12, 1999); Yon Kagegama, "Tokyo Auto Show Highlights," *Associated Press* (October 24, 2001).

[6] Edward T. Hall, *Beyond Culture* (New York: Doubleday, 1976).

[7] Quotes from "Lost in Translation," *The Wall Street Journal* (May 18, 2004), pp. B1, B6.

[8] F. Lee, "Being Polite and Keeping Mum: How Bad News Is Communicated in Organizational Hierarchies," *Journal of Applied Social Psychology* 23 (1983), pp. 1124–1149.

[9] See Elizabeth W. Morrison, "Employee Voice Behavior: Integration and Directions for Future Research," *The Academy of Management Annals* 5 (2011), pp. 373–412.

[10] Ibid.

[11] See Elizabeth W. Morrison and Frances Milliken, "Organizational Silence: A Barrier to Change and Development in a Pluralistic World," *Academy of Management Review* 25 (2000), pp. 706–725, and Elizabeth W. Morrison and Frances Milliken, "Speaking Up, Remaining Silent: The Dynamics of Voice and Silence in Organizations, 40 (2003), pp. 1353–1358; Elizabeth W. Morrison, "Employee Voice Behavior: Integration and Directions for Future Research," *The Academy of Management Annals* 5 (2011), pp. 373–412.

[12] Ibid.

[13] Ibid.

[14] D. A. Whetten and K. S. Cameron, *Developing Management Skills* (New York: Prentice Hall, 2006).

[15] Variation on Epictetus.

[16] Scott D. Williams, "Listening Effectively." Accessed June 1, 2013, at www.wright.edu/~scott.williams/LeaderLetter/listening.htm

[17] Ibid.

[18] "Giving Feedback: Keeping Team Member Performance High, and Well Integrated." Accessed June 2, 2013, at www.mindtools.com/pages/article/newTMM_98.htm

[19] See Susan Ashford, Ruth Blatt, and Don VandeWalle, "Reflections on the Looking Glass: A Review of Research on Feedback-Seeking Behavior in Organizations," *Journal of Management* 29 (2003), pp. 773–799.

[20] Ibid.

[21] See Susan Ashford and Anne Tsui, "Self-Regulation for Managerial Effectiveness: The Role of Active Feedback Seeking," *Academy of Management Journal* 34 (1991), pp. 251–280.

[22] See Jason J. Dahling, Samantha L. Chau, and Alison O'Malley, "Correlates and Consequences of Feedback Orientation in Organizations" *Journal of Management* 38 (2012), pp. 531–546.

[23] B. G. Linderbaum and P. E. Levy, "The Development and Validation of the Feedback Orientation Scale (FOS), *Journal of Management* 36 (2010), pp. 1372–1405; M. London and J. W. Smither, "Feedback Orientation, Feedback Culture, and the Longitudinal Performance Management Process," *Human Resource Management Review* 12 (2002), pp. 81–100.

[24] See Jason J. Dahling, Samantha L. Chau, and Alison O'Malley, "Correlates and Consequences of Feedback Orientation in Organizations," *Journal of Management* 38 (2012), pp. 531–546.

Chapter 12

[1] See Ahmad N. Azim and F. Glenn Boseman, "An Empirical Assessment of Etzioni's Topology of Power and Involvement within a University Setting," *Academy of Management Journal* 18:4 (December 1975); Herbert C. Kelman, "Compliance, Identification, and Internalization: Three Processes of Attitude Change," *The Journal of Conflict Resolution* 2:1 (March 1958): pp. 51–60; and Cameron Anderson, Oliver John, and Dacher Keltner, "The Personal Sense of Power," *Journal of Personality* 80:2 (April 2012).

[2] See Richard M. Emerson, "Power-Dependence Relations," *American Sociological Review* 27:1 (1962); see also David Mechanic, "Sources of Power of Lower Participants in Complex Organizations," *Administrative Science Quarterly* 7:3 (December 1962).

[3] See Mechanic (1962), op. cit.

[4] See Emerson (1962), op. cit. see also Lisa A. Mainiero, "Coping with Powerlessness: The Relationship of Gender and Job Dependency to Empowerment-Strategy Usage," *Administrative Science Quarterly* 31 (1986); Blake E. Ashforth, "The Experience of Powerlessness in Organizations," *Organizational Behavior and Human Decision Processes* 43 (1989); and R. Blauner, *Alienation and Freedom: The Factory Worker and His Industry* (Chicago: University of Chicago Press, 1964).

[5] Cameron Anderson and Jennifer L. Berdahl, "The Experience of Power: Examining the Effects of Power on Approach and Inhibition Tendencies," *Journal of Personality and Social Psychology* 83 (2002), pp. 1362–1377.

[6] See Ashforth (1989), op. cit.

[7] Jack W. Brehm, *A Theory of Psychological Reactance* (New York: Academic Press, 1966).

[8] See Mary Parker Follett, "The Basis of Authority," in L. Urwick (ed.), *Freedom and Coordination: Lectures in Business Organisation by Mary Parker Follett* (London: Management Publications Trust, Ltd., 1949) pp. 34–46.

[9] See John R. P. French, Jr., and Bertram Raven, "The Bases of Social Power," in D. Cartwright (ed.), *Studies in Social Power* (Ann Arbor, MI: Institute for Social Research, 1959), pp. 259–269.

[10] See Bertram H. Raven, "The Bases of Power: Origins and Recent Developments," *Journal of Social Issues* 49:4 (1993), p. 233.

[11] See French and Raven (1959), op. cit.

[12] See Chester Barnard, *The Functions of the Executive* (Cambridge, MA: Harvard University Press, 1938).

[13] See Bill McKelvey, "Emergent Strategy via Complexity Leadership: Using Complexity Science and Adaptive Tension to Build Distributed Intelligence," in Mary Uhl-Bien and Russ Marion (eds.), *Complexity Leadership, Volume I: Conceptual Foundations* (Charlotte, NC: Information Age Publishing, 2008), pp. 225–268.

[14] See Bernard M. Bass, *Leadership, Psychology, and Organizational Behavior* (New York: Harper, 1960). See also French and Raven (1959), op. cit.; Erin Landells and Simon L. Albrecht, "Organizational Political Climate: Shared Perceptions about the Building and Use of Power Bases," *Human Resource Management Review* (2012), doi:10.1016/j.hrmr.2012.06.014.

[15] See Richard M. Emerson, "Power-Dependence Relations," *American Sociological Review* 27:1 (1962).

[16] See Paul Hersey, Kenneth H. Blanchard, and Walter E. Natemeyer, "Situational Leadership, Perception, and the Impact of Power," *Group and Organization Studies* 4 (1979); see also Bertram Raven, "Social Influence and Power," in I. D. Steiner and M. Fishbein (eds.), *Current Studies in Social Psychology* (New York: Holt, Rinehart, Winston, 1965), pp. 371–381.

[17] See L. E. Greiner and V. E. Schein, *Power and Organization Development: Mobilizing Power to Implement Change* (Reading, MA: Addison-Wesley Publishing Company 1988). See also Hersey, Blanchard, and Natemeyer (1979), op. cit.; and Landells and Albrecht (2012), op. cit.

[18] See Rob Cross, "A Smarter Way to Network," *Harvard Business Review* (July–August 2011).

[19] See Herbert C. Kelman, "Compliance, Identification, and Internalization: Three Processes of Attitude Change," *Journal of Conflict Resolution* 2:1 (March 1958), p. 53.

[20] See Bennett J. Tepper, Michelle K. Duffy, and Jason D. Shaw, "Personality Moderators of the Relationship between Abusive Supervision and Subordinates' Resistance," *Journal of Applied Psychology* 86:5 (2001), pp. 974–983.

[21] See Bennett J. Tepper, Mary Uhl-Bien, Gary Kohut, Steven Rogelberg, Daniel Lockhart, and Michael Ensley, "Subordinates' Resistance and Managers' Evaluations of Subordinates' Performance," *Journal of Management* 32:2 (2006), pp. 185–209.

[22] Ibid.

[23] See Tepper, Duffy, and Shaw (2001), op. cit.

[24] See B. J. Tepper, C. A. Schriesheim, D. Nehring, R. J. Nelson, E. C. Taylor, and R. J. Eisenbach, "The Multi-Dimensionality and Multi-Functionality of Subordinates' Resistance to Downward Influence Attempts," paper presented at the annual meeting of the Academy of Management, San Diego, CA (1998).

[25] See Dean C. Ludwig and Clinton O. Longenecker, "The Bathsheba Syndrome: The Ethical Failure of Successful Leaders," *Journal of Business Ethics* 12:4 (1993), pp. 265–273.

[26] Useful reviews include a chapter in Robert H. Miles, *Macro Organizational Behavior* (Santa Monica, CA: Goodyear, 1980); Bronston T. Mayes and Robert W. Allen, "Toward a Definition of Organizational Politics," *Academy of Management Review* 2 (1977), pp. 672–677; Dan Farrell and James C. Petersen, "Patterns of Political Behavior in Organizations," *Academy of Management Review* 7 (1982), pp. 403–412; and D. L. Madison, R. W. Allen, L. W. Porter, and B. T. Mayes, "Organizational Politics: An Exploration of Managers' Perceptions," *Human Relations* 33 (1980), pp. 92–107.

[27] See Philip Selznick, "Foundations of the Theory of Organizations," *American Sociological Review* 13 (1948), pp. 25–35; and Philip Selznick, *Leadership in Administration* (New York: Harper and Row, 1957).

[28] See Chu-Hsiang Chang (2009), op. cit.

[29] See Landells and Albrecht (2012), op. cit.

[30] Ibid.

[31] Ibid.

[32] See A. Drory, "Perceived Political Climate and Job Attitudes," *Organization Studies* 14 (1993), pp. 59–71. See also G. R. Ferris, Darren C. Treadway, Pamela L. Perrewe, Robyn L. Brouer, Ceasar Douglas, and Sean Lux, "Political Skill in Organizations," *Journal of Management* 33 (2007). See also Chu-Hsiang Chang (2009), op. cit.

33 See Landells and Albrecht (2012), op. cit.

34 See Daniel J. Brass, "Taking Stock of Networks and Organizations: A Multilevel Perspective," *Academy of Management Journal* 47:6 (2004).

35 See Gerald R. Ferris, Sherry L. Davidson, and Pamela L. Perrewe, *Political Skill at Work* (Palo Alto, CA: Davies-Black Publishing, 2005).

36 See J. Nahapiet and S. Ghoshal, "Social Capital, Intellectual Capital, and the Organizational Advantage," *Academy of Management Review*, 23:2 (1998), p. 243.

37 See Daniel J. Brass, "Taking Stock of Networks and Organizations: A Multilevel Perspective," *Academy of Management Journal* 47:6 (2004); E. Bueno, P. Salmador, and O. Rodriguez, "The Role of Social Capital in Today's Economy, "*Journal of Intellectual Capital* 5 (2004), pp. 556–574; and H. C. Sozen, "Social Networks and Power in Organizations: A Research on the Roles and Positions of Junior Level Secretaries in an Organizational Network, *Personnel Review* 41 (2012), pp. 487–512.

38 See R. S. Burt, *Structural Holes: The Social Structure of Competition* (Cambridge, MA: Harvard University Press, 1992).

Chapter 13

1 See Edwin P. Hollander and James W. Julian, "Contemporary Trends in the Analysis of Leadership Processes," *Psychological Bulletin* 71 (1969), pp. 387–397. See also Gary Yukl, *Leadership in Organizations,* 8th ed. (Boston: Pearson, 2013).

2 See Edwin P. Hollander, "Emergent Leadership and Social Influence," in L. Petrullo and B.M. Bass (eds.), *Leadership and Interpersonal Behavior* (New York: Holt, Rinehart & Winston, 1961), pp. 30–47; see also Edwin P. Hollander, "Processes of Leadership Emergence," *Journal of Contemporary Business* 3 (1974), pp. 19–33.

3 See Gail Fairhurst and Mary Uhl-Bien, "Organizational Discourse Analysis (ODA): Examining Leadership as a Relational Process," *The Leadership Quarterly* 23:6 (2012), pp. 1043–1062.

4 See D. Scott DeRue and Susan J. Ashford, "Who Will Lead and Who Will Follow? A Social Process of Leadership Identity Construction in Organizations," *Academy of Management Review* 35 (2010), pp. 627–647.

5 Ibid.

6 See K. Y. Chan and F. Drasgow, "Toward a Theory of Individual Differences and Leadership: Understanding the Motivation to Lead," *Journal of Applied Psychology* 86 (2001), pp. 481–498; and R. Kark and D. van Dijk, "Motivation to Lead, Motivation to Follow: The Role of the Self-Regulatory Focus in Leadership Processes," *Academy of Management Review* 32 (2007), pp. 500–528.

7 D. Eden and U. Leviatan. "Implicit Leadership Theory as a Determinant of the Factor Structure Underlying Supervisory Behavior Scales," *Journal of Applied Psychology* 60 (1975), pp. 736–741; and R. Lord and C. Emrich, "Thinking Outside the Box by Looking Inside the Box: Extending the Cognitive Revolution in Leadership Research," *The Leadership Quarterly* 11 (2001), pp. 551–579.

8 Based on L. R. Offermann, John K. Kennedy, Jr., and P. W. Wirtz. "Implicit Leadership Theories: Content, Structure, and Generalizability, *The Leadership Quarterly* 5 (1994), pp. 43–58.

9 J. Meindl, S. Erlich, and J. Dukerich, "The Romance of Leadership," *Administrative Science Quarterly* 30 (1985), pp. 78–102.

10 M. Uhl-Bien and R. Pillai, "The Romance of Leadership and the Social Construction of Followership," in B. Shamir, R. Pillai, M. Bligh, and M. Uhl-Bien (eds.), *Follower-Centered Perspectives on Leadership: A Tribute to the Memory of James R. Meindl* (Charlotte, NC: Information Age Publishers, 2007, pp. 187–209).

11 M. Carsten, M. Uhl-Bien, B. West, J. Patera, and R. McGregor, "Exploring Social Constructions of Followership, *The Leadership Quarterly* 21:3, (2010), pp. 543–562.

12 M. Carsten, M. Uhl-Bien, and L. Huang, "How Followers See Their Role in Relation to Leaders: An Investigation of Follower Role Orientation," working paper, University of Nebraska (2013).

13 See Bradley Kirkman, Gilad Chen, Jiing-Lih Harh, Zhen Xiong Chen, and Kevin Lowe, "Individual Power Distance Orientation and Follower Reactions to Transformational Leaders: A Cross-Cultural Examination," *Academy of Management Journal* 52 (2009), pp. 744–764.

14 Carsten et al. (2013), op. cit.

15 T. Sy, "What Do You Think of Followers? Examining the Content, Structure, and Consequences of Implicit Followership Theories," *Organizational Behavior and Human Decision Processes 113*:2 (2010), pp. 73–84.

16 Based on T. Sy, "What Do You Think of Followers? Examining the Content, Structure, and Consequences of Implicit Followership Theories," *Organizational Behavior and Human Decision Processes* 113:2 (2010), pp. 73–84.

17 G. B. Graen and M. Uhl-Bien, "Relationship-Based Approach to Leadership: Development of Leader-Member Exchange (LMX) Theory of Leadership over 25 Years: Applying a Multi-Level Multi-Domain Perspective," *The Leadership Quarterly* 6 (1995), pp. 219–247.

18 See B. Tepper, "Abusive Supervision in Work Organizations: Review, Synthesis and Research Agenda," *Journal of Management* 33 (2007), pp. 261–289.

19 G. C. Homans, "Social Behavior as Exchange," *American Journal of Sociology* 63 (1958), pp. 597–606.

20 A. W. Gouldner, "The Norm of Reciprocity: A Preliminary Statement," *American Sociological Review* 25 (1960), pp. 161–177.

21 E. P. Hollander, "Conformity, Status, and Idiosyncrasy Credit," *Psychological Review* 65 (1958), pp. 117–127.

159

[22] C. A. Gibb, "The Sociometry of Leadership in Temporary Groups," *Sociometry* 13:3, pp. 226–243; and C. A. Gibb, "Leadership," in G. Lindzay (ed.), *Handbook of Social Psychology,* Vol. 2, (Reading, MA: Addison-Wesley, 1954), pp. 877–917.

[23] R. Bolden, "Distributed Leadership in Organizations: A Review of Theory and Research," *International Journal of Management Reviews* 13:3 (2011), pp. 251–269; and R. Bolden, G. Petrov, and J. Gosling, "Distributed Leadership in Higher Education: Rhetoric and Reality," *Educational Management Administration & Leadership* 37:2 (2009), pp. 257–277.

[24] See Mary Uhl-Bien, Russ Marion, and Bill McKelvey, "Complexity Leadership Theory: Shifting Leadership from the Industrial Age to the Knowledge Era," *The Leadership Quarterly* 18:4 (2007), pp. 298–318.

[25] See J.L. Denis, A. Langley, and V. Sergi, "Leadership in the Plural," *The Academy of Management Annals* 6 (2012), pp. 211–283.

[26] Ibid.

[27] C. L. Pearce, "The Future of Leadership: Combining Vertical and Shared Leadership to Transform Knowledge Work," *Academy of Management Executive* 18:1 (2004), pp. 47–59; and C. L. Pearce and J. A. Conger (eds.), *Shared Leadership: Reframing the Hows and Whys of Leadership* (Thousand Oaks, CA: Sage Publications, 2003).

[28] C. Pearce and C. Manz, "The New Silver Bullets of Leadership: The Importance of Self- and Shared Leadership in Knowledge Work," *Organizational Dynamics* 34:2 (2005), pp. 130–140.

Chapter 14

[1] See Gary Yukl, *Leadership in Organizations*, 8th ed. (New York: Pearson, 2013).

[2] See Timothy Judge, Joyce Bono, Remus Ilies, and Megan Gerhardt, "Personality and Leadership: A Qualitative and Quantitative Review," *Journal of Applied Psychology* 87 (2002), pp. 765–780.

[3] See Mark Van Vugt, Robert Hogan, and Robert Kaiser, "Leadership, Follower and Evolution: Some Lessons from the Past," *American Psychologist* 63 (2008), pp. 182–196. See also Timothy Judge and Ronald Piccolo, "The Bright and Dark Sides of Leader Traits: A Review and Theoretical Extension," *Leadership Quarterly* 20 (2009), pp. 855–875.

[4] See Edward Fleishman, "The Description of Supervisory Behavior Fleishman," *Personnel Psychology* 37 (1953), pp. 1–6. See also A. Halpin and B. Winer, "A Factorial Study of the Leader Behavior Descriptions," in R. Stogdill and A. E. Coons (eds.), *Leader Behavior: Its Description and Measurement* (Columbus, OH: Bureau of Business Research, Ohio State University, 1957); J. K. Hemphill and A. E. Coons, "Development of the Leader Behavior Description Questionnaire," in R. Stogdill and A.E. Coons, (eds.), *Leader Behavior: Its Description and Measurement* (Columbus, OH: Bureau of Business Research, Ohio State University, 1957), pp. 6–38.

[5] See Yukl (2013), op. cit.

[6] Ibid.

[7] See R. Arvey, Z. Zhang, B. Avolio, and R. Krueger, "Developmental and Genetic Determinants of Leadership Role Occupancy among Women." *Journal of Applied Psychology* 92 (2007), pp. 693–706.

[8] See Martin Evans, "The Effects of Supervisory Behavior on the Path-Goal Relationship," *Organizational Behavior and Human Performance* 5 (1970), pp. 277–298. See also Robert House, "Path Goal Theory of Leadership: Lessons, Legacy and a Reformulated Theory," *Leadership Quarterly* 7 (1996), pp. 323–352; R. J. House and T. R. Mitchell, "Path-Goal Theory of Leadership," *Contemporary Business* 3 (1974), pp. 81–98.

[9] For documentation, see Fred E. Fiedler and Linda Mahar, "The Effectiveness of Contingency Model Training: A Review of the Validation of Leader Match," *Personnel Psychology* 32 (Spring 1979), pp. 45–62; Fred E. Garcia, Cecil H. Bell, Martin M. Chemers, and Dennis Patrick, "Increasing Mine Productivity and Safety Through Management Training and Organization Development: A Comparative Study," *Basic and Applied Social Psychology* 5.1 (March 1984), pp. 1–18; Arthur G. Jago and James W. Ragan, "The Trouble with Leader Match Is That It Doesn't Match Fiedler's Contingency Model," *Journal of Applied Psychology* 71 (November 1986), pp. 555–559; and R. Ayman, M. M. Chemers, and F. E. Fiedler, "The Contingency Model of Leadership Effectiveness: Its Levels of Analysis," *The Leadership Quarterly* 6.2 (Summer 1995), pp. 147–168.

[10] See Jerry Hunt, "Transformational/Charismatic Leadership's Transformation of the Field: An Historical Essay," *Leadership Quarterly* 10 (1999), pp. 129–144; and Russ Marion and Mary Uhl-Bien, "Leadership in Complex Organizations," *Leadership Quarterly* 12 (2001), pp. 389–418.

[11] See Max Weber, *The Theory of Social and Economic Organizations* (New York: Free Press, 1947).

[12] See Katherine Klein and Robert House, "On Fire: Charismatic Leadership and Levels of Analysis," *Leadership Quarterly* 6 (1995), pp. 183–198.

[13] Ibid.

[14] See B. Angle, J. Nagarajan, J. Sonnenfeld, and D. Srinivisan, "Does CEO Charisma Matter? An Empirical Analysis of the Relationships Among Organizational Performance, Environmental Uncertainty and Top Management Team Perceptions of CEO Charisma," *Academy of Management Journal 49* (2006), pp. 161–174; Yukl (2013), op. cit.; H. Tosi, V. Misangyi, A. Fanelli, D. Waldman, and F. Yammarino, "CEO Charisma, Compensation and Firm Performance," *Leadership Quarterly* 15 (2004), pp. 405–420.

[15] See Jean Lipman-Blumen, *The Allure of Toxic Leaders* (Oxford, UK: Oxford University Press, 2005).

[16] See G. Hofstede, *Culture's Consequences: Comparing Values, Behaviors, Institutions, and Organizations Across Nations* (Thousand Oaks, CA: Sage, 2001); and B. Kirkman, G. Chen, J-L. Fahr, Z. Chen, and K. Lowe, "Individual Power Distance Orientation and Follower Reactions to Transformational Leaders: A Cross-Level, Cross-Cultural Examination," *Academy of Management Journal* 52 (2009), pp. 744–764.

[17] See James MacGregor Burns, *Leadership* (New York: Harper & Row, 1978).

[18] See Ram de la Rosa, "Book Synopsis: Leadership—James McGregory Burns" (January 23, 2012), http://ramdelarosa.blogspot.com/2012/01/book-synopsis-leadership-james.html (accessed January 14, 2013).

[19] See J. Ciulla, "Leadership Ethics: Mapping the Territory," *The Business Ethics Quarterly* 5 (1995), pp. 5–24; and J. Ciulla, "Introduction to Volume I: Theoretical Aspects of Leadership Ethics," in J. Ciulla, M. Uhl-Bien, and P. Werhane (eds.), *Leadership Ethics* (London: Sage, 2013).

[20] See Scott London, "Book Review: Leadership" (2008), www.scottlondon.com/reviews/burns.html (accessed January 12, 2013).

[21] See Yukl (2013), op. cit.; and Bernard M. Bass, *Leadership and Performance Beyond Expectations* (New York: Free Press).

[22] B. Bass, "Two Decades of Research and Development in Transformational Leadership," *European Journal of Work and Organizational Psychology* 8 (1999), pp. 9–32.

[23] This sentence taken from Bradley Kirkman, Gilad Chen, Jiing-Lih Harh, Zhen Xiong Chen, and Kevin Lowe, "Individual Power Distance Orientation and Follower Reactions to Transformational Leaders: A Cross-Cultural Examination," *Academy of Management Journal* 52 (2009), pp. 744–745.

[24] See B. Bass and B. Avolio, "Multifactor Leadership Questionnaire, Form 5x," www.mindgarden.com/products/mlq.htm (accessed July 12, 2013).

[25] Ibid.

[26] See K. Dirks and D. Ferrin, "Trust in Leadership: Meta-Analytic Findings and Implications for Research and Practice," (2002), pp. 611–628; T. Judge and R. Piccolo, "Transformational and Transactional Leadership: A Meta-Analytic Test of Their Relative Validity," *Journal of Applied Psychology*, 89 (2004), pp. 755–768; K. Lowe, K. G. Kroeck, and N. Sivasubramaniam, "Effectiveness of Correlates of Transformational and Transactional Leadership: A Meta-Analytic Review of the MLQ Literature," *Leadership Quarterly* 7 (1996), pp. 385–425; and G. Wang, I-S. Oh, S. Courtright, and A. Colbert, "Transformational Leadership and Performance Across Criteria and Levels: A Meta-Analytic Review of 25 Years of Research," *Group and Organization Management* 36 (2011), pp. 223–270.

[27] See M. Kets de Vries and D. Miller, "Narcissism and Leadership: An Object Relations Perspective," *Human Relations* 38 (1985), pp. 583–601; Dirk Van Dierendonck, "Servant Leadership: A Review and Synthesis," *Journal of Management* 37 (2011), pp. 1228–1261; and J. Ciulla, "Leadership Ethics: Mapping the Territory," *The Business Ethics Quarterly* 5 (1995), pp. 5–24.

[28] See Warren Bennis, *On Becoming a Leader* (Reading, MA: Addison-Wesley, 2009).

[29] See Richard Osborn, Jerry Hunt, and Larry Jauch, "Toward a Contextual Theory of Leadership," *The Leadership Quarterly* 13 (2002), pp. 797–837.

[30] See Melanie Mitchell, *Complexity: A Guided Tour* (Oxford, UK: Oxford University Press, 2009).

[31] See Yasmin Merali and Peter Allen, "Complexity and Systems Thinking," in Peter Allen, Steve Maguire, and Bill McKelvey (eds.), *The Sage Handbook* of *Complexity and Management* (London: Sage, 2011), p. 41.

[32] See Gary Hamel, "Moon Shots for Management," *Harvard Business Review* (February 2009), pp. 91–98.

[33] See Charles C. Heckscher, "Defining the Post-Bureaucratic Type," in Charles Heckscher and Anne Donnellon (eds.), *The Post-Bureaucratic Organization: New Perspectives on Organizational Change* (Thousand Oaks, CA: Sage, 1994), pp. 14–62.

[34] See Edwin Olson and Glenda Eoyang, Facilitating Organizational *Change: Lessons from Complexity Science.* (SanFrancisco: Jossey-Bass/Pfeiffer, 2001).

[35] See Mary Uhl-Bien, Russ Marion, and Bill McKelvey, "Complexity Leadership Theory: Shifting Leadership from the Industrial Age to the Knowledge Era," *The Leadership Quarterly* 18 (2007), pp. 298–318.

[36] See Mary Uhl-Bien and Russ Marion, "Complexity Leadership in Bureaucratic Forms of Organizing: A Meso Model," *The Leadership Quarterly* 20 (2009), pp. 631–650.

[37] See Uhl-Bien and Marion (2007), op. cit.; and Uhl-Bien and Marion (2009), op. cit.

[38] See Joanne Ciulla, Mary Uhl-Bien, and Patricia Werhane, *Leadership Ethics* (London: Sage, 2013); and Mary Uhl-Bien and Melissa Carsten, "How to Be Ethical When the Boss Is Not," *Organizational Dynamics* 36 (2007), pp. 187–201.

[39] See Joanne Ciulla, "Introduction to Volume I: Theoretical Aspects of Leadership Ethics," in Joanne Ciulla, Mary Uhl-Bien, and Patricia Werhane (eds.), *Leadership Ethics* (London: Sage, 2013); and Joanne Ciulla, "Leadership Ethics: Mapping the Territory," *The Business Ethics Quarterly* 5 (1995), pp. 5–24. See also J. Ciulla, "Leadership Ethics: Mapping the Territory," *The Business Ethics Quarterly* 5 (1995), pp. 5–24; and Joanne Ciulla, *Ethics: The Heart of Leadership* (New York: Praeger, 2004).

[40] See Milton Friedman, "The Social Responsibility of Business Is to Increase Its Profits," *New York Times Magazine* (Sept. 13, 1970).

[41] See M. Porter and M. Kramer, "Creating Shared Value," *Harvard Business Review* (Jan.–Feb. 2011), pp. 63–77. See also "Conscious Capitalism," www.consciouscapitalism.org (accessed July 13, 2013).

[42] Based on Louis W. Fry, "Toward a Paradigm of Spiritual Leadership," *The Leadership Quarterly* 16 (2005), pp. 619–622; and Louis W. Fry, Steve Vitucci, and Marie Cedillo, "Spiritual Leadership and Army Transformation: Theory, Measurement, and Establishing a Baseline," *The Leadership Quarterly* 16.5 (2005), pp. 835–862.

[43] See Dirk Van Dierendonck, "Servant Leadership: A Review and Synthesis," *Journal of Management* 37 (2011), pp. 1228–1261; and Dirk Van Dierendonck, "The Servant Leadership Survey: Development and Validation of a Multidimensional Measure," *Journal of Business and Psychology* 26 (2011), pp. 249–267.

[44] Ibid.

[45] Dirk Van Dierendonck, "The Role of the Follower in the Relationship Between Empowering Leadership and Empowerment: A Longitudinal Investigation," *Journal of Applied Social Psychology* 42 (2012), pp. E1–E20; J. Arnold, S. Arad, J. Rhoades, and F. Drasgow, "The Empowering Leadership Questionnaire: The Construction and Validation of a New Scale for Measuring Leader Behaviors," *Journal of Organizational Behavior* 21 (2000), pp. 249–269; B. Kirkman and B. Rosen, "A Model of Work Team Empowerment," in R. W. Woodman & W. A. Pasmore (eds.), *Research in Organizational Change and Development*, Vol. 10 (Greenwich, CT: JAI Press, 1997), pp. 131–167; and B. Kirkman and B. Rosen, "Beyond Self-Management: Antecedents and Consequences of Team Empowerment," *Academy of Management Journal* 42 (1999), pp. 58–74.

[46] See M. Ahearne, J. Mathieu, and A. Rapp, "To Empower or Not to Empower Your Sales Force? An Empirical Examination of the Influence of Leadership Empowerment Behavior on Customer Satisfaction and Performance," *Journal of Applied Psychology* 90 (2005), pp. 945–955; and X. Zhang and K. Bartol, "Linking Empowering Leadership and Employee Creativity: The Influence of Psychological Empowerment, Intrinsic Motivation, and Creative Process Engagement," *Academy of Management Journal* 53 (2010), pp. 107–128.

[47] See M. Brown, L. Trevino, and D. Harrison, "Ethical Leadership: A Social Learning Perspective for Construct Development and Testing," *Organizational Behavior and Human Decision Processes* 97 (2005), pp. 117–134.

[48] See M. Schminke, A. Arnaud, and M. Kuenzi, "The Power of Ethical Work Climates," *Organizational Dynamics* 36 (2007), pp. 171–186.

[49] See Brown, Trevino, and Harrison (2005), op. cit.

[50] See R. Piccolo, R. Greenbaum, D. Den Hartog, and R. Folger, "The Relationship Between Ethical Leadership and Core Job Characteristics," *Journal of Organizational Behavior* 31 (2010), pp. 259–278; D. Mayer, M. Kuenzi, and R. Greenbaum, "Examining the Link Between Ethical Leadership and Employee Misconduct: The Mediating Role of Ethical Climate," *Journal of Business Ethics* 95 (2010), pp. 7–16.

Chapter 15

[1] This treatment and many analyses of corporate culture are based on Edgar Schein, "Organizational Culture," *American Psychologist* 45 (1990), pp. 109–119; and E. Schein, *Organizational Culture and Leadership* (San Francisco: Jossey-Bass, 1985).

[2] For a recent treatment, see Ali Danisman, C. R. Hinnings, and Trevor Slack, "Integration and Differentiation in Institutional Values: An Empirical Investigation in the Field of Canadian National Sport Organizations," *Canadian Journal of Administrative Sciences* 23.4 (2006), pp. 301–315.

[3] Schein (1990).

[4] See www.dellapp.us.dell.com.

[5] This example was reported in an interview with Edgar Schein, "Corporate Culture Is the Real Key to Creativity," *Business Month* (May 1989), pp. 73–74.

[6] Schein (1990).

[7] Aetna. (2001–2013). "Culture." Accessed June 19, 2013, at http://qawww.aetna.com/working/why/culture.html.

[8] Schein (1990).

[9] For an extended discussion, see J. M. Beyer and H. M. Trice, "How an Organization's Rites Reveal Its Culture," *Organizational Dynamics* (Spring 1987), pp. 27–41.

[10] A. Cooke and D. M. Rousseau, "Behavioral Norms and Expectations: A Quantitative Approach to the Assessment of Organizational Culture," *Group and Organizational Studies* 13 (1988), pp. 245–273.

[11] Mary Trefry, "A Double-Edged Sword: Organizational Culture in Multicultural Organizations," *International Journal of Management* 23 (2006), pp. 563–576; and J. Martin and C. Siehl, "Organization Culture and Counterculture," *Organizational Dynamics* 12 (1983), pp. 52–64.

[12] Accessed June 19, 2013, at www.apple-history.com.

[13] See R. N. Osborn, "The Culture Clash at BofA," Working Paper, Department of Management, Wayne State University, 2008.

[14] For a recent discussion of the clash of corporate cultures, see George Lodorfos and Agyenim Boateng, "The Role of Culture in the Merger and Acquisition Process: Evidence from the European Chemical Industry," *Management Decision* 44 (2006), pp. 1405–1410.

[15] Jean Louis Barsoux, "Start Slow, End Fast—Jean Louis Barsoux Offers Advice on Working in Multicultural Teams," *Financial Times* (July 8, 1994), p. 12.

[16] Osborn (2008); and Osawa Juro, "Japan Investors: Why No Women, Foreigners in the Board Room," *Wall Street Journal*, June 30, 2010, accessed June 19, 2013, at http://blogs.wsj.com/japanrealtime/2010/06/30/japan-investors-why-no-womenforeigners-in-the-boardroom.

[17] Taylor Cox Jr., "The Multicultural Organization," *Academy of Management Executive* 2.2 (May 1991), pp. 34–47.

[18] See Schein (1985), pp. 52–57, and Schein (1990).

[19] For a discussion from a different perspective, see Anat Rafaeli and Michael G. Pratt (eds.), *Artifacts and Organizations: Beyond Mere Symbols* (Mahwah, NJ: Erlbaum, 2006).

[20] For early work, see T. Deal and A. Kennedy, *Corporate Culture* (Reading, MA: Addison-Wesley, 1982); and T. Peters and R. Waterman, *In Search of Excellence* (New York: Harper & Row, 1982), whereas more recent studies are summarized in Joanne Martin and Peter Frost, "The Organizational Culture War Games: The Struggle for Intellectual Dominance," in Stewart R. Clegg, Cynthia Hardy, and Walter R. Nord (eds.), *Handbook of Organization Studies* (London: Sage, 1996), pp. 599–621.

[21] Schein (1990).

[22] See www.montereypasta.com for the original quotes; www.montereygourmetfoods.com for updated information; and www.fundinguniverse.com/company-histories/monterey-pasta-company for a more complete history until 2003.

[23] H. Gertz, *The Interpretation of Culture* (New York: Basic Books, 1973).

[24] See Rafaeli and Pratt (2006) and Beyer and Trice (1987).

[25] H. M. Trice and J. M. Beyer, "Studying Organizational Cultures through Rites and Ceremonials," *Academy of Management Review* 3 (1984), pp. 633–669.

[26] J. Martin, M. S. Feldman, M. J. Hatch, and S. B. Sitkin, "The Uniqueness Paradox in Organizational Stories," *Administrative Science Quarterly* 28 (1983), pp. 438–453.

[27] For a recent study, see John Barnes, Donald W. Jackson, Michael D. Hutt, and Ajith Kumar, "The Role of Culture Strength in Shaping Sales Force Outcomes," *Journal of Personal Setting and Sales Management* 26.3 (2006), pp. 255–269. This tradition of strong cultures goes back to work by Deal and Kennedy (1982) and Peters and Waterman (1982).

[28] Wikipedia.org (2013, June 15), "One World Trade Center," accessed June 20, 2013, at http://en.wikipedia.org/wiki/One_World_Trade_Center; and News24.com, "Twin Tower Replacement to Be Impressive" (2011, August 5), accessed June 20, 2013, at www.news24.com/World/News/Twin-Tower-replacementto-be-impressive-20110805.

[29] Trice and Beyer (1984).

[30] J. Collins, *How Do the Mighty Fall* (New York: HarperCollins, 2009).

[31] R. N. Osborn and D. Jackson, "Leaders, River Boat Gamblers or Purposeful Unintended Consequences," *Academy of Management Journal* 31 (1988), pp. 924–947.

[32] For an interesting twist, see John Connolly, "High Performance Cultures," *Business Strategy Review* 17 (2006), pp. 19–32; a more conventional treatment may be found in Martin, Feldman, Hatch, and Sitkin (1983).

[33] Martin and Frost (1996).

[34] This section was originally based on R. N. Osborn and C. C. Baughn, *An Assessment of the State of the Field of Organizational Design* (Alexandria, VA: U.S. Army Research Institute, 1994).

[35] For example, see Gerard J. Tellis, Jaideep C. Prabhu, and Rajesh C. Chandy, "Radical Innovation Across Nations: The Preeminence of Corporate Culture," *Journal of Marketing* 73.1 (2009), pp. 3–23.

[36] Richard N. Osborn, James G. Hunt, and Lawrence R. Jauch, *Organization Theory: Integrated Text and Cases* (Melbourne, FL: Krieger, 1985).

[37] Ibid. (1985); and W. Richard Scott and Gerald F. Davis, *Organizations and Organizing: Rational and Open Systems* (Englewood Cliffs, NJ: Prentice Hall, 2007).

[38] H. Talcott Parsons, *Structure and Processes in Modern Societies* (New York: Free Press, 1960).

[39] See B. Bartkus, M. Glassman, and B. McAfee, "Mission Statement Quality and Financial Performance," *European Management Journal* 24.1 (2006), pp. 66–79; J. Peyrefitte and F. R. David, "A Content Analysis of the Mission Statements of United States Firms in Four Industries," *International Journal of Management* 23.2 (2006), pp. 296–305; Terri Lammers, "The Effective and Indispensable Mission Statement," *Inc.* 7.1 (August 1992), p. 23; and I. C. MacMillan and A. Meshulack, "Replacement versus Expansion: Dilemma for Mature U.S. Businesses," *Academy of Management Journal* 26 (1983), pp. 708–726.

[40] Osborn, Hunt, and Jauch (1985).

[41] See Jeffery Pfeffer, "Barriers to the Advance of Organization Science," *Academy of Management Review* 18.4 (1994), pp. 599–620; and Richard M. Cyert and James G. March, *A Behavioral Theory of the Firm* (Englewood Cliffs, NJ: Prentice-Hall, 1963). A historical view of organizational goals is also found in Charles Perrow, *Organizational Analysis: A Sociological View* (Belmont, CA: Wadsworth, 1970), and in Richard H. Hall, "Organizational Behavior: A Sociological Perspective," in Jay W. Lorsch (ed.), *Handbook of Organizational Behavior* (Englewood Cliffs, NJ: Prentice-Hall, 1987), pp. 84–95.

[42] W. Richard Scott and Gerald F. Davis, *Organizations and Organizing: Rational and Open Systems* (Englewood Cliffs, NJ: Prentice-Hall. 2007); Stewart R. Clegg and Cynthia Hardy, "Organizations, Organization and Organizing," in Clegg, Hardy, and Nord (eds.), *Handbook of Organizational Studies* (1996), pp. 1–28; and William H. Starbuck and Paul C. Nystrom, "Designing and Understanding Organizations," in P. C. Nystrom and W. H. Starbuck (eds.), *Handbook of Organizational Design: Adapting Organizations to Their Environments* (New York: Oxford University Press, 1981).

[43] See Osborn, Hunt, and Jauch (1985) for the historical rates, and for differences in survival rates by time of formation in the development of a technology, see R. Agarwal, M. Sarkar, and R. Echambadi, "The Conditioning Effect of Time on Firm Survival: An Industry Life Cycle Approach," *Academy of Management Journal* 25 (2002), pp. 971–985.

[44] J. Karpoff, D. S. Lee, and Gerald Martin, "A Company's Reputation Is What Gets Fried When Its Books Are Cooked" (2007). Accessed June 24, 2013, at www.washington.edu/news/2006/11/16/ a-companys-reputation-is-what-gets-fried-when-itsbooks-get-cooked-2.

[45] J. Kerr and J. Slocum, "Managing Corporate Culture through Reward Systems," *Academy of Management Executive* 19.4 (2005), pp. 130–138.

Chapter 16

[1] The bulk of this chapter was originally based on Richard N. Osborn, James G. Hunt, and Lawrence R. Jauch, *Organization Theory: Integrated Text and Cases* (Melbourne, FL: Krieger, 1985). For a more recent but consistent view, see Lex Donaldson, "The Normal Science of Structural Contingency Theory," in Stewart R. Clegg, Cynthia Hardy, and Walter R. Nord (eds.), *Handbook of Organizational Studies* (London: Sage Publications, 1996), pp. 57–76. For a more advanced treatment, see W. Richard Scott and Gerald F. Davis, *Organizations and Organizing: Rational and Open Systems* (Englewood Cliffs, NJ: Prentice-Hall. 2007).

[2] Osborn, Hunt, and Jauch (1985).

[3] For reviews, see Scott and Davis (2007); Osborn, Hunt, and Jauch (1985); Clegg, Hardy, and Nord (1996).

[4] For related reviews, see Scott and Davis (2007); Osborn, Hunt, and Jauch (1985); Clegg, Hardy, and Nord (1996).

[5] Rhys Andrews, George A. Boyne, Jennifer Law, and Richard M. Walker, "Centralization, Organization Strategy, and Public Service Performance," *Journal of Public Administration Research and Theory* 19.1 (2009), pp. 57–81.

[6] See C. Bradley, "Succeeding by (Organizational) Design," *Decision: Irelands Business Review* 11.1 (2006), pp. 24–29; and Osborn, Hunt, and Jauch (1985), pp. 273–303, for a discussion of centralization/decentralization.

[7] For reviews of structural tendencies and their influence on outcomes, also see Scott and Davis (2007); and Clegg, Hardy, and Nord (1996).

[8] See P. R. Lawrence and J. W. Lorsch, *Organization and Environment: Managing Differentiation and Integration* (Homewood, IL: Richard D. Irwin, 1967).

[9] Osborn, Hunt, and Jauch (1985).

[10] For a good discussion of the early use of matrix structures, see Stanley Davis, Paul Lawrence, Harvey Kolodny, and Michael Beer, *Matrix* (Reading, MA: Addison-Wesley, 1977).

[11] Lawrence and Lorsch (1967).

[12] See Osborn, Hunt, and Jauch (1985); and Scott and Davis (2007).

[13] Chris P. Long, Corinee Bendersky, and Calvin Morrill, "Fair Control: Complementarities Between Types of Managerial Controls and Employees' Fairness Evaluations," *2008 Academy of Management Proceedings* (2008), pp. 362–368.

[14] This discussion of organizational design was initially based on R. N. Osborn, J. G. Hunt, and L. Jauch, *Organization Theory Integrated Text and Cases* (Melbourne, FL: Krieger, 1984), pp. 123–215. For a more advanced treatment, see W. Richard Scott and Gerald F. Davis, *Organizations and Organizing: Rational and Open Systems* (Englewood Cliffs, NJ: Prentice-Hall, 2007).

[15] This section is based on R. N. Osborn, "The Evolution of Strategic Alliances in High Technology," Working Paper, Detroit: Department of Business, Wayne State University (2007); R. N. Osborn and J. G. Hunt, "The Environment and Organization Effectiveness," *Administrative Science Quarterly* 19 (1974), pp. 231–246; and Osborn, Hunt, and Jauch (1984). For a more extended discussion, see P. Kenis and D. Knoke, "How Organizational Field Networks Shape Interorganizational Information Rates," *Academy of Management Journal* 27 (2002), pp. 275–294.

[16] See R. N. Osborn and C. C. Baughn, "New Patterns in the Formation of U.S. Japanese Cooperative Ventures," *Columbia Journal of World Business* 22 (1988), pp. 57–65.

[17] Max Weber, *The Theory of Social and Economic Organization,* translated by A. M. Henderson and H. T. Parsons (New York: Free Press, 1947).

[18] Stephen Cummings and Todd Bridgman, "The Strawman: The Reconfiguration of Max Weber in Management Textbooks and Why it Matters," *2008 Academy of Management Proceedings* (2008), pp. 243–249.

[19] Ibid.

[20] These relationships were initially outlined by Tom Burns and G. M. Stalker, *The Management of Innovation* (London: Tavistock, 1961).

[21] See Mintzberg (1983).

[22] Ibid.

[23] See Osborn, Hunt, and Jauch (1984) for an extended discussion.

[24] See Peter Clark and Ken Starkey, *Organization Transitions and Innovation—Design* (London: Pinter Publications, 1988).

SIXTH EDITION

CRIMINOLOGY

A Sociological Understanding

Steven E. Barkan

University of Maine

PEARSON

Boston   Columbus   Indianapolis   New York   San Francisco   Upper Saddle River
Amsterdam   Cape Town   Dubai   London   Madrid   Milan   Munich   Paris   Montréal   Toronto
Delhi   Mexico City   São Paulo   Sydney   Hong Kong   Seoul   Singapore   Taipei   Tokyo

Editorial Director: Vernon Anthony
Acquisitions Editor: Gary Bauer
Editorial Assistant: Kevin Cecil
Director of Marketing: David Gesell
Senior Marketing Manager: Mary Salzman
Senior Marketing Coordinator: Alicia Wozniak
Program Manager: Megan Moffo
Project Management Team Lead: JoEllen Gohr
Production Project Manager: Jessica H. Sykes
Procurement Specialist: Deidra Skahill

Senior Art Director: Diane Ernsberger
Text Designer: PreMedia Global
Cover Art: Robert Eaton/Alamy
Media Project Manager: April Cleland
Full-Service Project Management: Cindy
    Sweeney/S4Carlisle Publishing Services
Composition: S4Carlisle Publishing Services
Printer/Binder: RR Donnelley
Cover Printer: RR Donnelley
Text Font: Minion Pro

Library of Congress Cataloging-in-Publication Data

Barkan, Steven E.
    Criminology: a sociological understanding/Steven E. Barkan.—6th ed.
        p. cm.
    Includes bibliographical references and index.
    ISBN-13: 978-0-13-345899-2 (alk. paper)
    ISBN-10: 0-13-345899-7 (alk. paper)
    1. Crime—Sociological aspects.   2. Criminology.   I. Title.
HV6025.B278 2014
364—dc23

                                                        2013046850

3   16

ISBN 13: 978-0-13-345899-2
ISBN 10:   0-13-345899-7

Dedication

To Barb,
Dave,
and Joe,
and in memory of my parents

Brief Contents

Contents

PART 2
Explaining Crime

Contents   xii

▼

PART 4

Controlling and Preventing Crime

Chapter 16   Policing: Dilemmas of Crime Control in a Democratic
Society   327

Chapter 17   Prosecution and Punishment   350

This sixth edition has been thoroughly revised. It includes the latest crime and criminal justice statistics available as the book went to production, and it discusses the latest research on crime and criminal justice issues that had appeared by that time, with dozens of new references added and some older ones deleted. This edition continues the popular features of the previous one, including the chapter-opening *Crime in the News* vignettes ripped from the headlines (almost all new from 2013) that engage students' attention and demonstrate the text's relevance for real-life events and issues; the *Crime and Controversy* and *International Focus* boxes, several of them new or revised for this edition, that respectively highlight crime and justice issues within the United States and abroad; and the *What Would You Do?* feature at the end of each chapter that presents hypothetical scenarios on real-world situations faced by criminal justice professionals and average citizens alike.

Major changes or additions to specific chapters include the following:

Chapter 3. The Measurement and Patterning of Criminal Behavior

- New examples of crime-reporting problems at colleges and universities
- New discussion in the *Crime and Controversy* box of a possible connection between reduced lead paint exposure and the decline in crime rates
- New discussion of possible effects of climate change on crime rates

Chapter 5. Classical and Neoclassical Perspectives

- New discussion of routine activities theory's explanation of relationship between unemployment and changes in crime rates

Chapter 6. Biological and Sociological Explanations

- New material on brain abnormalities and antisocial behavior
- New material on fish oil and antisocial behavior
- New material on child malnutrition and later antisocial behavior
- New discussion of the relevance of biological research on prenatal difficulties and on poverty for efforts to reduce crime

Chapter 7. Sociological Theories: Emphasis on Social Structure

- New material on physical disorder and quality of life
- New *International Focus* box
- Expanded discussion of the prospects for subcultural explanations
- New material on structural explanations and female victimization

Chapter 8. Sociological Theories: Emphasis on Social Process

- New section on evaluation of learning theories
- New material on animal rights activism and techniques of neutralization
- New material on social schemas and theoretical integration

Chapter 10. Violent Crime: Homicide, Assault, and Robbery

- New *International Focus* box
- New material on women as victims of serial killers
- Revised and expanded discussion of workplace violence
- New section on elder abuse
- Revised section on firearms and violence
- Updated discussion of Virginia's gun-carrying laws in *Crime and Controversy* box

Chapter 11. Violence Against Women

- Revised section on defining rape/sexual assault and domestic violence
- New material on prevalence rates for rape/sexual assault and domestic violence
- Updated discussion of military rape/sexual assault in *Crime and Controversy* box
- New material on gang rapes by teenaged boys
- New material on stalking and on cyberstalking

Chapter 13. White-Collar and Organized Crime

- New material on price-fixing and on false advertising
- New material on workplace hazards

- Revised estimates of deaths from unsafe products
- New discussion of gender and involvement in white-collar crime
- New section on patterning of white-collar crime by race/ethnicity and social class
- New *International Focus* box

Chapter 15. Consensual Crime

- New discussion of drug war's impact on African-Americans and Latinos
- New material on legalization of marijuana in the United States

- New *International Focus* box
- New section on the sex trafficking controversy
- New material on drinking by high school students
- Expanded *Crime and Controversy* box

Chapter 16. Policing: Dilemmas of Crime Control in a Democratic Society

- Expanded discussion of Japanese police in *International Focus* box
- Revised discussion of impact of additional police on crime rates
- New material on focused deterrence involving juvenile gangs

Welcome to this sociological introduction to the field of criminology! This book emphasizes the need to understand the social causes of criminal behavior in order to be able to significantly reduce crime. This approach is similar to the approach followed in the field of public health. In the case of a disease such as cancer, we naturally try to determine what causes it so that we can prevent people from contracting it. Although it is obviously important to treat people who already have cancer, there will always be more cancer patients unless we discover its causes and then do something about these causes. The analogy to crime is clear: Unless we discover the causes of crime and do something about them, there will always be more criminals.

Unfortunately, this is not the approach the United States has taken during the past few decades. Instead, it has relied on a "get tough" approach to the crime problem that relies on more aggressive policing, longer and more certain prison terms, and the building of more and more prisons. The nation's prison and jail population has soared and has reached more than 2.2 million despite a small recent decrease. Many criminologists warn that the surge in prisoners has set the stage for a crime increase down the line, given that almost all of these prisoners will one day be returned to their communities, many of them penniless, without jobs, and embittered by their incarceration.

In offering a sociological understanding of crime, this book suggests that the "get tough" approach is shortsighted because it ignores the roots of crime in the social structure and social inequality of society. To reduce crime, we must address these structural conditions and appreciate the role that factors such as race and ethnicity, gender, and social class play in criminal behavior. Students in criminology courses in sociology departments will especially benefit from the sociological understanding that this book offers. But this understanding is also important for students in courses in criminal justice or criminology departments. If crime cannot be fully understood without appreciating its structural context, students in all these departments who do not develop this appreciation have only an incomplete understanding of the reasons for crime and of the most effective strategies to reduce it.

Although street crime has declined since the early 1990s, it remains a national problem, as the residents of high-crime communities know all too well. Meanwhile, white-collar crime continues to cost tens of billions of dollars and thousands of lives annually, even as it receives far less attention than mass murder, terrorism, and everyday violent and property crime.

In presenting a sociological perspective on crime and criminal justice, this book highlights issues of race and ethnicity, gender, and social class in every chapter and emphasizes the criminogenic effects of the social and physical features of urban neighborhoods. This sixth edition continues to include certain chapters that remain uncommon in other criminology texts, including Chapter 2: Public Opinion, the News Media, and the Crime Problem; Chapter 11: Violence Against Women; Chapter 14: Political Crime; and Chapter 18: Conclusion: How Can We Reduce Crime? In addition, the book's criminal justice chapters, Chapter 16: Policing: Dilemmas of Crime Control in a Democratic Society and Chapter 17: Prosecution and Punishment, continue to address two central themes in the sociological understanding of crime and criminal justice: (1) the degree to which race and ethnicity, gender, and social class affect the operation of the criminal justice system and (2) the extent to which reliance on the criminal justice system can reduce the amount of crime. These two themes, in turn, reflect two more general sociological issues: the degree to which inequality affects the dynamics of social institutions and the extent to which formal sanctions affect human behavior.

Supplements

Instructor Supplements

MyTest and *TestBank* represent new standards in testing material. Whether you use a basic test bank document or generate questions electronically through MyTest, every question is linked to the text's learning objective, page number, and level of difficulty. This allows for quick reference in the text and an easy way to check the difficulty level and variety of your questions. MyTest can be accessed at www.Pearson-MyTest.com.

PowerPoint Presentations Our presentations offer clear, straightforward outlines and notes to use for class lectures or study materials. Photos, illustrations, charts, and tables from the book are included in the presentations when applicable.

Other supplements are:

- Instructor's Manual with Test Bank
- Test Item File for ingestion into an LMS, including Blackboard and WebCT.

To access supplementary materials online, instructors need to request an instructor access code. Go to **www.pearsonhighered .com**/irc, where you can register for an instructor access code. Within 48 hours after registering, you will receive a confirming email, including an instructor access code. Once you have received your code, go to the site and log on for full instructions on downloading the materials you wish to use.

Pearson Online Course Solutions

Criminology: A Sociological Understanding is supported by online course solutions that include interactive learning modules, a variety of assessment tools, videos, simulations, and current event features. Go to www.pearsonhighered.com or contact your local representative for the latest information.

Alternate Versions

eBooks This text is also available in multiple eBook formats including Adobe Reader and CourseSmart. CourseSmart is an exciting new choice for students looking to save money. As an alternative to purchasing the printed textbook, students can purchase an electronic version of the same content. With a *CourseSmart* eTextbook, students can search the text, make notes online, print out reading assignments that incorporate lecture notes, and bookmark important passages for later review. For more information, or to purchase access to the *CourseSmart* eTextbook, visit **www.coursesmart.com.**

Acknowledgments

The first edition of this book stated my personal and intellectual debt to Norman Miller and Forrest Dill, and I continue to acknowledge how much I owe them. Norman Miller was my first undergraduate sociology professor and quickly helped me fall in love with the discipline. He forced me to ask questions about society that I probably still haven't answered. I and the many other students he influenced can offer only an inadequate "thank you" for caring so much about us and, to paraphrase a verse from a great book, for training us in the way we should go. Forrest Dill was my mentor in graduate school and introduced me to criminology and the sociology of law and to the craft of scholarship. His untimely death about three decades ago continues to leave a deep void.

My professional home since graduate school has been the Sociology Department at the University of Maine. I continue to owe my colleagues there an intellectual debt for sharing and reaffirming my sense of the importance of social structure and social inequality to an understanding of crime and other contemporary issues. They continue to provide a warm, supportive working environment that often seems all too rare in academia.

I also wish to thank the editorial, production, and marketing staff at Prentice Hall for their help on all aspects of the book's revision. In particular, the assistance of development editor Elisa Rogers on this edition was indispensable, as was Gary Bauer's faith in the vision underlying the book. In addition, thanks go to Jessica Sykes for her help and patience during the various stages of the book's production.

I also wish to thank the reviewers who read the fifth edition and provided very helpful comments and criticism. Any errors that remain, of course, are mine alone. These reviewers are: Theodore Curry, University of Texas—El Paso; Melissa Deller, University of Wisconsin—Whitewater; Robert W. Greene, University of Wisconsin—Whitewater ; Tammy Kochel, Southern Illinois University—Carbondale; Karen S. Miller, West Virginia Wesleyan College; Mark A. Mills, Glenville State College; and Paul Odems, St. John's University—Queens

Finally, as in my first five editions, I acknowledge with heartfelt gratitude the love and support that my wife, Barbara Tennent, and my sons, Dave and Joe, bring to my life. They put up with my need to write, my quirks, and my reactions to the success and failure of our favorite sports teams more than any husband and father has a right to expect.

The sixth edition of this book is again dedicated to my late parents, Morry and Sylvia Barkan, who instilled in me respect for learning and sympathy for those less fortunate than I. As I continue to think about them after so many years, I can only hope that somewhere they are smiling with pride over this latest evidence of their legacy.

About the Author

Steven E. Barkan is professor of sociology at the University of Maine, where he has taught since 1979. His teaching and research interests include criminology, sociology of law, and social movements. He was the 2008–2009 president of the Society for the Study of Social Problems and had previously served as a member of the SSSP Board of Directors, as chair of its Law and Society Division and Editorial and Publications Committee, and as an advisory editor of its journal, *Social Problems*. He also previously served as a member of the council of the Sociology of Law Section of the American Sociological Association and served on its student paper award committee as well as that of the ASA Crime, Law, and Deviance Section. He currently serves on the council of Alpha Kappa Delta, the sociology honor society, and is Vice President/President-elect of the Text and Academic Authors Association.

Professor Barkan has written many journal articles dealing with topics such as racial prejudice and death-penalty attitudes, views on police brutality, political trials, and feminist activism. These articles have appeared in the *American Sociological Review, Journal for the Scientific Study of Religion, Journal of Crime and Justice, Journal of Research in Crime and Delinquency, Justice Quarterly, Social Forces, Social Problems, Sociological Forum, Sociological Inquiry, Sociological Perspectives,* and other journals. He has also authored another text, *Law and Society: An Introduction,* with Prentice Hall.

Professor Barkan welcomes comments from students and faculty about this book. They may e-mail him at barkan@maine .edu or send regular mail to Department of Sociology, 5728 Fernald Hall, University of Maine, Orono, Maine 04469–5728.

Timeline of Major Criminological Theories

Chapter 5

Year			
	1764	Classical Theory (Utilitarianism)	Cesare Beccaria
		Neoclassical Theories	
	1968	Rational Choice Theory	Gary Becker
	1985		Derek B. Cornish
			Ronald V. Clarke
	1970s	Deterrence Theory	
	1979	Routine Activities Theory	Lawrence E. Cohen
			Marcus Felson

Chapter 6

Year			
	1796	Phrenology	Franz Gall
	1876	Atavism	Cesare Lombroso
	1939	Biological Inferiority	Earnest Hooton
	1949	Body Shapes (Somatology)	William Sheldon
	1960s–1970s	Contemporary Explanations	

Chapter 7

Year			
	1942	Social Disorganization Theory	Clifford R. Shaw, Henry D. McKay
	1987	Deviant Places Theory	Rodney Stark
	1938	Anomie Theory	Robert K. Merton
	1992	General Strain Theory	Robert Agnew
	1955	Status Frustration Theory	Albert K. Cohen
	1958	Focal Concerns Theory	Walter B. Miller
	1960	Differential Opportunity Theory	Richard Cloward, Lloyd Ohlin
	1958, 1967	Subculture of Violence Theory	Marvin Wolfgang, Franco Ferracuti
	1999	Code of the Street Theory	Elijah Anderson

Chapter 8

Year			
	1939	Differential Association Theory	Edwin H. Sutherland
	1956	Differential Identification Theory	Daniel Glaser
	1973, 1977	Social Learning Theory	Albert Bandura
	1966	Differential Reinforcement Theory	Robert L. Burgess Ronald L. Akers
	1956, 1961	Containment Theory	Walter Reckless
	1957	Neutralization and Drift Theory	Gresham M. Sykes David Matza
	1969	Social Bonding Theory	Travis Hirschi
	1990	Self-Control Theory	Michael Gottfredson Travis Hirschi
	2004	Control Balance Theory	Charles R. Tittle
	2002	Coercive Control and Social Support Theory	Mark Colvin Francis T. Cullen
	1979	Integrated Strain-Control Theory	Delbert S. Elliott
	1987	Interactional Theory	Terence P. Thornberry
	1993	Life-Course-Persistent Theory	Terrie E. Moffitt
	1993	Age-Graded Theory	Robert J. Sampson John H. Laub

Chapter 9

Year			
	1951 1963	Labeling Theory	Edwin Lemert Howard S. Becker
	1938 1958 1969	Conflict Theory	Thorsten Sellin George Vold Austin T. Turk
	1916 1952 1964 1974	Radical Theory	Willem Bonger Jerome Hall William Chambliss Richard Quinney
	1988 1989	Feminist Theories	Kathleen Daly Meda Chesney-Lind Sally S. Simpson

mom&paparazzi / Splash News/Newscom

1 Criminology and the Sociological Perspective

· ·

Crime in the News

On December 14, 2012, a young man entered the Sandy Hook Elementary School in Newtown, CT, and began fatally shooting everyone he saw. His victims included 6 adults and 23 children. Their deaths shocked the nation and ignited a heartfelt reflection on violence in America. More than 3,900 U.S. residents nonetheless were to die from gun violence within the next five months. One of these victims was Jerrick Jackson, 46, who was shot at his home in Atlanta, GA, during a robbery in May 2013. The robbers took Jackson's wallet and his fiancée's purse and then shot him after he tried to prevent them from going upstairs where his fiancée's daughter was in her bedroom. The robbers used the fiancée's debit card at a store nine hours later.

Source: Nocera 2013.

· ·

These many deaths remind us that violence and other street crime continue to trouble people across the nation. Although the U.S. crime rate has actually declined since the early 1990s, the prison and jail population stands at more than 2.3 million, the highest rate of incarceration in the Western world. The criminal justice system costs more than $250 billion annually, compared to only $36 billion in the early 1980s. Why do we have so much violence and other crime? What can we do to reduce our crime rate? What difference do police and prisons make? Could our dollars be spent more wisely? How serious is white-collar crime? Is the war on drugs working? What role do race and ethnicity, social class, and gender play in criminal behavior and in the response of the criminal justice system to such behavior? These are just a few of the questions this book tries to answer.

The rationale for the book is simple. Crime is one of our most important social problems and also one of the least understood. Most of our knowledge about crime comes from what we read in newspapers or see on TV or the Internet. From these sources, we get a distorted picture of crime and hear about solutions to the crime problem that ultimately will do little to reduce it. These are harsh accusations, to be sure, but they are ones with which most criminologists probably agree.

A major reason crime is so misunderstood is that the popular sources of our knowledge about crime say little about its social roots. Crime is not only an individual phenomenon but also a social one. Individuals commit crime, but their social backgrounds profoundly shape their likelihood of doing so. In this sense, crime is no different from other behaviors sociologists study. This basic sociological understanding of crime has an important social policy implication: if crime is rooted in the way our society is organized, then crime-reduction efforts will succeed only to the extent that they address the structural roots of criminality.

This book presents a sociological understanding of crime and criminal justice, an approach commonly called sociological criminology. As we will see later, for most of its history virtually all criminology was sociological criminology, and this two-word term would have been redundant. This view of criminology gave explicit attention to issues of poverty and race and ethnicity, as well as to the structure of communities and social relationships. As John Hagan (1994), a former president of the American Society of Criminology, once observed, a sociological criminology is thus a *structural* criminology. It takes into account the social and physical characteristics of communities and the profound influence of race and ethnicity, social class, and gender.

In the past few decades, criminology has moved away from this structural focus toward individualistic explanations, as the fields of biology and psychology are vying with sociology for prominence in the study of crime. These fields enliven the discipline and have expanded criminology's interdisciplinary focus. However, they ultimately fail to answer three of the most central questions in criminology: (1) Why do crime rates differ across locations and over time? (2) Why do crime rates differ according to the key dimensions of structured social inequality: race and ethnicity, social class, and gender? (3) How and why is the legal response to crime shaped by

▼

race and ethnicity, social class, and gender and by other extralegal variables? Only a sociological criminology can begin to answer these questions, which must be answered if we are to have any hope of seriously reducing crime and of achieving a just legal system.

A sociological criminology is not only a structural criminology. To be true to the sociological perspective, it should also be a criminology that debunks incorrect perceptions about crime and false claims about the effectiveness of various crime-control strategies. In addition, it should expose possible injustice in the application of the criminal label.

These themes appear throughout the book. Part 1, Understanding Crime and Victimization, introduces the sociological perspective and discusses public beliefs about crime and criminal justice. It also discusses what is known about the amount and social patterning of crime and victimization. Part 2, Explaining Crime, critically reviews the major explanations of crime and criminality and discusses their implications for crime reduction. These explanations are integrated into the chapters contained in Part 3, Criminal Behaviors. These chapters discuss the major forms of crime and ways of reducing them. The fourth and final part of the book, Controlling and Preventing Crime, explores among other things two important issues for a sociological understanding of the criminal justice system: (1) To what degree do race and ethnicity, class, and gender unjustly affect the chances of arrest, conviction, and imprisonment? (2) To what degree do arrest and punishment reduce criminal behavior? The concluding chapter of the book presents a sociological prescription for crime reduction.

Our sociological journey into crime and criminal justice begins by reviewing the sociological perspective and discussing the mutual relevance of sociology and criminology. We look briefly at the development of sociological criminology and at its approaches to crime and criminal justice and review some key legal terms and concepts.

▶ The Sociological Perspective

Above all else, the sociological perspective stresses that people are *social beings* more than mere individuals. This means that society profoundly shapes their behavior, attitudes, and life chances. People growing up in societies with different cultures tend to act and think differently from one another. People within a given society growing up in various locations and under diverse socioeconomic circumstances also tend to act and think differently. We cannot understand why people think and behave as they do without understanding their many social backgrounds.

This perspective derives from the work of Émile Durkheim (1858–1917), a French sociologist and a founder of the discipline, who stressed that social forces influence our behavior and attitudes.

In perhaps his most famous study, Durkheim (1952 (1897)) found that even suicide, normally regarded as the most individualistic act possible, has social roots. Examining data in France and elsewhere, he found that suicide rates varied across locations and across different kinds of people. Protestants, for example, had higher suicide rates than did Catholics. Durkheim explained these differences by focusing on structural characteristics, in particular the level of social integration, of the locations and people he studied. People in groups with high social integration, or strong bonds to others within their group, have lower suicide rates. His analysis remains a classic study of the influence of social structure on individual behavior such as suicide.

What exactly is social structure? Briefly, social structure refers to how a society is organized in terms of social relationships and social interaction. It is both *horizontal* and *vertical*. Horizontal social structure refers to the social and physical characteristics of communities and the networks of social relationships to which an individual belongs. Vertical social structure is more commonly called social inequality, and refers to how a

▼ The sociological perspective emphasizes that people are social beings more than individuals. This means that society shapes our behavior, attitudes, and life chances.

© jon11 /Fotolia

society ranks different groups of people. In U.S. society, social class, race and ethnicity, and gender are key characteristics that help determine where people rank and whether some are "more equal" than others.

Sociologist C. Wright Mills (1959) emphasized that social structure lies at the root of private troubles. If only a few individuals, he wrote, are unemployed, then their private troubles are their own fault. But if masses of individuals are unemployed, structural forces must account for their bad fortune. What people may define as private troubles are thus more accurately described as public issues, wrote Mills. Their personal troubles result from the intersection of their personal biography with historical and social conditions. Mills referred to the ability to understand the structural and historical basis for personal troubles as the sociological imagination. Once people acquire a sociological imagination, they are better able both to understand and to change the social forces underlying their private troubles.

As Mills's comments suggest, sociology's emphasis on the structural basis for individual behavior and personal troubles often leads it to challenge conventional wisdom. Max Weber (1864–1920), another founder of sociology, echoed this theme when he noted that one of sociology's most important goals was to uncover "inconvenient facts" (Gerth and Mills 1946). As Peter Berger (1963) observed in his classic book, *Invitation to Sociology*, the "first wisdom" of sociology is that things are not always what they seem; sociological research often exposes false claims about reality and taken-for-granted assumptions about social life and social institutions. Berger referred to this sociological tendency as the debunking motif.

iStock/Getty Images

▲ A job-seeker consults a bulletin board listing some employment possibilities. C. Wright Mills considered unemployment a public issue that results from structural problems in society.

Review and Discuss

What do we mean by the *sociological perspective*? How does this perspective help us to understand the origins of crime and possible ways of reducing crime?

The Mutual Relevance of Sociology and Criminology

With this brief discussion of the sociological perspective in mind, the continuing relevance of sociology for criminology immediately becomes clear. Perhaps most important, crime, victimization, and criminal justice cannot be fully understood without appreciating their structural context. Using Mills's terminology, crime and victimization are public issues rather than private troubles. They are rooted in the social and physical characteristics of communities, in the network of relationships in which people interact, and in the structured social inequalities of race and ethnicity, social class, and gender. Reflecting this point, many of criminology's important concepts, including anomie, relative deprivation, and social conflict, draw from concepts originally developed in the larger body of sociology. Moreover, research methodology originating in sociology provides the basis for much criminological research.

Criminology is just as relevant for its parent field of sociology because of the structural basis for criminality. If crime and victimization derive from community characteristics, social relationships, and inequality, criminological insights both reinforce and advance sociological understanding of all these areas. Crime, victimization, and legal punishment are certainly important negative life chances for people at the bottom of the socioeconomic ladder. More than most other subfields in sociology, criminology shows us how and why social inequality is, as Elliott Currie (1985: 160) once put it, "enormously destructive of human personality and of social order." By the same token, positions at the top of the socioeconomic ladder contribute to a greater probability of white-collar crime that results in little or no punishment. Again, perhaps more than most other sociological subfields, criminology illuminates the privileges of those at the top of the social hierarchy.

Another major dimension of inequality, gender, also has important consequences for criminality and victimization and, perhaps, legal punishment. Criminological findings have contributed to the larger body of sociological knowledge about the importance of gender

(Renzetti 2013). More generally, the study of crime has furthered understanding of many standard sociological concepts, such as alienation, community, inequality, organization, and social control (Short 2007).

Review and Discuss

In what ways are the disciplines of sociology and criminology relevant for each other?

The Rise of Sociological Criminology

Many of the themes just outlined shaped the rise of sociological criminology in the United States during the twentieth century. Because Part 2 discusses the development of criminological theory in greater detail, here we simply sketch this history to underscore the intellectual connection between criminology and sociology. Before we do so, it will be helpful to review some basic concepts.

All societies have social norms or standards of behavior. Behavior that violates these norms and arouses negative social reactions is called deviance. In most traditional societies studied by anthropologists, the norms remain unwritten and informal and are called customs. These customs are enforced through informal social control (society's restraint of norm-violating behavior) such as ostracism and ridicule. People obey customs because they believe in them and because they fear the society's informal sanctions. In large, modern societies, many norms tend to be more formal, meaning that they tend to be written or codified. These formal norms are called laws. Social control is also more formal and takes the form of specialized groups of people (legislators, police officers, judges, and corrections officials) who create laws, interpret them, and apprehend and punish law violators. With these concepts in mind, we now trace the rise of sociological criminology.

For much of recorded history, people attributed crime and deviance to religious forces. Individuals were said to commit these behaviors because God or, in polytheistic societies, the gods were punishing or testing them. During the Middle Ages, deviance was blamed on the devil. In the eighteenth century, the *classical school* of criminology stressed that criminals rationally choose to commit crime after deciding that the potential rewards outweigh the risks. In view of this, said classical scholars, legal punishment needed to be severe enough only to deter potential criminals from breaking the law.

During the nineteenth century, scholars began to investigate the causes of criminal behavior through scientific investigation. Perhaps, the first such criminologist was Adolphe Quetelet (1796–1874), a Belgian astronomer and mathematician who gathered and analyzed crime data in France. Crime rates there, he found, remained fairly stable over time and, further, were higher for young adults than for older ones and higher among men and the poor than among women and the nonpoor.

Later in the century, Émile Durkheim began providing his major contributions. He stressed the primacy of social structure over the individual and thus established the sociological paradigm. He also observed that deviance will always exist because social norms are never strong enough to prevent *all* rule breaking. Even in a "society of saints," he said, such as a monastery, rules will be broken and negative social reactions aroused. Because Durkheim (1962 (1895)) thought deviance was inevitable, he considered it a *normal* part of every healthy society and stressed its functions for social stability. The punishment of deviance, he said, clarifies social norms and reinforces social ties among those doing or watching the punishing. Durkheim further argued that deviance is necessary for social change to take place. A society without deviance, he said, would be one with no freedom of thought; hence, social change would not be possible. A society, thus, cannot have social change without also having deviance.

Quetelet's and Durkheim's interest in the social roots of crime gave way to interest in its biological roots, as physicians and other nineteenth-century researchers began to investigate the biological basis for criminal behavior. Although their methodology was seriously flawed and many of their views were racist, their perspective influenced public and scholarly thinking on crime. The recent rise of biological explanations of crime indicates their continuing popularity for understanding criminal behavior.

At the end of the nineteenth century, famed African-American scholar W. E. B. DuBois (1899) disputed a biological basis for crime in his renowned book *The Philadelphia Negro*, in which he attributed the relatively high crime rates of African-Americans to negative social conditions rather than to biological problems. His analysis of crime in Philadelphia is today regarded as an early classic of sociological criminology (Gabbidon and Greene 2013). DuBois was also one of the first social scientists to write about possible racial discrimination in arrest and sentencing. Another African-American scholar, Ida B. Wells-Barnett (2002), documented perhaps the most extreme use of law in this regard in an 1892 pamphlet titled *Southern Horrors*, an indictment of lynch law. She wrote the pamphlet after three of her friends were lynched in Memphis, Tennessee, where Wells-Barnett co-owned a newspaper named *Free Speech*. After she editorialized against these and other lynchings, whites threatened to lynch her and other *Free Speech* staff and forced the newspaper to shut down.

The sociological study of crime advanced further at the University of Chicago after the turn of the twentieth century. Scholars there noticed that high crime rates in Chicago's inner-city neighborhoods stayed stable from one year to the next, even as certain immigrant groups moved out and others moved in. They attributed these crime rates to certain social and physical conditions of the neighborhoods, including their stark poverty and residential instability, that reflected a breakdown in conventional social institutions.

One student of the Chicago sociologists was Edwin Sutherland, who soon became a towering figure in the development of sociological criminology. Sensitive to the criminogenic (crime-causing) conditions of urban neighborhoods, Sutherland was especially interested in how and why these conditions promote criminality and emphasized the importance of peer influences in his famous *differential association theory*. He further developed the concept of *white-collar crime* and was sharply critical of the illegal and harmful practices of the nation's biggest corporations. At the heart of his sociological criminology was a concern for issues of race, poverty, and political and economic power.

At about the same time, Robert K. Merton, a Columbia University sociologist, developed his *anomie theory* of deviance. Borrowing heavily from Durkheim, Merton attributed deviance to the poor's inability to achieve economic success in a society that highly values it. His theory was perhaps the most "macro" of all the early structural theories of crime and remains influential today.

During the 1970s, a new *social control* or *social bonding theory* of criminal behavior rose to prominence. Drawing on Durkheim, this theory emphasized the criminogenic effects of weak bonds to social institutions. Although this theory focused on social relationships, it was less of a macro-structural theory than its social disorganization and anomie forebears.

The 1960s and early 1970s were also a turbulent era marked by intellectual upheaval in several academic disciplines, perhaps most of all sociology. Some sociologists asserted that society was rooted in conflict between the "haves" and "have-nots" in society. In the study of crime and deviance, *labeling* and *conflict theories* emphasized bias and discrimination in the application of criminal labels and in the development of criminal laws. Shortly thereafter, new feminist understandings of gender and society began to make their way into criminology, as feminists criticized the male bias of traditional criminological theories and called attention to the gendered nature of crime and victimization.

Today all of these sociological approaches inform the study of crime and criminal justice. As this textbook will indicate, sociological criminology's emphasis on the structural origins of crime and on the impact of race/ethnicity and poverty continues to guide much contemporary theory and research. To aid your understanding of sociological perspectives on crime, we now discuss some important concepts in the study of crime and deviance.

▼ This photo shows students running away after National Guard troops opened fire on demonstrators at Kent State University on May 4, 1970. The 1960s and early 1970s were a turbulent era that stimulated the use of labeling and conflict theories in the study of crime and deviance.

© Everett Collection Historical / Alamy

► Crime, Deviance, and Criminal Law

Edwin Sutherland (1947) defined criminology as the study of the making of laws, of the breaking of laws, and of society's reaction to the breaking of laws. Put another way, criminology is the scientific study of the creation of criminal law, of the causes and dynamics of criminal behavior, and of society's attempt through the criminal justice system and other efforts to punish, control, and prevent crime. Note that criminology as a social science differs from crime-scene investigation, or *forensic science*, featured in *CSI* and other TV shows.

The term *crime* has already appeared many times in this chapter, but what actually is crime? Most simply, crime is behavior that is considered so harmful that it is banned by a criminal law. Though straightforward, this definition begs some important questions. For example, how harmful must a behavior be before it is banned by a criminal law? Is it possible for a behavior to be harmful but not banned? Is it possible for a behavior to be banned but not very harmful? Who decides what is or is not harmful? What factors affect such decisions?

▲ Killing in wartime is considered necessary and even heroic, but killing in most other circumstances is considered a crime (homicide).

As these questions indicate, the definition of crime is not all that straightforward after all. Instead, it is problematic. In sociology, this view of crime derives from the larger study of deviant behavior, of which crime is obviously one very important type. Recall that deviance is a behavior that violates social norms and arouses negative social reactions. Durkheim's monastery example, given earlier, raises an interesting point. Behavior considered deviant in a monastery, such as talking, would be perfectly acceptable elsewhere. This illustrates that deviance is a *relative* concept: whether a given behavior is judged deviant depends not on the behavior itself but on the circumstances under which it occurs. Consider murder, the most serious of interpersonal crimes. As a behavior, murder involves killing someone. We consider this act so horrible that sometimes we execute people for it. Yet if soldiers kill someone in wartime, they are doing their job, and if they kill several people in a particularly heroic fashion, they may receive a medal. The behavior itself, killing, is the same, but the circumstances surrounding it determine whether we punish the killer or award a medal.

Whether a given behavior is considered deviant also depends on where it occurs, as the monastery example reminds us. What is considered deviant in one society may be considered acceptable in another. Another way of saying this is that deviance is *relative in space*. As just one example, anthropologists have found that sexual acts condemned in some societies are often practiced in others (Goode 2011).

Deviance is also *relative in time:* within the same society, what is considered deviant in one time period may not be considered deviant in a later period, and vice versa. For example, the use of cocaine, marijuana, and opium was very common (and legal) in the United States just over a century ago, even though all three drugs are illegal today. Many over-the-counter medicines contained opium for such problems as depression, insomnia, and various aches and pains. Marijuana was used to relieve migraines, menstrual cramps, and toothaches. Many over-the-counter products, including Coca-Cola, contained cocaine. Coke was popular when it hit the market in 1894 because it made people feel so good when they drank it (Goode 2011).

By saying that deviance is a relative concept, we emphasize that deviance is not a quality of a behavior itself but, rather, the result of what other people think about the behavior. This was a central insight of sociologist Howard S. Becker (1963: 9), who famously wrote that "deviance is not a quality of the act the person commits, but rather a consequence of the application by others of rules or sanctions to an 'offender.' The deviant is one to whom that label has been successfully applied; deviant behavior is behavior that people so label."

Becker's observation alerts us to two possibilities. First, some harmful behaviors, such as white-collar crime, may not be considered deviant, either because "respectable" people do them, because they occur secretly, or because people know about them but do not deem them harmful.

Second, some less harmful behaviors, such as prostitution, may still be considered deviant because people are morally opposed to them or do not like the kinds of people (poor, nonwhite, etc.) who are doing them.

Consensus and Conflict in the Creation of Criminal Law

The previous discussion raises two related questions about criminal laws: (1) Why do criminal laws get established? (2) Whom do criminal laws benefit? In criminology, consensus and conflict theories of crime, law, and society try to answer these questions. These views derive from related perspectives in the larger field of sociology.

Consensus theory originates in Durkheim's work. It assumes a consensus among people from all walks of life on what the social norms of behavior are and should be. Formal norms, or laws, represent the interests of all segments of the public. People obey laws not because they fear being punished but because they have internalized the norms and regard them as appropriate to obey. When crime and deviance occur, they violate these widely accepted norms, and punishment of the behavior is necessary to ensure continuing social stability.

Conflict theory (discussed further in Chapter 9) derives from the work of Karl Marx and Friedrich Engels and is generally the opposite of consensus theory. It assumes that members of the public disagree on many of society's norms, with their disagreement reflecting their disparate positions based on their inequality of wealth and power. Laws represent the views of the powerful, not the powerless, and help them stay at the top of society's hierarchy and keep the powerless at the bottom. Behavior labeled criminal by laws is conduct by the poor that threatens the interests of the powerful. The powerful may commit very harmful behaviors, but because they determine which laws are created, their behaviors are often legal, or at least not harshly punished even if they are illegal.

▲ When Coca-Cola was first manufactured in 1894, it contained cocaine, contributing in no small measure to its instant popularity.

© Archive Images / Alamy

These two theories have important implications for how we define and understand crime. In consensus theory, crime is defined simply as any behavior that violates a criminal law, to recall our earlier straightforward definition. Criminal law in turn is thought to both represent and protect the interests of all members of society. In conflict theory, the definition of crime is more problematic: it is just as important to consider why some behaviors *do not become* illegal as to consider why others *are* illegal. A conflict view of crime, law, and society thus defines crime more broadly than does a consensus view. In particular, it is willing to consider behaviors as crimes in the larger sense of the word if they are harmful, even if they are not illegal.

Both theories have their merits. The greatest support for consensus theory comes from criminal laws banning the criminal behaviors we call *street crime,* which all segments of society condemn and which victimizes the poor more than the wealthy. Although the historical roots of some of these laws lie in the conflict between rich and poor, today they cannot be said to exist for the protection of the wealthy and powerful. The greatest evidence for conflict theory perhaps comes from corporate misconduct, which is arguably more socially harmful than street crime but is less severely punished. Both kinds of behavior are discussed in the chapters ahead.

Goals of Criminal Law

Criminal law in the United States and other Western democracies ideally tries to achieve several goals. Because criminal law is obviously an essential component of the criminal justice system, perhaps its most important goal is to *help keep the public safe from crime and criminals or,* to put it another way, *to prevent and control crime and criminal behavior.*

A second goal of criminal law is to *articulate our society's moral values and concerns,* a goal that consensus theory emphasizes. Ideally, criminal law bans behaviors that our society considers immoral or wrong for other reasons. Murder is an obvious example here. More controversially, criminal law also bans the use of certain drugs, prostitution, and some other behaviors that people voluntarily commit and for which there may be no unwilling victims. We call these behaviors *consensual* or *victimless* crimes, and critics say that society's effort to ban them amounts to "legislating morality" and may in fact do more harm than good (Brownstein 2013).

A third goal of criminal law and the larger criminal justice system is to *protect the rights and freedoms of the nation's citizenry* by protecting it from potential governmental abuses of power. This is what is meant by the *rule of law* that is so fundamental to a democracy and is lacking in authoritarian nations where police and other government agents take away their citizens' freedom and otherwise abuse them. This consideration helps us to understand why reports of torture and abuse by U.S. personnel of persons captured in the Iraq War a decade ago aroused so much concern: the alleged abuse was committed

Photo courtesy of Washington Post via Getty Images

▲ Reports of abuse and torture of Iraqi detainees by U.S. personnel aroused much controversy, in part because critics said these incidents violated international law.

by personnel of a democratic nation and violated the rules of international law governing the treatment of military prisoners and detainees (Cole 2009).

An Overview of Criminal Law

We turn now from this basic understanding of criminal law to its origins and current aspects. Law in the United States has its origins in English common law, which began during the reign of Henry II in the twelfth century. Over the centuries, England developed a complex system of law that specified the types of illegal behaviors, the punishment for these behaviors, and the elements that had to be proved before someone could be found guilty of a crime. English judges had great powers to interpret the law and in effect to make new *case law*. As a result, much of English law derived from judges' rulings rather than from legislatures' statutes.

During this time the jury was developed to replace ordeals as the chief way to determine a defendant's guilt or innocence. However, the jury's power was limited because jurors could be punished if they found a defendant innocent. Its power and importance grew considerably in 1670 after William Penn was arrested and tried for preaching about Quakerism. When the jurors refused to convict him, the judge imprisoned and starved them. In response, an English court ruled that juries could not be punished for their verdicts. This ruling allowed juries to acquit defendants with impunity and strengthened their historic role as protectors of defendants against arbitrary state power (Barkan 1983).

When English colonists came to the New World beginning with the Pilgrims, they naturally brought with them English common law. Several grievances that led to the Revolutionary War centered on England's denial of jury trials for colonial defendants, its search and seizure of colonial homes and property, and its arbitrary use of legal punishment. After the Revolution, the new nation's leaders wrote protections from these and other legal abuses into the Constitution and the Bill of Rights.

Legal Distinctions in Types of Crime

Most U.S. jurisdictions still retain common law concepts of the types of crime and the elements of criminal law violation that must be proved before a defendant can be found guilty. One distinction is made between *mala in se* crimes and *mala prohibita* crimes, with the former considered more serious than the latter. *Mala in se* (evil in themselves) crimes refer to behaviors that violate traditional norms and moral codes. This category includes the violent and property crimes that most concern the public. *Mala prohibita* (wrong only because prohibited by law) crimes refer to behaviors that violate contemporary standards only; examples include illegal drug use and many white-collar crimes (Worrall and Moore 2014).

Another distinction is between felonies and misdemeanors. Felonies are crimes punishable by more than one year in prison, and misdemeanors are crimes punishable by less than one year. Most people convicted of felonies and then incarcerated are sent to state prisons (or, if convicted of a federal crime, to federal prisons), whereas most people convicted of misdemeanors and then incarcerated serve their sentences in local jails, which also hold people awaiting trial.

Criminal Intent

For a defendant to be found guilty, the key elements that must be proved are *actus reus* and *mens rea*. *Actus reus* (actual act) refers to the actual criminal act of which the defendant is accused. For a defendant to be found guilty, the evidence must indicate beyond a reasonable doubt that he or she committed a criminal act. *Mens rea* (guilty mind) refers to criminal intent. This means that the state must show that the defendant intended to commit the act. Although the concept of criminal intent is complex, it generally means that the defendant committed a criminal act knowingly. If the defendant is too young or mentally incapable of understanding the nature and consequences of the crime, criminal intent is difficult to prove. By the same token, the defendant must have also broken the law willingly. This generally means that the defendant was not in fear of her or his life or safety at the time of the crime. If someone holds a gun to your head and forces you to shoplift (admittedly an unlikely scenario), you do not have criminal intent.

The concept of *mens rea* also covers behaviors in which someone acts recklessly or negligently and injures someone else, even though he or she did not intend the injury to happen. If you accidentally leave an infant inside a car on a hot day and the infant becomes ill or dies, you can be found guilty of a crime even though you did not intend the infant to suffer. If you try to injure someone but end up accidentally hurting someone else instead, you can still be found guilty of a crime even though you did not intend to hurt that person.

Legal Defenses to Criminal Liability

Defendants may offer several types of excuses or justifications as defenses against criminal accusations (Worrall and Moore 2014).

Accident or Mistake   One possible defense is that the defendant committed the act by *accident* or *mistake*. If you are driving a car in the winter at a safe speed but skid on the ice and hit a pedestrian, your act is tragic but probably not criminal. If, however, you were driving too fast for the icy conditions and then skid and hit a pedestrian, you might very well be held responsible.

Ignorance   Another defense is that the defendant committed a criminal act out of *ignorance*. Here it is generally true, as the popular slogan says, that "ignorance of the law is no excuse," because people are assumed to be aware of the law generally. However, the law does exempt *mistakes of fact* that occur when someone engages in an illegal activity without being aware it is illegal. If someone gives you a package to mail that, unknown to you, contains illegal drugs or stolen merchandise, you commit a mistake of fact when you mail the package and are not criminally liable.

Duress   Another defense to criminal prosecution is duress, which is usually narrowly defined to mean fear for one's life or safety. During the Vietnam War, several antiwar protesters arrested for civil disobedience claimed in their trials that they were acting under duress of their consciences. However, judges almost always excluded this defense from the jury's consideration (Barkan 1983).

Self-Defense   A common defense to prosecution is self-defense to prevent an offender from harming you or someone nearby. However, if you injure your would-be attacker more than legitimate self-defense would reasonably have required, you may be held liable.

The issue of self-defense has arisen in cases of abused women who kill their husbands or other male partners (Lemon 2013). Often, such a killing occurs when the husband or partner is sleeping, turned the other way, or otherwise not threatening the woman at that instant. Several women who killed their batterers in this manner have claimed they were acting out of self-defense, even though they were not afraid for their lives at the moment they committed the homicide. Traditionally, the law of self-defense does not apply to this situation, and many judges still refuse to permit this defense. However, some courts have expanded the self-defense concept to cover these circumstances.

Entrapment   Another possible defense is *entrapment*, which generally refers to a situation in which someone commits a crime only because law enforcement agents induced the offender to do so. For example, suppose you are living in a dormitory and have never used marijuana. A new resident of the dorm offers you a joint, but you turn him down. Over the next couple of weeks, he repeatedly tries to get you to smoke marijuana and finally you give in and take a joint. As you begin to smoke it, your friend, who in fact is an undercover narcotics officer, stuns you by arresting you for illegal drug use. Because you had no history of marijuana use and agreed to try some only after repeated pleas by the undercover officer, you may have a good chance of winning your case, assuming a prosecutor goes forward with it, with an entrapment defense.

Insanity   A final, very controversial defense is the *insanity* defense. Despite the attention it receives, few criminal defendants plead insanity, diminished capacity, or related mental and emotional states, and abolition of the insanity defense would not affect the operation or effectiveness of the criminal justice system (Walker 2011). This issue aside, if a defendant does not have the capacity (e.g., knowing right from wrong) to have criminal intent at the time he or she commits a criminal act, the person is not assumed to have the necessary *mens rea*, or guilty mind, for criminal liability.

Review and Discuss

What are any three legal defenses to criminal liability? Do you think these defenses should exist, or do you think they have been exploited by criminal defendants?

▶ Research Methods in Criminology

Like any natural, physical, or social science, theory and research lie at the heart of criminology. Theories and hypotheses must be developed and then tested. Again like the other social and natural sciences, criminological research often asks whether one variable (e.g., attachment to one's parents) influences another variable (e.g., delinquency). The variable that does the influencing is called the independent variable, and the variable that is influenced is called the dependent variable. Research typically tests whether the independent variable is associated with the dependent variable (e.g., whether the degree of adolescents' attachment to their parents is related to the extent of their delinquency). This book discusses the latest criminological research findings in every chapter. To help understand how crime is studied, this section briefly reviews the major types of research in criminology.

Surveys

One of the most important types of research in criminology (and sociology) is survey research. A survey involves the administration of a questionnaire to some group of respondents who are interviewed either

▼ Telephone surveys have become very common in criminology and other social sciences.

© contrastwerkstatt/Fotolia

face-to-face in their homes or another location, by telephone, through the mail, or online. However a survey is conducted, it enables a researcher to gather a good deal of information about the respondents, although this information is often relatively superficial.

Often the group of respondents interviewed is a random sample of an entire population of a particular location, either the whole nation, a state, a city, or perhaps a campus. The process of selecting a random sample is very complex but is functionally equivalent to flipping a coin or rolling two dice to determine who is in, and not in, the sample. The familiar Gallup poll is a random sample of the adult population of the United States. Even if the size of a national random sample like this poll might be as small as 400, its results will accurately reflect the opinions and behaviors of the entire U.S. adult population, if we could ever measure them. This means we can generalize the results of a random sample to the entire population.

Other surveys are carried out with nonrandom samples. For example, a researcher might hand out a questionnaire to a class of high school seniors or first-year college students. Although we cannot safely generalize from these results to the population, some very well-known studies in criminology rely on such *convenience* or *captive audience* surveys.

In criminology, surveys are used primarily to gather three kinds of information. The first kind involves public opinion on crime and the criminal justice system. Depending on the survey, respondents may be asked about their views on several issues, including the death penalty, spending to reduce crime, their satisfaction with the local police, or the reasons they believe people commit crime. The second kind of information gathered involves self-report data, primarily from adolescents, on crime and delinquency. Respondents are asked to indicate, among other things, how many times in the past they have committed various kinds of offenses. The third kind of information concerns criminal victimization. Respondents are asked whether they have been victimized by various crimes and, if so, are further asked about certain details about their victimization. We will discuss all these types of information in the chapters ahead.

Review and Discuss

What three kinds of information do criminological surveys gather?

Experiments

Experiments are very common in psychology, but less so in criminology and sociology. Subjects typically are assigned randomly either to an experimental group, which is subjected to an experimental condition, or to a control group for comparison. Many experiments take place in the laboratory. A common laboratory experiment with criminological implications concerns the effects of violent pornography. An experimental group of subjects may watch violent pornographic films, while a control group watches nonviolent films. Researchers test both groups before and after the experiment to see whether the subjects in the experimental group became more violent in their attitudes toward women than those in the control group. If they find such evidence, they can reasonably conclude that watching the pornographic films prompted this shift in attitudes.

Certain problems exist with the conclusions drawn from such laboratory experiments. First, even if an experimental effect is found, it might be only a short-term effect rather than a long-term effect. Second, an effect found in the artificial setting of a laboratory will not necessarily be found in a real-world setting. Third, most subjects in laboratory experiments conducted by social scientists are college students, typically in lower-level classes. College students are younger than most people not in college and obviously differ in many ways, and experimental effects found among college students may not necessarily pertain to other people.

Some experiments, called *randomized field experiments* or *randomized field trials*, occur outside a laboratory. Such experiments in criminology go back to the 1950s, and there is growing interest in what has been called "experimental criminology" (Welsh et al. 2013). Randomized field experiments have been used to test the effectiveness of various treatment and prevention programs, and they have also been used to help understand the causes of crime. As just one example of such experiments, police have increased their foot patrol in randomly selected high-crime areas. Subsequent crime rates in these areas have been found to be lower than rates in other high-crime areas in which foot patrol did not increase. The randomized nature of these studies permits the conclusion that the increased foot patrol did, in fact, reduce criminal behavior (Sorg et al. 2013).

Qualitative Research: Observing and Intensive Interviewing

Many classic studies have resulted from researchers spending much time and effort observing various groups. These observational studies are also called *field studies* or *ethnographies*. Two of the most famous such accounts in sociology are the late Elliott Liebow's *Tally's Corner* (1967), a study of urban African-American men, and *Tell Them Who I Am: The Lives of Homeless Women* (1993), which provides a rich account of urban women living on the streets. Classic field studies in criminology and deviance include William Foote Whyte's (1943) *Street Corner Society*, a study of leadership in a Chicago gang, and Laud Humphreys's (1975) *Tearoom Trade*, a study of male homosexual sex in public bathrooms.

Criminologists have also observed the police. Typically, trained researchers ride in police cars and observe the police as they deal with suspects, victims, witnesses, and other people (Weidner and Terrill 2005). These studies illuminate police behavior and provide important data on several issues, including why police decide to arrest or not to arrest suspects and the extent to which they engage in police brutality. One potential problem with these and other observational studies is that the people being observed—in this case, the police—may change their normal behavior when they know they are being watched.

Another type of qualitative research in criminology involves intensive interviewing of criminal offenders. Some studies interview convicted offenders who are either still imprisoned or on probation or parole. In a recent example, Heith Copes and Lynne M. Vieraitis (2009) interviewed 59 federal prison inmates, 23 men and 36 women, convicted of identity theft. Among other questions, they asked the inmates to discuss how they obtained the identity information they stole. Other interview studies involve offenders who are still on the streets. As you might expect, this type of study poses several difficulties. Active criminals might not want to cooperate because they fear the interviewer could be an undercover police officer or might report what is heard to the police; interviewers may also face a legal or ethical obligation to report serious crimes. Some offenders may also pose a danger to the interviewer. Nonetheless, criminologists have published several fascinating studies of active robbers, burglars, carjackers, drug dealers, female and male gang members, and other types of offenders (Jacobs 2012; Jacques and Reynald 2012; Miller 2008; Steffensmeier and Ulmer 2005).

Increasingly, intensive interviewing has been combined with surveying in longitudinal studies, in which the same people are studied over time. Criminology has a growing number of investigations in which researchers interview children or teenagers and their parents and then reinterview them periodically for one or two decades or even longer. Juvenile and criminal police and court records are often also consulted. Major longitudinal studies are being conducted in cities such as Chicago, Philadelphia, Pittsburgh, and Rochester, New York. The federal government also sponsors national longitudinal studies that focus on delinquency or that focus on education, health, or other issues but include measures of delinquency; these studies, too, have been important sources of information for criminological research. Longitudinal studies have greatly contributed to the understanding of crime over the life course (see Chapter 8) and are invaluable for the testing of many theories of crime and delinquency.

If criminal offenders have been interviewed at great length, so have criminal victims. Heart-rending accounts of the experiences of women survivors of rape, sexual assault, and domestic violence helped bring these crimes to public attention beginning in the 1970s. Since that time, victims of these and other types of crimes have been interviewed at length (Cobbina 2013; Huey et al. 2013). In a related type of study, interviews of urban residents have helped to illuminate their complex concerns about crime and incivility and have yielded a poignant picture of how the threat of crime and the prospect of being arrested affect their daily lives. Qualitative research, whether in the form of observation or intensive interviewing, cannot readily be generalized to

▼

other segments of the population, but it has nonetheless provided richer accounts of the motivation, lives, and behavior of criminals than any other research method has yielded. Several ethnographic studies of urban areas, such as Elijah Anderson's (2000) sensitive account of inner-city culture, do not touch on crime directly, but still provide important perspectives that help us understand why street crime is so common in these areas.

Research Using Existing Data

Criminologists often analyze data that have been recorded or gathered by government agencies and other sources. For example, criminologists may code data from the case files of criminal defendants to determine whether defendants' race or ethnicity, social class, or gender affects their likelihood of conviction and imprisonment. They also often combine Census data with government-produced crime and victimization statistics to assess how the social characteristics of neighborhoods, cities, and counties affect crime and victimization; some studies also use Census data to determine how the social characteristics of states affect imprisonment rates, the number of executions, and other criminal justice responses to crime (Brown 2013).

Comparative and Historical Research

Two final types of research that combine several of the kinds already mentioned are comparative and historical research. Comparative research usually means cross-cultural or international research. Different nations' varying rates of crime and imprisonment reflect differences in the nations' social structure and culture (Chon 2013; Rogers and Pridemore 2013). By examining other nations' experiences, we can better understand our own situation. International Focus boxes throughout this book highlight the comparative approach.

Historical research is also important. Much of the work of the three key founders of sociology—Émile Durkheim, Max Weber, and Karl Marx—was historical. Societies change over time, as do their rates of criminal and other behavior. For example, murder rates in Western nations were much higher a few centuries ago than they are now. By looking at crime in history, we can better understand our own situation today and the possibilities for change. Most chapters in this book discuss historical research.

▶ Conclusion

Viewed from a sociological perspective, crime is a public issue rooted in the way society is organized, not a private trouble rooted in the personal failures of individuals. Accordingly, a sociological criminology highlights the role played by social structure, broadly defined, in criminal behavior, victimization, and the legal response to crime. It emphasizes the criminogenic social and physical conditions of communities and stresses the impact of social inequalities based on race and ethnicity, social class, and gender. It also challenges commonsense perceptions of crime and the legal order and offers prescriptions for dealing with crime that address its structural roots.

The primary aim of this book is to develop your sociological imagination, to allow you to perceive, perhaps a little more than you do right now, the structural basis for crime, victimization, and criminal justice. As you develop your sociological imagination, it is hoped that you will understand yourself, or at least your friends and loved ones, a little better than you do now. As C. Wright Mills (1959: 5) observed some fifty years ago, the idea that individuals can understand their own experience only by first understanding the structural and historical forces affecting them is "in many ways a terrible lesson (and) in many ways a magnificent one." It is terrible because it makes us realize that forces affecting our behavior and life chances are often beyond our control; it is magnificent because it enables us to recognize what these forces are, and perhaps, therefore, to change them.

Welcome to the world of sociological criminology. Enjoy the journey you are about to make!

Summary

1. The popular sources of our knowledge about crime say little about its social roots. A sociological understanding of crime and criminal justice emphasizes the need to address the structural roots of crime for crime-reduction efforts to succeed.

2. The sociological perspective states that our social backgrounds influence our attitudes, behaviors, and life chances. Sociologist C. Wright Mills stressed that people's private troubles are rooted in the social structure. A sociological approach often challenges conventional wisdom by exposing false claims about reality and taken-for-granted assumptions about social life and social institutions.

3. Criminology and sociology are mutually relevant. Criminology grew largely out of sociology, and today each discipline addresses concepts and theories and uses methodology that are all relevant for the other discipline.

4. Sociological criminology arose from the writings of Émile Durkheim in France in the late nineteenth century and then from the work of social scientists at the University of Chicago in the early twentieth century. Somewhat later in that century, the pioneering efforts of Edwin Sutherland contributed further to the prominence of sociological criminology. Today several sociological theories of crime vie for scholarly popularity.

5. A sociological approach suggests that the definition of crime is problematic because some behaviors may be harmful but not criminal, and others may be criminal but not very harmful. This view of crime derives from the larger study of deviant behavior, which sociologists consider relative in time and space, given that whether a behavior is considered deviant depends on the circumstances under which it occurs.

6. Consensus and conflict theories of criminal law try to answer two related questions: (1) Why do criminal laws get established? and (2) Whom do criminal laws benefit? Consensus theory assumes that laws represent the interests of all segments of the public, whereas conflict theory assumes that laws represent the views of the powerful and help them stay at the top of society's hierarchy and keep the powerless at the bottom.

7. For a defendant to be found guilty of a crime, criminal intent, among other things, must be proved. This means that the defendant must have committed a criminal behavior knowingly and willingly. Legal defenses to criminal liability include accident or mistake, ignorance, duress, self-defense, entrapment, and insanity.

8. Research methods in criminology include surveys, experiments, observing and intensive interviewing, the use of existing data, and comparative and historical research.

Key Terms

actus reus 10
common law 9
conflict 8
consensus 8
crime 7
criminal intent 10
criminogenic 6
criminology 7
customs 5
debunking motif 4
dependent variable 11

deviance 5
duress 10
felony 10
generalize 12
independent variable 11
laws 5
longitudinal studies 13
mala in se 10
mala prohibita 10
mens rea 10
misdemeanor 10

norms 5
private troubles 4
public issues 4
self-defense 10
social control 5
social inequality 3
social structure 3
sociological criminology 2
sociological imagination 4
sociological perspective 3
survey 11

What Would You Do?

1. Suppose you are a single parent with two young children and are living in a large city. Like many of those urban residents, you and your neighbors are very concerned about the crime and drug trafficking you see in your neighborhood. Some of your neighbors have moved out of the city, but most have stayed, and some have even joined a neighborhood watch group. You can afford to move out of the city, but it would be a severe financial strain to do so. Do you think you would decide to move out of the city, or would you stay? Explain your response. If you stayed, would you join the neighborhood watch group? Why or why not?

2. Suppose you are the college student described in this chapter who smokes your first marijuana joint only after repeated appeals by another dormitory student who turns out to be an undercover police officer. You know you were entrapped, but you also realize that if you decide not to plead guilty and take the case to trial, your entrapment defense might not work and you will face harsher punishment than if you had pled guilty. Would you plead guilty, or would you plead not guilty and argue that the officer entrapped you? Explain your response.

AP Photo/Bob Child

2 Public Opinion, the News Media, and the Crime Problem

· ·

Crime in the News

It was May 2013, and the residents of the small town of Waterville, Ohio, were still in shock after a home invasion that involved the fatal shooting of a young man living inside the house. As police searched for three suspects, the victim's neighbors still could not believe what happened. One neighbor said, "It's kind of unbelievable to think someone's been murdered right across the street from you." Another neighbor added, "I turned all my lights on outside last night, [and] I made sure all the doors are locked and things like that that I'm not normally worried about."

Source: Wildstein 2013.

· ·

Think about why you are taking this criminology course. If you are like many students, you may be taking it because you needed some credits and this course fit into your schedule. Or you might be interested in becoming a probation officer, a juvenile caseworker, a police officer, a prison guard, or a lawyer. Perhaps you even want an academic career in crime and criminal justice. Some students may be taking the course because they broke the law in the past (hopefully not in the present!). Conversely, some may be crime victims themselves or friends or relatives of crime victims. Still others may simply be interested in and even fascinated by crime and criminals. A final group may consider crime a serious social problem and want to know why crime occurs and what can be done about it.

Now think about why you have taken courses in other subject areas: math, biology, English literature, or even many of the social sciences. It may have been to fulfill general education or major requirements, to prepare you for a career, to help you learn more about an interesting topic, or—be honest—to fill a convenient time slot in your schedule.

It is doubtful that you took these courses because you were concerned about their subject matter or because you were worried about the subject matter somehow affecting you. A criminology course differs in this sense because its subject matter is very real to students. They hear about crime from the news media and see many crimes portrayed in TV programs and the movies. They come into their criminology courses with real concerns about crime and even fears that they or their friends and relatives will become crime victims. Like the residents of Waterville, Ohio, and so many other communities, they worry about being unsafe.

In this respect, students are no different from average citizens, as most of us hold strong opinions about crime and criminal justice. But where do these beliefs come from? How accurate are the sources of our beliefs and, for that matter, our beliefs themselves? What does social science research reveal about these matters? To return to a theme of Chapter 1, how does our location in society affect our beliefs? This chapter attempts to answer these questions and to indicate the major findings on public opinion about crime. Before we do so, though, some historical context is in order.

▶ A Brief Look Back

Although crime is a major concern for many people today, it has been considered a serious problem throughout U.S. history. As the President's Commission on Law Enforcement and Administration of Justice reported in 1967, "There has always been too much crime. Virtually every generation since the founding of the Nation and before has felt itself threatened by the spectre of rising crime and violence" (Pepinsky and Jesilow 1984:21).

In the nineteenth century, for example, the major East Coast cities were plagued by repeated mob violence beginning in the 1830s, hastening the development of the modern police force. Teenage gangs roamed the streets and attacked innocent bystanders, and newspaper stories about crime were common (Roth 2011).

Moving ahead to the next century, the 1920s were a "crime boom" decade with headlines such as "Cities Helpless in the Grip of Crime" and "The Rising Tide of Crime." An American Bar Association committee declared in 1922, "Since 1890 there has been, and continues, a widening, deepening tide of lawlessness in this country, sometimes momentarily receding, to swell again into greater depth and intensity." A New York newspaper agreed: "Never before has the average person, in his place of business, in his home or on the streets, had cause to feel less secure. Never before has a continuous wave of crime given rise to so general a wave of fear" (Wright 1985).

This brief history reminds us that crime has always been considered a serious problem. Although we worry about it today, Americans have always worried about it, and their anxiety has been fueled by news media coverage. This concern helps drive policy decisions about crime and criminal justice. But what if public concern is at least partly the result of misleading media coverage? We explore this issue in the next section.

▲ This wanted poster for the notorious outlaw Billy the Kid reminds us that crime has been considered a serious problem throughout U.S. history.

▶ Public Opinion and Crime Policy

As you undoubtedly learned before you entered college, the most defining feature of a democracy is that citizens elect their leaders by majority vote. A related feature, say scholars of democratic theory, is that policy decisions by public officials should reflect public opinion (Dye 2013).

Critics have challenged this view on several grounds. A first criticism is that public officials are influenced more by a small, wealthy, powerful elite than by the general public (Domhoff 2014). To the extent this criticism might be true, public policy development differs from the idealized version of democratic theory.

A second criticism is that majority opinion may violate democratic principles of fairness, equality, and justice. Support for slavery before the Civil War is just one of many examples that could be cited from U.S. history. Public opinion that violates democratic principles should not influence public policy.

A final challenge to democratic theory is that public opinion is often inaccurate. Europeans used to believe that the earth was flat, but that did not make it flat. In today's world, many people get their information from the news media, but the news media often distort reality (Glassner 2010). Expert opinion may also influence our views, but even expert opinion may be inaccurate. In the late 1800s, some of the most respected U.S. physicians believed that women should not go to college. These "experts" believed that the rigors of higher education would upset women's menstrual cycles and that they would not do well on exams during "that time of the month" (Ehrenreich and English 2005)! Fortunately, we have moved beyond these foolish beliefs, but the damage they did back then to women's opportunities for higher education was real.

What relevance does all this have for public opinion about crime? People have many concerns and strong opinions about crime and criminal justice. Their views may influence criminal justice policy decisions and, in particular, promote tougher penalties for serious crime. But what if these views are sometimes misinformed? What if public concern about crime stems partly from sensational news media coverage of violent crime and alarmist statements by politicians? Moreover, what if antidemocratic attitudes such as racial prejudice affect public views about crime? These possibilities raise some troubling questions about the influence of public opinion on criminal justice policy in a democratic society.

The remainder of this chapter addresses these possibilities. A major goal is to emphasize the problems involved in allowing public opinion on a complex topic such as crime to influence policy without careful evaluation of all available evidence.

Review and Discuss

What are three criticisms or challenges to democratic theory? What is the relevance of these challenges to public opinion about crime?

▶ News Media Coverage of Crime and Criminal Justice

To stimulate your thinking about these issues, complete this minisurvey on certain aspects of crime and criminal justice in the United States:

1. What percentage of convicted felony defendants are found guilty by a jury instead of by a judge? Answer: _____
2. How much of the average police officer's time is spent fighting crime (i.e., questioning witnesses, arresting suspects) as opposed to other activities? Answer: _____
3. About how many people die each year from homicides? Answer: _____
4. About how many people die each year from taking illegal drugs? Answer: _____
5. What percentage of all felonies in a given year lead to someone being convicted of a felony and imprisoned? Answer: _____
6. In terms of race and social class, who is the typical criminal in the United States? Answer: _____

If your answers are similar to many of my own students' answers, you would have said the following:

1. Between 30 percent and 60 percent of convicted felons are found guilty at a jury trial.
2. About 60 percent or more of police officers' time is spent fighting crime.
3. At least 50,000 to 100,000 people die each year from homicides.
4. At least 30,000 to 50,000 people die annually from use of illegal drugs.
5. About one-third of all felonies in a given year lead to someone being imprisoned for committing the felony.
6. The typical criminal, despite many exceptions, is poor and nonwhite.

Now compare your answers to what the best available evidence tells us:

1. Fewer than 10 percent of convicted felons are found guilty at jury trials, with most found guilty as a result of plea bargaining (Neubauer and Fradella 2014).
2. Only about 10 to 20 percent of police officers' time is spent fighting crime; the remainder is spent on directing traffic, responding to traffic accidents, and other relatively mundane matters (Dempsey and Forst 2014).
3. About 14,000–15,000 people die each year from homicides (Federal Bureau of Investigation 2012).
4. About 17,000 people die each year from taking illegal drugs (Mokdad et al. 2004).

5. Well under 10 percent of all felonies in a given year lead to someone being imprisoned for committing the felony (Walker 2011).

6. The profile of the typical criminal, if one includes very common crimes such as employee theft and other kinds of white-collar crime, is certainly not restricted to those who are poor and nonwhite (Simon 2012).

Many students have trouble believing these findings, but each is based on sound evidence that later chapters will discuss. For now, let us assume that these findings are accurate and that public opinion and perceptions on these and other crime and criminal justice matters may sometimes be mistaken. Where do these perceptions come from? Where did you acquire the information that led to your answers? Research suggests that the major source of your information is the news and popular media (Surette 2011).

▲ Despite the importance of juries, fewer than 10 percent of felony convictions occur as the result of jury trials. Instead, most convictions occur as the result of plea bargaining.

Overdramatization of Crime

If so many people rely on the media for their knowledge about crime, it is important that the media depict crime accurately. But how accurate is the media's depiction of crime? To begin our answer to this question, pretend that you are a newspaper editor or a TV news director. Why might it be in your interest to devote a lot of stories to crime and drugs? The answer is obvious: these stories have great potential for capturing readers' or viewers' attention and even increasing their numbers, and thus for advancing your career. Now pretend that you are in charge of nightly programming for one of the TV networks. Which types of events hold the most promise for boosting your network's ratings: Violent street crime or white-collar crime? Police chases of violent criminals or traffic citations? Jury trials or plea bargains? The answer is again obvious. Like the news media, the networks' TV schedules will naturally feature the most dramatic kinds of crime and criminal justice activities, as will theatrical films dealing with criminal justice.

Scholarly investigations of media crime coverage find that the news media do, in fact, overdramatize crime. This occurs in several related ways, as we shall now discuss.

Crime Waves

The first way the media overdramatize crime is through crime waves, in which a city's news media suddenly devote much attention to a small number of crimes and create a false impression that crime is rampant. In an early study, Felix Frankfurter, a future Justice of the U.S. Supreme Court, and Roscoe Pound, dean of Harvard Law School, examined the manufacture of a crime wave in Cleveland, Ohio, in January 1919, when the city's Ohio newspapers sharply increased their number of crime stories even though police reports of crime had increased only slightly (Frankfurter and Pound 1922). Frankfurter and Pound criticized the press for alarming the public and for pressuring Cleveland officials to ignore due process rights guaranteed by the U.S. Constitution. In a more recent and widely cited study, Mark Fishman (1978) documented a media crime wave in 1976 by New York City newspapers, which extensively covered a few crimes against the elderly. Although these crimes were not in fact increasing, the media coverage alarmed the public.

Often the media's crime coverage continues to be heavy even though the crime rate may be declining. For example, murder stories on the TV networks' evening newscasts surged, thanks in part to the O. J. Simpson murder case, by 721 percent from 1993 to 1996 (Kurtz 1997). This heavy crime coverage heightened fears that crime was soaring even though the U.S. homicide rate had actually dropped by 20 percent during that time, prompting one TV news reporter to comment, "The myth of rapidly rising crime is so widespread that almost every report(er) believes it's true. I'm as guilty as anyone" (Williams 1994).

▲ Despite popular belief, the view that several trick-or-treaters have died from eating poisoned Halloween candy is a myth.

In a related phenomenon, the media may devote much attention to very uncommon crimes or even report stories of crimes that never happened. Victor E. Kappeler and Gary W. Potter (2005) describe several such examples. No doubt you have heard of children stricken by poisoned Halloween candy. Such stories surfaced in the mid-1970s when the media reported that several children had died from poisoned candy. However, later investigation confirmed only two deaths, neither involving a stranger giving poisoned candy to a trick-or-treater. In one death, a child died after supposedly eating Halloween candy laced with heroin, but it was later discovered that he had found the drug in his uncle's home. In the other, an 8-year-old boy ate candy laced with cyanide by his father. The truth of both boys' deaths received far less coverage than the initial reports of trusting trick-or-treaters murdered by strangers.

No doubt you have also seen faces of missing children, believed to be kidnapped by strangers, on milk cartons and in heavily publicized news reports. Various government reports indicate that between 1.5 million and 2.5 million children are reported missing each year. However, most missing children are in fact runaways. The relatively few abducted children are usually taken by a parent in a custody battle, and only about 300 are abducted by strangers annually. Although even one child abducted by a stranger is too many, the real number of such children is much smaller than most people think.

Kappeler and Potter (2005) term a final example the "serial killer panic of 1983–85," when many news stories appeared about serial killers who murder people at random. A front-page article in the *New York Times* called serial killing a national epidemic, accounting for roughly 20 percent, or 4,000, of all the yearly U.S. homicides back then (Lindsey 1984). Many other news reports repeated the *Times*'s estimate. However, a later study put the annual number of serial killings at no more than 400 and perhaps as few as 50 (Jenkins 1988). The higher end of the estimate is still only one-tenth the size of the earlier 4,000 figure. Serial killers do exist and must be taken seriously, but they do not appear to be quite the menace the media had us believe.

Overreporting of (Violent) Crime

A second way the news media overdramatize crime is simply by reporting so many stories about it. Crime stories rank third in airtime on local newscasts, trailing only traffic and weather and gaining more time than sports (Pew Research Center 2013).

The news media's overreporting tends to focus on violent crime, especially homicide. As the old saying goes, "If it bleeds, it leads." This focus occurs even though most crimes are *not* violent (see Chapter 3). As a result, the media give the most coverage to the crimes that occur the least.

As criminologist Mark Warr put it, "If I were an alien and I came to this planet and I turned on the television, I would think that most crimes were . . . violent crimes, when in fact those are the least common crimes in our society" (Williams 1994). Much research supports this view, with homicide generally accounting for more than one-fourth of all TV and newspaper crime stories, even though it represents less than 1 percent of all crime (Feld 2003).

Review and Discuss

In what ways do the news media overdramatize crime? How and why do crime waves contribute to overdramatization?

Crime Myths

A myth is "a belief or set of beliefs, often unproven or false, that have accrued around a person, phenomenon, or institution" (Random House Webster's College Dictionary 2000). False beliefs about crime are therefore called crime myths (Kappeler and Potter 2005). We have just seen that the media contribute to two such myths—that crime is rampant and overly violent—by overdramatizing crime in the ways described. Other aspects of the media's crime coverage generate additional myths.

Racial and Ethnic Minorities

Racial and ethnic minorities have often been the subjects of distorted treatment in media coverage. Several historical examples abound. During the 1870s, whites became concerned about competition from Chinese immigrants for scarce jobs. As a result, labor unions and newspapers began to call attention to the use of opium, then a legal drug, by Chinese immigrants in opium dens. The Chinese were falsely said to be kidnapping white children and turning them into opium addicts. A few decades later, the press began to feature concerns about cocaine, then also a legal drug, saying that its use would make African-Americans more

▲ Crime stories in TV broadcasts and newspapers pay disproportionate attention to African-American and Latino offenders.

© Michael Matthews - Police Images / Alamy

cunning, extraordinarily strong, and invulnerable to bullets. A few decades after that, press reports claimed that marijuana use would make Mexican-Americans violent (Musto 2002)! We may laugh at such beliefs now, but back then they helped shape perceptions of people of color and helped prompt new laws to ban the use of opium, cocaine, and marijuana.

In modern evidence, TV news broadcasts and newspapers often overrepresent African-American and Latino offenders in their crime stories (Surette 2011). In a related problem, the news media often pay disproportionate attention to white crime victims: they feature more articles about white victims than actual crime statistics would justify, and these articles are longer than those about African-American victims. Moreover, even though most violent crime is intraracial (involving offenders and victims of the same race), newspapers tend to include stories with African-American offenders and white victims (Lundman 2003). Finally, African-American and Latino suspects are more likely than white suspects to be portrayed in a menacing context: in the physical custody of police, in a mug shot, or victimizing a stranger (Feld 2003). In all these ways, the media's racially tinged coverage exaggerates the involvement and menacing nature of people of color in crime (especially violence and drugs) and understates their victimization by it.

Youths

TV news shows and newspapers also disproportionately portray young people as violent offenders. In fact, the majority of crime stories on the local news focus on youth violence, even though only about 14 percent of violent crime is committed by teenagers and less than 1 percent of all teenagers are arrested annually for violent crime. The news media thus give a distorted picture of youths being heavily involved in violent crime. Perhaps for this reason, respondents in various polls say that teenagers commit most violent crime, which, as just noted, is far from the truth (Dorfman and Schiraldi 2001).

Virtuous Victims

Crime victims come from all walks of life. Many and perhaps most are fine, upright citizens who happened to be in the wrong place at the wrong time, but others are more disreputable and may even have contributed to their own victimization (see Chapter 4). Despite this diversity, the news media tend to give more coverage to crimes whose

▼ Newspaper reports contribute to public concern about crime.

© Jeff Greenberg / PhotoEdit

victims seem to be entirely innocent and even virtuous. These include small children and wealthy white women, even though such women have very low victimization rates. Critics say the media's attention to virtuous victims helps foster even greater public concern about crime (Kappeler and Potter 2005). One media observer put it this way: "Reporters, like vampires, feed on human blood. Tales of tragedy, mayhem, and murder are the daily stuff of front-page headlines and breathless TV newscasts. But journalists rarely restrict their accounts to the sordid, unadorned facts. If the victims of such incidents are sufficiently wealthy, virtuous or beautiful, they are often turned into martyred saints in the epic battle between good and bad" (Cose 1990:19).

Review and Discuss

What are any four crime myths promoted by news media coverage? How do these myths distort an accurate understanding of crime?

Other Problems in Media Coverage

Several other problems in the news media's crime coverage contribute to the misleading picture it provides (Kappeler and Potter 2005). These include (1) selecting people to be interviewed who support the reporter's point of view, (2) using value-laden language when referring to criminals ("preying on their victims" instead of more neutral terms), (3) presenting data that are misleading (e.g., reporting increases in the number of crimes without noting increases in population size), (4) neglecting various forms of white-collar crime, and (5) failing to provide the social and/or historical context for the information presented in a crime story.

A final problem is that the media sometimes deliver a biased or misleading picture of certain aspects of crime, with the possible result that the public misunderstands the crime. For example, the violent crime depicted in the media typically involves strangers, even though most violence is committed by friends or intimates. The media also neglect the role of gender in much violent crime. For example, the extensive media coverage of mass shootings in the United States, including the December 2012 mass murder of 26 staff and children at the Sandy Hook Elementary School in Newtown, CT, generally fails to indicate that all the offenders are males.

Media coverage of violence against women (rape and domestic violence) provides another example. Critics say this coverage is biased in several ways. First, the media tend to cover rapes by strangers, even though acquaintances and intimates commit most rapes. Second, reporters sometimes suggest that a woman somehow asked to be raped by emphasizing her "provocative" clothing or "careless" behavior. Third, although men commit the most serious violence against spouses (see Chapter 11), reporters often use vague terms such as a "stormy relationship" that imply either that both spouses were to blame or that no one was to blame. When women do abuse their husbands, these relatively few cases receive disproportionate media attention (Franiuk et al. 2008; Meyers 1996).

Effects of Media Coverage

We have seen that the media provide a misleading picture of crime involving several false beliefs: (1) crime is rampant, (2) crime is overly violent, (3) people of color are more heavily involved in crime and drugs and less likely to be crime victims, (4) teenagers are heavily involved in violent crime, and (5) crime victims are particularly virtuous. Although crime coverage varies among the news media, and in particular depends on whether the news outlet is a quality one or a more popular or tabloid type, one inescapable conclusion is that the image of crime that the public gains from the media is very distorted.

Public Ignorance

The media coverage responsible for this distorted image is thought to have several effects (Surette 2011). Perhaps, the most important is that many Americans are fairly ignorant about many aspects of crime and the criminal justice system, including the amount of crime, trends

Crime and Controversy SHOULD THE NEWS MEDIA DISCLOSE THE NAMES OF RAPE VICTIMS?

It is long-standing news-media practice *not* to disclose the name of any woman who tells police she was raped unless, as rarely happens, she agrees to be identified. This practice began in the 1970s when the new women's movement began to emphasize the seriousness of rape. So much shame surrounds this crime, anti-rape activists said, that media disclosure of rape victims' names would just add to the trauma of the rape itself. In support of this argument, studies of rape victims find that their major concern, and one that outranks fear of sexually transmitted disease, is that their names will become public. Proponents of withholding rape victims' names make at least one additional argument: A woman who thought her name would be known would be less willing to tell the police about her rape, making it more likely that her rapist would never be brought to justice and less likely that rape as a behavior can be deterred.

Although almost all media outlets follow the practice of nondisclosure, it has still been the subject of some debate. Observers who favor identifying rape victims make at least two points. First, if society has the right to know the name of an alleged rapist, they say, then it also has the right to know the name of his or her alleged victim; keeping the name secret might not be fair to the defendant, who has not yet been convicted of any crime. Second, the policy of withholding victims' names ironically reinforces the idea that rape should be considered shameful and embarrassing.

It is fair to say that both sides to this debate make good points. Should the news media disclose the names of women who report being raped or sexually assaulted? What do *you* think?

Sources: Kristof 2010; Tucker 2011.

---

in crime rates, and the likelihood of being arrested and imprisoned for committing crime. Media coverage should not bear the total blame for this ignorance, but because it is the public's major source of information on crime and criminal justice, the media shoulder a heavy responsibility.

An example of this effect is that the public may think crime is rising when it is actually falling. For example, 56 percent of Americans who said in a 2013 poll that gun crime was higher than twenty years earlier, even though gun crime had fallen sharply during those twenty years (Cohn et al. 2013), Similarly, public concern about illegal drugs during the mid-1980s soared after the publication of front-page newspaper articles and magazine cover stories on crack cocaine, even though use of this and other illegal drugs actually had been declining since the early 1980s (Beckett 1997).

Public Fear and Concern

A second effect of the media's overreporting of crime is greater public concern about crime, with some research finding that the more people watch local TV news and crime shows, the more they fear crime (Eschholz et al. 2003). Heightened public concern about crime in turn pressures prosecutors to take a hard line in cases involving serious violence and public officials to urge greater spending on crime and the tougher treatment of criminals (Pritchard and Berkowitz 1993). As one media critic put it, "Crime rhetoric has become desperate to the point of it being unthinkable for a candidate for major political office to dare pander to facts instead of fear" (Jackson 1994:15). Critics say that some public officials add to this problem by making alarmist and racially coded statements about the menace of crime (Shelden 2010).

Obscuring Underlying Forces

The media's focus on individual crimes and criminals obscures crime's underlying social and cultural forces, including neighborhood conditions. These forces are the subject of much of the rest of the book, but, as Chapter 1 indicated, they have to be understood and their importance for crime appreciated if the nation is to succeed in reducing the crime rate.

The text notes that Americans believe gun crime is on the rise even though this form of crime has been decreasing since the 1970s. This disconnect between public views and actual reality is not unique to the United States. People in the United Kingdom, too, think crime is rising when in fact the opposite has been true for many years.

UK violent crime rates in 2012 were about 50% lower than they were in the mid-1990s and as low as they were in the early 1980s. For the five years preceding 2013, homicides in the United Kingdom were down by 28 percent, and violent crime in general was down by 21 percent. Crime was even down in the highest crime-rate areas of the UK's two largest cities, London and Glasgow.

Despite this dramatic drop, two-thirds of British respondents in a 2012 national survey said that crime had been rising during the past decade. After reading about the drop in the crime rate, one UK resident wrote to a newspaper, "RUBBISH! Britain is worse than ever and soon will be even more." Other readers wrote that the British

government must be fudging the statistics. They simply refused to believe that crime could have been decreasing, probably because they were reading about it in newspapers and hearing about it from their TV sets every day.

The British experience of thinking crime is rising even when it is falling replicates the American experience. This international similarity underscores the text's point that media coverage and politicians' alarmist comments may unduly sway public views about crime. As one British news columnist observed, "Newspaper editors and broadcasters have always known what sells their products and rule No. 1 in the book is this: if it bleeds, it leads. . . . Politicians realize there are very few votes to be won in calm reassurance that things are, in one respect at least, improving. The prevailing mood is always that the world is going to hell in a handcart, and woe betide any political candidate who suggests otherwise."

Source: Fogg 2013.

Diversion from White-Collar Crime

Critics say the media's focus on street crime diverts attention from white-collar crime and reinforces negative feelings about poor people (Reiman and Leighton 2013). Although white-collar crime can be very harmful.

Racial and Ethnic Stereotyping

Finally, the media's exaggeration of the violent criminality of African-Americans and Latinos and its underplaying of their victimization reinforces negative stereotypes about these groups' violent tendencies (Bjornstrom et al. 2010). For example, whites tend to think they are more likely to be victims of crimes committed by people of color, even though most crimes against whites are committed by other whites (Dorfman and Schiraldi 2001). Similarly, 60 percent of a study's subjects who watched crime stories remembered seeing an offender when in fact one was never shown, and 70 percent of these subjects thought the offender was African-American (Gilliam and Iyengar 2000)!

Such a stereotyping in turn seems to contribute to white Americans' fear of crime. In an innovative study, Sarah Eschholz (2002) found that watching TV produced greater fear of crime among both African-American and white respondents in a large southeastern city: the more hours spent watching TV, the greater the fear of crime. At the same time, watching programs with higher proportions of African-American offenders produced greater fear of crime among white viewers, but not among African-American viewers.

Although more systematic research is needed, media crime coverage does seem to influence public beliefs and public policy in all the ways just described. To the extent that this is true, this coverage must be as accurate and objective as possible. For this reason, the evidence of the media's misleading portrayal of crime and criminals raises troubling questions for the key beliefs of democratic theory outlined at the start of this chapter.

Review and Discuss

What are any four effects of news media coverage of crime? If you were a newspaper editor or TV news director, how would you want crime covered?

▶ Research on Public Beliefs About Crime and Criminal Justice

We now turn from media coverage to specific public beliefs. A growing body of research addresses the nature and sources of public attitudes about crime and criminal justice. We look first at fear of crime, the belief for which there is probably the most research.

Fear of Crime

Take a moment and write down the things you do in your daily life to reduce your chances of becoming a crime victim. If you are like many students, you wrote that you usually lock the doors of your dormitory room, apartment, or house and also of your car (if you have one). You might also have written, especially if you are a woman, that you are careful where you walk alone at night or that you even refuse to walk alone. And you might even have written that you or your family has a gun at home or that you carry a weapon or other means of protection in case you are attacked.

Most of us take some of these precautions, which may be so routine that we do not even think about them. On some lofty intellectual level, we may realize that something like air pollution or price-fixing by large corporations might ultimately pose more danger to us than street crime or cost us more money. But we do not lock our doors to keep out air pollution, and we do not carry a gun or pepper spray to protect ourselves from price-fixing.

We worry about crime because it is so directly and personally threatening. We especially worry about crime by strangers, even though we often have more to fear from people we know than from strangers. In addition to the presence of strangers, other situational factors contribute to our fear of crime (Hughes et al. 2003). In particular, we are more afraid if we are in an unfamiliar location, in a setting at night, and alone. We are also more afraid if the people we encounter are young men than if they are women or older people of either sex.

It should not surprise you to learn that many people are afraid of becoming a victim of crime, with some more afraid than others. A standard question included in both the Gallup poll and the General Social Survey (GSS), a random sample of the noninstitutionalized U.S. population that has been conducted regularly since 1972, asks, "Are there any areas around here—that is, within a mile—where you would be afraid to walk alone at night?" In 2012, 33.7 percent of GSS respondents answered yes to this question.

This figure obscures the fact that some people fear crime more than other people. This variation stems from both structural factors and individual characteristics. Structural factors concern the social and physical characteristics of the locations in which people live, whereas individual characteristics include demographic variables, such as age, gender, and race, and crime-related factors, such as personal victimization and vicarious victimization (knowing someone who has been a crime victim). We now discuss research on both sets of factors.

Structural Factors

Research on structural factors focuses on community characteristics such as the level of social integration (e.g., how well people know their neighbors) of these communities, the quality of the living conditions of respondents' neighborhoods (e.g., whether the neighborhood is filled with abandoned buildings), and the proportion of people of color in respondents' neighborhoods. Fear is generally higher in neighborhoods with lower levels of social integration, more dilapidated living conditions, and higher proportions of nonwhites (Swatt et al. 2013).

As might be expected, urban residence also matters: the more urban an area, the greater the fear of crime. Figure 2–1 ■ indicates this with GSS data: big-city residents are much more likely than rural residents to be afraid to walk alone at night. Several reasons explain

▼ Fear of crime is generally higher in neighborhoods with dilapidated living conditions.

1000 Words/Shutterstock

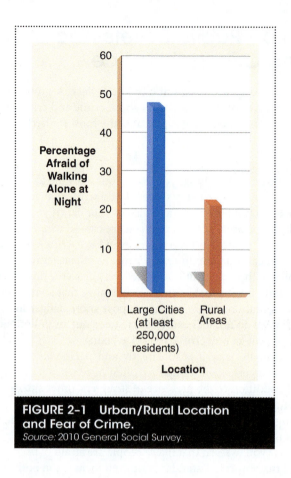

FIGURE 2-1   Urban/Rural Location and Fear of Crime.
Source: 2010 General Social Survey.

this urban–rural difference in fear of crime. First, big-city residents are more likely to perceive a higher crime rate where they live and in their cities as a whole. Second, big-city residents are more likely to reside amid dilapidated conditions, and these conditions suggest to them a higher crime rate.

Third, big-city residents fear crime because of the racial makeup of large cities. Residents of locations with high proportions of people of color, especially African-Americans, are more likely to fear crime than residents of locations that are mostly white. Additionally, whites who perceive that people of color live nearby are more afraid of crime than whites who perceive otherwise (Pickett et al. 2012). Because large urban areas typically have higher proportions of people of color, urban residents are more likely to fear crime. Surprisingly, crime rates of communities are only weakly related, if at all, to their residents' fear of crime; when we look at people in communities of similar sizes but with different crime rates, fear of crime does *not* seem to depend on a location's crime rate. This is because people generally do not know the actual crime rate of their place of residence.

Individual Characteristics

Demographic and other characteristics of individuals also influence their fear of crime. Before turning to these, note that one factor surprisingly does not seem to matter very much. If you asked your friends whether crime victims are more likely than nonvictims to fear crime, your friends would probably say yes. However, research results are mixed: some studies find that personal victimization heightens fear of crime, but others find no such effect or only a weak effect (Melde 2009).

One reason for these mixed results is that some of the demographic groups most afraid of crime have relatively low victimization rates. For example, although older people are much less likely than younger people to be crime victims, they feel physically vulnerable to attack and are thus more likely to fear crime (Rader et al. 2012). Similarly, women are more afraid of crime (see Figure 2–2 ■), even though they are less likely than men to be victims of crime other than rape and sexual assault.

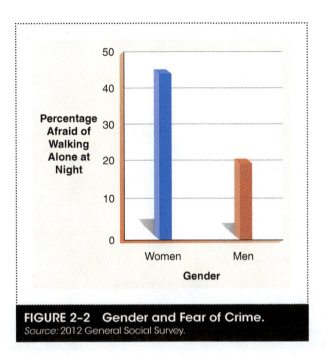

FIGURE 2-2 Gender and Fear of Crime.
Source: 2012 General Social Survey.

A third demographic variable influencing fear of crime is race/ethnicity, with African-Americans and Latinos more fearful than (non-Latino) whites (see Figure 2–3 ■). This difference results largely from the fact that African-Americans and Latinos are more likely than whites to live in large cities, which have high crime rates, and to reside in the high-crime areas of these cities. Because of this, they are more likely than whites to see themselves at risk for crime and are thus more fearful. Although fear of crime is highest among the age and gender subgroups *least* likely to be victimized, that pattern does not hold for race/ethnicity. As Chapter 4 discusses, African-Americans' and Latinos' fear of crime does square with harsh reality: they are indeed more likely than whites to be crime victims.

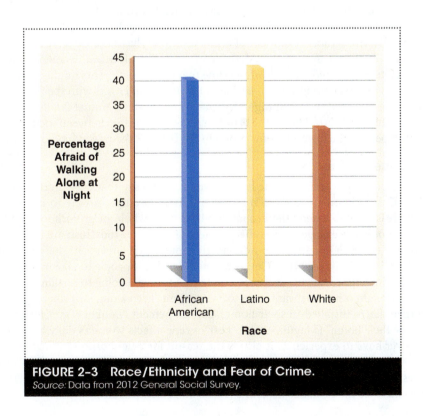

FIGURE 2-3 Race/Ethnicity and Fear of Crime.
Source: Data from 2012 General Social Survey.

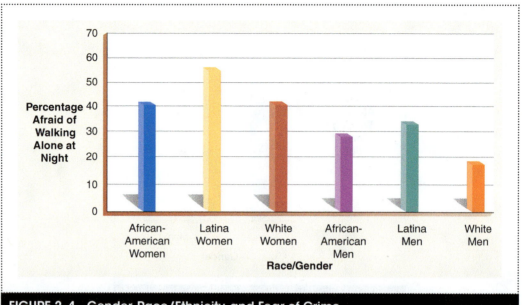

FIGURE 2–4   Gender, Race/Ethnicity, and Fear of Crime.
Source: Data from 2012 General Social Survey.

If gender and race both affect fear of crime, then African-American and Latino women should be especially concerned. To illustrate this, Figure 2–4 ■ reports fear of crime results for African-Americans, Latinos, and whites of both sexes. As expected, African-American and Latino women are much more likely than white men, the least afraid group, to fear walking alone in their neighborhoods at night. These results provide striking evidence of the sociological perspective's emphasis on the importance of social backgrounds.

We know less about fear of crime among other racial and ethnic groups. To help fill this gap, Ilhong Yun and colleagues (2010) studied fear of crime among almost 500 Chinese immigrants in Houston, Texas. Among other correlates, fear was higher among immigrants who were poorer and who perceived higher rates of crime in their own neighborhood. In a surprising finding, fear of crime was higher among younger immigrants than among older immigrants. The authors attributed the older immigrants' lower fear of crime to the emphasis the Chinese culture places on taking care of their elderly and to their elderly's consequent involvement in community activities. This type of culture helps reduce the fear of crime that older immigrants might otherwise have.

Social class is a final demographic variable linked to fear of crime, with the poor more afraid because they are more apt to live in high-crime areas. If we allow annual family income to be a rough measure of social class, Figure 2–5 ■ portrays the relationship between social class and fear of crime. As expected, the lowest income group in the figure is the most afraid of crime.

Consequences of Fear

What consequences does fear of crime have? Many scholars say that fear of crime weakens social ties within communities, leads to mistrust of others, prompts people to move away from high-crime areas, and threatens the economic viability of whole neighborhoods (Warr 2009). Although we should not exaggerate the effects of fear of crime, we must also not understate them. A large body of research documents how concern about crime affects our daily lives and influences crime policy (Meadows 2014). Concern over crime leads people to take many precautions. A 2007 Gallup poll found that 48 percent of U.S. residents "avoid going to certain places or neighborhoods they might otherwise want to go to," 31 percent "keep a dog for protection," 31 percent "had a burglar alarm installed in their home," and 23 percent "bought a gun for protection of themselves or their home" (Maguire 2013). Fear of rape affects women's daily behavior in ways that men never have to experience. It also is the reason for neighborhood watch groups across the nation and a burgeoning home security industry involving millions of dollars of products and services. In the area of criminal justice policy, public concern over crime underlies legislative decisions to increase the penalties for crime and to build new prisons.

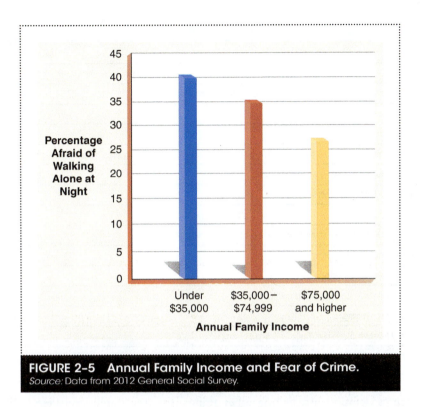

FIGURE 2-5   Annual Family Income and Fear of Crime.
Source: Data from 2012 General Social Survey.

In sum, fear of street crime has important consequences. This is true even if this fear is exaggerated by overdramatic media coverage and thus does not always reflect actual levels of crime. To paraphrase William I. Thomas and Dorothy Swaine Thomas (1928), if things are considered real, then they are real in their consequences. The consequences of fear of crime thus are very real for most of us, and especially for women, the elderly, and the residents (most of them people of color) of high-crime urban neighborhoods.

Review and Discuss

What are the structural and individual correlates of fear of crime? What are the consequences of fear of crime?

Seriousness of Crime

Which of the following crimes seems more serious to you: setting off a false fire alarm or taking $35 from an unlocked dormitory room? Stealing a car or stabbing a stranger with a knife? Being a prostitute or being *with* a prostitute?

Public judgments of the seriousness of crime are important for several reasons (Warr 2000). First, as part of a society's cultural beliefs, they reflect the value placed on human life and on personal property. Second, people's judgments of crime seriousness affect their own views of appropriate punishment for criminal offenders; the more serious we regard a specific crime, the more it concerns us and the more harshly we want it punished. Third, and perhaps most important, these judgments influence the penalties stipulated by legislators for violations of criminal laws and the sentences judges give to convicted offenders.

Thorsten Sellin and Marvin Wolfgang (1964) initiated the study of crime seriousness with a survey given to samples of judges, university students, and police officers. Each group was asked to assign a seriousness score to almost 150 offenses (the more serious the crime, the higher the score). Though obviously different in other respects, the three groups assigned similar scores to the various offenses. Wolfgang et al. (1985) later administered a survey of crime seriousness to a random sample of some 60,000 U.S. residents who were asked about more than 200 offenses. Table 2-1 presents the average seriousness scores they assigned to some of the offenses.

TABLE 2-1 Seriousness Scores for Selected Offenses

OFFENSE	SCORE
A person plants a bomb in a public building. The bomb explodes and 20 people are killed.	72.1
A man forcibly rapes a woman. As a result of her physical injuries, she dies.	52.8
A man stabs his wife. As a result, she dies.	39.2
A person runs a narcotics ring.	33.8
A person robs a victim of $1,000 at gunpoint. The victim is wounded and requires hospitalization.	21.0
A person breaks into a bank at night and steals $100,000.	15.5
A person steals a locked car and sells it.	10.8
A person sells marijuana to others for resale.	8.5
A person steals $1,000 worth of merchandise from an unlocked car.	6.5
A person turns in a false fire alarm.	3.8
A woman engages in prostitution.	2.1
A person is a customer in a house of prostitution.	1.6
A person smokes marijuana.	1.4
A person under 16 years old plays hookey from school.	0.2

Source: Wolfgang et al. 1985.

These scores demonstrate, among other things, that the public considers selling marijuana more serious than simply smoking it and, perhaps in a bit of sexism, a woman engaging in prostitution slightly more serious than a customer employing her services. Wolfgang and colleagues used the scores to determine why the public judges crimes as more or less serious. Violent crimes were considered more serious than property crimes, crimes against individuals more serious than crimes against businesses, and street crimes more serious than white-collar crimes.

Another important conclusion of this and other research on crime seriousness is that different demographic subgroups—for example, African-Americans and whites, women and men, the poor and nonpoor—generally agree on the seriousness of most crimes. This picture is very different from that in the fear-of-crime literature, where these subgroups do differ. Thus, although fear-of-crime research provides strong evidence for the impact of race and ethnicity, class, and gender, research on crime seriousness does not. Instead, its findings are thought to support a consensus view of crime, law, and society (Vogel and Meeker 2001). However, a very different picture emerges from the punitiveness literature, to which we now turn.

Punitiveness

Another public perception concerns judgments of appropriate punishment for convicted criminals, or punitiveness (Ramirez 2013). The General Social Survey asks, "In general do you think the courts in this area deal too harshly or not harshly enough with criminals?" In the 2012 GSS, 62.5 percent of respondents replied "not harshly enough." This figure and other evidence indicate that Americans are punitive regarding crime, even if they also favor rehabilitation and alternatives to imprisonment for certain kinds of crime and criminals (Applegate et al. 2009).

Many studies examine the public's punitiveness. Like judgments of crime seriousness, public sentencing preferences are fairly similar among major demographic subgroups. This similarity again supports consensus perspectives on crime and society and indicates to some scholars that government officials may appropriately consider the high degree of public punitiveness in formulating crime and criminal justice policies (Blumstein and Cohen 1980).

However, conclusions of consensus in public punitiveness may be premature for at least two reasons. First, although the public is generally punitive, religious fundamentalists, who interpret the Bible literally as the actual word of God, tend to hold more punitive views (Unnever and Cullen 2006). If so, a consensus on punitiveness among people of different religious beliefs cannot not be assumed.

Second and more important, significant racial differences exist in certain views on the treatment of criminals. For example, African-Americans are somewhat less punitive than whites, partly because they think the criminal justice system is biased (Johnson 2008). This difference is especially strong for the death penalty: in the 2012 GSS, only about 47 percent of African-Americans said they believed in the death penalty versus 71 percent of whites.

One additional set of findings is relevant, but also very troubling, for crime policy in a democracy: racial prejudice fuels support by whites for the harsher sentencing of offenders, both adult and juvenile (Pickett and Chiricos 2012; Unnever and Cullen 2012). If racial prejudice does motivate white punitiveness, then sentencing policy based on this support may be misguided. To return to our discussion on democratic theory, to the extent that public support for harsher sentencing is motivated by racial prejudice, it is inappropriate in a democratic society for officials to be influenced by such support.

The Death Penalty

A large segment of the punitiveness literature focuses on the death penalty. Because death is the ultimate punishment and because the death penalty is so controversial.

Most measures of death-penalty support rely on a single question, such as that used by the General Social Survey: "Do you favor or oppose the death penalty for persons convicted of murder?" Critics say a single question like this does not capture the full complexity of death-penalty opinion and, in particular, artificially inflates support for capital punishment. When people are given an alternative, such as "Do you favor the death penalty for persons convicted of murder, or do you favor life imprisonment without parole?" their support for the death penalty is much lower than when no alternative is given.

This methodological issue aside, the following kinds of people are more likely than their counterparts to support the death penalty: men, whites, older people, those with less education, Southerners, political conservatives, religious fundamentalists, and residents of areas with higher homicide rates and larger proportions of African-Americans (Unnever et al. 2008). Echoing the earlier point on harsher sentencing, death-penalty support is also higher among whites who are racially prejudiced (Unnever and Cullen 2012). This fact prompts Soss et al. (2003:416) to conclude, "White support for the death penalty in the United States has strong ties to anti-black prejudice." This point again raises troubling questions for crime policy in a democracy. It may also have implications for the constitutionality of the death penalty, which, according to the U.S. Supreme Court, rests partly on the fact that public support for capital punishment is so high (Egelko 2002). But if much of this support rests on anti-black prejudice, the Court's reliance on the amount of this support may be inappropriate.

Review and Discuss

Why might conclusions of consensus in public sentencing preferences be premature? Why do the findings on racial prejudice challenge the assumptions of democratic theory regarding public opinion and public policy?

Views About the Police

Scholars have also studied the public's views about other aspects of the criminal justice system, especially the police. In general, satisfaction with the police is lower, as you might expect, among people who have been stopped by the police for traffic violations and other issues; young people of color who have been stopped by police are especially likely to hold negative views of the police (Gau and Brunson 2010). It is also lower among people living in poor neighborhoods beset by crime and other problems (Reisig and Parks 2000). Certain demographic differences also stand out. Looking first at race and ethnicity, views about the police are more negative among African-Americans and Latinos than among whites (Weitzer 2013). For example, in a 2012 Gallup poll, only 32 percent of African-Americans reported a "great deal" or "quite a lot" of confidence in the police versus 57 percent of whites (Maguire 2013). Although very little research exists on the views about police held by members of other racial and ethnic groups, two studies of Alaska Natives and American-Indians in parts of Alaska found mixed results. In one study, their

▲ Public satisfaction with the police is lower among people who have been stopped by the police for traffic violations and other problems, and it is lower among people who live in high-crime neighborhoods.

© Radius Images/Corbis

views toward police were more positive than whites' views, but in the other study the reverse was true. Methodological differences between these two studies may have accounted for their opposite findings (Giblin and Dillon 2009; Myrstol 2005).

These racial and ethnic differences exist for at least two reasons. First, African-Americans and Latinos are more likely than whites to have negative experiences with the police (e.g., being stopped or insulted by police). Second, they are also more likely to live in high-crime neighborhoods where police–citizen relations are contentious (Sharp and Johnson 2009). Age and income differences also exist, with younger and poorer people holding more negative views on certain aspects of police performance.

A new line of research on views about police involves public approval of police use of force. Studies of this issue yield two related findings (Johnson and Kuhns 2009). First, whites are more likely than African-Americans to approve of the use of force by police. Second, racial prejudice partly motivates whites' approval of police use of force. This latter finding echoes a major finding from the punitiveness literature discussed in the previous section.

Perceptions of Criminal Injustice

Recent research has begun to focus on the extent and correlates of perceptions of *injustice* in the criminal justice system (Higgins et al. 2009; Unnever et al. 2011). Significant numbers of the public in national polls perceive that such injustice exists in various aspects of the criminal justice system (Maguire 2013). For example, about one-third of the public believes that the death penalty is applied unfairly, that the police do only a fair or poor job in treating everyone fairly, and that police brutality occurs in their area. Similarly, about half the public says that racial profiling is "widespread" when police stop motor vehicle drivers, and less than one-third think such profiling is justified.

A key finding by this research is that strong racial and ethnic differences exist in perceptions of injustice in the criminal justice system, with African-Americans and, to a smaller degree, Latinos more likely than non-Latino whites to perceive that such injustice exists (Gabbidon and Higgins 2009; Johnson 2008). Because perceptions of criminal injustice may contribute to tension between people of color and police and undermine the former's faith in the criminal justice system and larger society, the strong evidence of racial and ethnic differences in perceptions of criminal injustice presents a troubling portrait.

Views About Crime and Criminal Justice Spending

Because so much money is spent on the criminal justice system, scholars have begun to study public views about government spending priorities on crime and criminal justice. Although this research is still growing, two findings stand out. First, support by whites for greater spending to fight crime is motivated partly by racial prejudice against African-Americans (Barkan and Cohn 2005). This result again raises important questions about public opinion and crime policy in a democratic society like the United States. Second, although the public is often said to be punitive toward criminals, and survey evidence does support this conclusion, the public's spending priorities also indicate a strong preference for prevention and treatment measures (Applegate et al. 2009). When survey questions give the public an option between spending on more prisons and spending on prevention of crime and on the treatment of offenders, the public favors prevention and treatment at least as much as more prisons, and sometimes more so. To the extent the public favors prevention and treatment over incarceration, prison construction and other aspects of the "get tough" approach to crime of the last few decades may not reflect public views as much as is commonly thought.

A Final Word on Public Beliefs

There are many public beliefs about crime and criminal justice, and there is much research on them. Our discussion has only begun to summarize all the findings of this research. Nonetheless, one theme stands out: On many beliefs about and reactions to crime, Americans are divided along lines of race and ethnicity, social class, gender, age, and even location. In particular, prejudice against African-Americans and Latinos seems to make white Americans both more afraid of crime and more punitive toward it. In general, certain racial and ethnic differences in public beliefs about crime and criminal justice are so strong that it might not be exaggerating to say that racial and ethnic cleavages exist in American society on these beliefs.

This theme brings us back to the discussion in Chapter 1 of the sociological perspective, that our social backgrounds influence our behavior, attitudes, and life chances. Although most of this book is about the behavior we call crime, the discussion of public beliefs demonstrates that our social backgrounds also profoundly influence our attitudes about this behavior and about our nation's reaction to it.

▶ Conclusion

This chapter has now come full circle. It began with a critical discussion of decision making in a democratic society. We saw then that democratic theory neglects the possibilities of elite influence, public views that may violate democratic principles, and inaccurate public beliefs. It next examined distortion in news media coverage about crime and suggested, among other things, that the media often give a false picture of rising crime rates and a false impression of most crime as violent, and that they also exaggerate the involvement of racial and ethnic minorities in crime. Enough evidence exists on the effects of media coverage on public perceptions of crime to call into question the appropriateness of blindly basing criminal justice policy on public opinion.

We next reviewed the major findings on fear of crime and emphasized the effects on fear of dimensions of social inequality and social structure. Fear of crime is a social fact and thus has real and in many ways sad consequences for how people, especially women and the urban poor, live their daily lives.

The vast body of research on public beliefs about and reactions to crime and criminal justice was also reviewed. In a democracy, all these beliefs may have important implications for legislative and judicial policy. The evidence that racial prejudice shapes white Americans' views on the punishment of criminals, including the death penalty, calls into question the appropriateness of basing criminal justice policy on these views (Huddy and Feldman 2009).

A final issue involves measurement problems in assessing public opinion on crime and punishment, as these problems sometimes call into question our ability to gauge public opinion accurately enough for it to be used as a basis for criminal justice policy. In measuring death-penalty opinion, for example, recall that the use of a single question that lacks an alternative, such as life imprisonment without parole, artificially inflates estimates of public support. Yet the U.S. Supreme Court has relied on these inflated estimates in supporting the constitutionality of capital punishment. The Court's conclusion on this issue thus might not be justified. And to the extent that public support for the death penalty rests, as we have seen, partly on racial prejudice, the Court's conclusion may also not be appropriate.

As this chapter has tried to show, public opinion about crime and punishment is often an elusive target. But it is also a fascinating target, precisely because public sentiment about crime and punishment reflects our hopes and fears for society. As a product of our location in society, these hopes and fears further reflect the influence of our race/ethnicity, class, gender, and various aspects of the social structure and organization of the communities in which we live. For better or worse, then, public opinion will continue to affect public policy on crime and criminal justice. If this is true, enlightened policy making demands that social scientists continue their research on the sources and consequences of public opinion and that they continue to improve its measurement. It also requires accurate measures of the nature and incidence of crime itself. Appropriately, Chapter 3 turns to the measurement of crime.

Summary

1. Although crime concerns many Americans today, it has always been perceived as a major problem throughout the nation's history. Repeated mob violence during much of the nineteenth century alarmed the nation.

2. Democratic theory assumes that public opinion should influence the decisions of public officials. However, critics say that elite opinion is sometimes more influential than public opinion and that public opinion may also be mistaken and based on antidemocratic principles.

3. The news media are an important source of information for the public about crime and criminal justice. Yet the media paint a misleading picture of crime by manufacturing crime waves and by overdramatizing crime's more sensational aspects.

4. Crime myths propagated by the media include (1) crime is rampant, (2) crime is overly violent, (3) people of color are more heavily involved in crime and drugs and less likely to be crime victims, (4) teenagers are heavily involved in violent crime, and (5) crime victims are particularly virtuous.

5. Media crime coverage is thought to have several effects. These include public ignorance about crime and criminal justice, greater public concern about crime and hence increased pressure on prosecutors and public officials to take a hard line on crime, diversion of attention from white-collar crime, and reinforcement of racial and ethnic stereotyping.

6. Fear of crime, the subject of extensive criminological research, affects people's daily lives in several ways. It is higher among residents of big cities and of neighborhoods with higher proportions of nonwhites, and it is also higher among big-city residents and among women, the elderly, African-Americans, and the poor.

7. Public ratings of the seriousness of crime are important for legislative policy making and judicial decisions on punishment. These ratings reflect a consensus among demographic subgroups.

8. Americans hold a punitive view regarding how harshly criminals should be punished, but African-Americans are less punitive than whites, especially regarding the death penalty, and white punitiveness, including support for the death penalty, rests partly on racial prejudice.

9. As with other types of public beliefs on crime and justice, views about the police reflect differences based on race and ethnicity, age, location, and social class.

Key Terms

crime myths 23
crime waves 21
democratic theory 19
fear of crime 27
individual characteristics 27

news media 18
overdramatize 21
public opinion 19
public policy 19
punitiveness 32

racial prejudice 20
sentencing preferences 32
seriousness of crime 31
structural factors 27

What Would You Do?

1. You are the editor of a newspaper in a medium-size city. For most of the past two decades, your newspaper was the only major one in town. Just a year ago, however, another newspaper started up, and it is pretty much of the tabloid variety, with screaming headlines about drugs, robberies, and each of your city's occasional homicides. Your newspaper immediately began losing circulation to this upstart. Your publisher is putting pressure on you to respond with a lot more front-page crime coverage. What do you say to your publisher?

2. Suppose you live in a middle-class suburb of a large city. Almost all the residents of the suburb are white. On your way home from work late one afternoon, you drive by someone walking just a short distance from your home. You did not get a good look at the pedestrian, but you were able to notice that he was a young man with somewhat long hair, a scruffy beard, and a faded baseball cap. He may not have been white, but you are not sure. You cannot help feeling that he looked out of place in your neighborhood, but you realize your fears are probably groundless. Still, your pulse begins racing a bit. What, if anything, do you do?

© Mikael Damkier/Fotolia

3 The Measurement and Patterning of Criminal Behavior

• •

Crime in the News

In May 2013, the *Milwaukee Journal Sentinel* won a prestigious award for a series of articles documenting police misreporting of crime in Milwaukee. The newspaper found that the city's police had failed for several years to record thousands of serious crimes, including rapes, aggravated assaults, robberies, and burglaries, as the actual crimes they were. Instead, the police had reported these crimes, including many involving weapons and significant injuries, as more minor offenses. This practice meant that these crimes were missing from the count of serious crimes that the city transmitted to the federal government. These missing crimes thus artificially and misleadingly reduced the city's crime rate.

Source: Poston 2012. Milwaukee Sentinel Journal. 2013. "Journal Sentinel crime data probe wins Mollenhoff Award." May 14, 2013. Retrieved from: http://www.jsonline.com/watchdog/watchdogreports/journal-sentinel-crime-data-probe-wins-mollenhoff-award-for-investigative-reporting-c19uoto-207399601.html#ixzz2m4rQ1Nfz

• •

This news story from Milwaukee raises a very interesting and important question: How accurate are crime statistics? When the U.S. Congress investigated the Watergate scandal four decades ago that forced President Richard Nixon to resign, Republican Senator Howard Baker of Tennessee repeatedly asked about the president, "What did he know and when did he know it?" The Milwaukee story suggests that a similar question might be asked of the measurement of crime: What do we know and how do we know it? Accurate answers to this question are essential for the creation of fair criminal justice policy and sound criminological theory. For example, we cannot know whether crime is increasing or decreasing unless we first know how much crime occurs now and how much occurred in the past. Similarly, if we want to be able to explain why more crime occurs in urban areas than in rural areas, we first need to know the amount of crime in both kinds of locations.

Unfortunately, crime is very difficult to measure because usually only the offender and victim know about it. Unlike the weather, we cannot observe crime merely by looking out the window. On TV police shows or in crime movies, crimes are always discovered (otherwise there would be no plot). But real life is never that easy: because crime often remains hidden from the police, it is difficult to measure. Thus, we can never know with 100 percent accuracy how much crime there is or what kinds of people or organizations are committing crime and who their victims are.

At best we can measure crime in different ways, with each giving us a piece of the puzzle. When we put all these pieces together, we begin to come up with a more precise picture. Like many jigsaw puzzles lying around, however, some pieces might be missing. We can guess at the picture of crime, sometimes fairly accurately, but we can never know whether our guess is completely correct. Fortunately, the measurement of crime has improved greatly over the past few decades, and we know much more about crime than we used to. This chapter reports the state of our knowledge.

▶ Measuring Crime

Uniform Crime Reports

The primary source of U.S. crime statistics is the Uniform Crime Reports (UCR) of the Federal Bureau of Investigation (FBI). Begun in the 1930s, the UCR involves massive data collection from almost all the nation's police precincts. Each precinct regularly reports various crimes *known to the police*. The most extensive reporting is done on what are called Part I offenses, which the FBI considers to be the most serious: homicide (murder and nonnegligent manslaughter), rape, robbery, and aggravated assault, classified as violent crime; and burglary, larceny, motor vehicle theft, and arson, classified as property crime. The police tell the FBI whether each Part I crime has been *cleared by arrest*. A crime is considered cleared if anyone is arrested for the crime or if the case is closed for another reason, such as the death of the prime suspect. If someone has been arrested, the police report the person's race, gender, and age. The FBI also gathers data from the police on Part II offenses, which include fraud and embezzlement, vandalism, prostitution, gambling, disorderly conduct, and several others (see Figure 3–1 ■).

Part I Offenses

Criminal Homicide: (a) murder and nonnegligent manslaughter (the willful killing of one human being by another); deaths caused by negligence, attempts to kill, assaults to kill, suicides, accidental deaths, and justifiable homicides are excluded; (b) manslaughter by negligence (the killing of another person through gross negligence; traffic fatalities are excluded)

Rape: the penetration, no matter how slight, of the vagina or anus with any body part or object, or oral penetration by a sex organ of another person, without the consent of the victim

Robbery: the taking or attempting to take anything of value from the care, custody, or control of a person or persons by force or threat of force and/or by putting the victim in fear

Aggravated Assault: an unlawful attack by one person upon another to inflict severe bodily injury; usually involves use of a weapon or other means likely to produce death or great bodily harm. Simple assaults are excluded

Burglary: unlawful entry, completed or attempted, of a structure to commit a felony or theft

Larceny-Theft: unlawful taking, completed or attempted, of property from another's possession that does not involve force, threat of force, or fraud; examples include thefts of bicycles or car accessories, shoplifting, pocket-picking

Motor Vehicle Theft: theft or attempted theft of self-propelled motor vehicle that runs on the surface and not on rails; excluded are thefts of boats, construction equipment, airplanes, and farming equipment

Arson: willful burning or attempt to burn a dwelling, public building, personal property, etc.

Part II Offenses

Simple Assaults: assaults and attempted assaults involving no weapon and not resulting in serious injury

Forgery and Counterfeiting: making, altering, uttering, or possessing, with intent to defraud, anything false in the semblance of that which is true

Fraud: fraudulent obtaining of money or property by false pretense; included are confidence games and bad checks

Embezzlement: misappropriation of money or property entrusted to one's care or control

Stolen Property: buying, receiving, and possessing stolen property, including attempts

Vandalism: willful destruction or defacement of public or private property without consent of the owner

Weapons: carrying, possessing, etc. All violations of regulations or statutes controlling the carrying, using, possessing, furnishing, and manufacturing of deadly weapons or silencers. Attempts are included

Prostitution and Commercialized Vice: sex offenses such as prostitution and procuring

Sex Offenses: statutory rape and offenses against common decency, morals, etc.; excludes forcible rape and prostitution and commercial vice

Drug Abuse: unlawful possession, sale, use, growing, and manufacturing of drugs

Gambling

Offenses Against the Family and Children: nonsupport, neglect, desertion, or abuse of family and children

Driving Under the Influence

Liquor Laws: state/local liquor law violations, except drunkenness and driving under the influence

Drunkenness

Disorderly Conduct: breach of the peace

Vagrancy: vagabonding, begging, loitering, etc.

All Other Offenses: all violations of state/local laws, except as above and traffic offenses

Suspicion: no specific offense; suspect released without formal charges being placed

Curfew and Loitering Laws: persons under age 18

Runaways: persons under age 18

FIGURE 3-1 The Uniform Crime Reports.
Source: Federal Bureau of Investigation 2012.

▲ The FBI classifies the vandalism depicted here as one of many Part II offenses.

AP Photo/Ben Margot

In turn, each year the FBI reports to the public the official number of Part I crimes (i.e., the number the FBI hears about from the police) that occurred in the previous year for every state and major city in the United States. (Because of incomplete reporting of arson by police, the total number of arsons is not included in the UCR.) The FBI also reports the number of Part I crimes cleared by arrest and the age, race, and gender distribution of people arrested. This information makes UCR data valuable for understanding the geographical distribution of Part I offenses and the age, race, and gender of the people arrested for them. For Part II offenses, the FBI reports only the number of people arrested.

Table 3–1 presents UCR data for Part I crimes. Note that violent crime comprises about 12 percent of all Part I crimes and property crime about 88 percent.

For about three decades after the beginning of the publication of the UCR in the 1930s, the UCR and other official statistics (e.g., arrest records gathered from local police stations) were virtually the only data about U.S. crime. But in the 1960s and 1970s scholars of crime began to question their accuracy. Before reviewing the criticism, let us first see how crimes become *known to the police*, or official.

How a Crime Becomes Official

A crime typically becomes known to the police only if the victim (or occasionally a witness) reports the crime, usually by calling 911. Yet about 60 percent of all victims of violent and property crimes do *not* report these crimes. Because the police discover only 3 to 4 percent of all crimes themselves, many crimes remain unknown to the police and do not appear in the UCR count (Lynch and Addington 2007). When the police do hear about a crime, they decide whether to record it. Sometimes they do not believe the victim's account or, even if they do believe it, may not feel that it describes actual criminal conduct. Even if the police believe a crime has occurred, they may be too busy to do the necessary paperwork, particularly if the crime is not very serious. If the police do not record a crime, they do not report it to the FBI, and it does not appear in the UCR crime. For all these reasons, the number of crimes appearing in the UCR is much smaller than the number that actually occurs.

Even when the police do record a crime, an arrest is the exception and not the rule. Unless a victim or witness identifies the offender or the police catch him (or, much less often, her)

TABLE 3-1 Selected UCR Data, 2011

TYPE OF CRIME	NUMBER KNOWN TO POLICE	% CLEARED BY ARREST
Violent crime	1,203,564	47.7
Murder and nonnegligent manslaughter	14,612	64.8
Forcible rape	83,425	41.2
Aggravated assault	751,131	56.9
Robbery	354,396	28.7
Property crime	9,063,173	18.6
Burglary	2,188,005	12.7
Larceny–theft	6,159,795	21.5
Motor vehicle theft	715.373	11.9
Total offenses	10,266,737	22.0

Note: In 2012, the FBI changed its definition of rape. Previously the category of *forcible rape* was defined in part as "the carnal knowledge of a female forcibly and against her will." The forcible rape data in this table include only offenses reported under this older definition.
Source: Federal Bureau of Investigation 2012.

▼

in the act, they probably will not make an arrest. Unlike their TV counterparts, police do not have the time to gather evidence and interview witnesses unless the crime is very serious. As Table 3–1 indicates, the proportion of all Part I crimes cleared by arrest is shockingly small. This proportion does vary by the type of crime and is higher for violent crimes. Yet even for homicides, where there is the most evidence (a corpse), fewer than two-thirds are cleared by arrest.

Critique of UCR Data

Increased recognition some thirty years ago of all these problems led to several critiques of the validity of the UCR and other official measures. We discuss each problem briefly.

Underestimation of the Amount of Crime   The UCR seriously underestimates the actual number of crimes committed in the United States and in the individual states and cities every year. We explore the extent of this underestimation later in this chapter.

Diversion of Attention from White-Collar Crime   By focusing primarily on Part I crimes, the UCR emphasizes these crimes as the most serious ones facing the nation and diverts attention from white-collar crimes. As a result, the seriousness of the latter is implicitly minimized (Reiman and Leighton 2013).

Misleading Data on the Characteristics of Arrestees   UCR data may be more valid indicators of the behavior of the police than that of offenders. If so, the characteristics the UCR present for the people who get arrested may not accurately reflect those of the vast majority who escape arrest. This possibility is especially likely if police arrest practices discriminate against the kinds of people—typically poor, nonwhite, and male—who are arrested. To the extent this bias might exist, arrest data yield a distorted picture of the typical offender. To compound the problem, because white-collar criminals are even less likely than Part I criminals to get arrested, arrest data again mischaracterize the typical offender and divert attention from white-collar criminals.

Citizens' Reporting of Crime   The official number of crimes may change artificially if citizens become more or less likely to report offenses committed against them. For example, if the introduction of the 911 emergency phone number across the United States had its intended effect, more crime victims and witnesses started calling the police. If so, more crimes became known to the police and thus were reported to the FBI, artificially raising the official crime rate. Similarly, increases in UCR rapes since the 1970s probably reflect the greater willingness of rape victims to notify the police, not a real rise in the number of rapes (Baumer and Lauritsen 2010).

Police Recording Practices and Scandals   The official number of crimes may also change artificially because of changes in police behavior. This can happen in two ways. One way is through police crackdowns, involving sweeps of crime-ridden neighborhoods, on prostitution, drug trafficking, and other offenses. The number of crimes known to the police and the number of people arrested for them rise dramatically, artificially increasing the official rate of these crimes, even though the actual level of criminal activity might not have increased.

The second way crime rates reflect police behavior is more ominous: the police can change how often they record offenses reported to them as crimes. They can decide to record more offenses to make it appear that the crime rate is rising, with such "evidence" providing a rationale for increased funding, or they can decide to record fewer offenses to make it appear that the crime rate is falling, with such evidence indicating the local force's effectiveness at fighting crime. Police recording scandals of this nature have rocked several cities during the past two decades; these cities included Atlanta, Baltimore, New York City, and Philadelphia. The Milwaukee crime-reporting story that began this chapter provides possible evidence of another such scandal.

The Philadelphia scandal was especially notorious, as that city's police department was found to have downgraded or simply failed to record thousands of rapes and sexual assaults during the early 1980s. Police did not tell the victims they were doing this, and they did not try to capture the rapists (Fazlollah et al. 1999). In Atlanta, the city's police department had underreported crimes for several years, in part to help improve the city's image in order to boost tourism. Part of this

Jorge Salcedo/Shutterstock

▲ Victimizations of students just off campus are included in the crime tallies of some universities, but not in those of others. Critics also say that some universities address rape allegations through internal judicial proceedings to avoid alarming the public.

effort was aimed at helping Atlanta win the right to host the 1996 Summer Olympics. As part of this multiyear effort, thousands of 911 calls were apparently never answered (Hart 2004).

Different Definitions of Crimes   Police in various communities may have different understandings and definitions of certain crimes. Police in one area may thus be more likely than police elsewhere to record a given event as a crime. Even when they do record an event, police forces also vary in the degree to which they record the event as a more serious or a less serious crime, not because of any dishonesty, but because of normal variation in what they define as "serious."

School Reporting Practices   Although not a fault of the UCR per se, crime-reporting practices at collegiate and secondary school campuses have also come into question. Critics say some universities hide evidence of rapes and other crimes in internal judicial proceedings to avoid alarming the public and reducing admissions applications (Shapiro 2010). When university students are victimized just off campus, their crimes are included in the tallies of some campuses, but not in those of others. In a recent example of the general problem, Yale University was fined $165,000 by the federal government for failing to report four sexual assaults (Sander 2013) In a more serious example, the chancellor and police chief of Elizabeth City State University in North Carolina both resigned in May 2013 amid allegations that the school's police had failed to investigate and report dozens of alleged crimes, including 18 sexual assaults (Kingkade 2013).

NIBRS and Calls to the Police

The FBI's *National Incident-Based Reporting System* (NIBRS) will eventually replace the UCR. Under NIBRS, the police provide the FBI extensive information on many types of crimes. The information includes the relationship between offenders and victims and the use of alcohol and other drugs immediately before the offense. Previously, such detailed information had been gathered only for homicides in what are called the *Supplementary Homicide Reports* (SHR). Although NIBRS will still be subject to the same reporting and recording problems characterizing the UCR, the information it provides on crime incidents promises to greatly increase our understanding of the causes and dynamics of many types of crimes.

As another alternative to the UCR, some researchers advocate using *calls to police* to indicate the number and nature of crimes in a given community (Warner and Coomer 2003). When crime victims call the police, a dispatcher records their calls. Because these calls do not always find their way into the police records submitted to the FBI, they may provide a more accurate picture of the number and kinds of crimes. One problem is that not every call to the police represents an actual crime. Some callers may describe events that do not fit the definition of any crime, and others may call with falsified reports.

National Crime Victimization Survey

Another source of crime data is the National Crime Victimization Survey (NCVS), begun in the early 1970s under a slightly different name by the U.S. Department of Justice. The Justice Department initiated the NCVS to avoid the UCR problems just noted and to gather information not available from the UCR. This includes the context of crime, such as the time of day and physical setting in which it occurs, and the characteristics of crime victims, including their gender, race, income, extent of injury, and relationship with their offenders. Over the years, the NCVS has provided government officials and social scientists an additional database to determine whether various crime rates are changing and to test various theories of crime.

The NCVS interviews individuals from randomly selected households every six months for a period of three years. During 2011, about 143,000 individuals age 12 and older from 80,000 households were interviewed. Respondents are asked whether they have been a victim in the past half year of any of the following crimes: aggravated and simple assault, rape and sexual assault, robbery, burglary, various kinds of larcenies (including purse snatching and household larceny), and motor vehicle theft. The crimes are described rather than just listed. Notice that these crimes correspond to the Part I crimes included in the UCR, except that the UCR classifies simple assault as a Part II crime. The NCVS excludes the two remaining Part I crimes, homicide and arson (homicide victims obviously cannot be interviewed and too few household arsons occur), and all Part II crimes besides simple assault. The NCVS also does not ask about commercial crimes, such as shoplifting and burglary at a place of business, which the UCR includes. Finally, the NCVS includes sexual assaults short of rape, whereas the UCR excludes them.

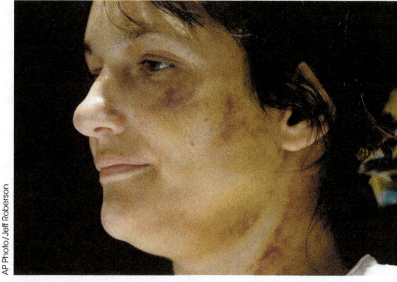

▲ The National Crime Victimization Survey collects important information in a large national survey from respondents who have been victims of various kinds of crimes.

For each victimization, the NCVS then asks residents additional questions, including the age, race, and gender of the victim and whether the victimization was reported to the police. For crimes such as robbery, assault, and rape in which the victim may have seen the offender, residents are also asked to identify the race and gender they perceived of the offender.

The NCVS estimates that about 22.9 million offenses of the kinds it covers occurred in 2011 (Truman and Planty 2012). Table 3–2 reports three kinds of data: (1) NCVS estimates of the number of victimizations for 2011, (2) the percentage of these incidents reported to the police, and (3) the number of corresponding official crimes identified by the UCR for that year. Because of the differences noted earlier in the coverage of the NCVS and the UCR, comparisons between them of crime frequency data are inexact and must be interpreted cautiously.

As you can easily see, many more victimizations occur than the UCR would have us believe, as only a surprisingly small proportion, about 40 percent overall, are reported to the police. The crimes not reported are *hidden* crimes and are often termed the "dark figure of crime" (Biderman and Reiss 1967). If, as most researchers believe, NCVS data are more reliable than UCR data,

TABLE 3–2 Number of Offenses, NCVS and UCR Data, 2011

TYPE OF CRIME	NCVS	% REPORTED TO POLICE	UCR
Violent crime	5,805,430	49	1,203,564
Homicide	—	—	14,612
Forcible rape[a]	243,800	27	83,425
Aggravated assault	1,052,080	67	751,131
Simple assault	3,952,780	43	
Robbery	556,760	66	354,396
Property crime	17,066,780	37	9,063,173
Burglary	3,613,190	52	2,188,005
Larceny–theft	12,825,510	30	6,159,795
Motor vehicle theft	628,070	83	715,373
Total offenses	22,872,210	40	10,266,737

[a]NCVS number for rape includes sexual assaults.
Source: Federal Bureau of Investigation 2012; Truman and Planty 2012.

the NCVS confirms suspicions that the U.S. street crime problem is much worse than official UCR data indicate.

Why do so many crime victims not report their victimization? Although specific reasons vary by the type of crime, many victims feel their experience was not serious enough to justify the time and energy in getting involved with the police. Some also feel the police would not be able to find the offender anyway. Victims of rape, domestic violence, and other crimes in which they know the offender also may fear further harm if they report what happened, and they may wish to avoid the publicity arising from talking to the police.

Although the number of victimizations reported in Table 3–2 is almost 23 million, the U.S. population is about 316 million (mid-2013). For this reason, the chances of becoming a crime victim should theoretically be fairly low. In some ways this is true for violent crime, because the NCVS estimates that your chances of becoming a victim of a violent crime in any given year are "only" about 2.3 percent (i.e., the number of violent-crime victimizations is about 23 per 1,000 persons age 12 or older). Your chances of becoming a victim of a property crime, however, are much higher: about 14 percent (Truman and Planty 2012).

These numbers obscure other figures. First, the risk of victimization varies greatly for the demographic subgroups of the population; depending on your race/ethnicity, social class, gender, and area of residence, you may be much more likely than average (or, if you are lucky, much less likely than average) to become a crime victim in any given year (see Chapter 4). Second, the annual risk of victimization adds up and over the course of a lifetime can become very high. In 1987, for example, the NCVS estimated the following lifetime risks of victimization: violent crime, 83 percent (i.e., 83 percent of the public would one day be a victim of violent crime) and property crime, 99 percent. Specific lifetime risks were as follows: robbery, 30 percent; assault, 74 percent; personal larceny, 99 percent; burglary, 72 percent; household larceny, 90 percent; and motor vehicle theft, 19 percent (Koppel 1987). Although victimization rates have declined since then, these figures indicate that many of us will become a victim of at least one violent or property crime during our lifetime and even of more than one crime.

Evaluating NCVS Data

The NCVS has at least two major advantages over the UCR (Lynch and Addington 2007). First, it yields a much more accurate estimate of the number of crimes. Because it involves a very large random sample of the U.S. population, reliable estimates of the number of victimizations in the population can be made. Second, NCVS information on the characteristics of victims and the context of victimization has furthered the development of theories of victimization (see Chapter 4). As this chapter discusses later, the NCVS also provides (through respondents' reported perceptions) a potentially more accurate portrait than UCR data of the race and gender of offenders.

Certain limitations of NCVS data also exist. A major one is that the NCVS itself underestimates the number of victimizations. Recall that the NCVS excludes commercial crime such as shoplifting and burglary at a business. In two underreporting problems, moreover, victims of several crimes may forget about some of them, and some respondents may decline to tell NCVS interviewers about their victimizations even though they remember them. This latter underreporting might be especially high for rape, domestic violence, and other crimes in which victims tend to know their offenders, because they may fear retaliation, wish the event to remain private, or even deem it an unfortunate episode and not a crime. Another reason for potential underestimating is that the NCVS interviews people in households. This means the survey excludes people such as the homeless and teenage runaways who do not live in households and who for various reasons tend to have higher victimization rates. Their exclusion reduces the amount of victimization the NCVS uncovers.

Although the NCVS underestimates some crimes, it might overestimate others. Respondents might mistakenly interpret some noncriminal events as crimes. They might also be guilty of *telescoping* by reporting crimes that occurred before the six-month time frame for the NCVS. Further, many of the assaults and larcenies they report are relatively minor in terms of the injury suffered or property taken. Despite possible overestimation, most researchers deem underestimation the more serious problem, and they think NCVS data on robbery, burglary, and motor vehicle theft provide a reasonably accurate picture of the actual number of these crimes in the nation (Lynch and Addington 2007).

▼

One final problem with the NCVS is similar to a problem with the UCR. Because the NCVS solicits information only on street crimes, not on white-collar crimes, it again diverts attention from the seriousness of white-collar crimes.

Self-Report Studies

A third source of information on crime comes from studies asking respondents about offenses they may have committed in a given time period, usually the past year. Some of these self-report studies use interviewers, and others use questionnaires that respondents fill out themselves. Self-report studies can be used to demonstrate the prevalence of offending—the proportion of respondents who have committed a particular offense at least once in the time period under study—and the incidence of offending—the average number of offenses per person in the study.

Although some self-report studies involve adult inmates of jails and prisons, most involve adolescents, who are asked not only about their offenses but also about various aspects of their families, friends, schooling, and other possible influences on their delinquency. High school students are often studied because they comprise a *convenience sample* (or *captive audience,* as it is also called) that enables researchers to gather much information fairly quickly and cheaply. High school samples also yield a high response rate. (Wouldn't you have wanted to fill out an interesting questionnaire in high school instead of listening to yet another lecture?)

A few notable self-report studies were undertaken beginning in the 1940s, but the impetus for these studies increased as the 1960s approached because of concern, discussed earlier, over the accuracy of official crime and delinquency data. In one of the most influential self-report studies in this early period, James F. Short Jr., and F. Ivan Nye (1957) surveyed a few thousand high school students and a smaller sample of youths in reform schools. They found that a surprising amount of delinquency had been committed by their nondelinquent students and concluded that delinquency was not confined to youths from lower- or working-class backgrounds.

Because of the information it provides on offenders and the influences on their offending, self-report research has permitted major developments in our understanding of delinquent and criminal behavior. One of its most important findings, as the Short and Nye study discovered, is the amount of delinquency that remains hidden from legal officials. Self-report studies thus underscore the extent of the dark figure of crime that the NCVS demonstrates. They remain very common today and often involve local or national longitudinal samples in which the same youths are studied over time and sometimes into adulthood. Other self-report surveys are *cross-sectional*, meaning their respondents are queried at only one point in time. A very popular self-report survey that involves both a cross-sectional design and a longitudinal follow-up of a sample of its respondents is *Monitoring the Future*, which is administered to secondary school students and young adults nationwide. Selected results for the high school senior class of 2011 appear in Figure 3–2 ■. As the results indicate, many high school seniors have broken the law, but far fewer have been arrested.

Critique of Self-Report Studies

A common criticism of self-report studies is that they focus on minor and trivial offenses: truancy, running away from home, minor drug and alcohol use, and the like. This focus was indeed true of most early self-report research, but recent studies ask their subjects about more serious offenses such as rape and robbery. The inclusion of these offenses has increased self-report research's ability to help us understand the full range of criminal behavior.

A second criticism is that self-report respondents sometimes fib about offenses they have committed. Investigations using lie detectors and police records verify the overall accuracy of respondents' answers (Morris and Slocum 2010), but some research has found that African-American youths are more likely than white youths to underreport their offending and that youths in general are likely to both overreport and underreport being arrested (Krohn et al. 2013). State-of-the-art self-report surveying, using self-administered computer surveys, appears to produce more accurate reports than traditional (paper-and-pencil) surveying, possibly because respondents are more likely to think their answers will remain confidential (Paschall et al. 2001).

A final criticism is that self-report studies join the UCR and NCVS in ignoring white-collar crime because their subjects—usually adolescents or, occasionally, adult jail and prison inmates—certainly do not commit this type of crime.

▼

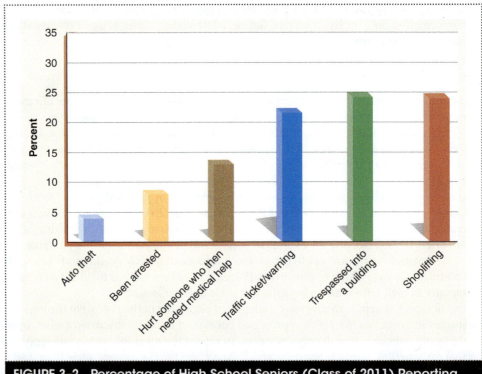

FIGURE 3–2 Percentage of High School Seniors (Class of 2011) Reporting Involvement in Selected Activities During Past Twelve Months.
Source: Johnston, et al. 2011.

Evaluating UCR, NCVS, and Self-Report Data

None of the three major sources of street-crime data is perfect, but which is the best depends on what one wants to know (Lynch and Addington 2007). For the best estimate of the actual number of crimes, NCVS data are clearly preferable to UCR data. Keep in mind, however, that NCVS data exclude homicide, arson, commercial crimes, and most of the Part II offenses in the UCR. For the best estimate of offender characteristics such as race and gender, self-report data, and victimization data may be preferable to UCR arrest data, which include few offender characteristics and may be affected by police biases. As we will see later, however, comparisons of type of offenders identified in all three data sources suggest that arrest data provide a fairly accurate portrait of offenders despite any bias affecting police arrest decisions.

Short of a superspy satellite circling Earth and recording each of the millions of crimes occurring every year or a video camera in every household and on every street corner recording every second of our behavior, the measurement of crime will necessarily remain incomplete. To return to our earlier metaphor, some pieces of the crime puzzle will always be missing, but we think we have enough of it assembled to figure out the picture. The three major sources of crime data we have discussed combine to provide a reasonably accurate picture of the amount of crime and the social distribution, or correlates, of criminality.

Review and Discuss

What are four criticisms of UCR data? In what ways are UCR data superior to and inferior to victimization and self-report data?

▼

► Recent Trends in U.S. Crime Rates

Crime rates rose sharply (UCR rates) during the 1960s and 1970s before declining during the early 1980s and then rising again during the late 1980s. They then began to fall sharply after the early 1990s before declining more slowly during the past several years (see Figures 3–3 ■ and 3–4 ■). for both UCR and NCVS data). Although the UCR and NCVS do not always exhibit the same crime-rate trends because of their different methodologies, the fact that both data sources show declining crime since the early 1990s provides confidence that crime has in fact decreased during this period.

Scholars and other observers have debated why crime fell so dramatically. Some cite changes in police practices and other aspects of the criminal justice system, whereas others cite social factors. The Crime and Controversy box discusses this debate.

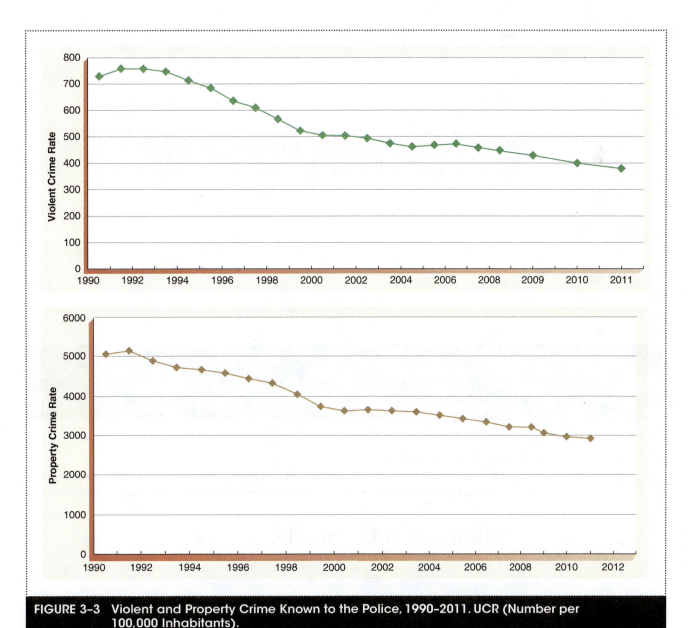

FIGURE 3-3   Violent and Property Crime Known to the Police, 1990–2011. UCR (Number per 100,000 Inhabitants).
Source: Federal Bureau of Investigation 2012.

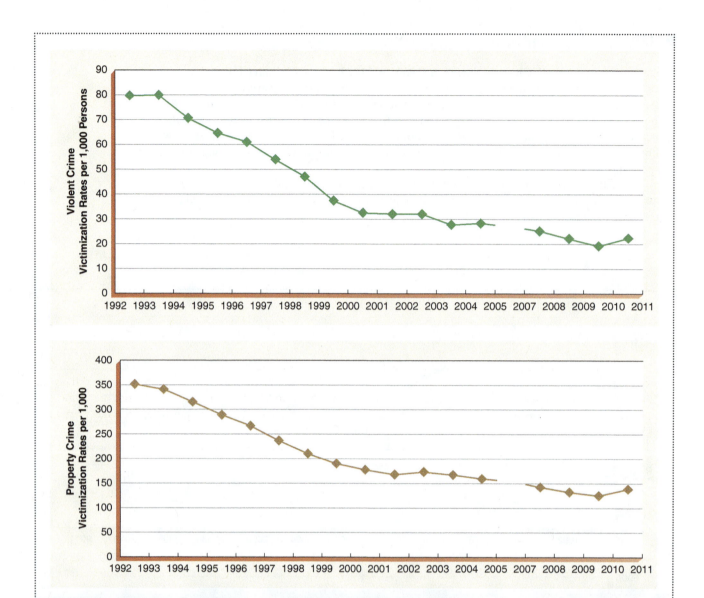

FIGURE 3-4 **Victimization Rates for Violent and Property Crime, 1993–2011, NCVS (per 1,000 Persons 12 or Older or 1,000 Households).**
Note: Because of changes in survey methodology, 2006 estimates for both violent and property crime were not comparable to earlier estimates and thus are omitted.
Source: http://www.bjs.gov/index.cfm?ty=nvat.

Review and Discuss

Why does the United States have higher crime rates than Japan and several other nations? How do international comparisons of crime rates reflect the sociological perspective?

▶ Patterning of Criminal Behavior

Crime rates vary according to location, season and climate, and demographic factors such as gender, race, and social class. This section discusses this patterning.

Geographical Patterns

International Comparisons

International comparisons of crime data are inexact. (See the International Focus box.) We have already seen that U.S. crime data are not totally reliable. Across the world, different nations have

Crime and Controversy WHY HAS THE CRIME RATE DROPPED SINCE THE EARLY 1990S?

The U.S. crime rate fell dramatically beginning in the early 1990s before declining more slowly during the past decade. Coming after a drastic rise in violent crime beginning in the late 1980s, the 1990s' crime decline was a pleasant surprise for Americans, but also the source of much controversy among criminologists and public officials over why it was occurring. This controversy was no mere intellectual exercise. If the reasons for the decline could be pinpointed, the nation would have gained some valuable information on effective policies and strategies to drive down the crime rate further or at least to keep it from rising again.

Debate over the reasons for the 1990s' crime decline falls into two camps, each centered on a very different set of factors. One side gives the bulk of the credit for the crime decline to the criminal justice system, specifically a get-tough-on-crime approach and smarter policing. According to this view, longer and more certain sentences prompted a rapidly increasing imprisonment rate during the 1990s that kept our streets safer by putting hundreds of thousands of criminals behind bars and by deterring potential offenders from committing crimes in the first place. *Zero-tolerance* policing in New York and other cities rid the streets of panhandlers and other minor offenders who had committed more serious crimes and sent a message of civility to other offenders and the general populace. At the same time, police targeting of neighborhoods rampant with drug crime, prostitution, and other offenses also proved effective.

The other side says that social and demographic factors explain most of the crime-rate decline. According to this view, the thriving economy during the 1990s lessened the motivation to commit crime, and a decline in the number of people in the crime-prone years of adolescence and young adulthood reduced the number of potential offenders. Also, the crack gang wars that fueled the rise in crime during the late 1980s and early 1990s finally subsided as the crack market stabilized. Proponents of this side of the debate also take issue with the arguments of the criminal justice advocates. Crime had risen during the 1980s, these proponents say, even though imprisonment had also risen, casting doubt on a presumed imprisonment–crime decline link during the 1990s. In addition, states that were the toughest on crime during the 1990s often did not experience the greatest crime declines. Although increasing imprisonment might have helped somewhat, they add, it has had harmful collateral consequences for many urban neighborhoods and has cost billions of dollars that could have been better spent on other efforts. Moreover, although new policing strategies might have helped, cities that did not use them also saw their crime rates drop. Although New York City used zero-tolerance policing and

had a huge drop in its crime rate, scholars continue to dispute the exact impact that this policing strategy had on the city's crime rate.

Chapters 16 and 17 return to this debate with a more complete discussion of the criminal justice factors that have been credited for the 1990s' crime drop, but the controversy over the reasons continues precisely because of its importance for determining the most effective crime-control strategies. If the first side to the debate is correct, then the United States would be wise to continue to put more and more people behind bars for a greater number of years and to have the police crackdown on minor offenses and on the serious offenses that terrorize high-crime neighborhoods. If the second side to the debate is correct, this criminal justice approach does more harm than good, and the dollars it incurs would be better spent on efforts that address the structural and individual factors that underlie crime and that are highlighted in a sociological approach to crime and crime control.

Ironically, it might be possible that neither side has a good explanation for the 1990s' crime decline, because Canada also experienced a significant crime decrease during the 1990s even though its rates of imprisonment and police employment both *decreased* and even though its economy did not fare particularly well. Although Canada, like the United States, did experience a drop in the number of people in their young crime-prone years, this drop was too small in either nation to account for very much of its crime decline.

One new explanation is attracting increasing attention: a decrease in environmental lead poisoning. According to this way of thinking, the huge switch to unleaded gasoline in the 1970s meant that fewer young children in that era had lead affecting their developing brains. When they reached their prime crime-age years 15–20 years later as older teenagers and young adults during the 1990s, they were thus less likely to break the law than the preceding generation. The drop in environmental lead during the 1970s, therefore, led to the drop in crime during the 1990s.

Despite this new explanation, the drop in the 1990s crime rate must remain a puzzle for now. As Franklin E. Zimring (2006:134), who called attention to the Canadian puzzle, wrote of the two nations' crime declines, "Much of the shared good news of recent history seems to elude easy explanations." No doubt criminologists and other scholars will continue to debate the reasons for the 1990s crime drop in the years ahead.

Source: Blumstein and Wallman 2006; Drum 2013; Goldberger and Rosenfeld 2008; Greenberg 2013; Rosenfeld et al. 2007; Zimring 2006.

Although international crime data are gathered by the United Nations and other organizations, the measurement of crime across the world is highly inconsistent. In some countries, such as the United States, Canada, and Great Britain, the government systematically gathers crime data through police reports and victimization surveys. In other nations, especially poor nations, crime reporting is haphazard or even virtually nonexistent. Some nations gather and provide arrest and conviction data, whereas others do not. Another problem is that various crimes are defined differently by different nations. For example, what constitutes an "official" rape in some nations may be very different from what constitutes a rape in the United States. Because of its nature, homicide is probably the crime most uniformly defined, and homicide data are believed to be the most consistent international data available about crime. For this reason, many researchers think international comparisons of crime rates should be restricted to homicide.

The three major sources of official international crime data include the International Criminal Police Organization (Interpol), the World Health Organization (WHO), and the United Nations. Although these sources differ in the crimes they cover and the definitions of crime they use, they all provide reasonably reliable data about homicide.

Interpol and the UN surveys use homicide data collected by appropriate agencies in various nations, whereas WHO uses nations' mortality data that identify homicide as the cause of death. WHO homicide data are considered more accurate than Interpol or UN data and thus tend to be the focus of international homicide research. At the same time, WHO homicide data exist for only about three dozen nations; these nations account for less than 20 percent of the world population, and their homicides account for less than 10 percent of world homicides. On the plus side, WHO data comprise virtually all the wealthy industrialized nations.

Victimization surveys, most of which are conducted in wealthy nations, are another source of international crime data and are becoming more popular (see Chapter 4). Similar to the NCVS, these surveys ask random samples of respondents about the extent and nature of their victimization by a wide variety of offenses. Although social and cultural differences make comparisons of international victimization data somewhat inexact, these data have nonetheless yielded valuable information on international differences in victimization rates.

Source: Bennett 2009; van Dijk 2012.

varying definitions and interpretations of criminal behavior and alternative methods of collecting crime data. Although these problems suggest caution in making international comparisons, these comparisons still provide striking evidence of the ways crime is patterned geographically.

Simply put, some nations have higher crime rates than others. In this regard, the United States has the highest homicide rate of any Western democratic nation. In the late 1980s it had one of the highest rates of other violent crimes, but by 2000 its violent-crime rate had lowered to about average; its property-crime rate also seems about average (van Dijk et al. 2008).

Scholars often attribute nations' crime rates to their cultures. In Japan, for example, one of the most important values is harmony: the Japanese are expected to be peaceable in their relations with each other and respectful of authority. Partly because such a culture inhibits people from committing crimes, Japan's crime rates remain relatively low despite its economic growth since World War II (Johnson 2007).

In contrast to Japan and some other nations, people in the United States are thought to be more individualistic and disrespectful of authority (Messner and Rosenfeld 2013). With the familiar phrase "look out for number one" as a prevailing philosophy, there is less emphasis in the United States on peaceable relations and less sense of social obligation. People do not care as much about offending others and are thus more likely to do so. The United States is also thought to have higher rates of violence than some other industrial nations because of its higher degree of inequality (Ouimet 2012).

Comparisons Within the United States

Crime rates within the United States also vary geographically. According to the UCR, the South and West have the highest rates of crime, and the Northeast and Midwest have the lowest rates. Community size also makes a huge difference; crime rates are higher in urban areas than they are in rural areas. Figure 3–5 ■ presents UCR data for crime rates per 100,000 broken down by community size. As you can see, violent- and property-crime rates in our largest cities (MSAs, or

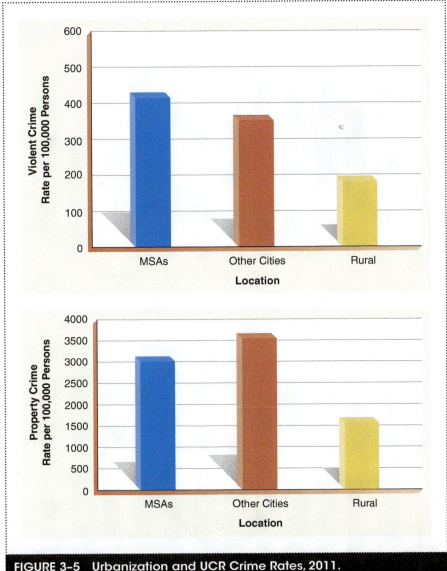

FIGURE 3-5 **Urbanization and UCR Crime Rates, 2011.**
Source: Federal Bureau of Investigation 2012.

metropolitan statistical areas) and other cities are higher than those in rural communities. Note, however, that urbanization does not automatically mean high crime rates. For example, some of the largest non-U.S. cities (e.g., Toronto, London, and Tokyo) have much lower homicide rates than those in much smaller U.S. cities.

Seasonal and Climatological Variations

Some of the most interesting crime data concern seasonal and climatological (weather-related) variations (see Figure 3–6 ■). For many people, summer can be very grim because violent crime is generally higher in the warmer months, although robbery remains high through January. Property crime also peaks in the summer.

Explanations for these patterns are speculative but seem to make some sense (Carbone-Lopez and Lauritsen 2013; Mares 2013). As you might already realize, the summer heat can cause tempers to flare, perhaps violently. We also tend to interact more when it is warmer, creating opportunities for violent behavior to erupt. In addition, people are outdoors and away from home more often in the summer, creating opportunities for various kinds of thefts. For example, there are more empty

▼ Crime is generally higher during the summer months, in part because people spend more time together outside their homes, creating greater opportunities for both violent crime and property crime to occur.

© david hancock / Alamy

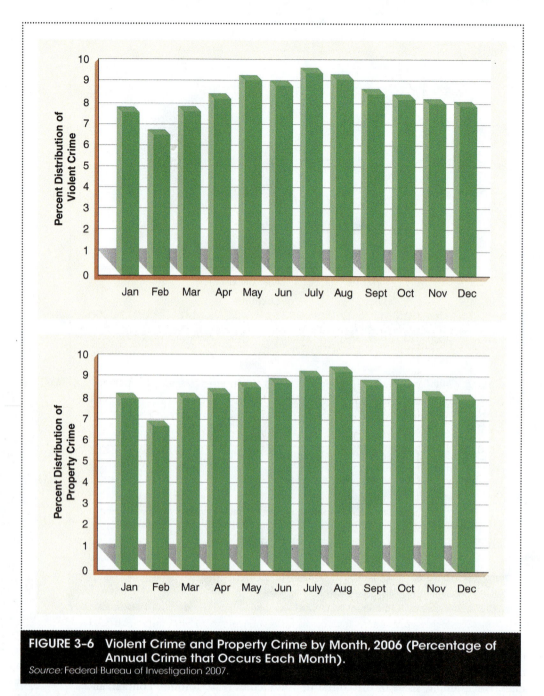

FIGURE 3–6   Violent Crime and Property Crime by Month, 2006 (Percentage of Annual Crime that Occurs Each Month).
Source: Federal Bureau of Investigation 2007.

homes to attract burglars. Those not on vacation are still more apt to leave windows open to let in fresh air, again making burglary more likely.

The seasonal research leads some scholars to predict that crime rates should rise, all things equal, as global warming raises the average temperature in the United States and around the globe (Agnew 2012; Mares 2013). When we hear about the dire effects of climate change, we do not usually think about rising crime rates, but the seasonal research does suggest that rising crime should be added to the list of concerns stemming from climate change.

▶ Social Patterns of Criminal Behavior

Gender and Crime

One of the key social correlates of criminal behavior is gender: women's crime rates are much lower than men's. Figure 3–7 ■ displays UCR arrest data broken down by gender. As you can

▼

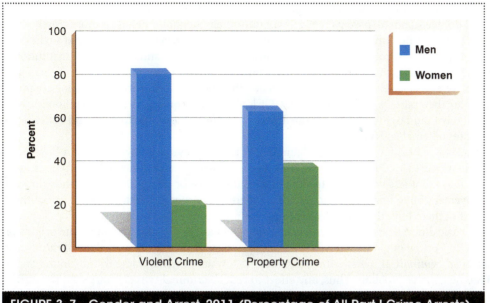

FIGURE 3–7 Gender and Arrest, 2011 (Percentage of All Part I Crime Arrests).
Source: Federal Bureau of Investigation 2012.

see, men account for about 80 percent of violent-crime arrests and 63 percent of property-crime arrests. It is possible, of course, that police bias may account for the high proportion of male arrests: perhaps the police are less likely to arrest women because they do not think women are very dangerous. However, victimization and self-report data reinforce the UCR's large gender difference. In the NCVS, victims identify men as about 86 percent of the lone offenders committing robbery and 77 percent of those committing aggravated assault (Rand and Robinson 2011). In self-report studies, males are also much more likely than females to commit the most serious offenses. Almost all scholars today acknowledge that women's rates of serious offending are much lower than men's rates, with this gender gap called "one of the few undisputed 'facts' in criminology" (Lauritsen et al. 2009:362).

Explaining Women's Low Crime Rates

In the past, many criminologists ignored female criminality. Some did discuss it, but their explanations emphasized women's biology (Griffin 2010). For example, one of the first scholars of crime, physician Cesare Lombroso (Lombroso 1920 (1903)), attributed women's low criminality to their natural passivity resulting from the "immobility of the ovule compared with the zoosperm". Followers of the great psychoanalytic thinker Sigmund Freud thought that women commit crime because of *penis envy:* jealous over not having penises, they strive to be more like men by committing crimes (and also by working outside the home). In an interesting twist, Otto Pollak (1950) argued that women's crimes often never show up in official statistics. The reason? Women are naturally deceitful and thus are good at hiding their behavior. The proof of such deceit? Women learn to hide evidence of their menstrual periods and also to fake orgasms!

The field of criminology now considers these early biological explanations outmoded and sexist. In the 1970s, women began to enter the field in greater numbers and, along with some male scholars, began to study the origins and nature of female crime and of crimes such as rape and family violence that especially victimize women. Several factors are now thought to account for women's low crime rates (Renzetti 2013).

A first explanation concerns the way we socialize girls and boys. Put briefly, we raise boys to be active, assertive, dominant, and to "fight like a man"—in other words, to be masculine. Because these traits are conducive to criminal behavior, especially violence, the way we raise boys increases their odds of becoming criminals. Conversely, we raise girls to be less assertive, less dominant, and more gentle and nurturing (Lindsey 2011). Because these traits are not conducive to criminal behavior, we in effect are raising girls not to be criminals.

AP Photo/Mike Wintroath

▲ Although women certainly commit crime, their crime rates are much lower than men's crime rates.

A second explanation concerns the opportunities provided to commit crime. Because of the traditional double standard, parents typically monitor their daughters' behavior more closely than their sons' behavior. Boys thus have more opportunity than girls to get into trouble, and so they do.

A third explanation concerns attachments to families, schools, and other social institutions. Some research indicates that these bonds are stronger for girls than for boys because of socialization. Girls, for example, feel more strongly attached than boys to their parents and thus are more likely to value their parents' norms and values. Girls also place more importance on schooling and are more likely than boys to emphasize obedience to the law. These attachments and beliefs lead to lower rates of female offending.

Yet another reason for girls' lower delinquency is that they have fewer ties than boys have to delinquent peers (McCarthy et al. 2004). Moreover, their greater attachment to parents and schools makes them less vulnerable to the negative influence of any delinquent friends they do have. Conversely, boys' lower attachment makes them more susceptible to the pressure of their peers, most of them boys themselves, to commit delinquency.

These basic differences in the way children are raised are key to understanding the origins of crime and how crime might be reduced. Put simply, *we are already doing a good job of raising our girls not to be criminals*. If men's crime rates were as low as women's, crime in the United States would *not* be a major problem. Thus, any effort to reduce criminality must start with the difference that gender makes. The more we know about the origins of both female criminality and law-abiding behavior, the greater our understanding will be of what it will take to lower the rate of male criminality.

These explanations of gender differences in crime rates all highlight sociological factors. Contemporary biological explanations highlight such factors as testosterone differences and evolutionary circumstances favoring male aggression. Chapter 6 discusses these explanations.

Are Girls and Women Becoming More Violent?

Before moving on, let us consider an important controversy that began in the mid-1970s when magazines and scholarly books began to stress that women's arrest rates were rising much faster than men's (Adler 1975; Deming 1977; Simon 1975). This increase was greeted with alarm and blamed, especially in the popular press, on the new women's liberation movement: because of this movement, females were said to be acting more like males. More recent writings also say that girls and women are "catching up" to boys and men in violent behavior (Garbarino 2006).

However, a series of scholarly studies since the 1970s has concluded that this belief is in fact a myth. Although female arrests have risen, that increase reflects an increase in decisions of police to arrest girls and women for violence, rather than an actual increase in their level of violence. Despite the impression conveyed by media reports of "mean girls," female rates of violent crime have been decreasing for many years (see Figure 3–8 ■) (Males and Chesney-Lind 2010; Stevens et al. 2011).

Review and Discuss

Why do women have lower crime rates than men? To what degree are changes in women's crime rates related to the contemporary women's movement?

Race, Ethnicity, and Crime

UCR data provide a complex picture of race and criminality in the United States. On the one hand, most criminals are white. In 2011, whites accounted for about 69 percent of all arrests, including 59 percent of violent-crime arrests, 68 percent of property-crime arrests, and at least two-thirds of arrests for forgery and counterfeiting, fraud, vandalism, drug abuse, liquor law offenses and drunkenness, and disorderly conduct (Federal Bureau of Investigation 2012). In terms of sheer numbers, whites commit most crime in the United States, and the typical criminal is white.

On the other hand, African-Americans commit a disproportionate amount of crime relative to their numbers in the population: even though they comprise only about 13 percent of the population, they account for 28 percent of all arrests, 38 percent of violent-crime arrests (including 50 percent of homicide arrests), and almost 30 percent of property-crime arrests (Federal

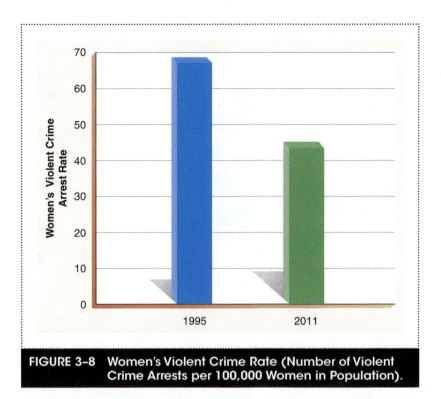

FIGURE 3–8 Women's Violent Crime Rate (Number of Violent Crime Arrests per 100,000 Women in Population).

Bureau of Investigation 2012). Another way of understanding racial differences in arrests is to examine racial arrest rates, or the number of each race arrested for every 100,000 members of that race. Figure 3–9 ■ displays these rates for African-Americans and whites. As you see, the African-American arrest rate for violent and property crime is much higher than the white arrest rate. Government statistical analysis estimates that nearly one-third of African-American males born in 2001 will one day go to prison, compared to less than 6 percent of white males (Bonczar 2003) (see Figure 3–10 ■).

The apparent disproportionate involvement of African-Americans in street crime is one of the most sensitive but important issues in criminology (Peterson 2012). As with gender, racial arrest statistics may reflect bias in police arrest practices more than racial differences in actual offending. Once again, however, NCVS data tend to support the UCR portrait of higher African-American crime rates. Recall that NCVS respondents are asked to report the perceived race of offenders for crimes—assault, rape, robbery—in which they saw their offender. Suggesting that African-Americans do have higher crime rates, the proportion of offenders identified by NCVS data as African-American is similar to the African-American proportion of UCR arrests (Walker et al. 2012). Self-report data find a similar racial difference in serious offending (Farrington et al. 2003). Notwithstanding possible racial bias in the criminal justice system, then, most scholars today agree that African-Americans are indeed more heavily involved in serious street crime (Haynie et al. 2008; Walker et al. 2012). For minor offenses, however, racial differences may be smaller than arrest statistics suggest.

Explaining African-American Crime Rates

If African-Americans do commit higher rates of serious street crime, why so? In the early 1900s, racist explanations blamed their supposed biological inferiority (Gabbidon and Greene 2013). Beginning in the 1960s, explanations focusing on a subculture of violence (e.g., attitudes approving violence) and on deficiencies in African-American family structure (e.g., absent fathers) became popular (Moynihan 1965; Wolfgang and Ferracuti 1967). Today many scholars consider the evidence for an African-American subculture of violence weak, but others continue to favor this explanation (see Chapter 7). The family structure explanations also remain popular, but evidence that father-absent households produce lawbreaking children is in fact inconsistent (see Chapter 8).

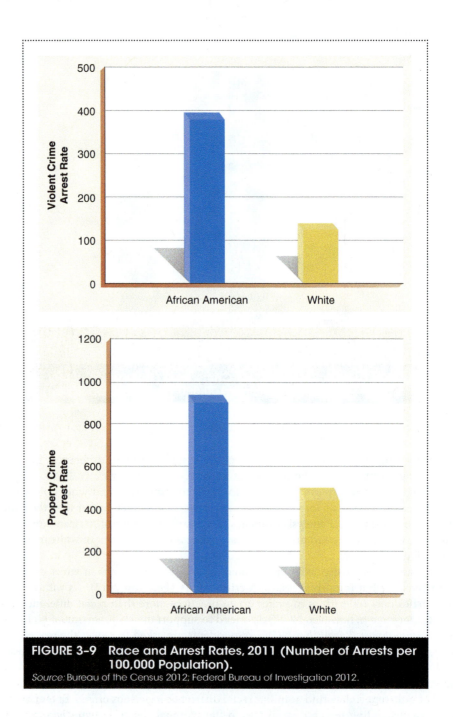

FIGURE 3-9   Race and Arrest Rates, 2011 (Number of Arrests per 100,000 Population).
Source: Bureau of the Census 2012; Federal Bureau of Investigation 2012.

Many criminologists instead cite the negative social conditions in which African-Americans and other people of color live (Peterson 2012). According to this view, "African Americans and other minorities exhibit higher rates of violence than do whites because they are more likely to reside in community contexts with high levels of poverty, unemployment, family disruption, and residential instability. . . . If whites were embedded in similar structural contexts, they would exhibit comparable rates of violence" (McNulty and Bellair 2003a:5). These structural conditions heighten crime because they weaken the influence of conventional social institutions such as family and schools and create frustration and hopelessness (Gabbidon and Greene 2013; Peterson 2012). The racial discrimination felt by African-Americans also matters because it is thought to cause anger and frustration that in turn result in criminal behavior (Unnever and Gabbidon 2011). Chapter 7 discusses these explanations further.

Before leaving the issue of race and crime, three additional points are worth mentioning. First, race is a *social construction*, something that we make up rather than something real (Gabbidon and Greene 2013). How, for example, do we determine whether someone is

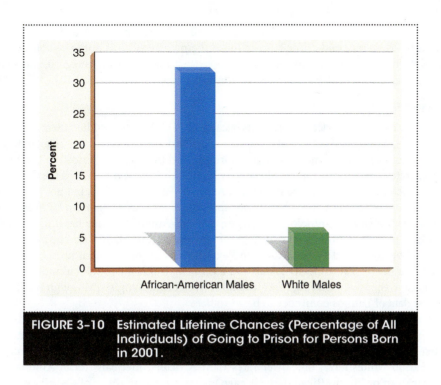

FIGURE 3-10 Estimated Lifetime Chances (Percentage of All Individuals) of Going to Prison for Persons Born in 2001.

African-American? In the United States, we usually consider people African-American if they have any African ancestry at all, even if most of their ancestry is white. Other countries follow different practices. This ambiguity in measuring race complicates any assessment of racial differences in offending.

Second, studies of racial differences in crime rates address street crime, not white-collar crime. If street criminals are disproportionately African-American and other people of color, white-collar criminals are almost always white. Despite the explanations of African-American criminality stressing a violent subculture, family structure problems, or poor living conditions, whites are quite capable of committing white-collar crime despite growing up in intact families and living in advantaged communities. In this regard, criminologists warn of the myth of the *criminal black man* that depicts a young African-American male as the prototypical serious criminal offender (Russell 2009; Young 2006). This myth, they say, obscures the domination of whites in white-collar crime and ignores the fact that whites, thanks to their large numbers, also account for the majority of street crime.

Third, although certain aspects of the African-American experience contribute to a higher crime rate, recent research finds that other aspects decrease African-Americans' criminal behavior. These aspects include relatively high levels of religiosity and low levels of alcohol use, strong family ties, and strong belief in the value of education. Sociologists Bradley R. Entner Wright and C. Wesley Younts (2009:348) say these "prosocial" aspects have been "virtually ignored in studies of race and crime," and they add that consideration of these aspects "contradicts the stereotypical caricature of African Americans as violent, aggressive, and crime prone."

Fourth, recall from Figure 3–9 that the African-American arrest rate for violent crime in 2011 was about 379 per 100,000, and for property crime it was 897 per 100,000. Although these numbers exceed those for whites, a more familiar way of understanding them is to say that for every 100 African Americans, about 0.38 are arrested every year for violent crime and 0.90 are arrested for property crime. That means that 99.62 of every 100 African-Americans are *not* arrested each year for violent crime, and 99.10 of every 100 African Americans are *not* arrested for property crime. Despite concern about African-American crime rates, then, the evidence is very clear that virtually all African-Americans are not arrested in any given year for Part I crimes.

Regardless, criminology must not shy away from acknowledging and explaining African-American street crime, because even the small absolute rates just cited translate into tens of thousands of crimes nationwide and devastate many urban neighborhoods. As Gary LaFree and Katheryn K. Russell (1993: 281) once put it, "[W]e must face the problem of race and crime directly, forthrightly, and with the most objective evidence we can muster collectively. Ignoring connections between race and crime has not made them go away." It is both possible and important to explain the race–crime connection in a nonracist manner. In this regard, the structural explanations mentioned earlier are especially promising (see Chapters 7 and 10).

Latinos and Other Groups

This section has discussed African-Americans because criminology has studied them far more than it has studied other people of color. This focus is understandable for several reasons. First, African-Americans historically were America's largest minority and the only one forced to live in slavery. Second, their rates of violent crime have been very high. Third, UCR data record the race of arrestees (white, African-American, Native American, Asian, or Pacific Islander), but not their ethnicity. Because Latinos may be of any race, they do not appear as a separate category in UCR arrest data.

As understandable as criminology's focus on African-Americans may be, it has nonetheless translated into neglect of other racial and ethnic groups, and the field knows much less about their criminal behavior and victimization and experiences in the criminal justice system. Now that Latinos are the largest minority group and a growing influence in the cultural and political life of the nation, they are receiving more attention from criminologists, although the lack of adequate arrest data of Latinos continues to be a problem.

That said, the available criminological knowledge does yield a fairly reliable picture of the extent of and reasons for Latino criminality (Miller et al. 2009; Miller 2012; Steffensmeier et al. 2010). First, Latinos (focusing on adolescents) have higher serious crime and victimization rates than non-Latino whites have, but lower rates than African-Americans have. Among Latinos, people of Mexican or Puerto Rican descent have higher rates than those of Cuban descent, who tend to be wealthier. Second, Latinos' crime rates are generally explained by the fact that they tend, like African-Americans, to live amid structural criminogenic conditions, including poverty, unemployment, and rundown urban neighborhoods. Native American crime rates are also higher than white rates and for similar structural reasons (Lanier and Huff-Corzine 2006; Painter-Davis 2012), while Asian-American crime rates appear lower than white rates, perhaps because of Asians' strong family structures and lower use of drugs and alcohol (McNulty and Bellair 2003b).

One interesting question is why Latinos have lower violent-crime rates than African-Americans. Scholars cite several reasons for this difference (Vélez 2006). First, Latino neighborhoods and individuals are less poor than their African-American counterparts and have lower rates of other structural problems, including unemployment and single-parent households. Second, Latino communities have higher numbers of immigrants, and immigrants tend to have lower crime rates than U.S.-born residents living in similar socioeconomic circumstances. Third, Latino communities have better relations than African-American communities with the police, local politicians, and bank officials, and these better relations help for many reasons (e.g., the provision of economic and legal resources) to reduce crime rates. Fourth, Latino neighborhoods are less racially segregated than African-American neighborhoods and less physically isolated from white neighborhoods. Latino neighborhoods can thus more easily avoid certain problems created by racial segregation and are also "in a better position to protect themselves from crime because they benefit from the spillover of nearby more affluent and socially organized neighborhoods" (Vélez 2006:101).

▼ Latinos have higher rates of street crime than non-Latino whites but lower rates than African-Americans.

Nancy Honey/Getty Images

Immigrants

The findings that immigrants have relatively low rates of crime, the second reason just noted, merit further discussion here. Contrary to what many Americans might assume, a research shows that immigrants have lower rates of crime than nonimmigrants (MacDonald et al. 2013; Zatz and Smith 2012). According to María B. Vélez (2006:96), at least two factors help explain why "the presence of immigrants in a neighborhood helps to control crime." First, immigrant neighborhoods tend to have high numbers of residents owning or working in the many small businesses (e.g., restaurants) that such neighborhoods need. Second, these neighborhoods also tend to have strong social institutions like churches and schools. For several reasons, the stable employment and strong institutions that thus characterize these neighborhoods help to reduce crime. Other scholars point to the relatively high rates of married households among Latino immigrants as a possible reason for their lower crime rates. Drawing on all this research, some criminologists credit the increased immigration of the 1990s for contributing to the crime rate decline during that decade, and they point out that the evidence of a crime-*reducing* effect of immigration challenges conventional wisdom (Zatz and Smith 2012).

Interestingly, some research finds that second-generation immigrants commit more crime than new immigrants and that third-generation immigrants commit more crime than second-generation ones (Sampson 2008). Thus, crime among immigrant families rises the longer they have been in the United States. This may happen for several reasons (Press 2006). First, immigrants' children may become embittered and abandon their parents' optimism as they experience ethnic discrimination and economic problems. Second, they have time to learn the U.S. culture and in particular two aspects of this culture: (1) its affinity for drugs, flashy possessions, and other temptations that may attract young people into criminal behavior and (2) its "look out for number one" ideology that is thought more generally to contribute to U.S. crime. In short, as two scholars put it, "The children and grandchildren of many immigrants—as well as many immigrants themselves the longer they live in the United States—become subject to economic and social forces that increase the likelihood of criminal behavior" (Rumbaut and Ewing 2007:11).

Review and Discuss

Why do African-Americans have higher crime rates than whites? Is it racist to claim that this racial difference in crime exists?

Social Class and Crime

Most people arrested and imprisoned for street crime are poorly educated with low incomes: about two-thirds of prisoners lack even a high school diploma. Sociologists have long been interested in the association between social class and criminality, and they developed several theories of crime from the 1920s through the 1950s to explain why poor people have higher crime rates (see Chapters 7 and 8).

In the 1960s, many sociologists began to argue that the overrepresentation of the poor in the criminal justice system stemmed more from class bias than from real differences in offending. Some scholars proclaimed the long-assumed relationship between social class and criminality a myth (Tittle et al. 1978). While conceding the possibility of class bias, other scholars challenged this new view (Braithwaite 1981; Hindelang et al. 1979). Addressing the debate, a president of the American Society of Criminology warned that a failure to recognize the importance of class would leave criminology impoverished (Hagan 1992). Another sociologist wryly observed that "social scientists somehow still knew better than to stroll the streets at night in certain parts of town or even to park there . . . [and they] knew that the parts of town that scared them were not upper-income neighborhoods" (Stark 1987:894). Supporting these latter views, self-report studies find that poor youths, especially those whose families live in extreme poverty and chronic unemployment, do have higher rates of serious offending (Bjerk 2007).

However, if we consider white-collar crime along with street crime, there probably is no relationship between social class and criminality. Although very poor individuals have higher rates of serious street crime, middle- and upper-class persons clearly have the monopoly on white-collar crime. Explanations of underclass involvement in street criminality focusing on poverty, unemployment, and related structural conditions cannot account for white-collar criminality.

Review and Discuss

Is the relationship between social class and criminality a myth, or does an actual relationship exist? What is the evidence for and against the existence of an actual relationship?

Age and Crime

As you probably realize by now, criminologists disagree on all sorts of issues involving the measurement and patterning of crime. Age, however, is one area in which there is widespread agreement: "The view that involvement in crime diminishes with age is one of the oldest and most widely accepted in criminology" (Steffensmeier and Allan 2000:803). Simply put, street crime is disproportionately committed by young people. As Figure 3–11 ■ shows, the 15-to-24 age bracket accounts for only about 14 percent of the population, but 38 percent of all arrests. Crime peaks at ages 17 or 18 and then declines, especially beyond young adulthood. Despite minor variations depending on the type of crime, this pattern holds true whether one looks at UCR arrests, the perceived age of offenders reported to NCVS interviewers, or self-report data. White-collar crime is once again a different matter because older people commit most of it; teenagers and young adults are too young to be in a position to commit such a crime.

Explaining the Age–Crime Relationship

Why is street crime primarily a young person's phenomenon, and why does it decline after adolescence and young adulthood? Several factors seem to be at work (Steffensmeier and Allan 2000). First, adolescence is a time when peer influences and the desire for friendships are especially strong. To the extent that peers influence one's own delinquent behavior, it is not surprising that adolescence is a peak time for offending. As we move into adulthood, our peer influences diminish, and our peers become more law-abiding than they used to be. As a result, we become more law-abiding as well (Warr 2002).

Second, adolescents, as you well know, have an increasing need for money that part-time jobs or parental allowances may not satisfy. For at least some adolescents, crime provides a means to obtain financial resources. If this is true, one reason crime declines after moving into adulthood might be that our incomes rise as we get full-time jobs. Third, our ties to society strengthen as we become young adults. We acquire full-time jobs, usually get married and have children, and in general start becoming full-fledged members of society. These bonds to society give us an increasing sense of responsibility and stake in conformity and thus reduce our likelihood of committing crime (Benson 2013).

We also become more mature as we leave adolescence; we are no longer the youthful rebels who think everything our parents say and want us to do is ridiculous. We begin to realize that many of the indiscretions of our youth may have been fun and daring but were clearly illegal.

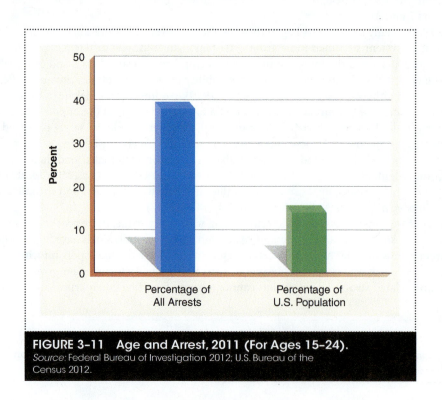

FIGURE 3–11   Age and Arrest, 2011 (For Ages 15–24).
Source: Federal Bureau of Investigation 2012; U.S. Bureau of the Census 2012.

What we were ready to excuse back then, we cannot excuse now. "Yes, I did _____ [fill in the blank] when I was a teenager," you might tell your own children, "but I don't want you doing that!" They'll inevitably see this remark as a sign of your hypocrisy; you'll regard it as a sign of your maturity.

An understanding of the age–crime relationship helps us understand shifts in a nation's crime rate. An increased birth rate will, some fifteen years later, begin to lead to an increased number of people in the 15-to-25 crime-prone age group. All other things being equal, the nation's crime rate should rise as the number of people in this age group rises. If the birth rate later declines, then as these young people move into their less crime-prone middle age and are replaced by fewer numbers of youths, the crime rate should decline. One reason U.S. crime rates probably rose during the 1960s was the entrance of the baby-boom generation born after World War II into the 15-to-25 age group (Ferdinand 1970); one reason they fell during the 1990s may have been a declining number of people in that age group owing to a lower birth rate two decades earlier (Goldberger and Rosenfeld 2008).

▲ Young people commit more street crimes than do older people.

Gender, Race, and Age Combined

In Chapter 2 we saw that race and gender combine to produce higher fear among African-American women. In this chapter we have seen that males have higher rates of serious crime than females, African-Americans have higher rates than whites, and young people have higher rates than older people. These patterns suggest that young African-American males should have especially high rates of serious offending and older white women very low rates. Table 3–3 reports homicide arrest rates (per 100,000 persons) for various gender, race, and age combinations. Notice first that the younger age group has higher arrest rates than the older age group for each gender and race combination. Now look just at the 18-to-24 age group. Notice that within each race males have higher arrest rates than females, and within each gender African-Americans have higher arrest rates than whites. The same patterns hold true for the older age group. This all works out so that African-American men between the ages of 18 and 24 have the highest rate in the table, 175.8, and white women 25 and older have the lowest rate, 0.8, a huge difference. The patterns displayed in Table 3–3 once again provide powerful evidence of the sociological perspective's emphasis on the importance of social backgrounds for behavior.

TABLE 3–3 Gender, Race, Age, and Arrest Rates for Homicide, 2008 (per 100,000 persons)

CATEGORY	RATE
Age 18–24	
African-American males	175.8
African-American females	10.8
White males	20.4
White females	2.5
Age 25 and older	
African-American males	37.8
African-American females	3.5
White males	5.4
White females	0.8

Source: Cooper and Smith 2011.

► Chronic Offenders and Criminal Careers

One of the most important findings of self-report studies, especially those studying the same persons over time, is that roughly 6 percent of adolescents are responsible for most of the serious crimes committed by the entire group of adolescents (Benson 2013). Although many young people break the law, their offenses are usually minor ones. However, a small number commit many offenses each, particularly the more serious offenses, and persist in their offending over time. These chronic offenders often continue their offending into adulthood as they enter criminal careers. Career criminality is more common among those with low education and bleak job prospects, characteristics most common of the urban underclass. Although some scholars feel that offending does not continue long into adulthood and thus dispute the existence of criminal careers, most accept the concept as a valid characterization of a small number of offenders.

Knowledge of the age patterning of crime and of the existence of career criminals has important implications for efforts to reduce crime. The "three strikes and you're out" legislation popular a decade or more ago required life imprisonment for people convicted of a third felony. Because imprisonment would continue long after the criminality of most offenders would have declined anyway as they aged, critics said this legislation would increase prison overcrowding, but do little to reduce crime (see Chapter 17). Another effort involves identifying youths at risk for becoming career criminals so that they can be targeted for innovative treatment and punishment (Visher 2000). However, the prediction of career criminality can be inaccurate, with many *false positives* (people falsely predicted to be career criminals) resulting. Efforts to target career criminals remain beset by various legal and ethical dilemmas.

► Conclusion

This chapter has discussed both the importance and the complexity of measuring crime. Accurate measurement is critical for efforts to understand the origins of crime and how best to reduce it. If we measure crime inaccurately, we may miss important factors that underlie it and thus ways of reducing it.

All the major sources of crime statistics have their advantages and disadvantages. UCR data help us to understand the geographical distribution of crime, but they greatly underestimate the actual number of crimes and are subject to possible police bias. They also tell us relatively little about the social context of crime and victimization and about the characteristics of victims. NCVS data provide the best estimate of the actual number of crimes and provide solid information on the context of victimization and the characteristics of victims, but even they underestimate certain crimes and exclude others. Self-report data provide important information about offenders, including the many influences on their behavior, but are generally limited to adolescents. Inclusion of serious offenses in the most recent self-report studies has made them even more valuable.

Because none of these sources covers white-collar crime, they reinforce impressions that white-collar crime is less serious than street crime. But together they provide a reasonably good picture of street crime in the United States. The picture is of a relatively small number of violent crimes and a much larger number of property crimes. Despite continuing debate, the picture of street crime is also one of offenders who tend to be male, nonwhite, and especially African-American, poor, and young. Regarding gender, something about being a female in our society inhibits criminality, and something about being a male promotes it. Continued research on the reasons for this gender difference holds promise for crime reduction. The racial and class distribution of street crime alerts us not only to the effect of race and class on criminality but also to the structural factors accounting for this effect. These factors can and must be explored without resorting to explanations that smack of racial or class prejudice.

Now that we have some idea of the extent of street crime and of the characteristics of offenders in the United States, it is almost time to turn to explanations of such crime. But first we explore further in Chapter 4 the characteristics of crime victims and the theories and consequences of victimization.

▼

Summary

1. Accurate measurement of crime is essential to understand geographical and demographic differences in crime rates and gauge whether crime is rising or falling. The nation's sources of crime data provide a good picture of the extent and distribution of crime, but this picture is also necessarily incomplete.

2. The UCR is the nation's official crime source and is based on police reports of crime to the FBI. Problems with the UCR include the fact that (1) many crime victims do not report their victimization to the police; (2) citizens may become more or less likely to report crimes to the police; (3) changes in police behavior, including whether and how they record reported crimes, may affect UCR statistics; and (4) police in different communities may have different definitions and understandings of certain crimes.

3. The NCVS measures the nature and extent of victimization. Begun in the early 1970s, it has since provided a valuable source of information on all these issues. Although it does not cover commercial crime and its respondents do not always disclose their victimizations, it provides a more accurate picture than the UCR of the amount of crime.

4. Self-report studies focus mainly on adolescents and measure the extent of their offending. By asking respondents about many aspects of their lives and backgrounds, self-report studies have been invaluable for the development and testing of criminological theory.

5. Crime is patterned geographically, climatologically, and socially. International differences in crime rates reflect aspects of nations' cultures and their degree of inequality. In the United States, crime is higher in cities than in rural areas and generally higher in the South and West than in the East and Midwest. Several types of violent and property crime are more common in warmer months. Despite much debate, serious street-crime rates seem much higher among men than among women, higher among African-Americans and Latinos than among non-Latino whites, and higher among the poor than the nonpoor.

6. Chronic offenders, who represent a small percentage of youths, commit the majority of serious offenses committed by all youths. Some chronic offenders continue their criminality past young adulthood. Efforts to predict such career criminals have been inaccurate, making it difficult to identify youths at risk for a career of crime.

Key Terms

chronic offenders 62
climatological 51
criminal careers 62
incidence 45
international comparisons 48
measurement 38

National Crime Victimization
   Survey (NCVS) 42
patterning 48
prevalence 45
property crime 38
seasonal 51

self-report studies 45
subculture of violence 55
underreporting 44
Uniform Crime Reports (UCR) 38
victimization 43
violent crime 38

What Would You Do?

1. It's a dark, chilly night in October, and you are walking to your car from the mall. In your arms is a box containing a DVD player you bought for a close friend's birthday. Suddenly you are grabbed around your neck from behind. A male voice says, quietly but ominously, "I don't want to hurt you. Just put the box on the ground and move away." Terrified, you comply. As the man picks up the box and runs off, you look in his direction in the darkened parking lot but see only his back. You take out your cell phone to call 911, but as you do so you begin to think the police probably won't be able to catch the robber and reflect that the DVD player cost only $70 anyway. Do you call 911? Why or why not?

2. You are the night manager of a convenience store. Normal closing time is 10:00 P.M., but it has been a slow night and you are pretty tired. It's now 9:50 P.M. The owner has told you it's okay to close a few minutes early when business is slow, so you have just locked the glass door and are cleaning up inside so that you can leave in a few more minutes. You're startled to hear a knock on the door. Looking through the door, you see two young men motioning to let them in. Something about them frightens you, but you don't know what it is. Do you unlock the door for them? Why or why not? Would your response have been different if the two people at the door had been middle-aged women?

AP Photo/Damian Dovarganes

4 Victims and Victimization

. . . .

Crime in the News

California is trying to find its crime victims. Many convicted offenders there are required to pay restitution to their victims. However, the state in May 2013 was holding onto millions of dollars because it did not know the addresses of the victims to whom the money is owed. That is because county courts and prosecutors' offices are failing to forward victims' addresses to the state office that administers the restitution program. Because of this problem, about half of all crime victims are estimated to be going without their lawful restitution.

Source: Noyes 2013

. . . .

B efore the 1960s, we knew little about crime victims and their families and friends. Criminals monopolized public concern and scholarly research, while crime victims were forgotten. Victims began to attract more attention in the late 1960s as the growing crime rate and urban unrest heightened interest in law and order. The courts, it was said, were giving too many rights to criminals and not enough to their victims. This concern helped put victims on the public agenda. At about the same time, feminists began to address rape as a major crime. One focus of their efforts was the psychological consequences of rape, and another was the experience of rape victims in the criminal justice system after they brought charges. Somewhat later, domestic violence against women began to receive similar attention. The study of victims, or victimology, had begun.

The growing interest in victims led to the initiation of the National Crime Survey, now known as the National Crime Victimization Survey (NCVS). As Chapter 3 noted, the NCVS has greatly increased our understanding of victims and victimization. Several other victimization surveys in the United States and other nations have added to this understanding, and today the field of victimology is flourishing. This chapter discusses what we know about victims and victimization.

▶ Defining Victims and Studying Victimization

No doubt you and people you know have worried about becoming a victim of a crime such as robbery, burglary, assault, rape, or theft of something from your car or dorm room/apartment. Have you ever worried about becoming a victim of price-fixing or false advertising? Would you even know if you had been a victim? Have you worried about being a victim of air or water pollution? Have you ever worried about eating bacteria-laden poultry or meat, taking unsafe medicine, or driving an unsafe car? If you or someone you know has ever taken ill or been injured in the workplace, did it occur to you that this might constitute crime victimization?

What exactly is a crime victim? Presumably one definition is someone who suffers because of a crime. But what if someone or, worse yet, many someones suffer from behavior that does not violate the law and thus is not a crime? To take one example, pharmaceutical companies sometimes send unsafe drugs that are prohibited in the United States to poor nations. Because no U.S. law prohibits the drug companies from sending their products elsewhere, they do not commit any crime. But this noncriminal behavior still causes death and illness, especially in children, every year (Coleman 2006).

Another example involving children concerns various corporations that once sent infant formula to poor nations, where it was sold or distributed as free samples to new mothers. Seeing a potential source of great profit, these corporations stressed the ease of formula feeding. Unfortunately, the mothers were often illiterate and could not understand the directions for preparing formula. They mixed it with dirty water that had not been boiled and sterilized and, to save money, often gave their babies less formula than required. Thinking the baby bottle had magical properties, some mothers even let their infants suck on empty bottles. Many infants acquired intestinal ailments, became severely malnourished, or even died. An international protest campaign and boycott began and lasted several years until the companies finally ceased "their lucrative but deadly practices (Viano 1990:xvi)." In the larger sense of the word *victim*, these children were clearly victims, but technically not crime victims, because no crime had been committed.

As this brief discussion suggests, people can be victimized in many ways, but only sometimes are they victims of actual crimes. They can be victims of legal behavior by the kinds of multinational corporations mentioned previously, but this does not make them crime victims. They can also be victims of illegal behavior by corporations. This does make them victims of criminal behavior, but they are not the kinds of victims to whom our hearts go out. We certainly do not usually hear about them in the news media, and they might not even be aware of their victimization. Finally, people can be victims of violations of civil liberties and human rights, including government surveillance, torture, and genocide. If we expand the definition of victims and victimization even further, we may talk about people as victimized by poverty, institutional racism, or institutional sexism. The term *institutional* implies that the very structure of society is one that inherently oppresses, subtly or more overtly, the poor, women, and people of color.

When we move away from individual victims of street crimes to mass victims of white-collar crime, violations of human rights, and the like, we are talking about *collective victimization*, much of it international in scope. Unfortunately, collective victimization is a neglected topic. Because victimology has focused on street crimes, we know far more about victimization by such crimes than we do about victimization by other kinds of crimes and by legal but harmful behaviors.

No universally accepted definition of crime victim exists. Defining victims as people suffering from street crimes or, more broadly, as those hurt by harmful corporate practices, institutional racism, and the like is ultimately a matter of personal preference. As one victimology expert has observed, "The key question becomes 'Which suffering people get designated as victims, and which don't, and why?' The answer is important, since it determines whether or not public and private resources will be mobilized to help them out, and end their mistreatment" (Karmen 1990:11).

Since the beginning of victimology about four decades ago, the answer has been that victims are those people suffering from street crimes. Because street crime is a serious problem, especially in poor urban neighborhoods, the victimization it causes certainly merits scholarly attention. Reflecting the victimology literature, this chapter deals mostly with street crime. But keep in mind that victimization by white-collar crime also deserves the concern of the public, elected officials, and social scientists.

▲ Certain corporations used to market infant formula heavily in poor nations, where it was not used properly. Many infants died or became seriously ill. Because no crime had been committed, these children were not crime victims.

AP Photo

Review and Discuss

Does it make sense to consider people who suffer from the legal behavior of corporations and from poverty to be crime victims? Why or why not?

▶ The Patterning of Victimization

According to the NCVS, roughly 2 percent of Americans age 12 and older experience a violent crime annually, while 14 percent of U.S. households experience a property crime (Truman and Planty 2012). (Recall that NCVS violent crime includes aggravated and simple assault, rape and sexual assault, and robbery, but not homicide, and NCVS property crime includes burglary, motor vehicle theft, and other thefts, but not commercial thefts.) These figures obscure the fact that victimization, like the crime rates discussed in Chapter 3, is patterned geographically and socially. Although differences between the NCVS and UCR make comparisons of victimization data to crime data inexact, victimization patterns do resemble those for crime: The locations and people with the highest crime rates usually also have the highest victimization rates.

Geographical Patterns

Victimization rates as measured by the NCVS differ across the United States. Western and Midwestern residents have higher victimization rates for violent crime than other regions, while Western households experience the highest victimization rates for property crime. Meanwhile, urban areas have higher victimization rates than suburban or rural areas (see Figure 4–1 ■).

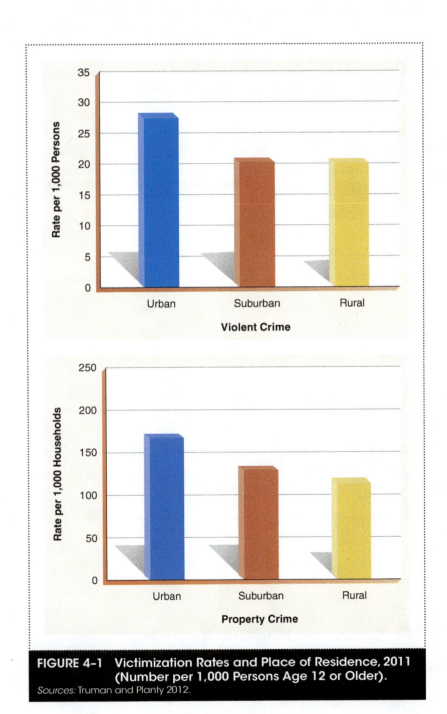

FIGURE 4–1 Victimization Rates and Place of Residence, 2011 (Number per 1,000 Persons Age 12 or Older).
Sources: Truman and Planty 2012.

Social Patterns

Victimization rates also vary by the demographic characteristics of people. Table 4–1 displays the relevant data for violent crime and property crime. Our discussion centers on these data and also on other information not reported in the table.

Gender, Race, and Ethnicity

For the combined measure of violence reported in Table 4–1, males have a higher victimization rate than females. Males are especially likely to be homicide victims; there are about 3.5 male homicide victims for every 1 female victim. However, women experience almost all the rape victimization reported to NCVS interviewers and almost all the assaults by family members and other intimates (see Chapter 11). Because some women probably decline to tell the NCVS about rape/sexual assault and domestic violence they have experienced, the actual violence victimization rate for women would be higher than the NCVS estimates appearing in the table.

Looking at race and ethnicity, violent crime victimization is by far the highest for Native Americans and lowest for Asians and Pacific Islanders. African-Americans and Latinos have slightly higher victimization rates than non-Latino whites. The difference between African-Americans and whites is much greater for homicide, as African-Americans are about five times more likely than whites to be homicide victims (see Figure 4–2 ■).

TABLE 4-1 Victimization by Violent Crime and Property Crime, 2011 (Victimizations per 1,000 Persons Age 12 or Older for Violent Crime or per 1,000 Households for Property Crime)

VARIABLE	VIOLENT CRIME	PROPERTY CRIME
Sex		
Male	25.4	—
Female	19.8	—
Age		
12–17	37.7	—
18–24	49.0	—
25–34	26.5	—
35–49	21.9	—
50–64	13.0	—
65 or older	4.4	—
Race and Ethnicity		
African-American[a]	26.4	159.0
Asian/Pacific Islander[a]	11.2	117.8
Latino	23.8	173.4
Native American[a]	45.4	272.5
White[a]	21.5	126.3
Family income		
Less than $7,500	52.9	243.8
$7,500–$14,999	52.5	208.7
$15,000–$24,999	32.4	171.5
$25,000–$34,999	22.5	145.8
$35,000–$49,999	18.1	148.2
$50,000–$74,999	19.9	133.8
$75,000 or more	18.0	117.7

[a] Non-Latino
Source: Truman and Planty 2012.

▼

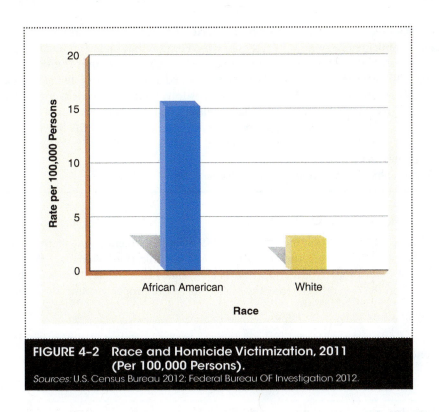

FIGURE 4-2 Race and Homicide Victimization, 2011 (Per 100,000 Persons).
Sources: U.S. Census Bureau 2012; Federal Bureau OF Investigation 2012.

International Focus THE INTERNATIONAL CRIME VICTIM SURVEY

Chapter 3 noted that the international crime data apart from homicide are not very reliable. For this reason, the initiation of the International Crime Victims Survey (ICVS), sponsored by the United Nations, in the 1980s was an important development for the understanding of international crime and victimization. The aim of the ICVS is to collect international victimization data so that the nations' crime rates and victimization patterns can be compared. Since its inception, the ICVS has become a valuable source of information for crime and victimization in many parts of the world. ICVS data have been collected in several waves: 1988, 1991, 1995, 1999, and 2003/04; a few nations were also surveyed in 2010. Most of the industrialized Western democracies and several developing nations have been included in one or more waves of the survey.

The ICVS asks respondents whether they were the victims during the previous year of any of several different crimes. For reporting purposes, the ICVS divides these crimes into two categories. *Contact crime* includes robbery, sexual offenses (sexual assaults and offensive sexual behavior), and physical assaults and threats. *Property crime* includes theft of cars, theft from cars, vandalism to cars, motorcycle theft, bicycle theft, burglary (completed and

attempted), and theft of personal property. The ICVS also combines these two categories into an overall measure of victimization. The ICVS reports both *prevalence* rates (the percentage of people victimized at least once in the previous year) and *incidence* rates (the number of crimes experienced by every 100 people).

Although ICVS data have been used to compare nations' victimization rates, questions remain about the validity of such comparisons. These questions stem from the fact that different nations may use different survey and sampling techniques and that the nations' different cultural understandings may affect responses to the identical questions asked in every nation.

With this caveat in mind, the ICVS has revealed some very interesting findings concerning the ranking of the United States relative to that of all thirty industrialized nations in the survey (2003/04 data). For overall victimization, the U.S. prevalence rate was only average, with 17.5 percent of Americans reporting at least one victimization during the previous year. Ireland had the dubious honor of ranking at the top with a prevalence of 21.9 percent, whereas Portugal, Japan, and Northern Ireland tied with the lowest rate, 9.1 percent.

continued

The United States is popularly considered a very violent country, and it does have the highest homicide rate of any industrialized nation. However, it ranks only about average overall for other types of violence. To be more specific, it ranked in the bottom third for robbery, at the top (tied with several other nations) for sexual offenses, and sixth for physical assaults. Northern Ireland ranked first for physical assault, while Japan ranked last.

Despite the different victimization rates and other differences among these nations, the demographic victimization patterns reported for the United States are also found in other countries. For example, higher victimization rates exist for urban residents than for rural residents, for young people than for older people, and for men (excluding rape and domestic violence) than for women. The international similarity of these patterns underscores the impact of urbanism, age, gender, and the like on the risk for victimization.

Source: van Dijk 2012; van Dijk et al. 2008.

Family Income

Table 4–1 shows some important income-based differences in violent-crime victimization rates. Generally, the lower the income, the higher the rate of victimization. Figure 4–3 ■ displays this trend graphically. For property crime, income is also related to victimization (see Table 4–1) in the same manner: the lower the income, the higher the rate of property-crime victimization.

Age

Figure 4–4 ■ displays the striking difference that age makes in violent victimization. Paralleling age differences in crime rates discussed in Chapter 3, young people are much more likely than older people to be violent-crime victims. In this regard, recall from Chapter 2 that, although people 65 and older are more fearful than younger people of crime, their victimization is much lower.

Race, Gender, and Age Combined

In Chapter 2 we saw how race and gender combine to produce higher fear of crime among African-American women, and in Chapter 3 we saw how race, gender, and age combine to produce higher serious crime rates among young African-American men. In this chapter we have seen that violence victimization rates are higher for men than for women, for African-Americans than for whites, and for the young than for the old. Is it possible that gender, race, and age combine to produce especially high victimization rates for African-American men and very low ones for older white women? The answer is yes. To illustrate, Table 4–2 reports homicide victimization rates for various age, race, and gender categories. In each age group, African-American males are

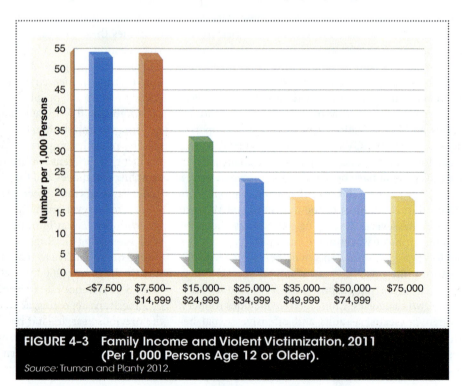

FIGURE 4-3 Family Income and Violent Victimization, 2011 (Per 1,000 Persons Age 12 or Older).
Source: Truman and Planty 2012.

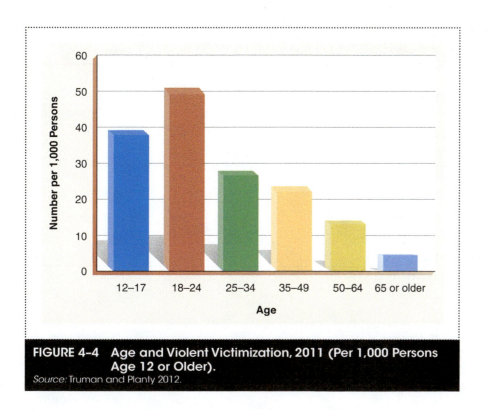

FIGURE 4–4 Age and Violent Victimization, 2011 (Per 1,000 Persons Age 12 or Older).
Source: Truman and Planty 2012.

the most likely and white females the least likely of the four race–gender categories to be homicide crime victims. The highest rate, 91.1 for African-American men 18 to 24 years old, is almost forty-six times greater than the lowest rate, 2.0, for white women 25 and older.

To reinforce the impact of race and gender on homicide victimization, Figure 4–5 ■ displays the rates for the 18-to-24 age group. Within each gender, African-Americans are much more likely than whites to be killed; within each race, males are much more likely than females to be killed. Race and gender certainly affect our chances of dying a violent death.

Review and Discuss

How do violent victimization rates differ by gender, age, race, and family income? Why do these different rates exist?

Victim-Offender Relationship

Strangers Versus Nonstrangers

Recall that the NCVS asks respondents who report aggravated or simple assault, rape or sexual assault, or robbery victimization whether they knew the offender. This information yields a valuable portrait of the victim-offender relationship. This might surprise you, but strangers commit *only about 41 percent* of these offenses combined, with the remainder committed by family members, friends, and acquaintances. This 41 percent figure for NCVS violence obscures a striking gender difference (see Table 4–3): Strangers commit 52 percent of men's victimizations but only 27 percent of women's victimizations. Conversely, nonstrangers commit 74 percent of women's victimizations, but only 48 percent of men's victimizations. Women are thus about 2.7 times more likely to be attacked by someone they know than by a

▼ Young people have higher violent-crime victimization rates than do older people.

TABLE 4-2 Age, Race, Gender, and Homicide Victimization, 2008 (per 100,000 persons)

CATEGORY	RATE
Age 18–24	
African-American males	91.1
African-American females	12.2
White males	11.4
White females	2.6
Age 25 and older	
African-American males	38.4
African-American females	5.8
White males	5.0
White females	2.0

Source: Cooper and Smith 2011.

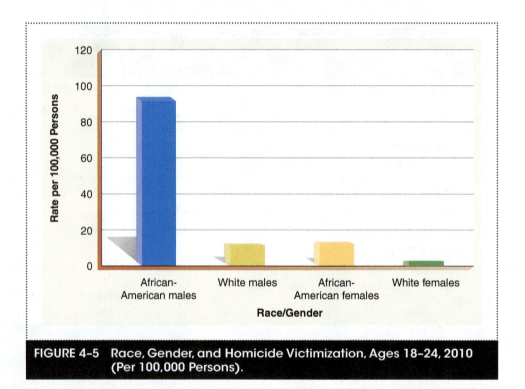

FIGURE 4-5 Race, Gender, and Homicide Victimization, Ages 18–24, 2010 (Per 100,000 Persons).

TABLE 4-3 Percentage of Violent Victimizations Committed by Strangers, 2011

	GENDER OF VICTIM	
TYPE OF CRIME	FEMALE	MALE
Aggravated assault	37	61
Simple assault	22	49
Robbery	45	61
Rape or sexual assault	29	39[a]
Total Victimizations	27	52

Note: [a] Number should be interpreted cautiously because of few sample cases.

Source: Bureau of Justice Statistics. Generated using the NCVS Victimization Analysis Tool at www.bjs.gov.

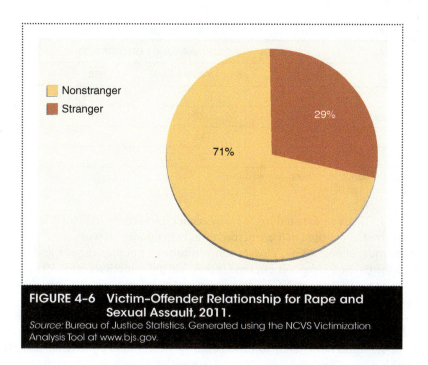

FIGURE 4–6   Victim–Offender Relationship for Rape and Sexual Assault, 2011.
Source: Bureau of Justice Statistics. Generated using the NCVS Victimization Analysis Tool at www.bjs.gov.

stranger. This pattern is no less true of rape and sexual assault: 71 percent of these offenses reported by women to NCVS interviewers were committed by nonstrangers, compared to only 29 percent committed by strangers (see Figure 4–6 ■). Chapter 11 further discusses this harsh reality of rape and sexual assault.

Intimate-Partner Violence

The majority of the nonstrangers who commit violence are friends or acquaintances, but a significant minority are *intimate partners:* spouses, ex-spouses, partners (boyfriends or girlfriends), or ex-partners. *Intimate-partner violence* (IPV) refers to any rape or sexual assault, robbery, or aggravated or simple assault committed by someone with such a relationship to the victim. We discuss IPV further in Chapter 11, but for now note that the NCVS estimates that about 851,000 IPV victimizations occurred in 2011, with almost three-fourths of these committed against women (Bureau of Justice Statistics 2013). Women are thus much more likely than men to suffer violence by intimate partners.

Perceived Race, Gender, and Age of Offenders

Chapter 3 noted that NCVS respondents who have been violent-crime victims report that the race, gender, and age distribution of offenders is similar to that found in UCR arrest data: disproportionately young, nonwhite, and male. Table 4–4 includes the relevant NCVS data for race. Although whites account for the majority of all offenses, the proportion of offenders perceived as African-American exceeds their proportion (13 percent) in the national population. This is especially true for robbery; African-Americans are perceived as committing 42 percent of all single-offender robberies.

Review and Discuss

To what extent are victims of violence harmed more by nonstrangers than by strangers? What does this pattern imply for efforts to reduce criminal victimization?

Again paralleling UCR arrest data, NCVS victims perceive that most offenders (78 percent) in all lone-offender violent crimes combined are male; this figure rises to 86 percent for the specific crime of robbery. Although victims' perceptions of offenders' ages are inexact, they also perceive that most of their offenders are young, once more

▼ Many women experience intimate violence from husbands, ex-husbands, boyfriends, or ex-boyfriends.

TABLE 4–4 Perceived Race of Offender in Lone-Offender Victimizations, NVCS

TYPE OF CRIME	PERCEIVED RACE OF OFFENDER (%)			
	WHITE	AFRICAN AMERICAN	OTHER	UNKNOWN
All violent crimes	58	23	7	12
Rape or sexual assault1	54	32	2[a]	12[a]
Robbery	37	42	10[a]	12[a]
Assault	61	20	7	12

[a] Estimate is based on about 10 or fewer sample cases.
Source: Rand and Robinson 2011.

replicating what UCR arrest data tell us: For all violent crimes involving one offender for which an age was perceived, more than half are perceived as being under 30 years old.

Some of the most important NCVS data concern the races of the offender and of the victim. A key myth in the public perception of crime is that African-American offenders prey on white victims (see Chapter 2). However, NCVS data reveal a very different pattern; they show that most violent crime is *intraracial*, meaning that it occurs within the same race. Contradicting the myth, about 77 percent of white victims of lone offenders who perceive the offender's race identify it as white, and only about 18 percent identify it as African-American. White victims of violence, then, are about 4.3 times more likely to be attacked by whites than by African-Americans. FBI data confirm this pattern for homicide; about 83 percent of white homicide victims are killed by whites and about 14 percent are killed by African-Americans (see Figure 4–7 ■). Robbery is the most *interracial* (i.e., between the races) crime; NCVS data indicate that about one-third of white victims are robbed by African-American offenders.

Crime Characteristics

The NCVS contains much information on various crime characteristics, including the use of alcohol and other drugs, the time and place of occurrence of crime, the use of weapons, and the extent of self-protection and resistance by victims (Rand and Robinson 2011).

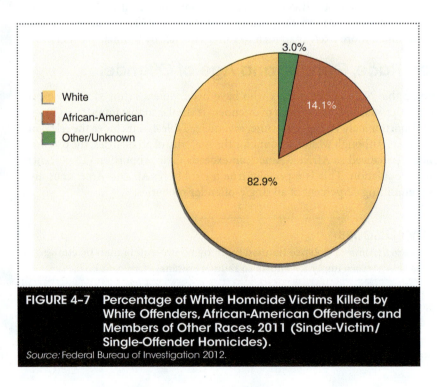

FIGURE 4–7 Percentage of White Homicide Victims Killed by White Offenders, African-American Offenders, and Members of Other Races, 2011 (Single-Victim/Single-Offender Homicides).
Source: Federal Bureau of Investigation 2012.

TABLE 4–5 Place of Occurrence for Violent Crime, NCVS (Percentage of All Incidents)

PLACE	PERCENTAGE
At victim's home	18
On street away from victim's home	14
School building or property	13
Near home	11
In or near someone else's home	9
Parking lot or garage	7
Other commercial building	9
On street near home	6
Apartment yard, park, field, playground	2
Public transportation	1
Other	7

Source: Rand 2011.

Use of Alcohol and Other Drugs

Chapter 15 discusses this topic in greater detail, but it is worth noting here that NCVS crime victims report rather heavy involvement of alcohol and drugs in the commission of violent crimes. Victims report that offenders were under the influence of alcohol or drugs in almost half of all the violent crimes in which they could distinguish whether these substances had been used (2008 data).

Time and Place of Occurrence

About 43 percent of violent crimes and also 43 percent of property crimes occur at night (6:00 P.M.–6:00 A.M.). However, some crimes are especially apt to occur at night: 56 percent of all rapes and sexual assaults occur then, as do 65 percent of all motor vehicle thefts. The largest proportions of violent crime occur at or near the victim's home, on school property, and on the street away from the victim's home (see Table 4–5). About 32 percent of all crimes involving non-strangers occur in the victim's home, compared to only 5 percent of crimes involving strangers.

Use of Weapons

According to NCVS respondents, weapons are used in about 20 percent of all violent crimes, including 18 percent of assaults and 40 percent of robberies. About one-third of the weapons are firearms, and another 25 percent are knives. The remainder includes blunt objects such as a club or rock.

Victim Self-Protection and Resistance

NCVS findings indicate that most violent-crime victims do not passively let the crime occur; almost 60 percent try to stop the crime. Of these, about one-fourth struggle with or threaten the offender, 16 percent run away or hide, and 13 percent try to persuade the offender not to commit the crime. Victims who use such measures say they helped the situation about two-thirds of the time, hurt the situation 6 percent of the time, both helped and hurt the situation 6 percent of the time, and neither helped nor hurt the situation 10 percent of the time.

▶ Explaining Victimization

These data provide useful information about crime victims and their victimization, but they do not tell us why people are victimized in the first place. When we attempt to explain criminal *behavior*, we are trying to explain at least two phenomena: Why do some locations have higher crime rates than others, and why are some individuals more likely than others to commit crime? Theories of crime attempt to answer these questions and are presented in several following chapters. When we try to explain criminal *victimization*, we ask similar questions: Why do some locations have higher victimization rates than others, and why are some individuals more likely than others to become crime victims? In answering these questions, victimologists highlight the opportunities for victimization.

Lifestyle and Routine Activities Theory

The most popular theory of victimization addresses the lifestyles and routine activities of individuals. This theory stems from two theories, lifestyle theory and routine activities theory, which developed about the same time in the late 1970s. Although they have somewhat different emphases, they both assume that "the habits, lifestyles, and behavioral patterns of potential crime victims enhance their contact with offenders and thereby increase the chances that crimes will occur" (Miethe and Meier 1990:244). The theories today are often treated as components of one larger theory.

Lifestyle theory stresses that some lifestyles put people more at risk for becoming crime victims (Zaykowski and Gunter 2013). These lifestyles include spending time outside home in places such as bars and nightclubs or just out on the street. This increases the chance of becoming a crime victim: an argument may break out in a bar; a robber may see an easy target. Recognizing that victimization is often committed by nonstrangers, the theory further assumes that people are more apt to become victims if they spend time with people who themselves commit high numbers of crimes. This helps explain why young people have the highest victimization rate for violent crime: They spend much time with other young people, who as a group commit the highest rates of violence, and thus sometimes place themselves in harm's way.

Routine activities theory argues that people engage in regular (hence the word *routine*) activities that increase their risk for victimization (Hollis et al. 2013). For victimization to occur, three components must coincide: (1) the presence of an attractive target (property or people), (2) the presence of a likely offender, and (3) the absence of *guardianship* (i.e., people who might observe and stop the crime from being committed). Thus, as more attractive targets emerge over time (e.g., more empty homes because of increased vacation travel or a rise in single-person households), victimization should increase. As more motivated offenders emerge (perhaps because of increasing unemployment), victimization should also increase.

Research testing lifestyle and routine activities theories uses measures such as the average number of nights a week spent walking alone at night or going to bars. This research finds that both theories help explain the occurrence of various types of victimizations against various kinds of people in various locations (Marcum 2010). Studies of college students are illustrative, as they find that students who eat out and or party more often are more likely to be victims of theft and/or sexual assault (Hines et al. 2012).

Studies like these suggest that some people engage in behavior that puts them at more risk for criminal victimization. By focusing on victims' behavior, lifestyle and routine activities theories might therefore imply that victims to some degree are responsible for their own victimization. The Crime and Controversy box discusses this issue of victim precipitation further.

▼ One reason for the high victimization rate of young people is that they spend time with other young people, who as a group commit relatively high rates of violence.

Tracy Whiteside/Shutterstock

Deviant Lifestyles and Victimization

A related idea from lifestyle and routine activities theories is that some people increase their chances of becoming crime victims by committing crimes themselves (Berg et al. 2012). As Topalli et al. (2002:237) observe, "One of criminology's dirty little secrets is that much serious crime, perhaps most, takes place beyond the reach of the criminal law because it is perpetrated against individuals who themselves are involved in lawbreaking."

This happens for several reasons. First and not surprisingly, criminals tend to spend time in high-crime areas and with other criminals. Second, their crimes may prompt a victim or the victim's family or friends to retaliate by attacking the offender. Such retaliation is especially likely when victims are criminals themselves (such as drug dealers), because calling the

Health care experts urge people not to smoke cigarettes or eat high-fat foods. To the extent that people ignore such advice, it is fair to say that they bear some responsibility and even blame for any health problems that develop.

Are crime victims also to blame for becoming victims? Because lifestyle and routine activities theories explain crime "not in the actions or numbers of motivated offenders, but in the activities and lifestyles of potential victims" (Meier and Miethe 1993:473), they imply that people would be safer from crime if they changed their behavior. Taken to an extreme, they imply we would all be safer if we never left our homes. By venturing outside, we decrease our guardianship and make ourselves and our homes attractive targets for motivated offenders. People who engage in deviant lifestyles and commit crimes increase their own risk for victimization. It might be possible, of course, for people to change certain risky lifestyles and to cut back on any criminal behavior they might commit. But most of us do not really have anything to change in these areas and thus can do little else to reduce our victimization. We need to go to work every day, and we are not about to stop engaging in leisure activities, including vacations, outside our homes. We cannot just hide under our beds. That said, it *is* true that we could be more careful at times. Leaving the keys in the car might be a mistake. And perhaps some of us could reduce our barhopping.

However, there are some crimes in which victims do seem to play an active role in their own victimization. In 1958, Marvin Wolfgang developed the idea of *victim-precipitated* homicide, in which the eventual victim is the one who was the first to use physical force, including a weapon. The person he (men are usually the ones involved) attacks fights back, perhaps with a weapon, and kills the victim. The victim, in short, precipitates his own death. Although not meant to excuse homicide, the concept of victim-precipitated homicide does point to an element of victim responsibility. In his study of 588 homicides, Wolfgang found that about one-fourth were victim precipitated. Depending on how precipitation is defined, other evidence indicates that some victims also precipitate assaults, robberies, and other crimes. This is especially true when women kill their male partners: Almost half of such killings are precipitated by a physical attack by the man on the woman.

Wolfgang's student, Menachem Amir, applied the victim-precipitated concept to rape not too long after Wolfgang developed it for homicide. Amir defined victim-precipitated rape as any rape that results when a woman engages in sexual relations and then changes her mind or behaves in any way, including accepting a drink, that could be construed as indicating her interest in having sex. Using this definition, Amir concluded that about one-fifth of the rapes he studied in Philadelphia, Pennsylvania, were precipitated by the victim.

As feminists began to study rape in the 1970s, they found Amir's notion of victim-precipitated rape repugnant. It implied that women were at fault for being raped and that rapists simply could not control themselves. It also put the burden for avoiding rape on women and fed common myths about the nature of rape. These myths make it very difficult for a rapist to be convicted if there is any evidence that the woman was wearing attractive clothing, had previously been sexually active, or in any other respect could be construed as somehow consenting to sexual activity. It may well be true that some homicide victims start the chain of events leading to their deaths, but it is quite different to say that women precipitate or bear any responsibility for their rapes.

Sources: Amir 1971; Karmen 2013; Meier and Miethe 1993; Wolfgang 1958.

police is not a viable option: If they report the crime, they obviously risk arrest, and they might not be taken seriously anyway. Third, because offenders cannot call the police, other offenders know this and act accordingly. Finally, criminals often have things that other criminals want. As Topalli et al. (2002:345) note for one type of offender, "Drug dealers recognize that their inability to go the police, coupled with their possession of cash and drugs, makes them attractive robbery targets."

Several studies confirm that offending does, in fact, increase victimization. Much of this research focuses on adolescents and finds that those who belong to gangs, who have been arrested for violence or drugs, or who report a history of delinquency are more likely to be victims of homicide or other crimes than youths with no such involvements (Zaykowski and Gunter 2013).

Drinking and drug use are also thought to contribute to victimization (Waller et al. 2012). Use of alcohol and other drugs may lead people to provoke other individuals, to engage in other risky behavior, and to be less on guard for potential victimization. It may also make them more attractive targets for potential offenders, who recognize that someone under the influence of alcohol or other drugs might be relatively easy to victimize. The studies of college students mentioned earlier find that students who drink more often and/or use marijuana or cocaine are more likely to become victims of theft and physical and sexual assault.

Review and Discuss

How does routine-activities theory help us understand why criminal victimization occurs? What does this theory imply for efforts to reduce crime?

Physical Proximity and Victimization

Our individual behavior does matter for victimization, but so does where we live. Cities have thousands of specific locations or places within them: street corners and intersections, homes, and commercial buildings. Because of their social and economic conditions, some areas of cities have higher crime and victimization rates than other areas (see Chapter 7).

Research finds that about 3–5 percent of all a city's locations account for at least 50 percent of the city's crime, and that the vast majority of locations have little or no crime (Braga 2012). If people live in or near these high-crime locations, commonly called hot spots, they are more likely to be victimized even if they do not have victimization-prone lifestyles. By the same token, people who live in or near hot spots and who have such lifestyles are especially likely to be victimized.

One factor that helps turn locations into hot spots is the presence of bars and taverns (Pridemore and Grubesic 2013). Assaults in and outside bars are common because of the use of alcohol. Further, the people going to bars are attractive targets to robbers, as routine activities theory would predict, because they carry credit cards and/or large amounts of money and sometimes make themselves vulnerable by drinking too much.

Review and Discuss

Why do some locations have much higher crime victimization rates than other locations? What does an understanding of location victimization rates imply for efforts to reduce crime?

Individual Traits

Routine activities, lifestyle, and proximity explanations are *situational* explanations: They all "stress how the context or situation influences vulnerability to crime" (Schreck et al. 2002:159).

▼ The presence of bars and taverns helps turn some urban locations into hot spots for street crime.

Although lifestyle theory does highlight potential victims' behavior, it says little about *why* certain people are more likely to adopt risky lifestyles or put themselves at increased risk for victimization for other reasons. Recent efforts to address this issue focus on some individual traits that make some people more likely than others to become crime victims.

Low Self-Control and Lack of Social Relationships

The first two traits are *low self-control* and *lack of social relationships* (Franklin et al. 2012; Stewart et al. 2004). Low self-control, characterized by impulsiveness and a desire for immediate gratification, leads some people to engage in risky behavior that brings them pleasure in the short run, but negative consequences in the long run. The concept of low self-control was originally developed to explain offending (see Chapter 8), but it also seems useful for explaining victimization. The second trait is a lack of close social relationships. People without family ties may be more inclined and have more opportunity to engage in various types of activities, such as going out to bars, that increase their victimization risk.

Childhood Problems

Another individual factor that increases one's risk for victimization is a history of childhood problems, including behavioral disturbance, sexual abuse, harsh physical punishment, and parental conflict (McIntyre and Widom 2011). All these factors predict greater violent victimization during adolescence, in large part because they first lead to violent offending, which then increases the risk for victimization. Childhood problems may also lower self-control and impair social relationships; if so, this would be another reason why they increase victimization.

Mental Disorder

Mental disorder is another individual trait that may increase victimization. Although many stereotypes of the mentally ill exist, it is true that their social relationships "may often become strained as family members and other seek to manage and control" their behavior (Silver 2002:191). Their social relationships, then, become "conflicted relationships" (p. 193) that lead to violence against the mentally ill.

Puberty

Recent studies have pinpointed the onset of early puberty as a risk factor for adolescent victimization (Haynie and Piquero 2006; Schreck et al. 2007). Puberty is thought to have this effect for at least three reasons. First, it raises the likelihood of offending (see Chapter 6), which, as we have seen, is itself a risk factor for victimization. Second, it prompts adolescents to spend more time with older adolescents away from home and in situations where victimization can and does occur. Third, it leads to emotional distress; teens with such distress act in a way that angers other teens and provokes them to commit violence against the distressed teens.

Repeat Victimization

Sometimes an individual or household that has already been victimized by crime is victimized one or more times again at a later date. The general explanations of victimization outlined earlier help explain why certain individuals and households are more prone to such *repeat victimization*. People who lead more risky lifestyles, including offending themselves, are more likely to be victimized in the first place, but also to be victimized again (Fagan and Mazerolle 2011). Individuals and households in or near hot spots are also more likely to be victimized initially and then again.

Repeat victimization is a fairly common occurrence. The NCVS has predicted that almost three-fourths of violent crime victims and almost all property crime victims will be victimized more than once (Koppel 1987). In a study of the National Youth Survey (NYS), a nationwide longitudinal sample of adolescents, 85 percent of respondents reported being victimized more than once, with more than half being victimized by an average of two offenses in any one year. The study concluded that "repeat victimization is the norm, not the exception, in the period from adolescence through early adulthood" (Menard 2000:571). At the same time, repeat victimization was concentrated in a small proportion of *chronic victims*, 10 percent of all adolescents, who account for more than half of all victimizations and who are disproportionately male and members of ethnic minority groups.

Explaining Demographic Variation in Victimization

Theories of victimization help explain the demographic patterns of victimization we have seen. For example, if lifestyles affect victimization, then it is not surprising that young people have much higher rates of victimization than the elderly, because they are much more likely to spend time away from home, especially in bars, nightclubs, and other high-risk areas, and are also more apt to engage in deviant lifestyles. Men are also more likely than women to spend time away from home and to engage in deviant lifestyles. This similarity between young people and men underscores why young males have such particularly high rates of victimization. African-Americans and Latinos are more likely than non-Latino whites to live in disadvantaged, high-crime areas and thus more likely to become crime victims. Their higher rate of offending for serious crimes also increases their victimization risk. The same logic applies to people with low family incomes. Given all these factors, it is no surprise that young African-American males have a high victimization rate and that older white females have a low one. Finally, adolescents who become chronic victims likely help secure their fates by having lifestyles and offending rates that are especially conducive to victimization (Menard 2000).

Lifestyle and routine activities theories are less applicable, however, to violence in the home. Because these theories focus on predatory crime outside the home, they assume that activities outside the home increase the likelihood of such victimization: "Time spent in one's home generally decreases victim risk, while time spent in public settings increases risk" (Meier and Miethe 1993:466). Because intimate-partner violence often occurs inside the home, it cannot be attributed to routine activities or lifestyles conducive to victimization. If this is true, these theories of victimization apply less to women than to men, because a greater proportion of women's victimization is by intimate partners. For obvious reasons, the theories are also irrelevant for physical and sexual abuse of children, because children cannot be considered to engage in lifestyles or routine activities conducive to such abuse. Finally, these theories also do not apply to victimization by most white-collar crime.

Review and Discuss

How do theories of victimization help explain demographic differences in victimization rates? Why are these theories less relevant for family violence than for victimization that occurs outside the home?

Victimization of College Students and the Homeless

The explanations we have just reviewed will help us to understand some aspects of the criminal victimization of college students and the homeless, even if these two groups have little or nothing else in common.

College Students

We saw earlier that many college students lead lifestyles that increase their chances of becoming crime victims. The NCVS compiled the average annual violent victimization rates (rape or sexual assault, robbery, aggravated or simple assault) of college students from 1995 to 2002 (Baum and Klaus 2005). Table 4–6 presents these rates and shows that about 61 of every 1,000 college students (or 6.1 percent) are victims of violence every year on the average. Because there were about 7.9 million college students in the study's time period, this rate translates to an average annual

TABLE 4-6 Average Annual Violent Victimization Rates of College Students and Nonstudents, NCVS, 1995–2002 (Per 1,000 Persons Age 18 to 24)

	COLLEGE STUDENTS	NONSTUDENTS
All individuals	60.7	75.3
Gender		
Male	80.2	79.2
Female	42.7	71.3
Race or ethnicity[a]		
White	64.9	81.2
African American	52.4	83.2
Other	37.2	43.1
Latinos	56.1	55.9

[a] Racial categories do not include Latinos. Other includes Asians, Native Hawaiians, Pacific Islanders, Alaska Natives, and American Indians considered together.
Note: Rates include rape or sexual assault, robbery, and aggravated or simple assault.
Source: Baum and Klaus 2005.

total of about 479,000 victimizations. Many of these victimizations are simple assaults; if we omit them from the figures, the victimization rate for serious violence (rape or sexual assault, robbery, aggravated assault) drops to 22.3 per 1,000 students, or about 176,000 victimizations, still a very large number.

Male students have a higher victimization rate (in fact twice as high) than female students have (see Table 4–6). The actual gender difference may be smaller than what the NCVS indicates because, as noted earlier, the NCVS may underestimate victimization by rape or sexual assault and by domestic violence. The NCVS college study determined the annual rate of rape or sexual assault victimization for women to be 6.0 per 1,000, but another national study from roughly the same time period determined the rate to be 35 per 1,000, equivalent to 350 rapes annually on a campus with 10,000 women (Fisher et al. 2000).

Chapter 3 noted that crime rates have declined since the 1990s. NCVS data show that the national violent crime victimization rate is now about half the rate that held true when these college data were gathered. We do not yet know whether college violence is also down by half, but let us suppose it is for the sake of argument. Using our earlier figures, that would mean that today's violent-crime victimization rate for college students is about 30 per 1,000 and that the rape/sexual assault rate is between 3 and 18 per 1,000. There are now about 13.5 million full-time college students, including 7.5 million women. Our assumed violent-crime victimization rates for today's students would yield an estimated 405,000 victimizations annually for all violent crime; an estimated 150,000 victimizations for serious violence; and an estimated range of between 22,500 and 135,000 victimizations for rape and sexual assault.

In other figures in Table 4–6, note that the victimization rate for African-American students is slightly lower than that for white students and that both groups' rates are higher than those for students of other races (primarily American Indians and Asians). White students have a very high victimization rate for simple assault. If we omit simple assaults and just consider serious violence, then African-American students emerge with the highest victimization rate (27.5), followed fairly closely by white students (21.6), and those of other races (18.8). Note also that college students overall have a lower victimization rate than nonstudents in the 18-to-24 age group. Although many college students have lifestyles that put them at risk for violent victimization, it is evident that nonstudents in the same age bracket have lifestyles or other risk factors, such as proximity to high-crime areas, that make them even more vulnerable to victimization.

The Homeless

Recall from Chapter 3 that the NCVS excludes groups such as the homeless who do not live in households and who have high victimization rates. If the lifestyles of college students puts some of them at risk for crime victimization, homelessness itself might be considered a lifestyle that makes the homeless extremely vulnerable to victimization. They tend to live in high-crime areas and, given their common mental and physical weaknesses, cannot defend themselves and thus lack the guardianship emphasized by routine activities theory. For these reasons, the homeless have been called "invisible victims" (Huey 2012).

The few studies we have on the homeless does find high rates of victimization. A study of homeless women in Los Angeles found that about one-third had been victims of violence during the preceding year (Wenzel et al. 2001). An earlier study of 150 homeless adults in Birmingham, Alabama, found that 35 percent of the sample had been victims of violence or theft in the preceding year (Fitzpatrick et al. 1993); this proportion was four times higher than the NCVS's estimate for the general population at the time of the study and three times higher than that for the poorest income bracket.

Another study, of 200 homeless women in New York City, found troubling racial differences in victimization and fear of crime (Coston 1992). The sample included 102 people of color and 98 whites. Sixty percent of the former group had been victimized by crime, usually robbery or

▲ Many college students engage in lifestyles, including drinking, that increase their chances of becoming crime victims.

assault, while living on the street, compared to only 48 percent of the latter group. People in the former group were also more likely to feel highly vulnerable to future victimization. In terms of victimization and fear of crime, race appears to make a difference in the world of the homeless, just as it does for the vast majority of Americans with a roof over their heads.

Research is beginning to document the consequences of criminal victimization for the homeless. As we shall see in the next section, victimization can have several kinds of consequences, but these are especially severe for the homeless in view of their high rates of victimization and lack of resources to help them cope with their victimization. Homeless people who are victimized by crime are more likely to consume higher amounts of alcohol and to use other drugs, and they are also more likely to experience depression and other mental health consequences (Perron et al. 2008; Tyler et al. 2013).

▶ Costs and Consequences of Victimization

As just indicated, crime victims suffer several types of consequences: medical, financial, psychological, and behavioral. Some are injured and require medical attention; some may even have to miss work or other major life activities. Victims of property crime obviously lose money and property. Victims of various crimes may also suffer psychological and/or behavioral problems. We look first at economic and medical costs and consequences and then at psychological and behavioral effects.

Economic and Medical Costs and Consequences

Information on the economic and medical costs of victimization comes from the NCVS, UCR, and other sources. Because these sources use different methodologies and measure different crimes, cost information is inexact but nonetheless indicates the serious impact of crime on victims and their families. The most significant economic and medical costs and consequences are as follows:

- The crimes the NCVS covers (robbery, rape, assault, personal and household theft, burglary, and motor vehicle theft) cost crime victims in 2008 an estimated $17.4 billion in *direct costs* (Rand and Robinson 2011). Direct costs means loss to the victim of any money or property stolen or damaged, medical expenses, and any wages lost because of missed work. The average violent crime cost victims $238; the average property crime cost $993. Other estimates that include offenses, such as drunk driving and commercial crime, that the NCVS omits put the annual total of direct costs at more than $100 billion (Miller et al. 1996). *Indirect costs* for victimization (lost productivity, medical care for long-term physical and mental health, police expenses, and victim services) can run into the thousands of dollars for crimes such as rape and robbery. If the quality-of-life cost of consequences such as pain and suffering are taken into account (and not all scholars agree that such costs should be considered or can even be measured), the total cost of victimization may be more than $1 million for homicide, close to $90,000 for rape, and $10,000 for some other crimes, or about $450 billion overall (Miller et al. 1996).

- Only 14 percent of 2008 NCVS victims who had money or property stolen recovered all of it, and 71 percent recovered none of it.

- About 7 percent of all NCVS violent- and property-crime victims lost time from work, usually a week or less. Almost one-fifth of victims of motor vehicle theft lost time from work.

- Violent victimization during adolescence has long-term income consequences because of its psychological consequences (discussed later). Teens who experience such a victimization are more likely by adulthood to have lower educational and occupational achievement and thus lower incomes. Because violent victimization during adolescence is highest for urban males of color, its long-term income consequences are greatest for "individuals already lacking social and economic resources. . . . (E)xposure to criminal violence may play a role in the reproduction of social and economic failure among the disadvantaged" (Macmillan 2000:575).

- More than one-third of NCVS robbery victims and more than one-fifth of assault victims are physically injured. Almost half of victims who need medical care obtain it at a hospital or emergency clinic, while 10 percent obtain it at a doctor's office and 16 percent at the scene of the crime.

Psychological Consequences

Before the beginning of victimology, criminologists did not study the psychological consequences of criminal victimization. Over the past 20–30 years, psychologists and other scholars have conducted in-depth interviewing of crime victims to get a picture that goes far beyond the dry economic and medical data just discussed. For some people and for some types of crimes, victimization can be especially traumatic.

In this context, rape has probably been studied more than any other crime, and it has both moderate and serious consequences that can have a lifelong impact (Brown et al. 2009; Malan et al. 2011). We have already seen in Chapter 2 that rape plays a large role in women's high fear of crime. Women victimized by rape often suffer additional psychological effects, including mild depression and loss of self-esteem. These symptoms begin to subside a few months after the rape for most women, but can last much longer for others. Sexual dysfunction, the refusal or inability to engage in sexual relations, is also common. Some research finds that about 20 percent of rape survivors attempt suicide, and 40 to 45 percent consider it. Drug abuse, including alcoholism, is also common, perhaps especially among women victimized as children by rape or other sexual abuse. Many rape survivors may experience *post-traumatic stress disorder* (PTSD), and some also experience depression and other serious psychological disorders.

Studies of victims of other crimes find similar psychological symptoms, although violent crimes appear to have more serious psychological consequences than do property crimes (Menard 2002). Victims of burglary, robbery, and nonsexual assault exhibit higher levels than nonvictims of fear, vulnerability, anxiety, loss of confidence, sleep difficulties, and other similar symptoms. They also can develop PTSD.

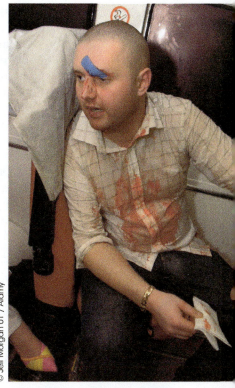

▲ Victims of violent crime may experience various psychological symptoms, including post-traumatic stress disorder.

An interesting question is whether crimes committed by strangers have more serious psychological consequences than those committed by nonstrangers. Most studies of this issue have examined rape and found that rapes committed by both kinds of offenders generally have the same impact. However, the evidence is again a bit mixed, and some research suggests that rapes are especially traumatic when committed by nonstrangers (Lurigio and Resick 1990).

Some research has begun to examine *indirect victimization* among relatives and neighbors of crime victims. In general, relatives of homicide victims suffer as least as much grief as that felt by anyone who loses a loved one. These relatives, as well as partners of rape victims, also experience symptoms similar to those of victims of violent crimes, including PTSD (Riggs and Kilpatrick 1990). Neighbors of property-crime victims are more likely to move to another area, while neighbors of violent-crime victims are not more likely to do so, perhaps because the violence they learn about is committed by someone the victim knew and thus is not threatening to the neighbor (Xie and McDowall 2008).

A final line of research has addressed whether crime victims' views about crime and justice change as a result of being victimized. Somewhat surprisingly, this body of research finds that victims are generally not more likely than nonvictims to hold punitive attitudes toward criminals. Disputing the common saying that "a liberal is someone who has not been mugged," this research also finds that victims are no more likely than nonvictims to hold conservative political beliefs (Unnever et al. 2007).

Social and Behavioral Consequences

Criminal victimization may also have several behavioral consequences. In particular, victims of violence at various ages become more likely themselves to commit crime or use drugs, or both, at later ages. This effect is especially strong for physical and sexual abuse during childhood and adolescence (Widom et al. 2013). *Vicarious* physical victimization by one's family members or friends also matters: Adolescents whose family members or friends have been physically victimized may become more likely themselves to engage in delinquency because of the strain they feel (Agnew 2002).

Although most research on the behavioral consequences of victimization focuses on individuals, some scholars also address the behavioral consequences for neighborhoods where crime and victimization flourish (Hipp 2010). A key consequence involves a neighborhood's cohesion and *informal control* (also called *informal surveillance*), that is, the daily efforts by neighbors to watch out for one another and in this and other ways to ensure a community with high levels of social integration that help keep crime in check. Crime and the fear it generates weaken cohesion and informal control by, among other effects, keeping people inside, reducing their involvement in local voluntary organizations, and even forcing some people to move away. The result is a vicious cycle: Crime and victimization undermine cohesion and informal control, and the weakened cohesion and control increase crime and victimization.

Other research on the consequences of victimization focuses on social relationships. As might be expected, child and adolescent sexual and physical abuse often makes it difficult for an abuse survivor to engage in stable romantic and platonic relationships (Widom et al. 2013). Because such relationships can be important for our psychological well-being, this difficulty compounds the original problems caused by the history of abuse.

Review and Discuss

What are the major consequences that crime victims suffer? To what extent do these consequences differ by age, gender, social class, and race and ethnicity?

▶ Victims in the Criminal Justice System

A growing body of literature addresses the experiences of victims in the criminal justice system. Much of this literature concerns women who have been raped and who are said to be assaulted a second time in the criminal justice system. The reasons for such a *second victimization* derive from popular myths about rape (see Chapter 11). In the past, many police, prosecutors, and judges believed these myths; and although their attitudes have improved, some criminal justice professionals still greet women's reports of rape with some skepticism (Patterson 2011). In spite of the fact that many states have passed laws to protect women during prosecutions and trials of their offenders, the burden is still on women to prove they did not give consent. Myths about domestic violence also still abound (see Chapter 11), and the criminal justice system has had to adapt to accommodate the needs and concerns of domestic violence victims, most of whom are women.

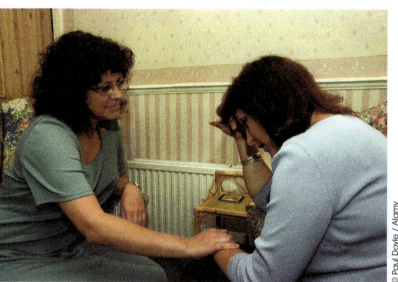

▼ Many jurisdictions have established victim-witness advocate programs to help victims during the various stages of the criminal justice process.

© Paul Doyle / Alamy

More generally, scholars and elected and criminal justice officials have begun to recognize that crime victims of all stripes feel shut out of the criminal justice process and otherwise have needs that must be addressed (Karmen 2013). Several kinds of services and programs for victims have begun across the United States, and some jurisdictions have developed *victim-witness advocate programs* involving court professionals to help steer victims through the morass of the criminal justice system. Many areas have also begun social service and victim restitution programs to help victims deal with the economic and psychological impacts of their victimization.

In another innovation, judges have begun to ask victims to submit victim-impact statements to consider as the judges decide on the appropriate sentence for convicted offenders. Victim involvement in sentencing is meant to increase victims' satisfaction with the criminal justice process. Evidence indicates that these statements tend to increase victims' satisfaction with how their cases are handled, but that they do not make it more likely that judges will assign harsher sentences to convicted defendants (Roberts 2009). However, some research has found that prison inmates were less likely to be paroled if their files contained victims' letters protesting parole and if their victims attended their parole hearings (Morgan 2005). Experimental evidence also suggests that victim-impact testimony may make jurors in capital (death penalty) cases more likely to decide a defendant should be executed (Paternoster and Deise 2011).

A related concept to the victim-impact statement is the *victim-impact panel*. This concept was introduced in 1982 by Mothers Against Drunk Driving to allow people arrested for drunk driving to hear about the harm and trauma suffered by victims of DUI (driving under the influence) traffic accidents. The usual panel consists of four or five victims who each talk for several minutes about how DUI affected their lives. A study in Georgia investigated whether DUI offenders who attended a victim-impact panel were less likely than those who did not (because their DUI occurred before the panels began) to engage in DUI again (Rojek et al. 2003). The researchers found that only about 16 percent of the offenders who attended a panel were rearrested for DUI within five years, compared to about one-third (33.5 percent) of those who did not attend a panel.

Victims and Criminal Case Outcomes

The increasing attention to victims has motivated research on how their behavior and demographic characteristics affect criminal prosecutions and trials by influencing the decisions of prosecutors, judges, and juries. Prosecutors prefer cases with *good victims*: those who, according to a prosecutor of sexual assault cases, "are well-educated and articulate, and are, above all, presentable to a jury" (Bryden and Lengnick 1997:1247). In contrast, *bad victims* have a prior criminal record or other history of disreputable behavior and have engaged in conduct that may be perceived as provoking the defendant. Because these victims are seen as less credible and their victimization may be considered less serious, prosecutors are less likely to bring their cases to indictment. If their cases do go to trial, they are less likely to end in a conviction (Baumer et al. 2000). Even dead victims—that is, those who were murdered—can be good or bad victims from the prosecutor's perspective: prosecutors are more likely to seek the death penalty in homicide cases when victims are of high social status and in other respects "respectable" (Phillips 2009).

Turning to demographic characteristics, research on the effects of victims' gender and age on case processing and outcomes is inconsistent. However, the race of the victim does seem to matter for homicide and rape cases, in which defendants are treated more harshly in terms of indictment and conviction when victims are white (Baumer et al. 2000).

Other research examines the impact of the victim–offender relationship on the processing of criminal cases, with much of this research focusing on rape and sexual assault (Spohn and Holleran 2001; Tasca et al. 2013). Two findings from this research stand out. First, rapes and sexual assaults by strangers are more likely than those by nonstrangers to lead to arrest, prosecution, and conviction, because the victim's declaration that she did not give consent is more likely to be believed. Second, the impact of victims' behavior and reputation on the likelihood that charges will be filed is higher for cases in which the victim knew the defendant. Because prosecutors fear that the defendant will argue that the victim gave her consent, they are more apt to drop a case if the victim's character or conduct might be called into question.

▶ Victimization by White-Collar Crime

Victimization research focuses on street crime and not on white-collar crime. Because the NCVS does not ask about white-collar crime, its wealth of information on the injuries and economic costs of street-crime victims is lacking for their white-collar-crime counterparts. The neglect of white-collar crime victims is unfortunate because the financial losses, injuries and illnesses, and even deaths that people suffer from white-collar crime are greater than those suffered from street crime (see Chapter 13).

A few studies have aimed to fill the gap. A national survey found that between 15 and 33 percent of U.S. adults have been victims of one type of white-collar crime, fraud, which costs Americans more than $40 billion yearly (Rebovich and Layne 2000). Yet only one-fifth of fraud victims report their victimization to police, district attorneys, or consumer protection agencies. Another study found that more than half of Tennessee residents had suffered fraud victimization during the past five years (Copes et al. 2001).

Some studies document the psychological cost of white-collar crime. One research team interviewed forty-seven people, many of them elderly, who lost funds when a savings and loan company collapsed because of criminal conduct by its officers and employees (Shover et al. 1994:86–87). Forty percent of the sample lost large sums of money, and many remained angry and/or depressed several years later. One victim said she has thought about it "every day. Every day for eight years. I go to bed with it. I get up with it. I think of it through the day. And my husband . . . I haven't seen my husband smile in eight years. . . . Really, it destroyed our life. We're not happy people anymore." Ironically, many victims blamed themselves for what happened as much as they blamed the savings and loan officials. The researchers concluded that "some victims of white-collar crime endure enormous long-term pain and suffering" similar to that experienced by victims of street crime.

▶ Conclusion

Victims of street crime remain a prime subject for social science research and for government action. The social pattern of victimization is disturbingly similar to the pattern for criminality: It is concentrated among the poor, nonwhite, and young sectors of society. Although women are less likely to be victimized than men overall, they face the threat of rape and intimate violence as a daily social fact and generally are more likely than men to be victimized by intimates and other people they know.

The most popular theories of victimization imply that changes in our behavior would reduce our risk for victimization. This is true to an extent, but some behaviors are easier to change than others. We can reduce our visits to bars and taverns, which seem to be special locations for victimization, but we cannot simply shut ourselves in our homes and hide under our beds. These theories further imply that victims are responsible for their victimization. Taken to an extreme, victims might even be said to precipitate their victimization. This may be true for some homicides, but it is an antiquated and even dangerous concept when applied to rape. Unless we want to say that women precipitate their rapes by simply knowing men and spending time with them, an absurd notion, the idea of women's involvement in their rapes must be abandoned.

In looking at public opinion about crime, the extent and patterning of criminal behavior, and the patterning and consequences of criminal victimization in this and the previous two chapters, one theme that emerges is inequality. The groups at the bottom of the socioeconomic ladder—the poor, people of color, the young—are most likely to fear crime and have the highest rates of both criminality and victimization. Gender presents somewhat of an exception to this link: Although women, who have less social and economic power than men, are much more likely to fear crime, they have a much lower offending rate and a lower victimization rate. The way we socialize females and males explains much of this pattern. The last three chapters have also stressed the importance of white-collar crime. The focus of media, scholarly, and government attention on street crime is certainly important and well deserved, but the neglect by all three sources of white-collar crime is not.

Summary

1. Although there are many kinds of victimizations, the study of victims and victimization in criminology has usually been limited to victimization by street crime. Victimization by white-collar crime has been neglected.

2. Victimization is patterned geographically and sociodemographically, with most of the patterns similar to those for criminality. Victimization rates are lower for whites, women (except for rape and domestic violence), older people, and the nonpoor than for their counterparts. Victimization rates for young African-American males are especially high.

3. NCVS data also show that alcohol and other drugs are involved in much criminal victimization, that weapons are used in about one-fifth of all violent crime, and that most victims try to avoid being victimized by struggling with the offender or trying to run away or hide. NCVS data also show that many nonstrangers commit violent crime and commit the majority of violent crime against women.

4. Lifestyle and routine activities theories emphasize that what people do in their daily lives can increase or decrease their chances of becoming crime victims. These theories help to explain some of the sociodemographic patterns of victimization. College students who spend a lot of time in bars, drink a lot, or misuse other substances increase their chances of victimization.

5. Criminal victimization costs victims nationwide billions of dollars in direct costs every year and perhaps tens of billions of dollars in indirect costs. It also takes a psychological toll, with depression, post-traumatic stress disorder, and other symptoms not uncommon. Behavioral changes may include increased abuse of alcohol and other drugs and increased violent offending. White-collar crime may have consequences similar to those of street crime, but only a few studies have documented these effects.

6. The criminal justice system is increasingly trying to accommodate the needs and desires of crime victims. Victim-witness advocate programs and compensation for victimization are now common throughout the nation. Many judges also ask victims to file victim-impact statements to help the judges decide on the appropriate sentences for convicted offenders.

Key Terms

crime characteristics *74*

crime victim *65*

hot spots *78*

inequality *86*

lifestyle theory *76*

psychological consequences *83*

routine activities theory *76*

victim-impact statements *84*

victim–offender relationship *71*

victim precipitation *76*

victimization *65*

victimology *65*

What Would You Do?

1. A friend from one of your classes confides that over the weekend another student began to attack her sexually. She was able to stop him by threatening to call the police, and he left her room in a fit of anger. Do you advise your friend to call the campus police about this attempted sexual assault? Why or why not?

2. Suppose you are a judge in a case in which the defendant was convicted of aggravated assault. He got into an argument with another man in a bar and beat him so severely that the victim suffered two broken bones in his arm. At your request, the victim files a victim-impact statement that indicates his arm may have suffered some permanent damage. How much, if at all, will the victim's statement affect the sentence you hand out to the defendant? Explain your answer.

5   Classical and Neoclassical Perspectives

· ·

Crime in the News

In May 2013, a 67-year-old Vietnam War veteran in Fort Myers, Florida, was watching a professional basketball game when a robber burst into his home and began hitting him in the face with a metal rod as part of a robbery. The veteran later recalled that he was hit "about five, six times. I mean he could have killed me. . . . (B)lood was streaming down my face." The man later needed 22 stitches to close up his wound. It could have been worse, as the victim conceded: "My head hurts, it throbs, but it doesn't hurt as bad as I thought it would." He had one bit of advice for the public: "When someone knocks on your door, make sure you know who the hell is there."

Source: Johnson 2013.

· ·

W hy did this terrible crime happen? Why did the robber decide to commit it? What can be done to prevent this type of crime and the many other types of crime that we read or hear about virtually every day?

A central task of criminology is to explain why crime occurs. Your author once had a student who said the devil caused most crime. Her classmates snickered when they heard this. Undaunted, the student added that the way to reduce crime would be to exorcise the devil from the bodies it possessed. More snickers. I said I respected her religious beliefs, but noted that modern criminological theory does not blame the devil and does not think exorcism would help.

As this story illustrates, assumptions of what causes crime affect what we think should be done to reduce it. If we blame the devil, our crime-reduction efforts will center on removing the devil's influence. If we hold biological or psychological problems in individuals responsible, our efforts will focus on correcting these problems. If we hold poverty and inadequate parenting responsible, our efforts will center on reducing poverty and improving parenting skills. If we instead think criminals are simply depraved and that the criminal justice system is too lenient to keep them from committing crime, our efforts will focus on adding more police, increasing prison terms, and building more prisons. To develop the most effective approach, we must first know why crime occurs.

Contemporary theories of crime differ widely in their assumptions and emphases. In the social and behavioral sciences, sociology has contributed the most to understanding crime, with psychology and economics also making important contributions. Of the remaining sciences, biology has long been interested in crime. This chapter highlights neoclassical explanations, rooted in economic thinking, that emphasize the rationality of crime and criminals, whereas the next chapter discusses biological and psychological explanations. The three subsequent chapters discuss explanations from sociology. After reading these chapters, you should have a good understanding of the reasons for crime that the various disciplines favor, of the strengths and weaknesses of the explanations they offer, and of the possible solutions to crime these explanations suggest.

▶ Understanding Theories of Crime

Theories of crime try to answer at least one of three questions: (1) Why are some individuals more likely than others to commit crime? (2) Why are some categories or kinds of people more likely than others to commit crime? (3) Why is crime more common in some locations than in other locations? Biological and psychological explanations tend to focus on the first question, whereas neoclassical and sociological explanations tend to focus on the last two questions.

These explanations also differ in other ways. Neoclassical explanations, as we shall soon see, assume that criminals act with free will, whereas the other explanations assume that people are influenced to commit crime by certain internal and external forces. To be more precise, biological and psychological explanations place the causes of crime inside the individual, whereas sociological explanations place these causes in the social environment outside the individual. Put another way, biology and psychology focus on the *micro*, or smaller, picture, and sociology focuses on the *macro*, or larger, picture. This distinction reflects long-standing differences in understanding human behavior. It does not mean that a macro approach is better than a micro approach, and neither does it mean the reverse. The approach you favor depends on whether you think it is more important to understand the smaller picture or the larger one.

Nevertheless, the approaches' different focuses do have different implications for efforts to reduce crime. If the fault for crime lies within the individual, then to reduce crime we must change the individual. If the fault instead lies in the social environment, then we must change this environment. And if neoclassical perspectives are correct, crime can be reduced by measures that convince potential criminals that they are more likely to be arrested and punished severely.

To help understand the distinction between the micro and macro orientations of biology/psychology and sociology, respectively, let us leave criminology to consider two related eating disorders, anorexia (undereating or starvation) and bulimia (self-induced regurgitation after eating). What causes these disorders? Psychologists and medical researchers cite problems in the individuals with the disorders. Psychologists emphasize low self-esteem, feelings of inferiority, and lack of control, whereas medical researchers stress possible biochemical imbalances (Keel and Forney 2013). These individual-level explanations are valuable, and you may know someone with an eating disorder who was helped by a psychologist or a physician.

▼ Actress Jamie-Lynn Sigler, who played the daughter in *The Sopranos*, struggled with an eating disorder that began during high school. Whereas psychologists attribute eating disorders to low self-esteem and other psychological problems, sociologists highlight the cultural emphasis on slender female bodies.

© Everett Collection In / Alamyr

A sociological explanation takes a different stance. Recognizing that eating disorders disproportionately affect young women, sociologists say a cultural emphasis on slender female bodies, evidenced by Barbie dolls and photos in women's magazines, leads many women to think they are too heavy and to believe they need to diet. Inevitably, some women will diet to an extreme and perhaps not even eat or else force themselves to regurgitate (Forney and Ward 2013). This type of explanation locates the roots of eating disorders more in society than in individual anorexics or bulimics. No matter how often psychologists and physicians successfully treat such women, other women will always be taking their place as long as the emphasis on female thinness continues. If so, efforts to cure eating disorders may help individual women, but ultimately will do relatively little to reduce the eating disorder problem.

Returning to criminology, if the roots of crime are biological and psychological problems inside individuals, then to reduce crime we need to correct these problems. If the roots of crime instead lie more in criminogenic features of the social environment, then new criminals will always be emerging and the crime problem will continue unless we address these features.

That said, it is also true that most people do not commit crime even if they experience a criminogenic social environment, just as most women do not have eating disorders despite the cultural emphasis on thinness. To understand why certain people do commit crime (or why certain women have eating disorders), individual-level explanations are necessary. To reiterate, whether you favor micro or macro explanations of crime (or of eating disorders) depends on whether you think it is more important to understand the smaller picture or the larger one.

It is time now to turn to the many theories of crime. The term *theories* can often make students' eyes glaze over. Perhaps yours just did. That is why this chapter began by stressing the need to understand *why* crime occurs if we want to reduce it. If you recognize this need, you also recognize the importance of theory. As you read about the various theories in the chapters ahead, think about what they imply for successful efforts to reduce crime.

▶ From Theology to Science

Our excursion into the world of theory begins by reviewing the historical change from theology to science in the understanding of crime.

God and Demons as Causes of Crime and Deviance

Like many folk societies studied by anthropologists today, Western societies long ago had religious explanations for behavior that violated their norms. People in ancient times were thought to act deviantly for several reasons: (1) God was testing their faith, (2) God was punishing them, (3) God was using their behavior to warn others to follow divine rules, and (4) they were possessed by demons (McCaghy et al. 2008). In the Old Testament, the prophets communicated God's unhappiness to the ancient Hebrews with behavior that today we would call mad and even violent. Yet they, and Jesus after them in the temple, were regarded as divinely inspired. Ancient Greeks and Romans, who believed in multiple gods, had similar explanations for madness.

From ancient times through the Middle Ages, witches—people who supposedly had associated with or been possessed by the devil—were a special focus of attention. The Old Testament mentions witches several times, including the commandment in Exodus (22:18), "Thou shalt not suffer a witch to live." Witches also appear in ancient Greek and Roman literature. Biblical injunctions against witches took an ominous turn in Europe from the 1400s to the 1700s, when some 300,000 "witches," most of them women, were burned at the stake or otherwise executed.

Perhaps, the most famous witch-hunting victim was Joan of Arc, a military hero for France in its wars with England, whom the English burned at the stake in May 1431. Other witches put to death, often by the Roman Catholic Church that dominated continental Europe, were what today we would call healers, midwives, religious heretics, political protesters, and homosexuals. In short, anyone, and especially any woman, who violated church rules could have been branded a witch (Demos 2009).

As this brief summary suggests, religion was the dominant source of knowledge in the Western world through the Middle Ages. Religion was used to explain norm-violating behavior, but it was also used to explain natural, physical, and social phenomena too numerous to mention. Science was certainly not unknown in the West, but it played a secondary role to religion as people sought to understand the social and physical worlds around them. They widely believed that God controlled all human behavior and that the church's authority was to be accepted without question. Although they learned these basic beliefs from childhood as part of their normal socialization, it is also true that the persecution of alleged witches would have made people afraid to question the primacy of the church. Regardless of the reason, religion was the ruling force during the Middle Ages, and science was hardly even in contention.

The Age of Reason

This fundamental fact of Western life through the Middle Ages began to change during the seventeenth and eighteenth centuries, when religious views began to give way to scientific explanations. This period marked the ripening in Europe of the Age of Reason, or the Enlightenment, which developed a new way of thinking about natural and social phenomena that eventually weakened religion's influence. Enlightenment philosophers included such famous figures as René Descartes (1596–1650), Thomas Hobbes (1588–1679), John Locke (1632–1704), and Jean-Jacques Rousseau (1712–1778), all of whom are still read today along with many others. As innumerable works have discussed (Israel 2011), these political philosophers influenced Western thought in many profound ways, and their ideas are reflected in the Declaration of Independence and other documents crucial to the founding of the United States.

The views of the Enlightenment philosophers differed in several important respects. For example, Rousseau thought that human nature was basically good, Hobbes thought that human nature was basically bad, and Locke thought that it was neither good nor bad as people were born with a "blank slate" and thereafter shaped by their experiences and social environments. Yet as Enlightenment philosophers, they shared certain fundamental assumptions that helped shape the classical school of criminology to be discussed shortly.

▼ Tens of thousands of women considered to be witches were executed in Europe from the 1400s to the 1700s.

© Historical image collection by Bildagentur-online / Alamy

One of these assumptions was that God had left people to govern their own affairs through the exercise of free will and reason. In this Enlightenment view, people rationally calculate the rewards and risks of potential actions and adopt behavior promising the greatest pleasure and least pain. To ensure that people not act too emotionally, Enlightenment thinkers stressed the need to acquire an education to develop reasoning ability.

Although this and other Enlightenment views represented significant advances beyond the philosophy of the Middle Ages, this more "enlightened" way of thinking did not extend to the criminal justice system. Europeans suspected of crimes during the Age of Reason were often arrested on flimsy evidence and imprisoned without trial. Torture was commonly used in continental Europe to force people to confess to their alleged crime and to name anyone else involved. In England, the right to jury trials for felonies should have lessened the use of torture. However, English defendants convicted by juries risked losing their land and property to the king. Many defendants thus refused jury trials, only to suffer a form of torture known as *pressing* (finally abolished in 1772), in which a heavy weight was placed on the defendant's body. Some were crushed to death instantly, but others lasted a few days until they either confessed or died. If they managed to die without confessing, their families kept their land and property (Roth 2011).

Although torture was less common in England despite the use of pressing, the death penalty was often used, with more than 200 crimes, including theft, punishable by death. Common citizens could be found guilty of treason for plotting the death of the king, servants for plotting the death of their master, and women for plotting the death of their husband. Execution was a frequent punishment for such "treason," with the "traitors" sometimes disemboweled or dismembered before they were killed.

Justice was severe during this period, but it was also *arbitrary*, as different judges would hand out very different punishments for similar crimes. This occurred for at least two reasons (Cullen and Agnew 2011). First, many laws were very vague, and various judges interpreted these laws differently. Second, some judges took bribes to mete out weaker punishments, or even none at all. People who could not afford these bribes were thus punished more severely.

The Classical School of Criminology

Against this frightening backdrop of torture and arbitrary justice, Italian economist and political philosopher Cesare Beccaria (1738–1794) wrote a small, path-breaking book on crime, *Dei Delitti e Delle Pene (On Crimes and Punishments)*, in 1764 (Beccaria 1819 (1764)). Essentially a plea for justice, Beccaria's treatise helped found what is now called the classical school of criminology, also called *utilitarianism* (see Table 5–1). Beccaria was appalled by the horrible conditions in the European criminal justice system at that time. Like other Enlightenment thinkers, he believed that criminals and noncriminals alike act rationally and with free will, calculating whether their behavior will cause them more pleasure or more pain. Influenced by Hobbes, Beccaria also believed that the state needed to ensure that people's natural impulses would stay controlled.

For this to happen, he wrote, the criminal justice system needed to perform effectively and efficiently. But because people think and act rationally, they will be deterred by a certain degree of punishment, and harsher punishment beyond that is not needed. The criminal justice system thus needed only to be punitive enough to deter people from committing crime, and not more punitive than this level. This reasoning led Beccaria to condemn torture and other treatment of criminals as being much crueler than this more humane standard. He also opposed executions for most crimes and believed that judges should ordinarily hand out similar punishments for similar crimes.

As should be clear, Beccaria believed that the criminal justice system exists primarily to deter criminal behavior rather than to avenge the harm that criminals do. He thought that legal punishment is most effective in deterring crime if it is *certain* and *swift*. The criminal justice system thus needs to be efficient in two respects. It needs to ensure that criminals believe they have a strong chance of being arrested and punished, and it needs to ensure that any arrest and punishment happen quickly. In focusing on certainty and swiftness, Beccaria explicitly minimized the importance of the severity of punishment, which he thought far less important than the certainty of punishment for deterring crime. As he put it, "The certainty of a small punishment will make a stronger impression, than the fear of one more severe, if attended with the hopes of escaping" (Beccaria 2006(1764):25).

▼

TABLE 5–1 Classical and Neoclassical Theories in Brief

THEORY	KEY FIGURE(S)	SYNOPSIS
Classical Theory (Utilitarianism)		
	Cesare Beccaria Jeremy Bentham	People act with free will and calculate whether their behavior will cause them more pleasure or more pain. Legal punishment needs to be severe enough only to deter individuals from committing crime, and not beyond that.
Neoclassical Theories		
Rational Choice Theory	Gary Becker Derek B. Cornish Ronald V. Clarke	Offenders commit crime because of the benefits it brings them. In deciding whether to commit crime, they weigh whether the potential benefits exceed the potential costs. Because offenders do not always have the time or ability to gather and analyze all relevant information relevant for their decision, their decision making is sometimes imperfect.
Deterrence Theory	—	Potential and actual legal punishment can deter crime. General deterrence refers to the deterrence of potential offenders because they fear arrest and/or punishment; specific deterrence refers to the deterrence of convicted offenders because they do not want to experience arrest and/or punishment once again.
Routine Activities Theory	Lawrence E. Cohen Marcus Felson	Crime and victimization are more likely when three factors are simultaneously present: (1) motivated offenders, (2) attractive targets, and (3) an absence of guardianship. Crime trends can be explained by changes in levels of attractive targets and of guardianship.

Beccaria is widely regarded as the father of modern criminology, and his treatise is credited with leading to many reforms in the prisons and criminal courts (Cullen and Agnew 2011). However, some critics claim that this credit is at least partly undeserved (Newman and Marongiu 1994). They note that, although Beccaria has been lauded for opposing torture and the death penalty, his treatise actually contains many ambiguous passages about these punishments. Moreover, the criminal justice reforms with which he has been credited were actually already being implemented before he wrote his treatise. Yet even these critics concede that Beccaria's views greatly influenced legal systems in Europe and affected the thinking of John Adams, Benjamin Franklin, Thomas Jefferson, and the writers of the U.S. Constitution. And it is certainly true that Beccaria's classical belief that "offenders are rational individuals who choose to engage in crime" forms "the foundation of our legal system" today (Cullen and Agnew 2011:23).

The other great figure of the classical school was English philosopher Jeremy Bentham (1748–1832). Like Beccaria, Bentham felt that people weigh whether their behavior is more apt to cause them pleasure or pain and that the law was far more severe than it needed to be to deter such rational individuals from behaving criminally. His writings inspired changes in the English criminal law in the early 1800s and helped shape the development of the first modern police force in London in 1829. They also influenced the creation of the modern prison. Before the time of Bentham, Beccaria, and other legal reformers, long-term incarceration did not exist; jails were intended only for short-term stays for suspects awaiting trial, torture, or execution. The development of the prison in the early 1800s thus represented a major change in the punishment of criminals.

Although the classical school of criminology led to important reforms in the criminal justice system throughout Europe, critics then and now have said that its view of human behavior was too simplistic. Even though individuals sometimes weigh the costs and benefits of their actions, other times they act emotionally. Also, although people often do act to maximize pleasure and to reduce pain, they do not always agree on what is pleasurable. Classical reformers also assumed that the legal system treated all people the same and overlooked the possibility that race or ethnicity, social class, and gender might make a difference.

▼ Jeremy Bentham was one of the founders of the classical school of criminology; he felt that the severity of legal punishment should be limited to what was necessary to deter crime.

Review and Discuss
How were criminals treated during the Age of Reason? How may the classical school of criminology be considered a reaction to this treatment?

The Rise of Positivism

Notice that we have said nothing about the classical school's views on the causes of crime, other than its belief that some people choose to commit crime when they decide as rational actors that the benefits outweigh the risks. Beccaria did acknowledge that a crime like theft results from "misery and despair" among people who are living "but a bare existence." This implied that poor people may reach a different decision than wealthier people in considering the potential risks and rewards of committing theft, and thus that poverty is a cause of this type of crime, but Beccaria did not develop this implication in his book. As Cullen and Agnew (2011:23) note, then, the explanation of crime beyond the rational calculation of its risks and rewards does "not form a central part of classical theory."

As this observation suggests, classical scholars largely failed to consider that forces both outside and inside individuals might affect their likelihood of breaking the law. This view was the central insight of a new way of thinking, positivism, which came to dominate the nineteenth century and derived from the great discoveries in the physical sciences of Galileo, Newton, and others. These discoveries indicated to social philosophers the potential of using science to understand not only the physical world but also the social world.

French social philosopher Auguste Comte (1798–1857) founded the positive school of philosophy with the publication of his six-volume *Cours de Philosophie Positive (Course in Positive Philosophy)* between 1830 and 1842. Comte argued that forces beyond an individual's control determine human behavior. Biologists and psychologists generally locate these forces inside the individual, whereas sociologists find them outside the individual. Research in biology, psychology, and sociology that attempts to explain what causes crime is all positivist in its orientation, even though these disciplines' perspectives differ in many other ways.

▼ Charles Darwin's theory of evolution established the credibility of science for understanding human behavior and helped usher in scientific explanations of criminal behavior.

Ralf Hettler/Getty Images

The rise of science as a mode of inquiry was cemented in 1859 with the publication of Charles Darwin's *Origin of Species*, in which he outlined his theory of evolution, and in 1871 with the publication of his book on human evolution, *Descent of Man*. The idea that science could explain the origin and development of the human species was revolutionary. It spawned great controversy at the time of Darwin's publications and is still attacked today by people who accept the biblical story of creation. However, Darwin's theory eventually dominated the study of evolution and also established the credibility of science for understanding human behavior and other social and physical phenomena.

Since the time of Comte and Darwin, positivism has guided the study of crime and other human behaviors. Although positivist research has greatly increased our understanding of the origins of crime, critics charge it with several shortcomings (Bernard et al. 2009). First, positivism accepts the state's definition of crime by ignoring the possibility that society's ruling groups define what is criminal. Positivism thus accepts the legitimacy of a social system that may contain serious injustices. Second, in arguing that external and internal forces affect individual criminal behavior, positivism sometimes paints an overly deterministic model of human behavior that denies free will altogether. Third, positivism assumes that criminals are different from the rest of us not only in their behavior, but also in the biological, psychological, and social factors determining their behavior. Noncriminals are thus normal, and criminals are abnormal and even inferior. As self-report studies indicate, however, the line between criminals and noncriminals might be very thin, with "noncriminals" very capable of breaking the law. Despite these criticisms, positivism remains the dominant approach in criminology. This is true for virtually all biologists and psychologists who study crime, but also true, despite notable exceptions, for most sociologists.

▶ Neoclassical Perspectives

We now turn to neoclassical explanations of crime. They are called *neoclassical* because they all ultimately rest on the classical view that criminals are rational individuals who choose to commit crime after calculating the potential risks and rewards of doing so. The three neoclassical explanations we discuss all share this fundamental assumption, even if they differ in other respects. They should thus be viewed as "close cousins" with certain different emphases that ultimately all manifest the classical view just described. As such, they are often said to have revived classical theory.

Rational Choice Theory

Contemporary rational choice theory assumes that potential offenders choose whether to commit crime after carefully calculating the possible rewards and risks. An individual commits crime after deciding that the rewards outweigh the risks but does not commit crime after deciding that the risks outweigh the rewards.

Although the roots of rational choice theory lie in the classical school, its modern inspiration comes from economic models of rational decision making and more generally from a growing emphasis in sociology and other fields on the rationality of human behavior (Ritzer and Stepinsky 2014). In criminology, the introduction of rational choice theory is widely credited to a very influential journal article published more than four decades ago by Gary S. Becker (1968), a famed economist at the University of Chicago. Becker wrote that choosing whether to commit crime is akin to choosing whether to buy almost any product that consumers purchase. Following what is now termed Becker's *expected utility model*, if individuals decide that the expected utility, or monetary value, of committing a crime exceeds the expected utility of not committing a crime, they decide as rational actors to commit it. Conversely, if they decide that the expected utility of not committing a crime exceeds the expected utility of committing it, they decide not to commit it. In making these decisions, potential offenders consider several factors, including (1) their possible opportunities for earning money from legitimate occupations, (2) the amount of legitimate money they might earn, (3) the amount of money they might gain from committing crime, (4) the possibility of being arrested for committing crime, and (5) the possibility of being punished if arrested.

In addition to considering all these factors, people committing crime resemble consumers in at least one other respect, added Becker. Consumers use whatever information they have to decide how to spend their money. Sometimes they make good decisions, and sometimes they make bad decisions, but whatever decisions they do make are based on a calculation of the relative benefits and costs of the decision. Criminals are no different. They decide whether to commit crime based on whatever information they have; sometimes they make good decisions from their perspective (i.e., they commit a financially beneficial crime and get away with it), and sometimes they make bad decisions (i.e., they get caught).

In likening decisions to commit crime to decisions to purchase a product, Becker explicitly stated that sociological concepts like anomie and differential association (see Chapter 1) are *unimportant* for these decisions. As two scholars have summarized Becker's view on this issue, "As an economic purist, he asserts provocatively that there is little reason for theorizing that treats offenders as if they have a special character that leads them to crime. Becker extends his logic to conclude that the most prominent theories of motivation in criminology are not needed; basic economics addresses their problem sufficiently. Criminal offenders are normal, reasoning economic actors responding to market forces" (Hochstetler and Bouffard 2010:20–21).

Becker's expected utility model was initially popular but also controversial. Subsequent development of rational choice theory retained Becker's emphasis on the overall rationality of crime, but did not try to reduce

▼ Contemporary rational choice theory assumes that potential offenders take into account other possible benefits of crime beyond monetary gain, including fun, excitement, and prestige.

© jedi-master/Fotolia

decisions to commit crime to a simple matter of economics. Still, most work using a rational choice perspective takes motivation to commit crime as a "given": it assumes there will always be people motivated to commit crime and that no special explanation is needed of why some people are more motivated than others to do so. This assumption leads rational choice studies to examine how individuals reach decisions to commit crime and the circumstances that affect their decision making, rather than on why they are motivated to commit crime at all. In doing so, these studies focus on decisions to commit a particular crime at a particular time and in a particular place (*event decisions*), not on decisions to commit crime in the first place (*involvement decisions*). Sociological explanations may help understand the latter decisions, many rational choice theorists acknowledge, but rational choice explanations are needed to help understand decisions to commit a specific crime under specific circumstances.

This approach was developed and popularized by two very influential theorists in contemporary rational choice theory, Derek B. Cornish and Ronald V. Clarke (Clarke and Cornish 1985; Clarke and Cornish 2001; Cornish and Clarke 1986). As these authors note, criminology had previously neglected the actual decision-making processes of criminals. In contrast, their rational choice perspective focuses specifically on these processes, as it assumes that offenders choose to commit crime because it brings them benefits. Given this assumption, their rational choice perspective "explains the conditions needed for specific crimes to occur, not just why people become involved in crime. It makes little distinction between offenders and nonoffenders and emphasizes the role of crime opportunities in causation" (Clarke and Cornish 2001:23).

In addition to these elements, Cornish and Clarke emphasized that potential offenders take into account other possible benefits of crime beyond monetary gain, including fun, excitement, and prestige. They also emphasized that offenders do not always have the time or ability to gather all information relevant to their decision, and neither do they always have the time and ability to analyze this information completely and accurately. To this extent, criminal offenders are acting with *limited* or *bounded* rationality, as their decision making is often imperfect. Nonetheless, offenders still make decisions that appear rational to them at the time they make them.

Like other rational choice theorists, Cornish and Clarke (2001) focus on event decisions, mentioned just earlier. Event decisions have at least five stages: (1) preparing to commit a crime, (2) selecting a target, (3) committing the crime, (4) escaping, and (5) aftermath of the crime. Involvement decisions have three stages: (1) committing crime for the first time (*initiation*), (2) continuing to commit crime (*habituation*), and (3) ceasing to commit crime (*desistance*). For a comprehensive understanding of crime, the factors affecting all these decisions must be fully understood.

In explaining these decisions, the rational choice perspective emphasizes two related concepts: (1) *situational factors* (aspects of the immediate physical setting, such as street lighting and the presence or absence of surveillance cameras) and (2) the *opportunities* that exist, or fail to exist, for an offender to commit crime without fear of arrest or other negative consequences. According to Cornish and Clarke, this emphasis in turn leads the rational choice perspective to regard criminals as not very different from noncriminals, as it argues that even normally law-abiding people may turn to crime if the need and temptation are great enough and if the opportunity presents itself.

Evaluating Rational Choice Theory

Rational choice theory has made major contributions to the understanding of criminal behavior by focusing on offenders' decision making. Studies of active (i.e., not incarcerated) robbers, burglars, and other offenders find that they do indeed often plan their crimes by taking into account their chances of being caught and also their chances of being put in danger by victims who resist the crime (McCarthy and Hagan 2005). Burglars make sure no one is home before they break into a house, and robbers make sure that no police or bystanders are around before they hold someone up (Bernasco and Block 2009). White-collar criminals in the world of corporations seem to plan their crimes very carefully (Piquero et al. 2005). In all these ways, offenders act rationally and proceed only if they perceive that the potential benefits outweigh the potential risks, just as rational choice theory assumes.

The focus of rational choice theory on the criminal event, and especially on the situational factors and opportunities that affect decisions to commit crime, has made a major contribution. It reminds us that criminals do make choices, that criminal behavior is more likely if opportunities for it exist, and that these opportunities must be addressed for crime to be reduced. This focus underlies the work on situational crime prevention that is discussed later in this chapter.

▼

Despite these contributions, rational choice theory has been criticized for exaggerating the rationality of criminal offenders, who often do not think or act as deliberately as rational choice theory implies. Evidence of this problem comes from the studies of active burglars and robbers just mentioned (Shover and Copes 2010). Although, as was noted, many offenders plan their crimes to some degree and try to ensure that they do not get caught, many other offenders actually give very little thought, if any, to this prospect. As one scholar put it, they "simply do not think about the possible legal consequences of their criminal actions before committing crimes" (Tunnell 1990:680). Some offenders also have a fatalistic attitude and go ahead and commit a crime even if they think they might be arrested (Tunnell 1996). Research on offenders and prisoners also indicates that one-third to one-half all offenders were under the influence of alcohol and/or drugs at the time of their offense (Mumola and Karberg 2006; Rand et al. 2010), making it difficult or impossible to think carefully about the possible consequences of their actions. Further, many crimes are obviously violent crimes, and these crimes often tend to be very emotional in nature. People committing them act from strong emotions, such as anger and jealousy, and thus are not able to carefully consider the consequences of their actions as they strike out against someone. For all these reasons, many offenders do not act in the rather careful, deliberate manner that rational choice theory assumes.

Deterrence Theory

Because rational choice theory assumes that criminals weigh the risks of their actions, it implies they can be deterred from committing crime if the potential risks seem too certain or too severe. To turn that around, theoretical belief in the law's deterrent impact is based on a rational choice view of potential criminals. As two scholars have observed, "What makes deterrence work is that human beings are both rational and self-interested beings. Persons make rational assessments of the expected costs and benefits of making numerous decisions—buying a house or car, changing jobs, committing a crime—and choose the line of behavior that is most beneficial (profitable) and least costly" (Paternoster and Bachman 2001:14). For obvious reasons, then, rational choice theory is closely aligned with deterrence theory, which assumes that potential and actual legal punishment can deter crime. In fact, the two theories are often considered synonymous (Matsueda et al. 2006). Their assumptions underlie the "get tough" approach, involving harsher punishment and more prisons, that the United States has used since the 1970s to fight crime.

Types of Deterrence

In addressing the deterrent effect of the law, scholars distinguish several types of deterrence. A first distinction is between absolute deterrence and marginal deterrence. Absolute deterrence refers to the effect of having some legal punishment (arrest, incarceration, and so forth) versus the effect of having no legal punishment. The law certainly has a very strong absolute deterrent effect; if the criminal justice system did not exist, crime would be much higher, or so most scholars believe. In the real world, of course, we usually do not have to worry about the criminal justice system disappearing short of a natural or human disaster. Thus, questions of deterrence are actually questions of marginal deterrence, which refers to the effect of increasing the severity, certainty, and/or swiftness of legal punishment.

A second distinction is between general and specific deterrence. *General deterrence* occurs when members of the public decide not to break the law because they fear legal punishment. To take a traffic example, we may obey the speed limit because we do not want to get a speeding ticket. Specific deterrence (also called *individual deterrence*) occurs when offenders *already punished* for lawbreaking decide not to commit *another* crime because they do not want to face legal consequences again. Remaining with our traffic example, if we have already received a speeding ticket or two and are close to losing our license, we may obey the speed limit because we do not want to suffer further consequences.

A final distinction is between objective and subjective deterrence. Objective deterrence refers to the impact of *actual* legal punishment, whereas subjective deterrence refers to the impact of people's *perceptions* of the certainty and severity of legal punishment. Deterrence theory predicts that people are deterred from crime by actual legal punishment that is certain and severe and also by their own perceptions that legal punishment will be certain and severe.

Taking a Closer Look at Deterrence

In considering how much marginal deterrent impact the criminal law might have, it is important to keep in mind several factors affecting the size of any impact that can be expected.

A first consideration concerns the *type of criminal offense*. Simply put, some types of crime might be more deterrable than other types of crime. A well-known distinction here is between instrumental offenses, those committed for material gain with some degree of planning, and expressive offenses, those committed for emotional reasons and with little or no planning. William Chambliss (1967), who popularized this distinction, thought that instrumental crimes are more deterrable than expressive crimes because they are relatively unemotional and planned. Because the people committing expressive crimes are by definition acting emotionally, they often do not take the time to think about the legal consequences of their actions. All things equal, then, marginal deterrence should be higher for instrumental crimes than for expressive crimes, and it might in fact be very low for these latter offenses.

A second consideration, according to Chambliss (1967), is whether offenders have high or low commitment to criminal behavior. Professional criminals such as "cat burglars" are very skilled and also very committed to their way of life; drug addicts are also very committed, because of their addiction, to using illegal drugs. In contrast, amateur criminals such as teenagers who take a car on a joy ride are less committed to criminal behavior. Chambliss said that offenders with higher commitment to their crime are less likely to be deterred by legal punishment.

A final consideration is whether a crime tends to occur in public, such as robbery, or in private, such as domestic violence and some illegal drug use. Public crimes, precisely because they are public and thus potentially more noticeable, are more deterrable by legal punishment, all things equal, than private crimes.

Putting all these considerations together, expressive crimes are less deterrable than instrumental crimes; high-commitment offenders are less deterrable than low-commitment offenders; and private crimes are less deterrable than private crimes. Efforts that try to increase marginal deterrence by making arrest more certain and/or by making punishment harsher are thus likely to have only a relatively small deterrent effect on expressive crimes, on crimes involving high-commitment offenders, and on private offenses. These relatively undeterrable crimes involve many violent and property offenses.

This pessimistic appraisal of the expected size of any marginal deterrent effect becomes even more pessimistic when we recall the studies of active burglars and robbers, discussed earlier, that focus on their decision making. Although these individuals are committing instrumental offenses, recall that many of them do not really think about their chances of getting caught. Others do think about their chances of getting caught but plan their crimes so that they will not be arrested. Still others have a fatalistic attitude and commit a crime with the expectation of being arrested. All these offenders are relatively undeterrable by legal punishment. Also recall that up to half of all offenders are on drugs and/or alcohol at the time of their offense; they, too, are undeterrable by legal punishment. Many offenders, then, do not think or act in the way they must think or act for marginal deterrence to have a relatively large impact (Shover and Copes 2010).

Additional considerations add even further to this pessimistic appraisal (Walker 2011). First, arrest and imprisonment have become so common in the United States, especially among young males in large cities, that scholars think these legal sanctions have lost the stigma they used to have (Hirschfield 2008). Rather, these sanctions have become an expectation, and, if this is true, not a deterrent. Second, arrest and imprisonment may increase the feelings of masculinity of urban youths: they become more "macho" and are more likely to reoffend for that reason (Rios 2009). Third, increased penalties and other deterrence-oriented criminal justice policies are not always implemented as legislators might have expected. For example, prosecutors might not charge an offender with the maximum charge because of prison overcrowding. If these deterrent policies are not fully implemented, then their deterrent impact cannot be expected to be very high.

Fourth, the chances of arrest and imprisonment are so low that it would be surprising if legal sanctions did have a high deterrent impact. Recall from Chapter 3 that victims of violent and property crime report only about 40 percent of their victimizations to the police, and that police make an arrest in only about one-fifth percent of the crimes known to them. Putting these figures together yields a rough arrest rate of only 8 percent for all violent and property crime. Less than one-fifth of these arrests result in a felony conviction and imprisonment, resulting in a risk of imprisonment of less than 2 percent of all violent and property crime. On TV crime shows, the

International Focus MANDATORY PENALTIES IN INTERNATIONAL PERSPECTIVE

A hallmark of the "get tough" approach that has guided U.S. criminal justice policy since the 1970s is the use of mandatory penalties. These include additional prison time for crimes involving the use of guns; long, automatic prison terms for drug crimes and violent crimes; and additional prison time for repeat offenders. These penalties have been intended to deter potential criminal offenders and simply to keep those already convicted locked up for longer durations.

Despite these goals, a large body of research has found that mandatory penalties have had only a small impact, and probably no impact, on the crime rate. This small or nil impact partly reflects the several reasons discussed in the text for why the general deterrent impact of law is usually low or nonexistent. In addition to these reasons, mandatory penalties are not consistently applied. Recognizing that the prison system is already overcrowded, prosecutors often avoid mandatory penalties by charging defendants with lesser crimes. They also reduce the charges because defendants facing long, automatic prison terms have little incentive to forgo jury trials, which are long and expensive. As Samuel Walker (2011:163) notes, "An increase in the severity of the potential punishment creates pressure to avoid its actual application."

The conclusion that mandatory penalties in the United States do not work as intended would be reinforced if it were also found in other nations. However, no other Western nation has enacted mandatory penalties to the extent found in the United States. A few nations do have these penalties to some degree, including Australia, Canada, England and Wales, and South Africa. The effects of mandatory penalties in these nations have been studied, and these studies find that prosecutors and judges find ways to circumvent the harsh penalties. They also find that harsher penalties, including mandatory penalties, do not reduce crime.

For example, the Sentencing Advisory Council in Australia's state of Victoria concluded, "Ultimately, current research in this area indicates that there is a very low likelihood that a mandatory sentencing regime will deliver on its [deterrent] aims." The Canadian Sentencing Commission similarly observed, "Evidence does not support the notion that variations in sanctions . . . affect the deterrent value of sentences. In other words, deterrence cannot be used with empirical justification, to guide the imposition of sentences." The National Research Institute of Policy in Finland concluded, "Can our long prison sentences be defended on the basis of a cost/benefit assessment of their general preventative effect? The answer of the criminological expertise was no."

These international assessments on mandatory penalties and general deterrence reinforce the conclusion from U.S. research that mandatory penalties and other harsher punishments have little or no general deterrent effect. This body of research in the United States and elsewhere leads deterrence expert Michael Tonry (2009:65) to observe, "There is no credible evidence that the enactment or implementation of such sentences has significant deterrent effects."

Sources: Tonry 2009; Walker 2011.

"perp" usually gets what is coming to him, but in the real world of crime, the perp actually has an incredibly low risk of arrest and punishment. This risk is so low that a strong deterrent effect of the law cannot be expected.

Research on Deterrence

All these considerations suggest that the size of the marginal deterrent effect of legal punishment is likely to be relatively small. Research on deterrence generally confirms this pessimistic expectation (Apel and Nagin 2011). Most research has focused on the certainty of punishment (the likelihood of being arrested) and on the severity of punishment (whether someone is incarcerated and, if so, for how long).

Early research found that states with high certainty rates, measured as the number of arrests divided by the number of known crimes, had lower crime rates, as deterrence theory would predict. Some early studies also found that states with more severe punishment again had lower crime rates (Gibbs 1968; Tittle 1969). Although these findings indicated a marginal deterrent effect, some scholars challenged this interpretation and instead argued that crime rates affect certainty and severity (Decker and Kohfeld 1985; Pontell 1984). In this way of thinking, called the system capacity argument, areas with high crime rates have lower arrest rates for two reasons: their police are "extra" busy, and their police also realize that too many arrests would overburden

▼

the criminal justice system. For these reasons, areas with high crime rates end up with low certainty rates. Similarly, areas with high crime rates also have lower severity of punishment because their prisons are too full to handle their many offenders. Prosecutors and judges both realize this, and prosecutors seek reduced charges and judges impose shorter sentences.

More recent research on deterrence has been much more methodologically sophisticated than the early research, and Chapters 16 and 17 discuss it in further detail. Suffice it to say here that the recent evidence generally finds that arrest and punishment (or, to be more precise, increases in the probability of being arrested and more severely punished) have only a weak general or specific deterrent effect on crime and delinquency, and perhaps no effect at all (Apel and Nagin 2011). A recent review concluded that "there is little credible evidence that changes in sanctions affect crime rates" (Tonry 2008:279). To the extent that a deterrent effect does exist, it exists more for the certainty of punishment than for the severity of punishment.

Various kinds of evidence suggest that the severity of punishment especially has little or no deterrent effect. For example, although deterrence theory predicts that higher imprisonment rates should produce lower crime rates, this pattern often does not occur: sometimes crime rates decline when imprisonment rates rise, as deterrence theory would predict, but sometimes crime rates decline only slightly, do not change at all, or even increase. During the late 1980s, U.S. imprisonment rates rose, but so did crime rates. Although crime rates finally declined after the early 1990s as imprisonment rates continued to rise, crime declined less in states with the greatest increase in imprisonment rates than in states with lower increases in imprisonment rates. Also, deterrence theory predicts that when penalties for certain crimes are made harsher, the rates of these crimes should decline, but once again this often does not happen (Walker 2011).

What about specific deterrence? Although it seems obvious that offenders who are arrested and imprisoned should reoffend less because of their punishment, evidence of this specific deterrent effect is mixed at best. There is even evidence of an opposite effect: that punishment *increases* the chances that offenders will break the law again (Bales and Piquero 2012; Listwan et al. 2013). A recent review of the literature on this issue concluded that "most studies of the impact of

 Crime and Controversy THREE STRIKES LAWS STRIKE OUT

Beginning in the 1990s, several states enacted so-called "three strikes" laws in an effort to reduce the crime rate. These laws required life imprisonment or, at the least, a very long prison sentence for offenders convicted of their second or third felony. A major reason given for these laws was that they would send a message to potential offenders and thus deter them from committing their third felony, and perhaps even their first or second felony.

The introduction of these laws provided criminologists an opportunity to test their deterrent impact. Drawing on deterrence theory, they gathered and analyzed various kinds of data to test the hypothesis that three strikes laws would reduce the street crime rate.

A central conclusion that emerges from this body of research is that the three strikes laws had no discernible deterrent effect on criminal behavior. During the 1990s, violent crime dropped throughout the nation, but it dropped at a greater rate in states that did *not* enact three strikes laws than in states that did enact them. Moreover, studies of specific states that enacted three strikes laws found that crime

did not fall at a greater rate in those states after the laws came into effect. Some studies even find that homicides *increased* after three strikes laws were enacted, perhaps, because offenders who are committing their third (or fourth, etc.) felony do not want to risk life imprisonment and thus decide to kill their victim to make it more difficult to arrest and convict them.

If three strikes laws have not reduced crime, they have increased the number of prison inmates, especially those who are African-American, serving life sentences or very long terms. Many of these inmates will stay in prison long after they would have "aged out" of crime, imposing a considerable financial cost not only from the cost of keeping them in prison, but also from the geriatric medical care many of them need. Three strikes laws thus provide important evidence against deterrence theory, and they also illustrate the financial costs that the "get tough" policy since the 1970s has incurred.

Sources: Kovandzic et al. 2004; Marvell and Moody 2001; Sutton 2013; Walker 2011.

imprisonment on subsequent criminality find [either] no effect or a criminogenic effect" (Nagin et al. 2009:121). The authors added that this conclusion "casts doubt on claims that imprisonment has strong specific deterrent effects" (p. 115).

As suggested earlier, it should not be very surprising that deterrence research casts doubt on the size of general and specific deterrent effects. For deterrence to occur, criminals must calculate their behavior, as rational choice and deterrence theories assume they do. This assumption is critical for deterrence theory, because if criminals did not weigh the risks of their behavior, then the threat of arrest and punishment could not deter them. Yet, as we have seen, studies of active offenders do not provide much support for this assumption (Shover and Copes 2010). Although some crimes, such as corporate crime, involve careful planning and weighing of all risks, many other crimes typically do not involve such efforts, and many "street crime" offenders do not think and act in the ways that rational choice and deterrence theories assume. Most criminals are smart enough to avoid committing a crime in front of a police station or elsewhere where they might be detected, but in other places many apparently do not worry about being arrested and punished. For this reason, increases in the penalties for crimes do not seem to deter them.

Some research also documents the deterrent effect of internal punishment (e.g., guilt, shame, embarrassment, and conscience) and of informal sanctions such as the disapproval of friends and loved ones (Nagin and Pogarsky 2001). However, such evidence says nothing about the deterrent effect of *legal* punishment (Akers and Sellers 2013).

In sum, deterrence research suggests that the general and specific deterrent effects of legal sanctions are small or nonexistent. Certain policing strategies do seem to deter some types of crime (see Chapter 16), but strategies involving harsher punishment generally do not seem to deter crime. Although deterrence theory might sound appealing at first glance, then, deterrence is more of a dream than a reality in the real world of crime.

bikeriderlondon/Shutterstock

▲ Increases in penalties for crime do not seem to deter criminals, who do not act in the ways that rational choice and deterrence theories assume.

Routine Activities Theory

A third and very influential neoclassical perspective is routine activities theory (also called *routine activity theory*). This theory was introduced in Chapter 4 as an explanation of criminal victimization patterns. To briefly recall that discussion, routine activities theory assumes that crime is more likely when three factors are simultaneously present: (1) motivated offenders, (2) attractive targets, and (3) an absence of guardianship (such as police, bystanders, and even a dog). Because the theory also assumes that offenders are more likely to decide to commit crime when they have attractive targets and when there are no guardians, it reflects rational choice assumptions of criminal decision making and is considered a neoclassical theory.

Routine activities theory was introduced in 1979 by Lawrence E. Cohen and Marcus Felson (1979) and elaborated in later writings. Cohen and Felson wrote that for crime to happen, offenders, targets, and the absence of guardians must all converge at the same time and in the same location. Because routine activities of everyday life affect the likelihood of this convergence, when people's routine activities change, crime rates change as well. Like rational choice theory, routine activities theory further assumes there will always be a supply of motivated offenders, and it does not try to explain why some people are more motivated than others to commit crime, nor why motivation to commit crime might change as other social changes occur. The theory instead focuses on changes in the supply of attractive targets and in the presence or absence of guardianship as key variables affecting changes in crime rates. Because these variables affect the opportunity for offenders to commit crime, or what Cohen and Felson (1979:592) call the "criminal opportunity structure," routine activities theory is often considered an *opportunity theory* of crime.

Cohen and Felson reasoned that routine activities inside or near one's home result in less victimization than activities that occur away from home. When people are at home, they are safer from burglary, because they provide guardianship for their home, and they are also safer from robbery and other predatory crimes, because they are not out in public providing attractive targets for motivated offenders. Cohen and Felson also reasoned that as smaller and more expensive consumer items go on the market, people are more likely to have these items in their homes or on their persons when away from home, making them attractive targets for offenders. The authors then used these two sets of reasoning to help understand two important trends in crime and victimization: (1) differences in criminal victimization rates for various categories of people, such as young versus old; and (2) why U.S. crime rates increased during the 1960s even though poverty and unemployment fell and median income and education levels rose during that decade.

For example, they hypothesized that young people should have higher victimization rates than older people because they spend so much more time away from home, and that is exactly what data from national victimization surveys find (see Chapter 4). They also hypothesized that single-person households should suffer higher burglary rates than multiple-person households because they are have less guardianship (i.e., they are more likely to be empty at any one time or to have fewer people at home when someone is there), and that is also what victimization data find.

Turning to the 1960s crime rate increase, Cohen and Felson argued that this increase resulted from the simultaneous increase in suitable targets and decrease of guardianship during that decade. Regarding guardianship, for example, many more women began working outside the home during the 1960s, and many more residences were occupied by only one person. These two facts meant that many more homes began to be empty most of the day as people went to work. Not surprisingly, burglary rates increased dramatically during the 1960s. Regarding target availability, Cohen and Felson found that the sales of consumer goods increased greatly during the 1960s, as did the sale of smaller and more valuable goods (i.e., smaller televisions). These trends provided "more suitable property available for theft" (p. 599), and more such theft occurred.

Cohen and Felson concluded that that crime results in part from the activities that so many people ordinarily enjoy. As they put it, "It is ironic that the very factors which increase the opportunity to enjoy the benefits of life also may increase the opportunity for predatory violations. For example, automobiles provide freedom of movement to offenders as well as average citizens and offer vulnerable targets for theft. . . . Rather than assuming that predatory crime is simply an indicator of social breakdown, one might take it as a by product of freedom and prosperity as they manifest themselves in the routine activities of everyday life" (p. 605).

Evaluating Routine Activities Theory

In the more than three decades since its introduction, routine activities theory has proven very popular and has stimulated much research (Akers and Sellers 2013). It is popular because it seems to explain important aspects of differences in crime rates among different categories of people and among different locations, and because it also seems to explain important aspects of changes in crime rates over time.

For example, crime is ordinarily higher during the summer than other times of the year (see Chapter 3). Routine activities theory provides an explanation for this trend. Homes are more likely to be empty during the summer as people travel, and homes' windows are more likely to be open. These two facts make homes more vulnerable to burglary during the summer. During the summer, people are also more likely to be out in public, increasing their vulnerability to crimes like robbery and assault. Routine activities theory also helps explain why rising unemployment is surprisingly associated with lower rates of crime: fewer people (the unemployed and their families) are away from home, resulting in fewer targets for robbers and other offenders, and more people stay at home, resulting in guardianship against potential burglary (D'Alessio et al. 2012). The theory also helps us understand why locations in cities with high numbers of bars and taverns have higher rates of robbery and assault (Pridemore and Grubesic 2013). People visiting these establishments are attractive targets because they tend to carry relatively large sums of money or credit/debit cards, and because they lack personal guardianship once they become inebriated. As routine activities theory would predict, the presence of these establishments contributes to higher rates of crime and victimization.

The popularity of routine activities theory has increased as various works have added to the original insights of Cohen and Felson. Certain studies have deepened understanding of the factors that contribute to target availability and the absence of guardianship (Reynald 2011). For example, adolescents with strong bonds to their parents reduce their target availability because they are more likely to stay home and not venture out to places where they might encounter motivated offenders (Schreck and Fisher 2004). Other work has extended the theoretical scope of routine activities theory. Although the theory was originally developed to explain victimization, some scholars have used it to explain offending. In their way of thinking, individuals' routine activities can make it more or less likely that they will have the opportunity to offend. When they do have this opportunity, they are more likely to commit crime. For example, adolescents who spend more time away from home and who are not involved in youth activities at school or elsewhere have more opportunity to get in trouble, and so they do (Osgood and Anderson 2004).

Routine activities theory has been criticized for ignoring the factors that motivate offenders to commit crime (Akers and Sellers 2013). In their original formulation, Cohen and Felson readily conceded this neglect but argued the importance of considering the factors on which they did focus: target suitability and the absence of guardianship.

Situational Crime Prevention

One of the major contributions of routine activities theory, along with rational choice theory, has been the stimulation of work on situational crime prevention, or efforts in specific locations that aim to "reduce exposure to motivated offenders, decrease target suitability, and increase capable guardianship" (Marcum 2010:54; Smith and Clarke 2012). These efforts try to reduce the opportunities for committing crime by accomplishing all three of these goals. Examples include installing or increasing lighting and camera surveillance on city streets or in public parks, and providing and installing better security systems for motor vehicles, commercial buildings, and homes. Another example is *hot-spot policing*, which involves intensive police patrol of high-crime areas (see Chapter 16) (Braga and Weisburd 2012).

One concern regarding these efforts is that crime might simply be displaced to other locations and to other victims. However, recent reviews conclude that displacement is not a problem (Johnson et al. 2012). Sometimes it does occur, but just as often the opposite consequence (*diffusion of benefits*) happens, in which crime is reduced in nearby locations. Moreover, when displacement does occur, the additional crime elsewhere is lower than the crime that was displaced, resulting in a lower crime rate overall.

▶ Conclusion

Classical and neoclassical perspectives all assume that individuals commit crime when they decide that the potential gains outweigh the potential costs. They ultimately attribute crime to the choices offenders make about their own behavior, and they explicitly or implicitly state that increasing the risk of legal punishment should reduce crime. Crime policies based on these views aim to affect offending decisions by making punishment more certain and more severe.

However, the decision making of potential criminals often does not follow the rational choice model. With the exception of certain situational crime prevention measures, increasing the certainty and severity of punishment thus does not hold great promise for reducing crime. Moreover, the world of classical and neoclassical perspectives is largely devoid of social inequality. To the extent that inequality helps generate criminality, these perspectives ignore significant sources of crime. Despite these criticisms, neoclassical perspectives still provide an important understanding of crime from the offender's perspective, and they have stimulated contemporary efforts in situational crime prevention that show promise in reducing crime.

Neoclassical perspectives are important for at least one other reason. Their emphasis on the rationality of criminals, belief in the deterrent power of law, and lack of emphasis on the social causes of crime are all reflected in the "get tough" approach that has guided U.S. criminal justice policy since the 1970s. Among other changes, this approach has involved mandatory incarceration and longer prison terms, which most criminologists think do little to reduce crime and cause many other problems (see Chapter 17) (Clear 2010). Sound social policy must always be based on good theory,

▼ Situational crime prevention involves efforts in specific locations to reduce the opportunity for criminal behavior. Camera surveillance on city streets is an example of this type of crime prevention.

© florisvis/Fotolia

and the neoclassical perspectives are good theories in many ways. But the "get tough" approach is based on assumptions from these perspectives that do not stand up well upon closer inspection. Criminals often do not act as rationally as rational choice theory assumes, and deterrence does not work nearly as well as deterrence theory assumes. Moreover, the advocates of the "get tough" approach tend to minimize or deny the role played by poverty and other structural problems in criminal behavior. Cullen and Agnew (2006:460) say this denial "ignores the rather substantial body of research showing that inequality and concentrated disadvantage are related to street crime."

Summary

1. To reduce crime most effectively, we must first understand why crime occurs. Biological and psychological explanations place the causes of crime inside the individual, whereas sociological explanations place the causes of crime in the social environment. To reduce crime, biology and psychology thus suggest the need to correct problems inside the individual, whereas sociology suggests the need to correct problems in the social environment.

2. Historically, deviance and crime were first attributed to angry gods and fiendish demons. The Age of Reason eventually led to more scientific explanations, especially those grounded in positivism, which attributes behavior to forces inside and outside the individual. The classical school of criminology arose with the work of writers such as Beccaria and Bentham, who believed that because people act to maximize pleasure and reduce pain, the legal system need only be sufficiently harsh to deter potential criminals from breaking the law.

3. Classical and neoclassical perspectives assume that potential criminals calculate whether lawbreaking will bring them more reward than risk and that increases in the certainty and severity of punishment will thus decrease their likelihood of engaging in crime. However, research finds that most criminals are not as calculating as rational choice theory assumes and that harsher and more certain legal punishment generally has only a weak or inconsistent effect on crime rates, or no effect at all.

Key Terms

absolute deterrence *97*

certainty *99*

classical school *92*

deterrence theory *97*

Enlightenment *91*

expressive offenses *98*

general deterrence *97*

instrumental offenses *98*

marginal deterrence *97*

objective deterrence *97*

positivism *94*

rational choice theory *95*

routine activities theory *101*

severity *99*

situational crime prevention *103*

specific deterrence *97*

subjective deterrence *97*

system capacity argument *99*

What Would You Do?

1. You are a policy advisor to a member of your state legislature. The legislature will soon be voting on a bill that would double the maximum prison term for anyone convicted of armed robbery. Your boss knows that you took a criminology course and has even seen this book proudly displayed on a bookcase in your office. She knows that the bill is very popular with the public, but wonders if it will really do much good and asks you to write a policy recommendation for her to read. What will you recommend to her? What will be the reasons for your recommendation?

2. You are a policy adviser to the mayor of a medium-sized city. A recent spurt of nighttime robberies has alarmed the city's residents and prompted the police to suspend vacation leave until the offenders can be arrested. Based on what you have read in this chapter, what would you advise the mayor to do to reduce the robbery problem in the city?

© Image Source/Corbis

6 Biological and Psychological Explanations

Crime in the News

After two young men allegedly set off bombs at the April 2013 Boston Marathon that killed four people and wounded more than 200 others, a natural question was, "Why did they do it?" In the wake of the bombings, some observers speculated that one or both suspects had neurological deficiencies that helped lead to their deadly acts. They noted that children's brains may develop problems if their mothers smoke or drink during pregnancy, if the children are exposed to lead, or if they are abused. These and other problems hinder normal brain development, and the lack of normal brain functioning in turn makes violent and antisocial behavior more likely later in life. Perhaps the Boston bombing suspects' deadly acts arose at least in part from neurological abnormalities that began in early childhood. One of the suspects had a 3-year-old daughter, and some observers wondered whether the suspect might have had a genetic problem that was passed down to his daughter, putting her at risk for antisocial behavior as she grew older.

Sources: Raine 2013b; Shapiro 2013.

This news story reminds us that scientists have long been interested in the biological basis for violent behavior. Accordingly, this chapter examines biological and psychological explanations of criminal behavior. As Chapter 5 explained, these two sets of explanations attribute crime primarily to traits inside the individual, whereas sociological explanations attribute crime primarily to aspects of the social environment.

▶ Biological Explanations

As the previous chapter also noted, positivism arose during the nineteenth century as a result of great advances by Darwin and other scientists. When applied to crime, the positivist approach attempts to locate the forces inside and external to individuals that affect whether they will engage in criminal behavior. The first positivist research on crime was primarily biological (Rafter 2008). Biological explanations enjoy a renewed popularity today, as the news story that begins this chapter illustrates, but remain controversial because of their social policy implications. We will examine older and contemporary biological explanations and then review the controversy. These explanations are summarized in Table 6–1.

TABLE 6-1 Biological Explanations in Brief

THEORY	KEY FIGURE(S)	SYNOPSIS
Nineteenth-Century Views		
Phrenology	Franz Gall	A specific region of the brain governs criminal behavior. Because this region is largest in criminals, skull dimensions provide good evidence of criminal tendencies.
Atavism	Cesare Lombroso	Criminals are evolutionary accidents who resemble primitive people more than modern people.
Early Twentieth-Century Views		
Biological Inferiority	Earnest Hooton	Criminals are biologically inferior, and the primary cause of crime is biological inferiority. The government should sterilize or exile criminals.
Body Shapes (Somatology)	William Sheldon	Body shapes affect personalities and thus criminality. Endomorphs are heavy and relatively noncriminal; mesomorphs are muscular and prone to violence; and ectomorphs are thin and introverted.

(continued)

TABLE 6-1 Biological Explanations in Brief (continued)

THEORY	KEY FIGURE(S)	SYNOPSIS
Contemporary Explanations		
Heredity and Genetics	—	Criminality is inherited. A genetic tendency for criminal behavior is passed from parents to children.
Neurochemical Factors	—	High levels of testosterone contribute to male criminality; premenstrual syndrome contributes to female criminality. Low levels of serotonin contribute to violent behavior.
Diet and Nutrition	—	Among other nutritional problems, high levels of sugar and refined carbohydrates contribute to aggressive behavior.
Pregnancy and Birth Complications	—	Pregnancy and birth complications impair central nervous system functioning and thus produce antisocial behavior.
Early Puberty	—	Adolescents of either sex who experience early puberty are more likely to commit delinquent acts and engage in other antisocial behavior.

▶ Nineteenth-Century Views

Phrenology

One of earliest biological explanations of crime, phrenology, concerned the size and shape of the skull and was popular from the mid-1700s to the mid-1800s (Rafter 2008). An Austrian physician, Franz Gall (1758–1828), was its major proponent. Gall thought that three major regions of the brain govern three types of behavior and personality characteristics: intellectual, moral, and lower. The lower type was associated with criminal behavior and would be largest in criminals. Because phrenologists could not directly measure the three brain regions, they reasoned that the size and shape of the skull corresponded to the brain's size and shape. They thus thought that skull dimensions provided good evidence of criminal tendencies.

Phrenology was popular initially but never really caught on. We now know, of course, that the brain cannot be measured by measuring the skull. But perhaps the most important reason phrenology faded was that its biological determinism clashed with the Enlightenment emphasis on free will, still popular in the early 1800s. The determinism of positivism did not become widely accepted until decades later.

Cesare Lombroso: Atavism

Cesare Lombroso (1835–1909), an Italian physician, is generally considered the founder of the positivist school of criminology. Influenced by Darwin's work on evolution, Lombroso thought criminals were *atavists*, or throwbacks to an earlier stage of evolution, and said criminal behavior stemmed from atavism. In essence, criminals were evolutionary accidents who resembled primitive people more than modern (i.e., nineteenth-century) people. Lombroso's evidence for his theory came from his extensive measurements of the bodies of men in Italian prisons that he compared to his measurements of the bodies of Italian soldiers, his control group. He concluded that the prisoners looked more like primitive men than like modern men, because, among other measurements, their arms were abnormally long, their skulls and jaws abnormally large, and their bodies very hairy. Lombroso published his atavist theory in 1876 in his famous book, *L'Uomo Delinquent (The Criminal Man)* (Lombroso 1876).

Given the intense interest in evolution from Darwin's work, Lombroso's discovery attracted much attention and his atavist theory of crime became very popular. However, Lombroso's research was methodologically flawed (Bernard et al. 2009). Because the Italian criminal justice system then was hardly a fair one, many of the prisoners he measured probably had not actually committed crimes. His control group probably included people who had committed crimes without being imprisoned, as is still true today. Many differences he found between his prisoners and control group subjects were too small to be statistically significant. Lombroso may have also unconsciously measured his subjects in ways that fit his theory. Even if we assume for the sake of argument that his prisoners did look different, their imprisonment may have resulted more from reactions to their unusual appearance than from their criminality. Finally, some of the traits Lombroso described characterize Sicilians, who have long been at the bottom of Italy's socio-economic ladder. Lombroso's prisoners might have looked like atavists not because his theory made any sense, but because the traits he identified as atavistic happened to be ones belonging to Sicilians.

By the end of his career, Lombroso had modified his view of atavism. Although he continued to think the most serious criminals were atavists, he reasoned that this group comprised only about one-third of all offenders. The remainder were criminals who developed brain problems long after birth and occasional criminals whose behavior stemmed from problems in their social environment. Two of Lombroso's students, Raffaele Garofalo (1852–1934) and Enrico Ferri (1856–1929), carried on his views and made their own contributions to the development of criminology. Garofalo continued to emphasize biological bases for crime, while Ferri stressed that social conditions also play a role. Both scholars attacked the classical view of free will and crime and argued for a more positivist, determinist view of crime causation.

As the founder of modern positive criminology, Lombroso left a lasting legacy; his assumption that criminals are biologically different continues to guide today's biological research on crime. Not surprisingly, his atavist theory has long been discredited. In 1913, English psychiatrist Charles Goring (1870–1919) published his book *The English Convict*. Goring measured the body dimensions of 3,000 English prisoners and of the members of a large control group. He did not find the differences that Lombroso found and thus found no support for atavism. This latter conclusion prompted Lombroso's theory to fall out of favor.

Lombroso on Women

Chapter 3 noted that few criminologists studied women criminals until fairly recently. Lombroso was one of these few. That is the good news. The bad news is that his explanation of female criminality, reflecting the sexism of his time, rested on antiquated notions of women's biology and physiology. Lombroso published *The Female Offender* in 1895. In it he wrote that women were more likely than men to be atavists and that "even the female criminal is monotonous and uniform compared with her male companion, just as in general woman is inferior to man" (Lombroso 1920 (1903)). He also thought that women "have many traits in common with children," that their "moral sense is deficient," and that "they are revengeful, jealous."

In view of these terrible qualities, how did Lombroso explain why women commit so little crime? He reasoned that women were naturally passive and viewed their "defects (as) neutralized by piety, maternity, want of passion, sexual coldness, weakness and an undeveloped intelligence." A woman who managed to commit crime despite these crime-reducing traits must be, thought Lombroso, "a born criminal more terrible than any man," as her "wickedness must have been enormous before it could triumph over so many obstacles" (Lombroso 1920 (1903):150–152). Although most modern criminologists consider Lombroso's views hopelessly outdated, his emphasis on women's physiology and supposed biological nature remained influential in the study of women's crime for many years (Chesney-Lind and Jones 2010).

Early Twentieth-Century Views

Earnest Hooton: Biological Inferiority

After Goring's 1913 refutation of Lombroso's atavism theory, criminologists temporarily abandoned the idea that criminals were physiologically different. Then in 1939, Harvard University anthropologist Earnest Hooton (1887–1954) revived interest in physiological explanations with the publication of two books that reported the results of his measurement of 14,000 male prisoners and 3,200 control group subjects (Hooton 1939a, 1939b). Compared to the control group, prisoners tended to have, among other things, low foreheads, crooked noses, narrow jaws, small ears, long necks, and stooped shoulders. Not one to mince words, Hooton labeled criminals "organically inferior" and "low-grade human organisms" and concluded that the "primary cause of

▼

crime is biological inferiority. . . . The penitentiaries of our society are built upon the shifting sands and quaking bogs of inferior human organisms" (Hooton 1939b:130). He further concluded that criminals' body shapes influenced the types of crime they committed. Murderers tended to be tall and thin, for example, whereas rapists were short and heavy. Men with average builds did not specialize in any particular crime because they, like their physical shape, had no specific orientation.

Hooton's belief in the biological inferiority of criminals led him to urge the government to reduce crime by undertaking "the extirpation of the physically, mentally, and morally unfit, or . . . their complete segregation in a socially aseptic environment" (Hooton 1939a:309). Put more simply, Hooton was advocating that the government sterilize criminals or exile them to reservations (Rafter 2004).

His research suffered from the same methodological flaws as Lombroso's, including the assumptions that all of his prisoners had committed crimes and that all of his control group subjects had not committed crime. It is also doubtful that his control group adequately represented the general population, because a majority were either firefighters or members of the Massachusetts militia. Given their occupations, their physical fitness and size may well have differed from those of the population at large. Because of these and other weaknesses, Hooton's work did not become popular, especially with the onset of World War II and the "extirpation" of the millions of people whom the Nazis considered biologically inferior.

William Sheldon: Body Shapes

Although assumptions of biological inferiority grew less fashionable, interest in physiology and criminality continued. In 1949, William Sheldon (1898–1977) published a book that outlined his theory of somatology, which assumes that people's body shapes affect their personalities and hence the crimes they commit (Sheldon 1949). Sheldon identified three such body types, or *somatotypes* (see Figure 6–1 ■). *Endomorphs* are heavy, with short arms and legs; they tend to be relaxed and extroverted and relatively noncriminal. *Mesomorphs* are athletic and muscular; they tend to be aggressive and particularly apt to commit violent crimes and other crimes requiring strength and speed. Finally, *ectomorphs* are thin, introverted, and overly sensitive. Sheldon compared 200 male delinquents in an institution to a control group of some 4,000 male college students. Compared to the students, the delinquents tended to be mesomorphic, as Sheldon predicted.

Although Sheldon's theory held some appeal, his research suffered from the same methodological flaws that characterized the work of Lombroso, Hooton, and other early biologists (Bernard

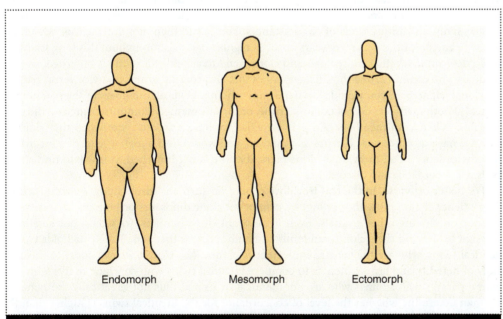

Endomorph   Mesomorph   Ectomorph

FIGURE 6–1   William Sheldon's Three Body Shapes.
Source: Adapted from Sheldon (1949).

et al. 2009). In addition, even if Sheldon's delinquent subjects were more mesomorphic, he could not rule out the possibility that their muscular, athletic bodies made it more probable that they worried juvenile justice officials and hence were more likely to be institutionalized. These many flaws, coupled with memories of the Holocaust, minimized the popularity of Sheldon's somatological theory of crime (Rafter 2007).

Contemporary Explanations

Although the early biological explanations of crime suffered from methodological and other problems, biological theories are now experiencing a resurgence thanks in part to developments in molecular genetics (Beaver and Walsh 2011; DeLisi and Beaver 2014; Raine 2013a). We discuss some of the major explanations in this section.

Family, Heredity, and Genes

Biologists and medical researchers have long noticed that crime tends to "run in families," and they assume that criminal tendencies are inherited. To these researchers, crime is analogous to disease and illness. Just as many cancers, high cholesterol and heart disease, and other medical problems are often genetically transmitted, so, they say, is criminal behavior and, for that matter, other behavioral problems such as alcoholism and schizophrenia. Work on heredity, genes, and crime now occupies a central place in biology and crime research, with much of it using sophisticated techniques from the field of molecular genetics.

Early Research   The first notable study of family transmission of crime was Richard Dugdale's 1877 study of a rural New York family named Jukes (Dugdale 1877). Noticing that six Jukes were behind bars, Dugdale researched their family tree back 200 years and found that about 140 of 1,000 Jukes had been imprisoned. Because he had no control group, however, Dugdale could not determine whether the Jukes's level of criminality was higher than that of other families. Henry H. Goddard's 1912 study of the descendants of Martin Kallikak was somewhat sounder in this regard (Goddard 1912). Kallikak had fathered children through two different women in the late 1700s. Goddard found a higher proportion of crime and other problems in one set of Kallikak's descendants than in the other. Despite the interesting comparison, learning and environmental factors may explain Goddard's findings better than heredity. The "deviant" set of Kallikak's descendants, for example, lived in poverty, whereas the "normal" set lived in wealth.

Twin Studies   The ideal way to study heredity and crime would be to take individuals at birth, clone them genetically, and randomly assign them and their clones to different families across the country living in various kinds of circumstances. You would then monitor the individuals' and clones' behavior for the next forty years or so. At regular intervals throughout this long study, you would determine whether individuals and clones tend to act alike. If crime is inherited, then individuals who commit crime should have clones that also commit crime, and vice versa. For each individual–clone pair, you would thus determine whether (1) both members of the pair commit crime, (2) both members do not commit crime, or (3) one member commits crime and the other does not. When both members of a pair act alike, we have concordance; when they don't act alike, we have discordance. If crime is inherited, you would find a higher level of concordance than discordance in all individual–clone pairs; if crime is not inherited, you would find similar levels of concordance and discordance.

For better or worse, in the real world we cannot do such an "ideal" study. *Jurassic Park* and other science fiction notwithstanding, we cannot yet clone dinosaurs or humans, despite recent advances in cloning other animals. Even if we could clone humans, we would not be allowed to assign babies and their clones randomly to families across the land. The same holds true for identical twins, who are the genetic equivalent of clones. The closest we can come to this ideal study of heredity and crime, then, is to compare identical twins who continue to live with their natural parents with siblings who are not identical twins and thus not genetically the same. We can then determine whether the level of concordance for the identical twins is higher than that for the other siblings. Researchers have performed many such studies and usually find higher concordance among the identical twins than among the other siblings. This evidence is widely interpreted as supporting a strong genetic basis for crime (Raine 2013a).

However, other reasons may account for the concordance. Compared to other siblings, identical twins spend more time together, tend to have the same friends, are more attached to each other, and tend to think of themselves as alike. They are also more likely than other siblings to be treated the same by their parents, friends, and teachers. All these likenesses produce similar attitudes and behaviors between identical twins, including delinquency and crime (Guo 2005).

Adoption Studies   To rule out environmental reasons for concordance, some researchers study identical twins separated shortly after birth and raised by different sets of parents. Because the twins do not live together, any concordance must stem from genetic factors. However, identical twins separated at birth are very rare, and too few studies exist to infer a genetic basis for crime. Their results are also mixed: some find a high level of concordance and others do not. Moreover, most of the identical twins in these studies who were reared "separately" were usually raised by parents who were close family members or neighbors. The twins thus lived in roughly the same environments, with many of them even spending a lot of time with each other. Because the twins were not really raised that separately after all, any concordance found may simply reflect their similar environments and not their genetic sameness (Lewontin 2010).

▲ Studies of identical twins suggest that criminal tendencies are genetically transmitted, but other similarities between the twins, including the amount of time they spend together, may account for their similar behaviors.

Other researchers look at non-twin siblings who, through adoption, are raised by different sets of parents. In this kind of study, researchers determine whether natural parents who are criminals tend to have children adopted and raised by other parents who are also criminals, and whether natural parents who are not criminals tend to have adopted children who also are not criminals. These studies usually find that the criminality of natural parents is statistically related to the criminality of their adopted children. For example, a study of about 4,000 adopted Danish males found criminal conviction rates of 24.5 percent among those with natural parents who had been convicted of a crime versus only 14.7 percent among those with natural parents who had not been convicted (Mednick et al. 1987).

Although many researchers interpret such evidence as support for a genetic basis for crime, others argue that siblings in adoption studies are often adopted several months after birth and thus experience similar environmental influences before adoption at a critical stage of their development. These influences might thus account for any similarity found later between their behavior and their natural parents' behavior. Another problem is that adoption agencies usually try to find adoptive parents whose socioeconomic status and other characteristics match those of the natural parents. The resulting lack of random assignment in adoption studies creates a bias that may account for the statistical relationships found (Moffitt and Caspi 2006).

Molecular Genetics   Given the methodological problems in twin and adoption studies, the best evidence for a genetic basis for criminal behavior comes from studies in molecular genetics. Techniques in molecular genetics allow researchers to determine whether individuals possess specific genes and then to determine whether these genes are associated with a greater probability of committing violent and other antisocial behavior and of having certain traits, such as low self-control, that help lead to criminal behavior (Boisvert et al. 2013). Research has identified a number of these genes (Barnes and Jacobs 2013; DeLisi et al. 2010; Guo et al. 2008; Simons et al. 2012). For example, mutations in a gene called MAOA have been implicated in high-risk behavior, including criminal behavior. This gene regulates a hormone called serotonin, which normally has a calming effect. Individuals with the mutated version of the gene are less responsive to serotonin and thus more aggressive. Several studies find that young males with mutated MAOA are more likely to be violent, more likely to be in juvenile gangs, and more likely to be arrested and imprisoned (Beaver et al. 2009; Beaver et al. 2013).

Evolutionary Biology   An essentially genetic explanation of crime comes from the field of *evolutionary biology*, which discusses how evolutionary needs tens of thousands of years ago favored certain behavioral traits that survived through natural selection and thus may account for behavioral tendencies today. If so, these tendencies are genetically based. Several evolutionary explanations of crime exist, but a brief discussion of just one should indicate their general perspective. This explanation assumes that rape provided an evolutionary advantage to some men, called *cads*, because it helped ensure the transmission of their genes into future generations (Thornhill and Palmer 2000). These men practiced what is called an *r strategy* by producing many children and then spending little time with them. Men (called *dads*) who practiced a *k strategy* produced fewer children because they were married or otherwise limited themselves to consensual sex. Presumably, cads who committed rapes thousands of years ago transmitted their genetic disposition to rape (and also to commit other antisocial behavior) into some men today. Critics fault this theory for several reasons, including its oversimplification of human history and its implication that rape was evolutionarily advantageous, which gives rape a positive slant (Travis 2003). Anthropological evidence also finds that children of rape victims are often killed by their mothers or other individuals, which obviously prevents their father's genes from being transmitted (Begley 2009).

Chromosomal Abnormalities   Before leaving the world of genetics, we should touch briefly on the issue of abnormal chromosomes. As you might remember from your biology classes in high school and college, each person normally has 23 pairs of chromosomes, or 46 chromosomes altogether. The twenty-third pair determines the sex of the child at the moment of conception. Two X chromosomes (XX) mean the fetus will be female, and one X chromosome and one Y chromosome (XY) mean it will be male. Although sperm usually carry either one X or one Y chromosome, occasionally a sperm will carry two Xs, two Ys, neither an X nor a Y (designated O), or both an X and a Y. The chromosome pattern that results in a fertilized egg will be either XXX, XYY, XO, or XXY, respectively.

The pattern that most interests some criminologists is XYY, which was discovered in 1961 and is found in fewer than one of every 1,000 men. Compared to normal, XY men, XYY men are more likely to be tall with long arms and severe acne and to have low intelligence. The relatively few studies of XYY men find that they are considerably more likely than normal XY men to be arrested or imprisoned, mainly for petty thefts (Carey 1994). Because the XYY abnormality is so rare, however, sample sizes in these studies are very small. Some scholars who view the XYY abnormality as a cause of crime attribute this link to the low intelligence of XYY men. However, other scholars think that the arrests and imprisonment of XYY men are more the result of bias against their unusual and even menacing appearance. In any event, because the XYY abnormality is so rare, at most it explains only a very minuscule fraction of crime.

Brain Abnormalities

Relatively new technologies, such as positron emission tomography (PET) and magnetic resonance imaging (MRI), have enabled scientists to study the brain as never before. Researchers have used these technologies to study a possible link between certain brain abnormalities and criminal behavior. According to a recent review, this new line of research shows that "brain impairment in several areas, particularly the frontal lobe, is associated with violence and antisocial behavior" (Raine et al. 2013:58). The review's authors said brain impairment has this effect partly because it lowers people's ability to control their impulses, to appreciate the consequences of their actions, and to be concerned about the welfare of potential victims.

Neurochemical Factors

The human body is filled with many kinds of substances that act as chemical messengers to help its various parts perform their functions. Because these functions include behavior, biologists have tried to determine the role chemical substances might play in crime. Two substances that have received considerable attention are hormones and neurotransmitters.

Hormones: Testosterone and Male Criminality   In the human body, endocrine glands secrete hormones into the blood, which then transports them throughout the body. After arriving at their intended organs or tissue, hormones enable certain functions to occur, including growth, metabolism, sex and reproduction, and stress reaction. A popular modern biological explanation of crime centers on testosterone, the "male hormone." As Chapter 3 noted, men commit much more crime than women. And as you undoubtedly already know, men also have more testosterone than women. Combining these two basic sex differences, some scholars argue that testosterone, or, to be more precise, variation in the amount of testosterone, is an important cause of male criminality. Testosterone differences explain not only why men commit more crime than women, but also why some men commit more crime than other men.

Ample evidence exists of a correlation between testosterone level and aggression or criminality (Booth et al. 2006). In the animal kingdom, testosterone has often been linked to aggression; among humans, the sex difference both in testosterone and in crime is obvious. Many studies also find that males with records of violent and other offending have higher testosterone than males with no such records (Mazur 2009; Montoya et al. 2012). Higher testosterone is said to increase aggression, risk taking, and impulsiveness, and thus also low self-control, all important components of delinquency and crime.

However, several methodological problems indicate that the testosterone explanation might be weaker than these findings suggest. Consider, for example, the common assumption that testosterone produces aggression throughout the animal kingdom. Although this link is

© magann/Fotolia

▲ A popular biological explanation assumes that higher levels of testosterone make it more likely that males will engage in criminal behavior, especially violent crime.

commonly found, it is also true that in many animal species, among them guinea pigs and lions, females are more aggressive than males even though they have lower testosterone. Moreover, neuroendocrinologists who study hormones and behavior caution against extrapolating from animal studies to human behavior (Nelson 2011). Although hormones strongly affect many behaviors of lower animals, including primates, the human central nervous system and the social environment are so complex that simple endocrine influences cannot be assumed.

The evidence among humans of testosterone-induced offending is also open to question (Sapolsky 2012). Although many studies have found a link between testosterone and aggression or offending, other studies have found no such link. Moreover, a correlation among human males between high testosterone and high offending does not necessarily mean that testosterone affects offending. Methodologically, it is just as plausible that offending affects testosterone or that some third factor leads to both high testosterone and high offending (Nelson 2011). In the animal kingdom, for example, aggression and dominance lead to high testosterone in certain species. Although this has not been widely investigated among humans, delinquency and adult criminality may lead to feelings of dominance and thus to higher testosterone (Miczek et al. 1994a). The sex difference in testosterone and criminality is also obviously subject to other interpretations. As Chapter 3 discussed, gender-role socialization produces different behaviors in girls and boys and different opportunities for offending. To most sociologists, a testosterone-based explanation of the gender difference in crime seems much less plausible than one based on social and structural factors.

In view of these problems, a significant effect of testosterone on human aggression cannot be assumed. A review commissioned for the National Academy of Sciences concluded that the testosterone–aggression correlations often found among human males "are not high, they are sometimes difficult to replicate, and importantly, they do not demonstrate causation. In fact there is better evidence for the reverse relationship (behavior altering hormonal levels). .. . [W]inning—even in innocuous laboratory competitions—can increase testosterone" (Miczek et al. 1994b).

Hormones: PMS and Crime by Women Another hormonal explanation focuses on women's crime. In some women, hormonal changes in the days before menstruation appear to be linked to increased stress, tension, lethargy, and other problems. These women are said to suffer from premenstrual syndrome, or PMS. Thinking that this emotional condition might lead to aggression and other offending, some researchers study whether crime by women tends to occur in their premenstrual phase. If PMS were not related to women's crime, their offending would occur

▼

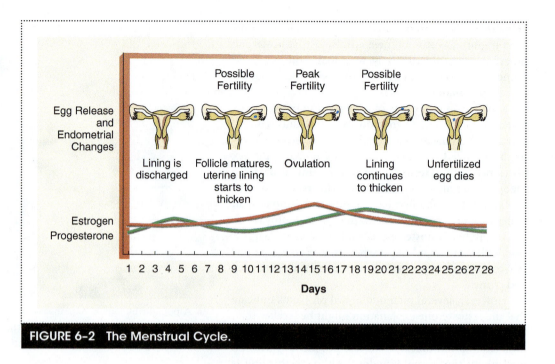

FIGURE 6-2   The Menstrual Cycle.

randomly throughout their menstrual cycles. If PMS did lead women to offend, their deviance would tend to occur during their premenstrual phases (see Figure 6–2 ■). To study this possibility, researchers ask women in prison to think back to when they committed the offense for which they were arrested and to remember the dates of their menstruation. From this information researchers can determine whether offenses occurred randomly throughout the women's cycles or instead were concentrated in their premenstrual phases.

One early researcher in this field, Katharina Dalton (1961), found such a concentration, with about half of prisoners she studied reporting committing their offenses in the eight-day period immediately preceding and during menstruation. Dalton attributed their criminality to their emotional condition and increased lethargy and clumsiness during this time: Their emotional condition prompted them to commit the crimes, and their lethargy and clumsiness made it more difficult for them to avoid detection and arrest. To support her view of women's physical ineptitude, Dalton noted that half of women drivers involved in serious auto accidents are also in the eight-day premenstrual–menstrual phase. Such findings have led some attorneys representing women defendants to claim PMS as a defense (Solomon 1995). In England in 1980, for example, one woman murdered her boyfriend by driving her car into him, and another killed a coworker in a London pub. Both claimed that PMS led to their violence, and both received probation instead of imprisonment.

As you might expect, the PMS explanation for women's crime is very controversial. Many scholars feel that it takes us back to the days of "raging hormones," when women were considered unfit to be airplane pilots, to be president of the United States, and to hold other positions because they could not be trusted to act rationally during "that time of the month." Beyond these ideological concerns, the PMS research is also methodologically flawed (Katz and Chambliss 1995). It assumes that women can accurately remember when menstruation occurred; even a few days' error can place their crime outside the premenstrual phase. Some women are very regular and can remember the dates of their menstruation, but others cannot. More important, stress and other problems can disrupt women's cycles. If the stress of committing a crime or the stress leading up to the crime hastens menstruation, it may appear artificially that the crime occurred during a woman's premenstrual phase only because menstruation occurred sooner than normal. In recalling Dalton's finding that half of all women drivers in serious accidents were in the eight-day premenstrual–menstrual phase of their cycles, consider that half of all women passengers involved in accidents are also in the same phase. As Janet Katz and William J. Chambliss (1995:290) aptly put it, "Unless we wish to argue that the passenger's lethargy somehow caused the accident, it would appear that the trauma of the accident triggered menstruation, not vice versa."

Neurotransmitters

The human nervous system consists of billions of cells called *neurons* and bundles of neurons called *nerves*. Nerves carry messages from the brain throughout the body and messages from the body back to the brain and spinal cord. Certain neurons called *receptors* are found in the sense organs of the body, such as the eye. Receptors send messages, or impulses, through nerves back to the brain. After obtaining these messages, the brain sends instructions for particular actions back to various parts of the body. Neurons transmit impulses to each other across synapses with the aid of chemical substances called neurotransmitters. In studying aggression, scientists have been particularly interested in one specific neurotransmitter, *serotonin*, mentioned earlier

In animal studies, low levels of serotonin are linked with higher levels of aggression. Many studies of humans have found low levels of serotonin in violent offenders (Raine 2013a). Although the serotonin–aggression research is intriguing, it suffers from some of the methodological problems already discussed, including the possibility that serotonin levels result from aggression rather than the reverse, which make it premature to assume a strong role for serotonin in human aggression. Some studies even find *higher* levels of serotonin in aggressive individuals. A review concluded that "serotonin is not a very discriminating marker for violence" (Wallman 1999:24).

Diet and Nutrition

In late 1978, a San Francisco city supervisor named Dan White allegedly murdered George Moscone, the city's mayor, and Harvey Milk, a city supervisor and gay activist. The murders shocked the Bay Area. People even stopped shopping for Christmas presents for several days as the whole community shared in collective grief. When White was tried for the two murders, his attorney claimed he had been eating too much junk food. The sugar and various additives in the food supposedly deepened his depression and reduced his ability to tell right from wrong. White's "Twinkie defense" worked: He was convicted only of manslaughter, not first-degree murder. His conviction on the lower charge outraged Bay Area residents (Weiss 1984).

As this example indicates, diet and nutrition might play a role in aggression and crime. Researchers investigate this role with two kinds of studies. In the first kind, they control the levels of various nutrients given to animal or occasionally human subjects and then compare the behavior of these subjects to control groups. In the second kind, they compare the diet and nutrition of offenders, usually juveniles, to those of nonoffenders. From this body of evidence, several diet and nutritional factors have been identified as producing aggression and other forms of offending: high amounts of sugar and refined carbohydrates, excessive levels of chemical additives, and deficiencies in vitamin B and other vitamins. Yet this research, too, suffers from several methodological problems that cast doubt on its findings, including small samples, possibly spurious findings, and ambiguity in defining offending (Curran and Renzetti 2001). Moreover, several studies of diet and nutrition do not find them linked to antisocial behavior. A review concluded that diet and nutrition have at most a "relatively minor" effect on criminality (Kanarek 1994:535).

Since that review was written, however, several studies have found that fish oil supplements help reduce aggressive behavior (Rocque et al. 2012). If additional research confirms these studies' findings, then diets or supplements rich in fish oil might hold significant promise for crime reduction.

Although diet and nutrition may have no more than a minor effect, if that, on criminality among adults, *malnutrition* during early childhood may have long-lasting effects in this regard (Raine et al. 2013). A growing number of studies show that malnourished children are more likely to engage in antisocial behavior during childhood and in delinquency and crime when they reach adolescence and adulthood. Malnutrition is thought to have this effect because it causes abnormalities in the rapidly growing brains of young children.

▼ Although many people probably think that high levels of sugar and refined carbohydrates contribute to aggressive behavior, research on this issue is inconclusive.

© ZUMA Press, Inc. / Alamy

Pregnancy and Birth Complications

Some of the most interesting biological research concerns the effects of pregnancy and birth complications. These complications are often referred to as *perinatal* problems. Poor nutrition and the use of alcohol, tobacco, and other drugs during pregnancy are thought to harm fetal development, with potentially long-lasting effects on central nervous system (CNS) functioning that in turn can lead to antisocial behavior. Many studies find that children born to women who smoke or use other drugs, including alcohol, during pregnancy are more likely to commit violence and other crimes by the time they reach adulthood (Paradis et al. 2011; Raine 2013a). CNS functioning can also be impaired by complications during difficult births; such complications may also increase the potential for later criminal behavior (Raine 2013a).

Although this body of research suggests a biological role in offending, other interpretations are possible. In particular, pregnancy and birth complications may often be the fault of mothers who fail to observe standard advice for promoting fetal health and development. If so, they may very well practice inadequate parenting after birth, making spurious the presumed relationship between offending and pregnancy and birth complications. To rule out this possibility, research must take parenting practices into account. Some studies of cigarette smoking during pregnancy have done this, and they still find that the mother's offspring are more likely to commit crime later on (Gibson et al. 2000). This result increases confidence that smoking during pregnancy was the cause of their criminality, but studies using a wider range of parenting behaviors are still necessary.

Early Puberty

A growing body of research finds that adolescents who experience early puberty are more likely to commit delinquent acts and other antisocial behavior (Harden and Mendle 2012; Jackson 2012). This effect is thought to occur for at least three reasons. First, early puberty prompts adolescents to associate with older adolescents who have already experienced puberty and, for this reason, to have more opportunity to get into trouble. Second, some early maturers resent the fact that they now look like adults but are not given the freedom by their parents to act like adults. Illegal behavior thus provides them a way to act out their resentment by rebelling against their parents. Third, some early maturers experience depression and other psychological problems that may prompt them to act in antisocial ways. To the extent that early puberty is a risk factor for both offending and victimization (see Chapter 4), parents, educators, and public health officials need to keep it in mind in addressing the needs of adolescents in their familial and professional capacities.

Evaluation of Biological Explanations

Many scholars are enthusiastic about biological explanations. Modern biological theory, they say, has been unfairly stigmatized by the crude early work of Lombroso, Hooton, and others (Wright et al. 2008). This stigma has resulted in "misguided prejudice" among many criminologists toward biological explanations (DeLisi et al. 2010:82). A former president of the American Society of Criminology, Francis T. Cullen (2011:310–311) says that criminologists should "embrace biosocial theory," and he adds that "we can no longer pretend that biology is not intimately implicated in human behavior and thus in criminal behavior."

Most sociologists who study crime are somewhat less enthusiastic but still recognize that "biological explanations have come to occupy a new place of respectability in criminology . . . [and] are taken more seriously today than at any other time since the early part of the 20th century" (Akers and Sellers 2009:53).

Biological criminologists increasingly advocate a blend of biology and sociology in what is termed a *biosocial perspective.* In this way of thinking, biological traits interact with environmental influences to produce crime: biological factors may predispose individuals to crime, but the extent and timing of their influence depend on environmental factors (Beaver and Walsh 2011). For example, biological factors such as a mutated MAOA gene may be more likely to lead to crime if an individual comes from a family environment characterized by poor parenting or from a disadvantaged neighborhood; conversely, individuals with a biological predisposition to crime may be less likely to actually commit it if they come from a warm, loving home (Barnes and Jacobs 2013). If so, and reflecting a *dual hazard* hypothesis, individuals are most likely to commit crime if they have a biological predisposition for it and if they come from negative family environments (Cullen and Agnew 2011). Biosocial criminologists point out that their perspective is compatible with a sociological framework, as it stresses the importance of the social environment for criminality (Ledger 2009).

Despite the growing popularity of biosocial explanations, sociologists and other criminologists continue to have some concerns. One problem is that crime is simply too diverse. Even if biological factors account for some violent aggression, they cannot explain most criminal behavior. Among other problems, they cannot easily account for the *relativity* of deviance; that is, they cannot explain why someone with a biological predisposition to violence turns to street crime instead of, say, football or any other activity involving physical violence. As Charles H. McCaghy et al. (2008) point out, violence in a bar fight makes you a criminal, whereas violence in wartime makes you a hero. A biological explanation of violence is thus not the same thing as a biological explanation of *criminal* violence.

A second problem concerns *group-rate differences*. As we have seen in earlier chapters, sociologists try to understand the reasons for different crime rates among different groups or locations and for changes in crime rates. For example, they are more interested in why big cities have higher crime rates than rural areas than in why a particular individual in a big city commits a crime. Biological explanations cannot easily account for group-rate differences. Take the fact that the United States has a much higher homicide rate than Canada and Western European nations. How would you explain this biologically? Is it really conceivable that Americans are different biologically from Canadians, the English, Germans, or Danes in a way that leads to more homicide in the United States? Can the high crime rates of big cities as compared to rural areas really be attributed to biological problems in big-city residents? Can biological explanations account for why

Crime and Controversy DOES ABORTION LOWER THE CRIME RATE?

A controversy erupted a decade ago when two economists proposed that almost half of the 1990s crime decline was the result of the large increase in abortions two decades earlier in the wake of the U.S. Supreme Court's famous 1973 *Roe v. Wade* decision. The drop in crime began, they said, when the children who were not born because of the abortion increase, much of it found among poor, unmarried teenagers, would have reached their late teenage years, when offending reaches its peak. The states that first legalized abortion before *Roe v. Wade* were the first to see their crime rates drop. States with the highest abortion rates after *Roe v. Wade* also had larger crime decreases than states with lower abortion rates.

The economists' claims met with immediate skepticism from criminologists and provoked concern from both sides of the abortion debate. Criminologists said the 1990s crime-rate decline stemmed from factors far more important than the rise in abortions two decades earlier. These included the thriving economy during the 1990s, a stabilization in gang wars over the sale and distribution of crack that began in the mid-1980s, and perhaps more effective policing and community-based crime-control strategies.

Criminologists have since noted some weaknesses of the economists' study that ignited the controversy. For example, adolescent property-crime rates began to decline only in 1994, about a decade after what would have been expected if the legalization of abortion in 1973 had been responsible, and adolescent violent-crime rates were increasing during the 1980s at the very time they would have been expected to decline because of abortion's legalization. Moreover, African-American youths experienced the greatest increase in violence, even though African-American women were more likely than women of other races to receive abortions after *Roe v. Wade*.

Empirical efforts to replicate the original abortion–crime findings have also been inconsistent. Several studies have found that legalized abortion did not lower the crime rate; some have found it did lower the crime rate; and some have even found that it raised the crime rate. These mixed results indicate that a link between legalized abortion and higher crime rates cannot be assumed, but they also promise that the abortion–crime controversy is not about to fade away.

Sources: Berk et al. 2003; Chamlin et al. 2008; Donohue and Levitt 2001; Hay and Evans 2006; Kahane et al. 2008.

▲ It probably sounds silly to suggest that a biological problem leads corporate executives to break the law. Given our society's prejudices, however, it might not sound silly to suggest that a biological problem leads poor people, and especially persons of color, to commit violent crime.

street crime rose in the United States during the 1960s and fell in the 1990s? Even if they might explain why some individuals commit crime, biological explanations cannot easily account for different crime rates among groups or locations or for changes in crime rates.

Another concern about biological explanations involves their social policy implications. One implication is that to reduce crime we must correct the biological deficiency that causes it. Thanks to drugs, gene therapy, and other scientific advances, it might be possible to correct these deficiencies (DeLisi et al. 2010; Raine 2013a), but these measures remain rather frightening to some observers, who fear they could open the door to genetic screening of people of various ages for criminogenic genes and even detainment of those with these genes (Anderson 2013).

In a final problem, people found to have a biological predisposition for criminality may inevitably be regarded as biologically different and even biologically inferior. History is replete with acts of genocide, lynchings, hate crime, and other actions taken against people deemed biologically inferior to some ruling group, with their supposed inferiority justifying the inhumane treatment. In the early decades of the twentieth century, the *eugenics* movement in the United States led to the involuntary sterilization of some 70,000 people, almost all of them poor and many of them-African American; one of the rationales for eugenics was a desire to reduce crime (Rocque et al. 2012). Not too long thereafter, Nazi Germany slaughtered millions of Jews and others who were thought to be inferior to the Aryan race. The "evidence" gathered by American eugenicists of biological inferiority reinforced Nazi ideology (Kuhl 1994).

If, then, we find that a biological trait makes certain people more likely to be criminals, history tells us these groups can then be considered biologically inferior and in need of special, even inhumane, treatment, even if no biologists today advocate such treatment. These groups are usually the poor and people of color, because biological research on crime has centered on street crimes committed by the poor while ignoring the white-collar crimes committed by wealthier people. It might sound silly even to suggest that a defective gene or hormonal imbalance leads corporate executives to engage in price-fixing or to market unsafe products. Yet, given our society's prejudices, it might not sound as silly to suggest that a biological problem leads poor people to commit violent crime. Given continuing racial and ethnic prejudice, we must be very careful in interpreting the findings of contemporary research on biology and crime.

Proponents of biosocial criminology vigorously defend it against all these criticisms and argue for the importance of their perspective. As a recent review advocated, "Neuroscience is shining light on the mechanisms of nature and nurture that underscore human existence and human behavior. This scientific advance has already infiltrated criminology. If not now then very soon, biosocial theory, an area once completely marginalized and ridiculed within criminology, will become the definite statement of crime" (DeLisi et al. 2010:83). As should be clear, the value of biosocial explanations will remain a major source of vigorous controversy in criminology for some years to come.

At least two strands of biological research hold promise for reducing crime without raising the problems just noted (Rocque et al. 2012). First, to the extent that the prenatal difficulties discussed earlier predict later offending, then it may be possible to reduce crime with social policies aimed at reducing smoking and alcohol use during pregnancy and at improving prenatal health care and nutrition. It is especially important for these policies to focus on low-income mothers, who are more likely to experience prenatal difficulties. Second, research increasingly suggests that poverty for many reasons results in children having neurological and cognitive deficits that can have consequences well into adolescence and adulthood. One of these consequences is antisocial behavior, including juvenile delinquency and adult criminality. The biological research documenting these deficits provides an important rationale for reducing poverty in order to reduce crime.

Review and Discuss

What concerns do many sociologists and criminologists have about biological explanations of criminal behavior? How valid do you think these concerns are?

▼

► Psychological Explanations

Psychology offers a valuable explanation of individual behavior, but says little about the larger social and structural forces also at work. In the area of crime, sociology and psychology together provide a more comprehensive explanation than either discipline can provide separately. Sociology tries to explain why certain groups and locations have more crime than others, and psychology tries to explain why a few people with or without these backgrounds commit serious crime, whereas most do not (Bartol and Bartol 2014; Moore 2011). This section examines the major psychological explanations (see Table 6–2) while leaving learning approaches, which are compatible with a sociological framework, for Chapter 8.

Psychoanalytic Explanations

Modern psychoanalytic explanations say delinquency and crime arise from internal disturbances developing in early childhood because of interaction problems between parents and children. These explanations derive from the work of Sigmund Freud (1856–1939), the founder of psychoanalysis (Freud 1935 (1920); Freud 1961 (1930)). Although Freud focused more on mental disorders than on criminal behavior, later theorists drew on his work to explain delinquency and crime.

Freud and his followers see mental disorders as arising from a conflict between society and the instinctive needs of the individual. The individual personality consists of three parts: the id, the ego, and the superego. The id, present at birth, consists of instinctual desires that demand immediate gratification: infants get hungry and do not take no for an answer if not fed soon enough. Eventually the ego develops and represents the more rational part of personality. Children learn that they cannot always expect immediate gratification of their needs. The superego comes later and represents the internalization of society's moral code. This is the individual's conscience and leads the individual to feel guilty or ashamed for violating social norms. The development of these three parts of the personality is generally complete by about age 5.

Freud thought that people are inherently pleasure seeking because of the id, but that too much pleasure seeking can translate into antisocial behavior. The ego and superego thus need to restrain the id. This happens in mentally healthy individuals because the three parts of the personality coexist harmoniously. A lack of balance can result when a child's needs are not met because of parental deprivation, neglect, or overly harsh discipline. If the superego then becomes too weak to control the id's instinctive impulses, delinquency and crime result. They can also result if the superego is too strong, when individuals feel overly guilty and ashamed. The rational part of the personality, the ego, realizes that if individuals commit a crime they will be punished and thus reduce their guilt. Given this realization, the ego leads the person to break the law.

Psychoanalytic explanations have been valuable in emphasizing the importance of early childhood experiences for later behavior, but their value for understanding crime is limited for several reasons (Akers and Sellers 2013). First, they suggest that antisocial behavior is mentally disordered behavior, which is not true for most individuals. Second, they neglect social factors and overemphasize childhood experiences; although these are undoubtedly important, later life-cycle

TABLE 6-2 Psychological Explanations in Brief

THEORY	KEY FIGURE(S)	SYNOPSIS
Psychoanalytic Explanations	Sigmund Freud	The individual personality consists of the id, ego, and superego. Delinquency and crime result if the superego is too weak to control the id, or if the superego is so strong that individuals feel overly guilty and ashamed.
Moral Development	Lawrence Kohlberg	Children experience several stages of moral development. Incomplete moral development is a major reason for criminal and other antisocial behavior.
Intelligence (IQ)	—	Low intelligence (IQ) produces criminality, in part because low intelligence impairs moral reasoning and the ability to appreciate the consequences of one's actions.
Personality Explanations	Terrie A. Moffitt	Personality problems during childhood contribute to delinquency during adolescence and criminality during adulthood.

influences are also important (see Chapter 8). Finally, psychoanalytic research relies on case histories of individuals under treatment or on samples of offenders in juvenile institutions, adult prisons, or mental institutions. This methodology ignores the possibilities that the subjects might not represent the vast majority of offenders not under treatment or institutionalized and that any mental or emotional problems in the institutionalized subjects may be the result, and not the cause, of their institutionalization.

Before we leave psychoanalytic explanations, a comment on their view of women's criminality is in order. Although Freud is widely regarded as one of the greatest thinkers of the last two centuries, his views on women reflected the sexism of his day (Klein 1995). Freud viewed child rearing as women's natural role and thought that females who could not adjust to this role suffered from "penis envy" and hence mental disorder. To compensate for the lack of a penis, some women, he thought, tried to act like men in desiring careers. Extending Freud's views to delinquency and crime, Freudian scholars later attributed most girls' delinquency to their sexual needs. In a traditional Freudian framework, then, women and girls with mental disorders or histories of crime and delinquency need to be helped to adjust to their natural child-rearing roles. Thanks to critiques by feminist scholars, this view of female criminality lost popularity in the 1970s.

▲ Although psychoanalytic explanations have helped highlight the influence of early childhood experiences on later behavior, their value for understanding crime is limited for several reasons.

Moral Development and Crime

Since the time of Jean Piaget (1896–1980), psychologists have been interested in children's mental and moral development. Piaget thought that children experience four stages of mental development. The *sensorimotor* period lasts until the age of 2 and involves learning about their immediate environment and developing their reflexes. The *preoperational* period lasts from ages 2 to 7 and consists of learning language, drawing, and other skills. A stage of *concrete operations* lasts from ages 7 to 11 and involves learning logical thinking and problem solving. The final *formal operations* stage occurs during ages 11 to 15 and concerns dealing with abstract ideas (Singer and Revenson 1997).

Following in Piaget's footsteps, psychologist Lawrence Kohlberg (1969) developed his theory of moral development, the ability to distinguish right from wrong and to determine the ethically correct course of action in complex circumstances. Kohlberg theorized that individuals pass through several stages in which they develop their ability to reason morally. In the early stages, children's moral reasoning is related solely to punishment: correct behavior is behavior that keeps them from getting punished. In later stages, as adolescents, they begin to realize that society and their parents have rules that deserve to be obeyed in and of themselves, not just to avoid punishment. They also realize that exhibiting the behaviors expected of them will lead others to view them positively. In the final stages of moral development, during late adolescence and early adulthood, people recognize that universal moral principles supersede the laws of any one society. Individuals reaching this stage may decide to disobey the law in the name of a higher law.

Kohlberg further theorized that not everyone makes it through all the stages of moral development. In particular, some people's moral development stops after only the early stages. Because their view of right and wrong is limited to what avoids punishment, they have not developed what many of us would call a conscience and may well engage in harmful behavior as long as they think they will not get punished for it. Kohlberg thus thought that incomplete moral development was a major reason for criminal and other antisocial behavior.

One problem with tests of Kohlberg's theory is the familiar chicken-and-egg question of causal order. Even if offenders do have a lower level of moral reasoning than nonoffenders, their offending may have affected their moral reasoning rather than the reverse. They might have begun to violate the law for other reasons, such as peer pressure or hostility toward their parents, and then adjusted their moral reasoning to accommodate their illegal behavior to minimize any guilt or shame.

Intelligence and Crime

Researchers have long blamed crime on low intelligence (IQ). Studies in the early twentieth century found low IQs among prisoners and juveniles in reform schools. Scholars later criticized this research on methodological grounds, and it lost popularity by the 1930s. In the late

1970s, however, a study by Travis Hirschi and Michael Hindelang (1977) renewed interest in the IQ–crime relationship. After determining from many studies that delinquents' IQ scores were about eight points lower than nondelinquents' scores on the average, the authors concluded that low IQ is an important cause of delinquency. More recent studies also link delinquency to low IQ (Kennedy et al. 2011), and some scholars go as far as to say that IQ is a stronger predictor of delinquency than either race or social class (Herrnstein and Murray 1994).

Several reasons might explain a possible causal link between IQ and delinquency (Hirschi and Hindelang 1977; Lynam et al. 1993). First, youths with low intelligence do poorly in school. Poor school performance in turn leads to less attachment to school and thus to higher rates of delinquency. Second, such youths also experience lower self-esteem and turn for support to youths with similar problems; because some of their new friends are involved in delinquency, they become delinquent themselves. Third, low intelligence leads to a lower ability to engage in moral reasoning and to delay gratification, increasing the likelihood of offending. Fourth, adolescents with low intelligence are less able to appreciate the consequences of their actions and to be more susceptible to the influence of delinquent friends.

▲ Although some research finds a link between low IQ and high levels of delinquency, methodological problems cast doubt on the validity of this finding.

Although a presumed low IQ–delinquency link sounds sensible, it has proven very controversial for several reasons (Nisbett 2009). The first is methodological. Without question, the early IQ research was rife with methodological problems, and serious questions remain regarding whether IQ tests measure native (inborn) intelligence or instead reflect the effects of schooling and familiarity with white, middle-class experiences. Recent IQ studies are more carefully designed, but some still use samples of offenders in adult prisons or juvenile institutions. Because incarcerated offenders represent only a very small proportion of all offenders, we cannot safely generalize these studies' findings to the entire offender population. In another issue, many researchers say the presumed IQ–delinquency link is not as strong as its proponents think and may not even exist at all. One study found that the effect of IQ on delinquency was weak initially and became spurious when other predictors of delinquency were taken into account (Cullen et al. 1997).

Race, IQ, and Crime

Contemporary research on IQ and crime also has troubling racial overtones that echo the first uses of the IQ test in the early twentieth century. Several studies find African-American–white differences in IQ scores, with the average scores of African-Americans about ten to fifteen points below those for whites. Some researchers think this difference reflects the lower natural intelligence of African-Americans and further think it explains why they commit more street crimes than whites do (Herrnstein and Murray 1994).

Suppose we accept the assumptions guiding this research linking IQ, race, and crime: (1) IQ tests are valid measures of natural intelligence, (2) African-Americans are intellectually inferior to whites, (3) low natural intelligence produces higher rates of delinquency and crime, and (4) low natural intelligence is perhaps the major reason for high rates of street crime by African-Americans. What do these beliefs imply about efforts to reduce such crime? Because these assumptions discount social factors, they suggest, first of all, that efforts to reduce social inequality and other structural problems would do relatively little to reduce African-American crime rates. They also imply that to reduce African-American crime rates, we have to improve African Americans' innate intelligence. But to say that intelligence is innate suggests that efforts to raise it will probably be useless; if so, we can do little to reduce African-American crime. If we cannot reduce it, perhaps all we can do is to deter African-Americans from committing crime by putting even more of them in prison.

This is certainly a pessimistic appraisal and perhaps a bit simplistic, but is it warranted? Not if the assumptions turn out to be questionable or even false, which is precisely what many critics charge (Menard and Morse 1984; Nisbett 2009). If the IQ test is culturally biased, as many critics say, then African-Americans' lower IQ scores reflect their poorer schooling and the fact that they are not white and often not middle class. In sum, race–IQ–crime assumptions are highly questionable at best and patently false at worst, with dangerous racial and class overtones. Although ruling out the presumed intelligence–criminality link in the race–IQ–crime chain may be premature, history tells us we must tread very cautiously in this area.

Review and Discuss

What does the research on intelligence and crime tell us? What are the methodological and other critiques of this line of research?

Personality and Crime

Some of the most important work today in psychology and crime focuses on personality. Early studies administered Rorschach (ink blot) tests or personality inventories to samples of incarcerated juvenile and adult offenders and to control groups of nonoffenders. Although this research found personality differences between offenders and nonoffenders, several problems limited the value of this finding (Akers and Sellers 2013). First, because most of this research examined institutionalized offenders, the offenders' personality problems may have been the result of their institutionalization and not the cause. Second, the personality–offending link that was found might have resulted from an effect of offending on personality traits rather than the reverse. Third, because many studies did not control for socioeconomic status, education, and other characteristics, their correlation between personality and criminality may have been spurious. These problems led many criminologists to discount the importance of personality traits for criminality (Andrews and Wormith 1989).

Much contemporary research avoids these problems by using random samples of the population and longitudinal data to clarify cause and effect. Important longitudinal research efforts in New Zealand and elsewhere follow individuals from infancy or adolescence into adulthood (see the International Focus box). Many of these studies focus on childhood temperament, which produces behavioral problems during childhood and also delinquency during adolescence and crime during adulthood. The long list of temperament problems includes such things as attention deficits, impulsiveness, hyperactivity, irritability, coldness, and suspiciousness. Although most children with temperament problems do not end up committing serious delinquency, the ones with the worst problems are more likely to become delinquent and to continue to commit crime during adulthood. Further, most serious delinquents are thought to have had childhood temperament problems (Loeber et al. 2008; Viding et al. 2011). Strong links between certain personality traits and delinquency and crime have been found in several nations, for both genders, and among several racial and ethnic groups (Caspi et al. 1994; Thornberry 2009).

The new wave of personality research has led many criminologists to recognize the importance of personality and to begin to incorporate personality traits more explicitly into sociological theories of crime (Agnew et al. 2002; Jones et al. 2011; Van Gelder and De Vries 2012). The new personality research has important implications for reducing crime because it points to childhood temperament problems as an important contributor to criminality. If these problems do matter, then efforts such as preschool and early family intervention programs that address them may also reduce delinquency and crime (Rocque et al. 2012; Welsh and Farrington 2012). Moreover, to the extent that temperament problems are more common among children raised in poverty and in disadvantaged neighborhoods, the new personality research also highlights the need to address these aspects of the social environment to reduce crime.

Two related problems still characterize the new personality research. First, personality explanations of crime, like their biological counterparts, cannot adequately account for the relativity of deviance: They cannot explain why individuals psychologically predisposed to thrill seeking or violence undertake criminal actions instead of legal ones (McCaghy et al. 2008). Some people

New Zealand has been the site not only of the making of the award-winning *Lord of the Rings* movies, but also of some of the best-designed research on the biological, psychological, and developmental (family-based) causes of delinquency and crime. The researchers involved are psychologists Avshalom Caspi and Terrie A. Moffitt and their colleagues in New Zealand and elsewhere. The basis for much of their research is the Dunedin Multidisciplinary Health and Development Study, a longitudinal investigation begun in the 1970s. The researchers began studying more than 1,000 children born in 1972 and 1973 in New Zealand's province of Dunedin when they were 3 years old and have studied them again periodically into their adulthood, gathering several kinds of medical, psychological, and sociological information each time. At the outset of the study, they also obtained perinatal data for when the subjects were born.

Caspi, Moffitt, and colleagues found correlations in one study between various personality characteristics and delinquency among their subjects and also a sample of Pittsburgh youths. The New Zealand data for this study were gathered when the youths were 18 years old. For both sexes, delinquency (as measured by self-reports) was higher in youths with the following traits: aggression (is willing to hurt or frighten others), alienation (feels victimized and betrayed), stress reaction (feels nervous and vulnerable or worries a lot), and social potency (is forceful and decisive). Delinquency was also lower in youths with these traits: traditionalism (favors high moral standards), harm avoidance (dislikes excitement and danger), and control (is reflective and cautious).

In other research, the New Zealand researchers have taken advantage of their study's longitudinal design and have found that behavioral, personality, and other problems during childhood predict several types of problems by adolescence and then young adulthood, including conflict in interacting with others, delinquency, employment problems, and domestic violence. They have also found that boys at age 13 with neuropsychological problems, such as poor language processing, poor memory, and difficulty in linking visual information to motor coordination, developed higher rates of delinquency, even after controlling for socioeconomic status. The researchers concluded that these neuropsychological problems impair communication between children and their parents, teachers, and peers and hamper school performance. These problems in turn promote delinquency.

According to Caspi, Moffitt, and their colleagues, their findings have important implications for preventing crime because childhood neuropsychological, personality, and behavioral problems often stem from issues in the social or family environment that can be prevented. These issues include poor nutrition during pregnancy, alcohol or drug use during pregnancy, birth complications, childhood head injuries, exposure to lead and other toxic substances, and inadequate parenting. Thus, efforts that successfully address all these problems will also help address the crime problem.

Sources: Caspi 2000; Moffitt 2003; Moffitt 2006; Odgers et al. 2008.

---

with the impulsiveness trait mentioned previously, for example, may pursue car racing or parachute jumping as careers or hobbies; others may choose crime. Personality explanations do not help us understand why a person chooses one behavior instead of another. Second, because so many people with personality problems do not break the law, conclusions from the personality–crime research should be interpreted cautiously.

Despite these problems, the new longitudinal personality research has succeeded in highlighting the importance of childhood temperament problems for later criminality. By doing so, it has also pointed to the need for social policies to reduce these problems once they emerge and, better yet, to prevent them from emerging at all.

Evaluation of Psychological Explanations

In certain respects, psychological explanations complement sociological ones by filling in the smaller picture of crime that sociology's larger, structural approach leaves empty. Some psychologists criticize the "antipsychological bias" they see in sociological criminology (Andrews and Bonta 2010). Although somewhat valid, this charge is also too severe. Sociologists certainly look beyond the individual, but many of their structural explanations for crime rest on social psychological states such as frustration and alienation (see Chapter 7). Many of the social process theories favored by sociologists (see Chapter 8) also rest on psychological concepts such as learning and role modeling. And personality traits are making their way, however belatedly, into sociological theories (Agnew et al. 2002; Simons et al. 2007).

Despite the contributions of some psychological approaches to the understanding of crime, several issues remain (Bernard et al. 2009). First, psychological studies historically have often used small, unrepresentative samples of offenders in prisons or mental institutions. Even if these offenders are psychologically different, the difference may be the result of their institutionalization and not the cause. Second, psychological studies generally disregard structural factors such as poverty and cannot easily account for variations in crime by group and location or for changes in crime rates.

Third, although these studies offer interesting statistical correlations, their causal order remains unclear. In this regard, the recent longitudinal studies of childhood temperament and later delinquency have been very valuable because their research design permits a conclusion that temperament problems precede initial delinquency, even if delinquency might later in turn affect temperament. Finally, psychologists of crime join their biological counterparts in rarely studying crimes by white-collar offenders, even though these crimes result in much injury and death. The fact that researchers and the public are attracted to suggestions of psychological problems in common criminals but not in white-collar criminals may reflect stereotypical views of the poor and people of color, who are much more likely to commit street crime than white-collar crime.

Abnormality or Normality?

Psychological approaches also suggest that criminals are psychologically abnormal and that crime thus results from psychological abnormality. Normal people do not commit crime; abnormal people do. As Chapter 1 noted, Émile Durkheim wrote that crime and deviance are indeed normal, meaning that they occur in every healthy society because people will always violate the norms of any society. Building on Durkheim's perspective, sociological criminology sees crime and deviance arising from normal social structures, institutions, and processes. Because psychological explanations assume that individuals have problems that lead them to commit crime, they imply that the way to reduce crime is to cure the few aberrant individuals who commit it. As we saw with eating disorders, a sociological perspective suggests that there will always be other deviants to take their place given the social and structural forces at work.

It may also be mistaken to view most criminals as psychologically abnormal. A person can commit horrible violence and still be psychologically normal in other respects. Studies after World War II of prison guards in Nazi concentration camps found them to be good husbands and fathers who performed well on various psychological tests. Despite their apparent psychological normality, they were able to commit some of the worst crimes known to humanity.

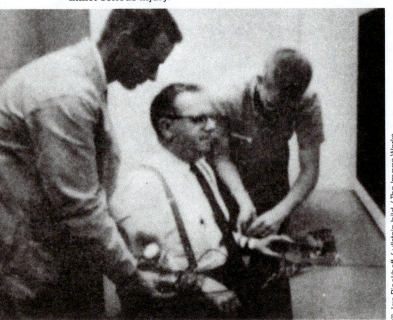

▼ This photo shows part of Stanley Milgram's famous experiment involving electric shock and learning. His experiment indicated that psychologically normal people will follow orders and inflict serious injury.

© Jan Rieckhoff / ullstein bild / The Image Works

Two famous psychological experiments are telling in this regard. The first took place in the early 1960s when Yale University psychologist Stanley Milgram (1974) recruited Yale students and residents of Bridgeport, Connecticut, to participate in a learning experiment. Subjects were told to apply electric shock to "learners" who performed poorly in word-pair tests. Unknown to the subjects, no electric shock was actually used, and the learners were all actors. Although they even screamed in pain and pleaded for the subjects to stop, the subjects proved all too ready to shock them. Because Milgram's experiment showed that psychologically normal people would follow orders and inflict serious injury on innocent people, it attracted wide attention and remains controversial to this day.

The other experiment was conducted at Stanford University. Psychologist Philip Zimbardo (1972) randomly assigned male student volunteers to be either guards or prisoners in a mock prison in the basement of a psychology building. Within a day, the guards began to treat the prisoners harshly, and within a few days some prisoners began suffering symptoms of a nervous breakdown. One prisoner even had to be convinced he was really a student. Because all the students had initially passed screening tests for mental disorder and drug and alcohol abuse and then were randomly assigned, the guards' abuse and prisoners' breakdowns could not have stemmed from any preexisting problems. Instead, their abnormal behaviors arose from the structural conditions and role expectations of the mock prison experience that led normal people to behave unacceptably.

Both of these experiments indicated that "normal" people are very capable of committing violent and abusive behavior under certain circumstances. Although people with mental disorders are at greater risk for committing violence (Rocque et al. 2012; Silver and Teasdale 2005), most people who commit violence do not have mental disorders.

Review and Discuss

The question of abnormality versus normality lies at the heart of much psychological research on criminal behavior. Do you think many criminals are psychologically abnormal?

▶ Conclusion

The explanations discussed in this chapter focus on the individual and attribute crime to individual biological or psychological traits. Ultimately, your view of the world influences the value you find in these explanations. If you think that people are responsible for their own behavior, then you will probably prefer the neoclassical views discussed in the previous chapter. If you think that behavioral problems arise primarily from individual failings, then you will probably prefer one or more of the explanations discussed in this chapter. If instead you think that behavioral problems derive primarily from problems in the larger society, then you will probably prefer sociological explanations discussed in the next few chapters. Although there is certainly room for more than one way to understand criminality, the explanation adopted has important implications for efforts to reduce crime.

Rational choice views attribute crime to the choices individuals make about their own behavior. Crime policies based on these views aim to affect these choices by making punishment more certain and more severe. However, it is unclear whether the decision making of potential criminals follows the rational choice model, as well as whether increasing the certainty and severity of punishment can reduce crime rates significantly. Moreover, the world of rational choice and deterrence theory is largely devoid of social inequality and social structure. To the extent that these social factors generate criminality, the rational choice model ignores important sources of crime.

Biological and psychological explanations both ultimately locate the origins of crime inside the individual. These explanations generally minimize the importance of social and structural factors. Even if the biological evidence were more conclusive, sociologists would continue to be troubled by its implications for social policy on crime. Several psychological approaches are more compatible with a sociological framework, but still minimize the importance of social factors.

Historically, biological research and, in its work on intelligence, psychological research have had damaging consequences for women, the poor, and people of color. Sensitivity to this history demands that biological and psychological evidence of criminality be interpreted cautiously.

These problems aside, biological and psychological research has made a valuable contribution in stressing the importance of early childhood for later delinquency and criminality. For example, certain approaches in both biology and psychology focus on childhood problems stemming from poor prenatal health and nutrition and inadequate parenting. These approaches suggest that programs focusing on families at risk for both sets of problems can achieve significant crime reduction. Because this risk is greatest for families living in poverty, this line of biological and psychological work complements sociological attention to the criminogenic effects of poverty and other structural conditions in the social environment explored in the next chapter. Chapter 8 examines social process theories in sociology that stress negative childhood social experiences, which again are more common for families living in poverty. Despite their differences, then, contemporary efforts in biology, psychology, and sociology all underscore the crime-reduction potential of well-designed and well-funded efforts that address the causes and consequences of poverty.

Summary

1. Biological explanations go back to phrenology in the early nineteenth century and Lombroso's theory of atavism several decades later. Explanations today focus on genetic transmission, neurochemical factors, diet and nutrition, and pregnancy and birth complications. To reduce crime, biological explanations imply the need to change the biological factors that produce it. They do not account well for group and location differences in crime rates and for the relativity of deviance. Because biological explanations historically were used to support racist ideologies, caution should be exercised in interpreting the findings of contemporary research on biology and crime.

2. Psychological explanations of crime include those emphasizing disturbances arising from negative early childhood experiences, inadequate moral development, low intelligence, and personality problems. Among other problems, these explanations generally minimize the importance of social factors, they cannot easily account for variations in crime by group or location for changes in crime rates, and they suggest that criminal behavior represents psychological abnormality. Research testing these explanations also often uses small, unrepresentative samples of offenders in prisons or mental institutions. Recent research using longitudinal data to investigate the impact of early childhood temperament problems is providing valuable evidence that such problems do predict later delinquency and crime.

Key Terms

abnormality *124*
atavism *107*
concordance *110*
discordance *110*
ego *119*
heredity *110*

id *119*
IQ *120*
moral development *120*
neurotransmitters *115*
personality *122*
phrenology *107*

premenstrual syndrome *113*
psychoanalytic *119*
somatology *109*
superego *119*
temperament *122*
testosterone *112*

What Would You Do?

1. You are working in a day care center that serves toddlers from working-class and middle-class backgrounds alike. On average, the working-class children seem more hyperactive than the middle-class children, but not very much so. One day, a university researcher approaches the manager of the day care center and requests permission to study the children to determine whether a relationship exists between their behavior and any personality problems they may have. The manager asks whether you think the researcher should be allowed to conduct this research. How do you respond?

2. The text notes that early childhood temperament problems can predict later delinquency and criminality. You are a teacher for grades 1 and 2 in a large city. The children are mostly African-American or Latino and generally come from working-class families. Most are well behaved, but a few seem off the wall. Having worked in a school serving a wealthier neighborhood mostly populated by white families, you do not think your current children's behavior is very much out of the ordinary. One day school administrators propose giving all your school's children a battery of tests to determine which of them have temperament problems. The children targeted by the tests will receive special education and counseling for the next year. The principal organizes a meeting of all the teachers to hear their reactions to this proposal. What will your reaction be? Why?

© Laiotz/Fotolia

7 Sociological Theories: Emphasis on Social Structure

Crime in the News

It was Mother's Day 2013, and thousands of people in a high-crime area of Boston marched 3.6 miles in the seventeenth annual Mother's Day Walk for Peace. The march is held every year to remember Bostonian deaths from street violence. One woman walked in memory of her godson, who had been slain seven months earlier. "We're tired of the violence occurring on the streets of Boston," she said. "Too many young men and women are losing their lives for no reason." Another woman walked in memory of her nephew, who was stabbed to death nine months earlier. She said sadly, "His birthday is next month, but he'll never turn 25. That's the reason I'm here. For him and for all the mothers." She added, "This is a difficult task for my sister. This is the first Mother's Day without him. . . . I can't even imagine the depth of her pain."

Source: Fox 2013.

We begin this chapter with two mental exercises. (1) Pretend you could wave a magic wand and create a community that would have a lot of street crime. What kind of community would this be? How would it look? Write down four or five characteristics that immediately come to mind. (2) Now pretend that you could take an individual and clone her or him at birth. One grows up in a poor urban area and the other in a wealthy suburb. Who would be more likely to commit street crimes?

Your list for Exercise 1 probably looks something like many urban neighborhoods: poverty, overcrowding, unemployment, run-down housing and schools. Is this correct? If so, your answer to Exercise 2 was undoubtedly the individual in the urban area. Is this correct again? If these were your answers, you recognize that there is something about poor urban areas that leads to more street crime. This "something" is what sociologists call structural conditions or structural problems. Although we must avoid stereotyping urban areas as evil and suburbs as angelic, the sociological evidence on the structural problems of urban areas supports your hypotheses.

As we saw in Chapter 6, individual-level theories of crime cannot easily account for why some locations and groups have higher crime rates than others. Many criminologists thus highlight the role played by social structure or, as it is more popularly called, *social environment*, in these differences, advocating what they call the "big picture" (Rosenfeld 2011). As Chapter 1 indicated, social structure refers not only to the physical features of communities, but also to the way society is organized: the distribution of social and economic resources and the nature of social relationships. Specific aspects of the social structure are sometimes called *structural conditions* and include such things as the levels of poverty and unemployment and the amount of crowded housing. Structural conditions are social forces external to the individual that affect behavior and attitudes. These forces help explain why crime and other behaviors vary across locations and groups.

A structural approach helps us understand why poor urban areas have higher street-crime rates than wealthy suburbs. Although most urban residents still do not commit street crimes, structural conditions like the ones you listed in the mental exercise help explain why street crime is more likely in poor urban areas. All other things being equal, individuals growing up in poor urban environments are more likely to commit street crime than are ones raised in more affluent locations. The structural conditions of the community matter more than the particular individuals living in it.

► The Legacy of Durkheim

Sociologists have recognized the impact of social structure on deviance and crime since Émile Durkheim's work more than a century ago. As Chapter 1 noted, Durkheim emphasized the influence of structural forces on individual behavior such as suicide. As a member of the conservative intellectual movement that arose after the French Revolution, Durkheim felt that human nature is basically selfish, with individuals having unlimited aspirations that, if left unchecked by a strong society, would result in chaos (Durkheim 1952 (1897)).

Durkheim emphasized two related mechanisms, socialization and social ties, by which society was able to hold individual impulses in check. Through socialization, we learn social norms and become good members of society. The ties we have to family, friends, and others further help socialize us, integrate us into society, and control our aspirations. Thus, a strong set of norms—or, to use Durkheim's term, a strong *collective conscience*—and solid social ties are both necessary for a stable society. A weakening in either of these elements destabilizes society and leads to many problems. This view lies at the heart of the "Durkheimian tradition" in sociology (Ritzer and Stepinsky 2014).

Durkheim's most notable application of this theory was to suicide (see Chapter 1). Although suicide is commonly considered the result of individual unhappiness, Durkheim found that suicide rates were influenced by external forces. For example, they tended to be higher in times of rapid social change, when traditional norms become less applicable to new circumstances. Normlessness, or anomie, sets in. Aspirations that previously were controlled are now unlimited, leaving people feeling more adrift. They realize that not all their aspirations can be fulfilled, and the resulting frustration leads some to commit suicide.

Durkheim used a similar argument to explain why Protestants have higher suicide rates than Catholics. Protestants are not less happy than Catholics, which an individual-level explanation might propose. Instead, said Durkheim, Catholic doctrine is stricter than Protestant doctrine and thus better controls the aspirations of its adherents. Catholics also have clearer norms on which to rely for comfort in times of trouble, whereas Protestants are left more to fend for themselves. Finally, Catholic doctrine condemns suicide in no uncertain terms; Protestant doctrine is less clear on the subject. Because of these factors, suicide rates are higher among Protestants than among Catholics.

Durkheim also explained that unmarried people have higher suicide rates than married people because of the former's lack of social ties. He reasoned that people with fewer ties have fewer sources of support in times of personal trouble and so have higher suicide rates.

These two structural conditions, anomie and low social integration, thus contribute to higher suicide rates. Obviously, not everyone in a society marked by anomie or low integration commits suicide. Individual-level explanations remain necessary to explain the specific suicides that do occur, but they cannot explain why suicide rates are higher for some groups and locations than others. Although Durkheim focused on suicide and only tangentially on crime, we will see in this and the next chapters that theorists have since applied his general views to various kinds of criminal behavior.

A modern literary application of Durkheim's (and the nineteenth-century conservative movement's) view of human nature and society appears in William Golding's (1954) famous novel *Lord of the Flies*, which you might have read in high school. To summarize a complex story far too simplistically, a group of young boys from England is stranded on an island after a plane crash. They have left their society behind and with it the norms, institutions, and social bonds that governed their behavior. Not sure how to proceed, they begin to devise new norms to deal with their extraordinary

▼ The boys in the novel *Lord of the Flies*, about the ages of those pictured here, became savages after they were stranded on an island and were no longer living in their former society.

© Mina Chapman/Corbis/Glow Images

situation, but their backgrounds as well-behaved youngsters do them no good after the ripping away of their society. Slowly but surely they become savages, as the book calls them again and again, and the story ends in murder. Echoing the view of Durkheim and other conservative intellectuals, Golding's bleak vision of human nature remains compelling, if controversial, and is reflected in many contemporary treatments of crime.

Review and Discuss

How and why did Durkheim's work contribute to a structural understanding of deviance and crime? How does the book *Lord of the Flies* reflect this understanding?

TABLE 7-1 Social Structure Theories in Brief

THEORY	KEY FIGURE(S)	SYNOPSIS
Social Ecological Theories		
Social disorganization	Clifford R. Shaw Henry D. McKay	High neighborhood crime rates due to weakened norms, social bonds, and conventional social institutions; evidence of social disorganization includes dilapidation and high rates of poverty and divorce.
Deviant places	Rodney Stark	High neighborhood crime rates due to high rates of density, poverty, coexistence of residential and commercial property, transience, and dilapidation.
Anomie and Strain Theories		
Anomie	Robert K. Merton	Crime results from the failure to achieve the cultural goal of economic success through the institutional means of working.
General strain	Robert Agnew	Negative emotions and thus delinquency result from the failure to achieve desired goals, from the removal of positive stimuli, and from the introduction of negative stimuli.
Subcultural Theories		
Status frustration	Albert K. Cohen	Delinquency results from the failure of lower-class boys to do well in school because of its middle-class values.
Focal concerns	Walter B. Miller	Delinquency results from several lower-class subcultural focal concerns: trouble, toughness, smartness, excitement, fate, and autonomy.
Differential opportunity	Richard Cloward Lloyd Ohlin	Whether individuals respond to their lack of access to legitimate means with criminal behavior depends on their access to illegitimate means.
Subculture of violence	Marvin Wolfgang Franco Ferracuti	High rates of urban violence result from a subculture of violence that favors violent responses to insults and other interpersonal conflicts.
Code of the street	Elijah Anderson	A variation of a subculture-violence approach that emphasizes the use and threat of violence to maintain respect; the need for respect results from the despair and alienation in which the urban poor live.

▼

We now turn to the major sociological theories of crime that emphasize aspects of the social structure. A summary of these theories appears in Table 7–1.

► Social Disorganization and Social Ecology

Durkheim and other members of the conservative intellectual movement were concerned about industrialization and the rapid growth of large cities in the nineteenth century. To these thinkers, society was changing from rural communities with close, personal relationships to larger, urban communities with impersonal relationships. These types of societies are less able to exert social control over individual behavior, leading to more deviance, crime, and other problems.

This view guided the work of U.S. social scientists who began to study crime and deviance in the late 1800s and early 1900s. Many of these scholars had grown up in small, rural communities with a strict Protestant upbringing condemning various acts of deviance as sins. In Chicago and other cities, they saw drinking, prostitution, and other deviance being committed by poor people, many of them Catholic immigrants. The social scientists' concern over urban crime was thus heightened by their bias against urban areas, Catholics, and immigrants and by their religious beliefs that drinking and other acts were sins. They viewed these "sins" as evidence of a sickness in society stemming from individuals' moral failings.

Although this social pathology school faded by the 1930s, a new approach emerged at the University of Chicago that emphasized structural causes of urban crime over moral failings. In particular, it attributed crime in certain neighborhoods to social disorganization, or a breakdown in social bonds and social control and on the accompanying confusion regarding how to behave (Akers and Sellers 2013). (In this sense the "society" in Lord of the Flies suffered from extreme social disorganization.) These were neighborhoods in transition, with poor immigrants and others moving in and long-standing residents moving out. High divorce rates, dilapidated housing, and other problems characterized these neighborhoods. In such conditions, these theorists thought, high crime rates were inevitable.

The concept of social disorganization first appeared in the work of W. I. Thomas and Florian Znaniecki (1927), who documented the troubles faced by Polish immigrants in Chicago, a huge, bustling city very different from the small, rural farms in their home country. These were stable areas where little change took place, whereas Chicago was undergoing rapid change in the early 1900s. In such a setting, the immigrants found their old ways not working as well; their children faced new, alien influences and weakened familial and other traditional sources of social control. Delinquency and crime thus became much more common in Polish neighborhoods in Chicago than they had been in the old country.

At about the same time, other social scientists at the University of Chicago, most notably Robert E. Park and Ernest W. Burgess, developed an ecological analysis of Chicago neighborhoods. Just as the relationship of plants and animals to their physical environment can be studied, said Park and Burgess, so can that of people to their environment. Their type of analysis has since been called a social ecology approach. Park and Burgess (Park et al. 1925) divided Chicago into five concentric zones, radiating from the central part of the city at the center of the circles to the outlying areas of Chicago on the outer circle. They found these zones differing widely in their physical and social characteristics. The outer areas had wealthier homes and more spacious streets, for example, whereas the inner zones had poorer, more crowded housing and other symptoms of social disorganization.

Clifford R. Shaw and Henry D. Mckay

This ecological model influenced the work of Clifford R. Shaw and Henry D. McKay (1942), who studied delinquency rates in Chicago from 1900 to 1933. Shaw and McKay noted that the ethnic and racial backgrounds of inner-zone residents changed during this period. In the early 1900s, inner-zone residents came from English, German, and Irish backgrounds. By the 1920s, these residents had given way to Polish and other Eastern European immigrants, who in turn began to be replaced in the 1930s by African-Americans migrating from the South. After painstakingly compiling data from some 56,000 juvenile court records on male delinquency in Chicago for this period, Shaw and McKay found that delinquency remained highest in the inner zones regardless of which ethnic groups lived there. They also found that the ethnic groups' delinquency fell after they moved to the outlying areas.

Shaw and McKay concluded that personal characteristics of the ethnic groups could not logically explain these two related phenomena. Instead, the social disorganization of the inner zones had to be at work. In such a climate, informal social control weakens, and deviant values emerge to flourish alongside conventional values. Adolescents grow up amid these conflicting values. Most adopt conventional values, but some adopt deviant beliefs, especially when influenced by delinquent peers. Shaw and McKay rejected the idea that crime was due to biological or psychological deficiencies of the people living in high-crime areas, feeling instead that crime was a normal response to negative social conditions. Although they acknowledged that individual-level factors help explain whether particular adolescents commit delinquency, Shaw and McKay argued that adolescents commit more delinquency if they are living in less advantaged neighborhoods because of these neighborhoods' social disorganization.

Evaluation of Social Disorganization Theory

Shaw and McKay's social disorganization theory was popular for some time, but later gave way to several methodological critiques (Bursik 1988; Kornhauser 1978). The most devastating criticism concerned their reliance on official records for measuring delinquency rates, as middle-class delinquents may not show up in official records, while bias against the poor and people of color may increase their appearance in official records. In a related criticism, scholars also noted that social disorganization theory cannot explain middle-class delinquency, because the middle classes do not, almost by definition, live in conditions of social disorganization.

Shaw and McKay were also faulted for imprecision in their concept of social disorganization. At times they engaged in circular reasoning by taking criminality as an indicator of disorganization. They also underestimated the amount of social organization in cities' inner zones. Rich ethnographic studies of inner-city neighborhoods find they can have high amounts of social order and social integration (Suttles 1968; Whyte 1943). In view of these and other problems, the causal power of the social disorganization model eventually came to be considered rather weak.

The Revival of Social Disorganization Theory

Since the mid-1980s, however, sociologists have rediscovered social disorganization theory and found it a powerful tool for explaining variation in crime and victimization across groups and locations (Kubrin and Weitzer 2003a; Pratt and Gau 2010; Steenbeek and Hipp 2011). In response to the methodological critiques of Shaw and McKay's work, recent research uses self-report and victimization data (to avoid the problems of official crime measures) and more sophisticated, neighborhood-level measures of social disorganization than were available to Shaw and McKay.

Although the results of the new research depend on the type of crime examined and the way variables are measured, it generally finds crime and victimization highest in communities with (1) low participation in voluntary organizations; (2) few networks of friendship ties; (3) low levels of *collective efficacy*, or community supervision of adolescents and of other informal social control mechanisms; and (4) high degrees of residential mobility, population density, single-parent homes, dilapidated housing, and poverty (Bellair and Browning 2010; Pratt and Cullen 2005; Sampson 2013; Steenbeek and Hipp 2011). These findings provide new and very strong empirical support for Shaw and McKay's decades-old theory, even if the findings may partly reflect the influence of crime on social disorganization rather than the reverse (Hipp 2010).

Consistent with Shaw and McKay's view, the new research assumes that social disorganization increases crime and delinquency because it weakens a neighborhood's social relationships and thus its informal social control, and also because it increases adolescents' associations with delinquent peers (Warner 2007). One reason for the latter effect is that social disorganization weakens the quality of parenting in a community. Poorer parenting in turn puts children at greater risk for delinquency because it weakens the parent–child bond and makes it more likely that children will spend time with delinquent peers (Hay et al. 2006).

Other Ecological Work

The revival of social disorganization theory reflects a growing and more general interest in the impact of ecological factors on community crime rates (Sampson 2013). This growing interest departs from the individual-level focus of biological and psychological explanations: "Instead of

▼

looking for what is wrong with people, these researchers are looking for what is wrong with society" (Turk 1993:355). Interestingly, some evidence suggests that high-risk neighborhoods (with high levels of social disorganization and economic deprivation) can lead even "well-adjusted children to become adolescent delinquents," to borrow from the title of a study of delinquency in Pittsburgh (Wikström and Loeber 2000). This study found that male delinquency was more common in more disadvantaged neighborhoods, but, perhaps more tellingly, it also found that neighborhood disadvantage affected whether individual risk factors translate into delinquency. Although high-risk boys were more delinquent no matter what type of neighborhood they lived in, average-risk and even low-risk boys were more delinquent when they lived in more disadvantaged neighborhoods. High-risk neighborhoods also have negative consequences for former prisoners, as recent research finds that released prisoners who settle in disadvantaged neighborhoods are more likely than those who settle in more advantaged neighborhoods to commit new crimes (Stahler et al. 2013; Tillyer and Vose 2011). The disadvantaged neighborhoods lack resources, including treatment clinics, job placement centers, and stable personal networks, that would help ex-offenders, and they also include other offenders with whom ex-offenders could get into trouble.

Extreme Poverty and Crime

As should be clear, a key emphasis of contemporary ecological work is the effect of extreme poverty (also termed economic deprivation) on community crime rates. At least two reasons explain why poverty might increase neighborhood criminality (Mears and Bhati 2006). Shaw and McKay thought that poverty fosters crime at the community level only because it first generates social disorganization and hence undermines traditional social control mechanisms. In this sense they considered the ecological effect of poverty on crime to be *indirect*. Although not rejecting this assumption, some scholars say that poverty also has a *direct* effect. In this view, some people, called the underclass, live in a continuing cycle of *concentrated disadvantage* characterized by extreme poverty, housing segregation, and racial and ethnic discrimination. As a result of these conditions, some members of the underclass commit violence and other crime out of frustration, anger, or economic need (Sampson and Wilson 1995).

Most ecological studies find the expected poverty–crime relationship. In some, an initial relationship disappears when social disorganization factors are held constant, supporting Shaw and McKay's view of how poverty generates crime. In other studies, concentrated disadvantage continues to predict crime even when social disorganization is taken into account, supporting the "direct" view of the causal process. Although these new ecological studies do not agree on how extreme poverty generates crime, they nonetheless underscore its importance for community differences in criminality (Akins 2009; Hipp and Yates 2011; Pyrooz 2012; Sampson 2013; Strom and MacDonald 2007).

One reason the poor become angry and frustrated might be their realization that other people in society have more money. This realization leads them to experience relative deprivation: It is one thing to be poor if everyone else is; it is another to be poor if many others are not (Hipp 2007; Webber 2007). Supporting this view, a study found that Houston adolescents who thought they were economically deprived compared to their friends, relatives, and the national population had lower feelings of self-worth and, as a result, higher rates of violent and property crime and drug use (Stiles et al. 2000). At the macro level, relative deprivation should be higher in poor neighborhoods located near affluent ones than in poor neighborhoods farther away, because people in the former neighborhoods see the wealth and possessions of richer residents more often than do their counterparts in the latter neighborhoods. If this is true, they should also be more angry and frustrated and, as a result, more likely to commit crime. Crime rates should thus be higher in poor neighborhoods bordering affluent areas than in poor neighborhoods farther away. Some studies find that this is indeed the case (Peterson and Krivo 2009).

The evidence on economic deprivation and community crime rates helps explain the relatively high crime rates of people of color (Painter-Davis 2012). As Chapter 3 noted, it is possible to acknowledge and explain these groups' higher rates without resorting to biological and other racially biased explanations. The new ecological work on economic deprivation and crime provides one such explanation, suggesting that a primary reason is these groups' poverty, the seriously disadvantaged communities in which many live, and their resulting frustration and hostility. All these factors in turn generate violent crime and other offenses (Bellair and McNulty 2005;

This chapter emphasizes that crime is more common in urban neighborhoods characterized by extreme poverty and other indicators of concentrated disadvantage. These neighborhoods are often rife with signs of physical disorder: graffiti, litter, abandoned cars, dilapidated stores and housing, public drinking, homeless people begging for a living, and so forth. Does such a disorder contribute to their high crime rates? If so, then one way to reduce crime is to literally clean up the neighborhoods and remove the physical disorder that is an important component of urban blight.

This is precisely the view, popularly called *broken windows theory*, of scholars James Q. Wilson and George L. Kelling. In 1982 they penned an influential article in *The Atlantic Monthly* that argued that signs of disorder—such as a broken window—send a signal to potential criminals that neighborhood residents do not care about what happens in their surroundings, making crime more likely. The New York City police force embraced the theory during the 1990s when it formulated a zero-tolerance policing strategy aimed at getting petty criminals, vagrants, and other such nuisance people off the streets. The strategy was widely credited for lowering New York's crime rate, although many scholars think this credit is undeserved (see Chapter 16).

Since then, broken windows theory itself has come under careful scrutiny. A basic issue is whether it can be proved that physical disorder does, in fact, raise the crime rate. Because physical disorder is worse in the neighborhoods with the worst concentrated disadvantage, it is difficult to isolate the effects of the disorder from those of the other neighborhood problems. Crime may even produce disorder rather than the reverse, or both problems may stem from the same source, such as the poverty of the neighborhoods.

Most research investigating these possibilities has found only weak or even no evidence for the validity of the broken windows theory. For example, a study of 2,400 city blocks in Chicago found only a weak correlation between physical disorder and violent crime that disappeared, except for robbery, when poverty and other factors were taken into account. This study concluded that crime and disorder both stem from the neighborhood structural characteristics, especially concentrated poverty. On the other hand, a study using Colorado Springs, Colorado, data did conclude that physical disorder induces crime, as broken windows theory predicts.

Critics say that broken windows theory and its implied anticrime strategy—to reduce physical disorder—take attention away from more important causes of crime such as extreme poverty, persistent unemployment, and racial discrimination. Given the importance of determining the most effective crime-control strategies, debate over broken windows theory will undoubtedly continue to engage scholars and criminal justice policy makers.

Whether or not physical disorder affects the crime rate, recent research finds that it may affect residents' quality of life. Allison T. Chappell and colleagues surveyed 746 residents in two large Southeastern cities. Among other things, respondents were asked to assess how much physical disorder (littering, etc.) characterized their neighborhoods, and they were also asked various questions about how happy they were with their lives. Holding other variables constant, the authors found that perceived physical disorder reduced the residents' self-reported quality of life. Reducing physical disorder, then, may raise residents' quality of life, whether or not it lowers their neighborhoods' crime rates.

Source: Chappell et al. 2011; Gau and Pratt 2008; Harcourt and Ludwig 2007; Sampson and Raudenbush 2001; Yang 2010.

Peterson and Krivo 2005). A complementary explanation has to do with the kinds of places in which many people of color live. We now discuss this view in some detail.

Kinds of Places Versus Kinds of People

The revival of an ecological focus reflects the belief of many scholars that kinds of places matter more than kinds of people (Kubrin and Weitzer 2003a). Recalling Shaw and McKay's central finding that neighborhoods can continue to have high crime rates despite changes in the kinds of people who live there, Rodney Stark (1987:893) observed that "*there must be something about places as such* that sustains crime" (emphasis his). Drawing on ecological and other approaches, Stark then advanced thirty propositions, many of them focusing on neighborhood physical features, that offer a compelling ecological explanation for the high crime and delinquency of particular urban neighborhoods and more generally of the cities containing them. His view has since been referred to as the *theory of deviant places*.

In one proposition, Stark assumed that the denser a neighborhood, the greater the likelihood that "good kids" will come into contact with "bad kids," increasing the pressures on the former to break the law. This helps explain why cities have more serious delinquency than other areas: adolescents who step out the door can easily find other teenagers. In suburbs and especially rural areas where housing is much more spread out, it is more difficult to get together with friends, especially if a car ride is necessary. In other propositions, Stark noted that poor urban neighborhoods contain many overcrowded homes, which generate family conflict and lead their inhabitants, especially adolescents, to spend extra time outside the home to have some elbow room. Once outside, they are freer to associate with delinquent peers, with more delinquency again resulting. The presence of convenience stores and other places to hang out in urban neighborhoods aggravates this problem, because these places can become targets for crime or at least foster communication about committing crime elsewhere. All these factors in turn increase these neighborhoods' criminality.

AP Photo/Charles Rex Arbogast

▲ Rodney Stark's theory of deviant places argues that crowded neighborhoods contribute to higher rates of street crime.

Taken together, Stark's propositions and other research on kinds of places provide a powerful ecological basis for the high crime rates of urban neighborhoods (Stucky and Ottensmann 2009). They suggest that normal people get caught in a vicious cycle of structural conditions that generate delinquency and crime, just as the normal people in Zimbardo's and Milgram's experiments (Chapter 6) committed abnormal behavior. Stark's theory and other ecological perspectives thus explain why neighborhoods can continue to have high crime rates even when some people move from the neighborhoods and others move in. They also provide yet another racially unbiased explanation of the high crime rates of African-Americans and other people of color. As Stark (1987:905–906) noted, the particularly high crime rates of non-Southern African-Americans can be seen as "the result of where they live," for example, the inner zones of cities. These areas, said Stark, are "precisely the kinds of places explored in this essay—areas where the probabilities of *anyone* committing a crime are high" (emphasis his). In the South, African-Americans tend to live in rural areas and thus have lower crime rates than their northern counterparts. Kinds of places matter more than kinds of people.

Notice that we are *not* saying that kinds of people make *no* difference. Ecological theories do not mean we should "stop seeking and formulating 'kinds of people' explanations" (Stark 1987: 906) to explain why some individuals in damaging ecological conditions commit crime, whereas most do not. Chapter 8 discusses such explanations.

Whether you prefer kinds of places or kinds of people explanations depends on which level of analysis makes the most sense to you. Ecological theories remind us that, no matter what kinds of people we have in mind, their criminality would be lower if they grew up and lived in communities lacking the many structural conditions generating crime. We do not have to be stranded like the boys in *Lord of the Flies* to realize that where we live strongly affects our values and behavior, including crime. To return to a mental exercise that began this chapter, a clone growing up amid overcrowding, extreme poverty, and other disadvantaged structural conditions will often turn out very different from its match growing up in a more advantaged area.

Review and Discuss

What does the new ecological work on crime and victimization generally tell us about the factors that make crime more common?

▶ Anomie and Strain Theory

Durkheim felt that anomie, or strain, results when people's aspirations become uncontrolled and unfulfilled. Although Durkheim discussed how anomie can lead to suicide, it remained to

Columbia University sociologist Robert K. Merton to connect anomie to other forms of deviance. In his 1938 paper "Social Structure and Anomie," perhaps the most famous in the criminology literature, Merton discounted the assumption, popular then and still today, that criminality is rooted in biological impulses. He argued instead that "certain phases of social structure generate the circumstances in which infringement of social codes constitutes a 'normal' response" (Merton 1938:672). Assuming that most crime is committed by poor people, he intended his anomie theory to explain the high rates of crimes by the poor.

Merton reasoned as follows: Every society includes cultural goals and institutional means (norms) about how to reach these goals. These two dimensions are usually in harmony, meaning that, more often than not, members of society can reach the cultural goals, or at least have some hope of reaching them, by following certain socially approved means. A lack of harmony, or anomie, between the goals and the means results when either too much emphasis is given to goals or the means are inadequate to reach the goals.

In the United States, Merton reasoned, there is too much emphasis on the goal of economic success. As a result, U.S. residents often find they cannot fulfill "the American dream" unless they commit illegal activity. This problem is greatest for the poor in the United States, said Merton, because they also lack the ability, because of their poverty, to achieve economic success through the approved means of working. The strain they feel is heightened because they live in a society where it is widely believed that all people can pull themselves up by their bootstraps. Given this ideology, they are especially likely to feel frustrated. In response to their strain, the poor may either accept or reject the cultural goals of economic success and the legitimate means (working) of becoming economically successful. These possibilities result in the logical adaptations to anomie depicted in Table 7–2.

The first adaptation is *conformity*. Even given anomie, most poor people continue to accept the goal of economic success and the means of working; in short, they continue to be law-abiding members of society. Merton said it is not surprising that so many people continue to conform, because otherwise there could be no social order. Conformity is, of course, not deviant behavior, but a logical and by far the most common adaptation to anomie.

The second adaptation is *innovation*. Here people continue to accept the goal of economic success, but reject the means of working and undertake new means, or innovate, to achieve success. Unlike conformity, innovation thus involves illegal behavior, of which theft, fraud, and other economic crimes are prime examples. If we were to think about good grades as another kind of success, then cheating would be an example of innovation.

The third adaptation is *ritualism*. Here people reject the goal of economic success, but continue to accept the means of working. Examples include "bureaucrats" who come to work day after day as a ritual, not to achieve economic success. Though a logical adaptation to anomie, ritualism is not deviant per se and certainly not illegal, and Merton spent little time discussing it.

Retreatism is the fourth adaptation. Here people reject both the goal of economic success and the means of working. In effect, they give up. Merton included in this category alcoholics, drug addicts, and hobos.

The fifth and final adaptation is *rebellion*. People who rebel not only reject both the goal of economic success and the means of working, but also try to bring about a new society with different, more egalitarian goals. These are the radicals and revolutionaries of society who often break the law in an attempt to transform it.

TABLE 7–2 Merton's Adaptations to Anomie

ADAPTATION	CULTURAL GOALS	INSTITUTIONAL MEANS
1. Conformity	Accept	Accept
2. Innovation	Accept	Reject
3. Ritualism	Reject	Accept
4. Retreatism	Reject	Reject
5. Rebellion	Reject/substitute	Reject/substitute

▼

Like social disorganization theory, Merton's anomie theory provides a structural explanation of criminality that assumes that problems in the way society is set up produce deviance among normal but poor people. In social disorganization theory, these problems involve structural conditions at the neighborhood level that generate deviance by weakening traditional social control mechanisms. In anomie theory, these issues involve a disjunction at the societal level between the goal of economic success and the means of working that generates deviance by creating strain. Although the theories disagree on how and why economic deprivation leads to deviance, they nonetheless locate the roots of deviance in the social structure, not in the properties or failings of individuals.

Evaluation of Anomie Theory

Anomie theory (or *strain theory*, as it is often called) provides an important structural explanation for some crimes by the poor in the United States, but it falls short in other respects (Akers and Sellers 2013). Many scholars question Merton's assumption that the poor commit more crime than the nonpoor, and they fault its failure to address either middle-class delinquency or the many serious white-collar offenses committed by the "respectable" elements of society. They also fault the theory for not explaining the violent crimes of homicide, assault, and rape, which do not readily fit into any of Merton's logical adaptations. Innovation applies to crimes such as theft that are committed for financial gain, but the motivation for these violent crimes is usually not financial. Instead, it is anger, jealousy, or the thrill of "doing evil" (Katz 1988). For rape, it is also contempt for women and perhaps sexual gratification (Brownmiller 1975; Felson and Krohn 1990). Even much theft is often done more for thrills than for money. Because the power of a theory of crime depends to a large degree on the number of different crimes it can explain, anomie theory's inability to explain most violent crimes and other noneconomic offenses is a serious failure.

Merton's retreatism adaptation is also problematic. He assumed that most alcoholism, drug addiction, and vagrancy occur when poor people reject both economic success and working. They are double failures who give up on society and withdraw from it. However, research since Merton's time finds that much alcohol and drug use occurs as a result of noneconomic factors such as peer influences (Goode 2012). Merton's explanation also overlooks the alcohol and drug abuse found among the nonpoor, including very successful occupational groups such as physicians. College friends of yours who have used marijuana and other illegal drugs might disagree with Merton's assumption that they have given up on making money by getting a good education and working!

Anomie theory also fails to explain why people choose one adaptation over another, and, more generally, cannot explain why, given anomie, some people commit crime and others do not. Finally, several tests of anomie theory have not supported it. In these studies, researchers measured adolescents' aspirations and expectations. Anomie theory predicts that strain and thus delinquency should be highest among juveniles with high aspirations and low expectations and among juveniles with the largest gap between their aspirations and expectations. However, empirical tests do not support these hypotheses (Elliott et al. 1985).

Defense and Extension of Anomie Theory

In response to these criticisms, anomie theory supporters have revised and extended it to explain some of the crimes that Merton's original formulation did not cover. They have also defended the theory against its critics (Adler and Laufer 1995; Agnew 2000). A first argument focuses on the issue of social class and offending. Even if Merton may have exaggerated class differences in delinquency by relying on official records, his assumption of these differences appears to be supported at least for serious offenses (see Chapter 3). The anomie concept can

▼ Robert K. Merton's anomie theory assumes that drug users are retreatists, or double failures. This explanation overlooks the use of marijuana and other drugs by people who want to be financially successful and who accept the need to work hard to achieve such success.

AP Photo/Albuquerque Journal, Mike Stewart

▲ Institutional anomie theory argues that crime results from several key cultural values, including an exaggerated emphasis on economic success.

also be extended to cover middle-class delinquency and white-collar crime; given the intense importance in the United States of economic success, middle-class adolescents, and corporate executives may still feel they do not have enough wealth and possessions and thus break the law (Passas 1990).

This view forms the basis for an influential extension of Merton's theory by Steven F. Messner and Richard Rosenfeld (2013), whose *institutional anomie theory* argues that crime in the United States results from several key cultural values, including achievement, individualism, universalism, and the fetishism of money. To achieve the American dream, people eagerly pursue economic success in a society whose universal ideology is that anyone, rich or poor, has a chance for success. Because economic success is so important, Americans often judge one another's merit by how much wealth and possessions they have. Because this creates intense pressures for the most economic success possible, many people, rich or poor, feel they lack enough money and turn to crime. At the same time, the exaggerated emphasis on monetary success makes the economic institution more prominent than other social institutions, such as the family and schools. This effect weakens these traditional social control institutions, making crime even more likely. For all these reasons, U.S. society itself is criminogenic, or, as Messner and Rosenfeld (p. 1) put it, a "society organized for crime." This in turn means, they say, that the "American Dream thus has a dark side that must be considered in any serious effort to uncover the social sources of crime" (p. 10). The same values that make the American dream attainable also make crime not only possible but likely.

A second argument of anomie theory supporters addresses the empirical tests of the theory. In these tests, strain is typically measured by examining the difference between expectations and educational or occupational aspirations. These aspirations, the theory's supporters say, are not the same as the *economic* aspirations that Merton addressed. Eventual economic success might be more important to adolescents than their eventual education or occupational status. Supporting this view, a study of Seattle adolescents found delinquency more related to the imbalance between their economic goals and educational expectations than to the imbalance between their educational goals and expectations (Farnworth and Leiber 1989).

General Strain Theory

A very influential extension of Merton's views is Robert Agnew's (1992; 2007) *general strain theory* (GST) of delinquency, which broadens strain theory's focus beyond economic goals and success. Agnew argued that adolescent strain results not only from failure to achieve economic goals, but also from failure to achieve noneconomic goals, the removal of positive stimuli (e.g., the death of a loved one, the ending of a romantic relationship), and the introduction of negative stimuli (e.g., arguments with parents, insults by teachers or friends). Events occurring closely in time cause more stress than events occurring far apart. Repeated stress leads to several negative emotions, including anger, frustration, and unhappiness. Of these, anger is particularly likely to occur when adolescents blame others for their misfortune. Because anger increases the desire for revenge and inhibits self-control, it, along with other negative emotions, can increase delinquency and drug use. Whether someone does engage in crime depends on a variety of factors, including the individual's social support networks, relationships with delinquent friends, parental upbringing, and personal characteristics such as self-esteem.

The many tests of GST generally support it (Botchkovar et al. 2009; Moon et al. 2009). Various kinds of strain predict delinquency, including the death or serious injury of a family member or friend; a change in school or residence; victimization by physical and sexual abuse and other crimes; and unemployment. Additionally, ex-prisoners who experienced more strain during their confinement—for example, they experienced more assaults and had worse relationships with prison guards—are more likely to commit new crimes than ex-prisoners who experienced less strain (Listwan et al. 2013).

Importantly, Agnew (1999) has also used GST to explain variation in crime and delinquency across communities. If strain produces anger at the individual level, he reasoned, negative social conditions should also produce strain, and in turn anger and frustration, at the macro level. Thus, the neighborhoods with the worst social conditions should have the most angry and frustrated residents and thus the most crime. This perspective nicely supplements the ecological emphasis on concentrated disadvantage discussed earlier.

Despite the empirical support for GST, more research is needed on several issues. A first issue concerns the reasons that strain leads to delinquency. For example, although the theory highlights the role played by anger, not all types of strain produce anger, and not all studies find that anger produces delinquency (Tittle et al. 2008). Another issue concerns whether gender differences exist in the response to strain. For example, some studies have found that females are less likely than males to react to strain with anger and more likely to react with guilt or depression (Kaufman 2009). This raises the further point that it is still unclear "why some individuals are more likely than others to react to strain with delinquency" (Agnew et al. 2002:43).

GST and the other recent defenses, revisions, and extensions of anomie or strain theory have revived it as an important explanation. Additional research is needed to assess the importance of strain at the community and individual levels for crime and delinquency.

 ## International Focus STRAIN, IMMIGRATION, AND RIOTING IN SWEDEN

Strain theory in its various formulations emphasizes that crime results from the frustration and anger stemming from poverty, discrimination, and other strains. Rioting in Sweden in May 2013 illustrates this dynamic.

Sweden is normally a peaceful nation. It has a low poverty rate and provides an extensive range of goods and services to its citizens. Amid such tranquility, the May 2013 riots were shocking, but a look at their background indicates that they were not very surprising, especially if we keep in mind strain theory's assumptions.

The rioting was carried out mostly by young immigrants, who ran through cities and towns across the nation and set fire to cars, schools, and other buildings. A news report called the rioting "a spasm of destructive rage rarely seen in a country proud of its normally tranquil, law-abiding ways." The rioting, the report continued, "left Swedes wondering what went wrong in a society that has invested so heavily in helping the underprivileged."

On the face of it, Sweden's immigrants, many of them fleeing from armed conflict in Middle Eastern and Northern African nations, live a fairly good life, thanks to Sweden's famed social welfare system. Sweden had welcomed immigrants, who, along with their children, make up 15 percent of the nation's population. But at the time of the riots, immigrants' unemployment rate

was twice as high as the national rate of 8 percent, and almost one-third of immigrants under age 25 were unemployed. The extremely high unemployment rate of Sweden's young immigrants helps explain their rioting, as it constituted a significant source of strain. As the principal of an elementary school for immigrant children commented, "They don't get work, and they feel excluded from society."

Interestingly, a generation gap was apparent in the Swedish immigrant community after the rioting, as older immigrants condemned the violent actions of their younger counterparts, with one older immigrant saying, "There is no excuse for this violence." A young immigrant countered this sentiment, saying, "Our parents say we should be thankful. They feel thankful themselves because they lived through wars. But those of us who were born here have nothing to compare our lives with."

The Swedish rioting came on the heels of immigrant rioting in Britain in 2011 and in France in 2005. In all these riots, immigrants were protesting their high unemployment, feelings of discrimination, and other grievances. Strain theory does not excuse their actions, but it does help explain why they occurred at all.

Source: Higgins 2013.

Why should anomie theory be considered a structural theory? How does general strain theory build on anomie theory?

▶ Subcultural Theories

Recall that Merton's theory does not explain why some people unable to achieve economic success turn to crime, whereas others do not. Shaw and McKay gave an early clue to one of the processes involved when they noted that juveniles in socially disorganized neighborhoods grow up amid conflicting values, some of them law-abiding and some of them lawbreaking. Delinquency results when juveniles adopt the latter values. Beginning in the 1950s, scholars began to discuss various kinds of subcultures through which adolescents and others learn that it is acceptable to break the law. Explicitly or implicitly, most of these theorists traced these subcultures' origins to poverty and other kinds of strain.

Albert K. Cohen: School Failure and Delinquent Subcultures

Extending Merton's anomie theory into noneconomic behavior, Albert K. Cohen (1955) developed the notion of a delinquent subculture in his influential book, *Delinquent Boys*. Like Merton, Cohen assumed that lower-class boys have high delinquency rates. He observed that much, and perhaps most, delinquency, such as fighting and vandalism, is noneconomic or nonutilitarian and that even delinquency involving theft—shoplifting, burglary, and the like—is often done more for thrills than for economic reasons. As a result, this delinquency cannot result from anomie as Merton conceived it.

Cohen adapted Merton's concept of strain but reasoned that a major adolescent goal involves making a favorable impression on others and thus feeling good about oneself. However, the school experience of lower-class boys makes it difficult to achieve this goal because schools are dominated by middle-class values such as courtesy and hard work. Having not been raised with these values, lower-class boys do poorly in school and experience status frustration, or strain. To reduce their frustration, they turn to a delinquent gang subculture to regain status and respect. This subculture includes values, including hedonism and maliciousness, that help promote delinquency. *Hedonism*, or pleasure seeking, involves the immediate, impulsive gratification of the need for fun and excitement, whereas *maliciousness* involves a desire to hurt, and even delight in hurting, others. For obvious reasons, both values can lead gang members to pursue illegal activities. Their primary motive is not to acquire money or possessions, but rather to gain status in the eyes of their peers and to improve their self-esteem by defying authority.

Notice that Cohen's book is entitled *Delinquent Boys*. What about girls? For the most part, Cohen ignored them because he considered delinquency primarily a lower-class male phenomenon. He thought girls were not delinquent because they care less than boys about how well they do in school. Instead, they attach more importance to romantic relationships because they consider marriage their major goal in life. Girls' delinquency, Cohen thought, stems more from a poor romantic life than from poor school performance.

Evaluation of Cohen's Status Frustration Theory

When Cohen wrote his book in 1955, relatively little research on gang delinquency had been done since Shaw and McKay's work. Cohen's book helped change that, and delinquency research burgeoned in the ensuing years. Ironically, much of this research challenged Cohen's assumptions and conclusions (Bernard et al. 2009).

A first criticism should by now be familiar: Cohen overlooked middle-class delinquency, which his theory cannot explain. A second criticism concerns his assumption that most delinquency

▲ Albert K. Cohen thought that poor school performance leads to status frustration that, in turn, leads to involvement in a delinquent gang subculture to regain status and respect.

© Marmaduke St. John / Alamy

is nonutilitarian. Some researchers argue that delinquency is more utilitarian, or economically motivated, than Cohen assumed. The involvement of many urban gangs these days in drug trafficking is aimed more at making money than at finding cheap thrills. Critics also take issue with Cohen's explanation of why school failure leads to delinquency. Although the association between school failure and delinquency is a common finding in the literature, processes other than status frustration might be at work (see Chapter 8).

Another criticism is that Cohen failed to explain why many boys doing poorly in school do *not* become delinquent. Critics also charged that by placing more emphasis on delinquent subcultures than on the structural conditions in which poor adolescents live, Cohen implicitly blamed lower-class adolescents for their problems. A final criticism is that Cohen's view of girls and their delinquency was based on outmoded, sexist views.

Walter B. Miller: Focal Concerns

Three years after the publication of Cohen's book, Walter B. Miller (1958) published an influential article on lower-class subcultures and delinquency. Like Cohen, Miller emphasized that juveniles learn values conducive to delinquency from their subculture, but his views differed as to the nature of the subculture. While Cohen attributed delinquency to involvement in a delinquent gang subculture after failure in school, Miller attributed it to the lower-class subculture itself. He thought that lower-class boys are exposed to this subculture, and are hence likely to commit delinquent acts, whether or not they do well in school.

Miller termed the values of the lower-class subculture focal concerns and thought that they contribute to delinquency. In order of importance, Miller presented the focal concerns as follows (see Figure 7–1 ■):

1. **Trouble.** Miller wrote that an interest in "trouble" characterizes lower-class culture. Adults usually want their children to stay out of trouble, but lower-class adolescents sometimes gain prestige with their friends by getting into trouble.

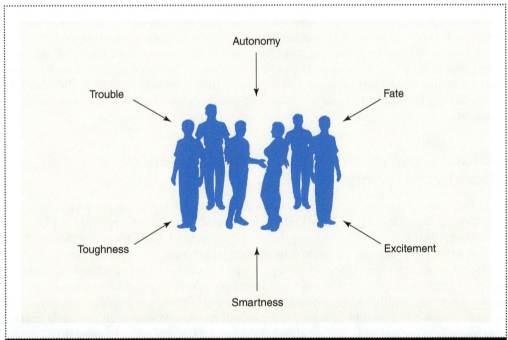

FIGURE 7–1   Focal Concerns. Walter Miller felt that lower-class boys grow up amid several focal concerns that they learn from their subculture. These focal concerns, he thought, help explain their high rates of delinquency.
Source: Based on Miller 1958.

2. **Toughness.** This concern evokes the John Wayne image of the strong, silent, brave cowboy adept at fighting and involves, Miller said, preoccupation with masculinity and extreme homophobia (hatred of homosexuals). Miller believed it arises from the fact that many lower-class boys are raised in female-headed households and thus lack adequate male role models.

3. **Smartness.** To be "smart" in the lower-class subculture is to outwit others and to avoid being outwitted yourself. It involves the ability to achieve a goal by the use of wits rather than physical force. Boys grow up outwitting each other in various activities, including the mutual trading of insults.

4. **Excitement.** Miller wrote that many aspects of lower-class life revolve around excitement and thrills. On weekends people typically drink, gamble, go out on the town, and have sex. Many men are involved in physical fights. Miller believed that the pursuit of excitement on weekends arises in part from boring lives led the rest of the week.

5. **Fate.** Lower-class people have a particularly fatalistic outlook on life, said Miller. Whether they succeed or fail is due less to their own efforts than to good luck or bad luck. This helps account for their high interest in gambling, he said.

6. **Autonomy.** This focal concern involves a rejection of authority and distaste for anyone trying to control one's behavior. Autonomy helps justify the violation of laws and other rules.

If adolescents grow up in a subculture valuing trouble, toughness, smartness, excitement, fate, and autonomy, said Miller, it is no surprise that they often end up being delinquent: By conforming to their culture, they violate the larger society's legal norms. Delinquents are thus normal adolescents who have learned from their subculture several attitudes that justify breaking the law.

Evaluation of Miller's View

Miller's analysis has been subject to some withering criticism (Bernard et al 2009). The most pointed is that his discussion of lower-class culture "blames the victim" by ignoring the dire effects of economic deprivation. Much research since Miller's article also finds that poor and middle-class adolescents have similar values and attitudes: Middle-class boys appear to value excitement, toughness, autonomy, and other focal concerns as much as their poorer counterparts do (Cernkovich 1978). Moreover, to the extent that middle-class delinquency exists, Miller's theory cannot readily account for it because it attributes the focal concerns conducive to delinquency to the lower class. Miller also engaged in circular reasoning. He identified delinquent boys' focal concerns by observing their behavior and then used these concerns to explain their behavior. Finally, Miller's thesis, like Cohen's work, ignored female delinquency and thus was necessarily incomplete.

Richard Cloward and Lloyd Ohlin: Differential Opportunity Theory

Recall that Merton's anomie theory fails to explain why people facing anomie choose a specific adaptation. Richard Cloward and Lloyd Ohlin (1960) extended Merton's formulation to address this problem with their differential opportunity theory. Merton stressed that society provides *differential access to legitimate means*—working—to achieve monetary success. The nonpoor have such access; the poor often do not. Cloward and Ohlin argued that there is also *differential access to illegitimate means*, or illegitimate opportunity structures. Given anomie, the type of adaptation one pursues depends on which illegitimate opportunities are available in a particular neighborhood. Where organized crime is a powerful presence, adolescents will gravitate toward it. In especially deprived areas where drug use and addiction are already rampant, adolescents will start using drugs.

The neighborhoods' deviant activities in turn reflect their social organization and resulting subculture. Some neighborhoods have a *criminal subculture*. These tend to be well-organized, highly integrated neighborhoods with adults who have become well-to-do through illegitimate means (e.g., organized crime). Adolescents look up to these adults as role models and turn to various forms of property crime themselves, just as middle-class youths who spend time with businesspeople may desire a business career. Delinquent gangs in these communities thus specialize in highly organized, well-planned criminal activities. Other adolescents live in disorganized neighborhoods in which a *conflict subculture* exists. Organized crime does not flourish, and there are few successful adult criminals to befriend impressionable adolescents. Because youths in these communities lack both legitimate and illegitimate opportunities, they join gangs and engage in high amounts of random, and often spontaneous, violence. Regardless of their type of neighborhood, some youths find it difficult to join gangs or fail to do well after they join and then drop out of the gang. These youths are *double failures*, and among them a *retreatist subculture* develops that involves heavy drug and alcohol use.

Evaluation of Differential Opportunity Theory

Cloward and Ohlin's theory was immediately popular and helped prompt many of the antipoverty programs of the 1960s. Its emphasis on differential access to illegitimate opportunities remains important in helping to explain various types of deviance and crime. However, it too has been criticized for neglecting middle-class delinquency and white-collar crime. Although some research supports Cloward and Ohlin's idea that gangs specialize in various illegitimate activities determined by neighborhood social organization, the type of specialization does not always correspond with their criminal, conflict, and retreatist typology. Many gangs also combine several different kinds of illegitimate activities (e.g., drug use and theft) and thus are unspecialized. In another criticism, urban adolescent drug users often do not appear to be the double failures depicted by Cloward and Ohlin. Instead, as noted earlier regarding Merton's view, they use drugs for other reasons.

Showing the contemporary relevance of differential opportunity theory, a recent study of Chicago neighborhoods found violence to be particularly high, relative to other crimes, in neighborhoods that had the highest levels of social disorganization. Reasoning that these were precisely the neighborhoods with conflict subcultures as discussed by Cloward and Ohlin, the authors of the study concluded that this finding supported Cloward and Ohlin's theory (Schreck et al. 2009).

Marvin Wolfgang and Franco Ferracuti: The Subculture of Violence

About the time that Miller published his influential article, Marvin Wolfgang (1958:329) said that a subculture of violence explains the high level of violence among poor, urban males. This subculture "does not define personal assaults as wrong or antisocial." Instead, it is a subculture in which "quick resort to physical aggression is a socially approved and expected concomitant of certain stimuli." Wolfgang later expanded on this view in a book with Franco Ferracuti (Wolfgang and Ferracuti 1967). The two authors reasoned that when insults and other interpersonal conflicts occur, lower-class males often respond with physical force, whereas middle-class males tend to walk away. Echoing Miller's emphasis on lower-class males' obsession with masculinity, they thought this aggressive response stems from the need of lower-class males to defend their honor and masculinity.

Evaluation of the Subculture of Violence Theory

As the discussion of race and crime in Chapter 3 indicated, the subculture of violence theory is very controversial. Early research found that the urban poor disapprove of violence as much as other demographic subgroups do (Ball-Rokeach 1972; Erlanger 1974), and more recent research finds that African-Americans are no more likely than whites to approve of violence (Cao et al. 1997; Sampson and Bartusch 1999). Although the disproportionate involvement of young urban males in street violence seems beyond dispute (see Chapter 3),

▼ Some scholars say that a subculture of violence, involving a physical response to insults and other interpersonal problems, characterizes urban neighborhoods.

© Kayte Deioma / PhotoEdit

this does not automatically mean that their behavior stems from a subculture of violence, as Wolfgang and Ferracuti argued. Their reasoning, like Miller's, is a bit circular: they infer a subculture of violence from the high level of violence among young urban men and then attribute the violence to the subculture they have inferred.

These criticisms notwithstanding, a growing body of work supports Wolfgang and Ferracuti's basic theme, but places it squarely in the context of the structural problems discussed earlier in this chapter. According to this view, urban violence stems from the combined stresses of economic deprivation, urban living, and racial discrimination, all of which lead to a subculture characterized by a desire for self-respect and angry aggression (Baron et al. 2001; Bernard 1990; Sampson and Wilson 1995). These factors in turn increase the willingness to use violence in interpersonal confrontations, especially as younger adolescents come under the influence of older adolescents and young adults who reject conventional values (Harding 2010).

Elijah Anderson: The Code of the Street

The most influential contemporary view on the subcultural basis for violence comes from sociologist Elijah Anderson (2000), one of the most sensitive observers of urban life. Based on his years of ethnographic research in Philadelphia, Anderson documented a *code of the street* among young urban African-Americans that arises from their despair and alienation and that helps explain their interpersonal violence. Its most central feature is the need and striving for respect. "People are being told day in and day out that they are not respectable," Anderson said. "This is the message young black people get every day from the system. If you perceive that you're getting those kinds of messages, it may be that you will crave respect—you've got to get it from a turnip if you can. So every encounter becomes an opportunity for salvaging respect" (Coughlin 1994:A8).

To help command respect, Anderson said, young urban men often adopt a certain "look" involving the way they dress, move, and talk; this persona helps deter verbal and physical assaults by other men and is an essential aspect of the conception of manhood in inner cities. Displaying nerve by initiating physical and verbal attacks is another way for a young male to prove his manhood and gain respect. Striving for respect in these ways thus leads masculinity in urban areas to take on an especially violent tone.

Distrust of the police and courts also helps explain urban violence, Anderson added. Like the frontier settlers of an earlier era, young urban males feel they cannot count on the legal system for help and deem it necessary to use violence to defend themselves, their families, and friends. Gang wars over drugs and the availability of ever more powerful firearms all make an explosive situation even more volatile.

Anderson's work on the code of the street has stimulated many additional studies. Although his analysis was based on his fieldwork in Philadelphia, many studies since have found a similar code in other poor urban areas (Matsuda et al. 2013; Stewart and Simons 2010). This replication reinforces Anderson's conclusions and suggests that the code of the street is an important feature of poor urban areas generally that helps explain their level of violence.

Prospects for Subcultural Explanations

A particular strength of Anderson's framework is that it presents a subcultural basis for urban violence that derives from the structural problems and conditions of urban areas. This clear structural underpinning and the richness of his discussion have revived subcultural explanations in the field of criminology. As a result, research has begun to stress the combined impact of structural problems and cultural influences on crime rates (Harding 2010; Kubrin and Weitzer 2003b; Warner 2003). This new body of research also supports Anderson's view that distrust of the police leads some urban residents to turn to violence to resolve confrontations rather than call the police (Wilkinson et al. 2009).

Despite the revival of subcultural explanations, much work remains in this area. For example, a recent study of Kentucky adolescents found that acceptance of violence as a solution to problems—i.e., belief in a subculture of violence—predicted the youths' involvement in general offending. However, it did not predict their involvement in violent offending. Because the subculture of violence perspective suggests that this type of subculture especially makes violent behavior more likely, the authors of the study concluded that it "poses significant challenges to the predictive validity of the subculture of violence premise" (McGloin et al. 2011:785). As this conclusion suggests, the subculture of violence thesis will continue to arouse criminologists' interest for some time to come.

Review and Discuss

Evaluate the value of the various subcultural theories of crime. To what extent do you agree with Anderson's "code of the street" thesis? Explain your answer.

▶ Structural Theories and Gender

What if the stranded children in William Golding's *Lord of the Flies* had been girls instead of boys? Would they have become as savage as the boys? Would they have committed murder? If not, is Golding's view of human behavior really only a view of male behavior? Could he have written the same book with girls as the protagonists?

As these questions indicate, Golding's neglect of gender limits the value of his book, however powerful it is in other respects. The same neglect characterizes the structural theories of crime discussed in this chapter. Although social class and race lie at the heart of these theories, gender remains invisible. The work of the many scholars of anomie or strain, social disorganization, and subcultural theories was limited not only to lower-class delinquency and crime but also to male delinquency and crime. Hence, these theories may explain only male offending.

To address this neglect, scholars have begun to test the theories with samples of female offenders. They generally find that the theories do help explain variation in female offending, although they differ on whether the factors emphasized in the various theories have stronger effects on female offending or on male offending, if either (Agnew 2009; Zahn and Browne 2009). Supporting an *economic marginality hypothesis*, studies find that the poverty resulting from women's low-paying jobs and increasing divorce rates plays a very important role in female offending, most of which involves petty property crime (Hunnicutt and Broidy 2004).

Although structural theories do seem to apply to female offending, they are less helpful in understanding why there is much less female offending than male offending. For example, because women's incomes are much lower than men's on the average, they should experience more anomie than men and thus, if Merton is correct, be more likely than men to commit crime (Leonard 1995). However, we know women commit less crime. Also, although contemporary ecological work stresses, as we have seen, the criminogenic effects of urban living conditions, concentrated disadvantage, and racial discrimination, males commit most of the crime in disadvantaged urban neighborhoods even though females experience the same strain-producing conditions. In this regard, Lisa Broidy's (2001) finding that girls are less apt than boys to have their strain-induced anger translate into delinquency may explain why similar structural conditions do not yield similar levels for both genders of crime and delinquency.

The structural conditions that underlie criminal behavior also underlie criminal victimization (see Chapter 4). An interesting question, then, is whether these conditions help explain female victimization as well as they explain male victimization. A recent study examining various individual, family, and neighborhood found that "most risk factors for violent victimization are similar across gender and crime type" (Lauritsen and Carbone-Lopez 2011:538). At the same time, neighborhood poverty predicted victimization more strongly for men than for women, while the percentage of female-headed households predicted victimization more strongly for women than for men.

▼ Structural theories help explain why some women are more likely than other women to commit crime. However, they do not help explain why female crime rates are lower than male crime rates.

© Marmaduke St. John / Alamy

In what ways do structural theories ignore gender differences in criminal offending? Do you think these theories help us understand why these gender differences exist?

► Conclusion

The structural theories presented in this chapter are distinctively sociological. They invoke Durkheim's classic view that external forces affect individual behavior and attitudes and remind us that normal people may be compelled to commit criminal behavior. This does not mean that we should excuse such behavior, but it does mean that we should be sensitive to the structural conditions underlying crime as we try to reduce it.

Social disorganization theory has recently been revived, and with good reason. Its focus on the criminogenic conditions of urban neighborhoods is perhaps more timely than ever, and its emphasis on kinds of places over kinds of people is an important corrective to continuing beliefs that crime is due to moral or other failings of individual offenders. Its recent revival in contemporary ecological work represents a major theoretical development with significant policy implications. Perhaps most important, it provides a nonracist explanation for the high crime rates of poor urban areas.

Merton's anomie theory has also been revived and calls attention to the strain and subsequent deviance produced by failure to reach economic and other goals. Such strain is heightened in a society whose ideology stresses equal opportunity for all. Anomie theory thus allows us to see that certain values of U.S. society are ironically criminogenic. The very ideology that drives many people to seek their fortunes legally drives others, poor or rich, to seek theirs illegally.

Subcultural theories were developed to help explain how and why structural conditions lead to crime and delinquency. Although they remind us that crime is a learned behavior, some come close to stereotyping the poor and blaming them totally for their behavior. Recent work that provides a strong structural underpinning for the subculture of urban areas provides an important corrective to these problems and is growing in popularity as an explanation for these areas' high crime rates.

All these theories try to explain crime and delinquency by the poor. This focus is both their blessing and their curse. Although it is important to explain why poor people disproportionately commit serious street crime, it is also important to recognize that wealthier people commit serious crimes themselves and to explain why they do so. Strain theory begins to provide part of the explanation for white-collar crime, but the other theories do not. Finally, all three theories suffer from their neglect of gender. Although females and males both experience social disorganization and anomie and both live in deviant subcultures, if they exist, males remain far more likely than females to commit serious crime and delinquency. None of the structural theories discussed in this chapter adequately accounts for this fact.

A final problem is that most people experiencing the structural problems presented in this chapter still do *not* commit serious crime and delinquency, whereas some not experiencing these problems do commit them. Structural theories cannot easily explain such individual variation. Several sociological theories have been developed to help us understand the more micro-level social processes that lead some individuals to commit crime and deviance. Chapter 8 discusses these theories.

Summary

1. Structural theories emphasize that crime is the result not of individual failings or abnormalities, but of certain physical and social aspects of communities, the distribution of social and economic power, and the nature of relationships among individuals and groups. They stress that normal people are led to commit crime because of these factors and that any individuals will be more likely to commit crime if they are subject to these factors. Structural explanations are particularly useful for explaining variation in crime rates across social groups and locations.

2. Structural theories are the legacy of Émile Durkheim, who focused on social integration and socialization as sources of individual behavior and attitudes. Durkheim argued that individual suicides are the result of normlessness and lack of social integration.

3. Shaw and McKay's social disorganization theory recognized that some urban areas continue to have high crime rates even after their residents are displaced by other types of residents. They said that the multiple social and economic problems of some neighborhoods create social disorganization that leads to conflicting values and weakens conventional social institutions. Crime and delinquency rates are thus higher in areas with greater social disorganization. Although social disorganization theory eventually fell out of favor, its recent revitalization has enriched criminological theory.

4. Merton's anomie theory stressed that U.S. culture is characterized by an exaggerated emphasis on economic success. Individuals living in poverty who cannot achieve economic success experience normlessness. Their possible adaptations in reaction to this strain include conformity, innovation, ritualism, retreatism, and rebellion. Although anomie theory, too, eventually fell out of favor, it has also been revitalized, especially with the advent of general strain theory.

5. Several subcultural theories attempt to explain why certain structural conditions lead to crime and deviance. Albert Cohen theorized that lower-class boys turn to delinquency because they lose self-esteem after doing poorly in school, where middle-class values conflict with their own. Walter Miller identified several focal concerns that guide the behavior of boys living in poverty and push them into delinquency. Richard Cloward and Lloyd Ohlin emphasized differential access to illegitimate opportunities afforded by different subcultures of poor urban areas, whereas Marvin Wolfgang emphasized the role played by a subculture of violence in the genesis of crime in nonwhite urban areas. In general, all these views come close to stereotyping the poor and blaming them for their deviance, but recent work provides a strong structural basis for subcultural problems and is attracting popularity as a reasonable explanation for the high crime rates of urban areas.

6. Structural theories generally ignore female crime and delinquency and cannot adequately explain gender difference in the rates of crime and delinquency. Some research does indicate that structural explanations help explain variation in female offending.

Key Terms

anomie *129*
aspirations *129*
concentric zones *131*
differential opportunity *142*
economic deprivation *133*
focal concerns *141*
kinds of people *134*

kinds of places *134*
relative deprivation *133*
social disorganization *131*
social ecology *131*
social integration *129*
socialization *128*
social pathology *131*

social structure *128*
social ties *129*
status frustration *140*
strain *135*
subculture of violence *143*
underclass *133*

What Would You Do?

1. Suppose you are driving a young child through a blighted urban neighborhood. After the child asks, "What happened here?" what do you tell her? How, if at all, would your answer reflect the structural understanding emphasized in this chapter?

2. Recall that part of Stark's theory of deviant places says that youths who step out of their homes are more likely to break the law because they have greater opportunity to do so. Because they are more likely to encounter peers in urban neighborhoods when they do step out, urban neighborhoods have more delinquency than rural areas. If you were the parent of an adolescent in a middle-class urban neighborhood, would you let your teen go out with friends on weekend nights whenever she or he wanted to? Would you have a curfew? Explain your answers.

8 Sociological Theories: Emphasis on Social Process

▼

• •

Crime in the News

High school students were graduating in spring 2013, and news stories showed that young people in the nation's low-income neighborhoods can beat the odds and not end up in a life of crime and other problems. In Atlanta, Georgia, a young woman, Chelsea, graduated as valedictorian of her class despite living with her family in homeless shelters and even in their car during much of her childhood. Chelsea recalled, "I would just have to open my book in the dark and use a cell phone light, and do what I had to do." She was helped by a devoted mother, who, according to a news report, "read to her children a lot, took them to the library and put a large emphasis on education."

Farther north, a young woman named Megan was graduating from high school in Saco, Maine, despite a childhood spent in foster and group homes after being removed from her drug-addicted mother at age 7. During her first year of high school, she was taken in by a teacher and her family, who provided Megan loving support thereafter. The teacher "really took me under her wing," Megan recalled. She said that the members of her informally adopted family were "great role models," and that they were "very, very supportive" and "always there no matter what."

Source: Collins 2013; Georgantopoulos 2013.

• •

I n Chapter 7, we said the behavior of the boys in *Lord of the Flies* arose from their extreme anomie and social disorganization. There are other ways to explain their behavior. We could talk instead about how they influenced each other to be violent. Or we could say their island lacked the law-abiding influence of parents, schools, and religion. The explanation in Chapter 7 emphasized social structure. The explanations just listed emphasize social processes such as peer influences, socialization, and social interaction. These processes help explain why many people turn to crime, but they also provide clues about why people like Chelsea and Megan in the Crime in the News feature can manage to beat the odds.

Such social process explanations see crime arising more from the interaction of individuals than from the way society is organized. Although structural and social process explanations both make sense, some scholars favor the macro view of structural approaches, whereas others favor the micro view of social process perspectives. The popularity of the latter view stems from scholarly recognition that most people living in criminogenic structural conditions do *not* commit serious crime. If this is true, then it is important to understand the social processes leading some people in these conditions to commit crime and others not to do so.

While conceding the importance of criminogenic social processes, structural theorists still stress the underlying influence of structural problems in society or in specific neighborhoods. They argue that poor individuals would commit less street crime if they were living in more advantaged locations. A healthy tension exists today between the two approaches' proponents, with some scholars favoring integrated theories combining factors from both views. For a comprehensive explanation of crime, structural and social process factors are both necessary. We would have less crime if not for the structural conditions producing it, and we would have less crime if not for certain social processes increasing individuals' likelihood of committing crime. Efforts to reduce crime need to keep these basic facts in mind.

▼ Social processes such as peer influences, socialization, and social interaction affect our chances of becoming or not becoming criminal offenders. The more law-abiding friends we have, the more likely we are to be law-abiding ourselves.

© diego cervo/Fotolia

▼

This chapter reviews the major social process theories of criminal behavior. Helping to explain their popularity, these theories incorporate ideas compatible with both sociological and psychological explanations. A summary of the social process theories discussed in this chapter appears in Table 8–1.

TABLE 8-1 Social Process Theories in Brief

THEORY	KEY FIGURE(S)	SYNOPSIS
Learning Theories		
Differential association	Edwin H. Sutherland	Techniques of and attitudes regarding criminal behavior are learned within intimate personal groups; a person becomes delinquent from an excess of definitions favorable to the violation of law over definitions unfavorable to the violation of law.
Differential identification	Daniel Glaser	People pursue criminal behavior to the extent they identify with members of reference groups who engage in criminal behavior.
Social learning	Albert Bandura	Aggressive tendencies are learned through a process of rewards for such tendencies and imitation of aggressive behavior.
Differential reinforcement	Robert L. Burgess Ronald L. Akers	Criminal behavior and attitudes are more likely to be learned if they are rewarded by friends and/or family; when the rewards for criminal behavior outweigh the rewards for conforming behavior, differential reinforcement occurs and the criminal behavior is learned.
Control Theories		
Containment	Walter Reckless	Inner containments (e.g., a positive self-concept and tolerance for frustration) and outer containments (e.g., family influences) help prevent juvenile offending.
Neutralization and drift	Gresham M. Sykes David Matza	Before committing delinquent acts, adolescents develop techniques of neutralization, or rationalizations, to minimize any guilt they might feel from breaking the law; specific techniques include denial of responsibility, denial of injury, denial of the victim, condemnation of the condemners, and appeal to higher loyalties.
Social bonding	Travis Hirschi	Delinquency and crime are more common among individuals with weakened social bonds to conventional social institutions such as the family and school.
Self-control	Michael Gottfredson Travis Hirschi	Criminal behavior results from low self-control, which in turn results from ineffective parenting.
Control balance	Charles R. Tittle	People are more likely to engage in deviance when they are either very controlling or very controlled than when they have a balance of control.
Coercive control and social support	Mark Colvin Francis T. Cullen	Coercion at either the micro or macro level promotes criminal behavior, while social support at either level reduces it.
Life-Course Theories		
Integrated Strain Control	Delbert S. Elliott	Weak social bonds, strain, and delinquent peers contribute to delinquency; adolescents with weak bonds and strain are particularly vulnerable to the delinquent peers' influence. Strain may weaken even strong bonds and thus increase delinquent peer associations and delinquency.
Interactional	Terence P. Thornberry	Weak social bonds and delinquent peers contribute to delinquency; delinquency and delinquent peer associations may also weaken social bonds and increase delinquency further.
Life-course-persistent	Terrie E. Moffitt	Some individuals' antisocial behavior is serious; persists adolescence-limited through the life course, and begins during childhood because of neuropsychological and other problems. A much greater number of individuals' antisocial behavior occurs only during adolescence, is relatively minor, and is a way of expressing their growing maturity and independence from parents.
Age graded	Robert J. Sampson John H. Laub	Weak social bonds, inadequate parenting, and delinquent peers contribute to criminality, but turning points in the life course, such as marriage and employment, often lead to desistance from crime.

► Learning Theories

Sociologists consider socialization critical for social order. As Chapter 7 noted, Émile Durkheim emphasized the need for people to internalize the norms and values of society and learn how to get along with each other. In this way, society forms a "moral cocoon" around us and we become social beings who care about the welfare of others and the well-being of society as a whole (Collins 1994:194). Socialization makes this possible. Accordingly, almost every introduction to sociology text has an early chapter extolling the virtues of socialization and emphasizing its importance during childhood and adolescence and beyond.

Just as most people learn to obey society's norms, however, others learn that it is okay to violate these norms. They learn these deviant norms and values from their delinquent peers and immediate environments, and perhaps also from the mass media. Learning theories of crime see criminality as the result of the socialization process we all experience. Because of their individual circumstances, some people learn and practice behaviors that the larger society condemns. Not surprisingly, children growing up in neighborhoods rife with crime often end up committing crime themselves. Middle-class kids often engage in shoplifting, vandalism, and other delinquency because of the influence of delinquent friends. White-collar executives learn to consider price-fixing and other financial crimes a normal and necessary part of doing business.

Learning theories start where structural theories leave off. Structural theories tell us why various attitudes and feelings arise that promote criminality. Learning theories tell us how people come to adopt these views and how and why these views result in crime, a process that a recent study called "learning to be bad" (Simons and Burt 2011:553). Several learning theories exist, and certain nuances distinguish them from one another. But they agree much more than they disagree, and all view crime and delinquency as a consequence of "wrong" socialization. In showing how individuals are socialized to commit crime, learning theories join with structural approaches in presenting a positivist view of crime that stresses the influences of external forces on the individual.

Edwin H. Sutherland: Differential Association Theory

Seven decades ago, sociologist Edwin Sutherland (1883–1950) presented the most famous learning theory of crime, which he termed differential association theory, in his text, *Principles of Criminology* (Sutherland 1939). As noted in Chapter 1, Sutherland is a towering figure in the sociological study of crime. As a sociologist, he thought biological and psychological approaches presented a false picture of crime and criminals as abnormal. The work of Shaw and McKay and other Chicago sociologists had sensitized Sutherland to the consequences of growing up in neighborhoods abounding in crime and delinquency. While Shaw and McKay aimed to explain why certain urban areas have high crime rates, Sutherland tried to explain why and how some people in such areas turn to crime while others do not. Sutherland later applied his theory to professional thieves and argued that differential association with different types of thieves (e.g., shoplifters, professional burglars, or pickpockets) influences what kind of thief someone becomes. He also applied it to white-collar criminals, who learn that it is okay to violate the law in a business climate that justifies lawbreaking to maximize profit (Sutherland 1940).

Sutherland presented his final version of differential association in a 1947 revision of his text (Sutherland 1947). His theory contained nine propositions that have appeared in most criminology textbooks since then:

1. **Criminal behavior is learned.** Sutherland declared that criminal behavior is not inherited biologically or otherwise the result of any biological traits.

2. **Criminal behavior is learned in interaction with other persons in a process of communication.** Here Sutherland said that the learning of criminal behavior occurs through interpersonal interaction.

3. **The principal part of the learning of criminal behavior occurs within intimate personal groups.** Following Tarde, Sutherland asserted that people learn crime from people who are close to them emotionally. He implied that criminal behavior is not learned from the mass media.

▼ The late James Gandolfini was the star of the television show *The Sopranos*. Sutherland's theory of differential association assumes that criminal tendencies are learned from close friends and not from the mass media, including TV crime shows like *The Sopranos*.

© ZUMA Press, Inc. / Alamy

4. **When criminal behavior is learned, the learning includes (a) the techniques of committing the crime, which are sometimes very complicated, sometimes very simple; and (b) the specific direction of motives, drives, rationalizations, and attitudes.** This proposition says that the learning of criminal behavior involves mastering how to commit the crime and also deviant attitudes that justify committing it.

5. **The specific direction of motives and drives is learned from definitions of the legal codes as favorable or unfavorable.** Gaining knowledge of criminal behavior also involves learning whether to define laws as worthy of obedience or deserving of violation.

6. **A person becomes delinquent because of an excess of definitions favorable to the violation of law over definitions unfavorable to the violation of law.** This is the heart of Sutherland's differential association theory. People will break the law if they develop more lawbreaking attitudes than law-abiding attitudes.

7. **Differential association may vary in frequency, duration, priority, and intensity.** Associations do not affect one's views equally. Police come into frequent contact with criminals, but do not usually adopt these criminals' attitudes (Shoemaker 2010). In this proposition, Sutherland noted that the effects of associations vary according to four dimensions. *Frequency* simply means how often one spends time with friends. *Duration* means how much time on the average one spends with them during each association. *Priority* refers to how early in life the associations occur, and *intensity* means how much importance one places on one's associations. Although these dimensions often overlap, associations will likely have the greatest impact on one's views if they are of high frequency and duration, occur early in life, and involve people whose views and friendship one values highly.

8. **The process of learning criminal behavior by association with criminal and anticriminal patterns involves all the mechanisms that are involved in any other learning.** Here Sutherland emphasized that socialization into crime includes the same processes involved in socialization into law-abiding behavior.

9. **Although criminal behavior is an expression of general needs and values, it is not explained by these general needs and values, because noncriminal behavior is an expression of the same needs and values.** Sutherland believed that motives are not sufficient to explain crime. For example, the desire for money motivates some people to break the law, but motivates most people to get a good education and work hard. Similarly, jealousy may lead some people to commit murder, but most people who are jealous do not commit murder. Thus, other forces must also be at work.

Evaluation of Differential Association Theory

Along with Merton's anomie theory, Sutherland's theory of differential association is the most notable historically in the sociological study of crime (Akers and Sellers 2013). By explicitly linking crime to learning and socialization, Sutherland emphasized its social nature and thus countered explanations emphasizing biological abnormalities. By stressing the importance of differential associations, he helped to explain variation in offending among people experiencing similar structural conditions. And by extending his theory to white-collar crime, Sutherland helped understand how and why the wealthy commit their share of criminal behavior. For all these reasons, differential association theory has been called a "watershed in criminology" (Matsueda 1988:277).

Perhaps, the major reason for its historical importance is that so much research supports its emphasis on the importance of learning and peer influences for lawbreaking (Augustyn and McGloin 2013; Megens and Weerman 2012). As a review observed, "No characteristic of individuals known to criminologists is a better predictor of criminal behavior than the number of delinquent friends an individual has. The strong correlation between delinquent behavior and delinquent friends has been documented in scores of studies from the 1950s up to the present day" (Warr 2002:40). Peer networks also help explain gender and racial/ethnic differences in offending, as males, African-Americans, and Latinos have greater numbers of delinquent peers than females and whites, respectively (Haynie and Payne 2006). There is even evidence that antisocial individuals tend to have romantic relationships with other deviant individuals and that these relationships then foster more involvement in deviant activities

(Seffrin et al. 2009). Supporting one of Sutherland's assumptions, recent research also shows that many criminal offenders were drawn into and taught crime by a mentor in much the same way that someone working in a lawful occupation may benefit from the help of a mentor (Morselli et al. 2006).

Despite its important contributions, differential association theory has been criticized (Miller et al. 2010). A first criticism, and perhaps the most important, concerns causal order. Staying for a moment with delinquency, which comes first, associating with delinquent peers or one's own delinquency? It is possible that someone's delinquency produces friendships with delinquent peers rather than the reverse. People become delinquent for reasons other than differential association, but once they do, they find themselves spending more time with other delinquents, the reverse of what Sutherland and other learning theorists assume. To investigate this problem, some studies use longitudinal data and find a reciprocal relationship: Having delinquent peers influences delinquency, as differential association and other learning theories assume, and then delinquency increases involvement with delinquent peers. However, some research finds that the effect of delinquency on delinquent-peer associations is greater than that of the associations on delinquency (Matsueda 1988). Although the general importance of delinquent-peer associations seems beyond dispute, this research suggests that the exact nature of this relationship remains to be determined.

In a second criticism, Sutherland may have erred in talking about the influence of friends' definitions, or attitudes, favorable to violating the law while neglecting other influences of the friends' behavior. We might do what our friends do, not because we have adopted their attitudes, but simply because we want them to like us or because we find their behavior rewarding. We can adopt their behavior without necessarily adopting any deviant attitudes they might have. This view of the learning of crime supports other learning theories (discussed later) more than it does Sutherland's (Warr 2002). However, recent research does suggest that peer attitudes to matter for one's own chances of delinquency (Megens and Weerman 2012).

A third criticism concerns Sutherland's implication that crime is committed in groups or, if done alone, is still influenced by "intimate personal groups." Differential association theory applies well to many crimes and especially to juvenile offenses such as shoplifting, vandalism, and drug use, in which peer influences loom large. But many criminal behaviors do not fit this pattern: They are committed by lone individuals and also do not stem from attitudes and techniques learned from friends. For example, most murders are committed by people acting alone, who cannot be said to have learned from their friends that it is acceptable to commit murder. Most rapes are similarly committed by lone offenders who cannot be said to have learned attitudes approving rape from their friends. Rape might derive from attitudes in the larger culture condoning rape (see Chapter 11), but this sort of explanation differs from Sutherland's emphasis on intimate personal groups.

Some critics also point to difficulties in testing differential association theory. As implied earlier, empirical tests of the theory usually examine the effects of the number of delinquent friends. To measure this variable, scholars might ask, "In the last year, how many of your friends have engaged in" shoplifting, marijuana use, and the like. But this focus differs from Sutherland's emphasis on the number of definitions favorable and unfavorable to violating the law. This concept is much more difficult to measure than the number of delinquent friends (Bernard et al. 2009). In another problem, some research finds that "recent rather than early friends have the greatest effect on delinquency" (Warr 1993:35). This finding suggests that Sutherland had his *priority* dimension backward, because he thought that earlier friendships have the greatest effect.

▼ Differential association theory is very applicable to juvenile crimes such as shoplifting, in which peer influences play an important role, but it is much less applicable to crimes such as homicide that are committed by lone individuals who are not reacting to peer influences.

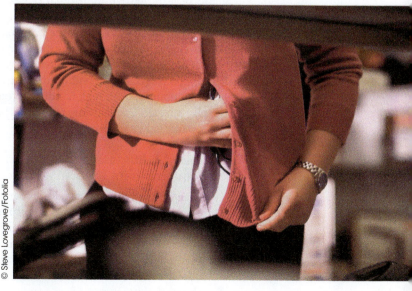

© Steve Lovegrove/Fotolia

Finally, because Sutherland's focus was on male delinquency, he did not consider whether differential association works the same for females. Some studies suggest that it may not (Agnew 2009; Giordano 2009). Although girls often have more intimate relationships than boys do, their friends tend to be less delinquent than boys' friends are. Their relationships are thus less likely than boys' to promote delinquency. To put it another way, peer relationships may be a stronger determinant of male delinquency than of female delinquency, even if they do account for female delinquency. To the extent that this is true, Sutherland's theory applies more to males than to females. Despite this problem, differential association theory nonetheless helps explain the gender difference in criminality because females have fewer delinquent peers than males do.

These criticisms notwithstanding, differential association theory remains important for calling attention to the influence of peers and learning on delinquency. Notice that Sutherland did not say much about the processes by which individuals adopt deviant attitudes through differential associations. Other subsequent learning theories discuss some of these processes. We turn briefly to these theories.

Review and Discuss

What are the key assumptions of Sutherland's differential association theory?

Other Learning Theories

Daniel Glaser: Differential Identification Theory

Sociologist Daniel Glaser's (1956) *theory of differential identification* rests on the notion of *reference groups*, or groups whose values, attitudes, and behavior you admire and wish to copy. These can be groups to which you already belong, such as your circle of friends, or groups to which you do not belong, such as the clique of high school students who are the well-dressed school leaders, or even a popular music group. If your reference groups happen to be ones engaging in criminal or deviant behavior, you are more apt to engage in such behavior yourself.

As Glaser (1956:440) summarized his central thesis, "A person pursues criminal behavior to the extent that he identifies himself with real or imaginary persons from whose perspective his criminal behavior seems acceptable" (italics deleted). In contrast to differential association theory and the other learning theories discussed later, differential identification theory stressed that learning of criminal behavior can occur without actually interacting with the influencing group.

Albert Bandura: Social Learning Theory

Psychologist Albert Bandura (1973) developed his social learning theory of aggression more than forty years ago. He argued that aggressive tendencies are learned rather than inborn. We may see our friends or parents act aggressively, and we may see violence on TV and in other aspects of our popular culture. All these influences help us learn that aggression is acceptable behavior. In developing his theory, Bandura drew on a rich body of psychological research on classical and operant conditioning, which stresses that learning occurs from the association of a stimulus with a response (classical conditioning) or because of the rewarding of a particular behavior (operant conditioning). Although Bandura recognized the importance of rewards for learning behavior, he also stressed that learning can occur just through modeling, or imitating behavior, without any rewards being involved.

Robert L. Burgess and Ronald L. Akers: Differential Reinforcement Theory

In an influential 1966 article, Robert L. Burgess and Ronald L. Akers (1966) presented their *differential reinforcement theory of crime*. Akers (1977) developed this theory further in later work and, borrowing Bandura's term, named it a *social learning theory*. Burgess and Akers argued that criminal behavior and attitudes are more likely to be learned if they are reinforced, or rewarded, usually by friends, family, or both. When the rewards for criminal behaviors outweigh the rewards for alternative behaviors, differential reinforcement occurs and the criminal behavior is learned. Although Burgess and Akers granted that much learning of criminal behavior occurs within the intimate personal groups emphasized by Sutherland, they said such learning can also stem from the influence of school authorities, police, the mass media, and other nonprimary group sources. These sources all provide rewards and punishments that influence the learning of behavior. As revised and extended by Akers, social learning theory is the dominant learning theory today and, in his words, "is more strongly and consistently supported by empirical data than any other social psychological explanation of crime and deviance" (Akers and Jensen 2006:37).

Evaluation of Learning Theories

As should be clear, learning theories in criminology are very popular, and much research has confirmed that involvement with delinquent peers is associated with a higher degree of one's own delinquency. That said, certain problems raise questions about the strength of learning theories.

As noted in discussing differential association theory, one problem concerns the actual causal order governing the association between delinquent peers and one's own delinquency that is so often found. A second problem concerns the exact reasons for any influence that delinquent peers might have on one's own delinquency. Do these peers' attitudes affect one's own attitudes? Does an individual commit delinquency primarily to win the favor of these peers? Are we more likely commit delinquency when with delinquent peers mainly because we are "hanging out" in unstructured situations in which opportunities for crime exist? As these questions suggest, the actual reasons for the criminogenic effects of delinquent peers remain to be determined (Megens and Weerman 2012; Thomas and Mcgloin 2013). Finally, not all criminal behavior can be said to stem from peer influences. As also noted in discussing differential association theory, for example, many individuals committing homicide and rape cannot be said to have learned from friends that it is acceptable to commit these crimes.

Despite these problems, learning theories remain, to repeat, extremely popular in criminology today. Our peers matter greatly during our formative adolescent years, even if criminologists do not yet know exactly how and why they matter.

► Control Theories

Theories of behavior, including theories of crime and deviance, are often based on assumptions about human nature. As Chapter 7 noted, Durkheim and other conservative thinkers of the 1800s thought that society needed to restrain individual impulses because human nature was selfish. Other thinkers have presented a less pessimistic view. The most notable statement is probably that of English philosopher John Locke in his 1690 work, *An Essay Concerning Human Understanding* (see Chapter 5). Locke believed that humans are naturally neither good nor bad and instead are born with a blank slate into which ideas are placed by experience.

Learning theories of crime share this view. Recall their basic assumption that individuals learn to be criminals. This view implies that individuals will *not* commit crime unless they first learn criminal attitudes and behaviors. This in turn implies that the individual is a blank slate who would generally not become a criminal without first learning about crime from society. With this assumption of human nature, learning theories thus ask: Why do people become criminals?

Control theories of crime take a different view of human nature and ask a different question about crime. Like the nineteenth-century conservative thinkers, they assume that people are naturally selfish and capable of committing crime and other antisocial behavior. Given this view, the key question control theories try to answer is not why people become criminals, but rather why people do *not* become criminals.

In answering this question, control theorists discuss two kinds of controls: personal and social (Reiss 1951). Personal controls concern such things as individual conscience, commitment to law, and a positive self-concept. Social controls concern attachments to and involvement in conventional social institutions such as the family, schools, and religion. Weak personal controls often result from weakened social controls. The basic argument is that a positive self-concept and other personal controls combine with strong attachments to conventional social institutions to keep individuals from becoming criminals. When either or both types of control weaken, individuals are freer to become criminals. In this regard, *Lord of the Flies* is a vivid example of the effects of weakened social attachments.

Walter Reckless: Containment Theory

In the 1950s and 1960s, sociologist Walter C. Reckless (Reckless 1961; Reckless et al. 1956) developed his containment theory of delinquency, which stressed that inner and outer containments help prevent juvenile offending. *Inner containments* include a positive self-concept, tolerance for frustration, and an ability to set realistic goals; *outer containments* include institutions such as the family. Both types of containments are necessary, said Reckless, to keep juveniles from succumbing to internal pushes and external pressures and pulls that might otherwise prompt them to break the law. *Internal pushes* are social–psychological states, such as the need for immediate gratification, restlessness, and a hostile attitude. *External pressures* are structural problems and include poverty, unemployment, and other social conditions. *External pulls* are forces such as delinquent peers that draw or pull individuals into crime and delinquency.

Evaluation of Containment Theory

Critics of containment theory raise several issues. One is the familiar chicken-and-egg question. Although youths with delinquent records may have lower self-concepts, these may stem from their official label of delinquency (see Chapter 9) and not be the cause of the delinquency. It is also questionable whether a positive self-concept is the most important factor preventing delinquency, as containment theory asserts: Other factors, such as peer relationships and family influences, may be more important (Shoemaker 2010). Finally, empirical research does not always find the presumed link between self-concept and delinquency.

Gresham M. Sykes and David Matza: Neutralization and Drift Theory

Assume you believe there should be speed limits for cars. Now consider all the times you and your friends drive a car past the speed limit. You might be worried about getting a ticket, but do you ever feel a tiny twinge of guilt now and then? If so, why do you exceed the speed limit? Do you justify to yourself that it is acceptable to do so? If you don't feel any guilt, why not? Whether or not you feel guilty, do you reason that the speed limit is too low and that no one will get hurt if you exceed it?

As these questions suggest, law-abiding people may accept the validity of laws but violate them anyway. Part of this process involves justifying to themselves why it is okay to break the law, especially when they might feel guilty or ashamed for doing so. The theories discussed so far generally ignore this issue. Differential association theory suggests that the individual passively succumbs to peer influences to commit crime. Other learning theories say that the individual more actively calculates whether potential rewards for crime outweigh the risks. Yet even these theories generally disregard any guilt accompanying such calculations. Most control theories also allow little or no role for guilt or shame because they assume that people are naturally selfish.

Guilt and shame lie at the center of *neutralization* theory, developed by Gresham M. Sykes and David Matza (1957) in a classic article. They wrote that adolescents need to neutralize any guilt or shame they feel before committing delinquent acts by developing at least one of five rationalizations, or *techniques of neutralization*, about why it is okay to break the law. These rationalizations precede delinquency and comprise an important part of the definitions favorable to law violation stressed by differential association theory. The five techniques of neutralization follow:

1. **Denial of Responsibility.** Here adolescents say they are not responsible for the delinquent acts they intend to commit. Their behavior is due to forces beyond their control, such as abusive parents or deviant friends. Teenagers who drink or use illegal drugs with their friends may say that peer pressure made them do it.

2. **Denial of Injury.** Here adolescents reason that no one will be hurt by their intended illegal behavior. Borrowing a car for a joy ride is just fun-loving mischief, not a crime; because the owner will get the car back or at least has insurance, no one gets hurt. A large department store will not miss any items that are shoplifted.

3. **Denial of the Victim.** Even if offenders concede that they are about to harm someone or something, they may reason that their target deserves the harm. Robin Hood felt it acceptable

to rob from the rich and give to the poor. Shoplifters reason that the store has "ripped them off," so now it is their turn to rip off the store. People about to commit hate crimes say their targets are less than human and deserve to be beaten. Men who beat their wives/girlfriends say they should have kept the children more quiet, should not have looked at another man, or should have had dinner ready on time.

4. **Condemnation of the Condemners.** Here offenders question the motives and integrity of police, parents, teachers, and other parties who condemn the offenders' behavior: The police are corrupt, so it's okay for me to break the law. My parents used marijuana when they were my age, so why can't I?

5. **Appeal to Higher Loyalties.** Here offenders reason that their illegal behavior is necessary to help people dear to them. Members of gangs may conclude that loyalty to the gang justifies their taking part in illegal activities committed by the gangs. Poor people may steal food to help their starving families.

Matza (1964) later expanded the idea of neutralization with his drift theory of delinquency. (Sykes and Matza's views today are commonly referred to as *neutralization and drift theory*.) Matza argued that delinquents are not constantly delinquent and instead drift into and out of delinquency. Techniques of neutralization make their delinquency possible, but so do *subterranean* values from the larger culture such as daring and excitement, a belief that aggression is sometimes necessary, and the desire for wealth and possessions. Although these values often underlie conforming behavior, they can also lead to deviant behavior, especially when peer influences help channel these values into illegal activity.

Evaluation of Neutralization and Drift Theory

Sykes and Matza's ideas have been popular, but they have also been criticized. Some scholars say that adolescents who are serious offenders do not feel guilty and have nothing to neutralize (Topalli 2005). Moreover, although several studies find that offenders do rationalize their behavior, it is difficult to prove that this happened *before* they broke the law, as Sykes and Matza assumed. Techniques of neutralization may thus be "after-the-fact rationalizations rather than before-the-fact neutralizations" (Hirschi 1969:207). In another criticism, Sykes and Matza believed that delinquents do not hold different values and are not chronic offenders because they drift into and out of delinquency. However, some offenders are chronic (see Chapter 3) and do appear to hold values different from those of nondelinquents.

Despite these criticisms, many scholars defend neutralization and drift theory, with some research finding that most adolescents do disapprove of violence and other offending and thus indeed must neutralize guilt or shame before engaging in delinquent acts. This research "does much to provide support for the arguments of Sykes and Matza" (Agnew 1994:573).

A recent study of animal rights activists supported this conclusion, as it found that the activists engaged in various techniques of neutralization to justify the illegal activities such as arson they sometimes perform (Liddick 2013). The study's author found that the activists also sometimes used an additional neutralization not included in Sykes and Matza's original list: *appeal to a higher moral principle.* This particular rationalization is commonly cited by civil disobedients breaking the law in an attempt to change existing social, economic, or political conditions (see Chapter 14).

Review and Discuss

What are the five techniques of neutralization discussed by Sykes and Matza? How have some scholars criticized their view of deviance and crime?

Travis Hirschi: Social Bonding Theory

Have you ever refused to join your friends in illegal behavior because you were worried about what your parents might think or about how it might affect your school record? Do you know people whose religious beliefs have led them to avoid drinking, using illegal drugs, or having sex? As these examples suggest, our bonds to conventional social institutions such as family, schools, and religion may keep us from committing deviant behavior. This is the central view of Travis Hirschi's *social bonding theory* (also called *social control theory*), which may be the most popular criminological theory today and certainly the most popular control theory. First presented in a 1969 book, Hirschi's (1969) theory has since stimulated many investigations.

Hirschi began his book by stating that human nature is selfish. Given this view, he said, the key question is why people do *not* commit crime. Drawing on Durkheim, his answer was that their bond to society's institutions keeps them from breaking the law. When that bond is weakened, they feel freer to deviate and crime results. Social bonding theory presents a social process or micro complement to the structural or macro view of social disorganization theory. If the latter theory says that crime flourishes in neighborhoods with weakened social institutions, social bonding theory argues that crime is more common among individuals with weakened bonds to the same institutions. Four elements of social bonds exist.

1. **Attachment.** Attachment is the most important social bond element and refers to the degree to which we care about the opinions of others, including parents and teachers. The more sensitive we are to their views, the less likely we are to violate norms, both because we have internalized their norms and because we do not want to disappoint or hurt them. The opposite is also true: The less sensitive we are to their views, the more likely we are to break the law.

2. **Commitment.** This refers to an individual's investment of energy and emotion in conventional pursuits, such as getting a good education. The more committed people are in this sense, the more they have to lose if they break the law. People with low commitment to conventional pursuits thus are more likely to deviate.

3. **Involvement.** This is the amount of time an individual spends on a conventional pursuit. The argument here is that the more time spent, the less the opportunity to deviate.

4. **Belief.** This refers to acceptance of the norms of conventional society. People who believe in these norms are less likely to deviate than are those who reject them. Hirschi noted that all four elements are related, so that someone with a strong tie in one element tends to have strong ties in the others. For example, people who are strongly attached to parents and schools also tend to believe in conventional norms.

Hirschi tested his hypotheses with a sample of about 4,000 male junior and senior high school students from the San Francisco Bay area. He asked them many questions about their delinquency and the four social bond elements just outlined, including their feelings about their parents and teachers, the amount of time they spent on various school activities, and what they thought about conventional pursuits such as getting a good education. His analysis yielded considerable support for his theory. For example, youths who felt very close to their parents were less likely to be delinquent than youths who felt more distant.

▼ Strong parent–child attachment and other indicators of high-quality parenting are associated with lower delinquency.

© szeyuen/Fotolia

Social bonding theory has won wide acclaim, with support for it found in dozens of studies of delinquency (Lilly et al. 2011). These studies generally find that delinquency is lower among teens who feel close to their parents, who like their teachers, who value their schooling and take part in school activities, and who believe in the conventional rules of society.

Social Bonding Theory and the Context of Delinquency

Most of the research inspired by social bonding theory focuses on the family, school, and religious contexts of delinquency. We examine these briefly to indicate the theory's impact and application.

The Family To study the role played by the family in delinquency, researchers distinguish between family structure and family functioning. Family structure refers to the way the family is set up or organized, whereas family interaction or *family functioning* refers to the nature of the interaction and relationships within the family.

Regarding family structure, the most studied component is *family disruption* in the form of a household headed by a single parent, usually the mother, because of divorce, birth out of wedlock, or, less commonly, the death of a parent. Because there is only one parent to supervise the children and father role models are lacking for sons, such households are popularly thought to contribute to delinquency. Supporting this view, many studies find that children from single-parent households are indeed more at risk for serious juvenile offending (Fomby and Sennott 2013; Kierkus and Hewitt 2009). Yet some studies do not find this presumed relationship once these households' low income is taken into account or find it limited to *status offenses*, such as truancy and running

International Focus SOCIAL BONDING IN THE LAND OF THE RISING SUN

Japan has long had the lowest crime rate in the industrialized world, or nearly so. The 2004–2005 International Crime Victims Survey (ICVS) found that 9.9 percent of Japanese had been victimized by crime in the previous year; this figure ranked Japan as next to last among the thirty industrialized nations included in the ICVS. By contrast, 17.5 percent of U.S. residents had been victimized. Japan ranked lowest in assaults and threats, with only 0.6 percent reporting being assaulted or threatened during the past year; the U.S. rate was seven times higher at 4.3 percent. Japan is thus a very safe nation, even though its popular culture—films, TV shows, and so on—depicts a great deal of violence and its history is filled with war, murders of peasants, political assassinations, and other violence.

Given this background, why is Japan's crime rate so low? According to Hirschi's social bonding theory, the stronger an individual's bonds to conventional social institutions such as the family and schools are, the less likely the individual will be to break the law. Does Hirschi's view help understand Japan's low crime rate?

In explaining its low rate, several scholars emphasize the Japanese culture, in particular the value it places on *group-belonging*. From birth the Japanese are taught that the group is more important than the individual. The family, the school, and the workplace are the subjects of great respect and authority in Japanese culture. In school, individual achievement is not as important as a whole classroom's achievement. At home, Japanese families are known for their high levels of love and harmony. Children sleep with their parents from birth until they are about 5 years old. When they misbehave, parents punish them by locking them out of the house, whereas U.S. children are often punished by being "grounded," or kept within the house. As scholar David H. Bayley says, "The effect is that

American children are taught that it is punishment to be locked up with one's family; Japanese children are taught that punishment is being excluded from one's family."

The emphasis on group-belonging in Japan promotes two other emphases, harmonious relationships and respect for authority. All three emphases contribute to especially strong social bonding in Japan and hence to its lower crime rates. Japanese children grow up strongly attached to their parents and teachers and very committed to obeying social norms. In contrast, U.S. children grow up much more independently, because U.S. culture emphasizes individualism rather than group-belonging. The ties U.S. children feel to parents, schools, and other conventional social institutions are weaker than those felt by Japanese children. With weaker bonds, U.S. adolescents are thus freer, as social bonding theory predicts, to violate social norms, which means they are freer to commit crime and delinquent acts.

Although some observers credit Japan's low crime rate to its criminal justice system, Japan's experience does seem to underscore the value of the social bond for reducing crime. It suggests that significant crime reduction could be achieved in the United States if children were more respectful of their parents and teachers and if family relationships were more harmonious. Are these qualities beyond the scope of social policy? For better or worse, the U.S. culture is not likely to become more similar to the Japanese culture. Japan's example suggests that it is possible to have an industrial society with low crime rates, but it also implies the difficulty of implementing the Japanese model in the United States. In this regard, family intervention programs for U.S. families at greatest risk for conflict may be an effective strategy for reducing crime.

Sources: Bayley 1996; Komiya 1999; Schneider and Silverman 2013; van Dijk et al. 2008.

away from home, or to drinking and drug use (Rankin and Kern 1994). These studies conclude that if children from single-parent households are more likely to be delinquent, it is because their families are poor, not because their families have only one parent.

Reflecting the impact of social bonding theory, most scholars believe that family interaction is more important than family structure for delinquency. Many studies link strong parent–child attachment and other indicators of quality parenting to lower delinquency. To turn that around, delinquency is more often found among children with cold and distant relationships with their parents and among children whose parents do not supervise them adequately (Farrington 2011). Children with such relationships are more apt to reject their parents' values and rules, as Hirschi thought, but are also more vulnerable to their friends' delinquent influences (Warr 2005).

In related research, harsh or erratic discipline and especially physical and sexual abuse are also thought to contribute to delinquency (Farrington 2011; Mersky et al. 2012). In contrast, *authoritative* (also called *firm but fair*) parenting, which involves clear but fair rules and positive feedback and little or no spanking, seems to prevent delinquency, in part because it leads to greater internalization of parental values. Conversely, harsh discipline may lower children's affection for their parents and, as Hirschi noted, increase their delinquency potential. In addition, because corporal punishment teaches children that violence is an acceptable solution to interpersonal conflict, it may ironically lead to violent aggression in adolescence and adulthood, especially when the punishment becomes abusive (Boutwell et al. 2011; Simons and Wurtele 2010).

These negative family influences are especially found among children born to teenage mothers. Their families tend to be unstable (male partners moving in and out), to have low incomes, and to live in disadvantaged neighborhoods, and the mothers are more likely to practice ineffective parenting. All these reasons are thought to explain why their children are more at risk for abuse and neglect, low school achievement, aggressive behavior during childhood, and delinquency during adolescence (Farrington et al. 2012).

Review and Discuss

If parents want to reduce their children's chances of growing up to be delinquents, what type of discipline should they practice? Why?

Schools   A large literature on schooling and delinquency also exists. Supporting social bonding theory views, adolescents with poor grades and negative attitudes about their teachers, their schools, and the importance of education are more likely to be delinquent than youths with good grades and positive attitudes (Gottfredson et al. 2012; Payne 2012). Adolescents who are less involved in school extracurricular activities are also more likely to be delinquent. Once again, though, questions remain on causal order, as it is possible that delinquency and delinquent peers affect students' perceptions of their schools and involvement in school activities.

Social bonding theory's explanation of the relationship between various school factors and delinquency relationships is different from that of strain theory. As you might recall from Chapter 7, Albert Cohen's status frustration theory argued that school failure leads to frustration and hence to delinquency to resolve that frustration. Social bonding theory instead argues that failure in and negative attitudes about school prompt youths to reject the conformist values of school and the legitimacy of school authorities to tell them how to behave, with frustration playing no role.

An interesting controversy is whether dropping out of school promotes or reduces delinquency. The Crime and Controversy box discusses this issue further.

Religion   Following Durkheim (1947 (1915)), sociologists have long considered religion an important force for social stability. Accordingly, many think that religious belief and practice (*religiosity*) should help to prevent delinquent and criminal behavior, as social bonding theory would predict.

A growing body of research finds that youths who are more religious are indeed less likely to be delinquent, although the effect may be stronger for drinking, drug use, and sexual behavior than for other kinds of delinquency (Adamczyk 2012; Landor et al. 2011; Salas-Wright et al. 2012). Extending the relationship to adults, studies of national and local data link religiosity to reduced criminality during adulthood (Evans et al. 1995; Petts 2009). Other national research even

▼

Crime and Controversy   DOES DROPPING OUT
OF SCHOOL PROMOTE OR REDUCE DELINQUENCY?

Most people would probably think that youths who drop out of school are at greater risk for committing delinquency. They have more time to spend with their friends and thus have more opportunity to get into trouble. Also, if strong bonds to school help reduce delinquency, as social bonding theory assumes, then teens who drop out of school should be at greater risk for delinquency because they eliminate all their school bonds.

However, Albert Cohen's status frustration theory, discussed in the text, predicts that dropping out should reduce delinquency. Because Cohen thought delinquency arises from poor school performance that leads to status frustration, a logical prediction from his theory is that dropping out of school should reduce this frustration and thus reduce delinquency. The best studies that test this hypothesis take into account the age at which students drop out and also why they drop out (poor grades, problems at home, financial problems, etc.), and they also control for important variables

such as social class and prior delinquency. However, these studies report very inconsistent results: Some studies find that dropping out increases delinquency, some studies find that dropping out decreases delinquency, and some studies find that dropping out does not affect delinquency.

It is also possible that dropping out and delinquency are both the result of other problems, including having a mother who had her first child when she was a teenager and having a history of antisocial behavior since childhood, as recent research has found. To the extent this is true, the statistical correlations that are sometimes found between dropping out and delinquency may be spurious. As one study observed, "This finding suggests that concern about the event of dropout may be misplaced. Instead, attention must be focused on the process that leads to dropout and criminal involvement; this process seems to begin to take place at an early age."

Sources: Bjerk 2012; Jarjoura 1993; Sweeten et al. 2009.

---

suggests that religiosity reduces premarital sex among never-married adults (Barkan 2006). At the macro level, violent crime is lower in rural counties with more churches per capita than in those with fewer churches (Lee 2006).

One problem in interpreting the religiosity–delinquency relationship is that teens who crave excitement tend to be bored with religion, and are hence less religious and also more likely to commit delinquency. If so, the relationship may be at least partially spurious (Cochran et al. 1994). However, a test of this possibility with national longitudinal data found that religiosity had a nonspurious effect on delinquency, in part because it increased disapproval of delinquency and the proportion of law-abiding friends (Johnson et al. 2001).

Evaluation of Social Bonding Theory

The research just discussed gives ready evidence of social bonding theory's importance. The theory has also been lauded for helping to understand gender and age differences in delinquency. Girls are less delinquent than boys in part because they are more attached to family and school, more likely to hold conventional beliefs, and more closely supervised by their parents (Agnew 2009). Turning to age, recall that criminality decreases as adolescents become adults (Chapter 3). One reason for this is that many young adults marry, join the workforce, and otherwise become more involved in conventional society. As social bonding theory predicts, these new conventional social bonds help reduce their criminality (Farrington 2003).

Still, critics note several problems with the theory. First, relationships between social bonding and delinquency in the research tend to be rather weak, suggesting that various social bonds may not matter as much as the theory assumes (Lilly et al. 2011). Some research also finds that social bonds are more weakly related to serious delinquency than they are to minor delinquency, suggesting that the theory explains minor offending better than it explains serious offending.

Another problem concerns the familiar chicken-and-egg question of causal order. If, for example, youths with weak parental attachment are more delinquent than those with strong parental attachment, does this mean that parental attachment influences

▼ Greater religiosity is associated in several studies with lower rates of juvenile delinquency and adult criminality.

ColorBlind/Getty Images

delinquency or that delinquency influences parental attachment? Fortunately, there are studies investigating this issue with longitudinal data (Liska and Reed 1985; Stewart et al. 2002). Significantly, they find a reciprocal relationship: Weak social bonds help produce delinquency, but delinquency also weakens social bonds. These findings do support social bonding theory, but they also indicate that the reason for some of the statistical support is the reverse of what the theory assumes.

Two final criticisms exist. First, the theory's concepts of commitment and involvement cannot easily be distinguished from each other: It is difficult to imagine someone spending a lot of time on a conventional pursuit who is not also committed to it (Krohn 2000). For example, is time spent on homework best seen as a measure of involvement in school or as a commitment to the importance of education? Second, the theory cannot easily explain certain geographical differences in crime (Bohm and Vogel 2011). If, say, Texas has a higher delinquency rate than Maine, it is doubtful that Texan children are less attached than Maine children to their parents.

In sum, Hirschi's social bonding theory has been very influential and for very good reasons. At the same time, questions remain about several issues, including the strength and direction of the social bond–criminality relationship that is so often found.

Review and Discuss

How does Hirschi's view of human nature relate to his social bonding theory of crime and deviance? In his theory, what are the four elements of the bonds that individuals have to their society?

Michael Gottfredson and Travis Hirschi: Self-Control Theory

In 1990, Hirschi coauthored a book with Michael Gottfredson that revised social control theory to present a "general theory of crime," as the book was entitled (Gottfredson and Hirschi 1990). They argued that all crime stems from one problem: the lack of self-control, which results from ineffective child rearing and lasts throughout life. People with low self-control act impulsively and spontaneously, value risk and adventure, and care about themselves more than they do about others. They are thus more likely than people with high self-control to commit crime, because all types of crime, said the authors, are spontaneous and exciting and require little skill. This is as true for white-collar crime as for petty theft and assault. Self-control, or more precisely, low self-control, thus "explains all crime, at all times" (p. 117). Low self-control often continues into adulthood and thus explains adult criminality as well as juvenile delinquency. In stressing low self-control, Gottfredson and Hirschi explicitly minimized or ruled out the effects of other problems such as economic deprivation and peer influences. They thus declared that the only hope to reduce crime lies in improving child rearing. Policies focusing on structural causes of crime and on criminal opportunities will, they said, have little effect.

▼ Low self-control, including the tendency to act impulsively and to care about oneself more than others, develops during childhood and results from inadequate parenting.

PhotoAlto/Frederic Cirou/Getty Images

Self-control theory, as their theory has come to be called, has generated much research, most of which finds that individuals with low self-control are indeed more likely to commit various kinds of offenses and to have other kinds of problems as well (Rocque et al. 2013; Steketee et al. 2013). Studies also find that differences in self-control help to understand the gender difference in criminality: Males have less self-control than females and partly for this reason they commit more delinquent acts (Agnew 2009). As Chapter 4 noted, some research also finds that low self-control helps make people more vulnerable to being victimized by crime (Holtfreter et al. 2008). In another area, a recent study found that low self-control makes it more likely that suspects will be hostile toward police and thus be arrested (Beaver et al. 2009).

Evaluation of Self-Control Theory

Although self-control theory is very popular, it, too, has been criticized (Akers and Sellers 2013; Piquero and Piquero 2010). One problem is that it engages in circular (or *tautological*) reasoning: Because crime is considered evidence of low self-control, crime is being used to explain itself. To help avoid this problem, most tests of the theory use attitudinal measures of low self-control, such as losing one's temper and thinking only about short-term consequences, but critics say the theory remains somewhat tautological nonetheless.

A second problem is that the actual effects of low self-control are not very strong (Pratt and Cullen 2000) and that it overstates its case in claiming that low self-control is the only factor that matters for delinquency and crime. Contrary to this assumption, factors such as peer influences also matter and may even be more important than low self-control (Akers and Sellers 2013), and neuropsychological problems may also matter (DeLisi and Beaver 2014).

Two additional problems concern other assumptions of the theory. Contrary to its assumption that low self-control and its effects on criminal behavior last throughout life, ample evidence exists that people can gain self-control and that those with a history of offending can "straighten out" when they reach adulthood, thanks to marriage, employment, and other such influences (Benson 2013; Na and Paternoster 2012). The theory's assumption that ineffective child rearing is the sole source of low self-control has also been questioned. At the individual level, low self-control may also stem from neuropsychological deficits (Boutwell and Beaver 2010). At the structural level, low self-control results from living in socially disorganized neighborhoods—those with high levels of poverty and low levels of collective efficacy (see Chapter 7) (Gibson et al. 2010).

A final criticism focuses on Gottfredson and Hirschi's assumption that all crime, including white-collar crime, is spontaneous and unskilled. To the contrary, many crimes do not fit this description, in particular corporate and other business crime, which involves much planning and skill (Geis 2000). Although low self-control may explain some types of crime, it does not appear to explain white-collar crime.

In sum, self-control theory helps explain some criminal and delinquent behavior, and the empirical support for it has been "fairly impressive" (Pratt and Cullen 2000:951). However, it does not seem to offer the all-powerful general theory of crime its authors intended and claimed.

Review and Discuss

What are any three problems associated with self-control theory? In your opinion, to what degree does self-control theory offer a better understanding of delinquency and crime than the other theories presented in this chapter?

Charles R. Tittle: Control Balance Theory

Another control theory is Charles R. Tittle's (2004) *control balance theory*, which has been applauded as "one of the most important theoretical contributions to the sociology of deviance" (Braithwaite 1997:77). Tittle observed that some people, by virtue of their roles and personal qualities, can exercise considerable control over other people. At the same time, some people are more easily controlled by other people. When people are either very controlling or very controlled, Tittle said, they are more likely to engage in deviance than when their *control ratio*, the degree to which they exercise control versus the degree to which they experience control, is in balance. Thus, people with a *control surplus*, such as corporate executives, tend to commit crime, albeit of the white-collar variety, and those with a *control deficit*, such as the urban poor, also tend to commit crime, in this case violent and property crime.

Why does control ratio make a difference? Tittle assumed that people want to be as autonomous as possible. If they have a control deficit, they break the law to achieve more control over their lives, if only by victimizing someone else, and to lessen the feelings of humiliation and inferiority arising from their control deficit. If they have a control surplus, they break the law because they greedily want even more control and because they realize that the control they exert reduces their risk of sanctions for lawbreaking.

Tests of control balance theory generally support it (Baron 2010; Piquero and Piquero 2006). In one study, 146 college students were asked to read several scenarios in which individuals engaged in various deviant activities and then to indicate the likelihood that they would do the same. The students were also asked several questions to measure the amount of control they exercised and the amount of control they experienced. Supporting Tittle's theory, students with control surpluses and control deficits were both more likely than those with a control balance to indicate that they would engage in the deviant activities (Piquero and Hickman 1999).

Mark Colvin and Francis T. Cullen: Coercive Control and Social Support Theory

A final control theory is Mark Colvin and Francis T. Cullen's *coercive control and social support theory* (Colvin et al. 2002). Coercion is defined as "a force that compels or intimidates an individual to act because of the fear or anxiety it creates" (Colvin et al. 2002:19) and can be micro (e.g., someone threatens or humiliates you) or macro (e.g., poverty) in nature. Social support is defined as "assistance from communities, social networks, and confiding partners in meeting the instrumental and expressive needs of individuals" (p. 20) and can also be micro or macro in nature. The theory argues that coercion causes crime and that social support reduces or prevents it. Coercion promotes criminal behavior because it first leads to anger, frustration, alienation, weaker self-control and social bonds, and then to a belief that actions to avenge coercion are acceptable. Social support reduces crime because it helps people meet their emotional and practical needs. People are more or less likely to commit crime based on the amount of coercion and social support they experience.

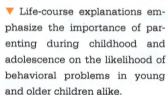
▼ Life-course explanations emphasize the importance of parenting during childhood and adolescence on the likelihood of behavioral problems in young and older children alike.

Studies support this theory (Baron 2009; Unnever et al. 2004). One study used involved data on almost 2,500 students from six middle schools in Virginia. The students were asked to indicate the extent of their exposure to four types of coercion: (1) parental coercion (e.g., corporal punishment), (2) peer coercion (e.g., being bullied), (3) neighborhood coercion (e.g., whether they considered their neighborhood dangerous), and (4) school coercion (e.g., whether they considered their school dangerous). Supporting the theory, students with high scores on three types of coercion (all except peer coercion) were more likely to be delinquent and to be so partly because coercion weakened their parental and school bonding and made them more likely to favor revengeful actions after being coerced (Unnever et al. 2004).

▶ Life-Course Theories

Learning and control theories typically focus on delinquency during adolescence. Aided by the growth of longitudinal data, however, criminologists have begun to pay attention to the onset and termination of antisocial behavior, delinquency, and crime at different stages over the life course: infancy, childhood, adolescence, young adulthood, and beyond. These criminologists have formulated and tested *life-course theories* (also called *developmental theories*), and their theories and research are together called *life-course criminology* (Benson 2013). Criminologists who favor this perspective come from biological, psychological, and sociological backgrounds, and their work draws on many of the explanations presented in this and the previous two chapters, while also drawing from important work in developmental psychology.

Their research addresses many questions, some of which we have already encountered, and include (1) Why are some children more at risk for engaging in antisocial behavior, including delinquency and crime? (2) To what degree do childhood behavioral problems predict similar problems during adolescence? (3) Why do some juvenile delinquents continue their criminal ways well into adulthood, whereas most desist after leaving their teenage years? (4) Why are delinquency and crime highest in middle

Designpics/Glow Images

to late adolescence, and why do they decline thereafter? (5) Which factors matter more for delinquency at different stages of adolescence? (6) Which factors help explain why some adolescents and adults who have been involved in crime later decide to desist from it? and (7) How does the importance of all these factors differ by gender or race and ethnicity?

In explaining the onset of offending, life-course research identifies many of the *risk factors* we have already reviewed: extreme poverty, inadequate parenting, poor family relationships and school performance, delinquent peers, and unemployment (Farrington et al. 2012). Two insights from this research are especially valuable. First, many children with these risk factors do *not* end up committing delinquent acts because various events and processes during the life course— better parenting, positive school experiences, supportive friendships with law-abiding peers— may intervene. Second, criminal offenders may *desist* from crime because of certain *turning points*, such as marriage and employment, that increase social attachments, promote conventional beliefs, reduce the opportunity for offending (for example, by keeping someone busy at home or at work), and minimize the influence of criminal peers.

Specific Life-Course Theories

Several life-course theories exist and share many features while having different emphases. Brief summaries of a few life-course theories follow.

Delbert S. Elliott: Integrated Strain-Control Theory

Delbert S. Elliott and colleagues (Elliott et al. 1979, 1985) formulated one of the most popular life-course theories, which they termed an *integrated strain-control* theory. Elliott and colleagues integrated strain, social learning, and social control theories into their approach, which they considered a better explanation of delinquency than any one of the three theories by itself.

In their view, childhood socialization affects whether bonds to society become weak or strong. Weak bonds are more likely for children living in very poor and otherwise socially disorganized areas. During adolescence, youths achieve success or failure in schooling and other conventional activities, with failure causing further strain. Peer influences become very important during this time. Adolescents with weak bonds to their parents and schools and experiencing strain from failure in conventional activities are particularly vulnerable to the criminogenic influence of delinquent peers. Failure and strain may also weaken the strong bonds that some adolescents initially have and prompt these adolescents to spend more time with delinquent friends and thus to engage in delinquent acts themselves. Thus, although delinquency most often results from weak bonds in childhood that then lead to associations with delinquent peers, even strong childhood bonds may weaken because of adolescent strains and open the door to delinquent peer associations and delinquency itself.

Terence P. Thornberry: Interactional Theory

Another life-course perspective is Terence P. Thornberry's (1987, 2009) *interactional theory*. This theory is similar to integrated strain-control theory, as it emphasizes that strong childhood bonds to parents reduce the risk for delinquency and weak bonds raise this risk, in particular by increasing associations with delinquent peers. But Thornberry adds that delinquency and association with delinquent peers can weaken parental and school bonds in a type of vicious cycle that increases delinquency even further. Thornberry also argues that the relative importance of parental and school bonds and peer associations for delinquency changes as youths become older. During early adolescence, parental bonds matter more, and during middle adolescence, school bonds and peer associations matter more. More generally, Thornberry emphasizes that parental and school bonds can change as other aspects of a youth's life change.

With colleague Marvin D. Krohn, Thornberry also used his theory to explain why antisocial behavior emerges at different stages of the life course (Thornberry and Krohn 2005). During childhood and early adolescence (up through age 11), youngsters who develop behavior problems tend to do so for several reasons: (1) they live in disadvantaged neighborhoods, (2) their parents' child rearing is inadequate, (3) they do poorly in school, and (4) and they associate with misbehaving friends. Such youths are at great risk for continuing their antisocial behavior well into adolescence, where it can take on very serious forms. During middle adolescence (ages 12 to 16), some teens who had previously been well behaved nonetheless begin to misbehave in relatively minor ways (e.g., drinking, experimental drug use, shoplifting), and they do so partly because of negative peer associations that they develop during this time. As these teens leave middle adolescence, they tend to end their minor misbehavior.

During young adulthood, a relatively small number of individuals who had not really misbehaved earlier nonetheless begin to break the law. These tend to be individuals who had certain personal problems when they were younger that did not translate into delinquency because they were protected by strong parental and school bonds. When they reach young adulthood, however, they leave this protective environment, and negative peer influences may now have an impact. These individuals may also encounter employment and relationship problems, and these, too, may lead them to commit crime.

Terrie E. Moffitt: Life-Course-Persistent/Adolescence-Limited Theory

Terrie E. Moffitt's (1993, 2006) influential *life-course-persistent/adolescence-limited theory*, related to her longitudinal research reviewed in Chapter 6, attempts to explain the onset and patterning of two distinct types of antisocial behavior. As the theory's name implies, it assumes that antisocial behavior either persists across the life course or instead is limited to adolescence. Individuals whose antisocial behavior is life-course persistent begin to misbehave during childhood and continue to do so well into adulthood. To recall some terminology from Chapter 1, they are *chronic criminals*. According to the theory, these individuals suffer from neuropsychological problems that often begin during the prenatal period and then lead to psychological problems during childhood and in turn to serious misbehavior. Life-course-persistent offenders also tend to grow up in disadvantaged neighborhoods and to suffer from inadequate parenting.

In contrast, adolescence-limited offenders begin their offending during adolescence and largely end it once they leave adolescence. They drink, engage in experimental drug use, and commit minor forms of delinquency as a way of expressing their growing maturity and independence from their parents. In a sense, their offending is a normal pattern of behavior during this stage of life that is heavily influenced by peer associations. As they leave adolescence, they end their pattern of minor offending partly because they take on new adult responsibilities, such as employment and marriage. In general, adolescence-limited offenders come from more advantaged social backgrounds and had parents who practiced effective parenting.

Some critics question Moffitt's assumption that offenders fall only into the two categories she has identified (Lilly et al. 2011). For example, life-course-persistent offenders may not be as homogeneous as Moffitt assumes, as some commit serious offenses and others commit only minor offenses. Similarly, some adolescence-limited offenders commit serious offenses, even if most commit only minor offenses. These criticisms notwithstanding, Moffitt's taxonomy has helped direct criminological attention to chronic offenders and to the reasons for their persistent offending over much of the life course.

Robert J. Sampson and John H. Laub: Age-Graded Theory

Another influential theory is John H. Laub and Robert J. Sampson's *age-graded theory* (Laub et al. 2006; Sampson and Laub 1993). Laub and Sampson recognize the importance of the many factors outlined in other life-course perspectives, in particular bonds to parents and school during childhood and adolescence, the quality and effectiveness of parenting, and the influence of one's friends. However, they especially emphasize that key events over the life course act as turning points in helping individuals to desist from crime. These turning points during adulthood include marriage, stable employment, and military service. Individuals with a history of offending who enter adulthood and then get married and land a stable job, for example, may well stop their criminal behavior.

In emphasizing that such turning points can lead to desistance from crime, Laub and Sampson take issue with the idea that serious antisocial behavior that begins in childhood necessarily persists throughout the life course. In this regard, they challenge key assumptions of Moffitt's theory and of Gottfredson and Hirschi's self-control theory discussed earlier. Supporting Laub and

Sampson's view, research finds that marriage and parenthood tend to inhibit criminality (Bersani and Doherty 2013; Doherty and Ensminger 2013). However, if one's spouse also has a history of criminal behavior, marriage has less of a protective effect in this regard and perhaps none at all (van Schellen et al. 2012). The extent to which marriage is a turning point, then, depends on the character of a person's spouse.

A recent study challenged one of Laub and Sampson's conclusions, that military service reduces criminality, from their analysis of the data collected during the World War II era. This conclusion left unclear whether military service per se reduces offending or whether only military service during World War II reduced offending. Using data on youths from the Vietnam War era, Wright et al. (2005) found that youths who served in Vietnam were more likely after leaving the military to use drugs and commit crime than their counterparts who did not serve in the military. Thus, although service in World War II may have been a positive turning point that led to desistance from crime, service in Vietnam was a negative turning point that led to increased drug use and criminal behavior.

The Promise and Problem of Theoretical Integration

Because life-course theories often combine factors highlighted in other theories, they are often considered *integrated theories*. Many scholars favor theoretical integration because they feel that neither a social process nor a structural approach can adequately explain crime by itself: Social process theories cannot easily account for structural variation in criminality, and structural theories cannot easily account for individual variation in crime among people living in similar structural conditions. A more comprehensive understanding of crime thus might be achieved by integrating social process and structural factors.

Several integrated theories of crime have been developed (Akers and Sellers 2013), and an example of an integrated model appears in Figure 8–1 ■. In recent examples of models that combined structural and social process factors, Ronald L. Simons and colleagues (Simons et al. 2005) found that high-quality, authoritative parenting is more common in neighborhoods with high levels of collective efficacy and that both authoritative parenting and collective efficacy reduce delinquency. They also found a stronger deterrent effect of authoritative parenting on delinquency in neighborhoods with high levels of collective efficacy than in those with low levels. Similarly, Dana L. Haynie and colleagues (2006) found that economically disadvantaged neighborhoods have higher rates of violence in part because they provide greater opportunities for youths to associate with violent peers.

More limited integrated models that combine only social process factors also exist. Combining social bonding and self-control theories, a study of teen offenders found that those with low self-control had weakened social bonds to family and school and, for that reason, were more

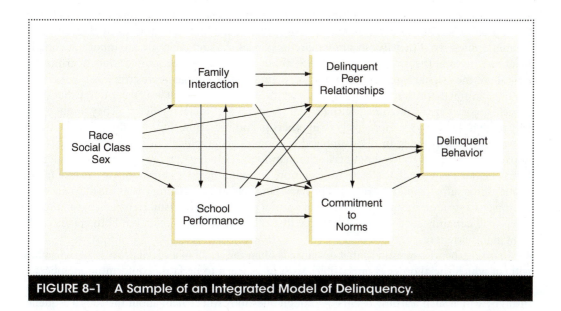

FIGURE 8–1   A Sample of an Integrated Model of Delinquency.

likely to have a greater history of delinquency (Longshore et al. 2005). Similarly, combining social learning and self-control theories, another study found that teens with low self-control were more likely to develop ties to delinquent peers and, partly for this reason, to be more delinquent (Chapple 2005).

In a recent formulation, Ronald L. Simons and Callie Harbin Burt (2011) sought to integrate certain strands of thought from social bonding, learning, and social disorganization theories. In particular, they said that bad parenting, deviant peers, and negative community conditions such as high crime rates and low collective efficacy produce higher criminality because they all promote the same criminogenic *social schemas*. In their words, these schemas include "a hostile view of people and relationships, a preference for immediate rewards, and a cynical view of conventional norms" (p. 553). These views form a "criminogenic knowledge structure" that leads people to be more likely to commit crime because they come to perceive that "illegal actions are warranted, necessary, and justified" (p. 554).

As surprising as it might seem, some scholars dispute the value of integrated theories. Self-control theory proponent Travis Hirschi (1989), for example, believes theoretical integration does more harm than good. In his view, some theories are so different that to integrate them yields a "theoretical mush" (Akers 1989:24) that weakens their ability to explain crime. Even scholars who favor theoretical integration concede that it may nonetheless reduce the "clarity and strength" of the theories that are integrated (Thornberry 1989:56). In contrast, other scholars think theoretical integration can be useful if the theories to be integrated complement each other. This is particularly true, said learning theorist Ronald L. Akers (1989:28), for structural theories and social learning theory because "social learning is the basic process by which the structural variables specified in the macro-level theories have an effect on deviant behavior." Akers also notes the compatibility of social learning and social control theories.

As should be clear, theoretical integration in criminology holds much promise but is not without some risk. Future work will determine if it leads to useless "mush" or instead to a more comprehensive explanation of crime and delinquency. In this regard, life-course criminology offers a very promising approach to understand a myriad of issues regarding the onset and termination of crime and other antisocial behavior at different stages of our lives.

Review and Discuss

What are the advantages and disadvantages of integrated theories of criminality? What are the major questions that life-course and developmental theories try to answer?

▶ Conclusion

Social process theories of crime emphasize learning, socialization, human interaction, and other social processes. They help us understand why some individuals are more likely than others to commit crime even if they live in similar circumstances. As such, they are an important complement to structural theories, which say much about the social and economic roots of crime, but little about the mechanisms through which structural conditions generate crime.

If structural theories err by forgetting about the individual, then it is also fair to say that social process theories err by often neglecting social structure and social inequality. They might tell us why some individuals are more likely than others to commit crime, but they do not explicitly tell us why individuals living in disadvantaged economic, geographical, or other structural conditions are also more likely to commit crime than individuals living in more advantaged conditions. It may be, for example, that street crime is more common in poor communities because family relationships suffer from the stresses of poverty, but such an explanation traces the ultimate cause of crime to a structural condition instead of a social process mechanism. Debate between the two camps will certainly continue, as well it should: Both have much to offer, but both are also deficient in important respects.

Learning theories remind us that deviance is often the result of a social process, socialization, without which social order is impossible. Most of us learn to be fairly conforming members of society, but some of us learn to be criminals. Different learning theories discuss different mechanisms by which such learning occurs. Although questions still remain about the causal sequence involved and other important problems, the emphasis of learning theories on socialization and on peer influences is one of the most important themes in criminology today.

Control theories assume a pessimistic view of human nature. People are basically selfish and hedonistic and will deviate unless controlled by society. Although different control theories focus on different kinds of constraints, all assume that there would be social chaos without these constraints. Hirschi's social bonding theory has been the most influential formulation, with his emphasis on the parent–child bond receiving the most attention. Although the theory has been criticized, it has greatly expanded our knowledge of the micro origins of criminal behavior and helps to explain the gendered patterning of criminal behavior.

Increasingly popular, life-course and developmental theories combine insights from biology, psychology, and sociology to examine the many factors affecting the onset, persistence, and termination of antisocial behavior over the many stages of our lives. Though not without some faults, integrated theories promise to offer a more comprehensive explanation of criminal behavior than any one theory can offer by itself.

We now turn to our final chapter on theory, in which we look at *critical* perspectives that challenge fundamental ideas in criminology and that also spend much more time than any of the theories already discussed on the social reaction to crime. Social inequality lies at the heart of these perspectives, so they are of special interest for the themes of this book. At the same time, some of these perspectives have been criticized by traditional criminologists at least as much as traditional criminology has been, and we will explore the controversy they generate.

Summary

1. Social process theories take up where social structural theories leave off. The latter cannot explain why some individuals living in criminogenic structural circumstances are led to commit crime, whereas most individuals in these same circumstances remain law-abiding citizens.

2. Learning theories say that criminal behavior is the result of socialization by peers and others with deviant values and lifestyles. Edwin Sutherland's differential association theory is the most influential learning theory. His basic emphasis on learning and peer pressure has received much empirical support over the decades, although his theory has been criticized for several reasons, including the possibility that involvement in delinquency may influence associations with delinquent peers.

3. Control theories derive from Durkheim. They assume a selfish human nature and argue that individuals must be constrained by internal and external controls from following their natural impulses and committing antisocial behavior, including crime. Sykes and Matza's neutralization and drift theory assumes that adolescents rationalize that it is acceptable to break the law before actually committing delinquency in order to lessen any guilt or shame they might otherwise feel.

4. Hirschi's 1969 social bonding theory is the most influential control theory. It argues that strong social bonds to family and schools help prevent delinquency. Research inspired by social bonding theory finds that social bonds to parents, schooling, and religion all help reduce delinquency. This theory, too, is subject to causal order questions. Hirschi and Gottfredson's more recent self-control theory has also generated much interest but also much controversy, thanks in part to the authors' declaration that low self-control is by far the most important reason for all criminal behavior.

5. Tittle's control balance theory states that deviance results when people are very controlling or very controlled. The reason for this is that people want to be as autonomous as possible. Those with control deficits break the law to achieve more control over their lives, and those with a control surplus break the law because they desire even more control.

6. Life-course criminology focuses on the onset and termination of crime and delinquency stages over the life course. This perspective emphasizes developmental problems in infancy and childhood that create antisocial behavior that may continue into adolescence and even beyond. It also emphasizes that criminality lessens as people move into adulthood because

of increasing stakes in conformity through strengthened bonds to family, work, and other conventional social institutions.

7. Some criminologists favor theoretical integration in which concepts or whole theories are blended to yield what is intended to be a more comprehensive and therefore better explanation of criminality. Others feel that theoretical integration reduces the clarity of the theories and their ability to explain crime.

Key Terms

attachment *158*

containment *156*

conventional social institutions *155*

delinquent peers *151*

differential association *151*

drift *157*

family interaction *159*

family structure *159*

learning theories *151*

life course *164*

personal controls *155*

self-control *162*

social bonds *158*

social controls *155*

socialization *151*

social learning *154*

theoretical integration *167*

What Would You Do?

1. You have a son in first grade. It is about halfway through the school year. Your son has always been rambunctious, but lately his attention span and behavior seem even worse. You think this has happened because two of his new classmates are wild boys themselves. What do you do?

2. Your daughter, the oldest of your three children, just started ninth grade. She has always been a nice, well-behaved young woman, but one day you notice an empty can of beer when you are cleaning out her backpack. You confront her with the can and she says in an angry voice, "It's no big deal!" You want her to know that you trust her, but you also don't want her to be drinking. You are worried that if you come down too hard on her, your relationship with her will deteriorate. You are also worried that if you don't come down hard enough, she won't get the message. What do you do?

AP Photo/Daniel Portnoy

9 Sociological Theories: Critical Perspectives

· ·

Crime in the News

In May 2013, Jeffrey Deskovic, 40, received an M.A. in criminal justice from the John Jay College of Criminal Justice in New York City. He did so after spending 16 years in prison after being convicted at age 16 of a rape and murder he did not commit. Although DNA found at the scene of the crime did not match his DNA, he confessed to the crime after extensive questioning by the police. Deskovic recalled, "They wore me down after interrogating me for seven and a half hours. I didn't have an attorney present, my parents didn't know where I was, I wasn't given anything to eat." He finally was released from prison in 2006 after evidence emerged that exonerated him, and then decided to get his degree. With money acquired from a legal settlement in his case, he started a foundation to help other inmates who, like himself, were convicted and imprisoned despite being innocent. As Deskovic explained, "I need to feel like I'm making some sort of a difference so I can make some sense out of what happened to me."

Source: Siegal 2013.

· ·

Despite their many differences, the sociological theories examined in the preceding two chapters are similar in several ways. They are all *positivist* theories: They try to explain why crime occurs and they locate its causes in the immediate social environment or in the whole society. These theories do not ask how particular behaviors and people come to be defined as crimes and criminals, and they disregard how social networks and social institutions respond to crime. They also do not wonder how and why some people such as Jeffrey Deskovic are mistaken as criminals. Although many of the theories suggest the need for social reforms to reduce crime, none urges the drastic overhaul of society's social and economic foundations. In these various ways, these sociological theories might all be called *traditional theories*.

Critical perspectives on crime take a different view. Because they highlight the ways in which people and institutions respond to crime and criminals, they are often called *social reaction* theories. Although critical perspectives differ in many respects, they all consider the definition of crime *problematic*, meaning that the definition of a behavior as a crime and the defining of individuals as criminals are both something to explain. In explaining how these definitions originate, critical perspectives emphasize the concept of power and the inequality based on differences in power. Depending on the theory, power differences are based on social class, race or ethnicity, or gender. Whatever the source of the difference, the theories hold that behaviors by people or groups with power are less likely to be considered crimes than behaviors by those without power. The unfortunate story of Jeffrey Deskovic illustrates the importance of understanding how people come to be defined as criminals.

The various critical perspectives became popular in the 1960s and 1970s, a turbulent era highlighted by the civil rights movement, the Vietnam antiwar movement, and the beginning of the contemporary women's movement. Many sociology graduate students and younger sociology faculty took part in these movements, all of which questioned the status quo and emphasized the discriminatory and other damaging practices of social institutions. The civil rights movement and black power movements called attention to the racism pervading all aspects of society. The antiwar movement charged the U.S. government with committing genocide abroad and lying to its own citizens at home. The women's movement began to challenge the many inequities based on gender. "Question authority" and "don't trust anyone over 30" became rallying cries for a whole generation. Against this backdrop, it was perhaps inevitable that younger sociologists began to question traditional views of society, including those of crime. They wondered whether the chances of arrest and imprisonment had less to do with the crime itself and more to do with the suspect's race, social class, and gender.

TABLE 9-1 Critical Perspectives in Brief

THEORY	KEY FIGURE(S)	SYNOPSIS
Labeling Theory		
	Edwin Lemert	Deviance is not a quality of the act a person commits; some people and behaviors are more likely than others to be labeled deviant; the deviant label may lead to continued deviance.
	Howard S. Becker	
Conflict and Radical Theories		
Conflict	Thorsten Sellin	Law and crime result from conflict among the various groups in society, not just economic classes.
	George Vold	
	Austin T. Turk	
Radical	Willem Bonger	The wealthy use the legal system to protect their dominance and to suppress the poor; the criminal law and justice system reflects the interests of the powerful.
	Jerome Hall	
	William Chambliss	
	Richard Quinney	
Feminist Theories		
	Kathleen Daly	Crime cannot be fully understood and explained without appreciating the important role that gender plays; feminist theories can and should be used to reduce gender inequality in the areas of crime and criminal justice, as well as in the larger society.
	Meda Chesney-Lind	
	Sally S. Simpson	

This chapter discusses the major critical perspectives on crime. Labeling theory was the first critical perspective of the 1960s and was soon followed by various conflict theories. Feminist views on crime developed in the mid-1970s, in part because labeling and conflict theories neglected gender. Although all these theories stress the social reaction to crime, they also aim to explain the origins of crime. However, their explanations differ in important ways from those advanced by traditional theories. A summary of the critical perspectives discussed in this chapter appears in Table 9–1. We begin our discussion with labeling theory.

▶ Labeling Theory

Labeling theory, which has been called "one of the most significant perspectives in the study of crime and deviance" (Matsueda 2001:238), addresses three major issues: (1) the definition of deviance and crime, (2) possible discrimination in the application of official labeling and sanctions, and (3) the effect of labeling on continued criminality.

The Relativist Definition of Crime and Deviance

We start with labeling theory's definition of deviance. Traditional theories of deviance and crime adopt an *absolutist* definition of deviance as something real that is inherent in behavior. In contrast, labeling theory adopts a relativist definition (see Chapter 1), by assuming that nothing about a given behavior automatically makes it deviant. In this view, deviance is not a property of a behavior, but rather the result of how others regard the behavior. Howard S. Becker (1963:9), one of the originators of labeling theory, presented the theory's definition of deviance in perhaps the most widely quoted passage in the deviance and criminality literature in the last fifty years:

> Social groups create deviance by making the rules whose infraction constitutes deviance, and by applying those rules to particular people and labeling them as outsiders. From this point of view, deviance is not a quality of the act the person commits, but rather a consequence of the application by others of rules or sanctions to an "offender." The deviant is one to whom that label has been successfully applied; deviant behavior is behavior that people so label.

To illustrate this view, recall Chapter 1's discussion of murder, widely regarded as the most serious crime because it involves the taking of a human life. Labeling theory would say there

altrendo images/Getty Images

▲ Labeling theory assumes that wealthy, white people are less likely than other categories of people to be arrested or to suffer other legal sanctions.

is nothing inherent in murder that makes it deviant. Rather, murder is considered deviant because of the circumstances under which it occurs. Much killing occurs in wartime, but people who do the most killing in wars may receive medals, not arrest records. We deem it acceptable and even necessary to kill in wartime, so we do not call it murder, as long as the rules of war are followed. A police officer who kills an armed criminal in self-defense does not murder. Capital punishment also involves killing, but again, most of society does not consider an execution a murder.

The Imposition of the Deviant Label

In addition to defining deviance in an unusual way, labeling theory also discusses how *official labeling* (i.e., the identification of certain people as deviants and criminals) occurs. Traditional theories accept the accuracy of official labeling such as arrest and imprisonment. Labeling theory challenges this view and says that some people and behaviors are more likely than others to be labeled deviant. Simply put, people in power impose definitions of deviance on behaviors committed by people without power, with the poor and people of color more likely to suffer legal punishment, including arrest, conviction, and incarceration.

William Chambliss's (1973) famous discussion of the Saints and the Roughnecks provides a classic example of labeling theory's view. The Saints were eight extremely delinquent male high school students in a particular town. They drank routinely, committed truancy, drove recklessly, and engaged in petty theft and vandalism. One of their favorite activities was going to street construction sites at night and removing warning signals; they would then hide and watch cars bottom out in potholes and other cavities. As their name implies, the Saints, despite their behavior, were considered "good kids." They came from middle-class families and were never arrested because their offenses were dismissed as harmless pranks. When they grew into adulthood, they went to graduate and professional schools and became doctors, lawyers, and the like. The six Roughnecks fared much differently. They were also very delinquent and got into many fights, but caused less monetary damage than the Saints did. They came from poor families and were often in trouble with the police because everyone viewed them as troublemakers. When they grew into adulthood, they ended up in low-paying jobs and even prison.

Chambliss's analysis suggests that our impressions of people affect how likely they are to be officially labeled. Since the 1960s, many studies have examined whether *extralegal* factors such as race or ethnicity, social class, gender, and appearance affect the chances of arrest, imprisonment, and other official labeling. Overall, the evidence is inconsistent. Early studies found these variables to have the effects predicted by labeling theory, but later research found that official labeling was affected primarily by *legal* factors such as the weight of the evidence and the seriousness of the offense. Debate on the importance of extralegal factors continues to be among the most heated in the criminology literature (see Chapters 16 and 17). A reasonable view, shared by many but not all scholars, is that extralegal factors matter much less than legal factors. Race and ethnicity, social class, and gender do make a difference, but in more variable and subtle ways than depicted by labeling theory (Walker et al. 2012).

The evidence of only a fairly weak effect of extralegal factors leads many critics to dismiss labeling theory; they say that most people who are officially labeled have, in fact, committed the behavior for which they are labeled. Labeling proponents just as quickly point to the evidence supporting the theory, such as the wrongful conviction and imprisonment of Jeffrey Deskovic highlighted in the news story that began this chapter. Regardless of where the weight of the evidence lies, it is fair to say that labeling theory generated a new focus fifty years ago on the social reaction to crime and the operation of the legal system that continues to influence the study of crime and delinquency.

▼

The Negative Consequences of Labeling

One of the most important sociological principles is that our interaction with others shapes our conception of ourselves and affects our behavior. Labeling theorists build on this view to present a similar dynamic. They stress that labeling someone deviant can produce a deviant self-image that prompts the person to commit more deviance. Frank Tannenbaum (1938:21), a historian of crime, called this process the dramatization of evil and said it "plays a greater role in making the criminal than perhaps any other experience." A person labeled deviant, said Tannenbaum, "becomes the thing he is described as being." Howard S. Becker (1963:31) highlighted a similar view twenty-five years later, noting that the "experience of being caught and publicly labeled as a deviant" is "one of the most crucial steps" leading to a deviant career, with "important consequences for one's further participation and self-image."

If labeling promotes continued deviance, says the theory, then official labeling by the legal system is counterproductive. In this view, arrest and imprisonment have the ironic effect of increasing deviance by generating a deviant self-image. The person labeled not only comes to accept the label, but also finds others treating her or him like a criminal. As a result, conventional opportunities and friendships are blocked: Jobs are hard to get with a criminal record, and friendships with law-abiding people are difficult to achieve. In a self-fulfilling prophecy, the social–psychological and practical consequences of official labeling thus lead to deviance amplification, or the commission of continued deviance and the adoption of a deviant lifestyle.

Labeling theory's focus is not on the initial act or two leading someone to be officially labeled, and labeling theory does not try to explain why these initial acts occur. In Edwin Lemert's (1951) term, these acts are examples of primary deviance and occur among wide segments of the population. We all transgress now and then: Some youths shoplift, others commit vandalism, and still others use illegal drugs. But suppose a youth, say a 15-year-old male, is caught vandalizing or using an illegal drug. His arrest, fingerprinting, and other legal measures make him think of himself as a young criminal. Parents, friends, teachers, and even the whole neighborhood hear about his crime. He is now labeled a troublemaker, and people look at him differently. Perhaps, some of his friends are even told not to spend time with him, and he might have trouble finding an after-school job for extra money. If some other offense occurs in the neighborhood, the youth might be suspected. He becomes angry and resentful and figures if they are all going to treat him this way, why not act this way? Secondary deviance, or continued deviance, follows.

Although this is admittedly a melodramatic scenario, it lies at the heart of labeling theory. Experimental evidence shows how deviance can reduce opportunities to succeed in the law-abiding world. In a study of fictitious job applications, Devah Pager (2009) had pairs of male college students apply for jobs in Milwaukee. The students were articulate and well dressed, but one in each pair claimed he had spent time in prison for cocaine possession. The applicants with the (supposed) criminal record were called back by the employers only half as often as those with a clean record. Reflecting racial discrimination, African-American applicants without a criminal record were slightly less likely than white applicants with a criminal record to be called back.

Other studies also show that official labeling can reduce educational and employment opportunities. A record of juvenile delinquency reduces the likelihood of graduating from high school and hurts employment chances into young adulthood (Sweeten 2006), while incarceration during adulthood severely reduces employment opportunities after release from prison (Western 2006). These problems in turn are widely thought to increase the likelihood of continued criminality (Clear 2010).

▼ Labeling theory assumes that an arrest, conviction, or other criminal label produces several consequences that often lead someone to commit additional deviance.

© Mikael Karlsson / Alamy

In arguing that official labeling increases future criminality, labeling theory directly challenges deterrence theory's view (see Chapter 5) that official labeling has the opposite effect (specific deterrence). The two theories also disagree on the effects of official labeling on the offender's perceptions. Labeling theory argues that labeling causes or increases a deviant self-image, whereas deterrence theory argues that it increases the offender's perceived risk of arrest and aversion to arrest and punishment.

Review and Discuss

To what extent does labeling have negative consequences for the people who are labeled?

Evaluation of Labeling Theory

Labeling theory has certainly generated much controversy over the years, and scholars have criticized it since its inception (Akers 1968). Several criticisms are worth noting (Bernburg 2010). First, labeling theory paints an overly passive view of the individual as quietly succumbing to the effects of the deviant label. Second, the theory implies that a life of crime, or secondary deviance, does not develop unless official labeling first occurs, even though many individuals end up with a life of crime without ever being labeled. Third, the theory fails to explain primary deviance and thus ignores the effects of family and peer relationships and more macro factors on deviance and crime.

Next, some critics take issue with labeling theory's prescription for reducing crime and delinquency. Because the theory stresses that official labeling promotes continued deviance, many labeling theorists urge caution in using the law to fight crime except for the most serious offenders. Critics, especially deterrence theory proponents, charge that following such a policy would increase crime and delinquency rather than reduce it. Finally, radical criminologists also criticize labeling theory. While liking its general perspective, they nonetheless charge it with focusing on "nuts, sluts, and perverts," or deviance by the powerless, and ignoring crimes by the powerful. They also criticize the theory for ignoring the sources of the power inequalities that affect the making of laws and the likelihood of official labeling for criminal behavior (Liazos 1972; Taylor et al. 1973).

These criticisms notwithstanding, what does the research say about labeling theory's central assumption that formal labeling produces more, not less, criminality? Several early studies found that labeling neither produced a deviant self-image nor increased (secondary) deviance, and their findings initially reduced labeling theory's popularity and influence. However, some recent research provides more support for labeling theory's belief in the negative effects of formal labeling. In particular, recent studies find that recidivism (repeat offending) is (1) higher among offenders who spend more time in prison than among similar offenders who spend less time in prison (Baay et al. 2012), (2) also higher among offenders sentenced to prison than among similar offenders who receive only probation (Bales and Piquero 2012), (3) and higher among juveniles who are arrested than among juveniles with similar offense histories who are not arrested (Restivo and Lanier 2013). This recent research prompts many scholars to conclude that official labeling does tend to produce more criminality rather than to deter it (Bales and Piquero 2012; Jackson and Hay 2013; Restivo and Lanier 2013).

However, other recent research finds that imprisonment, the most severe form of official labeling, does *not* produce more criminality compared to noncustodial sanctions like probation or at most has only a small such effect (Loeffler 2013; Nagin et al. 2009). This body of research suggests that labeling theory's assumption concerning secondary deviance may be overstated. To the extent that official labeling does produce secondary deviance, this consequence probably tends to occur more often among juvenile offenders, who are at a more impressionable age, than among adult offenders. At least for juveniles, then, recent studies "provide confirmation of the idea that formal labeling will result in increases of future delinquent behavior" and "attest to the value of the labeling approach for explaining criminal and delinquent behavior" (Restivo and Lanier 2013:17, 22).

Some scholars note that official labeling promotes deviance for some people and deters it for others. If this is true, they say, then research must clarify the circumstances under which

Crime and Controversy   HOW SHOULD WE DEAL WITH JUVENILE OFFENDERS?

Labeling theory spawned new concern over the negative consequences of labeling, especially for adolescents who get into trouble with the law. Sociologists warned that treating juveniles like common criminals would only make them more likely to continue breaking the law. During the 1960s and 1970s, states across the nation heeded this warning and began to *divert* from the juvenile justice system adolescents who had committed minor delinquency or status offenses (running away from home, truancy, etc.). Instead of going into juvenile court and youth centers, these offenders stayed out of the system and experienced other sanctions, such as undergoing counseling, making restitution to their victims, or having their behavior monitored by juvenile probation officers or sometimes by their parents.

A rough consensus of studies since the 1970s is that diversion produces modest *decreases* in recidivism (repeat offending). Because it costs much less money to divert juvenile offenders than to place them in youth centers, diversion remains a popular legal sanction for adolescents, especially those charged with minor offenses.

However, as the public became more concerned about juvenile crime in the late 1970s, sentiment about juvenile delinquency began to change. Thinking that juvenile court sentencing is generally too lenient, many observers urged that the cases of serious juvenile offenders be transferred to adult criminal court, and states began to do so. Critics replied that even serious juvenile offenders are still too young to be able to fully comprehend their actions and, if tried as adults, would turn out worse than if they were processed through the juvenile justice system. This transfer movement eventually extended in many states to juveniles accused of property crime rather than just serious violent crime. Today twenty-seven states even permit children under the age of 13 to be tried as adults.

A major goal of treating juvenile offenders as adults is to reduce juvenile crime. However, there is little evidence that the transfer movement has had this general deterrent effect. There is even evidence, as labeling theory would predict, that juvenile offenders whose cases are handled by the (adult) criminal court have higher recidivism rates than those whose cases are retained by juvenile court, even when factors like the seriousness of the offense are taken into account. These results indicate that transferring juvenile cases to adult court ironically has the opposite effect of what is intended. As one of these studies concluded, "(G)et-tough policies that transfer juvenile cases to criminal court may backfire and have a criminogenic rather than deterrent effect."

Sources: Bishop 2006; Deitch et al. 2009; Johnson et al. 2011; Lanza-Kaduce et al. 2005.

---

labeling has one effect or the other. In this regard, some studies find that continued deviance is more likely when offenders perceive that the police and courts are treating them unfairly or disrespectfully (Sherman 1993); when offenders have few social ties to family, employment, and other social institutions (McCarthy and Hagan 2003); and, among juveniles, when offenders have a closer relationship with their parents (Jackson and Hay 2013).

John Braithwaite (2001) argues that the type of shaming, or social disapproval, involved in labeling makes a crucial difference for continued deviance. Braithwaite distinguishes between *disintegrative shaming* and *reintegrative shaming*. Disintegrative shaming, or stigmatization, occurs when offenders are treated like outcasts and no effort is made to forgive them and to involve them in community affairs. It promotes continued deviance because it humiliates and angers offenders, denies them legitimate opportunities, and forces them to associate with criminal peers. Reintegrative shaming occurs when efforts are made to bring offenders back into the community. Such shaming reduces continued deviance, partly because it encourages offenders to feel ashamed, and is most common

▼ The Japanese are much more likely than Americans to think criminals can change for the better.

© Mark Richards / PhotoEdit

in *communitarian* societies marked by a high degree of concern for the welfare of others. One such society is Japan, where social networks readily support offenders and try to reintegrate them into the community.

Despite many pessimistic assessments of labeling theory's value, research findings that legal sanctions do contribute to additional delinquency (see Crime and Controversy box) "attest to the viability of the labeling approach for explaining secondary deviance" (Bernburg and Krohn 2003:1314). The new emphasis on informal labeling and on the conditions under which labeling increases or decreases deviance has further reinvigorated the theory and increased its importance for contemporary criminology.

Restorative Justice

Labeling theory's views in general, and Braithwaite's views in particular, are reflected in a new *restorative justice* movement that has been gaining popularity in recent years (Toews 2013). Reflecting a philosophy that goes back to ancient times, restorative justice focuses on restoring the social bond between the offender and the community. In contrast to the *retributive model* guiding U.S. crime policy, which emphasizes punishment of the offender, restorative justice emphasizes the needs of the victim and of the community and, perhaps above all, the need to reintegrate the offender into the community. Often involving meetings between offenders, their victims, and community members, restorative justice is a more personal process that encourages offenders to take responsibility for their actions. A major goal of these efforts is to accomplish the reintegrative shaming that Braithwaite advocates.

Restorative justice has been tried in some areas of the United States and also in nations such as Australia, Canada, Japan, and New Zealand. It is also popular among native peoples in the United States and Canada and in some socialist nations. Although restorative justice practices differ, they include such things as *victim impact panels*, in which victims talk with offenders about their feelings as victims; *family group conferences* involving family members of both offenders and victims; *sentencing circles* involving offenders' and victims' relatives, friends, and other associates; and *citizen reparative boards* that determine the conditions of probation for convicted offenders (Dobrow 2012).

The key question, of course, is whether restorative justice works. Does it reduce repeat offending, does it reduce community fear of crime, and does it enhance victims' satisfaction with the criminal justice system? Unfortunately, restorative justice is still too new for definitive answers to these questions. However, it does seem to increase victim satisfaction with the justice process and reduce their fear of revictimization by the same offender. Some studies also indicate that offenders who participate in restorative justice procedures are less likely to reoffend than control groups of offenders who experience more typical criminal justice outcomes (Armour 2012). In the United States, restorative justice has probably been used most often for juvenile offenders who commit relatively minor offenses. Whether it would work for more serious juvenile offenders and for their adult counterparts remains an important question.

Review and Discuss

On balance, does the empirical evidence support labeling theory's various assumptions, or does it fail to support them?

▶ Conflict and Radical Theories

Conflict and radical theories take up where labeling theory leaves off. They argue that law is a key part of the struggle between powerful interests and the powerless: to preserve their dominance, the powerful use the law to control the powerless. This argument applies to both the formation of law and the operation of the legal system. In contrast, traditional theories stress the positive functions of law. They see law needed by every modern society to maintain social order, given that there will always be people deviating. Law and the criminal justice system are thus designed to benefit all of us, not just the powerful.

Consensus and Conflict Perspectives in Sociology

This contrast between conflict/radical theories and traditional theories reflects a more general division in sociology between functional or consensus perspectives and conflict perspectives. Following the Durkheimian sociological tradition, consensus perspectives stress that social institutions help create social stability. In contrast, conflict theory says that social institutions serve the interests of the powerful in society and are dysfunctional for many other members of society.

Conflict theory lies at the heart of the *conflict tradition* in sociology, which goes back to the work of the German social philosopher and political activist Karl Marx (1818–1883), his collaborator Friedrich Engels (1820–1895), and the German sociologist Max Weber (1864–1920) (Ritzer and Stepinsky 2014). As is well known, Marx and Engels distinguished classes based on the ownership of the means of production—land, technology, factories, tools, and the like. In capitalist society, the two major classes are the bourgeoisie (sometimes called the ruling class), who own the factories and other modern means of production, and the proletariat, who work for the bourgeoisie. The bourgeoisie's primary interest is to maintain its dominance by exploiting and oppressing the proletariat; the proletariat's primary interest is to eliminate its oppression by overthrowing the bourgeoisie. Weber recognized economic classes, but, unlike Marx and Engels, he also recognized *status groups* with different amounts of power. Some status groups derive from their placement in the economic system, but others are based on religion, ethnicity, urban versus rural residence, and other noneconomic factors. Weber's concept of power and conflict is thus more multidimensional than that of Marx and Engels.

Conflict Perspectives in Criminology

Because law is an important social institution, the debate between consensus and conflict views inevitably entered the field of criminology. In the 1960s and 1970s, the civil rights, Vietnam antiwar, and other social movements affected a new generation of scholars interested in crime. They saw law used again and again to repress African-Americans in the South and to harass antiwar protesters, and began to consider whether the criminal law and justice system similarly oppress or otherwise harm the powerless. These scholars looked back to Marx, Engels, and Weber for inspiration and developed two strands of thought, *conflict theory* and *radical theory*.

Conflict theory, is more Weberian in orientation. It considers law and crime the result of conflict among various kinds of groups in society, not just economic classes. Austin T. Turk's (1969) book *Criminality and Legal Order* is perhaps the most important statement of this perspective. He argued that the powerful impose the label of crime on the powerless to help reinforce their political power. From this vantage point, Turk developed a theory of criminalization that spelled out how criminal labels are applied. For example, criminalization is more likely when the subordinate groups are less sophisticated.

Turk's Weberian orientation followed in the footsteps of earlier scholars Thorsten Sellin and George Vold. Sellin (1938) discussed immigration and crime in a short report, *Culture Conflict and Crime*. Because some behaviors considered acceptable in immigrant cultures are illegal in the eyes of the larger U.S. society, he said, many crimes they commit should be seen as the result of culture conflict. In a famous example, Sellin wrote about a Sicilian father in New Jersey who killed a teenage boy for having sex with his daughter. Because Sicilian culture approved this way of defending family honor, the man was surprised to be arrested!

Vold (1958) presented a *group conflict* theory of crime in his important book, *Theoretical Criminology*. He said that groups with legislative power have the power to decide which behaviors will be illegal and that crime stems from the conflict among various interest groups. Vold also argued that juvenile gangs arise from conflict between young people's values and those of the adult culture. Finally, he believed his theory was especially relevant for crimes involving political protest, labor disputes, and racial and ethnic hostility (see Chapter 14).

Evaluation of Conflict Theory

Conflict theory helps to explain the origins of some criminal laws and types of crime. In both areas, it seems especially relevant for crimes committed as part of social movement unrest, including labor strife, and for behaviors such as abortion, drug and alcohol use, and other consensual crimes on which people have many different views (see Chapter 15). However, as Vold himself conceded, it seems less relevant for conventional street crimes such as murder, assault, robbery, and burglary. Laws prohibiting these behaviors are meant to protect all segments of society, not just the powerful, who suffer less than the poor from these crimes. In another area, conflict theory shares labeling theory's view on unfairness in the labeling process. However, evidence of these disparities is inconsistent, and scholars continue to disagree on their extent.

Some of the best evidence for conflict theory comes from historical studies. One such study was Joseph R. Gusfield's (1963) book *Symbolic Crusade*, which discussed the origins and dynamics of the *temperance* (prohibition) movement of the late 1800s and early 1900s. As his book's title implies, Gusfield saw the temperance movement as a symbolic attack of one group on another group. The movement was composed mostly of devout middle-class, small-town, or rural Protestants who considered alcohol use a sin. They disliked the drinking by poor Catholic immigrants in urban areas. To the minds of temperance advocates, these people had several strikes against them: They were poor, they were Catholic, they were immigrants, and they were urban residents. The temperance attack on their drinking is thus best seen as a symbolic attack against their poverty, religion, immigrant status, and urban residence. Rural Protestants, who dominated state legislatures and the Congress, were able to amend the U.S. Constitution to prohibit alcohol.

Radical Theories in Criminology

Conflict theory was the first strand of thought that the new generation of scholars began developing in the 1960s. The second line of thinking was more Marxian than Weberian and views law and crime as the result of conflict between capitalists and workers, or the ruling class and the poor. This perspective has been variously called "critical," "new," "radical," "dialectical," "socialist," and "Marxist" criminology. Although these labels indicate certain differences, all these approaches basically adopt a Marxian approach to the study of crime and law (DeKeseredy and Dragiewicz 2012). For the sake of simplicity, the term *radical theory* will refer to all these theories. Their primary views all stem from the work of Marx and Engels, to whom we now return.

Marx and Engels on Crime and Law

In contrast to other topics, Marx and Engels actually wrote relatively little about law and even less about crime, and what they did write is scattered throughout their various essays and books (Cain and Hunt 1979). They thought that law helps the ruling class in at least two ways: (1) it emphasizes and preserves private property, almost all of which belongs to the ruling class, and (2) it gives everyone various legal rights and thus appears to provide "equal justice for all." In promoting an appearance of legal equality, the law pacifies the powerless by making them feel good about the status quo and obscuring the true nature and extent of their oppression.

Marx and Engels presented several contrasting views of crime. In some of their writing, they depicted crime as stemming from the misery accompanying capitalism and as a necessary, logical response by the poor to the conditions in which they live. At other times, however, they depicted crime as political rebellion by the poor against their exploitation and an expression of their hostility toward the ruling class. And sometimes they harshly depicted criminals as a *lumpenproletariat*, or "the social scum, the positively rotting mass" composed of vagabonds, pimps, prostitutes, pickpockets, and the like (Marx and Engels 1962 (1848)). As might be evident from their language, Marx and Engels felt that the *lumpenproletariat* hindered the chances of a proletarian revolution.

Willem Bonger: Capitalism, Egoism, and Crime

Despite Marx and Engels's occasional concern with crime and law, for a long time Marxists neglected these subjects. Dutch criminologist Willem Bonger (1876–1940) was a major exception. Bonger (1916) argued in his book *Criminality and Economic Conditions* that a cultural emphasis on altruism characterized pre-capitalist, agricultural societies. In such societies, everyone was poor and looked out for each other's welfare. The development of capitalism led to a very different situation, because as an economic system it emphasizes competition for profit above all. Competition in turn means that someone wins and someone loses: Your success comes at the expense of someone else's failure.

This leads to a cultural emphasis on egoism and greed that makes people willing to break the law for economic gain and other advantages even if others get hurt. Bonger thought this was true for all social classes, not just the poor, but also noted that the poor are driven to crime by

International Focus   CRIME AND THE ECONOMY IN CHINA, VIETNAM, AND RUSSIA

Many radical criminologists blame capitalism for much of the crime the United States suffers: Crime results from the economic deprivation caused by capitalism and also from the selfish individualism that accompanies capitalism. If they are right, then as communist nations move toward a capitalist economy, crime of many types should increase. The experience of China, Vietnam, and Russia supports this prediction.

In 1984 the Communist Party in China initiated economic reforms to reduce government control over business activity as a move toward a market (capitalist) economy began. During the next few years, China's official crime rate rose sharply. Keeping in mind that official crime statistics in China may be even less reliable than those in the United States, China's rate quadrupled between 1985 and the early 1990s, and its serious crime rate (homicide, rape, aggravated assault, robbery, theft, and fraud) quintupled during that time. Political corruption in China is also thought to have soared during this period of economic change. The former director of international law enforcement research for China's Ministry of Public Security attributed the rising crime rate to the social changes and growing unemployment accompanying China's move to a market economy.

A crime increase also followed Vietnam's move toward a market economy. In the wake of this effort, theft, drug use and trafficking, delinquency, smuggling, and business-related crime grew into major problems. Experts blamed the growth in crime on problems related to the move toward capitalism. As a Vietnamese social scientist explained, "Inequality and unemployment have increased, education and health care are no longer free, so Vietnamese people are losing the social protection they once had."

Russia's crime rate also increased when it, too, began moving toward a market economy after the Soviet Union dissolved in the late 1980s. Its homicide rate doubled by 2000, and its rates of other crimes also soared. Homicide rates rose more rapidly in Russian regions that fared worse economically than in regions that did better economically. A study of Russia's crime rate increase concluded, "Unfortunately, it appears that increases in and high levels of violence are a price Russians must pay for a path chosen by their leaders and others."

The growth in crime problems in all three nations was doubtless the result of several factors. Their shift to market economies may have prompted greater inequality and selfish individualism, but it also involved other kinds of social changes. Following Durkheim, the resulting anomie, or normlessness, accompanying these changes may well be another factor accounting for rising crime in all three nations. Nevertheless, the experience of China, Vietnam, and Russia does support radical criminology's view that capitalism may be criminogenic.

Sources: Broadhurst et al. 2013; Mel and Wang 2007; Mitton 2007; Pomfret 1999; Pridemore 2007; Sato 2009; Ward 1995.

---

economic necessity. Although the wealthy commit crimes, he said, they escape legal punishment, because the law in capitalist societies is intended to help dominate the poor. Attributing crime to capitalism, Bonger thought it would largely disappear under socialism, which places much more importance on altruism. Supporting one of Bonger's views, a study of 100 nations found that their degree of capitalism was positively related to their homicide rates (Antonaccio and Tittle 2007).

Review and Discuss

According to Bonger, why does capitalism promote crime?

Jerome Hall: The Law of Theft

Almost four decades after Bonger published his book, historian Jerome Hall (1952) presented a Marxian analysis of the law of theft in his influential book *Theft, Law, and Society*. This book discussed how the modern concept of theft developed in England some 500 years ago. England was then emerging from a feudal, agricultural society into a mercantile economy. When a merchant sold goods to another merchant or landowner, poor people, or *carriers,* working for the merchant transported these goods on a horse-drawn cart. Because carriers were thought to technically own the goods while transporting them, they had the legal right to keep the goods for themselves, with no crime committed.

Fearing being fired or physically attacked, most carriers simply transported their goods, but some did decide to keep them. Merchants naturally detested this practice, but the poor, by far the vast majority of English people, supported it. Eventually, the issue reached the courts, and English judges established a new crime in the landmark 1473 *Carrier's Case* by ruling that carriers could no longer keep the goods. This decision, said Hall, protected the mercantile class's interests. Although today we all agree that carriers should not keep goods they are delivering (if you buy a flat-screen TV, you would certainly not want the truck driver to keep it!), the origins of this particular concept of theft do fit a Marxian perspective.

William Chambliss: The Law of Vagrancy

In 1964, William Chambliss authored a similar analysis of the development of vagrancy laws long ago. Before the 1340s, no law in England prohibited begging or loitering. Then the bubonic plague struck England in 1348 and killed about half of the population. With fewer people left to work on their land, landowners would have to pay higher wages. The passage of the first vagrancy law in 1349 aimed to prevent this by making it a crime for people to beg and to move from place to place to find employment. Both provisions in effect increased the size of the labor force, keeping wages lower than they would have been otherwise.

Chambliss (1964:69) said this law was "designed for one express purpose: to force laborers . . . to accept employment at a low wage in order to insure the land-owner an adequate supply of labor at a price he could afford to pay." In the following centuries, Chambliss said, vagrancy laws were revived from time to time to benefit the mercantile class. Although some critics say Chambliss's analysis over-emphasizes the economic motivation for vagrancy law development (Adler 1989), it remains a classic application of radical theory.

Contemporary Radical Views on Crime and Law

As radical perspectives on crime and law developed during the 1960s and 1970s, scholars drew on the work of Marx and Engels, Bonger, Hall, Chambliss, and others. Much of the new work was historical, but a good deal of it also looked at the law and crime in the contemporary United States and other nations, with the major emphasis on the formation of law and the punishment of criminals. Reflecting more general Marxist theory, radical work on law and crime is often categorized according to whether it embraces *instrumental* or *structural* Marxist views. The first radical scholars in the 1970s took an instrumental view, whereas more recent radical scholars espouse structural views.

Instrumental Marxism considers the ruling class a small, unified group that uses the law to dominate the poor and to advance its own interests. According to Richard Quinney (1974:16), a noted proponent of this view, law is simply "an instrument of the state and ruling class to maintain and perpetuate the existing social and economic order." *Structural Marxism* says this view is simplistic. If law were just a means of oppression, its proponents ask, how can such advantages as civil liberties and unemployment insurance exist? Their answer is that the ruling class is less unified than instrumental Marxists think, as ruling class members disagree over important issues and compete among themselves for political and economic power. The state and its legal order must thus be "relatively autonomous" to ensure the long-term interests of capitalism by providing legal rights and other benefits that keep the public happy (Chambliss and Seidman 1982). Thus these benefits are sham, not real, because they serve in the long run to preserve capitalist interests.

A Common Agenda   Despite their different views, radical criminologists generally agree on a common set of beliefs (DeKeseredy and Dragiewicz 2012; Paternoster and Bachman 2001). First, a few people in capitalist societies have most of the wealth and power and the mass of people have little. Second, the wealthy use their power and the legal system to protect their dominance and to keep the poor and people of color in their place. Third, the criminal law reflects the

▲ Today's vagrancy laws originated during the 1348 bubonic plague that killed half of England's population. The first vagrancy law was enacted the next year to force people to work. By increasing the size of the labor force in this manner, the law kept wages lower than they would otherwise have been.

© SCPhotos / Alamy

interests of the powerful and not those of the general public. Fourth, criminals are normal people who commit crime because they are poor. Fifth, a harsh criminal justice system will not reduce crime because it does not address the causes of crime; instead, it will only worsen the lives of the poor. Finally, the criminal justice system must become fairer, and social and economic reform must occur.

Evaluation of Radical Criminology

Some traditional criminologists vigorously attack radical criminology. One scholar called the "new criminology" the "old baloney" and accused it of sentimentality in glorifying predatory crime by the poor (Toby 1980). Critics challenge radical criminology on other grounds (Arrigo and Williams 2010). Most generally, they say that radical criminologists unfairly malign the United States and other democracies and overlook the oppressive nature of authoritarian nations. Because crime also exists in these societies, say

▲ Radical criminologists believe that the wealthy use the legal system to keep the poor and people of color in their place.

the critics, it is unfair to blame capitalism for crime, and it is utopian to think crime would disappear if socialism replaced capitalism. Critics also say that radical criminology exaggerates the importance of class relations in the genesis of crime and ignores the many other factors at work (Akers and Sellers 2013).

In response, radical criminologists fault this criticism for focusing on instrumental Marxist approaches, which characterized the early work of radical criminologists in the 1970s, and for neglecting structural Marxist views, which themselves criticize instrumental views. They thus claim that criticism by traditional criminologists focuses on a particular type of radical criminology that is no longer popular even in radical circles (Lynch and Michalowski 2006).

In sum, radical criminology has been harshly attacked and just as staunchly defended. Although some early radical views of crime presented an instrumental Marxist view that even other Marxists find too simplistic, more recent formulations present a richer understanding of crime and law formulation under capitalism. Marxist historical work on the development of the police, prisons, and other mechanisms of legal control has been especially useful (Harring 1993). Although not usually grounded in Marxism, the studies of inequality and crime discussed in Chapter 7 nonetheless support the basic thrust of radical criminology. Plentiful evidence of disparity in the legal treatment of street and white-collar crime also supports radical views (Reiman and Leighton 2013). However, radical theory has been less successful in presenting a "radical" explanation of street crime that differs substantially from the structural explanations discussed in Chapter 7 (Akers and Sellers 2013). Like conflict theory, radical theory's view on the origins of laws and operation of the criminal justice system seems less relevant for street crime than for consensual offenses and political criminality.

The debate between radical and traditional criminologists has cooled since the 1970s, but sharp differences of opinion remain. Although one critic concluded in 1979 that radical criminology's "capacity for contribution is exhausted" because of its "theoretical and empirical poverty" (Klockars 1979:478–479), a radical criminologist observed in 1993 that "Marxist criminology is healthier than it has ever been" (Greenberg 1993:21). Two decades later, radical and traditional criminologists continue to dispute the validity of radical criminology, even if the debate has become less heated.

Left Realism and Peacemaking Criminology

Before leaving radical criminology, we should address two recent developments. Recall that traditional criminologists criticized instrumental Marxist approaches for dismissing the seriousness of street crime. In the 1970s and 1980s, feminist criminologists also took instrumental Marxism to task for neglecting rape and family violence. These developments led some British criminologists in the 1980s to develop a radical approach to crime termed "left realist criminology," or left realism (DeKeseredy and Schwartz 2012). This approach was a response to the "left idealism" of instrumental Marxists who viewed street crime as political rebellion and the result of the alienation caused by capitalism. The left realists instead insisted that crime causes real distress, not only for the poor and people of color, but also for women victimized by rape and family violence. Given this reality, left realists say, crime prevention and control are essential. They champion measures similar to those advanced by liberal observers, including improving the socioeconomic conditions underlying crime, community policing, victim compensation, and using imprisonment only for criminals posing a real threat to society. However, some left realists have also called for increased police surveillance and more punitive treatment of criminals (Matthews and Young 1992). In turn, some radical criminologists criticize left realism for being too willing "to inflict punishment as a tool of social justice" and for deflecting blame for crime away from the capitalist system (Menzies 1992:143).

Another recent development in radical criminology is peacemaking criminology, which combines Gandhism, Marxism, Buddhism, and other humanistic strains of thought (Pepinsky 2012). Peacemaking criminology views crime as just one of the many forms of suffering that characterize human existence. To reduce such suffering, people must find inner peace and develop nonviolent ways of resolving conflict, including both crime and war. These efforts must involve a fundamental transformation of our social institutions so that they no longer cause suffering and oppression. Peacemaking criminologists also say that the criminal justice system is too authoritarian and violent to reduce crime and advocate using alternative types of punishment such as restitution and community service.

Review and Discuss

What are the elements of the common agenda of radical criminology? What kinds of evidence support the views of radical criminology and what kinds of evidence fail to support these views?

▶ Feminist Theories

Previous chapters have noted that theories of crime developed before the 1970s were essentially theories of male crime, because scholars either ignored girls and women altogether or else discussed them in stereotypical ways. This combination of neglect and ignorance impoverished criminological theory. Thus, one of the most exciting developments in criminology is the growth of feminist theory and research that focuses on women and girls (Renzetti 2013).

An Overview of Feminist Perspectives in Criminology

Just as there are many radical theories in criminology, so are there many feminist perspectives. Jody Miller and Christopher W. Mullins (2009) summarize several assumptions and beliefs that distinguish feminist theories and the work of feminist scholars from traditional theories and work in criminology. Two of these are particularly important for the discussion here. First, crime cannot be fully understood and explained without appreciating the important role that gender plays. Second, feminist theories can and should be used to reduce gender inequality in the areas of crime and criminal justice, as well as in the larger society.

Within this broad framework, feminist theories all highlight women's subordinate status, but feminist scholars differ in their explanations for this status and in their recommendations to improve it. *Liberal feminists* attribute gender differences in crime rates to gender differences in socialization and also call attention to gender discrimination in the criminal justice system. They advocate changes in socialization to reduce male criminality and reforms in the criminal justice system to reduce the gender discrimination found there. *Marxist feminists* say that women's subordination results from the development of capitalism, which forced women to depend on men for economic support. Women's subordination under capitalism is also thought to increase the amount of rape and other violence they suffer.

Radical feminists argue that patriarchy precedes capitalism and that gender relations are more important than class relations. Instead of viewing violence against women as a by-product of capitalism, radical feminists see such violence as a primary means by which men in all societies maintain and extend their dominance over women. *Socialist feminists* consider capitalism and patriarchy equally important. In their view, the interaction of class and gender relations affects the opportunities available to people and thus both their likelihood of committing crime and being victimized by crime. Finally, scholars who favor *multicultural* (or *multiracial*) *feminism* consider race and ethnicity, class, and gender simultaneously (Renzetti 2013). In their view, crime by and victimization of women of color can thus be understood only if we consider the intersection of gender, race and ethnicity, and class. Work on the gender–race–class intersection is one of the most important developments in contemporary criminology.

The Scope of Feminist Theory and Research

Whatever particular perspective it adopts, feminist work in criminology generally addresses four areas: (1) the victimization of women, (2) gender differences in crime, (3) explanations of women's criminality, and (4) women's experiences and gender discrimination in the criminal justice system (Griffin 2010; Renzetti 2013).

The Victimization of Women

The first feminist work in the 1970s focused mostly on the victimization of women by rape and sexual assault, and domestic violence, which previously had received little attention. As Chapter 4 noted, a major accomplishment of this work was simply to bring these crimes to public attention. To do so, feminist criminologists began to document the extent of these crimes and their psychological and behavioral consequences. They also stressed the involvement of male intimates and other nonstrangers in these crimes, and they emphasized that women were not to blame for being victimized by them. (Chapter 11 discusses rape and sexual assault and domestic violence further.)

An important focus of feminist work on victimization, and one that provides a bridge to its work on women's criminality, is the role played by sexual abuse in girls' delinquency (Estrada and Nilsson 2012). Although both girls and boys suffer physical abuse, girls are much more likely than boys to be sexually abused, and their history of sexual abuse "is at the heart of much of girls' and women's lawbreaking" (Chesney-Lind 2004:265).

Gender Differences in Crime

A second area inspired by feminist work is often called the *gender-ratio* issue and seeks to understand why female rates of serious offending are so much lower than men's rates (or, conversely, why men's rates are so much higher). Chapter 7 noted that structural theories do not explain why women living in criminogenic conditions are less likely than their male counterparts to turn to crime. As that chapter discussed, certain social process theories do help explain this gender difference (Agnew 2009; Augustyn and McGloin 2013).

Masculinity and Crime

A significant focus of work on the gender-ratio issue emphasizes the effects of masculinity. As Chapter 3 noted, we are already doing a good job of raising girls not to become criminals. The crime problem that concerns us is really the *male* crime problem: If our national crime rates were no higher than women's crime rates, crime would concern us much less.

▼ Feminist perspectives focus on many aspects of women's criminality, including the problems that women inmates face in jail and prison.

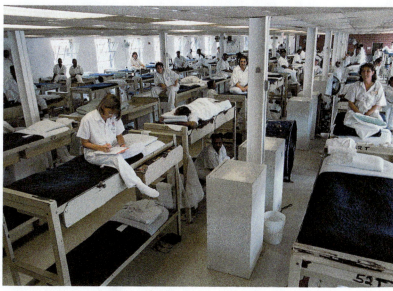

© Robin Nelson / PhotoEdit

▲ Girls are socialized in ways that develop nurturing values and other traits that make it less likely they will commit crime.

Recognizing this fact, some scholars consider "maleness" and masculinity to be criminogenic conditions. To reduce crime, they argue, male socialization and notions of masculinity must be changed and male dominance reduced (Messerschmidt and Tomsen 2012). This argument applies not only to rape, domestic violence, and other crimes that especially target women, but also to other street crimes and even to white-collar crime. Masculinity brings with it attitudes, values, and behavior that underlie a wide range of criminal activities.

Admittedly, some might regard women's low criminality merely as an unintended silver lining of their subordinate status, lack of freedom and opportunity, and socialization into feminine values. If so, their low criminality might not be something to praise. But neither is it something to overlook, because it might offer some insight into how we can lower men's criminality. In this regard, Ngaire Naffine (1995) argued that the nurturing values produced by female socialization should be welcomed as important, positive traits, not as evidence of weakness, passivity, and dependency. Reflecting this view, Kathleen Daly and Meda Chesney-Lind (1988:527) wrote that they see "some cause for hope" in the gender difference in crime:

> Of whatever age, race, or class and of whatever nation, men are more likely to be involved in crime, and in its most serious forms. . . . A large price is paid for structures of male domination and for the very qualities that drive men to be successful, to control others, and to wield uncompromising power. . . . Gender differences in crime suggest that crime may not be so normal after all. Such differences challenge us to see that in the lives of women, men have a great deal more to learn.

The mass media, public officials, and criminal justice professionals have ignored the essential link between masculinity and crime. They say little about the need to change masculinity and lessen male dominance if we want to be serious about reducing crime. When mass shootings occur, the killers are always males, but this essential fact goes ignored. The growing body of theory and research on masculinity and crime suggests an important but neglected avenue for public policy on the crime problem.

Review and Discuss

Why do men and boys commit more serious crime than women and girls? What are some of the social process and socialization factors that account for this difference?

Explanations of Women's Criminality

Because traditional criminological theories focused mostly on males and were tested primarily with data about males, feminist criminologists ask whether these theories also apply to females. This third area is often called the *generalizability* issue. In this regard, Chapters 7 and 8 noted that certain structural and social process theories help explain variation in female offending, even if specific factors identified by these theories may be more important for one gender than the other. Traditional theories of (male) crime thus once again seem to apply generally to female criminality (Agnew 2009).

Other work goes beyond the generalizability issue in seeking to understand such things as the gendered nature of criminal behavior, the impact of gender stratification in offender networks on how crime happens, and the impact of families' gender processes on delinquency. We look at examples of research in these areas.

Doing Gender   A first line of inquiry, on the gendered nature of crime and the impact of gender stratification in offender networks, reflects the idea that female and male offenders "do gender" (West and Zimmerman 1987), as do women and men in other walks of life, in their daily activities in order to accomplish femininity and masculinity. In this regard, Jody Miller (1998) studied active (i.e., not imprisoned) robbers in St. Louis. Although both genders committed robbery for the same motives—money, possessions, and thrills—the ways they committed robbery differed, Miller found. Men generally robbed men instead of women and routinely threatened their victims with a gun and often hit them.

In contrast, women robbers more often targeted women instead of men and rarely used a gun to rob them. Sometimes they would show a knife, but only rarely would they stab them. Instead they typically hit, shoved, or beat up their female victims. When women robbed men, they usually used a gun in view of the men's greater size and strength. They also would pretend to be sexually interested in the men, either as prostitutes or just as women out to have a good time, and then rob the men when their guard, and sometimes their pants, were down. Miller concluded that all these differences reflected "a gender-stratified environment in which, on the whole, males are perceived as strong and women are perceived as weak" (p. 42).

Miller and Scott H. Decker (2001) also studied female gang members and found that gendered notions of behavior and gender stratification within the gangs shaped the girls' involvement in gang activities. Specifically, the girls were less likely than boys to take part in gang fighting and other dangerous gang activities. When the girls met up with rival gang members, they usually avoided fighting, but when a fight did occur, they typically used fists or sometimes knives, but not guns. Their reluctance to fight and to use guns when fighting stemmed from their understanding of gender roles. As one girl put it, "We ain't no supercommando girls!" (p. 127). Two other girls concurred: "Girls don't be up there shooting unless they really have to" and "We ladies, we not dudes for real . . . we don't got to be rowdy, all we do is fight" (p. 127).

This body of work provides striking evidence that the behavior of active robbers and gang members is influenced by their understanding of gender roles and by gender stratification in their criminal networks. Both types of female and male offenders "do gender" in the ways described and thus accomplish femininity and masculinity, respectively.

Power-Control Theory   A second line of inquiry examines the gendered processes of family life that increase or decrease delinquency. The major perspective here is John Hagan and associates' (Hagan et al. 1987) *power-control theory*, which highlights the roles played by both gender and class. This theory distinguishes between *patriarchal* and *egalitarian* households. In patriarchal households, the father works outside the home and the mother stays at home to take care of the children. The parents subscribe to traditional gender roles and teach those to their children. Boys learn the criminogenic masculine values discussed earlier, and girls learn anticrime feminine values. Reflecting her own situation, the mother controls her daughters' behavior much more than her sons' behavior. All these factors produce relatively high gender differences in delinquency.

In egalitarian households, both father and mother work outside the home in positions of authority. As a result, both sons and daughters receive less maternal supervision and, given their mothers' workplace autonomy, are encouraged to be more independent. Mothers treat their daughters more like their sons, increasing their daughters' potential for delinquency. The gender difference in delinquency in these households will thus be smaller than in patriarchal households where daughters are much more controlled.

Tests of power-control theory yield mixed results (Blackwell 2000). Supporting the theory, they generally find that working-class patriarchal families control their children more than do middle-class egalitarian families. However, contrary to the theory, they often do not find patriarchal families exhibiting greater gender differences in delinquency. Critics also fault the theory for ignoring criminogenic factors such as harsh punishment and negative school experiences and for assuming that the mother's employment leads to greater delinquency (Akers and Sellers 2013). They say this assumption smacks of the backlash to feminism underlying earlier arguments blaming increased female criminality on the women's movement (see Chapter 3). There is also little evidence linking maternal employment to increased delinquency (De Coster 2012). Hagan and colleagues (McCarthy et al. 1999) conceded some of this criticism and revised their theory to argue that maternal employment decreases male delinquency by reducing sons' exposure to patriarchal attitudes.

▼

Women in the Criminal Justice System

The fourth general area of feminist work addresses the experiences of women offenders and professionals in the criminal justice system. Many studies document the abuse and other problems that women prison and jail inmates face and the kinds of discrimination that women lawyers, police officers, and prisons guards also face (Muraskin 2012); Chapter 16 discusses women police further.

Other studies focus on possible gender differences in the probability of arrest, sentencing, and other criminal justice outcomes. Three hypotheses on these differences have been developed. The *chivalry* hypothesis predicts that girls and women will be treated more leniently than boys and men. The *evil woman* hypothesis predicts the opposite: Because female criminality is so rare, a woman committing crime looks that much more terrible by comparison. Conflict and labeling theories would also expect more punitive treatment of women given their subordinate status to men. A third hypothesis, *equal treatment*, predicts that gender will not affect legal processing.

Empirical tests of these hypotheses are examined in Chapters 16 and 17. For now, it seems fair to say that the empirical evidence is inconsistent. Although all three hypotheses receive support in one study or another, the most recent and best-designed studies yield the following conclusions (Freiburger and Hilinski 2013):

- Women are less likely than men to be imprisoned for similar crimes.

- If imprisoned, women generally receive shorter sentences than men, although the evidence of this difference is inconsistent.

- The effect of gender on incarceration is weak compared to the effects of legally relevant variables such as prior criminal record and offense severity.

- Some but not all studies find that African-American and Latina women receive less chivalry than white women in sentencing decisions.

Review and Discuss

What are the four major areas that comprise the scope of feminist theory and research? According to recent research on girls' lives and delinquency, what factors inhibit the chances of girls becoming delinquent, and what factors raise the chances of girls becoming delinquent?

A Final Word on Feminism

Feminist work in criminology represents one of the most important advances in the field. At the same time, it is only about thirty to thirty-five years old, whereas the field of criminology has been around for more than a century if we go back to its early biological explanations. Historically, then, feminist criminology is still relatively new. Nonetheless, as Claire Renzetti (2013:1–2) concludes, "in a relatively short period of time, feminist criminologists have made a substantial impact on criminological theory and research methods; on curriculum, pedagogy, and the campus climate for faculty and students; and on the practice of law and criminal justice."

▶ Conclusion

We are now leaving the world of theory, but will visit it again during the next several chapters on types of criminal behavior. Recall that we must understand the reasons for crime in order to reduce it. The theories reviewed in the past five chapters suggest several avenues for reducing crime.

Neoclassical theories suggest the need to increase the probability of arrest, to have harsher legal punishments, and to undertake situational crime prevention. Although situational crime prevention shows promise, the vast majority of studies show that efforts to reduce crime by relying on deterrence do not work and are very expensive. Although criminals often act and think in the ways that rational choice and deterrence theories assume, they also often fail to act in these ways. Hence, efforts to reduce crime must rely on other explanations of criminality if they are to succeed.

Biological theories suggest the need to change the biological factors involved in criminality. This, of course, is difficult and fraught with ethical and political problems. The "softer" biosocial view is that social factors such as poverty and stress trigger genetic and other biological predispositions toward crime. It might be possible to change these social factors, many of which are featured in sociological theories of crime. Biological explanations highlighting pregnancy and birth complications are also compatible with a sociological perspective, because many of these complications could be minimized or prevented with improved social and health programs and policies.

Psychological explanations focusing on personality also hold some promise for reducing crime, although ethical and practical questions remain about identifying children with temperament problems. Still, if our society can do something about the social factors underlying temperament problems—poverty, inadequate child rearing, and the like—then we should be able to reduce crime.

Structural theories in sociology point to several conditions underlying many types of crime: economic deprivation and inequality, overcrowding and dilapidated housing, and other aspects of what is sometimes called social disorganization. The physical and economic problems of urban living combine to produce especially high street criminality. Although we might not be able to reduce the emphasis on the American dream that leads people from many walks of life to commit crime, we might be able to address the other structural conditions producing street crime.

Social process theories highlight the importance of proper parenting, harmonious family relationships, associations with conventional peers, and positive school experiences for reducing the potential for delinquency and later criminality. Public-policy efforts designed to address family and school problems thus hold great potential for crime reduction.

In this chapter we discussed critical perspectives on crime and criminal justice. Although these theories' focus on the social reaction to crime represents their most distinctive contribution to criminology, they also have something to say about why crime occurs. Labeling theory contends that extralegal factors affect legal processing and that legal processing creates increased deviance by inducing deviant self-images and reducing conventional opportunities. To the extent that legal processing may sometimes have unintended effects, as research indicates, we must be careful that attempts to control juvenile and adult offenders through the law do not increase the likelihood of future offending.

Conflict and radical theories attribute several types of crime and criminal laws to the self-interest of powerful groups in society. As with labeling theory, the empirical evidence for conflict and radical theories is inconsistent. While some scholars dismiss the theories, others consider them valuable. Conflict and radical theories echo certain structural theories in calling attention to the criminogenic effects of social inequality. Radical theories, of course, suggest the need to eliminate capitalism if we want to reduce crime significantly. Although that is not about to happen, this view underscores the reductions in crime that would occur if social inequality were diminished, even if capitalism itself remained.

Feminist perspectives alert us to the inadequacy of a criminology that ignores women or discusses them stereotypically. Feminist work stresses that certain features of a patriarchal society help account for both women's criminality and women's victimization, and it highlights the criminogenic effects of masculinity and the price women, men, and society pay for male dominance. In this regard, one of the most effective things we could do to reduce street crime and women's victimization would be to reduce male dominance and to change male socialization and notions of masculinity. Such change, of course, will not come soon and might even be impossible to achieve to any significant degree. However, as feminists emphasize, masculinity and male dominance can no longer be ignored as major causes of street crime and victimization.

We now turn to several types of criminal behavior, beginning with interpersonal violence. Here we will see the influence of masculinity and male domination, inequality, and several of the other factors discussed by the theories of crime and delinquency we have reviewed.

▼

Summary

1. The traditional theories reviewed in previous chapters do not discuss the social reaction to crime, which critical theories do discuss. In explaining this reaction, these theories highlight the concept of power and the inequality based on differences in power.

2. Labeling theory addresses three major issues: (1) the definition of deviance and crime, (2) possible discrimination in the application of official labeling and sanctions, and (3) the effect of labeling on continued criminality. It adopts a relativist definition of deviance, saying that deviance is not a property of a behavior, but rather the result of how others regard that behavior, and it claims that extralegal factors such as gender and appearance affect the chances of being officially labeled. It also states that labeling acts to increase deviant behavior in the future. Empirical support for labeling theory's views is inconsistent, but recent efforts to revive and revise the theory, such as Braithwaite's work on reintegrative shaming, hold some promise.

3. Conflict and radical theories argue that law is a key part of the struggle between powerful interests and the powerless. To preserve their dominance, the powerful use the law to control the powerless. This argument applies to both the formation of law and the operation of the legal system.

4. Conflict theory focuses on group and culture conflict and helps to explain the origins of some criminal laws and types of crime. It seems especially relevant for crimes committed as part of social movement unrest, but less relevant for conventional street crimes. As with labeling theory, the empirical evidence for conflict theory's assumptions of disparities in legal processing is inconsistent.

5. Radical theories are generally Marxian in orientation and take several forms. However, they all share a common set of beliefs that are critical of the economic structure of U.S. society to which they attribute much street crime. They also emphasize the more lenient treatment of white-collar crime, which they say is the best evidence of social class disparities in the criminal justice system. Critics say that radical criminologists unfairly malign the United States, overlook the oppressive nature of socialism and communism, and exaggerate the importance of economic factors in the genesis of crime. Radical criminologists say that this criticism attacks oversimplified versions of radical theory. Like conflict theory, radical theory's views seem less relevant for street crime than for consensual offenses and political criminality.

6. Several feminist perspectives on crime and society exist, but they all generally address three areas: (1) the victimization of women, (2) gender differences in crime and explanations of women's criminality, and (3) gender discrimination in the criminal justice system. Feminist work on rape and domestic violence began in the 1970s and has brought these crimes to public attention. Feminist-inspired work also finds that traditional theories of crime help explain gender differences in crime and variation among women in criminality. A line of inquiry here highlights the criminogenic functions of masculinity and the anticrime implications of femininity. Gender seems to affect legal processing in complex ways, but it does appear that women's criminal sentences are somewhat more lenient owing to their child-rearing responsibilities.

Key Terms

bourgeoisie *179*
conflict *173*
consensus *179*
criminalization *179*
critical perspectives *172*
culture conflict *179*
deviance amplification *175*

dramatization
   of evil *175*
feminist *173*
labeling *173*
left realism *184*
Marxism *183*
peacemaking criminology *184*

primary deviance *175*
proletariat *179*
relativist definition *173*
ruling class *179*
secondary deviance *175*
shaming *177*

What Would You Do?

1. Pretend you are again a high school student and have heard through the grapevine that a student who recently moved into your high school district and is in two of your classes was once arrested for armed robbery. The student's behavior seems okay, but he does have a rough edge to him and tends to keep to himself. You find yourself feeling kind of sorry for him, but you also wonder whether the rumor is true. At lunch in the cafeteria, he usually sits by himself as people whisper to each other when they walk by him. One day the cafeteria is crowded, but you notice an empty seat next to the new student. Do you sit next to him? Why or why not?

2. Suppose you have two friends, Susan and Joshua, who have been married for three years. They had their first child, William, about four months ago. Now you're out shopping with the whole family at the local mall as the holiday season approaches. Knowing that Susan has been concerned about gender roles as long as you have known her, you tell the proud parents that you'd like to buy William a baby doll. Susan says with delight, "Oh, how thoughtful!" But Joshua is less happy and even angry. "I won't have my son playing with a girl's toy!" he almost shouts. Susan looks at him in horror. What do you do?

AP Photo/The Roanoke Times, Matt Gentry

10   Violent Crime: Homicide, Assault, and Robbery

. . . .

Crime in the News

In two separate weekends in June 2013, many people lost their lives to violence in Baltimore and Chicago. In Chicago, 9 people died from gunfire and 47 more were wounded during Father's Day weekend. "Across the city," said one news report, "reminders of the bloody weekend literally stained Chicago's streets."

During the following weekend in Baltimore, 8 people were fatally shot, and at least 12 others were wounded by gunfire. A relative of one of the victims lamented, "I'm scared to come out the door. I'm in fear for my grandkids to come out here."

Source: Fenton et al. 2013; Nickeas et al. 2013.

. . . .

People fear senseless violence more than any other crime. It is the stuff of TV movies and the type of crime the news media favor, and it is the reason we lock our doors at night, buy firearms for protection, and build more prisons. Violent crime makes us afraid and drives public policy. The weekends of violence in Baltimore and Chicago remind us of the enormity of violence in the United States and of the need to understand why it occurs so that we can prevent it before it happens.

Much violence occurs between strangers, but much also occurs between acquaintances, friends, and even loved ones. Women and children are especially likely to be victims of non-stranger violence, such as rape and other forms of sexual and physical abuse. To emphasize this point and to underscore the seriousness of the crimes suffered, two chapters are devoted to violent crime. This chapter features homicide, assault, and robbery, and several special topics related to violence, while the next chapter discusses rape, sexual assault, and domestic violence. Continuing our earlier emphasis, the discussion in each chapter highlights the criminogenic effects of inequality and masculinity.

Both chapters focus on interpersonal violence, defined as the "threat, attempt, or actual use of physical force by one or more persons that results in physical or nonphysical harm to one or more other persons" (Weiner et al. 1990:xiii). *Nonphysical harm* here refers to fear, anxiety, and other emotional states. Thus, an armed robbery involving no physical injury would still be considered an act of interpersonal violence because it frightens the victim. The adjective *interpersonal* rules out such things as pollution, unsafe products, and dangerous workplaces, which kill and harm many thousands of people each year. These practices are often called *corporate violence* because corporations commit them, but they do not involve interpersonal physical force. Another type of violence involving such acts as terrorism, sabotage, and genocide is often called *political violence*. Although most political violence is interpersonal, its special nature places it under the broader category of political crime. Later chapters discuss corporate and political violence.

▶ Homicide and Assault

The subject of countless mystery novels, TV shows, and films, homicide captures the attention of the public, news media, and criminologists more than any other crime. Partly because of the presence of a corpse, homicides are also far more likely than other crimes to become known

▼

▲ Homicide captures the attention of the public, news media, and criminologists more than any other crime.

to the police. Hence we have more information about and a greater understanding of homicide than of any other crime.

Defining Homicide and Assault

The FBI's list of Part I crimes included in its Uniform Crime Reports (UCR) begins with murder and nonnegligent manslaughter. This category refers to the willful killing of one human being by another and excludes deaths caused by gross negligence, suicide, and justifiable homicide. *Justifiable homicide* refers to the killing of armed and dangerous felons by police or private citizens.

The criminal law divides murder and nonnegligent manslaughter into four subcategories: (1) first-degree murder, (2) second-degree murder, (3) voluntary manslaughter, and (4) involuntary manslaughter. The placing of a killing into one of these subcategories depends on the offender's intent and the amount and nature of the physical force that results in death. Traditionally, *first-degree murders* are committed with malice aforethought, meaning that the offender planned to kill someone and then did so. The popular term for this category, *premeditated murder*, has been extended in the past few decades to include *felony murders*, in which the commission of a felony such as rape, robbery, or arson causes someone's death. Thus, if an arsonist sets fire to a building and someone inside dies, even though that was not intended to happen, the arsonist may be charged with felony murder and hence first-degree murder. *Second-degree murders* refer to deaths in which an offender intended to do serious bodily harm short of killing the victim, but the victim died anyway. Deaths resulting from a "depraved heart" or extremely reckless conduct can also lead to second-degree murder charges. *Manslaughter* refers to killings considered less serious or less blameworthy but still not justifiable. *Voluntary manslaughter* alludes to killings committed out of intense emotion such as anger or fear. *Involuntary manslaughter* refers to killings committed because offenders have acted recklessly, as when a parent shakes a crying infant and accidentally kills the baby. Traffic fatalities constitute most involuntary manslaughter cases.

In practice, these four subcategories overlap, and it is often difficult to know which one best describes a particular killing. Prosecutors have great latitude in deciding which charge to bring against a murder defendant. Their decision depends heavily on whether the evidence will indicate beyond a reasonable doubt the intent, amount, and nature of physical force required for a particular charge. Sometimes other factors, such as the race of the offender and the victim, also influence, however unwittingly, the prosecutor's decision (see Chapter 17).

The UCR defines two types of assault. *Aggravated assault* is "an unlawful attack by one person upon another for the purpose of inflicting severe or aggravated bodily injury." Aggravated assault involves the use of a weapon or other "means likely to produce death or great bodily harm." *Simple assaults* are assaults "where no weapon is used and which do not result in serious or aggravated injury to the victim." Only aggravated assaults are included in the FBI's Part I crimes, but both types of assault are included in the National Crime Victimization Survey (NCVS).

The major difference between homicide and aggravated assault is whether the victim dies. Because of the greater reliability of homicide data, most of our discussion focuses on homicide, but still pertains to aggravated assault. We will rely heavily on the UCR (from which all data are for 2011 unless otherwise indicated; see Federal Bureau of Investigation (2012)) for our understanding of homicide, because victimization surveys are obviously irrelevant.

Patterning and Social Dynamics of Homicide

Race, Gender, and Age of Offenders and Victims

The race and gender makeup of homicide offenders and victims is very instructive. As depicted in Table 10–1, approximately half of offenders and victims are African-American, even though

TABLE 10-1 Race and Sex of Murder Offenders and Victims, 2011 (percentage)

VARIABLE	OFFENDERS[a]	VICTIMS[a]
Race		
White	45	46
African-American	52	50
Other	2	3
Sex		
Male	89	78
Female	11	22

Note: [a]Percentages are based on homicides for which information is known.
Source: Federal Bureau of Investigation 2012.

African-Americans comprise only about 13 percent of the U.S. population. Homicide is largely an intraracial crime: for single-offender, single-victim homicides, 92 percent of African-American murder victims are murdered by African-American offenders, and 85 percent of white murder victims are murdered by white offenders.

Turning to gender in Table 10–1, men are much more likely than women both to murder and be murdered. As these data suggest, homicide is a "distinctively masculine matter" (Polk 1994:5). When women murder men, the majority kill a current or former husband or boyfriend who has been physically and/or sexually abusing them. That said, women are still much more likely than men to be murdered by a current or former spouse or partner (intimates). Almost 37 percent of all female murder victims are killed by male intimates, whereas less than 3 percent of male victims are killed by female intimates (Federal Bureau of Investigation 2012).

Young people are also disproportionately likely both to murder and be murdered. Although only about 14 percent of the population is in the 15-to-24 age bracket, 45 percent of all homicide arrests in 2011 were of people in this age range. Their victims also tend to be in this range.

Geographic Patterns

As with much other crime, homicide is also patterned geographically. The homicide rate (number of homicides per 100,000 residents) is 10.1 in the nation's largest cities (population over 250,000) versus only 2.9 in towns with populations under 10,000 (see Figure 10–1 ■).

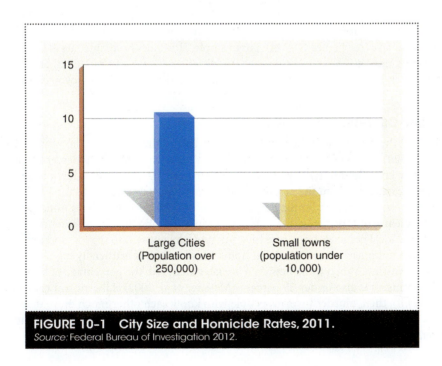

FIGURE 10-1   City Size and Homicide Rates, 2011.
Source: Federal Bureau of Investigation 2012.

▲ Despite the impression given by this upscale neighborhood in Charleston, South Carolina, the South historically has had the nation's highest regional rate of homicide. Some scholars think that this fact arises from a southern subculture of violence in which disputes that might fade away in other regions become deadly in the South.

The South Looking at different regions of the United States, homicide rates are highest in the South (5.5) and lowest in the Northeast (3.9), with the Midwest and West in between (4.5 and 4.2, respectively). The South historically has had the nation's highest regional homicide rate. The most popular explanation for this is that the South has a regional subculture of violence in which disputes that might fade away in other regions become deadly. Southerners are thought to have a code of honor that demands responses, ones that are violent if necessary, to insults and other slights (D'Antonio-Del Rio et al. 2010).

This subculture arose for several reasons. The first is the South's history of slavery, which, as a violent institution, made the South accustomed to the use of violence in everyday life. The South's history of lynching is presumed to have had a similar effect (Messner et al. 2005). A second reason is the South's warmer temperatures. As Chapter 3 indicated, higher temperatures seem associated with greater violence. Southerners may have originally been more violent because of their warmer temperatures, but over time this violence became part of their culture. A third reason is that the South's initial economy hundreds of years ago was primarily herding, not farming. Because animals that are herded make such tempting targets for potential rustlers, herders must be very willing to protect their herds with any means necessary, including violence. Thus, Southerners hundreds of years ago became oriented to violence for this reason.

Some scholars attribute the South's high homicide rate not to a subculture of violence, but instead to its level of economic deprivation, which is higher than in other regions (Parker 1989). Although some scholars also attribute the South's high homicide rate to its gun-ownership rate, the South also has the highest rate of aggravated assault; this fact suggests there is more serious violence in the South regardless of the presence of guns.

International Comparisons Homicide is also patterned geographically across nations. In this regard, the United States has the highest homicide rate of the world's industrialized nations (see Figure 10–2 ■). Here it is useful to compare the homicide rates of U.S. cities with those of other cities of similar size (see Figure 10–3 ■). For example, Houston's homicide rate is six times greater than Toronto's rate. It is worth noting that the difference between the United States and other nations is much larger for homicide than it is for other types of serious violence; we revisit this issue later.

The Victim–Offender Relationship

According to the UCR, the relationship between the victim and offender was unknown for 44 percent of 2011 homicide victims. Of the remaining victims, about 79 percent were killed by someone they knew, and only 21 percent were murdered by a stranger. Most of the "unknown relationship" cases arise from the fact that police often report homicides to the FBI before an arrest occurs. In such unsolved homicides, the victim–offender relationship is initially recorded as unknown. When arrests occur later, new information, including the victim–offender relationship, is added to the local police station's case files, but typically not sent to the FBI and not reported by the UCR. The unknown category in UCR homicide data is thus artificially high because this information is missing. When these new data are later analyzed, the percentage of homicides committed by strangers is also under 25 percent (Messner et al. 2002). Like violent crime in general (see Chapter 4), then, murder involves people who know each other much more than it involves strangers; murder victims are three times more likely to be killed by someone they know than by a stranger.

▼

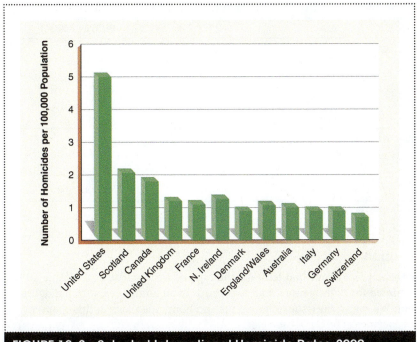

FIGURE 10-2 Selected International Homicide Rates, 2009 (homicides per 100,000 population).

Source: United Nations Office on Drugs and Crime 2013.

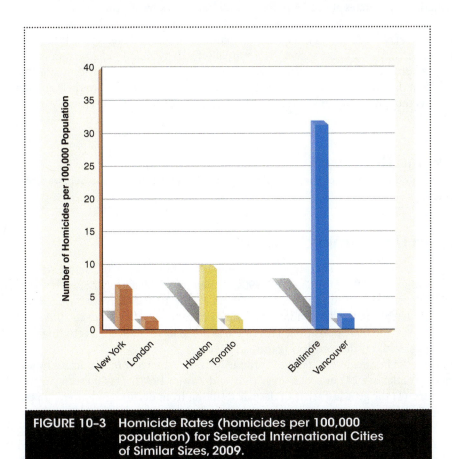

FIGURE 10-3 Homicide Rates (homicides per 100,000 population) for Selected International Cities of Similar Sizes, 2009.

Source: Davenport 2013; Federal Bureau of Investigation 2012; Statistics Canada 2012.

TABLE 10-2 Homicide and Type of Weapon Used, 2011

WEAPON	PERCENTAGE
Firearms	68
Handguns	49
Shotguns	3
Rifles	3
Other or unknown type of firearm	13
Knives and cutting instruments	13
Personal (hands, fists, feet)	6
Blunt objects	4
Others	9

Source: Federal Bureau of Investigation 2012.

Type of Weapon

Another important fact about homicides is the type of weapon used (see Table 10–2). In 2011, firearms accounted for slightly more than two-thirds of all homicides, with handguns accounting for 49 percent. We revisit the issue of handguns and homicides later in this chapter.

Circumstances Leading to Homicides

We have seen that most homicides involve the use of handguns and other firearms among people who know each other. With this profile in mind, it is not surprising that the typical U.S. murder is a relatively spontaneous event arising from an argument that gets out of hand and escalates into lethal violence, usually involving a handgun. Early research by Marvin Wolfgang (1958) found that the victim precipitates about 25 percent of all homicides by starting the argument or being the first to use physical force. Depending on how precipitation is defined, some studies find that more than half of all homicides are victim precipitated (Felson and Steadman 1983). In a typical scenario, the victim insults and angers the eventual offender. The offender responds in kind and may even use physical force. The victim reacts with another verbal or physical attack and soon is killed. Often the offender, the victim, or both, have been drinking before their encounter, and alcohol use is thought to play a key role in the violence and death that eventually occur (Kuhns et al. 2011).

Review and Discuss

How does an understanding of the type of weapons involved in homicides help us understand why homicides occur?

Trends in U.S. Homicide Rates

The U.S. homicide rate rose sharply after the mid-1960s into the 1970s, before declining after 1980 and rising after 1985 into the early 1990s. It then dropped sharply before leveling off and then declining more slowly during the past few years. Figure 10–4 ■ displays the trend since 1980.

According to the UCR, 14,612 homicides occurred in the United States in 2011, for a rate of 4.7 homicides per 100,000 population. This rate was much lower than the beginning of the 1990s and in fact was as low as the rate during the early 1960s.

The post-1985 homicide rise stemmed primarily from an increase in homicides by and against young males (under age 24) in urban areas (Fox and Zawitz 1998). This increase stemmed from several factors: (1) the growing sense of despair resulting from declining economic opportunities in urban areas during the 1980s; (2) increased drug trafficking in inner cities because of the declining economic opportunities; and (3) the increased possession and use of powerful handguns in urban areas, partly because of drug-trafficking battles (Ousey and Lee 2007; Sampson and Wilson 1995). The drop in the homicide rate after the early 1990s reflects the general decline in crime since then. As Chapter 3 discussed, scholars attribute this crime decline to various social and economic factors, including a strong economy, declining numbers of people in the high-crime 15-to-25 age

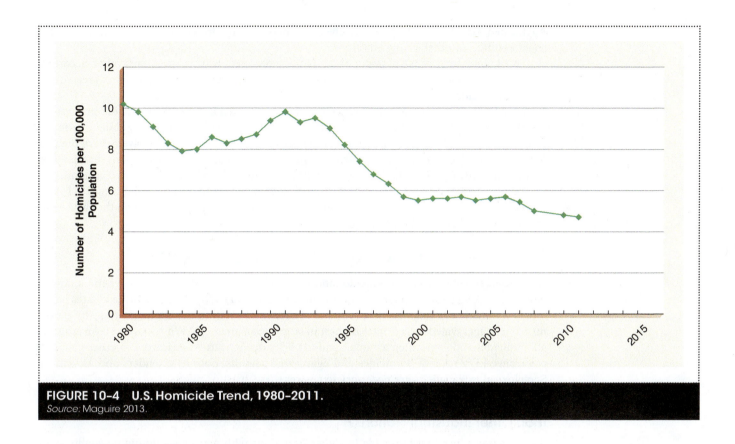

FIGURE 10-4 U.S. Homicide Trend, 1980–2011.
Source: Maguire 2013.

group, and fewer gang wars over drug trafficking. Most criminologists think the rising incarceration rate during this period played only a small role in the decline in homicides. For example, Richard Rosenfeld (2006) found that rising imprisonment accounted for only about 25 percent of the homicide drop during the early 1990s, meaning that social and economic factors had much more of an impact. He estimated that each prevented homicide cost more than $13 million in annual prison costs and suggested that this sum would prevent more homicide and other crime if it were instead spent on drug treatment, preschool programs, and other prevention efforts.

One additional factor may have helped reduce homicides since the early 1990s and possibly prevented many homicides even when the homicide rate was increasing before then. This factor is improved emergency medical technology and care. Although 5.6 percent of aggravated assaults in 1960 ended in death and thus became homicides, only 1.7 percent had the same result in 1999. As sociologist Anthony Harris observed, "People who would have ended up in morgues 20 years ago are now simply treated and released by a hospital, often in a matter of a few days" (Tynan 2002:A2). Harris and colleagues (2002) estimate that the number of homicides would be three to four times greater without the medical advances.

Aggravated Assault

Our discussion of homicide and aggravated assault has centered on homicide because its data are the most reliable and because the two crimes are generally so similar except for the fate of the victim. This discussion of aggravated assault is thus much briefer and presents the most important information for understanding this crime.

First, the trend data for homicide and social and geographical patterning of homicide apply generally to aggravated assault. The rate of aggravated assault declined after the early 1990s along with homicide, as we would expect, and the racial, ethnic, gender, age, and geographical patterning for homicide offending and victimization also apply to aggravated assault. Aggravated assaults are disproportionately committed by men, by people of color, by young people, and in the South and major urban centers.

Second, the dynamics of aggravated assault resemble those for homicide, an unsurprising conclusion given that the major difference between the two crimes is whether the victim dies.

Aggravated assaults tend to be relatively spontaneous events in which the assailant acts out of anger, revenge, or other strong emotions.

Third, many aggravated assaults, about half, involve people who know each other, according to the NCVS, whereas about half percent involve strangers. This latter percentage is greater than that for homicide.

Fourth, perhaps the major difference between aggravated assault and homicide involves the use of weapons. Although about two-thirds of homicides involve a firearm, only about one-fourth of aggravated assaults involve firearms (Truman 2011). The much greater involvement of firearms in homicides reflects the fact that firearms are much more lethal than other weapons. Because firearm victims are more likely to die, their assaults are more likely to become classified as homicides.

Finally, the FBI reported that about 751,000 aggravated assaults occurred during 2011, for a rate of 241 per 100,000 residents. This rate was more than 40 percent lower than the early 1990s and as low as the rate in the late 1970s.

Explaining Homicide and Aggravated Assault

An adequate explanation of homicide (and also aggravated assault) must answer the following questions arising from the central facts about this crime: (1) Why does the United States have a higher homicide rate than any other industrial nation? (2) Within the United States, why are homicide and aggravated assault rates highest in large urban areas? (3) Why do men commit almost all homicides and aggravated assaults? and (4) Why do African-Americans and other people of color have high rates of homicides and aggravated assaults, both as offenders and as victims? Sociological explanations are necessary to answer these questions.

Why Does the United States Have a Higher Homicide Rate than Other Industrial Nations?

Several studies find that homicide is higher in nations with greater economic inequality, measured as the difference between rich and poor, and greater levels of poverty (Ouimet 2012). The fact that the United States has more inequality than other industrial nations may be one reason for its higher homicide rate.

The difference between the United States and other industrial nations is much larger for homicide than for other types of serious violence, for which the U.S. ranking, according to the International Crime Victims Survey (ICVS), is only about average (see Chapter 4). A major reason for the especially high U.S. homicide rate is probably its very high rate of handgun ownership compared to these other nations (Hoskin 2001; Zimring and Hawkins 1997). The much greater use of handguns by assailants in the United States than elsewhere increases the chance that their intended victims will die. What would have been an aggravated assault in another nation thus becomes a homicide in the United States.

A third reason for the high U.S. homicide rate, and its historically high rate of serious violence, might be historical. Historian Richard Maxwell Brown (1990) argued that the expansive use of violence in the United States, beginning with the War for Independence against England and continuing with the Civil War, massacres of Native Americans, and lynchings of African-Americans, among other experiences, helped integrate violence into the American character: "We have resorted so often to violence that we have long since become a trigger-happy people. Violence is clearly rejected by us as a part of the American value system, but so great has been our involvement with violence over the long sweep of our history that violence has truly become part of our unacknowledged (or underground) value structure" (Brown 1990:15).

Although this argument is appealing, other nations such as Japan and Scotland had very violent pasts but have much lower homicide rates today than the United States. In effect, they have succeeded in overcoming their violent pasts, even if the United States has not. Thus, although the violent U.S. past may be one factor, other forces must also be at work. The high level of inequality seems to be one such factor. Another might be the U.S. cultural emphasis on strong individualism and distrust of authority, values that may undermine nonviolent attempts to settle interpersonal disputes.

Review and Discuss

Why is the United States more violent than many other industrial nations?

▼

Why Are U.S. Homicides and Aggravated Assaults More Common in Urban Areas than Elsewhere?

Social disorganization and anomie and strain theories (see Chapter 7) help explain why urban areas have higher rates of homicide and aggravated assault than other areas: The population density, household overcrowding, dilapidated living conditions, weak social institutions, and concentrated disadvantage (e.g., extreme poverty and high unemployment) of many urban neighborhoods contribute to their high rates of violence. As Elliott Currie (1985:160) noted, "(H)arsh inequality is . . . enormously destructive of human personality and of social order. Brutal conditions breed brutal behavior." In addition to these problems, urban communities also have high numbers of bars, taverns, and other settings where violence is apt to occur, as routine activities theory would predict (Pridemore and Grubesic 2013). Recent research suggests that the subcultures of urban neighborhoods also matter: The most disadvantaged neighborhoods respond with a code of honor featuring an exaggerated emphasis on respect and manhood that often translates into violence (Stewart and Simons 2006) (see Chapter 7).

Why Do Men Commit Almost All Homicides and Aggravated Assaults?

Chapter 9 emphasized the violent nature of masculinity. This gender difference takes on critical importance in adolescence as males become bigger and stronger and are more likely than females to commit various acts of violence (see Table 10–3). Gender differences in homicide thus stem from gender differences in nonlethal violence.

Poverty interacts with masculinity to explain why poor men have higher rates of homicide and aggravated assault than wealthier men. Masculinity means many things: academic and economic success, breadwinning for one's family; competitiveness, assertiveness, and aggressiveness; lack of emotionality; the willingness to "fight like a man" when necessary (Kimmel and Messner 2013).

International Focus THE "CHAIN SAW CONGRESSMAN" AND OTHER HIGH-LEVEL VIOLENCE IN BRAZIL

This chapter concerns interpersonal violence among common citizens, but an outbreak of protests in Brazil in June 2013 served as a reminder that government officials are also responsible for violence and death in many nations across the world.

During that month, tens of thousands of people began protesting across Brazil against a variety of problems they saw besetting their nation. Among their concerns were rising taxes, deteriorating public services, and the billions of dollars being spent for Brazil to host the 2014 World Cup soccer championship and the 2016 Summer Olympics. But another concern was a history of financial cooperation and interpersonal violence committed by members of Brazil's national Congress.

One of these legislators, nicknamed the "chain saw congressman," had been elected to Congress even though he was suspected of arranging for a political foe to be murdered with a chain saw. According to a news report, "When he ran for office, it was common knowledge that he was investigated for operating a death squad in a remote corner of the Amazon, employing tactics like throwing victims into vats of acid or dismembering them with chain saws."

He was later convicted and sentenced to prison. Another legislator had also taken office under a cloud of suspicion after ordering the murder of a member of Congress so that he could take her place. This legislator was also found guilty after entering Congress and sentenced to prison.

The protesters in Brazil had had enough of this type of criminal behavior and the other problems that led to their demonstrations. As one protester explained, "Congress thinks they are the owners of the country. And they are not." Another protester said of the demonstrations, "I think we desperately need this, that we've been needing this for a very, very long time."

The example of Brazil reminds us that interpersonal violence can occur in all walks of life. Sometimes government officials are responsible for mass violence against their political opponents and other individuals. Chapter 14 discusses such *political violence* further. Although most violence is not committed for political reasons, the political nature of some violence underscores the fact that violence is committed for many reasons and to accomplish many goals.

Source: Associated Press 2013; Romero 2013.

TABLE 10-3 Proportion of High School Seniors (Class of 2011) Reporting Involvement in Various Violent Acts in Past 12 Months (percentage saying at least once)

ACTIVITY	MALES	FEMALES
Fought with group of friends against another group	18	13
Got into serious fight in school or at work	14	7
Hurt someone badly enough to need bandages or a doctor	19	5
Used a weapon to get something from a person	4	1
Hit instructor or supervisor	4	1

Source: Johnston et al. 2013.

In many societies, a man's socioeconomic standing affects the way he expresses these ways of "being a man." As James W. Messerschmidt (1993:87–88) put it, "'Boys will be boys' differently, depending upon their position in social structures and, therefore, upon their access to power and resources."

Men at the middle and top of the socioeconomic ladder engage in a masculine behavior pattern involving economic competition and various forms of nonphysical dominating behavior (Messerschmidt and Tomsen 2012). In contrast, men at the bottom of the ladder are more apt to engage in *opposition masculinity* involving physical competition, violence, and drinking (Hobbs 1994). They are much more likely to regard insults and slights as major offenses meriting violent responses and thus to commit *confrontational homicides*. This violence permits these males to demonstrate their masculinity and to gain the respect their low economic standing denies them.

Review and Discuss

Why do men commit almost all serious violent crime? To what extent do you think the gender difference in crime is biologically caused?

Why Do African-Americans and Other People of Color Have High Rates of Homicide and Aggravated Assault?

As Darnell F. Hawkins (2003) notes, this question has long been emotional and contentious, in part because some researchers in the past responded in a racist manner by claiming that African-Americans have an inborn disposition to be violent, are biologically inferior, or both. This problem has made criminologists hesitant "to engage in discussions of the extent and causes of racial differences in crime and violence" (Hawkins 2003:xxi).

As discussed in previous chapters, a nonracist explanation of violent crime by African-Americans emphasizes certain criminogenic structural and ecological factors and their social–psychological effects: (1) the anger and frustration arising from racial discrimination and from economic deprivation; (2) the stress, social disorganization, and other criminogenic conditions that are especially severe in urban neighborhoods with the multiple problems social scientists call *concentrated disadvantage*; (3) negative family and school experiences; and (4) the influence of deviant peers and the "code of the street" that is especially common in these neighborhoods. These reasons all "come together" for African-Americans, and particularly young African-American males, more than for any other group (Kaufman 2005; McNulty and Bellair 2003; Stewart and Simons 2006).

▼ Males at the bottom of the socioeconomic ladder are more likely than wealthier males to engage in opposition masculinity involving physical competition, violence, and drinking.

© shockpix.com / Alamy

As Chapter 3 noted, these explanations for the high levels of African-American violence also appear to apply to the high levels found among Latinos and Native Americans (Painter-Davis 2012; Phillips 2002). Compared to non-Latino whites, both these groups are much more likely to live amid extreme poverty and the other structural and ecological conditions conducive to violent crime. The conditions on many Native American reservations are thought to be especially desperate, accounting for their high rates of violent crime and victimization.

Violence by Women

Most research on homicide and other violence explicitly or implicitly concerns men because men commit most violent crime. The studies we have of women's violence suggest that it has the same roots—extreme poverty, negative family and school experiences, and disadvantaged neighborhoods—as men's violence (Baskin and Sommers 1998; Kruttschnitt and Carbone-Lopez 2006; Steffensmeier and Haynie 2000). Much of the research on women's violence focuses on African-American women, whose violent crime rate is much higher than that for white women and sometimes exceeds that for white men, even though it remains much lower than that for African-American men.

In his study of the "code of the street," Elijah Anderson (2000) noted that young African-American women seek respect as much as their male counterparts and in the same manner: through displays of bravado, verbal insults, and a willingness to use violence to settle disputes. Despite these similarities, young African-American women's violence lags behind that of their male counterparts because of gender socialization. When young urban women feel the need to retaliate violently, Anderson said, they typically enlist the aid of a brother, uncle, or cousin. When they do fight themselves, they rarely use guns because, as women, they do not feel a "macho" need to do so. Jody Miller and Scott H. Decker's (2001) research on female gang members found a similar phenomenon: Girls fought less often than boys because of their gender socialization, and they also used guns less often.

Recall that when women commit homicide their victims are usually men who have been abusing them. This pattern holds true for women of color as well as for white women. Coramae Richey Mann (1990:198) wrote that African-American female homicide offenders are part of a *subculture of hopelessness*: "By the time these women reach age 30 or more, they feel the full impact of the hopelessness of their lives. When the last straw is broken, they finally strike back at the closest living representative of their plight."

An explanation of women's homicide by Robbin S. Ogle and colleagues (1995) supports Mann's view. They argued that women, like men, experience significant stress in their lives. Both sexes react to stress with anger, but men direct theirs at external targets through violence, whereas women tend to internalize theirs as guilt, hurt, and self-doubt. This leads to "overcontrolled personalities" that ordinarily commit no violence, but occasionally become overwhelmed and "erupt in extreme violence" such as homicide. The targets of this violence are often the men who abuse women and sometimes even a woman's own children.

PhotoEdit, Inc.

▲ Several structural, ecological, and cultural factors help account for African-American violent crime rates. These factors also help explain violent crime by Latinos and Native Americans.

Review and Discuss

Why do you think women commit violence? How are the reasons for their violence similar to the reasons for men's violence, and how do these reasons differ from those for men's violence?

▶ Robbery

When people say they fear crime, they often have robbery (or mugging) in mind. What do we know about this crime?

Defining Robbery

Robbery is "the taking or attempting to take anything of value from the care, custody, or control of a person or persons by force or threat of force or violence and/or by putting the victim in fear" (Federal Bureau of Investigation 2012). As this definition implies, robbery involves both theft and interpersonal violence. The latter component distinguishes robbery from other property crimes and prompts both the UCR and NCVS to classify it as a violent crime. UCR robbery data include both personal and commercial (e.g., in convenience store) robberies, whereas the NCVS covers only personal robberies. This difference leads the two data sources to give us slightly different pictures of robbery, but together they give us a better understanding of robbery than either source provides alone.

Extent and Patterning of Robbery

The UCR reports a lower number of robberies than the NCVS (Federal Bureau of Investigation 2012; Truman and Planty 2012). The UCR reported 354,396 robberies of all types in 2011, a drop of almost 50 percent from the early 1990s. The NCVS estimates that 556,760 personal robberies occurred in 2011. Of all the UCR robberies, about 29 percent were cleared by arrest.

Like homicide and assault, robbery is primarily a young person's crime: Persons under the age of 25 account for almost two-thirds of all robbery arrests. Robbery is also much more common in large urban areas than elsewhere (see Figure 10–5 ■). Again like homicide and assault, robbery is disproportionately committed by men and by African-Americans. Men comprised 88 percent of all robbery arrests in 2011, and African-Americans comprised almost 56 percent. As Table 10–4 indicates, men, African-Americans, and Latinos are also disproportionately likely to be victims of robberies. Reflecting the victimization pattern for violent crime noted in Chapter 4, robbery victimization is also highest among young people and among people from low-income backgrounds.

In an important difference between robbery and other violent crime, robbery is somewhat more likely to be committed by a stranger than by someone the victim knows. According to the NCVS, about 55 percent of personal robberies in 2011 for which the victim/offender relationship was known involved a stranger, and almost 46 percent involved someone the victim knew. This latter figure masks a gender difference: about 55 percent of female victims were robbed by someone they knew, compared to only 39 percent of male victims.

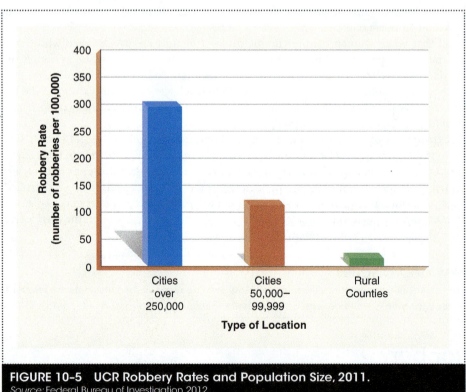

FIGURE 10-5 UCR Robbery Rates and Population Size, 2011.
Source: Federal Bureau of Investigation 2012.

TABLE 10-4 Robbery Victimization Rates by Race//Ethnicity, Gender, and Age, 2010 (per 1,000 persons 12 and older)

VARIABLE[a]	RATE
Race and Ethnicity	
African-American	3.6
Latino	2.7
White	1.4
Two or more races	5.2
Gender	
Male	2.4
Female	1.4
Age	
18–20	5.9
21–24	3.7
25–34	2.5
35–49	1.5
50–64	1.3

Note: [a]Table includes only those categories with sufficient numbers of sample cases.
Source: Truman 2011.

Types of Robbers

Just as there are several types of murderers, there are also several types of robbers. John Conklin (1972) developed the standard classification. A first type is *professional robbers*. These people carefully plan their robberies, carry guns, and often work in groups. Their targets include "big scores" such as stores, banks, or other commercial targets. A second type is *opportunist robbers*, who commit robberies when the opportunity presents itself. They are usually young males who choose vulnerable targets, such as people walking alone at night, and they get relatively little money from each robbery. The third type is *addict robbers*, who rob to acquire money to buy illegal drugs. They generally plan their robberies less carefully than professional robbers, but more carefully than opportunistic robbers. *Alcoholic robbers* are the final type; they commit robberies when they are drunk and trying to get money to buy more alcohol. Their robberies are rarely planned and usually involve no firearms.

Explaining Robbery

Robbery is a violent crime committed for economic gain. As such, robbery is a prototypical example of *innovation* in Merton's anomie theory: In a society placing so much value on economic success, the poor often feel pressured to achieve this success through illegitimate means. Robbery is one of the crimes they commit.

This chapter's explanations for homicide and aggravated assault also apply to robbery. Like these other crimes, robbery stems from the criminogenic features of many urban neighborhoods, including extreme poverty, dilapidated living conditions, and other evidence of social disorganization (Cancino et al. 2009). Routine activities theory also helps explain robbery because robbery victimization is higher among people who put themselves at risk, for example, by going out more often at night instead of staying home (Groff 2007). Further, certain locations promote robbery because they provide attractive targets without guardianship (Braga

▼ Because robbery is committed for economic gain, it is an example of innovation in Robert Merton's anomie theory.

© MIXA / Alamy

et al. 2011). For example, the advent of automated teller machines (ATMs) helped increase robbery rates because they provided a location where a lone target could be expected to have a fair amount of money. The growth of convenience stores has increased commercial robberies for similar reasons. Routine activities theory also stresses the importance of attractive targets, and many robberies have occurred during the last decade because the growth of cell phones and then smart phones provided attractive targets for robbers.

So far we have implied that the motivation for robbery is primarily economic. Other scholars take a different view. Jack Katz (1991) argued that the amount of money robbers obtain is too small for economic gain to be their primary motivation. If it were, he said, they would engage in more lucrative illegal activities such as drug trafficking or illegal gambling. Instead, robbers' primary goal is to sustain a "badass" identity involving "the portrayal of a personal character that is committed to violence beyond calculations of legal, material, or even physical costs to oneself" (p. 285). This motivation makes persistent robbers willing to risk arrest and renders them relatively immune to any deterrent effects that the threat of legal punishment might have. A related motivation is robbers' desire to look "cool" and "hip" through the spending of huge sums of money. To keep up this appearance, they often need money quickly and thus commit robberies with little concern for, or even attention to, the possible consequences (Jacobs and Wright 1999).

These motivations reflect the emphasis on respect so characteristic of the code of the streets in urban areas, discussed earlier. Katz (1991:298) observed that urban adolescents learn the need to use violence and exert a "fierceness of will" and "humiliating dominance" when faced with insults and assaults by peers. More than most crimes, robbery embodies these characteristics. Although most urban adolescents do not become robbers, those who do reflect their socialization into the code of the streets. As Elijah Anderson (2000) observed, masculinity is a fundamental part of this code. Although Katz (1991) did not stress the point, masculinity is thus fundamental to his own argument on the nature of robbery and helps explain why robbers are almost always men.

Review and Discuss

Should robbery be best understood as a crime that is done for economic gain or as one done for thrills and other reasons?

► Special Topics in Violent Crime

This section examines some additional kinds of violence—mass murder and serial killing, workplace violence, hate crime, and child and elder abuse—as well as two controversial issues—mass media and violence, and guns and gun control. The entire next chapter is devoted to the very important topic of violence against women, in view of its great importance and the amount of research on it.

Mass Murder and Serial Killing

The December 2012 fatal shootings of 26 schoolchildren and staff at the Sandy Hook Elementary School in Newtown, CT, reminded us of the horror of mass murder. Mass murder and serial killing are both examples of *multiple murder*, or *multicide*, in which several victims die either all at once or in a much longer time span. Although both types of multicide are thankfully uncommon, they shock us and attract major headlines when they occur.

Much has been written about mass murder and serial killing, and we have room here only for a brief summary of the research on these subjects (DeFronzo et al. 2007; Fox et al. 2012). *Mass murder* involves the taking of several lives at once or within a very short time frame. There is no clear definition of how many lives must be taken or how short the time frame must be. Two lives would ordinarily not be enough for this term to be used; eight to ten lives would ordinarily suffice. Many scholars think that at least four people must be killed for an event to be labeled a mass murder (Alvarez and Bachman 2003). The mass murder of 32 students and faculty at Virginia Polytechnic and State University (Virginia Tech) in April 2007 certainly exceeded this standard.

The very short time frame for mass murder distinguishes it from *serial killing*, which involves the methodical taking of a human life one at a time over a period of days, weeks, months, and even years. Once again, there is no clear definition of how many lives must be taken, but many scholars think at least three separate killings must happen for serial murder to have occurred (Alvarez and Bachman 2003).

Mass Murder

Mass murder usually takes place at one of a low number of locations: a home, a workplace, a school, or, more rarely, a shopping mall or other public area. When mass murder occurs in a home, the offender is almost always a close male relative of the victims. Typically, such men feel at the end of their ropes and kill out of despair and hopelessness, often committing suicide afterward. Mass murder in the workplace violence typically occurs because an employee or ex-employee is outraged over a firing or some perceived slight or other problem. Mass murder in schools, perhaps most infamously illustrated by the April 1999 killings at Columbine High School in Littleton, Colorado, also occurs because of perceived injustice. The students who commit mass murder typically feel harassed by other students for any number of things that often lead some students to be teased or ridiculed. The two students who committed the Columbine massacre were both seen as "nerds" and outcasts and hung out with other such students in a group called the Trench Coat Mafia. Their massacre was an act of revenge on the people and school that they felt had caused them so much suffering (Fox et al. 2012).

Mass murderers are almost always males, as was certainly true of the Sandy Hook, Virginia Tech, and Columbine killers. Although girls and women suffer the same indignities and problems as boys or men do and sometimes even worse, they do not respond with mass murder and, as we have seen in previous chapters, they also do not respond nearly as often as males with other acts of violence. As always, gender differences in socialization must be kept in mind as we try to understand the problem of violence in America, whether we talk about mass murder or about more everyday acts of violence.

Most mass murderers, regardless of where they commit their horrible crimes, feel aggrieved by family members, workplace associates, or school peers and teachers and perhaps by life in general. However, this sense of grievance does not sufficiently explain mass murder, as many people certainly feel aggrieved and yet do not commit mass murder. Thus, a sense of grievance may be a necessary condition for mass murder but does not by itself explain why mass murder occurs.

Some dynamics of mass murder are also apparent from studies of various examples of this crime (Fox et al. 2012). First, firearms are definitely the weapon of choice, and it is not an exaggeration to say that mass murder would not be possible without firearms. Second, most mass murderers plan their crime for days or weeks in advance. They compile their arsenal, plan the sequencing and locations of their attack, and determine other courses of action to help ensure their horrific plan will succeed. Mass murderers often also choose particular individuals or categories of individuals (e.g., women) that they perceive as responsible for their problems. Innocent bystanders may also be shot and killed, but most mass murderers have selected specific individuals or types of individuals as targets long before they start their rampage. In this regard, mass murderers seem to select women disproportionately for execution. Some experts think they do so because they are both *misogynistic* (hating women) and *homophobic* (hating gays), and that mass murder is, for them, a way of proving their manhood, especially if they have also experienced shame or humiliation in their personal lives (Herbert 2007).

Serial Killing

In contrast to mass murderers, serial killers tend to murder strangers, and these strangers are typically prostitutes, the homeless, and runaway youths and other individuals whom serial killers perceive as "easy targets." As Alex Alvarez and Ronet Bachman (2003:131) note, "Prostitutes, for example, are used to getting into vehicles with total strangers and driving to secluded areas. This behavior, of course, makes them very vulnerable to victimizations of many kinds, including serial killing." Regardless of their exact backgrounds, women are especially targeted by serial killers: women comprised about 70 percent of all victims of serial murder from 1985 to 2010, even though women comprised only 22 percent of all homicide victims during that period (Hargrove 2010).

Scholars distinguish several types of serial killers based on their motivation (Holmes and Holmes 2001). *Hedonistic lust killers* commit their murders for sexual pleasure, and may even have sex with a corpse. *Thrill killers* also kill for sexual pleasure, but obtain their

▼ Serial killer Danny Rolling, nicknamed the Gainesville Ripper, was convicted and executed in 2006 after murdering eight people, including five university students in Gainesville, FL in August 1990.

AP Photo/File

pleasure by torturing or humiliating their victims before they die. *Comfort killers* commit their crimes for financial gain, while *power-control killers* commit their murders for the (nonsexual) satisfaction they obtain from dominating and then killing their victims. *Mission killers* are, as the name implies, "on a mission" to end the lives of types of people (e.g., prostitutes) whom they regard as immoral or inferior. Finally, *visionary killers* are psychotic and hear voices that tell them to kill.

This last type of serial killer notwithstanding, many scholars think it a mistake to regard most serial killers as mentally ill, however horrible their crimes may be. As Alvarez and Bachman (2003:133) observe, "By definition, we want to believe that anyone who can kill, mutilate, and perhaps eat other human beings must be crazy. This is a natural reaction . . . [but] this conception of serial killers as crazy is not accurate. Most serial killers are not found to suffer from a psychosis and can typically distinguish right from wrong." Serial killers do tend to be *sociopaths,* in that they exhibit *antisocial personality disorder* traits such as lack of conscience and remorse and a desire for manipulation, but, as James Alan Fox and Jack Levin (2005:112) note, this is a "disorder of character rather than that of the mind."

So why do they do it? Ultimately, there is no easy answer to this question. Many scholars attribute serial killing, and also mass murder, to childhood problems, including head injuries or brain trauma, parental neglect, and physical and/or sexual abuse (Begley 2007). Although some combination of these factors has been found in the backgrounds of many serial killers, these are common problems, and most everyone with them certainly does *not* become a serial killer. Thus, childhood problems by themselves do not explain why a few individuals commit serial murder years later. In a more sociological explanation, a recent study found that serial killers disproportionately grew up in the South, supporting the idea that they were influenced by the subculture of violence found in that region that was discussed earlier (DeFronzo et al. 2007). Despite many studies of serial killers, however, a good explanation for serial killing remains elusive.

Review and Discuss

Do you think mass murder and serial killing reflect psychological abnormality among the individuals who commit these crimes? Why or why not?

Workplace Violence

"Going postal" entered the U.S. lexicon some time ago as disgruntled workers, some of them U.S. Post Office employees, went into their workplaces with handguns or other firearms and took a deadly toll on their bosses, coworkers, and former bosses and coworkers. Other workplace violence occurs when strangers enter to commit a robbery or when estranged lovers come to confront their partners, sometimes with deadly force. Some workplace violence is random; in one example, a man who was angry over a broken door in his apartment building shot and killed the maintenance man and then shot and killed two more people at a nearby McDonald's and Burger King (Spangler 2000). Still other workplace violence is committed against people, such as police, who are performing their jobs but not technically in a workplace.

The Extent and Nature of Workplace Violence

Whatever its source, workplace violence is very common and the subject of growing research (Piquero et al. 2013). NCVS data paint a disturbing picture (Harrell 2011). In 2009 (the latest year for which data were available at this writing), an estimated 572,000 acts of nonfatal violence occurred in the workplace (i.e., against people 16 or older at work or on duty). This figure comprised about one-fourth of all violent victimizations of employed people in this age group. Simple assaults comprised almost four-fifths of this violence, while rapes and sexual assaults, robberies, and aggravated assaults comprised slightly more than one-fifth of the violence. Another 521 people were murdered in the workplace in 2009. Robbers committed more than one-third (38 percent) of workplace homicides from 2005 through 2009; workplace associates (co-workers, customers, etc.) committed one-fifth of workplace homicides; and relatives and acquaintances committed 8 percent of these homicides.

As high as the 2009 rate of workplace violence was, it was actually only about two-thirds as high as the 2002 rate and only one-fourth as high as the 1993 rate. This decline in workplace violence reflects the decline in U.S. violence of all types since the early 1990s.

Some additional facts about workplace violence are worth noting (Harrell 2011):

- Law enforcement officers, security guards, and bartenders experience the highest rates of nonfatal workplace violence.
- Firearms are used in 5 percent of nonfatal workplace violence but account for 80 percent of workplace homicides.
- The rates of workplace violence are higher for males than for females, and higher for Native Americans and whites than for African-Americans, Asians and Pacific Islanders, and Latinos.
- Victims perceive that offenders were using drugs and/or alcohol in one-fourth of workplace violence.
- Males account for four-fifths of victims of workplace homicides.

We earlier commented on the number of homicides and aggravated assaults that are committed by people the victim knows. This important fact for these types of violence also holds true for workplace violence: nonstrangers commit about 59 percent of workplace violence against females and 47 percent of workplace violence against males. Notice the gender difference here: women are more likely than men to experience workplace violence from someone they know, just as they are more likely to be murdered or robbed by someone they know. Table 10–5 provides further information about gender and the victim/offender relationship in workplace violence. As the table indicates, female employees are more likely than male employees to experience violence by people they know from both outside the workplace and inside the workplace.

Hate Crime

Hate crimes are committed against individuals or groups or their property (destruction and theft) because of their race, ethnicity, religion, national origin, disability, or sexual orientation. The key factor distinguishing hate crime from "normal" violent crime is the motive of the offender(s). If the offender's motivation includes prejudice or hostility based on the victim's race, religion, and the like, it is a hate crime.

Defined this way, hate crimes have always been with us. In the United States, they go back at least to the 1600s, when Puritans in Massachusetts Bay Colony hanged Quakers (Brinton 1952). Although the term *hate crime* had not yet been coined in the days of slavery, the lynchings of African-Americans, the killings of Native Americans, and the racial hostility underlying these acts classifies them as hate crimes carried out on a massive scale.

Although whites are sometimes the victims of racially motivated hate crime, most hate crime is committed by dominant or established groups against people perceived as different, many of them without power or at least statistically in the minority. In U.S. history, whites have committed hate crime against people of color, long-time citizens against immigrants, Protestants against Catholics, non-Jews against Jews, and heterosexuals against homosexuals. Sometimes hate crime

TABLE 10-5 Victim/Offender Relationship for Victims of Workplace Violence, by Sex, 2005–2009

	PERCENT OF WORKPLACE VIOLENCE	
VICTIM/OFFENDER RELATIONSHIP	FEMALE	MALE
Intimate Partner or Other Relative[a]	2.4	1.4
Acquaintances	19	12
Work Relationships (customer, client, co-worker, etc.)	32	26
Unknown relationship	6	8
Stranger	41	53

Note: [a]Based on a small number of sample cases.

Source: Harrell 2011.

▼

takes the form of mob violence. Between 1830 and 1860, the major U.S. cities were racked by dozens of riots, many of them begun by native white Protestants who attacked African-Americans, immigrants, Mormons, Catholics, and other non-WASP groups (Feldberg 1998).

Most hate crimes, however, are committed by organized groups or by individuals, not by mobs. Perhaps, the most notorious U.S. example is the Ku Klux Klan (KKK), which committed many of the lynchings of African-Americans and also terrorized Catholics, Jews, and other groups. Although the KKK is commonly associated with the South, it has had a strong presence elsewhere in the United States. During the 1920s, it numbered some 550,000 members in New England and held rallies across the region. Franco-Americans were a major target because their immigrant status and Catholic religion angered the Protestants who made up the KKK. During the rallies, Franco-Americans would darken their houses and hide under beds and in closets (Doty 1994). A newer hate group is neo-Nazis, including Skinheads (Travis and Hardy 2012). Skinhead gangs, typically composed of working-class young men and also some women, first formed in England in the 1970s, but spread to the United States, Germany, and other European nations by the 1980s. A specific type of hate crime, violence against lesbians and gay men, has attracted particular attention in recent years, especially after the brutal murder of Matthew Shepard in Wyoming in October 1998. Two men lured Shepard to a remote area, beat him with a gun, and tied him to a ranch fence in freezing temperatures. He was found after 18 hours and died a few days later (Swigonski et al. 2001).

Because members of hate groups are, not surprisingly, difficult to study, we know relatively little about their social backgrounds or motivation beyond their racism or other prejudice. Sociologist Kathleen Blee (2002) interviewed thirty-four women in racist hate groups. Most of the women came from middle-class backgrounds and were not abused as children, and many worked in professional jobs. Although men tended to join the groups because of their racism and anti-Semitism, women joined for other reasons and then became more racist and anti-Semitic because of their participation.

Hate crime is vastly underreported, and the true number of hate crimes remains unknown. The FBI's count in the UCR is probably a serious underestimate, but the 2011 UCR listed 6,222 incidents of hate crime, involving 7,254 separate offenses, 5,731 offenders, and 7,713 victims (persons, businesses, other targets). The FBI's total included 4 homicides, 7 rapes, 895 aggravated assaults, and 1,595 simple assaults. Racial prejudice motivated 47 percent of all single-bias incidents; sexual-orientation bias motivated 21 percent; religious bias motivated 20 percent; and ethnicity or national origin bias motivated another 12 percent (see Figure 10–6 ■). About 64 percent of the offenses were crimes against persons, while 36 percent were crimes

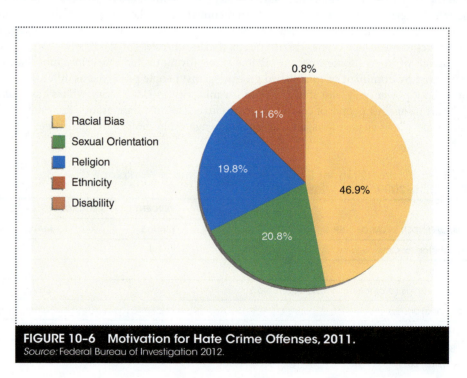

FIGURE 10-6 Motivation for Hate Crime Offenses, 2011.
Source: Federal Bureau of Investigation 2012.

against property (Federal Bureau of Investigation 2012). The NCVS estimates a much higher figure of hate crimes, almost 150,000 in 2009. For the 2003–2009 period, NCVS victims of hate crime reported that 58 percent of their victimizations were motivated by racial prejudice, 30 percent by ethnic prejudice, 15 percent by sexual-orientation prejudice, 12 percent by religious bias, and 10 percent by disability bias (Langton and Planty 2011). Victims notified police less than half (45 percent) the time.

Child Abuse and Elder Abuse

Two of the most tragic forms of violence in the United States and elsewhere are committed against children and the elderly. This violence takes two forms: *physical abuse* and *sexual abuse*. Children and elders can also suffer from neglect, psychological abuse, and other problems, and these are often included in discussions of child abuse and elder abuse. We include these other problems here while acknowledging that they do not involve actual violence. Our discussion begins with child abuse before turning to elder abuse.

Child Abuse

We will never know how many children are abused each year. The major reason is that children are usually unlikely to report their abuse. The youngest ones, infants, obviously cannot even talk, and toddlers are little better. But even older children, say age 7, do not report their abuse for several reasons: They do not typically define their abuse as abuse, they may feel their parents have the right to hit them, they may feel they deserved to be hit and thus blame themselves, they may fear parental retaliation, or they may not know how or where to report the abuse. As a result, most child abuse remains hidden, and children can only hope that a teacher, nurse, physician, or other adult will notice their bruises and injuries.

We do have some idea of how many abused children there are, but this estimate represents only the tip of the iceberg for the reasons just stated. Each year the U.S. Department of Health and Human Services (HHS) gathers data from child protective service agencies across the nation. Using this information, HHS estimated that almost 700,000 different children were victims of child abuse in 2011 (Administration on Children Youth and Families 2012). An estimated 1,570 children died from abuse or neglect. The total abuse figure included the following specific types of abuse:

- 118,825 cases of physical abuse
- 61,472 cases of sexual abuse
- 60,832 cases of psychological abuse
- 531,413 cases of general neglect
- 15,074 cases of medical neglect

Explaining Child Abuse   Although many theories of child abuse highlight psychological disorders in the adults who abuse their children, sociological approaches instead emphasize the structural and cultural factors that help explain child abuse. Following the theme of this book, we focus here on these factors.

One factor is inequality: Because of their size, intellectual immaturity, and lack of economic resources, children are a powerless group, perhaps the most powerless of all. Sociologically, it is thus no accident, and perhaps even inevitable, that children will suffer violence and other abuse at the hands of adults (Gil 1979). This and earlier chapters have also emphasized that people are more likely to commit violence when they are very poor, and child physical abuse appears to be more common in poorer families than in wealthier families (English 1998). If so, this income patterning underlines yet another alarming consequence of poverty, even if most poor parents do not abuse their children. A key mechanism here is *stress* (Bakalar 2012). Many studies document that poverty can be a source of enormous stress as parents cope with paying bills, crowded housing conditions, and other problems. Given such stress, tempers often flare, with children a convenient target. Even in the best of circumstances, children often annoy parents; in worse circumstances, parents are annoyed more often and more intensely and can go over the edge.

Another important factor in child physical abuse is whether parents were abused themselves as children: Such parents are more likely to abuse their own children in a tragic vicious cycle (Widom et al. 2013). A particular explanation for physical abuse derives from the frequent use in the United States of spanking to discipline children. Reflecting the old saying, "spare the rod and spoil the child," many parents spank their children regularly, with national survey evidence indicating that two-thirds of 3-year-olds are spanked at least once monthly (Smith 2010). Even if parents intend spanking for good purposes, it is still a violent act. Unfortunately, there is a very thin line between a "good, hard spanking" and physical abuse. Once parents are accustomed to using any force against a child, it is inevitable that undue force, or abuse, will occur. Coupled with the vulnerability of children, cultural approval of violence against them in the form of spanking makes child physical abuse inevitable.

Turning to child sexual abuse, psychological explanations center on such factors as men's craving for love and affection, extreme jealousy and authoritarianism, and various personality disorders (Rowan 2006). A sociological explanation of child sexual abuse emphasizes power and gender inequality. Because the most typical episode of sexual abuse involves an adult man and a young girl, the power and gender inequality dimensions are apparent. These dimensions become especially important in incest, where fathers and stepfathers assume that their daughters are their sexual property (Russell 1984). Beyond this structural explanation, we cannot forget that girls and women in our society are still regarded as sex objects existing for men's pleasure. This belief contributes to our high levels of child sexual abuse and adult rape.

Elder Abuse

We have seen that child abuse occurs in part because children's young age and small size make them "easy targets" for being abused. At the other end of the age spectrum, a similar dynamic helps explain elder abuse: many elders experience physical and mental infirmities, social isolation, and other problems that also make them easy targets for being abused (Johannesen and Logiudice 2013).

Elder abuse is less studied than child abuse, rendering estimates of elder abuse less reliable than we would like (Jackson and Hafemeister 2013). Unlike child abuse, the federal and state governments do not systematically gather data about elder abuse. However, enough data do exist for the National Center on Elder Abuse (2013) to provide various kinds of information about this problem:

1. About 10 percent of elders experience at least one form of elder abuse annually, with about 90 percent of these cases committed by family members—adult children, spouses and partners, and other relatives—of the victims.

2. Only about 7 percent of all elder abuse cases become known by the police or other relevant authorities.

3. Several risk factors increase the likelihood that a family member will abuse an elder: (a) a history of drug or alcohol abuse, (b) a history of a mental or emotional disorder, and (c) a feeling of being overwhelmingly stressed by caregiving responsibilities for an elder.

4. Dementia is a special problem among the elderly and also a major risk factor for elder abuse. More than 5 million people over age 65 have some type of dementia, and almost half of those over age 85 have dementia; about half of all elders with dementia are abused in some way.

5. Although, as we have seen, family members commit most elder abuse, such abuse also occurs in nursing homes and other facilities, with 44 percent of nursing home residents in one study saying they had been abused.

The effects of elder abuse are devastating (National Center on Elder Abuse 2013). Elders who are abused are much more likely to die than elders who are not abused. Abused elders also experience higher levels of psychological distress and other health problems, including chronic pain and high blood pressure. The medical costs stemming from physical injuries accompanying some elder abuse amount to more than $5 billion annually.

Mass Media and Violence

Violence portrayed in the mass media, particularly on TV shows and in Hollywood movies and many video games, is often blamed for the U.S. violent-crime problem, especially violence committed by juveniles. The key question is whether mass-media violence is a symptom of a violent culture or a cause of our violence. Both possibilities might be true: The United States might have mass-media violence because of its historical emphasis on violence, but mass-media violence in turn might promote additional violence in real life.

Much research establishes a strong statistical connection between mass-media violence and violent attitudes, behavior, or both, but causality is hard to prove (Kaplan 2012; Leshner et al. 2013). Several lines of research exist. The most common study involves having children, teenagers, or college students watch violent videos; often a control group watches a nonviolent video. Typically, researchers measure the subjects' violent attitudes before and after they watch the videos by, for example, asking them how they would behave in various scenarios or whether they would approve of violence depicted in certain scenarios. When children are the subjects, researchers often watch them play before and after they view the videos. Regardless of the type of study, researchers typically find that viewing violent videos increases subjects' violent attitudes, behavior, or both.

At least two problems limit the value of such studies

▲ Although many studies suggest that violence on TV and in the movies contributes to real-life violence, the actual effect of media violence remains unclear.

(Leshner et al. 2013). First, because the studies are necessarily short term, they can find only short-term effects. Whether viewing violence has long-term effects, especially on criminal violence and not just on aggression, remains unclear. Second, because these are experimental studies, the effects occurring in the "laboratory" may not occur in the real world, where many other influences come into play.

Another line of research involves surveying children and teenagers and asking them how much TV, or how much violent TV, they watch, or how often they play violent video games. Their amount of time watching TV or playing the games is then compared to their involvement in violent delinquency and other aggression. Researchers often find a statistical correlation between watching TV and committing aggression, and they conclude that watching TV or playing violent video games increases aggression. However, this correlation might be spurious. Youths might both watch TV or play violent video and commit violence because they are interested in violence for other reasons. If so, both behaviors stem from this interest, and it cannot be said that watching TV causes their aggression (Leshner et al. 2013).

The various problems in the research on mass media and violence make it difficult to conclude that the media have a strong effect on actual violence. One critic even said that the notion that mass-media violence causes interpersonal violence amounts to nothing more than "hollow claims" (Rhodes 2000:19). A conservative conclusion is that mass-media violence may have an effect on real-life violence (Glymour et al. 2008), but that this effect is small and eclipsed by other influences. In view of the possible censorship involved in any legislative attempts to control the mass media, we should remain skeptical of mass-media effects until the empirical evidence becomes compelling. Even then, censorship remains an important issue that should be addressed.

Review and Discuss

What is the evidence for and against the proposition that mass-media violence plays a large role in real-life violence?

Firearms, Crime, and Violence

Already very controversial, the issue of firearms, crime, and violence received new attention after the December 2012 massacre of the Sandy Hook Elementary School children and staff. Because the gunman was armed with a semi-automatic assault rifle and two handguns and had an

▲ Handguns and handgun control remain one of the most controversial issues in criminal justice today.

apparent history of mental illness, much of the ensuing debate focused on assault weapons and mass shootings and on keeping firearms out of the hands of people with mental disorders (Young 2013).

As valuable as this debate was, it was misplaced for at least three reasons. First, almost all gun violence and other kinds of violence are committed by people who are *not* mentally ill (Young 2013) (see Chapter 6). Second, almost all firearm-related homicides occur via "ordinary" violence, not via mass shootings. To illustrate, an estimated 547 people died in mass shootings in the United States from 1983 to 2012; in a much smaller period, 2000–2010, almost 131,000 people died in all firearm-related homicides (Leshner et al., 2013). As a government review summarized these very different numbers, "Mass shootings are a highly visible and moving tragedy, but represent only a small fraction of total firearm-related violence" (Leshner et al. 2013:32). Third, and recalling this chapter's earlier discussion of the involvement of handguns in homicide, most firearm-related homicides and other gun violence in the United States involve handguns, not assault weapons. Combining all these circumstances, the focus of any debate over guns in America should therefore be on handguns and ordinary violence and other crime.

There is at least one thing that all sides to this debate can agree on: Americans own many, many more firearms per capita than the residents of any other nation (Leshner et al. 2013). Altogether, Americans own about 300 million firearms, one-third of which are handguns. These firearms are found in 43 percent of the nation's households. The big question, and one on which there is certainly huge disagreement, is whether these handguns and other firearms make us safer or less safe overall. Many scholars say handguns make us less safe, while some scholars and certainly the National Rifle Association say handguns make us safer. A major focus of this dispute is whether handgun ownership by law-abiding citizens raises or lowers their risk of becoming victims of gun crimes and other crimes.

Gun-control opponents think handgun ownership by law-abiding citizens lowers their risk of crime. This is the "more guns, less crime" thesis (Lott 2000). According to this argument, offenders are deterred from committing robbery, burglary, and other crimes if they think or know that their potential targets have a handgun. The more that citizens own guns, then, the lower the crime rate.

Gun-control proponents reply that the presence of a handgun increases shootings and homicides by turning a disagreement or mere assault into a homicide or nonlethal gun shooting (Hoskin 2001). In regard to this "situational dynamics" view, recall this chapter's earlier observation that most homicides occur between people who know each other, often after an argument arising out of a minor dispute or as part of ongoing family violence. According to gun-control proponents, the presence of a handgun in law-abiding households thus greatly increases the chances that a gun will be used against a victim by someone he or she knows: if no handgun were present, the offender would have to use a less lethal weapon, and a homicide would be less likely.

Several kinds of evidence suggest that handgun ownership does, in fact, increase the risk of homicide. At the micro level, a widely cited study compared households with guns with households without guns in the same neighborhoods and matched by age, sex, and race of household members (Kellerman et al. 1993). The researchers found that the households with guns were 2.7 times more likely to have someone in the house murdered, usually by a family member or close friend. This was true even when the researchers controlled for the use of alcohol or illegal hs and a history of domestic violence. At a more macro level, another study analyzed the relationship between state rates of firearm ownership and homicide victimization. States with higher rates of firearm ownership had higher homicide victimization rates. Importantly, there was no relationship between firearm ownership and non-firearm homicide victimization (Miller et al. 2007). Finally, and as noted earlier, the United States has a much higher homicide rate than other industrial nations even though its rate of other serious violence is only about average among these nations. This fact points to the high U.S. handgun ownership rate as the reason for the high U.S. homicide rate (Zimring and Hawkins 1997).

Crime and Controversy PACKING HEAT IN THE LAND OF JEFFERSON

What would you think if you were eating at a restaurant and you saw a table full of diners wearing handguns in plain view? This was a sight that confronted Virginians a decade ago, and it was a sight that prompted much debate over the wisdom and effects of "packing heat" out in the open.

The controversy began when the police in one Virginia town received a report in July 2004 that six men were sitting at a restaurant, all of them wearing guns. Four police hurried to the scene, only to be told by the men that they had a right to carry their guns in public. Much to many people's surprise and to some people's dismay, Virginia state law allows such a practice. At least three times that summer, members of the Virginia Citizens Defense League were seen carrying guns tied to their hips. Two of them were college students who had their guns taken by the police, who returned them the next day when they realized the students had broken no law. Police in various jurisdictions were then informed that carrying guns in public was perfectly legal under Virginia law. Ironically, Virginia, like many other states, requires a permit to carry a concealed weapon, but not to carry one out in the open.

The situation arose from a quirk in the Virginia statute that bans the open carrying of firearms, but then defines firearms in a manner that excludes handguns, which, as a result, are not considered firearms under state law. A law that took effect on July 1, 2004, also contributed to the controversy: The law forbids any local gun-control regulation, and its enactment did away with local regulations that prohibited open carrying.

Virginia again made the news in early 2010 when it enacted a law that lets persons with concealed weapons permits take their guns into restaurants that serve alcohol, provided they do not also drink. The state senator who sponsored the bill said he wanted to enable women who carry guns in their purses to be safe when they eat at a Red Lobster restaurant, which he used as an example. A woman state senator who opposed the bill said, "I've really never been afraid for my life at the Red Lobster." Opponents said it would be difficult to enforce the no-drinking provision in the law, as gun-carrying diners could drink without anyone knowing they had guns because the guns would be concealed. A comment on a blog about the new law stated, "This is just what we need in Virginia. This law will ensure that the waiters and the cooks get the orders right."

By 2013, at least one Virginia restaurant had decided to capitalize on the state's "open carry" law by naming every Wednesday "Open Carry Wednesday" and providing a 10 percent discount to every customer wearing a licensed firearm who visits the restaurant on that day of the week. Although many customers applauded the discount, at least one couple told the owner they would not eat there again. A sign at the restaurant said, "Guns are welcome on the premises. Please keep all firearms holstered unless the need arises. In such case, judicious marksmanship is greatly appreciated by all!"

Sources: Helderman 2010; Jackman 2004; Rothstein 2013.

Even if handguns make homicides more likely, they may still help victims defend themselves or their property once a crime has begun and thus prevent criminals from completing their crimes. The use of handguns and other firearms for such self-protection is called *defensive gun use* (DGU). Estimates of annual DGU in the United States come from the NCVS and other surveys and range widely from about 100,000 incidents annually to a 3 million, with the actual number probably somewhere between these two extremes (Leshner et al. 2013). The lower end of this range represents only a very small percentage of all violent crime, suggesting to some scholars that gun ownership provides little help (McDowall and Wiersema 1994). The higher end of the range suggests to other scholars that gun ownership provides significant help (Kleck and Gertz 1995). These scholars also find that gun use in general helps reduce the risk of victim injury compared to other self-protective measures (Tark and Kleck 2004).

Reflecting the complexity of this evidence, a recent review concluded that the effectiveness of DGU and other victim self-protection "is likely to vary across types of victims, types of offenders, and circumstances of the crime, so further research is needed, both to explore these contingencies and to confirm or discount earlier findings" (Leshner et al. 2013:16). The review added that even if DGU does prevent victim death or injury, handgun ownership may cause enough injury or death through the situational dynamics described earlier so as to "cancel or outweigh the beneficial effects" (p. 16) of DGU.

To return to the "big question" raised earlier, do handguns make us safer or less safe over-all? The answer is not very simple. On the one hand, the widespread prevalence of handguns in American households almost certainly contributes to thousands of homicides and nonlethal shootings every year that would not occur without a handgun's presence and helps explain why the United States is the most deadly of the world's democracies. On the other hand, DGU does occur and helps prevent crimes and victim injuries, even if the actual amount and effectiveness of DGU remain to be determined. Putting this body of evidence together, handguns make us both safer in some ways and less safe in other ways. Proponents and opponents of handgun ownership will both find support for their viewpoints in this complex evidence. A fair conclusion, and one with which most criminologists would probably agree, is that handguns do both good and harm but do far more harm than good.

Review and Discuss

Do handguns make people safer or less safe? If effective gun control were possible, would it greatly reduce the number of gun-related crimes? Explain your answer.

▶ Reducing Violent Crime

Although violent crime has declined since the early 1990s, it is still much more common than most Americans would want. What can be done to reduce it? Recall the explanations of violent crime stressed in this chapter: economic deprivation, criminogenic urban conditions, masculin-ity, racial discrimination, and inadequate and abusive parenting, among others. A sociological ap-proach to reducing violent crime focuses on all these causes. Programs that might reduce poverty and joblessness, lessen urban blight, and improve the quality of parenting all hold potential for significant reductions in violent crime (see Chapter 18). Although they certainly have not been in fashion, such programs are essential if we want to make a dent in violent crime. To the extent that racial discrimination against African-Americans and other people of color heightens their angry aggression and use of violence, successful efforts to reduce such discrimination would also help reduce violent crime.

A final focus for reducing violent crime must be masculinity. If men's violence rates were as low as women's rates, the U.S. violent-crime rate would be much, much lower. We must begin to raise our sons differently from the way we have been raising them. If we continue to accept the notions that "boys will be boys" and that they need to learn to "fight like a man," we are ensuring that interpersonal violence will continue.

What History Tells Us

None of these roots of violent crime will be easy to eliminate, but if we do not begin to address them, our nation will continue to have much violent crime. Lest we despair too much over our situation, history tells us that reductions in violent crime *are* possible. Homicide rates in Europe were much higher in the Middle Ages than now, historians say (Pinker 2012). Amsterdam's rate in the mid-1400s was about 47 per 100,000, compared to about 1.5 per 100,000 in the early 1800s. Medieval England's rate was about ten times higher than it is now and about twice as high as the current U.S. rate.

Most homicides in medieval England took place among farmers in their fields who fought over scarce resources (e.g., land) and over insults to honor they took very seriously. Because the courts were seen as slow and expensive, violence was a preferred way to resolve disputes. More generally, medieval people in England and other nations lived in a culture that "accepted, even glorified, many forms of brutality and aggressive behavior" (Gurr 1989:21). Knives and quar-terstaffs, the heavy wooden stick used by Little John of Robin Hood fame, were their weapons of choice. The major reason for the drop in homicide rates in England and other European nations in the 1500s and 1600s was the development of a "civilizing process" marked by the rise of "courtly manners" and an increase in the use of courts to resolve private disputes (Elias 1978 (1939)).

A similar process later occurred in the United States, where the homicide rate peaked in the mid-1800s and then fell after the Civil War through the early 1900s, even though cities were growing rapidly. Scholars attribute this homicide decrease in the face of urban growth to the greater control that factories exerted over people's behavior, to the spread of public schools, and to the growth of the YMCA and other institutions that stressed moral behavior (Butterfield 1994). Looking at the historical decrease in homicides until the 1960s, historian Eric Monkkonen saw some hope: "What we are finding is that violence is not an immutable human problem. . . . The good news is violence can go down. The bad news is, we need to learn how to make it happen" (Butterfield 1994:16).

If history tells us that violence can go down, it also tells us that this will not happen if we do not provide economic opportunity for the poor and people of color. For example, despite the general decrease in U.S. homicide rates after the Civil War period, the African-American homicide rate did not decrease during this time, as African-Americans continued to experience racial discrimination and declining economic opportunity (Lane 1986). Their rates finally did drop in the late 1940s and early 1950s, when increasing employment opportunities in factories and offices lowered African-American unemployment rates. Later in the 1950s, however, these unemployment rates rose as factories closed or moved from northern cities, and the urban decay that we see today accelerated. Not surprisingly, African-American homicide rates rose as a result (Lane 1989).

▶ Conclusion

Violent crime remains one of the most serious problems in the United States. The fact that some groups—the poor, people of color, women—are more vulnerable to violent crime in general, or to specific types of violent crime, underscores the consequences of economic, racial, and gender inequality in U.S. society. Presenting a sociological understanding, this chapter emphasized that the roots of violent crime generally lie in the social environment. Even if we could somehow eliminate the violent individuals among us, others will soon take their place unless we also do something about the structural and cultural problems that make violence so common. A sociological understanding of violent crime thus underscores the need to reduce economic and racial inequality and to reshape masculinity if we want to reduce violent crime significantly (Currie 2010).

Another important theme of this chapter was that people we know, and in some cases know very well, account for much of the violence against us: Nonstrangers commit most homicides and many assaults. In Chapter 11 we examine several kinds of violence that women are especially likely to suffer from men they know, including spouses and partners.

Summary

1. Interpersonal violence involves the use or threat of physical force against one or more other people. This definition excludes two other types of violence, corporate and political violence, which also cause death, injury, and other harm, but are conceptually distinct from everyday interpersonal violence such as homicide, assault, and robbery.

2. Homicides include first- and second-degree murders and voluntary and involuntary manslaughter. In practice, these four categories often overlap, and it is sometimes difficult to determine which category best describes a particular homicide.

3. Homicide and aggravated assault are patterned socially and geographically. Homicide rates are disproportionately high among African-Americans, men, urban residents, and Southerners.

4. Certain characteristics of homicides are relevant. Regarding the victim–offender relationship, most homicide victims knew the person who killed them. Homicides tend to be relatively spontaneous, emotionally charged events involving handguns.

5. Inequality and extreme poverty, cultural beliefs including masculinity, and other reasons rooted in the social environment help explain why the United States has the highest homicide rate among industrialized nations, why homicides are more common in urban areas than elsewhere within the United States, why men commit most homicides and aggravated assaults, and why African-Americans and other people of color have disproportionately high homicide rates. Structural reasons also generally account for why some women commit violence while most do not.

6. Robbery is a crime that many Americans fear most of all. Like homicide and assault, it is patterned socially and geographically. Structural factors and a search for thrills help account for differences in robbery rates, and factors drawn from routine activities theory help account for differences in robbery victimization.

7. Mass murder and serial killing receive heavy media attention but are actually relatively rare events. Men commit most of these crimes, but accurate understanding of why specific individuals commit these crimes remains elusive. Almost one-fifth of violence occurs in the workplace, most often by strangers committing robberies. When coworkers "go postal" and go on shooting sprees in their workplaces, these incidents receive heavy media coverage.

8. TV shows, films, and other components of the mass media are filled with violence, much of it graphic, and many scholars and much of the public believe that mass-media violence is a prime contributor to violence by youths and other individuals. Although many studies find a correlation between exposure to mass-media violence and actual involvement in violent behavior, scholars disagree among themselves whether this correlation means that mass-media violence is, in fact, an important cause of real-life violence.

9. The issue of gun control is one of the most controversial in society at large and in the field of criminology, with scholars disagreeing among themselves on whether guns make people safer or less safe.

10. The homicide rate has decreased dramatically since several centuries ago. History tells us that increased economic opportunities for the poor and people of color are necessary to decrease their relatively high homicide rates.

Key Terms

assault *194*

child abuse *211*

elder abuse *211*

homicide *193*

interpersonal violence *193*

intraracial *195*

manslaughter *194*

masculinity *201*

mass media *212*

robbery *204*

victim–offender relationship *196*

What Would You Do?

1. Suppose you are driving a car on a city street and begin to stop for a traffic light. As you do so, you notice a burly, somewhat unkempt man come walking toward you rather quickly from the sidewalk. You naturally find yourself becoming tense as you see the man approaching. He may simply need some help, he may want to ask you for money, or he may want to steal your car. You have only a few more seconds until he reaches your window. What do you do?

2. This chapter included a discussion of guns and gun control. Pretend you are the mayor of a medium-sized city. A recent spate of robberies has captured a good deal of attention on local TV news shows and in the city's major newspaper. The public is clamoring for your office to do something about the robberies. A member of the city council introduces a resolution to allow private citizens to carry concealed handguns for their protection. What would your response be?

© ZUMA Press, Inc. / Alamy

11 Violence Against Women

· ·

Crime in the News

In April 2013, the University of Arizona held a march and rally as part of the campus's annual "Take Back the Night" to protest rape and sexual assault and to support survivors of sexual violence. Several people at the rally told of their own experiences of being sexually assaulted. After hearing their stories, one student commented, "I've never been to Take Back the Night. I wasn't really sure what to expect. Once people started talking about their own experiences I got really emotional. Some of the people that spoke, I really care about, and I didn't think I would start crying but I started crying. I almost didn't come, but I'm glad I did because it was a great experience."

Source: Burgoyne 2013.

· ·

B efore the 1970s, sexual assault and domestic violence were hardly ever discussed inside or outside the college classroom, even though they had been occurring for centuries. Then these crimes began to capture the attention of the modern women's movement, which was still in its early stages. Because of the feminist movement, there are now countless numbers of scholarly studies and popular accounts of sexual assault and domestic violence. Many college courses now consider these crimes, and many campuses, as the Crime in the News story illustrates, have Take Back the Night marches and rallies, Rape Awareness Weeks, and other events. This chapter discusses the major findings from the burgeoning research on violence against women and continues the book's emphasis on the sociological roots of criminal behavior.

▶ Overview: The Gendered Nature of Violent Crime

Women, like men, are victims of the major violent crimes examined in Chapter 10: homicide, aggravated assault, and robbery. For all these crimes, their rates of victimization are much lower than men's rates. However, there are two types of violent crime for which women's rates of victimization are much higher than men's rates: (1) rape and sexual assault and (2) domestic violence, or violence committed by intimates (current or former spouses and partners). In NCVS data, women were the victims in 86 percent of all rape and sexual assaults in 2011, in 79 percent of all nonlethal violence (aggravated and simple assault, robbery, rape and sexual assault) committed by intimates, and in 92 percent of all serious nonlethal violence (aggravated assault, robbery, rape and sexual assault) committed by intimates (Bureau of Justice Statistics 2013). In line with intimate violence figures, women were also the victims in 79 percent of all homicides committed by an intimate in 2011 (Federal Bureau of Investigation 2012). All these numbers yield a central conclusion: Women are the primary targets in rape and sexual assault and domestic violence precisely because they are women.

Sociologically, this is not surprising. Socially, economically, and physically, women have less power than men. As Chapter 10's discussion of hate crime against people of color and other subordinate groups illustrated, powerless groups are often the victims of violence by those with power. Sexual assault and domestic violence are no different. We cannot understand violence against women unless we recognize men's social, economic, political, and physical dominance and women's lack of such dominance. It is no accident that men are almost always the ones who commit rape and sexual assault and domestic violence or that women are their targets. Given this context, rape and sexual assault and domestic violence may even be regarded as the equivalent of hate crimes against women.

▶ An International Problem

As we look around the globe, violence against women is a worldwide phenomenon of "epidemic proportions," according to international organizations (Cheng 2013). These organizations estimate that almost one-third of women worldwide have been physically and/or sexually assaulted by a former or current spouse or partner and that 7 percent of women worldwide have also been sexually assaulted by a nonintimate. In addition to these forms of violence, female genital mutilation, a routine practice in many countries, affects an estimated 140 girls and women worldwide (World Health Organization 2013).

▲ Violence against women is an international problem. About one-third of women across the world have been victims of rape, sexual assault, or domestic violence.

In Pakistan, women in police custody are often sexually and physically abused. In Kuwait, male employers routinely rape their foreign maids. About half of married men in Northern India say they have physically or sexually abused their wives (Martin et al. 1999). In Uganda, more than half of women have been victims of physical and/or sexual violence, while the government does little to prevent it or to punish the men who commit it. One young woman recalled her beatings after she got married: "At first all he did was beat me, and then he began to have sex with me by force as well. When I told him to wear a condom because I suspected he had been sleeping with other women, he would beat me some more. . . . I know that even if I go to the Local Council, they won't do anything; the same thing happens to my friends and nothing is done when they report it" (Amnesty International 2010b:12).

In India and Pakistan, dowry deaths claim the lives of thousands of women annually (Thekaekara 2012). Brides in those two nations are supposed to pay the groom money or goods. If they do not, the groom often beats his wife, or he and his relatives murder her. To hide their crime, they often burn the woman with kerosene and claim she caught fire accidentally in the kitchen. Police then accept bribes from the husband and/or his relatives to pretend the murder was an accident. A Pakistani human rights attorney once noted, "These cases are some of the most horrifying and gruesome human rights abuses in the world." Although they are common in Pakistan, she said they reflect a more general international problem: "It is really, at bottom, simply about violence and cruelty to women. That is not a story unique to Pakistan" (Sennott 1995:1).

The nations mentioned in these examples are neither wealthy nor industrialized, but international human rights groups emphasize that violence against women is very common in the industrialized world as well, as this chapter will illustrate for the United States. Amnesty International reports that emergency service agencies in the United Kingdom receive one phone call each minute about domestic violence. A woman there explained why she finally called the police after being beaten by her partner for eight years:

> I really don't know what it was that evening that made me decide to call the police, but I always say it was the sight of cleaning up my own blood. People have asked me why I didn't just leave, but my partner made lots of threats to me which he always carried out. I was very, very frightened of him. So you get to the point where you live with it, it becomes a normal pattern of life, you adapt, you cope, you hide it. (Amnesty International 2004b:1)

Some of the worst abuses of women occur in wartime. In one of the first books on rape, Susan Brownmiller (1975) wrote that wartime rape has been occurring for centuries. In nations that are dissimilar geographically and culturally, such as Mexico and Bosnia, women have been routinely raped and genitally mutilated over the past two decades during ethnic and political conflicts. After a war began in eastern Congo in 1998 between rebels and government forces, the latter routinely used rape as a weapon to quell the rebellion. It is estimated that over the next five years, soldiers raped almost one-third of eastern Congolese women, leaving thousands of them with vaginal fistula (a medical term for an abnormal duct or passage resulting from an injury or disease) and unable to work or to have sex or children (Wax 2003). Another epidemic of wartime rape occurred in Sudan during bloody ethnic conflict that racked the Darfur region of that Northern African nation in 2003 and 2004. A government-sponsored militia known as the *Janjaweed* (translated as "armed men on horses") attacked village after village and routinely raped the women they found there, often in front of their husbands and other villagers (Amnesty International 2004a).

Rape and battering in the United States are thus part of a larger, international pattern of violence against women that also includes murder, torture, sexual slavery, incest, genital mutilation, and involuntary sterilization. Jane Caputi and Diana E. H. Russell (1992:15) termed these acts *sexist terrorism*. They are directed against women because they are women and the acts are motivated by "hatred, contempt, pleasure, or a sense of ownership of women." In its most severe form, such violence involves what Caputi and Russell called femicide, or the murder of women. They likened femicide and other antiwomen violence to the lynchings of African-Americans that were designed to reinforce white dominance over African-Americans. In a similar fashion, they wrote, men's violence against women helps maintain their dominance over them. Femicide goes back at least to the witch hunting in medieval Europe that killed some 300,000 people, most of them poor women (Demos 2009). The gendered nature of these witch killings led one scholar to call them "part of the ongoing attempt by men . . . to ensure the continuance of male supremacy" (Hester 1992:36). In the modern era, women in the United States and elsewhere are murdered by men who have been battering them. In other countries they are also killed during ethnic and political conflicts or because they violate rigid cultural codes of sexuality. Whatever the reason and the context, women are murdered or assaulted because they are women. Men are not killed or assaulted for the same reasons.

▶ Defining Rape/Sexual Assault and Domestic Violence

Put most simply, rape may be defined as sexual intercourse (vaginal, anal, or oral penetration) without the consent of the victim, while sexual assault may be defined as sexual contact without the consent of the victim that does not include intercourse. Force or the threat of force is often involved in rape and sexual assault; however, sexual contact of someone who is under the influence of alcohol or other drugs or otherwise unable to give consent is also considered rape when penetration occurs or sexual assault when it does not occur.

Domestic violence, or battering, may be defined as physical and sexual attacks committed by intimates: spouses or ex-spouses, boyfriends or girlfriends, and ex-boyfriends or ex-girlfriends. This form of violence is also called *intimate-partner violence* (IPV) or more simply, *intimate violence*. IPV includes aggravated assaults, in which a weapon is used or a serious injury occurs; simple assaults, in which no weapon is used and only a minor injury occurs; and rape and sexual assault; and robbery; some discussions of IPV limit themselves to just aggravated and simple assaults. Although the definition of domestic violence allows for men to be battered, most domestic violence, and almost all serious domestic violence is committed against women, as we have already seen. One problem with defining domestic violence as physical and sexual attacks is that doing so excludes psychological abuse, which is often as harmful or even more harmful than physical abuse. Because there is much more research on physical abuse than on psychological abuse by intimates, most of our discussion addresses the physical dimension.

▼ Intimate-partner violence, or domestic violence, includes aggravated assaults, simple assaults, rape and sexual assault, and robbery.

AP Photo/Al Grillo

The Nordic nations of Denmark, Finland, Norway, and Sweden are widely regarded as among the wealthiest and most progressive in the world, with a strong record of gender equality throughout their societies. Despite this reputation, rape remains a serious problem in these nations that is compounded by the failure of their governments to take it seriously. A recent Amnesty International report declared that "rape and other forms of sexual violence remain an alarming reality that affects the lives of many thousands of girls and women every year in all Nordic countries." The report went on to discuss many ways in which the Nordic governments compound the problem.

For example, Denmark's rape laws fall short of international human rights standards in at least two respects. First, they provide lower penalties for men who have sex with women who are in a helpless state, for example, because of mental illness or drug use, because physical force was not used or threatened; if a husband rapes his wife who is in a helpless state, there are no penalties. According to the Danish Minister of Justice, "It is not natural to call it a 'rape,' if the perpetrator has not used physical coercion or has not threatened the victim or placed that victim in a state where that person is unable to resist." Second, the laws allow for reduced penalties if a rape is committed by a husband against a wife even when she is not in a helpless state. The government was reconsidering this latter problem at the time of this writing.

Finland's rape laws take into account the seriousness of the violence used against a woman and include a category called "coercion into sexual intercourse." The average prison term for this type of rape is only seven months, even though the "coercion" often involves very serious violence. Two examples illustrate this problem. In one case, a man raped a woman in a restaurant bathroom after banging her head against the wall, twisting her arm behind her, and covering her mouth with his hand to prevent her from screaming. He was convicted of coercion into sexual intercourse and received a seven-month sentence that was suspended. In a second case, a case "where a woman was held captive for several days, raped repeatedly and denied her medication," according to Amnesty International, also resulted in a prosecution and conviction only for coercion into sexual intercourse.

In these and other ways, the Nordic nations fail to protect women who are raped or otherwise sexually abused. The Amnesty International report called on their governments to take several measures to help their women, including: (1) adopting legal definitions of rape that conform to international human rights standards, (2) undertaking education and other preventive efforts to reduce rape, and (3) improving the quality of the investigation and judicial handling of rape cases.

Source: Amnesty International 2010a.

► Extent of Rape/Sexual Assault and Domestic Violence

Rape and Sexual Assault

When the U.S. women's movement turned its attention to rape in the early 1970s, it documented the role that rape played in women's daily lives. Thus Susan Griffin (1971:26) began her classic essay, "Rape: The All-American Crime," by saying, "I have never been free of the fear of rape. From a very early age I, like most women, have thought of rape as a part of my natural environment—something to be feared and prayed against like fire or lightning. I never asked why men raped; I simply thought it one of the many mysteries of human nature."

Research since the early 1970s confirms the magnitude of the rape problem. The NCVS estimates that almost 244,000 rapes and sexual assaults occurred in 2011 against people age 12 or older. Of this number, about 86 percent were committed against females for a rate of 1.6 per 1,000 women; 68 percent of these were committed by someone the woman knew and only 28 percent by a stranger (see Table 11-1).

While the NCVS focuses on crimes in the past year, other U.S. national and local surveys estimate how many women have been raped at some point in their lifetime (*prevalence rates*). The U.S. Centers for Disease Control and Prevention (CDC) conducted such a survey in 2010 (Black et al. 2011). Almost one-fifth (18.3 percent) of the women in the survey, equal to some 22 million women nationwide, reported that they had been raped in their lifetime; more than one-fourth (27.2 percent) reported having been sexually assaulted. Another survey, the National Violence against Women Survey (NVAW), similarly found that 18 percent of women had been raped at least once in their lifetime (Tjaden and Thoennes 2000). These sets of findings indicate

TABLE 11-1 Victim–Offender Relationship for Rape and Sexual Assault (percentage of all offenses committed against women), NCVS, 2011

OFFENDER	PERCENTAGE
Nonstranger	68
Intimate	19
Friend or acquaintance	48
Stranger	28
Unknown	4

Source: Bureau of Justice Statistics 2013.

that almost one-fifth of U.S. women have been raped and that more than one-fourth have been sexually assaulted. Both national surveys also found that nonstrangers committed more than 80 percent of the rapes reported by respondents.

A study of a random sample of 420 women in Toronto found an even higher rape prevalence rate. Melanie Randall and Lori Haskell (1995) supervised face-to-face interviews with the subjects that lasted about two hours each. Of the 420 women, 56 percent reported at least one experience of forced or attempted forced sexual intercourse, with 83 percent of these rapes committed by someone they knew. When Randall and Haskell included other forms of sexual assault, including unwanted sexual touching of the breasts or genitals, two-thirds of the subjects reported at least one completed or attempted sexual assault, including rape. The researchers concluded that "it is more common than not for a woman to have an experience of sexual assault during her lifetime" (p. 22).

Review and Discuss

How common are rape and sexual assault? How might the way the answer to this question is determined affect the estimates that are found?

Intimate Rape and Sexual Assault

Table 11-1 shows from NCVS figures that intimates accounted for 19 percent of all rapes and sexual assaults in 2011. The CDC survey just mentioned found that intimates had committed about half of the rapes and one-fourth of the sexual assaults committed against women. The NVAW survey also mentioned found that intimates, including dates, committed 62 percent of the rapes its respondents reported. The Toronto study found that intimates committed 30 percent of all sexual assaults occurring after a woman reached the age of 16.

Taking all these studies together, a fair estimate is that intimates commit at least one-fifth and perhaps more than half of the rapes and sexual assaults of women. Such rapes are especially likely to occur in marriages or relationships that also include battering: In the Toronto study, half of the women reporting a physical assault by an intimate had also been sexually assaulted by the same man. Intimate rapes, whether or not they occur without other physical violence, are often more traumatic for women than stranger rapes for at least two reasons. First, they cause a woman to feel betrayed and to question whether she can trust *any* man. Second, women raped by husbands or boyfriends they live with often have to continue living with them (Bergen 2006).

Review and Discuss

How does an understanding of the victim–offender relationship help us understand why rapes occur?

Domestic Violence

What about domestic violence? The best evidence indicates that domestic violence is even more common than rape. According to the NCVS, about 121,000 aggravated assaults and 391,000 simple assaults were committed by intimates against women in 2011, or about 512,000

Crime and Controversy "ALL I SEE IS BLOOD": RAPE AND BATTERING IN THE MILITARY

Women who serve our country in the military often find that the greatest threat to their safety comes from the men with whom they serve. As the title of a news report put it, "they fear ambush, snipers—and an enemy within." From 2002 to 2006, more than 500 military women in Afghanistan or Iraq reported being raped or sexually assaulted by U.S. military personnel; the actual number was probably much greater than this, since many women keep quiet about being attacked because they fear retaliation and because they do not think the military will take any action.

Members of the military reported 3,374 sexual assaults to authorities in 2012. However, anonymous surveys of military personnel indicated that 26,000 such assaults occurred that same year, with most of the assault victims not reporting them.

A decade ago, the *Denver Post* conducted one of the first investigative reports of sexual assault and domestic violence in the military. This report, published in November 2003, documented thousands of rapes and acts of battering of women at military bases in the United States and elsewhere. The *Post* began its investigation after dozens of women cadets in the U.S. Air Force Academy came forward in February 2003 with reports that they had been raped or sexually assaulted by other cadets. The Academy, they said, did little or nothing to their offenders, while they, the victims, were intimidated and even punished for reporting the crimes. The *Post's* investigation found that sexual assault and battering were rampant throughout the armed forces.

According to the *Post* report and more recent investigations, many military women keep quiet about their victimization, but when they do report it, military officials usually treat the offenders with kid gloves, if they investigate the cases at all. As the *Post* observed, "The obstacles to pursuing justice are wrenching. Many (victims) fear retaliation, damage to their careers and being portrayed as disloyal. And those who do report are often punished, intimidated, ostracized or told they are crazy by their superiors."

Many women told the *Post* that the crimes committed against them and the callous responses of military officials amounted to a betrayal of trust. One woman, who was raped on a South Korea base by an army sergeant, said,

"These people were supposed to be my family. All through basic training, that's what you're taught. Now I know that's not true."

Women veterans testify to the emotional trauma caused by their rape and battering. One woman, Rebekah, who was assaulted by her captain in Iraq, recalled, "The first two days after the incident, I just got physically ill. I just kept throwing up. After two days with the medics, I came back to the unit. But after that happened, I was so paranoid. It screwed me up for a while." Another woman, Sharon, was a combat medic during Operation Desert Storm in 1991 when she was gang-raped by fellow soldiers after being drugged. Although her rapists threatened to kill her if she reported what happened, she did so anyway, only to hear the military police officer respond, "What did you expect, being a female in Saudi Arabia?" In 1999 she suffered an emotional breakdown and was diagnosed with post-traumatic stress disorder.

A third woman, Marian, was 18 and just out of basic training when she was gang-raped by her drill sergeant and four other soldiers. In addition to the repeated rapes, they fractured several bones including her spine, urinated on her, and burned her with cigarettes. Her assailants were never brought to justice. Years later, she was continuing to have many serious health problems arising from her gang rape and beating when she was diagnosed with cervical cancer and given just a few years to live. Her will specifies that if her daughters join the military, they will not inherit any of her money. She will also not display the American flag: "When I looked at the American flag, I used to see red, white, and blue. Now, all I see is blood."

Congressional hearings in Spring 2013 focused new attention on sexual assault in the military. Although Pentagon officials promised increased efforts to reduce sexual assaults and to prosecute those accused of committing them, these promises were undercut by revelations that two military officers responsible for addressing sexual assaults had themselves been accused of sexually assaulting women.

Source: Cassata and Baldor 2013; Harris 2007; Schmitt 2004; Vanden Brook and Zoroya 2013.

---

overall for a rate of about 3.9 assaults per 1,000 women. The CDC survey found that one-third of U.S. women, or about 39 million women overall, have been physically assaulted by an intimate partner, and that 4 percent, or 4.7 million women, are assaulted annually by their partners. The NVAW survey concluded that 22 percent of women are assaulted in their lifetime by a partner, including 1.3 percent in the past year (Tjaden and Thoennes 2000).

This body of evidence suggests that one-fifth and one-third of U.S. and Canadian women have been assaulted by a husband or other male intimate. This evidence leads domestic violence

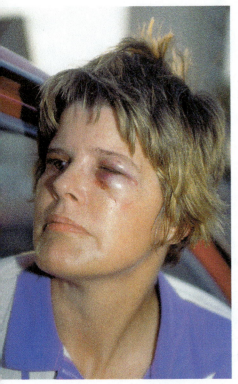

scholar Angela Browne to conclude that women "are more likely to be attacked and injured by a male partner than any other category of person. They are also more likely to be killed by a male partner than any other category of person" (Reynolds 1987:A18).

▶ Social Patterning of Rape/Sexual Assault and Domestic Violence

Age

The NCVS has reported detailed sociodemographic patterns for a combined measure of intimate-partner violence (IPV) that includes rape and sexual assault, aggravated and simple assault, and robbery (Catalano 2012a). Because robberies comprise only 12 percent or less of the total measure, the patterns revealed by NCVS IPV data safely apply to rape/sexual assault and domestic violence. With this in mind, rape/sexual assault and battering are, like many other crimes, more common among some demographic subgroups than others. One of the biggest risk factors is age: Young women are much more likely than older women to experience IPV (see Figure 11–1 ■).

Social Class

Many discussions emphasize that rape/sexual assault and battering transcend social class boundaries. Although this is true, the NCVS does find that the poorest women have rates of IPV six times higher than those for women in the highest income bracket (see Figure 11–2 ■). This social class difference underscores an important consequence of economic inequality in society.

That said, it remains true that rape/sexual assault and battering also occur among the middle and upper classes. As the notorious case of O. J. Simpson illustrates, men in all walks of life commit these crimes. In 1989 police responding to a "domestic dispute"

▲ The National Crime Victimization Survey estimates that male intimates commit tens of thousands of assaults against women every year.

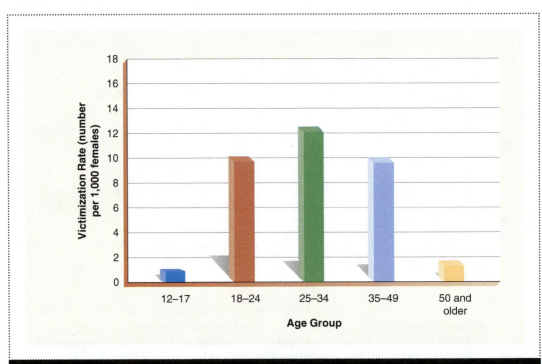

FIGURE 11–1   Age and Intimate-Partner Violence Committed Against Women, 2010.
Source: Catalano 2012.

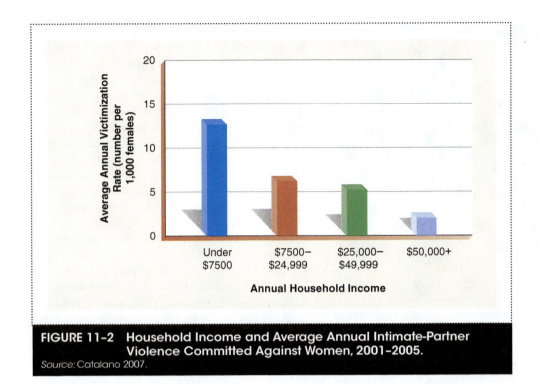

FIGURE 11–2 Household Income and Average Annual Intimate-Partner Violence Committed Against Women, 2001–2005.

Source: Catalano 2007.

saw his wife, Nicole Brown Simpson, "her lip bloodied, face swollen and eye blackened," running across the lawn and collapsing. At that point she screamed, "He's going to kill me, he's going to kill me!" When the police asked her who, she said, "O. J." (McGrory 1994:12).

Studies of college students reinforce this point: 5 percent of women college students nationwide report being raped during the past year, and experts estimate that at least one-fifth of college women are raped or sexually assaulted during their years in college (Paul et al. 2013). In various studies, between 8 percent and 14 percent of male college students report committing a rape, and between 25 percent and 60 percent report committing a sexual assault (Mouilso and Calhoun 2013). These men include campus leaders, athletes, and fraternity members (Schwartz et al. 2001). The college student evidence led Diana Scully (1995:2007) to conclude that "sexual aggression is commonplace in college dating relationships."

Race and Ethnicity

Racial differences in IPV against women also appear to exist. In 2010, rates of IPV victimization were higher for African-American women (7.8 victimizations per 1,000 women) than for white women (6.2) or Latina women (4.1) (Catalano 2012a). Although these differences are fairly small, Native American women have an especially high rate of IPV. A 2007 report by Amnesty International estimated that one-third of Native American women will be raped at least once in their lifetime, compared to only half that for non-Native American women (Amnesty International 2007). The higher rates for African-Americans and Native Americans probably stem from several factors, including (1) these groups' greater poverty, (2) their greater likelihood of living in high-crime areas, and (3) a lack of adequate legal help and social service provision for IPV survivors (Benson et al. 2004; Stark 2004).

Many women of color face particular problems in seeking help from rape crisis centers, battered women's shelters, social service agencies, the police, and other sources (Huisman 1996; Potter 2006). A major problem is that the antirape and battered women's movements were begun by white feminists and over the years have included few women of color. As a result, rape crisis centers and battered women's shelters continue to be relatively absent in inner cities and other areas, such as Native American reservations, where women of color live. For women in the United States who do not speak English, another problem is the language barrier (Klevens et al. 2007). Even when rape

© morgan hill / Alamy

▲ Native American women experience especially high rates of intimate partner violence.

crisis centers and battered women's shelters do exist, they do not always have interpreters to whom these women can talk. The same problem applies when a non-English-speaking woman calls the police for help. Many times her husband or partner may speak English better than she and thus be able to convince the police there is no real problem. Sometimes the husband or partner even has to translate the woman's words to the police; as you might expect, they cannot be trusted to tell the police what the woman is saying. For immigrant women and undocumented workers, the problem is even worse. In addition to the language barrier, these women also face possible legal problems, including deportation or arrest, should they seek help from the police or social service agencies.

Certain racial or ethnic groups also have cultural traditions that make battered or raped women especially reluctant to seek help (Huisman 1996; Klevens et al. 2007; Rasche 1988). For example, a strong norm on Native American reservations is that one does not seek help outside one's own community. In addition to this obstacle, reservations are usually in isolated rural areas, and a woman may not be able to get off the reservation even if she wants to get help. If she decides to seek help on the reservation, it is likely that law enforcement officers and social service agency workers know her and/or her abuser. In Asian-American communities, hostility toward the larger, white society may inhibit women from reporting their victimization. The particularly high respect in Asian-American families for men leads to the same inhibition.

Another problem affecting many women of color is fear of and hostility toward the police. A good deal of evidence suggests that people of color of either sex are more likely than whites to distrust the police (see Chapter 2). This feeling may lead women of color to be less likely than white women to call the police in cases of battering or rape. One additional problem facing battered African-American women is that the police may have more trouble noticing bruises on their bodies than they would on white women's bodies (Rasche 1988).

Review and Discuss

What special problems do women of color face in regard to intimate violence?

Explaining Rape/Sexual Assault and Battering

A basic issue in explaining rape/sexual assault and battering is whether the crimes are more psychological or sociological in origin. A psychological perspective assumes that many and even most rapists and batterers have psychological problems that predispose them to commit their crimes. A noted proponent of this view is A. Nicholas Groth (1979:5), who wrote, "Rape is always a symptom of some psychological dysfunction, either temporary and transient or chronic and repetitive." Although more than three decades have passed since Groth wrote this, this view remains popular within the field of psychology (Corvo and Johnson 2013; Young et al. 2012). In contrast, a sociological approach emphasizes the structural and cultural roots of rape/sexual assault and battering. Adopting this view, Diana Scully (1995:199) said it is wrong to assume that "individual psychopathology is the predisposing factor that best explains the majority of sexual violence against women." This assumption, she said, overlooks the social sources of this violence and implies that it is "unusual or strange" (p. 204), rather than a common phenomenon of everyday life.

In evaluating this debate, recall from Chapter 6 that psychologically normal people are very capable of committing antisocial and even violent behavior. Although it might be difficult to understand how psychologically normal men could rape and batter, there is ample evidence that such men commonly commit these crimes. Although no one will deny that some rapists, batterers,

▼

and other criminals have mental disorders, these individuals comprise only a small proportion of all criminals. The remainder are as psychologically normal as you or people you know.

Support for this view comes from the evidence on the prevalence of rape and battering. If these crimes are so common, it becomes very difficult to argue that they stem from psychological abnormality, unless we want to assume that 20 to 30 percent or more of all men are psychologically abnormal. That, of course, would be silly. Instead, these figures indicate that structural and cultural forces must be at work.

Gender and Economic Inequality

A key force here is gender inequality. Feminist scholars see rape and battering as inevitable consequences of patriarchy, or male dominance. These crimes reflect women's social and economic inequality and allow men to exert and maintain their power over women (Valenti 2013a). This does not mean that all men rape or batter women, but that a gender-based analysis of violence against women is necessary.

Anthropological evidence supports this view. Peggy Reeves Sanday (1981) studied 95 tribal societies on which a wide variety of information had been gathered. In forty-seven of these societies, rape was unknown or rare, and in eighteen, rape was common. She then compared the two types of societies and found that women in the rape-prone tribes had less decision-making and other power than did women in the rape-absent tribes. A similar study by Rae Lesser Blumberg (1979) focused on women's economic power in sixty-one preindustrial societies. Beatings of women by male partners were more common in societies in which women had less economic power.

Some U.S. evidence complements this anthropological evidence, but the evidence is complex overall (Vieraitis et al. 2007). Studies using city and state data usually find that rape rates are higher where women have lower levels of income and education, but some also find that rape rates are higher where women have higher levels of employment and occupational prestige. Complicating matters further, studies often also find that rape rates are higher where women have greater equality relative to men (e.g., when relative measures, such as women's income divided by men's income, are used). This latter evidence is interpreted as supporting a *backlash hypothesis* that violence against women is higher when men feel threatened by women's growing equality compared to what men already have. The U.S. ecological evidence, then, does suggest that gender inequality matters for rape rates, but also that it matters in a complex manner that future research will have to clarify.

If gender inequality might contribute to rape, so does economic inequality. In her classic essay, Susan Griffin (1971) observed that women become convenient scapegoats for the anger some men feel over their low socioeconomic status: "For every man there is always someone lower on the social scale on whom he can take out his aggressions. And that is any woman alive." In this regard, recall the discussion in Chapter 10 of masculinity and violence. We saw that men with low socioeconomic status use violent, "opposition" masculine behavior against each other to gain the respect their low status deprives them of. A similar argument holds for their interaction with women; rape/sexual assault and battering allow them to take out on women their frustration over their economic inequality and to prove their masculinity (Petrik et al. 1994).

Supporting this view, several studies find higher rape rates in areas with greater rates of economic deprivation (Martin et al. 2006). In a study of the fifty states, Larry Baron and Murray A. Straus (1987) found that states with higher economic inequality had higher rape rates. The authors concluded that "rape may be a way for some men to assert their masculinity in the absence of viable avenues of economic success" (p. 843).

▼ Anthropological evidence supports the view that gender inequality helps to explain violence against women.

Penny Tweedie/Getty Images

Cultural Myths Supporting Rape and Battering

If economic and gender inequality make rape and battering inevitable, so do cultural beliefs that either minimize the harm these crimes cause or somehow blame women for their victimization (Valenti 2013b). Because these beliefs distort reality, they are often called cultural myths. The myths about the two crimes are similar in many ways, but for clarity's sake receive separate discussions here.

Rape Myths

Two of the most common rape myths are that women like to be raped and "ask" to be raped by their dress, behavior, or both (Deming et al. 2013). Regarding the first myth, one of the most famous scenes in U.S. cinema occurs in *Gone with the Wind*, when Rhett Butler carries a struggling, resisting Scarlett O'Hara upstairs to have sex with her—in short, to rape her. The next scene we see takes place the following morning, when Scarlett awakens with a satisfied, loving smile on her face.

Unfortunately, traditional psychoanalytic views of women support the idea that they want to be raped. Psychoanalyst Karen Horney (1973:24) once wrote, "The specific satisfactions sought and found in female sex life and motherhood are of a masochistic nature. . . . What the woman secretly desires in intercourse is rape and violence, or in the mental sphere, humiliation." Another psychoanalyst, Ner Littner (1973), distinguished between "professional victims" of rape and "true victims." The former unconsciously want to be raped and thus act unknowingly in a way that invites rape, whereas the former do not unconsciously want to be raped. Although psychoanalysts have begun to abandon such notions, they remain common in both psychoanalytic and popular circles (Melton 2010).

Decades after *Gone with the Wind*, attitudes have changed, but many men still believe that women enjoy being forced to have sex and thus do not take her no for an answer. Despite the anti-rape movement's dictum that "no means no," this cultural myth is still very much with us. The traditional dating ritual demanding that men "make the first move" feeds into this myth. So does the traditional component of masculinity that says men are more masculine, or "studs," if they have a lot of sex. As we saw from the studies of approval by male college students for hypothetical rapes, many men, even those who do not rape, find the idea of forcing a woman to submit to them to be sexually stimulating. This notion combines with the cultural myth that women enjoy being forced to have sex to produce tragic consequences for women and their loved ones.

The other myth is that women "ask" or "deserve" to be raped by the way they dress and/or behave and thus precipitate their own victimization. In this view, if a woman dresses attractively, drinks, walks into a bar by herself, or hitchhikes, she wants to have sex. If a rape then occurs in these circumstances, it is thought that she really wanted it to happen anyway or at least was asking for it to happen. Either way, she bears some blame for the rape. As writer Tim Beneke (2013:566) puts it, "A woman who assumes freedoms normally restricted to a man (like going out alone at night) and is raped is doing the same thing as a woman who goes out in the rain without an umbrella and catches a cold. Both are considered responsible for what happens to them." In turn, the man who rapes her is held only partly responsible, or perhaps not even responsible at all.

This reaction is especially common if the woman has been sexually active in the past. Unless a woman in any of these circumstances suffers physical injuries in addition to the rape, it is often assumed that she consented to have sex and thus was not raped. Many people believe a "real rape" has not occurred unless all the following are true: (1) An injury or other evidence indicates forced intercourse, (2) the woman has not been sexually active, and (3) the woman did not dress or act

▼ One myth about rape is that a woman who dresses attractively wants to have sex. If a rape then occurs in these circumstances, it is thought that she really wanted it to happen anyway or at least was "asking" for it to happen.

© godfer/Fotolia

in any way that might suggest she wanted to have sex (Deming et al. 2013). This way of thinking ignores the fact that women are often raped without visible injuries. Often they do not physically resist the rape out of fear of even worse consequences or out of paralysis induced by the sheer terror of the situation.

These rape myths start early in life. A study of Rhode Island students in sixth through ninth grades found more than half saying it is okay for a man to force a woman to have sex if they have been dating at least six months. About a fifth said it is acceptable for him to force her to have sex if he has spent money on her on a date. About half said a woman who dresses "seductively" and walks alone at night is asking to be raped. More than 80 percent said rape is okay when a couple is married, and almost a third said it "would not be wrong" for a man to rape a sexually active woman (Hood 1995; White and Humphrey 1995).

As this evidence suggests, rape myths are part of the larger culture and, as such, are learned from this culture. During 2012 and 2013, several gang rapes by teenage boys occurred in the United States and Canada, perhaps most notoriously in Steubenville, Ohio, where the victim was unconscious. After these rapes, the alleged offenders proudly shared photos of what they had done. Commenting on their actions, Jessica Valenti (2013c), a feminist critic of rape, observed, "Boys across North America didn't get the idea to rape and humiliate their female peers out of thin air; they learned it. Yes, rape is illegal; in theory, we take it seriously. But in reality, rape jokes are still considered funny, women are told that what they wear has some bearing on whether or not they'll be attacked, and the definition of rape is still not widely understood." She added, "That's why whenever we blame a woman for being attacked—when we speculate what she was wearing, suggest she shouldn't have been drinking or that she stayed out too late—we're making the world safer for rapists."

Domestic Violence Myths

Myths about battering also abound (Policastro and Payne 2013). One myth blames battered women for being hit and says that they must have done something to anger their male partners. This myth is akin to the victim-precipitation myth that women ask to be raped. Feeding into this myth, a batterer often says he hit his wife or partner only because she did something to provoke him.

Another myth is that, because many women do not leave their batterers or call the police, the battering cannot be that bad. If it were bad, the reasoning goes, then they would leave or call for help. This myth distorts reality in at least two ways. First, most battered women *do* try to leave their batterers or at least call the police. Second, when women do not leave, they typically have many practical reasons for being hesitant to leave or to otherwise seek help. Perhaps, you even know a woman who has been beaten but who has not tried to end the relationship or call the police. Did you ever wonder why she did not take either action? Let's examine her possible reasons (Kim and Gray 2008).

First, there is often nowhere to go, especially if a woman has children. Battered women's shelters are only a short-term solution and are often filled to capacity. Relatives or friends may be able to house a battered woman and her children for a while. However, this again is only a short-term solution, and many women cannot find a relative or friend to stay with. Second, the question of money applies particularly to wives and other women living with their batterers: Because many battered women have no income independent of their husband's or partner's, economically they simply cannot afford to leave.

Next, women may fear that if they do try to leave their batterer, he will track them down and hurt them even worse than before. They may fear the same consequence if they call the police. Unfortunately, this fear is often warranted (DeKeseredy and Schwartz 2009; Ornstein and Rickne 2013). Studies indicate that at least 50 percent of women who do try to leave their batterers are harassed or further assaulted and that more battered women are killed while trying to leave their abusers

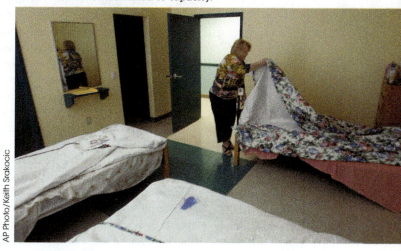

▼ Battered women's shelters are of great help to women who experience domestic violence, but are also only a short-term solution and are often filled to capacity.

AP Photo/Keith Srakocic

than at any other time (Browne 2004). As family violence researcher Angela Browne observed, "If a woman attempts to end or ends the relationship, there's often an escalation in violence just at that point because the man believes he's losing the woman" (Elias 1994:10). Echoing these views, one batterer said about beating his wife, "Every time, Karen would have ugly bruises on her face and neck. She would cry and beg me for a divorce, and I would tell her, 'If I can't have you for my wife, you will die. No one else will have you if you ever try to leave me'" (Browne 1995:232). In this context, the O. J. Simpson case again serves as a reminder. As sociologist Saundra Gardner (1994:A9) wrote at the time, "Nicole Simpson left. Not only did she leave, she took legal action and divorced her husband. And, she is dead."

Another reason battered women stay is that many continue to love their batterers. Most relationships and marriages begin in love, and battered women often continue to love their batterers and to hope things will improve. Feeding this hope, many batterers are very apologetic after hitting their wives or girlfriends and say it won't happen again. It is also true that women often blame themselves for being battered, just as rape survivors often blame themselves for being raped, feeling they should not have "dressed that way," led the guy on, and so forth. In short, battered women often accept the myth that the battering is their fault. Helping this to happen, a man might tell a woman he's battering her for any number of reasons: The kids are noisy, the dinner was cold, she allegedly looked at another man. He thus tries to get her to think it was her fault she had to be hit, and she often believes him. If she does blame herself for being battered, she is less apt to try to leave or call the police.

Finally, experts on women's violence talk about a sense of *learned helplessness* that some women develop from repeated battering (Walker 1984). This self-defense mechanism helps a battered woman cope by giving up any hope of improvement and by becoming passive.

With all these reasons in mind, the surprising thing might be that so many battered women *do* try to leave or call the police. Certainly, if a woman takes neither action, it should not be assumed that the battering "can't be that bad."

Review and Discuss

What are any three cultural myths that help explain the amount of rape and battering in the United States today?

Other Factors and Perspectives

Gender and economic inequality and cultural myths help explain why rape and battering occur, but other factors also matter. Specific factors highlighted by researchers include the overuse of alcohol, unemployment and other stressful life events, and male peer support (Armstrong et al. 2006; DeKeseredy et al. 2006; Fisher et al. 2010). Thus, rape and battering stem not only from the inequality and myths stressed in a feminist perspective on violence against women but also from other sources.

Disputing a feminist perspective, Richard B. Felson (2006; Felson and Lane 2010) contends that violence against women is not qualitatively different from violence against men. By this he means that the same factors that explain violence against men also explain violence against women, and that patriarchy, misogyny, and other concepts basic to a feminist perspective play no role in violence against women. As an analogy, he says that although the Nazis killed millions of women, it would be a mistake to say they did so out of sexism because they also killed millions of men. Thus Felson (2006:21) asks, "Perhaps this same kind of selective focus affects our understanding of violence against women today. Are the offenders sexist or just violent men? Are women victimized because of their gender, or because they make up half the population?" His answer is that "sexism plays at most a trivial role in rape and in physical assault on wives. Typically, men who commit these crimes commit other crimes as well, and their backgrounds and attitudes toward women are similar to those of other criminals." In this *violence perspective*, then, violence against women is no different from violence against men in its origins and dynamics, and the feminist perspective has no basis.

Feminist scholars dispute Felson's violence perspective (Brush et al. 2007). Among other objections, they say it ignores the gendered nature of violence against women, including the fact that so much of it is committed by male intimates, and the roots of violence against women in male dominance. Although Felson's argument has forced feminist scholars to sharpen their own arguments, it seems beyond question, as this chapter observed at the outset, that women are raped and battered precisely because they are women and that violence against women is in many ways qualitatively different from violence against men. The issue of battered men, to which we now turn, again reflects the tension between the violence and feminist perspectives on the violence women experience.

▶ Battered Men: Fact or Fiction?

The violence perspective also assumes that men are assaulted by their wives and girlfriends as often as women are assaulted by their husbands and boyfriends. If this is true, there is nothing special about the battering of women because both sexes commit violence against the other sex, and women victims should not be singled out for extra attention. This in turn implies that the physical harm men do to women is less reprehensible because women inflict the same kind of harm on men. As you might expect, this issue is the source of a heated debate among criminologists and other observers.

Murray A. Straus (1993; 2006), a noted family violence researcher, says that the prevalence of violence by wives against husbands (and, by extension, female intimate partners against other men) is at least as great as that by husbands against wives. About 12 percent of each sex commits at least one act of violence (contained in a Conflict Tactics Scales [CTS] list ranging from slapping to using a knife or gun) against a spouse in a given year. Studies using the CTS to examine dating relationships also report such gender equivalence in battering (Marshall and Rose 1990).

In his early work, Straus argued that this gender similarity obscures important differences that make domestic violence a far more serious problem for women (Straus 1980). One difference is that a woman's violence is usually in self-defense or the result of being battered, whereas a man's violence is meant simply to injure and dominate his wife or partner. Another difference is that women tend to commit more minor acts of violence (e.g., slapping or pushing), whereas men tend to commit more serious acts (e.g., beating or using a weapon). Men are also much more likely to repeat their violence. In another difference, even when women and men both slap or punch, the man's greater strength allows him to inflict a far more severe injury. A final difference is that male batterers tend to be especially likely to hit a pregnant partner.

In his later work, Straus abandoned this argument. Instead, he concluded that women often initiate violence against their husbands and are not acting in self-defense or in response to a history of battering, and he has called for more research on this topic (Straus 2006). The title of one his articles called their violence a "major social problem" (Straus 1993). This assertion of *gender symmetry in intimate-partner violence*, as it is often called, has received considerable attention in the popular media and has often been cited as evidence that the attention given to the battering of women is at least partly misdirected because it ignores the battering of men (Kay 2013).

Critics sharply criticize the gender symmetry claim as yet another myth that obscures the true nature of IPV (DeKeseredy 2006; Johnson 2006). Ironically, the reasons for their criticism echo those that Straus noted in his early work, that is, most women's "violence" against men is best considered self-defense or the result of repeated battering and men injure women far more than women injure men (Allen et al. 2009). Among other things, critics also say that CTS measures ignore the context of violence and do not include rapes and other acts that men inflict. Another problem is that some CTS measures are overly broad. For example, one measure is "bit, kicked, or hit with fist." A woman who bites gets the same score as a man who uses his fist (Dobash et al. 1992).

Perhaps, the most important evidence against the gender symmetry claim comes from victimization surveys such as the NCVS, which, contrary to CTS studies, finds that about 80–85 percent of all intimate violence is committed against women (Catalano 2012a; Lauritsen and Heimer 2008). Drawing on such evidence, reviews conclude that evidence overall fails to support the gender symmetry claim (Kimmel 2002; Saunders 2002).

Michael P. Johnson (2006) says the different findings about gender symmetry in IPV stem from different sampling strategies and different measurement of IPV. He adds that different types of IPV exist, including *intimate terrorism*, in which one individual (almost always a man) is extremely violent and controlling, and *situational couple* violence, in which both partners commit

▲ In 2009, Erin Andrews, a sideline reporter for ESPN, was stalked by a man who spied on her in hotel rooms and posted videos on the Internet of her unclothed body.

relatively minor and limited violence and neither partner is controlling. The studies that find gender symmetry, he says, typically rely on representative surveys of the population, but these surveys have high refusal rates (many people refuse to answer the questions), and the people who refuse are likely those who are either committing or experiencing the most serious IPV. For this reason, these surveys underestimate the serious, one-sided violence men commit and overestimate gender symmetry. Johnson urges future research on the issue to explicitly recognize that IPV is not a "unitary phenomenon" (p. 1015).

Scholars and other observers will no doubt continue to debate the belief that the battering of men is as bad as the battering of women. For now, it seems fair to say that male battering is certainly not fiction, but that it is also not the huge problem that some observers assert. Claims of gender symmetry in IPV are not justified and do an injustice to the tens of thousands of women each year who fear for their lives from men they once loved and from men they sometimes continue to love despite the violence they experience.

▶ Stalking

In 2009, Erin Andrews, a sideline reporter for ESPN, was stalked by a man who spied on her in hotel rooms. He filmed her through peepholes he made and posted videos of her unclothed body on the Internet. He was later arrested and sentenced to thirty months in prison (Dillon 2010).

Although rape, sexual assault, and battering are the most serious forms of violence that target women because of their gender, stalking, or the persistent following, observing, and/or harassment of an individual, "has come to be seen as a new and increasingly prevalent form of criminal behavior" (Mullen and Pathé 2002:275). Although this behavior has undoubtedly existed for many years, only since the early 1990s have the public and media come to recognize it as a serious problem and criminal laws have been passed against it. Although celebrities of either sex can be stalked by persons of either sex, stalking has become generally seen as a violent crime that a man does against a woman. A common goal is to intimidate the woman into staying in a romantic relationship (Fleming et al. 2012).

How common is stalking against women? Perhaps the best evidence comes from the NCVS, in which respondents were asked in 2006 whether they had experienced any of the following behaviors at least twice:

- Unwanted phone calls
- Unwanted letters or emails
- Following or spying on the victim
- Appearing at places without a legitimate reason
- Waiting at places for the victim
- Leaving unwanted presents
- Spreading rumors about the victim, including on the Internet

If a respondent reported experiencing any one of these behaviors at least twice and also reported being afraid as a result, the NCVS reasoned the person had been stalked. Based on this measure, the NCVS concluded that 1.5 percent of Americans 18 or older, amounting to 3.3 million people, had been stalked in the prior year (Catalano 2012b). This overall figure masked a gender difference: 2.2 percent of women reported being stalked, compared to only 0.8 percent of men. Translating these percentages into actual numbers, women comprised about 75 percent of all the stalking victims, and men only 25 percent.

The national CDC survey discussed earlier also measured stalking with items similar to those used by the NCVS. The CDC survey found that about 16 percent of American women and 5 percent of men had been stalked in their lifetimes (Black et al. 2011). These figures translated to about 19 million women and almost 6 million men. A similar gender difference was found in stalking in just the past year: 4.3 percent of women compared to 1.3 percent of men.

Combining all these figures, it seems safe to say that women are about three times as likely as men to be stalked. If so, stalking is yet another crime that is gendered to women's distinct disadvantage.

Stalking is also fairly common in college and university settings. A national survey of 4,500 college women found that slightly more than 13 percent of these students, who were surveyed during the spring semester, reported being stalked at least once since the beginning of the academic year about seven months earlier (Fisher et al. 2002). Four of every five stalking victims knew their offender, but they reported less than one-fifth of their stalking incidents to campus security or local police.

Another study of college students focused just on *cyberstalking*, a specific form of stalking involving electronic devices and/or the use of social media and other aspects of the Internet. The authors studied the prevalence of cyberstalking among a random sample of 974 students at a large Midwestern university (Reyns et al. 2012). Almost 41 percent of the students reported having ever been cyberstalked. Here again a gender difference emerged: 46 percent of female students had been cyberstalked, compared to 32 percent of male students. Another, though slight, gender difference existed in cyberstalking offending: 7 percent of male students admitted they had cyberstalked someone, compared to 4 percent of female students. The authors called for replications of their study at other colleges and universities to determine the amount of cyberstalking at campuses in general.

Whatever form it takes, stalking can last for many months and may produce anxiety, sleeplessness, and psychological trauma (Ornstein and Rickne 2013). Besides the fear they often feel, victims also perceive that they have little or no control over what happens and that the criminal justice system offers little help. An important question about stalking is how often it actually results in a physical attack on the victim. Although more research is needed, it is estimated that 30 to 40 percent of stalking victims are eventually attacked, with this risk being the highest for stalking by an intimate or ex-intimate (Mullen and Pathé 2002). In 15 percent of all stalking incidents reported in the national college women survey, the offender threatened the victim, attempted to harm her, or actually harmed her (Fisher et al. 2002).

▶ Reducing Violence Against Women

Along with crime rates generally, IPV against women has decreased dramatically since the early 1990s. The IPV rate for women was 16.1 per 1,000 in 1995 but only about one-third of that, 5.9, in 2010 (Catalano 2012a). Experts attribute this decline to greater awareness of such violence, to improved services for battered and raped women, and to improved policing, despite the problems that still exist in these areas. Although the decline in IPV is welcome, several policies and measures would help reduce it even further.

If violence against women is a consequence of gender inequality, to reduce it we must first reduce male dominance. As Melanie Randall and Lori Haskell (1995:27) put it, "Understanding the causes and context of sexual [and physical] violence in women's lives, and examining how and why it continues to happen on a massive scale, means calling into question the organization of sexual inequality in our society." Similarly, if economic inequality precipitates violence against women, then efforts to reduce poverty should also reduce violence against women. Reducing male dominance and economic inequality are, of course, easier said than done. But unless these underlying causes are addressed, rape and battering will surely continue.

A related solution focuses on the nature of masculinity. As Chapter 10 stressed, the violent nature of masculinity underlies much violent crime. If men in the United States and elsewhere learn to be violent, it is no surprise that they commit violence against women as well as against men. To reduce violence against women, we must begin to change the way we raise our boys.

In another area, one of the major accomplishments of the women's movement has been the establishment of rape crisis centers and battered women's shelters. These have been an invaluable aid to women who have been raped and/or battered. There is a need for even more crisis centers and shelters in urban and rural areas alike. To this end, more money should be spent to expand the network of existing rape crisis centers and battered women's shelters.

One final possible solution to violence against women lies in the criminal justice system. Compared to forty years ago, police, prosecutors, and judges are more likely to view rape/sexual assault and domestic violence as real crimes, not just as private matters in which the woman is to blame. That said, many of these legal professionals still subscribe to the myths discussed earlier (Alderden and Ullman 2012). Efforts to educate criminal justice officials on the true nature of intimate violence continue to be needed, as are efforts involving collaboration between criminal justice officials and community groups (Visher et al. 2008).

Other problems include the fact that women who are raped and battered often face a difficult time if they choose to bring charges. If they testify on the witness stand, defense attorneys often question their character and try to vigorously suggest that they share the blame for their victimization. More women might bring charges if this line of questioning were limited or prohibited.

Recognizing this, just about all states now have *rape-shield* laws that restrict the use of a woman's sexual history in rape cases. However, the degree of this restriction varies from state to state. Some states prohibit any such evidence unless it concerns a prior sexual relationship between the defendant and his accuser, whereas other states allow this evidence if the judge decides it is relevant. Many states allow evidence of a woman's sexual history if it might show that sexual activity with a third person accounted for any semen that was found. All states permit evidence of a sexual history with the defendant.

Arresting Batterers: Deterrence or Escalation?

Does arresting domestic violence offenders make it more or less likely that they will batter again? The answer to this question is important for both theoretical and practical reasons. Theoretically, it addresses the more general issue of the degree to which arrest, prosecution, and punishment deter criminal behavior. Practically, it holds important implications for how we can best protect battered women. If arresting batterers does indeed help keep them from battering again, as deterrence theory would predict, then batterers should be routinely arrested. However, if arrest increases the chances for future battering, as labeling theory might predict, then arresting batterers may put battered women even more at risk. What does the research say?

In a widely cited investigation of this issue in Minneapolis in the early 1980s, the government sponsored a study in which police randomly did one of the following when called to the scene of a battering: (1) arrested the batterer, (2) separated him from his wife or partner for 8 hours, or (3) advised the batterer as the officer saw fit, but did not arrest or separate him. Researchers then compared the battering recidivism (repeat offending) rate in the three groups. They found that arrest produced the lowest recidivism rate in the six months after the police were called (Sherman and Berk 1984). The finding that arrest worked prompted many jurisdictions across the country to begin arresting battering suspects routinely, even when their victims did not want an arrest to occur (Sherman and Cohn 1989).

However, the Minneapolis experiment suffered from methodological problems that cast doubt on its conclusions (Sherman 1992). For example, its measurement of recidivism neglected the seriousness of repeat offending in terms of injury and hospitalization. In another problem, it examined recidivism only for the six-month follow-up period. It is possible that arrest may reduce recidivism during this period, but increase it beyond this period. Further, because Minneapolis differs from other cities in its racial composition and other factors, its results were not necessarily generalizable to other locations.

These concerns led the government to sponsor several replication experiments in other cities: Charlotte, North Carolina, Colorado Springs, Colorado, Miami, Milwaukee, and Omaha, Nebraska (Sherman 1992). In two of the cities, arrest generally reduced future battering, but in the other three cities, arrest often increased battering after first decreasing it. The effects of arrest depended to a large extent on certain offender characteristics. In three of the cities, arrest reduced recidivism by employed offenders, but increased it by unemployed offenders. In one city, arrest increased recidivism by unmarried offenders, but did not increase it among married offenders.

Lawrence W. Sherman (1992), the primary architect of the Minneapolis study, noted that the equivocal results of the replication studies leave police and other officials with some major policy dilemmas. Because arrest apparently increases battering in some cities but reduces it in others, we cannot tell whether a city will experience an increase or a decrease. As Sherman observed, "Cities that do not adopt an arrest policy may pass up an opportunity to help the victims of domestic violence. But cities that do adopt arrest policies—or have them imposed by state law—may catalyze more domestic violence than would otherwise occur" (p. 19).

Further, because arrest may increase battering by unemployed men but reduce it among employed men, mandatory arrest policies may protect women whose husbands or partners work, but harm those whose husbands or partners do not work. As Sherman noted, "Even in cities where arrest reduces domestic violence overall, as an unintended side effect it may increase violence against the poorest victims" (p. 19). Another dilemma arises from the finding in some cities that arrest reduces battering in the short term, but increases it in the long term. With such evidence in mind, it becomes difficult to know whether arrest would do more harm than good.

Mandatory arrest policies raise other issues as well (Chesney-Lind 2002; Humphries 2002). First, because these policies increase the number of arrests for domestic violence, they can be very costly in terms of prosecutorial and court resources. This effect can undermine the intent of mandatory arrest. For example, after domestic violence prosecutions increased in Milwaukee during the mid-1990s, such cases took much longer to process and convictions for domestic violence decreased, as did victims' satisfaction with the handling and outcome of their cases. The researchers who uncovered these unintended effects concluded, "Good intentions do not always result in good public policy. Arresting more batterers does not necessarily result in more prosecutions" (Davis et al. 2003:280).

Second, mandatory arrest policies lead to more women being arrested for domestic violence even though their violence is much less serious than men's violence. Women's arrests may trigger child-custody actions and other difficulties. Third, mandatory arrest, as we have seen, may put some women in more danger. Fourth, mandatory arrest deprives victims of any role in the decision to arrest even though they may have good reasons for not desiring an arrest: It might put them more at risk for future battering, for example, or affect their family's financial stability. For his part, Sherman (1992) concluded from all the evidence that mandatory arrest laws should be repealed where they now exist, especially in locations with high unemployment rates.

Kathleen J. Ferraro (1995) believes that arrest helps define battering as a real crime, but she also fears that police will enforce mandatory arrest policies more against poor people and people of color than against wealthy whites. Although arrest may be needed, she said, to help women in great danger, battering and other violence against women will be reduced only to the extent that the patriarchy underlying these crimes is also reduced. The criminal justice system may deal with individual batterers, but more will take their place as long as patriarchy continues to exist.

A recent study analyzed the arrest issue with NCVS data. It found that arrest did not reduce repeated domestic violence, but it also found that victims' reporting of domestic violence to the police did reduce repeated violence. The researchers concluded that "the best policies for deterrence will be those that encourage victims and third parties to report violence by intimate partners to the police" (Felson et al. 2005:563). As should be clear, the appropriate legal handling of batterers will remain an important issue for some time to come.

Review and Discuss

Do you think men who abuse their female partners should always be arrested? Why or why not?

▶ Conclusion

This chapter continued the Chapter 10 emphases on the huge amount of violence by nonstrangers, on the inequality lying at the heart of much of this violence, and on the psychological normality of the offenders who commit violence. As long as the structural and cultural forces responsible for violence, including violence against women, continue to exist, the crimes resulting from them will continue as well.

Violence against women is an international problem that manifests itself in the United States through rape, battering, and other behaviors. Although it is true that most men do not rape and batter, it is also true that rape and battering are two of the most dire consequences of patriarchy and gender inequality. It might not be too much of an exaggeration to say that men who do rape and batter are fulfilling, in an extreme and terrible way, certain notions of masculinity. We certainly must hold individual men responsible for their violence against women, but at the same time we must also seek to reduce gender inequality and change the norms of masculinity if we want to reduce this violence. Because women have much more to fear from men they know than from men who are strangers, it is not enough to focus on making the streets safer for women. The problem goes far beyond popular conceptions of strangers lurking in alleyways.

It is time now to leave interpersonal violence to turn to property crime. We will return to the issue of violence in later chapters on white-collar crime, where we discuss corporate violence, and on political crime, where we examine political violence. These chapters will show that violence takes many forms and is even more common than this and the previous chapter indicated.

Summary

1. Violence against women is an international problem in poor and wealthy nations alike. Human rights organizations estimate that one-third of women worldwide have been sexually or physically abused. Other forms of violence against women include murder, torture, genital mutilation, and involuntary sterilization.

2. Rape and battering are two common crimes within the United States. Various studies estimate that 20 to 30 percent of U.S. women will be raped or sexually assaulted at least once in their lifetime and that the same proportion of women will be physically assaulted by a husband or intimate partner.

3. Rape and battering seem more common among people who are young adults and who are poor or near-poor. The evidence on racial or ethnic differences in rape and battering is inconsistent, but substantial differences do not seem to exist. If they do exist, they are likely due to the greater poverty and other criminogenic circumstances in which people of color are more likely than non-Latino whites to live.

4. A sociological understanding of rape and battering emphasizes gender and economic inequality. Cultural myths also matter and include such ideas as a woman "asking" to be raped or a woman not leaving her batterer because his behavior is not that bad.

5. One of the most heated controversies in the study of domestic violence is the issue of battered males. The best evidence indicates that women are far more likely than men to be battered.

6. A study in the early 1980s in Minneapolis suggested that the mandatory arrest of batterers would reduce battering. Replications of this study suggested that the issue is much more complex, and it is not clear whether mandatory arrest overall helps battered women to be safer or less safe.

Key Terms

battering 222
cultural myths 230
domestic violence 222
dowry deaths 221

femicide 222
genital mutilation 221
male dominance 229
patriarchy 229

rape 222
sexual assault 222
stalking 234

What Would You Do?

1. Your friend Susan went to a movie with a guy she had met in one of her classes. Afterward they went out to get a bite to eat and then he took her back to her dorm room. She invited him in and they began to kiss, when suddenly he forced himself on her, threatened her with bodily harm if she screamed, and raped her. Paralyzed with fear, she kept quiet and did not fight back. The next morning she tells you what happened. She wonders what she might have done to provoke him, and she also fears that no one will believe her story. What do you advise her to do or not to do? Why?

2. Suppose one of your neighbors, a good friend, confesses that her husband recently hit her because she was late putting dinner on the table. She says this was "only the second time" that he had hit her and urges you not to say or do anything about it. Although you want to respect your friend's wishes, you also worry about her safety. What do you do?

Socialstock / SuperStock

12 Property Crime and Fraud

- -

Crime in the News

Even a police officer's house may not be safe. The headline in May 2013 said it all: "Burglars Steal Police Officer's Gun." On a Saturday night, two people allegedly broke into the officer's home in the central Iowa town of State Center and stole his handgun and other property. The police later arrested two suspects on several charges of theft, burglary, and possession of stolen property.

Source: Alexander 2013.

- -

A s this news story reminds us, property crime can happen anywhere and to anyone. Legendary folk singer Woody Guthrie used to sing that some people rob you with a gun, while others rob you with a fountain pen. As his words imply, crimes for economic gain occur in different ways. The next two chapters discuss these crimes. We look at property crime and several types of fraud in this chapter and at white-collar crime and organized crime in the next chapter. Although these types of crime differ greatly, they all aim to improve the offender's financial status. Most property criminals are not as desperate as the proverbial parent who steals bread to feed a starving child, but they are still fairly poor. In contrast, white-collar criminals are often wealthy, with their crimes smacking more of greed. To the extent that this is true, the motivation of white-collar criminals is perhaps more shameful than that of property criminals. As we will see, white-collar criminals also cause more financial loss, injury, and death than do property criminals.

Nevertheless, as Chapter 2 pointed out, the public fears property crime far more than white-collar crime. There is no doubt that property crime is very costly. The FBI estimates that almost $16 billion in property is stolen annually, including cash, jewelry, clothing and furs, motor vehicles, office equipment, televisions and stereos, firearms, household goods, and livestock (Federal Bureau of Investigation 2012). The National Crime Victimization Survey (NCVS) estimates that property crime costs the nation more than $16 billion annually in total economic loss (property loss, medical expenses, time lost from work) (Maston 2011). By any measure, property crime is a serious problem. We thus need to understand the causes and dynamics of the many types of property crime that exist.

▶ Defining Property Crime

There are many types of property crime. The FBI classifies four types—burglary, larceny–theft, motor vehicle theft, and arson—as Part I offenses and several others as Part II offenses. Most of this chapter's discussion focuses on the Part I offenses. The following definitions come from the Uniform Crime Reports (UCR).

Burglary is attempted or completed "unlawful entry of a structure to commit a felony or a theft." Most burglarized structures are homes and businesses.

Larceny–theft (hereafter *larceny*) is attempted or completed "unlawful taking, carrying, leading, or riding away of property from the possession or constructive possession of another." Larceny's key feature is that it involves stealth, but does not involve force, the threat of force, or deception. It is a miscellaneous category that includes such behaviors as shoplifting, pickpocketing, purse snatching, the theft of contents from autos, and bicycle theft, but it excludes property crimes involving deception, such as embezzlement, fraud, and forgery.

Burglary, larceny, and *robbery* (see Chapter 10) all involve theft. How something is stolen determines what kind of crime is committed. For example, if someone stops you at gunpoint on a street and demands your purse, wallet, or any jewelry you might be wearing, this is a robbery because it involves the use or threat of physical force. The involvement of physical force in robbery classifies it as a violent crime even though it is committed for economic gain. If someone runs down the street and grabs your purse or snatches a gold chain from your neck before you realize what is happening and then runs away, this is larceny. If he pickpockets your wallet, it is also larceny.

If someone steals an object from a store while the store is open for business, this is larceny (shoplifting) because the person had the right to be in the store. If the offender breaks into the store at night and steals the same object, it is a burglary. If someone breaks into your house and steals an object, this is also a burglary. If you invite someone into your house and he or she steals the same object, it is larceny. If you answer the doorbell and someone holds you up at gunpoint, it is a robbery. In one other area of confusion, if someone steals your car's hubcaps, CD player, or cell phone, this is larceny. But if the offender takes the whole car, it is motor vehicle theft.

To return to our definitions, *motor vehicle theft* is, as the name implies, the attempted or completed theft of a motor vehicle. Such vehicles include cars, trucks, buses, snowmobiles, and motorcycles, but exclude boats, farming equipment, airplanes, and construction equipment. About 80 percent of all motor vehicle thefts involve cars, including minivans and SUVs.

Arson, the final Part I property crime, is "any willful or malicious burning or attempt to burn, with or without intent to defraud, a dwelling house, public building, motor vehicle or aircraft, personal property of another, etc." To be counted by the UCR, arson must definitely be proved. Fires of unknown or suspicious origins are not counted. The FBI did not classify arson as a Part I crime until 1979. The reporting system is still not fully in place, as many law enforcement agencies do not submit arson reports for all twelve months or are spotty when they do report it. For these reasons, the FBI does not include arson in its estimate of the annual crime rate.

The UCR's Part II offenses include several other property crimes, all of which involve deception of some kind. *Forgery* and *counterfeiting* involve "making, altering, uttering, or possessing, with intent to defraud, anything false in the semblance of that which is true." *Fraud* involves "obtaining money or property by false pretenses." *Buying, receiving, and possessing stolen property* is another Part II property offense and is just what its name implies. We will take a further look at forgery, fraud, and stolen property offenses later. A final Part II property offense is *embezzlement*, defined as the "misappropriation or misapplication of money or property entrusted to one's care, custody, or control." This crime is examined in Chapter 13.

▶ Extent of Property Crime

Although the UCR and NCVS provide different estimates of the amount of property crime, they both indicate how common it is. Table 12–1 reports UCR and NCVS estimates for burglary, larceny, and motor vehicle theft. With so much property crime, it is not surprising that the risk of becoming a property-crime victim adds up over time. The NCVS estimates that 72 percent of U.S. households will suffer at least one burglary over a twenty-year period (Koppel 1987).

TABLE 12-1 Number of Property Crimes, UCR and NCVS Data, 2011

TYPE OF CRIME	UCR	NCVS
Burglary	2,188,005	3,613,190
Larceny–theft	6,159,795	12,825,510
Motor vehicle theft	715,373	628,070
Total crimes	9,063,173	17,066,770

Source: Maguire 2013.

Although the UCR and NCVS report somewhat different pictures of trends in property crime, they both agree that this form of crime has declined greatly since the early 1990s. Property crime has declined not only in the United States, but also in most other Western nations (Farrell et al. 2011). What accounts for this decline? No one is sure, but experts offer several possible reasons: *target hardening* (discussed later), involving the greater use of alarm systems and other measures; less cash being carried because of the greater use of credit and debit cards; and the fact that people probably stay at home more to watch cable TV and videos (Farrell et al. 2011; Felson and Boba 2010). Some of the possible reasons for the more general crime decline since the early 1990s, such as demographic changes in the population, may also apply to U.S. property crime (see Chapter 3).

▶ Patterning of Property Crime

Like violent crime, property crime in the United States is patterned both geographically and demographically. Let's look first at geographical differences and then at demographic (gender, race, class, age) differences.

Figure 12–1 ■ displays regional differences in UCR property crime for the United States; property crime is highest in the South and lowest in the Northeast. Figure 12–2 ■ displays UCR urban–rural differences in property crime. Like violent crime, property crime is lowest in rural areas.

Turning to demographic differences, property crime tends to be a young person's offense; people under 25 years of age account for 51 percent of all property-crime arrests. Self-report data from high school seniors indicate that various kinds of theft and property damage are very common during adolescence (see Table 12–2).

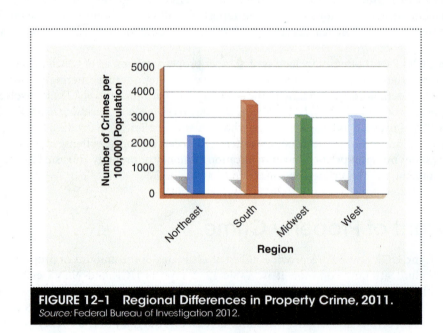

FIGURE 12-1   Regional Differences in Property Crime, 2011.
Source: Federal Bureau of Investigation 2012.

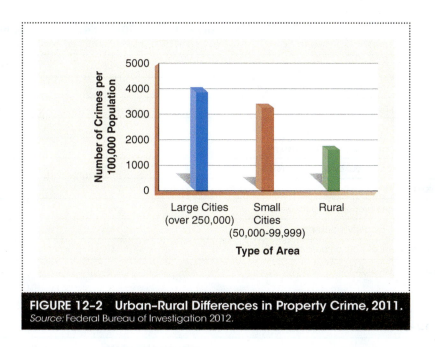

FIGURE 12-2 Urban–Rural Differences in Property Crime, 2011.
Source: Federal Bureau of Investigation 2012.

As Table 12–2 indicates, male high school seniors are more likely than female seniors to commit the various property crimes. This gender difference also appears in UCR arrest data for all ages: males account for about 84 percent of all burglary arrests, 82 percent of all motor vehicle theft arrests, 82 percent of all arson arrests, and 57 percent of all larceny arrests (2011 figures). The male proportion of larceny arrests is lower than for the other crimes because females are more involved in one type of larceny, shoplifting, than they are in other crimes. As the high school survey reported in Table 12–2 indicates, however, more males than females shoplift. Male shoplifters steal more items, and also more expensive items, than do female shoplifters and are also more likely to be professional shoplifters instead of amateurs (discussed later).

According to arrest data, the typical property offender is white, although African-Americans are disproportionately represented (see Table 12–3). Although the UCR and NCVS do not report the social class backgrounds of property offenders, it is safe to say that the typical property offender comes from a low-income background.

▶ Social Organization of Property Crime

A rich literature describes the social organization of property crime. Social organization refers to the roles that different property criminals play and the social networks that support their criminal ways. This literature makes a useful distinction between amateur theft and professional theft (Hepburn 1984) similar to that for robbery (see Chapter 10). *Amateur* criminals (also called *opportunistic* or *occasional* criminals) comprise the vast majority of property offenders. Most are in their teens or early twenties; they are unskilled and commit crimes when the opportunity arises, rather than planning them far in advance. In another defining feature, their illegal profit from any one property crime is relatively small.

▼ Although men are more likely than women to shoplift, store personnel monitor female customers' behavior more closely because they believe women are more likely than men to shoplift.

AP Photo/Joseph Kaczmarek

TABLE 12-2 Proportion of High School Seniors (Class of 2011) Reporting Involvement in Various Property Crimes in Last 12 Months (percentage saying at least once)

ACTIVITY	MALE	FEMALE
Taken something from a store without paying for it	25	22
Taken something not belonging to you worth under $50	31	19
Taken something not belonging to you worth over $50	12	4
Taken a car without owner's (nonrelative) permission	5	3
Taken part of a car without owner's permission	5	2
Gone into a house or building when not supposed to be there	29	18
Set fire to someone's property on purpose	4	1
Damaged school property on purpose	16	6
Damaged property at work on purpose	6	1

Source: Johnston et al. 2013.

TABLE 12-3 Race and Property Crime Arrests, 2011 (Percentage of All Arrests)

CRIME	AFRICAN-AMERICAN	WHITE
Burglary	32	67
Larceny–theft	29	69
Motor vehicle theft	34	64
Arson	21	72

Source: Federal Bureau of Investigation 2012.

In contrast, professional property criminals are older and more skilled at what they do. They plan their offenses carefully, and the illegal profit from each crime can be high. Often they learn their craft from other professional criminals who serve as tutors by introducing them into the world of professional crime. Professional property criminals excite our imagination. Cat burglars and other professional thieves have been the subject of many movies and books over the years. We treat them somewhat like Robin Hood: Although intellectually we condemn their crimes, we secretly admire their brave daring, perhaps because of our own longing for economic success.

The amateur–professional distinction helps us understand the different types of offenders committing the different property crimes. In a classic study of shoplifting, Mary Owen Cameron (1964) categorized shoplifters as snitches and boosters. Most shoplifters are snitches, or amateurs, who steal merchandise of little value that they keep for themselves. Boosters, some 10 percent of all shoplifters, are skilled professionals who sell their stolen goods to fences or pawnshops.

Motor vehicle theft exhibits a similar distinction between amateur and professional offenders. Most analysts divide motor vehicle theft into two kinds, joyriding or professional theft (Clarke and Harris 1992). Joyriding is committed primarily by teenage boys working in groups as amateur motor vehicle thieves. As their name implies, these joy riders steal cars for a lark, take them for a short ride, and then dump them, often before the owner even knows the car is gone. They target unlocked cars with the key in the ignition or else crudely break into locked cars and hot-wire them. Because they abandon their stolen vehicles so soon, it is difficult to arrest them. Professional car thieves are older and more skilled. They can get into very secure vehicles, drive them away, and quickly dismantle them for parts in *chop shops* or otherwise deposit them into a very sophisticated auto resale market where they will be sold for a tidy profit. These professionals are so skilled that they are rarely discovered and arrested.

How does the distinction between amateur and professional criminals help us understand the nature and dynamics of property crime?

Burglary

The literature on the social organization of burglary is especially extensive. Although the image of a solitary professional cat burglar crawling up buildings and breaking into heavily guarded structures has been the stuff of many movies and books, most burglars are not nearly so skillful or specialized. They enter buildings through unlocked doors or windows or break into them in crude, unskilled ways. Most burglars do not specialize in burglary and instead commit other crimes over the long haul, but some do specialize in burglary for short periods (Wright and Decker 1994). Unlike the legendary cat burglar, many burglars work in groups of two or more, evidently feeling there is safety in numbers.

Beyond these generalizations, burglars differ in other ways. Mike Maguire (1982) identified three categories of burglars: low level, middle range, and high level. *Low-level* burglars are adolescents and young adults who get together to commit spontaneous, unskilled burglaries as a lark. They typically spend only a few minutes in the residence they enter and steal only small amounts of money and videos and other items popular in their age group. They do not think of themselves as criminals and lack access to fences and other members of what might be called the *burglary support system*.

Middle-range burglars tend to be older than low-level ones and more apt to spend time searching for attractive targets. They tend to act alone and often choose suburban areas featuring wealthy, isolated homes. They are more skilled than low-level burglars and more able to defeat home security systems. Middle-range burglars spend a fair amount of time in the residences they enter in order to find the most valuable items.

High-level burglars are the most skilled of all and tend to act in groups of two or more. They spend a lot of time planning their burglaries and are ready and willing to travel long distances to their targets. They also plan how to dispose of the items they steal through fences and other parts of the burglary support network. Neal Shover (1991) likened their burglary method to "military commando operations."

To determine how the experiences of female and male burglars differ, Scott Decker and associates (1993) interviewed 105 urban residential burglars, 18 women and 87 men, and found some interesting similarities and differences. Female and male burglars were similar in their extent of drug and alcohol use and in their degree of specialization in burglary. Compared with the male burglars, however, female burglars began their crimes at a later age, were more likely to commit burglaries with other burglars, and were less likely to have been convicted of burglary. Additional studies of women burglars are needed to determine how they compare to male burglars and to yield a more complete understanding of the genesis and dynamics of burglary overall.

Tipsters and Fences

The burglary literature also describes the support system for burglars involving tipsters and fences (Shover 1973). *Tipsters* let burglars know of safe, attractive targets. They come not only from the criminal world, but also from legitimate occupations: Unscrupulous attorneys, repair people, police, bartenders, and the like, all tip off burglars about residences and businesses ripe for the taking. No one really knows how many tipsters exist or how much of a role they play in burglary, but it is safe to say that they often help middle-range and high-level burglars.

If you were to enter a home and steal an expensive stereo system and valuable jewels and silver, what would you do with these items? You might keep the stereo, but want to get rid of the jewels and silver in return for money. How would you dispose of the latter items? You cannot just walk into a jewelry store and say you found the items. It might also sound suspicious if you say they were in your family and you need money to pay your bills. As these problems suggest, burglars often need *fences* to dispose of their stolen goods and give them money in return

© Jeff Greenberg / PhotoEdit

▲ Burglars tend to target homes that are less visible to possible scrutiny by neighbors and people passing by.

(Cromwell and McElrath 1994). Fences sell the stolen goods to customers, many of whom are in legitimate occupations and recognize the shady nature of their transaction, but still want to buy the stolen goods for much less than they would otherwise cost. The world of professional burglars thus cannot exist without the help of otherwise law-abiding citizens.

Darrell J. Steffensmeier (1986) sees fences as working "in the shadow of two worlds," to quote the subtitle of his book on fencing. One world is that of any legitimate businessperson, whose activities a fence's functions resemble. Financial success in both fencing and legitimate business depends on marketing and management skills and on the ability to be reliable and punctual. As noted, fences also deal with law-abiding customers, further placing them in the world of legitimate business. The other world is the criminal world. The fence not only engages in illegal activity, but also interacts with many types of criminals.

Decision Making in Burglary

Another topic in the burglary literature is burglars' decision-making processes. Studies try to get into the minds of burglars to see how and why they decide whether to commit a crime and how they proceed once they decide to commit it. Most studies draw on in-depth interviews of small samples of burglars (Cromwell 1994; Tunnell 2006; Wright et al. 1995).

As Chapter 5 noted, these studies disagree on whether burglars pay much attention to their risk of arrest and imprisonment. On other points there is some consensus. In choosing a geographic area in which to commit a crime, burglars (and also other property criminals) rely on their knowledge of the area from their noncriminal activities. Once they choose an area, they tend to select homes less visible to neighbors and homes they believe to be unoccupied. As the police and news media remind us, burglars look for signs, including accumulating mail and newspapers, that people are away on vacation. Some burglars even scan newspaper obituaries to determine when homes will be empty while families attend funeral services. Other homes at risk are those whose residents are away at work or school for long periods.

▶ Property-Crime Victimization: Costs and Circumstances

To understand property crime further, we now examine its costs and the circumstances under which it occurs. The costs of property crime are both economic and psychological and are especially high for burglary. Homeowners and businesses spend tens of millions of dollars annually on elaborate security systems, firearms, and other items to prevent burglaries and protect themselves from intruders. Although burglary rates have been declining, this spending continues apace, and burglary remains very costly. The UCR estimates that burglary victims lost $4.2 billion in 2011, with an average loss per burglary of $2,185. Almost three-fourths of reported burglaries are residential; the remainder are commercial.

Although burglary typically does not threaten its victims with injury, it still violates their privacy and sense of "personal space." Accordingly, about one-third of burglary victims become depressed, lose sleep, or suffer other similar problems. Female burglary victims are more likely than male victims to report being afraid and upset, whereas male victims are more apt to report being angry or annoyed. Women burglary victims who live alone are the most likely to feel

TABLE 12-4 Average Property Loss by Type of Larceny, UCR, 2011

TYPE OF LARCENY	AMOUNT LOST
Thefts from buildings	$1,443
Motor vehicle contents	818
Pocket picking	539
Purse snatching	412
Coin machines	368
Bicycles	367
Shoplifting	199

Source: Federal Bureau of Investigation 2012.

afraid, evidently reflecting their concern over their physical vulnerability and the possibility of rape (Burt and Katz 1984; Shover 1991).

The NCVS has compiled some interesting figures on residential burglaries (Maston and Klaus 2010). Burglaries are slightly more likely to occur during the day than at night. Burglary victimization rates are much higher for poorer households; those with annual incomes under $7,500 are three times more likely to be burglarized than those with incomes of at least $75,000. In about one-fourth of all burglaries, a household member was at home, either asleep or doing various activities; another one-fourth were at work or on the way to or from work. Half of all burglaries are reported to the police, although this figure depends on the value of cash and/or property that was stolen: 84 percent of burglaries involving an economic loss of at least $1,000 are reported to the police, compared to less than 25 percent of burglaries with loss less than $100. When burglaries are reported, the police fail to visit the burglarized home 11 percent of the time; when they do visit the home, they arrive within ten minutes about one-third of the time, and within an hour three-fourths of the time.

Other property crimes are also costly. Turning to larceny, the UCR estimates that each 2011 larceny cost its victim an average $987, for a total loss from reported larcenies of almost $5.4 billion. Because so many larcenies are not reported, the true property loss is undoubtedly much higher. As Table 12–4 indicates, the amount per larceny varies widely by the type of larceny.

Motor vehicle theft also adds up to billions of dollars annually. The FBI reported the value of motor vehicles stolen in 2011 was almost $4 billion, or $6,089 per vehicle. According to the NCVS, most motor vehicle theft occurs at night and either near the victim's home or in a parking lot or garage. In recent years, motor vehicle theft has become a worldwide phenomenon that the International Focus box discusses in more detail.

The average arson in 2011 cost $13,196 in property loss, for a total loss of $600 million. About 46 percent of all arson involved buildings; 24 percent involved motor vehicles and other mobile property; and 30 percent involved other types of property, such as crops and fences.

▶ Explaining Property Crime

Explanations of property crime echo theories discussed in previous chapters. We first review several explanations of property crime generally and then turn to explanations of specific crimes.

Cultural Emphasis on Economic Success

An important reason for property crime lies in the U.S. culture, which emphasizes economic success above other goals. As the discussion of anomie and the American dream in Chapter 7 indicated, the high emphasis on economic success underlies economic crime. The poor want more because they have not fulfilled the American dream; the rich want more because one can never have enough in a society that stresses economic success.

▲ Many motor vehicle thefts involve young men who take cars for quick, thrilling joyrides. Because of the speed involved, sometimes these joyrides end in tragedy.

To explore this argument further, consider auto theft. Both as a status symbol and as a vehicle for transportation, cars are a vital part of our culture and economy. Auto manufacturers spend billions of dollars annually on advertising, with many of their ads targeting young men and stressing the excitement and even the sex appeal of owning a car. Against this backdrop, if you are a young man who cannot afford a car, you might well be tempted to steal one. With so many cars around, it is very easy to find one to steal. Given their advertisement-induced fascination with cars, many young men "borrow" them for a quick thrill (Kellett and Gross 2006). Other auto thieves are more economically motivated. Because cars are so expensive and have to be repaired so often, these thieves realize they can make a lot of money by stealing cars and either reselling them or dismantling them to sell their parts for repairs. For several reasons, then, auto theft is an inevitable property crime in our society.

Although this cultural emphasis seems to matter, it is also true that social class affects the way people break the law for economic gain. An important principle of criminology is that people have differential access to illegitimate means or, to put it another way, different opportunities for illegal gain (Cloward and Ohlin 1960). Poor people commit property crimes because they are not in a position to engage in complex financial schemes or to sell unsafe products. Wealthy people would not dream of breaking into a house or robbing someone on a street, but think nothing of defrauding the government, private citizens, and other parties in any number of ways.

Techniques of Neutralization

Chapter 8 noted that offenders engage in techniques of neutralization, or rationalizations, to justify their illegal behavior. Another underpinning of property crime is the rationalizations property offenders use: *A store or other business is ripping us off or charging us too much, so we will rip it off. Everyone else does it, so why not me? The business is so big and rich, it won't miss what I take.* Although most of us have not stolen a car or burglarized a home, many of us have done other things like shoplifting or taking items from hotels and motels, with many rationalizations for why our crimes are not really crimes.

Fencing

Rationalizations play an important role in fencing, as illustrated in Darrel J. Steffensmeier's (1986; 2005) account of the experiences of a fence he called Sam Goodman (an alias). Goodman was close to 60 years old when Steffensmeier met him in January 1980 while Sam was serving a three-year prison term for receiving stolen property. Sam denied he was a thief: "A thief is out there stealing, breaking into people's places. . . . A fence would not do that. A fence is just buying what the thief brings, he is not the one crawling in windows" (1986:238–239). Sam also thought his fencing did burglary victims little harm because most of them would have insurance pay for their losses, and he likened fencing to legitimate businesses. As Steffensmeier (1986:243) put it, "Sam is in his store every day of the week. He buys and sells things, waits on customers, transports merchandise, and advertises in the yellow pages."

Sam also emphasized that his work benefited many people. The Red Cross sent him victims of fires to pick out home furnishings, and he then billed the Red Cross for what they chose. At Christmas he gave church groups household goods for poor families and toys for children. He added that many legitimate businesses deceive their customers, citing funeral directors who persuade the bereaved to buy expensive caskets and building contractors who exaggerate the effectiveness of security systems. As Sam put it, "Your fence really isn't much more crooked than your average businessman, who are many times very shady" (p. 243).

In May 2012, federal authorities arrested 19 people in Kansas, New Jersey, and New York for allegedly smuggling stolen SUVs to West Africa. These arrests came on the heels of several dozen arrests earlier in the year for smuggling stolen motor vehicles abroad. Like so many things in the world today, motor vehicle theft is becoming globalized. Two international developments account for this increasing problem.

The first development is the rise of drug trafficking from Mexico and other nations south of the border into the United States. Of the ten urban areas with the highest amount of motor vehicle theft, seven are on or near the border with Mexico. Drug trafficking groups use the stolen vehicles to carry illicit drugs, weapons, and cash from drug sales into and out of the United States, and they also sell the stolen vehicles to help finance their drug trafficking.

The second development is the fall of the Soviet Union in 1991. This historic event freed the former Soviet nations to move toward capitalist economies. As they did so, they increased their demand for luxury cars and other vehicles, creating a market for vehicles stolen from other nations. Demand for imported stolen vehicles has also increased in other parts of the world, including the Middle East, parts of Africa, and China. The vehicles these nations receive come from the United States, western Europe, and Japan. The number of stolen vehicles that are exported to other nations is estimated to be 500,000 annually. About 200,000 come from the United States, 20,000 from Canada, and as many as 300,000 from western Europe.

Several groups ironically benefit from the massive exporting of stolen vehicles. Automobile insurance companies raise their rates to cover the loss of the vehicles and may increase their profits as a result. The companies that ship the stolen vehicles across oceans and other bodies of water also make a profit. Auto manufacturers also profit by selling new cars to the people whose vehicles were stolen. Finally, the economy of the nation from which a stolen vehicle is exported profits when the people responsible for the theft spend the illegal income they receive for their crime.

Certain "practical" conditions contribute to the exportation of stolen vehicles. First, many vehicles are driven across national borders each day, making it relatively easy to drive a stolen one across a border. Second, customs officials rarely examine the huge containers routinely carried on cargo ships. Third, many used cars are legally shipped from one nation to another, and stolen car rings are able to set up their activities as legitimate enterprises of this type. Fourth, the content and appearance of motor vehicle documents differ greatly from one nation to the next and are obviously written in different languages. These problems make it difficult for customs officials to know whether the documents are forged or changed. Fifth, officials in the countries receiving stolen vehicles are often corrupt and take bribes to look the other way. Sixth, motor vehicle theft is simply not a high priority for law-enforcement officials in the poor countries that receive stolen vehicles, because these nations face much more serious crime. For all these reasons, international trafficking in stolen vehicles is flourishing and shows no signs of abating.

Sources: Binagman 2010; Clarke and Brown 2003; Sherman 2012.

Review and Discuss

How does an understanding of techniques of neutralization help us understand the behavior and motivation of fences and other people involved in property crime?

Economic Deprivation and Unemployment

The explanation of property crime so far has highlighted cultural factors. Structural factors (see Chapter 7) also matter, as research links economic deprivation and urban living conditions to such crime (Kikuchi and Desmond 2010; Thompson and Uggen 2012). A related body of research examines the effects of unemployment on property crime by comparing areas or individuals with different unemployment rates (Andresen 2012; Phillips and Land 2012). Despite many reasons to expect a strong unemployment–property crime link, research findings are inconsistent. Some find the expected link, others do not, and some studies have even found higher unemployment related to less property crime. Methodological differences appear to account for these inconsistent findings. In particular, individual-level studies find a link more often than community studies do.

In a related puzzle, property crime does not always rise when the economy sours, which might ordinarily be expected, and often even declines. For example, and as noted earlier, property crime rates have declined since the early 1990s and have continued to decline even after the deep economic recession began in 2008. An explanation for this counter-intuitive trend comes from the routine activities and lifestyles literature (Felson and Boba 2010). Although unemployment may increase the motivation to commit property crime, it may also reduce the opportunities for property crime. For example, in areas and times of high unemployment, fewer people will be working or, because of their reduced incomes, vacationing, eating out, or engaging in other leisure activities. For these reasons, they will be more likely to be at home, ironically making their homes safer from burglars and themselves safer from robbers.

Complicating the issue, a recent study suggested that consumer sentiment about the economy might matter more for property crime than objective indicators such as the unemployment rate. Richard Rosenfeld and Robert Fornango (2007) found that property-crime rates between 1970 and 2003 rose when consumer sentiment as measured by the government was more pessimistic, and declined when sentiment was more optimistic. Drawing on this study and other recent research, Rosenfeld (2009:302) concluded, "Property crime rises during economic downturns and falls during recoveries."

Routine Activities and Social Process Factors

As the discussion of unemployment implied, the routine activities/lifestyles literature provides yet another explanation for property crime. Simply put, certain activities and lifestyles put people more at risk for burglary, larceny, and motor vehicle theft. For example, people whose homes are vacant for long periods because of work or vacationing are more apt to suffer burglaries, and those who often walk on crowded streets are more likely to become the victims of pickpockets or purse snatchers. Property crime rates are often higher when the weather is warm simply because more people are away from home, and, as just discussed, lower when unemployment is high because more people are staying home.

Social process factors such as learning and negative family and school influences also contribute to property crime. As Chapter 8 indicated, a large body of literature documents the effects of criminal peer influences, dysfunctional family environments, and negative school experiences on criminality, including property crime.

Property Crime for Thrills

In a novel formulation, Jack Katz (1988) argued that much violent and property crime is done for excitement and thrills. He described property offenses as sneaky thrill crimes that offenders commit because they are excited by the idea of stealing and by the prospect of obtaining objects they desire. Katz's view is both commended for calling attention to the importance of thrills and emotion for criminal behavior and criticized for overstating this importance (Hagan 1990; Turk 1991). Nevertheless, his theory helps explain why young males have especially high rates of property crime: they are more "seduced" than adults and women by objects that they want to steal, for example, motor vehicles (McCarthy 1995).

Importantly, Katz also found that, although socioeconomic status did not affect whether someone was *attracted* to an object he or she did not own, it did affect the likelihood of considering *stealing* the object. Whether people act illegally on their material seductions, then, may well depend on their social class. As Bill McCarthy (1995:533) put it, "People desire goods regardless of their structural conditions, whereas only those lacking (economic) opportunities are more willing to consider future theft if seduced."

A Look at Shoplifting

The several kinds of explanations just discussed—cultural emphasis on economic success, techniques of neutralization, routine activities, and sneaky thrills—all help explain why property crime occurs. A discussion of shoplifting will emphasize this point.

Shoplifting is very common. The high school survey reported in Table 12–2 indicated that almost one-fourth of seniors had shoplifted in the last year. It is estimated that 8 to 10 percent of all shoppers shoplift, that about $13 billion in merchandise is stolen annually, and that the number of shoplifting incidents each year falls between 225 million and 300 million (Grannis 2009; Hayes International 2009). Most shoplifters, even professional ones, would condemn anyone robbing a store cashier at gunpoint of $10 or $20, yet they rationalize their own behavior. If you have friends who have shoplifted, you might have heard some of these justifications: The store charges them too much, makes them wait in line too long, treats them impersonally, or is so big it won't miss the shoplifted items. Like Sam the fence, shoplifters see crime and deviance as something other people do, even though the estimated annual loss from shoplifting runs into the billions of dollars.

▲ Shoplifters rationalize their criminal behavior: The store charges them too much, makes them wait in line too long, treats them impersonally, or is so big it will not miss the shoplifted items.

Why else is shoplifting so common? For one reason, it is exciting, especially for the many adolescent shoplifters who act in groups of two or more to see what they can get away with. But cultural, gender, and social class forces also explain adolescent shoplifting. The teen subculture is so consumer oriented that youths feel pressured to steal items they cannot afford. This consumer subculture is a natural outcome of the cultural emphasis in the larger society on possessions and appearance. This emphasis leads girls to be especially interested in shoplifting cosmetics and clothes. For teens of both sexes, shoplifting stems from "the bombarding of young people with images of looks and goods attainable only with money many of them do not have" (Chesney-Lind and Sheldon 1992:44).

Routine activities theory also helps explain why shoplifting is so common (Dabney et al. 2004). One reason shoplifting rose in the 1960s was the rapid development of large department and discount stores and especially of shopping malls, which did not exist before the late 1950s and early 1960s. For obvious reasons, it is easier to shoplift in large stores and malls than in smaller establishments. Large stores and malls thus presented the combination of motivated offenders, attractive targets, and lack of guardianship that, as routine activities theory stresses, results in crime and victimization. The rise in shoplifting was both predictable and inevitable.

▶ Reducing Property Crime

Property crime has declined since the early 1970s, according to the NCVS. Popular efforts today to reduce property crime even further focus on the criminal justice system, on making it more difficult for property criminals to gain access to their targets, and on neighborhood watch groups.

The Criminal Justice System

Beginning in the 1970s, the United States began relying heavily on longer and more certain prison terms to reduce violent and property crime as the nation became "addicted to incarceration," as the title of one book put it (Pratt 2008). As noted earlier in this chapter and in Chapter 5, however, many property criminals do not weigh their chances of arrest and imprisonment as they decide whether to commit a crime or else commit a crime only when they think they will not be arrested. We also saw in Chapter 3 that only 18.6 percent of reported property crime is cleared by arrest. Because so much property crime is not reported to the police in the first place, the actual percentage of property crime that is cleared by arrest is much less than 18.6 percent. Because many property criminals tend not to think and act in a way that makes their crimes deterrable, and because so few are arrested anyway, efforts to reduce property crime by increasing prison terms hold little or no potential for success (Shover and Copes 2010). Certain proactive policing strategies might help, and Chapter 16 discusses those further.

Situational Prevention

Another popular response to property crime has been *situational prevention* strategies such as camera surveillance at street intersections, improved lighting, and requiring exact change on buses. Situational prevention occurs at both the individual and community levels. Michael Tonry (2009:8) says "there is no doubt that situational prevention methods . . . can reduce crime rates, especially for kinds of crime that are often committed impulsively."

Target Hardening

At the individual level, situational prevention especially focuses on burglary and motor vehicle theft and takes the form of target hardening: efforts to make residences and businesses more difficult to burglarize, and motor vehicles less vulnerable to theft of the vehicle and/or of its contents. These efforts include stronger locks, burglar alarms, and other home security measures, all of which can reduce burglaries; and alarm systems, keyless locks, and other devices to make it more difficult to break into vehicles and to drive them away.

Target hardening seems to work (Farrell et al. 2011; Lee and Wilson 2013). At the same time, it is difficult to know exactly how effective target hardening actually is. As one review put it, "the evidence has not always been compelling" (Bernasco 2009:185). For example, British data show that window locks and deadbolt locks on doors appear to lower the risk of burglary: Only 2.5 percent of households with these simple security measures are burglarized annually, compared to 22.5 percent of those without any locks (Felson and Clarke 2010). However, these households may differ in other respects that affect their burglary risk, making it difficult to draw any firm conclusions (Bernasco 2009).

Despite the inconsistent evidence, a growing consensus is that target hardening has indeed helped reduce property crime rates (Farrell et al. 2011). This is perhaps especially true for motor vehicle theft. As a recent review noted, "Vehicles are now more difficult to steal than ever before as people have begun to take proactive measures to protect their vehicles by purchasing alarms, clubs, and other security devices" (Cherbonneau and Wright 2009:214). Vehicles are also now being manufactured with sophisticated security systems and keyless entry systems. An additional target-hardening device is the electronic immobilizer, which is required on vehicles in Australia, Canada, and Europe and is becoming more common in the United States. This device involves a computer chip on the key that prevents thieves from jump-starting the vehicle. Evidence indicates that these vehicles indeed have a lower rate of theft than vehicles without the device. However, there is some evidence that thieves have simply switched to vehicles without the device and are finding ways to defeat it and steal the vehicle anyway. Ironically, increased security devices for vehicles may make vehicle theft more of a professional crime than it used to be, because the new measures often frustrate the efforts of joy riders to steal cars.

Two effective burglary deterrents are simply the presence of someone at home and a dog, both of which provide *guardianship*, to recall a key term from routine activities theory. As Paul Cromwell (1994:43) observed, "Large dogs represent a physical threat to the burglar, and small ones are often noisy, attracting attention to his or her activities." Active burglars interviewed by Cromwell named dogs as the second most effective burglary deterrent, or "no go" factor, topped only by the presence of someone at home. One burglar said, "I don't mess with no dogs. If they got dogs, I go someplace else" (p. 44). Supporting this point, a study of college students at nine campuses found that theft victimization was lower for those who owned dogs than for those without a dog (Mustaine and Tewksbury 1998). The Crime and Controversy box discusses the issue of attacks by dogs on property criminals and innocent citizens.

▼ One of the most effective deterrents to burglary is a dog. Large dogs pose physical threats to burglars, and small dogs may yap and attract attention.

Steve Barkan

Community Prevention

In addition to target hardening, situational prevention at the community level has also been used. This form of prevention focuses on streets and whole neighborhoods. Examples of community-level situational strategies include better street lighting, camera surveillance, and the reconfiguring of physical space to establish clearer sight lines. These measures have generally proven successful, although more research is needed to determine exactly how effective they are in reducing property crime (Eck and Guerette 2012).

Another form of community prevention also appears to be successful, and that is the establishment of neighborhood watch organizations (*neighborhood watch*). Although early studies questioned the effectiveness of neighborhood watch, a recent review of the research on this issue found a 16-percent drop in crime in areas where neighborhood watch was used compared to areas where it was not used (Bennett et al. 2006). The review's authors cautioned that most but not all of the studies they reviewed found this crime-reduction effect and said that more studies of neighborhood watch's effectiveness are needed. They also called for more research on the exact factors affecting whether a particular watch program is effective or ineffective.

Crime and Controversy VICIOUS DOGS AND PROPERTY CRIME

A dog can be a very good deterrent to burglary. One reason many people own a dog is to provide them some protection against burglars and other criminals and, in this way, to give themselves a feeling of security. For better or worse, many of the dogs that people own for protection are those with aggressive tendencies, such as a Doberman, Rottweiler, pit bull, or German shepherd. These dogs may provide excellent protection against burglars, but on occasion they have attacked innocent people without provocation and seriously injured or even killed them.

One question that arises from such tragic incidents is the dog owner's legal liability. Owners can be sued for harboring a dangerous dog, and homeowner insurance companies are increasingly charging larger premiums for homes in which dogs from certain breeds reside, or refusing to cover such homes altogether. But some dog owners have also been criminally prosecuted after their dog has attacked someone without provocation. In a case that won national media attention, a San Francisco resident, Diane Whipple, was mauled to death in 2001 by her neighbors' two large dogs, both Presa Canario, a breed known for its ferocity. The attack, which lasted several minutes, occurred as Whipple was returning home, and the dogs bolted from their apartment. Their owner tried to stop them but to no avail. She and her husband, both lawyers, were arrested and indicted with various homicide charges. The trial judge called their dogs "a canine time bomb that would at some inevitable point explode with disastrous consequences."

Both defendants were found guilty of involuntary manslaughter and sentenced to the maximum four years in state prison allowed under state law.

In a more recent incident, a dog owner in Everett, WA, was charged with a felony—owning a dangerous dog—in July 2013 because her pit bull terrier and boxer attacked five people a year earlier after escaping from their yard and going on a rampage. A police officer killed the pit bull, and the boxer was captured and eventually euthanized. The owner had previously received a notice from the police warning her that the dogs were potentially dangerous.

What if a dog attacks a burglar? Although most jurisdictions have statutes that stipulate legal punishment for vicious, unprovoked attacks by dogs and that allow for these dogs to be put to death, these statutes typically exclude attacks on intruders or other people posing a threat to the dog's owner. For example, New York State law stipulates that a dog owner may be found guilty of a Class A misdemeanor if the dog "shall without justification kill or cause the death of any person who is peaceably conducting himself or herself in any place where he or she may lawfully be." However, the law exempts owners whose dog "was coming to the aid or defense of a person during the commission or attempted commission of a murder, robbery, burglary, arson, (or) rape in the first degree."

Sources: Animal Legal & Historical Center 2013; Associated Press 2004; Cantley and U'Sellis 2013; Hefley 2013.

In sum, certain forms of situational prevention appear to help reduce property crime. Beyond these efforts, what else can we do? A sociological prescription for crime reduction would involve the cultural emphasis on economic success, economic deprivation, and social process factors. Perhaps, it is too much to hope that the United States will soon decrease its emphasis on economic success and conspicuous consumption, but it is possible that public policy can do something about the economic deprivation, urban conditions, family dysfunction, and other by now familiar factors that set the stage for much property and other crime. Chapter 18 returns to this issue.

Review and Discuss

Evaluate the desirability and effectiveness of target hardening as a means of reducing property crime.

▶ Fraud

Another type of economic crime in addition to property crime is fraud. Fraud involves deceit or trickery used for financial gain or for some other material advantage. Many types of crime fall under the broad category of fraud. We have saved these types of crime for last because they serve as a bridge between the property crime already discussed and the white-collar crime examined in Chapter 13. Many fraud cases could easily be considered white-collar crime, as they are committed by businesses and wealthy professionals as part of their occupations. We will keep most of our discussion of these types of fraud until Chapter 13 and will instead focus here on selected types of fraud committed by individuals but not as part of their occupations. These characteristics indicate that these types of fraud should not be classified as white-collar crime, although their proper classification is often difficult to determine.

Identity Theft

Identity theft involves acquiring someone else's credit card number, Social Security number, bank account information, or other information that is then used for illegal economic gain, including the draining of an individual's bank account. The arrival of the Internet, as many people know all too well, increased identity theft by enabling hackers to access credit card numbers from individuals' purchases or from company databases. The Federal Trade Commission estimates that 9 million Americans experience identity theft annually, while the NCVS estimates that 8.6 million households, or 7 percent of all households, have someone who experiences identity theft annually (Langton 2011; Reyns 2013). These figures both suggest that the number of Americans who experience identity theft each year ranges between 8 million and 9 million. The NCVS further estimates that the total annual financial loss to individuals from identity theft exceeds $13 billion (Langton 2011). In addition to this loss, businesses also experience more than $40 billion annually in financial loss from identity theft (Woolsey and Schulz 2013). All these figures indicate that identity theft is both widespread and costly.

Two specific types of identity theft involve check fraud and credit card fraud. *Check fraud* is a common crime, especially with the advent of high-speed printers, scanners, and other equipment to produce counterfeit checks. It is estimated that check fraud costs at

▼ Credit card fraud amounts to at least $3.5 billion annually in the United States and involves lost or stolen cards, the theft of card numbers from the Internet, or their acquisition through deceptive phone calls or from someone's mail or trash.

Reuben Schulz/Getty Images

least $1 billion annually and involves more than 1 million fraudulent checks used or deposited each day (Abagnale 2005; Schmidt 2010). In the days before modern technology, check fraud was less common and relied on the stealing of checks, a practice still in use today. Edwin Lemert's (1953) classic study of check forgers at that time distinguished two types of check forgers: *naive* and *systematic*. The former were the equivalent of amateur property criminals in that they worked alone and committed their crimes with relatively little skill, whereas the latter were more like professional property criminals in that they worked in groups and had fairly elaborate schemes for stealing and using checks.

A crime similar to check fraud is *credit card* (including *debit card*) *fraud*, which amounts to at least $3.5 billion annually in the United States and $7.6 billion worldwide (BusinessWire 2011). This type of fraud usually involves lost or stolen cards, the theft of card numbers from the Internet (described later), or their acquisition through deceptive phone calls or from someone's mail or trash. As with motor vehicles, the abundance of credit cards provides tempting targets for motivated criminals. Some robbers or burglars acquire credit cards along with money and then use the cards until the victim informs the credit card company of the theft.

Tax Fraud

Tax fraud, or *tax evasion,* involves the intentional failure to pay all taxes owed. The Internal Revenue Service refers to this problem as the *tax gap*, the difference between taxes that are legally owed and revenue that is actually collected, with almost all of this gap due to fraud. The IRS estimates that the tax gap in 2006 (the last year for which it has an estimate at this writing) was $450 billion, or about 17 percent of all taxes due by April 15. Of this amount, $65 billion was eventually collected through enforcement and voluntary compliance, yielding a net tax gap of $385 billion (Internal Revenue Service 2012). This amount is far greater than the total value of all losses from the other property crimes and types of fraud described in this chapter. Because of who is involved, tax fraud could easily also be considered white-collar crime. It is discussed here to reinforce the fact that economic crime is found in all walks of life.

It is difficult for the average person whose taxes are withheld from paychecks to cheat the IRS. Much tax fraud thus arises from the failure to report self-employment income and also from the claiming of false deductions (Braithwaite 2009). A common example of the former practice is the failure of restaurant employees to report their tips. But much more self-employment income is hidden from the IRS by small businesses and self-employed individuals, both blue collar (such as a plumber) and white collar (such as a physician). Much, and perhaps most, of such income belongs to middle- and upper-class professionals. However, the IRS has little way of knowing their income and thus must rely on them to report their incomes honestly. Many do not. Because of their occupations, investments, and other aspects of their status, many are also in a position to claim phony deductions that might sound plausible for them, but implausible for less wealthy people. Some also hide their assets in offshore bank accounts and undertake other sophisticated schemes.

Corporations also commit much tax fraud. In 1991 the U.S. General Accounting Office estimated that two-thirds of all U.S. corporations fail to report some of their income (The New York Times 1991). The IRS's 2006 estimate of the tax gap listed $67 billion in unpaid corporation income tax.

Despite the enormity of tax fraud, our society does not condemn it. In fact, more than one-tenth of Americans say that tax cheating is OK to do (Linn 2013). Nobody likes the IRS, so "ripping it off" is considered acceptable. As a technique of neutralization, we reason that because our taxes are so high it is okay to lower the tax bite through fraudulent means. The IRS gets so much money each year that it will not miss the relatively small sum of money we individually keep from it. We criticize, as we should, crimes such as burglary and larceny, but readily minimize the harm of tax fraud that costs many times more than these crimes combined.

Insurance Fraud

Another type of fraud is *insurance fraud,* which is estimated to cost between about $100 billion and $400 billion annually (Insurance Information Institute 2013). Even the lower end of this range is about six times greater than the FBI's estimate of the loss due to the street property crimes that worry us much more. The billions of dollars lost to insurance fraud do not come from us at gunpoint, but are costly nonetheless, as they raise the average household's insurance premiums by more than $1,000 per year (South Carolina Attorney General's Office 2013). As with tax evasion, many otherwise law-abiding citizens think insurance fraud is acceptable. In national survey evidence, 24 percent of Americans approve of increasing an insurance claim to compensate for the cost of the deductible, and 18 percent approve of increasing a claim to compensate for the cost of past premiums (Insurance Information Institute 2013). This latter percentage rises to 23 percent for men in the 18–34 age range. In an interesting gender difference, only 8 percent of women in this age range approve of this type of insurance fraud.

Several types of insurance fraud exist. One type involves arson to collect fire insurance. Health insurance fraud is also very costly and is covered in Chapter 13 as a type of white-collar crime because it so often involves medical professionals. Another common type of insurance fraud involves cars and other motor vehicles. Auto insurance fraud, as it is usually called, amounts to about $5 billion to $7 billion annually (Insurance Information Institute 2013). In New York City, about one-third of auto insurance claims are estimated to be partly or totally fraudulent. These claims raise the cost of the average auto insurance policy paid by the city's residents, who are estimated to pay an extra $240 million in auto insurance as a result (Estrin 2013).

Auto insurance fraud occurs in several ways: (1) "paper" accidents in which no accident occurred but false reports are filed to collect insurance money, (2) minor accidents (e.g., the side-swiping of an innocent driver's car) deliberately committed to collect insurance, (3) staged accidents in which cars already damaged are driven to the same location so the drivers could pretend an accident occurred, (4) exaggeration of whiplash and other injuries after real accidents occurred, (5) abandoning or hiding a car and pretending it was stolen, and (6) arriving at the scene of an accident and pretending one has been injured (Estrin 2013).

After Hurricane Katrina hit Louisiana and Mississippi in August 2005, much insurance and related fraud occurred to claim some of the $5 billion made available for hurricane relief and rebuilding. Thousands of people committed at least $1 billion of fraud to get some of these funds. Some falsely claimed to be hurricane victims, and some falsely claimed to be helping real victims (Cohen 2007). Although much of the fraud was committed by ordinary citizens, some was also traced to public officials, small business owners, and employees of the Federal Emergency Management Agency and the Army Corps of Engineers.

Review and Discuss

Does tax and insurance fraud occur for the same reasons as burglary and larceny? Why or why not?

Computer Fraud and Computer Crime

ATTENTION—FBI E-MAIL HOAX ALERT!! The FBI has become aware of e-mails being generated with the subject line "FBI Investigation" and implying the e-mail originated from the FBI. The e-mail requests the recipient's assistance by purchasing merchandise via the Internet. This e-mail is fictitious, and its origin is being investigated. The FBI would never direct someone to expend personal funds in furtherance of an investigation. If you've received the e-mail, please contact the FBI at www.ifccfbi.gov.

This warning appeared on the FBI's home page in July 2004 and is just one example of the many types of *computer crime* (also called *cybercrime*) that plague the Internet and affect so many people in the United States and abroad (Brenner 2012). Not long ago, this type of crime hardly existed, because personal computers were still rare before the 1990s. But just as the invention of automobiles more than a century ago enabled a new type of crime, motor vehicle theft, so the rapid growth of personal computer ownership and the Internet has enabled many types of crimes that could not have been imagined a generation ago. Now that computers and the Internet are ubiquitous, so are opportunities for many types of offenses involving them.

With so many offenses, computer crime does not fit neatly into any crime category. For example, a man who makes a woman's acquaintance in a chat room and then rapes or robs her when he finally meets her is not just a computer criminal. Instead, his computer-related act is a violent crime. There are also reports that some juvenile gangs are planning their meetings, fights, and other activities over the Internet, but most of us would not call them computer criminals. As we have seen, much fraud involves computers, e-mail, and the Internet, so computer crime could easily fall into the earlier identity theft section. But because of its growing importance, we examine computer crime here in a separate category.

Much computer crime involves *hacking*, in which, as you know, someone breaks into a Web site or acquires information from someone's computer. Often

▲ Computer crime is a growing problem and involves such offenses as hacking and phishing.

the goal is identity theft: to steal someone's credit card number, social security number, or other information that can then be used to acquire money, other valuables, or important information fraudulently. Sometimes hacking is just done for thrills. A behavior related to hacking is *phishing*, which involves the use of e-mail or instant messaging to gain sensitive information. A popular type of phishing involves e-mails that purportedly come from a bank or other financial institution and ask the target to provide information so that a supposed account problem can be corrected. These e-mails look incredibly real and have fooled many people; it is estimated that phishing victimizes more than 9 million people annually with a loss of $650 million (Consumer Reports 2010, 2013). Bank of America, Facebook, and PayPal are among the companies' names most commonly used by phishers. Another example of computer misconduct involves *malware*, malicious software that affects a computer's performance. Almost 60 million people have a malware infection annually, and it costs them almost $4 billion to correct their problems (Consumer Reports 2013).

There are far too many examples of hacking and phishing to list here, but one notorious example involved the January 2007 hacking of the TJ Maxx and Marshall's clothing stores. Information was obtained on 46 million credit and debit cards that had been used beginning more than two years earlier (Kerber 2007). Eleven people from more than three different nations were accused of hacking into the accounts of these and other stores. The ringleader was eventually sentenced to a twenty-year prison term.

Other computer crime involves infringement of copyright laws and plagiarism. Term-paper mills, which a generation ago consisted of stacks of old papers in an offender's room that he or she would sell, now exist at any number of sites on the Internet. A click of a mouse button can access these sites, and a quick (and expensive) credit card purchase allows a user to download some very well-written, and other not so well-written, term papers. As you know, students can also use the Internet to access electronic journal indexes; a quick click and drag of a mouse or touchpad can copy parts of these articles into a student's term paper. Some instructors are becoming more reluctant to assign the traditional term paper because such plagiarism is now so easy to do.

Cybercrime is difficult to control for many reasons, including the fact that it is often difficult to determine the identity of the person committing the crime. Someone can certainly wreak havoc over the Internet from halfway around the world. Hackers and other sophisticated computer criminals are very skilled and can keep one step ahead of investigators. They may eventually be discovered and apprehended, but in the meantime they will have done much damage.

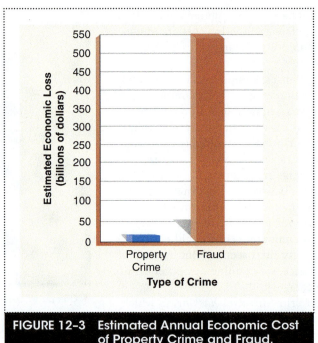

FIGURE 12-3   Estimated Annual Economic Cost of Property Crime and Fraud.

The Cost of Fraud

It is instructive to compare the cost of "street" property crime—burglary, larceny, motor vehicle theft, and arson—with that of the types of fraud just discussed. Recall that property crime costs the nation about $16 billion annually. Now recall the annual estimates of losses from the various types of fraud: (1) identity theft, $53 billion from individuals and businesses combined; (2) tax fraud, $385 billion; and (3) insurance fraud, $100 billion to $400 billion. Taking the lower end of this last estimate, fraud amounts to at least $538 billion annually. This amount dwarfs the $16 billion lost to the property crime that worries us so much more (see Figure 12–3 ■).

► Conclusion

Several theories and factors introduced in previous chapters help explain property crime, especially by the poor. Anomie, economic deprivation, and social process and routine activities factors all contribute to the higher involvement of the poor in robbery, burglary, and related crimes. We also cannot underestimate the role of gender, given that males account for the majority of larceny and more than 80 percent of other serious property crime. We previously explained this basic gender difference in terms of what masculinity means in modern U.S. society. Involvement in most of the property crimes in this chapter also demands the various traits that we associate with masculinity. The role that race plays is a bit more complex. Most property criminals are white, but African-American involvement in property crime exceeds the African-American proportion of the population. This latter fact once again underscores the criminogenic conditions in which many African-Americans live.

The criminals in many property crimes can be divided into two basic types. Amateurs are the vast majority of all property criminals, but professionals steal more on the average because of their higher skills, greater willingness to take risks, and more frequent criminal involvement. People and organizations committing tax and insurance fraud could also be divided along these lines, with many white-collar criminals sounding and behaving very much like fences and other professional property criminals. Chapter 13 discusses this point further.

If nothing else, this chapter showed that economic crime in the United States is rampant. Many people have doubtless stolen or damaged property at some time in their lives. This is especially true if we include employee theft and other crimes to be discussed in Chapter 13. The poor commit the economic crimes we fear the most, but the middle class and the wealthy also commit many economic crimes. As emphasized at the outset, the kind of economic crime we commit depends on our opportunities. To recall Woody Guthrie's famous line, quoted at the beginning of this chapter, "some people rob you with a gun, while others rob you with a fountain pen." The next chapter examines the many forms of white-collar crime committed by the wealthy and respectable elements, individuals and businesses alike, of our society.

Summary

1. The legendary folk singer Woody Guthrie's observation that some people rob you with a gun while others rob you with a fountain pen reminds us that many types of economic crime exist. Property crime tends to be committed by the poor or near-poor, whereas white-collar crime tends to be committed by the wealthy.

2. The major forms of property crime are burglary, larceny, motor vehicle theft, arson, and fraud. The first four types cost their victims more than $15 billion annually. Property crime is least common in the Northeast and in rural areas. Most of it is committed by males. Although whites commit the majority of property crime, African-Americans have disproportionately high rates.

3. Most property criminals are amateurs who tend to commit their crimes with little skill and planning and for little economic gain. Professional property criminals are much more skilled, commit their crimes with more planning, and reap much greater economic gain.

4. The external support system for burglars includes tipsters and fences. Tipsters include other criminals, but also people in legitimate occupations, who inform burglars of attractive targets. Fences sell the stolen merchandise, sometimes to otherwise law-abiding citizens.

5. Many types of fraud exist. Check forgery involves the writing of bad checks and is committed by both amateur and professional forgers. Its modern equivalent is credit card fraud. Before welfare reform in the mid-1990s, welfare fraud involved no more than 4 percent of people on welfare and amounted to $1 billion. In contrast, tax fraud amounts to almost $300 billion annually and involves many wealthy people and large organizations.

6. Insurance fraud is also common and costs tens of billions of dollars annually. A major type is auto insurance fraud, which adds an estimated $200 to the insurance premium for the average car.

7. Explanations of property crime include a cultural emphasis on economic success and conspicuous consumption, the use of techniques of neutralization, economic deprivation, routine activities and social process factors, and the desire for excitement and thrills.

8. Harsher criminal justice measures, target hardening, and neighborhood watch groups have been touted to reduce property crime, but the evidence does not indicate that they are very effective. The factors emphasized in sociological explanations of property crime should be addressed to reduce property crime beyond its current levels.

9. Computer crime plagues the Internet and affects people worldwide. Many forms of computer crime exist, helping to make such crime difficult to control.

Key Terms

amateur theft *243*

booster *244*

decision-making processes *246*

fencing *248*

fraud *254*

identity theft *254*

joyriding *244*

professional theft *243*

rationalization *248*

sneaky thrill crimes *250*

snitch *244*

social organization *243*

support system *245*

target hardening *252*

tax fraud *255*

What Would You Do?

1. The text points out that a surprisingly high proportion of residential burglaries in which a household member saw the intruder is committed by someone the household member knew. Suppose you are the parent of a 16-year-old boy. One day you are returning from a trip to the supermarket and notice that your front door is ajar. You figure you must not have closed it properly and go inside. Suddenly you see a friend of your son looking in a kitchen drawer. He stammers that he was looking for paper and a pencil to leave a note for your son, but you notice some jewelry on the counter next to him. You demand that he leave the house immediately, and he goes without protest. Which of the following, if any, will you now do? (1) Call the police. (2) Call the boy's parents. (3) Tell your son. Explain your answers.

2. Suppose Joe from work says you can buy some expensive stereo equipment cheap. The equipment is almost brand new, he says. When you ask why he's selling the equipment at such a low price, he replies that someone gave it to him. When you ask why, he just shrugs his shoulders and says you don't want to know. Do you buy the stereo equipment? Why or why not?

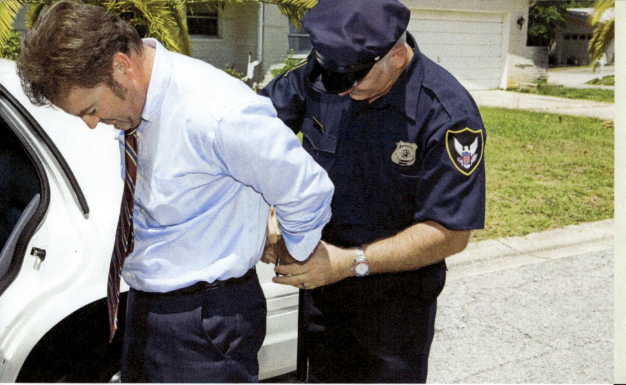

Lisa F. Young/Shutterstock

13 White-Collar and Organized Crime

LEARNING OBJECTIVES

1. *Define white-collar crime*
2. *Distinguish pilferage from embezzlement*
3. *List the annual monetary cost of health care fraud*
4. *Explain why unnecessary surgery occurs*
5. *Define corporate violence*
6. *List the estimated number of annual deaths from pollution*
7. *Compare the annual estimate monetary cost of street crime and of white-collar crime*
8. *Compare the annual estimated number of deaths from street crime and from white-collar crime*

Crime in the News

Coal mining is a dangerous activity, but events in 2013 indicated that some of the danger stems from neglect by coal-mining companies. In February 2013, two miners were killed in separate machinery accidents at the same West Virginia coal mine. Seventeen additional miners had been injured in various accidents at the mine in the previous twelve months. It was later revealed that federal authorities had cited the mine more than 1000 times during this same period for many kinds of safety violations, including improper ventilation and missing carbon monoxide and fire detectors. After the two deaths, state authorities cited the mine for 45 additional safety violations, including and allowing the accumulation of unsafe levels of potentially explosive coal dust. The day after the second death, a state official issued a "fatal alert" that urged the state's mines to follow all safety standards and procedures.

Source: Pope 2013.

A bout forty years before these coal mine deaths and injuries, 125 people died in the mining company of Buffalo Creek, West Virginia, when a 20-foot-high flood surged into a peaceful valley of several thousand homes, destroying everything in its path. The water had built up behind an artificial dam composed of the mine waste, or slag, which remains after coal has been mined and washed. After days of torrential rain, the 132 million gallons of "black water" used to wash the coal finally broke through the dam and destroyed Buffalo Creek in seconds (Erikson 1976).

The sad thing is that this tragedy could have been prevented. Despite the rain and flood, this was entirely a human disaster, not an act of God. The danger the dam posed to the people of Buffalo Creek was certainly no secret; they themselves had worried about its safety. Although the dam violated safety regulations, no one from the mining company was indicted or prosecuted for homicide. Nor were the 125 deaths it caused added to the list of homicides known to the police in 1972, the year the flood occurred. The company did pay $13.5 million to the flood survivors to settle a lawsuit, but this was an amount the company could easily afford because it was owned by a large corporation.

Some forty years later, the Buffalo Creek disaster remains a poignant example of corporate wrongdoing that may have been repeated in the mine disasters described in the Crime in the News feature. Many aspects of the disaster are common to other corporate misconduct: reckless behavior by corporate officials in the name of profit; their denial of any wrongdoing; death, injury or illness, and property loss; and little or no legal punishment. Despite growing awareness of these problems, the public, elected officials, and the news media remain much more concerned about street crime.

This chapter discusses white-collar crime and organized crime. Their grouping within the same chapter reflects the fact that much white-collar crime is committed by organizations (corporations and small businesses) whose motivations and strategies are similar in many ways to those characterizing organized crime. In addition, white-collar crime and organized crime both have dire economic consequences and endanger the health and safety of people across the country.

▶ White-Collar Crime

As cities grew rapidly in nineteenth-century Europe and the United States because of industrialization, public concern over the "dangerous classes" of the poor in these cities also grew (Shelden 2008). Industrialization fueled this concern, but it also ironically spawned a new type of crime that was much less visible and mostly ignored. This was the crime of a new form of business organization, the industrial corporation, that changed the face and economy of the United States after the Civil War. In this period, the oil, steel, railroad, and other industries brought the United States squarely into the Industrial Revolution. Men such as Andrew Carnegie (steel), J. P. Morgan (banking), John D. Rockefeller (oil), and Jay Gould, Leland Stanford, and Cornelius Vanderbilt (railroads) acquired massive fortunes. They are still honored today as the pioneers of the Industrial Revolution and as philanthropists who donated hundreds of millions of dollars to worthy causes.

Yet most of them repeatedly broke the law or at a minimum engaged in questionable business practices. Although some call these men "captains of industry," others call them "robber barons" (Josephson 1962). Their crimes included bribery, kickbacks, and other complex financial schemes, and their industries established factories and other work settings with inhumane working conditions. In the early 1900s, the muckrakers bitterly criticized business and political corruption and condemned the cruel treatment of workers. Ida M. Tarbell (1904) wrote a scathing history of Rockefeller's Standard Oil Company; Upton Sinclair (1990 (1906)) wrote a famous novel, *The Jungle* (1990 [1906]), that discussed the horrible sanitary and work conditions in the U.S. meatpacking industry; and Lincoln Steffens (1904) wrote a classic book on political corruption, *The Shame of the Cities.*

At about the same time, sociologist Edward A. Ross (1965 (1907)) authored a book about the corrupt and dangerous practices of corporate leaders, whom he called "criminaloids." Like the muckrakers, he noted that the actions of industrial leaders and their corporations often caused great financial and physical harm, even if they did not violate any criminal laws. Ross blamed corporate wrongdoing on the intense pursuit of profit that he saw as the hallmark of industrialization and capitalism.

© B Christopher / Alamy

▲ Andrew Carnegie was one of the pioneers of the Industrial Revolution in the United States after the Civil War and a very generous philanthropist. Most of the leading financial and industrial figures of this era repeatedly broke the law or at least engaged in questionable business practices. Their crimes included bribery, kickbacks, and other complex financial schemes, and their industries established factories and other work settings with inhumane working conditions.

Edwin Sutherland and White-Collar Crime

Despite the work of the muckrakers and sociologist Ross, criminologists continued to focus on street crime. In the 1940s, however, Edwin Sutherland wrote some important works about *white-collar crime,* a term he coined. Sutherland (1949) studied the seventy largest U.S. corporations and found that they had violated antitrust, false advertising, bribery, and other laws 980 times, or 14 each on the average. Their crimes were deliberate, repeated, extensive, and harmful. He wrote that any common criminal committing this number of offenses would be considered a habitual offender and harshly punished by the law. Many of the corporations had been charged with engaging in crimes during World Wars I and II, including illegal profiteering, the manufacture of defective military parts, the sale of rancid food to the army, and the sale of munitions and other war materials to Germany. This history led Sutherland to observe that "profits are more important to large corporations than patriotism, even in the midst of an international struggle which endangered Western civilization" (p. 174). The widespread corporate lawbreaking also led him to question the assumption of "conventional theories that crime is due to poverty or to the personal and social pathologies connected with poverty" (p. 25).

Defining White-Collar Crime

In one of criminology's most famous definitions, Sutherland (1949:9) said white-collar crime is "a crime committed by a person of respectability and high social status in the course of his occupation." Sutherland's definition has two major components. First, the crime must be committed by someone of "respectability and high social status"; Sutherland's definition thus excluded crime by blue-collar workers. Second, the crime must be committed "in the course of" one's occupation. Thus, a wealthy corporate executive who murders a lover would not have committed white-collar crime. Like Ross and the muckrakers, Sutherland stressed that behavior of respectable persons can be very harmful even if it does not violate any criminal laws.

Over the years, Sutherland's definition of white-collar crime has been criticized and revised (Payne 2013). Some early critics argued that behavior that does not violate criminal law should not be considered a crime, no matter how harmful it may be. Others said his definition excluded crimes by blue-collar workers and businesses that, notwithstanding the color of the collar, share many features of crimes committed by persons of high social status. One other problem arose from Sutherland's own application of his definition. Although his definition focused on

▼

crime committed by an individual, his 1949 book *White-Collar Crime* focused almost entirely on crime by corporations, or *corporate crime.* This inconsistency led to some confusion over whether white-collar crime is something individuals do or something corporations and other businesses do (Geis 1995).

Contemporary Views

Given the complexity of white-collar crime, many substitute terms have been proposed over the years and many categories of white-collar crime developed. Given the popularity of Sutherland's coinage, most scholars continue to favor *white-collar crime,* but many favor other terms and definitions. Marshall Clinard and Richard Quinney (1973) divided white-collar crime into two types, occupational and corporate. Occupational crime is committed by individuals in the course of their occupation for *personal* gain, whereas corporate crime is committed by corporations. Corporate executives obviously plan and commit the crime, but they do so for their corporations' financial gain. Although they may then benefit along with their corporations, their primary intention is to benefit the corporation. While liking Clinard and Quinney's typology, some scholars prefer the name organizational crime over the term *corporate crime* (Shover and Scroggins 2009). This term emphasizes that crime can be done by and on behalf of organizations, many of them corporations, but some of them small businesses, including blue-collar businesses such as auto-repair shops.

We will use the typology of *occupational and organizational crime.* With this typology in mind, sociologist James W. Coleman (2006:6) defines white-collar crime (borrowing from the National White Collar Crime Center) as "illegal or unethical acts . . . committed by an individual or organization, usually during the course of legitimate occupational activity, by persons of high or respectable social status for personal or organizational gain." One advantage of this definition is that it includes harmful but legal behavior. Thus, the term *corporate crime* is typically used to cover harmful corporate behavior whether or not it violates any criminal law.

Review and Discuss

What are some of the conceptual problems in defining white-collar crime? What do you think is the best definition of such crime?

Occupational Crime: Lawbreaking for Personal Gain

Employee Theft: Pilferage and Embezzlement

If you are or ever have been employed, write down everything you have taken without permission from your workplace without paying for it: pens and pencils, dishes or glassware, food, and so forth. Next to each item, note its approximate value. Now write down how much cash you might have taken. Finally, if you ever were paid for more hours than you worked because you misreported your time, write down the amount you were overpaid. Now add up the value of all the items on your list to yield the total value of *employee theft* you have committed. Even if the average employee theft per student were only, say, $20, that would still mean that students at a 10,000-student campus would in effect have stolen $200,000 from their workplaces.

As this exercise might indicate, employee theft is very common and, indeed, has been called a "widespread, pervasive, and costly form of crime" (Langton et al. 2006:539). About three-fourths of all workers are thought to steal from their employers at least once, with half of these stealing more than once (DeMers 2013). The annual amount of employee theft is estimated at $15 billion (National Retail Federation 2012). Consumers pay in the long run for employee theft because businesses raise their prices to help compensate for it.

Pilferage   Employee theft may be divided into *pilferage* and *embezzlement.* Pilferage involves the theft of merchandise, tools, stationery, and other items. The most common reason for pilferage is employee's dissatisfaction with pay, working conditions, and treatment by supervisors and the company itself. Another reason is what might be called the *workplace culture.* In many workplaces, employees develop informal norms of what is acceptable and not acceptable to steal. These norms generally dictate that expensive, important company property should not be stolen, but that inexpensive, less important property is up for grabs. The workplace culture also includes techniques of neutralization (see Chapter 8) that help employees rationalize their theft: They do not pay us enough, they treat us too harshly, the business won't miss the property we take.

Many types of items are stolen through pilferage. Pens, pencils, paper clips, cell phones, food, cleaning supplies, toilet paper—just about anything an employee can get away with is fair game. Even body parts: In March 2004, two UCLA employees were placed on leave and criminally investigated for allegedly selling body parts from dozens of cadavers donated to the university's medical school over a five-year period (Ornstein 2004).

Embezzlement The second type of employee theft is embezzlement, which involves the theft of cash and the misappropriation or misuse of funds. In a classic study, Donald R. Cressey (1971 (1953)) observed that embezzlers have financial problems they want to keep secret because of their embarrassment or shame. To use Cressey's term, their financial problems are *nonshareable*. They typically rationalize that they are only borrowing the money or that their company will not miss the funds. An individual act of embezzlement ranges from the tens of dollars to the millions. In a million-dollar example, the manager of the Missouri State University bookstore pleaded guilty in March 2013 to several charges of embezzling more than $1 million from his employer. After he was accused of embezzlement, authorities found $81,000 in cash in his office desk drawer (DeSantis 2013).

Although embezzlement is usually a solo activity, a new type, collective embezzlement, emerged in the 1980s in the savings and loan and other financial industries (Rosoff et al. 2010). This scandal involved the stealing of company funds by top executives who often worked in groups of two or more and conspired with "outsiders" such as real estate developers and stock brokerage executives. A common activity was the practice of "land flips" by selling each other land back and forth, with each transaction involving a higher price in a process that artificially inflated the land's value. The executives also spent millions of dollars of company money on artwork and worldwide travel and took salaries and fees that exceeded federal limits. Their collective embezzlement led to the failure of more than 450 savings and loans institutions and the criminal conviction of some 2,300 defendants. This embezzlement is estimated to cost the federal government at least $500 billion by 2030 (Calavita et al. 1997).

Professional Fraud: Focus on Health Care

Physicians, lawyers, and other professionals are in a tempting position to defraud their patients, clients, and the government. Their work is private and complex, and it is difficult for investigators to know when fraud occurs. They are also more autonomous than most other workers and able to work without someone looking over their shoulder. Their patients and clients thus cannot know whether their bills are truthful and accurate. As one example, lawyers sometimes bill their clients for more time than they actually put in or even charge them for work never done. The clients, of course, have no way of knowing this.

Most professions practice *self-regulation* by establishing rules for their members' behavior. Unfortunately, this is often like the proverbial fox guarding the chicken coop. Regulations often allow professionals great latitude in their behavior, and enforcement and punishment are often lax. Professionals also rationalize wrongdoing just as other kinds of criminals do. This allows them to view their crimes as justifiable and even necessary, however illegal they may be. The particular rationalizations depend on the profession and the type of crime involved, but all of them help ease any guilt professionals might feel from breaking the law.

Health care fraud, which is estimated at between $77 billion and $259 billion annually (Insurance Information Institute 2013), has received perhaps the most attention of any professional fraud (Payne 2013). This

▼ The fraud committed by physicians and other health care professionals is estimated at between $77 billion and $259 billion annually.

auremar/Shutterstock

fraud is committed by physicians, pharmacists, medical equipment companies, nursing homes, medical testing laboratories, home health care providers, medical billing services, and ambulance services. Several types of health care fraud exist, but they often involve overbilling Medicare and other insurance. These types include (1) exaggerating charges, (2) billing for services not rendered for a real patient, (3) billing for services for fictitious or dead patients, (4) "pingponging" (sending patients to other doctors for unnecessary visits), (5) family "ganging" (examining all members of a family when only one is sick), (6) "churning" (asking patients to come in for unnecessary office visits), (7) "unbundling" (billing a medical procedure or piece of equipment as many separate procedures or equipment parts), (8) providing inferior products to patients, (9) paying kickbacks and bribes for referrals of patients, (10) falsifying medical records to make an individual eligible for benefits, (11) billing for inferior products or for items never provided, (12) falsifying prescriptions, and (13) inflating charges for ambulance services (Cohen 1994).

Review and Discuss

What are three types of health care fraud? Why does such fraud occur? To what degree do techniques of neutralization help us understand the origins of such fraud?

Unnecessary Surgery

Another common medical practice is unnecessary surgery. What is considered unnecessary, of course, is often a matter of interpretation. Physicians and patients naturally want to err on the side of caution and often decide on surgery as the safest course of action to treat a disease or injury. However, studies have determined that a surprising amount of surgery, tens of thousands of cases a year and perhaps more than 2 million annually, exceeds any reasonable exercise of caution and is clearly unnecessary (Eisler and Hansen 2013). The major reason unnecessary surgery occurs is that physicians profit from it. An estimated 12,000 to 16,000 people die from medical complications resulting from these surgeries (Reiman and Leighton 2013).

Financial Fraud

The collective embezzlement discussed earlier is just one example of financial crime in financial institutions and corporations. Some of this crime is committed for the benefit of the companies and is thus discussed later in the organizational crime section, but other financial crime is committed for personal gain. In addition to collective embezzlement, another financial crime is *insider trading*. Here a company executive, stockbroker, or investment banker with special knowledge of a company's economic fortunes (such as a proposed merger) buys or sells stock in that company before this information is shared with the public. Lifestyle celebrity Martha Stewart's prison term in 2004 for lying to investigators arose from an insider trading scandal involving a friend who was convicted of insider trading (White 2003).

Police and Political Corruption: Violations of Public Trust

Another form of occupational crime is corruption by police and politicians, who violate the public trust by accepting bribes and kickbacks and by occasionally engaging in extortion and blackmail. Such public corruption was the subject of Lincoln Steffens's *The Shame of the Cities,* mentioned earlier. In the twentieth century it reached into the upper echelons of mayors' and governors' offices, police administration, Congress, and the White House. We will explore political corruption further in Chapter 14 and police corruption in Chapter 16.

Organizational Criminality and Corporate Crime

Much white-collar crime is committed for the sake of corporations and other businesses. The primary intent of the persons committing the crime is to benefit the organization for which they work. They know, of course, that if they help their business, the business will "help" them. But their primary goal of helping the business classifies their crime as organizational, not occupational, although this classification becomes somewhat tricky when the owner of a business is involved.

Much organizational crime is committed by legitimate businesses that defraud the public or commit other harms as part of their business practice. Auto-repair shops are notorious in this regard. Auto-repair fraud (overcharging and unnecessary or faulty repairs) costs more than an estimated $20 billion annually (Fleck 2002; Payne 2013). Other organizational crime involves illegitimate businesses that are fraudulent from the outset and have the sole purpose of defrauding the public. Examples include phony home improvement businesses, contests, and charities.

We now come to crime by corporations, which, because of their size and scope, commit great harm (Reiman and Leighton 2013). Corporate crime has continued long after Sutherland first wrote about it. During the mid-1970s, the federal government accused almost two-thirds of Fortune 500 corporations of violating the law and almost one-fourth of these were convicted of (or did not contest) at least one criminal or civil offense (U.S. News & World Report 1982). During the 1990s, more than 100 top corporations were criminally fined after pleading guilty or no contest to criminal charges

▲ Auto repair fraud consists of overcharging for repairs and unnecessary or faulty repairs. This type of business fraud costs more than an estimated $20 billion annually.

involving behavior such as price-fixing, environmental law violations, and the marketing of drugs to doctors without Food and Drug Administration's approval (Mokhiber and Weissman 1999). During the 2000s, major financial scandals broke involving Enron and many other corporations that exaggerated their assets. Major pharmaceutical companies paid hundreds of millions of dollars to settle accusations that they overcharged Medicaid by illegally failing to offer it their lowest prices or marketed drugs for uses that the FDA had not approved (Abelson 2004; Farrell 2004). In 2009, two pharmaceutical companies were fined almost $4 billion for illegal marketing of drugs. A news report observed, "Marketing fraud cases against pharmaceutical companies have become almost routine, with almost every major drug maker having been accused of giving kickbacks to doctors or shortchanging the Medicaid program on prices" (Harris 2009:B4).

Corporate crime takes two general forms: *financial* and *violent.* The major distinction between the two is whether people are injured or killed by corporate misconduct. We will first examine financial crime by corporations and then discuss the violence they commit.

Corporate Financial Crime

The economic cost of corporate crime is enormous. A 1982 investigation estimated that financial crime by corporations, including price-fixing, false advertising, bribery, and tax evasion, costs the public $200 billion per year (U.S. News & World Report 1982). In 2013 dollars, this amount would be about $483 billion. Several types of corporate financial crime exist.

Corporate Fraud, Cheating, and Corruption A first type of corporate financial crime involves fraud, cheating, bribery, and other corruption not falling into the antitrust or false advertising categories that we examine later. Much of this fraud and corruption parallels what individuals do for personal gain as occupational crime. The difference here is that the fraud and corruption are performed primarily for the corporation's benefit, not for the benefit of the corporate executives engaging in these crimes.

Fraud and corruption, including conspiracy, securities fraud, and wire fraud, were widely suspected in the financial crisis involving the collapse of several huge financial and securities firms in 2008 and 2009 (Cohan 2010). These companies insured or invested heavily in subprime (high-risk) mortgages and collapsed when the housing market bottomed out and mortgage owners could no longer pay off their loans. In the wake of their collapse, reports indicated that executives at some of the companies had deceived creditors and investors about the companies' poor financial health and/or violated certain regulatory laws in taking such unnecessary risks in their investments. As the headline of one news column put it, these executives were "looters in loafers" (Krugman 2010).

▲ Financier Bernard Madoff used a *Ponzi scheme* for some fifteen years to enrich himself and other people who worked with him. This scheme defrauded thousands of investors of an estimated $50 billion. Madoff pleaded guilty in February 2009 to eleven felonies and was sentenced to a 150-year prison term.

While this financial crisis was occurring, the case of the notorious financial investor, Bernard Madoff, emerged. Madoff was discovered to have been using a *Ponzi scheme* (in which new investments are used to pay the interest on old investments) for some fifteen years to enrich himself and other people who worked with him. His scheme defrauded thousands of investors of an estimated $50 billion. Madoff eventually pleaded guilty to eleven felonies and was sentenced to a 150-year prison term (Henriques and Healy 2009).

There have been many other examples of high-finance fraud over the decades, but those that came to light in the early 2000s stand out for their enormity and audacity. Many of them involved accounting fraud, as numerous companies exaggerated their assets during the economic boom and stock market bubble of the late 1990s to artificially inflate the value of their stock. In doing so, they violated securities laws by defrauding their investors. When their scandalous behavior came to light and their stock value plummeted, many of their workers lost their jobs, and countless investors lost billions of dollars, including funds in their pension plans.

The most notorious accounting scandal involved Enron, a global energy company that had been the darling of Wall Street. In December 2000 its stock sold for $84 a share and the company employed some 20,000 people worldwide. Fewer than twelve months later, it was worth less than a dollar a share after the company revealed that it had overstated earnings and hidden losses, with the total sum surpassing $1 billion. A month later it filed for bankruptcy and laid off more than 4,000 workers. The plummeting of its stock cost investors tens of billions of dollars (Behr and Whitt 2002). More than thirty people involved in the Enron scandal were eventually indicted, including its top executives, both of whom were convicted. Other corporations implicated in financial scandals at the same time were Adelphia, Halliburton, Rite Aid, and WorldCom. Top executives at Rite Aid, the national drugstore chain, were convicted of various charges relating to the hiding of operating losses, including bribing some employees and intimidating others to remain quiet (Johnson 2004).

Price-Fixing and Restraint of Trade A second type of corporate financial crime involves antitrust violations. If corporations conspire to set high prices for goods and services rather than allowing the free market to work, consumers pay more than they should. Such price-fixing thus constitutes a form of theft from the public, which costs about $60 billion annually (Simon 2012). Also, if one company buys out all the others, does not have to worry about competition and can raise its prices without fear of losing sales to another company. This action, too, constitutes a theft from the public as restraint of trade violates antitrust law. Restraint of trade goes back to the post–Civil War period, when Standard Oil and other corporations bought up competitors or used questionable practices to prevent others from springing up or to drive them out of business. Congress passed the 1890 Sherman Antitrust Act to counter such behavior. One additional type of restraint of trade prohibited by antitrust laws involves *anticompetitive agreements,* in which a manufacturer sells its products only to retailers who agree not to sell rival manufacturers' products. Although some of the fines and legal settlements for price-fixing and other antitrust crimes range in the millions of dollars, the corporations involved are usually so wealthy that these financial penalties scarcely worry them.

Perhaps the most celebrated price-fixing scandal was uncovered in 1959–1960 and involved General Electric, Westinghouse, and twenty-seven other heavy electrical equipment manufacturers that controlled 95 percent of the electrical industry (Geis 1987). These companies' executives conspired over several years to fix prices on $7 billion of electrical equipment, costing the public about $1.7 billion in illegal profit. After pleading guilty in 1961, seven of the electrical executives received thirty-day jail terms for their conspiracy, and twenty-one others got suspended sentences. These were obviously light sentences compared to what a typical property criminal might get for stealing only a few dollars. In somewhat stiffer punishment, the corporations were fined a

Bryan Smith/ZUMApress/Newscom

total of $1.8 million. This sum amounted to only $1 of every $1,000 the corporations stole from the public and still left them holding almost $1.7 billion in illegal profit. Of the total fines, GE's share came to $437,000. This might be a lot of money for you to pay, but for GE it was the equivalent of someone with an annual income of $175,000 paying a $3 fine. To bring this down to more meaningful figures, if you had an income of $17,000 and knew that your punishment for robbing a bank would be only 30 cents, would you rob the bank?

In a more recent example of price-fixing, in May 2013 a judge ordered Dow Chemical to pay $1.2 billion in damages after a jury concluded that Dow had fixed prices on polyurethane foam materials used in motor vehicles and household products (Cameron 2013). Although this sum was certainly much higher than the fines paid by the electrical companies in the price-fixing scandal just discussed, it is worth noting that Dow Chemical's total assets at the time of this judgment were about $70 billion and that its 2012 revenue was $57 billion. The damages that Dow was ordered to pay thus equaled only about 2 percent of either figure, leaving Dow with tens of billions of dollars left over.

False Advertising   Another common corporate financial crime is false advertising. Advertisers obviously do their best to sell their products and engage legally in exaggerated claims, or *puffery*. A particular product, for example, may claim to be the best of its kind or, as in the case of cigarettes and beer, imply that using it will make you popular. But much advertising goes beyond puffery and makes patently false and illegal claims. Such deceptive advertising is very common, with the cosmetic, food, pharmaceutical, and many other industries accused of it (Jackson and Jamieson 2007).

A recent example of false advertising involved the Kellogg's cereal company, which agreed in May 2013 to pay $4 million to settle a lawsuit alleging that the company had falsely advertised that its Frosted Mini-Wheats could improve children's cognitive abilities (Bachman 2013); the company admitted no wrongdoing. Although its $4 million settlement was not a small sum, it is worth noting that Kellogg's total assets were about $15 billion at the time of this settlement and its annual revenue about $14 billion. The $4 million settlement thus equaled only about two-tenths of 1 percent of either figure, leaving Kellogg's, like Dow, with billions of dollars left over.

Another type of false advertising involves *bait-and-switch* advertising, in which a store advertises a low-priced item that is not actually available or available only in small quantities. The item is gone when customers come in to buy it, and the sales clerk switches them to a more expensive product in the same line.

Corporate Violence: Threats to Health and Safety

If you heard that corporations kill many more people each year than all murders combined, would you believe it? Even if corporations are corrupt, you may be thinking, they do not murder. Yet their actions do, in fact, kill more people each year than all murders combined. It is difficult for any of us to believe that corporations maim and kill. We equate violence with interpersonal violence, which dominates public discussion, fills us with fear, and even controls our lives. Corporate violence, in contrast, is less visible and has been called "quiet violence" (Frank and Lynch 1992:1). The term *corporate violence* refers to actions by corporations that cause injury, illness, and even death. These lives are lost in the name of profit, as corporations pursue profits with reckless disregard for the health, safety, and lives of their workers, consumers, and the general public (Reiman and Leighton 2013).

Workers and Unsafe Workplaces   As the Crime in the News story on coal mining that began this chapter illustrates, many workers die or become injured or ill every year because of hazardous occupational conditions; others suffer long-lasting psychological effects. Some hazardous workplace conditions violate federal and state laws, whereas others are technically not illegal but still pose dangers to workers. Most hazardous conditions involve worker exposure to various toxic substances that cause cancer and serious respiratory illnesses. Working with dangerous equipment and in dangerous circumstances also causes injury and death.

It does not have to be this way, as the mining problems discussed in the news story indicate. Although some jobs and workplaces are inevitably hazardous, the primary reason for the nation's high rate of occupational injury, illness, and death is that corporations disregard their workers' health and safety in the name of profit. Moreover, the government has lax rules on workplace conditions and does relatively little to enforce the ones that do exist.

Estimates of the problem　Exact data on workplace illness, injury, and death are difficult to determine for several reasons (Reiman and Leighton 2013). First, it is often difficult to establish that illness and death are work-related. Second, the U.S. Bureau of Labor Statistics, a major source of workplace data, gathers data only from workplaces with at least eleven employees. Its annual count of the number of workplace injuries is thought to miss from 33 to 69 percent of the actual number of injuries (Leigh et al. 2004). Third, corporations and smaller businesses often hide workplace injuries and illnesses.

Not surprisingly, estimates of annual workplace illness and disease, injury, and death vary widely, but reasonable estimates include the following: (1) 50,000 deaths from illness/disease; (2) almost 4,700 deaths from injury; and (3) almost 3 million injuries and illnesses (AFL-CIO 2013; Reiman and Leighton 2013; Simon 2012). Because of underreporting and other measurement problems, the true toll of work-related death, illness, and injury may well be much higher. It is unknown how many of workplace-related deaths, injuries, and illnesses could have been prevented if companies had maintained safe workplaces, but is fair to say that almost all the deaths from illness/disease and at least some of the deaths from injuries could have been prevented. These deaths probably number about 50,000 overall annually.

Examples of the problem　Sometimes the harm done to workers is immediate and visible, as the coal-mine deaths at the beginning of this chapter again illustrate. In another example, an explosion at a fertilizer plant in West, Texas, in April 2013 killed 14 people and seriously injured some 200 other people. Although the components of fertilizer can be very explosive under certain conditions, the fertilizer company had previously been cited several times for various safety and reporting violations. In effect, as two critics of these violations declared, the explosion at the fertilizer plant "wasn't an accident" (Dreier and Cohen 2013).

Usually, however, the harm done to workers takes much more time to kill them. The coal-mining industry is a prime example. Long-term breathing of coal dust leads to several respiratory problems, including black lung disease, which has killed more than 76,000 miners during the past half-century and still kills about 1,500 annually. Mine safety advocates blame many of these deaths on coal companies' repeated violations of ventilation and other safety standards designed to help prevent black lung disease. As an attorney who represents miners in black-lung lawsuits commented, "As a whole in the industry, ventilation is a joke in underground mines" (Estep and Cheves 2013).

The asbestos industry has also killed many workers. Beginning in the late 1960s, medical researchers began to discover that asbestos, long used as a fire retardant in schools, homes, and other buildings and as an insulator in high-temperature equipment, can cause asbestosis, a virulent lung disease. Because this disease takes a long time to develop, it is estimated that more than 200,000 people, mostly asbestos workers, but also consumers, will eventually die from asbestos-related cancer and lung disease within the next few decades (Brodeur 1985).

"Where's the crime?" you might be asking. What if no one happened to know that asbestos was dangerous? If this were the case, then asbestos deaths would be a tragic problem, but not one for which the industry should be blamed. Unfortunately, there is plenty of blame, and even murderous criminal neglect, to go around. It turns out that the asbestos industry began to suspect at least as early as the 1930s that asbestos was dangerous, as it saw its workers coming down with serious lung disease. Instead of reporting their suspicions to the appropriate federal and state authorities, asbestos companies kept quiet and settled workers' claims out of court to avoid publicity (Lilienfeld 1991). For more than thirty years, they continued to manufacture a product they knew was dangerous. During that time, workers continued to handle asbestos, and asbestos was put into many schools and other new buildings. It is no

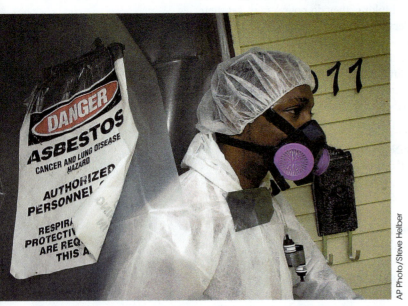

▲ The asbestos industry hid the dangers of asbestos for several decades.

Crime and Controversy　HARVEST OF SHAME: PESTICIDE POISONING OF FARM WORKERS

Each year in the United States, thousands of farm workers most of them Mexican American, are exposed to pesticides used in the fruit and vegetable fields in which they work. According to one report "Pesticide exposure causes farmworkers to suffer more chemical-related injuries and illnesses than any other workforce in the nation."

In our most populous state, California, about 75,000 tons of pesticides are used in fields annually to control the many types of insects that could decimate crops. Many of these pesticides cause cancer and/or damage the nervous and reproductive systems. Often the pesticides are sprayed by helicopter. Sometimes the wind blows the pesticide spray hundreds of yards until it reaches an area where farm workers are picking crops. One farmworker explained what happens after being exposed to pesticides: "As a strawberry picker, I have worked near many pesticide applications. First we smell the pesticides. Then our eyes burn, our noses run and our throats hut."

When farm workers are sickened by pesticides, they have the right to apply for workers' compensation. Because many speak little English, however, they might not know about workers' comp, and some who are aware of it still fear having anything to do with the government. They also realize they would lose time from work if they get involved with the workers' compensation process and even fear losing their jobs. For all these reasons, they often get no help at all in paying their medical expenses. Because they so often do not report pesticide exposure, the actual number of workers sickened by pesticide drifts is probably much higher than the number indicated in official reports.

Farm workers are not the only people harmed by pesticide drifts. Children, who are especially vulnerable to pesticide-caused medical problems, are often exposed to pesticide drift at school or on their way to or from school. Many California counties have "protection zones" that restrict how close to a school pesticide spraying can occur, but eleven counties have no such zones, while six counties have rules that apply only if classes are in session. An Associated Press investigation found "that over the past decade, hundreds, possibly thousands, of schoolchildren in California and other agricultural states have been exposed to farm chemicals linked to sickness, brain damage, and birth defects."

In spring 2009, two children were waiting for their school bus when a pesticide cloud from a vineyard across the street drifted over and drenched them. One of the children later recalled, "And then I told the bus driver that I wasn't feeling good, like I was feeling sick. My head hurt, I wanted to throw up and everything."

Sources: Burke 2007; Carrillo 2011; Farmworker Justice 2013; Khokha 2010; Reeves et al. 2003.

---

exaggeration to say that the companies' concern for profit was and will be responsible for more than 200,000 deaths and that the asbestos industry was guilty of "corporate malfeasance and inhumanity . . . that is unparalleled in the annals of the private-enterprise system" (Brodeur 1985:7).

Consumers and Unsafe Products　Even if you work in a safe workplace, you are not necessarily safe from corporate violence. Every year companies market dangerous products that injure us, make us sick, and even kill us. The Consumer Product Safety Commission (CPSC) (2013) estimates that consumer products are associated with 35,900 deaths and more than 38 million injuries annually. Meanwhile, the U.S. Centers for Disease Control and Prevention (CDC) (Centers for Disease Control and Prevention 2013) estimates that each year about 3,000 people die and 128,000 are hospitalized from eating contaminated food. Combining the two agencies' estimates, about 39,000 people die each year from consumer products, including food. Because not all deaths and injuries from products and contaminated food come to the government's attention, the number of deaths from these sources is very likely higher than 39,000.

The exact number of these deaths that stem from corporate misconduct is unknown. For example, a death may result from a product that is unsafe as manufactured, but it may also result from a product that had merely aged past safe use (e.g., an old toaster with a frayed electric cord); a death may also occur because someone using a safe product made a mistake or was careless. Similarly, a death from contaminated food may stem from a company's food processing violation, but it may also occur because a consumer prepared or handled food carelessly. These possibilities mean that the exact amount of the 39,000 (or likely higher number of) deaths caused by corporate misconduct cannot be determined. For the sake of argument, and using just the CPSC and CDC estimates, we will assume that one-tenth of the deaths from consumer products stem from unsafe products when manufactured and that half the deaths from contaminated food stem from corporate misconduct. These admittedly rough assumptions yield an estimated 5,100 annual deaths from unsafe products and contaminated food.

Whatever the actual number of such deaths, it remains true that people do die from products that were unsafe as manufactured and from food that was contaminated because of company processing violations. In regard to unsafe products, children seem to be at special risk. About three dozen infants have died in recent years in accidents involving cribs whose sides drop down (Callahan 2010). An earlier news report concluded that seventeen companies "kept quiet about products that were seriously injuring children until the government stepped in" (O'Donnell 2000:1A). These products included cribs and infant carriers, and the injuries included amputated fingers, broken bones, and skull fractures. Some of the companies had received thousands of complaints from parents and had investigated their products' safety, but they hid the evidence of their products' dangers from the government.

Three industries posing a great danger to consumers are the automobile, pharmaceutical, and food industries. In each of these industries, companies have known their products were dangerous but sold them anyway to consumers.

The automobile industry Beginning in late 2009, news reports indicated that certain Toyota models were subject to sudden acceleration that may have caused 89 deaths since 2000. Toyota eventually recalled millions of vehicles and paid a fine of $16.4 million (but without admitting any wrongdoing) for delay in reporting the problem to the federal government for four months. The Department of Transportation said Toyota had "knowingly hid a dangerous defect for months from U.S. officials and did not take action to protect millions of drivers and their families" (Maynard 2010:A1; Thomas 2010).

The complexity of motor vehicles means that some defects are inevitable. But as the Toyota example suggests, there have been many tragic cases in which automobile manufacturers knew of safety defects that killed and injured many people, but decided not to do anything in order to save money.

The most infamous case is probably that of the Ford Pinto, which was put on the market in 1971 even though Ford knew the Pinto's gas tank could easily explode in minor rear-end collisions. Ford did a cost–benefit analysis to determine whether it would cost more money to fix each Pinto, at $11 per car, or to pay settlements in lawsuits after people died or burned in accidents. Ford determined that it would cost $49.5 million to settle lawsuits from the 180 burn deaths, 180 serious burn injuries, and 2,100 burned cars it anticipated would occur, versus $137 million to fix the 12.5 million Pintos and other Fords with the problem. Because not fixing the problem would save Ford about $87 million, Ford executives decided to do nothing, even though they knew people would die and be seriously burned. About 500 people eventually did die (although one estimate puts the number at "only" some two dozen) when Pintos were hit from behind, often by cars traveling at relatively low speeds, before the Pinto was finally recalled (Cullen et al. 2006).

Ford was responsible for more deaths and injuries beginning a few years earlier because of faulty automatic transmission that slipped from park into reverse. Drivers would put their cars in park and leave the engine running while they got out to get groceries from the trunk and to do other tasks. The transmission would shift unexpectedly into reverse, causing the car to roll backward and hit or run over the driver. By 1971 Ford was receiving six letters per month on this problem, but did nothing. In fact, for years it denied that its vehicles had any reversal problem at all. Instead of ordering a recall, the Department of Transportation allowed Ford in 1980 to send warning stickers to owners of all Ford vehicles manufactured between 1966 and 1979. Because many original owners had sold their cars, about 2.7 million owners of used Fords never received the stickers. At least eighty people died in Ford reversal accidents from 1980, when the stickers were mailed, to 1985. By this time, an estimated 207 deaths and 4,597 injuries had occurred from Ford vehicles rolling backward onto people (Consumer Reports 1985; Kahn 1986).

Ford claimed that its vehicles were no worse than any other manufacturer's and blamed the problem on drivers' failure to actually put their cars in park initially. Unfortunately for Ford, although the National Highway Traffic Safety Administration (NHTSA) recorded the eighty deaths from Ford cars between 1980 and 1985, it recorded only thirty-one similar fatalities for General Motors, Chrysler, and American Motors combined. Unless we are to assume that Ford drivers were somehow more inept than others at putting their vehicles into park, the Ford transmission had to be at fault. Ford eventually corrected the problem.

In another Ford problem, thousands of Ford drivers began reporting in the 1980s that their cars were stalling on highways and when making left turns. Although Ford told the government that this problem was not due to any defect, its officials and engineers knew that the cars did, in fact, have a significant defect: an ignition system that would become too hot and then shut off the engine. Determining that it would cost almost half a billion dollars to fix the problem in millions of cars, Ford kept quiet about the defect for nine years, even as it led to serious car accidents, some of them fatal. Ford finally fixed the problem (Labaton and Bergman 2000).

The pharmaceutical industry   The pharmaceutical industry has also put profits above people by knowingly marketing dangerous drugs. As one scholar wrote, "Time after time, respected pharmaceutical firms have shown a cavalier disregard for the lives and safety of the people who use their products" (Coleman 2006:83).

One example of pharmaceutical misconduct involved Eli Lilly and Company, which in the 1980s put a new arthritis drug, Oraflex, on the market overseas. Shortly after taking the drug, at least twenty-six people died. These patients' doctors reported the deaths to Lilly. Because the patients were usually elderly, any individual physician could not assume that Oraflex was the cause of death. After getting several reports of such deaths, however, a responsible company would have told the government, conducted more tests, and perhaps taken the drug off the market. Lilly instead kept the deaths a secret, and the Food and Drug Administration allowed Lilly to market the drug in the United States in April 1982. More deaths took place, and Lilly pleaded guilty in August 1985 to deceiving the government. By this time, Oraflex had killed at least 62 people and made almost 1,000 more seriously ill. Lilly's total legal punishment was a $25,000 fine for the company and a $15,000 fine for one of its executives (Coleman 2006).

In another example, the Wyeth company withdrew two diet drugs from the market after many reports of heart valve damage associated with using the drugs and allegations that the company had hid evidence of the problem. Wyeth eventually paid more than $1 billion to settle class-action lawsuits (Feeley and McCarty 2004).

One of the most notorious examples of pharmaceutical corporate violence involved the A. H. Robins Company and its Dalkon Shield IUD, or intrauterine device (Hicks 1994). Robins distributed more than 4 million Dalkon Shield IUDs between 1971 and 1975 in 80 nations, including 2.2 million in the United States, after falsifying safety tests. The IUD turned out to be a time bomb ticking inside women because its "tail string" carried bacteria from the vagina into the uterus, where it caused pelvic inflammatory disease for thousands of women, leading to sterility, miscarriage, or, for at least eighteen U.S. women, death. More than 100,000 U.S. women became pregnant despite using the IUD. Sixty percent of these women miscarried, and hundreds of those who did not miscarry gave birth to babies with severe defects, including blindness, cerebral palsy, and mental retardation; other women had stillborn babies. After finally recalling the IUD in 1974, Robins continued to sell it overseas for up to nine months. The company eventually paid more than $400 million to settle numerous lawsuits. Like other corporations, wrote Morton Mintz (1985:247), a former investigative reporter for the *Washington Post,* A. H. Robins "put corporate greed before welfare, suppressed scientific studies that would ascertain safety and effectiveness, (and) concealed hazards from consumers." He added that "almost every other major drug company" has done similar things, often repeatedly.

The food industry   A third industry that has put profit over people is the food industry. Historically, one of the worst food offenders is the meatpacking industry. Upton Sinclair, in his muckraking novel *The Jungle,* wrote that rats routinely would get into meat in meatpacking plants. Workers used poisoned bread to try to kill the rats. The meat sold to the public thus included dead rats, rat feces, and poisoned bread. Sinclair's novel led to the Federal Meat Inspection Act in 1906 (Frank and Lynch 1992).

Despite this act and other regulations, some meatpacking companies still endanger our health, thanks in large part to lax federal monitoring of the meat industry. A 2010 report concluded that "beef containing harmful pesticides, veterinary antibiotics and heavy metals is being sold to the public because federal agencies have failed to set limits for the contaminants or adequately test for them" (Eisler 2010:A1). In just three examples of tainted meat, a Louisiana meat company recalled 468,000 pounds of meat products in April 2013 for suspected contamination of listeria, a potentially fatal bacterial disease (Brasted 2013); four Los Angeles companies were charged in 2004 with violating federal food safety laws for, among other actions, selling meat containing rat feces (Rosenzweig 2004); and a Georgia meat company that supplies schools, supermarkets, and restaurants across the nation had been cited for safety violations hundreds of times during the previous three years (Petersen and Drew 2003).

The Public and Environmental Pollution   No doubt some pollution of the air, land, and water is inevitable in an industrial society. If people become ill or die from it, that is unfortunate, but unavoidable. But much of our pollution *is* preventable. Federal environmental laws are weak or nonexistent, corporations often violate the laws that do exist, federal monitoring and enforcement of these laws are lax, and the penalties for environmental violations are minimal (Payne 2013). As a result, an estimated 20 percent of U.S. landfills and incinerators, 25 percent of drinking water systems, and 50 percent of wastewater treatment facilities violate health regulations (Armstrong 1999).

The consequences of these problems are illness, disease, and death. For many reasons, it is difficult to determine how many people die or become ill each year from pollution, but it is clear that pollution causes many deaths and illnesses every year. A study by the American Cancer Society that followed 500,000 people for sixteen years found that air pollution contributes to both heart disease and lung cancer and is as dangerous as secondhand smoke or being overweight or a former smoker (Pope et al. 2004). Scientists estimate that air pollution kills between 50,000 and 100,000 Americans and more than 300,000 Europeans each year from the heart disease, cancer, and respiratory diseases it causes (BBC News 2005; National Oceanic and Atmospheric Administration 2013; Reiman and Leighton 2013). The key question, and one very difficult to answer, is: How many of these deaths could be prevented if corporations acted responsibly and put people above profit? A conservative estimate of annual pollution deaths in the United States due to corporate crime and neglect would be 35,000.

In this regard, an investigative report deplored several major corporations, including General Motors, Standard Oil, and Du Pont, for engaging in a "sad and sordid commercial venture" by conspiring from the beginning of the automobile age to manufacture and market gasoline containing lead, a deadly poison, even though the companies knew there were safe alternatives. Along the way they suppressed evidence of the health dangers of lead. More than sixty years after it was first used, lead was finally banned as a gasoline additive in 1986. By that time, lead-related heart disease was killing an estimated 5,000 Americans yearly (Kitman 2000).

Another environmental problem is the dumping of toxic waste. The United States produces close to 300 million tons of toxic waste each year, and as much as 90 percent of this is disposed of improperly into some 600,000 contaminated sites across the nation (Simon 2012). Perhaps the most infamous toxic-waste dumping crime occurred in an area known as Love Canal, near Niagara Falls, New York. For years a chemical company had dumped toxic wastes at Love Canal—and then it donated the land to the Niagara Falls School Board in 1953. The school board sold the land to a developer, and houses were eventually built on top of the toxic waste. Eventually, the waste leaked into the surrounding land and water, causing birth defects, miscarriages, and other health problems. By the 1980s, more than 500 families had to leave their homes, which were later destroyed. The company had also dumped toxic wastes in several other communities (Levine 1982).

The underlying motive for much of the pollution and environmental problems discussed in this section is profit. Companies make more money when they do not take measures to reduce the pollution they emit or to safely dispose of their toxic waste. A terrible example of this dynamic occurred in April 2010, when an oil rig owned by BP, the British global energy company, exploded in the Gulf of Mexico. The resulting oil spill lasted several months and became the largest oil spill in U.S. history. Reports several weeks after the explosion indicated that BP officials may have chosen to save money by using an inferior type of casing for the oil well. The casing was known to be more likely to release certain gases, and gas leaks were widely thought to have caused the explosion (Urbina 2010).

Review and Discuss

What are the ways in which corporations cause illness, injury, and/or death?

Economic and Human Costs of White-Collar Crime

Many criminologists believe that white-collar crime costs us more in lives and money than street crime (Reiman and Leighton 2013). We can collect the various figures presented in this chapter on the costs of both types of crime to see why they feel this way.

We will start with the value of property and money stolen annually from the public, government, and/or private sector by street crime and white-collar crime. Our figure for street crime is $16 billion, the FBI's estimate of the annual loss from all property crime and robbery. For white-collar crime, we will add several estimates presented earlier in this and the previous chapter: (1) $483 billion (the *U.S. News & World Report* estimate in today's dollars) for the cost of all corporate crime, including price-fixing, false advertising, tax evasion, and various types of fraud; (2) $77 billion in health care fraud (lower-end estimate); and (3) $15 billion in employee theft. These amounts add up to $575 billion annually. As you can see in Figure 13–1 ■, this amount towers over the annual loss from street crime. Many forms of tax fraud (see Chapter 12) could also be considered white-collar crime, and if they were included in the estimation of white-collar crime costs, the total estimate would be many billions of dollars larger.

Now we will do a similar calculation for the number of people killed each year by street crime (murder and non-negligent manslaughter) and white-collar crime and misconduct. The UCR's estimate for 2011 homicides was 14,612. For white-collar crime (and misconduct), we again use the estimates presented earlier in this chapter and previous chapters: (1) 50,000 workplace-related deaths from disease/illness and injury; (2) 5,100 deaths from unsafe products and contaminated food; (3) 35,000 deaths from environmental pollution; and (4) 12,000 deaths from unnecessary surgery (lower-end of the earlier estimate). Adding these figures together, about 102,100 people a year, admittedly a very rough number, die from corporate and professional crime and misconduct. As Figure 13–2 ■ illustrates, this number far exceeds the number of people murdered each year.

Explaining White-Collar Crime

In many ways, white-collar criminals are not that different from street criminals. Both groups steal and commit violence, even if their methods differ in ways already discussed. In addition, certain explanations of street crime also apply to white-collar crime. At the same time, there are obvious differences between the two types of crime and their respective offenders. To help understand why white-collar crime occurs, it is useful to examine its similarities with and differences from street crime. Because so many types of white-collar crime exist, our discussion will focus on the most serious type, corporate crime.

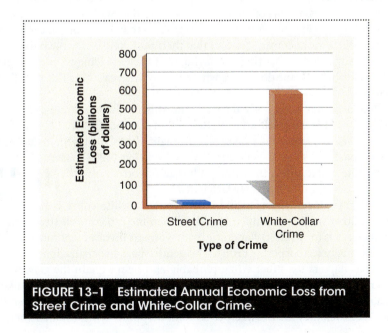

FIGURE 13–1 Estimated Annual Economic Loss from Street Crime and White-Collar Crime.

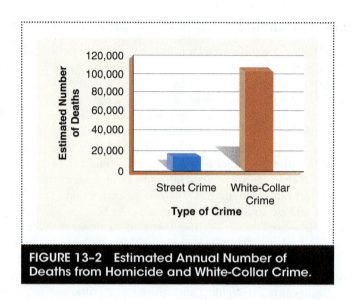

FIGURE 13–2 Estimated Annual Number of Deaths from Homicide and White-Collar Crime.

Similarities with Street Crime

A basic similarity between white-collar crime and street crime is that both types of crime involve stealing and violence. To again recall Woody Guthrie's line at the beginning of Chapter 12, some people rob you with a gun, while others rob you with a fountain pen (or, in the modern era, a computer). Beyond this basic similarity, both types of crime also share some other features and dynamics.

Like street criminals, white-collar criminals do not usually break the law unless they have both the opportunity and the motivation to do so (Payne 2013; Wang and Holtfreter 2012). But the opportunity for corruption and other white-collar crime differs across occupations and industries. This helps us understand why some occupations and industries have more crime than others. For example, financial corruption is probably much less common among professors than among businesspeople, physicians, and politicians. Are professors that much more virtuous than these other professionals? Professors would certainly like to think so! But, to be objective, we have to concede that the reason might simply be that professors have much less opportunity than the other professionals to make a buck through illegal means.

Also like street criminals, white-collar criminals use many techniques of neutralization to justify their crimes and other misconduct. At the corporate level, executives and middle managers see their behavior as necessary to compete in very competitive markets. Despite massive evidence to the contrary, corporate executives deny again and again that their workplaces harm their workers, that their products harm consumers, and that their pollutants harm the public. We will never know if they actually believe what they are saying or if they are lying to protect themselves and their companies. Probably, some do believe what they say, whereas others know full well the harm they have caused.

Another similarity has been hotly debated, and this is whether white-collar criminals join with street criminals in lacking self-control. Recall that Michael Gottfredson and Travis Hirschi (1990) put lack of self-control at the root of all criminality (see Chapter 8), including white-collar crime. This view has been sharply challenged. As Gilbert Geis (1995) observed, "For most scholars who study white-collar crime, the idea that low self-control holds the key to such offenses as antitrust conspiracies seems exceedingly farfetched."

A final similarity concerns gender and involvement in white-collar crime. We have seen in previous chapters that women are much less likely than men to commit street crime. The same gender difference exists for white-collar crime, with women's involvement much lower than men's involvement, especially for corporate crime. The gender-based socialization differences emphasized in previous chapters for street crime probably also help explain the gender difference for white-collar crime. Opportunity matters as well: because women are much less likely than men to be corporate executives, their opportunities for corporate crime are much lower. Because their opportunities are lower, they are less likely to commit corporate crime (Steffensmeier et al. 2013).

Differences from Street Crime

So far we have discussed factors that help explain both white-collar crime and street crime and one factor, lack of self-control, that does not seem to apply to corporate crime. Other reasons for street crime also do not apply to corporate crime. Consider, for example, the view, rejected by most sociologists, that violent and other street criminals suffer from biological or psychological abnormalities. Although corporate executives are responsible for more deaths each year than all the murderers in our midst, it would probably sound silly to say they have some biological or psychological abnormality that causes them to allow people to die.

Turning to sociological explanations of conventional crime, it would also sound silly to say that corporate executives fleece the public because as children they grew up amid social disorganization, suffered negative family and school experiences, and consorted with delinquent friends. Corporate executives are, after all, successful. They have achieved the American dream, and one reason for this is that many were raised in the best of surroundings and went to the best schools. Nor can we blame their present economic circumstances. As Sutherland (1949) noted more than sixty years ago, we cannot attribute the crime of corporate executives to economic deprivation because they are, by definition, wealthy to begin with.

Cultural and Social Bases for White-Collar Crime

To explain the behavior of white-collar criminals, then, we must look beyond explanations stressing individual failings and instead consider a combination of structural and cultural forces. Here we again go back to Sutherland (1949), who said that white-collar crime stems from a process of differential association in which business offenders learn shared views on the desirability of their criminal conduct. Most contemporary scholars of white-collar crime agree with his view, especially where corporate crime is concerned, because many corporations develop "subcultures of resistance" that encourage corporate lawbreaking to enhance corporate profits (Braithwaite 1989). Here the views of top management matter greatly. According to one business professor, "Of all the factors that lead to corporate crime, none comes close in importance to the role top management plays in tolerating, even shaping, a culture that allows for it" (Leaf 2002:67).

Many scholars also blame white-collar crime on an insatiable thirst for money and the power accompanying it. This greed in turn arises from the stress placed in our society on economic success (Passas 1990). Even if we are already wealthy, we can never have enough. The pursuit of profit in a capitalist society can be ruthless at times, and individuals and organizations will often do whatever is necessary to acquire even more money, wealth, and power.

Lenient Treatment

Another reason corporate crime occurs is the lenient treatment afforded corporate criminals. As an article in *Fortune* magazine, the well-known business publication, put it, "The double standard in criminal justice in this country is starker and more embedded than many realize. Bob Dylan was right: Steal a little, and they put you in jail. Steal a lot, and you're likely to walk away with a lecture and a court-ordered promised not to do it again" (Leaf 2002:62). This lenient treatment involves several components (Benson and Simpson 2009).

Weak or Absent Regulations First, regulations forbidding corporate misconduct are either weak or nonexistent. Part of the reason for this is that corporations, whether you like them or not, are very powerful and influential and are often able to prevent or water down regulatory legislation. Also, because federal and state regulatory agencies are woefully underfunded and understaffed, much corporate misconduct goes undetected.

Difficulty of Proving Corporate Crime Second, corporate crime is difficult to prove and punish even when it is suspected. A major reason for this is again corporate

▼ Despite some recent publicized prosecutions of prominent individuals accused of corporate crime, the legal treatment of corporate criminals continues to be fairly lenient.

AP Photo/Dennis Cook

power. Simply put, corporations have more resources, including sheer wealth and highly paid, skilled attorneys, than do enforcement agencies and district attorney offices. A regulatory agency or district attorney bringing charges against a major corporation is like David fighting Goliath. In the Bible, David won, but in the contemporary world of corporate crime, Goliath usually wins. Regulatory agencies and district attorneys often have to settle for promises by corporations that they will stop their misconduct, which they often do not even admit they were doing (Rosoff et al. 2010).

The complexity of corporate crime is also a factor in the difficulty of proving it. As prosecutors realize, juries often find it difficult to understand complicated financial transactions and shenanigans. It is also often difficult to determine when and how a law or regulation was violated, who made the decision to violate it, and whether the alleged offender acted with criminal intent. For all these reasons, in many cases criminal indictments and prosecutions never occur.

Weak Punishment The third component of lenient treatment of white-collar criminals is weak punishment (Pontell 2010). As a business writer for the *New York Times* noted, "It's an all-too-familiar pattern: a corporation—usually a big name, with broad business and political influence—gets enmeshed in scandal. Shocking revelations portray a pattern of wrongdoing. The damages run into the billions . . . and then, not very much happens. Not many people go to jail, and if they do, it's not for very long" (Eichenwald 2002:A1). The writer then recounted several corporate scandals; although the companies involved in the scandals paid millions of dollars in fines, not a single senior executive was imprisoned.

As this writer noted, most corporate violations that are punished involve fines, not imprisonment. Although the fines may run into hundreds of thousands or even tens of millions of dollars, they are the proverbial drop in the bucket for the people or corporations who must pay them. We saw this earlier with the electrical price-fixing scandal of 1961 and with the contemporary examples involving Dow Chemical and Kellog's. In another recent example, Bank of America was fined $10 million in 2004 for delaying the delivery of documentation on possible securities trading violations (Countryman 2004). The Securities and Exchange Commission (SEC) said this fine was the largest it had ever imposed for this type of offense. The fine was a certainly lot of money in absolute terms. However, Bank of America took in $48 billion in revenue in 2003 and cleared a profit of $10.8 billion, and its total assets were almost $1 trillion. Thus, the fine amounted to 0.02 percent of its revenue, less than 1 percent of its profit, and 0.001 percent of its assets. Even after paying the fine, Bank of America still had assets of almost $1 trillion. All these examples make clear that fines for corporations have little impact and are often seen as just the cost of doing business.

Imprisonment also has little impact on corporate criminals and other high-status offenders because it only rarely occurs and involves a light sentence (either no prison time or just a short sentence) when it does occur (Pontell 2010). This remains true despite some relatively long prison sentences handed out in the aftermath of the Enron scandal. Part of the reason for this problem is the high-powered attorneys and other resources that wealthy defendants can afford and the unwillingness of judges to regard them as real criminals deserving actual punishment. Another part of the reason is that the law often does not provide in a stiff prison term. For example, the executives convicted of crimes in the savings and loan scandal discussed earlier each stole at least $100,000, but received an average of only 36 months in prison. In contrast, burglars (who generally steal only a few hundred dollars' worth of goods) receive a sentence of almost 56 months (Calavita et al. 1997). In California, only 38 percent of physicians and other persons convicted of Medicaid fraud were incarcerated, compared to 79 percent of grand-theft defendants, even though the economic loss from Medicaid fraud was ten times greater than the loss from grand theft (Tillman and Pontell 1992).

Lack of News Media Coverage

A final factor contributing to corporate crime is that the news media gloss over the damage it causes. This is unfortunate, because the threat of publicity can deter such crime (Scott 1989). Morton Mintz (1992), the former *Washington Post* investigative reporter cited earlier, attributed the media's neglect to cowardice, friendships, libel risks, and its "pro-business orientation." Although Mintz conceded that the press was covering corporate crime more than in the past (and, more than a decade after his statement, probably more now in the aftermath of the Enron scandal and others), he said it was still guilty of a "pro-corporate tilt" that led to a lack of adequate coverage of corporate crime and other misconduct.

Race/Ethnicity and Social Class

Earlier we noted the relevance of gender helps explain who commits both street crime and white-collar crime, with women less likely than men to engage in either type of crime. Race/ethnicity and social class, however, operate differently for white-collar crime than they do for street crime. Previous chapters noted that low-income people and people of color are more likely than wealthier whites to engage in street crime. The opposite is true for white-collar crime and especially for corporate crime, for which wealthy whites are almost always the offenders. Just as (lack of) opportunity helps explain why women are less involved in corporate crime, so does it help explain why low-income people and people of color are similarly less involved. Simply put, they are not corporate executives and thus lack the opportunity to commit corporate crime. Because they do have this opportunity, wealthy whites are the people committing corporate crime.

Review and Discuss

Why, generally, does white-collar crime occur?

Reducing White-Collar Crime

To reduce corporate and other white-collar crime, several measures are necessary (Payne 2013; Piquero and Schoepfer 2010). To list but a few, federal and state regulatory agencies must be provided much larger budgets so they will become at least somewhat stronger Davids against corporate Goliaths. The media would have to focus as much or more attention on corporate and other white-collar crime as they now do on street crime. More severe punishment might also work. Because the major corporations can easily afford to pay even millions of dollars in fines, these would have to be increased substantially to have a noticeable deterrent effect. Because so few corporate executives and other high-status offenders are threatened with imprisonment, many scholars think the increased use of even short prison terms may induce these offenders to obey the law (Pontell 2010). Agreeing with this view, a writer for *Fortune* magazine observed that "the problem will not go away until white-collar thieves face a consequence they're actually scared of: time in jail" (Leaf 2002:62).

Other observers say that stiffer fines and greater use of imprisonment will not work and will lead only to further problems, including overburdening a legal system already stretched beyond its means. These observers think that self-regulation and compliance strategies emphasizing informal sanctions, such as negative publicity campaigns, would ultimately reduce corporate crime more effectively (Braithwaite 1995). However, Henry Pontell and Kitty Calavita (1993) think this approach would not have prevented the 1980s savings and loan fraud, partly because savings and loan executives looted their own institutions and would thus not have cared about their institutions' reputations.

▶ Organized Crime

When the public demands goods or services, organized crime is all too ready to provide them. Sometimes this is true even if the products and services are legal. For example, organized crime is thought to be involved in several legitimate businesses, including trash-hauling operations, the vending and amusement machine industries, and the toxic-waste dumping industry (Abadinsky 2013; Lyman and Potter 2011; Nussbaum and Troncone 2009).

Despite its involvement in these kinds of businesses, however, organized crime's primary source of income remains illegal activities and products: drugs, prostitution, pornography, gambling, loan sharking (loaning money at extraordinarily high interest rates), and extortion (obtaining money through threats). Throughout its history, organized crime has flourished because it has catered to the public's desires and has had the active or passive cooperation of political, legal, and business officials. The rest of this section explores these themes.

History of Organized Crime

If by organized crime we mean coordinated efforts to acquire illegal profits, then organized crime has existed for centuries. The earliest example of organized crime is piracy, in which pirates roamed the high seas and plundered ships. Piracy was common among ancient Phoenicians on the Mediterranean Sea and, many centuries later, among Vikings in what is now western Europe. In the 1600s, buccaneers—Dutch, English, and French pirates—began plundering ships carrying goods to and from the Spanish colonies in the New World and then branched out to colonies farther north. By the end of the 1600s, pirates openly traded their plunder with merchants in Boston, New York, Philadelphia, and other port cities in what is called the "golden age of piracy." The merchants bought the pirated booty at low cost and sold the pirates food and other provisions. Royal governors and other public officials took bribes to look the other way, with corruption especially rampant in the New York colony.

Eventually, merchants realized that they could get greater profits by trading with England rather than with pirates, and by the late 1720s piracy had faded. "At that point," wrote criminologists Dennis J. Kenney and James O. Finckenauer (1995:70), "the markets for pirate goods dried up, and the public demand for their services and support for their existence disappeared." The merchants who once traded with pirates now called them a public menace. One lesson of the golden age of piracy is that "colonial piracy flourished only because the colonists wanted it to" (Kenney and Finckenauer 1995:70). Piracy's success depended on the willingness of merchants to trade with pirates, the public's willingness to buy the pirates' plunder from the merchants, and the readiness of political officials to take bribes. The situation today with organized crime is not much different.

Organized crime began anew in New York City in the early 1800s, where almost 1 million people—most of them poor, half of them immigrants, and many of them unemployed—lived crammed into two square miles. Amid such conditions, stealing and other crime were inevitable. Young women were forced to turn to prostitution, and young men formed gangs, enabling them to commit crime more effectively and protecting them from the police. These gangs were the forerunners of today's organized crime groups and, like the pirates before them, had a cozy relationship with public officials. Crooked city politicians used them at polling places to stuff ballot boxes and intimidate voters (Kenney and Finckenauer 1995).

By the end of the century, the gangs in New York and elsewhere had developed into extensive operations, many of them involving vice crime such as prostitution and gambling. The ethnic makeup of these organized crime groups reflected the great waves of immigration into the United States during the nineteenth century. Most immigrants settled in the nation's major cities and faced abject poverty and horrible living conditions. As cities grew and the vice trade developed, it was inevitable that many immigrants would turn to organized crime to make ends meet. Irish Americans were the first to take up organized crime and eventually became very dominant in many cities. Later in the century, Italians and Jews immigrated into the country in enormous numbers and soon got their share of the vice trade, working closely, as the Irish had before them, with politicians, police, and various legitimate businesses. In the twentieth century, African-Americans, Asian-Americans, and Latinos became more involved in organized crime. Although many scholars question whether the United States has been, as popularly thought, one big "melting pot" of various ethnic and racial groups, organized crime ironically is one area in which diverse groups have pursued economic opportunity and the American dream (O'Kane 1992).

If New York and other city gangs were the forerunners of organized crime, the nineteenth-century robber barons were the role models (Abadinsky 2013). To extend our earlier discussion, railroad baron Leland Stanford bribed members of Congress and other officials to gain land grants and federal loans for his Central Pacific Railroad. John D. Rockefeller's Standard Oil Company forced competitors out of business with price wars and occasionally dynamite. The Du Pont family, which made its fortune on gunpowder, cornered its market after the Civil War with bribery and explosions of competing firms. These and other examples are evidence of the corruption and violence characterizing much of U.S. business history. Organized crime since the nineteenth century is merely its latest manifestation.

The robber baron analogy indicates that organized crime and corporate crime might be more similar than we think. Taking up this theme, many scholars see little difference between the two (Abadinsky 2013). Both kinds of crime involve careful planning and coordinated effort

▼

to acquire illegal profits. Both rely on active or passive collusion of public officials and on public willingness to buy the goods and services they provide. Although organized crime is more willing to use interpersonal violence to acquire its profits, corporate crime, as we saw earlier, can also be very violent.

Organized crime's power and wealth increased enormously during Prohibition (Okrent 2011). Before this era, organized crime was primarily a local phenomenon with little coordination across cities. Bootlegging demanded much more coordination, because it involved the manufacture, distribution, and sale of alcohol. Organized crime groups in different cities now had to coordinate their activities, and organized crime became more organized to maximize the enormous profits from bootlegging. At the same time, rival gangs fought each other to control bootlegging turf. Politicians and federal and local law enforcement officials were all too willing to take bribes. For these reasons, Prohibition fueled the rise and power of organized crime. Bribery of politicians and police was common in cities such as Chicago, where organized crime acquired enormous influence.

After Prohibition ended, organized crime's primary source of income for several decades was gambling. Starting in the 1960s, it moved more into the illegal drug trade, which now provides an important source of organized crime's annual income, estimated between $50 billion and $150 billion in the United States, with gambling a fairly distant second. Due in large part to drug trafficking, organized crime in recent years has taken on an international focus, with cocaine smuggled into the United States from Colombia and elsewhere.

Alien Conspiracy Model and Myth

One of the most controversial scholarly issues in U.S. organized crime today is whether it is controlled by a highly organized, hierarchical group of some twenty-four Italian *families*. This view, often called the alien conspiracy model or the *Mafia mystique,* was popularized in important congressional hearings beginning in the 1950s (Albanese 2000). It was later featured in the various *Godfather* films and many other movies and books, and lived again in the TV series *The Sopranos.* In addition to specifying a hierarchical, Italian-dominated structure of organized crime, the model argues that organized crime was largely unknown before Italians immigrated to the United States in the late 1800s. It also assumes that organized crime exists because immigrants, first Italians and later Asians and others, corrupt righteous U.S. citizens and prey on their weaknesses.

Despite its popularity, the alien conspiracy model is best regarded as a myth (Kappeler and Potter 2005). In emphasizing Italian domination, this particular myth ignores the long history of organized crime before Italian immigration and overlooks the involvement of many other ethnic and racial groups. It also diverts attention from organized crime's roots in poverty, in the readiness of citizens to pay for the goods and services it provides, and in the willingness of politicians, law enforcement agents, and legitimate businesses to take bribes and otherwise cooperate with organized crime.

As the history of organized crime indicates, the public, politicians, and other officials are not very righteous after all. This is still true today. As Gary W. Potter (1994:147) observed, "It is a fallacy that organized crime produces the desire for vice. Organized crime doesn't force people to gamble, snort cocaine, or read pornography. It merely fills an already existing social gap. The law has made organized crime inevitable because it denies people legal sources for those desired goods and services."

Nor does organized crime seduce honest politicians, police, and other officials and owners of legitimate businesses. Instead, these keepers of the public trust are often very willing to take bribes and otherwise cooperate with organized crime. In a Seattle, Washington, study, William Chambliss (1988) found organized crime, business leaders, politicians, and police working hand

▼ According to the alien conspiracy model, U.S. organized crime is controlled by a small group of Italian families. This model was depicted in the popular TV series, The Sopranos, shown here.

V.O. Press/ZUMA Press/Newscom

Japan is famed for having a relatively low street crime rate among the world's industrial nations. While that may be so, it is paradoxically one of the world's leaders in organized crime.

Organized crime members in Japan are called the yakuza. The yakuza, according a news report, have "deep-rooted ties" with Japanese corporations, especially the construction industry, with Japanese banks reportedly helping to finance business relationships between construction companies and the yakuza.

The reason for the yakuza's involvement in construction is simple: money. Japan's construction involves 30 million yen (about $387 billion in 2013 dollars) annually. Before the Japanese government began cracking down on the yakuza's construction efforts just a few years ago, it was taking in between 2 and 3 percent of these dollars, or as much as $12 billion annually.

The yakuza are thought to number nearly 83,000 members across Japan and to control various enterprises with an annual value of $242 billion. Ironically, Japan's defeat in World War II helped fuel the rise of the yakuza. When the company tried to rebuild after the war, the yakuza broke up strikes and in this and other ways helped ensure that construction companies would keep wages and other labor costs to a minimum.

In addition to using front companies for construction projects, today's yakuza also bring in money by providing "protection" for legitimate construction companies. By 2013, there were signs that various yakuza's gangs had started fighting each other and had increased their violence toward construction executives who refused to pay for their "protection." As the head of a construction company explained, "The yakuza have a hand in all sorts of industries, and working with them is just a part of doing business in this city. But times are changing. We used to have a sort of harmony with these bosses. They were enforcers, protectors who asked for our money to smooth out permits and deals, but who kept the battles to themselves. Now they're out of control."

Source: Cain 2013; Tabuchi 2010.

in hand. In a study of organized crime in "Morrisburg," a pseudonym for an East Coast city of 98,000, Potter (1994:101–102) concluded, "It is quite clear to anyone walking the streets of 'Morrisburg' that the political fix is in and extends from the cop on the beat to the most senior political officials." Such corruption, he noted, "is critical to the survival of organized crime. In fact, organized crime could not operate at all without the direct complicity and connivance of the political machinery in its area of operation" (p. 149).

Like Chambliss and other organized crime researchers, Potter also found legitimate businesses cooperating with organized crime in Morrisburg and noted, "The close interrelationships between legitimate and illicit businesses have been documented time and again in every local study of organized crime groups" (p. 135).

Chambliss, Potter, and other scholars also argue that the alien conspiracy model exaggerates the hierarchical nature of organized crime and the degree to which it is Italian-dominated. Instead, they say, organized crime today is best seen as a loose confederation of local groups consisting of people from many different ethnic backgrounds. Organized crime's decentralized, fluid structure permits it to adapt quickly to the ebb and flow of the vice trade and government's efforts to control it.

Controlling Organized Crime

Organized crime has been around for so long because it provides goods and services that the public desires. For this reason, it will not go away soon. Here the debate over the alien conspiracy model has important implications for how we should try to control organized crime and even for whether any effort will succeed. If the alien conspiracy model is correct, arrests and prosecutions of selected organized crime "bosses" should eliminate its leadership and thus weaken its ability to entice the public to use its goods and services and various officials to take bribes. The government has used this strategy at least since the days of Al Capone.

If, however, organized crime has a more fluid, decentralized structure whose success depends on public and official readiness to cooperate with its illegal activities, this strategy will not work. As long as public demand for illicit goods and services remains, the financial incentives for organized crime will also remain. And as long as politicians, police, and the business community are eager to cooperate, organized crime will be able to operate with impunity. Organized crime, in short, is too much a part of our economic, political, and social systems for the law enforcement strategy to work well (Albanese 2000).

To reduce organized crime's influence, then, we first must reduce public demand for its illicit goods and services. For better or worse, this is probably a futile goal. If so, a more effective way to fight organized crime might be to admit defeat and to legalize drugs, gambling, and prostitution, because the laws against these crimes have ironically generated opportunities for organized crime to realize huge financial gains (Kappeler and Potter 2005). Legalizing these crimes would be a very controversial step (see Chapter 15), but would at least lessen organized crime's influence. Legalization might weaken organized crime in an additional way, because current enforcement of the laws in fact strengthens organized crime. The reason is that organized crime figures who get arrested tend to be the smallest, weakest, and most inefficient operators. Their removal from the world of organized crime allows the stronger and more efficient organized crime figures to gain even more control over illicit goods and services. They can also charge more for the goods and services they provide, increasing their profits even further (Kappeler and Potter 2005).

Of course, legalization of drugs and other illicit products and activities is not about to happen soon. Given that fact, another way to fight organized crime would be to concentrate on the cooperation given it by politicians, police, and legitimate businesses. Unfortunately, this would entail a law enforcement focus that has not really been tried before. It is unlikely that the government would want to take this approach, given that in some ways it would be investigating itself.

One final way to weaken organized crime would be to provide alternative economic opportunities for the young people who become involved in it each year. Thus, if we could effectively reduce poverty and provide decent-paying, meaningful jobs, we could reduce the attractiveness of organized crime to the new recruits it needs to perpetuate itself. Unfortunately, there are no signs that our nation is eager to launch a new "war on poverty" with the same fervor that has guided our war against drugs and other illicit goods and services that now make so much money for organized crime.

Review and Discuss

The text says that organized crime has often had the cooperation of political, legal, and business officials. What evidence does the text provide for this allegation?

▶ Conclusion

There once was an editorial cartoon depicting two men. One was middle-aged, dressed in a slick business suit, and listed as a corporate executive; the other was young and shabbily dressed with unkempt hair and a day-old beard. Under the cartoon was the question: Who's the criminal? This chapter has attempted to answer this question. By any objective standard, white-collar crime causes more financial loss, injury and illness, and death than street crime. However, street crimes remain the ones we worry about. We lock our doors, arm ourselves with guns, and take many other precautions to protect ourselves from muggers, rapists, burglars, and other criminals. These are all dangerous people, and we should be concerned about them. Because white-collar crime is more indirect and invisible than street crime, it worries us far less, no matter how much harm it causes. White-collar crime is less visible partly because of its nature and partly because of press inattention. One consequence of its invisibility is that white-collar crime victims often do not realize that they are being victimized.

As a result, most white-collar crime remains hidden from regulatory agencies and law enforcement personnel. If someone poisoned a bottle of aspirin or other consumer product, the press would publicize this crime heavily. We would all be alarmed and refuse to buy the product, and its manufacturer would probably take it off retail shelves. Meanwhile, we use dangerous products that kill many people each year because we are unaware of their danger. Even when we are aware of two other kinds of corporate violence, unsafe workplaces and environmental pollution, there is often little we can do. Workers have to go to work each day to pay their bills. Locked doors will not keep out air, water, or land pollution. The same is true for economic white-collar crime that steals from the public: locked doors, guns, and mace will not protect the average family of four from losing $1,000 to price-fixing each year.

White-collar crime remains an elusive concept. As used here, it encompasses petty workplace theft by blue-collar workers as well as complex financial schemes by wealthy professionals and major corporations. The inclusion of crime by blue-collar workers and businesses takes us far from Sutherland's original focus on corporate and other crime by high-status offenders. But it does remind us that crime takes on a variety of forms and involves many otherwise law-abiding people who would denounce robbers and burglars, but see nothing wrong with occasionally helping themselves to a few items from their workplaces or cheating a customer now and then.

However, given the power and influence of corporations, wealthy professionals, and other high-status offenders, it is important to keep their behavior at the forefront of the study of white-collar crime. As Sutherland reminded us, crime is not just something that poor nonwhite people do. And as he also reminded us, the harm caused by corporate and other high-status crime greatly exceeds the harm caused by the street crime of the poor. Sutherland and other like-minded scholars are not saying we should minimize the problem of street crime. This would not be fair to its many victims, most of them poor and many of them people of color. But they are saying that it is time to give white-collar crime the concern and attention it so richly deserves.

Organized crime has certainly received much attention over the decades and for good reason. It is a powerful influence in U.S. life and, as least as depicted in film and on TV, has colorful characters ready to commit violence. Although we know much about organized crime, this does not mean it is very possible to weaken it. As long as people continue to desire the goods and services organized crime provides, this type of crime will remain with us.

If white-collar crime has still received relatively little scholarly and other attention, political crime has received even less. This crime again challenges traditional views of criminality and forces us to question the nature and legitimacy of law when lawbreaking is committed by the government itself or by members of the public, acting not for personal gain, but for a higher end. We will examine this fascinating topic in Chapter 14.

Summary

1. In 1949, Edwin Sutherland examined lawbreaking by major U.S. corporations. Despite his pathbreaking work, the study of white-collar crime lagged until the 1970s. Sutherland defined white-collar crime as "a crime committed by a person of respectability and high social status in the course of his occupation." There has been much discussion of the value of this definition. A useful typology of white-collar crime distinguishes between occupational crime and organizational crime.

2. A major type of occupational crime is employee theft, composed of pilferage and embezzling. Much of this crime occurs because of the dissatisfaction of employees with their pay and various aspects of their working conditions. The savings and loan scandal of the 1980s involved a new form of crime called collective embezzlement, in which top executives stole from their own institutions.

3. Professional fraud occurs for many reasons, among them the fact that professional work is autonomous and self-regulated. Professionals who commit fraud invoke many techniques of neutralization. A very common type of professional fraud is health care fraud, which costs the nation about $100 billion annually. Unnecessary surgery costs about 12,000 lives per year.

4. Blue-collar businesses and corporations also commit financial crimes. The auto-repair industry is notoriously rife with fraud that costs consumers billions of dollars annually. Financial fraud by corporations received much attention in the beginning of this decade thanks to accounting scandals at Enron and other major corporations. These scandals resulted in the loss of thousands of jobs and of tens of billions of dollars held by investors. Corporate

financial fraud takes several forms, including accounting improprieties, price-fixing and other antitrust violations, and false advertising. Financial fraud of all types by corporations may amount to almost $400 billion annually, and the total economic cost of all economic crime reaches more than $800 billion.

5. Corporate violence refers to actions by corporations that cause injury, illness, or death. Examples of corporate violence include unsafe workplaces, unsafe products, and environmental pollution. The number of annual estimated deaths in the United States from white-collar crime of all types is more than 118,000.

6. Many of the factors implicated in street crime (e.g., extreme poverty, negative childhood experiences, and low self-control) do not seem to explain white-collar crime by corporate executives and other high-status professionals. Instead, white-collar crime arises from an insatiable thirst for money and power, a workplace culture that condones lawbreaking, and a system of lax law enforcement.

7. Although many scholars and other observers think that longer and more certain prison terms would significantly deter white-collar crime in general and corporate crime in particular, other observers think this strategy would prove ineffective and overburden a legal system that is already stretched beyond its means.

8. Organized crime goes back to the days of pirates and exists because it provides citizens goods and services they desire. The popular image of organized crime dominated by a few Italian families and corrupting innocent individuals is a myth. Instead, organized crime is relatively decentralized and composed of many groups of different ethnicities and other backgrounds.

Key Terms

alien conspiracy model *281*
collective embezzlement *265*
corporate crime *264*
corporate violence *269*
embezzlement *265*
goods *279*

muckrakers *263*
occupational crime *264*
organizational crime *264*
pilferage *264*
piracy *280*
price-fixing *268*

professional fraud *265*
restraint of trade *268*
services *279*
white-collar crime *263*

What Would You Do?

1. One day you are hired for a summer job as a cashier in the clothing section of a large department store in a tourist area. At any one time, there are four cashiers working in your section. Because the hours of all the cashiers are staggered, over the next two weeks you meet a dozen other cashiers who were all hired just for the summer. By the end of this period, you have also become aware that most of them have stolen clothing from the store by taking the security tags off articles of clothing and putting the articles in their backpacks. Just about everyone but you has taken a couple of shirts and one or two pairs of pants. Because your store is so large and so busy, it is likely that the store will not realize what is happening until long after the summer is over, if then. Would you join the other cashiers in taking clothing, tell the store manager, or do nothing? Explain your answer.

2. You are working full-time in a summer job in a hamburger joint so that you can afford to pay your tuition for the fall semester at the state university. One day you notice that someone forgot to put a shipment of raw meat into the freezer immediately after arrival, as store regulations require, and instead let it lie around for several hours. Concerned that the meat may not be safe to eat, you notify the store manager. The manager says the meat is probably safe to eat and that, if he throws it out, the cost would come out of his salary. He then instructs you and one of your coworkers to put the meat in the freezer. What do you do? Why?

AP Photo/Joe Kohen

14 Political Crime

Crime in the News

Eight University of Michigan students were arrested in April 2013 for blocking a busy intersection just off campus. They were among a group of about 50 people protesting in favor of in-state tuition for undocumented Michigan residents. The protesters chanted, "Education, not deportation," as they stood in a circle in the intersection and police directed traffic around them. After police told the protesters to vacate the intersection or risk arrest, most of them complied with this order, except for the eight who remained behind and submitted to arrest. One of the students explained why he decided to do so: "The cause is worthy enough. The students who can't get in here deserve our support."

Source: Lichterman 2013.

The behavior for which the University of Michigan protesters were arrested was very different from the crimes covered in earlier chapters. Those crimes were either committed for economic gain (property crime or white-collar crime) or out of hatred, anger, jealousy, and other emotions (violent crime). The CSUN activists had none of these reasons in mind. Instead, their motivation was *ideological:* They aimed to call attention to the denial of in-state tuition for undocumented Michigan residents. The behavior for which they were arrested was a *political crime.* Political crime has existed for centuries and takes many forms. People like the University of Michigan protesters commit political crime, but so do governments. And although the Michigan traffic blockage was a relatively benign, if disruptive, act of civil disobedience, the unforgettable attacks on 9/11 were obviously very deadly acts of terrorism. This chapter discusses these and the many other types of political crime. As we will see, political crime often plays a key role in the struggle between government and dissenters.

▶ Defining Political Crime

Like *white-collar crime,* political crime is an ambiguous term. For example, we could say that all crimes are political crimes because all crimes by definition violate criminal laws passed by legislative bodies. However, this conceptualization would render the term *political crime* meaningless. As another example, political officials, as we will see, often take legal actions that violate standards of human decency and democracy. Should we consider their actions political crimes? Should social problems such as hunger, poverty, corporate violence, and institutionalized sexism and racism be considered political crimes, as some scholars argue? Should African-Americans and other poor people of color languishing in our prisons for street crime be considered political prisoners, as some radicals argued a generation ago (Lefcourt 1971)? Were the urban riots of the 1960s political revolts or just common violence? What about politicians who take bribes and are otherwise corrupt for personal gain? Are their crimes political crimes?

None of these questions is easy to answer. A major part of the struggle between any government and its dissenters is to influence public views of the legitimacy and necessity of actions taken by both sides. The state does its best to frame its own actions, however harmful, as necessary to protect the social order from violent and even irrational individuals. Meanwhile, dissenters call attention to the evils of state policies and frame their own activities, even if illegal, as necessary for a more just society. Public officials call an urban uprising a riot, whereas dissenters call it a revolt. Against this backdrop, any attempt to define and categorize political crime is itself a political act. Omitting harmful, unethical, and even illegal actions by the state risks obscuring behaviors that are often far worse than what any common criminal does. In contrast, calling any state policy or social condition that oppresses some deprived group (the poor, women, people of color) a political crime might dilute the concept's analytic power.

As with white-collar crime, it seems best to take an eclectic view of political crime that encompasses what many people mean by the concept without being overly broad. A reasonable definition of political crime might then be *any illegal or socially harmful act aimed at preserving or changing the existing political and social order.* This is not a perfect definition because it leaves open, for example, the question of who defines whether a given act is "socially harmful," but it does get at what most scholars mean by political crime (Ross 2012). Although the actual behavior involved in political crime (e.g., killing) may be very similar to that involved in conventional crimes, the key difference is that political crime is performed for ideological reasons. Thus tax evasion intended for personal gain is fraud, whereas nonpayment of taxes to protest U.S. military or taxation policy is a political crime. A killing during a robbery is a homicide, whereas a killing by an act of terrorism is a homicide but also a political crime.

Major Categories of Political Crime

Let us further divide political crime into two major categories: crime by government and crime against government. *Crime by government,* also called *state crime* or *state criminality* (Rothe and Kauzlarich 2010), aims to preserve the existing order and includes (1) political repression and human rights violations (genocide, torture, assassination, and other violence; surveillance and infiltration; and arrest, prosecution, and imprisonment), (2) unethical or illegal experimentation, and (3) the aiding and abetting of corporate crime. Many governments, including the United States and other democracies, commit some or all of these crimes, which occur inside or outside their national borders. A fourth type of crime by government is *political corruption.* As Chapter 13 noted, many scholars place this corruption in the occupational crime category. But because political corruption violates the public trust by enhancing the wealth and influence of political officials, other scholars consider it a form of political crime, especially when it involves conspiracies of people at the highest levels of government, such as in the Watergate and Iran–Contra scandals (discussed later).

Crime against government aims to change the existing order and includes (1) terrorism, assassination, and other political violence, (2) nonviolent civil disobedience, and (3) espionage and treason. It might be more accurate to call this category "crime against government and other established interests." For example, although much illegal protest is directed against government, as it was during the Vietnam War, much is also aimed against corporations and other targets. Illegal protest by organized labor, nuclear arms opponents, and animal rights activists are just a few that fall into this category.

With these broad categories of political crime in mind, we now explore its nature and extent by turning to specific examples.

► Crime by Government

Political Repression and Human Rights Violations

In an ideal world, all societies would be democratic and egalitarian, treating their citizens and those of other nations with dignity and respect. This ideal world has never existed. History is replete with governments that have used both violent and legal means to repress dissent and to preserve inequality. The worst offenders are typically totalitarian regimes, but even democratic governments, including the United States, have engaged in various types of repression, including mass murder. To do justice to all victims of repression would take too much space, but several examples should give you an idea of its use in both totalitarian and democratic societies.

Genocide

The ultimate act of repression is genocide (Hagan and Kaiser 2011). Genocide, a term coined during World War II, refers to the deliberate extermination of a group because of its race, religion, ethnicity, or nationality. By definition, genocide is the worst crime by government of all and is often called a *crime against humanity.* The most infamous example of genocide, of course, is the Holocaust: the Nazi slaughter of 6 million Jews during World War II, more than two-thirds of all the Jews in Europe, and up to 6 million other people, including Poles, Slavs, Catholics, homosexuals, and gypsies (Kokh and Polian 2012). In the late 1800s, Russia also committed Jewish genocide by murdering hundreds of Jews in massacres called *pogroms.* More than 2 million Russian Jews fled their homeland for the safety of the United States, Palestine, and other areas (Klier and Lambroza 1992). In yet another act of genocide, about 1 million Armenians died from thirst, starvation, or attacks by roving tribes after Turkey forced them into the surrounding desert in 1915 (Balakian 2003).

Genocide did not end with the Nazis. In the last decade, the mass murder of Africans in Sudan by a militia group called the Janjaweed amounted to genocide. Political unrest in the western region of Darfur led the Sudanese government to pay the Janjaweed to quell the rebellion. The Janjaweed did so through mass terror, including murder, rape, torture, and the burning of whole villages. By July 2004, more than 1 million Africans had been displaced and hundreds of thousands died from murder and starvation (Hagan and Kaiser 2011). A decade earlier, political violence in two other regions of the world, Bosnia in eastern Europe and Rwanda in Africa, also led to tens of thousands of deaths and repeated charges of genocide (Lynch 1995; Post 1994). And during the late 1970s, the Khmer Rouge regime of dictator Pol Pot slaughtered hundreds of thousands of Cambodians (Martin 1994).

Genocide is typically linked to totalitarian governments, but democracies can also commit it. Here the U.S. treatment of Native Americans is widely cited. When Europeans first came to this continent, about 1 million Native Americans lived here. Over the decades, tens of thousands were killed by white settlers and then U.S. troops, while many others died from disease introduced by the Europeans. Deaths from these two sources reduced the Indian population to less than 240,000 by 1900. Many historians and other scholars say the killings constituted genocide against American Indians (Johansen 2005).

▲ During World War II, the Nazis imprisoned Jews and other groups in concentration camps such as this one and eventually slaughtered some 6 million Jews and 5 million to 6 million other people.

The term *genocide* was used again during the Vietnam War years. The Vietnam War killed some 58,000 U.S. soldiers and other personnel and almost 2 million Vietnamese. The United States dropped four times as many tons of bombs, many targeting civilian populations, as the Allies had dropped over Germany in World War II. Some were strictly antipersonnel in nature, sending out small nails able to shred muscles and body organs but not able to dent military equipment, or steel pellets able to penetrate flesh but not trucks (Branfman 1972). Many bombs contained napalm, a jellied gasoline that would ignite when dropped from the plane, splatter across a wide area, and burn anything it touched. Often the "anything" was children and other civilians. In 1968, U.S. troops massacred up to 200 civilians at My Lai village. Although this massacre received wide attention after it was publicized, Vietnam veterans later revealed many other civilian massacres that never came to light (Tirman 2011).

Review and Discuss

The text mentions that some critics claimed that the United States was committing genocide during the Vietnam War. How valid is this charge?

Torture, Assassination, and Related Violence

Governments often resort to political violence that stops short of genocide. This violence includes torture and beatings; assassination, execution, and mass murder; and related actions, including forced expulsion. This is government rule by terror and is called state terrorism (Robaina 2013). One of the most notorious examples of state terrorism of the last century occurred under Soviet Union dictator Joseph Stalin in the 1930s and 1940s. In that period, a purge of Communist Party leaders who might have threatened Stalin's reign resulted in the execution of thousands as Stalin's secret police terrorized the Soviet citizenry (Tzouliadis 2008).

State terrorism did not end with Stalin. International human rights groups have documented thousands of government-sponsored murders, beatings, and related violence across the world. In Latin America, the Middle East, Africa, and elsewhere, dissenters are kidnapped, tortured, and murdered, and government troops have raped women routinely. These human rights violations are once again much more common under totalitarian regimes than in democratic societies, but, as we will see shortly, the United States has seen its share of government violence over the years.

Governments also assassinate selected dissenters whom they perceive as special threats. As just one example, in the late 1970s peasants and other poor citizens in El Salvador began demanding that the government provide land, jobs, and other help to the poor. Many Roman Catholic priests and nuns supported the protesters. One of the most vocal clergy was Archbishop Oscar Arnulfo Romero, who was assassinated by government troops in March 1980. His death became a rallying cry for dissident forces for several years (Goldston 1990).

Government Violence in the United States   The United States has also seen its share of political violence committed against dissenters, especially those in the labor movement. One of the several labor massacres remembered by history occurred in Ludlow, Colorado, in April 1914, at a tent city of striking miners and their families evicted from their company-owned homes. On Easter night, April 20, company guards and National Guard troops poured oil on the tents, set them afire, and machine-gunned the families as they fled from the tents. Thirteen children, one woman, and five men died from bullet wounds or smoke inhalation (McGovern and Guttridge 1972).

During the 1960s, violence against Southern civil rights activists by police, state troopers, and white civilians was common. Several dozen civil rights workers were murdered and hundreds more beaten. The murdered included Southern blacks as well as Northerners who had come to help the movement. Other violence greeted civil rights demonstrators engaging in protest campaigns, especially those in Selma, Alabama, in April and May 1963 and in Birmingham, Alabama, in March 1965. In Birmingham, police clubbed nonviolent demonstrators, attacked them with police dogs, and swept them away with powerful fire hoses. In Selma, state troopers again clubbed the demonstrators with nightsticks, attacked them with police horses, and used tear gas. Both episodes shocked the nation and helped win passage of federal civil rights legislation (Branch 1998).

The kind of official violence used against Southern civil rights activists was much less common during the Vietnam antiwar movement, but some still occurred. On May 4, 1970, National Guard troops fired into an antiwar rally at Kent State University in Ohio, killing four students and wounding nine others. Several of the students were just watching the rally or walking to classes (Davies 1973). Ten days later, campus protest not related to the war brought police and state troopers onto the campus of Jackson State College, a historically black college in Mississippi. At one point they fired rifles, shotguns, and submachine guns into a dormitory, killing two students and wounding twelve others (Spofford 1988).

At the federal level, the U.S. government has conspired in or otherwise supported the torture and murder of dissidents and the assassination of political leaders in other nations in the last half century. During the Vietnam War, for example, the Central Intelligence Agency (CIA) established the notorious Operation Phoenix program that arrested, tortured, and murdered some 40,000 Vietnamese civilians (Chomsky and Herman 1979). Following orders of the White House and State Department, the CIA has supported coups that deposed and often killed national leaders in countries such as Chile, the Dominican Republic, Guatemala, Iran, and South Vietnam. These assassinations and coups often plunged these nations further into civil war or led to despotic governments that terrorized their citizenry (Moyers 1988).

Since 2001, U.S. military and civilian personnel have also participated in the torture and abuse of an unknown number of persons of Middle Eastern backgrounds, both during the wars in Iraq and Afghanistan and in the effort to stop international terrorism (Cole 2009; Miles 2009). The U.S. government also engaged in a policy called *extraordinary rendition*. Under this policy, the CIA arrested or kidnapped suspected terrorists in several nations and transported them, blindfolded and shackled, to secret CIA prisons in the Middle East and eastern Europe, where they were reportedly tortured (Clarke 2012). All these policies aroused outrage around the world when they came to light.

Surveillance, Infiltration, and Disruption

In George Orwell's (1949) classic novel *1984*, Big Brother was always watching, and citizens had no freedom of movement. Orwell's novel remains a frightening indictment of societies that today still have police and other agents spy on the citizenry, infiltrate dissident groups, and harass and disrupt their activities.

One cornerstone of democracy is freedom of movement and lawful dissent. Yet from the 1940s to the 1970s in the United States, the FBI, CIA, and other federal, state, and local law enforcement agencies systematically and illegally spied on hundreds of thousands of U.S. citizens who were lawfully involved in civil rights, antiwar, and other protests (Finan 2007). These agencies also infiltrated many dissident groups and did their best to disrupt their activities. The FBI's efforts were part of its counterintelligence program called COINTELPRO, begun in 1941 to target the Communist and Socialist Workers parties. During the 1960s, the FBI turned its attention to the civil rights, antiwar, and other social movements that began during that decade. Using wiretaps and informants, it monitored the activities of tens of thousands of citizens, some of them leaders of these movements, but most of them unknown except to their families and friends. Perhaps, the most famous target of FBI harassment was the great civil rights leader, Martin Luther King, Jr. The FBI bugged motel rooms in which King stayed to gather evidence of alleged extramarital affairs and at one point wrote him anonymously, urging him to commit suicide before this evidence became public (Garrow 1981).

▲ During the Vietnam War, the FBI and other intelligence groups spied on thousands of antiwar dissidents involved in lawful protest and sometimes infiltrated groups opposed to the war.

After the terrorist acts of 9/11, the U.S. government increased its surveillance of people suspected of terrorism, and in 2013 it was revealed that the National Security Agency has been engaging in a massive, "data-mining" domestic surveillance program involving the phone calls, emails, and social media use of tens of millions of Americans. Critics say the government surveillance erodes civil liberties and has a chilling effect on activities protected by the First Amendment. The Crime and Controversy box reviews this debate.

Review and Discuss

In a democracy like the United States, is it legitimate for police and other law enforcement agents to conduct surveillance against and to infiltrate dissenting groups? To what degree does your response depend on whether the dissenting groups have indicated that they intend to break the law and/or to commit violence?

Legal Repression

A favorite repression strategy in totalitarian nations is to arrest and imprison dissidents. The aim here is to use the guise of law to legitimate political repression, even though the arrests and prosecutions are based on trumped-up charges. Stalin's reign of terror involved many *show trials* that depicted his opponents as dangerous threats to law and order. Yet repressive uses of the law also occur in democratic societies, where officials hope that arrests and prosecutions will prompt the public to view dissidents as common criminals. They also hope to intimidate dissidents and their movements and force them to spend large amounts of time, money, and energy on their legal defense.

U.S. history has been filled with legal repression (Finan 2007). To cite one example, federal law prohibited virtually all criticism of World War I. Arrests and prosecutions of some 2,000 labor radicals and socialists during the war muffled dissent and destroyed the Industrial Workers of the World, a radical labor union. After the war ended, federal agents raided homes, restaurants, and other places in thirty-three cities across the country and arrested some 10,000 radicals in what became known as the *Palmer raids,* named after the U.S. attorney general at the time. Legal repression was also used during the Southern civil rights movement of the 1960s, when thousands of activists were arrested and jailed on trumped-up charges, forced to spend large sums of money on their defense, and subjected to beatings and the very real possibility of death in Southern

A fundamental dilemma of any democratic society is how best to strike the right balance between keeping the society safe and keeping the society free. This dilemma became a national controversy after the 9/11 terrorist attacks. In their wake, the federal government arrested thousands of people of Middle Eastern backgrounds living in the United States. They were detained in secret locations for months, and many were not permitted to contact family or friends or even an attorney. Many also had no charges filed against them, and the government refused to reveal their names or locations of detainment. When some were allowed to meet with an attorney, the government monitored their communication in violation of attorney–client privilege.

Forty-five days after 9/11, Congress passed—with hardly any debate—the so-called Patriot Act that greatly expanded the powers of the federal government to combat terrorism. President George W. Bush quickly signed the bill. The act was 342 pages long and most members of Congress did not read it all (or at all). Among other provisions, it gave the FBI the power to gain access to anyone's medical, library, or student records without having to show probable cause or acquire a search warrant. It also expanded the power of law enforcement agents to conduct wiretapping and other surveillance.

In the months that followed, the government increased its surveillance of individuals and groups suspected not only of terrorist activity but also of dissent in general. In one case, a 60-year-old retired telephone company worker said at a gym that "Bush has nothing to be proud of. He is a servant of the big oil companies and his only interest in the Middle East is oil." Shortly afterward, FBI agents visited the man to question him about his statement. FBI agents also questioned many other people about statements and activities such as displaying artwork critical of the government, which is protected by the First Amendment.

The government's detainment of Middle Eastern individuals, the Patriot Act, and the other actions taken in the wake of 9/11 aroused enormous controversy. Civil liberties advocates denounced the erosion of civil liberties, and many cities across the country passed resolutions calling for reforms to the act or its outright elimination. Defenders of the government's actions said they were necessary to keep America safe from terrorism. The war of words escalated when U.S. Attorney General John Ashcroft questioned the patriotism of his critics in testimony before the Senate Judiciary Committee.

Further fuel was provided for civil liberties advocates' fears in March 2007, when it was disclosed that the FBI "may have violated the law or government policies as many as 3,000 times since 2003 as agents secretly collected the telephone, bank and credit card records of U.S. citizens and foreign nationals residing here," according to a news report. Six hundred of the violations were called "serious misconduct" because they involved the use of national security letters, equivalent to subpoenas but not approved by a judge, issued by the FBI. Civil liberties advocates became even more alarmed when it was revealed in June 2013 that the National Security Agency has been conducting a massive domestic surveillance program of the phone calls and electronic communications of tens of millions of Americans.

The civil liberties debate in the aftermath of 9/11 goes to the heart of fundamental questions regarding crime and society. As terrorism will be with us for many years to come, so will the questions about the extent to which a government in a free society should curtail the civil rights and liberties of its residents and citizens.

Source: Cohen and Wells 2004; Cole and Lobel 2007; Robinson 2013; Smith 2007.

jails. Convictions by white judges and juries were a foregone conclusion. Several Southern cities used mass arrests and prosecutions to thwart civil rights protest campaigns. By avoiding police violence, these cities' efforts seemed reasonable and even won plaudits from the press and federal officials (Barkan 1985).

Unethical or Illegal Experimentation

In the concentration camps of World War II, Nazi scientists performed some hideous experiments in the name of science (Lifton 2000). In a typical experiment, they would strip camp prisoners naked and leave them outside in subfreezing temperatures to see how long it would take them to freeze to death. These experiments outraged the world community when they came to light.

This outrage did not prevent similar government-sponsored experiments from occurring in the United States during the next few decades. This is a strong charge, to be sure, but the evidence supports the accusation. Perhaps, the most notorious experiment began before the Holocaust and lasted forty years. In 1932 the U.S. Public Health Service identified some 400 poor, illiterate African-American men in Tuskegee, Alabama, who had syphilis, a deadly venereal disease that was incurable at the time. To gather information on the progression of this disease, the government decided to monitor these men for many years. When a cure for syphilis, penicillin, was discovered in the 1940s, the government decided to withhold it from the men to avoid ruining the study. They remained untreated for three more decades, when the press finally revealed the Tuskegee experiment in 1972. During that time, their wives who caught syphilis from them also remained untreated, as did any of their children born with syphilis (Washington 2006). After the experiment was disclosed in 1972, commentators compared it to the worst Nazi experiments and charged that it would not have occurred if the subjects had been white and wealthy.

The Tuskegee experiment was not the only one in which the U.S. government treated U.S. citizens as human guinea pigs. Congressional and other investigations since the 1970s have revealed many secret experiments conducted by the military and the CIA over the years. Many of these involved radiation. From 1946 to 1963, for example, the military subjected up to 300,000 soldiers and civilians to radiation during atomic bomb tests in Nevada and elsewhere. Many times soldiers were made to stand near the sites of the bomb tests; in others, nuclear fallout was spread in the air over civilian populations in the Southwest (Kershaw 2004). The exposed groups ended up with abnormally high levels of leukemia and cancer, and medical records of their exposure either disappeared or were destroyed.

During that period, federal agencies also injected people with plutonium, uranium, and radium or gave them high doses of X-rays. These "government guinea pigs" included prisoners, mentally retarded individuals, and others who were not fully informed of the nature of the experiments (Lee 1995). In Idaho, radioactive iodine was added to land and drinking water. The CIA conducted its own medical experiments, one of them involving spiking army scientists' drinks with LSD. Two days later one of the scientists jumped from a hotel window and died. The CIA hid the true circumstances of his death from his family for more than two decades (Thomas 1989).

State-Corporate Crime

Chapter 13 indicated that much corporate crime occurs because of the government's inability or unwillingness to have stronger regulations and more effective law enforcement. Along this line, some scholars have discussed episodes in which government agencies and corporations *cooperate* to commit illegal or socially harmful activities. Such state-corporate crime represents the intersection of corporate crime and crime by government (Rothe and Kauzlarich 2010).

A notorious example of state–corporate criminality was the January 1986 explosion of the *Challenger* space shuttle that killed six astronauts and schoolteacher Christa McAuliffe. When people around the nation watched in horror as the *Challenger* exploded, little did they know that the explosion was, as Ronald C. Kramer (1992:214) noted, the "collective product of the interaction between" the National Aeronautics and Space Administration (NASA) and Morton Thiokol, Inc., the corporation that built the flawed O-ring seals that caused the explosion. After the United States finally reached the moon in the late 1960s, support for NASA began to dry up. The space shuttle program became its salvation. However, NASA was under orders to implement the program at relatively low cost. As a result, said Kramer, "NASA began to promise the impossible in order to build the shuttle and save the agency" (p. 220).

This pressure mounted in the 1980s as the Reagan administration became eager to use the shuttle system for commercial and military purposes. In July 1982, President Reagan declared the shuttle system "fully operational," meaning that all bugs had

▼ The explosion of the *Challenger* space shuttle resulted from the failure of NASA and Morton Thiokol officials to heed warnings about problems with the O-ring seals.

AP Photo/Bruce Weaver

International Focus CRACKING DOWN ON DIGITAL DISSENT IN VIETNAM

The digital age has made it very easy for dissenters across the world to express opposition to their governments via emails, blogging, and other electronic activities. In response, some governments have tried to restrict their citizens' access to electronic media and, failing that, have arrested and imprisoned people for dissenting via electronic media. Vietnam stands out in this regard.

Vietnam's Communist government controls all traditional news and popular media, but it has found it difficult to control the Internet. Although the government has tried to block access to Web sites that it deems too critical of the government, electronic activists have been able to defeat these measures.

Their success has in turn led the government to arrest some of them. One of these arrested dissidents is Truong Duy Nhat, a journalist who retired from his job to write a blog in which he criticized the Vietnamese government for corruption and called on its leaders to resign. That criticism led to his arrest in May 2013. Two additional people were arrested shortly afterward for also criticizing the government online, with seven-year prison terms the possible outcome. By mid-2013, Vietnam had sentenced 46 electronic activists to prison, compared to 40 in all of 2012. In January 2013, the government convicted five bloggers and nine other dissidents for allegedly plotting to overthrow the government. The group's prison terms ranged from 3 to 13 years. One of the bloggers said before their trial, "I have done nothing contrary to my conscience." He added that the government was "trampling on the eternal good morals of the Vietnamese nation."

Reporters Without Borders, an international group, ranks Vietnam near the bottom of the world's nations in press freedom. Vietnam also ranks third in the world for the number of Internet activists behind bars, trailing only China and Oman.

Source: Brady 2013; Mydans 2013.

been eliminated and it was ready to deploy. However, the president's declaration was premature because NASA had not finished developing the shuttle. His declaration nonetheless led to "relentless pressure on NASA to launch shuttle missions on an accelerated schedule" (Kramer 1992:221). This pressure in turn led NASA officials to overlook evidence of problems in the O-ring design.

Morton Thiokol was also to blame for the *Challenger* disaster. Thiokol tests in the 1970s indicated problems with the O-ring seal design. The company reported these problems to NASA but said they were no cause for concern. Engineers at NASA's Marshall Space Flight Center reported similar problems in the late 1970s, more than six years before the disaster. One 1978 memo warned that the O-ring seal design could produce "hot gas leaks and resulting catastrophic failure" (Kramer 1992:225). Although Marshall managers initially did not tell higher NASA officials about these concerns, in 1982 they finally did classify the O-ring seals as a hazard, but called them an "acceptable risk." In 1985, Marshall and Thiokol engineers repeatedly warned that the O-ring design could cause a catastrophe. High-level officials at both NASA and Thiokol ignored these warnings and certified the O-ring seals as safe. To do otherwise would have scuttled the shuttle and reduced Thiokol's profits.

The launch of the *Challenger* was set for January 28, 1986. With very cold weather predicted, Thiokol engineers became concerned that the O-rings would become brittle and even more risky. On January 27 they alerted Marshall officials, who pressured Thiokol officials into overriding their engineers' concerns and into recommending that the launch proceed. The *Challenger* went up the next day and seconds later exploded in a ball of flame, killing everyone on board.

Political Corruption

Political corruption is committed either for personal economic gain or for political influence. We look at each of these types in turn.

Personal Economic Gain

Officials at the local, state, and national levels of government may misuse their offices for personal economic gain, most often by accepting bribes and kickbacks for favors they give businesses and individuals. These favors include approving the purchase of goods and services from certain companies and awarding construction contracts to other companies. This form of graft goes back at least to the nineteenth century, when public officials in the major U.S. cities were notorious for corruption, documented by muckraker Lincoln Steffens in his famous 1904 book *The Shame of the Cities,* in which he detailed corruption in many cities, including Chicago, Minneapolis, New York, Philadelphia, Pittsburgh, and St. Louis. Perhaps the worst offender was William March "Boss" Tweed, the head of New York City's Democratic Party organization after the Civil War. Tweed and his associates robbed New York of up to $200 million (almost $5 billion in today's dollars) in a ten-year span, as more than two-thirds of every municipal contract went into their pockets (Hershkowitz 1977).

One of the most infamous national scandals, Teapot Dome, occurred during President Warren G. Harding's administration in the early 1920s. Secretary of the Interior Albert B. Fall took bribes in 1922 of more than $400,000 (more than $5.5 million in today's dollars) for leasing government-owned oil fields to private oil companies. Fall then resigned in 1923 to join one of the companies. He was

▲ The governor of Illinois, Rod Blagojevich, was impeached and removed from office in 2009 after being arrested on federal charges of bribery and other corruption.

convicted in 1929 of accepting a bribe, fined $100,000, and sentenced to one year in prison. Harding's attorney general was tried but not convicted in 1926 for other corruption. In yet another scandal, the director and legal adviser of Harding's Veterans Bureau were accused of embezzling bureau funds. The director was convicted and imprisoned, and the legal adviser committed suicide (Noggle 1965).

Four decades ago, Vice President Spiro Agnew was forced to resign his office because of his own political corruption. During the 1960s, Agnew was a Baltimore County executive and then Maryland's governor. During this period, he and other officials took kickbacks from contractors and engineering and architectural firms to approve various construction projects. Agnew continued to receive these kickbacks while he was governor and later vice president. He eventually resigned in 1971 and pleaded no contest to one charge of income tax evasion. His punishment was a $10,000 fine and three years' probation (Cohen and Witcover 1974).

Any number of more recent political corruption scandals could be cited, but one example involved the governor of Illinois, Rod Blagojevich, who was impeached and removed from office in 2009 after being arrested on federal charges of bribery and other corruption (Long and Pearson 2009). Four years later, a former member of Congress from Arizona, Richard G. Renzi, was convicted in June 2013 of bribery and extortion charges after helping to shape a federal land exchange while still in Congress that netted him hundreds of thousands of dollars (Bresnahan 2013).

Political Power and Influence

Officials may also misuse their office for political power and influence. There are too many examples of such corruption, including campaign fraud, to recount here, but the most celebrated examples of the last half-century, the Watergate and Iran–Contra scandals, do deserve some mention.

The well-known Watergate scandal began with a mysterious burglary in June 1972 at Democratic Party headquarters in the Watergate office complex and hotel in Washington, DC, and two years later toppled President Nixon and many of his chief aides and cabinet members, including the U.S. attorney general. It involved illegal campaign contributions running to the millions of dollars from corporations and wealthy individuals, dirty tricks against potential Democratic nominees for president, lie after lie to Congress and the public, obstruction of justice, and the secret wiretapping of people critical of Nixon presidency (Bernstein and Woodward 1974).

A decade later, the Iran-Contra scandal had the potential to topple the Reagan presidency. It involved key figures in the upper levels of the U.S. government, including the CIA director and National Security Council advisers, who allegedly helped supply weapons to Iran in exchange for the release of hostages held in Lebanon. The money gained from the Iranian arms sales was then used illegally to help arm the Contras in Nicaragua, a group of right-wing rebels trying to overthrow the left-wing, democratically elected Nicaraguan government. The arming of the Contras in this manner violated congressional prohibitions on Contra funding. Some of the illegal funds for the Contras also came from drug smuggling in Latin America that was aided and abetted by military and CIA officials. There is strong evidence that President Reagan knew of and approved the arms sale to Iran despite his denials, and several officials later lied to Congress (Arnson 1989).

▶ Crimes against Government

The torture, experimentation, and other crimes just discussed account for only one side of the political crime picture. The other side consists of crimes by individuals and organizations opposed to government and other established interests. The motivation for their criminality is largely ideological: They want to change the existing order (Ross 2012). The strong political convictions underlying their illegal behavior lead some scholars to call them "convictional criminals" (Schafer 1974). These political criminals can be on the left or the right side of the political spectrum, and they can be violent or nonviolent. They usually act as members of organized protest groups, but they can also act alone.

Whatever form it takes, crime against government is an important part of the dissent occurring in most societies. Some of the most important people in world history—Socrates, Jesus, Joan of Arc, Sir Thomas More, Mahatma Gandhi, and Martin Luther King, Jr., to name just a few—were political criminals who were arrested, tried, imprisoned, and, in some cases, executed for opposing the state. Though condemned at the time, their illegality contributed to the freedom of thought many societies enjoy today, as Durkheim (1962 (1895)) recognized long ago. History now honors them for opposing oppression and arbitrary power.

Of course, not all crime against government is so admirable. History is also filled with terrorism and other political violence in which innocent victims die, as America learned firsthand on 9/11. Other illegal dissent has evoked very different reactions at the time it occurred. During the civil rights movement, for example, many white Southerners condemned civil rights protest as anarchy and communism, whereas most Northerners saw Southern governments and police as the real criminals. Vietnam antiwar protest aroused similar passions pro and con. What people think about a particular crime against government obviously depends on their own ideological views. Some of us may liken political criminals to common lawbreakers, whereas others may consider them heroes. Americans and people across the world condemned the 9/11 terrorists, but some Middle Eastern residents deemed them martyrs for a just cause.

Mass Political Violence: Rebellion, Riots, Terrorism

Individuals and groups often commit terrorism and other political violence to change the status quo. Although it is tempting to think of this violence as irrational acts of demented minds, its motivation and purpose are very rational: to force established interests to grant social and political reforms or even to give up power altogether. In this sense, mass political violence is no less rational, and its users no more deranged, than the government violence discussed earlier. Just as the people ordering and committing government violence know exactly what they are doing, so do those committing violence against government (Midlarsky 2011).

Not surprisingly, mass political violence has deep historical roots. Peasant revolts were common in preindustrial Europe, with labor riots replacing them after industrialization. Agrarian revolts also marked early U.S. history. Two you might remember from your history classes are Shays' Rebellion in Massachusetts in 1786–1787 and the Whiskey Rebellion in Pennsylvania in 1794. There were also farmer revolts after the Civil War and in the early 1900s. Historian Richard Maxwell Brown (1989:45) wrote that these agrarian revolts "formed one of the longest and most enduring chronicles in the history of American reform—one that was often violent."

Violent labor strife was common in the many strikes in the United States after the Civil War. Workers often turned to violence to protect themselves when police and company guards used violence to suppress strikes, but they also rioted and used other violence to force concessions. One of the most violent labor groups was the Molly Maguires, a secret organization of Irish miners in 1870s Pennsylvania who murdered company officials and committed terrorism. They took their name from an Irish folk hero said to have led a peasant revolt in the 1600s (Broehl 1964).

Over the years African-Americans have also used violence to improve their lot. The first slave uprising occurred in New York City in 1712, with several more occurring before slavery ended with the Civil War. The most famous took place in Virginia in 1831 and was led by Nat Turner, whose rebellion involved more than sixty slaves who killed some sixty whites, including the family of Turner's owner. Twenty of the slaves, including Turner, were later hanged, and some 100 other slaves who had not participated in the revolt were also murdered by vengeful whites (Oates 1983).

African-Americans also rioted in major U.S. cities in the twentieth century. This was a change from the past, when many cities in the 1800s and early 1900s were the scenes of race riots begun by whites, who typically encountered no resistance as they beat and slaughtered African-Americans (Feldberg 1980). Beginning in the early 1900s, African-Americans began to fight back when attacked by white mobs in cities such as Chicago and Washington, DC, in 1919 and Detroit in 1943. In the 1960s, urban violence assumed a new character as African-Americans struck out against white-owned businesses, white police, and the National Guard in many cities. These riots were met with lethal force and a massive legal response, but led to increased federal funding to urban areas and other gains for African-Americans (Button 1989). Many scholars view these riots as small-scale political revolts stemming from blacks' anger over their poverty and other aspects of racial oppression by a white society (Baldassare 1994).

Political scientist Richard E. Rubenstein (1970) wrote that the United States has long been characterized by a "myth of peaceful progress," which assumes that deprived groups have historically made social and economic gains by working within the electoral system. Looking at the expanse of U.S. history, Rubenstein said the myth of peaceful progress is just that—a myth: "For more than two hundred years, from the Indian wars and farmer uprisings of the eighteenth century to the labor–management and racial disturbances of the twentieth, the United States has experienced regular episodes of serious mass violence related to the social, political and economic objectives of insurgent groups" (p. 7). Against this historical backdrop, he said, the 1960s' urban riots and other episodes of insurgent violence over the years are hardly atypical; instead they are understandable as normal, if extreme, responses to racial and economic deprivation.

Terrorism

If revolts and riots are often hard for us to understand, terrorism is even more baffling because it usually involves the killing and maiming of innocent bystanders. Wartime violence is understandable, if tragic, because the soldiers being killed and wounded are appropriate targets. But the innocent lives lost through terrorism are senseless killings. This was the common reaction in the United States after the 9/11 attacks and after the April 1995 bombing of the Oklahoma City Federal Building by U.S. citizens linked to right-wing militia (Serrano 1998).

It is tempting to view 9/11 and other terrorism as irrational, demented acts, but such a view would obscure the rational, political purposes of terrorism, which is best seen as a strategy, however horrible and desperate, for achieving political goals (Dugan and Chenoweth 2012). This understanding of terrorism is reflected in its definition: "The use of unexpected violence to intimidate or coerce people in the pursuit of political or social objectives" (Gurr 1989:201). The motivation here is to frighten or demoralize one's political targets or the public at large.

Several types of terrorism exist (Gurr 1989). A first type is *state terrorism,* which involves the use of police and other government agents to repress their citizenry through violent means. As we saw, state terrorism is common in totalitarian nations, but has also occurred in the United States. A second type is *vigilante terrorism,* initiated by private groups against other private groups to preserve the status quo. Much vigilante terrorism takes the form of the hate crime discussed in Chapter 9. Bombings of abortion and family planning clinics and the murders of physicians performing abortions in the 1990s were other examples of vigilante terrorism. Many feminists also consider rape and battering to be a form of vigilante terrorism against women.

▼ This photo of the World Trade Center after the September 11 attack reminds us of the horror of terrorism. However irrational terrorism might seem, it is best seen as a strategy for achieving political goals.

AP Photo/HO

A third type of political terrorism, and the one falling under the crime against government rubric now being discussed, is *insurgent terrorism,* which is designed to bring about political change. The violence involved includes bombings, shootings, kidnappings, and hijackings, and its targets include public figures and the general public, public buildings, and buses and other means of transportation. The Oklahoma City federal building bombing was a particularly deadly example of insurgent terrorism.

This example notwithstanding, the terrorism that now most concerns Americans originates in the Middle East. The 9/11 terrorism is an example of the fourth type of terrorism, *transnational terrorism* (also called *global terrorism*), that is committed by residents of one or more nations against human and property targets in another nation. In addition to 9/11, other examples of transnational terrorism in the world in recent decades include bombings of buses, public buildings, and other targets by Palestinian nationalists in Israel.

Review and Discuss

What are the four major types of terrorism? Why should terrorism be considered *political* violence?

Political Assassination

A related form of political violence is political assassination, or the murder of public figures for political reasons. Political assassinations are often part of a larger campaign of political terrorism, but they are also sometimes committed by lone individuals bearing a political grudge. Murders of public figures are considered political assassinations only if they are politically motivated. If someone kills a public figure out of jealousy or because of mental illness, it is not a political assassination and thus not a political crime. Like terrorism, political assassination has a long history. One of its most famous victims was Roman dictator Julius Caesar, who was killed by a group that included his friend Brutus and memorialized in Shakespeare's famous play. Moving much further forward in European history, the assassination of Archduke Ferdinand of Austria in 1914 helped start World War I. In the United States, the assassination of Abraham Lincoln was an early tragic example.

The list of public figures assassinated since the 1960s is dismaying. It includes Medgar Evers, Southern civil rights leader; Indira Gandhi, prime minister of India; John F. Kennedy; Robert Kennedy; Martin Luther King, Jr.; Malcolm X; Yitzhak Rabin, prime minister of Israel; and Anwar Sadat, president of Egypt. Two lesser known figures, San Francisco Mayor George Moscone and Supervisor Harvey Milk, were assassinated in late November 1978 by a former supervisor with personal and political grudges. Other notable figures were also the targets of assassination attempts: former Georgia governor George Wallace, President Gerald Ford (twice), and President Ronald Reagan.

▼ President John F. Kennedy (right) and his brother Robert (left) were both gunned down by assassins during the 1960s.

Rolls Press/Popperfoto/Getty Images

Civil Disobedience

Civil disobedience is the violation of law for reasons of conscience and is usually nonviolent and public (Lovell 2009). In the classic act of civil disobedience, protesters violate a law they consider morally unjust and wait to be arrested. Political and legal philosophers have long debated the definition and justification of civil disobedience in a democratic society, but this debate lies beyond our scope. Instead, we sketch the history of civil disobedience in the United States to give some idea of its use to bring about social change.

History of Civil Disobedience

The idea of civil disobedience goes back at least to ancient Greece. After the death of King Oedipus, according to Greek mythology, his two sons killed each other in a battle for the throne. The new king, Creon, considered one of the sons a traitor and ordered that he not be given a proper burial. His sister, Antigone, thought this order violated divine law and defiantly buried the son. In response, Creon sentenced her to death. She soon disappeared, and Greek mythology differs on whether she was executed, committed suicide, or fled (Bushnell 1988). The ancient Greek philosopher Socrates was also sentenced to death for defying the state by teaching unorthodox religious views. After his sentence, he declined several opportunities to escape from prison and eventually committed suicide by drinking a cup of hemlock (Stone 1989). Antigone and Socrates remain symbols of courageous, conscientious resistance to unjust state authority.

Civil disobedience also appears in the Bible. In the New Testament, Jesus' disciples disobeyed government orders to stop their teachings because they felt their loyalty was to God rather than to the state. Jesus himself can also be regarded as a civil disobedient who died for refusing state orders to stop his religious teaching. The conflict between religious belief and state decrees recurred during the medieval period, when Sir Thomas More was executed for adhering to his religious faith. More was lord chancellor, the highest judicial authority in England, from 1529 to 1532. During that time King Henry VIII wanted a divorce so that he could marry Anne Boleyn. The pope refused to grant permission. More resigned his post to protest the king's actions. Two years later he was imprisoned for refusing to take an oath that the king ranked higher than other rulers, including the pope, and he was beheaded in July 1535 (Kaufman 2007).

Disobedience to the law for religious reasons continued during colonial America, as pacifist Quakers refused to pay taxes to support the colonial effort in the war against England (Brock 1968). Depending on how civil disobedience is defined, many of the colonists' acts of resistance to British rule can also be considered civil disobedience.

A major event in the history of civil disobedience occurred in 1849 with the publication of Henry David Thoreau's (1969) famous essay on the subject. Thoreau had spent a night in jail in 1846 for refusing to pay taxes to protest slavery and the Mexican War, and the essay arose from a public lecture he gave in 1848 to justify his tax resistance. It is one of the most famous essays in U.S. history and profoundly influenced such important literary and political figures as Leo Tolstoy, Mahatma Gandhi, and Martin Luther King, Jr. The abolitionist period during which Thoreau wrote was marked by civil disobedience against the 1850 Fugitive Slave Law. Abolitionists were arrested for helping slaves escape in the South and for obstructing their capture or freeing them once imprisoned in the North (Friedman 1971). Two decades later, suffragist Susan B. Anthony voted in November 1872 in violation of a federal law prohibiting people (including all women) from voting when they had no right to vote. At her June 1873 trial in Canandaigua, New York, the judge refused to let her say anything in her defense and ordered the jury to find her guilty. Anthony was allowed to give a statement before sentencing that attracted wide attention and ended with the stirring words, "I shall earnestly and persistently continue to urge all women to the practical recognition of the old revolutionary maxim, 'Resistance to tyranny is obedience to God'" (Barry 1988).

Moving forward almost a century, nonviolent civil disobedience was the key strategy of the Southern civil rights movement. Rosa Parks's heroic refusal to move to the back of the bus was only the beginning of civil disobedience aimed at protesting and ending segregation. Southern blacks were arrested for sitting-in at segregated lunch counters, libraries, and movie theaters and for "kneeling-in" at segregated churches. They were also arrested countless times for peacefully marching after being unfairly denied parade permits. One such arrest landed Martin Luther King, Jr., in jail in Birmingham, Alabama, where he wrote an essay, "Letter from Birmingham City Jail" (King 1969), which rivals Thoreau's essay in its fame and impact.

The civil rights movement's use of nonviolent civil disobedience inspired similar protest by other social movements of the 1960s and the decades since. There are too many instances to detail here, but some of the most dramatic occurred during the Vietnam War when devout Catholics burned draft files. Wearing clerical clothing or otherwise dressed neatly, they went into about thirty draft board offices across the country, seized their files, took them outside and then poured blood on them or burned them, and they prayed while they waited to be arrested. These events involved more than 150 Catholic priests, nuns, and lay Catholics and destroyed more than 400,000 draft files (Bannan and Bannan 1974).

Other examples of civil disobedience abound. A decade ago, many people broke the law and were arrested for protesting the U.S. government's intention to invade Iraq in March

▼ In 1955, Rosa Parks was arrested in Montgomery, AL for refusing to move to the back of a city bus. Her act of civil disobedience helped spark the Southern civil rights movement.

2003, and close to 2,000 protesters were arrested at the Republican National Convention in New York in August 2004. As the Crime in the News story that began this chapter illustrated, college students have also committed civil disobedience in regard to campus issues.

Review and Discuss
What were Henry David Thoreau's and Martin Luther King, Jr.'s arguments justifying civil disobedience?

Espionage and Treason

A final category of crime against government is espionage and treason. Espionage, or spying, has been called the world's "second oldest profession" and has probably been with us for thousands of years (Knightley 1987). In the Old Testament, Moses sent spies into Canaan. During the Revolutionary War, George Washington used many spies, including the celebrated Nathan Hale, to obtain information on British forces. Espionage remains the stuff of James Bond movies and countless spy thrillers. Today, many governments employ spies, and spying by the United States and the Soviet Union was a virtual industry during the Cold War (Kessler 1988).

Treason involves the aiding and abetting of a country's enemy by, for example, providing the enemy military secrets or other important information that puts the country at risk. Historically, the terms *treason* and *traitor* have been used rather loosely to condemn legitimate dissent falling far short of treacherous conduct. During much of the Vietnam War, for example, much of the country considered antiwar protest unpatriotic at best and traitorous at worst (DeBenedetti and Chatfield 1990). Similar charges were made against early critics of the war in Iraq and as late as 2007 against Democrats in Congress who opposed continued funding for the war (Conte 2007).

The most famous traitor in U.S. history is certainly Benedict Arnold, the decorated Revolutionary War general who conspired in 1780 to surrender the West Point military base he commanded to the British. Today his name in the United States is synonymous with treason.

When citizens spy on their own country, espionage and treason become the same. Some do so for ideological reasons, and some for money and other personal reasons (Hagan 1989). One of the most controversial cases of espionage for ideological reasons involved the 1953 execution of Ethel and Julius Rosenberg for allegedly conspiring as members of the Communist Party to supply the Soviet Union with U.S. atomic bomb secrets. In a case of espionage for money, CIA operative Aldrich Ames spied for the Soviet Union as a "mole" from 1985 to 1994 and was paid or promised more than $4 million for his efforts. He gave the KGB, the Soviet CIA counterpart, the names of dozens of Soviet citizens whom the CIA had recruited. The Soviets executed ten of these people and imprisoned others. Aldrich also supplied the KGB with information about hundreds of CIA operations. He was later sentenced to life in prison (Adams 1995).

▶ Explaining and Reducing Political Crime

Political crime is perhaps best seen as a consequence of power. Crime by government and other established interests is crime by those with power. Crime against government and other established interests is crime by those without power. The history of nations around the world indicates that governments are ready to use violence, the law, and other means to intimidate dissenters and the masses at the bottom of society. Powerful individuals within government are similarly ready to use their offices for personal economic gain and political influence.

By the same token, the history of nations also indicates that the lack of power motivates crime and other dissent against government. Explanations of why people dissent fall into the sociological subfield of social movements. Some of these explanations emphasize social–psychological factors, whereas others emphasize structural ones (Tilly and Wood 2012). Social–psychological explanations emphasize emotions and other psychological states that motivate people to engage in protest. Thus, people are considered more apt to protest when conditions worsen and they become more upset or when they compare themselves to more successful groups and feel relatively deprived. Structural explanations focus on *micro-structural* factors such as preexisting friendship and organizational ties: People having friends or belonging to organizations already involved in social movements are considered more likely to join themselves. Another type of structural explanation, *political opportunity* theory, stresses that movements are more likely to arise when changes in the national government promise it will prove receptive or vulnerable to movement challenges.

In explaining terrorism, we might be tempted to believe that anyone who is able to commit such random, senseless violence must be psychologically abnormal or at least have certain psychological problems. However, this does not appear to be the case. "Most terrorists are no more or less fanatical than the young men who charged into Union cannonfire at Gettysburg or those who parachuted behind German lines into France. They are no more or less cruel and cold-blooded than the Resistance fighters who executed Nazi officials and collaborators in Europe, or the American GI's ordered to 'pacify' Vietnamese villages" (Rubenstein 1987:5). As Chapter 6 discussed, people can commit extreme violence without necessarily being psychologically abnormal.

The Social Patterning of Political Crime

So far we have said little about the race, class, and gender of the people who commit either crime by government or crime against government. Understanding political crime as a function of power helps us in turn to understand the sociodemographic makeup of the people who commit this crime. Simply put, their race, class, and gender often mirror those of the powerful and powerless in any particular society.

Thus, in the United States and other Western nations, crime by government is almost always committed by white men of middle- or upper-class status, if only because privileged white men occupy almost all positions of political power in these societies. It is true that working-class soldiers, police, and other individuals, often nonwhite and occasionally female, carry out repression and other government crimes, but they do so in Western nations under orders from privileged white men. In non-Western nations, men are in positions of power, and race is sometimes less of a factor depending on the nation involved. However, in such nations ethnicity and/or religion often become more important, and the privileged men with political power usually belong to the dominant ethnicity or religion in the nation. Such men are thus responsible for the government crime that occurs.

The targets of government crime are typically those without power; in non-Western and Western nations alike, this often means the poor and people belonging to subordinate races, ethnicities, and religions. Which sociodemographic factor becomes most important in determining government crime targets depends on the particular society. For the Nazis, religion, nationality, and ethnicity were what mattered. They considered people not belonging to the Aryan "race" to be less than human and thus suitable targets for genocide. Jews had the same skin color as Nazis, but not the "correct" religion. In the United States, however, skin color has often mattered, as a similar dehumanization process made it possible for white Europeans to target Native Americans for slaughter and Africans for slavery. Race has also played an important role in determining the targets of vigilante terrorism and other hate crimes.

Whether race, class, or gender affects the targets of government repression in the United States has depended on the specific social movement that the government wishes to repress. The targets of repression during the labor movement were obviously working-class people, men and women, usually white but sometimes black or of other races. In the South, the victims of government crime during the civil rights movement were obviously black, although whites who supported the movement were also arrested, attacked, and sometimes murdered. During the Vietnam antiwar movement, however, the targets of surveillance and other government crime were often middle- and upper middle-class whites, because many of them were involved in the movement (DeBenedetti and Chatfield 1990). People from these social-class backgrounds were also the targets of government surveillance of Central American protest groups in the 1980s and gay rights groups in the early 1990s.

The targets of U.S. government experimentation often come from the ranks of the poor and nonwhite, but not always. It is difficult to imagine the government deciding to conduct the equivalent of the Tuskegee syphilis experiment on the children of corporate executives. Likewise, because most soldiers are from the working class, the soldiers upon whom the government conducted its radiation and other tests did not come from the ranks of the wealthy. Yet when the government spread nuclear fallout into the air and groundwater, everyone was vulnerable, white or black, male or female, rich or poor.

We have seen that most crime against government is committed by members of various social movements. Not surprisingly, the kinds of people who are the targets of government crime are usually those who commit crimes against government. What we have said about the racial, class, and gender makeup of the targets of government crime thus applies to the makeup of the perpetrators of crime against government. In non-Western nations, they are usually the poor or members of subjugated ethnicities and religions. In Western nations, including the United States, their specific makeup depends on the particular social movement. Thus, the abolitionists and women's suffragists who broke the law were white and middle class, while labor movement activists who broke the law were working class and mostly white, but sometimes of color. In nonlabor social movements, U.S. activists tend to be fairly well educated and at least middle class.

Reducing Political Crime

Compared to the literature on reducing the kinds of crimes discussed in earlier chapters, reducing crime by or against government receives less attention. Part of the reason for this inattention is that the political crime literature is relatively scant to begin with. Another reason is that political crime is so universal, both historically and cross-nationally, that it almost seems natural and inevitable. If, as we have argued, political crime is best understood as a function of power, then to reduce political crime we must reduce the disparities of power that characterize many societies. At a minimum, this means moving from authoritarian to democratic rule.

As we have seen, however, even democracies have their share of political crime, and the U.S. historical record yields little hope that crime by government and by political officials will soon end. The historical record also indicates that dissenters will turn to civil disobedience and other illegal activities as long as they perceive flawed governmental policies. One way to reduce their political crime, then, would be to reduce poverty, racial discrimination, military adventurism, and other conditions and policies that promote dissent. It would be more difficult, and even antidemocratic, to change governmental policies in such a way as to placate right-wing militia and other groups and individuals committed to terrorism and hate crime. At a minimum, responsible political officials from all sides of the political spectrum must state in no uncertain terms their opposition to these activities.

Countering Terrorism

The 9/11 attacks and other examples of transnational terrorism before and since have stimulated much thinking on how best to combat this form of political violence. For better or worse, however, the *counterterrorism* literature is filled with disagreement. Many counterterrorism experts support a combined law enforcement and military approach that emphasizes military strikes, arrests, and harsh prison terms (Maras 2013); this is the approach the United States used, along with abuse and torture, after 9/11. Terrorist groups in the Middle East and elsewhere have remained strong despite the measures. Some terrorism experts think a law enforcement and military approach may ironically strengthen terrorist groups by giving them more resolve and by winning them at least some public sympathy. As Laura Dugan (2009:447) writes, "Most terrorist organizations are unlikely to be deterred by traditional sanctions, especially because they are often wholly willing to exchange their lives or their freedom to strike a blow against their enemies."

Another way to combat terrorism is to address the problems underlying the grievances that terrorists have. The key question, of course, is whether doing so would only encourage terrorists to commit more random violence. And it is obviously not possible to appease the many Middle Eastern terrorists who detest the American way of life without doing away with America itself or at least drastically changing our culture. That said, some experts cite American imperialism as a major reason that much of the world, including terrorists, dislikes the United States (Rubenstein 1987). Eliminating U.S. intervention overseas, they feel, could thus help to reduce terrorism.

▶ Conclusion

Political crime is part of the perpetual struggle between established interests, especially the state, and forces for social change. Because of the ideological issues and goals so often at stake, political crime differs in many ways from the other kinds of crime to which criminology devotes far more attention.

Crime by government takes many forms, including political repression involving torture and other violence. Political repression is almost a given in totalitarian societies, but occurs surprisingly often in and by democratic nations such as the United States. It is tempting to dismiss U.S. repression as historically abnormal, but there has been so much of it over the years that it would be wrong to succumb to such a temptation. To say that the United States is not as repressive as totalitarian nations is of small comfort. Our own Declaration of Independence, after all, speaks eloquently of God's gift to humanity of "certain unalienable rights" including "life, liberty, and the pursuit of happiness." The Pledge of Allegiance we have recited throughout our lives speaks of "one nation, under God, indivisible, with liberty and justice for all." U.S. government repression takes us far from these democratic ideals, as our country has too often denied its own citizens, and those living elsewhere, their liberty, their happiness, and even their lives. Surely we should aspire to a higher standard than this.

If much crime by government deprives its opponents of liberty and justice, the goal of a good amount of crime against government is to secure these elusive states. The United States and other nations have a long history of mass political violence and nonviolent civil disobedience aimed at producing fundamental social change. Whether or not we agree with the means and/or the goals of such lawbreaking, history would be very different if people had refrained from it. The "myth of peaceful progress" notwithstanding, change often does not come unless and until aggrieved populations resist their government. Often their protest is legal, but sometimes it is illegal and even deadly. Although it is easy to dismiss terrorism, assassination, and other political violence as the desperate acts of fanatical minds, it would be neither correct nor wise to obscure the political motivation and goals of politically violent actors. This is true even of terrorism on the scale of 9/11, however much we detest the destruction of that day and the people who caused it.

Political crime raises some fascinating questions about the nature of law, order, and social change in democratic and nondemocratic societies. Unless some utopian state is finally reached, governments and their opponents will continue to struggle for political power. If history is any guide to the future, this struggle will inevitably include repression by the government and lawbreaking by its opponents. Whatever form it takes, political crime reminds us that what is *legally* right or wrong sometimes differs from what is *morally* right or wrong. For these and other reasons, political crime deserves more attention than it has received from criminologists and other social scientists.

Summary

1. Political crime is any illegal or socially harmful act aimed at preserving or changing the existing political and social order. It takes on many forms and falls into two major categories, crime by government and crime against government.

2. A major form of crime by government involves political repression and human rights violations. The ultimate act of repression is genocide, which has resulted in the deaths of millions of people over the last century. Governments also commit torture and murder against dissenters that stops short of genocide but is deadly nonetheless. Other acts of government oppression include surveillance and the use of the law to quell dissent.

3. Governments have also used illegal or unethical experimentation. The Nazis performed hideous experiments in concentration camps, but the U.S. government has also sponsored experiments involving syphilis and radiation that resulted in much death and illness.

4. State–corporate crime involves cooperation between government agencies and corporations that results in illegal or harmful activities. A major example involved the *Challenger* space shuttle that exploded because of defective O-rings.

5. Many political officials have engaged in political corruption for personal economic gain by taking bribes or kickbacks, with some notable scandals involving people at the highest reaches of government. Vice President Spiro Agnew was forced to resign his office when it was discovered that he had received kickbacks as the governor of Maryland and also as vice president. Corruption scandals regarding political influence include the Watergate and Iran–Contra scandals.

6. A major form of crime against government involves mass political violence that takes the form of rebellion, rioting, or terrorism. The United States and many other nations have experienced such violence throughout much of their history. Of the several types of terrorism, the one that most concerns Americans is transnational (or global) terrorism.

7. Civil disobedience is the violation of law for reasons of conscience. In the classic act of civil disobedience, protesters violate a law that is felt to be unjust and then wait to be arrested. The idea of civil disobedience goes back to ancient Greece and is a recurring theme in U.S. history. Two essays on civil disobedience by Henry David Thoreau and Martin Luther King, Jr., are among the most famous writings in U.S. history.

8. Two final forms of political crime are espionage and treason, which have also been common in the history of many nations. In U.S. history, the most famous spy is Nathan Hale, and the most famous traitor is Benedict Arnold.

9. The counterterrorism literature is divided over the potential effectiveness of a military and law enforcement approach to combat terrorism. This approach may work to some extent, but leaves untouched the roots of terrorism and may endanger civil liberties. It may also give terrorists more resolve and win them some public support. Although some experts thus believe that strategies focusing on the social problems that lead to terrorism could reduce this form of violence, others say that such efforts are too weak and would encourage terrorists to commit further violence.

Key Terms

civil disobedience *298*
COINTELPRO *291*
espionage *300*
genocide *288*
Iran–Contra scandal *295*

political crime *287*
political violence *296*
repression *288*
state–corporate crime *293*
state terrorism *289*

terrorism *297*
treason *300*
Watergate scandal *295*

What Would You Do?

1. You are a member of the jury in a trial involving four people who poured their own blood on a nuclear submarine to protest the proliferation and possible use of nuclear weapons. After committing their act of protest, they waited to be arrested. They are accused of trespassing and defacing government property. They admit to this in court, but say their actions were necessary to call attention to the threat of nuclear war. As a juror, do you vote to find them guilty or not guilty? Explain your answer.

2. Suppose that someday you are elected to the U.S. House of Representatives. During your second term in office, the president seeks an expansion of the powers of the FBI to combat terrorism by giving it the right to subject suspected terrorists to what the president calls "mild" psychological and physical punishment, including sleep and food deprivation and minor electric shocking. A physician would supervise any such treatment. Do you vote for the bill that would allow the FBI to undertake these actions? Why or why not?

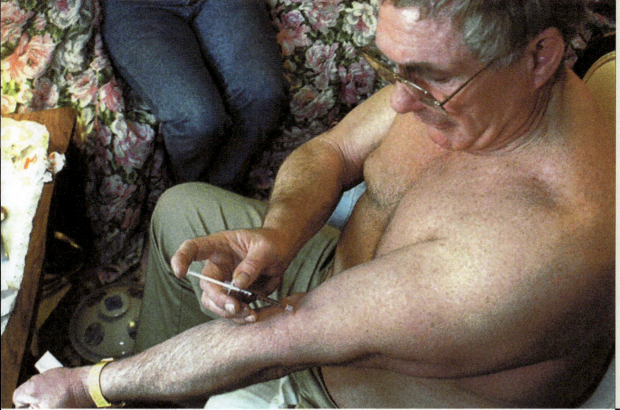

AP Photo/Andrew Sullivan

15 Consensual Crime

. . . .

Crime in the News

A broken brake light led a University of Georgia student to be arrested in July 2013, but not for anything having to do with the brake light. The student was driving along when a police officer pulled him over because of the light. The officer then smelled marijuana in the car and asked the student if he had been smoking. When the student denied using the drug, the officer did a "probable cause" search of his car and found some marijuana and a pipe. The officer then arrested the student for possession, a misdemeanor offense.

Source: Mannion 2013.

. . . .

What should be done about illegal drugs? What should be done about other illegal behaviors, such as prostitution and much gambling, in which people engage voluntarily? Drugs, prostitution, and gambling raise the important issue of whether and to what degree the law should be used to enforce notions of how morally proper people should behave. Reasonable people hold very different views on these behaviors. Many oppose them for moral or pragmatic reasons and think the law should be used to punish their participants. Other people think individuals should have the right in a free society to engage in some or all of these consensual behaviors.

This chapter examines the debate over the major consensual crimes: drug use, prostitution and pornography, and gambling. We will discuss why people engage in them, and we will explore possible alternatives to the current criminalization of these behaviors. Two general themes will guide the discussion. First, consensual crime laws are often arbitrary and even illogical. For example, some gambling is legal, whereas other gambling is illegal, and some of the most harmful drugs are the legal ones. Second (and using drugs as the prime example), the laws against consensual crimes may do more harm than good.

▶ Overview of the Consensual Crime Debate

The crimes we have studied so far involve unwilling victims. *Consensual crimes* (also called *vice crimes, public order crimes,* or *victimless crimes*) are distinct because they involve people who participate in these behaviors willingly. Some scholars say people should be free in a democratic society to engage in these behaviors, however unwise these behaviors may be, as the state should not enforce morality. Other scholars say people engaging in these behaviors do not just hurt themselves. Illegal drug use and gambling, for example, may also hurt the offenders' families and even lead to other crimes involving unwilling victims. If so, consensual crimes are less a matter of morality than of protecting society.

Critics of laws against these behaviors reply that families are often hurt by many things a family member may do, including starting a business that fails, clogging one's arteries with "fat food," and other normal, legal practices. Just as the law cannot begin to prohibit these practices, so it should not prohibit other practices that sound less socially acceptable. They also emphasize that laws against these behaviors might do more harm than good (Meier and Geis 2006). Among other things, these laws may (1) increase police and other official corruption, (2) lead consensual offenders to commit other types of crime that they would not commit if their behaviors were legal, (3) generate public disrespect for the law, (4) divert much time, money, and energy from fighting more serious crime to futile efforts to stop what so many people want to do, (5) prompt law enforcement agencies to engage in wiretapping and other possible violations of civil liberties, and (6) provide much of the revenue for organized crime, which is all too willing to supply the goods and services prohibited by consensual crime laws but remaining in demand by large segments of the population (see Chapter 13).

We now explore these issues further by looking more closely at the major consensual crimes, starting with drug use.

▶ Illegal Drug Use

Illegal drug use and trafficking continue to be the most publicized consensual crimes in the United States. We hear from public officials and news media accounts of a drug crisis, and many statistics about the drug problem exist. The federal, state, and local governments spend an estimated $51 billion yearly on criminal justice expenses (law enforcement, courts, corrections) related to illegal drugs (Drug Policy Alliance 2013; Miron and Waldock 2010). More than 60 percent of male arrestees test positive for an illegal drug (Lobel and Christian 2013). In many of our cities, drug dealers operate openly at street corners and drug gangs control entire neighborhoods.

Amid public concern over illegal drugs, it is easy to get caught up in a frenzy of mythology and misinformation and lose sight of carefully gathered, scientific evidence. Perhaps nowhere is this truer than for the drug problem. As Samuel Walker (2011:304) observes, "Public hysteria over drugs and drug-related crime inhibits sensible discussion of policy."

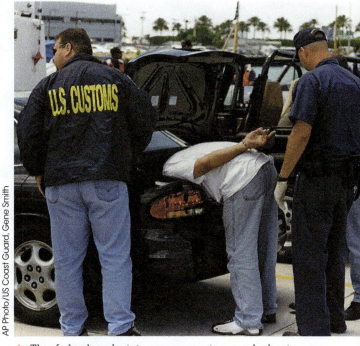

AP Photo/US Coast Guard, Gene Smith

▲ The federal and state governments spend about $49 billion annually on law enforcement expenses related to illegal drugs.

Drug Use in History

Drug use in contemporary life is hardly a new phenomenon. In fact, a society with little or no drug use is rare in human history (Goode 2012). Primitive people during the Stone Age drank alcohol; South American Indians have chewed coca leaves containing cocaine since before the time of the Incas; people in ancient China, Greece, and India smoked marijuana; Mexican Indians have chewed hallucinogenic mushrooms since before the time of the Aztecs (Goode 2008).

Drug use was very common in the United States in the late nineteenth century (Musto 2002). Dozens of over-the-counter products containing opium, and its derivatives (such as morphine) were used across the country by people with headaches, toothaches, menstrual cramps, sleeplessness, depression, and other problems. About 500,000 Americans, many of them middle-aged, middle-class women, were addicted to opium at the turn of the twentieth century. These addicts were not considered criminals because their drugs were legal and readily available. Instead, they were considered unfortunate individuals in need of help. Only slightly less popular was cocaine, which was used in many over-the-counter products and as an anesthetic for some surgeries. It was also a major ingredient in Coca-Cola, which was first marketed in 1894 and, not surprisingly, became very popular. Marijuana, another common drug, was used as a painkiller by people with menstrual cramps, migraine headaches, and other aches and pains.

Contemporary U.S. Drug Use

Drug use is certainly common in the United States today. To illustrate this, let us first define a psychoactive drug as any substance that physiologically affects our behavior by changing our mood, emotion, perception, or other mental states. Defined this way, each of the following substances is a psychoactive drug or contains a drug: beer, wine, and other alcohol; Coca-Cola, Pepsi, and other colas; coffee and tea; chocolate; cigarettes and other tobacco products; cocaine and crack; heroin; No-Doz and other over-the-counter products that help us stay awake; Valium and other antianxiety drugs; and Prozac and other antidepressant drugs.

As this list makes clear, most of us use drugs at one time or another, and many of us use at least some of these drugs daily. Some drugs, such as caffeine (found, of course, in coffee, colas, chocolate, and many other products) are "good drugs": Their use is socially acceptable, celebrated in advertising, and very much a part of our culture. Alcohol, too, would fall into this category, despite recognition of its contribution to drunk driving, domestic violence, rape, and other crimes. Cigarettes (tobacco) were another "good drug" not too long ago and are still the subject of much advertising, but have become much less socially acceptable since the 1970s. Other drugs are "bad drugs": Their use is not only socially unacceptable but also illegal, and we view users of these drugs much more negatively than someone who drinks coffee or has a beer every day. Both good and bad drugs can cause physiological and/or psychological dependence, as anyone smoking a pack of cigarettes or drinking several cups of coffee daily can attest.

▲ The United States is a nation of drug users, even if many of the drugs we use, such as nicotine in tobacco, are legal.

ONOKY - Fabrice LEROUGE/Getty Images

Prevalence of Legal Drug Use

It is no exaggeration to say that the United States is a nation of drug users, even if we disregard such common products as aspirin, Tylenol, and cold and allergy medications. A few figures help illustrate this point (Goode 2012; Johnston et al. 2013; U.S. Census Bureau 2012). Starting with legal drugs, more than 80 percent of Americans use coffee and other caffeine products regularly, with the average person consuming about 16 pounds of caffeine yearly from all sources. Physicians write about 250 million prescriptions annually for psychoactive drugs such as Valium. One-fifth of adults, or 45 million people, smoke cigarettes. Smokers include 20 percent of high school seniors and 18 percent of college students.

Turning to alcohol, two-thirds of adults drink alcohol occasionally or regularly, and one-sixth of adults binge drink at least four times each month. About one-fourth of students in grade 8 have drunk alcohol during the past year; this figure rises to 64 percent for high school seniors. About one-fourth of seniors have also engaged in binge drinking during the past two weeks. More than 80 percent of college students have drunk alcohol during the past year; almost three-fourths have drunk alcohol during the past month; 40 percent have been drunk in the past month; and more than one-third have engaged in binge drinking during the past two weeks.

Prevalence of Illegal Drug Use

We have just seen that legal drug use (including by minors) is commonplace. Illegal drug use is less common but far from rare: *About 47 percent of people of age 12 or older, or some 121 million individuals, have used an illegal drug at least once in their lifetime* (Substance Abuse and Mental Health Services Administration 2012). Americans spend more than $100 billion on these drugs annually (Office of National Drug Control Policy 2012). This amount includes $38 billion on cocaine and crack, $11 billion on heroin, and $34 billion on marijuana. The proportion of the U.S. population using selected illegal drugs in 2011 appears in Table 15-1, with the data taken from the annual National Survey on Drug Use and Health that is administered to people of age 12 or older. To look at just a few numbers in the table, 42 percent of the population have used marijuana, while 15 percent have used cocaine. These figures represent a good deal of illegal drug use, but a more valid indicator of *serious* (i.e., current) drug use, as opposed to experimental or occasional use, involves people who used a drug in the past month. Only 9 percent of the population of age 12 or older had used an illicit drug in the past month, with marijuana the drug of choice. Past-month use is only 2 percent for psychotherapeutic drugs (painkillers, tranquilizers, etc.) and 1 percent or less for other illegal drugs.

Most of these percentages are higher for people 18 to 25 years old than for the general population of 12 and older, which obviously includes young teenagers and much older people who are unlikely to use illegal drugs. Yet even in the 18–25 population, current illegal drug use other than marijuana is uncommon. In contrast, 61 percent of the 18-to-25 group drank alcohol in the past month, and 40 percent "used" tobacco. Alcohol and tobacco use is thus more

TABLE 15-1 Prevalence (Percentage) of Illegal Drug Use, 2011 (National Survey on Drug Use and Health)

	AGE 12 AND OLDER			18–25		
	EVER USED	PAST YEAR	PAST MONTH	EVER USED	PAST YEAR	PAST MONTH
Any illicit drug	47	15	9	57	35	21
Marijuana	42	12	7	52	30	19
Psychotherapeutic	20	6	2		13	5
Cocaine or crack	15	2	1	14	5	1
Hallucinogens	14	2	<1	18	7	2
Heroin	2	<1	<1	1	<1	<1

Source: Substance Abuse and Mental Health Services Administration 2012.

common—and, statistically speaking, much more of a problem—than illegal drug use for this and the other age groups.

A Drug Crisis?

Scholars dispute whether these data on illegal drug use show a nation in a drug crisis (Goode 2012). Stressing that illegal drug use other than marijuana is low, some say the data do *not* show a crisis, and they add that illegal drug use has declined since a generation ago. In terms of sheer numbers, they say, if there is a nationwide drug crisis, it is a crisis of alcohol and tobacco, not of illegal drugs.

Other observers say that this portrait of low illegal drug use is misleading for two reasons (MacCoun and Martin 2009). First, the low percentages for drugs other than marijuana still translate into millions of people. For example, the 1 percent of the 12 and older population using cocaine in the past month (Table 15-1) translates into about 1.4 million monthly users. Thus, although illegal drug use is low in percentage terms, it is high in absolute numbers. Whether you think illegal drug use is "low" or "high" thus depends on whether you think percentages or actual numbers are better measures of such use.

Second, the national self-report surveys that provide this portrait exclude people whose illegal drug use is especially high: youths in juvenile detention centers, the homeless, runaway teenagers, and high school dropouts, all of whom are concentrated in our largest cities. The national surveys also obviously include many people living in smaller towns and rural areas, where illegal drug use is less common. For these reasons, the national portrait of low illegal drug use overlooks high use of cocaine/crack, heroin, and some other drugs in many poor, urban neighborhoods. Thus, although there might not be a drug crisis for the national population, there *is* one for "America's have-nots," as sociologist Elliott Currie (1994:3) called them. As Currie observed, "Serious drug abuse is not evenly distributed: it runs 'along the fault lines of our society.' It is concentrated among some groups and not others, and has been for at least half a century" (pp. 4–5).

▼ National self-report surveys of drug use exclude people whose illegal drug use may be especially high, such as the homeless, prisoners, and runaway teenagers.

nicholas belton/Getty Images

Review and Discuss

It is often said that the United States has a "drug culture." What evidence does the text give that such a culture exists?

Explaining Illegal Drug Use

Structural and social process factors help explain illegal drug use. As Currie's comment indicates, much of the illegal drug problem is an urban phenomenon reflecting the many urban problems that also prompt high rates of other crimes. Accordingly, scholars attribute today's urban drug use to economic decline in U.S. cities after World War II and especially during the 1970s and 1980s. Unemployment soared during these decades for urban youths, federal aid to the poor decreased, and poverty rates increased. Amid such growing economic despair, it is not surprising that drug abuse also worsened in inner cities during this period. As Currie (1994:123–124) observed, the "drug crisis of the 1980s flourished in the context of an unparalleled social and economic disaster that swept low-income communities in America in ways that virtually ensured that the drug problem would worsen." When crack was introduced during the mid-1980s, the most blighted urban neighborhoods saw the highest levels of crack sales and use. Amid the despair and frustration created by economic deprivation (see Chapter 7), illegal drug use induces psychoactive effects that provide temporary relief. Drug dealing is another response to this frustration because of the high income it promises.

Peers and families also matter for illegal drug use. Not surprisingly, many studies confirm peers' use of drugs as an important influence on one's own use, and also note the importance of inadequate parenting and other family problems (Levinthal 2012). As Chapter 8 discussed, peer influences are greater in neighborhoods with chronic joblessness and poverty because families there are weaker. Delinquency and crime are higher in these neighborhoods, and so is illegal drug use.

It is also true that illegal drug use creates more illegal drug use in a vicious cycle: In poor, urban neighborhoods, drug use and drug trafficking make neighborhoods even more blighted, and this consequence in turn leads to more drug use (Currie 1994). In a related problem, addicted parents are especially unable to keep their own kids from using drugs. Because their families are likely to be poor and jobless, their children may well turn to drug dealing as a source of income. All these factors create a drug spiral from which there is little escape as long as economic deprivation continues.

If this sociological explanation makes sense, it is shortsighted to view drug abuse by the urban poor mainly as an individual problem with biochemical and psychological roots. Such a view ignores the systematic social inequality lying at the heart of the problem. Urban drug abuse occurs, wrote Currie (1994:122), because it helps in many ways "to meet human needs that are systematically thwarted by the social and economic structures of the world the users live in." Urban drug abuse, then, is best regarded not as a decadent, aberrant act, but rather as "a predictable response to social conditions that destroy self-esteem, hope, solidarity, stability, and a sense of purpose" (Currie 1994:123).

Gender and Illegal Drug Use

Gender also helps explain illegal drug use. Increased scholarly attention to women's illegal drug use has provided a more complete picture of drug use than previously existed. What has the research found?

The best evidence is that women tend to use illegal drugs somewhat less than men do. According to the National Survey on Drug Use and Health, 42.9 percent of women have used an illegal drug sometime in their lives, compared to 51.4 percent of men. About 6.5 percent of women report illegal drug use in the past month, compared to 11.1 percent of men (Substance Abuse and Mental Health Services Administration 2012). Women's illegal drug use appears to arise from the same structural and social process factors underlying men's use, as female users resemble male users in their economic and family backgrounds (Berenson and Rahman 2011; Sommers et al. 2000).

However, certain gender differences also exist. Females are more likely than males to use illegal drugs to cope with depression and other psychological distress, often stemming from sexual abuse, whereas men are more likely to use illegal drugs for excitement (Chesney-Lind and Pasko 2013). One other gender difference in motivation for illegal drug use is financial. Because they have fewer job opportunities than men and more often have children to support, young women face economic crisis more often than young men do, making illegal drug use more likely.

A final gender difference concerns the reaction to women who use illegal drugs during pregnancy. In the 1980s and early 1990s, the news media and public officials sounded an alarm about illegal drug use during pregnancy. Prosecutors charged dozens of drug-using pregnant women with child abuse or drug trafficking, and the term *crack babies* became a household word. In response, several scholars noted that (1) the much more common use of alcohol, tobacco, and even caffeine during pregnancy was at least as dangerous to the fetus as illegal drug use; (2) prosecuting pregnant women for using illegal drugs would discourage them from seeking prenatal medical

▼

care or drug treatment; and (3) prosecutions of "crack mothers" obscured the many other problems these women faced (Humphries et al. 1995). Prosecutions of this nature continue to occur and continue to prompt scholarly criticism. As two scholars recently observed, these prosecutions "undermine maternal and fetal health" and divert attention from a lack of social supports for pregnant women and their children (Flavin and Paltrow 2010:231).

The Drugs–Crime Connection

One question that comes up repeatedly is whether drugs cause crime. Although many people believe that drugs are a major cause of crime, we have seen in previous chapters that popular beliefs do not always square with scientific evidence. Keeping this in mind, what does the evidence say about the drugs–crime connection?

Before we can answer this question, we must first be clear on what we mean when we say that drugs "cause" crime (Zilney 2011). We could mean that drugs cause crime because of their physiological and psychological effects on drug users. Or, we could mean that people using illegal drugs commit other crimes, such as robbery, burglary, and prostitution, to get money to help pay for their drug habits. Or, finally, we could mean that drug traffickers go to war against each other to control "turf" for drug sales. One thing is clear: A very strong correlation exists between illegal drug use and other types of crime. People who regularly use illegal drugs tend to commit more crime than people using illegal drugs less often or not at all.

Does this mean that illegal drug use causes crime? Not necessarily. At least two reasons cast doubt on a simple drug–crime causal relationship. First, most illegal drug use is experimental or recreational, and very few of the millions of illegal drug users each year go on to commit other kinds of crime. Second, the drugs–crime correlation might mean that drug use leads to other crime, but it might also mean that committing other crime leads to drug use, say because you get involved with other offenders who already use drugs. The correlation may even be spurious: Perhaps the same factors, such as economic deprivation and inadequate parenting, lead to both drug use and other criminality.

Scholars have examined these possibilities with juvenile offenders and young adults. Although the evidence is complex, a rough consensus is that much of the illegal drugs–crime connection is indeed spurious, with both kinds of illegal behavior the result of the various structural and social process factors examined in this and previous chapters (Faupel et al. 2013). It also seems that delinquency more often precedes drug use rather than the reverse: Adolescents begin to commit delinquent acts and then start using drugs, perhaps because of the influence of delinquent friends or because their delinquency worsens their relationship with their parents (Menard et al. 2001). Once that process has started, illegal drug use does seem to increase the likelihood of future offending. The drugs–crime connection is thus best explained partly as a spurious correlation and partly as one indicating that crime causes drug use. The "illegal drug use causes crime" belief thus turns out to be largely a myth (Kappeler and Potter 2005).

What about drugs leading to crime because of their physiological and psychological effects? Although anecdotal evidence suggests that people using certain illegal drugs can become violent, there does not appear to be a systematic, cause-and-effect relationship (Boyum et al. 2011). Any such violence tends to occur only rarely and is committed primarily by individuals with histories of emotional problems or antisocial behavior. Some drugs, notably marijuana and opiates, reduce violent behavior. Ironically, the one psychoactive drug consistently linked to interpersonal violence is a legal drug, alcohol: "Indeed, of all psychoactive substances, alcohol is the only one that has been shown in behavioral experiments to commonly (not inevitably) increase aggression" (Boyum et al. 2011:371).

Illegal drug users do commit crimes to get money to pay for their drug habit. Yet here the drug–crime connection is not due to the illegal drug use itself, but rather due to the fact that the drugs being used are illegal. When drugs are illegal, simple supply-and-demand economics dictates that their prices will be higher than if they were legal. Their users, most of them very poor, cannot afford to pay for them unless they steal the necessary funds. Such theft thus results from the laws against the drugs, not from the drugs themselves (MacCoun and Martin 2009).

This logic also applies to drug users who commit crime because they start associating with other drug users and, in general, become more involved in the criminal community. Although this might sound a bit simplistic, if the drugs they were using were not illegal, they would not start associating with other criminals. To the extent that they then would not become involved in the criminal community, they would not commit other crimes. Even here, then, the drugs–crime connection is the result of the laws against drugs, rather than the drugs themselves.

When people talk about drugs causing crime, they often mean the violence between drug gangs that can harm innocent bystanders (Joe-Laidler and Hunt 2012). Once again, such violence, as horrible as it is, results from the fact that the drugs the gangs are selling are illegal, not from the drugs themselves. We do not see such violence from the "traffickers" of legal drug products such as coffee and cigarettes (large supermarkets, convenience stores, etc.), who, because their products are legal, can instead rely on advertising, competitive pricing, and friendly service.

To summarize, the answer to the question of whether drugs cause crime is yes, if we are talking about alcohol, and generally no, if we are talking about illegal drugs. To the extent that illegal drugs are connected to crime, the connection results primarily from laws against these drugs, rather than from their physiological or social effects. Ironically, the war against drugs aggravates one of the very problems it is intended to stop (Faupel et al. 2013).

Review and Discuss

What is the evidence for and against the argument that drugs cause crime?

The Legalization Debate

Earlier we outlined the debate over laws against consensual crimes. One dimension of the debate is *philosophical:* In a democratic society people should be free to engage in self-destructive behavior, and it is arbitrary and even hypocritical for a society to decide which such behaviors it will allow and prohibit. A second dimension is more *social-scientific:* Consensual crime laws do more harm than good, or so some scholars think. Perhaps, nowhere is the debate over consensual crime laws more important—and also more controversial—than on the issue of illegal drugs.

▼ Marijuana smoking causes less death and illness than consuming the typical U.S. high-fat diet of red meat, ice cream, and other such foods.

© ACE STOCK LIMITED / Alamy

The Philosophical Argument

We first explore the philosophical argument against drug laws, which is a libertarian position: In a free society, people should be allowed to engage in risky behavior, including drug use (Bandow 2012). For example, eating the all-too-typical U.S. diet of red meat, butter, ice cream, and other fat-laden food causes far more death and illness—with incalculable social harm from increased health care costs, lost economic productivity, and the tears of bereaved spouses and children—than does drug use. If our society allows such a diet, why should it not allow drug use?

Like most nations, the United States has obviously not adopted this position. Instead, it has decided to permit the use of many drugs and ban the use of many other drugs. For practical purposes, then, the philosophical question becomes: Which drugs should the state prohibit, and which drugs should the state allow?

Any answer to this question has to be arbitrary, because any drug is potentially harmful if taken in large enough doses. Someone downing a bottle of aspirin causes more personal, familial, and social harm (medical costs, lost economic productivity, etc.) than someone smoking a marijuana joint or even snorting a typical amount of cocaine, but the state is not about to prohibit aspirin use. Moreover, sometimes the harm a drug causes has little to do with whether it is permitted or prohibited. Surely, however, we can distinguish more harmful drugs from less harmful drugs and prohibit the former while allowing, however grudgingly, the latter. Yet even here our decisions have less to do with the harm of the drugs than with various political and social factors, including how many people use the drug, the extent to which it is ingrained in our culture, and the influence of the organizations manufacturing and selling the drug.

To explore this issue further, let us consider two groups of drugs. Our first group consists of alcohol and tobacco (nicotine), both legal drugs when used by those beyond a certain age. Our second group consists of cocaine, heroin, marijuana, and all other illegal drugs. How many people die in the United States each year from taking these two groups of drugs? Death is not the only harm drugs cause, of course, but

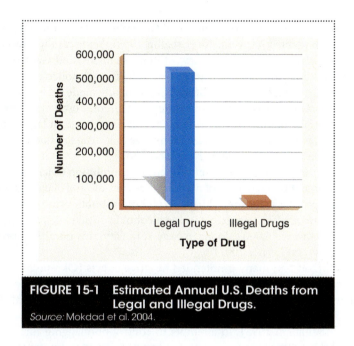

FIGURE 15-1   Estimated Annual U.S. Deaths from Legal and Illegal Drugs.
Source: Mokdad et al. 2004.

it is their ultimate harm and can be counted by federal agencies (Mokdad et al. 2004). The deadliest drug of all is tobacco, which kills about 435,000 people each year from lung cancer, emphysema, heart disease, and other illnesses. Next on the list is alcohol, with almost 102,000 people dying each year from alcohol-induced liver disease and other illness, alcohol-related motor vehicle accidents, and homicides committed under the influence of alcohol. Tobacco and alcohol together thus kill approximately 537,000 people every year.

In contrast, the physiological effects of all illegal drugs kill about 17,000 people annually (Mokdad et al. 2004). Many of these deaths occur not from the physiological effect of the drug itself, but from the fact that it has been laced with other toxic substances or from the fact that the user overdoses because the drug's potency is greater than expected. No deaths occur from marijuana use. Although constant use of high doses of marijuana might in the long run have health effects similar to those of tobacco, very few people use this much marijuana for that long. This does not mean that marijuana is a safe drug, only that it is not a lethal one. Figure 15-1 ■ depicts the disparity in the deaths caused by legal and illegal drugs, respectively.

It might be argued that illegal drugs would kill more people if they were legal because more people would then use them (Goode 2012). If so, the disparity in Figure 15-1 ■ might indicate the success of the laws prohibiting illegal drugs. We discuss this argument later, but for now simply ask, If the legal drugs kill far more than the illegal ones, where is the logic behind our drug laws? The answer is that there is little logic here. Tobacco is legal not because it is safe—far from it—but because so many people for so long have smoked cigarettes and because tobacco companies provide thousands of jobs to people in the South and millions of dollars in campaign contributions to members of Congress. Although tobacco does not distort perception and motor skills as many other psychoactive drugs do, it is nonetheless a slow, deadly poison. If it were just now invented by a small, entrepreneurial company, the Food and Drug Administration would never approve its sale and use. Alcohol is legal not because it is safe—again, far from it—but because so many people for so long have drunk alcohol that it is an integral part of our culture, and because the alcohol industry spends millions of dollars each year advertising its drug's supposed ability to help people be popular and to have a good time.

Review and Discuss

Summarize the philosophical debate regarding laws against consensual behaviors.

The Social Science Argument

The social science dimension of the drug law debate considers the very important question of whether drug laws do more harm than good (Becker and Murphy 2013; Brownstein 2013).

When then-U.S. Surgeon General Jocelyn Elders in December 1993 proposed considering drug legalization, a firestorm greeted her remarks (Labaton 1993). Yet several prominent people, including noted conservatives William F. Buckley, Milton Friedman, and George Schultz, as well as the then-mayors of Baltimore and San Francisco and the former police chiefs of Minneapolis, Minnesota, New York City, and San Jose, California, had already made the same proposal or have made it since. The Global Commission on Drug Policy (2011), composed of the former presidents of four nations and several other prominent individuals, has also called for legalization. These and other drug war critics, including some scholars, all believe that drug laws do far more harm than good and thus should be abolished or extensively modified.

In making their case, legalization proponents often cite Prohibition (Dickinson 2013). In 1920, a constitutional amendment banned alcohol manufacture and sale and began the Prohibition era. Although alcohol use probably declined during Prohibition, bootlegging was still widespread, with many otherwise law-abiding people obtaining alcohol in speakeasies and elsewhere. When Prohibition began, there were 15,000 saloons in New York City; this number more than doubled to 32,000 within a few years (Lerner 2007).

Worse yet, Prohibition had many unintended negative effects (Okrent 2011). The potential illegal profits from bootlegging were so enormous that organized crime decided to provide this service and in a few short years became much wealthier and more powerful, with Al Capone, the famous organized crime leader, making $200 million a year (equivalent to more than $2 billion in today's dollars) (Rorabaugh 1995). In attempts to control bootlegging turf, organized crime groups fought each other with machine guns and engaged in drive-by shootings. Police and other parts of the criminal justice system devoted much time, energy, and money to stopping the bootlegging. Many police were wounded or killed by organized crime members. Thus, even though Prohibition probably decreased alcohol use and some of the deaths associated with drinking, it caused even more deaths—of organized crime figures, innocent bystanders, and police—and made the nation more murderous overall. As sociologist Gary F. Jensen (2000:31) concluded, "Despite the fact that alcohol consumption is a positive correlate of homicide. . . . Prohibition and its enforcement increased the homicide rate." Prohibition also increased official corruption, as police, politicians, and other public servants took bribes to look the other way. Finally, several thousand Americans probably died from drinking "bad liquor" during Prohibition, as they could never know exactly what was in their beverage (Lerner 2007). Prohibition, in short, was a disaster, and the nation repealed the Prohibition amendment in 1933.

In recalling Prohibition, legalization proponents make the following points. First, drug laws, as we have already seen, create the very crime and other problems they are intended to stop. Addicts commit robberies and other crimes to obtain money to support their habit, drug gangs terrorize neighborhoods with deadly violence to control turf, and people taking illegal drugs become involved in the criminal community and then commit other crimes themselves. Police enforcing drug laws also come in the line of fire, with some police shot, including sometimes fatally, every year as a result. Drug laws are also responsible for most of the 17,000 annual deaths from using illegal drugs. These deaths largely result from the adulteration of the drugs with various toxic substances and from their users' willingness to take the drugs in an unsafe manner (e.g., smoking crack instead of snorting cocaine) to get the most intense "high" because of the drugs' expense. If the drugs were legalized with some government regulation, many of these deaths would be prevented. The drugs would not be adulterated, and their lower expense would allow users to take them in a safer manner.

Second, drug laws cost more than $50 billion annually, as we have seen, though millions of people still use illegal drugs. This money could be better spent on prevention and treatment programs that ultimately would be more effective in lowering drug abuse. Third, in a related point, the drug war fills our prisons and jails with hundreds of thousands of people who would otherwise not be there. In 2011, for example, more than 1.5 million arrests occurred for drug abuse violations (including some 663,000 for marijuana possession) in the United States, a figure almost three times greater than the number of arrests for violent crime (homicide, rape, robbery, aggravated assault) (Federal Bureau of Investigation 2012). The large number of drug arrests has flooded the nation's prisons and jails over the past few decades (see Figure 15-2 ■) and forced the criminal justice system to release violent criminals who pose much more of a threat to society.

Fourth, drug laws are good for organized crime. As happened during Prohibition, drugs are a major source of organized crime's money and influence (see Chapter 13). Fifth, drug laws create opportunities for official corruption throughout the criminal justice system. Bribery of police and thefts

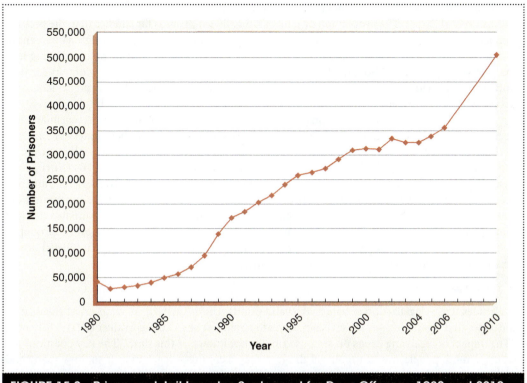

FIGURE 15-2 Prison and Jail Inmates Sentenced for Drug Offenses, 1980 and 2010.
Source: The Sentencing Project. 2013.

by police of confiscated drugs are common. Over the years, police forces in major cities have been plagued with many scandals involving officers taking bribes from drug dealers, robbing dealers, or selling confiscated drugs themselves. Most of this corruption would disappear if drugs were legalized.

Sixth, if illegal drugs were legalized and sold like any other product, they could be taxed like any other product. The taxes on the drugs would add an estimated $47 billion annually to federal and state revenues (Miron and Waldock 2010). Much or all of this money could, if we wished, be used for drug treatment and prevention programs.

Seventh, the drug war has had a disproportionate impact on African-Americans and Latinos, who are much more likely than non-Latino whites to be arrested for illegal drug possession even though they do not use illegal drugs more often than whites do. Chapters 16 and 17 explore this impact in further detail.

Eighth and last, enforcement of drug laws often involves the use of informants, wiretapping, and other legally distasteful procedures. Drug testing in the workplace and in the schools has become commonplace. Like many other consensual crime laws, drug laws, say their critics, thus threaten the nation's civil liberties by turning us all into "a society of suspects" (Wisotsky 1995).

Argument against Legalization   Opponents of legalization concede some of these points but argue that drug laws have indeed reduced the use of illegal drugs, even if many people still use them (Goode 2012). They predict that many more people would use illegal drugs if they were made legal, leading to more drug addicts and much more of the death and disease that we now see with tobacco and alcohol. Although they concede that these two drugs would be illegal in an ideal world, they say we should not compound the problem by legalizing other drugs. The increase in drug abuse after legalization would be especially great in the nation's inner cities. As Currie (1994:188) observed, "If consumption increased, it would almost certainly increase most among the strata already most vulnerable to hard-drug use—thus exacerbating the social stratification of the drug crisis."

Rebuttal by Legalization Proponents   Legalization proponents counter that it is by no means certain that more people would use illegal drugs if they were made legal. Illegal drugs are so easy to get now that anyone who wants to use them already does. If people are not using them now, it is because they dislike drugs or fear their effects, not because the drugs are illegal.

Support for this argument comes from a federally funded national survey of high school seniors (Johnston et al. 2013). The proportion of seniors using illegal drugs is far smaller than the proportion feeling they could obtain the drugs fairly or very easily. For example, although 84 percent of seniors in 2011 reported they could easily obtain marijuana, only 36 percent reported using it in the past year. Similarly, although 33 percent of the seniors said they could easily obtain cocaine, only 3 percent had used it in the past year. These data suggest to legalization proponents that people who do not use illegal drugs now also would not use them if they were legalized.

To support their views, legalization proponents point to marijuana use. When marijuana was decriminalized in many states in the 1970s, marijuana use did not go up in these states as compared to other states that did not decriminalize it; in fact, marijuana use declined nationally. Marijuana use in the Netherlands also declined after it was decriminalized there in the 1970s (Korf 2001). A study that compared marijuana use in Amsterdam, the largest city in the Netherlands, and San Francisco, where marijuana use is subject to arrest and prosecution despite that city's reputation, concluded, "Our findings do not support claims that criminalization reduces cannabis use and that decriminalization increases cannabis use" (Reinarman et al. 2004:841). Legalization opponents counter that what might be true for marijuana might not hold true for other illegal drugs, which are much more enticing and addictive (Currie 1994).

A Final Word

Both sides to the legalization debate make valid points. Unfortunately, we cannot test their views unless we first legalize drugs, which is not about to happen soon. Thus, as Walker (2011:330) notes, "The impact of legalizing drugs on serious crime is not known at this time." The key questions are whether more people would use illegal drugs if they were made legal, and, if so, how many and at what social cost. Assuming for the sake of argument that there would be some increased use, the question then becomes whether this risk is worth taking to obtain the benefits of legalization. A former governor of New Mexico, Gary Johnson, thought the risk was worth it: "There are going to be new problems under legalization. But I submit to you they are going to be about half of what they are today under the prohibition model" (Kelley 1999:A7). Because the war on drugs has been so ineffective and has cost billions of dollars and led to other problems, alternatives like legalization deserve the careful consideration for which the Surgeon General called two decades ago. In this regard, the United States has begun legalizing, however slowly, marijuana. As of mid-2013, marijuana is now legal in two states, Colorado and Washington, although federal law still prohibits its use. The U.S. Conference of Mayors has also called for the decriminalization of marijuana. In addition, the use of marijuana for medical purposes (*medical marijuana*) is now legal in 18 states and Washington, DC. The Crime and Controversy box examines the issue of medical marijuana further.

Review and Discuss

What are the arguments for and against legalizing some of the drugs that are now illegal? Do you think any illegal drugs should be made legal? Why or why not?

Harm Reduction and Drug Courts

Many drug experts who think legalization goes too far, and even those who favor some form of it, think our nation should adopt a harm reduction policy regarding illegal drug use and drug offenders (McKeganey 2012). Under this policy, drug use is treated as a public health problem and not as a crime problem: drug users are treated not as criminals but as persons in need of medical, psychological, and other help. Among other measures, sterile needles would be made available to known drug users to reduce the spread of AIDS and other diseases. A harm reduction approach allows much more money to be spent on drug prevention and treatment programs and much less on law enforcement. Several European nations have adopted harm reduction policies along these lines.

In the United States, harm reduction has been much slower to develop, but there are signs of some change. In the late 1990s, for example, Baltimore adopted some harm reduction measures (Gammage 1997). One-ninth of Baltimore's adult population was addicted to heroin or other illegal drugs. Aided by a $25 million contribution from a philanthropist, Baltimore funded drug treatment and other efforts, including needle exchange, to deal with its drug problem. The city estimated that every nonviolent drug offender who was imprisoned was costing taxpayers about $20,000 a year,

Crime and Controversy POT SHOPS AND THE MEDICAL MARIJUANA DEBATE

An important dimension of the controversy over the legal war against drugs involves the issue of marijuana used for medical purposes, especially for the following illnesses or conditions: AIDS, cancer pain, the severe nausea resulting from chemotherapy, epilepsy, glaucoma, and multiple sclerosis.

Two key questions, of course, are whether marijuana is an effective drug for any or all of these medical problems and, if so, whether it is more effective than legal medications. Many medical experts say yes to both questions, but other experts say no. The Institute of Medicine, one of the four National Academies that provide independent advice to the federal government on scientific and medical issues, issued a report that assessed the health benefits of marijuana. The report found that marijuana can indeed relieve the symptoms of several illnesses and diseases, but it also found that existing prescription medicines are generally more effective in providing relief. For patients who have AIDS or who suffer from chemotherapy-induced nausea and whose symptoms are unrelieved by existing medicines, the report said that marijuana would be a suitable treatment. It found that marijuana could help reduce some of the eye pressure caused by glaucoma, but it also concluded that the health risks of long-term marijuana use outweighed this particular benefit.

The report found that smoking marijuana may pose a threat of lung cancer, and it cautioned that marijuana should be smoked only by patients who are terminally ill or who suffer debilitating symptoms unrelieved by existing medicines. For other patients, the report recommended that cannabinoids, the chemical components of marijuana, could be usefully combined with existing medicines to provide additional benefits beyond those achieved by these medicines alone. The report recommended rigorous assessment of the potential health benefits of cannabinoids through clinical trials that would involve the delivery of these components through means other than smoking. In one other finding, the report concluded that there is no evidence that the medical use of marijuana would increase its use by the general population.

The debate over medical marijuana has gone beyond the scientific domain and into the public arena. Eighteen states and the District of Columbia now permit the use of medical marijuana under certain circumstances. In California and some locations, "pot shops" have emerged to sell marijuana to people who need it for medical reasons. Critics say the shops often sell marijuana to people without a medical need for it. A news report in 2010 said that California "allowed the pot industry to grow so out of control that at one point Los Angeles had more medical marijuana shops than Starbucks."

The rapid rise of pot shops has led federal authorities to try to shut them down, and many shops have been forced to close since 2011. In June 2013, the government sent warning letters to dozens of other pot shops in Southern California threatening arrest or foreclosure if the shops remained open. Medical marijuana and pot shops will certainly continue to arouse much controversy for some time to come.

Sources: Associated Press 2013; Mack and Joy 2000; Volz 2010.

International Focus   WHAT HAPPENED AFTER PORTUGAL DECRIMINALIZED DRUG POSSESSION?

In 2000, Portugal abolished criminal penalties for possession of any drug, including cocaine, heroin, and marijuana. Portugal's experience provides a natural experiment for assessing whether decriminalizing drugs leads to more drug use or less drug use, or whether it might not affect drug use at all.

The evidence is complex, as there are many dimensions of drug use that can be analyzed. Some evidence, though, is suggestive. During the first five years after decriminalization, teenaged drug use in Portugal declined, and so did HIV infections from sharing needles. At the same time, the number of drug addicts who sought help for their addiction

continued

increased by 41 percent, perhaps because they no longer had to fear criminal penalties. In other evidence, the number of heroin addicts in the country declined from about 100,000 before decriminalization to 55,000 by 2008. On the other hand, the percentage of adults using drugs has risen slightly in Portugal since decriminalization. Although this latter trend at first glance could be blamed on decriminalization, the percentage of adult drug users has also risen in other European nations that still criminalize drugs, and Portugal's increase is not higher than these other nations' increase.

Any definitive conclusion regarding Portugal must await the passage of time and the gathering and analysis of new data. Overall, though, the available evidence does not suggest that Portugal's policy of decriminalization in 2000 has increased drug use compared to the rest of Europe. To that extent, decriminalization in Portugal has succeeded in reducing criminal justice time and money spent on drug possession without increasing drug use.

Sources: Berger 2013; Ferreira 2010; Hughes and Stevens 2010; Hughes and Stevens 2012; Szaalavitz 2009.

but would cost only about $3,000 to $4,000 in a treatment program. In early 2004, Baltimore's approach became state policy in Maryland after the passage of a bill that authorized the diversion of nonviolent drug offenders into drug treatment programs instead of prison, at a savings of millions of dollars annually. Several other states, including Arizona, California, and Texas, adopted similar programs (Wagner 2004). Harm reduction efforts are no panacea for drug use, but they do seem to help reduce drug use while costing much less than arrest and incarceration (Ritter and Cameron 2006).

A complementary harm reduction approach involves the use of drug courts, which typically sentence drug users to drug treatment and counseling rather than to jail. This approach again saves money and is thought to hold much more potential for weaning users from drugs. Drug courts have become more popular in recent years. In the mid-1990s there were only twelve in the nation, but now they operate in virtually every state and number in the hundreds. Research evidence indicates that they provide a promising, cost-effective alternative to prison for helping nonviolent drug offenders (Rossman et al. 2011; Stinchcomb 2010). Critics feel they still treat drug users as criminals and rob offenders of their rights to due process and privacy because they often require a defendant to plead guilty to be allowed to enter a drug treatment program (Cole 1999). They also say that not everyone who uses drugs needs treatment, because the use of marijuana and other drugs ordinarily does not cause serious problems. In a final criticism, critics fear that drug courts may, because of their lower expense, ironically lead to more arrests for drug use, increasing the harm caused by the war against drugs.

▶ Sexual Offenses: Prostitution and Pornography

Prostitution

Prostitution is often called the world's oldest profession, and it might well be. It existed in ancient Mesopotamia, where priests had sex with women whose religious duty was to help procreate the species. In ancient Greece, legal brothels (houses of prostitution) were common. One class of prostitutes served the needs of Greek political officials, and another class served the common citizenry. Prostitution also flourished in ancient Rome. In the Old Testament, prostitution "was accepted as a more or less necessary fact of life and it was more or less expected that many men would turn to prostitutes" (Bullough and Bullough 1977:137–138). Licensed brothels providing much tax revenue were found throughout Europe during the Middle Ages. The church disapproved but still tolerated the practice as one that prevented more wanton lust. In the 1500s, however, brothels were shut down across Europe when the church and political officials became alarmed by the possibility that prostitutes were spreading syphilis. Brothels and certainly prostitution did not disappear, and in the 1700s and 1800s many European cities permitted licensed brothels and required regular medical exams of their employees (Bullough and Bullough 1987).

Prostitution was also common in the United States in the 1800s, as poor young women chose it as one of the few jobs available to them (Bullough and Bullough 1987). Individual prostitutes solicited business at street corners and respectable hotels and businesses throughout many cities, and camps of prostitutes would travel to railroad construction sites and other locations where men lacking wives or other female partners would be found. Railroad workers visiting prostitutes would hang their red signal lamps outside the women's tents so that they could be found in case they were needed suddenly for railroad work. The term *red-light district* comes from the red glow illuminating the prostitutes' encampments on busy nights. Earlier, during the Civil War, men in either side's army were potential customers for prostitutes. The modern term *hooker* comes from the prostitutes who had sex with soldiers under the command of Union General Joseph Hooker.

Through the early 1900s many U.S. cities had legal brothels, which were often segregated in certain parts of the cities. A moral crusade against brothels, carried out by the same white, middle-class Protestants behind the temperance movement, began in the United States about 1910 and sounded the alarm about prostitution's influence on middle-class girls lured into sexual depravation by the promise of lots of money for little time and effort. The crusade was especially strong in Chicago, and its brothels ceased business by late 1912. Dozens of other cities shut down their brothels during the next six years (Hobson 1987).

Despite the bans on brothels, some have continued their business over the years. In Nevada, brothels are legal outside the counties containing Las Vegas and Reno, and these *ranches,* as they are called, are a favorite tourist attraction for men. Some illegal brothels in other states have also received their share of publicity. During World War II, Sally Stanford ran a fancy brothel in San Francisco, where the customers included many of the city's

▲ Prostitution is often called the world's oldest profession; it was legal in brothels in many U.S. cities through the early 1900s. Today it is legal only in certain parts of Nevada.

leading politicians, law enforcement officers, and businessmen. Stanford required regular health exams of her employees to guard against venereal disease, and her rather luxurious enterprise ensured that the employees would not suffer the various problems that streetwalkers often experience. Stanford later became mayor of a town across the bay from San Francisco and published her autobiography with a major publishing house (Stanford 1966). Another elegant brothel was run in the 1980s by Sydney Biddle Barrows in a posh New York City neighborhood. Barrows, a descendant of the *Mayflower* settlers, quickly became known as the Mayflower Madam after her brothel was uncovered. She eventually also published her autobiography (Barrows and Novak 1986).

Explaining Prostitution

Most prostitutes are women, and the majority of the 57,345 arrests in 2011 for prostitution and commercialized vice were of women (Federal Bureau of Investigation 2012). The men arrested are usually male prostitutes serving a male clientele. Pimps are only occasionally arrested, and male customers of female prostitutes hardly at all, notwithstanding the widely publicized 1995 arrest of British actor Hugh Grant for "lewd conduct" in a car with a California prostitute. Although the exact number is difficult to determine, the United States has an estimated 70,000 full-time female prostitutes; they each have an average of 700 male sex partners annually, for a yearly total of about 50 million acts of prostitution (Brewer et al. 2000).

Prostitution is widely disliked because it involves sex in exchange for money or other economic gain. Not surprisingly, our negative attitudes toward prostitution apply much more to (female) prostitutes than to their (male) customers, many of whom are middle-class businessmen and other so-called respectable individuals. Over the years, critics have condemned prostitutes as immoral women with uncontrolled sexual desire, but they have said little about their customers. Scholars have studied why women become prostitutes, yet few, if any, studies exist of why men become their customers. The message is that it is normal for men, often in a sort of rite of passage, to have sex with a prostitute, but abnormal for women to take money for sex with these men.

Many scholars say that prostitution symbolizes the many ways society victimizes women (Kissila and Daveya 2010; Miller 2009). It is no accident, they say, that most prostitutes are poor. Poor women turn to prostitution because they lack the income alternatives available to men, even poor men. Also, prostitution is a particularly tempting option if money is needed to support an illegal drug habit. Women also commit prostitution because, in a society that continues to regard women as "sex objects" that exist for the pleasure of men, female prostitution is inevitable and perhaps even a logical extension of "normal" female–male relationships in which men continue to be dominant. Further, many young women turn to prostitution as a tragic, complex psychological response to long histories of incest and other childhood and adolescent sexual abuse and family disorder (Chesney-Lind and Pasko 2013). In prostitution, then, we see a striking manifestation of the many ways women suffer in a sexist society.

Some scholars also note that prostitution, however disagreeable to many people, still provides several important functions for prostitutes and their customers (McCaghy et al. 2008). For prostitutes, their behavior is a source of income. For their customers, prostitution is a sexual outlet for those who have no other sexual alternatives. Some of these are men who lack female partners because they are at locations, such as military bases, where few women live; others lack partners because of a physical disability or other problem; still others lack partners because they have unusual sexual desires. In 1937, sociologist Kingsley Davis (1937) proposed that prostitution even lowers the divorce rate by providing married men unhappy with their marital sex with a love-free sexual outlet. Otherwise, a married man might have to have an affair and could more easily fall in love with another woman.

The Legalization Debate

As with drugs, various observers debate whether prostitution should be legalized, with their arguments echoing some of those at the center of the drug debate. Proponents say that legalizing prostitution would reduce some of the problems now associated with it, whereas opponents fear that legalization would increase prostitution and victimize women even further (Miller 2009; Weitzer 2011a).

Proponents offer both philosophical and social-scientific arguments. Philosophically, prostitution is an act involving two individuals consenting to the behavior. Although many people do not like the idea of exchanging sex for money, this is ultimately a moral view on which the state should not legislate. Other people, including athletes and models, "sell their bodies." Some women and men go out on dates in which, even today, the man still expects sex in return for showing the woman a good time and spending lavishly on their evening together. Any sex that then occurs is thus not too different from what the law bans.

Perhaps more important, say legalization proponents, the problems associated with prostitution stem from the laws against it and would be reduced greatly, and perhaps eliminated, if it were decriminalized. Sometimes prostitutes are beaten and robbed by their customers, and sometimes customers are robbed by prostitutes or their pimps. Prostitution also is a source of money for organized crime and helps spread AIDS and other venereal disease. All these problems would be reduced if prostitution were legalized and regulated like any other business. In short, we should adopt and improve on the licensed brothel model common in the United States for much of its history and now common in many parts of Nevada and in several western European nations. Under this model, regular health exams could be required to check for venereal disease, and the use of condoms could be required to reduce the spread of venereal disease. In addition, hundreds of millions of dollars of tax money would be added to federal, state, and local government revenues. Moreover, the time, energy, and money the criminal justice system now spends on the 50,000+ prostitute arrests each year would be more wisely used against the truly violent criminals who are real threats to public safety.

Opponents of legalization take issue with many of these arguments. Some say prostitution is so immoral that society should not implicitly condone it by making it legal. Other opponents with a more feminist orientation say that, because prostitution inherently victimizes the women who engage in it, any effort to legalize it and thus possibly expand the number of prostitutes would only victimize more women. The brothel model might work to some degree, they add, but the problems associated with prostitution would still continue.

The Sex Trafficking Controversy

Sex trafficking involves the forcing of girls and young women (and occasionally males) into prostitution or sexual slavery. It is difficult to imagine that anyone could not abhor sex trafficking except for the people who profit from it economically and the men who enjoy having sex with prostitutes or sexual slaves. Even so, sex trafficking is the source of considerable controversy among scholars and activists.

On one side are concerned organizations and individuals, including scholars, who emphasize that sex trafficking is a worldwide problem involving tens of thousands of girls and women who are kidnapped or otherwise forced into prostitution and sometimes shipped from their home country to another nation (Kara 2010; Kristof 2012). Estimates of the number of these girls and women range as high as 4.5 million, with the number forced into the United States as high as 100,000 (Grant 2013; Yen 2008). Sex-trafficking activists have been very vocal in calling attention to this problem and

▼

lobby national officials in many countries to crack down on it. Many activists consider prostitution automatically to be sexual exploitation; as the title of a recent book puts it, prostitution is "not a choice, not a job" (Raymond 2013). Many activists also say that legalizing prostitution would help promote sex trafficking.

On the other side are people, some of them scholars and some of them current or former sex workers, who say the sex trafficking problem has been exaggerated (Grant 2013; O'Brien et al. 2013). While stating plainly that they themselves detest sex trafficking, they also say that the number of girls and women forced into prostitution and sexual slavery is far smaller than the number claimed by sex-trafficking activists. As sociologist Ronald Weitzer (2011b:1337) states, "While no one would claim that sex trafficking is fictional, many of the claims made about it are wholly unsubstantiated." These observers add that most sex workers have not been forced into prostitution and that their lives in general are far better, if also far from ideal, than the image conveyed by sex-trafficking activists. They add that legalizing and regulating prostitution would help to reduce sex trafficking.

▲ The popularity of pornography reflects a more general widespread interest among many Americans in nudity and sexual encounters.

Pornography

Like prostitution, pornography has been around since ancient times. The term comes from the Greek word *pornographos* and literally means "writings about prostitutes." As the history of the term suggests, pornography, which for now is defined as sexually explicit materials, was common in ancient Greece and Rome and especially popular in ancient India and Japan. It persisted through the Middle Ages, but lost popularity in the West because of rigid Judeo-Christian views on sexuality. Like prostitution, the church tolerated pornography but did not approve it. Pornography remained uncommon in the United States until the late 1800s, when it became more popular amid the great social and economic upheaval after the Civil War (Kendrick 1987; Richlin 1992).

The years since have seen various federal, state, and local efforts to ban or control the distribution of pornography. These efforts were filled with controversy over the definition of pornography and over questions of censorship in a democratic society. Finally, in 1973 the U.S. Supreme Court said that pornography could be considered obscene and therefore banned (1) if an average person applying current community views would conclude that the work appealed to the "prurient" interest, (2) if the work depicts sexual conduct in a "patently offensive way," and (3) if the work taken as a whole lacks "serious literary, artistic, political, or scientific value" (*Miller v. California*, 413 U.S. 15). As critics pointed out, even this definition raised more questions than it answered. For example, who is an "average person"? Who should decide whether the way a work depicts sexual conduct is "patently offensive" or, alternatively, just unpleasant or even appealing? Who should decide whether a work lacks serious literary or other value? What if a few people think it has such value and most do not? How much value constitutes *serious* value?

In 1987 the Court modified its 1973 ruling when it noted that a work could be judged obscene and thus banned if a "reasonable person," applying a national standard, would conclude that the work lacked any social value (*Pope v. Illinois*, 107 S. Ct. 1918). This ruling still left unanswered several questions, including who is a "reasonable person" and how we know what the national standard would be (Albanese 1996).

Defining and Debating Pornography

As the questions about the Supreme Court rulings suggest, one of the most important issues regarding pornography is how to define it. Related to this issue is the question of censorship. Just as beauty is in the eye of the beholder, so may be pornography. Some of the greatest works in art history depict nudes in paintings or sculpture. Many of these were considered pornographic by various secular or religious authorities at the time of their creation. Some books now hailed as literary masterpieces, such as James Joyce's *Ulysses,* were considered obscene and even banned when they were first published. If pornography is defined as sexually explicit or sexually arousing material, then even the most benign works have the potential to be considered pornographic. In the 1950s, for example, adolescent boys would look at pictures of seminude women in *National Geographic* to become sexually aroused. Not surprisingly, some religious groups considered the pictures pornographic and urged the magazine to omit them. Four decades later, a classic episode in the 1990s TV comedy *Seinfeld* began with one of the characters, George, telling his friends that he had been caught by his mother in the act of masturbating while reading *Glamour* magazine. As these examples indicate, any effort to ban pornography, no matter how disgusting the vast majority of the public finds certain kinds of pornography, inevitably raises the question of censorship (Bauder 2007).

Those in favor of banning pornography say that censorship is not an issue. Even in a democratic society, they note, some speech is prohibited without it being considered censorship. People may not shout "fire" in a crowded theater, nor may they libel or slander other individuals. Given these exceptions to the First Amendment, they say that banning pornography is not a question of censorship, but rather one of protecting society (Kammeyer 2008).

The kind of protection urged depends on why one opposes pornography in the first place. Two otherwise very different groups, religious moralists and antipornography feminists, have been especially vocal in criticizing pornography and calling for its ban. Religious moralists condemn the sexual aspect of pornography. Representing traditional Judeo-Christian views, they feel that sexual pleasure is a means to an end—reproduction of the species—and not an end in itself. Depictions of nudity and sexual behavior thus violate their religious views, which prompt them to feel that pornography both offends and threatens society's moral order.

Many feminists also call for the banning of pornography, but for very different reasons. To them pornography, like rape, is not about sex but rather about male domination and violence against women (Cornell 2000). It is no accident, say these feminists, that virtually all pornography depicts women rather than men and that, when men are also depicted, they usually dominate women sexually and/or violently. Whether or not it involves violence, pornography expresses contempt for women and degrades them as sexual objects existing solely for men's pleasure. Perhaps the worst aspect of pornography, say many feminists, is that it contributes to rape by reinforcing men's beliefs that women like or need to be raped. As Robin Morgan (1977:169) asserted almost four decades ago in a now-famous phrase, "Pornography is the theory, and rape the practice."

In criticizing pornography, some feminists distinguish between violent pornography, which depicts sexual violence against women, and erotica, which depicts respectful nudity and consensual, loving sexual interaction between adults. They also distinguish violent pornography from nonviolent pornography, which falls short of the respect and loving nature of erotica, but does not include violence against women. Other feminists make no such distinctions; they consider nudity such as that appearing in *Playboy* or *Penthouse* little better than violent pornography. They would thus ban virtually any pornography. Other feminists feel that this goes too far and believe only the most violent pornography should be banned. Still other feminists criticize pornography, but oppose its banning because they worry about the censorship issue. They and other free-speech advocates fear that any bans on pornography would inevitably extend to erotica and even to feminist depictions of the nature of rape, prostitution, and crimes involving women.

Pornography and Rape

Does pornography cause rape or other violence against women, as many feminists charge? Anecdotal evidence indicates that the homes of convicted rapists often contain a good deal of violent pornography. Some people interpret such evidence as proof of a pornography–rape causal connection, but it may simply mean that men with violent sexual attitudes are likely both to read and view violent pornography and to rape women. Several studies show that men (usually male college students) who view violent pornography in laboratory experiments often, but not always, exhibit short-term increases in aggressive attitudes toward women and in acceptance of rape myths (Donnerstein et al. 1987). However, these laboratory studies do not necessarily mean that pornography actually causes men to go out and rape in real life.

A recent review of these and other studies concluded that pornography does not cause rape and argued that "it is time to discard the hypothesis that pornography contributes to increased sexual assault behavior" (Ferguson and Hartley 2009:323). As Chapter 11 indicated, there are many structural and cultural sources of rape, and pornography is probably more a symptom of these structural and cultural conditions than an independent cause of rape. However, even if pornography does not cause rape, much pornography, depending on how it is defined, degrades women by portraying them as men's sexual playthings. No matter what pornographers try to tell us, women are far more than collections of attractive body parts. Unfortunately, many men, subscribing to antiquated notions of masculinity and femininity, cannot see beyond these limits.

Certainly, opponents of pornography are not about to stop their efforts to ban offensive sexual material. However repugnant many people find much pornography, though, the civil liberties issues raised by calls for its prohibition demand that we proceed with the greatest caution in this area. Judging from the other consensual crimes already discussed, any outright ban on pornography may well prove futile. For better or worse, there is simply too much interest in pornography, however it is defined, for such a ban to work well and too many individuals and organizations willing to provide it, especially in the modern era of the Internet.

Review and Discuss

Do you think pornography helps cause rape? Why or why not?

▶ Gambling

Like the other behaviors discussed in this chapter, gambling has a very long history punctuated by laws designed to regulate the conduct of society's poor (Meier and Geis 2006). In ancient Egypt, authorities prohibited gambling because they worried it would distract workers from mining and other labor. A similar concern prompted the kings of England and France in the late twelfth century to prohibit gambling for the poor, while allowing it for the nobility. Several centuries later, vagrancy laws expanded in England in 1743 to forbid certain types of gambling. Additional legislation in 1853 further outlawed most of the types of betting in which the English poor were involved, although they flouted the law and continued to bet anyway.

In the U.S. colonies, Massachusetts Bay Puritans considered gambling a sin and banned it in 1638, but gambling eventually became very popular in the colonies (Fenster 1994). Lotteries were the game of choice, as lottery revenue helped finance the construction of public buildings and early universities such as Harvard and Yale. Lotteries eventually fell prey to corruption and were abolished during the 1800s. In their place grew illegal betting, most commonly in the form of bookmaking and *numbers running,* in which people bet on the last few numbers of stock exchange and other numerical indicators. Over the years, illegal gambling has provided much of the revenue for organized crime and fueled corruption by police, politicians, and other public officials.

Most U.S. residents gamble at one time or another, and many gamble repeatedly. About 85 percent of Americans say they have gambled at least once in their lives, and 60 percent say they have gambled in the past year (MayoClinic.com 2004). Estimates say that more than 20 million Americans either have gambling problems or are at risk for developing them and put the number of addicted gamblers between 2 million and 5 million. One study concluded that gambling addiction costs the nation $5 billion each year in lost wages, bankruptcy, and legal fees for divorce and other problems (Arnold 1999). It is not an exaggeration to say we are a "nation of gamblers" suffering from "gambling fever," as the titles of gambling studies put it (Fenster 1994; Welles 1989). We spend more than $1 trillion every year on legal gambling at casinos, horse- and dog-racing tracks, state lotteries, and church bingo, and probably tens of billions on illegal gambling, much of it sports related, and on gambling on the Internet (Lange 2007).

The Growth of Gambling

For better or worse, gambling has become increasingly legal (Dombrink 2009). As Walker (2011:295) noted, "The legal status of gambling in the United States has undergone a massive change in recent years. The old moralistic objections to gambling have collapsed as many states have created lotteries and authorized casino gambling." After more than a century of no legal lotteries, most states now have them, and land- and water-based casinos can be found around the country. Reflecting the growth in legal gambling and police decisions to de-emphasize control of illegal gambling, gambling arrests have dropped dramatically in the last few decades, from some 123,000 in 1960 to only 8,596 in 2011 (Federal Bureau of Investigation 2012).

At least three reasons explain the growth of legal gambling (Rosecrance 1988). First, the United States in general has become more tolerant in the last few decades of the various consensual or vice crimes. Given such a relaxation of attitudes, legalization of gambling was probably inevitable. Second, and perhaps more important, states and cities have turned to lotteries and casinos as sources of much-needed revenue. The lotteries are very profitable for the states, with the odds against winning many millions to one. A third reason for casino growth lies in decisions by various Native American tribes to start casinos on their reservations, again as a source of much-needed revenue; two very successful Connecticut casinos, Foxwoods and Mohegan Sun, are prime examples.

The Gambling Debate

Despite the growing acceptance and legalization of gambling, religious groups warn against it. In addition to worrying about the money people lose from legal gambling and the harm done to their families, they view gambling as an immoral attempt to get something for nothing, which destroys personal character (Kennedy 2004). The position of the United Methodist Church is representative: "Gambling is a menace to society, deadly to the best interests of moral, social, economic, and spiritual life, and destructive of good government" (Keating 2004). Despite the religious condemnation of gambling, however, many churches and synagogues (as well as other nonprofit organizations) have long held regular bingo or beano games to raise funds.

This inconsistency aside, their concern over legal gambling's economic harm is worth restating. There is little question that the growth of lotteries and casinos has increased the number of gamblers and the amount of money spent on gambling (Dombrink 2009). Noting that the poor and near-poor are the major players of state lotteries, many observers charge that lotteries and casinos exploit the poor and worsen their financial condition (Lange 2007). Still others point to compulsive gambling that ravages hundreds of thousands of families, even if compulsive gamblers comprise only a minuscule fraction of all gamblers, and they worry that the growth of casinos will only worsen this problem (Bortz 2013).

As these warnings attest, gambling, like the other behaviors in this chapter, cannot be truly victimless. But it is a choice that people make, and critics of laws against gambling and other risky consensual behaviors question whether we should stop people from making unwise choices. So much gambling occurs anyway, they add, that there is little hope of banning it effectively. Despite the problems it may cause, the growing legalization of gambling may be keeping some gambling revenue from organized crime, and the great decrease in gambling arrests has freed up scarce criminal justice resources for more important crime fighting. Like the other behaviors discussed in this chapter, gambling remains an activity that provides thrills and excitement for millions of people, even as it causes some of them to suffer. For better or worse, gambling is here to stay, and its legalization, however distasteful to some, may lead to more good than harm.

Review and Discuss

The text argues that there may be no logical distinction between the types of gambling that are legal and the types that are illegal. Do you agree? Why or why not?

► Reducing Consensual Crime

We have seen that consensual crime laws generally do not work and may even do more harm than good. Because drug use, prostitution, pornography, and gambling have been around for centuries, they are not about to disappear, and the historical record provides little hope that we can do much about them. That said, economic deprivation does seem to underlie some illegal drug use and much prostitution. To the extent that this is true, efforts to reduce poverty hold much potential for reducing these two crimes. Unfortunately, because current approaches to these two crimes, including the legal war against drugs and education and treatment programs for drug users, ignore their structural roots in economic inequality, they ultimately offer little promise for reducing these crimes.

For better or worse, one way to reduce consensual criminal behaviors is to legalize the behaviors, as was done for alcohol use with the repeal of Prohibition in 1933. People would still engage in the behaviors, as they do now, but they would no longer be committing a crime when they do so. The problems of the consensual behaviors discussed in this chapter would continue, but the problems caused by the enforcement of the laws against these behaviors would diminish or disappear altogether. This is a basic rationale of the legalization argument for all consensual crimes. Legalization may be a risky solution and may even be entirely wrongheaded but, as Surgeon General Elders said in 1993 about the drug problem, it at least deserves careful consideration, which it has not yet received in the United States.

▶ Conclusion

The behaviors we call consensual or vice crimes have existed since ancient times and will doubtless continue far into the future. Illegal drug use, prostitution, pornography, and gambling occur because many people desire them. This is a fact. The question is what, if anything, society should do about this fact.

One problem with consensual crime laws is that the distinction between legal and illegal behavior can be blurry and artificial. We prohibit some drugs, but allow the use of others such as alcohol and tobacco that kill hundreds of thousands annually and cost tens of billions of dollars in health care costs, lost economic productivity, and other expenses. We prohibit prostitutes from selling their bodies for sex, but pay athletes, models, and other people large sums of money to sell their bodies. We allow some forms of gambling but prohibit others, with no logical reason for why some are allowed but others are banned. We try to ban pornography even as reasonable people disagree on what is pornographic and what is merely erotic.

Vice behavior raises some fascinating philosophical and social-scientific questions regarding the role of the state and the nature of individual freedom. The major philosophical question is how far the state should go in prohibiting people from engaging in consensual behavior that may harm themselves or indirectly harm others. The major social-scientific question is whether laws against consensual behaviors do more harm than good. There are many things wrong and even counterproductive about our current approach to illegal drugs, prostitution, pornography, and gambling. Unfortunately, it is easier to note these problems than to come up with workable solutions. Should we pour even more time, money, and energy into fighting consensual crimes? Or should we instead consider a radically different approach such as legalization? Reasonable people will debate these questions for many years to come.

Summary

1. The debate over consensual crime centers on two issues. First, to what degree should the state prohibit consensual behaviors that may directly harm their participants and indirectly harm the participants' family and friends? Second, do the laws against consensual behaviors do more harm than good?

2. Drug use has been common throughout human history, and it is not an exaggeration to say that the United States is a nation of drug users. Many types of legal drugs exist, and almost everyone uses them. Illegal drug use is also very common, although most such use is of marijuana and is often experimental or occasional, rather than frequent or habitual. National surveys of illegal drug use obscure its high concentration in poor, urban areas.

3. Economic deprivation, peer influences, and dysfunctional families account for much illegal drug use. Although women use illegal drugs slightly less often than men do, they are more likely to use drugs because of depression and a history of sexual abuse.

4. Illegal drug use and criminal behavior are highly correlated, but this does not necessarily mean that drug use causes criminal behavior. Much of the relationship between using drugs

and committing crimes is spurious, because both behaviors result from the same kinds of structural and social process factors. The drug–crime connection is clearest for alcohol, which in U.S. culture produces violent behavior.

5. All drugs can be dangerous, at least in large quantities, and the state must decide which drugs it will ban and which it will allow. Two legal drugs, tobacco and alcohol, cause many more deaths than all the illegal drugs combined. The laws against certain drugs are said by critics to do more harm than good. The harms they have in mind include the many criminal behaviors resulting from the fact that the drugs are illegal, many of the deaths associated with using illegal drugs, the billions of dollars spent on the legal war against drugs, the bolstering that the illegality of drugs gives to organized crime, the corruption of police and other public servants and individuals resulting from the illegality of certain drugs, and the use of legally unsavory investigative procedures such as wiretapping. If the laws against certain drugs were repealed, it is uncertain whether and how much use of those drugs would increase. Harm reduction involving drug treatment alternatives to imprisonment is gaining a foothold in the United States.

6. Prostitution is called the world's oldest profession, and legal brothels existed for much of U.S. history and still operate in many parts of Nevada. Economic deprivation and a history of sexual abuse underlie the decisions of many women to turn to prostitution. Prostitution is said to perform several important functions for prostitutes and their customers. It gives prostitutes a source of income and their customers a sexual outlet.

7. A key issue in the nation's response to pornography is that pornography is very difficult and perhaps impossible to define precisely. Attempts to outlaw pornography raise important issues of censorship in a free society. Although many people believe that pornography causes rape, empirical evidence of such a causal connection is not conclusive.

8. Like other consensual behaviors, gambling, both legal and illegal, is very common. Thanks to lotteries and casinos, legal gambling has grown rapidly in recent decades. Critics of gambling laws say it is not clear why some gambling is legal and some is illegal.

9. Because drug use, prostitution, pornography, and gambling are historically and currently very common, society can do little to eliminate these behaviors. The legal war against them has not proved effective. In 1933 the United Stated repealed Prohibition because it decided that Prohibition was causing more harm than good. Critics of consensual crime laws say that the nation should carefully consider whether to maintain these laws.

Key Terms

bribery *314*
brothel *318*
casino *323*
erotica *322*

harm reduction *316*
legalization *314*
moral crusade *319*
more harm than good *306*

nonviolent
    pornography *322*
sex trafficking *320*
violent pornography *322*

What Would You Do?

1. You have a 16-year-old daughter and a 14-year-old son. Most days they are involved in after-school activities, but sometimes they both come home right after school and are by themselves until you and your spouse come home from work. One day you leave work early and go home because you are not feeling well. When you get home and go upstairs, you think you smell marijuana, an odor with which you are familiar because you used to smoke it occasionally in college. You knock on your daughter's bedroom door and open it right away without waiting to hear her reply. Inside you see your daughter and son, who were obviously sharing a joint, which your son is now frantically trying to hide in a cup of soda. What do you do and say?

2. You are 51 years old and living in the suburbs. Your daughter and her best friend go to different colleges out of state, but they are now home for Christmas break. One day you overhear your daughter talking with her friend when you come home unexpectedly, and you are shocked to hear the friend telling your daughter that she is now a call girl a few times a month, meeting men at a four-star hotel near her college, to help pay her tuition. Your daughter sounds very upset to hear the news. What, if anything, do you do or say?

© Marmaduke St. John / Alamy

16 Policing: Dilemmas of Crime Control in a Democratic Society

···

Crime in the News

In June 2013, the city council of Jasper, Texas, voted unanimously to fire two white police officers for alleged brutality against an African-American woman. The woman was at a police station after being arrested for an unpaid traffic ticket, and, according to a news report, video surveillance at the station showed one officer pushing the woman and another officer "slamming" her head against a countertop. After the vote to fire the officers, Jasper's mayor stated, "The law is the law for everyone, and just because you have a badge on doesn't mean you have the right to break the law, or do something wrong."

Source: San Juan 2013; Stewart 2013.

···

T his Crime in the News story is a striking reminder that the police have great powers over us and may make arrests and use physical force when necessary. Sometimes, they make mistakes, and sometimes they act consciously or unconsciously out of racial and other biases. The role and power of police are central issues in the study of crime. How far should the police go in a democracy in their efforts to control crime? Should they be allowed to search our cars or homes without permission? Should they be allowed to threaten suspects to get them to confess? Many U.S. Supreme Court rulings limit police powers, and questions such as these lie at the heart of contemporary debate over police and crime.

In a famous distinction, law professor Herbert L. Packer (1964) outlined two competing models of the criminal justice system. These crime-control and due process models, as Packer labeled them, reflect the tensions of crime-control in a democratic society. As its name implies, the crime-control model's key concerns are the apprehension and punishment of criminals, and it stresses the criminal justice system's need to capture and process criminals in the most efficient manner possible. In contrast, the due process model stresses the need of the criminal justice system to protect suspects from honest mistakes or deliberate deception and bias by police and other criminal justice actors. These two models have long been in tension as the United States decides how best to deal with crime.

▶ Crime Control in a Democratic Society

This tension goes to the heart of fundamental questions in criminology. Simply put, the more crime control we want, the less due process we can have; the more due process we want, the less crime control we can expect. In a classic book about police, Jerome H. Skolnick (1966) referred to this problem as a "dilemma of democratic society." This dilemma is perhaps best illustrated by using an exaggerated example of the crime-control model. Consider a society with no due process. In such a society, the police can arrest suspects without probable cause, torture them to extract confessions, and throw them in jail and even execute them without a trial. Suppose further that this system of "justice" applies not just to political dissidents but also to the most common criminals, such as pickpockets, who could have their arms amputated. Crime in such a society would likely be very low because people would live in terror of doing anything wrong, however minor.

Of course, no reasonable U.S. crime-control advocate proposes such an exaggerated model. The question then becomes which balance to strike between the polar opposites of the crime-control and due process models. Do we err on the side of crime control and sacrifice individual freedom, or do we err on the side of due process and perhaps sacrifice public safety? Crime might well be lower in the exaggerated model. But is this the kind of society we want? Émile Durkheim (1962 (1895)) noted long ago that a society (such as the United States) valuing freedom of thought will also have high levels of deviance: if people are free to think individually, they will also feel free to violate social norms. As one criminologist observed, "Crime may be one of the prices we pay for the individualism that we have in this society" (Rosen 1995:109). The dilemma of crime control in a democratic society becomes one of deciding what kind of society we want to have.

▲ In a democratic society, a key question is how much power to give to the police to preserve law and order.

In considering this dilemma, it is important to keep in mind that a democracy that can be relatively crime free; several democratic nations have lower crime rates than the United States (see Chapter 3), even though they do not follow the U.S. tough crime-control model. These nations have less crime than the United States in part because they have lower inequality and do more to help children most at risk for committing delinquent acts and crime when they get older. In the long run, these nations point to directions the United States could pursue to lower its own crime rate.

The Ideal of Blind Justice

So far, we have been discussing the problem of civil liberties as a democracy like the United States considers how to deal with crime. But if one of the cornerstones of democracy is freedom, another is equality. In the legal system, this means that justice should be *blind* to personal differences—that is, people should be treated the same regardless of their race, ethnicity, social class, gender, or other extralegal characteristics. Crime control in a democratic society thus also raises the problem of civil rights. As we try to control crime, we have to be careful that citizens are not singled out because of who they are instead of what they did and how they did it. If one dilemma of crime control in a democratic society involves striking the right balance between public safety and individual freedom, another dilemma concerns striking the right balance between public safety and equality of treatment. Civil rights advocates and *law and order* champions often have different views on where this balance should be struck.

A Preview of the Discussion

This and the next chapter explore some aspects of these two basic dilemmas of crime control in democratic society. We will discuss the major issues facing the police, courts, and prisons as they try to control crime and the issues facing our society as it uses the criminal justice system to deal with crime. We will also discuss the evidence on inequality in crime control and explore how aspects of the social structure affect how the criminal justice system operates. Anticipating the book's final chapter on reducing crime, we will, in addition, critically examine the effectiveness of our criminal justice system. Our view will stress what Packer (1968) called "the limits of the criminal sanction." Simply put, the amount of crime control tolerable in a democratic society can ultimately do little to prevent criminality. Given this reality, "get tough" approaches to crime will do little to reduce crime; efforts to address the roots of crime hold more promise.

This chapter begins our discussion with a look at police. We begin by reviewing the history of police and then discuss sociological research on police behavior and the impact of policing.

► Development of the Modern Police Force

The concept of police goes back to ancient times. Ancient Egypt, Mesopotamia, and Rome all used police forces to maintain public order (Mosse 1975). Although this sounds like a benign function, the police forces in effect were private bodyguards whose primary purpose was to protect the societies' rulers from uprisings and other threatening conduct by the masses.

In eleventh-century England, a system of community policing called the *frankpledge* developed, in which groups of ten families, called *tithings,* were required to maintain order within each tithing. Ten tithings living on a particular noble's estate were called a *hundred.* The noble appointed an unpaid constable to monitor their behavior; one of his main duties was to control poaching on the noble's land. Several hundred eventually constituted a *shire,* or county, which were put under the charge of a *shire reeve,* the root of the modern term *sheriff.* Eventually, English units of government called *parishes* developed and appointed unpaid constables to watch out for disorderly conduct and perform various services such as trash collection. The constables in turn appointed watchmen as assistants (Critchley 1972).

By the early 1800s, the constable system was no longer working. London was the scene of repeated riots and crime by the poor. There were too few constables who were too poorly trained to handle these problems. A call began for a larger, more organized police force to quell the social chaos, but some people worried that this step would endanger individual freedom. Finally, Prime Minister Sir Robert Peel persuaded Parliament in 1829 to establish the first paid, specialized police force in London, whose police soon became known as *bobbies* because of Peel's influence. London was divided into small districts called *beats,* and police were given jurisdiction over specific beats.

The development of police forces in the United States followed the English model. In the colonial era, the constable and watch system was typical. As in England, by the early 1800s this system had outlived its usefulness. Cities were growing rapidly and were the scenes of repeated mob violence in the decades preceding the Civil War, most of it instigated by bands of white youths who preyed on immigrants and African-Americans. This violence prompted calls for organized police forces similar to London's. In 1838, Boston created a daytime police force to complement the night watchmen, and then in 1844, New York City established the first full-time force. Within a decade, most big U.S. cities had gone the same route. Although Northern cities developed police forces because they feared mob violence, Southern cities developed them because they feared slave revolts. In Southern cities police forces evolved from the "slave patrols" that tracked down runaway slaves (Shelden 2008).

These early U.S. police forces were notoriously corrupt and brutal and were of little help against crime. Many police officers drank heavily while they patrolled and used their nightsticks freely on suspects, most of them poor immigrants, who were widely considered by "respectable society" to be "dangerous classes" in need of careful monitoring (Shelden 2008). Police forces grew in size beginning in the 1870s to deal with thousands of strikes by workers across the country against their pitiful wages and wretched living and working conditions. In the early 1900s, cities began to reform their police departments by developing a professional model of policing in which police were hired on their qualifications and properly trained to carry out their jobs efficiently and honestly. As we will see later, police brutality and corruption may be less common today than a century ago, but they are still a problem.

Review and Discuss

How and why did the modern police force develop? Do the operation and behavior of today's police forces resemble those of their historical counterparts? Why or why not?

► Working Personality and Police Behavior

Police spend a surprisingly low amount of their time responding to 911 calls, questioning witnesses, arresting suspects, and performing other aspects of crime control. Only about 20 percent of police time is spent on these activities, with most police time spent on activities such as directing traffic, responding to traffic accidents, and other much more mundane matters (Kappeler and Potter 2005).

The police nonetheless remain afraid for their safety, especially in urban areas. They realize that anyone they confront, even in a routine traffic stop, poses a potential threat of injury and even death. As a result, they are constantly on the alert for any signs that their safety is in danger when they interact with citizens. The fact that these citizens are not exactly happy when being questioned by police (and often become downright hostile) only heightens an officer's concern. The importance of this basic feature of policing cannot be underestimated because it has important implications for all other aspects of police behavior.

In his classic book on policing, Jerome H. Skolnick (1966) developed the very influential concept of the police officer's working personality. Skolnick said the work people do affects the way they view the world and even their personalities. The working personality of the police, wrote Skolnick, stems from the danger of their job. This inevitably makes police suspicious of and even hostile toward the public and reinforces police solidarity, or mutual loyalty. The public's hostility toward the police reinforces police solidarity and creates among police an "us against them" mentality. These and other aspects of policing prompt police officers to develop a working personality that is authoritarian, cynical, and suspicious, which prompts them to be ready and willing to use violence when they feel it is necessary.

▲ Many citizens are hostile to the presence of police. In turn, police are constantly on alert for any signs that their own lives are in danger.

This foundation for police behavior is dramatically illustrated in a classic article by George L. Kirkham (1984), a criminology professor who became a police officer. In the classroom, Kirkham often criticized police behavior. Many of his students were police, and they told him that he "could not possibly understand what a police officer has to endure in modern society until I had been one myself" (p. 78). At the age of 31, Kirkham took up their challenge and, after completing police academy training, joined the Jacksonville, Florida, police force and quickly began to learn his "street lessons."

As a professor, Kirkham had always thought that police exaggerated the disrespect they encountered from the public. On his first day on the beat in Jacksonville, Kirkham learned how wrong he had been. He wrote, "As a college professor, I had grown accustomed to being treated with uniform respect and deference by those I encountered. I somehow naively assumed that this same quality of respect would carry over into my new role as a policeman . . . [but] quickly found that my badge and uniform . . . only acted as a magnet which drew me toward many individuals who hated what I represented" (p. 81).

In one of his first encounters, Kirkham asked a drunk to leave a bar. Smiling at the man, Kirkham asked him, "Excuse me, sir, but I wonder if I could ask you to step outside and talk with me for just a minute?" Kirkham described what happened next: "Without warning . . . he swung at me, luckily missing my face and striking me on the right shoulder. I couldn't believe it. What on earth had I done to provoke such a reaction?" (p. 81).

In the weeks that followed, fear "became something which I regularly experienced," Kirkham wrote (p. 82). In one incident in which he and his partner tried to arrest a young male in a poor neighborhood, an ugly crowd threatened their safety. Kirkham felt a "sickening sensation of cold terror" as he put out a distress call on his police car radio and grabbed a shotgun to protect himself and his partner. He wrote, "How readily as a criminology professor I would have condemned the officer who was now myself, trembling with fear and anxiety and menacing an 'unarmed' assembly" with a shotgun (p. 83). Circumstances, he noted, "had dramatically changed my perspective, for now it was my life and safety that were in danger, my wife and child who might be mourning" (p. 84). Kirkham wrote later in the article that as a criminology professor he could always take his time to make decisions, but as a police officer he was "forced to make the most critical choices in a time frame of seconds, rather than days: to shoot or not to shoot, to arrest or not to arrest, to give chase or let go" (p. 85).

What explains the working personality of police? How does the working personality of police help us understand their behavior?

Police Misconduct: Brutality

The picture Kirkham and other observers present of policing helps explain why police brutality and corruption occur. We look first at brutality, more neutrally called the excessive, unjustified, or undue use of force.

A defining feature of the police is that they are authorized to use physical force when necessary to subdue suspects (Westley 1970). As we have seen, the police are often in tense situations in which their safety and lives might be on the line. They confront suspects who are often hostile and who often insult them. Tempers flare. Inevitably, police will use force when none was needed or will sometimes use more force than was needed to subdue a suspect. The result is police brutality.

Measuring Excessive Force

No one really knows how many cases of police use of excessive force occur each year (Fyfe 2002). Usually its only witnesses are the police and their victims. Their solidarity usually leads the police to keep quiet about these incidents. The victims are often reluctant to lodge a complaint because they feel they will not be believed or it will not do any good. When interviewed by the press, many young African-American and Latino males say they have been hassled and physically abused by police (Rivera 2012).

Surveys The two primary methods of measuring excessive force are surveys and direct observation. A prominent survey for this purpose is the Police–Public Contact Survey (PPCS), a random sample of more than 60,000 persons of age 16 or older interviewed nationwide, with the last survey conducted in 2008 (Eith and Durose 2011). Almost 17 percent of the sample, equivalent to 40 million people, had face-to-face contact with the police during the previous year, mostly for traffic stops or after they were in a traffic accident or had reported a crime.

▼ A defining feature of the police is that they are authorized to use physical force when necessary to subdue suspects.

AP Photo/Wally Santana

All these respondents were asked whether the police used or threatened any force against them. About 1.4 percent responded yes regarding their most recent police contact, with almost three-fourths (74 percent) further considering the force excessive. Putting all these numbers together, slightly more than 1.0 percent of all police contacts in 2008, involving some 417,000 people, involved perceived excessive force (including threats). In an interesting gender difference, males comprised about 53 percent of all police contacts, but 68 percent of all contacts involving police use of force (see Figure 16-1 ■). This difference may indicate police bias against males, but it may also reflect the possibility that males behave more aggressively than females toward a police officer.

One problem with the estimate of 417,000 cases of excessive force is that the individual may have been wrong in thinking the force was excessive. The true number of cases of excessive force may thus be somewhat lower than the survey implies. However, excessive force is probably more common in contacts involving criminal suspects. For this group, 9.6 percent of the most recent police contacts involved the use of force, compared to the 1.4 percent of all the most recent police contacts listed earlier. If the overall 74 percent figure for excessive force applies to suspects (admittedly a rough guess), then slightly more than 7 percent of suspects ($9.6 \times .74 = 7.1$) experienced excessive force, compared to only 1.0 percent of all police contacts. In this regard, the PPCS's sample excluded the nation's

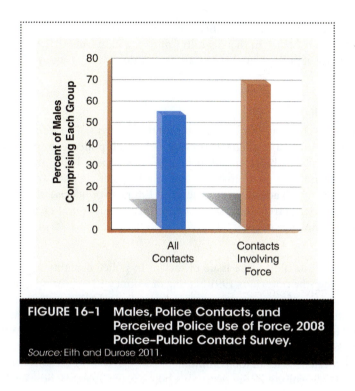

FIGURE 16-1   Males, Police Contacts, and Perceived Police Use of Force, 2008 Police-Public Contact Survey.
Source: Eith and Durose 2011.

more than 2 million jail and prison inmates, who may be particularly likely to have experienced excessive force.

The PPCS assessed police use of force during just the past year. A decade earlier, a Gallup poll assessed lifetime prevalence of (perceptions of) police brutality by asking whether respondents had "ever been physically mistreated or abused by the police" (Blumberg 1994). Five percent of the respondents, equivalent to more than 8 million adults, answered yes. As with the PPCS, it is possible that at least some of the respondents were behaving in a way that justified the police behavior in question.

Direct Observation   Police behavior, including excessive force, has also been measured via direct observation by trained researchers. One of the earliest and still best such studies occurred in the summer of 1966, when thirty-six observers funded by the federal government accompanied police officers in Boston, Chicago, Illinois, and Washington, DC, on their patrols for seven weeks. The observers recorded several kinds of information on the 3,826 encounters that officers had with suspects and other citizens. Some of this information concerned brutality. In the seven-week study, the observers found 37 cases of brutality involving 44 citizens. Because the police knew they were being observed, it is possible that more brutality would have occurred had they been unobserved. Typically, the police committing brutality falsely claimed they were acting in self-defense, and some even carried guns and knives to plant on suspects to support these bogus claims (Reiss 1980b).

Albert J. Reiss (1980b), the study's director, later discussed whether these 37 cases represented a high or low level of brutality. Because there were 3,826 encounters in the study, "only" 1 percent (37 ÷ 3,826) involved brutality (a figure strikingly similar to the PPCS estimate discussed just above). Of the 10,564 citizens in these encounters, "only" 0.4 percent (44 ÷ 10,564), or 4 out of 1,000, were beaten. However, said Reiss, because many of these encounters were with victims or witnesses, who are not the "logical" targets of police violence, a better denominator is the number of suspects, 1,394, whom the police encountered. Using this figure, the brutality rate rises to 44 of 1,394, or 3.16 percent. Reiss concluded from this figure that police brutality in large cities is "far from rare" (p. 288). This is especially true if we keep in mind that Reiss's police knew they were being observed and might have been on their best behavior. Moreover, even 3.16 percent translates to large numbers of cases. If we venture to apply this rate to the roughly 12.4 million people arrested in 2011 for all offenses, then about 392,000 people (3.16 percent of 12.4 million) were victims of police brutality in that year. In California alone, about 1.18 million people were arrested. Our estimate of police brutality in California would thus be about 37,300, or 102 per day.

Explaining Excessive Force

One important factor affecting the amount of brutality across police forces is their culture and operating philosophy (Terrill et al. 2003). In cities in which police administrators make it very clear that brutality will not be tolerated, brutality rates appear lower than in cities in which administrators make no such proclamations. Police killings of civilians are also less common in police departments in which administrators set clear limits on police use of force (Fyfe 1993). The philosophies and policies of individual police departments thus seem to have an important effect on how much police violence occurs.

Racism and Police Brutality   The issue of racism in police brutality remains highly controversial. Many consider the notorious 1991 beating of Rodney King beating by Los Angeles police to be typical: King was African-American, and the police who beat him were white. African-Americans have long listed brutality as one of their major grievances against the police, and beatings of African-American suspects were widely blamed for igniting many of the 1960s urban riots (Kerner Commission 1968). After King's beating, many observers deplored the racial pattern in the brutality he experienced as all too common.

How true is this allegation? To the extent that police brutality exists, how much of it is directed at African-Americans or Latinos because of their race or ethnicity? The PPCS data discussed earlier exhibit an ambiguous picture. Whereas only 1.2 percent of whites and 1.6 of Latinos with police contact experienced use of force, 3.4 percent of African-Americans with police contact experienced use of force. However, among those who did experience use of force, race/ethnicity did not affect whether they considered the force excessive. This latter finding does not support the view that African-Americans or Latinos are more likely than whites to be victims of police brutality.

Although African-Americans and perhaps Latinos are more likely to experience police use of force in general, this fact does not necessarily indicate police racial/ethnic bias. Some scholars believe that the many instances each year of police excessive force against people of color simply reflect their urban locations. African-Americans and Latinos in large cities may suffer police violence not because of police racism, but because they are the suspects that police encounter, and suspects in general are at risk for brutality. They might be suspects because our society denies them full equality (see Chapters 7 and 10), but that does not necessarily mean that racism motivates the police brutality they suffer.

Evidence for this view comes from the 1966 Reiss study discussed earlier. Although Reiss's observers recorded brutality for 31.6 of every 1,000 suspects, this rate broke down to 41.9 for every 1,000 white suspects and 22.6 for every 1,000 black suspects (Reiss 1980b). The risk of white suspects for brutality was thus twice as great as that of black suspects. Reiss's observers also found no evidence that white police were more likely to beat black suspects than white suspects. (Keep in mind, however, that Reiss's police knew they were being watched and thus might not have beaten suspects they normally would have beaten.) Although Reiss readily acknowledged that white officers were racially prejudiced, in his study he concluded that racism did not motivate the use of excessive force by the white police against African-Americans.

Reiss's view is certainly not the final word on the subject of police brutality and racism, but it does reinforce the complexity of the issue. The police are least as likely

▼ Among respondents in the Police-Public Contact Survey (PPCS) who experienced police use of force, African-Americans and Latinos were not more likely than whites to say the force was excessive.

© A. Ramey / PhotoEdit

as the general public to hold racially biased views, and perhaps more so (Gatto et al. 2010). The key question is whether these views lead white police to treat whites and people of color differently.

Racism and Police Use of Deadly Force Scholars have also considered whether racism affects police use of deadly force. As with brutality, a disproportionate number of the civilians killed by police, 50 percent, are African-American or Latino (Mumola and Noonan 2010). Espousing a *community violence hypothesis,* many scholars think this fact simply reflects the disproportionate number of felons and other suspects who are people of color (Fyfe 1993). Espousing a *conflict hypothesis,* other scholars think it reflects police racism, with one scholar asserting that police have "one trigger finger for whites and another for African Americans" (Takagi 1974:30).

Which view is correct? Here again, the evidence is complex and ambiguous. Supporting the community violence view, several studies find that police killings of civilians are highest in areas with high violent-crime rates, and that white officers tend to kill white suspects and black officers tend to kill black suspects. Such findings suggest that "the application of deadly force by officers is not racially motivated" (Sorensen et al. 1993:429). Supporting the conflict view, however, other studies find that police killings of civilians are highest in areas with the greatest racial inequality and with higher proportions of African-Americans (Jacobs and O'Brien 1998). These results suggest that the "police response in these areas is higher than is warranted by the levels of violent crime" (Sorensen et al. 1993:437).

Review and Discuss

To what extent does racial bias play a role in the use of violence by police?

Police Violence against Women Despite the news story that began this chapter, women are less likely than men to be the victims of police brutality as it is usually defined. Of the 44 citizens beaten by police in Reiss's study, only two, both African-Americans, were women. Several reasons probably account for women's low incidence of brutality victimization. Compared to men, few women are suspects (and thus less at risk than men for brutality) because their crime rates are far lower than men's. Because of socialization differences in aggressiveness, when women do become suspects they are probably less likely than male suspects to act belligerently and thus are less likely to arouse police ire. It is also possible that police may be reluctant to hit female suspects because of notions of chivalry or embarrassment.

Although women's gender may protect them from police beatings, it subjects them to police sexual violence (PSV). Such violence includes rape and other sexual assaults and unnecessary strip searches and body cavity searches by male officers. Criminologists Peter B. Kraska and Victor E. Kappeler (1995) examined newspaper accounts of PSV between 1991 and 1993 and federal lawsuits between 1978 and 1992 alleging PSV. Their research revealed 124 cases of PSV, with many more, they assumed, not reaching press or judicial attention. About 30 percent of the cases involved rape and other sexual assaults; 56 percent, strip and body cavity searches; and 15 percent, violations of privacy such as voyeurism.

The authors blamed PSV on at least three factors. The first is male officers' sexist ideology, which, as Chapter 11 noted, helps explain sexual violence against women in general. The remaining factors are more structural. The first of these concerns the "extreme power differential between policemen and female citizens" (Kraska and Kappeler 1995:106), which is even greater than the normal power differential underlying sexual violence in our society. The second structural factor concerns the "situational opportunity of the police to commit acts of PSV" (p. 107). Just as police are corrupt because they have many opportunities to be corrupt (see the following section), so do they commit PSV because they have opportunities to do so. As Kraska and Kappeler (p. 107) put it, "The police possess exceptional access to women, often in situations with little or no direct accountability."

Police Misconduct: Corruption

The observers in Reiss's 1966 government study also noticed police corruption as they accompanied officers on their patrols. More than one-fifth of the officers engaged in at least one act of corruption, including taking bribes and stealing objects from stores they were checking (Reiss

▼

1980a). The police in Reiss's study may even have been less corrupt than usual because they knew they were being observed.

Perhaps, the most famous investigation was conducted in 1972 by the Knapp Commission (1973). The commission was established after New York City police officer Frank Serpico disclosed corruption by his fellow officers and then was set up by some of them and almost murdered. The commission found corruption throughout New York's police force that stemmed primarily from illegal drug trafficking and gambling. It divided corrupt officers into meat-eaters and grass-eaters. The former were a small percentage of all corrupt officers who pursued corruption aggressively and made the most money. Grass-eaters were more passive in their corruption and made less money, but lay at the heart of the problem by making corruption respectable, keeping quiet about the corruption, and threatening any officer who disobeyed this "code of silence" with physical injury or worse. One such officer was Serpico.

Police corruption arises from structural roots similar to those motivating brutality. The nature of police work fuels police perceptions that the public not only dislikes the police, but also fails to appreciate the hard job they do. Combine these perceptions with the many opportunities for police to obtain money through bribes and other forms of corruption and you inevitably end up with much corruption. This sort of explanation suggests that the problem of such "blue-coat crime" extends far beyond a "few rotten apples" and instead reflects a "rotten barrel" that will remain even if the "apples" are removed from the force. As a former Philadelphia police officer put it, "[P]olice corruption results from a system where honest police recruits are placed into a dishonest police subculture" (Birch 1984:120). As Chapter 15 discussed and as the Knapp Commission documented, illegal drug trafficking, gambling, and other consensual crimes are responsible for most of this corruption. This was true more than a century ago and remains true now. Legalizing these behaviors should reduce the corruption by drying up the opportunities police have for acquiring money illegally.

Police Scandals

Sometimes police brutality, corruption, and other misconduct become so rampant that, when discovered, they take on a new life as a full-fledged police *scandal* that reminds us of the dangers of having out-of-control police in a democratic society. One of the worst scandals occurred in Los Angeles and was revealed in early 2000. Months earlier, an LA police officer, Rafael Perez, had been arrested for stealing drugs. In return for a plea bargain, he told authorities that dozens of LA antigang police and supervisors in the city's Rampart Division and elsewhere had engaged in massive corruption, brutality, and other wrongdoing. Their acts included many beatings, several unjustified police shootings, the planting of weapons on their victims, the planting of illegal drugs on other citizens to justify false arrests, false testimony at trials, and the stealing of drugs and money. More than seventy officers eventually were investigated for either engaging in these acts or for covering them up.

In one case, Perez said he saw an officer plant a gun on a dying suspect and a supervisor delay an ambulance so that the officers involved in the unjustified shooting would have time to make up a story. In another act, police allegedly shot an unarmed man who was in handcuffs. In still another act, police allegedly used a suspect as a battering ram by banging his head on a wall when he would not lead police to a gun they were trying to find. Sometimes officers even reportedly had "shooting parties" in which they got awards for wounding or killing people. Because of the scandal, dozens of criminal convictions were overturned (Glover and Lait 2000a; Glover and Lait 2000b).

A similar scandal came to light a few years earlier in Philadelphia. There a group of police engaged in practices similar to those in Los Angeles, including false testimony, beatings, and planted evidence. About 300 convictions were overturned because of the scandal (Fazlollah 1997).

Review and Discuss

Why does police corruption occur? To what extent does the major blame lie with a few corrupt officers versus the nature of policing itself?

► Police Discretion: To Arrest or Not to Arrest?

Officials make decisions at every stage of the criminal justice system. Police decide whether to arrest someone once they have identified a suspect. Once a person is arrested, a prosecutor decides whether to prosecute the case and which charges to bring against the defendant. The judge determines whether to require bail and how much bail should be required. A judge or jury decides whether to find the defendant guilty, and the judge determines how severe the sentence for a convicted offender will be. Such discretionary justice helps the criminal justice system remain flexible and individualized, but it also opens the system to the possibility of disparate treatment of suspects and defendants based on their race, social class, gender, and other extra-legal variables.

The first stage of discretionary justice is the police officer's decision to arrest or cite someone for an alleged offense. As Shakespeare might have put it, to arrest or not to arrest, that is the discretion. The police arrest only a small percentage of all the suspects they encounter (Dempsey and Forst 2014). What factors influence the chances of arrest? The two most important factors are the seriousness of the alleged offense and the strength of the evidence. Another factor is the relationship between the offender and victim. Arrest is more likely if the alleged offender and victim are strangers than if they know each other. Yet another factor is the *complainant's preference:* Arrest is more likely when complainants (i.e., victims) prefer arrest than when they do not. A final factor is the suspect's *demeanor:* suspects who are hostile toward the police are more likely to be arrested than respectful suspects (Engel et al. 2000).

Race, Ethnicity, And Arrest

Perhaps the most controversial issue in police discretion is whether arrest practices are racially discriminatory, an issue introduced in Chapter 3. In 2011, 28 percent of all persons arrested were African-American, a figure that rose to 38 percent for violent crimes and 50 percent and 56 percent for homicides and robberies, respectively (Federal Bureau of Investigation 2012). Because African-Americans comprise only 13 percent of the total population, there is ready evidence of disproportionate arrest of African-Americans. The Uniform Crime Reports had not yet started reporting arrest information for Latinos at the time of this writing, but they, too, are thought to be arrested disproportionately (Walker et al. 2012).

The major debate is whether these groups' disproportionate arrests reflect police/ethnic racial prejudice, including unconscious bias, or, instead, simply their disproportionate involvement in street crime (see Chapter 3). The research evidence, as we will now see, is both complex and ambiguous.

A Review of the Evidence

There is ample evidence that police routinely harass African-Americans and Latinos by stopping and questioning them for no apparent reason and by verbally abusing them (Brunson and Weitzer 2009; Stewart 2007). This practice is called *racial profiling,* or, more caustically when applied to traffic violations, *DWB (driving while black).* The Crime and Controversy box takes a further look at racial profiling.

If the police do engage in racial profiling involving harassment and traffic offenses, does that also mean they are more likely to *arrest* people of color for criminal offenses? Reiss's 1966 police observation study found police arresting a greater proportion of African-American suspects than white suspects, but it attributed this disparity to three reasons other than police racism: (1) African-Americans tended to be suspected of more serious crimes than whites, (2) African-American suspects were more hostile than white suspects toward police, and (3) complainants (who were usually African-American) in cases involving black suspects preferred arrest more often than did the (mostly white) complainants in cases involving white suspects (Black 1980). Other observation studies reach similar conclusions (Riksheim and Chermak 1993). Whether police might again be on their best behavior because they are being watched is an important question in interpreting these studies' results.

Further support for a conclusion of nonracism in arrest comes from the similarity of racial disparity in arrest data to that found in self-report and victimization studies. As Chapter 3 noted,

▼

In the United States, there are as many police forces as there are cities and towns, and they all have many different styles and sets of procedures. As a result, there is little standardization among U.S. police regarding training, equipment, or procedures. The situation is very different in Japan, because the Japanese police force is a branch of the national government called the National Police Agency (NPA). This allows the Japanese police to be more standardized than their U.S. counterparts. They all receive the same type of training and are expected to conform to the same sets of rules. At the same time, Japanese police are much more oriented toward community policing than most U.S. police are, because they operate at the level of the immediate neighborhood.

A key feature of the Japanese model of policing is a type of mini police station located in neighborhoods across the country. The mini station in urban neighborhoods is called the *koban,* and the mini station in rural areas is called the *chuzaisho.* Both sets of police stations are small operations. The *koban* usually has fewer than fifteen officers per shift and the *chuzaisho* is staffed by one officer.

The police at either kind of station integrate law enforcement with community service functions, and they typically solicit community input on crime and other problems. To do this, they often make house calls and use these calls to allow them and citizens to get to know one another better. They keep petty cash funds to help the homeless and other people in need of money, and their mini stations often include counseling rooms in which specially trained officers sit down to talk with families or individuals in need of help.

Another difference between U.S. and Japanese police lies in police decision making. In the United States, police management style follows a top–down model in which police supervisors command the officers under them and make almost all policy decisions. In Japan, police decision making is more consensual. Police officials still make decisions, but are expected to be aware of what the average officer thinks and to take rank-and-file views into account.

Compared to their U.S. counterparts, the Japanese police enjoy two significant advantages. One is the respect and gratitude of the public. In the United States, a cultural value of autonomy and distrust of authority underlies the hostility with which much of the public views police. In Japan, a cultural value of respect for authority and of harmonious relations prompts the Japanese citizenry to respect the police and to regard them as important public servants.

The other advantage enjoyed by the Japanese police is their nation's low crime rate. The high U.S. crime rate puts pressure on police to see themselves as law enforcement officers first and foremost and to view the public with suspicion. It also leads the U.S. public to see the police as inefficient and harassing. In contrast, the low Japanese crime rate allows the police to act more as public servants than as law enforcers and reinforces the public's positive view of police and policing in that nation.

Some critics take issue with this positive view of the Japanese police. They say that Japan has a low crime rate not because of the police, but despite the police. According to this criticism, Japan's police are not very skilled at solving crimes: rather than doing the usual investigation with which Americans are familiar, Japanese police rely heavily on suspects to confess. According to one critic, "the dependence on confessions means Japanese detectives are not used to building cases and proving guilt."

Sources: Adelstein 2010; Parker 2001; Parry 2012.

---

self-report surveys and the National Crime Victimization Survey (NCVS) indicate disproportionate involvement in crime by people of color, including African-Americans. To the extent that these crime measures are more valid measures of crime than the Uniform Crime Reports (UCR), they bolster the conclusion that racial disparities in arrest do not reflect police racism.

Other evidence disputes this conclusion. For one thing, the proportion of African-Americans arrested exceeds the proportion of offenders identified by victims in the NCVS as being African-American (see Figure 16–2 ■). This difference suggests to some observers that African-Americans are disproportionately likely to be arrested (Reiman and Leighton 2013). However, whether this is due to police racism or to some other factors (e.g., the nature of the crimes or even the possibility that victims are more likely to report crimes to the police when their offenders are black) remains unclear.

Better evidence for actual racial bias in arrest would come from observational studies. Although the observational studies cited earlier found no racial bias in arrest, others have found such evidence (Walker et al. 2012). Further, despite the finding in some studies that African-American suspects' hostile demeanor helps account for their greater likelihood of arrest, their

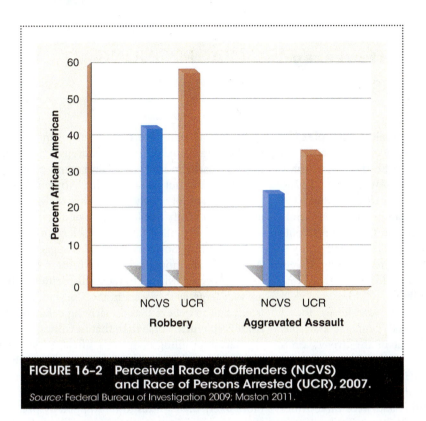

FIGURE 16–2 Perceived Race of Offenders (NCVS) and Race of Persons Arrested (UCR), 2007.
Source: Federal Bureau of Investigation 2009; Maston 2011.

demeanor may stem from hostile treatment by police and even from the arrest itself. Thus, "arrest may cause disrespect as much as disrespect causes arrest" (Sherman 1980:80).

In a more subtle form of police discrimination, race/ethnicity affects the strength of the evidence needed for arrest: Police tend not to arrest whites unless the evidence against them is fairly strong, whereas they often arrest African-Americans and Latinos even when the evidence is fairly weak (Hagan and Zatz 1985; Petersilia 1983).

Where do all these findings leave us? A fair conclusion is that police arrest practices are racially biased to a degree, but that racial/ethnic disparities in arrest reflect disproportionate racial involvement in crime more than police bias (Kochel et al. 2011; Walker et al. 2012). As with police brutality, some arrests are undoubtedly racially motivated, but overall the higher arrest rates for African-Americans and other people of color "are not substantially the result of bias" (Tonry 1994:71). This conclusion notwithstanding, the evidence that does exist of racial and ethnic bias in arrest and also the use of brutal and deadly force is troubling in a society whose Pledge of Allegiance professes "liberty and justice for all."

Race, Arrest, and the War on Drugs

So far we have explored racial and ethnic discrimination in arrest by focusing on the proportion of African-Americans, Latinos, and whites who get arrested. This focus led to the conclusion of a lack of substantial bias in arrest. A much harsher conclusion is reached if we focus on arrests for one type of crime, illegal drug use (Alexander 2012; Tonry 2012). *Simply put, even though African-Americans and Latinos are no more likely than whites to use illegal drugs, they have been much more likely than whites to be arrested for the use of illegal drugs.* This disparity began in the mid-1980s, when the government intensified its legal war on drugs. This was mainly a war against crack cocaine, which African-Americans tend to

▼ African-Americans and Latinos are much more likely than non-Latino whites to be arrested for possessing illegal drugs even though they are not more likely to use illegal drugs.

The evidence on racial profiling by police is complex but suggests that the police do engage in profiling. Much of the evidence concerns traffic stops, with the typical study comparing the proportion of African-American or Latino drivers who are stopped, ticketed, searched, and/or arrested with the proportion of people from these racial/ethnic backgrounds in the general population (i.e., the residents of a city or state or the drivers on a particular road or highway). If people of color are overrepresented among drivers who receive such treatment, this is evidence of a racial disparity that may reflect racial profiling.

Investigations in Maryland and New Jersey found strong evidence of profiling. In Maryland, for example, African-Americans were 17 percent of the drivers on a major highway but 77 percent of all the drivers stopped by state troopers. The New Jersey investigation found that state troopers had targeted African-American and Latino drivers for alleged traffic violations and were three times more likely to search their cars than those of white drivers they stopped. A study of drivers in St. Louis, Missouri, also found evidence of racial profiling, with African-American drivers more likely than white drivers to experience searches after being stopped.

In the 2008 PPCS discussed earlier in the text, equal proportions of African-American, Latino, and white drivers reported being stopped by police, but among all drivers stopped, African-Americans (12.3 percent) and Latinos (5.8 percent) were more likely than whites (3.9 percent) to be searched by police. African-Americans (4.7 percent) were also more likely than whites (2.4 percent) to be arrested during traffic stops. These findings may not necessarily indicate racial and ethnic profiling, because the survey did not assess whether African-Americans and Latinos were more likely than whites to display behavior or evidence to justify a police search or arrest.

This is a methodological problem in most studies of racial profiling. Some evidence also suggests that African-Americans are more likely than whites to exceed the speed limit. However, when the racial disparities in traffic stops are very large, as they were in the Maryland investigation, it is difficult to believe that the driving behavior of people of color is so much worse than that of whites.

Racial profiling may also affect which citizens get stopped and frisked while walking down the street or simply hanging out. An investigation in New York City found that African-Americans and Latinos were much more likely than whites to be stopped by police and, once stopped, to be frisked. However, once stopped, they were not more likely to be arrested. In making these stops, police gave as the most common reasons "furtive movements" and "casing a victim or location." Because the three groups had the same arrest rates once stopped, the data strongly suggested that police were especially suspicious of the behavior of African-Americans and Latinos simply because of their race/ethnicity.

Sources: Baker 2010; Lundman and Kaufman 2003; Lundman and Kowalski 2009; Rojek et al. 2012; Tomaskovic-Devey and Warren 2009.

---

use and sell. In contrast, whites prefer powder cocaine. Taking their cue from the congressional, media, and public concern over crack, police departments focused their efforts in poor African-American neighborhoods and ignored the use and sale of powder cocaine and other illegal drugs in wealthier white neighborhoods. The problem was aggravated by federal penalties that involved the same sentence for selling only 5 grams of crack as for selling 500 grams of powder cocaine.

Accordingly, drug arrests since the 1980s have had a huge racial impact, with African-Americans, most of them young males, accounting for more than one-third of all drug arrests. This figure held true in 2011, when African-Americans still comprised 32 percent of all drug arrests (Federal Bureau of Investigation 2012). As Figure 16–3 ■ illustrates, the African-American arrest rate for drug offenses that year was almost 3 times higher than the white rate.

The racial discrimination suggested by these figures troubles many observers. As Alfred Blumstein (1993:4–5), a former president of the American Society of Criminology, observed, "What is particularly troublesome . . . is the degree to which the impact [of the drug war] has been so disproportionately imposed on nonwhites. There is no clear indication that the racial differences in arrest truly reflect different levels of [drug] activity or of harm imposed." Calling the war on drugs "a major assault on the black community," Blumstein commented, "One can be reasonably confident that if a similar assault was affecting the white community, there would be a strong and effective effort to change either the laws or the enforcement policy" (p. 5). In addition to arrest, the drug war has also had a significant racial impact on incarceration, an issue examined further in Chapter 17.

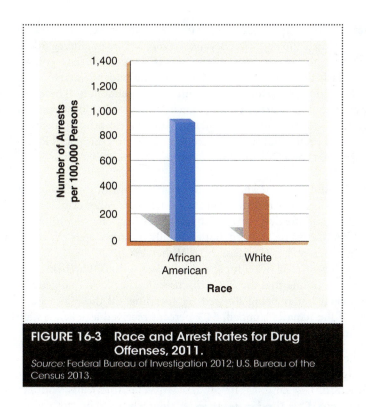

FIGURE 16-3 Race and Arrest Rates for Drug Offenses, 2011.
Source: Federal Bureau of Investigation 2012; U.S. Bureau of the Census 2013.

Ecological Evidence for Racial Discrimination in Policing

The example of the war on drugs shows that racial discrimination in policing occurs if the police target a behavior popular among a subordinate racial group while ignoring similar behavior popular among wealthier whites. Similar discrimination occurs if police resources are focused more on communities with high proportions of people of color than on those with lower proportions but similar crime rates. Drawing on Hubert Blalock's (1967) *racial-threat theory,* the idea here is that dominant groups (whites) feel more threatened as the size and power of minority groups grow, and they respond with legal measures and other actions to protect their dominant status.

Supporting this view, several studies find police force size and police expenditures higher in cities with higher proportions of African-Americans, even after controlling for crime rates (Kent and Jacobs 2005). Research also finds that increases in the 1960s and 1970s in spending on police resources were highest in cities with the greatest increases in black population, even with crime rates held constant (Jackson 1989).

Review and Discuss

To what degree does racial prejudice affect police decisions to arrest suspects? Explain your answer.

Gender and Arrest

The issue of gender discrimination in arrest is perhaps less controversial than its racial counterpart but no less interesting. In 2011, 74 percent of all people arrested were men, and more than 80 percent of people arrested for violent crimes (including 88 percent of those arrested for homicide and robbery) were men (Federal Bureau of Investigation 2012). Although these high percentages reflect heavier male involvement in crime (see Chapter 3), they may also reflect more lenient treatment of women by police. This is the view of the *chivalry hypothesis,* which says that male police do not arrest female suspects because of notions of chivalry: They feel that women need to be protected, not punished; that arrest would harm them and their families; and that women do not pose a threat to society (see Chapter 9). Police may also be reluctant to arrest women because they do not want to have to use physical force on a woman who resists arrest. A contrasting *evil woman hypothesis* predicts the opposite: Because women are normally regarded as more virtuous than men, a woman suspected of a crime might seem that much worse by comparison, prompting police to be particularly likely to arrest her. What does the evidence say?

Here we have to consider juvenile and adult arrests separately. The evidence for juvenile arrests is fairly clear that girls are disproportionately arrested or otherwise brought to the attention of juvenile authorities for *status offenses,* such as running away from home, parental curfew violations, and premarital sexual intercourse (Chesney-Lind and Pasko 2013). This discrimination arises from the traditional *double-standard* view that girls need protection more than boys do.

The evidence for adults is somewhat complex. Female prostitutes, of course, are far more likely than their male customers to be arrested, but the evidence for other crimes appears to depend on suspects' race and age and the degree to which female suspects act "femininely." Women are generally less likely than men to be arrested, but especially or only if they cry or otherwise conform to traditional female stereotypes (DeFleur 1975; Visher 1983).

Although receiving a traffic ticket for speeding is less serious than being arrested for a criminal offense, it is worth noting that the PPCS discussed earlier found no gender difference in the chance of being ticketed after being stopped for speeding. Of the males stopped, 55.9 percent received a ticket; of the females stopped, 54.9 percent received a ticket, a statistically insignificant difference. However, males were slightly more likely than females (3.5 percent compared to 1.4 percent) to be arrested after a traffic stop.

▶ Impact of Policing on Crime

Do police make a difference in crime? On the face of it, this is an absurd question. Of course police make a difference in crime. If we had no police, we would probably have chaos. But when we ask whether police make a difference in crime, we are not posing an all-or-nothing alternative. Instead, we are asking whether more police (once some minimal threshold is reached) are more effective than fewer police in controlling crime, whether more arrests (again assuming a minimal threshold) are more effective than fewer arrests, and whether certain police practices are more effective than other practices. Answers to these questions obviously have important criminal justice policy implications. What does the evidence say?

Do Additional Police Deter Crime?

Early studies concluded that larger police forces do not in and of themselves deter crime, but more recent studies reach the opposite conclusion. As Robert Apel and Daniel S. Nagin (2011:240) observe in their review of this evidence, "(P)utting more police officers on the street—either by hiring new officers or by allocating existing officers in ways that put them on the street in larger numbers or for longer periods of time—has a substantial deterrent effect on serious crime."

Other scholars think the evidence is less clear than this assessment (Paternoster 2010). They note that crime rates after the early 1990s fell in some U.S. cities as their police forces grew, but that crime rates fell in other cities even though their police forces did *not* grow. They also observe that crime rates fell in Canada during the 1990s even though the size of its police force actually declined. This inconsistent evidence leads Raymond Paternoster (2010:795–796) to conclude that it is "only *probably* true" that additional police reduce crime, and that "while the number of police can influence the amount of crime a city experiences, we do not know how much it matters, and other things seem to matter a great deal as well."

Samuel Walker (2011) cautions against placing too much faith in larger police forces *per se.* Even when additional police are hired by a city, he says, the actual presence of police at a given place and at a given time hardly increases. Further, many violent crimes involve people who know each other and also occur indoors, where the police cannot see them and cannot prevent them. Even when more police are added, the risk of detection and arrest for public crimes such as robbery still remains low. Finally, as noted in Chapter 5, many criminals give little thought to their chances of arrest, and those who do so assume they can get away with it.

How Police Are Used

Walker's (2011) caution suggests that *how* police are used is at least as important as whether they are used in the first place. In this regard, there is growing evidence on the effectiveness of *directed police patrol* (also called *hot spots policing*), in which the police focus their attention on *hot spots* of crime, the relatively few locations at which most of a city's serious street crime occurs. Studies find that additional police patrol of hot spots reduces crime in these locations compared to locations where additional patrol does not occur (Braga and Weisburd 2012; Sorg et al. 2013).

Related research involves directed patrol in hot spots for *gun crime.* Here an experiment in Kansas City was telling. The experiment involved intensive efforts to take handguns from people who had them illegally. In a high-crime area of Kansas City, police officers trained in detecting concealed firearms stopped cars and pedestrians for legitimate reasons. They found many illegal handguns on the people they stopped. Gun seizures rose by 60 percent, and gun crimes dropped by 49 percent (Sherman and Rogan 1995). Other studies also find that police targeting of gun crimes in this manner helps reduce these crimes (Wellford 2011).

▲ Directed police patrolling, in which the police focus on hot-spot locations for crime, appears to be able to reduce the amount of crime at these locations.

Another related effort involves "focused deterrence" strategies targeted at juvenile gangs. In these strategies, police and community leaders sit down with gang leaders and other gang members and remind them in no uncertain terms of the legal consequences for committing violence. These strategies also appear to be effective in reducing gang violence (Engel et al. 2013; Telep and Weisburd 2012).

Crackdowns

If hot spots and focused deterrence policing can reduce crime, what about an even more intense police presence in the form of a police crackdown? Here police suddenly saturate a small area and arrest drug pushers, prostitutes, gang members, and others committing visible crime. For better or worse, research on crackdowns suggests that they offer little hope for reducing crime. Most studies find that crackdowns reduce drug trafficking and other crime in the target areas only for a short time or perhaps not at all (Sherman et al. 1998). Often the drug trafficking and other crimes are simply displaced to other neighborhoods. Crackdowns thus appear to be at best a quick fix to the crime problem with no long-term effects, and have had little success in the war against drugs. As Elliott Currie (1994:206) put it, "On balance, it is not that crackdowns make no difference, but that, especially where drug dealing is heaviest and most widespread, any effects they have are likely to be short-lived."

Zero-Tolerance Policing

Beginning in the 1990s, several police departments, especially New York City's, began to use an ongoing, aggressive style of zero-tolerance policing that falls short of a crackdown, but is more intense than directed policing. It involves frequent traffic stops, "stop and frisk" questioning of some 700,000 supposedly suspicious persons each year, and frequent arrests for disorderly conduct, vagrancy, and other minor offenses. Such visible, aggressive policing may lower crime rates by increasing the chances that criminals get arrested and by deterring potential criminals from offending. By reducing *incivilities* such as disorderly youth and public drunkenness, it may also prompt potential offenders to think that residents care what happens in their neighborhoods and again deter them from offending (Kelling and Coles 1998).

Zero-tolerance policing raises important civil liberties questions; complaints of racial harassment by police increased after zero-tolerance policing was begun in New York City and continue to this day (Goldstein 2013; Herbert 2000; Staples 2012). Moreover, zero-tolerance policing may not live up to its advocates' claims. For example, although New York's crime rate declined after it introduced zero-tolerance policing, crime rates also declined in many other large cities where zero-tolerance policing was not used.

Actual research on New York's zero-tolerance policing yields mixed results. Some studies conclude it did not reduce New York's crime rate at all (Greenberg 2013; Harcourt and Ludwig 2007), while other studies conclude it had small, inconsistent effects on the city's crime rates that were "fleeting" (Rosenfeld and Fornango 2012:23) and that "substantial crime reductions" would probably have occurred even without it (Messner et al. 2007:377). However, a study of a similar policy, *proactive policing* (measured as the number of arrests for drunk driving and disorderly conduct divided by the number of police officers), in cities across the country found a link between such policing and lower robbery rates (Kubrin et al. 2010). The study's authors nonetheless cautioned that "whatever the deterrent effects of proactive or any other policing style might prove to be, policy decisions need to be informed not only by considerations of crime control but by the fundamental values of a democratic society" (Kubrin et al. 2010:85).

Review and Discuss

Would a change in policing strategy help to reduce the crime rate? Why or why not?

Does Arrest Make a Difference?

When we ask whether arrest makes a difference in crime rates, we are not talking about some arrests versus no arrests; instead we are considering more arrests versus fewer arrests. A common line of investigation determines an arrest or *certainty* ratio for states or cities by dividing a location's number of annual arrests by its official number of crimes for that location. The resulting ratio provides a rough measure of the chances that a crime will lead to an arrest.

A *police deterrence* hypothesis would predict that locations with higher certainty ratios should have lower crime rates than locations with lower ratios. This correlation is usually found, but it is difficult to interpret because of the chicken-and-egg question: Which comes first, the certainty of arrest or the crime rate? Although a deterrence view would interpret this correlation as support for its perspective, it is also possible that crime rates affect certainty rates. In this view, police in areas with low crime rates will be able to devote more resources to solving the few crimes they do have and thus be able to solve more crimes through arrest, creating high certainty ratios. Conversely, police in areas with high crime rates will simply not have the time or resources to investigate many crimes, resulting in low certainty ratios. These possibilities support a *system capacity* argument (see Chapter 5) and are at least as compelling as deterrence views. If so, the evidence on certainty ratios and crime rates cannot be interpreted as supporting the deterrence hypothesis.

To investigate these possibilities, studies looking at certainty ratios and crime rates over time are necessary. Several such studies find little or no impact of arrest certainty (or, to be more precise, changes in arrest certainty) on crime rates. A review concluded that these studies "provide little, if any, evidence consistent with the general deterrence perspective" (Chamlin 1991:188). However, a later study indicated that arrest certainty does make a difference. Stewart J. D'Alessio and Lisa Stolzenberg (1998) studied arrests and the number of crimes in greater Orlando, Florida over a 184-day period. The number of daily arrests ranged from 8 to 104, with an average of almost 54 per day. The authors concluded that "as the number of arrests made by police increases, criminal activity decreases substantially the following day" (p. 748), probably because word gets around after an arrest and deters potential offenders from committing a crime.

A fair conclusion from the arrest-deterrence literature is that arrests reduce crime only to the extent that potential offenders become more concerned about being arrested. This might happen because they hear about an arrest, as in the Orlando study, or because they see more police out and about, as the directed patrol research discussed in the last section suggests.

Community Policing

Community policing (also called *problem-oriented policing*) has become more popular. In this style of policing, police work closely with community groups and residents on various activities designed to reduce crime, including youth programs, cleanup projects, meetings with juvenile gangs, and replacing car patrol with foot patrol. These strategies allow police officers and citizens to get to know each other better and humanize the police to the citizenry. In return, citizens are more likely to trust the police, to report crimes to them, and to work with them on community projects. Foot patrol also allows officers to notice trash and other neighborhood incivilities that contribute to fear of crime and to bring these incivilities to the attention of local officials (Peak and Glensor 2012).

Several comprehensive community policing programs have been implemented in several cities, and research shows that these programs generally reduce crime at least to a modest degree (Reisig 2011; Weisburd et al. 2010). As Walker (2011:347) concludes from this body of research, "Focused, problem-oriented policing programs that involve partnerships and utilize a range of strategies can reduce serious crime."

Legal Technicalities and Police Effectiveness

Many critics charge that the Warren Court's rulings in the 1960s forced the police to fight crime with one hand tied behind their backs. Suspects and defendants now have too many rights, the critics say, forcing the police not to arrest them or prosecutors to release them. In either case, public safety suffers as the law shackles police and prevents them from doing their job. Reduce the controls on police and they will be able to arrest more criminals and otherwise do a better job of keeping the public safe.

The two Court rulings most under attack are the ones that developed the exclusionary rule and the *Miranda* warning. In the first case, the Court ruled in *Mapp v. Ohio* (367 U.S. 643 [1961]) that evidence obtained by police in violation of the Fourth Amendment of the Constitution cannot be used in court. In the second case, the Court ruled in *Miranda v. Arizona* (384 U.S. 436 [1966]) that police must advise suspects that they may remain silent, that anything they say may be used against them, and that they have the right to have an attorney present during questioning.

How valid is the argument that these rules restrict arrests, let criminals go free, and raise our crime rates? Several considerations suggest that it is not valid at all. For example, because so few offenders are arrested at all (see Chapter 3), even if the police could arrest more people if legal technicalities were reduced, these extra arrests would probably have little effect on the crime rate.

Moreover, legal technicalities do not even seem to inhibit arrests. The clear conclusion from many studies is that very few suspects are freed because of the exclusionary rule. Of more than 500,000 felony arrests in California between 1976 and 1979, for example, prosecutors dismissed only 4,130 cases, or less than 1 percent, because of illegally obtained evidence (Fyfe 1983). This type of evidence leads Walker (2011:113) to conclude, "The exclusionary rule does not let 'thousands' of dangerous criminals loose on the streets, and it has almost no effect on violent crime."

The *Miranda* warning also has not impeded the police. Walker (2011) points out that most suspects confess anyway, because the evidence against them is often substantial and they want to plea bargain to reduce their sentence. Police also have various ways of getting around the *Miranda* warning. They are required to give suspects the warning only when they are about to ask them questions. If a suspect confesses or provides other information before questioning has begun, this evidence is admissible. Some officers also continue questioning suspects even after they give the *Miranda* warning and eventually wear them down, sometimes leading to confessions by innocent people (Hoffman 1998; Shipler 2012). Walker (2011:117) concludes that "repeal or modification of the *Miranda* warning will not result in more convictions."

Impact of Policing on Crime Revisited

Overall, the literature on police, arrest, and crime rates suggests that intelligent policing strategies can reduce crime rates. These strategies include directed patrol and community policing, but they do not include crackdowns. The simple addition of police officers may reduce crime, but the extent and consistency of this effect remain unclear. In any event, how any additional officers are deployed probably matters more than the actual number of officers. Zero-tolerance policing might also work, but the mixed results overall leave its actual impact unclear, and such policing may lead to abuse of police powers and worsen civilian–police relationships, if New York City's experience is any indication.

It is less clear how these policing strategies can reduce the many crimes of violence, including much homicide and assault, rape, domestic violence, and child abuse, that typically occur behind closed doors among people who know each other. Also, these policing strategies certainly leave white-collar crime untouched, which should not be forgotten in this discussion. Another problem is money. Even if additional police and the greater use of directed patrol can reduce some crime, the financial cost of each deterred crime is large and perhaps prohibitive. For example, a study of police in New York City subway and trains stations determined that each reduced felony resulting from greater police patrol cost the city some $125,000 in today's dollars (Chaiken et al. 1975). Finally, intensified police efforts at crime control also raise serious civil liberties questions for a democratic society.

▶ Women and People of Color in Police Forces

In a democratic society in which everyone is held equal under the law, everyone should also be equal *in* the law. All citizens, regardless of gender, race, or ethnicity, should have the same opportunity to become police officers and should be treated equally if and when they do join the police. Because police are our first line of defense in creating order under law, anything less than equitable recruitment and treatment is unacceptable. Thus, another dilemma of crime control in a democratic society is ensuring that equality prevails in the recruitment of police and in their treatment once on the job.

With these ideals in mind, how equitable is our law enforcement institution? Not too long ago, few people of color and hardly any women were on our police forces. In the past few decades, more women and people of color have joined police forces, and conditions for them on the job have improved. As the old saying goes, however, the more things change, the more they stay the same. People of color and women still face obstacles in joining police forces and in their treatment by other officers and opportunities for advancement once they are on the job.

Let's look first at race and ethnicity issues in police work. On the eve of World War II more than a half century ago, only 1 percent of all U.S. police officers were people of color. This figure rose to 2 percent in 1950, almost 4 percent in 1960, and about 6 percent by 1970. One result of the urban riots of the 1960s was increased pressure for the recruitment of more people of color. Coupled with new affirmative-action hiring regulations, recruitment of people of color into police forces accelerated in the 1980s. Today about 20 percent, or one-fifth, of all sworn officers in the United States are people of color, although their proportion varies greatly from one city to another (Walker et al. 2012). This variation reflects differences not only in city racial composition, but also in the cities' police recruitment policies and efforts.

Once they are on the police force, people of color face obstacles that their white counterparts do not (Dempsey and Forst 2014). They tend to be denied prestigious positions on special anticrime units and undercover patrols and are far less likely than their white peers to be promoted. Their chances for promotion are greatest in cities with the largest populations of people of color. In addition, the racial prejudice of many white officers often contaminates their relationships with officers who are not white. African-American officers in Los Angeles and elsewhere have reported bigoted comments and discriminatory treatment by white officers.

Women police officers also face discrimination, but of a different sort (Dempsey and Forst 2014). Women comprise fewer than 15 percent of all police officers, but policing is still seen as "men's work" in many police departments. Women officers thus confront many of the same problems that women entering other male-dominated occupations have faced, including sexual harassment. But

▼ Women and people of color have joined police forces in increasing numbers, but still face many obstacles.

© Dwayne Newton / PhotoEdit

because police work sometimes involves dangerous confrontations with suspects, women officers face the additional burden of overcoming widespread doubts about their ability to handle themselves during such incidents. Studies of this issue find women officers at least as capable as male officers in persuading or subduing suspects to submit to arrest (Harrington and Lonsway 2004).

Research on African-American and other women officers of color indicate that they face a double burden of both racism and sexism (Martin 2004). In an early example, an African-American officer, Cheryl Gomez-Preston, was transferred to the largest precinct in Detroit in 1982, only to receive from fellow officers written racial slurs such as "n——bitch," "die, bitch," and "go back to Africa." When she went to her commanding officer to tell him about these notes, he responded by showing her pictures of nude women in pornographic magazines. Once, when she and six other officers were chasing an armed robbery suspect, the other officers failed to back her up when she confronted the suspect as he tried to pull out his gun. Gomez-Preston eventually sued the Detroit Police Department for sexual harassment and won a jury award of $675,000 (Gomez-Preston and Trescott 1995).

Criminologist Susan E. Martin (2004) wrote that, historically, white women have been "put on a pedestal" by being considered frail and in need of male protection. In contrast, African-American women have been considered very capable of performing physical labor. These stereotypes contribute to differences in the tasks assigned to African-American and white female officers. In particular, white women are more likely than African-American women to be given station house duties instead of more dangerous street patrol assignments. On patrol, white male officers typically back up white female officers, but often fail to back up African-American female officers, as Gomez-Preston's experience illustrates. In the station house, women of both races encounter hostility from male officers, but African-American women experience more problems than white women. Martin found that African-American women officers resent the preferential treatment that their white counterparts receive, and white women accept many of the racially stereotyped views that white male officers espouse. All these differences contribute to deep divisions between African-American and white women in police forces and prevent them from acting together to fight sexism in policing.

▶ Conclusion

Policing in a democratic society is filled with dilemmas. First and foremost, the police must enforce the law while staying within it. The delicate balance between police powers and democratic rights remains a hotly debated topic. The evidence is clear, however, that judicial restrictions on police powers do not hamper police officers' ability to fight crime and protect public safety. Directed patrol does appear to reduce crime, but cost and civil liberties questions remain significant issues. Problem-oriented policy also appears to reduce crime, but cost again is a significant issue.

In a democratic society, police also need to exercise their discretion without regard to race, gender, or other extralegal variables. Experts continue to disagree on whether police practices in arrest and brutality differ by race/ethnicity and gender. Certainly, there is evidence to support very different conclusions. A fair conclusion, but one with which partisans on either side of the discretion debate will disagree, is that race/ethnicity and gender play a small but significant role in police behavior.

Regardless of this issue, it is clear that, for better or worse, the police pay more attention to crimes by the poor than by the wealthy. Historically, the police arrested and beat up workers who were protesting horrible wages and working conditions, but they did not arrest company officials for their mistreatment of their workers. In contemporary times, the police arrest poor street criminals, but largely ignore wealthy white-collar criminals. This social class difference in today's policing reflects larger social and institutional priorities, including the public's concern over street crime and lack of concern over its white-collar counterpart.

We now turn to the remaining stages of the criminal justice system and continue focusing on the two major themes introduced in this chapter: the extent to which race or ethnicity, gender, and class biases affect the exercise of legal discretion and the ability of the criminal justice system to control crime.

Summary

1. Herbert Packer's crime-control and due process models remind us that democratic societies face difficult questions of maintaining order while remaining a free society. Because the police have great powers over civilians, it is important, but very difficult, for society to strike the correct balance between crime control and due process. It is also important for a democratic society to ensure that the criminal justice system treats people the same regardless of their race, ethnicity, social class, gender, or other extralegal characteristics.

2. A major impetus for the development of the modern police force in England and later the United States was mob violence and the general unruliness of what were called the "dangerous classes." Early U.S. police forces were notoriously corrupt and brutal and of little help against crime.

3. The nature of police work contributes to a working personality of police officers that tends to be authoritarian, cynical, and suspicious. It also contributes to a strong feeling of loyalty among police officers and an "us against them" mentality in their relations with the public.

4. Although tens of thousands of acts of excessive force by police may occur annually, these acts comprise a very small proportion of all police–citizen encounters. Although the evidence is complex, it does not appear that racial prejudice plays a large role in the excessive force experienced by African-Americans. To the extent that prejudice plays any such role, policing is not as blind as it should be in a democracy.

5. Police corruption in the form of bribery and other illegal behavior arises from the nature of police work and from the opportunities available to police to be corrupt. Scholars believe that police corruption extends beyond a few "rotten apples" to the entire culture of policing.

6. Legal factors such as the strength of the evidence play the largest role in decisions by police to arrest suspects. The evidence on racial bias in arrests is again very complex, but such bias does not appear to play a substantial role. The legal war against drugs has had a strong racially discriminatory effect, given that African-Americans and Latinos are being arrested for drug offenses far out of proportion to their actual use of illegal drugs.

7. The evidence on gender bias and arrest is also complex. Whether women receive favorable treatment depends on whether they act femininely and perhaps also on their race. White women seem more likely than black women to avoid arrest for similar offenses.

8. Additional police do not appear to deter crime in and of themselves. What appears more important is how additional police are deployed, with directed policing in high-crime areas a promising strategy. Aggressive, zero-tolerance policing has won much acclaim in the popular media, but research on its crime-reduction effects is very mixed.

9. Community policing is another popular crime-control strategy. It appears to produce more positive civilian perceptions of the police, but studies of its effectiveness in lowering the crime rate yield mixed results.

10. The *Miranda* ruling and the exclusionary rule are two examples of legal technicalities that are popularly thought to hamper the police. However, studies of this possible effect do not confirm this belief.

11. Women and people of color have joined the ranks of police forces in recent decades, but they continue to face many kinds of obstacles in their workplaces. Black women officers face a double burden of being both black and female that hampers their ability to achieve respect and promotions in their careers.

Key Terms

brutality *332*	crackdown *343*	discretion *337*
community policing *344*	crime control *328*	discrimination *346*
constable *330*	democratic society *328*	double burden *347*
corruption *335*	deterrence *344*	due process *328*

What Would You Do?

1. It's Saturday morning and you just began a 400-mile trip to visit some close friends in a nearby state for the weekend. Although the speed limit is 65 mph, you're cruising along at about 75. Even so, many cars have already passed you. Suddenly you see some flashing lights in your rearview mirror. You pull over, and the officer approaches your car and asks to see your license, registration, and proof of insurance. The officer then tells you that you were going 75. When you begin to protest that you were probably the slowest car on the road, the officer gets angry, tells you to be quiet, and asks for permission to search your car. What is your reaction?

2. You're a server at a local restaurant and have been waiting on a table occupied by two police officers eating lunch. When they finish, you bring them the check. One of the officers says, "You don't expect us to pay that bill, do you?" and they both get up to leave. What do you do?

© Ocean/Corbis

17 Prosecution and Punishment

· ·

Crime in the News

Damon Thibodeaux is lucky to be alive. In September 2012, he was released from prison in Louisiana after spending more than 15 years in solitary confinement on death row for a murder he did not commit. In 1996 he confessed to the rape and murder of his 14-year-old step-cousin after police had interrogated him for nine hours overnight. There was no physical evidence linking him to the crime, and it was later discovered that the victim had not been raped. During the interrogation, Thibodeaux denied at least nine times that he had committed the murder, but he finally confessed to the murder at the crack of dawn in what a news report called an "almost catatonic" state. His confession statement included details of the crime scene that police gave him but that turned out to be inaccurate. After he was released from prison, Thibodeaux explained why he confessed: "At that point I was tired," Thibodeaux said, "I was hungry. All I wanted to do was sleep, and I was willing to tell them anything they wanted me to tell them if it would get me out of that interrogation room." Fifteen years later, DNA evidence finally exonerated Thibodeaux. Leading to his release.

Source: Blackmon 2012.

· ·

Policing is only the first stage of the criminal justice process. After an arrest, the prosecutor determines whether to prosecute the case or to drop it, and the judge decides how much bail to require. If the decision is to prosecute, the prosecutor then determines what charges to bring against the defendant. The defendant must decide whether to plead guilty, which most do, or to plead not guilty and have a trial. At the end of the trial a jury or judge decides on the verdict. If the defendant pleads guilty or is found guilty after a trial, the judge next determines the punishment. Here the judge must first decide whether to incarcerate the defendant. If the decision is to incarcerate, the judge must also determine the length of the sentence.

No doubt you are already familiar with these basic stages of the legal process. But notice that decisions are made at every stage, with each creating the possibility of mistakes and/or bias for or against defendants because of their race or ethnicity, gender, social class, or other extralegal factors. The Damon Thibodeaux case described in the Crime in the News story is just one example of the injustice that can result. Much of this chapter examines the extent to which mistakes and bias exist. As with arrest, we will see that the evidence is very complex.

Another major issue in criminal justice today is whether a "get tough" approach involving mandatory sentences and longer prison terms can reduce crime. This chapter examines this issue. Most criminologists think this approach is short-sighted, even as many politicians and members of the public favor tougher treatment of criminals involving longer prison terms and the building of more prisons.

This chapter, then, continues the themes of the last chapter on policing: the extent to which social inequality affects the exercise of legal discretion and the extent to which reliance on the criminal justice system can reduce crime. These are arguably the two most important issues for a sociological understanding of criminal justice and they deserve our full attention.

▶ Criminal Courts and the Adversary System

The United States has long been said to have an adversary system of criminal justice. The adversary model is one of combat. Like the knights of old, prosecutor and defense attorney fight each other with all the weapons at their disposal. Their weapons are not lances or swords, but rather their legal

▼ The adversary system, in which a prosecutor and defense attorney are said to vigorously contest the evidence at a trial refereed by a judge, is largely a myth.

skills and powers of oratory, with which they vigorously contest the evidence as the judge referees their fight. The fate of the defendant lies in the balance, just as the fate of the proverbial "fair maiden" lay in the balance in the old, and probably sexist, knightly tales of mortal combat.

This exciting image of the courtroom process is the setting for many novels, films, and TV shows. Unfortunately, the adversary system is largely a myth. Although the most serious and/or publicized cases do follow the adversary model, most cases involve poor, unknown defendants. Few of these run-of-the-mill defendants can afford expensive attorneys and instead are forced to go with overworked and underpaid public defenders or court-appointed attorneys who usually provide them only perfunctory representation. Not surprisingly, most of these defendants plead guilty.

This was the central finding of work by sociologists and other scholars that began in the 1960s, as researchers studied how the criminal courts really worked, not how they claimed to work. A series of scholarly articles and books and journalistic accounts documenting the lack of equal justice and adversarial justice came out in rapid succession.

Normal Crimes and the Fate of Poor Defendants

In one of the most influential studies, David Sudnow (1965) developed the concept of the *normal crime* and applied it to cases involving poor defendants. He argued that prosecutors and public defenders develop the same idea of what constitutes a typical or "normal" crime based on the strength of the evidence, the seriousness of the charges, and the defendant's prior record. These assumptions allow them to classify particular crimes as either serious or minor cases and to quickly dispose of them through guilty pleas by agreeing on appropriate punishment for the defendant.

Sudnow concluded that the courts feature much more cooperation than combat between prosecutors and public defenders. Other work extended his view to private counsel assigned by judges to represent poor defendants and even to private defense attorneys paid by defendants. Abraham S. Blumberg (1967) said that the latter sell out their clients in a "confidence game" in which they do little for their clients, but pretend to do a lot. Their object is to collect their fees while minimizing the time spent on any one case. Blumberg further termed defense attorneys "double agents" for cooperating with prosecutors to obtain guilty pleas instead of vigorously defending their clients.

In short, this early body of work charged that poor but innocent defendants were being railroaded into pleading guilty by lawyers who cared more for courts' administrative needs and their own professional needs than for their clients' well-being. Urban courts were depicted as assembly lines in which the typical defendant, accused of a misdemeanor or minor felony, spends at most a few moments with a public defender or assigned counsel before pleading guilty. Public defenders and assigned counsel were depicted as undertrained and overworked and urban courtrooms as dismal, dirty, and crowded settings (Downie 1972; Mather 1973). These works were especially critical of rampant plea bargaining, which was said to deny defendants due process: "A lawyer who knows next to nothing about his client or the facts of the crime with which he is charged barters away a man's right to a trial, and, along with it, the presumption that a defendant is innocent until proved guilty" (Downie 1972:23).

Prosecutors, the Courtroom Work Group and Plea Bargaining

This early body of work was soon followed by a new wave of scholarship, much of it by political scientists, that refined our understanding of the flow of criminal cases after arrest. It stressed that heavy caseloads burden prosecutors, public defenders and other defense attorneys, and judges alike.

Recognizing this, the courtroom work group consisting of all three parties realizes that the best thing for everyone is to resolve the case as quickly as possible through a guilty plea. Plea bargaining thus accounts for at least 90 percent of all guilty verdicts in many jurisdictions, and judge or jury trials are relatively rare (Eisenstein and Jacob 1977).

For prosecutors, who simply cannot afford to prosecute all the cases the police hand them, plea bargaining ensures convictions and helps process huge caseloads as quickly as possible. Prosecutors usually do not proceed with a case without being fairly confident that a jury would find the defendant guilty. They thus drop up to half of all felony arrests because of weak evidence or lack of cooperation from victims and other witnesses. To decide which cases to drop or plea bargain, prosecutors determine whether the case is a strong one from their perspective.

▲ Like other members of the courtroom work group, judges recognize that plea bargaining expedites the processing of large caseloads.

Several elements make up such a case: (1) a serious offense (e.g., murder compared to simple assault); (2) an injured victim; (3) strong evidence, including eyewitnesses or recovered weapons or stolen property; (4) the defendant's use of a weapon; (5) defendants with serious prior records; and (6) a "stand-up" victim whom "the jury would believe and consider undeserving of victimization" (Myers 2000:452). Ideally, these are victims who are articulate, who have no criminal background, who did not know their offender, and who did nothing to cause their victimization. If victims do not fit this profile or are unwilling to cooperate, prosecutors often drop the charges altogether or reduce them as part of a plea bargain.

The cases remaining after this initial screening are those in which the evidence is strongest and the charges the most serious. These are the best cases from the prosecutor's standpoint because most of these defendants are probably guilty of the crime for which they were arrested. Given this likelihood, the new scholarship said, plea bargaining does not constitute the miscarriage of justice that earlier critics had cited. If anything, it helps defendants because they cannot be certain what sentence they would receive if they insisted on their right to a jury trial and were then found guilty. Recognizing this, most defendants in fact favor guilty pleas. Guilty pleas also resolve their cases much sooner, which shortens the time until defendants can resume their normal lives. Because defense attorneys realize all this, they are usually very willing to plea bargain instead of taking the case to trial (Eisenstein and Jacob 1977).

The new scholarship further challenged critics' charges that plea bargaining lets serious offenders off too lightly. When the courtroom work group determines the sentence for serious offenses and chronic offenders, little actual bargaining over the sentence occurs, because the courtroom work group already knows what the sentence will be. Suspects guilty of serious crimes thus receive stiff sentences even if they plead guilty (Feeley 1979). These sentences are at least as harsh as those for similar crimes in other Western nations and often harsher (Kappeler and Potter 2005).

Although the new scholarship took a more benign view of plea bargaining than did the earlier critiques, it still supported their view that courtroom work groups usually fail to vigorously contest the guilt of defendants. For better or worse, the adversary model is largely a myth for most criminal cases.

Review and Discuss

How does the concept of the courtroom work group help us understand why so much plea bargaining occurs? Do you think plea bargaining is good or bad? Why?

▶ Punishment, Social Structure, and Inequality

Since the time of Émile Durkheim, punishment has been central to sociological theories of law and society. Durkheim (1933 (1893)) thought that punishment reinforced social stability by clarifying social norms and uniting conventional society against the deviants who are punished. He further argued that the social structure of a society helps determine the type of punishment it adopts. In small, traditional societies, the *collective conscience*, or society's shared norms and values, is extremely strong. When deviance occurs, these societies engage in repressive law marked by harsh physical punishment of deviants. In contrast, because the collective conscience is weaker in larger, modern societies, these societies deal with deviance through restitutive law marked by an interest in restoring relationships to their previous state. Restitution, such as payments to aggrieved parties, becomes a primary punishment. Such societies also develop prisons as a substitute for physical punishment (Durkheim 1983 (1901)).

Although some scholars question Durkheim's view of social evolution and punishment, his basic theme that a society's social structure influences its type of punishment remains compelling (Garland 1990). It is a basic theme of the broad category of conflict and radical theories (see Chapter 9). These theories see the inequality in society as a central influence on the type and severity of punishment and view legal punishment as a way for the ruling class to preserve its power by controlling the poor, people of color, and other subordinate groups.

Economic Conditions and Punishment

The classic statement on social structure and punishment is that of George Rusche and Otto Kirchheimer (1939), who contended that imprisonment increases when unemployment increases. Higher unemployment, they said, generates anger and rebellion. To counter this, the ruling class puts more of the poor behind bars when unemployment rises. This action helps intimidate the poor from rebelling and also reduces their labor supply, leaving fewer of them to compete for scarce jobs. The greater job prospects that result reduce the poor's anger and thus their potential for revolt.

Research on Unemployment and Imprisonment

Several studies have since tested Rusche and Kirchheimer's view. The evidence is inconsistent. Some studies have found that unemployed defendants are more likely than their employed counterparts to be imprisoned and that incarceration is higher in locations with higher unemployment (Chiricos and Delone 1992), but other studies have not found the presumed relationship or have found it in some locations but not in others (Nobiling et al. 1998).

These mixed results suggest that Rusche and Kirchheimer overestimated the importance of unemployment and underestimated the importance of other factors affecting incarceration rates (Sutton 2004). However, Raymond J. Michalowski and Susan M. Carlson (1999) found that the unemployment–imprisonment relationship is stronger for some periods of U.S. history than for others and speculated that the inconsistent findings reflect the fact that various studies have used data from various periods of U.S. history. Yet a study of business cycles and imprisonment in fifteen Western democracies did not find the presumed unemployment–imprisonment link once certain political and institutional factors were taken into account (Sutton 2004). As these contradictory findings suggest, the link between unemployment and incarceration remains unproven.

Research on the Postbellum South

Another line of research on economic conditions and punishment focuses on the African-American experience in the postbellum (post–Civil War) South. Much of this research is inspired by Blalock's (1967) *racial-threat theory* (see Chapter 16). Supporting the theory, imprisonment of African-Americans for various offenses increased steadily during this period as Southern whites feared that the freed slaves would gain political and economic power (Myers 1990). Lynchings increased when African-American economic gains relative to whites were greatest and when the price of cotton was falling and threatening employment (Tolnay and Beck 1995). Imprisonment rates and sentence lengths of young African-American males accused of rape in Georgia also increased when cotton prices fell. Ironically, the increased imprisonment of African-American males for rape probably reduced their lynchings for the same accusation (Myers 1995).

Most contemporary work on punishment, social structure, and inequality focuses on class, racial/ethnic, and gender differences in prosecution and sentencing. Many studies analyze data on samples of individual defendants, but some analyze macro-level data from states, cities, and

Crime and Controversy SHOULD FELONS LOSE THE RIGHT TO VOTE?

When they are sentenced to prison or jail, convicted criminals lose certain rights, most importantly their freedom. In recent years the loss of another right, voting, has become a controversial social, political, and policy issue. All but two states, Maine and Vermont, prohibit prison inmates from voting if they were convicted of a felony. The key difference among states regarding felony disenfranchisement occurs after felons are released from prison. Fifteen states, including Maine and Vermont, permit felons to vote once they are released from prison, but the other 35 states prohibit them from voting for various amounts of time after they leave prison.

The estimated number of felons and ex-felons who are prohibited from voting 5.85 million equal to about 2.4 percent of all U.S. adults. This figure includes 2.2 million African-American citizens, equivalent to almost 8 percent of all African-Americans of voting age. In three states (Florida, Kentucky, and Virginia), more than 20 percent of African-Americans of voting age are not allowed to vote because of a felon record.

Felony disenfranchisement became an issue in the 2000 and 2004 presidential elections, but also raises larger questions of criminal justice policy. In 2000, 600,000 ex-felons were not allowed to vote in Florida. Because George Bush was deemed by the U.S. Supreme Court to have won Florida and its electoral votes (and thus the presidential election) by the narrowest of margins, 537 votes, the exclusion of felons from the voting booths took on enormous importance. Most of the felons were African-American, and most would probably have voted for Bush's opponent, Vice President Al Gore, had they been allowed to vote. Because Bush won Florida by so few votes, the felon vote would certainly have enabled Gore to win Florida and, with it, the presidency.

Florida's experience raises the issue of the political impact of prohibiting felons from voting. In a comprehensive study of this issue, Jeff Manza and Christopher Uggen found that felony disenfranchisement has affected the outcome of at least seven U.S. Senate elections and helped to ensure a Republican majority in the Senate in the early 1980s and mid-1990s. Other evidence suggests that felony disenfranchisement laws reduce voting even among people still allowed to vote, because going to the polls on election day is often a family event. If a member of the family is not allowed to vote, that person's spouse or partner may therefore not bother to vote.

The prohibition of felon voting also has important implications for criminal justice policy. Because hundreds of thousands of prisoners are released back into society each year, it is important that their reentry go as smoothly as possible to help keep them from committing new crimes. Many scholars feel that by refusing to let felons vote, society sends the wrong message and only embitters these ex-convicts. If they have served their sentences and paid their debt to society, these scholars say, then they should be allowed to vote. Presenting a different view, other observers say that felons should permanently forfeit their right to vote because they have indicated their disdain for society's rules and a lack of respect for society itself.

Sources: Chung 2013; Manza and Uggen 2008.

---

other areas. This body of work is both important and complex, and we explore it here in some detail, looking first at social class and then at race/ethnicity and gender.

Social Class and Legal Outcomes

To test whether social class influences legal outcomes, researchers examine the conviction and imprisonment rate and the average sentence length of criminal defendants. Although most of these defendants are poor, this research finds that the poorest defendants do not fare worse than less poor defendants after offense seriousness, prior record, and other factors are held constant (Myers 2000). Some observers view this lack of class differences in sentencing as contradicting conflict theory views (Chiricos and Waldo 1975).

Other scholars challenge this conclusion. Because most defendants are from lower- and working-class backgrounds, these scholars argue, there is too little income variation among them to allow class differences in outcomes to emerge, and there are too few middle- and upper-income defendants accused of street crimes with whom to compare them. Wealthy people, after all, rarely commit robbery, burglary, auto theft, or the like. Tests of class differences in sentencing and other outcomes are therefore meaningless (Shelden 1982). Further, wealthy defendants are certainly far more able than poor defendants to contest the evidence, because they can afford to hire highly skilled attorneys, private investigators, and other experts. In this manner, wealthy defendants are much more able to vigorously contest the evidence as envisioned by the adversary model. As Herbert Jacob (1978:185–186) observed,

> Those few defendants who are not poor can often escape the worst consequences of their involvement. . . . They can afford bail and thus avoid pretrial detention. They can obtain a private attorney who specializes in criminal work. They can usually obtain delays that help weaken the prosecution case. . . . They can enroll in diversion programs by seeking private psychiatric treatment or other medical assistance. They can keep their jobs and maintain their family relationships and, therefore, qualify as good probation risks. They can appeal their conviction (if, indeed, they are convicted) and delay serving their sentence.

Here the prosecution of O. J. Simpson beginning in 1994 is instructive. Simpson was accused of two ghastly murders. Most poor defendants in his situation would have pleaded guilty or had a much shorter and more perfunctory trial handled by a lone public defender. Simpson's "dream team" defense cost $10 million, hundreds of thousands of dollars of which helped pay for expert forensic and DNA witnesses who effectively challenged the credibility of the evidence against the wealthy, celebrated defendant, who was found not guilty (Barkan 1996).

The clearest class disparity in legal outcomes is seen by comparing poor defendants accused of street crime with much wealthier defendants accused of white-collar crime (Reiman and Leighton 2013). To recall a study mentioned in Chapter 13, Robert Tillman and Henry N. Pontell (1992) compared sentences received in California by Medicaid fraud defendants (physicians and other health care professionals) and grand theft defendants. Only 38 percent of the former were incarcerated, compared to 79 percent of the latter, even though the median economic loss from Medicaid fraud was ten times greater than the loss from grand theft.

Some may argue, of course, that street crimes should be treated more harshly than white-collar crimes because the public is so much more concerned about them. Notwithstanding this argument, the fact remains that criminal courts are "fundamentally courts against the poor" (Jacob 1978:185). The reason for this, wrote James Eisenstein and Herbert Jacob (1977:289), is that "the behaviors most severely punished by governmental power are those in which persons on the fringes of American society most readily engage. . . . Crimes (especially white-collar crimes) committed by other segments of the population attract less public attention, less scrutiny from the police, and less vigorous prosecution."

▼ Criminal defendants who are wealthy are much more able than poor defendants to afford bail, to hire a skilled defense attorney, and to pay for investigators.

AP Photo/Masahiko Yamamoto

Community Context of Social Class and Sentencing

Most studies of social class and sentencing for street crime use individual-level data. Recent research has begun to explore a possible relationship at the community level. Prosecutors and judges may feel that defendants from poorer neighborhoods pose a greater threat than defendants who come from less poor neighborhoods. If so, the former defendants should receive harsher sentences than the latter defendants. Testing this hypothesis, John Wooldredge (2007) analyzed the sentences of almost 3,000 convicted felony defendants in Ohio. He found that defendants were indeed more likely to receive a prison term if they came from poorer neighborhoods, but that neighborhood disadvantage was unrelated to the sentence length among those who were incarcerated. Research on juveniles similarly finds that those from poorer neighborhoods are more likely than those from wealthier areas to be incarcerated (Rodriguez 2013).

Review and Discuss

To what extent does social class affect legal outcomes?

Impact of Race and Ethnicity

Much research examines whether race and ethnicity influence the decisions of prosecutors, judges, and juries (Ulmer 2012). We look first at research on prosecutorial decisions and then at studies of conviction and sentencing.

Prosecutorial Decisions

Several studies have explored whether race/ethnicity affects prosecutorial decisions to drop charges against defendants, or to bring more serious charges against defendants whose cases are not dropped. The evidence is mixed; some studies do find white defendants more likely than African-American and Latino defendants to have their charges dropped or reduced (Hartley et al. 2007), but other studies do not find this dynamic (Shermer and Johnson 2010) or find worse outcomes specifically for young African-American males but not for race/ethnicity more generally (Wooldredge 2012).

In another type of racial discrimination, some studies have found that prosecutors bring more serious charges in homicide and rape cases when whites were victims than when African-Americans were victims (Myers 2000). For example, people accused of killing whites are more likely to be indicted for first-degree murder, and thus are more likely to receive the death penalty if convicted, than people accused of killing African-Americans. The charges in homicide and rape cases tend to be the most severe when African-Americans are accused of victimizing whites. Such findings "raise the disturbing possibility that some prosecutors define the victimization of whites, especially when African-Americans are perpetrators, as more serious criminal events than the comparable victimization of African-Americans" (Myers 2000:451).

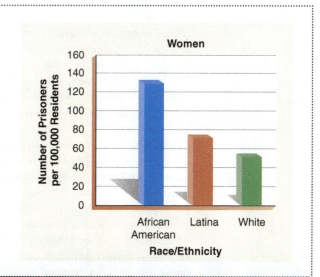

▲ Some studies find that defendants accused of killing white victims are more likely to be indicted for first-degree murder than those accused of killing members of other races. These defendants are also more likely to receive the death penalty.

Conviction and Sentencing

African-Americans and Latinos in the United States are far more likely than non-Latino whites to be in prison. In 2011, about 38 percent of all prison inmates were African-Americans and 23 percent were Latinos, even though these groups comprise only 13 and 14 percent of the U.S. population respectively. Incarceration rates (the number of inmates per 100,000 residents of each

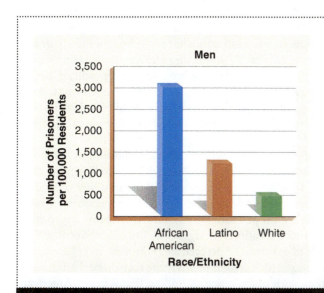

FIGURE 17–1 Race, Ethnicity, Gender, and Imprisonment Rates, 2011 (Federal and State Prisoners).
Note: The African-American and white categories exclude Latinos.
Source: Carson and Sabol 2012.

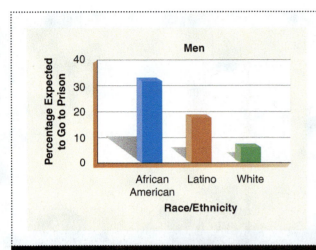

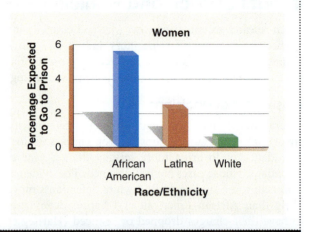

FIGURE 17-2 Race, Ethnicity, Gender, and Lifetime Likelihood of Going to Prison.
Note: The black and white categories exclude Hispanics.
Source: Bonczar 2003.

race) present an even more vivid picture of racial disparity (see Figure 17–1 ■). The rate for African-Americans and Latinos of both sexes is much higher than that for whites. These rates reflect the chances of going to prison sometime in one's lifetime, which again are much higher for African-Americans and Latinos than for whites (see Figure 17–2 ■).

Do these large racial and ethnic disparities reflect systematic racial/ethnic discrimination in the criminal justice system, especially at the sentencing stage, or do they simply reflect disproportionate involvement of African-Americans and Latinos in street crime? Once again the evidence is very complex, and scholars dispute what it is saying. Several, but by no means all, recent studies find that African-American, Latino, and Native American defendants are more likely than white defendants to be sentenced to prison after conviction, and some find that they also receive longer prison terms (Bales and Piquero 2012; Doerner and Demuth 2010; Franklin 2013a, 2013b; Walker et al. 2012). Other studies find that African-Americans are treated more harshly than whites in these ways, but that Latinos are treated the same as whites (Brennan and Spohn 2009). Yet other studies find few or no racial/ethnic differences in sentencing outcomes (Harris et al. 2009; Reitler et al. 2013).

Race-related factors other than the defendant's own race have also been studied. One of these factors is the victim's race, as several studies, especially of rape and capital (death sentence) offenses, uncover more punitive sentencing when whites are victims than when African-Americans are victims (Sorensen and Wallace 1999). A second factor is the seriousness of the crime, as harsher sentencing for African-Americans and Latinos seems to be more likely in less serious crimes than in more serious crimes (Chen 2008). Reflecting a liberation hypothesis, the idea here is that in the most serious cases, there is little room for prosecutorial or judicial discretion to affect the sentence, because a severe sentence is clearly in order. In less serious cases, however, more discretion is possible, and thus greater opportunity exists for racial bias. Less serious cases thus "liberate" judges to use their discretion and also, perhaps, to base sentencing decisions on racial prejudice.

A third factor is the structural and social makeup of states and local communities. Supporting Blalock's (1967) racial-threat hypothesis noted earlier, some (but again, not all) studies find harsher sentencing in states and counties with higher proportions of African-Americans after controlling for crime rates and other relevant variables. African-American imprisonment rates are higher in states and counties with higher proportions of African-Americans, and death-penalty sentences are also more common in such locations (Bridges et al. 1987; Jacobs et al. 2005).

Looking at all the evidence, how much of a difference do race and ethnicity make? Evidence on racial/ethnic discrimination in the juvenile justice system seems more consistent than the evidence for the adult criminal justice system, with much research finding that African-American and Latino youths receive harsher treatment than white youths at the various stages of the juvenile justice process even after relevant legal factors are taken into account (Hayes-Smith and Hayes-Smith 2009; Rodriguez 2013; Shook and Goodkind 2009).

The evidence on the adult criminal justice system is less clear (Walker et al. 2012). As already noted, some studies find racial/ethnic discrimination in sentencing, and some do not. Some find that African-Americans and Latinos are both treated more harshly than whites, and some find that only one of these two groups receives harsher treatment (Freiburger and Hilinski 2013; Spohn and Sample 2013). To the extent that racial/ethnic discrimination does occur in sentencing, it occurs primarily for young males, and perhaps especially for young African-American males, and not among females (Brennan and Spohn 2009; Steffensmeier and Demuth 2006; Warren et al. 2012). Complicating the picture further, racial/ethnic discrimination is more often found for the decision to incarcerate (the in/out decision) than for sentence lengths among those incarcerated. It is also more often found, as we have seen, for less serious offenses than for more serious offenses.

▲ The evidence on racial and ethnic discrimination in criminal sentencing is very complex. A fair conclusion is that race and ethnicity sometimes play a small but significant role in sentencing and other court outcomes.

Discrimination also sometimes appears in the way judges determine sentences: Some studies find that judges place more emphasis on prior record and/or on offense seriousness when defendants are African-American or Latino than when they are white (Walker et al. 2012).

So what should we conclude about race and ethnicity and sentencing from all the research? For better or worse, no clear picture quickly emerges. As Walker and colleagues (2012:333) concede, "a definitive answer to the question, 'Are racial minorities sentenced more harshly than whites?' remains elusive. Although a number of studies have uncovered evidence of racial discrimination in sentencing, others have found that there are no significant racial differences?. . . . [D]iscrimination against racial minorities is not universal but is confined to certain types of cases, certain types of settings, and certain types of defendants."

To return to the issue of disproportionate imprisonment of African-Americans and Latinos, many criminologists think this situation largely reflects the disproportionate involvement of these two groups in serious street crime (Harris et al. 2009; Tonry and Melewski 2008). As Alfred Blumstein (2009:183) argues, any racial discrimination "cannot account for more than a fraction of" the racial disproportionality in the criminal justice system. To address this disproportionality, he says, "will require larger changes in the society outside the criminal justice system (p. 183)." Other criminologists think that racial bias and other race-related factors do play a large role in producing the disproportionate incarceration, especially in certain states. As sentencing expert Marc Mauer (2009:3) says, "Thus, while greater involvement in some crimes is related to higher rates of incarceration for African-Americans, the weight of the evidence to date suggests that a significant proportion of the disparities we currently observe is not a function of disproportionate criminal behavior."

The Drug War Revisited

Although the research on racial/ethnic discrimination in adult sentencing is rather inconsistent, it is very consistent for two specific types of sentencing. The first is the death penalty, for which the evidence consistently indicates pervasive racial discrimination. We discuss this evidence later in this chapter. The other type of sentencing derives from the war on drugs, which, as we saw in Chapter 16, has targeted African-Americans and Latinos, and especially young African-American and Latino males, far out of proportion to their actual illegal drug use. That chapter noted the disproportionate arrests of African-Americans and Latinos for illegal drug use and sale. Not surprisingly, they are also disproportionately imprisoned.

The drug war's focus on crack cocaine and its much higher penalties for crack than for similar amounts of powder cocaine account for much of these proportions. As Chapter 16 noted, the legal penalties for crack are much harsher than for powder cocaine, even though the two drugs are identical pharmacologically. Given racial differences in the use of crack and powder, it was inevitable that African-Americans would be imprisoned in greater numbers and for longer periods than whites when the nation began cracking down on crack in the 1980s.

This is exactly what happened. In states across the nation, the African-American prison admission rate (number of African-Americans imprisoned per 100,000 African-Americans in the population) increased by a much greater amount than the white prison admission rate during the 1980s and 1990s. Today African-Americans comprise almost 45 percent of all state prisoners sentenced for drug offenses (Carson and Sabol 2012). Partly reflecting this disparity, some one-third of young African-American males (ages 20 to 29) nationally are under correctional supervision, meaning that they are either in prison, in jail, or on probation or parole. In some cities more than half of young African-American males are under correctional supervision (Mauer 2009). Of all men born between 1965 and 1969, 20 percent of African-Americans had gone to prison by 1999, compared to only 3 percent of whites. The figure for African-American males rises to 30 percent of those without a college education and, astoundingly, almost 60 percent of those who had dropped out of high school (Western 2006). The war against drugs, whether intended or not, is clearly racially discriminatory.

Review and Discuss

To what extent do race and ethnicity affect conviction and sentencing?

Gender and Sentencing

Gender disparity is readily evident in imprisonment, with men comprising 93 percent of all prison inmates in the United States (Carson and Sabol 2012). Earlier chapters noted that men are much more likely than women to commit serious offenses, and this fundamental gender difference in criminality undoubtedly accounts for most of the gender differences in imprisonment. However, gender may still affect sentencing. Perhaps, women would be more likely to be imprisoned were it not for the chivalry of prosecutors and judges. Perhaps, there are crimes for which women are more likely than men to be imprisoned. What does the evidence say?

The data on gender and sentencing parallel those for gender and arrest (see Chapter 16). In the juvenile justice system, girls are treated more harshly than boys for status offenses, but a bit less harshly for more serious offenses. Nonwhite girls are less likely than their white counterparts to benefit from chivalrous treatment (Chesney-Lind and Pasko 2004).

In the adult criminal justice system, the best-designed studies generally find that women are 10 to 25 percent less likely than men with similar offenses and prior records to be incarcerated (Brennan and Spohn 2009; Griffin and Wooldredge 2006), but generally do not find that gender affects the sentence length for people who are incarcerated. This difference stems from prosecutors' and judges' beliefs that women are less of a threat than men to society, that their families and children would suffer if they were incarcerated, that they are less blameworthy than men for the crimes they committed, and that they have more community ties. Some scholars view these reasons as evidence of "warranted disparity in judicial decision making" involving women and men (Daly 1994:268).

▼ Women appear 10 to 25 percent less likely than men with similar offenses and prior records to be incarcerated.

© Robin Nelson / PhotoEdit

► Impact of Punishment on Crime

During the past few decades, a "get tough" attitude has guided the U.S. approach to crime (Tonry 2012). The federal government and states and cities across the country have established longer prison terms and mandatory minimum prison terms for many crimes. The war on drugs that began in the mid-1980s involved drastic crime-control efforts in our large cities and was targeted largely at African-Americans. Beginning in 1994, two dozen states and the federal government enacted "three strikes and you're out" legislation requiring that defendants convicted of a third felony receive very long sentences, including life imprisonment. The death penalty has also been part of the "get tough" approach, with the number of death row inmates rising from 134 in 1973 to 3,158 at the end of 2010, despite a slight drop in the preceding years. The U.S. "get tough" approach stands out in the Western world; as Michael Tonry (2004:viii) observed, "[P]ractices that many Americans endorse—capital punishment, three-strikes laws, prison sentences measured in decades or lifetimes—are as unthinkable in other Western countries as are lynchings and public torture in America." (The International Focus box discusses a different approach to crime control undertaken by Denmark and the Netherlands.)

The result of these "get tough" efforts has been an enormous increase in the United States in the number of people incarcerated in our jails and prisons. These new prison admissions have swelled already overcrowded prisons far beyond capacity and forced states to spend billions of dollars on new prisons. As Figure 17–3 ■ illustrates, the number of federal and state prisoners quintupled from 1980 through 2011, rising from just over 300,000 in 1980 to about 1.6 million in 2011 despite a slight decline beginning two years earlier. The number of people in jail more than quadrupled during this period, from about 180,000 to about 740,000 in 2012. The number on probation or parole also quadrupled. Combining all these statuses, the number of adults under correctional supervision (in prison or jail or on probation or parole) rose from 1.84 million in 1980 to 7.3 million in 2008 before falling to just under 7.0 million in 2011. In fact, the United States has the highest incarceration rate of any Western nation, with 716 of every 100,000 Americans behind bars in 2011 (Glaze and Parks 2012). Despite this fact, the United States also has, as we know, higher crime rates than those of many other Western nations.

The "get tough" approach reflects the widespread belief among the public and politicians alike that harsher and more certain punishment deters crime (the deterrence argument) and protects society by keeping dangerous criminals behind bars (the incapacitation argument) As we have seen earlier in this book, however, what people believe about crime and criminal justice sometimes turns out to be a myth. What, then, does the evidence say about the effect of harsher punishment on crime rates? The conclusion here is clear: *Harsher punishment does not reduce crime to any considerable degree, and it does not do so cost-efficiently.* This conclusion is probably shared by most criminologists and is supported by many kinds of evidence (Doob and Webster 2003; Walker 2011). Let's examine this evidence, looking first at deterrence and then at incapacitation.

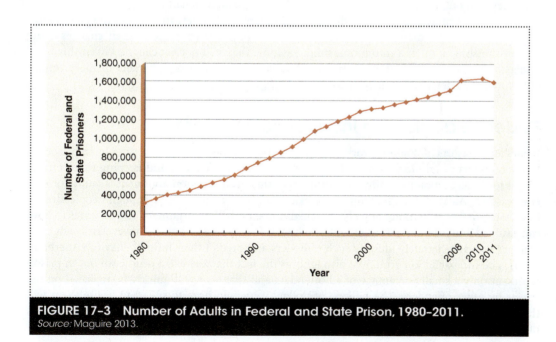

FIGURE 17–3   Number of Adults in Federal and State Prison, 1980–2011.
Source: Maguire 2013.

Evidence against a Deterrent Effect

First, decreases in crime rates have not always accompanied the huge increases in incarceration over the past two decades. For example, even though incarceration rose throughout the 1980s, the violent-crime rate also rose after the mid-1980s. Although the crime rate fell throughout the 1990s as incarceration continued to rise, factors other than incarceration seem to explain the drop in the crime rate then (see Chapter 3).

Second, at the state level only a weak and inconsistent relationship exists between severity of punishment (e.g., length of prison terms) and crime rates. Many states with longer prison terms have higher crime rates than states with shorter terms. As with similar research on arrest rates (see Chapter 16), even when a long sentence–low crime rate relationship expected from a deterrence viewpoint is found, this does not necessarily mean that harsh sentences deter crime. Using a *system capacity* argument, it is just as likely that states with lower crime rates and presumably less crowded prisons can afford to keep their prisoners behind bars for longer periods (Pontell 1984).

Third, and perhaps most tellingly, decreases in crime rates do not generally occur after the establishment of harsher penalties for various crimes. For example, laws mandating minimum or harsher sentences for gun crimes do not generally lower the rates of these crimes (Walker 2011). In a comprehensive investigation of this topic, Thomas B. Marvell and Carlisle E. Moody (1995) studied the effects of firearm sentence enhancement (FSE) laws in all forty-four states that established them since the 1960s. In a few states, FSE laws apparently decreased crime rates, but in some other states they had the opposite effect. The authors concluded that "on balance the FSE laws do little nationwide to reduce crime or gun use" (p. 274). The popular "three-strikes" laws also have not lowered crime rates and are even thought by some scholars to have raised homicide rates because offenders committing their third strike have apparently not wanted to leave any witnesses alive whose testimony could put the offenders in prison for life (Kovandzic et al. 2004).

Fourth, the dramatic increase in prisoners during the past two decades has forced the early release of convicted offenders already there. If harsher punishment makes a difference, these offenders should have higher rates of repeat offending (recidivism) than offenders convicted of similar crimes who are not released early. However, studies of this issue find that released offenders do not generally have higher recidivism rates than their counterparts who stay in prison, and they sometimes even have lower recidivism rates. As labeling theory predicts, longer stays in prison may embitter offenders and increase their exposure to the prison's criminal subculture. These and other problems make some offenders more crime prone when they leave prison than when they went in (Nagin et al. 2009).

In many respects, it is not so surprising that harsher punishment does not deter crime. When people commit violent offenses, they usually do so fairly spontaneously (see Chapter 5). At the time they lash out, they are not carefully weighing the possible penalties for their actions. Property offenses are more planned, allowing time for potential offenders to consider the prison term they may receive. Yet many property offenders either pay little attention to their chances of arrest or punishment or, at a minimum, simply assume they will not get caught. Given this basic understanding of violent and property crimes, it would be surprising if harsher or more certain punishment did deter criminal behavior.

Evidence against an Incapacitation Effect

If harsher punishment does not work, perhaps we could at least keep society safer by imprisoning larger numbers of criminals, especially chronic, hard-core offenders and keeping them off the streets for longer amounts of time. Unfortunately, this incapacitation argument is faulty for several reasons (Walker 2011). It assumes, for example, that we do not have enough people already in prison, but our prisons are already stretched to the limit. This argument also assumes that we can easily identify the dangerous offenders who need to be incapacitated. However, it is not clear whether we can accurately identify such offenders and predict their future behavior (Auerhahn 2006). The incapacitation argument also ignores the fact that any extra people we put in prison represent only a small percentage of all offenders and that they will quickly be replaced on the streets by other offenders. The billions of dollars we would have to spend to house them will thus be largely wasted. Finally, the incapacitation argument overlooks the fact that the dangerous offenders it addresses must be caught in the first place, which may not happen given the low arrest rates for crimes of all types.

International Focus   PUNISHING CRIMINALS IN DENMARK AND THE NETHERLANDS

The U.S. response to crime has focused on harsher imprisonment of criminals. Although this policy is politically popular, it arguably has done very little, if anything, to reduce crime. In Europe, various nations have confronted rising crime with very different measures and have rates of imprisonment (number of inmates per 100,000 population) up to ten times lower than the U.S. rate. Let's take a look at the European experience and focus on Denmark and the Netherlands.

Europe in general is far more pessimistic than the United States about the effectiveness of imprisonment. Almost all European criminal justice officials surveyed by the Helsinki Institute think prison often makes offenders worse and that alternative sanctions should be used whenever possible. They also acknowledge that prisons are very expensive and that prison overcrowding increases the chances that prisoners will come out of prison worse than when they went in.

These views lead Europe to favor probation and community service as alternatives to prison. Although these are not a cure-all for crime, say two criminologists, they "are at least as successful as sentences of imprisonment on several important counts, and . . . lack many of the drawbacks of imprisonment." The experience of Denmark and the Netherlands illustrates the European approach.

Denmark began to face a growing crime problem in the 1960s, which continued into the next decade. According to H. H. Brydensholt of Denmark's Prison and Probation Administration, the increase in crime stemmed from several reasons, including growing industrialization, rising youth drug use, and increasing unemployment. In response, Denmark devised a multifaceted response in 1973 that in many ways was the opposite of U.S. crime policy. It replaced longer indeterminate sentences (e.g., 3 to 7 years) with shorter fixed ones, reduced the length of prison terms and the number of offenses (especially nonviolent property offenses) leading to imprisonment, and reallocated funds from prisons to community-based corrections. These measures reduced the number of Danish prisoners during the next several years.

Denmark had several reasons for wanting to reduce imprisonment. First, it considered imprisonment a harsh measure because it stigmatized inmates and hurt their families. Second, it feared that imprisonment would lessen inmates' self-respect and increase their aggressiveness and other problems. Third, it considered imprisonment too harsh a penalty for many nonviolent property offenses. Finally, Denmark realized that it would be prohibitively expensive to put more people in prison.

The Netherlands' view of and experience with imprisonment is similar to Denmark's. Like Denmark, it considers imprisonment a costly, ineffective alternative to be avoided whenever possible, and it favors relatively short prison terms for offenders who need to be imprisoned. Although the number of Dutch prisoners has risen since the 1960s because of growing crime rates, the Dutch policy of short prison terms has kept this number from rising as high as it would have otherwise.

The United States is admittedly very different from Denmark, the Netherlands, and other European nations. Even so, their experience reminds us that it is possible to address crime without resorting to the "get tough" approach the United States has been following. This approach has cost the United States tens of billions of dollars that could be spent on crime prevention and alternatives to incarceration that would be at least as effective and less expensive.

Sources: Bijleveld and Smit 2005; Brydensholt 1992; Downes 2007; Ebbe 2013; Joutsen and Bishop 1994.

Putting all these factors together, incarcerating a much larger number of offenders (*gross incapacitation*) might reduce the crime rate, but only by a very small amount. This is what happened during the 1990s, when the number of prison and jail inmates increased by 67 percent. Although this increase cost tens of billions of dollars, its incapacitation effect accounted for no more than one-fourth of the crime drop during the 1990s (Spelman 2006). Empirical research confirms that the actual crime reduction stemming from gross incapacitation is very small and not cost-efficient. For example, Bruce Western (2006) found that a 10 percent rise in the incarceration rate produces a decrease of 1 percent in the crime rate. This means that the United States would have to imprison an additional 150,000 inmates (10 percent of the current 1.5 million in prison) to reduce the crime rate by only 1 percent. Because each inmate costs about $31,286 annually to house (Henrichson and Delaney 2012), these new inmates would cost about $4.7 billion annually. And because prisons are filled beyond capacity, many new prisons would have to be built to house them, at a cost of many more billions of dollars.

Figures like these lead many criminologists to sharply question the wisdom of the "get tough" policy that relies on incapacitation. As Samuel Walker (2011:160) observes, "The evidence indicates no clear link between incarceration and crime rates. Moreover, gross incapacitation locks up many low-rate offenders at a great dollar cost to society." Elliott Currie (1985:88) is equally pessimistic: "No one seriously doubts that a modicum of crime can be prevented by incapacitating offenders. . . . [But] the potential reduction in serious crime is disturbingly small, especially when balanced against the social and economic costs of pursuing this strategy strenuously enough to make much difference to public safety."

Ironically, the massive increase in incarceration of the past few decades may eventually make the crime problem worse for at least two reasons (Clear 2008). First, the hundreds of thousands of extra offenders now behind bars or with prison and jail records include many minor offenders. Their experiences in the criminal justice system may embitter them and reduce their employment chances, and thus make them more likely to commit additional and more serious crime (Listwan et al. 2013). Second, the increase in incarceration is also damaging our urban communities, as the imprisonment of so many of their young men weakens the communities' families and other social institutions (DeFina and Hannon 2013). When these men, some 700,000 every year, return to their communities after being released from prison, their criminal orientation may be a bad influence on some community residents. By intensifying the communities' social disorganization in these ways, massive incarceration may ironically raise their crime rates and worsen the very problem it has been trying to stop (Hipp and Yates 2009; Western and Wildeman 2009).

Ultimately, then, "get tough" measures involving harsher punishment do little, if anything, to reduce our crime rate, no matter how much common sense and popular opinion tell us otherwise, and any crime reduction they achieve is very small, costs billions of dollars, and causes many kinds of "collateral consequences" for the nation's cities (Foster and Hagan 2009). To reduce crime, another approach is required. Chapter 18 sketches what such an approach might look like.

Review and Discuss

To what extent does legal punishment prevent potential criminal behavior?

▶ The Death-Penalty Debate

The themes of this chapter—discrimination in sentencing and the deterrent effect of punishment—come together in the debate over the death penalty, which produces passions pro and con as perhaps no other issue in criminal justice. The number of death row inmates has risen dramatically since the early 1970s despite a recent decrease (see Figure 17–4 ■). Let's look at the death-penalty debate in detail.

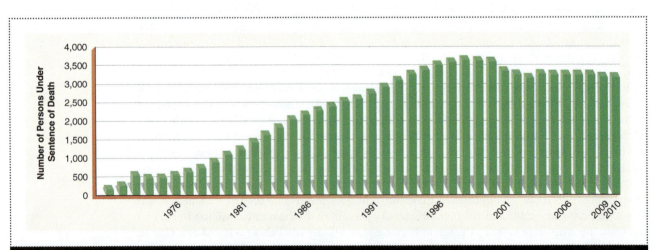

FIGURE 17–4 Persons Under Sentence of Death, 1973–2010.
Source: Maguire 2013.

Death-penalty proponents make at least three arguments: (1) people convicted of heinous murders deserve to be executed, (2) the death penalty saves the money that would be spent on years of confinement were the offender to serve a life sentence, and (3) the death penalty sends a message to potential murderers and thus has a general deterrent effect on homicide.

Death-penalty opponents, probably including most criminologists, attack all these arguments. The first argument, that vicious murderers deserve to be executed, raises philosophical and religious issues that are beyond the scope of this book. Whether it is moral for the state to take a life, even that of a vicious murderer, is a philosophical or religious question, not a sociological one. But criminologists do point out that the United States is the only remaining Western nation to use the death penalty, the rest having decided long ago that civilized nations should not commit what opponents call *legal murders* against those who have murdered. As a slogan of death-penalty opponents asks: Why do we kill people to show that killing people is wrong?

▲ The death penalty remains one of the most controversial issues in criminal justice today.

Cost of the Death Penalty

The second argument, that the death penalty saves money, is an appropriate one for social scientists to address. Here the evidence is clear: The death penalty actually costs more than life imprisonment in constant dollars. Keeping someone in prison for life, say forty years, would cost about $31,286 per year in constant dollars, as noted earlier, or $1.25 million overall. Because someone's life is at stake, death-penalty cases are especially complicated from pretrial motions through sentencing and appeals, with the state usually having to pay for all costs at least through appeals to state courts. Although the cost of death-penalty cases varies by state, each capital case on the average costs $1 million to $2 million *beyond* the cost of a noncapital case ending with a life sentence (Dieter 2013). With 3,158 people on death row at the end of 2010, the death-penalty cost to the states that sentenced them to death is almost $3.2 billion and perhaps as high as $6.4 billion.

General Deterrence and the Death Penalty

The third argument, that the death penalty has a general deterrent effect, is one that social scientists have tested for several decades. With few exceptions (Land et al. 2009), studies find that the death penalty does not have this effect (Bohm 2012; Kovandzic et al. 2009). This conclusion comes from several kinds of studies. Some of the earliest research compared the homicide rates of states with and without the death penalty. Contrary to the general-deterrence argument, states with the death penalty do not have lower homicide rates than those without it. States that eliminated the death penalty a few decades ago did not see their homicide rates rise compared with states that retained the death penalty. Conversely, states that established the death penalty did not see their homicide rates decrease compared with states that did not have the death penalty.

Scholars have also examined the consequences of well-publicized executions. If the death penalty does deter homicide, homicide should go down in the month or so after stories about these executions appear in the press. Although a few studies find this effect (Stack 1987), most find no effect (Peterson and Bailey 1991). Some studies even show that homicide actually increases after executions occur. This is called the brutalization effect. The argument here is that executions desensitize the public to the immorality of killing and thus increase the likelihood that some people will decide to kill. Executions may also increase homicide as a sort of imitation (Bowers and Pierce 1980).

In a demonstration of this effect, John K. Cochran and colleagues (1994) studied the aftermath of a September 1990 execution in Oklahoma, the first execution in the state in twenty-five years.

In the three years following the execution, the general Oklahoma homicide rate did not change. There was, however, "an abrupt and lasting increase in the level of stranger homicides" (p. 129), which on the average rose by one per month. A replication of their study found that newspaper coverage of executions outside Oklahoma also increased other kinds of homicides in Oklahoma (Bailey 1998). Such evidence indicates that capital punishment may increase the number of homicides rather than reduce them. A study of California executions found that both effects may occur: The California executions apparently decreased felony murders (i.e., murders committed in the course of committing another felony), but increased stranger murders stemming from an argument (Cochran and Chamlin 2000).

It would be surprising if the death penalty did deter homicide. Most people who commit violence do not weigh the punishment they might receive before they strike. Most homicides are fairly spontaneous events, and offenders certainly do not pause to mull over their chances of being executed before they kill their victims. Felony murders are somewhat less spontaneous because offenders (usually armed robbers) have "at least a tacit understanding that lethal force may be necessary during the commission of the crime" (Cochran and Chamlin 2000:690). If so, this may account for the finding in the California study just cited. This finding notwithstanding, the vast majority of studies do not find a general-deterrent effect of executions on homicide.

Arbitrariness and Racial Discrimination in the Application of the Death Penalty

In addition to challenging the arguments of death-penalty proponents, opponents of the death penalty cite other problems with capital punishment. Many of these have to do with the way the death penalty is applied. In 1972, the U.S. Supreme Court ruled 5 to 4 in *Furman* v. *Georgia* (408 U.S. 238) that capital punishment as it was then practiced violated the Eighth Amendment's prohibition of cruel and unusual punishment. The Court found that jurors in capital cases had few standards to guide their decision to impose the death penalty, leading them to impose death sentences in some murder cases but not in others that were equally appalling. Far from logical and rational, the capital punishment process was, the Court declared, both capricious and arbitrary and held the potential for racial discrimination.

In the wake of *Furman*, states revised their death-penalty laws and procedures to reduce arbitrariness in the application of the penalty. Some mandated death sentences for any convictions of first-degree murder, and others devised a system of *bifurcated* juries that would first decide on the guilt of the defendant and then decide whether to impose the death penalty. In this second phase, juries would have to consider both *aggravating* (e.g., the murder was committed while the defendant was committing another felony) and *mitigating* (e.g., the defendant had no prior history of criminality) factors as they determined whether a death sentence was appropriate.

In a series of decisions in 1976, the Supreme Court struck down the mandatory death-penalty statutes, but upheld in *Gregg* v. *Georgia* (428 U.S. 153) the statutes establishing bifurcated juries and aggravating and mitigating factors. Social scientists since that time have studied whether the new, post-*Furman* system of capital punishment has continued to exhibit the same arbitrariness, capriciousness, and racial discrimination that motivated the *Furman* decision (Smith 2000).

Continuing Arbitrariness

On the issue of arbitrariness the evidence is clear: Throughout the country, defendants accused of similar murders are treated differently for no logical reasons (Bohm 2012). Some are charged with capital murders, whereas others are not. Some receive the death penalty after conviction, whereas others do not. Even within the same state, murder defendants are more likely to receive the death penalty in some jurisdictions than in others. Although such disparities inevitably exist in the criminal justice system for all kinds of crimes, they have even more ominous implications when a defendant's life is at stake. Researchers conclude that the capital punishment process is akin to a lottery system and that "being sentenced to death is the result of a process that may be no more rational than being struck by lightning" (Paternoster 1991:183).

Here again the 1994–1995 O. J. Simpson case is illustrative. Simpson was accused of the extremely vicious murders of two people. Many aspects of the alleged murders fit circumstances that often lead California prosecutors to ask for the death penalty when they charge defendants. Simpson's prosecutors chose not to ask for the death penalty in his case. Legal observers attributed this to Simpson's celebrity and assumed that the prosecutors thought a jury would never convict such a famous, well-liked defendant if they knew he could be executed. Thus Simpson did not face the death penalty, even though many poor, unknown defendants accused of far less vicious murders have faced it and continue to face it.

Racial Discrimination

Another line of research has focused on racial discrimination. Several studies have found one type of racial discrimination in the application of the death penalty: The lives of white victims are seemingly valued more than the lives of African-American victims (Paternoster and Brame 2008; Sorensen and Wallace 1999). Prosecutors in homicide cases are more likely to impose a first-degree murder charge (the only charge for which the death penalty is allowed) and also to seek the death penalty after conviction when the victim is white than when the victim is African-American. Further, among defendants indicted for first-degree murder, death sentences from juries are also more likely when the victim is white than when the victim is African-American. Some evidence indicates that death sentences are particularly likely when the victim is both white and female (Williams et al. 2007). Although not all studies find that the victim's race makes a difference (Berk et al. 2005), the bulk of the evidence does indicate that death sentences are more likely when the victim is white. A recent study also found that death sentences are more likely when victims are relatively wealthy and otherwise "respectable" members of society (Phillips 2009).

The evidence for harsher treatment of African-American defendants once the race of the victim is held constant is less consistent. Some studies find African-American defendants more likely to be indicted for first-degree murder and also to receive the death penalty eventually, but some studies do not find this difference. When this difference is found, African-American offenders who murder white victims are much more likely than other combinations to be charged with first-degree murder, to have the death penalty sought by prosecutors, and to receive death sentences after conviction. Several scholars conclude that racial discrimination on the basis of the defendant's race has declined or even disappeared after *Furman,* but that discrimination on the basis of the victim's race has continued (Bohm 2012).

Quality of Legal Representation of Capital Defendants

Another criticism of the death penalty addresses the quality of legal representation of capital defendants (Bohm 2012; Perez-Pena 2000). Recall that almost all criminal defendants are poor and receive inadequate legal representation. This is no less true for defendants facing the death penalty. Capital cases are extraordinarily complex and can cost hundreds of thousands of dollars to defend. Most public defenders and assigned counsel simply are not equipped to handle them and have little time to do so. They thus do not raise evidentiary and other issues at trial that may be grounds for later appeals, and they certainly do not have the funds and other resources to mount an effective defense in the first place.

Similar problems affect the appeals process after defendants are sentenced to death. Because almost all of them cannot afford to hire private counsel to launch an appeal, they must rely on assigned counsel. Once again, public attorneys are usually less able to handle death-penalty appeals than are more experienced, and much more expensive, private attorneys. Once appeals are denied by state courts, the defendant's only recourse lies in the federal courts. At this level, public funding for defense counsel is not available. The defendant thus must usually rely on volunteer attorneys, but very few attorneys are willing to serve in this capacity. Those who do volunteer their time usually do not have the resources to put forward the best appeal possible.

Sometimes defense attorneys in death-penalty cases are downright incompetent or corrupt. Some fail to present witnesses or evidence or do so ineptly, and some have even fallen asleep during the trials of their clients. Others have questionable legal credentials: In one death-penalty case,

▼

the attorney was a former leader of the Ku Klux Klan, and in another case the attorney was facing disbarment at the same time the trial of his client was occurring. According to various studies, 25 percent of Kentucky death row inmates were represented by attorneys who were later disbarred or who resigned to avoid this fate, 13 percent of Louisiana defendants who had been executed were represented by attorneys who had been disciplined for various kinds of misconduct, and 33 defendants sentenced to death in Illinois had lawyers who were later disbarred or suspended (Berlow 1999; Johnson 2000b; Perez-Pena 2000).

In short, defendants facing the death penalty receive inadequate representation at all levels of the legal process even though their lives are at stake. This is especially true in the South, where most death-penalty cases occur; few capable attorneys there are willing to take on capital cases. When they do so, their regular legal practice might suffer because of hostility from the public and other legal professionals.

Wrongful Executions

A final criticism of the death penalty centers on the possibility of wrongful executions. Mistakes do occur in criminal justice, either out of honest errors or downright prejudice. It is estimated that between 1 percent and 6 percent of all felony convictions are mistaken (Huff 2002; Webster 2012; Zalman et al. 2008). If a person is mistakenly found guilty, he or she can be released from prison once the mistake is discovered. But if that person is executed, he or she obviously cannot be brought back to life. Evidence of mistaken convictions abounds. At least 350 defendants during the twentieth century were convicted of potentially capital crimes even though they were probably or certainly innocent. Of these defendants, 139 received the death penalty and 23 were executed (Radelet et al. 1992). At least 381 homicide defendants had their convictions overturned between 1963 and the late 1990s because prosecutors presented false evidence or hid evidence they knew would favor the defendant (Berlow 1999). And, as the Crime in the News story that began this chapter reminds us, 143 death row inmates (as of November 2013) have been released from prison since the early 1970s after new evidence, sometimes gathered by college and graduate students, established their innocence or raised serious doubts about their guilt.

Although these inmates won their freedom and their lives, it is estimated that at least a dozen people who have been executed during the past four decades were probably innocent of the capital crime for which they were sentenced to death (Bohm 2012). One of these was Cameron Todd Willingham, who was executed in Texas in 2004 for setting a fire to his home that killed his three daughters. According to later investigations, his court-appointed attorneys often seemed incompetent, and a major witness was a jail inmate and drug addict who claimed that Willingham had confessed to him. Most damning, forensic evidence strongly indicated that his house fire was an accident, not arson (Grann 2009). Another wrongful execution was probably that of Gary Graham, executed in 2000 in Texas for murdering a drug dealer. No physical evidence linked Graham to the murder. A witness's testimony was the only evidence against him, and two witnesses who could have cleared Graham were never called by his attorney to testify (Miller 2000). Yet another was Wilburn Henderson, convicted of the 1980 murder of a furniture store dealer in a robbery. The evidence against Henderson was so thin that an appellate court overturned his conviction and ordered a new trial; the court's decision listed several other suspects, including the victim's husband, who had abused the victim and wondered aloud the day before she died where she would want to be buried. Henderson was again found guilty at his second trial and executed in 1998 (Mills et al. 2000).

Why are innocent people sometimes convicted of murder and sentenced to death? According to legal writer Alan Berlow (1999:68), the reasons "range from simple police and prosecutorial error to the most outrageous misconduct, such as the framing of innocent people, and everything in between: perjured testimony, erroneous eyewitness testimony, false confessions (including the confessions of innocent defendants), racial bias, incompetent defense counsel, and overzealous police officers and prosecutors." Damon Thibodeaux's, discussed at the beginning of this chapter, typifies some of these reasons. So does the case of Rolando Cruz, convicted in 1985 of the murder, rape, and kidnapping of a 10-year-old girl who was abducted from her home in a Chicago suburb by a man who kicked in her front door. Cruz was sentenced to die even though no physical evidence linking him to the rape and murder was introduced at his trial. DNA evidence later implicated another man who confessed to the crimes, and four police officers and three former prosecutors were eventually indicted for perjury and obstruction of justice in Cruz's case. He was released from prison after serving more than ten years on death row (Berlow 1999).

The possibility of wrongful convictions and executions and other problems in the application of the death penalty have led the American Bar Association and other organizations to call for a moratorium on executions. In early 2000, revelations that thirteen innocent men had been put on death row in Illinois led the state's governor, George Ryan, a Republican, to impose a moratorium on executions until it could be established that Illinois death-penalty cases were free from error or bias. His action led to calls for moratoriums in other states (Johnson 2000a). Ryan eventually commuted the sentences of all 167 death row inmates in Illinois because of his concern over the possibility of wrongful executions. When he did so, he declared, "Our capital system is haunted by the demon of error: error in determining guilt and error in determining who among the guilty deserves to die" (Wilgoren 2003:A1).

Review and Discuss

What are the arguments for and against the death penalty? Are you in favor of the death penalty? Why or why not?

▶ Conclusion

This chapter's focus on the prosecution and punishment of criminals completes our brief overview of the criminal justice system. Many issues were omitted for lack of space, but we did deal with the most important ones for a sociological understanding of crime and criminal justice: the inequality of legal outcomes and the crime-reduction effects of legal punishment.

We saw that structural context often shapes post-arrest legal decision making. In particular, we reviewed the extensive literature on class, racial and ethnic, and gender discrimination in sentencing. We saw that disparities do exist in many jurisdictions and at different stages of the legal process, even if legal factors exert the major influence on sentencing. There is thus evidence here to support both consensus and conflict views of law and criminal justice. Whether the system is fair or not overall is up to you to decide. What we have tried to provide is a sociological lens through which to view the evidence so that you can draw your own conclusions.

The chapter also reviewed the evidence on the crime-reduction effect of harsher sentences and reached a pessimistic conclusion: "Get tough" approaches offer little hope of reducing crime. This, of course, has been the dominant approach to the crime problem in the past few decades, as politicians continue to compete to show who is toughest on criminals. Amid all the calls for cracking down on criminals, it is easy to forget that the social policy may not always have its desired effects. The best evidence indicates that recent social policy on crime and drugs has failed in its most important professed goal, that of reducing the crime problem.

The United States holds the dubious honor of having a high crime rate even though it also has the highest imprisonment rate of all Western nations and longer prison terms than most of these nations. A quadrupling of imprisonment since 1980 has not lowered the crime rate, and a very punitive war on drugs has neither reduced the drug trade appreciably nor lowered drug use. Instead, they have swelled the number and occupation of our jails and prisons, cost us billions of dollars that could have been put to better use, and otherwise done much more harm than good. There must be a better way.

We have now come full circle. Near the beginning of the book, Chapter 2 tried to show that public opinion on crime and politicians' calls for cracking down on crime have little to do with actual crime-rate trends. Later chapters discussed explanations of crime and examined its nature and dynamics. More recently, we have considered the extent of discrimination in the criminal justice system and questioned whether a "get tough" approach is the most promising way to tackle the crime problem. This approach cannot and does not work for several reasons, not the least of which have to do with the sociological causes and nature of criminality that earlier chapters presented. Now that we have reached the end of the book, we will spend a few pages in the final chapter spelling out a sociological prescription for crime reduction.

Summary

1. The United States is popularly thought to have an adversary system of criminal justice. However, courtrooms feature much more cooperation than combat between prosecutors and defense attorneys. Sociological and journalistic accounts beginning in the 1960s painted a picture of criminal courts as assembly lines in which poor defendants did not receive justice.

2. Research beginning in the 1970s said that plea bargaining was an inevitable and not unwelcome dynamic for all sides to criminal court proceedings. For the prosecutor, it helps ensure convictions, whereas for the defendant it helps to some extent to minimize sentence severity, even though defendants accused of the most serious crimes still receive severe sentences.

3. Since the time of Durkheim, the study of punishment has been of particular interest to criminologists and law and society scholars. Much research has explored whether unemployment at the micro and macro levels increases the likelihood of incarceration, but evidence for this linkage is inconsistent. Historical research on the incarceration and lynchings of African-Americans in the post–Civil War South supports the presumed link between punishment and economic problems and unemployment. Although research on social class and criminal case outcomes does not find that social class makes a difference, there is too little income variation among criminal defendants to adequately test this hypothesis.

4. The evidence on racial and ethnic biases in sentencing is very complex, and scholars interpret this evidence in many different ways. To the extent that racial and ethnic discrimination in sentencing exists, it is most often seen in regard to the race of the defendant and for less serious crimes and for the in/out (incarceration) decision rather than for sentence lengths once the decision is made to incarcerate. Evidence for racial and ethnic discrimination in punishment is much stronger and clearer for drug offenses and capital cases.

5. The evidence on gender and sentencing indicates that women are somewhat less likely than men convicted of like crimes to be incarcerated. However, once the decision is made to incarcerate, gender does not appear to affect the length of prison terms.

6. The number of prison and jail inmates now is tens of thousands greater than two decades ago, but the huge increase in imprisonment does not seem to have had a large effect, if any, on the crime rate. The evidence indicates that imprisonment has neither a strong deterrent effect nor a strong incapacitation effect.

7. Research on the death penalty does not support the arguments of its proponents. In particular, the death penalty costs more than life imprisonment and does not deter homicide. It is also applied arbitrarily and in a discriminatory manner in regard to the race of the victim. In other problems, the legal representation of capital defendants is often of poor quality, and many wrongful convictions and even executions of such defendants in capital cases have occurred.

Key Terms

adversary system *351*
arbitrariness *366*
brutalization effect *365*
caseloads *352*
correctional supervision *360*
courtroom work group *353*

deterrence *361*
discretion *351*
incapacitation *361*
incarceration *354*
in/out decision *359*
liberation hypothesis *358*

plea bargaining *352*
repressive law *354*
restitutive law *354*
wrongful executions *368*

What Would You Do?

1. Suppose you are a juror in a homicide case for which the defendant could receive the death penalty if found guilty. As is true of the other jurors, you generally support the death penalty, but you also think it should be used only when there is clear and convincing evidence of the defendant's guilt and when the defendant committed a particularly vicious crime. In the case before you, the defendant is accused of fatally shooting a cashier during a robbery of a store after the cashier tried to grab the robber's gun. Although the robber ran from the store, an eyewitness who was in the store identified the defendant in a police lineup, but the murder weapon was never found. The prosecution's case rests almost entirely on the one eyewitness's testimony. Two other people shopping in the store at the time said they did not get a good look at the robber. Based on this description of the case, would you vote to convict the defendant and, if so, would you vote to execute him? Explain your answer.

2. You are a judge in a case in which a 22-year-old woman is on trial for possessing a small amount of heroin. She is employed part-time in a fast-food restaurant and has a 2-year-old daughter; the defendant's only previous arrest and conviction is for shoplifting when she was 18. The jury has found her guilty, and it is now your turn to impose the sentence. What sentence do you impose? Why?

© Huntstock, Inc / Alamy

18   Conclusion: How Can We Reduce Crime?

W̲e have reached the end of our journey into the world of sociological criminology. In this world, crime and victimization are rooted in the social and physical characteristics of communities and in the structured social inequalities of race/ethnicity, social class, and gender. While not excusing any criminal's action, our sociological imagination allows us to understand that any individual's criminality is just one example of a public issue affecting masses of people. Our sociological imagination also forces us to realize that to reduce crime we must address its structural and cultural roots. Even if we could somehow "cure" all the criminals, new ones will replace them unless the structural and cultural conditions underlying crime are changed.

The need to address these conditions becomes even more paramount when we consider the criminal justice system's inability to reduce the crime problem. As we saw in the last two chapters, increasing the certainty and severity of arrest and punishment offers only faint hope. The "get tough" approach to crime during the past few decades has had at most a small impact on the crime rate and has cost hundreds of billions of dollars. In addition to costing so much and achieving so little, the mass incarceration at the heart of the "get tough" approach has created many problems (as Chapter 17 noted) that are called *collateral consequences* (Petersilia and Reitz 2012; Sahl 2013; Tierney 2013; Turanovic et al. 2012). These consequences include (1) the release of some 700,000 ex-prisoners every year back into their home communities; (2) joblessness, drug addiction, and other problems among these ex-inmates; (3) the resulting prospect of many additional crimes committed by these former prisoners; (4) a generation of children raised with one parent in prison or jail; and (5) community-level problems including poverty, homelessness, and AIDS and other infectious diseases. All these problems suggest the need to look to a different type of strategy to reduce crime.

The field of public health offers one such strategy. If we tried to prevent a disease by only curing those having it and not attacking the underlying causes, that disease would certainly continue. Recognizing this, the public health model stresses the need to identify the social and other causes of disease so that efforts can be launched to target these causes (Schneider 2014). Unfortunately, the U.S. approach to crime has not followed this sensible strategy. Instead, it has focused on "curing" those "afflicted" with crime by arresting as many as possible and putting them behind bars, all to little avail, and creating many other problems in the process.

More than a decade ago, public health experts began to treat violent crime as a public health problem (Friedman 1994; Hemenway 2004; Kellerman 1996). Their aim was to uncover the social causes of violence so that these causes could be addressed by public policy. In the spirit of this approach, this chapter offers a sociological prescription for reducing crime.

▶ The Criminal Justice System Funnel

Before considering a sociological prescription for crime reduction, we will examine one more bit of evidence that underscores the cost-*ineffectiveness* of the "get tough" approach. This evidence concerns what is often called the criminal justice funnel. The funnel image comes from the fact that as we move from the number of crimes committed, the top of the funnel, to the number of offenders going to prison or jail, the bottom of the funnel, a sharp drop in numbers occurs at every stage of the criminal justice process. As the previous two chapters discussed, the reason for this is that decision makers at every stage of the process determine whether a crime, or someone suspected of the crime, filters down to the next level. Inevitably, these decisions "kick out" many crimes and suspects from the criminal justice system or at least from consideration for incarceration, so only a few remain by the time we get to prison and jail at the bottom of the funnel. Let's see how this happens.

As we saw in Chapter 3, many victimizations are not reported to the police. Of the crimes known to the police, only about one-fifth overall are cleared by arrest. What happens to the people arrested? Relatively few are convicted of felonies, and even fewer of these are sentenced to prison or jail. As we saw in Chapter 17, many cases are either dropped for lack of sufficient evidence or are plea bargained to a misdemeanor, for which incarceration is unlikely. Of those convicted of a felony, some receive probation and/or fines instead of imprisonment.

Now we will illustrate the criminal justice system funnel with some real data in Table 18–1 for 2006 (the latest year for which complete information was available at the time of writing). The data come from the National Crime Victimization Survey (NCVS), the Uniform Crime Reports (UCR), and government reports on the judicial processing of defendants. The table includes only

TABLE 18-1 The Criminal Justice System Funnel for UCR Part I Crime, 2006[a]

VARIABLE	TOTAL
NCVS victimizations	21,406,800
UCR offenses known to police	11,401,611
Number of arrests	2,151,820
Felony convictions in state and federal courts	435,629
Sentenced to prison or jail	320,908

Sources: Calculated from Durose et al. 2009; Maguire 2013.
[a]All figures include homicides and exclude arson.

the UCR Part I crimes of homicide, rape, aggravated assault, robbery, burglary, larceny, and auto theft. Thus, it excludes simple assaults, even though the NCVS reports them. Keep in mind that the NCVS itself excludes homicides, commercial burglaries, shoplifting, and other crimes included in the other figures in the table. The UCR's number of homicides has been added into the NCVS figure for total victimizations.

As you can see, we start with more than 21 million personal victimizations at the top of the funnel and end up with just 320,908 persons going to prison or jail at the bottom of the funnel. This number of incarcerated offenders represents only about 1.5 percent of the total number of victimizations estimated by the NCVS.

Perhaps the funnel effect for violent crimes is less severe. We consider this in Table 18–2, which presents the relevant data for the UCR violent crimes of homicide, aggravated assault, rape, and robbery. Once again, the NCVS figure in the table excludes simple assaults but includes homicides.

Here we start with more than 2.3 million personal violent victimizations at the top of the funnel and end up with 160,628 going to prison or jail. This number of incarcerated offenders represents about 6.8 percent of the total number of victimizations estimated by the NCVS. Although the drop throughout the violent crime funnel is a little less severe than the drop for the funnel combining violent and property offenses, it is still noticeable.

Besides making you want to live in a low-crime state or even move out of the country, what are the implications of the funnel effect for public policy on crime? One implication is that efforts concentrating on offenders and offenses at the bottom of the funnel will have only a limited impact, if that, on overall crime. Even if all people convicted of a violent felony each year were sentenced to prison for life, for example, they would still represent only a very small proportion of all people committing such felonies, leaving the crime rate essentially intact. This is true even if each person put into prison had committed more than one crime in a given year and therefore accounted for more than one of the crimes at the top of the funnel.

Suppose you decided you wanted to double the number of people going to prison for felonies. How much would that cost, and would the money be worth it? To answer these questions, let us go back to the data in Table 18–1. Suppose we wanted to double the number of people going to prison or jail. This would mean that, instead of about 1.5 percent of all victimizations leading to someone being incarcerated, we would now have about 3 percent. How much safer would you feel? Even if the people incarcerated had accounted for, say, five crimes each in a given year, you would be increasing the proportion of all crimes accounted for by imprisonment from 7.5 to 15 percent. This would still leave 85 percent of all crimes unaccounted for. Would you feel much safer? Even if we just tried to "fix" the violent crime funnel depicted

▼ Building even more prisons will cost the nation billions of dollars but will not reduce crime significantly.

© Bill Aron / PhotoEdit

TABLE 18-2 The Criminal Justice System Funnel for UCR Violent Crime, 2006[a]

VARIABLE	TOTAL
NCVS victimizations	2,317,840
UCR offenses known to police	1,418,043
Number of arrests	611,523
Felony convictions in state courts	208,260
Sentenced to prison or jail	160,628

Sources: Calculated from Durose et al. 2009; Maguire 2013.
[a]All figures include homicides and exclude arson.

in Table 18–2, doubling the number at the bottom would still leave the vast majority of violent crimes unaccounted for.

How much would it cost to double the small number of people at the bottom of the funnel depicted in Table 18–1 who are incarcerated? To keep things simple, say we would eventually have to double the number of prison cells because our prisons are already stretched beyond capacity. Because we now have about 1.5 million people in our prisons, we would have to build at least 1,500 more prisons, each containing 1,000 beds. With the cost of each such prison averaging about $100 million or more, the cost of prison construction alone would come to about $150 billion, with another $150 billion or so in interest on construction loans. Because it also costs about $31,000 per year to keep each person in prison, it would eventually cost an extra $47 billion annually, in constant dollars, to house the new prisoners.

Let's say further that to double the number of people going to prison each year, it would help to double the number of police. With about 660,000 local and state law enforcement officers in the United States, each costing an average of $100,000 in salary, benefits, and operating expenses, the cost of doubling the number of police would amount to an additional $66 billion. We would also have to build new courthouses, hire new prosecutors and other court personnel, and elect or appoint more judges, all at an expense that would easily run into the billions of dollars. We are now up to well over $260 billion in immediate and annual costs (excluding prison construction loan interest), just to double the proportion of victimizations leading to imprisonment from 1.5 to 3 percent. If you were a businessperson, how cost-effective would you consider this expenditure? If you ran your business this way, how long would you stay in business?

As this brief discussion suggests, it might make more sense to concentrate on the top of the funnel instead of on the bottom. To the extent this is true, we must focus more on crime prevention than on crime control and do so by addressing crime's structural and cultural roots. This is the view of many criminologists. Stressing perhaps the most important structural factor, Elliott Currie (1998:131) observed, "There is little question that growing up in extreme poverty exerts powerful pressures toward crime." It does so, he said, by impairing children's cognitive development, increasing their abuse and neglect, and hampering the quality of parenting in other respects. To reduce crime, he said, requires only that poverty be reduced, not eliminated. The next section outlines a reasonable crime-reduction strategy informed by sound social research on poverty and the other structural and cultural roots of criminal behavior.

Review and Discuss

About what percentage of all serious crime victimizations end up with someone going to prison or jail? How does this criminal justice funnel help us understand what might work or not work to reduce the crime rate?

▶ A Sociological Prescription for Crime Reduction

Earlier we outlined a public health approach to violence and other crime. A public health strategy emphasizes the need for prevention. Here the public health community stresses three kinds of prevention: primary, secondary, and tertiary (Moore 1995; Schneider 2014).

Primary prevention tries to prevent disease or injury from occurring at all by focusing on aspects of the social or physical environment that contribute to the disease or injury. Thus, public health advocates underscore poverty as a cause of poor health and toxic dump sites and other environmental hazards as a cause of cancer. A primary prevention approach to crime, then, addresses features of our society, culture, and local communities that contribute to our high crime rates. We discussed many of these features in Chapter 6.

Secondary prevention aims to identify practices and situations that put certain individuals at risk for illness or injury. Thus, public health advocates emphasize that poor children are especially at risk for serious childhood diseases because they often do not get needed vaccinations. To address this problem, public health workers champion high-profile government vaccination and public education efforts. A secondary prevention approach to crime, then, addresses the developmental processes, especially those in early childhood, that make crime even more likely among individuals living in criminogenic social environments. We discussed many of these processes in Chapter 7.

Finally, tertiary prevention occurs after an illness has begun or an injury has occurred and "seeks to minimize the long-term consequences" of the health problem (Moore 1995:247). When you visit a physician for an illness or injury, the physician is engaging in tertiary prevention. A tertiary prevention approach to crime, then, focuses on preventing recidivism, or repeat offending, by offenders and on protecting society from these offenders. This, of course, is how the United States has traditionally responded to crime. Although the last two chapters discussed the limitations of this approach, there are some criminal justice-related policies that should be considered.

The following proposals represent a reasonable approach to crime reduction. They rest on the vast body of criminological theory and research presented in previous chapters and are advocated by highly regarded criminologists (Barlow and Decker 2010; Currie 2010; Frost et al. 2010; Welsh 2012; Welsh and Farrington 2012). The proposals are grouped according to three categories: (1) social, cultural, and community; (2) developmental (social processes); and (3) criminal justice. These categories roughly correspond to primary, secondary, and tertiary prevention, respectively.

Physicians' prescriptions sometimes do not cure illnesses immediately or at all, and not every aspect of this sociological prescription for crime reduction may have its intended effects. Some of the proposals will undoubtedly sound like pipe dreams and will be difficult or almost impossible to achieve, either because we do not have the national will to accomplish them or because the issues they address are intractable. But even some success in achieving these proposals' objectives offers real hope to reduce crime. Most of the proposals speak generally to street crime; some speak to violence against women; a few speak to white-collar crime.

Social, Cultural, and Community Crime Prevention (Primary Prevention)

A primary prevention approach to U.S. crime recognizes the geographical and sociodemographic patterning of street crime outlined in earlier chapters. The most important elements of this patterning are these: (1) serious violent crime in the United States is among the highest of all Western nations and (2) serious street crime, both violent and property, in the United States is committed disproportionately by young people, the poor, males, urban residents, and African-Americans. Combining these characteristics, crime rates are highest among young, poor, urban, African-American men.

If we could wave a magic wand, we could probably reduce crime significantly, including white-collar crime, by giving our country a new value system. This value system would place less emphasis on economic success, individualism, and competition, and more emphasis on cooperation and multiple kinds of success. If Bonger (1916) and other critics of capitalism are correct (see Chapter 9), our capitalist economic system is responsible for many of the criminogenic values that need to be replaced. However, the United States is certainly not about to abandon capitalism and not about to adopt a new value system, although other industrial and nonindustrial nations, Western and non-Western alike, with lower crime rates all feature value systems that stress community and cooperation (Adler 1983; Clinard 1978; Johnson 2007).

If we had a magic wand, we could also reduce crime significantly by wiping out economic deprivation and racial discrimination. The high degree of economic deprivation in the United States is at least partly responsible for its high crime rate, and economic deprivation and racial discrimination help account for much of the relatively high criminality of urban African-Americans and Latinos.

Finally, if we could wave a magic wand, we could reduce crime significantly by eliminating the many aspects of masculinity that prompt males to be so much more crime prone than females. If the male crime rate were as low as the female rate, crime in the United States would probably not be considered a serious problem.

Unfortunately, of course, magic wands do not exist except at Hogwarts Castle and in the Land of Oz, and we are not about to overhaul U.S. values, abolish poverty and racial discrimination, and eliminate the worst aspects of masculinity in any of our lifetimes. More practical strategies that address the structural and cultural roots of crime are therefore necessary. The following proposals outline several such strategies.

1. **Undertake social policies to create decent-paying jobs for the poor, especially those in urban communities.** The U.S. poverty rate has grown since 2000. Even when the nation's economy was thriving during the middle and late 1990s, the economic situation of people at the bottom of the socioeconomic ladder remained dismal and even worsened (Mishel et al. 2013). Economic and social policies, therefore, must be developed to address their needs. Here employment policy is crucial, as research documents the connection between extreme poverty and crime (see Chapter 7). According to Elliott Currie (1985:263), "(A) commitment to full and decent employment remains the keystone of any successful anticrime policy." Currie noted that Western nations with lower violent-crime rates than the United States all have much more effective employment policies than the United States does. Employment reduces poverty, especially among the economic underclass; it increases an individual's bond to society and sense of responsibility; and it reduces family stress and enhances family functioning. If the United States can reduce poverty by enabling more people to work at decent-paying jobs, crime will eventually decrease. Specific policies to increase employment lie beyond the scope of this discussion, but they include large public expenditures for job training and public works jobs and tax and other incentives for corporations to develop stable employment in urban areas.

2. **Provide government economic aid for people who cannot find work or who find work but still cannot lift themselves out of poverty.** Many of the poor are working poor. They have jobs at or close to the minimum wage, which still leaves them far below the poverty line. Other members of the poor are women with young children. They either cannot afford to work because of high day care costs or are unemployable because they lack a high school degree and/or job skills. If we do not provide for our poor, we are certain to increase the chances that their children will grow up to commit crime.

3. **End racial segregation in housing.** Racial segregation in housing remains extensive and has serious consequences for African-Americans (Akins 2009; Peterson 2012). Among other consequences, it worsens their economic distress by trapping them in deteriorating neighborhoods with weakened social institutions and higher crime rates.

4. **Restore the social integration and strengthen the social institutions of urban neighborhoods.** This proposal stems from social disorganization theory (see Chapter 7). Any measures to strengthen the urban neighborhoods in these respects should concentrate on children and adolescents. Examples here would include youth recreation programs, increased involvement of parents in school activities, increased involvement of youths in church-based religious and social activities, and adult–youth mentoring in job skills, hobbies, and other areas.

▼ Unemployment lines indicate a social problem—the absence of a sufficient number of decent-paying jobs for the poor—that contributes to the crime rate.

© Tony Freeman / PhotoEdit

▲ Improving the physical conditions of urban neighborhoods should help to reduce street crime.

5. **Reduce housing and population density.** Crime is more likely when families live in apartment buildings, public housing projects, and other types of crowded housing than when they live more spread apart (Barkan 2000). New public housing for the poor should thus be larger and more dispersed geographically. If they desire, current residents of urban public housing projects and other dense housing should be able to move to such housing.

6. **Reduce urban neighborhood dilapidation.** Several scholars have emphasized the physical incivilities of urban neighborhoods as a cause of their high crime rates (Skogan 2008; Stark 1987). These incivilities include graffiti, broken windows, abandoned buildings, and strewn trash. Such dilapidation may prompt nondeviant neighborhood residents to move elsewhere and makes those remaining feel stigmatized and less willing to report victimization to the police. It also encourages potential offenders to commit crime, because they feel the residents care little about their neighborhoods. Dilapidation also decreases the odds that children will come to respect the need to obey laws and other social norms. Although the actual incivilities–crime connection remains in dispute (see Chapter 7), efforts that successfully clean up neighborhoods might reduce crime.

7. **Change male socialization practices so that notions of masculinity move away from violence and other criminogenic attitudes and values.** Although we are not about to change masculinity overnight, it is possible for parents to begin to raise their boys according to a different value system. Parents who try to do this, of course, inevitably face the influences of violent-toy advertising, of violent TV shows and movies, and of their sons' friends raised according to traditional masculine values. Despite these influences, parents' socialization practices do make a difference, and to the extent they begin to raise their boys away from traditional masculine emphases on violence and economic success, crime will be reduced.

8. **Reduce social and economic inequality between women and men.** To the extent that rape/sexual assault and domestic violence reflect women's economic and social subordination, reducing gender inequality should reduce these crimes. A complete discussion of policies addressing gender inequality is beyond our scope but would include, at a minimum, reducing the gender gap in wages and salaries and increasing career opportunities for women.

▼ To help reduce violent crime, it is important that we begin to raise our boys away from the traditional masculine emphasis on violence.

Review and Discuss

What are any three primary prevention measures that might reduce the crime rate?

Developmental Crime Prevention (Secondary Prevention)

A secondary prevention approach recognizes that serious crime is disproportionately committed by a small group of chronic offenders whose antisocial behavior began before adolescence. They tend to come from economically deprived, dysfunctional families characterized by parents whose relationships with each other and with their children are hostile rather than harmonious; by fathers (and stepfathers and boyfriends) who physically abuse mothers; by parents whose discipline of their children is either too permissive or too coercive; by parents who routinely spank and even physically and/or sexually abuse their children; and by parents with histories of criminality and of alcohol or other drug abuse (Welsh 2012). These offenders likely attended run-down, dysfunctional schools with overcrowded classrooms and outmoded books and equipment, and more often than not they got poor grades in these schools and were uninvolved in school activities. A secondary prevention approach thus recognizes that the seeds of juvenile delinquency and adult crime are planted long before delinquency and crime appear and that it is absolutely essential to focus prevention efforts on developmental experiences in early childhood that set the stage for later offending.

If we could again wave a magic wand, we would reduce crime by immediately transforming dysfunctional families into the kind advocated by Dr. Benjamin Spock in his classic guide *Baby and Child Care* (Spock and Needleman 2012). We would have parents who treat each other and their children with loving respect; who do not abuse alcohol or other drugs; who supervise their children's behavior, and especially their sons' behavior, carefully without being overbearing; and who discipline their children firmly but fairly, and with little or no spanking and certainly no physical or sexual abuse. If we could wave a magic wand, we would also immediately transform our schools, especially those in poor, urban communities, into better places of learning.

Although once again we have no magic wand, there are still several practical policies that could help our parents and our schools do a better job of keeping our children from developing antisocial and then delinquent and criminal tendencies (Farrington 2011; Welsh 2012). These policies include the following:

9. **Establish well-funded early childhood intervention programs for high-risk children and their families.** These critical programs should target multiple risk factors and should involve, among other things, preschool education, home visits, and parenting training. A growing amount of evidence indicates that intensive early intervention programs of this nature can reduce later delinquency and other behavioral problems.

10. **Provide affordable, high-quality child day care for all parents who need it to work outside the home and flexible work schedules to allow parents to spend more time with children.** These two policies would enable parents to be employed and help ensure that their children have good caretaking. Currently, the United States lags behind many European nations that already provide government-sponsored day care and flexible work schedules. Adoption of these policies would reduce structural (unemployment and poverty) and developmental (poor child rearing) problems that create criminality.

11. **Improve the nation's schools, especially in urban areas, where schools are beset by "savage inequalities" (Kozol 1991) that generate criminogenic conditions.** Dysfunctional schools should be thoroughly renovated and much better funded. In many areas, new schools should be built. New schools should be smaller than existing schools, and all schools should have small numbers of students in classes, with heavy involvement of community volunteers. Among other things, such measures will improve students' educational performance, strengthen their commitment to the educational process and their attachment to their teachers, and encourage them to become more involved in school activities. All these achievements should in turn lower their risk for delinquency and later criminality.

12. **Provide prenatal and postnatal nutrition and other health-related services.** To the extent that poor prenatal and

▼ A developmental focus on early childhood risk factors will help reduce delinquency and adult crime. In this regard, it is essential that we expand prenatal and postnatal nutrition and other health services.

AP Photo/The New Mexican, Kathy De La Torre

postnatal nutrition and other health problems impair children's neurological functioning, their chances for antisocial and thus later criminal behavior increase. United States prenatal and postnatal programs are currently inadequate, leaving many poor children at risk for neurological impairment.

13. **Expand the network of battered women's shelters and rape crisis centers.** These establishments have provided an invaluable service for women beaten and/or raped by husbands, boyfriends, and former husbands and boyfriends. However, their numbers and resources are currently inadequate to meet the need of the millions of women battered or raped each year. Expanding the network of shelters and centers would not only help protect these women from additional abuse, but would also reduce the likelihood that any children they might have will grow up in violent households.

Review and Discuss

What are any three secondary prevention measures that might reduce the crime rate?

Criminal Justice Approaches (Tertiary Prevention)

A tertiary approach to crime prevention that is grounded in sociological criminology recognizes the "limits of the criminal sanction," to use Herbert Packer's (1968) famous term. It acknowledges that only very limited crime reduction can be achieved by relying on law and criminal justice and that any crime reduction that can be achieved comes only at a great cost of dollars and threats to civil liberties and civil rights. At the same time, it recognizes that crime is a serious problem and that the public must be kept safe from dangerous offenders. Several of the following criminal justice–based proposals would help make society safer at lower financial, social, and political costs than are true of current strategies. Others might not affect crime rates, but at least would raise public trust and confidence in criminal justice and have it operate more in line with democratic ideals.

14. **Reduce reliance on imprisonment and put more emphasis on community corrections.** This model is used by many western European nations. The surge in U.S. imprisonment since 1980 has accomplished little but cost us much. Reducing reliance on imprisonment would free up significant dollars for community corrections approaches. There is increasing evidence that these approaches save money, do not lead to more recidivism than imprisonment, and might even lead to less recidivism if they are properly funded (Petersilia and Reitz 2012; Pew Center on the States 2012). Greater use of these programs would save money and keep society at least as safe as, and perhaps a bit safer than, imprisonment would. Probation and parole officers should have much smaller caseloads to permit more intensive supervision of offenders released into the community.

    Offenders considered for community corrections should be nonviolent drug and property offenders. Nationally, about half of all state prisoners have been convicted either of a drug offense, property offense, or consensual offense such as commercialized vice. Without threatening public safety, most of these offenders could be placed into community corrections at a savings of several billion dollars per year, even after paying for their community corrections costs. The dollars saved could be used for employment, early family intervention, and other policies that would reduce crime. For example, the money saved for each offender going into community corrections could fund one preschool teacher who could be involved with five to ten children at high risk for developmental problems. Reducing reliance on imprisonment would also mean that new prison construction could stop, saving tens of billions of dollars in future construction and maintenance costs. These funds could also be reallocated to primary and secondary crime-prevention programs.

15. **Make prisons and jails smaller, reduce overcrowding, and improve other decrepit prison and jail conditions.** Despite popular belief, conditions in many prisons and jails are substandard (Kappeler and Potter 2005). Current prison conditions do little to rehabilitate offenders and often make them worse. At a minimum, improving prisons would help reduce the extent

to which offenders worsen because of their prison experience and thus lead to a safer society. This reform should include the establishment of much better educational, vocational, and other rehabilitation programs in prisons. These programs appear to reduce crime and would be even more effective were they adequately funded (Cullen and Gilbert 2013).

16. **Eliminate "three strikes and you're out" and mandatory imprisonment policies.** These policies have swelled our prison population without lowering the crime rate. Given that criminality declines sharply with advancing age, people sent to prison for life after a third felony stay in prison for many more years after they would have stopped committing crime. In general, many prison terms could be shortened, saving prison costs and reducing prison overcrowding, without endangering public safety (Tonry 2009).

17. **Consider repealing at least some of the present drug laws.** These laws might do more harm than good. They have unfairly targeted the African-American and Latino communities, and they have cost billions of dollars in criminal justice expenses. The billions of dollars saved could be redirected to educational and treatment programs designed to prevent drug use from beginning and to halt drug use that has already started. Because of the very legitimate concerns raised by both proponents and opponents of drug decriminalization, a national debate must begin on what drug policies make the most sense.

18. **Eliminate the death penalty.** The death penalty has no general deterrent effect and costs at least twice as much as life imprisonment. It continues to be arbitrary and discriminatory in its application and to put at least some innocent people at risk for death. In a nonsociological area, serious questions can be raised about the morality of capital punishment in a society that professes to be civilized.

19. **Expand community policing and consider expanding directed police activity in crime hot spots.** A growing amount of evidence indicates that community policing and directed police activity in crime hot spots may reduce crime and that community policing reduces fear of crime and may help lessen the incivilities of urban neighborhoods. Because directed patrol may overburden the courts, jails, and prisons and raise civil liberties questions, such activity should be considered carefully before being undertaken.

20. **Increase the hiring of minority and female police officers and develop a zero-tolerance policy for the hostility and discrimination they now experience from other officers.** This proposal would increase the respect of minority urban residents for the police and strengthen police–community relations. Although the crime-reduction benefit from this proposal may be minimal, a democratic society should not tolerate discrimination within its law enforcement community.

21. **Reduce police brutality and racial profiling.** Police departments should develop zero tolerance for such behaviors and take every step possible to identify and remove the officers responsible for them. Again, these measures might not reduce crime, but they would at least protect the public from police misconduct and reduce citizen disrespect for and hostility toward the police.

22. **Increase gun-control efforts.** The huge number of handguns in the United States is an important reason for our high number of homicides. If we could wave a magic wand and make all handguns disappear, our homicide rates would drop significantly. Without a magic wand, however, there are far too many handguns and far too many people who want handguns for these weapons to be eliminated entirely, and the U.S. Supreme Court has said that private firearm ownership is protected by the Second Amendment. Given these facts, the best we can do is to undertake policies that limit the supply of handguns and otherwise make them safer for law-abiding citizens and offenders alike, especially youths. Several scholars have discussed such policies (Cook et al. 2011; Wellford 2011). Their proposals include: (a) heavily taxing guns and ammunition to make them too expensive for at least some people, and especially adolescents, to buy; (b) substantially raising the licensing fee for gun dealers to reduce their number; (c) requiring that new guns include safety measures to reduce accidental use; (d) increasing community policing to reduce fear of crime and hence citizens' perceptions that they need handguns for protection; and (e) removing guns from homes where domestic violence occurs.

23. **Increase intolerance for white-collar crime and political corruption.** This will be no easy task. Even so, several policies might help limit white-collar crime and political corruption, including greater media attention to the harm of such crime; greater expenditure of resources on preventing, detecting, and enforcing current laws; and the development of new laws. More certain punishment, especially imprisonment, for white-collar and governmental offenders should also work. Although this "get tough" approach has not been shown to work with common criminals, it may have more of a deterrent effect on potential white-collar and governmental offenders.

Review and Discuss

What are any three tertiary prevention measures that might reduce the crime rate?

We now stand at a crossroads. Although crime rates are much lower now than in the early 1990s, conditions for the U.S. poor have been worsening over the past few decades, and the nation was still emerging from a serious recession at the time of this writing. The good news is that several states have begun to realize that they can no longer afford to pay for their great numbers of prisoners resulting from the nation's "get tough" policy on crime. The bad news is that many states have also cut back on various programs that aid the children most at risk for an eventual life of crime, namely, those growing up in poor, single-parent households. If we wanted to ensure that crime will increase, we would do exactly what we have been doing in regard to the poor among us.

Michael Tonry (2004:vii) observed, "The United States has a punishment system that no one would knowingly have built from the ground up. It is often unjust, it is unduly severe, it is wasteful, and it does enormous damage to the lives of black Americans." Taking this view one step further, Elliott Currie (1985:278) said that if we wanted for some reason to design a society that would be especially violent, it would look very much like what we now have. It would be a society with high rates of inequality and high rates of unemployment among the young, which deprives them of participation in community life. It would be a society that allows thousands of jobs to leave whole communities, disrupting their social organization and forcing people to migrate in search of new jobs. It would also be a society that promotes "a culture of intense interpersonal competition" and emphasizes material consumption to such a degree that many people violate the law to reach this level, while others experience anger and frustration over their inability to live up to this lofty standard.

In the same vein, Jeffrey Reiman and Paul Leighton (2013) note that if we wanted for some reason to design a criminal justice system that would certainly fail, it would also look very much like the one we now have. It would be a system that bans many consensual behaviors and forces people committed to those behaviors to engage in other types of crime. It would also be a system in which arrest, prosecution, and punishment are somewhat arbitrary and in which wealthy individuals and organizations committing very harmful behaviors generally avoid legal sanctions. Both sets of dynamics, Reiman and Leighton said, lead to resentment among the relative few who end up under the control of criminal justice officials. Next, it would be a system in which the prison experience is more likely to make inmates worse than better and a system in which prisoners learn no marketable skills in prison and have no jobs awaiting them when they leave prison. Finally, it would be a system in which ex-offenders are shunned by conventional society, lose their right to vote, cannot find work, and otherwise are prevented from reintegrating themselves into the conventional social order.

If we are honest, we would admit that we live in a society whose fundamental structural and cultural features contribute heavily to our high crime rates. We would also admit that we know that the criminal justice system is not working and cannot be made to work to reduce crime. If we are serious about reducing crime, we will undertake some or all of the preventive measures just listed. They may not all succeed, but we certainly cannot do much worse than we have been doing. Dickens, Dostoyevsky, and other great writers have reminded us that how we treat the poor and the criminals among us is a sign of what kind of a people we are. If we are to be true to our democratic, egalitarian ideals, we must attack the social roots of the crime and victimization that plague us so. Anything else would betray the noble principles on which our nation was founded.

▼

► Conclusion

This chapter has proposed several measures that hold at least some promise for reducing the rates of many types of criminal behaviors. The basis for all the proposals is a vast body of research, discussed in earlier chapters, on the structural and cultural causes of crime and victimization.

Chapter 1 mentioned that a key goal of this book was to develop your sociological imagination about crime. We hope we have succeeded. A sociological criminology tells us much about the society in which we live. As C. Wright Mills (1959) observed, the knowledge that the sociological imagination gives us is both terrible and magnificent. Your new sociological imagination about crime may be terrible for indicating the power of the social forces underlying crime and victimization. But it is also magnificent for pointing you to the possibility of changing these forces so that we can, at long last, have a safer society.

Summary

1. A public health approach emphasizes the need to prevent crime from occurring. The "get tough" approach underlying U.S. crime policy during the past few decades has not succeeded in doing this and has cost tens of billions of dollars.

2. The criminal justice funnel highlights the fact that only a very small percentage of all serious crimes lead to the incarceration of the offender. The huge drop throughout all stages of the funnel underscores the cost-ineffectiveness of reliance on the criminal justice system to reduce crime.

3. A public health approach to crime control involves primary, secondary, and tertiary prevention. A sociological prescription for crime reduction comprises several policies and actions to accomplish each kind of prevention.

Key Terms

criminal justice funnel *373*
developmental experiences *379*

primary prevention *376*
public health model *373*

secondary prevention *376*
tertiary prevention *376*

What Would You Do?

1. You are the mayor of a large city that has a limited budget. Your police chief has put in a request for an additional $1 million to hire and equip several more police officers. Meanwhile, the head of your Child Services Division has also put in a request for about $1 million to hire several more caseworkers to work with families in which children are at risk for neglect and/or abuse. You probably do have $1 million to allocate to one of these requests. Which one do you select, and why?

2. You are the warden of a medium-security state prison that was built to house 1,000 inmates but now is holding 1,600 inmates. Reflecting national statistics, about half of your inmates are behind bars for committing nonviolent property, drug, or consensual offenses. Most of them would not be a threat to public safety were they to be released from prison, but some of them would be a threat, and there is probably little way of predicting successfully the inmates who would fall into either group. Of course, you have no power to release any inmates, but you have been asked to testify before your state legislature's Criminal Justice Committee about the possible effects of releasing at least some of the inmates back into the community to relieve the crowding at your prison. What do you say in your testimony?

Glossary

abnormality an abnormal biological or psychological condition said to be responsible for criminal behavior.

absolute deterrence the effect of having some legal punishment versus the effect of having no legal punishment.

actus reus the actual criminal act of which a defendant is accused.

adversary system the idealized model of the criminal justice process in the United States in which the prosecutor and defense attorney vigorously contest the evidence concerning the defendant's guilt or innocence.

agents provocateurs government agents who pretend to join a dissident group and then try to goad the group into committing violence or other illegal activity.

alien conspiracy model the belief that a small number of Italian-American "families" control organized crime in the United States.

amateur theft property crime committed by unskilled offenders who act when the opportunity arises.

anomie as developed by Émile Durkheim, a state of normlessness in society in which aspirations that previously were controlled now become unlimited. Robert Merton adapted this term to refer to the gap between the institutionalized goal in the United States of financial success and the institutionalized means of working.

arbitrariness the process occurring when legal outcomes are based on prejudice or other nonlegal criteria instead of legal factors, such as the seriousness of the crime and the strength of the evidence.

aspirations strong desires or longings. As used in extensions of Merton's anomie theory, aspirations refer to economic and other goals of adolescents that result in frustration when they are not realized.

assault an unlawful attack by one person on another to inflict bodily injury. Aggravated assault involves a serious injury or the use of a weapon. Simple assault involves only minor injuries and no use of a weapon.

atavism the belief, popularized by Cesare Lombroso, that criminals are born as throwbacks to an earlier stage of evolution.

attachment in Travis Hirschi's social control theory, the degree to which adolescents care about the opinions of conventional others, including parents and teachers, and feel close to them. The greater the attachment, the less the delinquency.

battering physical assaults and other physical abuse committed against a woman by a male intimate.

booster skilled, professional shoplifters who sell their stolen goods to fences or pawn shops.

bourgeoisie as used by Karl Marx and Friedrich Engels, the class in capitalist society that controls the means of production.

bribery the giving or accepting of money or other things of value in return for promises to grant favors to the party giving the bribe.

brothel a house of prostitution.

brutality a form of police misconduct involving the undue or excessive use of physical coercion to subdue a suspect or other citizen.

brutalization effect the possibility that executions increase the homicide rate.

caseloads the workload of prosecutors, defense attorneys, and judges.

casino a building used for gambling.

causal order the direction of the relationship between two variables.

certainty the likelihood of being arrested.

child abuse physical violence or sexual misconduct committed against children by their parents or other adults.

chronic offenders a small number of offenders who commit a disproportionate amount of serious crime and delinquency and who persist in their criminality.

civil disobedience the violation of criminal law for reasons of conscience.

classical school a school of thought popular in the eighteenth century in Europe. Its main assumptions were that criminals act rationally and that the severity of legal punishment should be restricted to the degree necessary to deter crime.

climatological as used in discussing the patterning of crime, refers to the variation of crime rates with climate and seasons of the year.

COINTELPRO a secret FBI program, aimed at disrupting and discrediting dissident groups and individuals, that reached its zenith during the 1960s and early 1970s.

collective embezzlement the stealing of company funds by top management. The term was first used to refer to one type of crime that characterized the U.S. savings and loan scandals of the 1980s.

common law the system of law originating in medieval England and emphasizing court decisions and customs.

community policing a style of policing in which police patrol neighborhoods on foot and try to help their residents solve community problems.

concentric zones the division of cities into geographical sectors radiating out from the city's center.

concordance a similarity of criminal behavior and other outcomes between identical twins.

conflict as used in sociology and criminology, refers to a theory that assumes that people disagree on norms and act with self-interest because of their disparate socioeconomic positions.

consensus as used in sociology and criminology, refers to a theory that people agree on norms despite their disparate socioeconomic positions.

constable an official appointed by medieval English nobles to control poaching and otherwise monitor the behavior of people living on the nobles' land.

containment as used in criminology, refers to a theory developed by Walter C. Reckless that stressed the inner and outer conditions that help prevent juvenile delinquency.

conventional social institutions structured patterns of behavior and relationships, such as the family, the educational system, and religion.

corporate crime an action by a corporation that violates the criminal law.

corporate violence activities or neglect by corporations that lead to injury, illness, or death.

correctional supervision placement in prison, jail, or on probation or parole.

corruption dishonest practices, especially when committed by public or corporate officials.

courtroom work group the "team" of prosecutor, defense attorney, and judge, all of whom are said to cooperate to expedite cases.

crackdown the short-term concentration of police resources in a specific neighborhood, usually to control a specific activity, such as drug possession and trafficking.

crime behavior that is considered so harmful that it is banned by a criminal law.

crime characteristics aspects of a crime, such as its location and the typical victim–offender relationship.

crime control the use of the criminal justice system to prevent and punish crime. The *crime-control model* refers to the belief that crime control is the primary goal of the criminal justice system.

crime myth a widespread but inaccurate belief about crime.

crime victim any person who unwillingly suffers a completed or attempted crime.

crime wave a sudden and often distorted focus of the news media on one or more types of criminal behavior.

criminal careers the continuation of criminal behavior past adolescence and young adulthood.

criminal intent having the desire to commit a crime.

criminal justice funnel the rapid drop from the number of actual crimes committed to the number of offenders incarcerated.

criminalization the process by which lawful behaviors are turned into criminal ones because of the enactment of new laws.

criminogenic crime causing.

criminology the study of the making of laws, the breaking of laws, and society's reaction to the breaking of laws.

critical perspectives views that challenge traditional understandings and theories of crime and criminal justice.

cultural myths as used in criminology, refers to false beliefs in society that make crimes such as rape and battering more likely.

culture conflict the clash of values and norms between different social groups, especially as it leads to the behavior of one group to be branded as criminal.

customs norms that are unwritten and informal.

debunking motif part of the sociological perspective; refers to the challenge sociology poses to conventional understandings of social institutions and social reality.

decision-making processes the ways judges and prosecutors determine what happens at various stages of the criminal justice system.

delinquent peers lawbreaking adolescents with whom a particular adolescent associates.

democratic society a society in which the people freely elect officials to represent their views and interests and in which they are free from arbitrary government power.

democratic theory the view that elected officials should represent the interests of all people in a democracy.

dependent variable an attitude or behavior that changes because of the influence of an independent variable.

deterrence in criminology, having a deterrent effect on crime.

deterrence theory the belief that the threat or application of legal punishment prevents criminal behavior.

developmental experiences aspects of childhood and adolescence that affect the likelihood of crime.

deviance behavior that violates accepted norms and arouses negative social reactions.

deviance amplification the process by which official labeling increases the likelihood of deviant behavior.

differential association Edwin Sutherland's concept for the process by which adolescents become delinquent because they are exposed to more lawbreaking attitudes than to law-abiding attitudes.

differential opportunities conditions or situations that are more or less favorable for the commission of crime.

discordance a difference in criminal behavior and other outcomes between identical twins.

discretion latitude in decision making.

double burden the difficulties faced by minority female police officers because of their race and gender.

dowry deaths murders of women in India and Pakistan because their families could not pay the expected dowry.

dramatization of evil the process by which deviant labels affect self-images and promote continued deviance.

drift the intermittent commission of delinquency.

due process rights granted to criminal defendants by the U.S. Constitution and judicial rulings.

duress threats or coercion on another to commit a crime.

economic deprivation poverty and economic inequality.

ego Sigmund Freud's term for the rational dimension of the personality that develops after the id.

embezzlement the stealing or misappropriation of funds entrusted to an employee.

Enlightenment an intellectual movement in the seventeenth and eighteenth centuries that challenged medieval religious beliefs.

erotica written or visual materials dealing with sexual behavior and often intended to arouse sexual desire.

espionage spying.

exclusionary rule a rule that prohibits evidence from criminal trials that was gathered in violation of judicial rulings; also includes other procedural rules governing the gathering of evidence.

expressive offenses crimes committed for emotional reasons and with little or no planning.

extralegal refers to race, ethnicity, gender, social class, and other nonlegal factors that may affect arrest, sentencing, and other legal decision making.

family interaction behavior and functioning within a family.

family structure the nature and pattern of statuses in a family.

fear of crime concern or worry over becoming a crime victim.

felony a serious criminal offense punishable by a prison term of more than 1 year.

femicide the murder of women and girls.

feminism the belief that women deserve to be men's equals in economic, political, and social power.

fencing the selling of stolen goods.

focal concerns Walter Miller's term for beliefs and values said to be characteristic of lower-class males that increase their likelihood of delinquency.

general deterrence deterrence that occurs when members of the public decide not to break the law because they fear legal punishment.

generalize to apply knowledge of particular cases to other, similar cases.

genital mutilation the excision of a clitoris.

genocide the systematic extermination of a category of people because of their race, ethnicity, or religion.

goods objects the public desires, several of which are provided by organized crime.

grass-eaters police who engage in minor bribery and other corruption.

handgun control efforts to restrict the supply and ownership of handguns.

harm reduction a public policy strategy in which drug use is treated as a public health problem and not as a crime problem.

hate crime violent or property crimes committed against the person or property of someone because of that person's race, ethnicity, religion, national origin, or sexual orientation.

heredity the genetic transmission of physical characteristics, behavior, and other traits.

homicide the unjustified killing of a human being.

hot spots specific locations in neighborhoods in which crime is especially common.

id Sigmund Freud's term for the instinctive, pleasure-seeking dimension of the personality that characterizes infancy.

incapacitation physically preventing a convicted offender from committing a crime; usually refers to incarceration.

incarceration the placing of a convicted offender in prison or jail.

incidence the average number of offenses per person in the time period under examination.

independent variable a sociodemographic characteristic or other trait that influences changes in a dependent variable.

individual characteristics personal traits that influence the likelihood of committing an inequality crime or becoming a crime victim.

in/out decision the determination of whether a convicted offender should be incarcerated.

instrumental offenses crimes committed for material gain and with some degree of planning.

international comparisons cross-national comparisons of crime rates.

interpersonal violence physically injurious acts committed by one or more people against one or more others.

intraracial within one race.

IQ intelligence as measured by standardized tests.

Iran–Contra scandal a scandal in the 1980s involving the illegal sale of weapons to Iran and the diverting of funds from that sale to Contra rebels in Nicaragua.

joyriding the temporary stealing of a car or other motor vehicle in order to drive or ride in it for thrills.

kinds of people the characteristics of individuals that generate criminality.

kinds of places the structural and physical characteristics of neighborhoods and other locations that generate criminality.

labeling defining a person or behavior as deviant.

laws written, formal norms.

learning acquiring attitudes, knowledge, and skills; in criminology, a process by which people become criminals.

learning theories explanations that emphasize that criminal behavior is learned.

left realism an approach to crime developed by radical criminologists in Great Britain that emphasizes the harm that crime causes and the need to take measures to reduce crime.

legalization the elimination of laws prohibiting certain behaviors, especially consensual crimes.

liberation hypothesis the view that racial discrimination in sentencing is more likely for defendants convicted of minor offenses than for those convicted of serious offenses.

life course infancy, childhood, adolescence, young adulthood, and older stages of life.

lifestyle theory the belief that certain leisure-time and other activities increase the chances of becoming a crime victim.

longitudinal studies research in which the same people are studied over time.

mala in se behaviors that are wrong in and of themselves.

mala prohibita behaviors that are wrong only because they are prohibited by law.

male dominance the supremacy of men in society.

manslaughter an unjustified killing considered less serious or less blameworthy than murder.

marginal deterrence the effect of increasing the severity, certainty, and/or swiftness of legal punishment.

Marxism a set of beliefs derived from the work of Karl Marx and Friedrich Engels that emphasizes the conflict of interests between people based on whether they own the means of production.

mass media modes of communication, such as television, radio, and newspapers.

measurement in criminology, the determination of the frequency of criminal behavior and of the characteristics of offenders and victims.

meat-eaters police who engage in serious forms of corruption.

mens rea a guilty mind; refers to an individual having criminal intent.

misdemeanor a relatively minor criminal offense punishable by less than 1 year in prison.

moral crusade a concerted effort to prevent and punish behavior considered immoral.

moral development the process by which children and adolescents develop their sense of morality.

more harm than good in the drug legalization debate, refers to whether drug laws result in more disadvantages than advantages.

muckrakers a group of early twentieth-century U.S. journalists and other social critics of political and corporate corruption and other misconduct.

National Crime Victimization Survey (NCVS) an annual survey of criminal victimization sponsored by the U.S. Department of Justice.

neurotransmitters chemical substances that help neurons transmit impulses to each other across synapses.

news media the members of the mass media transmitting information about current events.

nonviolent pornography sexually explicit materials that do not involve violent acts.

norms standards of behavior.

objective deterrence the impact of actual legal punishment.

occupational crime crime committed in the course of one's occupation.

organizational crime crime committed on behalf of an organization.

overdramate to exaggerate for the news media the frequency and seriousness of violent crime.

patriarchy male supremacy.

patterning the social distribution of criminal behavior according to certain characteristics of locations and of individuals.

peacemaking criminology an approach that combines several humanistic strains of thought to view crime as just one of the many forms of suffering that characterize human existence.

personality aspects of an individual's character, behavior, and other qualities.

phrenology the belief that the size and shape of the skull indicate the propensity for criminal behavior.

pilferage employee theft of workplace items, usually of small value.

piracy robbery at sea.

plea bargaining negotiations between prosecution and defense over the sentence the prosecutor will request in return for a plea of guilty by the defendant.

police sexual violence (PSV) violence committed by police against female suspects or other female civilians.

political crime any illegal or socially harmful act aimed at preserving or changing the existing political and social order.

political violence interpersonal violence committed to achieve a political goal.

politics of victimization the ideological implications of government efforts to help victims of street crime.

positivism the view that human behavior and attitudes are influenced by forces both external and internal to the individual.

premenstrual syndrome symptoms such as severe tension and irritability occurring in the premenstrual phase.

prevalence the proportion of respondents who have committed a particular offense at least once in the time period under study.

price-fixing the practice whereby businesses conspire to fix prices on goods and services rather than let the free market operate.

primary deviance the first deviant act that someone commits; in labeling theory, primary deviance is said not to lead often to continued or secondary deviance unless labeling occurs.

primary prevention efforts to prevent problems such as disease, injury, or crime by focusing on aspects of the social or physical environment that contribute to these problems.

private troubles individual problems that many people have that they think stem from their own failings or particular circumstances.

professional fraud fraud committed by physicians, attorneys, and other professional workers.

professional theft property crime committed by skilled offenders who carefully plan their offenses.

proletariat as used by Karl Marx and Friedrich Engels, the class in capitalist society that does not control the means of production.

property crime theft and other crime committed against property.

psychoanalytic refers to explanations of human motivation and behavior that derive from the work of Sigmund Freud.

psychological consequences mental and emotional effects; in criminology, particularly from criminal victimization.

public health model an approach to illness, injury, and other problems that emphasizes primary prevention.

public issues social problems resulting from structural and other problems in the social environment.

public opinion the views and attitudes of the public on important social, political, and economic issues.

public policy government efforts to deal with public issues and societal needs.

punitiveness public judgments of appropriate punishment for convicted criminals.

racial prejudice unfavorable views toward a certain category of people because of their race.

rape forced or nonconsensual sexual intercourse.

rational-choice theory the view that people plan their actions and weigh the potential benefits and costs of their potential behavior.

rationalization a justification or technique of neutralization that minimizes the guilt that criminal offenders may otherwise feel.

reinforcement the rewarding of behavior; a key concept in differential reinforcement theory, which argues that criminal behavior and attitudes are more likely to be learned when they are reinforced by friends and/or family.

relative deprivation the feeling that one is less well off than others.

relativist definition labeling theory's view that deviance is not a property of a behavior, but is rather the result of how others regard that behavior.

religious fundamentalism in Christianity and Judaism, the belief that the Bible is the actual word of God.

repression government suppression of dissent through violent or legal means.

repressive law Émile Durkheim's term for the punitive type of legal punishment that he thought characterizes traditional societies.

restitutive law Émile Durkheim's term for the compensatory type of legal punishment that he thought characterizes modern societies.

restraint of trade business practices that violate free market principles.

robbery taking or attempting to take something from one or more people by force or threat of force.

routine-activities theory the view that an individual's daily activities can affect his or her chances of becoming a crime victim.

ruling class the capitalist class or bourgeoisie.

seasonal of or relating to the seasons of the year; some crime rates vary from season to season and are thus said to be seasonal.

secondary deviance continued deviance; said by labeling theory to result from the labeling of primary deviance.

secondary prevention the identification of practices and situations that put certain individuals at risk for illness, injury, or criminality and efforts to address these risk factors.

self-control the restraining of one's impulses and desires.

self-defense violent or other actions committed to protect oneself or others.

self-referral a physician's referral of patients to medical testing laboratories that the physician owns or in which the physician has invested.

self-report studies surveys in which respondents are asked to report about criminal offenses they have committed.

sentencing preferences public views of appropriate legal punishment for given crimes.

seriousness of crime opinions regarding the importance or degree of harm associated with given crimes.

services the performance of activities that the public desires, several of which are provided by organized crime.

sexual assault nonconsensual or forced sexual contact that does not involve sexual intercourse.

severity whether someone is incarcerated and, if so, for how long.

shaming social disapproval.

sin a morally improper act.

situational crime prevention efforts in specific locations that aim to make it more difficult for offenders to commit crimes against potential victims.

sneaky thrill crimes offenses committed for the excitement.

snitch an amateur shoplifter.

social bond the connection among individuals or between individuals and social institutions such as families and schools.

social control society's restraint of norm-violating behavior.

social disorganization the breakdown of social bonds and social control in a community or larger society.

social ecology the relationship of people to their environment; in criminology, the study of the influence of community social and physical characteristics on community crime rates.

social inequality the differential distribution of wealth, power, and other things of value in a given society.

social integration the degree to which a community or society is characterized by strong or weak social bonds.

social learning the view that individuals learn criminal attitudes and behaviors from others who already hold these attitudes and behaviors.

social organization the pattern of relationships and roles in a society.

social pathology the view that crime and deviance are symptoms of individual and societal sickness.

social structure the pattern of social interaction and social relationships in a group or society; horizontal social structure refers to the social and physical characteristics of communities and the networks of social relationships to which an individual belongs, and vertical social structure refers to social inequality.

social ties social bonds.

socialization the learning of social norms, attitudes, and values.

sociological criminology the sociological understanding of crime and criminal justice, stressing the importance of social structure and social inequality.

sociological imagination the ability to attribute private troubles to problems in the larger social structure.

sociological perspective the belief that social backgrounds influence individuals' attitudes and behaviors.

somatology the belief that body size and shape influence criminality.

specific deterrence deterrence that occurs when offenders already *punished* for lawbreaking decide not to commit another crime because they do not want to face legal consequences again.

spurious a statistical relationship between two variables that exists only because the effects of a third variable have not been considered.

stalking state-corporate crime cooperation between government agencies and corporations to commit illegal or socially injurious activities.

state terrorism government rule by terror.

status frustration disappointment and feelings of dissatisfaction resulting from the failure to do well in school; said by Albert Cohen to lead to delinquency among lower-class boys.

strain anomie or frustration, stemming from the failure to achieve goals.

structural factors aspects of the social structure.

subculture of violence a set of attitudes, said to characterize poor urban communities, that approves the use of violence to deal with interpersonal problems and disputes.

subjective deterrence the impact of people's perceptions of the likelihood of arrest and punishment.

superego Sigmund Freud's term for the dimension of the personality that develops after the id and ego; this dimension represents society's moral code.

support system the network of tipsters and fences that help burglars carry out their burglaries and dispose of their stolen goods.

survey questionnaire administered to a set of respondents.

system capacity argument the belief that areas with high crime rates have low arrest rates because the police have many more crimes to investigate and also realize that too many crimes would overburden the criminal justice system.

tabula rasa blank slate; refers to the belief that human nature is neutral and can become good or bad because of society's influence.

target hardening efforts to make homes, stores, and other buildings less vulnerable to burglary and other crimes.

technicalities term, often pejorative, used for the rules governing the gathering of evidence against a criminal suspect.

temperament personality.

terrorism the indiscriminate use of violence to intimidate or coerce people to achieve social and political goals.

tertiary prevention efforts to treat people already having a problem, such as illness or injury; in criminology, refers to efforts to deal with people who have already committed a crime.

testosterone the so-called male hormone.

theoretical integration the combining of two or more theories to present a more comprehensive explanation of crime.

treason actions designed to overthrow one's government or otherwise weaken it severely.

underclass the group of people living in persistent poverty and unemployment.

underreporting the failure of crime victims to report crimes they have suffered or of respondents in self-report surveys to report crimes they have committed.

Uniform Crime Reports (UCR) the FBI's annual compilation of crime statistics.

victim-impact statement a written statement by a crime victim that discusses the effects of the victimization and sometimes makes recommendations for sentencing.

victim–offender relationship refers to whether the victim and offender knew each other before the victimization occurred.

victim precipitation activities by an eventual crime victim that initiate or further the events leading to the victim's victimization.

victimization the suffering of a crime.

victimology the study of victims and victimization.

violent crime interpersonal violence, especially homicide, rape, assault, and robbery.

violent pornography sexually explicit materials that depict violence.

Watergate scandal the scandal in the early 1970s that involved illegal activity committed during the 1972 presidential campaign and the subsequent obstruction of justice; the scandal led to several criminal prosecutions and the resignation of President Richard Nixon.

white-collar crime illegal or unethical acts committed by an individual or organization during the course of legitimate occupational activity.

working personality the personality associated with a particular occupation.

wrongful execution an execution of someone who in fact was innocent of the crime for which he or she was convicted.

zero-tolerance policing a style of aggressive policing that encourages arrests for even minor infractions of the law.

Chapter 1, Criminology and the Sociological Perspective

Anderson, Elijah. *Code of the Street: Decency, Violence, and the Moral Life of the Inner City.* New York: W.W. Norton, 2000.

Barkan, Steven E. "Jury Nullification in Political Trials." *Social Problems* 31 (1983): 28–45.

Becker, Howard S. *Outsiders: Studies in the Sociology of Deviance.* New York: Free Press, 1963.

Berger, Peter L. *Invitation to Sociology: A Humanistic Perspective.* Garden City, NY: Anchor Books, 1963.

Brown, Elizabeth K. "Foreclosing on Incarceration? State Correctional Policy Enactments and the Great Recession." *Criminal Justice Policy Review* 24 (2013): 317–337.

Brownstein, Henry H. *Contemporary Drug Policy.* New York: Routledge, 2013.

Chon, Don Soo. "Economic Development, Change of Age Distribution, and Stream Analogy of Homicide and Suicide: A Cross-National Assessment." *JQ: Justice Quarterly* 30 (2013): 169–193.

Cobbina, Jennifer E. "Victimization and Resistance Strategies Among Female Offenders." *Deviant Behavior* 34 (2013): 464–482.

Cole, David. *The Torture Memos: Rationalizing the Unthinkable.* New York: New Press, 2009.

Copes, Heith, and Lynne M. Vieraitis. "Understanding Identity Theft: Offenders Accounts of Their Lives and Crimes." *Criminal Justice Review* 34 (2009): 329–349.

Currie, Elliott. *Confronting Crime: An American Challenge.* New York: Pantheon Books, 1985.

DuBois, W. E. Burghardt. *The Philadelphia Negro: A Social Study.* New York: Benjamin Blom, 1899.

Durkheim, Emile. *The Rules of Sociological Method.* Edited by S. Lukes. New York: Free Press, 1962(1895).

———. *Suicide.* Translated by J. Spaulding and G. Simpson. New York: Free Press, 1952(1897).

Gabbidon, Shaun L., and Helen Taylor Greene. *Race and Crime.* Thousand Oaks, CA: Sage Publications, 2013.

Gerth, Hans, and C. Wright Mills. *From Max Weber: Essays in Sociology.* New York: Oxford University Press, 1946.

Goode, Erich. *Deviant Behavior.* Upper Saddle River, NJ: Prentice Hall, 2011.

Hagan, John. 1994. *Crime and Disrepute.* Thousand Oaks, CA: Pine Forge Press.

Huey, Laura, Georgios Fthenos, and Danielle Hryniewicz. "'If Something Happened, I Will Leave It, Let It Go and Move On': Resiliency and Victimized Homeless Women's Attitudes Toward Mental Health Counseling." *Journal of Interpersonal Violence* 28 (2013): 295–319.

Humphreys, Laud. *Tearoom Trade: Impersonal Sex in Public Places.* Chicago: Aldine, 1975.

Jacobs, Bruce A. "Carjacking and Copresence." *Journal of Research in Crime & Delinquency* 49 (2012): 471–488.

Jacques, Scott, and Danielle M. Reynald. "The Offenders' Perspective on Prevention: Guarding Against Victimization and Law Enforcement." *Journal of Research in Crime & Delinquency* 49 (2012): 269–294.

Lemon, Nancy K. D. *Lemon's Domestic Violence Law.* St. Paul, MN: West Academic Publishing, 2013.

Liebow, Elliot. *Tell Them Who I Am: The Lives of Homeless Women.* New York: Free Press, 1993.

———. *Tally's Corner.* Boston, MA: Little, Brown, 1967.

Miller, Jody. *Getting Played: African American Girls, Urban Inequality, and Gendered Violence.* New York: NYU Press, 2008.

Mills, C. Wright. *The Sociological Imagination.* London: Oxford University Press, 1959.

Nocera, Joe. "The Gun Report." *New York Times,* May 10, 2013. http://nocera.blogs.nytimes.com/2013/05/10/the-gun-report-may-10-2013/.

Renzetti, Claire. *Feminist Criminology.* New York: Routledge, 2013.

Rogers, Meghan L., and William Alex Pridemore. "The effect of poverty and social protection on national homicide rates: Direct and moderating effects." *Social Science Research* 42 (2013): 584–595.

Short, James F., Jr. "Criminology, Criminologists, and the Sociological Enterprise." In *Sociology in America: A History,* edited by C. Calhoun, 605–638. Chicago: University of Chicago Press, 2007.

Sorg, Evan T., Cory P. Haberman, Jerry H. Ratcliffe, et al. "Foot Patrol in Violent Crime Hot Spots: The Longitudinal Impact of Deterrence and Posttreatment Effects of Displacement." *Criminology* 51 (2013): 65–101.

Steffensmeier, Darrell J., and Jeffery T. Ulmer. *Confessions of a Dying Thief: Understanding Criminal Careers and Illegal Enterprise.* New York: Transaction Publishers, 2005.

Sutherland, Edwin H. *Principles of Criminology.* Philadelphia, PA: J.P. Lippincott, 1947.

Walker, Samuel. *Sense and Nonsense About Crime, Drugs, and Communities: A Policy Guide.* Belmont, CA: Wadsworth Publishing Company, 2011.

Weidner, Robert R., and William Terrill. "A Test of Turk's Theory of Norm Resistance Using Observational Data on Police-Suspect Encounters." *Journal of Research in Crime and Delinquency* 42 (2005): 84–109.

Wells-Barnett, Ida B. "Southern Horrors: Lynch Law in All Its Phases." In *African American Classics in Criminology & Criminal Justice,* edited by S. L. Gabbidon, H. T. Greene, and V. D. Young, 23–38. Thousand Oaks, CA: Sage Publications, 2002.

Welsh, Brandon C., Anthony A. Braga, and Gerben J. N. Bruinsma. *Experimental Criminology: Prospects for Advancing Science and Public Policy.* Cambridge: Cambridge University Press, 2013.

Whyte, William Foote. *Street Corner Society: The Social Structure of an Italian Slum.* Chicago: University of Chicago Press, 1943.

Worrall, John L., and Jennifer L. Moore. *Criminal Law and Procedure.* Upper Saddle River, NJ: Pearson, 2014.

Chapter 2, Public Opinion, the News Media, and the Crime Problem

Applegate, B. K., R. K. Davis, and F. T. Cullen. "Reconsidering Child Saving: The Extent and Correlates of Public Support for Excluding Youths from the Juvenile Court." *Crime & Delinquency* 55 (2009): 51–77.

Barkan, Steven E., and Steven F. Cohn. "Why Whites Favor Spending More Money to Fight Crime: The Role of Racial Prejudice." *Social Problems* 52 (2005): 300–314.

Beckett, Katherine. *Making Crime Pay: Law and Order in Contemporary American Politics.* New York: Oxford University Press, 1997.

Bjornstrom, Eileen E. S., Robert L. Kaufman, Ruth D. Peterson, et al. "Race and Ethnic Representations of Lawbreakers and Victims in Crime News: A National Study of Television Coverage." *Social Problems* 57 (2010): 269–293.

Blumstein, Alfred, and Jacqueline Cohen. "Sentencing of Convicted Offenders: An Analysis of the Public's View." *Law and Society Review* 14 (1980): 223–261.

Bohm, Robert M. *Deathquest: An Introduction to the Theory and Practice of Capital Punishment in the United States.* Cincinnati: Anderson Publishing Company, 2012.

Cohn, D'Vera, Paul Taylor, Mark Hugo Lopez, et al. "Gun Homicide Rate Down 49% Since 1993 Peak; Public Unaware." Washington, DC: Pew Research Center, 2013.

Cose, Ellis. "Turning Victims into Saints: Journalists Cannot Resist Recasting Crime into a Shopworn Morality Tale." *Times,* January 22, 1990: 19.

Dempsey, John S., and Linda S. Forst. *An Introduction to Policing.* Belmont, CA: Cengage Learning, 2014.

Domhoff, G. William. *Who Rules America: Challenges to Corporate and Class Dominance.* New York: McGraw Hill, 2014.

Dorfman, Lori, and Vincent Schiraldi. *Off Balance: Youth, Race and Crime in the News.* Washington, DC: Building Blocks for Youth, 2001.

Dye, Thomas R. *Understanding Public Policy*. Upper Saddle River, NJ: Prentice Hall, 2013.

Egelko, Bob. "Public Opinion Had Role in Court Ruling on Retarded." *San Francisco Chronicle*, June 30, 2002:A6.

Ehrenreich, Barbara, and Deirdre English. *For Her Own Good: Two Centuries of the Experts' Advice to Women*. New York: Anchor Books, 2005.

Eschholz, Sarah. "Racial Composition of Television Offenders and Viewers' Fear of Crime." *Critical Criminology* 11 (2002): 41–60.

Eschholz, Sarah, Ted Chiricos, and Marc Gertz. "Television and Fear of Crime: Program Types, Audience Traits, and the Mediating Effect of Perceived Neighborhood Racial Composition." *Social Problems* 50 (2003): 395–415.

Federal Bureau of Investigation. *Crime in the United States, 2011*. Washington, DC: Federal Bureau of Investigation, 2012.

Feld, Barry C. "The Politics of Race and Juvenile Justice: The "Due Process Revolution" and the Conservative Reaction." *Justice Quarterly* 20 (2003): 765–800.

Fishman, Mark. "Crime Waves as Ideology." *Social Problems* 25 (1978): 531–543.

Fogg, Ally. "Crime Is Falling. Now Let's Reduce the Fear of Crime." *Guardian*, April 24, 2013. http://web.ebscohost.com.prxy4.ursus.maine.edu/ehost/detail?vid=8&sid=20b24508-ed20-4b4e-9ba9-76e15ab706ff%40sessionmgr112&hid=126&bdata=JnNpdGU9ZWhvc3QtbGl2ZQ%3d%3d#db=cja&AN=85395936.

Franiuk, Renae, Jennifer Seefelt, and Joseph Vandello. "Prevalence of Rape Myths in Headlines and Their Effects on Attitudes Toward Rape." *Sex Roles* 58 (2008): 790–801.

Frankfurter, Felix, and Roscoe Pound. *Criminal Justice in Cleveland*. Cleveland: The Cleveland Foundation, 1922.

Gabbidon, Shaun L., and George E. Higgins. "The Role of Race/Ethnicity and Race Relations on Public Opinion Related to the Treatment of Blacks by the Police." *Police Quarterly* 12 (2009): 102–115.

Gau, Jacinta M., and Rod K. Brunson. "Procedural Justice and Order Maintenance Policing: A Study of Inner-city Young Men's Perceptions of Police Legitimacy." *JQ: Justice Quarterly* 27 (2010): 255–279.

Giblin, Matthew J., and Amber D. Dillon. "Public Perceptions in the Last Frontier: Alaska Native Satisfaction with the Police." *Journal of Ethnicity in Criminal Justice* 7 (2009): 107–120.

Gilliam, F. D., and S. Iyengar. "Prime Suspects: The Influence of Local Television News on the Viewing Public." *American Journal of Political Science* 44 (2000): 560–573.

Glassner, Barry. *The Culture of Fear: Why Americans Are Afraid of the Wrong Things*. New York: Basic Books, 2010.

Higgins, George E., Scott E. Wolfe, Margaret Mahoney, et al. "Race, Ethnicity, and Experience: Modeling the Public's Perceptions of Justice, Satisfaction, and Attitude Toward the Courts." *Journal of Ethnicity in Criminal Justice* 7 (2009): 293–310.

Huddy, Leonie and Stanley Feldman. 2009. "On Assessing the Political Effects of Racial Prejudice." *Annual Review of Political Science* 12: 423–447.

Hughes, Patricia Paulsen, David Marshall, and Claudine Sherrill. "Multidimensional Analysis of Fear and Confidence of University Women Relating to Crimes and Dangerous Situations." *Journal of Interpersonal Violence* 18 (2003): 33–49.

Jackson, Derrick Z. "Politicians' Crime Rhetoric." In *The Boston Globe*, 15. Boston, 1994. Newspaper article from October 21.

Jenkins, Philip. "Myth and Murder: The Serial Killer Panic of 1983–85." *Criminal Justice Research Bulletin* 3 (1988): 1–7.

Johnson, Devon. "Racial Prejudice, Perceived Injustice, and the Black-White Gap in Punitive Attitudes." *Journal of Criminal Justice* 36 (2008): 198–206.

Johnson, Devon, and Joseph B. Kuhns. "Striking Out: Race and Support for Police Use of Force." *JQ: Justice Quarterly* 26 (2009): 592–623.

Kappeler, Victor E., and Gary W. Potter. *The Mythology of Crime and Criminal Justice*. Prospect Heights, IL: Waveland Press, 2005.

Kristof, Nicholas D. "Is It Ever OK to Name Rape Victims?"*New York Times*, February 4, 2010. http://kristof.blogs.nytimes.com/2010/02/04/is-it-ever-ok-to-name-rape-victims/?scp=1&sq=naming%20rape%20victims&st=cse.

Kurtz, Howard. "The Crime Spree on Network News." *Washington Post*, August 12, 1997:D1.

Lindsey, Robert. "Officials Cite a Rise in Killers Who Roam US for Victims." *New York Times*, 1984: 1.

Lundman, Richard J. "The Newsworthiness and Selection Bias in News About Murder: Comparative and Relative Effects of Novelty and Race and Gender Typifications on Newspaper Coverage of Homicide." *Sociological Forum* 18 (2003): 357–386.

Maguire, Kathleen. "Sourcebook of Criminal Justice Statistics." 2013. Available at http://www.albany.edu/sourcebook/.

Meadows, Robert J. *Understanding Violence and Victimization*. Upper Saddle River, NJ: Prentice Hall, 2014.

Melde, Chris. "Lifestyle, Rational Choice, and Adolescent Fear: A Test of a Risk-Assessment Framework." *Criminology* 47 (2009): 781–812.

Meyers, Marian. *News Coverage of Violence Against Women*. Newbury Park, CA: Sage Publications, 1996.

Mokdad, Ali H., James S. Marks, Donna F. Stroup, et al. "Actual Causes of Death in the United States, 2000." *Journal of the American Medical Association* 291 (2004): 1238–1245.

Musto, David F. *"Drugs in America: A Documentary History."* New York: New York University Press, 2002.

Myrstol, B. "Making the Grade? Public Evaluation of Police Performance in Alaska." *Alaska Justice Forum* 22 (2005): 5–10.

Neubauer, David W., and Henry F. Fradella. *America's Courts and the Criminal Justice System*. Belmont, CA: Wadsworth, 2014.

Pepinsky, Harold E., and Paul Jesilow. *Myths that Cause Crime*. Cabin John, MD: Seven Locks Press, 1984.

Pew Research Center. *The State of the News Media 2013*. Washington, DC: Pew Research Center, 2013.

Pickett, Justin T., T. E. D. Chiricos, Kristin M. Golden, et al. "Reconsidering the Relationship Between Perceived Neighborhood Racial Composition and Whites' Perceptions of Victimization Risk: Do Racial Stereotypes Matter?" *Criminology* 50 (2012): 145–186.

Pickett, Justin T., and Ted Chiricos. "Controlling Other People's Children: Racialized Views of Delinquency and Whites' Punitive Attitudes Toward Juvenile Offenders." *Criminology* 50 (2012): 673–710.

Pritchard, David, and Dan Berkowitz. "The Limits of Agenda-Setting: The Press and Political Responses to Crime in the United States, 1950–1980." *International Journal of Public Opinion Research* 5 (1993): 86–91.

Rader, Nicole E., Jeralynn S. Cossman, and Jeremy R. Porter. "Fear of Crime and Vulnerability: Using a National Sample of Americans to Examine Two Competing Paradigms." *Journal of Criminal Justice* 40 (2012): 134–141.

Ramirez, Mark D. "Punitive Sentiment." *Criminology* 51 (2013): 329–364.

Reiman, Jeffrey, and Paul Leighton. *The Rich Get Richer and the Poor Get Prison: Ideology, Class, and Criminal Justice*. Upper Saddle River, NJ: Prentice Hall, 2013.

Reisig, Michael D., and Roger B. Parks. "Experience, Quality of Life, and Neighborhood Context: A Hierarchical Analysis of Satisfaction with Police." *Justice Quarterly* 17 (2000): 607–630.

Roth, Michael P. *Crime and Punishment: A History of the Criminal Justice System*. Belmont, CA: Wadsworth, 2011.

Sellin, Thorsten, and Marvin E. Wolfgang. *The Measurement of Delinquency*. New York: Wiley, 1964.

Sharp, Elaine B., and Paul E. Johnson. "Accounting for Variation in Distrust of Local Police." *JQ: Justice Quarterly* 26 (2009): 157–182.

Shelden, Randall G. *Our Punitive Society: Race, Class, Gender and Punishment in America*. Long Grove, IL: Waveland Press, 2010.

Simon, David R. *Elite Deviance*. Upper Saddle River, NJ: Pearson, 2012.

Soss, Joe, Laura Langbein, and Alan R. Metelko. "Why Do White Americans Support the Death Penalty?" *The Journal of Politics* 65 (2003): 397–421.

Surette, Ray. *Media, Crime, and Criminal Justice: Images, Realities, and Policies*. Belmont, CA: Wadsworth Publishing Co, 2011.

Swatt, Marc L., Sean P. Varano, Craig D. Uchida, et al. "Fear of Crime, Incivilities, and Collective Efficacy in Four Miami Neighborhoods." *Journal of Criminal Justice* 41 (2013): 1–11.

Thomas, William I., and Dorothy Swaine Thomas. *The Child in America: Behavior Problems and Programs*. New York: Knopf, 1928.

Tucker, Cynthia. "Why Don't We Name Victims of Rape?" *Atlanta Journal-Constitution*, 2011. http://blogs.ajc.com/cynthia-tucker/2011/07/13/why-dont-we-name-victims-of-rape/.

Unnever, James D., and Francis T. Cullen. "Christian Fundamentalism and Support for Capital Punishment." *Journal of Research in Crime and Delinquency* 43 (2006): 169–197.

———."White Perceptions of Whether African-Americans and Hispanics Are Prone to Violence and Support for the Death Penalty." *Journal of Research in Crime & Delinquency* 49 (2012): 519–544.

Unnever, James D., Francis T. Cullen, and Cheryl L. Jonson. "Race, Racism, and Support for Capital Punishment." In *Crime and Justice: A Review of Research*, edited by M. Tonry, 45–96. Chicago: University of Chicago Press, 2008.

Unnever, James D., Shaun L. Gabbidon, and George E. Higgins. "The Election of Barack Obama and Perceptions of Criminal Injustice." *JQ: Justice Quarterly* 28 (2011): 23–45.

Vogel, Brenda L., and James W. Meeker. "Perceptions of Crime Seriousness in Eight African-American Communities: The Influence of Individual, Environmental, and Crime-Based Factors." *Justice Quarterly* 18 (2001): 301–321.

Walker, Samuel. *Sense and Nonsense About Crime, Drugs, and Communities: A Policy Guide*. Belmont, CA: Wadsworth Publishing Company, 2011.

Warr, Mark. "Public Perceptions of and Reactions to Crime." In *Criminology: A Contemporary Handbook*, edited by J. F. Sheley, 13–31. Belmont, CA: Wadsworth Publishing Company, 2000.

———."Safe at Home." *Contexts* 8(3) 2009: 46–51.

Weitzer, Ronald. "The Puzzling Neglect of Hispanic Americans in Research on Police–Citizen Relations." *Ethnic and Racial Studies* 2013. DOI:10.1080/01419 870.2013.790984.

Wildstein, Eric. "Waterville Neighbors React to Home Invasion Murder." *WNWO*, May 19, 2013. http://www.northwestohio.com/news/story .aspx?id=899593#.UZrAXj_LUlY.

Williams, Scott. "ABC Special Takes the Scare Out of Life." *The Boston Globe* (1994): 72.

Wolfgang, Marvin E., Robert M. Figlio, Paul E. Tracy, et al. *The National Survey of Crime Severity*. Washington, DC: U.S. Department of Justice, 1985.

Wright, Kevin N. *The Great American Crime Myth*. Westport, CT: Greenwood Press, 1985.

Yun, Ilhong, Glen Kercher, and Sam Swindell. "Fear of Crime Among Chinese Immigrants." *Journal of Ethnicity in Criminal Justice* 8 (2010): 71–90.

Chapter 3, The Measurement and Patterning of Criminal Behavior

Adler, Freda. *Sisters in Crime: The Rise of the New Female Criminal*. New York: McGraw-Hill, 1975.

Agnew, Robert. "Dire Forecast: A Theoretical Model of the Impact of Climate Change on Crime." *Theoretical Criminology* 16 (2012): 21–42.

Baumer, Eric P., and Janet L. Lauritsen. "Reporting Crime to the Police, 1973–2005: A Multivariate Analysis of Long-Term Trends in the National Crime Survey (NCS) and National Crime Victimization Survey (NCVS)." *Criminology* 48 (2010): 131–185.

Bennett, Richard R. "Comparative Criminological and Criminal Justice Research and the Data that Drive Them." *International Journal of Comparative and Applied Criminal Justice* 33 (2009): 171–192.

Benson, Michael L. *Crime and the Life Course: An Introduction*, 2nd ed. New York: Routledge, 2013.

Biderman, Albert D., and Albert J. Reiss, Jr. "On Exploring the 'Dark Figure' of Crime." *Annals of the American Academy of Political and Social Science* 374 (1967): 1–15.

Bjerk, David. "Measuring the Relationship Between Youth Criminal Participation and Household Economic Resources." *Journal of Quantitative Criminology* 23 (2007): 23–39.

Blumstein, Alfred, and Joel Wallman. "The Crime Drop in America." Cambridge: Cambridge University Press, 2006.

Bonczar, Thomas P. *Prevalence of Imprisonment in the U.S. Population, 1974–2001*. Washington, DC: Bureau of Justice Statistics, U.S. Department of Justice, 2003.

Braithwaite, John. "The Myth of Social Class and Crime Reconsidered." *American Sociological Review* 46 (1981): 36–47.

Carbone-Lopez, Kristin, and Janet Lauritsen. "Seasonal Variation in Violent Victimization: Opportunity and the Annual Rhythm of the School Calendar." *Journal of Quantitative Criminology* 29 (2013): 399–422.

Cooper, Alexia, and Erica Smith. *Homicide Trends in the United States, 1980–2008*. Washington, DC: Bureau of Justice Statistics, U.S. Department of Justice, 2011.

Deming, Richard. *Women: The New Criminals*. Nashville: Thomas Nelson, 1977.

Drum, Kevin. "America's Real Criminal Element: Lead." *Mother Jones*, January–February, 2013. http://www.motherjones.com/environment/2013/01/lead-crime-link-gasoline.

Farrington, David P., Rolf Loeber, and Magda Stouthamer-Loeber. "How Can the Relationship Between Race and Violence be Explained?" In *Violent Crime: Assessing Race and Ethnic Differences*, edited by D. F. Hawkins, 213–237. Cambridge: Cambridge University Press, 2003.

Fazlollah, Mark, Michael Matza, Craig R. McCoy, et al. "Women Victimized Twice in Police Game of Numbers." *The Philadelphia Inquirer* (1999):A1.

Federal Bureau of Investigation. *Crime in the United States, 2011*. Washington, DC: Federal Bureau of Investigation, 2012.

Ferdinand, Theodore. "Demographic Shifts and Criminality: An Inquiry." *British Journal of Criminology* 10 (1970): 169–175.

Gabbidon, Shaun L., and Helen Taylor Greene. *Race and Crime*. Thousand Oaks, CA: Sage Publications, 2013.

Garbarino, James. *See Jane Hit: Why Girls Are Growing More Violent and What We Can Do About It*. New York: Penguin, 2006.

Goldberger, Arthur S., and Richard Rosenfeld. "Understanding Crime Trends: Workshop Report." Washington, DC: National Academies Press, 2008.

Greenberg, David F. "Studying New York City's Crime Decline: Methodological Issues." *Justice Quarterly* (2013). DOI:10.1080/07418825.2012.752026.

Griffin, Marie. "Feminist Criminology: Beyond the Slaying of Demons." In *Criminology and Public Policy: Putting Theory to Work*, edited by H. D. Barlow and S. H. Decker, 215–232. Philadelphia: Temple University Press, 2010.

Hagan, John. "The Poverty of a Classless Criminology—The American Society of Criminology 1991 Presidential Address." *Criminology* 30 (1992): 1–19.

Hart, Ariel. "Report Finds Atlanta Police Cut Figures on Crimes." *New York Times*, February 21, 2004:A1.

Haynie, Dana L., Harald E. Weiss, and Alex Piquero. "Race, the Economic Maturity Gap, and Criminal Offending in Young Adulthood." *JQ: Justice Quarterly* 25 (2008): 595–622.

Hindelang, Michael J., Travis Hirschi, and Joseph Weis. "Correlates of Delinquency: The Illusion of Discrepancy Between Self-Report and Official Measures." *American Sociological Review* 44 (1979): 995–1014.

Johnson, David T. "Crime and Punishment in Contemporary Japan." *Crime and Justice: A Review of Research* 36 (2007): 371–423.

Kingkade, Tyler. "ECSU Chancellor Willie Gilchrist Resigns Amid State Investigation Into Campus Crime Reporting." *The Huffington Post*, May 21, 2013. http://www.huffingtonpost.com/2013/05/21/ecsu-chancellor-willie-gilchrist_n_3308484.html.

Koppel, Herbert. *Lifetime Likelihood of Victimization*. Washington, DC: U.S. Department of Justice, Bureau of Justice Statistics, 1987.

Krohn, Marvin D., Alan J. Lizotte, Matthew D. Phillips, et al. "Explaining Systematic Bias in Self-Reported Measures: Factors that Affect the Under- and Over-Reporting of Self-Reported Arrests." *Justice Quarterly* 30 (2013): 501–528.

LaFree, Gary, and Katheryn K. Russell. "The Argument for Studying Race and Crime." *Journal of Criminal Justice Education* 4 (1993): 273–289.

Lanier, Christina, and Lin Huff-Corzine. 2006. "American Indian Homicide: A County-Level Analysis Utilizing Social Disorganization Theory." *Homicide Studies* 10 (1993): 181–194.

Lauritsen, Janet L., Karen Heimer, and James P. Lynch. "Trends in the Gender Gap in Violent Offending: New Evidence from the National Crime Victimization Survey." *Criminology* 47 (2009): 361–399.

Lindsey, Linda L. *Gender Roles: A Sociological Perspective*. Upper Saddle River, NJ: Prentice Hall, 2011.

Lombroso, Cesare. *The Female Offender*. New York: Appleton, 1920 (1903).

Lynch, James P., and Lynn A. Addington. "Understanding Crime Statistics: Revisiting the Divergence of the NCVS and the UCR." New York: Cambridge University Press, 2007.

MacDonald, John, John Hipp, and Charlotte Gill. "The Effects of Immigrant Concentration on Changes in Neighborhood Crime Rates." *Journal of Quantitative Criminology* 29 (2013): 191–215.

Males, Mike, and Meda Chesney-Lind. "The Myth of Mean Girls." *New York Times*, April 1, 2010:A23.

Mares, Dennis. "Climate Change and Crime: Monthly Temperature and Precipitation Anomalies and Crime Rates in St. Louis, MO 1990–2009." *Crime, Law and Social Change* 59 (2013): 185–208.

McCarthy, Bill, Diane Felmlee, and John Hagan. "Girl Friends Are Better: Gender, Friends, and Crime Among School and Street Youth." *Criminology* 42 (2004): 805–835.

McNulty, Thomas L., and Paul E. Bellair. "Explaining Racial and Ethnic Differences in Adolescent Violence: Structural Disadvantage, Family Well-Being, and Social Capital." *Justice Quarterly* 20 (2003a): 1–31.

———."Explaining Racial and Ethnic Differences in Serious Adolescent Violent Behavior." *Criminology* 41 (2003b): 709–748.

Messner, Steven F., and Richard Rosenfeld. *Crime and the American Dream*. Belmont, CA: Wadsworth Publishing Company, 2013.

Miller, H. V., W. G. Jennings, and L. L. Alvarez-Rivera. "Self-Control, Attachment, and Deviance Among Hispanic Adolescents." *Journal of Criminal Justice* 37 (2009): 77–84.

Miller, Holly Ventura. "Correlates of Delinquency and Victimization in a Sample of Hispanic Youth." *International Criminal Justice Review (Sage Publications)* 22 (2012): 153–170.

Milwaukee Sentinel Journal. 2013. "Journal Sentinel crime data probe wins Mollenhoff Award." May 14, 2013. http://www.jsonline.com/watchdog/watchdogreports/journal-sentinel-crime-data-probe-wins-mollenhoff-award-for-investigative-reporting-c19uoto-207399601.html#ixzz2m4rQ1Nfz.

Morris, Nancy A., and Lee Ann Slocum. "The Validity of Self-Reported Prevalence, Frequency, and Timing of Arrest: An Evaluation of Data Using a Life Event Calendar." *Journal of Research in Crime & Delinquency* 47 (2010): 210–240.

Moynihan, Daniel P. *The Negro Family: The Case for National Action*. Washington, DC: U.S. Department of Labor, 1965.

Ouimet, Marc. "A World of Homicides: The Effect of Economic Development, Income Inequality, and Excess Infant Mortality on the Homicide Rate for 165 Countries in 2010." *Homicide Studies* 16 (2012): 238–258.

Painter-Davis, Noah. "Structural Disadvantage and American Indian Homicide and Robbery Offending." *Homicide Studies* 16 (2012): 219–237.

Paschall, Mallie J., Miriam L. Ornstein, and Robert L. Flewelling. "African American Male Adolescents' Involvement in the Criminal Justice System: The Criterion Validity of Self-Report Measures in a Prospective Study." *Journal of Research in Crime and Delinquency* 38 (2001): 174–187.

Peterson, Ruth D. "The Central Place of Race in Crime and Justice: The American Society of Criminology's 2011 Sutherland Address." *Criminology* 50 (2012): 303–328.

Pollak, Otto. *The Criminality of Women*. Philadelphia, PA: University of Pennsylvania Press, 1950.

Poston, Ben. "Crimes Underreported by Police Include Robbery, Rape." *Milwaukee Journal Sentinel* (2012). http://www.jsonline.com/watchdog/watchdogreports/crimes-underreported-by-police-include-robbery-rape-e567cu0-167448105.html.

Press, Eyal. "Do Immigrants Make Us Safer?" *The New York Times Magazine*, December 3, 2006: 20+.

Rand, Michael R., and Jayne E. Robinson. *Criminal Victimization in the United States, 2008—Statistical Tables*. Washington, DC: Bureau of Justice Statistics, U.S. Department of Justice, 2011.

Reiman, Jeffrey, and Paul Leighton. *The Rich Get Richer and the Poor Get Prison: Ideology, Class, and Criminal Justice*. Upper Saddle River, NJ: Prentice Hall, 2013.

Renzetti, Claire. *Feminist Criminology*. New York: Routledge, 2013.

Rosenfeld, Richard, Robert Fornango, and Andres F. Rengifo. "The Impact of Order-Maintenance Policing on New York City Homicide and Robbery Rates: 1988–2001." *Criminology* 45 (2007): 355–384.

Rumbaut, Rubén G., and Walter A. Ewing. *The Myth of Immigrant Criminality and the Paradox of Assimilation: Incarceration Rates Among Native and Foreign-born Men*. Washington, DC: American Immigration Law Foundation, 2007.

Russell, Katheryn. *The Color of Crime*. New York: New York University Press, 2009.

Sampson, Robert J. "Rethinking Crime and Immigration." *Contexts* 7 (2008): 28–33.

Sander, Libby. "Yale U. Is Fined $165,000 Under Crime-Reporting Law." *Chronicle of Higher Education*, May 16 2013. http://chronicle.com/article/Yale-U-Is-Fined-165000/139343/.

Shapiro, Joseph. "Campus Rape Victims: A Struggle for Justice." *npr.org* February 24, 2010. http://www.npr.org/templates/story/story.php?storyId=124001493.

Short, James F., Jr., and F. Ivan Nye. "Reported Behavior as a Criterion of Deviant Behavior." *Social Problems* 5 (1957): 207–213.

Simon, Rita James. *Women and Crime*. Lexington, MA: Lexington Books, 1975.

Stark, Rodney. "Deviant Places: A Theory of the Ecology of Crime." *Criminology* 25 (1987): 893–911.

Steffensmeier, Darrell, and Emilie Allan. "Looking for Patterns: Gender, Age, and Crime." In *Criminology: A Contemporary Handbook*, edited by J. F. Sheley, 85–127. Belmont, CA: Wadsworth, 2000.

Steffensmeier, Darrell, Jeffery T. Ulmer, B. E. N. Feldmeyer, et al. "Scope and Conceptual Issues in Testing the Race-Crime Invariance Thesis: Black, White, and Hispanic Comparisons." *Criminology* 48 (2010): 1133–1169.

Stevens, Tia, Merry Morash, and Meda Chesney-Lind. "Are Girls Getting Tougher, or Are We Tougher on Girls? Probability of Arrest and Juvenile Court Oversight in 1980 and 2000." *JQ: Justice Quarterly* 28 (2011): 719–744.

Tittle, Charles R., Wayne J. Villemez, and Douglas A. Smith. "The Myth of Social Class and Criminality: An Empirical Assessment of the Empirical Evidence." *American Sociological Review* 43 (1978): 643–656.

Truman, Jennifer L., and Michael Planty. *Criminal Victimization, 2011*. Washington, DC: Bureau of Justice Statistics, U.S. Department of Justice, 2012.

Unnever, James D., and Shaun L. Gabbidon. *A Theory of African American Offending: Race, Racism, and Crime*. New York: Routledge, 2011.

van Dijk, J. J. M. "The International Crime Victims Survey: Latest Results and Prospects." *Newsletter European Society of Criminology* 11 (2012): 24–33.

van Dijk, Jan, John van Kesteren, and Paul Smit. *Criminal Victimisation in International Perspective: Key Findings from the 2004–2005 ICVS and EU ICS*. Devon, England: Willan Publishing, 2008.

Vélez, María B. "Toward an Understanding of the Lower Rates of Homicide in Latino versus Black Neighborhoods: A Look at Chicago." In *The Many Colors of Crime: Inequalities of Race, Ethnicity, and Crime in America*, edited by R. D. Peterson, L. J. Krivo, and J. Hagan, 91–107. New York: New York University Press, 2006.

Visher, Christy A. "Career Offenders and Crime Control." In *Criminology: A Contemporary Handbook*, edited by J. F. Sheley, 601–619. Belmont, CA: Wadsworth, 2000.

Walker, Samuel, Cassia Spohn, and Miriam DeLone. *The Color of Justice: Race, Ethnicity, and Crime in America*. Belmont, CA: Wadsworth Publishing Company, 2012.

Warner, Barbara D., and Brandi Wilson Coomer. "Neighborhood Drug Arrest Rates: Are They a Meaningful Indicator of Drug Activity? A Research Note." *Journal of Research in Crime and Delinquency* 40 (2003): 123–138.

Warr, Mark. *Companions in Crime: The Social Aspects of Criminal Conduct*. New York: Cambridge University Press, 2002.

Wolfgang, Marvin E., and Franco Ferracuti. *The Subculture of Violence*. London: Social Science Paperbacks, 1967.

Wright, Bradley R. Entner, and C. Wesley Younts. "Reconsidering the Relationship between Race and Crime: Positive and Negative Predictors of Crime among African American Youth." *Journal of Research in Crime and Delinquency* 46 (2009): 327–352.

Young, Vernetta. "Demythologizing the 'Criminalblackman': The Carnival Mirror." In *The Many Colors of Crime; Inequalities of Race, Ethnicity, and Crime in America*, edited by R. D. Peterson, L. J. Krivo, and J. Hagan, 54–66. New York: New York University Press, 2006.

Zatz, Marjorie S., and Hilary Smith. "Immigration, Crime, and Victimization: Rhetoric and Reality." *Annual Review of Law & Social Science* 8 (2012): 141–159.

Zimring, Franklin E. *The Great American Crime Decline*. New York: Oxford University Press, 2006.

Chapter 4, Victims and Victimization

Agnew, Robert. "Experienced, Vicarious, and Anticipated Strain: An Exploratory Study on Physical Victimization and Delinquency." *Justice Quarterly* 19 (2002): 603–632.

Amir, Menachem. *Patterns in Forcible Rape*. Chicago: University of Chicago Press, 1971.

Baum, Katrina, and Patsy Klaus. *Violent Victimization of College Students, 1995–2002*. Washington, DC: Bureau of Justice Statistics, U.S. Department of Justice, 2005.

Baumer, Eric P., Steven F. Messner, and Richard B. Felson. "The Role of Victim Characteristics in the Disposition of Murder Cases." *Justice Quarterly* 17 (2000): 281–307.

Berg, Mark T., Eric A. Stewart, Christopher J. Schreck, et al. "The Victim-Offender Overlap in Context: Examining the Role of Neighborhood Street Culture." *Criminology* 50 (2012): 359–390.

Braga, Anthony A. "High Crime Places, Times, and Offenders." In *Oxford Handbook of Crime Prevention*, edited by B. C. Welsh and D. P. Farrington, 316–336. New York: Oxford University Press, 2012.

Brown, Amy L., Maria Testa, and Terri L. Messman-Moore. "Psychological Consequences of Sexual Victimization Resulting from Force, Incapacitation, or Verbal Coercion." *Violence Against Women* 15 (2009): 898–919.

Bryden, D. P. and S. Lengnick. "Rape in the Cirminal Justice System." *Journal of Criminal Law and Criminology* 87 (1997): 1194–1384.

Bureau of Justice Statistics. "Generated using the NCVS Victimization Analysis Tool". 2013. Available at www.bjs.gov.

Coleman, James William. *The Criminal Elite: Understanding White-Collar Crime*. New York: Worth Publishers, 2006.

Cooper, Alexia and Erica Smith. *Homicide Trends in the United States, 1980–2008*. Washington, DC: Bureau of Justice Statistics, U.S. Department of Justice, 2011.

Copes, Heith, Kent R. Kerley, Karen A. Mason, et al. "Reporting Behavior of Fraud Victims and Black's Theory of Law: An Empirical Assessment." *Justice Quarterly* 18 (2001): 343–363.

Coston, Charisse Tia Maria. "The Influence of Race in Urban Homeless Females' Fear of Crime." *Justice Quarterly* 9 (1992): 721–729.

Fagan, Abigail A., and Paul Mazerolle. "Repeat Offending and Repeat Victimization: Assessing Similarities and Differences in Psychosocial Risk Factors." *Crime & Delinquency* 57 (2011): 732–755.

Federal Bureau of Investigation. 2012. *Crime in the United States, 2011*. Washington, DC: Federal Bureau of Investigation.

Fisher, Bonnie S., Francis T. Cullen, and Michael G. Turner. *The Sexual Victimization of College Women*. Washington, DC: National Institute of Justice and Bureau of Justice Statistics, U.S. Department of Justice, 2000.

Fitzpatrick, Kevin M., Mark E. La Gory, and Ferris J. Ritchey. "Criminal Victimization Among the Homeless." *Justice Quarterly* 10 (1993): 353–368.

Franklin, Cortney A., Travis W. Franklin, Matt R. Nobles, et al. "Assessing the Effect of Routine Activity Theory and Self-Control on Property, Personal, and Sexual Assault Victimization." *Criminal Justice & Behavior* 39 (2012): 1296–1315.

Haynie, Dana L., and Alex R. Piquero. "Pubertal Development and Physical Victimization in Adolescence." *Journal of Research in Crime and Delinquency* 43 (2006): 3–35.

Hines, Denise A., Jessica L. Armstrong, Kathleen Palm Reed, et al. "Gender Differences in Sexual Assault Victimization Among College Students." *Violence & Victims* 27 (2012): 922–940.

Hipp, John R. "A Dynamic View of Neighborhoods: The Reciprocal Relationship Between Crime and Neighborhood Structural Characteristics." *Social Problems* 57 (2010): 205–230.

Hollis, Meghan E., Marcus Felson, and Brandon C. Welsh. "The Capable Guardian in Routine Activities Theory: A Theoretical and Conceptual Reappraisal." *Crime Prevention & Community Safety* 15 (2013): 65–79.

Huey, Laura. *Invisible Victims: Homelessness and the Growing Security Gap.* Toronto: Toronto University Press, 2012.

Karmen, Andrew. *Crime Victims: An Introduction to Victimology.* Belmont, CA: Wadsworth, 1990.

———. *Crime Victims: An Introduction to Victimology.* Belmont, CA: Wadsworth Publishing Company, 2013.

Koppel, Herbert. 1987. *Lifetime Likelihood of Victimization.* Washington, D.C.: U.S. Department of Justice, Bureau of Justice Statistics, 1987.

Lurigio, Arthur J., and Patricia A. Resick. "Healing the Psychological Wounds of Criminal Victimization: Predicting Postcrime Distress and Recovery." In *Victims of Crime: Problems, Policies, and Programs,* edited by A. L. Lurigio, W. G. Skogan, and R. C. Davis, 50–68. Newbury Park, CA: Sage Publications, 1990.

Macmillan, Ross. "Adolescent Victimization and Income Deficits in Adulthood: Rethinking the Costs of Criminal Violence from a Life-Course Perspective." *Criminology* 38 (2000): 553–587.

Malan, Stefanie, Sian Hemmings, Martin Kidd, et al. "Investigation of Telomere Length and Psychological Stress in Rape Victims." *Depression & Anxiety (1091–4269)* 28 (2011): 1081–1085.

Marcum, Catherine D. "Routine Activity Theory: An Assessment of a Classical Theory." In *Criminological Theory: Readings and Retrospectives,* edited by H. Copes and V. Topalli, 43–55. New York: McGraw-Hill, 2010.

McIntyre, Jared Kean, and Cathy Spatz Widom. "Childhood Victimization and Crime Victimization." *Journal of Interpersonal Violence* 26 (2011): 640–663.

Meier, Robert F., and Terance D. Miethe. "Understanding Theories of Criminal Victimization." In *Crime and Justice: A Review of Research,* edited by M. Tonry, 459–499. Chicago: University of Chicago Press, 1993.

Menard, Scott. "The 'Normality' of Repeat Victimization from Adolescence Through Early Adulthood." *Justice Quarterly* 17 (2000): 543–574.

———. *Short- and Long-Term Consequences of Adolescent Victimization,* vol. February. Washington, DC: Office of Juvenile Justice and Delinquency Prevention, 2002.

Miethe, Terance D., and Robert F. Meier. "Opportunity, Choice, and Criminal Victimization: A Test of a Theoretical Model." *Journal of Research in Crime and Delinquency* 27 (1990): 243–266.

Miller, Ted, Marc Cohen, and Brian Wiersema. *Victim Costs and Consequences: A New Look.* Washington, DC: National Institute of Justice, U.S. Department of Justice, 1996.

Morgan, Kathryn. "Victims, Punishment, and Parole: The Effect of Victim Participation on Parole Hearings." *Criminology & Public Policy* 4 (2005): 333–360.

Noyes, Dan. "Millions Meant for California Crime Victims Goes Unpaid." *KGO_TV,* May 22, 2013. http://abclocal.go.com/kgo/story?section=news/iteam&id=9112950.

Paternoster, Ray, and Jerome Deise. "A Heavy Thumb on the Scale: The Effect of Victim Impact Evidence on Capital Decision Making." *Criminology* 49 (2011): 129–161.

Patterson, Debra. "The Linkage Between Secondary Victimization by Law Enforcement and Rape Case Outcomes." *Journal of Interpersonal Violence* 26 (2011): 328–347.

Perron, Brian Edward, Ben Alexander-Eitzman, David F. Gillespie, et al. "Modeling the Mental Health Effects of Victimization Among Homeless Persons." *Social Science & Medicine* 67 (2008): 1475–1479.

Phillips, Scott. "Status Disparities in the Capital of Capital Punishment." *Law & Society Review* 43 (2009): 807–838.

Pridemore, William Alex, and Tony H. Grubesic. "Alcohol Outlets and Community Levels of Interpersonal Violence: Spatial Density, Outlet Type, and Seriousness of Assault." *Journal of Research in Crime & Delinquency* 50 (2013): 132–159.

Rand, Michael R., and Jayne E. Robinson. *Criminal Victimization in the United States, 2008—Statistical Tables.* Washington, DC: Bureau of Justice Statistics, U.S. Department of Justice, 2011.

Rebovich, D., and J. Layne. *The National Public Survey on White Collar Crime.* Morgantown, WV: National White Collar Crime Center, 2000.

Riggs, David S., and Dean G. Kilpatrick. "Families and Friends: Indirect Victimization by Crime." In *Victims of Crime: Problems, Policies, and Programs,* edited by A. J. Lurigio, W. G. Skogan, and R. C. Davis, 120–138. Newbury Park, CA: Sage Publications, 1990.

Roberts, Julian V. "Listening to the Crime Victim: Evaluating Victim Input at Sentencing and Parole." *Crime and Justice: A Review of Research* 39 (2009): 347–412.

Rojek, Dean G., James E. Coverdill, and Stuart W. Fors. "The Effect of Victim Impact Panels on DUI Rearrest Rates: A Five-Year Follow-Up." *Criminology* 41 (2003): 1319–1340.

Schreck, Christopher J., Melissa W. Burek, Eric A. Stewart, et al. "Distress and Violent Victimization Among Young Adolescents." *Journal of Research in Crime & Delinquency* 44 (2007): 381–405.

Schreck, Christopher J., Richard A. Wright, and J. Mitchell Miller. "A Study of Individual and Situational Antecedents of Violent Victimization." *Justice Quarterly* 19 (2002): 159–180.

Shover, Neal, Greer Litton Fox, and Michael Mills. "Long-Term Consequences of Victimization by White-Collar Crime." *Justice Quarterly* 11 (1994): 75–98.

Silver, Eric. "Mental Disorder and Violent Victimization: The Mediating Role of Involvement in Conflicted Relationships." *Criminology* 40 (2002): 191–212.

Spohn, Cassia, and David Holleran. "Prosecuting Sexual Assault: A Comparison of Charging Decisions in Sexual Assault Cases Involving Strangers, Acquaintances, and Intimate Partners." *Justice Quarterly* 18 (2001): 651–688.

Stewart, Eric A., Kirk W. Elifson, and Claire E. Sterk. "Integrating the General Theory of Crime into an Explanation of Violent Victimization Among Female Offenders." *Justice Quarterly* 21 (2004): 159–181.

Tasca, Melinda, Nancy Rodriguez, Cassia Spohn, et al. "Police Decision Making in Sexual Assault Cases: Predictors of Suspect Identification and Arrest." *Journal of Interpersonal Violence* 28 (2013): 1157–1177.

Topalli, Volkan, Richard Wright, and Robert Fornango. "Drug Dealers, Robbery and Retaliation: Vulnerability, Deterrence and the Contagion of Violence." *British Journal of Criminology* 42 (2002): 337–351.

Truman, Jennifer L., and Michael Planty. *Criminal Victimization, 2011.* Washington, DC: Bureau of Justice Statistics, U.S. Department of Justice, 2012.

Tyler, Kimberly A., Sarah J. Gervais, and M. Meghan Davidson. "The Relationship Between Victimization and Substance Use Among Homeless and Runaway Female Adolescents." *Journal of Interpersonal Violence* 28 (2013): 474–493.

Unnever, James D., Francis T. Cullen, and Bonnie S. Fisher. " 'A Liberal Is Someone Who Has Not Been Mugged': Criminal Victimization and Political Beliefs." *JQ: Justice Quarterly* 24 (2007): 309–334.

U.S. Census Bureau. 2012. *Statistical Abstract of the United States: 2012* (http://www.census.gov/compendia/statab/). Washington, DC: U.S. Government Printing Office.

van Dijk, J. J. M. "The International Crime Victims Survey: Latest Results and Prospects." *Newsletter European Society of Criminology* 11 (2012): 24–33.

van Dijk, Jan, John van Kesteren, and Paul Smit. *Criminal Victimisation in International Perspective: Key Findings from the 2004–2005 ICVS and EU ICS.* Devon, England: Willan Publishing, 2008.

Viano, Emilio C. "Victimology: A New Focus of Research and Practice." In *The Victimology Handbook: Research Findgins, Treatment, and Public Policy,* edited by E. C. Viano, xi–xxiii. New York: Garland Publishing, Inc., 1990.

Waller, Martha W., Bonita J. Iritani, Sharon L. Christ, et al. "Relationships Among Alcohol Outlet Density, Alcohol Use, and Intimate Partner Violence Victimization Among Young Women in the United States." *Journal of Interpersonal Violence* 27 (2012): 2062–2086.

Wenzel, Suzanne L., Barbara D. Leake, and Lillian Gelberg. "Risk Factors for Major Violence Among Homeless Women." *Journal of Interpersonal Violence* 16 (2001): 739–752.

Widom, Cathy Spatz, Sally Czaja, Helen W. Wilson, et al. "Do the Long-Term Consequences of Neglect Differ for Children of Different Races and Ethnic Backgrounds?" *Child Maltreatment* 18 (2013): 42–55.

Wolfgang, Marvin E. *Patterns in Criminal Homicide.* Philadelphia, PA: University of Pennsylvania Press, 1958.

Xie, Min, and David McDowall. "Escaping Crime: The Effects of Direct and Indirect Victimization on Moving." *Criminology* 46 (2008): 809–840.

Zaykowski, Heather, and Whitney D. Gunter. "Gender Differences in Victimization Risk: Exploring the Role of Deviant Lifestyles." *Violence & Victims* 28 (2013): 341–356.

Chapter 5, Classical and Neoclassical Perspectives

Akers, Ronald L., and Christine S. Sellers. *Criminological Theories: Introduction, Evaluation, and Application.* New York: Oxford University Press, 2013.

Apel, Robert, and Daniel S. Nagin. "General Deterrence: A Review of Recent Evidence " In *Crime and Public Policy,* edited by J. Q. Wilson and J. Petersilia, 411–436. New York: Oxford University Press, 2011.

Bales, William, and Alex Piquero. "Assessing the Impact of Imprisonment on Recidivism." *Journal of Experimental Criminology* 8 (2012): 71–101.

Beccaria, Cesare. *On Crimes and Punishment.* Translated by E. D. Ingraham. Philadelphia, PA: Philip H. Nicklin, 1819 (1764).

———."An Essay on Crimes and Punishments." In *Criminological Theory: Past to Present: Essential Readings,* edited by F. T. Cullen and R. Agnew, 23–25. Los Angeles: Roxbury Publishing Company, 2006 (1764).

Becker, Gary S. "Crime and Punishment: An Economic Approach." *Journal of Political Economy* 76 (1968): 169–217.

Bernard, Thomas J., Jeffrey B. Snipes, and Alexander L. Gerould. *Vold's Theoretical Criminology*. New York: Oxford University Press, 2009.

Bernasco, Wim, and Richard Block. "Where Offenders Choose to Attack: A Discrete Choice Model of Robberies in Chicago." *Criminology* 47 (2009): 93–130.

Braga, Anthony A., and David L. Weisburd. "The Effects of Focused Deterrence Strategies on Crime: A Systematic Review and Meta-Analysis of the Empirical Evidence." *Journal of Research in Crime & Delinquency* 49 (2012): 323–358.

Chambliss, William J. "Types of Deviance and the Effectiveness of Legal Sanctions." *Wisconsin Law Review* Summer (1967): 703–719.

Clarke, Ronald V., and Derek B. Cornish. "Modeling Offenders' Decisions: A Framework for Research and Policy." *Crime and Justice: A Review of Research* 6 (1985): 147–185.

———. "Rational Choice." In *Explaining Criminals and Crime*, edited by R. Paternoster and R. Bachman, 23–42. Los Angeles: Roxbury Publishing Company, 2001.

Clear, Todd R. "Policy and Evidence: The Challenge to the American Society of Criminology: 2009 Presidential Address to the American Society of Criminology." *Criminology* 48 (2010): 1–25.

Cohen, Lawrence E., and Marcus Felson. "Social Change and Crime Rate Trends: A Routine Activity Approach." *American Sociological Review* 44 (1979): 588–607.

Cornish, Derek B., and Ronald V. Clarke. "The Reasoning Criminal: Rational Choice Perspectives on Offending." New York: Springer-Verlag, 1986.

Cullen, Francis T., and Robert Agnew. "Criminological Theory: Past to Present: Essential Readings." Los Angeles: Roxbury Publishing Company, 2006.

———. "Criminological Theory: Past to Present: Essential Readings." New York: Oxford University Press, 2011.

D'Alessio, Stewart J., David Eitle, and Lisa Stolzenberg. "Unemployment, Guardianship, and Weekday Residential Burglary." *JQ: Justice Quarterly* 29 (2012): 919–932.

Decker, Scott, and Carol Kohfeld. "Crimes, Crime Rates, Arrests, and Arrest Ratios: Implications for Deterrence Theory." *Criminology* 23 (1985): 437–450.

Demos, John. *The Enemy Within: 2,000 Years of Witch-Hunting in the Western World*. New York: Penguin Books, 2009.

Forney, K. Jean, and Rose Marie Ward. "Examining the Moderating Role of Social Norms between Body Dissatisfaction and Disordered Eating in College Students." *Eating Behaviors* 14 (2013): 73–78.

Gibbs, Jack P. "Crime, Punishment, and Deterrence." *Southwestern Social Science Quarterly* 48 (1968): 515–530.

Hirschfield, Paul J. "The Declining Significance of Delinquent Labels in Disadvantaged Urban Communities." *Sociological Forum* 23 (2008): 575–601.

Hochstetler, Andy, and Jeffrey A. Bouffard. "Classical and Rational Choice Perspectives." In *Criminological Theory: Readings and Retrospectives*, edited by H. Copes and V. Topalli, 19–35. New York: McGraw-Hill, 2010.

Israel, Jonathan I. *Democratic Enlightenment: Philosophy, Revolution, and Human Rights 1750–1790*. New York: Oxford University Press, 2011.

Johnson, Julian. "Fort Myers Man Beaten During Attempted Robbery." *WBBH-TV*, May 23, 2013. http://www.nbc-2.com/story/22412060/fort-myers-man-beaten-during-attempted-robbery#.UaJT2D_LUIY.

Johnson, Shane D., Rob T. Guerette, and Kate J. Bowers. "Crime Displacement and Diffusion of Benefits." In *The Oxford Handbook of Crime Prevention*, edited by B. C. Welsh and D. P. Farrington, 337–353. New York: Oxford University Press, 2012.

Keel, Pamela K., and K. Jean Forney. "Psychosocial Risk Factors for Eating Disorders." *International Journal of Eating Disorders* 46 (2013): 433–439.

Kovandzic, Tomislav V., John J. Sloan, III, and Lynne M. Vieraitis. "'Striking Out' as Crime Reduction Policy: The Impact of 'Three Strikes' Laws on Crime Rates in U.S. Cities." *Justice Quarterly* 21 (2004): 207–239.

Listwan, Shelley Johnson, Christopher J. Sullivan, Robert Agnew, et al. "The Pains of Imprisonment Revisited: The Impact of Strain on Inmate Recidivism." *JQ: Justice Quarterly* 30 (2013): 144–168.

Marcum, Catherine D. "Routine Activity Theory: An Assessment of a Classical Theory." In *Criminological Theory: Readings and Retrospectives*, edited by H. Copes and V. Topalli, 43–55. New York: McGraw-Hill, 2010.

Marvell, Thomas B., and Carlisle E. Moody, Jr. "The Lethal Effects of Three Strikes Laws." *Journal of Legal Studies* 30 (2001): 89–106.

Matsueda, Ross L., Derek A. Kreager, and David Huizinga. "Deterring Delinquents: A Rational Choice Model of Theft and Violence." *American Sociological Review* 71 (2006): 95–122.

McCaghy, Charles H., Timothy A. Capron, J. D. Jamieson, et al. *Deviant Behavior: Crime, Conflict, and Interest Groups*. Boston: Allyn & Bacon, 2008.

McCarthy, Bill, and John Hagan. "Danger and the Decision to Offend." *Social Forces* 83 (2005): 1065–1096.

Mumola, Christopher J., and Jennifer C. Karberg. *Drug Use and Dependence, State and Federal Prisoners, 2004*. Washington, DC: Bureau of Justice Statistics, U.S. Department of Justice, 2006.

Nagin, Daniel S., Francis T. Cullen, and Cheryl Lero Jonson. "Imprisonment and Reoffending." *Crime and Justice: A Review of Research* 38 (2009): 115–200.

Nagin, Daniel S., and Greg Pogarsky. "Integrating Celerity, Impulsivity, and Extralegal Sanction Threats into a Model of General Deterrence: Theory and Evidence." *Criminology* 39 (2001): 865–891.

Newman, Graeme, and Pietro Marongiu. "Penological Reform and the Myth of Beccaria." In *The Origins and Growth of Criminology: Essays on Intellectual History, 1760–1945*, edited by P. Beirne. Brookfield, VT: Dartmouth Publishing Company, 1994.

Osgood, D. Wayne, and Amy L. Anderson. "Unstructured Socializing and Rates of Delinquency." *Criminology* 42 (2004): 519–549.

Paternoster, Raymond, and Ronet Bachman. "Explaining Criminals and Crime: Essays in Contemporary Criminological Theory." Los Angeles: Roxbury Publishing Company, 2001.

Piquero, Nicole Leeper, M. Lyn Exum, and Sally S. Simpson. "Integrating the Desire-for-Control and Rational Choice in a Corporate Crime Context." *Justice Quarterly* 22 (2005): 252–280.

Pontell, Henry N. *A Capacity to Punish: The Ecology of Crime and Punishment*. Bloomington: Indiana University Press, 1984.

Pridemore, William Alex, and Tony H. Grubesic. "Alcohol Outlets and Community Levels of Interpersonal Violence: Spatial Density, Outlet Type, and Seriousness of Assault." *Journal of Research in Crime & Delinquency* 50 (2013): 132–159.

Rand, Michael R., William J. Sabol, Michael Sinclair, et al. *Alcohol and Crime: Data from 2002 to 2008*. Washington, DC: Bureau of Justice Statistics, U.S. Department of Justice, 2010.

Reynald, Danielle M. "Factors Associated with the Guardianship of Places: Assessing the Relative Importance of the Spatio-Physical and Sociodemographic Contexts in Generating Opportunities for Capable Guardianship." *Journal of Research in Crime & Delinquency* 48 (2011): 110–142.

Rios, Victor M. "The Consequences of the Criminal Justice Pipeline on Black and Latino Masculinity." *The ANNALS of the American Academy of Political and Social Science* 623 (2009): 150–162.

Ritzer, George, and Jeff Stepinsky. *Sociological Theory*. New York: McGraw Hill, 2014.

Roth, Michael P. *Crime and Punishment: A History of the Criminal Justice System*. Belmont, CA: Wadsworth, 2011.

Schreck, Christopher J., and Bonnie S. Fisher. "Specifying the Influence of the Family and Peers on Violent Victimization: Extending Routine Activities and Lifestyles Theories." *Journal of Interpersonal Violence* 19 (2004): 1021–1041.

Shover, Neal, and Heith Copes. "Decision Making by Persistent Thieves and Crime Control Policy." In *Criminology and Public Policy: Putting Theory to Work*, edited by H. D. Barlow and S. H. Decker, 128–149. Philadelphia, PA: Temple University Press, 2010.

Smith, Martha J., and Ronald V. Clarke. "Situational Crime Prevention: Classifying Techniques Using 'Good Enough' Theory." In *The Oxford Handbook of Crime Prevention*, edited by B. C. Welsh and D. P. Farrington, 291–315. New York: Oxford University Press, 2012.

Sutton, John R. "Symbol and Substance: Effects of California's Three Strikes Law on Felony Sentencing." *Law & Society Review* 47 (2013): 37–72.

Tittle, Charles R. "Crime Rates and Legal Sanctions." *Social Problems* 16 (1969): 409–423.

Tonry, Michael. "The Mostly Unintended Effects of Mandatory Penalties: Two Centuries of Consistent findings." *Crime and Justice: A Review of Research* 38 (2009): 65–114.

Tonry, Michael. 2008. "Learning from the Limitations of Deterrence Research." *Crime and Justice: A Review of Research* 37: 279–311.

Tunnell, Kenneth D. "Choosing Crime: Close Your Eyes and Take Your Chances." *Justice Quarterly* 7 (1990): 673–690.

———. "Let's Do It: Deciding to Commit a Crime." In *New Perspectives in Criminology*, edited by J. E. Conklin, 246–258. Boston: Allyn and Bacon, 1996.

Walker, Samuel. *Sense and Nonsense About Crime, Drugs, and Communities: A Policy Guide*. Belmont, CA: Wadsworth Publishing Company, 2011.

Chapter 6, Biological and Psychological Explanations

Agnew, Robert, Timothy Brezina, John Paul Wright, et al. "Strain, Personality Traits, and Delinquency: Extending General Strain Theory." *Criminology* 40 (2002): 43–71.

Akers, Ronald L., and Christine L. Sellers. *Criminological Theories: Introduction, Evaluation, and Application*. New York: Oxford University Press, 2009.

———. *Criminological Theories: Introduction, Evaluation, and Application.* New York: Oxford University Press, 2013.

Anderson, Lori. "Jailed, Because You Might Commit Crime." *Scotsman.com,* March 5, 2013. http://www.scotsman.com/news/lori-anderson-jailed-because-you-might-commit-crime-1-2918249.

Andrews, D. A., and James Bonta. *The Psychology of Criminal Conduct.* Cincinnati: Anderson Publishing Company, 2010.

Andrews, D. A., and J. Stephen Wormith. "Personality and Crime: Knowledge Destruction and Construction in Criminology." *Justice Quarterly* 6 (1989): 289–309.

Barnes, J. C., and Bruce A. Jacobs. "Genetic Risk for Violent Behavior and Environmental Exposure to Disadvantage and Violent Crime: The Case for Gene-Environment Interaction." *Journal of Interpersonal Violence* 28 (2013): 92–120.

Bartol, Curt R., and Anne Bartol. *Criminal Behavior: A Psychological Approach.* Upper Saddle River, NJ: Prentice Hall, 2014.

Beaver, Kevin M., Matt DeLisi, Michael G. Vaughn, et al. "Monoamine Oxidase A Genotype Is Associated with Gang Membership and Weapon Use." *Comprehensive Psychiatry* 51 (2009): 130–134.

Beaver, Kevin M., and Anthony Walsh. "The Ashgate Research Companion to Biosocial Theories of Crime." Burlington, VT: Ashgate Publishing, 2011.

Beaver, Kevin M., John Paul Wright, Brian B. Boutwell, et al. "Exploring the Association Between the 2-Repeat Allele of the MAOA Gene Promoter Polymorphism and Psychopathic Personality Traits, Arrests, Incarceration, and Lifetime Antisocial Behavior." *Personality & Individual Differences* 54 (2013): 164–168.

Begley, Sharon. "Don't Blame the Caveman." *Newsweek,* June 29, 2009: 52–62.

Berk, Richard A., Susan B. Sorenson, Douglas J. Wiebe, et al. "The Legalization of Abortion and Subsequent Youth Homicide: A Time Series Analysis." *Analyses of Social Issues & Public Policy* 3 (2003): 45–64.

Bernard, Thomas J., Jeffrey B. Snipes, and Alexander L. Gerould. *Vold's Theoretical Criminology.* New York: Oxford University Press, 2009.

Boisvert, Danielle, John Paul Wright, Valerie Knopik, et al. "A Twin Study of Sex Differences in Self-Control." *Justice Quarterly* 30 (2013): 529–559.

Booth, Alan, Douglas A. Granger, Allan Mazur, et al. "Testosterone and Social Behavior." *Social Forces* 85 (2006): 167–191.

Carey, Gregory. "Genetics and Violence." In *Understanding and Preventing Violence: Biobehavioral Influences,* vol. 2, edited by J. Albert J. Reiss, K. A. Miczek, and J. A. Roth, 21–58. Washington, DC: National Academy Press, 1994.

Caspi, Avshalom. "The Child Is Father of the Man: Personalities Continuities from Childhood to Adulthood." *Journal of Personality and Social Psychology* 78 (2000): 158–172.

Caspi, Avshalom, Terrie E. Moffitt, Phil A. Silva, et al. "Are Some People Crime-Prone? Replications of the Personality-Crime Relationship Across Countries, Genders, Races, and Methods." *Criminology* 32 (1994): 163–195.

Chamlin, M. B., A. J. Myer, and B. A. Sanders. "Abortion as Crime Control: A Cautionary Tale." *Criminal Justice Policy Review* 19 (2008): 135–152.

Chesney-Lind, Meda, and Nikki Jones. "Fighting for Girls: New Perspectives on Gender and Violence." Albany, NY: State University of New York Press, 2010.

Cullen, Francis T. "Beyond Adolescence-Limited Criminology: Choosing Our Future—The American Society of Criminology 2010 Sutherland Address." *Criminology* 49 (2011): 287–330.

Cullen, Francis T., and Robert Agnew. "Criminological Theory: Past to Present: Essential Readings." New York: Oxford University Press, 2011.

Cullen, Francis T., P. Gendreau, G. R. Jarjoura, et al. "Crime and the Bell Curve: Lessons from Intelligent Criminology." *Crime & Delinquency* 43 (1997): 387–411.

Curran, Daniel J., and Claire M. Renzetti. *Theories of Crime.* Boston: Allyn and Bacon, 2001.

Dalton, Katharina. "Menstruation and Crime." *British Medical Journal* 2 (1961): 1752–1753.

DeLisi, Matt and Kevin M. Beaver. *Criminological Theory: A Life-Course Approach.* Burlington, MA: Jones and Bartlett Learning, 2014.

DeLisi, Matt, Kevin M. Beaver, Michael G. Vaughn, et al. "Contemporary Perspectives on Biological and Biosocial Theories of Crime." In *Criminological Theory: Readings and Retrospectives,* edited by H. Copes and V. Topalli, 74–83. New York: McGraw-Hill, 2010.

Donohue, John J., and S. D. Levitt. "The Impact of Legalized Abortion on Crime." *Quarterly Journal of Economics* 116 (2001): 379–420.

Dugdale, Richard. *The Jukes: A Study in Crime, Pauperism, Disease, and Heredity.* New York: G.P. Putnam's Sons, 1877.

Freud, Sigmund. *A General Introduction to Psycho-Analysis.* Translated by J. Riviere. New York: Liveright, 1935 (1920).

———. *Civilization and Its Discontents.* Translated by J. Strachey. New York: Norton, 1961 (1930).

Gibson, Chris L., Alex R. Piquero, and Stephen G. Tibbetts. "Assessing the Relationship Between Maternal Cigarette Smoking During Pregnancy and Age at First Police Conact." *Justice Quarterly* 17 (2000): 519–542.

Goddard, Henry H. *The Kallikak Family: A Study in the Heredity of Feeblemindedness.* New York: Macmillan, 1912.

Guo, Guang. "Twin Studies: What Can They Tell Us About Nature and Nurture?" *Contexts* 4 (2005): 43–47.

Guo, Guang, Michael E. Roettger, and Tianji Cai. "The Integration of Genetic Propensities into Social-Control Models of Delinquency and Violence among Male Youths." *American Sociological Review* 73 (2008): 543–568.

Harden, K. Paige, and Jane Mendle. "Gene-Environment Interplay in the Association Between Pubertal Timing and Delinquency in Adolescent Girls." *Journal of Abnormal Psychology* 121 (2012): 73–87.

Hay, Carter, and Michelle M. Evans. "Has *Roe v. Wade* Reduced U.S. Crime Rates? Examining the Link Between Mothers' Pregnancy Intentions and Children's Later Involvement in Law-Violating Behavior." *Journal of Research in Crime and Delinquency* 43 (2006): 36–66.

Herrnstein, Richard J., and Charles Murray. *The Bell Curve: Intelligence and Class Structure in American Life.* New York: Free Press, 1994.

Hirschi, Travis, and Michael J. Hindelang. "Intelligence and Delinquency: A Revisionist Review." *American Sociological Review* 42 (1977): 571–587.

Hooton, Earnest A. *The American Criminal: An Anthropological Study.* Cambridge: Harvard University Press, 1939a.

———. *Crime and the Man.* Cambridge: Harvard University Press, 1939b.

Jackson, Dylan B. "The Role of Early Pubertal Development in the Relationship Between General Strain and Juvenile Crime." *Youth Violence & Juvenile Justice* 10 (2012): 292–310.

Jones, Shayne E., Joshua D. Miller, and Donald R. Lynam. "Personality, Antisocial Behavior, and Aggression: A Meta-Analytic Review." *Journal of Criminal Justice* 39 (2011): 329–337.

Kahane, L. H., D. Paton, and R. Simmons. "The Abortion-Crime Link: Evidence from England and Wales." *Economica* 75 (2008): 1–21.

Kanarek, Robin B. "Nutrition and Violent Behavior." In *Understanding and Preventing Violence: Biobehavioral Influences,* vol. 2, edited by J. Albert J. Reiss, K. A. Miczek, and J. A. Roth, 515–539. Washington, DC: National Academy Press, 1994.

Katz, Janet, and William J. Chambliss. "Biology and Crime." In *Criminology: A Contemporary Handbook,* edited by J. F. Sheley, 275–303. Belmont, CA: Wadsworth Publishing Company, 1995.

Kennedy, Tom D., Kent F. Burnett, and William A. Edmonds. "Intellectual, Behavioral, and Personality Correlates of Violent vs. Non-violent Juvenile Offenders." *Aggressive Behavior* 37 (2011): 315–325.

Klein, Dorie. "The Etiology of Female Crime: A Review of the Literature." In *The Criminal Justice System and Women: Offenders, Victims, and Workers,* edited by B. R. Price and N. J. Sokoloff, 30–53. New York: McGraw-Hill, Inc, 1995.

Kohlberg, Lawrence. *States in the Development of Moral Thought and Action.* New York: Holt, Rinehart and Winston, 1969.

Kuhl, Stefan. *The Nazi Connection: Eugenics, American Racism, and German National Socialism.* New York: Oxford University Press, 1994.

Ledger, Kate. "Sociology and the Gene." *Contexts* 8(3) (2009): 16–20.

Lewontin, R. C. *Biology as Ideology: The Doctrine of DNA.* Toronto: House of Anansi Press, 2010.

Loeber, Rolf, David P. Farrington, Magda Stouthamer-Loeber, et al. *Violence and Serious Theft: Development and Prediction from Childhood to Adulthood.* New York: Routledge, 2008.

Lombroso, Cesare. *The Criminal Man (L'uomo Delinquente).* Milan: Hoepli, 1876.

———. *The Female Offender.* New York: Appleton, 1920 (1903).

Lynam, Donald, Terrie E. Moffitt, and Magda Stouthamer-Loeber. "Explaining the Relation Between IQ and Delinquency: Class, Race, Test Motivation, School Failure, or Self-Control?" *Journal of Abnormal Psychology* 102 (1993): 187–196.

Mazur, Allan. "Testosterone and Violence Among Young Men." In *Biosocial Criminology: New Directions in Theory and Research,* edited by A. Walsh and K. M. Beaver, 190–204. New York: Routledge, 2009.

McCaghy, Charles H., Timothy A. Capron, J. D. Jamieson, et al. *Deviant Behavior: Crime, Conflict, and Interest Groups.* Boston: Allyn & Bacon, 2008.

Mednick, Sarnoff A., William F. Gabrielli, Jr., and Barry Hutchings. "Genetic Factors in the Etiology of Criminal Behavior." In *The Causes of Crime: New Biological Approaches,* edited by S. A. Mednick, T. E. Moffitt, and S. Stack, 74–91. New York: Cambridge University Press, 1987.

Menard, Scott, and Barbara J. Morse. "A Structuralist Critique of the IQ-Delinquency Hypothesis." *American Journal of Sociology* 89 (1984): 1347–1378.

Miczek, Klaus A., Margaret Haney, Jennifer Tidey, et al. "Neurochemistry and Pharmacotherapeutic Management of Aggression and Violence." In *Understanding and Preventing Violence: Biobehavioral Influences*, vol. 2, edited by J. Albert J. Reiss, K. A. Miczek, and J. A. Roth, 245–514. Washington, DC: National Academy Press, 1994a.

Miczek, Klaus A., Allan F. Mirsky, Gregory Carey, et al. "An Overview of Biological Influences on Violent Behavior." In *Understanding and Preventing Violence: Biobehavioral Influences*, vol. 2, edited by J. Albert J. Reiss, K. A. Miczek, and J. A. Roth, 1–20. Washington, DC: National Academy Press, 1994b.

Milgram, Stanley. *Obedience to Authority*. New York: Harper and Row, 1974.

Moffitt, Terrie, and Avshalom Caspi. "Evidence from Behavioral Genetics for Environmental Contributions to Antisocial Conduct." In *The Explanation of Crime: Context, Mechanisms, and Development*, edited by P.-O. H. Wikström and R. J. Sampson, 108–152. New York: Cambridge University Press, 2006.

Moffitt, Terrie E. "Life-Course-Persistent and Adolescence-Limited Antisocial Behavior: A Ten-Year Research Review and a Research Agenda." In *Causes of Conduct Order and Juvenile Delinquency*, edited by B. B. Lahey, T. E. Moffitt, and A. Caspi. New York: Guilford Press, 2003.

———. "A Review of Research on the Taxonomy of Life-Course Persistent Versus Adolescence-Limited Antisocial Behavior." In *Taking Stock: The Status of Criminological Theory*, vol. 15, *Advances in Criminological Theory*, edited by F. T. Cullen, J. P. Wright, and K. R. Blevins, 277–311. New Brunswick, NJ: Transaction Publishers, 2006.

Montoya, Estrella, David Terburg, Peter Bos, et al. "Testosterone, Cortisol, and Serotonin as Key Regulators of Social Aggression: A Review and Theoretical Perspective." *Motivation & Emotion* 36 (2012): 65–73.

Moore, Megan. "Psychological Theories of Crime and Delinquency." *Journal of Human Behavior in the Social Environment* 21 (2011): 226–239.

Nelson, Randy J. *An Introduction to Behavioral Endocrinology*. Sunderland, MA: Sinauer Associates, 2011.

Nisbett, Richard E. *Intelligence and How to Get It: Why Schools and Cultures Count*. New York: W.W. Norton, 2009.

Odgers, Candice L., Terrie E. Moffitt, Jonathan M. Broadbent, et al. "Female and Male Antisocial Trajectories: From Childhood Origins to Adult Outcomes." *Development & Psychopathology* 20 (2008): 673–716.

Paradis, Angela D., Garrett M. Fitzmaurice, Karestan C. Koenen, et al. "Maternal Smoking During Pregnancy and Criminal Offending Among Adult Offspring." *Journal of Epidemiology & Community Health* 65 (2011): 1145–1150.

Rafter, Nicole. "Somatotyping, Antimodernism, and the Production of Criminological Knowledge." *Criminology* 45 (2007): 805–833.

———. "Earnest A. Hooton and the Biological Tradition in American Criminology." *Criminology* 42 (2004): 735–771.

———. *The Criminal Brain: Understanding Biological Theories of Crime*. New York: New York University Press, 2008.

Raine, Adrian. *The Anatomy of Violence: The Biological Roots of Crime*. New York: Pantheon, 2013a.

———. "What Made the Boston Bombers Do It." *The Daily Beast*, May 3, 2013b. http://www.thedailybeast.com/articles/2013/05/03/what-made-the-boston-bombers-do-it.html.

Raine, Adrian, Michael Rocque, and Brandon C. Welsh. "Experimental Neurocriminology: Etiology and Treatment." In *Experimental Criminology: Prospects for Advancing Science and Public Policy*, edited by B. C. Welsh, A. A. Braga, and G. J. N. Bruinsma, 43–64. Cambridge: Cambridge University Press, 2013.

Rocque, Michael, Brandon C. Welsh, and Adrian Raine. "Biosocial Criminology and Modern Crime Prevention." *Journal of Criminal Justice* 40 (2012): 306–312.

Sapolsky, Robert M. *The Trouble with Testosterone: And Other Essays on the Biology of the Human Predicament, reprint edition*. New York: Scribner, 2012.

Shapiro, Eliza. "The Children of Killers." *Newsweek*, April 29, 2013. http://www.thedailybeast.com/newsweek/2013/04/29/the-aftermath-of-the-boston-bombings-behind-the-children-of-killers.html.

Sheldon, William. *Varieties of Delinquent Youth*. New York: Harper and Row, 1949.

Silver, Eric, and Brent Teasdale. "Mental Disorder and Violence: An Examination of Stressful Life Events and Impaired Social Support." *Social Problems* 52 (2005): 62–78.

Simons, Ronald L., Man Kit Lei, Eric A. Stewart, et al. "Social Adversity, Genetic Variation, Street Code, and Aggression: A Genetically Informed Model of Violent Behavior." *Youth Violence & Juvenile Justice* 10 (2012): 3–24.

Simons, Ronald L., Leslie Gordon Simons, Yi-fu Chen, et al. "Identifying the Psychological Factors that Mediate the Association between Parenting Practices and Delinquency." *Criminology* 45 (2007): 481–517.

Singer, Dorothy G., and Tracey A. Revenson. *A Piaget Primer: How a Child Thinks*. Madison, CT: International Universities Press, 1997.

Solomon, Lee. "Premenstrual Syndrome: The Debate Surrounding Criminal Defense." *Maryland Law Review* 54 (1995): 571.

Thornberry, Terence P. "The Apple Doesn't Fall Far from the Tree (or Does It?): Intergenerational Patterns of Antisocial Behavior—the American Society of Criminology 2008 Sutherland Address." *Criminology* 47 (2009): 297–325.

Thornhill, Randy, and Craig T. Palmer. *A Natural History of Rape: Biological Bases of Sexual Coercion*. Cambridge, MA: MIT Press, 2000.

Travis, Cheryl B. *Evolution, Gender, and Rape*. Cambridge, MA: MIT Press, 2003b.

Van Gelder, Jean-Louis, and Reinout E. De Vries. "Traits and States: Integrating Personality and Affect into a Model of Criminal Decision Making." *Criminology* 50 (2012): 637–671.

Viding, Essi, Michel Boivin, Nathalie M. G. Fontaine, et al. "Predictors and Outcomes of Joint Trajectories of Callous-Unemotional Traits and Conduct Problems in Childhood." *Journal of Abnormal Psychology* 120 (2011): 730–742.

Wallman, Joel. "Serotonin and Impulsive Aggression: Not So Fast." *The HFG Review* 3 (1999): 21–24.

Weiss, Mike. *Double Play: The San Francisco City Hall Killings*. Reading, MA: Addison-Wesley Publishing Co., 1984.

Welsh, Brandon C., and David P. Farrington. *The Oxford Handbook of Crime Prevention*. New York: Oxford University Press, 2012.

Wright, John P., Kevin M. Beaver, Matt DeLisi, et al. "Lombroso's Legacy: The Miseducation of Criminologists." *Journal of Criminal Justice Education* 19 (2008): 325–338.

Zimbardo, Philip G. "Pathology of Imprisonment." *Society* 9 (1972): 4–8.

Chapter 7, Sociological Theories: Emphasis on Social Structure

Adler, Freda, and William S. Laufer. "The Legacy of Anomie Theory." In *Advances in Criminological Theory*, vol. 6. New Brunswick, NJ: Transaction Publishers, 1995.

Agnew, Robert. "Foundation for a General Strain Theory of Crime and Delinquency." *Criminology* 30 (1992): 47–87.

———. "A General Strain Theory of Community Differences in Crime Rates." *Journal of Research in Crime and Delinquency* 36 (1999): 123–155.

———. "Sources of Criminality: Strain and Subcultural Theories." In *Criminology: A Contemporary Handbook*, edited by J. F. Sheley, 349–371. Belmont, CA: Wadsworth, 2000.

———. *Pressured into Crime: An Overview of General Strain Theory*. New York: Oxford University Press, 2007.

———. "The Contribution of 'Mainstream' Theories to the Explanation of Female Delinquency." In *The Delinquent Girl*, edited by M. A. Zahn, 7–29. Philadelphia, PA: Temple University Press, 2009.

Agnew, Robert, Timothy Brezina, John Paul Wright, et al. "Strain, Personality Traits, and Delinquency: Extending General Strain Theory." *Criminology* 40 (2002): 43–71.

Akers, Ronald L., and Christine S. Sellers. *Criminological Theories: Introduction, Evaluation, and Application*. New York: Oxford University Press, 2013.

Akins, Scott. "Racial Segregation, Concentrated Disadvantage, and Violent Crime." *Journal of Ethnicity in Criminal Justice* 7 (2009): 30–52.

Anderson, Elijah. *Code of the Street: Decency, Violence, and the Moral Life of the Inner City*. New York: W.W. Norton, 2000.

Ball-Rokeach, Sandra J. "The Legitimation of Violence." In *Collective Violence*, edited by J. James F. Short and M. E. Wolfgang, 100–111. Chicago: Aldine, 1972.

Baron, Stephen W., Leslie W. Kennedy, and David R. Forde. "Male Street Youths' Conflict: The Role of Background, Subcultural and Situational Factors." *Justice Quarterly* 18 (2001): 759–789.

Bellair, Paul E., and Christopher R. Browning. "Contemporary Disorganization Research: An Assessment and Further Test of the Systemic Model of Neighborhood Crime." *Journal of Research in Crime & Delinquency* 47 (2010): 496–521.

Bellair, Paul, and Thomas L. McNulty. "Beyond the Bell Curve: Community Disadvantage and the Explanation of Black-White Differences in Adolescent Violence." *Criminology* 43 (2005): 1135–1168.

Bernard, Thomas J. "Angry Aggression Among the 'Truly Disadvantaged.'" *Criminology* 28 (1990): 73–96.

Bernard, Thomas J., Jeffrey B. Snipes, and Alexander L. Gerould. *Vold's Theoretical Criminology*. New York: Oxford University Press, 2009.

Botchkovar, Ekaterina V., Charles R. Tittle, and Olena Antonaccio. "General Strain Theory: Additional Evidence Using Cross-Cultural Data." *Criminology* 47 (2009): 131–176.

Broidy, Lisa M. "A Test of General Strain Theory." *Criminology* 39 (2001): 9–35.

Brownmiller, Susan. *Against Our Will: Men, Women, and Rape.* New York: Simon and Schuster, 1975.

Bursik, Robert J., Jr. "Social Disorganization and Theories of Crime and Delinquency: Problems and Prospects." *Criminology* 26 (1988): 519–551.

Cao, Liqun, Anthony Adams, and Vickie J. Jensen. "A Test of the Black Subculture of Violence Thesis: A Research Note." *Criminology* 35 (1997): 367–379.

Cernkovich, Stephen A. "Value Orientations and Delinquency Involvement." *Criminology* 15 (1978): 443–458.

Chappell, Allison T., Elizabeth Monk-Turner, and Brian K. Payne. "Broken Windows or Window Breakers: The Influence of Physical and Social Disorder on Quality of Life." *JQ: Justice Quarterly* 28 (2011): 522–540.

Cloward, Richard A., and Lloyd E. Ohlin. *Delinquency and Opportunity: A Theory of Delinquent Gangs.* New York: Free Press, 1960.

Cohen, Albert K. *Delinquent Boys: The Culture of the Gang.* New York: Free Press, 1955.

Coughlin, Ellen K. "Mean Streets Are a Scholar's Lab." *Chronicle of Higher Education* September 21 (1994): A8–A9, A14.

Durkheim, Emile. *Suicide.* Translated by J. Spaulding and G. Simpson. New York: Free Press, 1952 (1897).

Elliott, Delbert S., David Huizinga, and Suzanne S. Ageton. *Explaining Delinquency and Drug Use.* Beverly Hills: Sage Publications, 1985.

Erlanger, Howard S. "The Empirical Status of the Subculture of Violence Thesis." *Social Problems* 22 (1974): 280–292.

Farnworth, Margaret, and Michael J. Leiber. "Strain Theory Revisited: Economic Goals, Educational Means, and Delinquency." *American Sociological Review* 54 (1989): 263–274.

Felson, Richard B., and Marvin Krohn. "Motives for Rape." *Journal of Research in Crime and Delinquency* 27 (1990): 222–242.

Fox, Jeremy C. "Mother's Day Walk Carries Message of Peace." *The Boston Globe,* May 12, 2013. http://www.bostonglobe.com/metro/2013/05/12/thousands-gather-dorchester-for-mother-day-march-for-peace/6gbsaRRyBs6nGSTfsx MByJ/story.html.

Gau, Jacinta M., and Travis C. Pratt. "Broken Windows or Window Dressing? Citizens' (in) Ability to Tell the Difference between Disorder and Crime." *Criminology & Public Policy* 7 (2008): 163–194.

Golding, William. *Lord of the Flies.* London: Coward-McCann, 1954.

Goode, Erich. *Drugs in American Society.* New York: McGraw-Hill, 2012.

Harcourt, Bernard E., and Jens Ludwig. "Reefer Madness: Broken Windows Policing and Misdemeanor Marijuana Arrests in New York City, 1989–2000." *Criminology & Public Policy* 6 (2007): 165–181.

Harding, David J. *Living the Drama: Community, Conflict, and Culture among Inner-City Boys.* Chicago: University of Chicago Press, 2010.

Hay, Carter, Edward N. Fortson, Dusten R. Hollist, et al. "The Impact of Community Disadvantage on the Relationship between the Family and Juvenile Crime." *Journal of Research in Crime and Delinquency* 43 (2006): 326–356.

Higgins, Andrew. "In Sweden, Riots Put an Identity in Question." *The New York Times,* May 27, 2013: A4.

Hipp, John R. "Income Inequality, Race, and Place: Does the Distribution of Race and Class Within Neighborhoods Affect Crime Rates?" *Criminology* 45 (2007): 665–697.

———. "A Dynamic View of Neighborhoods: The Reciprocal Relationship between Crime and Neighborhood Structural Characteristics." *Social Problems* 57 (2010): 205–230.

Hipp, John R., and Daniel K. Yates. "Ghettos, Thresholds, and Crime: Does Concentrated Poverty Really Have an Accelerating Increasing Effect on Crime?" *Criminology* 49 (2011): 955–990.

Hunnicutt, Gwen, and Lisa M. Broidy. "Liberation and Economic Marginalization: A Reformulation and Test of (Formerly?) Competing Models." *Journal of Research in Crime and Delinquency* 41 (2004): 130–155.

Katz, Jack. *Seductions of Crime: Moral and Sensual Attractions of Doing Evil.* New York: Basic Books, 1988.

Kaufman, Joanne M. "Gendered Responses to Serious Strain: The Argument for a General Strain Theory of Deviance." *JQ: Justice Quarterly* 26 (2009): 410–444.

Kornhauser, Ruth. *Social Sources of Delinquency.* Chicago: University of Chicago Press, 1978.

Kubrin, Charis E., and Ronald Weitzer. "New Directions in Social Disorganization Theory." *Journal of Research in Crime and Delinquency* 40 (2003a): 374–402.

Kubrin, Charis E., and Ronald E. Weitzer. "Retaliatory Homicide: Concentrated Disadvantage and Neighorhood Culture." *Social Problems* 50 (2003b): 157–180.

Lauritsen, Janet L., and Kristin Carbone-Lopez. "Gender Differences in Risk Factors for Violent Victimization: An Examination of Individual-, Family-, and Community-Level Predictors." *Journal of Research in Crime & Delinquency* 48 (2011): 538–565.

Leonard, Eileen. "Theoretical Criminology and Gender." In *The Criminal Justice System and Women: Offenders, Victims, and Workers,* edited by B. R. Price and N. J. Sokoloff, 54–70. New York: McGraw-Hill, Inc., 1995.

Listwan, Shelley Johnson, Christopher J. Sullivan, Robert Agnew, et al. "The Pains of Imprisonment Revisited: The Impact of Strain on Inmate Recidivism." *JQ: Justice Quarterly* 30 (2013): 144–168.

Matsuda, Kristy N., Chris Melde, Terrance J. Taylor, et al. "Gang Membership and Adherence to the 'Code of the Street.'" *Justice Quarterly* 30 (2013): 440–468.

McGloin, Jean Marie, Christopher J. Schreck, Eric A. Stewart, et al. "Predicting the Violent Offender: The Discriminant Validity of the Subculture of Violence." *Criminology* 49 (2011): 767–794.

Mears, Daniel P., and Avinash S. Bhati. "No Community Is an Island: The Effects of Resource Deprivation on Urban Violence in Spatially and Socially Proximate Communities." *Criminology* 44 (2006): 509–547.

Merton, Robert K. "Social Structure and Anomie." *American Sociological Review* 3 (1938): 672–682.

Messner, Steven F., and Richard Rosenfeld. *Crime and the American Dream.* Belmont, CA: Wadsworth Publishing Company, 2013.

Miller, Walter B. "Lower Class Culture as a Generating Milieu of Gang Delinquency." *Journal of Social Issues* 14 (1958): 5–19.

Moon, Byongook, Merry Morash, Cynthia Perez McCluskey, et al. "A Comprehensive Test of General Strain Theory: Key Strains, Situational- and Trait-Based Negative Emotions, Conditioning Factors, and Delinquency." *Journal of Research in Crime and Delinquency* 46 (2009): 182–212.

Painter-Davis, Noah. "Structural Disadvantage and American Indian Homicide and Robbery Offending." *Homicide Studies* 16 (2012): 219–237.

Park, Robert E., Ernest W. Burgess, and Roderick McKenzie. *The City.* Chicago: University of Chicago Press, 1925.

Passas, Nikos. "Anomie and Corporate Deviance." *Contemporary Crises* 14 (1990): 157–178.

Peterson, Ruth D., and Lauren J. Krivo. "Macrostructural Analyses of Race, Ethnicity, and Violent Crime: Recent Lessons and New Directions for Research." *Annual Review of Sociology* 31 (2005): 331–356.

———. "Segregated Spatial Locations, Race-Ethnic Composition, and Neighborhood Violent Crime." *THE ANNALS of the American Academy of Political and Social Science* 623 (2009): 93–107.

Pratt, Travis C., and Francis T. Cullen. "Assessing Macro-Level Predictors and Theories of Crime: A Meta-Analysis." *Crime and Justice: A Review of Research* 32 (2005): 373–450.

Pratt, Travis, and Jacinta M. Gau. "Social Disorganization Theory." In *Criminological Theory: Readings and Retrospectives,* edited by H. Copes and V. Topalli, 104–112. New York: McGraw-Hill, 2010.

Pyrooz, David C. "Structural Covariates of Gang Homicide in Large U.S. Cities." *Journal of Research in Crime & Delinquency* 49 (2012): 489–518.

Ritzer, George, and Jeff Stepinsky. *Sociological Theory.* New York: McGraw Hill, 2014.

Rosenfeld, Richard. "The Big Picture: 2010 Presidential Address to the American Society of Criminology." *Criminology* 49 (2011): 1–26.

Sampson, Robert J. "The Place of Context: A Theory and Strategy for Criminology's Hard Problems." *Criminology* 51 (2013): 1–31.

Sampson, Robert J., and Dawn Jeglum Bartusch. *Attitudes Toward Crime, Police, and the Law: Individual and Neighborhood Differences.* Washington, DC: National Institute of Justice, U.S. Department of Justice, 1999.

Sampson, Robert J., and Steve Raudenbush. *Disorder in Urban Neighborhoods: Does It Lead to Crime?* Washington, DC: National Institute of Justice, U.S. Department of Justice, 2001.

Sampson, Robert J., and William Julius Wilson. "Toward a Theory of Race, Crime, and Urban Inequality." In *Crime and Inequality,* edited by J. Hagan and R. D. Peterson, 37–54. Stanford: Stanford University Press, 1995.

Schreck, Christopher J., Jean Marie McGloin, and David S. Kirk. "On the Origins of the Violent Neighborhood: A Study of the Nature and Predictors of Crime-Type Differentiation across Chicago Neighborhoods." *JQ: Justice Quarterly* 26 (2009): 771–794.

Shaw, Clifford R., and Henry D. McKay. *Juvenile Delinquency and Urban Areas.* Chicago: University of Chicago Press, 1942.

Stahler, Gerald J., Jeremy Mennis, Steven Belenko, et al. "Predicting Recidivism for Released State Prison Offenders: Examining the Influence of Individual and Neighborhood Characteristics and Spatial Contagion on the Likelihood of Reincarceration." *Criminal Justice & Behavior* 40 (2013): 690–711.

Stark, Rodney. "Deviant Places: A Theory of the Ecology of Crime." *Criminology* 25 (1987): 893–911.

Steenbeek, Wouter, and John R. Hipp. "A Longitudinal Test of Social Disorganization Theory: Feedback Effects among Cohesion, Social Control, and Disorder." *Criminology* 49 (2011): 833–871.

Stewart, Eric A., and Ronald L. Simons. "Race, Code of the Street, and Violent Delinquency: A Multilevel Investigation of Neighborhood Street Culture and Individual Norms of Violence." *Criminology* 48 (2010): 569–605.

Stiles, Beverly L., Xiaoru Liu, and Howard B. Kaplan. "Relative Deprivation and Deviant Adaptations: The Mediating Effects of Negative Self-Feelings." *Journal of Research in Crime and Delinquency* 37 (2000): 64–90.

Strom, Kevin J., and John M. MacDonald. "The Influence of Social and Economic Disadvantage on Racial Patterns in Youth Homicide Over Time." *Homicide Studies* 11 (2007): 50–69.

Stucky, Thomas D., and John R. Ottensmann. "Land Use and Violent Crime." *Criminology* 47 (2009): 1223–1264.

Suttles, Gerald. *The Social Order of the Slum*. Chicago: University of Chicago Press, 1968.

Thomas, William I., and Florian Znaniecki. *The Polish Peasant in Europe and America*, vol. 2. New York: Knopf, 1927.

Tillyer, Marie Skubak, and Brenda Vose. "Social Ecology, Individual Risk, and Recidivism: A Multilevel Examination of Main and Moderating Influences." *Journal of Criminal Justice* 39 (2011): 452–459.

Tittle, Charles R., Lisa M. Broidy, and Marc G. Gertz. "Strain, Crime, and Contingencies." *JQ: Justice Quarterly* 25 (2008): 283–312.

Turk, Austin T. "Back on Track: Asking and Answering the Right Questions." *Law & Society Review* 27 (1993): 355–359.

Warner, Barbara D. "The Role of Attenuated Culture in Social Disorganization Theory." *Criminology* 41 (2003): 73–97.

———. "Directly Intervene or Call the Authorities? A Study of Forms of Neighborhood Social Control Within a Social Disorganization Framework." *Criminology* 45 (2007): 99–129.

Webber, Craig. "Reevaluating Relative Deprivation Theory." *Theoretical Criminology* 11 (2007): 97–120.

Whyte, William Foote. *Street Corner Society: The Social Structure of an Italian Slum*. Chicago: University of Chicago Press, 1943.

Wikström, Per-Olof H., and Rolf Loeber. "Do Disadvantaged Neighborhoods Cause Well-Adjusted Children to Become Adolescent Delinquents? A Study of Maile Juvenile Serious Offending, Individual Risk and Protective Factors, and Neighborhood Context." *Criminology* 38 (2000): 1109–1142.

Wilkinson, Deanna L., Chauncey C. Beaty, and Regina M. Lurry. "Youth Violence—Crime or Self-Help? Marginalized Urban Males' Perspectives on the Limited Efficacy of the Criminal Justice System to Stop Youth Violence." *The ANNALS of the American Academy of Political and Social Science* 623 (2009): 25–38.

Wolfgang, Marvin E. *Patterns in Criminal Homicide*. Philadelphia, PA: University of Pennsylvania Press, 1958.

Wolfgang, Marvin E., and Franco Ferracuti. *The Subculture of Violence*. London: Social Science Paperbacks, 1967.

Yang, Sue-Ming. "Assessing the Spatial-Temporal Relationship Between Disorder and Violence." *Journal of Quantitative Criminology* 26 (2010): 139–163.

Zahn, Margaret A., and Angela Browne. "Gender Differences in Neighborhood Effects and Delinquency." In *The Delinquent Girl*, edited by M. A. Zahn, 164–181. Philadelphia, PA: Temple University Press, 2009.

Chapter 8, Sociological Theories: Emphasis on Social Process

Adamczyk, Amy. "Understanding Delinquency with Friendship Group Religious Context." *Social Science Quarterly (Wiley-Blackwell)* 93 (2012): 482–505.

Agnew, Robert. "The Techniques of Neutralization and Violence." *Criminology* 32 (1994): 555–580.

———. "The Contribution of 'Mainstream' Theories to the Explanation of Female Delinquency." In *The Delinquent Girl*, edited by M. A. Zahn, 7–29. Philadelphia, PA: Temple University Press, 2009.

Akers, Ronald L. *Deviant Behavior: A Social Learning Perspective*. Belmont, CA: Wadsworth, 1977.

———. "A Social Behaviorist's Perspective on Integration of Theories of Crime and Deviance." In *Theoretical Integration in the Study of Deviance and Crime: Problems and Prospects*, edited by S. F. Messner, M. D. Krohn, and A. E. Liska, 23–36. Albany, NY: State University of New York Press, 1989.

Akers, Ronald L., and Gary F. Jensen. "The Empirical Status of Social Learning Theory of Crime and Deviance: The Past, Present, and Future." In *Taking Stock: The Status of Criminological Theory*, vol. 15, *Advances in Criminological Theory*, edited by F. T. Cullen, J. P. Wright, and K. R. Blevins, 37–76. New Brunswick, NJ: Transaction Publishers, 2006.

Akers, Ronald L., and Christine S. Sellers. *Criminological Theories: Introduction, Evaluation, and Application*. New York: Oxford University Press, 2013.

Augustyn, Megan Bears, and Jean Marie McGloin. "The Risk of Informal Socializing with Peers: Considering Gender Differences Across Predatory Delinquency and Substance Use." *JQ: Justice Quarterly* 30 (2013): 117–143.

Bandura, Albert. *Aggression: A Social Learning Analysis*. Englewood Cliffs, NJ: Prentice Hall, 1973.

Barkan, Steven E. "Religiosity and Premarital Sex During Adulthood." *Journal for the Scientific Study of Religion* 45 (2006): 407–417.

Baron, Stephen W. "Differential Coercion, Street Youth, and Violent Crime." *Criminology* 47 (2009): 239–268.

———. "Street Youths' Control Imbalance and Soft and Hard Drug Use." *Journal of Criminal Justice* 38 (2010): 903–912.

Bayley, David H. "Lessons in Order." In *Criminology: A Cross-Cultural Perspective*, edited by R. Heiner, 3–14. Minneapolis/St. Paul: West Publishing Co., 1996.

Beaver, Kevin M., Matt DeLisi, Daniel P. Mears, et al. "Low Self-Control and Contact with the Criminal Justice System in a Nationally Representative Sample of Males." *JQ: Justice Quarterly* 26 (2009): 695–715.

Benson, Michael L. *Crime and the Life Course: An Introduction*, 2nd ed. New York: Routledge, 2013.

Bernard, Thomas J., Jeffrey B. Snipes, and Alexander L. Gerould. *Vold's Theoretical Criminology*. New York: Oxford University Press, 2009.

Bersani, Bianca E., and Elaine Eggleston Doherty. "When the Ties That Bind Unwind: Examining the Enduring and Situational Processes of Change Behind the Marriage Effect." *Criminology* 51 (2013): 399–433.

Bjerk, David. "Re-examining the Impact of Dropping Out on Criminal and Labor Outcomes in Early Adulthood." *Economics of Education Review* 31 (2012): 110–122.

Bohm, Robert M., and Brenda Vogel. *A Primer on Crime and Delinquency Theory*. Belmont, CA: Wadsworth Publishing Co., 2011.

Boutwell, Brian B., and Kevin M. Beaver. "The Intergenerational Transmission of Low Self-Control." *Journal of Research in Crime & Delinquency* 47 (2010): 174–209.

Boutwell, Brian B., Cortney A. Franklin, J. C. Barnes, et al. "Physical Punishment and Childhood Aggression: The Role of Gender and Gene-environment Interplay." *Aggressive Behavior* 37 (2011): 559–568.

Braithwaite, John. "Charles Tittle's *Control Balance* and Criminological Theory." *Theoretical Criminology* 1 (1997): 77–97.

Burgess, Robert L., and Ronald L. Akers. "A Differential Association-Reinforcement Theory of Criminal Behavior." *Social Problems* 14 (1966): 128–147.

Chapple, Constance L. "Self-Control, Peer Relations, and Delinquency." *Justice Quarterly* 22 (2005): 89–106.

Cochran, John K., Peter B. Wood, and Bruce J. Arneklev. "Is the Religiosity–Delinquency Relationship Spurious? A Test of Arousal and Social Control Theories." *Journal of Research in Crime and Delinquency* 31 (1994): 92–123.

Collins, Kate Irish. "TA Senior Overcomes Hard Times and Road to Diploma." *Sun Chronicle*, May 22, 2013. http://www.keepmecurrent.com/sun_chronicle/news/ta-senior-overcomes-hard-times-on-road-to-diploma/article_be18da36-c311-11e2-8a4d-0019bb2963f4.html.

Collins, Randall. *Four Sociological Traditions*. New York: Oxford University Press, 1994.

Colvin, Mark, T. Cullen Francis, and Thomas Vander Ven. "Coercion, Social Support, and Crime: An Emerging Theoretical Consensus." *Criminology An Interdisciplinary Journal* 40 (2002): 19–42.

DeLisi, Matt, and Kevin M. Beaver. "Criminological Theory: A Life-Course Approach." Burlington, MA: Jones and Bartlett Learning, 2014.

Doherty, Elaine Eggleston, and Margaret E. Ensminger. "Marriage and Offending Among a Cohort of Disadvantaged African Americans." *Journal of Research in Crime & Delinquency* 50 (2013): 104–131.

Durkheim, Emile. *The Elementary Forms of Religious Life*. Translated by J. Swain. Glencoe, IL: Free Press, 1947(1915).

Elliott, Delbert S., Suzanne S. Ageton, and Rachelle J. Canter. "An Integrated Theoretical Perspective on Delinquent Behavior." *Journal of Research in Crime and Delinquency* 16 (1979): 3–27.

Elliott, Delbert S., David Huizinga, and Suzanne S. Ageton. *Explaining Delinquency and Drug Use*. Beverly Hills: Sage Publications, 1985.

Evans, T. David, Francis T. Cullen, R. Gregory Dunaway, et al. "Religion and Crime Reexamined: The Impact of Religion, Secular Controls, and Social Ecology on Adult Criminality." *Criminology* 33 (1995): 195–224.

Farrington, David P. "Developmental and Life-Course Criminology: Key Theoretical and Empirical Issues—The 2002 Sutherland Award Address." *Criminology* 41 (2003): 221–255.

———. "Families and Crime." In *Crime and Public Policy*, edited by J. Q. Wilson and J. Petersilia, 130–157. New York: Oxford University Press, 2011.

Farrington, David P., Rolf Loeber, and Maria M. Ttofi. "Risk and Protective Factors for Offending." In *The Oxford Handbook of Crime Prevention*, edited by B. C. Welsh and D. P. Farrington, 46–69. New York: Oxford University Press, 2012.

Fomby, Paula, and Christie A. Sennott. "Family Structure Instability and Mobility: The Consequences for Adolescents, Problem Behavior." *Social Science Research* 42 (2013): 186–201.

Geis, Gilbert. "On the Absence of Self-Control as the Basis for a General Theory of Crime: A Critique." *Theoretical Criminology* 4 (2000): 35–53.

Georgantopoulos, Mary Ann. "Homeless Teen Graduates as 2013 Valedictorian." *Metro.us*, May 27, 2013. http://www.metro.us/boston/news/national/2013/05/27/homeless-teen-graduates-as-2013-valedictorian/.

Gibson, Chris L., Christopher J. Sullivan, Shayne Jones, et al. " 'Does It Take a Village?' Assessing Neighborhood Influences on Children's Self-Control." *Journal of Research in Crime and Delinquency* 47 (2010): 31–62.

Giordano, Peggy. "Peer Influences on Girls' Delinquency." In *The Delinquent Girl*, edited by M. A. Zahn, 127–145. Philadelphia, PA: Temple University Press, 2009.

Glaser, Daniel. "Criminality Theories and Behavioral Images." *American Journal of Sociology* 61 (1956): 433–444.

Gottfredson, Denise C., Philip J. Cook, and Chongmin Na. "Schools and Prevention." In *The Oxford Handbook of Crime Prevention*, edited by B. C. Welsh and D. P. Farrington, 269–287. New York: Oxford University Press, 2012.

Gottfredson, Michael, and Travis Hirschi. *A General Theory of Crime*. Stanford: Sanford University Press, 1990.

Haynie, Dana L., and Danielle C. Payne. "Race, Friendship Networks, and Violent Delinquency." *Criminology* 44 (2006): 775–805.

Haynie, Dana L., Eric Silver, and Brent Teasdale. "Neighborhood Characteristics, Peer Networks, and Adolescent Violence." *Journal of Quantitative Criminology* 22 (2006): 147–169.

Hirschi, Travis. *Causes of Delinquency*. Berkeley: University of California Press, 1969.

———. "Exploring Alternatives to Integrated Theory." In *Theoretical Integration in the Study of Deviance and Crime: Problems and Prospects*, edited by S. F. Messner, M. D. Krohn, and A. E. Liska, 37–49. Albany, NY: State University of New York Press, 1989.

Holtfreter, Kristy, Michael D. Reisig, and Travis C. Pratt. "Low Self-Control, Routine Activities, and Fraud Victimization." *Criminology* 46 (2008): 189–220.

Jarjoura, G. Roger. "Does Dropping Out of School Enhance Delinquent Involvement? Results from a Large-Scale National Probability Sample." *Criminology* 31 (1993): 149–171.

Johnson, Byron R., Sung Joon Jang, David B. Larson, et al. "Does Adolescent Religious Commitment Matter? A Reexamination of the Effects of Religiosity on Delinquency." *Journal of Research in Crime and Delinquency* 38 (2001): 22–44.

Kierkus, Christopher A., and John D. Hewitt. "The Contextual Nature of the Family Structure/Delinquency Relationship." *Journal of Criminal Justice* 37 (2009): 123–132.

Komiya, Nobuo. "A Cultural Study of the Low Crime Rate in Japan." *British Journal of Criminology* 39 (1999): 369–390.

Krohn, Marvin. "Sources of Criminality: Control and Deterrence Theories." In *Criminology: A Contemporary Handbook*, edited by J. F. Sheley, 373–399. Belmont, CA: Wadsworth, 2000.

Landor, Antoinette, Leslie Simons, Ronald Simons, et al. "The Role of Religiosity in the Relationship Between Parents, Peers, and Adolescent Risky Sexual Behavior." *Journal of Youth & Adolescence* 40 (2011): 296–309.

Laub, John H., Robert J. Sampson, and Gary A. Sweeten. "Assessing Sampson and Laub's Life-Course Theory of Crime." In *Taking Stock: The Status of Criminological Theory*, vol. 15, *Advances in Criminological Theory*, edited by F. T. Cullen, 313–333. New Brunswick, NJ: Transaction Publishers, 2006.

Lee, Matthew R. "The Religious Institutional Base and Violent Crime in Rural Areas." *Journal for the Scientific Study of Religion* 45 (2006): 309–324.

Liddick, Don. "Techniques of Neutralization and Animal Rights Activists." *Deviant Behavior* 34 (2013): 618–634.

Lilly, J. Robert, Francis T. Cullen, and Richard A. Ball. *Criminological Theory: Context and Consequences*. Thousand Oaks, CA: Sage Publications, 2011.

Liska, Allen E., and Mark D. Reed. "Ties to Conventional Institutions and Delinquency: Estimating Reciprocal Effects." *American Sociological Review* 50 (1985): 547–560.

Longshore, Douglas, Eunice Chang, and Nena Messina. "Self-Control and Social Bonds: A Combined Control Perspective on Juvenile Offending." *Journal of Quantitative Criminology* 21 (2005): 419–437.

Matsueda, Ross L. "The Current State of Differential Association Theory." *Crime and Delinquency* 34 (1988): 277–306.

Matza, David. *Delinquency and Drift*. New York: Wiley, 1964.

Megens, Kim C. I. M., and Frank M. Weerman. "The Social Transmission of Delinquency: Effects of Peer Attitudes and Behavior Revisited." *Journal of Research in Crime & Delinquency* 49 (2012): 420–443.

Mersky, Joshua P., James Topitzes, and Arthur J. Reynolds. "Unsafe at Any Age: Linking Childhood and Adolescent Maltreatment to Delinquency and Crime." *Journal of Research in Crime & Delinquency* 49 (2012): 295–318.

Miller, J. Mitchell, J. Eagle Shutt, and J. C. Barnes. "Learning Theory: From Seminal Statements to Hybridization." In *Criminological Theory: Readings and Retrospectives*, edited by H. Copes and V. Topalli. New York: McGraw-Hill, 2010.

Moffitt, Terrie E. "Adolescence-Limited and Life-Course-Persistent Antisocial Behavior: A Developmental Taxonomy." *Psychological Review* 100 (1993): 674–701.

———. "A Review of Research on the Taxonomy of Life-Course Persistent Versus Adolescence-Limited Antisocial Behavior." In *Taking Stock: The Status of Criminological Theory*, vol. 15, *Advances in Criminological Theory*, edited by F. T. Cullen, J. P. Wright, and K. R. Blevins, 277–311. New Brunswick, NJ: Transaction Publishers, 2006.

Morselli, Carlo, Pierre Tremblay, and Bill McCarthy. "Mentors and Criminal Achievement." *Criminology* 44 (2006): 17–43.

Na, Chongmin, and Raymond Paternoster. "Can Self-Control Change Substantially Over Time? Rethinking the Relationship Between Self- and Social Control." *Criminology* 50 (2012): 427–462.

Payne, Allison Ann. "Communal School Organization Effects on School Disorder: Interactions with School Structure." *Deviant Behavior* 33 (2012): 507–524.

Petts, Richard J. "Family and Religious Characteristics' Influence on Delinquency Trajectories from Adolescence to Young Adulthood." *American Sociological Review* 74 (2009): 465–483.

Piquero, Alex R., and Matthew Hickman. "An Empirical Test of Tittle's Control Balance Theory." *Criminology* 37 (1999): 319–341.

Piquero, Nicole Leeper, and Alex R. Piquero. "Control Balance and Exploitative Corporate Crime." *Criminology* 44 (2006): 397–430.

———. "Overview of Self-Control Theory." In *Criminological Theory: Readings and Retrospectives*, edited by H. Copes and V. Topalli, 299–307. New York: McGraw-Hill, 2010.

Pratt, Travis C., and Francis T. Cullen. "The Empirical Status of Gottfredson and Hirschi's General Theory of Crime: A Meta-Analysis." *Criminology* 38 (2000): 931–964.

Rankin, Joseph H., and Roger Kern. "Parental Attachments and Delinquency." *Criminology* 32 (1994): 495–515.

Reckless, Walter C. "A New Theory of Delinquency and Crime." *Federal Probation* 25 (1961): 42–46.

Reckless, Walter C., Simon Dinitz, and Ellen Murray. "Self-Concept as an Insulator Against Delinquency." *American Sociological Review* 21 (1956): 744–756.

Reiss, Albert J. "Delinquency as the Failure of Personal and Social Controls." *American Sociological Review* 16 (1951): 196–207.

Rocque, Michael, Chad Posick, and Gregory M. Zimmerman. "Measuring Up: Assessing the Measurement Properties of Two Self-Control Scales." *Deviant Behavior* 34 (2013): 534–556.

Salas-Wright, Christopher, Michael Vaughn, David Hodge, et al. "Religiosity Profiles of American Youth in Relation to Substance Use, Violence, and Delinquency." *Journal of Youth & Adolescence* 41 (2012): 1560–1575.

Sampson, Robert J., and John H. Laub. *Crime in the Making: Pathways and Turning Points Through Life*. Cambridge: Harvard University Press, 1993.

Schneider, Linda, and Arnold Silverman. *Global Sociology: Introducing Five Contemporary Societies*. New York: McGraw-Hill, 2013.

Seffrin, Patrick M., Peggy C. Giordano, Wendy D. Manning, et al. "The Influence of Dating Relationships on Friendship Networks, Identity Development, and Delinquency." *Justice Quarterly* 26 (2009): 238–267.

Shoemaker, Donald J. *Theories of Delinquency: An Examination of Explanations of Delinquent Behavior*. New York: Oxford University Press, 2010.

Simons, Dominique A., and Sandy K. Wurtele. "Relationships Between Parents' Use of Corporal Punishment and Their Children's Endorsement of Spanking and Hitting Other Children." *Child Abuse & Neglect* 34 (2010): 639–646.

Simons, Ronald L., and Callie Harbin Burt. "Learning to Be Bad: Adverse Social Conditions, Social Schemas, and Crime." *Criminology* 49 (2011): 553–598.

Simons, Ronald L., Leslie Gordon Simons, Callie Harbin Burt, et al. "Collective Efficacy, Authoritative Parenting and Delinquency: A Longitudinal Test of a Model Integrating Community- and Family-Level Processes." *Criminology* 43 (2005): 989–1029.

Steketee, Majone, Marianne Junger, and Josine Junger-Tas. "Sex Differences in the Predictors of Juvenile Delinquency: Females Are More Susceptible to Poor Environments; Males Are Influenced More by Low Self-Control." *Journal of Contemporary Criminal Justice* 29 (2013): 88–105.

Stewart, Eric A., Ronald L. Simons, Rand D. Conger, et al. "Beyond the Interactional Relationship Between Delinquency and Parenting Practices: The Contribution of Legal Sanctions." *Journal of Research in Crime and Delinquency* 39 (2002): 36–59.

Sutherland, Edwin. "White-Collar Criminality." *American Sociological Review* 5 (1940): 1–12.

Sutherland, Edwin H. *Principles of Criminology*. Philadelphia, PA: Lippincott, 1939.
———. *Principles of Criminology*. Philadelphia, PA: J.P. Lippincott, 1947.

Sweeten, Gary, Shawn D. Bushway, and Raymond Paternoster. "Does Dropping Out of School Mean Dropping into Delinquency?" *Criminology* 47 (2009): 47–91.

Sykes, Gresham M., and David Matza. "Techniques of Neutralization: A Theory of Delinquency." *American Sociological Review* 22 (1957): 664–670.

Thomas, Kyle J., and Jean Marie Mcgloin. "A Dual-Systems Approach for Understanding Differential Susceptibility to Processes of Peer Influence." *Criminology* 51 (2013): 435–474.

Thornberry, Terence P. "Toward an Interactional Theory of Delinquency." *Criminology* 25 (1987): 863–891.

———. "Reflections on the Advantages and Disadvantages of Theoretical Integration." In *Theoretical Integration in the Study of Crime and Deviance: Problems and Prospects*, edited by S. F. Messner, M. D. Krohn, and A. E. Liska, 51–60. Albany, NY: State University of New York Press, 1989.

———. "The Apple Doesn't Fall Far from the Tree (or Does It?): Intergenerational Patterns of Antisocial Behavior—the American Society of Criminology 2008 Sutherland Address." *Criminology* 47 (2009): 297–325.

Thornberry, Terence P., and Marvin D. Krohn. "Applying Interactional Theory to the Explanation of Continuity and Change in Antisocial Behavior." In *Integrated Developmental and Life-Course Theories of Offending*, edited by D. P. Farrington, 183–209. New Brunswick, NJ: Transaction Publishers, 2005.

Tittle, Charles R. "Refining Control Balance Theory." *Theoretical Criminology* 8 (2004): 395–428.

Topalli, Volkan. "When Being Good Is Bad: An Expansion of Neutralization Theory." *Criminology* 43 (2005): 797–835.

Unnever, James D., Mark Colvin, and Francis T. Cullen. "Crime and Coercion: A Test of Core Theoretical Propositions." *Journal of Research in Crime and Delinquency* 41 (2004): 244–268.

van Dijk, Jan, John van Kesteren, and Paul Smit. *Criminal Victimisation in International Perspective: Key Findings from the 2004–2005 ICVS and EU ICS*. Devon, England: Willan Publishing, 2008.

van Schellen, Marieke, Anne-Rigt Poortman, and Paul Nieuwbeerta. "Partners in Crime? Criminal Offending, Marriage Formation, and Partner Selection." *Journal of Research in Crime & Delinquency* 49 (2012): 545–571.

Warr, Mark. "Age, Peers, and Delinquency." *Criminology* 31 (1993): 17–40.

———. *Companions in Crime: The Social Aspects of Criminal Conduct*. New York: Cambridge University Press, 2002.

———. "Making Delinquent Friends: Adult Supervision and Children's Affiliations." *Criminology* 43 (2005): 77–105.

Wright, John Paul, David E. Carter, and Francis T. Cullen. "A Life-Course Analysis of Military Service in Vietnam." *Journal of Research in Crime and Delinquency* 42 (2005): 55–83.

Chapter 9, Sociological Theories: Critical Perspectives

Adler, Jeffrey S. "A Historical Analysis of the Law of Vagrancy." *Criminology* 27 (1989): 209–229.

Agnew, Robert. "The Contribution of 'Mainstream' Theories to the Explanation of Female Delinquency." *The Delinquent Girl*, edited by M. A. Zahn, 7–29. Philadelphia, PA: Temple University Press, 2009.

Akers, Ronald L. "Problems in the Sociology of Deviance: Social Definitions and Behavior." *Social Forces* 46 (1968): 455–465.

Akers, Ronald L., and Christine S. Sellers. *Criminological Theories: Introduction, Evaluation, and Application*. New York: Oxford University Press, 2013.

Antonaccio, Olena, and Charles R. Tittle. "A Cross-National Test of Bonger's Theory of Criminality and Economic Conditions." *Criminology* 45 (2007): 925–958.

Armour, Marilyn. "Restorative Justice: Some Facts and History." *Tikkun* 27 (2012): 25–64.

Arrigo, Bruce A., and Christopher R. Williams. "Conflict Criminology: Developments, Directions, and Destinations Past and Present." *Criminological Theory: Readings and Retrospectives*, edited by H. Copes and V. Topalli, 401–412. New York: McGraw-Hill, 2010.

Augustyn, Megan Bears, and Jean Marie McGloin. "The Risk of Informal Socializing with Peers: Considering Gender Differences Across Predatory Delinquency and Substance Use." *JQ: Justice Quarterly* 30 (2013): 117–143.

Baay, Pieter, Marieke Liem, and Paul Nieuwbeerta. "Ex-Imprisoned Homicide Offenders: Once Bitten, Twice Shy?" The Effect of the Length of Imprisonment on Recidivism for Homicide Offenders." *Homicide Studies* 16 (2012): 259–271.

Bales, William, and Alex Piquero. "Assessing the Impact of Imprisonment on Recidivism." *Journal of Experimental Criminology* 8 (2012): 71–101.

Becker, Howard S. *Outsiders: Studies in the Sociology of Deviance*. New York: Free Press, 1963.

Bernburg, Jón Gunnar, and Marvin D. Krohn. "Labeling, Life Chances, and Adult Crime: The Direct and Indirect Effects of Official Intervention in Adolescence on Crime in Early Adulthood." *Criminology* 41 (2003): 1287–1318.

Bernburg, Jón Gunnar. "Labeling and Secondary Deviance." *Criminological Theory: Readings and Retrospectives*, edited by H. Copes and V. Topalli, 340–350. New York: McGraw-Hill, 2010.

Bishop, Donna M. "Public Opinion and Juvenile Justice Policy: Myths and Misconceptions." *Criminology & Public Policy* 5 (2006): 653–664.

Blackwell, Brenda Sims. "Perceived Sanction Threats, Gender, and Crime: A Test and Elaboration of Power-Control Theory." *Criminology* 38 (2000): 439–488.

Bonger, Willem. *Criminality and Economic Conditions*. Translated by H. P. Horton. Boston: Little, Brown, 1916.

Braithwaite, John. 2001. "Reintegrative Shaming." Pp. 242–251 in *Explaining Criminals and Crime: Essays in Contemporary Criminological Theory*, edited by R. Paternoster and R. Bachman. Los Angeles: Roxbury Publishing Company.

Broadhurst, Roderic, Brigitte Bouhours, and Thierry Bouhours. "Business and the Risk of Crime in China." *British Journal of Criminology* 53 (2013): 276–296.

Cain, Maureen, and Alan Hunt. "Marx and Engels on Law." New York: Academic Press, 1979.

Chambliss, William J. "A Sociological Analysis of the Law of Vagrancy." *Social Problems* 12 (1964): 67–77.

———. "The Saints and the Roughnecks." *Society* 11 (1973): 24–31.

Chambliss, William, and Robert Seidman. *Law, Order, and Power*. Reading, MA: Addison-Wesley Publishing Company, 1982.

Chesney-Lind, Meda. "Beyond Bad Girls: Feminist Perspectives on Female Offending." *The Blackwell Companion to Criminology*, edited by C. Sumner, 255–267. Oxford: Blackwell Publishing, 2004.

Clear, Todd R. "Policy and Evidence: The Challenge to the American Society of Criminology: 2009 Presidential Address to the American Society of Criminology." *Criminology* 48 (2010): 1–25.

Daly, Kathleen, and Meda Chesney-Lind. "Feminism and Criminology." *Justice Quarterly* 5 (1988): 497–538.

De Coster, Stacy. "Mothers' Work and Family Roles, Gender Ideologies, Distress, and Parenting: Consequences for Juvenile Delinquency." *Sociological Quarterly* 53 (2012): 585–609.

Deitch, Michele, Amanda Barstow, Leslie Lukens, et al. *From Time Out to Hard Time: Young Children in the Adult Criminal Justice System*. Austin, TX: LBJ School of Public Affairs, University of Texas at Austin, 2009.

DeKeseredy, Walter S., and Molly Dragiewicz. "Routledge Handbook of Critical Criminology." New York: Routledge, 2012.

DeKeseredy, Walter S., and Martin D. Schwartz. "Left Realism." *Routledge Handbook of Critical Criminology*, edited by W. S. DeKeseredy and M. Dragiewicz, 105–116. New York: Routledge, 2012.

Dobrow, Jason. "After the Crime: The Power of Restorative Justice Dialogues Between Victims and Violent Offenders." *Journal of Criminal Justice Education* 23 (2012): 550–552.

Estrada, Felipe, and Anders Nilsson. "Does It Cost More to Be a Female Offender? A Life-Course Study of Childhood Circumstances, Crime, Drug Abuse, and Living Conditions." *Feminist Criminology* 7 (2012): 196–219.

Freiburger, Tina L., and Carly M. Hilinski. "An Examination of the Interactions of Race and Gender on Sentencing Decisions Using a Trichotomous Dependent Variable." *Crime & Delinquency* 59 (2013): 59–86.

Greenberg, David F. "Introduction." *Crime and Capitalism: Readings in Marxist Criminology*, edited by D. F. Greenberg, 1–35. Philadelphia, PA: Temple University Press, 1993.

Griffin, Marie. "Feminist Criminology: Beyond the Slaying of Demons." *Criminology and Public Policy: Putting Theory to Work*, edited by H. D. Barlow and S. H. Decker, 215–232. Philadelphia, PA: Temple University Press, 2010.

Gusfield, Joseph R. *Symbolic Crusade: Status Politics and the American Temperance Movement*. Urbana, IL: University of Illinois Press, 1963.

Hagan, John, John Simpson, and A. R. Gillis. "Class in the Household: A Power-Control Theory of Gender and Delinquency." *American Journal of Sociology* 92 (1987): 788–816.

Hall, Jerome. *Theft, Law, and Society*. Indianapolis: Bobbs-Merrill, 1952.

Harring, Sidney L. "Policing a Class Society: The Expansion of the Urban Police in the Late Nineteenth and Early Twentieth Centuries." *Crime and Capitalism: Readings in Marxist Criminology*, edited by D. F. Greenberg, 546–567. Philadelphia, PA: Temple University Press, 1993.

Jackson, Dylan B., and Carter Hay. "The Conditional Impact of Official Labeling on Subsequent Delinquency: Considering the Attenuating Role of Family Attachment." *Journal of Research in Crime and Delinquency* 50 (2013): 300–322.

Johnson, Kristin, Lonn Lanza-Kaduce, and Jennifer Woolard. "Disregarding Graduated Treatment: Why Transfer Aggravates Recidivism." *Crime & Delinquency* 57 (2011): 756–777.

Klockars, Carl B. "The Contemporary Crises of Marxist Criminology." *Criminology* 16 (1979): 477–515.

Lanza-Kaduce, L., J. Lane, and D. M. Bishop. "Juvenile Offenders and Adult Felony Recidivism: The Impact of Transfer." *Journal of Crime & Justice* 28 (2005): 59–78.

Lemert, Edwin M. *Social Pathology*. New York: McGraw-Hill, 1951.

Liazos, Alexander. "The Poverty of the Sociology of Deviance: Nuts, Sluts, and Perverts." *Social Problems* 20 (1972): 103–120.

Loeffler, Charles E. "Does Imprisonment Alter the Life Course? Evidence on Crime and Employment from a Natural Experiment." *Criminology* 51 (2013): 137–166.

Lynch, Michael J., and Raymond J. Michalowski. *Primer in Radical Criminology: Critical Perspectives on Crime, Power and Identity*. Monsey, NY: Criminal Justice Press, 2006.

Marx, Karl, and Friedrich Engels. "The Communist Manifesto." *Marx and Engels: Selected Works*, vol. 2, 21–65. Moscow: Foreign Language Publishing House, 1962 (1848).

Matsueda, Ross L. "Labeling Theory: Historical Roots, Implications, and Recent Developments." *Explaining Criminals and Crime: Essays in Contemporary Criminological Theory*, edited by R. Paternoster and R. Bachman, 223–241. Los Angeles: Roxbury Publishing Company, 2001.

Matthews, Roger, and Jock Young. "Issues in Realist Criminology." London: Sage, 1992.

McCarthy, Bill, and John Hagan. "Sanction Effects, Violence, and Native North American Street Youth." *Violent Crime: Assessing Race and Ethnic Differences*, edited by D. F. Hawkins, 117–137. Cambridge: Cambridge University Press, 2003.

McCarthy, Bill, John Hagan, and Todd S. Woodward. "In the Company of Women: Structure and Agency in a Revised Power-Control Theory of Gender and Delinquency." *Criminology* 37 (1999): 761–788.

Mel, Jianming, and Mu Wang. "Social Change, Crime, and Criminology in China." *Crime & Justice International* 23 (2007): 14–21.

Menzies, Robert. "Beyond Realist Criminology." *Realist Criminology: Crime Control and Policing in the 1990s*, edited by J. Lowman and B. D. MacLean, 139–156. Toronto: University of Toronto Press, 1992.

Messerschmidt, James W., and Stephen Tomsen. "Masculinities." *Routledge Handbook of Critical Criminology*, edited by W. S. DeKeseredy and M. Dragiewicz, 172–185. New York: Routledge, 2012.

Miller, Jody. "Up It Up: Gender and the Accomplishment of Street Robbery." *Criminology* 36 (1998): 37–66.

Miller, Jody, and Scott H. Decker. "Young Women and Gang Violence: Gender, Street Offending, and Violent Victimization in Gangs." *Justice Quarterly* 18 (2001): 115–140.

Miller, Jody, and Christopher W. Mullins. "Feminist Theories of Girls' Delinquency." *The Delinquent Girl*, edited by M. A. Zahn, 30–49. Philadelphia, PA: Temple University Press, 2009.

Mitton, Roger. "Rise in Violent Crime Rattles Vietnam." *The Straits Times (Singapore)*, January 9, 2007: 1.

Muraskin, Roslyn. *Women and Justice: It's a Crime*. Upper Saddle River, NJ: Prentice Hall, 2012.

Naffine, Ngaire. *Gender, Crime and Feminism*. Brookfield, VT: Dartmouth Publishing Company, 1995.

Nagin, Daniel S., Francis T. Cullen, and Cheryl Lero Jonson. "Imprisonment and Reoffending." *Crime and Justice: A Review of Research* 38 (2009): 115–200.

Pager, Devah. *Marked: Race, Crime, and Finding Work in an Era of Mass Incarceration*. Chicago: University of Chicago Press, 2009.

Paternoster, Raymond, and Ronet Bachman. *Explaining Criminals and Crime: Essays in Contemporary Criminological Theory*. Los Angeles: Roxbury Publishing Company, 2001.

Pepinsky, Hal. "Peacemaking Criminology." *Routledge Handbook of Critical Criminology*, edited by W. S. DeKeseredy and M. Dragiewicz, 186–193. New York: Routledge, 2012.

Pomfret, John. "Chinese Crime Rate Soars as Economic Problems Grow." *The Washington Post*, January 21, 1999: A19.

Pridemore, William Alex. "Socioeconomic Change and Homicide in a Transitional Society." *The Sociological Quarterly* 48 (2007): 229–251.

Quinney, Richard. *Critique of Legal Order: Crime Control in Capitalist Society*. Boston: Little, Brown, 1974.

Reiman, Jeffrey, and Paul Leighton. *The Rich Get Richer and the Poor Get Prison: Ideology, Class, and Criminal Justice*. Upper Saddle River, NJ: Prentice Hall, 2013.

Renzetti, Claire. *Feminist Criminology*. New York: Routledge, 2013.

Restivo, Emily, and Mark M. Lanier. "Measuring the Contextual Effects and Mitigating Factors of Labeling Theory." *Justice Quarterly* 2013. DOI: 10.1080/07418825.2012.756115.

Ritzer, George, and Jeff Stepinsky. *Sociological Theory*. New York: McGraw Hill, 2014.

Sato, Yasunobu. "How to Deal with Corruption in Transitional and Developing Economies: A Vietnamese Case Study." *Journal of Financial Crime* 16 (2009): 220–228.

Sellin, Thorsten. *Culture Conflict and Crime*. New York: Social Science Research Council, 1938.

Sherman, Lawrence W. "Defiance, Deterrence, and Irrelevance: A Theory of the Criminal Sanction." *Journal of Research in Crime and Delinquency* 30 (1993): 445–473.

Siegal, Ida. "NY Man Exonerated of Rape, Murder Gets Master's Degree in Criminal Justice." www.nbcnewyork.com, May 29, 2013. http://www.nbcnewyork.com/news/local/Wrongly-Convicted-Man-Graduates-John-Jay-College-Masters-209281011.html.

Sweeten, Gary. "Who Will Graduate? Disruption of High School Education by Arrest and Court Involvement." *Justice Quarterly* 23 (2006): 462–480.

Tannenbaum, Frank. *Crime and the Community*. Boston: Ginn, 1938.

Taylor, Ian, Paul Walton, and Jock Young. *The New Criminology: For a Social Theory of Deviance*. London: Routledge and Kegan Paul, 1973.

Toby, Jackson. "The New Criminology Is the Old Baloney." *Radical Criminology: The Coming Crises*, edited by J. A. Inciardi, 124–132. Beverly Hills, CA: Sage Publications, 1980.

Toews, Barb. "Toward a Restorative Justice Pedagogy: Reflections on Teaching Restorative Justice in Correctional Facilities." *Contemporary Justice Review* 16 (2013): 6–27.

Turk, Austin T. *Criminality and Legal Order*. Chicago: Rand McNally, 1969.

Vold, George. *Theoretical Criminology*. New York: Oxford University Press, 1958.

Walker, Samuel, Cassia Spohn, and Miriam DeLone. *The Color of Justice: Race, Ethnicity, and Crime in America*. Belmont, CA: Wadsworth Publishing Company, 2012.

Ward, Dick. "Vietnam: The Criminal Justice Challenge of Moving Toward a Market Economy." *CJ International* 11 (1995).

West, Candace, and Don H. Zimmerman. "Doing Gender." *Gender and Society* 1 (1987): 125–151.

Western, Bruce. *Punishment and Inequality in America*. New York: Russell Sage Foundation Publications, 2006.

Chapter 10, Violent Crime: Homicide, Assault, and Robbery

Administration on Children Youth and Families. *Child Maltreatment 2011*. Washington, DC: U.S. Department of Health and Human Services, U.S. Government Printing Office, 2012.

Alvarez, Alex, and Ronet Bachman. *Murder American Style*. Belmont, CA: Wadsworth/Thomson Learning, 2003.

Anderson, Elijah. *Code of the Street: Decency, Violence, and the Moral Life of the Inner City*. New York: W.W. Norton, 2000.

Associated Press. "Brazil Protests Expand to Over One Million People." *CBSNews.com*, June 20, 2013. http://www.cbsnews.com/8301-202_162-57590383/brazil-protests-expand-to-over-one-million-people/.

Bakalar, Nicholas. "Childhood: More Abuse Seen in Areas of Fiscal Stress." *New York Times*, (2012) July 24: D6.

Baskin, Deborah R., and Ira B. Sommers. *Casualties of Community Disorder: Women's Careers in Violent Crime*. Boulder: Westview Press, 1998.

Begley, Sharon. "The Anatomy of Violence." *Newsweek*, April 30, 2007: 40–44.

Blee, Kathleen. *Inside Organized Racism: Women in the Hate Movement*. Berkeley: University of California Press, 2002.

Braga, Anthony A., David M. Hureau, and Andrew V. Papachristos. "The Relevance of Micro Places to Citywide Robbery Trends: A Longitudinal Analysis of Robbery Incidents at Street Corners and Block Faces in Boston." *Journal of Research in Crime & Delinquency* 48 (2011): 7–32.

Brinton, Howard H. *Friends for 300 Years*. New York: Harper and Row, 1952.

Brown, Richard Maxwell. "Historical Patterns of American Violence." *Violence: Patterns, Causes, Public Policy*, edited by N. A. Weiner, M. A. Zahn, and R. J. Sagi, 4–15. San Diego: Harcourt Brace Jovanovich, 1990.

Butterfield, Fox. "A History of Homicide Surprises the Experts: Decline in U.S. Before Recent Increase." *New York Times*, (1994) October 23: 16.

Cancino, Jeffrey M., Ramiro Martinez, and Jacob I. Stowell. "The Impact of Neighborhood Context on Intragroup and Intergroup Robbery: The San Antonio Experience." *The ANNALS of the American Academy of Political and Social Science* 623 (2009): 12–24.

Conklin, John. *Robbery and the Criminal Justice System.* Philadelphia, PA: Lippincott, 1972.

Currie, Elliott. *Confronting Crime: An American Challenge.* New York: Pantheon Books, 1985.

———. "On Being Right, But Unhappy." *Criminology & Public Policy* 9 (2010): 1–10.

D'Antonio-Del Rio, Julia M., Jessica M. Doucet, and Chantel D. Chauvin. "Violent and Vindictive Women: A Re-Analysis of the Southern Subculture of Violence." *Sociological Spectrum* 30 (2010): 484–503.

Davenport, Justin. "Murder Rate Hits 42-Year-Low in London." *London Evening Standard,* January 23, 2013. http://www.standard.co.uk/news/crime/murder-rate-hits-42yearlow-in-london-8462974.html.

DeFronzo, James, Ashley Ditta, Lance Hannon, et al. "Male Serial Homicide: The Influence of Cultural and Structural Variables." *Homicide Studies* 11 (2007): 3–14.

Doty, C. Stewart. "The KKK in Maine Was Not OK." *Bangor Daily News,* (1994) June 11-12: A11.

Elias, Norbert. *The Civilizing Process: The History of Manners.* New York: Urizen, 1978 (1939).

English, Diana J. "The Extent and Consequences of Child Maltreatment." *The Future of Children* 8 (1998): 39–53.

Federal Bureau of Investigation. *Crime in the United States, 2011.* Washington, DC: Federal Bureau of Investigation, 2012.

Feldberg, Michael. "Urbanization as a Cause of Violence: Philadelphia as a Test Case." *The Peoples of Philadelphia: A History of Ethnic Groups and Lower-Class Life, 1790–1940,* edited by A. F. Davis and M. H. Haller, 53–69. Philadelphia, PA: University of Pennsylvania Press, 1998.

Felson, Richard B., and Henry J. Steadman. "Situational Factors in Disputes Leading to Criminal Violence." *Criminology* 21 (1983): 59–74.

Fenton, Justin, Justin George, and Luke Broadwater. "Despair, Resolve in Baltimore After 20 Shot Over the Weekend." *Baltimore Sun,* June 24, 2013. http://articles.baltimoresun.com/2013-06-24/news/bs-md-ci-homicide-crisis-20130624_1_southwest-baltimore-east-baltimore-city-council-members.

Fox, James Alan, and Jack Levin. *Extreme Killing: Understanding Serial and Mass Murder.* Thousand Oaks, CA: Sage Publications, 2005.

Fox, James Alan, Jack Levin, and Kenna Quinet. *The Will to Kill: Making Sense of Senseless Murder.* Upper Saddle River, NJ: Prentice Hall, 2012.

Fox, James Alan, and Marianne W. Zawitz. *Homicide Trends in the United States.* Washington, DC: Bureau of Justice Statistics, U.S. Department of Justice, 1998.

Gil, David G. *Violence Against Children.* Cambridge, MA: Cambridge University Press, 1979.

Glymour, Bruce, Clark Glymour, and Maria Glymour. "Watching Social Science: The Debate About the Effects of Exposure to Televised Violence on Aggressive Behavior." *American Behavioral Scientist* 51 (2008): 1231–1259.

Groff, Elizabeth. "Simulation for Theory Testing and Experimentation: An Example Using Routine Activity Theory and Street Robbery." *Journal of Quantitative Criminology* 23 (2007): 75–103.

Gurr, Ted Robert. "Historical Trends in Violent Crime: Europe and the United States." *Violence in America: The History of Crime,* vol. 1, edited by T. R. Gurr, 21–54. Newbury Park, CA: Sage Publications, 1989.

Hargrove, Thomas. "Most Serial Killing Victims Are Women, FBI Reports." *San Angelo Standard-Times,* November 27, 2010. http://www.gosanangelo.com/news/2010/nov/27/most-serial-killing-victims-are-women-fbi/.

Harrell, Erika. *Workplace Violence, 1993–2009.* Washington, DC: Bureau of Justice Statistics, U.S. Department of Justice, 2011.

Harris, Anthony R., S. H. Thomas, G. A. Fisher, et al. "Murder and Medicine: The Lethality of Criminal Assault, 1960–1999." *Homicide Studies* 6 (2002): 128–166.

Hawkins, Darnell F. "Editor's Introduction." *Violent Crime: Assessing Race and Ethnic Differences,* edited by D. F. Hawkins, xiii–xxv. Cambridge: Cambridge University Press, 2003.

Helderman, Rosalind S. "Va. Senate Votes to Allow Guns in Restaurants." *Washington Post,* February 16, 2010. http://voices.washingtonpost.com/virginiapolitics/2010/02/va_senate_votes_to_allow_guns.html.

Herbert, Bob. "A Volatile Young Man, Humiliation and a Gun." *New York Times,* April 19, 2007: A27.

Hobbs, Dick. "Mannish Boys: Danny, Chris, Crime, Masculinity and Business." *Just Boys Doing Business? Men, Masculinities and Crime,* edited by T. Newburn and E. A. Stanko, 118–134. London: Routledge, 1994.

Holmes, Ronald M., and Stephen T. Holmes. *Murder in America, 2nd ed.* Thousand Oaks, CA: Sage Publications, 2001.

Hoskin, Anthony W. "Armed Americans: The Impact of Firearm Availability on National Homicide Rates." *Justice Quarterly* 18 (2001): 569–592.

Jackman, Tom. "Guns Worn in Open Legal, But Alarm Va." *Washington Post,* July 15, 2004: A1.

Jackson, Shelly L., and Thomas L. Hafemeister. *Understanding Elder Abuse: New Directions for Developing Theories of Elder Abuse Occurring in Domestic Settings.* Washington, DC: National Institute of Justice, 2013.

Jacobs, Bruce A., and Richard Wright. "Stick-Up, Street Culture, and Offender Motivation." *Criminology* 37 (1999): 149–173.

Johannesen, Mark, and Dina Logiudice. "Elder Abuse: A Systematic Review of Risk Factors in Community-Dwelling Elders." *Age & Ageing* 42 (2013): 292–298.

Johnston, Lloyd D., Jerald G. Bachman, and Patrick M. O'Malley. *Monitoring the Future: Questionnaire Responses from the Nation's High School Seniors 2011.* Ann Arbor, MI: Survey Research Center, Institute for Social Research, University of Michigan, 2013.

Kaplan, Arline. "Violence in the Media: What Effects on Behavior? (Cover Story)." *Psychiatric Times* 29 (2012): 1–11.

Katz, Jack. "The Motivation of the Persistent Robber." *Crime and Justice: A Review of Research,* vol. 14, edited by M. Tonry, 277–306. Chicago: University of Chicago Press, 1991.

Kaufman, Joanne M. "Explaining the Race/Ethnicity-Violence Relationship: Neighborhood Context and Social Psychological Processes." *Justice Quarterly* 22 (2005): 224–251.

Kellerman, Arthur L., et al. "Gun Ownership as a Risk Factor for Homicide in the Home." *New England Journal of Medicine* 329 (1993): 1084–1092.

Kimmel, Michael S., and Michael A. Messner. *Men's Lives.* Boston: Pearson, 2013.

Kleck, Gary, and Marc Gertz. "Armed Resistance to Crime: The Prevalence and Nature of Self-Defense with a Gun." *Journal of Criminal Law and Criminology* 85 (1995): 150–187.

Kruttschnitt, Candace, and Kristin Carbone-Lopez. "Moving Beyond the Stereotypes: Women's Subjective Accounts of Their Violent Crime." *Criminology* 44 (2006): 321–351.

Kuhns, Joseph B., David B. Wilson, Tammatha A. Clodfelter, et al. "A Meta-Analysis of Alcohol Toxicology Study Findings Among Homicide Victims." *Addiction* 106 (2011): 62–72.

Lane, Roger. *Roots of Violence in Black Philadelphia, 1860–1900.* Cambridge: Harvard University Press, 1986.

———. "On the Social Meaning of Homicide Trends in America." *Violence in America: The History of Crime,* vol. 1, edited by T. R. Gurr, 55–79. Newbury Park, CA: Sage Publications, 1989.

Langton, Lynn, and Michael Planty. *Hate Crime, 2003–2009.* Washington, DC: Bureau of Justice Statistics, U.S. Department of Justice, 2011.

Leshner, Alan I., Bruce M. Altevogt, Arlene F. Lee, et al. *Priorities for Research to Reduce the Threat of Firearm-Related Violence.* Washington, DC: The National Academies Press, 2013.

Lott, John R., Jr. *More Guns, Less Crime.* Chicago: University of Chicago Press, 2000.

Mann, Coramae Richey. "Black Female Homicide in the United States." *Journal of Interpersonal Violence* 5 (1990): 176–201.

Maguire, Kathleen. "Sourcebook of Criminal Justice Statistics." 2013. Available at: http://www.albany.edu/sourcebook/.

McDowall, David, and Brian Wiersema. "The Incidence of Defensive Firearm Use by U.S. Crime Victims, 1987 Through 1990." *American Journal of Public Health* 84 (1994): 1982–1984.

McNulty, Thomas L., and Paul E. Bellair. "Explaining Racial and Ethnic Differences in Serious Adolescent Violent Behavior." *Criminology* 41 (2003): 709–748.

Messerschmidt, James W. *Masculinities and Crime: Critique and Reconceptualization of Theory.* Lanham, MD: Rowman and Littlefield, 1993.

Messerschmidt, James W., and Stephen Tomsen. "Masculinities." *Routledge Handbook of Critical Criminology,* edited by W. S. DeKeseredy and M. Dragiewicz, 172–185. New York: Routledge, 2012.

Messner, Steven F., Robert D. Baller, and Matthew P. Zevenbergen. "The Legacy of Lynching and Southern Homicide." *American Sociological Review* 70 (2005): 633–655.

Messner, Steven F., Glenn Deane, and Mark Beaulieu. "A Log-Multiplicative Association Model for Allocating Homicides with Unknown Victim-Offender Relationships." *Criminology* 40 (2002): 457–479.

Miller, Jody, and Scott H. Decker. "Young Women and Gang Violence: Gender, Street Offending, and Violent Victimization in Gangs." *Justice Quarterly* 18 (2001): 115–140.

Miller, Matthew, David Hemenway, and Deborah Azrael. "State-Level Homicide Victimization Rates in the US in Relation to Survey Measures of Household Firearm Ownership, 2001–2003." *Social Science and Medicine* 64 (2007): 656–664.

National Center on Elder Abuse. "Statistics/Data." 2013. http://www.ncea.aoa.gov/Library/Data/index.aspx#problem. Government agency in Washington, DC.

Nickeas, Peter, David Jackson, Mitch Smith, et al. "Weekend Violence Leaves 9 Dead, 47 Shot." *Chicago Tribune*, June 17, 2013. http://articles.chicago tribune.com/2013-06-17/news/chi-chicago-crime-shooting-gun-violence-marquette-park_1_weekend-violence-little-village-neighborhood-day-sunday.

Ogle, Robbin S., Daniel Maier-Katkin, and Thomas J. Bernard. "A Theory of Homicidal Behavior Among Women." *Criminology* 33 (1995): 173–193.

Ouimet, Marc. "A World of Homicides: The Effect of Economic Development, Income Inequality, and Excess Infant Mortality on the Homicide Rate for 165 Countries in 2010." *Homicide Studies* 16 (2012): 238–258.

Ousey, Graham C., and Matthew R. Lee. "Homicide Trends and Illicit Drug Markets: Exploring Differences Across Time." *Justice Quarterly* 24 (2007): 48–79.

Painter-Davis, Noah. "Structural Disadvantage and American Indian Homicide and Robbery Offending." *Homicide Studies* 16 (2012): 219–237.

Parker, Robert Nash. "Poverty, Subculture of Violence, and Type of Homicide." *Social Forces* 67 (1989): 983–1007.

Phillips, Julie A. "White, Black, and Latino Homicide Rates: Why the Difference?" *Social Problems* 49 (2002): 349–374.

Pinker, Steven. *The Better Angels of Our Nature: Why Violence Has Declined*. New York: Penguin, 2012.

Piquero, Nicole Leeper, Alex R. Piquero, Jessica M. Craig, et al. "Assessing Research on Workplace violence, 2000–2012." *Aggression and Violent Behavior* 18 (2013): 383–394.

Polk, Kenneth. *When Men Kill: Scenarios of Masculine Violence*. Cambridge: Cambridge University Press, 1994.

Pridemore, William Alex, and Tony H. Grubesic. "Alcohol Outlets and Community Levels of Interpersonal Violence: Spatial Density, Outlet Type, and Seriousness of Assault." *Journal of Research in Crime & Delinquency* 50 (2013): 132–159.

Rhodes, Richard. "Hollow Claims About Fantasy Violence." *New York Times*, (2000) September 17: 19.

Romero, Simon. "Public Rage Catching Up with Brazil's Congress." The New York Times June 28, 2013: A1.

Rosenfeld, Richard. "Patterns in Adult Homicide: 1980–1995." *The Crime Drop in America*, edited by A. Blumstein and J. Wallman, 130–163. Cambridge: Cambridge University Press, 2006.

Rothstein, Ethan. "Guns & Gumbo: Leesburg Restaurant Encourages Customers to Open Carry." *Lessburg Today*, April 3, 2013. http://www.leesburgtoday.com/news/guns-gumbo-leesburg-restaurant-encourages-customers-to-open-carry/article_fa7f26b4-9c6b-11e2-8665-0019bb2963f4.html.

Rowan, Edward L. *Understanding Child Sexual Abuse*. Jackson, MS: University of Mississippi Press, 2006.

Russell, Diana. *Sexual Exploitation: Rape, Child Sexual Abuse, and Harassment*. Beverly Hills: Sage Publications, 1984.

Sampson, Robert J., and William Julius Wilson. "Toward a Theory of Race, Crime, and Urban Inequality." *Crime and Inequality*, edited by J. Hagan and R. D. Peterson, 37–54. Stanford: Stanford University Press, 1995.

Smith, Michael. "Spanking Kids Still Common in U.S." *MedPage Today*, August 23, 2010. http://www.medpagetoday.com/Pediatrics/DomesticViolence/21816.

Spangler, Todd. "Pa. Gunman Kills 2, Wounds 3 Seriously." *Boston Globe*, (2000) March 2:A9.

Statistics Canada. "Homicide in Canada, 2011." 2012. http://www.statcan .gc.ca/daily-quotidien/121204/dq121204a-eng.htm.

Steffensmeier, Darrell, and Dana Haynie. "Gender, Structural Disadvantage, and Urban Crime: Do Macrosocial Variables Also Explain Female Offending Rates?" *Criminology* 38 (2000): 403–438.

Stewart, Eric A., and Ronald L. Simons. "Structure and Culture in African American Adolescent Violence: A Partial Test of the 'Code of the Street' Thesis." *Justice Quarterly* 23 (2006): 1–33.

Swigonski, Mary E., Robin S. Mama, and Kelly Ward. *From Hate Crimes to Human Rights: A Tribute to Matthew Shepard*. New York: Harrington Park Press, 2001.

Tark, Jongyeon, and Gary Kleck. "Resisting Crime: The Effects of Victim Action on the Outcomes of Crimes." *Criminology* 42 (2004): 861–909.

Travis, Tiffani A., and Perry Hardy. *Skinheads: A Guide to an American Subclture*. Santa Barbara, CA: Greenwood, 2012.

Truman, Jennifer L. *Criminal Victimization 2010*. Washington, DC: Bureau of Justice Statistics, U.S. Department of Justice, 2011.

Truman, Jennifer L., and Michael Planty. *Criminal Victimization, 2011*. Washington, DC: Bureau of Justice Statistics, U.S. Department of Justice, 2012.

Tynan, Trudy. "Medical Improvements Lower Homicide Rate." *Washington Post*, August 12, 2002: A2.

United Nations Office on Drugs and Crime. *UNODC Homicide Statistics*. 2013. http://www.unodc.org/unodc/en/data-and-analysis/homicide.html.

Weiner, Neil Alan, Margaret A. Zahn, and Rita J. Sagi. "Introduction: What Is Violence?" in *Violence: Patterns, Causes, Public Policy*, edited by N. A. Weiner, M. A. Zahn, and R. J. Sagi, xi–xvii. San Diego: Harcourt Brace Jovanovich, 1990.

Widom, Cathy Spatz, Sally Czaja, Helen W. Wilson, et al. "Do the Long-Term Consequences of Neglect Differ for Children of Different Races and Ethnic Backgrounds?" *Child Maltreatment* 18 (2013): 42–55.

Wolfgang, Marvin E. *Patterns in Criminal Homicide*. Philadelphia, PA: University of Pennsylvania Press, 1958.

Young, Jeffrey. "Mental Health Solutions Alone Can't Thwart Gun Violence, Experts Say." *Huffington Post*, January 31, 2013. http://www.huffingtonpost .com/2013/01/31/mental-health-gun-violence_n_2583986.html.

Zimring, Franklin E., and Gordon Hawkins. *Crime Is Not the Problem: Lethal Violence in America*. New York: Oxford University Press, 1997.

Chapter 11, Violence Against Women

Alderden, Megan A., and Sarah E. Ullman. "Creating a More Complete and Current Picture: Examining Police and Prosecutor Decision-Making when Processing Sexual Assault Cases." *Violence Against Women* 18 (2012): 525–551.

Allen, Christopher T., Suzanne C. Swan, and Chitra Raghavan. "Gender Symmetry, Sexism, and Intimate Partner Violence." *Journal of Interpersonal Violence* 24 (2009): 1816–1834.

Amnesty International. *Darfur: Rape as a Weapon of War: Sexual Violence and Its Consequences*. London: Amnesty International, 2004a.

———. *It's in Our Hands: Stop Violence Against Women. Summary*. London: Amnesty International, 2004b.

———. *Maze of Injustice: The Failure to Protect Indigenous Women from Sexual Violence in the USA*. New York: Amnesty International, 2007.

———. *Case Closed: Rape and Human Rights in the Nordic Countries: Summary Report*. London: Amnesty International, 2010a.

———. *'I Can't Afford Justice': Violence Against Women in Uganda Continues Unpunished and Unchecked*. London: Amnesty International, 2010b.

Armstrong, Elizabeth A., Laura Hamilton, and Brian Sweeney. "Sexual Assault on Campus: A Multilevel, Integrative Approach to Party Rape." *Social Problems* 53 (2006): 483–499.

Baron, Larry, and Murray A. Straus. "Four Theories of Rape: A Macrosociological Analysis." *Social Problems* 34 (1987): 467–489.

Beneke, Tim. "Men on Rape." *Men's Lives*, edited by M. S. Kimmel and M. A. Messner. Upper Saddle River, NJ: Pearson, 2013.

Benson, Michael, John Wooldredge, Amy B. Thistlethwaite, et al. "The Correlation between Race and Domestic Violence Is Confounded with Community Context." *Social Problems* 51 (2004): 326–342.

Bergen, Raquel Kennedy. *Marital Rape: New Research and Directions*. Harrisburg, PA: National Resource Center on Domestic Violence, 2006.

Black, M. C., K. C Basile, M. J. Breiding, et al. *The National Intimate Partner and Sexual Violence Survey (NISVS): 2010 Summary Report*. Atlanta: Centers for Disease Control and Prevention, 2011.

Blumberg, Rae Lesser. "A Paradigm for Predicting the Position of Women: Policy Implications and Problems." *Sex Roles and Social Policy*, edited by J. Lipman-Blumen and J. Bernard. London: Sage Publications, 1979.

Browne, Angela. "Fear and the Perception of Alternatives: Asking 'Why Battered Women Don't Leave' Is the Wrong Question." *The Criminal Justice System and Women: Offenders, Victims, and Workers*, edited by B. R. Price and N. J. Sokoloff, 228–245. New York: McGraw-Hill, Inc, 1995.

———."Fear and the Perception of Alternatives: Asking 'Why Battered Women Don't Leave' Is the Wrong Question." *The Criminal Justice System and Women: Offenders, Prisoners, Victims, and Workers*, edited by B. R. Price and N. J. Sokoloff, 343–359. New York: McGraw Hill, 2004.

Brownmiller, Susan. *Against Our Will: Men, Women, and Rape*. New York: Simon and Schuster, 1975.

Brush, Lisa D., Angela Hattery, and Earl Smith. "On Violence Against Women (letters to the editor)." *Contexts* 6 (2007): 6–7.

Bureau of Justice Statistics. "NCVS Victimization Analysis Tool." 2013. http://www.bjs.gov/index.cfm?ty=nvat.

Burgoyne, Whitney. "UA Community Protest Against Sexual Violence at Take Back the Night." *Arizona Daily Wildcat*, April 24, 2013. http://www.wildcat .arizona.edu/article/2013/04/ua-community-protest-against-sexual-violence-at-take-back-the-night.

Caputi, Jane, and Diana E. H. Russell. "Femicide: Sexist Terrorism against Women." *Femicide: The Politics of Woman Killing*, edited by J. Radford and D. E. H. Russell, 13–21. New York: Twayne Publishers, 1992.

Cassata, Donna, and Lolita C. Baldor. "Military Sex-Assault Reports Up; Changes Ordered." *Washington Times*, May 7, 2013. http://www.washingtontimes.com/news/2013/may/7/military-sex-assault-reports-changes-ordered/?page=all.

Catalano, Shannan. *Intimate Partner Violence, 1993–2010*. Washington, DC: Bureau of Justice Statistics, U.S. Department of Justice, 2012a.

———. *Stalking Victims in the United States-Revised*. Washington, DC: Bureau of Justice Statistics, U.S. Department of Justice, 2012b.

———. Catalano, Shannan. 2007. *Intimate Partner Violence in the United States*. Washington, DC: Bureau of Justice Statistics, U.S. Department of Justice.

Cheng, Maria. "UN Agency Reports Domestic Violence at 'Epidemic' Levels." *Boston Globe*, June 21, 2013. http://www.bostonglobe.com/news/world/2013/06/20/third-world-women-suffer-domestic-violence/z1SnbnOc8UF9iLDItvK4DO/story.html.

Chesney-Lind, Meda. "Criminalizing Victimization: The Unintended Consequences of Pro-Arrest Policies for Girls and Women." *Journal of Research in Crime and Delinquency* 2 (2002): 81–90.

Corvo, Kenneth, and Pamela Johnson. "Sharpening Ockham's Razor: The Role of Psychopathology and Neuropsychopathology in the Perpetration of Domestic Violence." *Aggression and Violent Behavior* 18 (2013): 175–182.

Davis, Robert C., Barbara E. Smith, and Bruce Taylor. "Increasing the Proportion of Domestic Violence Arrests That Are Prosecuted: A Natural Experiment in Milwaukee." *Criminology & Public Policy* 2 (2003): 263–282.

DeKeseredy, Walter S. "Future Directions." *Violence Against Women* 12 (2006): 1078–1085.

DeKeseredy, Walter S., and Martin D. Schwartz. *Dangerous Exits: Escaping Abusive Relationships in Rural America*. New Brunswick, NJ: Rutgers University Press, 2009.

DeKeseredy, Walter S., Martin D. Schwartz, Danielle Fagen, et al. "Separation/Divorce Sexual Assault: The Contribution of Male Support." *Feminist Criminology* 1 (2006): 228–250.

Deming, Michelle E., Eleanor Krassen Covan, Suzanne C. Swan, et al. "Exploring Rape Myths, Gendered Norms, Group Processing, and the Social Context of Rape Among College Women: A Qualitative Analysis." *Violence Against Women* 19 (2013): 465–485.

Demos, John. *The Enemy Within: 2,000 Years of Witch-Hunting in the Western World*. New York: Penguin Books, 2009.

Dillon, Nancy. "Erin Andrews Alleged Stalker Michael Barrett Ordered to Serve Sentence in Atlanta Jail Near Her Home." *New York Daily News*, May 3, 2010. http://www.nydailynews.com/gossip/2010/05/03/2010-05-03_erin_andrews_alleged_stalker_michael_barrett_ordered_to_serve_sentence_in_atlant.html.

Dobash, Russell P., R. Emerson Dobash, Margo Wilson, et al. "The Myth of Sexual Symmetry in Marital Violence." *Social Problems* 39 (1992): 71–91.

Elias, Marilyn. "A Third of Women Hit by Male Partner." *USA Today*, July 07, 1994: 10.

Federal Bureau of Investigation. *Crime in the United States, 2011*. Washington, DC: Federal Bureau of Investigation, 2012.

Felson, Richard B. "Is Violence Against Women About Women or About Violence?" *Contexts* 5 (2006): 21–25.

Felson, Richard B., Jeffrey M. Ackerman, and Catherine A. Gallagher. "Police Intervention and the Repeat of Domestic Assault." *Criminology* 43 (2005): 563–588.

Felson, Richard B., and Kelsea Jo Lane. "Does Violence Involving Women and Intimate Partners Have a Special Etiology?" *Criminology* 48 (2010): 321–338.

Ferraro, Kathleen J. "Cops, Courts, and Woman Battering." *The Criminal Justice System and Women: Offenders, Victims, and Workers*, edited by B. R. Price and N. J. Sokoloff, 262–271. New York: McGraw-Hill, Inc, 1995.

Fisher, Bonnie S., Francis T. Cullen, and Michael G. Turner. "Being Pursued: Stalking Victimization in a National Study of College Women." *Criminology & Social Policy* 1 (2002): 257–308.

Fisher, Bonnie S., Leah E. Daigle, and Francis T. Cullen. "What Distinguishes Single from Recurrent Sexual Victims? The Role of Lifestyle-Routine Activities and First-Incident Characteristics." *Justice Quarterly* 27 (2010): 102–129.

Fleming, Kimberly N., Tamara L. Newton, Rafael Fernandez-Botran, et al. "Intimate Partner Stalking Victimization and Posttraumatic Stress Symptoms in Post-Abuse Women." *Violence Against Women* 18 (2012): 1368–1389.

Gardner, Saundra. "Real Domestic Tragedy Continues." *Bangor Daily News*, June 29, 1994: A9.

Griffin, Susan. "Rape: The All-American Crime." *Ramparts*, September 1971: 26–35.

Groth, A. Nicholas. *Men Who Rape: The Psychology of the Offender*. New York: Plenum Press, 1979.

Harris, Ron. "They Fear Ambush, Snipers-and an Enemy Within." *St. Louis Post-Dispatch*, June 4, 2007: A1.

Hester, Marianne. "The Witch-Craze in Sixteenth- and Seventeenth-Century England as Social Control of Women." *Femicide: The Politics of Woman Killing*, edited by J. Radford and D. E. H. Russell, 27–39. New York: Twayne Publishers, 1992.

Hood, Jane C. " 'Let's Get a Girl': Male Bonding Rituals in America." *Men's Lives*, edited by M. S. Kimmel and M. A. Messner, 307–311. Boston: Allyn and Bacon, 1995.

Horney, Karen. "The Problem of Feminine Masochism." *Psychoanalysis and Women*, edited by J. Miller. New York: Brunner/Mazel, 1973.

Huisman, Kimberly A. "Wife Battering in Asian American Communities: Identifying the Service Needs of an Overlooked Segment of the U.S. Population." *Violence Against Women* 2 (1996): 260–283.

Humphries, Drew. "No Easy Answers: Public Policy, Criminal Justice, and Domestic Violence." *Criminology & Public Policy* 2 (2002): 91–96.

Johnson, Michael P. "Conflict and Control: Gender Symmetry and Asymmetry in Domestic Violence." *Violence Against Women* 12 (2006): 1003–1018.

Kay, Barbara. "Male Victims of Domestic Abuse Continue to Suffer in Solitude." *National Post*, April 29, 2013. http://fullcomment.nationalpost.com/2013/04/29/barbara-kay-male-victims-of-domestic-abuse-continue-to-suffer-in-solitude/.

Kim, Jinseok, and Karen A. Gray. "Leave or Stay? Battered Women's Decision After Intimate Partner Violence." *Journal of Interpersonal Violence* 23 (2008): 1465–1482.

Kimmel, Michael S. " 'Gender Symmetry' in Domestic Violence: A Substantive and Methodological Research Review." *Violence Against Women* 8 (2002): 1332–1363.

Klevens, Joanne, Gene Shelley, Carmen Clavel-Arcas, et al. "Latinos' Perspectives and Experiences with Intimate Partner Violence." *Violence Against Women* 13 (2007): 141–158.

Lauritsen, Janet L., and Karen Heimer. "The Gender Gap in Violent Victimization, 1973–2004." *Journal of Quantitative Criminology* 24 (2008): 125–147.

Littner, Ner. "Psychology of the Sex Offender: Causes, Treatment, Prognosis." *Police Law Quarterly* 3 (1973): 5–31.

Marshall, Linda L., and Patricia Rose. "Premarital Violence: The Impact of Family of Origin Violence, Stress, and Reciprocity." *Violence and Victims* 5 (1990): 51–64.

Martin, Kimberly, Lynne M. Vieraitis, and Sarah Britto. "Gender Equality and Women's Absolute Status: A Test of the Feminist Models of Rape." *Violence Against Women* 12 (2006): 321–339.

Martin, Sandra L., Amy Ong Tsui, Kuhu Maitra, et al. "Domestic Violence in Northern India." *American Journal of Epidemiology* 150 (1999): 417–426.

McGrory, Brian. "Easy-Going Image, Violent Acts." *Boston Globe*, June 19, 1994: 12.

Melton, Heather. "Rape Myths: Impacts on Victims of Rape." *Female Victims of Crime: Reality Reconsidered*, edited by V. Garcia and J. Clifford. Upper Saddle River, NJ: Prentice Hall, 2010.

Mouilso, Emily R., and Karen S. Calhoun. "The Role of Rape Myth Acceptance and Psychopathy in Sexual Assault Perpetration." *Journal of Aggression, Maltreatment & Trauma* 22 (2013): 159–174.

Mullen, Paul E., and Michele Pathé. "Stalking." *Crime and Justice: A Review of Research* 29 (2002): 273–318.

Ornstein, Petra, and Johanna Rickne. "When Does Intimate Partner Violence Continue After Separation?" *Violence Against Women* 19 (2013): 617–633.

Paul, Lisa A., Kate Walsh, Jenna L. McCauley, et al. "College Women's Experiences with Rape Disclosure: A National Study." *Violence Against Women* 19 (2013): 486–502.

Petrik, Norman D., Rebecca E. Petrik Olson, and Leah S. Subotnik. "Powerlessness and the Need to Control." *Journal of Interpersonal Violence* 9 (1994): 278–285.

Policastro, Christina, and Brian K. Payne. "The Blameworthy Victim: Domestic Violence Myths and the Criminalization of Victimhood." *Journal of Aggression, Maltreatment & Trauma* 22 (2013): 329–347.

Potter, Hillary. "An Argument for Black Feminist Criminology: Understanding African American Women's Experiences with Intimate Partner Abuse Using an Integrated Approach." *Feminist Criminology* 1 (2006): 106–124.

Randall, Melanie, and Lori Haskell. "Sexual Violence in Women's Lives: Findings from the Women's Safety Project, a Community-Based Survey." *Violence Against Women* 1 (1995): 6–31.

Rasche, Christine E. "Minority Women and Domestic Violence: The Unique Dilemmas of Battered Women of Color." *Journal of Contemporary Criminal Justice* 4 (1988): 150–171.

Reynolds, Pam. "Thousands Are Locked in with the Danger." *Boston Globe* (1987) March 29: A18.

Reyns, Bradford W., Billy Henson, and Bonnie S. Fisher. "Stalking in the Twilight Zone: Extent of Cyberstalking Victimization and Offending Among College Students." *Deviant Behavior* 33 (2012): 1–25.

Sanday, Peggy Reeves. "The Socio-Cultural Context of Rape: A Cross-Cultural Study." *Journal of Social Issues* 37 (1981): 5–27.

Saunders, Daniel G. "Are Physical Assaults by Wives and Girlfriends a Major Social Problem? A Review of the Literature." *Violence Against Women* 8 (2002): 1424–1448.

Schmitt, Eric. "Military Women Reporting Rapes by U.S. Soldiers." *New York Times*, February 25, 2004: A1.

Schwartz, Martin, Walter S. DeKeseredy, David Tait, et al. "Male Peer Support and a Feminist Routine Activities Theory: Understanding Sexual Assault on the College Campus." *Justice Quarterly* 18 (2001): 623–649.

Scully, Diana. "Rape Is the Problem." *The Criminal Justice System and Women: Offenders, Victims, and Workers*, edited by B. R. Price and N. J. Sokoloff, 197–215. New York: McGraw-Hill, Inc, 1995.

Sennott, Charles M. "Rights Groups Battle Burning of Women in Pakistan." *Boston Globe*, (1995) March 18: 1.

Sherman, Lawrence W. *Policing Domestic Violence: Experiments and Dilemmas.* New York: Free Press, 1992.

Sherman, Lawrence W., and Richard A. Berk. "The Specific Deterrent Effects of Arrest for Domestic Assault." *American Sociological Review* 49 (1984): 261–272.

Sherman, Lawrence W., and Ellen G. Cohn. "The Impact of Research on Legal Policy: The Minneapolis Domestic Violence Experiment." *Law and Society Review* 23 (1989): 117–144.

Stark, Evan. "Race, Gender, and Woman Battering." *Violent Crime: Assessing Race and Ethnic Differences*, edited by D. F. Hawkins, 171–197. Cambridge: Cambridge University Press, 2004.

Straus, Murray A. "Victims and Aggressors in Marital Violence." *American Behavioral Scientist* 23 (1980): 681–704.

———. "Physical Assaults by Wives: A Major Social Problem." *Current Controversies on Family Violence*, edited by R. J. Gelles and D. R. Loseke, 67–87. Newbury Park, CA: Sage Publications, 1993.

———. "Future Research on Gender Symmetry in Physical Assaults on Partners." *Violence Against Women* 12 (2006): 1086–1097.

Thekaekara, Mari Marcel. "A Bride Burnt Every Hour: The Horror of Dowry Deaths." *New Internationalist,* February 7, 2012. http://newint.org/blog/majority/2012/02/07/dowry-deaths-in-india/.

Tjaden, Patricia, and Nancy Thoennes. *Full Report of the Prevalence, Incidence, and Consequences of Violence Against Women.* Washington, DC: National Institute of Justice and the Centers for Disease Control and Prevention, 2000.

Valenti, Jessica. "Rape-Still No Joke." *Nation* 296 (2013a): 4–6.

———. "Rape: As American as Apple Pie." *Nation* 296 (2013b): 5–5.

———. "In Rape Tragedies, the Shame Is Ours." *Nation* May 6, 2013c. http://www.thenation.com/article/173911/rape-tragedies-shame-ours#axzz2YBZr5rcz.

Vanden Brook, Tom, and Gregg Zoroya. "Why the Military Hasn't Stopped Sexual Abuse." *USA Today,* May 15, 2013. http://www.usatoday.com/story/news/2013/05/15/why-the-military-hasnt-stopped-sexual-abuse-/2162399/.

Vieraitis, Lynne M., Sarah Britto, and Tomislav V. Kovandzic. "The Impact of Women's Status and Gender Inequality on Female Homicide Victimization Rates: Evidence from U.S. Counties." *Feminist Criminology* 2 (2007): 57–73.

Visher, Christy A., Adele Harrell, Lisa Newmark, et al. "Reducing Intimate Partner Violence: An Evaluation of a Comprehensive Justice System-Community Collaboration." *Criminology & Public Policy* 7 (2008): 495–523.

Walker, Lenore E. *The Battered Woman Syndrome.* New York: Springer Publishers, 1984.

Wax, Emily. "Thousands in Congo Suffer Scars of Violent Wartime Rapes." *Boston Globe,* November 3, 2003: A8.

White, Jacquelyn W., and John A. Humphrey. "Young People's Attitudes Toward Acquaintance Rape." *Readings in Deviant Behavior*, edited by A. Theo and T. Calhoun, 161–168. New York: HarperCollins, 1995.

World Health Organization. "Female Genital Mutilation." 2013. http://www.who.int/mediacentre/factsheets/fs241/en/.

Young, Myla H., Jerald Justice, and Philip Erdberg. "A Comparison of Rape and Molest Offenders in Prison Psychiatric Treatment." *International Journal of Offender Therapy & Comparative Criminology* 56 (2012): 1103–1123.

Chapter 12, Property Crime and Fraud

Abagnale, Frank. *Check Fraud and Identity Theft.* 2005. http://www.abagnale.com/pdf/AbagnaleFraudBulletinVol6.pdf.

Alexander, David. "Burglars Steal Police Officer's Handgun." *Times-Republican,* May 23, 2013. http://www.timesrepublican.com/page/content.detail/id/560490/Burglars-steal-police-officer-s-gun.html.

Andresen, Martin A. "Unemployment and Crime: A Neighborhood Level Panel Data Approach." *Social Science Research* 41 (2012): 1615–1628.

Animal Legal & Historical Center. *Statutes/Laws: New York.* 2013. http://www.animallaw.info/statutes/stusnyagri_mkts_121.htm.

Associated Press. *Knoller, Convicted in Dog Mauling, Released from Prison.* 2004. http://www.sfgate.com/cgi-bin/article.cgi?f=/news/archive/2004/01/01/state0155EST0133.DTL.

Bennett, Trevor, Katy Holloway, and David Farrington. "Does Neighborhood Watch Reduce Crime? A Systematic Review and Meta-Analysis." *Journal of Experimental Criminology* 2 (2006): 437–458.

Bernasco, Wim. "Burglary." *The Oxford Handbook of Crime and Public Policy*, edited by M. Tonry, 165–190. New York: Oxford Univeristy Press, 2009.

Binagman, Jeff. "Bingaman Urges Administration to Crack Down on Vehicle Smuggling Across US-Mexico Border (press release)." 2010. http://bingaman.senate.gov/news/20100202-02.cfm.

Braithwaite, Valerie. "Tax Evasion." *The Oxford Handbook of Crime and Public Policy*, edited by M. Tonry, 381–405. New York: Oxford University Press, 2009.

Brenner, Susan W. *Cybercrime and the Law: Challenges, Issues, and Outcomes.* Boston: Northeastern University Press, 2012.

Burt, Martha R., and Bonnie L. Katz. "Rape, Robbery, and Burglary: Responses to Actual and Feared Victimization with Special Focus on Women and the Elderly." *Victimology* 10 (1984): 325–358.

BusinessWire. "U.S. Leads the World in Credit Card Fraud, States the Nilson Report." November 21, 2011. http://www.businesswire.com/news/home/20111121005121/en/U.S.-Leads-World-Credit-Card-Fraud-states.

Cameron, Mary Owen. *The Booster and the Snitch: Department Store Shoplifting.* New York: Free Press, 1964.

Cantley, Vanessa B., and Megan R. U'Sellis. "Beware of Dog." *Trial: The National Legal Newsmagazine* 49 (2013): 42–48.

Cherbonneau, Michael, and Richard Wright. "Auto Theft." *The Oxford Handbook of Crime and Public Policy*, edited by M. Tonry, 191–222. New York: Oxford University Press, 2009.

Chesney-Lind, Meda, and Randall G. Sheldon. *Girls, Delinquency, and Juvenile Justice.* Pacific Grove, Ca: Brooks/Cole Publishing Company, 1992.

Clarke, Ronald V., and Rick Brown. "International Trafficking in Stolen Vehicles." *Crime and Justice: A Review of Research* 30 (2003): 197–227.

Clarke, Ronald V., and Patricia M. Harris. "Auto Theft and Its Prevention." *Crime and Justice: A Review of Research*, vol. 16, edited by M. Tonry, 1–54. Chicago: University of Chicago Press, 1992.

Cloward, Richard A., and Lloyd E. Ohlin. *Delinquency and Opportunity: A Theory of Delinquent Gangs.* New York: Free Press, 1960.

Cohen, Sharon. "Katrina Fraud Stretches Far Beyond Gulf." *Washington Post,* April 2, 2007. http://www.washingtonpost.com/wp-dyn/content/article/2007/04/02/AR2007040200379.html.

Consumer Reports. "Social Insecurity: What Millions of Online Users Don't Know Can Hurt Them." *Consumer Reports*, June, 2010: 24–27.

———. "Consumer Reports Survey: How Safe Is Your Home Computer?" *Consumer Reports,* May 1, 2013. http://news.consumerreports.org/electronics/2013/05/consumer-reports-survey-asks-how-safe-is-your-home-computer.html.

Cromwell, Paul. "Burglary: The Burglar's Perspective." *Critical Issues in Crime and Justice*, edited by A. R. Roberts, 35–50. Thousand Oaks, CA: Sage Publications, 1994.

Cromwell, Paul, and Karen McElrath. "Buying Stolen Property: An Opportunity Perspective." *Journal of Research in Crime and Delinquency* 31 (1994): 295–310.

Dabney, Dean A., Richard C. Hollinger, and Laura Dugan. "Who Actually Steals? A Study of Covertly Observed Shoplifters." *Justice Quarterly* 21 (2004): 693–728.

Decker, Scott, Richard Wright, Allison Redfern, et al. "A Woman's Place Is in the Home: Females and Residential Burglary." *Justice Quarterly* 10 (1993): 143–162.

Eck, John E., and Rob T. Guerette. "Place-Based Crime Prevention: Theory, Evidence, and Policy." *The Oxford Handbook of Crime Prevention*, edited by B. C. Welsh and D. P. Farrington, 354–383. New York: Oxford University Press, 2012.

Estrin, Michael. "Six Shadiest Auto Insurance Fraud Schemes." *Fox Business,* April 2, 2013. http://www.foxbusiness.com/personal-finance/2013/04/02/six-shadiest-auto-insurance-fraud-schemes/.

Farrell, Graham, Andromachi Tseloni, Jen Mailley, et al. "The Crime Drop and the Security Hypothesis." *Journal of Research in Crime & Delinquency* 48 (2011): 147–175.

Federal Bureau of Investigation. *Crime in the United States, 2011.* Washington, DC: Federal Bureau of Investigation, 2012.

Felson, Marcus, and Rachel Boba. *Crime and Everyday Life.* Thousand Oaks, CA: Sage Publications, 2010.

Felson, Marcus and Ronald V. Clarke. 2010. "Routine Precautions, Criminology, and Crime Prevention." Pp. 106–120 in *Criminology and Public Policy: Putting Theory to Work*, edited by H. D. Barlow and S. H. Decker. Philadelphia: Temple University Press.

Grannis, Kathy. "Troubled Economy Increases Shoplifting Rates, According to National Retail Security Survey (press release)." *National Retail Federation,* June 16, 2009. http://www.nrf.com/modules.php?name=News&op=viewlive&sp_id=746.

Hagan, John. "The Pleasures of Predation and Disrepute." *Law & Society Review* 24 (1990): 165–177.

Hayes International. "Theft Surveys: Shoplifting." 2009. http://www .hayesinternational.com/thft_srvys.html.

Hefley, Diana. "Everett Woman Charged with Felony After Dogs Attack 5." *Herald*, July 5, 2013. http://www.heraldnet.com/article/20130705/ NEWS01/707059901#Everett-woman-charged-with-felony-after-dogs-attack-5%0A.

Hepburn, John. "Occasional Criminals." *Major Forms of Crime*, edited by R. Meier, 73–94. Beverly Hills: Sage Publications, 1984.

Insurance Information Institute. *Insurance Fraud*. 2013. http://www.iii.org/issues_ updates/insurance-fraud.html.

Internal Revenue Service. "IRS Releases New Tax Gap Estimates; Compliance Rates Remain Statistically Unchanged from Previous Study." Washington, DC: Internal Revenue Service, 2012.

Johnston, Lloyd D., Jerald G. Bachman, and Patrick M. O'Malley. *Monitoring the Future: Questionnaire Responses from the Nation's High School Seniors 2011*. Ann Arbor, MI: Survey Research Center, Institute for Social Research, University of Michigan, 2013.

Katz, Jack. *Seductions of Crime: Moral and Sensual Attractions of Doing Evil*. New York: Basic Books, 1988.

Kellett, Sue, and Harriet Gross. "Addicted to Joyriding? An Exploration of Young Offenders, Accounts of Their Car Crime." *Psychology, Crime & Law* 12 (2006): 39–59.

Kerber, Ross. "TJX Credit Data Stolen." *Boston Globe*, January 18, 2007: A1.

Kikuchi, George, and Scott A. Desmond. "A Longitudinal Analysis of Neighborhood Crime Rates Using Latent Growth Curve Modeling." *Sociological Perspectives* 53 (2010): 127–149.

Koppel, Herbert. *Lifetime Likelihood of Victimization*. Washington, DC: U.S. Department of Justice, Bureau of Justice Statistics, 1987.

Langton, Lynn. *Identity Theft Reported by Households, 2005–2010*. Washington, DC: Bureau of Justice Statistics, U.S. Department of Justice, 2011.

Lee, Seungmug, and Harry Wilson. "Spatial Impact of Burglar Alarms on the Decline of Residential Burglary." *Security Journal* 26 (2013): 180–198.

Lemert, Edwin M. "An Isolation and Closure Theory of Naive Check Forgery." *Journal of Criminal Law, Criminology and Police Science* 44 (1953): 301–304.

Linn, Allison. "Chat on Taxes? Not Cool, Say Most Americans." *Today.com*, February 27, 2013. http://www.today.com/money/cheat-taxes-not-cool-say-most-americans-1C8576287.

Maguire, Kathleen. *Sourcebook of Criminal Justice Statistics*. 2013. http://www .albany.edu/sourcebook/.

Maguire, Mike. *Burglary in a Dwelling*. London: Heinemann, 1982.

Maston, Cathy T. *Criminal Victimization in the United States—Statistical Tables*. Washington, DC: Bureau of Justice Statistics, U.S. Department of Justice, 2011.

Maston, Cathy T., and Patsy Klaus. *Criminal Victimization in the United States 2007—Statistical Tables*. Washington, DC: Bureau of Justice Statistics, U.S. Department of Justice, 2010.

McCarthy, Bill. "Not Just 'For the Thrill of It': An Instrumentalist Elaboration of Katz's Explanation of Sneaky Thrill Property Crimes." *Criminology* 33 (1995): 519–538.

Mustaine, Elizabeth Ehrhardt, and Richard Tewksbury. "Predicting Risks of Larceny Theft Victimization: A Routine Activity Analysis Using Refined Lifestyle Measures." *Criminology* 36 (1998): 829–857.

Phillips, Julie, and Kenneth C. Land. "The Link Between Unemployment and Crime Rate Fluctuations: An Analysis at the County, State, and National Levels." *Social Science Research* 41 (2012): 681–694.

Pratt, Travis C. *Addicted to Incarceration: Corrections Policy and the Politics of Misinformation in the United States*. Thousand Oaks, CA: Sage Publications, 2008.

Reyns, Bradford W. "Online Routines and Identity Theft Victimization: Further Expanding Routine Activity Theory beyond Direct-Contact Offenses." *Journal of Research in Crime and Delinquency* 50 (2013): 216–238.

Rosenfeld, Richard. "Crime Is the Problem: Homicide, Acquisitive Crime, and Economic Conditions." *Journal of Quantitative Criminology* 25 (2009): 287–306.

Rosenfeld, Richard, and Robert Fornango. "The Impact of Economic Conditions on Robbery and Property Crime: The Role of Consumer Sentiment." *Criminology* 45 (2007): 735–769.

Schmidt, Andy. *Rethinking Check Fraud: Taking a New Approach to an Old Fraud Type*. New York: Tower Group, 2010.

Sherman, Ted. "International Luxury Car Theft Ring Busted in Newark, 19 Arrested." *The Star-Ledger*, May 24, 2012. http://www.nj.com/news/index .ssf/2012/05/international_high-end_car_the.html.

Shover, Neal. "The Social Organization of Burglary." *Social Problems* 20 (1973): 499–514.

———. "Burglary." *Crime and Justice: A Review of Research*, vol. 14, edited by M. Tonry, 73–113. Chicago: University of Chicago Press, 1991.

Shover, Neal, and Heith Copes. "Decision Making by Persistent Thieves and Crime Control Policy." *Criminology and Public Policy: Putting Theory to Work*, edited by H. D. Barlow and S. H. Decker, 128–149. Philadelphia, PA: Temple University Press, 2010.

South Carolina Attorney General's Office. *Insurance Fraud*. 2013. http://www .scag.gov/insurance-fraud.

Steffensmeier, Darrell J. *The Fence: In the Shadow of Two Worlds*. Totowa, NJ: Rowman & Littlefield, 1986.

Steffensmeier, Darrell J., and Jeffery T. Ulmer. *Confessions of a Dying Thief: Understanding Criminal Careers and Illegal Enterprise*. New York: Transaction Publishers, 2005.

The New York Times. "Corporate Tax Cheating Seen." *The New York Times*, 1991 April 18: C6.

Thompson, Melissa, and Christopher Uggen. "Dealers, Thieves, and the Common Determinants of Drug and Nondrug Illegal Earnings." *Criminology* 50 (2012): 1057–1087.

Tonry, Michael. "Crime and Public Policy." *The Oxford Handbook of Crime and Public Policy*, edited by M. Tonry, 3–21. New York: Oxford University Press, 2009.

Tunnell, Kenneth D. *Living Off Crime*. Lanham, MD: Rowman & Littlefield, 2006.

Turk, Austin T. "Seductions of Criminology: Katz on Magical Meanness and Other Distractions." *Law and Social Inquiry* 16 (1991): 181–194.

Woolsey, Ben, and Matt Schulz. "Credit Card Statistics, Industry Facts, Debt Statistics." *CreditCards.com*, July 6, 2013. http://www.creditcards.com/ credit-card-news/credit-card-industry-facts-personal-debt-statistics-1276 .php#Identity-theft-fraud.

Wright, Richard, Robert H. Logie, and Scott H. Decker. "Criminal Expertise and Offender Decision Making: An Experimental Study of the Target Selection Process in Residential Burglary." *Journal of Research in Crime and Delinquency* 32 (1995): 39–53.

Wright, Richard T., and Scott Decker. *Burglars on the Job: Streetlife and Residential Break-ins*. Translated by next. Boston: Northeastern University Press, 1994.

Chapter 13, White-Collar and Organized Crime

Abadinsky, Howard. *Organized Crime*. Belmont, CA: Wadsworth, 2013.

Abelson, Reed. "How Schering Manipulated Drug Prices and Medicaid." *The New York Times*, July 31, 2004: C1.

AFL-CIO. *Death on the Job: The Toll of Neglect*. Washington, DC: AFL-CIO, 2013.

Albanese, Jay S. "The Mafia Mystique: Organized Crime." *Criminology: A Contemporary Handbook*, edited by J. F. Sheley, 265–285. Belmont, CA: Wadsworth, 2000.

Armstrong, David. "U.S. Lagging on Prosecutions." *The Boston Globe*, November 16, 1999: A1.

Bachman, Katy. "Kellogg's Agrees to Pay $4 Million to Settle Suit Over False Ad Claim." *Adweek*, May 29, 2013. http://www.adweek.com/news/advertising-branding/kelloggs-agrees-pay-4-million-settle-suit-over-false-ad-claim-149857.

BBC News. "Air Pollution Causes Early Deaths." February 21, 2005. http://news .bbc.co.uk/2/hi/health/4283295.stm.

Behr, Peter, and April Whitt. "Visionary's Dream Led to Risky Business." *The Washington Post*, July 28, 2002: A1.

Benson, Michael L., and Sally S. Simpson. *White-Collar Crime: An Opportunity Perspective*. New York: Routledge, 2009.

Braithwaite, John. "Criminological Theory and Organizational Crime." *Justice Quarterly* 6 (1989): 333–358.

———. "White Collar Crime." *White-Collar Crime: Classic and Contemporary Views*, edited by G. Geis, R. F. Meier, and L. M. Salinger, 116–142. New York: The Free Press, 1995.

Brasted, Chelsea. "Manda Recalls 468,000 Pounds of Various Products Following Possible Listeria Contamination." *The Times-Picayune*, April 13, 2013. http://www.nola.com/news/baton-rouge/index.ssf/2013/04/manda_recalls_ additional_46800.html.

Brodeur, Paul. *Outrageous Misconduct: The Asbestos Industry on Trial*. New York: Pantheon Books, 1985.

Burke, Garance. "Pesticide Drift from Nearby Farms Endangers Pupils, Calif. Data Show." *The Boston Globe*, May 27, 2007. http://www.boston.com/news/nation/ articles/2007/05/27/pesticide_drift_from_nearby_farms_endangers_pupils_ calif_data_show/.

Cain, Geoffrey. "Japan's Yakuza Gang Wars." *GlobalPost*, May 7, 2013. http://www. globalpost.com/dispatch/news/regions/asia-pacific/japan/130502/yakuza-fukuoka-gang-wars.

Calavita, Kitty, Robert Tillman, and Henry N. Pontell. "The Savings and Loan Debacle, Financial Crime, and the State." *Annual Review of Sociology*, vol. 23, edited by J. Hagan. Palo Alto: Annual Reviews, 1997.

Callahan, Trish. 2010. "Federal Safety Regulator Pledges to Ban Drop-Side Cribs" *Los Angeles Times* May 8: http://www.latimes.com/news/nationworld/nation/la-na-crib-20100508,0,3553984.story.

Cameron, Doug. "Dow Chemical Told to Pay $1.2 Billion." *The Wall Street Journal*, May 17 (2013): B3.

Carrillo, Patricia. "Salinas: Salad Bowl or Pesticide Bowl of the World?" *KQED*, September 21, 2011. http://blogs.kqed.org/ourxperience/2011/09/21/salinas-salad-bowl-or-pesticide-bowl-of-the-world/.

Centers for Disease Control and Prevention. *Estimates of Foodborne Illness in the United States*. 2013. http://www.cdc.gov/foodborneburden/.

Chambliss, William J. *On the Take: From Petty Crooks to Presidents*. Indianapolis: Indiana University Press, 1988.

Clinard, Marshall B., and Richard Quinney. *Criminal Behavior Systems*. New York: Holt, Rinehart and Winston, 1973.

Cohan, William D. "Will Wall Street Go Free?" *The New York Times*, May 27, 2010. http://opinionator.blogs.nytimes.com/2010/05/27/will-wall-street-go-free/?emc=eta1.

Cohen, Senator William S. "Gaming the Health Care System: Billions of Dollars Lost to Fraud & Abuse Each Year." Washington, D.C.: Senate Special Committee on Aging, 1994.

Coleman, James William. *The Criminal Elite: Understanding White-Collar Crime*. New York: Worth Publishers, 2006.

Consumer Product Safety Commission. *2012 Annual Report to the President and the Congress*. Washington, DC: U.S. Consumer Product Safety Commission, 2013.

Consumer Reports. "Fords in Reverse." *Consumer Reports*, September 1985: 520–523.

Countryman, Andrew. "Bank of America Unit Pays $10 Million." *Chicago Tribune*, March 11, 2004. http://articles.chicagotribune.com/2004-03-11/business/0403120019_1_banc-of-america-securities-sec-enforcement-director-stephen-cutler.

Cressey, Donald R. *Other People's Money: A Study in the Social Psychology of Embezzlement*. Belmont, CA: Wadsworth Publishing Company, 1971 (1953).

Cullen, Francis T., William J. Maakestad, and Gray Cavender. *Corporate Crime Under Attack: The Fight to Criminalize Business Violence*. Cincinnati: Anderson Publishing Company, 2006.

DeMers, Jayson. "5 Technologies to Help Reduce Employee Theft." *Huffington Post*, June 6, 2013. http://www.huffingtonpost.com/jayson-demers/5-technologies-to-help-re_b_3386245.html.

DeSantis, Nick. "Ex-Manager at Missouri State Bookstore Pleads Guilty to Embezzling $1-Million." *Chronicle of Higher Education*, March 26, 2013. http://chronicle.com/blogs/ticker/jp/ex-manager-at-missouri-state-bookstore-pleads-guilty-to-embezzling-1-million.

Dreier, Peter, and Donald Cohen. "The Texas Fertilizer Plant Explosion Wasn't an Accident." *The Huffington Post*, June 4, 2013. http://www.huffingtonpost.com/peter-dreier/texas-fertilizer-plant-explosion_b_3384739.html.

Eichenwald, Kurt. "The Criminal-less Crime." *The New York Times*, March 3, 2002: A1.

Eisler, Peter. "'Growing Concern' Over Marketing Tainted Beef." *USA Today*, April 15, 2010: A1.

Eisler, Peter, and Barbara Hansen. "Doctors Perform Thousands of Unnecessary Surgeries." *USA Today*, June 20, 2013. http://www.usatoday.com/story/news/nation/2013/06/18/unnecessary-surgery-usa-today-investigation/2435009/.

Erikson, Kai T. *Everything in Its Path: Destruction of Community in the Buffalo Creek Flood*. New York: Simon and Schuster, 1976.

Estep, Bill, and John Cheves. "After Decades of Decline, Black Lung on the Rise in Eastern Kentucky." *Lexington Herald-Leader*, July 6, 2013. http://www.kentucky.com/2013/07/06/2705218/after-decades-of-decline-black.html.

Farmworker Justice. *Pesticide Safety*. 2013. http://farmworkerjustice.org/content/pesticide-safety.

Farrell, Greg. "Pfizer Settles Fraud Case for $430M." *USA Today*, May 14, 2004: 1B.

Feeley, Jef, and Dawn McCarty. "Wyeth Wins One Case, Loses Another." *Daily Record (Morris County, NJ)*, July 29, 2004. http://www.dailyrecord.com/business/business1-wyethsuits.htm.

Fleck, Carole. "Avoid Car Repair Rip-Offs." *AARP Bulletin Online*, July/August, 2002. http://www.aarp.org/bulletin/consumer/Articles/a2003-06-30-carrepair.html.

Frank, Nancy K., and Michael J. Lynch. *Corporate Crime, Corporate Violence: A Primer*. New York: Harrow and Heston, 1992.

Geis, Gilbert. "The Heavy Electrical Equipment Antitrust Cases of 1961." *Corporate and Governmental Deviance: Problems of Orgnaizational Behavior in Contemporary Society*, edited by M. D. Ermann and R. J. Lundman, 124–144. New York: Oxford University Press, 1987.

———. "White-Collar Crime." *Readings in Deviant Behavior*, edited by A. Thio and T. Calhoun, 213–221. New York: HarperCollins College Publishers, 1995.

Gottfredson, Michael, and Travis Hirschi. *A General Theory of Crime*. Stanford: Sanford University Press, 1990.

Harris, Gardiner. "Pfizer Pays $2.3 Billion to Settle Marketing Case." *The New York Times*, September 3, 2009: B4.

Henriques, Diana B., and Jack Healy. "Madoff Goes to Jail After Guilty Pleas." *The New York Times*, March 13, 2009: A1.

Hicks, Karen M. *Surviving the Dalkon Shield IUD: Women v. the Pharmaceutical Industry*. New York: Teachers College Press (Columbia University), 1994.

Insurance Information Institute. *Insurance Fraud*. 2013. http://www.iii.org/issues_updates/insurance-fraud.html.

Jackson, Brooks, and Kathleen Hall Jamieson. *UnSpun: Finding Facts in a World of Disinformation*. New York: Random House, 2007.

Johnson, Carrie. "Former Rite Aid Chairman Gets 8 Years." *The Washington Post*, May 28, 2004: E3.

Josephson, Matthew. *The Robber Barons: The Great American Capitalists, 1861–1901*. New York: Harcourt, Brace, & World, 1962.

Kahn, Helen. "GAO Study Lists Remedies for Ford Park-Reverse Problem." *Automotive News*, June 23, 1986: 39.

Kappeler, Victor E., and Gary W. Potter. *The Mythology of Crime and Criminal Justice*. Prospect Heights, IL: Waveland Press, 2005.

Kenney, Dennis J., and James O. Finckenauer. *Organized Crime in America*. Belmont, CA: Wadsworth Publishing Company, 1995.

Khokha, Sasha. "'Pesticide Drift Eluding Efforts to Combat it." *National Public Radio*, 2010. http://www.npr.org/templates/story/story.php?storyId=123817702.

Kitman, Jamie Lincoln. "The Secret History of Lead." *The Nation*, March 20, 2000: 11–44.

Krugman, Paul. "Looters in Loafers." *The New York Times*, April 19, 2010: A23.

Labaton, Stephen, and Lowell Bergman. "Documents Indicate Ford Knew of Defect but Failed to Report It." *The New York Times*, September 12, 2000: A1.

Langton, Lynn, Nicole Leeper Piquero, and Richard C. Hollinger. "An Empirical Test of the Relationship Between Employee Theft and Low Self-Control." *Deviant Behavior* 27 (2006): 537–565.

Leaf, Clifton. "Enough Is Enough." *Fortune*, March 18, 2002: 60–68.

Leigh, Paul, James P. Marcin, and Ted R. Miller. "An Estimate of the U.S. Government's Undercount of Nonfatal Occupational Injuries." *Journal of Occupational and Environmental Medicine* 46 (2004): 10–18.

Levine, Adeline. *Love Canal: Science, Politics, and People*. Lexington, MA: Lexington Books, 1982.

Lilienfeld, David E. "The Silence: The Asbestos Industry and Early Occupational Cancer Research—A Case Study." *American Journal of Public Health* 81 (1991): 791–800.

Lyman, Michael D., and Gary W. Potter. *Organized Crime*. Upper Saddle River, NJ: Prentice Hall, 2011.

Maynard, Micheline. "U.S. Is Seeking a Fine of $16.4 Million Against Toyota." *The New York Times*, April 6, 2010: A1.

Mintz, Morton. 1992. "Why the Media Cover up Corporate Crime: A Reporter Looks Back in Anger." *Trial* 28: 72-77.

Mintz, Morton. *At Any Cost: Corporate Greed, Women, and the Dalkon Shield*. New York: Pantheon Books, 1985.

Mokhiber, Russell, and Robert Weissman. "Top 100 Corporate Criminals of the 1990s." *Mother Jones*, September 7, 1999. http://www.motherjones.com/news/feature/1999/09/fotc1.html.

National Oceanic and Atmospheric Administration. *Air Quality*. 2013. http://www.noaawatch.gov/themes/air_quality.php.

National Retail Federation. "Retail Theft Decreased in 2011, According to Preliminary National Retail Security Survey Findings." June 22, 2012. http://www.nrf.com/modules.php?name=News&op=viewlive&sp_id=1389.

Nussbaum, Alex, and Tom Troncone. "Big Profits from Illegal Dumping; Now We're Paying." *NorthJersey.com*, August 7, 2009. http://www.northjersey.com/news/environment/specialreports/The_mob_cleaned_up_Big_profits_from_illegal_dumping_now_were_paying.html?page=all.

O'Donnell, Jayne. "Suffering in Silence." *USA Today*, April 3, 2000: 1A.

O'Kane, James M. *The Crooked Ladder: Gangsters, Ethnicity, and the American Dream*. New Brunswick, NJ: Transaction Books, 1992.

Okrent, Daniel. *Last Call: The Rise and Fall of Prohibition*. New York: Scribner, 2011.

Ornstein, Charles. "Sale of Body Parts at UCLA Alleged." *Los Angeles Times*, March 6, 2004: A1.

Passas, Nikos. "Anomie and Corporate Deviance." *Contemporary Crises* 14 (1990): 157–178.

Payne, Brian K. *White-Collar Crime: The Essentials*. Thousand Oaks, CA: Sage Publications, 2013.

Petersen, Melody, and Christopher Drew. "New Safety Rules Fail to Stop Tainted Meat." *The New York Times*, October 9, 2003: A1.

Piquero, Nicole Leeper, and Andrea Schoepfer. "Theories of White-Collar Crime and Public Policy." *Criminology and Public Policy*, edited by H. D. Barlow and S. H. Decker, 188–200. Philadelphia, PA: Temple University Press, 2010.

Pontell, Henry N. "Wall St. Fraud and Fiduciary Responsibilities: Can Jail Time Serve as an Adequate Deterrent for Willful Violations?" *Testimony to Subcommittee on Crime and Drugs, Committee on the Judiciary, United States Senate* May 4, 2010.

Pontell, Henry N., and Kitty Calavita. "The Savings and Loan Industry." *Beyond the Law: Crime in Complex Organizations*, vol. 18, *Crime and Justice: A Review of Research*, edited by M. Tonry and J. Albert J. Reiss, 203–246. Chicago: University of Chicago Press, 1993.

Pope, C. Arden, III, R. T. Burnett, G. D. Thurston, et al. "Cardiovascular Mortality and Long-term Exposure to Particulate Air Pollution: Epidemiological Evidence of General Pathophysiological Pathways of Disease." *Circulation* 109 (2004): 71–77.

Pope, Stephen. "W.Va. Coal Mine Cited Over 160 Times in Year Before Two Fatal Accidents This Month." *Allvoices.com*, February 27, 2013. http://www.allvoices.com/contributed-news/14133380-wva-coal-mine-cited-over-160-times-in-year-before-two-miners-were-killed-this-month.

Potter, Gary W. *Criminal Organizations: Vice, Racketeering, and Politics in an American City*. Prospect Heights, IL: Waveland Press, Inc, 1994.

Reeves, Margaret, Anne Katten, and Marthua Guzmán. *Fields of Poison 2002: California Farmworkers and Pesticides*. San Francisco: Californians for Pesticide Reform, 2003.

Reiman, Jeffrey, and Paul Leighton. *The Rich Get Richer and the Poor Get Prison: Ideology, Class, and Criminal Justice*. Upper Saddle River, NJ: Prentice Hall, 2013.

Rosenzweig, Daniel. "4 Companies Are Charged with Food Safety Violations." *Los Angeles Times*, July 16, 2004. www.latimes.com/news/local/orange/la-me-taint16jul16,1,61136.story?coll=la-editions-orange.

Rosoff, Stephen M., Henry N. Pontell, and Robert Tillman. *Profit Without Honor: White Collar Crime and the Looting of America*. Upper Saddle River, NJ: Prentice Hall, 2010.

Ross, Edward A. *Sin and Society: An Analysis of Latter-Day Iniquity*. Gloucester, MA: P. Smith, 1965 (1907).

Scott, Donald W. "Policing Corporate Collusion." *Criminology* 27 (1989): 559–587.

Shelden, Randall G. *Controlling the Dangerous Classes: A Critical Introduction to the History of Criminal Justice, 2nd ed*. Upper Saddle River, NJ: Prentice Hall, 2008.

Shover, Neal, and Jennifer Scroggins. "Organizational Crime." *The Oxford Handbook of Crime and Public Policy*, edited by M. Tonry, 273–303. New York: Oxford University Press, 2009.

Simon, David R. *Elite Deviance*. Upper Saddle River, NJ: Pearson, 2012.

Sinclair, Upton. *The Jungle*. New York: New American Library, 1990 (1906).

Steffens, Lincoln. *The Shame of the Cities*. New York: McClure, Phillips, 1904.

Steffensmeier, Darrell J., Jennifer Schwartz, and Michael Roche. "Gender and Twenty-First-Century Corporate Crime: Female Involvement and the Gender Gap in Enron-Era Corporate Frauds." *American Sociological Review* 78 (2013): 448–476.

Sutherland, Edwin H. *White Collar Crime*. New York: Holt, Rinehart, and Winston, 1949.

Tabuchi, Hiroko. "Japan Pushing the Mob Out of Businesses." *The New York Times*, November 19, 2010: B1.

Tarbell, Ida M. *The History of the Standard Oil Company*. New York: McClure, Phillips, 1904.

Thomas, Ken. "89 Deaths May Be Linked to Toyota Recalls." *The Boston Globe*, May 26, 2010: B11.

Tillman, Robert, and Henry N. Pontell. "Is Justice 'Collar-Blind'?: Punishing Medicaid Provider Fraud." *Criminology* 30 (1992): 547–573.

U.S. News & World Report. "Corporate Crime: The Untold Story." *U.S. News & World Report*, September 6, 1982: 25.

Urbina, Ian. "BP Used Risker Method to Seal Well Before Blast." *The New York Times*, May 27, 2010: A1.

Wang, Xia, and Kristy Holtfreter. "The Effects of Corporation- and Industry-Level Strain and Opportunity on Corporate Crime." *Journal of Research in Crime & Delinquency* 49 (2012): 151–185.

White, Ben. "ImClone's Waksal Gets Maximum Jail Sentence." *The Washington Post*, June 11, 2003: A1.

Chapter 14, Political Crime

Adams, James. *Sellout: Aldrich Ames and the Corruption of the CIA*. New York: Viking Press, 1995.

Arnson, Cynthia. *Crossroads: Congress, the Reagan Administration, and Central America*. New York: Pantheon Books, 1989.

Balakian, Peter. *The Burning Tigris: The Armenian Genocide and America's Response*. New York: HarperCollins, 2003.

Baldassare, Mark. *The Los Angeles Riots: Lessons for the Urban Future*. Boulder, CO: Westview Press, 1994.

Bannan, John R., and Rosemary S. Bannan. *Law, Morality, and Vietnam: The Peace Militants and the Courts*. Bloomington: Indiana University Press, 1974.

Barkan, Steven E. *Protesters on Trial: Criminal Prosecutions in the Southern Civil Rights and Vietnam Antiwar Movements*. New Brunswick, NJ: Rutgers University Press, 1985.

Barry, Kathleen L. *Susan B. Anthony: Biography of a Singular Feminist*. New York: New York University Press, 1988.

Bernstein, Carl, and Bob Woodward. *All the President's Men*. New York: Simon and Schuster, 1974.

Brady, Brendan. "Amid Rising Dissent, Vietnam Cracks Down on Bloggers." *Time*, June 27, 2013. http://world.time.com/2013/06/27/amid-rising-dissent-vietnam-cracks-downs-on-bloggers/#ixzz2YfC5mpLj.

Branch, Taylor. *Pillar of Fire: America in the King Years, 1963–65*. New York: Simon and Schuster, 1998.

Branfman, Fred. *Voices from the Plain of Jars: Life Under an Air War*. New York: Harper and Row, 1972.

Bresnahan, John. "Former Rep. Rick Renzi Convicted in Corruption Trial." *Politico.com*, June 11, 2013. http://www.politico.com/story/2013/06/rick-renzi-guilty-on-17-counts-92619.html.

Brock, Peter. *Pioneers of the Peaceable Kingdom*. Princeton: Princeton University Press, 1968.

Broehl, Wayne G., Jr. *The Molly Maguires*. Cambridge: Harvard University Press, 1964.

Brown, Richard Maxwell. "Historical Patterns of Violence." *Violence in America: Protest, Rebellion, Reform*, vol. 2, edited by T. R. Gurr, 23–61. Newbury Park, CA: Sage Publications, 1989.

Bushnell, Rebecca W. *Prophesying Tragedy: Sign and Voice in Sophocles' Theban Plays*. Ithaca: Cornell University Press, 1988.

Button, James. "The Outcomes of Contemporary Black Protest and Violence." *Violence in America: Protest, Rebellion, Reform*, vol. 2, edited by T. R. Gurr, 286–306. Newbury Park, CA: Sage Publications, 1989.

Chomsky, Noam, and Edward S. Herman. *The Washington Connection and Third World Facism*. Boston: South End Press, 1979.

Clarke, Alan W. *Rendition to Torture*. New Brunswick, NJ: Rutgers University Press, 2012.

Cohen, David B., and John W. Wells. *American National Security and Civil Liberties in an Era of Terrorism*. New York: Palgrave Macmillan, 2004.

Cohen, Richard M., and Jules Witcover. *A Heartbeat Away: The Investigation and Resignation of Spiro T. Agnew*. New York: Viking Press, 1974.

Cole, David. *The Torture Memos: Rationalizing the Unthinkable*. New York: New Press, 2009.

Cole, David, and Jules Lobel. *Less Safe, Less Free: Why America Is Losing the War on Terror*. New York: New Press, 2007.

Conte, Andrew. "DeLay Says Top Dems Close to Treason." *Pittsburgh Tribune-Review*, April 24, 2007. http://www.pittsburghlive.com/x/pittsburghtrib/news/multimedia/s_504197.html.

Davies, Peter. *The Truth About Kent State: A Challenge to the American Conscience*. New York: Farrar, Straus, Giroux, 1973.

DeBenedetti, Charles, and Charles Chatfield. *An American Ordeal: The Antiwar Movement of the Vietnam Era*. Syracuse: Syracuse University Press, 1990.

Dugan, Laura. "Terrorism." *The Oxford Handbook of Crime and Public Policy*, edited by M. Tonry, 428–454. New York: Oxford University Press, 2009.

Dugan, Laura, and Erica Chenoweth. "Moving Beyond Deterrence: The Effectiveness of Raising the Expected Utility of Abstaining from Terrorism in Israel." *American Sociological Review* 77 (2012): 597–624.

Durkheim, Emile. *The Rules of Sociological Method*, Edited by S. Lukes. New York: Free Press, 1962 (1895).

Feldberg, Michael. *The Turbulent Era: Riot and Disorder in Jacksonian America*. New York: Oxford University Press, 1980.

Finan, Christopher M. *From the Palmer Raids to the Patriot Act: A History of the Fight for Free Speech in America*. Boston: Beacon Press, 2007.

Friedman, Leon. *The Wise Minority*. New York: Dial Press, 1971.

Garrow, David J. *The FBI and Martin Luther King, Jr*. New York: Penguin Press, 1981.

Goldston, James. *A Year of Reckoning: El Salvador a Decade After the Assassination of Archbishop Romero*. New York: Americas Watch Committee, 1990.

Gurr, Ted Robert. "Political Terrorism: Historical Antecedents and Contemporary Trends." *Violence in America: Protest, Rebellion, Reform*, vol. 2, edited by T. R. Gurr, 201–230. Newbury Park, CA: Sage Publications, 1989.

Hagan, Frank E. "Espionage as Political Crime? A Typology of Spies." *Journal of Security Administration* 12 (1989): 19–36.

Hagan, John, and Joshua Kaiser. "The Displaced and Dispossessed of Darfur: Explaining the Sources of a Continuing State-Led Genocide." *British Journal of Sociology* 62 (2011): 1–25.

Hershkowitz, Leo. *Tweed's New York: Another Look*. Garden City, NY: Anchor Books, 1977.

Johansen, Bruce E. *The Native Peoples of North America: A History*. Westport, CT: Praeger, 2005.

Kaufman, Peter Ives. *Incorrectly Political: Augustine and Thomas More*. Notre Dame: University of Notre Dame Press, 2007.

Kershaw, Sarah. "Suffering Effects of 50's A-Bomb Tests." *New York Times*, September 5, 2004: A1.

Kessler, Ronald. *Spy Versus Spy: Stalking Soviet Spies in America*. New York: Charles Scribner's, 1988.

King, Martin Luther, Jr. "Letter from Birmingham City Jail." *Civil Disobedience: Theory and Practice*, edited by H. A. Bedau, 72–89. New York: Pegasus, 1969.

Klier, John, and Shlomo Lambroza. *Pogroms: Anti-Jewish Violence in Modern Russian History*. Cambridge: Cambridge University Press, 1992.

Knightley, Phillip. *The Second Oldest Profession: Spies and Spying in the Twentieth Century*. New York: Norton, 1987.

Kokh, Alfred, and Pavel Polian. *Denial of the Denial, or the Battle of Auschwitz: The Demography and Geopolitics of the Holocaust*. Boston: Academic Studies Press, 2012.

Kramer, Ronald C. "The Space Shuttle Challenger Explosion: A Case Study of State-Corporate Crime." *White-Collar Crime Reconsidered*, edited by K. Schlegel and D. Weisburd, 214–243. Boston: Northeastern University Press, 1992.

Lee, Gary A. "U.S. Energy Agency Radiation Tests Involved 9,000, Study Says." *Washington Post*, February 10, 1995: A13.

Lefcourt, Robert. *Law Against the People*. New York: Vintage Books, 1971.

Lichterman, Joseph. "U-M Students Arrested in Protest for Undocumented Students." *Michigan Radio*, April 17, 2013. http://www.michiganradio.org/post/u-m-students-arrested-protest-undocumented-students.

Lifton, Robert Jay. *The Nazi Doctors: Medical Killing and the Psychology of Genocide*. New York: Basic Books, 2000.

Long, Ray, and Rick Pearson. "Impeached Illinois Gov. Rod Blagojevich Has Been Removed from Office." *Chicago Tribune*, January 30, 2009: A1.

Lovell, Jarret. *Crimes of Dissent: Civil Disobedience, Criminal Justice, and the Politics of Conscience*. New York: NYU Press, 2009.

Lynch, Colum. "Amnesty International Faults Rwanda War Crimes Tribunal." *The Boston Globe*, 14, 1995.

Maras, Marie-Helen. *Counterterrorism*. Burlington, MA: Jones and Bartlett, 2013.

Martin, Marie Alexandrine. *Cambodia: A Shattered Society*. Berkeley: University of California Press, 1994.

McGovern, George S., and Leonard F. Guttridge. *The Great Coalfield War*. Boston: Houghton Mifflin, 1972.

Midlarsky, Manus I. *Origins of Political Extremism: Mass Violence in the Twentieth Century and Beyond*. New York: Cambridge University Press, 2011.

Miles, Steven H. *Oath Betrayed: America's Torture Doctors*. Berkeley: University of California Press, 2009.

Moyers, Bill. *The Secret Government: The Constitution in Crisis*. Cabin John, MD: Seven Locks Press, 1988.

Mydans, Seth. "Activists Convicted in Vietnam Crackdown on Dissent." *New York Times*, January 10, 2013: A4.

Noggle, Burl. *Teapot Dome: Oil and Politics in the 1920s*. New York: Norton, 1965.

Oates, Stphen B. *The Fires of Jubilee: Nat Turner's Fierce Rebellion*. New York: New American Library, 1983.

Post, Tim. "Blood Bath." *Newsweek* February 14, 1994: 20–23.

Robaina, Celia Maria. "Mental Health Work with People Affected by State Terrorism in Uruguay: A Personal Reflection on 25 Years Work." *Intervention (15718883)* 11 (2013): 94–100.

Robinson, Eugene. "We Can Handle the Truth on NSA Spying." *Washington Post*, July 4, 2013. http://www.washingtonpost.com/opinions/eugene-robinson-we-can-handle-the-truth-on-nsa-spying/2013/07/04/76ef2c92-e408-11e2-a11e-c2ea876a8f30_story.html.

Ross, Jeffrey Ian. *An Introduction to Political Crime*. Bristol, England: The Policy Press, 2012.

Rothe, Dawn L., and David Kauzlarich. "State Crime Theory and Control." *Criminology and Public Policy: Putting Theory to Work*, edited by H. D. Barlow and S. H. Decker. Philadelphia: Temple University Press, 2010.

Rubenstein, Richard E. *Rebels in Eden: Mass Political Violence in the United States*. Boston: Little, Brown and Company, 1970.

———. *Alchemists of Revolution: Terrorism in the Modern World*. New York: Basic Books, 1987.

Schafer, Stephen. *The Political Criminal*. New York: The Free Press, 1974.

Serrano, Richard A. 1998. *One of Ours: Timothy McVeigh and the Oklahoma City Bombing*. New York: Norton.

Smith, R. Jeffrey. "FBI Violations May Number 3,000, Official Says." *Washington Post*, March 21, 2007: A7.

Spofford, Tim. *Lynch Street: The May 1970 Slayings at Jackson State College*. Kent, Ohio: Kent State University Press, 1988.

Stone, Isidor F. *The Trial of Socrates*. New York: Anchor Books, 1989.

Thomas, Gordon. *Journey into Madness: The True Story of Secret CIA Mind Control and Medical Abuse*. New York: Bantom Books, 1989.

Thoreau, Henry D. "Civil Disobedience." *Civil Disobedience: Theory and Practice*, edited by H. A. Bedau, 27–48. New York: Pegasus, 1969.

Tilly, Charles, and Lesley J. Wood. *Social Movements 1768–2012*. Boulder, CO: Paradigm Publishers, 2012.

Tirman, John. *The Deaths of Others: The Fate of Civilians in America's Wars*. New York: Oxford University Press, 2011.

Tzouliadis, Tim. *The Forsaken : An American Tragedy in Stalin's Russia*. New York: Penguin Press, 2008.

Washington, Harriet A. *Medical Apartheid: The Dark History of Medical Experimentation on Black Americans from Colonial Times to the Present*. New York: Doubleday, 2006.

Chapter 15, Consensual Crime

Albanese, Jay S. 1996. "Looking for a New Approach to an Old Problem: The Future of Obscenity and Pornography." Pp. 60–72 in *Visions for Change: Crime and Justice in the Twenty-First Century*, edited by R. Muraskin and A. R. Roberts. Upper Saddle River, NJ: Prentice Hall.

Arnold, Laurence. "Survey Finds Gambling Woes Could Affect 20 Million in US." *The Boston Globe*, March 19, 1999: A3.

Associated Press. "Los Angeles: Feds Continue Pot Shop Crackdown." *The Willits News* June 11, 2013. http://www.willitsnews.com/ci_23447217/feds-continue-pot-shop-crackdown-la-county.

Bandow, Doug. "The Most Important Election on November 6: More Americans Vote for Drug Peace." *The Huffington Post*, November 15, 2012. http://www.huffingtonpost.com/doug-bandow/the-most-important-electi_b_2135085.html.

Barrows, Sydney Biddle, and William Novak. *Mayflower Madam: The Secret Life of Sydney Biddle Barrows*. New York: Arbor House, 1986.

Bauder, Julia. *Censorship*. Detroit: Greenhaven Press, 2007.

Becker, Gary S., and Kevin M. Murphy. "Have We Lost the War on Drugs?" *The Washington Post*, January 4, 2013. http://online.wsj.com/article/SB10001424127887324374004578217682305605070.html.

Berenson, Abbey B., and Mahbubur Rahman. "Prevalence and Correlates of Prescription Drug Misuse Among Young, Low-Income Women Receiving Public Healthcare." *Journal of Addictive Diseases* 30 (2011): 203–215.

Berger, Lisa. "Drug Policy in Portugal: An Interview with Helen Redmond, LCSW, CADC." *Journal of Social Work Practice in the Addictions* 13 (2013): 216–222.

Bortz, Daniel. "Gambling Addicts Seduced By Growing Casino Accessibility." *US News & World Report*, March 28, 2013. http://money.usnews.com/money/personal-finance/articles/2013/03/28/gambling-addicts-seduced-by-growing-casino-accessibility.

Boyum, David A., Jonathan P. Caulkins, and Mark A. R. Kleiman. "Drugs, Crime, and Public Policy." *Crime and Public Policy*, edited by J. Q. Wilson and J. Petersilia, 368–410. New York: Oxford University Press, 2011.

Brewer, Devon D., John J. Potterat, Sharon B. Garrett, et al. "Prostitution and the Sex Discrepancy in Reported Number of Sexual Partners." *Proceedings of the National Academy of Sciences* 97 (2000): 12385–12388.

Brownstein, Henry H. *Contemporary Drug Policy*. New York: Routledge, 2013.

Bullough, Vern L., and Bonnie Bullough. *Sin, Sickness, and Sanity: A History of Sexual Attitudes*. New York: New American Library, 1977.

———. *Women and Prostitution: A Social History*. Buffalo: Prometheus, 1987.

Chesney-Lind, Meda, and Lisa Pasko. *The Female Offender: Girls, Women, and Crime*. Thousand Oaks, CA: Sage Publications, 2013.

Cole, David. "Doing Time-In Rehab: Drug Courts Keep Addicts Out of Jail." *The Nation*, 1999: 30.

Cornell, Drucilla. "Feminism and Pornography." New York: Oxford University Press, 2000.

Currie, Elliott. *Reckoning: Drugs, the Cities, and the American Future*. New York: Hill and Wang, 1994.

Davis, Kingsley. "The Sociology of Prostitution." *American Sociological Review* 2 (1937): 744–755.

Dickinson, Tim. "Ethan Nadelmann: The Real Drug Czar." *Rolling Stone*, June 6, 2013. http://www.rollingstone.com/culture/news/ethan-nadelmann-the-real-drug-czar-20130606.

Dombrink, John. "Gambling." *The Oxford Handbook of Crime and Public Policy*, edited by M. Tonry, 599–618. New York: Oxford University Press, 2009.

Donnerstein, Edward, Daniel Linz, and Steven Penrod. *The Question of Pornography: Research Findings and Policy Implications*. New York: Free Press, 1987.

Drug Policy Alliance. *The Federal Drug Control Budget*. Washington, DC: Drug Policy Alliance, 2013.

Faupel, Charles E., Alan M. Horowitz, and Greg S. Weaver. *The Sociology of American Drug Use, 3rd ed.* New York: Oxford University Press, 2013.

Federal Bureau of Investigation. *Crime in the United States, 2011*. Washington, DC: Federal Bureau of Investigation, 2012.

Fenster, Jim. "Nation of Gamblers." *American Heritage* 45 (1994): 34–45.

Ferguson, Christopher J., and Richard D. Hartley. "The Pleasure Is Momentary . . . The Expense Damnable?: The Influence of Pornography on Rape and Sexual Assault." *Aggression & Violent Behavior* 14 (2009): 323–329.

Ferreira, Susana. "At 10, Portugal's Drug Law Draws New Scrutiny." *Wall Street Journal—Eastern Edition* 256 (2010): A13.

Flavin, Jeanne, and Lynn M. Paltrow. "Punishing Pregnant Drug-Using Women: Defying Law, Medicine, and Common Sense." *Journal of Addictive Diseases* 29 (2010): 231–244.

Gammage, Jeff. "Baltimore Forges a Different Course on Drug Abuse." *The Philadelphia Inquirer*, December 29, 1997: A1.

Global Commission on Drug Policy. *War on Drugs: Report of the Global Commission on Drug Policy*. Rio de Janeiro: Global Commission on Drug Policy, 2011.

Goode, Erich. 2008. *Drugs in American Society, 7th ed.* New York: McGraw-Hill.

Goode, Erich. *Drugs in American Society, 8th ed.* New York: McGraw-Hill, 2012.

Goode, Erich. *Drugs in American Society, 7th ed.* New York: McGraw-Hill, 2008.

Grant, Melissa Gira. "Unpacking the Sex Trafficking Panic." *Contemporary Sexuality* 47 (2013): 1–6.

Hobson, Barbara Meil. *Uneasy Virtue: The Politics of Prostitution and the American Reform Tradition*. New York: Basic Books, 1987.

Hughes, Caitlin Elizabeth, and Alex Stevens. "What Can We Learn from the Portuguese Decriminalization of Illicit Drugs?" *British Journal of Criminology* 50 (2010): 999–1022.

———. "A Resounding Success or a Disastrous Failure: Re-examining the Interpretation of Evidence on the Portuguese Decriminalisation of Illicit Drugs." *Drug & Alcohol Review* 31 (2012): 101–113.

Humphries, Drew, John Dawson, Valerie Cronin, et al. "Mothers and Children, Drugs and Crack: Reactions to Maternal Drug Dependency." *The Criminal Justice System and Women: Offenders, Victims, and Workers*, edited by B. R. Price and N. J. Sokoloff, 167–179. New York: McGraw-Hill, Inc, 1995.

Jensen, Gary F. "Prohibition, Alcohol, and Murder: Untangling Counterveiling Mechanisms." *Homicide Studies* 4 (2000): 18–36.

Joe-Laidler, Karen, and Geoffrey P. Hunt. "Moving Beyond the Gang-Drug-Violence Connection." *Drugs: Education, Prevention & Policy* 19 (2012): 442–452.

Johnston, Lloyd D., Jerald G. Bachman, and Patrick M. O'Malley. *Monitoring the Future: Questionnaire Responses from the Nation's High School Seniors 2011*. Ann Arbor, MI: Survey Research Center, Institute for Social Research, University of Michigan, 2013.

Kammeyer, Kenneth C. W. *A Hypersexual Society: Sexual Discourse, Erotica, and Pornography in America Today*. New York: Palgrave Macmillan, 2008.

Kappeler, Victor E., and Gary W. Potter. *The Mythology of Crime and Criminal Justice*. Prospect Heights, IL: Waveland Press, 2005.

Kara, Siddharth. *Sex Trafficking: Inside the Business of Modern Slavery*. New York: Columbia University Press, 2010.

Keating, Raymond J. "Get Government Out of Gambling Business." *Newsday*, August 10, 2004. http://www.newsday.com/news/columnists/ny-vpkea 103924657aug10,0,5349844.column?coll=ny-news-columnists.

Kelley, Matt. "Governor Discusses Drug Legalization." *The Bangor Daily News*, October 5, 1999: A7.

Kendrick, Walter M. *The Secret Museum: Pornography in Modern Culture*. New York: Viking Press, 1987.

Kennedy, John W. "The New Gambling Goliath." *Christianity Today*, August, 2004: 50+.

Kissila, Karni, and Maureen Daveya. "The Prostitution Debate in Feminism: Current Trends, Policy and Clinical Issues Facing an Invisible Population." *Journal of Feminist Family Therapy* 22 (2010): 1–21.

Korf, Dirk J. *Trends and Patterns in Cannabis Use in the Netherlands*. 2001. http://www.parl.gc.ca/Content/SEN/Committee/371/ille/presentation/korf-e.htm.

Kristof, Nicholas D. "Financiers And Sex Trafficking." *New York Times*, April 1, 2012: A13.

Labaton, Stephen. "Surgeon General Suggests Study of Legalizing Drugs." *The New York Times*. New York, December 8, 1993: A23.

Lange, Mark. "The Gambling Scam on America's Poor." *The Christian Science Monitor*, May 2, 2007. http://www.csmonitor.com/2007/0502/p09s01-coop .html?s=hns.

Lerner, Michael A. *Dry Manhattan: Prohibition in New York City*. Cambridge, MA: Harvard University Press, 2007.

Levinthal, Charles F. *Drugs, Society and Criminal Justice*. Upper Saddle River, NJ: Prentice Hall, 2012.

Lobel, Greg, and Daniel Christian. "Study: Most Criminals Abuse Drugs, Lack Treatment." *USA Today*, May 23, 2013. http://www.usatoday.com/story/news/ nation/2013/05/23/half-of-men-arrested-used-drugs/2356033/.

MacCoun, Robert M., and Karin D. Martin. "Drugs." *The Oxford Handbook of Crime and Punishment*, edited by M. Tonry, 501–523. New York: Oxford University Press, 2009.

Mack, Alison, and Janet Joy. *Marijuana as Medicine? The Science Beyond the Controversy*. Washington, DC: National Academies Press, 2000.

Mannion, Brad. "UGA Student Charged with Marijuana Possession." *The Red & Black*, July 9, 2013. http://www.redandblack.com/crime/uga-students-face-possession-dui-charges/article_630d2a0a-e89d-11e2-a48f-001a4bcf 6878.html.

MayoClinic.com. *Compulsive Gambling*. 2004. http://www.mayoclinic.com/invoke. cfm?objectid=74AD9859-7FCC-46D0-851BEB27EE5CC91B.

McCaghy, Charles H., Timothy A. Capron, J.D. Jamieson, et al. *Deviant Behavior: Crime, Conflict, and Interest Groups*. Boston: Allyn & Bacon, 2008.

McKeganey, Neil. "Harm Reduction at the Crossroads and the Rediscovery of Drug User Abstinence." *Drugs: Education, Prevention & Policy* 19 (2012): 276–283.

Meier, Robert F., and Gilbert Geis. *Criminal Justice and Moral Issues*. New York: Oxford University Press, 2006.

Menard, Scott, Sharon Mihalic, and David Huizinga. "Drugs and Crime Revisited." *Justice Quarterly* 18 (2001): 269–299.

Miller, Jody. "Prostitution." *The Oxford Handbook of Crime and Public Policy*, edited by M. Tonry, 547–577. New York: Oxford University Press, 2009.

Miron, Jeffrey A., and Katherine Waldock. *The Budgetary Impact of Ending Drug Prohibition*. Washington, DC: Cato Institute, 2010.

Mokdad, Ali H., James S. Marks, Donna F. Stroup, et al. "Actual Causes of Death in the United States, 2000." *Journal of the American Medical Association* 291 (2004): 1238–1245.

Morgan, Robin. *Going Too Far*. New York: Random House, 1977.

Musto, David F. *Drugs in America: A Documentary History*. New York: New York University Press, 2002.

O'Brien, Erin, Sharon Hayes, and Belinda Carpenter. *The Politics of Sex Trafficking: A Moral Geography*. New York: Palgrave Macmillan, 2013.

Office of National Drug Control Policy. *What America's Users Spend on Illegal Drugs, 2000–2006.*. Washington, DC: Executive Office of the President, 2012.

Okrent, Daniel. *Last Call: The Rise and Fall of Prohibition*. New York: Scribner, 2011.

Raymond, Janice G. *Not a Choice, Not a Job: Exposing the Myths about Prostitution and the Global Sex Trade*. Dulles, VA: Potomac Books, 2013.

Reinarman, Craig, Peter D. A. Cohen, and Kaal L. Hendrien. "The Limited Relevance of Drug Policy: Cannabis in Amsterdam and in San Francisco." *American Journal of Public Health* 94 (2004): 836–842.

Richlin, Amy. "Pornography and Representation in Greece and Rome." New York: Oxford University Press, 1992.

Ritter, Alison, and Jacqui Cameron. "A Review of the Efficacy and Effectiveness of Harm Reduction Strategies for Alcohol, Tobacco, and Illicit Drugs." *Drug & Alcohol Review* 25 (2006): 611–624.

Rorabaugh, W. J. "Alcohol in America." *Drugs, Society, and Behavior, Annual Editions*, edited by E. Goode, 16–18. Guilford, CT: Dushkin Publishing Group, 1995.

Rosecrance, John D. *Gambling Without Guilt: The Legitimation of an American Pastime*. Pacific Grove, CA: Brooks/Cole Publishing Company, 1988.

Rossman, Shelli B., John Roman, Janine M. Zweig, et al. *The Multi-site Adult Drug Court Evaluation*. Washington, DC: Urban Institute, 2011.

Sentencing Project. *Drug Policy*. 2013. http://www.sentencingproject.org/template/ page.cfm?id=128.

Sommers, Ira, Deborah Baskin, and Jeffrey Fagan. *Working' Hard for the Money: The Social & Economic Lives of Women Drug Sellers*. 2000.

Stanford, Sally. *The Lady of the House*. New York: G.P. Putnam, 1966.

Stinchcomb, Jeanne B. "Drug Courts: Conceptual Foundation, Empirical Findings, and Policy Implications." *Drugs: Education, Prevention & Policy* 17 (2010): 148–167.

Substance Abuse and Mental Health Services Administration. *Results from the 2011 National Survey on Drug Use and Health: Summary of National Findings*. Rockville, MD: Substance Abuse and Mental Health Services Administration, 2012.

Szaalavitz, Maia. "Drugs in Portugal: Did Decriminalization Work?" *Time*, April 20, 2009. http://www.time.com/time/health/article/0,8599,1893946,00.html.

U.S. Census Bureau. *Statistical Abstract of the United States: 2012 (http://www .census.gov/compendia/statab/).* Washington, DC: U.S. Government Printing Office, 2012.

Volz, Matt. "Legalized Medical Marijuana Faces Backlash in Several States." *Bangor Daily News,* May 22–23, 2010: A1.

Wagner, John. "Ehrlich Advocates Drug Treatment Over Jail." *The Washington Post,* July 21, 2004: B3.

Walker, Samuel. *Sense and Nonsense About Crime, Drugs, and Communities: A Policy Guide.* Belmont, CA: Wadsworth Publishing Company, 2011.

Weitzer, Ronald. *Legalizing Prostitution: From Illicit Vice to Lawful Business.* New York: NYU Press, 2011a.

———. "Sex Trafficking and the Sex Industry: The Need for Evidence-Based Theory and Legislation." *Journal of Criminal Law & Criminology* 101 (2011b): 1337–1369.

Welles, Chris. "America's Gambling Fever." *BusinessWeek,* April 24, 1989: 112–117.

Wisotsky, Steven. "A Society of Suspects: The War on Drugs and Civil Liberties." *Drugs, Society, and Behavior, Annual Editions,* edited by E. Goode, 129–134. Guilford, CT: Dushkin Publishing Group, 1995.

Yen, Iris. "Of Vice and Men: A New Approach to Eradicating Sex Trafficking by Reducing Male Demand Through Educational Programs and Abolitionist Legislation." *Journal of Criminal Law & Criminology* 98 (2008): 653–686.

Zilney, Lisa Anne. *Drugs: Policy, Social Costs, Crime, and Justice.* Upper Saddle River, NJ: Prentice Hall, 2011.

Chapter 16, Policing: Dilemmas of Crime Control in a Democratic Society

Adelstein, Jake. *Tokyo Vice: An American Reporter on the Police Beat in Japan.* New York: Vintage, 2010.

Alexander, Michelle. *The New Jim Crow: Mass Incarceration in the Age of Colorblindness.* New York: The New Press, 2012.

Apel, Robert, and Daniel S. Nagin. "General Deterrence: A Review of Recent Evidence " in *Crime and Public Policy,* edited by J. Q. Wilson and J. Petersilia, 411–436. New York: Oxford University Press, 2011.

Baker, Al. "New York Minorities More Likely to Be Frisked." *The New York Times,* May 13, 2010: A1.

Birch, James W. "Reflections on Police Corruption." *'Order Under Law': Readings in Criminal Justice,* edited by R. G. Culbertson, 116–122. Prospect Heights, IL: Waveland Press, 1984.

Black, Donald. "The Social Organization of Arrest." *Police Behavior: A Sociological Perspective,* edited by R. J. Lundman, 151–162. New York: Oxford University Press, 1980.

Blalock, Hubert. *Toward a Theory of Minority-Group Relations.* New York: John Wiley, 1967.

Blumberg, Mark. "Police Use of Excessive Force: Exploring Various Control Mechanisms." *Critical Issues in Crime and Justice,* edited by A. R. Roberts, 110–126. Thousand Oaks, CA: Sage Publications, 1994.

Blumstein, Alfred. "Making Rationality Relevant—The American Society of Criminology 1992 Presidential Address." *Criminology* 31 (1993): 1–16.

Braga, Anthony A., and David L. Weisburd. "The Effects of Focused Deterrence Strategies on Crime: A Systematic Review and Meta-Analysis of the Empirical Evidence." *Journal of Research in Crime & Delinquency* 49 (2012): 323–358.

Brunson, Rod K., and Ronald Weitzer. "Police Relations with Black and White Youths in Different Urban Neighborhoods." *Urban Affairs Review* 44 (2009): 858–885.

Chaiken, Jan M., Michael W. Lawless, and Keith A. Stevenson. "The Impact of Police Activity on Subway Crime." *Urban Analysis* 3 (1975): 173–205.

Chamlin, Mitchell B. "A Longitudinal Analysis of the Arrest-Crime Relationship: A Further Examination of the Tipping Effect." *Justice Quarterly* 8 (1991): 187–199.

Chesney-Lind, Meda, and Lisa Pasko. *The Female Offender: Girls, Women, and Crime.* Thousand Oaks, CA: Sage Publications, 2013.

Critchley, Thomas A. *A History of Police in England and Wales.* Montclair, NJ: Patterson Smith, 1972.

Currie, Elliott. *Reckoning: Drugs, the Cities, and the American Future.* New York: Hill and Wang, 1994.

D'Alessio, Stewart J., and Lisa Stolzenberg. "Crime, Arrests, and Pretrial Jail Incarceration: An Examination of the Deterrence Thesis." *Criminology* 36 (1998): 735–761.

DeFleur, Lois B. "Biasing Influences on Drug Arrest Records: Implications for Deviance Research." *American Sociological Review* 40 (1975): 88–103.

Dempsey, John S., and Linda S. Forst. *An Introduction to Policing.* Belmont, CA: Cengage Learning, 2014.

Durkheim, Emile. *The Rules of Sociological Method,* Edited by S. Lukes. New York: Free Press, 1962 (1895).

Eith, Christine, and Matthew R. Durose. *Contacts between Police and the Public, 2008.* Washington, DC: Bureau of the Justice Statistics, U.S. Department of Justice, 2011.

Engel, Robin S., Marie Skubak Tillyer, and Nicholas Corsaro. "Reducing Gang Violence Using Focused Deterrence: Evaluating the Cincinnati Initiative to Reduce Violence (CIRV)." *Justice Quarterly* 30 (2013): 403–439.

Engel, Robin Shepard, James J. Sobol, and Robert E. Worden. "Further Exploration of the Demeanor Hypothesis: The Interaction Effects of Suspects' Characteristics and Demeanor on Police Behavior." *Justice Quarterly* 17 (2000): 235–258.

Fazlollah, Mark. "11 More Cleared Due to Scandal." *The Philadelphia Inquirer,* March 25, 1997: A1.

Federal Bureau of Investigation. *Crime in the United States, 2008.* Washington, DC: Federal Bureau of Investigation, 2009.

Federal Bureau of Investigation. *Crime in the United States, 2011.* Washington, DC: Federal Bureau of Investigation, 2012.

Fyfe, James J. "The NIJ Study of the Exclusionary Rule." *Criminal Law Bulletin* 19 (1983): 253–260.

———. "Police Use of Deadly Force: Research and Reform." *Criminal Justice: Law and Politics,* edited by G. F. Cole, 128–142. Belmont, CA: Wadsworth Publishing Company, 1993.

———. "Too Many Missing Cases: Holes in Our Knowledge About Police Use of Force." *Justice Research and Policy* 4 (2002): 87–102.

Gatto, Juliette, Michaël Dambrun, Christian Kerbrat, et al. "Prejudice in the Police: On the Processes Underlying the Effects of Selection and Group Socialisation." *European Journal of Social Psychology* 40 (2010): 252–269.

Glover, Scott, and Matt Lait. "Beatings Alleged to Be Routine at Rampart." *The Los Angeles Times,* February 14, 2000a: A1.

———. "Police in Secret Group Broke Law Routinely, Transcripts Say." *The Los Angeles Times,* February 14, 2000b: A1.

Goldstein, Joseph. "Recording Points to Race Factor in Stops by New York Police." *The New York Times,* March 22, 2013: A1.

Gomez-Preston, Cheryl, and Jacqueline Trescott. "Over the Edge: One Police Woman's Story of Emotional and Sexual Harassment." *The Criminal Justice System and Women: Offenders, Victims, and Workers,* edited by B. R. Price and N. J. Sokoloff, 398–403. New York: McGraw-Hill, Inc, 1995.

Greenberg, David F. "Studying New York City's Crime Decline: Methodological Issues." *Justice Quarterly* 2013. DOI:10.1080/07418825.2012.752026.

Hagan, John, and Marjorie S. Zatz. "The Social Organization of Criminal Justice Processing Activities." *Social Science Research* 14 (1985): 103–125.

Harcourt, Bernard E., and Jens Ludwig. "Reefer Madness: Broken Windows Policing and Misdemeanor Marijuana Arrests in New York City, 1989–2000." *Criminology & Public Policy* 6 (2007): 165–181.

Harrington, Penny, and Kimberly A. Lonsway. "Current Barriers and Future Promise for Women in Policing." *The Criminal Justice System and Women: Offenders, Prisoners, Victims, and Workers,* edited by B. R. Price and N. J. Sokoloff, 495–510. New York: McGraw Hill, 2004.

Herbert, Bob. "At the Heart of the Diallo Case." *The New York Times,* February 28, 2000: A23.

Hoffman, Jan. "As Miranda Rights Erode, Police Get Confessions from Innocent People." *The New York Times,* March 30, 1998: A1.

Jackson, Pamela I. *Minority Group Threat, Crime, and Policing.* New York: Praeger, 1989.

Jacobs, David, and Robert M. O'Brien. "The Determinants of Deadly Force: A Structural Analysis of Police Violence." *American Journal of Sociology* 103 (1998): 837–862.

Kappeler, Victor E., and Gary W. Potter. *The Mythology of Crime and Criminal Justice.* Prospect Heights, IL: Waveland Press, 2005.

Kelling, George L., and Catherine M. Coles. *Fixing Broken Windows: Restoring Order and Reducing Crime in Our Communities.* New York: The Free Press, 1998.

Kent, Stephanie L., and David Jacobs. "Minority Threat and Police Strength from 1980 to 2000: A Fixed-Effects Analysis of Nonlinear and Interactive Effects in Large U.S. Cities." *Criminology* 43 (2005): 731–760.

Kerner Commission. *Report of the National Advisory Commission on Civil Disorders.* New York: Bantam Books, 196.

Kirkham, George L. "A Professor's 'Street Lessons'." *'Order Under Law': Readings in Criminal Justice,* edited by R. G. Culbertson, 77–89. Prospect Heights, IL: Waveland Press, 1984.

Knapp Commission. *Knapp Commission Report on Police Corruption.* New York: George Braziller, 1973.

Kochel, Tammy Rinehart, David B. Wilson, and Stephen D. Mastrofski. "Effect of Suspect Race on Officers' Arrest Decisions." *Criminology* 49 (2011): 473–512.

Kraska, Peter B., and Victor E. Kappeler. "To Serve and Pursue: Exploring Police Sexual Violence Against Women." *Justice Quarterly* 12 (1995): 85–111.

Kubrin, Charis E., Steven F. Messner, Glenn Deane, et al. "Proactive Policing and Robbery Rates Across U.S. Cities." *Criminology* 48 (2010): 57–97.

Lundman, Richard J., and Robert L. Kaufman. "Driving While Black: Effects of Race, Ethnicity, and Gender on Citizen Self-Reports of Traffic Stops and Police Actions." *Criminology* 41 (2003): 195–220.

Lundman, Richard J., and Brian R. Kowalski. "Speeding While Black? Assessing the Generalizability of Lange et al.'s (2001, 2005) New Jersey Turnpike Speeding Survey Findings." *JQ: Justice Quarterly* 26 (2009): 504–527.

Martin, Susan E. "The Interactive Effects of Race and Sex on Women Police Officers." *The Criminal Justice System and Women: Offenders, Prisoners, Victims, and Workers*, edited by B. R. Price and N. J. Sokoloff, 527–541. New York: McGraw-Hill, 2004.

Maston, Cathy T. *Criminal Victimization in the United States—Statistical Tables*. Washington, DC: Bureau of Justice Statistics, U.S. Department of Justice, 2011.

Messner, Steven F., Sandro Galea, Kenneth J. Tardiff, et al. "Policing, Drugs, and the Homicide Decline in New York City in the 1990s." *Criminology* 45 (2007): 385–414.

Mosse, George L. *Police Forces in History*. Beverly Hills: Sage Publications, 1975.

Mumola, Christopher J., and Margaret E. Noonan. *Deaths in Custody: State and Local Law Enforcement Arrest-Related Deaths, 2003–2006—Statistical Tables*. Washington, DC: Bureau of Justice Statistics, U.S. Department of Justice, 2010.

Packer, Herbert L. "Two Models of the Criminal Process." *University of Pennsylvania Law Review* 113 (1964): 1–68.

———. *The Limits of the Criminal Sanction*. Stanford: Stanford University Press, 1968.

Parker, L. Craig. *The Japanese Police System Today: A Comparative Study*. Armonk, NY: M.E. Sharpe, 2001.

Parry, Richard Lloyd. "Japan's Inept Guardians." *The New York Times*, June 25, 2012: A19.

Paternoster, Raymond. "How Much Do We Really Know about Criminal Deterrence?" *Journal of Criminal Law & Criminology* 100 (2010): 765–823.

Peak, Kenneth J., and Ronald W. Glensor. *Community Policing and Problem Solving: Strategies and Practices*. Upper Saddle River, NJ: Prentice Hall, 2012.

Petersilia, Joan. *Racial Disparities in the Criminal Justice System*. Santa Monica: Rand Corporation, 1983.

Reiman, Jeffrey, and Paul Leighton. *The Rich Get Richer and the Poor Get Prison: Ideology, Class, and Criminal Justice*. Upper Saddle River, NJ: Prentice Hall, 2013.

Reisig, Michael D. "Community and Problem-Oriented Policing." *The Oxford Handbook of Crime and Criminal Justice*, edited by M. Tonry, 538–576. New York: Oxford University Press, 2011.

Reiss, Albert J., Jr. "Officer Violations of the Law." *Police Behavior: A Sociological Perspective*, edited by R. J. Lundman, 253–272. New York: Oxford University Press, 1980a.

———. "Police Brutality." *Police Behavior: A Sociological Perspective*, edited by R. J. Lundman, 274–296. New York: Oxford University Press, 1980b.

Riksheim, Eric, and Steven M. Chermak. "Causes of Police Behavior Revisited." *Journal of Criminal Justice* 21 (1993): 353–382.

Rivera, Ray. "Pockets of City See Higher Use of Force During Police Stops." *The New York Times*, August 16, 2012: A17.

Rojek, Jeff, Richard Rosenfeld, and Scott Decker. "Policing Race: The Racial Stratification of Searches in Police Traffic Stops." *Criminology* 50 (2012): 993–1024.

Rosen, Marie Simonetti. "A LEN Interview with Prof. Carl Klockars of the University of Delaware." *Annual Editions: Criminal Justice 95/96*, edited by J. J. Sullivan and J. L. Victor, 107–114. Guilford, CT: Dushkin Publishing Group, 1995.

Rosenfeld, Richard, and Robert Fornango. "The Impact of Police Stops on Precinct Robbery and Burglary Rates in New York City, 2003–2010." *Justice Quarterly*, 2012. DOI: 10.1080/07418825.2012.712152.

San Juan, Angel. "Two Jasper Officers Now on Paid Leave Pending Brutality Investigation." *KBMT*, June 8, 2013. http://www.12newsnow.com/story/22453433/jasper-woman-accuses-officers-of-police-brutality.

Shelden, Randall G. *Controlling the Dangerous Classes: A Critical Introduction to the History of Criminal Justice, 2nd ed.* Upper Saddle River, NJ: Prentice Hall, 2008.

Sherman, Lawrence W. 1980. "Causes of Police Behavior: The Current State of Quantitative Research." *Journal of Research in Crime and Delinquency* 17: 69–100.

Sherman, Lawrence W., Denise C. Gottfredson, Doris L. MacKenzie, et al. 1998. *Preventing Crime: What Works, What Doesn't, What's Promising*. Washington, DC: Office of Justice Programs, National Institute of Justice.

Sherman, Lawrence W., and Dennis P. Rogan. 1995. "Effects of Gun Seizures on Gun Violence: 'Hot Spots' Patrol in Kansas City." *Justice Quarterly* 12: 673–693.

Shipler, David K. "Why Do Innocent People Confess?" *The New York Times*, February 26, 2012: SR6.

Skolnick, Jerome H. *Justice Without Trial: Law Enforcement in Democratic Society*. New York: Wiley, 1966.

Sorensen, Jonathan R., James W. Marquart, and Deon E. Brock. "Factors Related to Killings of Felons by Police Officers: A Test of the Community Violence and Conflict Hypotheses." *Justice Quarterly* 10 (1993): 417–440.

Sorg, Evan T., Cory P. Haberman, Jerry H. Ratcliffe, et al. "Foot Patrol in Violent Crime Hot Spots: The Longitudinal Impact of Deterrence and Posttreatment Effects of Displacement." *Criminology* 51 (2013): 65–101.

Staples, Brent. "The Human Cost of 'Zero Tolerance.'" *The New York Times*, April 29, 2012: SR10.

Stewart, Eric A. "Either They Don't Know or They Don't Care: Black Males and Negative Police Experiences." *Criminology & Public Policy* 6 (2007): 123–130.

Stewart, Steve W. "Council Cans Cunningham & Grissom, Will Consult with DA on Possible Criminal Charges." *KJAS.com*, June 4, 2013: http://www.kjas.com/news/local_news/article_88294f32-cc6c-11e2-9c01-0019bb30f31a.html.

Takagi, Paul. "A Garrison State in a 'Democratic Society.'" *Crime and Social Justice* 1 (1974): 27–33.

Telep, Cody W., and David Weisburd. "What Is Known About the Effectiveness of Police Practices in Reducing Crime and Disorder?" *Police Quarterly* 15 (2012): 331–357.

Terrill, William, Eugene A. Paoline, III, and Peter K. Manning. "Police Culture and Coercion." *Criminology* 41 (2003): 1003–1034.

Tomaskovic-Devey, Donald, and Patricia Warren. "Explaining and Eliminating Racial Profiling." *Contexts* 8 (2009): 34–39.

Tonry, Michael. *Malign Neglect: Race, Crime, and Punishment in America*. New York: Oxford University Press, 1994.

———. *Punishing Race: A Continuing American Dilemma*. New York: Oxford University Press, 2012.

U.S. Census Bureau. *Statistical Abstract of the United States: 2012* (http://www.census.gov/compendia/statab/). Washington, DC: U.S. Government Printing Office, 2012.

Visher, Christy A. "Gender, Police Arrest Decisions, and Notions of Chivalry." *Criminology* 21 (1983): 5–28.

Walker, Samuel. *Sense and Nonsense About Crime, Drugs, and Communities: A Policy Guide*. Belmont, CA: Wadsworth Publishing Company, 2011.

Walker, Samuel, Cassia Spohn, and Miriam DeLone. *The Color of Justice: Race, Ethnicity, and Crime in America*. Belmont, CA: Wadsworth Publishing Company, 2012.

Weisburd, David, Cody W. Telep, Joshua C. Hinkle, et al. "Is Problem-Oriented Policing Effective in Reducing Crime and Disorder? Findings from a Campbell Systematic Review." *Criminology & Public Policy* 9 (2010): 139–172.

Wellford, Charles F. "Guns and Crime." *The Oxford Handbook of Crime and Criminal Justice*, edited by M. Tonry, 420–443. New York: Oxford University Press, 2011.

Westley, William A. *Violence and the Police*. Cambridge: MIT Press, 1970.

Chapter 17, Prosecution and Punishment

Auerhahn, Kathleen. "Conceptual and Methodological Issues in the Prediction of Dangerous Behavior." *Criminology & Public Policy* 4 (2006): 771–778.

Bailey, William C. "Deterrence, Brutalization, and the Death Penalty: Another Examination of Oklahoma's Return to Capital Punishment." *Criminology* 36 (1998): 711–733.

Bales, William D., and Alex R. Piquero. "Racial/Ethnic Differentials in Sentencing to Incarceration." *JQ: Justice Quarterly* 29 (2012): 742–773.

Barkan, Steven E. "The Social Science Significance of the O.J. Simpson Case." *Representing O.J.: Murder, Criminal Justice and Mass Culture*, edited by G. Barak, 36–42. Albany, NY: Harrow and Heston, 1996.

Berk, Richard, Azusa Li, and Laura J. Hickman. "Statistical Difficulties in Determining the Role of Race in Capital Cases: A Re-analysis of Data from the State of Maryland." *Journal of Quantitative Criminology* 21 (2005): 365–390.

Berlow, Alan "The Wrong Man." *The Atlantic Monthly*, November, 1999: 66–91.

Bijleveld, Catrien C. J. H., and Paul R. Smit. "Crime and Punishment in the Netherlands, 1980–1999." *Crime and Justice: A Review of Research* 33 (2005): 161–211.

Blackmon, Douglas A. "Louisiana Death-Row Inmate Damon Thibodeaux Exonerated with DNA Evidence." *The Washington Post*, September 28, 2012. http://www.washingtonpost.com/national/louisiana-death-row-inmate-damon-thibodeaux-is-exonerated-with-dna-evidence/2012/09/28/26e30012-0997-11e2-afff-d6c7f20a83bf_print.html.

Blalock, Hubert. *Toward a Theory of Minority-Group Relations*. New York: John Wiley, 1967.

Blumberg, Abraham S. "The Practice of Law as a Confidence Game: Organizational Cooptation of a Profession." *Law & Society Review* 1 (1967): 15–39.

Blumstein, Alfred. "Race and the Criminal Justice System." *Race and Social Problems* 1 (2009): 183–186.

Bohm, Robert M. *Deathquest: An Introduction to the Theory and Practice of Capital Punishment in the United States.* Cincinnati: Anderson Publishing Company, 2012.

Bonczar, Thomas P. 2003. *Prevalence of Imprisonment in the U.S. Population, 1974–2001.* Washington, DC: Bureau of Justice Statistics, U.S. Department of Justice.

Bowers, William J., and Glenn Pierce. "Deterrence or Brutalization: What Is the Effect of Executions?" *Crime and Delinquency* 26 (1980): 453–484.

Brennan, Pauline K., and Cassia Spohn. "The Joint Effects of Offender Race/Ethnicity and Sex on Sentence Length Decisions in Federal Courts." *Race and Social Problems* 1 (2009): 200–217.

Bridges, George S., Robert D. Crutchfield, and Edith E. Simpson. "Crime, Social Structure and Criminal Punishment: White and Nonwhite Rates of Imprisonment." *Social Problems* 34 (1987): 345–361.

Brydensholt, H. H. "Crime Policy in Denmark: How We Managed to Reduce the Prison Population." *Prisons Around the World: Studies in International al Penology*, edited by M. K. Carlie and K. I. Minor. Dubuque, IA: William C. Brown Publishers, 1992.

Carson, E. Ann, and William J. Sabol. *Prisoners in 2011.* Washington, DC: Bureau of Justice Statistics, U.S. Department of Justice, 2012.

Chen, Elsa Y. "The Liberation Hypothesis and Racial and Ethnic Disparities in the Application of California's Three Strikes Law." *Journal of Ethnicity in Criminal Justice* 6 (2008): 83–102.

Chiricos, Theodore G., and Miriam A. Delone. "Labor Surplus and Punishment: A Review and Assessment of Theory and Evidence." *Social Problems* 39 (1992): 421–446.

Chiricos, Theodore G., and Gordon P. Waldo. "Socioeconomic Status and Criminal Sentencing: An Assessment of a Conflict Proposition." *American Sociological Review* 40 (1975): 753–772.

Chung, Jean. *Felony Disenfranchisement: A Primer.* Washington, DC: The Sentencing Project, 2013.

Clear, Todd R. "The Effects of High Imprisonment Rates on Communities." *Crime and Justice: A Review of Research* 37 (2008): 97–132.

Cochran, John K., and Mitchell B. Chamlin. "Deterrence and Brutalization: The Dual Effects of Executions." *Justice Quarterly* 17 (2000): 685–706.

Cochran, John K., Mitchell B. Chamlin, and Mark Seth. "Deterrence or Brutalization? An Impact Assessment of Oklahoma's Return to Capital Punishment." *Criminology* 32 (1994): 107–134.

Currie, Elliott. *Confronting Crime: An American Challenge.* New York: Pantheon Books, 1985.

Daly, Kathleen. *Gender, Crime, and Punishment.* New Haven: Yale University Press, 1994.

DeFina, Robert, and Lance Hannon. "The Impact of Mass Incarceration on Poverty." *Crime & Delinquency* 59 (2013): 562–586.

Dieter, Richard C. *Testimony Submitted to the Nebraska Legislature: Judiciary Committee Hearings on the Death Penalty, March 13.* Washington, DC: Death Penalty Information Center, 2013.

Doerner, Jill K., and Stephen Demuth. "The Independent and Joint Effects of Race/Ethnicity, Gender, and Age on Sentencing Outcomes in U.S. Federal Courts." *JQ: Justice Quarterly* 27 (2010): 1–27.

Doob, Anthony N., and Cheryl Marie Webster. "Sentence Severity and Crime: Accepting the Null Hypothesis." *Crime and Justice: A Review of Research* 30 (2003): 143–195.

Downes, David. "Visions of Penal Control in the Netherlands." *Crime and Justice: A Review of Research* 36 (2007): 93–125.

Downie, Leonard, Jr. *Justice Denied: The Case for Reform of the Courts.* Baltimore: Penguin Books, 1972.

Durkheim, Emile. *The Division of Labor in Society.* London: The Free Press, 1933 (1893).

———. "Two Laws of Penal Evolution." *Durkheim and the Law*, edited by S. Lukes and A. Scull, 102–132. New York: St. Martin's Press, 1983 (1901).

Ebbe, Obi N. I. "Comparative and International Criminal Justice Systems." Boca Raton, FL: CRC Press, 2013.

Eisenstein, James, and Hebert Jacob. *Felony Justice: An Organizational Analysis of Criminal Courts.* Boston: Little, Brown and Company, 1977.

Feeley, Malcolm M. "Perspectives on Plea Bargaining." *Law and Society Review* 13 (1979): 199–209.

Foster, Holly, and John Hagan. "The Mass Incarceration of Parents in America: Issues of Race/Ethnicity, Collateral Damage to Children, and Prisoner Reentry." *The ANNALS of the American Academy of Political and Social Science* 623 (2009): 179–194.

Franklin, Travis W. "Race and Ethnicity Effects in Federal Sentencing: A Propensity Score Analysis." *Justice Quarterly* 2013a. DOI:10.1080/07418825.2013.790990.

———. "Sentencing Native Americans in US Federal Courts: An Examination of Disparity." *JQ: Justice Quarterly* 30 (2013b): 310–339.

Freiburger, Tina L., and Carly M. Hilinski. "An Examination of the Interactions of Race and Gender on Sentencing Decisions Using a Trichotomous Dependent Variable." *Crime & Delinquency* 59 (2013): 59–86.

Garland, David. *Punishment and Modern Society: A Study in Social Theory.* Chicago: University of Chicago Press, 1990.

Glaze, Lauren E., and Erika Parks. *Correctional Populations in the United States, 2011.* Washington, DC: Bureau of Justice Statistics, U.S. Department of Justice, 2012.

Grann, David. "Trial by Fire: Did Texas Execute an Innocent Man." *The New Yorker*, September 7, 2009. http://www.newyorker.com/reporting/2009/09/07/090907fa_fact_grann.

Griffin, Timothy, and John Wooldredge. "Sex-Based Disparities in Felony Dispositions Before Versus After Sentencing Reform in Ohio." *Criminology* 44 (2006): 893–923.

Harris, Casey T., Darrell Steffensmeier, Jeffrey T. Ulmer, et al. "Are Blacks and Hispanics Disproportionately Incarcerated Relative to Their Arrests? Racial and Ethnic Disproportionality Between Arrest and Incarceration." *Race and Social Problems* 1 (2009): 187–199.

Hartley, Richard D., Sean Maddan, and Cassia C. Spohn. "Prosecutorial Discretion: An Examination of Substantial Assistance Departures in Federal Crack-Cocaine and Powder-Cocaine Cases." *JQ: Justice Quarterly* 24 (2007): 382–407.

Hayes-Smith, Justin, and Rebecca Hayes-Smith. "Race, Racial Context, and Withholding Adjudication in Drug Cases: A Multilevel Examination of Juvenile Justice." *Journal of Ethnicity in Criminal Justice* 7 (2009): 163–185.

Henrichson, Christian, and Ruth Delaney. *The Price of Prisons: What Incarceration Costs Taxpayers.* New York: Vera Institute of Justice, 2012.

Hipp, John R., and Daniel K. Yates. "Do Returning Parolees Affect Neighborhood Crime?: A Case Study Of Sacramento." *Criminology* 47 (2009): 619–656.

Huff, C. Ronald. "Wrongful Conviction and Public Policy: The American Society of Criminology 2001 Presidential Address." *Criminology* 40 (2002): 1–18.

Jacob, Herbert. *Justice in America: Courts, Lawyers, and the Judicial Process.* Boston: Little, Brown and Company, 1978.

Jacobs, David, Jason T. Carmichael, and Stephanie L. Kent. "Vigilantism, Current Racial Threat, and Death Sentences." *American Sociological Review* 70 (2005): 656–677.

Johnson, Dirk. "Illinois Governor Hopes to Fix a 'Broken Justice'." *The New York Times*, February 19, 2000a: A7.

———. "Poor Legal Work Common for Innocents on Death Row." *The New York Times*, February 5, 2000b: A1.

Joutsen, Matti, and Norman Bishop. "Noncustodial Sanctions in Europe: Regional Overview." *Alternatives to Imprisonment in Comparative Perspective*, edited by U. Zvekic, 279–292. Chicago: Nelson-Hall Publishers, 1994.

Kappeler, Victor E., and Gary W. Potter. *The Mythology of Crime and Criminal Justice.* Prospect Heights, IL: Waveland Press, 2005.

Kovandzic, Tomislav V., John J. Sloan, III, and Lynne M. Vieraitis. " 'Striking Out' as Crime Reduction Policy: The Impact of 'Three Strikes' Laws on Crime Rates in U.S. Cities." *Justice Quarterly* 21 (2004): 207–239.

Kovandzic, Tomislav V., Lynne M. Vieraitis, and Denise Paquette Boots. "Does the Death Penalty Save Lives? New Evidence from State Panel Data, 1977 to 2006." *Criminology & Public Policy* 8 (2009): 803–843.

Land, Kenneth C., Raymond H. C. Teske, Jr., and Hui Zheng. "The Short Term Effects of Executions on Homicides: Deterrence, Displacement, or Both?" *Criminology* 47 (2009): 1009–1043.

Listwan, Shelley Johnson, Christopher J. Sullivan, Robert Agnew, et al. "The Pains of Imprisonment Revisited: The Impact of Strain on Inmate Recidivism." *JQ: Justice Quarterly* 30 (2013): 144–168.

Maguire, Kathleen. "Sourcebook of Criminal Justice Statistics." 2013. Available: http://www.albany.edu/sourcebook/. University at Albany, Hindelang Criminal Justice Research Center.

Manza, Jeff, and Christopher Uggen. *Locked Out: Felon Disenfranchisement and American Democracy.* New York: Oxford University Press, 2008.

Marvell, Thomas B., and Carlisle E. Moody. "The Impact of Enhanced Prison Terms for Felonies Committed with Guns." *Criminology* 33 (1995): 247–281.

Mather, Lynn M. "Some Determinants of the Method of Case Disposition: Decisionmaking by Public Defenders in Los Angeles." *Law and Society Review* 8 (1973): 187–215.

Mauer, Marc. "Racial Disparities in the Criminal Justice System." Testimony prepared for the House Judiciary Subcommittee on Crime, Terrorism, and Homeland Security, 2009.

Michalowski, Raymond J., and Susan M. Carlson. "Unemployment, Imprisonment, and Social Structures of Accumulation: Historical Contingency in the Rusche-Kirchheimer Hypothesis." *Criminology* 37 (1999): 217–249.

Miller, Mark. "A War Over Witnesses." *Newsweek*, June 26, 2000: 55.

▼

Mills, Steve, Maurice Possley, and Ken Armstrong. "Shadows of Doubt Haunt Executions." *Chicago Tribune*, December 17, 2000.

Myers, Martha A. "Economic Threat and Racial Disparities in Incarceration: The Case of Postbellum Georgia." *Criminology* 28 (1990): 627–656.

———. "The New South's 'New' Black Criminal: Rape and Punishment in Georgia, 1870–1940." *Ethnicity, Race, and Crime: Perspectives Across Time and Place*, edited by D. F. Hawkins, 145–166. Albany, NY: State University of New York Press, 1995.

———. "The Social World of America's Courts." *Criminology: A Contemporary Handbook*, edited by J. F. Sheley, 447–471. Belmont, CA: Wadsworth, 2000.

Nagin, Daniel S., Francis T. Cullen, and Cheryl Lero Jonson. "Imprisonment and Reoffending." *Crime and Justice: A Review of Research* 38 (2009): 115–200.

Nobiling, Tracy, Cassia Spohn, and Miriam DeLone. "A Tale of Two Counties: Unemployment and Sentence Severity." *Justice Quarterly* 15 (1998): 459–485.

Paternoster, Raymond. *Capital Punishment in America*. New York: Lexington Books, 1991.

Paternoster, Raymond, and Robert Brame. "Reassessing Race Disparities in Maryland Capital Cases." *Criminology* 46 (2008): 971–1007.

Perez-Pena, Richard. "The Death Penalty: When There's No Room for Error." *The New York Times*, February 13, 2000: WK3.

Peterson, Ruth D., and William C. Bailey. "Felony Murder and Capital Punishment: An Examination of the Deterrence Question." *Criminology* 29 (1991): 367–395.

Phillips, Scott. "Status Disparities in the Capital of Capital Punishment." *Law & Society Review* 43 (2009): 807–838.

Pontell, Henry N. *A Capacity to Punish: The Ecology of Crime and Punishment*. Bloomington: Indiana University Press, 1984.

Radelet, Michael L., Hugo Adam Bedau, and Constance E. Putnam. *In Spite of Innocence: Erroneous Convictions in Capital Cases*. Boston: Northeastern University Press, 1992.

Reiman, Jeffrey, and Paul Leighton. *The Rich Get Richer and the Poor Get Prison: Ideology, Class, and Criminal Justice*. Upper Saddle River, NJ: Prentice Hall, 2013.

Reitler, Angela K., Christopher J. Sullivan, and James Frank. "The Effects of Legal and Extralegal Factors on Detention Decisions in US District Courts." *JQ: Justice Quarterly* 30 (2013): 340–368.

Rodriguez, Nancy. "Concentrated Disadvantage and the Incarceration of Youth: Examining How Context Affects Juvenile Justice." *Journal of Research in Crime and Delinquency* 50 (2013): 189–215.

Rusche, George S., and Otto Kirchheimer. *Punishment and Social Structure*. New York: Columbia University Press, 1939.

Shelden, Randall G. *Criminal Justice in America: A Sociological Approach*. Boston: Little, Brown and Company, 1982.

Shermer, Lauren O'Neill, and Brian D. Johnson. "Criminal Prosecutions: Examining Prosecutorial Discretion and Charge Reductions in U.S. Federal District Courts." *JQ: Justice Quarterly* 27 (2010): 394–430.

Shook, Jeffrey J., and Sara A. Goodkind. "Racial Disproportionality in Juvenile Justice: The Interaction of Race and Geography in Pretrial Detention for Violent and Serious Offenses." *Race and Social Problems* 1 (2009): 257–266.

Smith, M. Dwayne. "Capital Punishment in America." *Criminology: A Contemporary Handbook*, edited by J. F. Sheley, 621–643. Belmont, CA: Wadsworth, 2000.

Sorensen, Jon, and Donald H. Wallace. "Prosecutorial Discretion in Seeking Death: An Analysis of Racial Disparity in the Pretial Stages of Case Processing in a Midwestern County." *Justice Quarterly* 16 (1999): 559–578.

Spelman, William. "The Limited Importance of Prison Expansion." *The Crime Drop in America*, edited by A. Blumstein and J. Wallman, 97–129. Cambridge: Cambridge University Press, 2006.

Spohn, Cassia, and Lisa L. Sample. "The Dangerous Drug Offender in Federal Court Intersections of Race, Ethnicity, and Culpability." *Crime & Delinquency* 59 (2013): 3–31.

Stack, Steven. "Publicized Executions and Homicide, 1950–1980." *American Sociological Review* 52 (1987): 532–540.

Steffensmeier, Darrell, and Stephen Demuth. "Does Gender Modify the Effects of Race-Ethnicity on Criminal Sanctioning? Sentences for Male and Female White, Black, and Hispanic Defendants." *Journal of Quantitative Criminology* 22 (2006): 241–261.

Sudnow, David. "Normal Crimes: Sociological Features of the Penal Code in a Public Defender's Office." *Social Problems* 12 (1965): 255–276.

Sutton, John R. "The Political Economy of Imprisonment in Affluent Western Democracies, 1960–1990." *American Sociological Review* 69 (2004): 170–189.

Tillman, Robert and Henry N. Pontell. 1992. "Is Justice 'Collar-Blind'?: Punishing Medicaid Provider Fraud." *Criminology* 30: 547–573.

Tolnay, Stewart E., and E. M. Beck. *A Festival of violence: An Analysis of Southern Lynchings, 1882–1930*. Urbana, IL: University of Illinois Press, 1995.

Tonry, Michael. *Thinking About Crime: Sense and Sensibility in American Penal Culture*. New York: Oxford University Press, 2004.

———. *Punishing Race: A Continuing American Dilemma*. New York: Oxford University Press, 2012.

Tonry, Michael, and Matthew Melewski. "The Malign Effects of Drug and Crime Control Policies on Black Americans." *Crime and Justice: A Review of Research* 37 (2008): 1–44.

Ulmer, Jeffrey T. "Recent Developments and New Directions in Sentencing Research." *Justice Quarterly* 29 (2012): 1–40.

Walker, Samuel. *Sense and Nonsense About Crime, Drugs, and Communities: A Policy Guide*. Belmont, CA: Wadsworth Publishing Company, 2011.

Walker, Samuel, Cassia Spohn, and Miriam DeLone. *The Color of Justice: Race, Ethnicity, and Crime in America*. Belmont, CA: Wadsworth Publishing Company, 2012.

Warren, Patricia, Ted Chiricos, and William Bales. "The Imprisonment Penalty for Young Black and Hispanic Males: A Crime–Specific Analysis." *Journal of Research in Crime & Delinquency* 49 (2012): 56–80.

Webster, Liz. "How Many Innocent People Have We Sent to Prison?" *The Nation*, June 18, 2012. http://www.thenation.com/article/168142/how-many-innocent-people-have-we-sent-prison?rel=emailNation#axzz2Z7zKlgI4.

Western, Bruce. *Punishment and Inequality in America*. New York: Russell Sage Foundation Publications, 2006.

Western, Bruce, and Christopher Wildeman. "The Black Family and Mass Incarceration." *The ANNALS of the American Academy of Political and Social Science* 621 (2009): 221–242.

Wilgoren, Jodi. "Governor Assails System's Errors as He Empties Illinois Death Row." *The New York Times*, January 12, 2003: A1.

Williams, Marian R., Stephen Demuth, and Jefferson E. Holcomb. "Understanding the Influence of Victim Gender in Death Penalty Cases: The Importance of Victim Race, Sex-Related Victimization, and Jury Decision Making." *Criminology* 45 (2007): 865–891.

Wooldredge, John. "Neighborhood Effects on Felony Sentencing." *Journal of Research on Crime and Delinquency* 44 (2007): 238–263.

———. "Distinguishing Race Effects on Pre-Trial Release and Sentencing Decisions." *JQ: Justice Quarterly* 29 (2012): 41–75.

Zalman, Marvin, Brad Smith, and Angie Kiger. "Officials' Estimates of the Incidence of "Actual Innocence" Convictions." *JQ: Justice Quarterly* 25 (2008): 72–100.

Chapter 18, Conclusion: How Can We Reduce Crime?

Adler, Freda. *Nations Not Obsessed with Crime*. Littleton, CO: Fred B. Rothman & Co, 1983.

Akins, Scott. "Racial Segregation, Concentrated Disadvantage, and Violent Crime." *Journal of Ethnicity in Criminal Justice* 7 (2009): 30–52.

Barkan, Steven E. "Household Crowding and Aggregate Crime Rates." *Journal of Crime and Justice* 23 (2000): 47–64.

Barlow, Hugh D., and Scott H. Decker. "Criminology and Public Policy: Putting Theory to Work." Philadelphia, PA: Temple University Press, 2010.

Bonger, Willem. *Criminality and Economic Conditions*. Translated by H. P. Horton. Boston: Little Brown, 1916.

Clinard, Marshall. *Cities with Little Crime: The Case of Switzerland*. Cambridge: Cambridge University Press, 1978.

Cook, Philip J., Anthony A. Braga, and Mark H. Moore. "Gun Control." *Crime and Public Policy*, edited by J. Q. Wilson and J. Petersilia, 257–292. New York: Oxford University Press, 2011.

Cullen, Francis T., and Karen E. Gilbert. *Reaffirming Rehabilitation, 2nd ed.* Waltham, MA: Anderson Publishing 2013.

Currie, Elliott. *Confronting Crime: An American Challenge*. New York: Pantheon Books, 1985.

———. *Crime and Punishment in America*. New York: Henry Holt, 1998.

———. "On Being Right, But Unhappy." *Criminology & Public Policy* 9 (2010): 1–10.

Durose, Matthew R., Donald Farole, and Sean P. Rosenmerkel. *Felony Sentences in State Courts, 2006 – Statistical Tables*. Washington, DC: Bureau of Justice Statistics, U.S. Department of Justice, 2009.

Farrington, David P. "Families and Crime." *Crime and Public Policy*, edited by J. Q. Wilson and J. Petersilia, 130–157. New York: Oxford University Press, 2011.

Friedman, Lucy N. "Adopting the Health Care Model to Prevent Victimization." *National Institute of Justice Journal* (1994) 228: 16–19.

Frost, Natasha A., Joshua D. Freilich, and Todd R. Clear. "Contemporary Issues in Criminal Justice Policy: Policy Proposals from the American Society of Criminology Conference." Belmont, CA: Wadsworth, 2010.

Hemenway, David. *Private Guns, Public Health*. Ann Arbor: University of Michigan Press, 2004.

Johnson, David T. "Crime and Punishment in Contemporary Japan." *Crime and Justice: A Review of Research* 36 (2007): 371–423.

Kappeler, Victor E., and Gary W. Potter. *The Mythology of Crime and Criminal Justice*. Prospect Heights, IL: Waveland Press, 2005.

Kellerman, Arthur. *Understanding and Preventing Violence: A Public Health Perspective*. Washington, DC: Office of Justice Programs, National Institute of Justice, 1996.

Kozol, Jonathan. *Savage Inequalities: Children in America's Schools*. New York: Crown, 1991.

Maguire, Kathleen. "Sourcebook of Criminal Justice Statistics." 2013. Available: http://www.albany.edu/sourcebook/.

Mills, C. Wright. *The Sociological Imagination*. London: Oxford University Press, 1959.

Mishel, Lawrence, Josh Bivens, Elise Gould, et al. *The State of Working America (12th ed.)*. Ithaca, NY: ILR Press, an imprint of Cornell University Press, 2013.

Moore, Mark H. "Public Health and Criminal Justice Approaches to Prevention." *Building a Safer Society: Strategic Approaches to Crime Prevention*, vol. 19, *Crime and Justice: A Review of Research*, edited by M. Tonry and D. P. Farrington, 237–262. Chicago: University of Chicago Press, 1995.

Packer, Herbert L. *The Limits of the Criminal Sanction*. Stanford: Stanford University Press, 1968.

Petersilia, Joan, and Kevin R. Reitz. *The Oxford Handbook of Sentencing and Corrections*. New York: Oxford University Press, 2012.

Peterson, Ruth D. "The Central Place of Race in Crime and Justice: The American Society of Criminology's 2011 Sutherland Address." *Criminology* 50 (2012): 303–328.

Pew Center on the States. *Time Served: The High Cost, Low Return of Longer Prison Terms*. Washington, DC: Pew Charitable Trusts, 2012.

Reiman, Jeffrey, and Paul Leighton. *The Rich Get Richer and the Poor Get Prison: Ideology, Class, and Criminal Justice*. Upper Saddle River, NJ: Prentice Hall, 2013.

Sahl, Joann. "Battling Collateral Consequences: The Long Road to Redemption." *Criminal Law Bulletin* 49 (2013): 383–437.

Schneider, Mary-Jane. *Introduction to Public Health*. Burlington, MA: Jones and Bartlett.

Skogan, Wesley G. 2008. "Broken Windows: Why—and How—We Should Take Them Seriously." *Criminology & Public Policy* 7 (2014): 195–201.

Spock, Benjamin, and Robert Needleman. *Dr. Spock's Baby and Child Care, 9th ed.* New York: Gallery Books, 2012.

Stark, Rodney. "Deviant Places: A Theory of the Ecology of Crime." *Criminology* 25 (1987): 893–911.

Tierney, John. "Prison and the Poverty Trap." *The New York Times*, February 19, 2013: D1.

Tonry, Michael. *Thinking About Crime: Sense and Sensibility in American Penal Culture*. New York: Oxford University Press, 2004.

———. "The Mostly Unintended Effects of Mandatory Penalties: Two Centuries of Consistent findings." *Crime and Justice: A Review of Research* 38 (2009): 65–114.

Turanovic, Jillian J., Nancy Rodriguez, and Travis C. Pratt. "The Collateral Consequences of Incarceration Revisited: A Qualitative Analysis of the Effects on Caregivers of Children of Incarcerated Parents." *Criminology* 50 (2012): 913–959.

Wellford, Charles F. "Guns and Crime." *The Oxford Handbook of Crime and Criminal Justice*, edited by M. Tonry, 420–443. New York: Oxford University Press, 2011.

Welsh, Brandon C. "The Case for Early Crime Prevention." *Criminology & Public Policy* 11 (2012): 259–264.

Welsh, Brandon C., and David P. Farrington. *The Oxford Handbook of Crime Prevention*. New York: Oxford University Press, 2012.

Name Index

Hickman, M., 164
Hicks, K. M., 273
Higgins, A., 139
Higgins, G. E., 34
Hilinski, C. M., 188, 359
Hindelang, M. J., 59, 121
Hines, D. A., 76
Hinkle, J. C., 345
Hipp, J. R., 58, 84, 132, 133, 364
Hirschfield, P. J., 98
Hirschi, T., 59, 121, 157, 162, 168, 276
Hobbs, D., 202
Hobson, B. M., 319
Hochstetler, A., 95
Hodge, D., 161
Hoffman, J., 345
Holcomb, J. E., 367
Holleran, D., 85
Hollinger, R. C., 251, 264
Hollis, M. E., 76
Hollist, D. R., 132
Holloway, K., 253
Holmes, R. M., 207
Holmes, S. T., 207
Holtfreter, K., 163, 276
Hood, J. C., 231
Hooton, E. A., 108, 109
Horney, K., 230
Horowitz, A. M., 311, 312
Hoskin, A. W., 200, 214
Hryniewicz, D., 13
Huey, L., 13, 81
Huff, C. R., 368
Huff-Corzine, L., 58
Hughes, C. E., 318
Hughes, P. P., 27
Huisman, K. A., 227, 228
Huizinga, D., 97, 137, 165
Humphrey, J. A., 231
Humphreys, L., 13
Humphries, D., 237, 311
Hunnicutt, G., 145
Hunt, A., 180
Hunt, G. P., 312
Hureau, D. M., 205
Hutchings, B., 111

I

Iritani, B. J., 77
Israel, J. I., 91
Iyengar, S., 26

J

Jackman, T., 215
Jackson, B., 269
Jackson, D., 193
Jackson, D. B., 116, 176, 177
Jackson, D. Z., 25
Jackson, P. I., 341
Jackson, S. L., 212
Jacob, H., 353, 356
Jacobs, B. A., 13, 111, 116, 206
Jacobs, D., 335, 341, 358
Jacques, S., 13
Jamieson, J. D., 91, 117, 122, 320
Jamieson, K. H., 269
Jang, S. J., 161
Jarjoura, G. R., 161
Jarjoura, R., 121
Jenkins, P., 22
Jennings, W. G., 58
Jensen, G. F., 155, 314
Jensen, V. J., 143
Jesilow, P., 19
Joe-Laidler, K., 312

Johannesen, M., 212
Johansen, B. E., 289
Johnson, B. D., 357
Johnson, B. R., 161
Johnson, C., 268
Johnson, D. T., 50, 376
Johnson, Devon., 33, 34, 369
Johnson, Dirk., 368
Johnson, J., 89, 228
Johnson, K., 177
Johnson, M. P., 223
Johnson, P., 228
Johnson, P. E., 34
Johnson, S. D., 103
Johnston, L. D., 202, 244, 308, 316
Jones, N., 54, 108
Jones, S., 163
Jones, S. E., 122
Jonson, C. L., 33, 101, 176, 362
Josephson, M., 363
Joutsen, M., 363
Joy, J., 317
Julia, M., 196
Junger, M., 162
Junger-Tas, J., 162
Justice, J., 228

K

Kahane, L. H., 117
Kahn, H., 272
Kaiser, J., 288, 289
Kammeyer, K. C. W., 322
Kanarek, R. B., 115
Kaplan, A., 213
Kaplan, H. B., 133
Kappeler, V. E., 22, 23, 24, 281, 283, 311, 331,
    335, 353, 380
Kara, S., 320
Karberg, J. C., 97
Karmen, A., 66, 77, 84
Katten, A., 271
Katz, B. L., 247
Katz, Jack, 137, 206, 250
Katz, Janet, 114
Kaufman, J. M., 139, 203
Kaufman, P. I., 299
Kaufman, R. L., 26, 340
Kauzlarich, D., 288, 293
Kay, B., 233
Keating, R. J., 324
Keel, P. K., 90
Kellerman, A., 373
Kellerman, A. L., 214
Kellett, S., 248
Kelley, M., 316
Kelling, G. L., 343
Kendrick, W. M., 321
Kennedy, J. W., 324
Kennedy, L. W., 144
Kennedy, T. D., 121
Kenney, D. J., 280
Kent, S. L., 341, 358
Kerber, R., 257
Kerbrat, C., 335
Kercher, G., 30
Kerley, K. R., 85
Kern, R., 160
Kershaw, S., 293
Kessler, R., 300
Kesteren, J., 50, 69, 159
Khokha, S., 271
Kidd, M., 83
Kierkus, C. A., 160
Kiger, A., 368
Kikuchi, G., 249

Kilpatrick, D. G., 83
Kim, J., 231
Kimmel, M. S., 201, 233
King, M. L., Jr., 299
Kingkade, T., 42
Kirchheimer, O., 354
Kirk, D. S., 143
Kirkham, G. L., 331
Kissila, K., 319
Kitman, J. L., 274
Klaus, P., 80, 247
Kleck, G., 215
Kleiman, M. A. R., 311
Klein, D., 120
Klevens, J., 227, 228
Klier, J., 288
Klockars, C. B., 183
Knightley, P., 300
Knopik, V., 111
Kochel, T. R., 339
Koenen, K. C., 116
Kohfeld, C., 99
Kohlberg, L., 120
Kokh, A., 288
Komiya, N., 159
Koppel, H., 44, 79, 241
Korf, D. J., 316
Kornhauser, R., 132
Kovandzic, T. V., 100, 229, 362, 365
Kowalski, B. R., 340
Kozol, J., 379
Kramer, R. C., 293, 294
Kraska, P. B., 335
Kreager, D. A., 97
Kristof, N. D., 25, 320
Krivo, L. J., 133, 134
Krohn, M. D., 45, 137, 162, 165, 178
Krugman, P., 267
Kruttschnitt, C., 203
Kubrin, C. E., 132, 134, 144, 344
Kuhl, S., 118
Kuhns, J. B., 34, 198
Kurtz, H., 21, 314

L

La Gory, M. E., 81
Labaton, S., 273
LaFree, G., 57
Lait, M., 336
Lambroza, S., 288
Land, K. C., 249, 365
Landor, A., 161
Lane, K. J., 232
Lane, L., J., 177
Lane, R., 217
Langbein, L., 33
Lange, M., 323, 324
Langton, L., 211, 264
Lanier, C., 58
Lanier, M. M., 176
Lanza-Kaduce, L., 177
Larson, D. B., 161
Laub, J. H., 166
Laufer, W. S., 137
Lauritsen, J., 51
Lauritsen, J. L., 41, 53, 145, 233
Lawless, M. W., 346
Layne, J., 85
Leaf, C., 277, 279
Leake, B. D., 81
Ledger, K., 117
Lee, A. F., 213, 214, 215
Lee, G. A., 293
Lee, M. R., 161, 198
Lee, S., 252

Subject Index